An Introduction to Database Systems

Bipin C. Desai

Concordia University

Montreal, Canada

West Publishing Company

St. Paul New York Los Angeles San Francisco

Copyeditor: **Sheryl Rose**
Interior Design: **David Corona Design**
Artwork: **Rolin Graphics**
Compositor: **The Clarinda Company**

50 W. Kellogg Boulevard
P.O. Box 64526
St. Paul, MN 55164-1003

Printed in the United States of America

97 96 95 94 93 92 91 90 8 7 6 5 4 3 2 1 0

Library of Congress Cataloging-in-Publication Data

Desai, Bipin C.
An introduction to database systems / Bipin C. Desai.
p. cm.
Includes bibliographical references.
ISBN 0-314-66771-7
1. Data base management. I. Title.
QA76.9.D3D465 1990
005.74—dc20 89-22627
CIP

In memory of my parents

Contents

[1]May be skipped without loss of continuity.

Preface

This textbook introduces the basic concepts of database systems. These concepts are presented through numerous examples in modeling and design. The material in this book is geared to an introductory course in database systems offered at the junior or senior level of Computer Science. It could also be used in a first year graduate course in database systems, focusing on a selection of the advanced topics in the latter chapters.

The Textbook Organization

The text is organized in a manner suitable for use in an undergraduate database course. The format of each chapter is as follows: introduction, concepts (illustrated with abundant examples), summary, key terms, exercises, bibliographic notes, and bibliographic references.

The key features of the text are its indepth coverage of the relational, network and hierarchical models as well as the extensive use of the E-R model. All these models are introduced and compared early in the text in Chapter 2 to provide the student with their essential features. Another aspect of the text is the self-contained nature of the material covered in each chapter. Coverage of the recent trends in database research with sections on knowledge representation, expert systems, deductive databases, the object approach and the object database is included. The text has been classroom tested in manuscript form and has incorporated the suggestions of expert reviewers.

Supplements

The following ancillary material is available, on request, from the publisher: instructor's manual, transparency masters and a floppy disk containing the implementation details of a sample data base application.

Objectives of the Text

The book's objective is to provide a conceptual understanding of the principles of database systems in a tutorial manner. Formal definitions are preceded by informal discussion allowing readers to gain an intuitive understanding of the concepts. Each chapter generally offers self-contained illustrative examples and can be studied independently. Since the intent is to present the concepts of the various database models, the details of the syntax of a particular implementation of a model are replaced by a uniform Pascal-like language wherever possible. Each chapter is summarized and offers numerous exercises of varying complexity.

In Chapter 1, the basic concepts of the database systems are introduced. The structure of a Database Management System and its components are presented. The interaction of the different classes of users with the database, and the database with the operating system are explained. Chapter 2 introduces the concepts of data modeling and association of data. The entity-relationship model is introduced; this model will be used throughout the text to present the various database design examples. An introduction to the relational, network and hierarchical models is also given. An implementation of the same database application example using these models along with a comparison is presented.

Chapter 3 deals with file organization and for most database courses it is optional and could be skipped without loss of continuity. Here the various file structures used in a database environment and their relative merits for retrieval and update operations are presented. The serial, sequential, indexed sequential and direct file structures to support primary key retrieval are focused on. The topic of retrieval based on secondary keys is presented using the inverted, multilist, and ring files. The use of the tree structured files using B^+-tree and B-tree is also considered.

Chapters 4 and 5 encompass the relational model, the relational operators of relational algebra, and relational calculus. The query languages based on these approaches (SQL, QUEL and QBE) are introduced. Chapter 6 focuses on the theory of relational database design. The basic normal forms and the process of normalization are demystified. The synthesis approach to relational database design and higher order normal forms are discussed in Chapter 7.

The CODASYL and hierarchical approaches are considered in a conceptual frame in Chapters 8 and 9. These two chapters could be skipped for a single semester course. If it is included, the material could easily be handled by a teaching assistant/tutor. The subject of query processing in a relational database system is addressed in Chapter 10. Methods for the estimation of the query processing costs and their minimization are examined.

The topics of recovery, concurrency, and database security and integrity are addressed in Chapters 11 through 13. The concepts of transactions and concurrency are introduced. The problems associated with the concurrent execution of transactions and the various schemes used to resolve them are presented in Chapter 11. Various methods of recovery from the loss of data are examined in Chapter 12. Methods of protecting the database are elaborated in Chatper 13.

Chapter 14 outlines the step by step approach used in designing a database application. Issues involved in the three level design are discussed. A number of suggested database design projects are given. The special problems that arise when a database is distributed over a number of sites connected via a communication network are elaborated in Chapter 15. Chapter 16 treats the advanced topics and may be omitted from a junior level course. Concepts of database machines are briefly examined in the final chapter.

The diagram on the following page is a suggested plan for a single semester course.

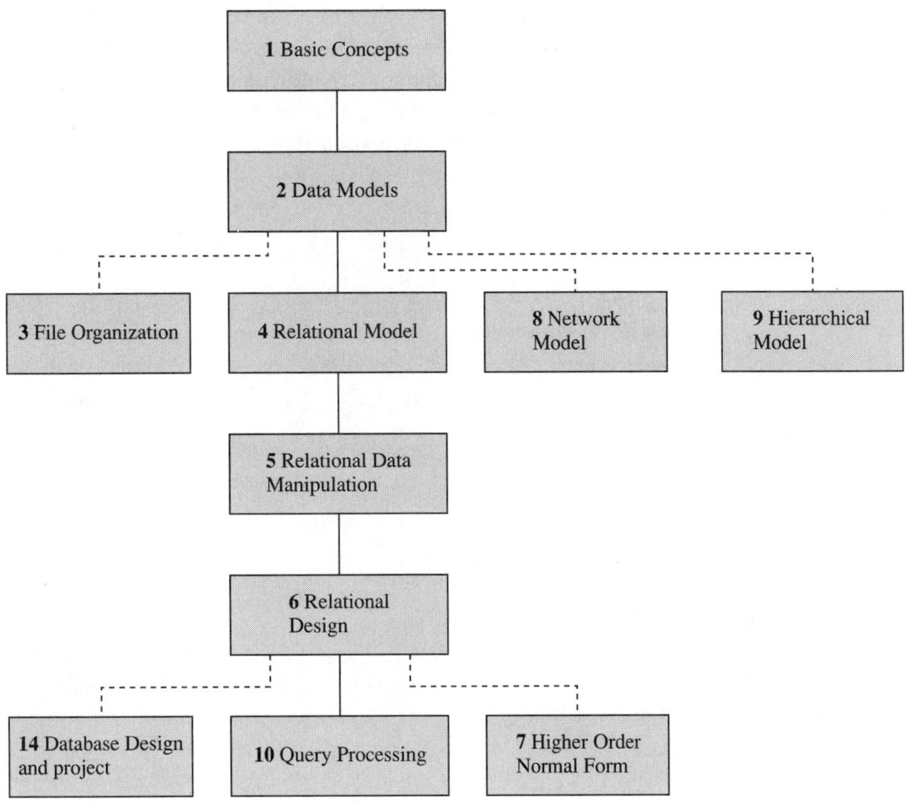

File Organization, Network Model and Hierarchical Model chapters are optional and could be skipped without loss of continuity. Alternatively, as is the practice at Concordia, the Network and Hierarchical Models are covered by a teaching assistant/tutor. It is suggested that the students be assigned a database design and implementation project and the chapter on Database Design and Query Processing could be covered concurrently. In a single term course, the instructor may choose to omit the database design project, Chapters 7 and 10.

When used in a second level or graduate course the latter chapters which deal with design and implementation issues such as concurrency, recovery, and security may be included. It is also the usual practice to discuss distributed database systems and recent trends in database systems in a second level course. Higher order normal forms and query processing techniques may be brought in at this level.

Acknowledgements

It is with great pleasure that the author acknowledges the contributions of a large number of people. The manuscript for the text, in its various stages, had been used by a large number of students over several terms in an introductory database course at Concordia. The author wishes to thank these students for their comments and questions. The author also wishes to acknowledge the initial contributions of Dr. P. Goyal in the formulation of chapters 3, 4, 5, 10, and 15. The informal discussions with P. Goyal, T. Narayanan, R. Kohli, Richard Pollock, and F. Sadri throughout this project were helpful. Special thanks are also due to Richard Pollock who spent endless hours reviewing this text in its various stages of completion and the very constructive comments provided.

The author gratefully acknowledges the contribution of these reviewers and their helpful suggestions:

John Atkins
West Virginia University

William Baker
Jamestown College

Mark Barnard
Marquette University

Anthony Q. Baxter
University of Kentucky

Helen Casey
Sam Houston State University

Maxine Cohen
SUNY—Binghamton

Lee D. Cornell
Mankato State University

Steven A. Demurjian
University of Connecticut

Herbert L. Dershem
Hope College

Kathleen Desmet
Marist College

James Diederich
University of California—Davis

Nelson Dinerstein
Utah State University

David A. Eichmann
University of Iowa

Alan L. Eliason
University of Oregon

Richard Epstein
George Washington University

Anil K. Garg
Southern Illinois University

Guy Johnson
Rochester Institute of Technology

V. S. Lakshmanan
University of Toronto

John B. Lane
Edinboro State College

Chung Lee
California State Polytecnic University

John Lowther
Michigan Technological University

A. Dale Magoun
Northeast Louisiana University

Ronald A. Mann
University of Louisville

Michael Mannino
University of Texas at Austin

Fatma Mili
Oakland University

Evelyn Rozanski
Rochester Institute of Technology

Sharon Salveter
Boston University

Peter Smith
California State University, Northridge

Arie Tzvieli
Louisiana State University

The author also wishes to express his sincerest appreciation and gratitude to the very helpful people at West. Among these are Jerry Westby, Liz Lee, Nancy Roth, and Patrick Fitzgerald.

Finally, there are some special people without whose support this project would have never come to fruition. The author wishes to thank. S.E.D. for the innumerable hours spent with the early editing of the manuscript and the continuing moral support provided. Special thanks to P.E.D. who contributed in the design of the UHL teams and invented its main characters. Last, but not least, thanks to L.M.D. and D.R.A.D. who helped keep the spirits up with their inquiries about the state of the 'book'.

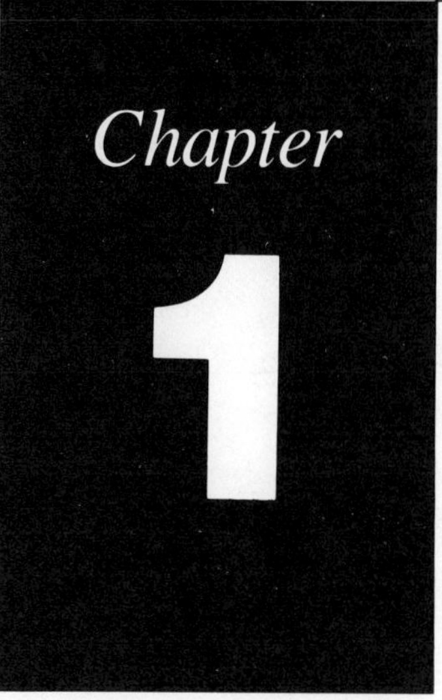

Basic Concepts

Contents

An organization must have accurate and reliable data for effective decision making. To this end, the organization maintains records on the various facets of its operations by building appropriate models of the diverse classes of objects of interest. These models capture the essential properties of the objects and record relationships among them. Such related data is called a **database.** A **database system** is an integrated collection of related files, along with details of the interpretation of the data contained therein.

A **database management system** (DBMS) is a software system that allows access to data contained in a database. The objective of the DBMS is to provide a convenient and effective method of defining, storing, and retrieving the information contained in the database. The DBMS interfaces with application programs, so that the data contained in the database can be used by multiple applications and users. In this chapter we look at the structure of a database management system, its main components and their interactions, and the different classes of users. The database system allows these users to access and manipulate the data contained in the database in a convenient and effective manner. In addition the DBMS exerts centralized control of the database, prevents fraudulent or unauthorized users from accessing the data, and ensures the privacy of the data.

1.1 Data Modeling for a Database

An organization is established to undertake one or several operations or projects. Typically, it is an environment with a single administrative control. Examples of an organization are a bank, conglomerate, government, hospital, manufacturer, or university. An organization may be a single venture such as a university located on a single campus under a single board of governors, or it may consist of a number of units, each of which could be considered a separate organization. An instance of the latter is a conglomerate, which is made up of various quasi-independent enterprises.

All organizations have some basic, common functions. Typically an organization needs to collect, process, store, and disseminate data for its human, financial, and material resources and functions. The functions performed by an organization depend on its nature and purpose and could include some of the following: payroll, accounts receivable and payable, sales reports and forecasts, design and manufacturing, course offerings, course enrollment, student transcripts, medical histories. The database system is an attempt to consolidate under a single administration the collection, storage, and dissemination of the data required for these operations.

The database is used to store information useful to an organization. To represent this information, some means of modeling is used. The components used in modeling are limited to the objects of interest to the organization and the relationships among these objects. One category of objects of concern to any organization is its personnel, and one relationship that exists within this category of objects is that of supervisor to employees. Another area in which the definition, management, and manipulation of a considerable amount of data is required is in computer-aided design (CAD) and computer-aided manufacturing (CAM). The objects in these applications consist of the specifications of various components and their interrelationships.

Each category of objects has certain characteristics or properties, called its attributes. Relationships have certain properties as well, represented as the attributes of the relationship. We briefly look at these components of modeling in this chapter and defer detailed discussion of data modeling to the next chapter.

1.1.1 Entities and Their Attributes

Entities are the basic units used in modeling classes of concrete or abstract objects. Entities can have concrete existence or constitute ideas or concepts. Each of the following is an entity: building, room, chair, transaction, course, machine, employee. An **entity type** or **entity set** is a group of similar objects of concern to an organization for which it maintains data. Examples of entity sets are transactions, concepts, job positions, courses, employees, inventories of raw and finished products, inventories of plants and machinery, students, academic staff, nonacademic staff, managers, flight crews, flights and reservations.

Identifying and classifying objects into entity sets can be difficult, because an object can belong to different entity sets simultaneously. A person can be a student as well as a part-time employee. Consider the modeling of a flight crew. It consists of a group of individuals employed by an organization who belong to the entity sets EMPLOYEE and PERSON. These individual members of the flight crew have different skills and functions. Some are assigned to the flight deck, others make up the cabin crew. In modeling we may decide simply to use the entity set EMPLOYEE and add the attribute *Skill* with possible values such as pilot, first officer, navigator, engineer, steward, purser, and stewardess. A *FLIGHT_CREW* can then be considered as a **relationship** among the instances of the entity set EMPLOYEE with appropriate value of *Skill*. Or we could consider creating entity sets PILOT, FLIGHT_ENGINEER, NAVIGATOR, and so forth for each distinct group of employees required in a flight crew. We can then set up a relationship, let us call it *FLIGHT_CREW*, among these entity sets.

One of the first steps in data modeling is to identify and select the entity sets that will best organize useful information for the database application (see Figure 1.1). Problems to be resolved include delimiting an entity and distinguishing and identifying occurrences of entities of the same type. In effect, entities such as bolts, electrons, trees, or cattle cannot be uniquely identified. However, with these types of entities, their number, density, weight, or other such attributes may be sufficient for modeling. For instance, we want to distinguish a #8-24 bolt that is two inches long from a #10-24 bolt of the same length. However, an instance of the former need not be distinguished from another instance of the same. Another problem to be resolved is the method of handling the changes that occur in an entity over time. An instance of the entity EMPLOYEE could successively be a junior engineer, an engineer, a senior engineer, and a manager.

To store data on an entity set, we have to create a model for it. For example, employees of an organization are modeled by the entity set EMPLOYEE. We must include in the model the properties or characteristics of employees that may be useful to the organization. Some of these properties are EMPLOYEE.*Name*, EMPLOYEE.*Soc_Sec_No* (Social Security number), EMPLOYEE.*Address*, EMPLOYEE.*Skill*, EMPLOYEE.*Annual_Salary*. Other properties, which are not deemed useful to the organization and not recorded, could be the color of the employees' hair or the size of the shoes they wear. The properties that characterize an entity set are called its

Figure 1.1 Identifying the requirements for database applications.

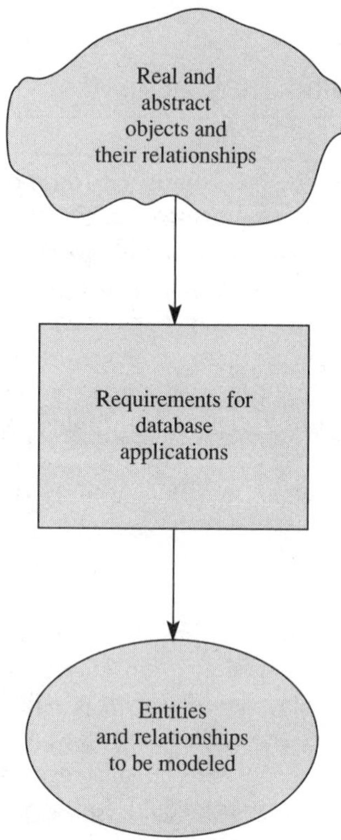

attributes (see Figure 1.2). An attribute is also referred to by the terms **data item, data element, data field, item, elementary item, or object property.** Figure 1.2 gives examples of entities relevant to a database application for an organization such as a hotel. In the figure an entity set is represented as a rectangle and each of its attributes is represented by an oval connected to the rectangle.

Attribute Values and Domains

The entity set EMPLOYEE is a classification whereby we view a set of persons employed by an organization. We record the details of each such person by recording the value of each attribute used in the classification. Therefore, we record facts about the person George Hall, who is an employee, by giving the values for the attributes used in modeling the entity set EMPLOYEE as shown in Figure 1.3. Having defined an entity set for the employees, we can represent the data for all the employees of the organization HOTEL PLEIN AIR by using the entity type EMPLOYEE. For each person employed by the hotel, we give the value for each of the attributes. In Figure 1.3, we associate the value George Hall with the attribute EMPLOYEE.*Name,* the value 787394510 with the attribute EMPLOYEE.*Soc_Sec_No,* the value 110 Woolsey Drive with the attribute EMPLOYEE.*Address,* and so forth.

Figure 1.2 Entity sets and their attributes.

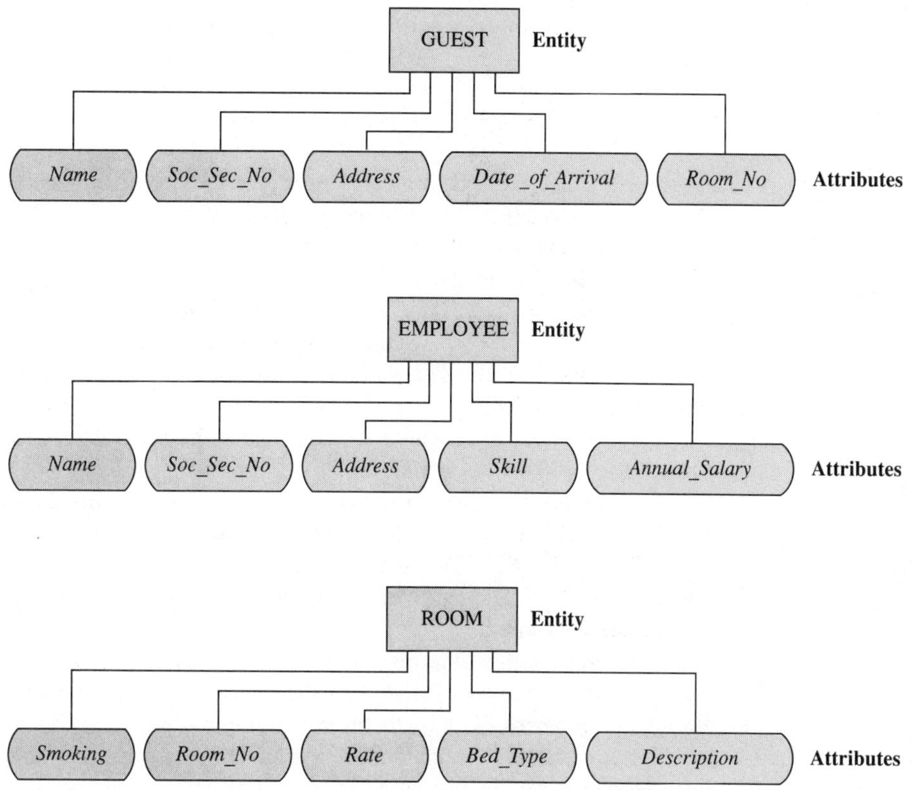

Each attribute of an entity set has a particular value. The set of possible values that a given attribute can have is called its **domain.** For example, the set of values that the attribute EMPLOYEE.*Soc_Sec_No* can assume is a positive integer of nine digits; similarly, the set of values that the attribute EMPLOYEE.*Annual_Salary* may take is a positive number ranging between 0.00 and 9,999,999.00. It is possible for different attributes to share a domain, as in the case of the attribute GUEST.*Soc_Sec_No*, which shares its domain with the attribute EMPLOYEE.*Soc_Sec_No*. If the EMPLOYEE.*Annual_Salary* were recorded in cents, then both the attributes EMPLOY-

Figure 1.3 An entity set, its attributes, and their values.

Entity set	**Attribute**	**Value**
EMPLOYEE	EMPLOYEE.*Name*	George Hall
	EMPLOYEE.*Soc_Sec_No*	787394510
	EMPLOYEE.*Address*	110 Woolsey Dr.
	EMPLOYEE.*Skill*	cook
	EMPLOYEE.*Annual_Salary*	42650.00

EE. *Annual_Salary* and EMPLOYEE.*Soc_Sec_No* would have a domain consisting of positive nine-digit integers. Although the set of values for the two attributes are identical, their domains are treated differently because we interpret the salary as a monetary unit and the Social Security number as an identifying number.

Keys

A **key** is a single attribute or combination of two or more attributes of an entity set that is used to identify one or more instances of the set. The attribute EMPLOYEE. *Soc_Sec_No* uniquely identifies an instance of the entity set EMPLOYEE. The value 787394510 for the attribute EMPLOYEE.*Soc_Sec_No* uniquely identifies the employee George Hall. A key would not be unique if an attribute such as EMPLOYEE.*Skill* were used. Such attributes identify more than one instance of the entity set EMPLOYEE. The value of cook for EMPLOYEE.*Skill* identifies all employees with this skill.

Two instances of an entity set could have the same values for all its attributes. In the case of the entity set GUEST, it is likely that the two guests Don Smith and David Smith, who are identical twins living at 123 New Brunswick Drive, are both registered as D. Smith. To distinguish such instances, we introduced the attribute GUEST.*Soc_Sec_No*. This attribute is unique and will identify an instance of the entity set GUEST. Such a unique entity identifier as GUEST.*Soc_Sec_No* is referred to as a **primary key.**

If we add additional attributes to a primary key, the resulting combination would still uniquely identify an instance of the entity set. Such augmented keys are called **superkeys:** a primary key is, therefore, a minimum superkey. It is possible that some existing attribute or combination of attributes of an entity set uniquely identifies an instance of the set. In this case, additional attributes need not be introduced. However, if no such attribute or combination of attributes exists, then in order to identify the object uniquely, an additional attribute needs to be introduced. Examples of such additional attributes are found in the introduction of identifiers such as car serial numbers, part numbers, customer and account numbers to uniquely identify cars, parts, customers and accounts, respectively. Instances of these entities would be harder to distinguish by their other attributes. Suppose that George Hall banks with the First National Bank. Even though each customer has a unique *Soc_Sec_No,* the bank uses a unique identifier called the *Account_Number* to identify each account. The fact that George Hall may have more than one account of the same type, for example, two current accounts, three savings accounts, and a mortgage account, necessitates such identification. The attribute *Account_Number* is a better choice for the primary key of the entity set ACCOUNT than the attribute *Soc_Sec_No.*

There may be two or more attributes or combinations of attributes that uniquely identify an instance of an entity set. These attributes or combinations of attributes are called **candidate keys.** In such a case we must decide which of the candidate keys will be used as the primary key. The remaining candidate keys would be considered **alternate keys.**

A **secondary key** is an attribute or combination of attributes that may not be a candidate key but that classifies the entity set on a particular characteristic. A case in point is the entity set EMPLOYEE having the attribute *Department,* which identifies by its value all instances of EMPLOYEE who belong to a given department. More

Figure 1.4 Relationships between entity sets.

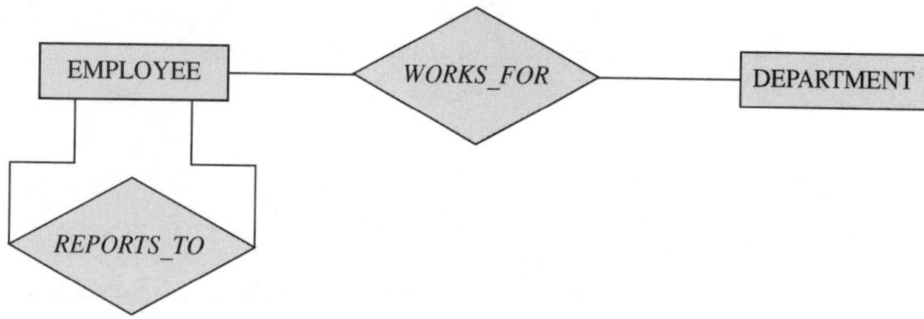

than one employee may belong to a department, so the *Department* attribute is not a candidate key for the entity set EMPLOYEE, since it cannot uniquely identify an individual employee. However, the *Department* attribute does identify all employees belonging to a given department.

1.1.2 Relationships

The **relationship set** is used in data modeling to represent an association between entity sets. This association could have certain properties represented by the attributes of the relationship set. A *Grade* is an attribute of the ENROLLMENT relationship set between the entity sets COURSE and STUDENT.

Each relationship set is named. The fact that an employee is assigned to a given department is indicated by the named relationship set *WORKS_FOR* between the entity sets EMPLOYEE and DEPARTMENT. Compare this with using the attribute *Department* as an attribute of EMPLOYEE. Figure 1.4 shows this relationship set as a diamond connected to the entity sets involved in the relationship. There could be a number of entity sets involved in a relationship and the same entity set could be involved in a number of different relationship sets. The relationship set *REPORTS_TO* in Figure 1.4 involves the same entity set EMPLOYEE and indicates that an employee reports to another employee, the supervisor. The same entity set EMPLOYEE is involved in both these relationship sets. We discuss the concept of relationships further in the next chapter.

1.2 Records and Files

The physical representation of an entity set is made by aggregating the attributes used to model the entity set. Such a representation is called a **record type.** An instance of a record type is a **record occurrence.** The usual practice is to group together in predetermined order the values of the attributes of an instance of an entity set and store them in an appropriate storage medium. Therefore,

[George Hall, 787394510, 110 Woolsey Drive, cook, 42650.00]

Figure 1.5 Storing records in a file.

George Hall	787394510	110 Woolsey Dr.	cook	42650.00
Denise Benoit	632749291	357 Joseph Blvd.	busboy	19700.00

is an example of a physical representation of an instance of the entity set EMPLOYEE. It represents an occurrence of the record type to which we refer by using the same name as the corresponding entity set, EMPLOYEE. The stored value of the attribute is referred to as an **attribute value, stored field,** or simply **field.** A **file** is a collection of identical record type occurrences pertaining to an entity set and is labeled to identify the entity set.

Two occurrences of the record type for the entity set EMPLOYEE may be stored in a file as shown in Figure 1.5. Only the values for the attributes of the record are stored and the interpretation of these values is left to the user or program using the file. Each record of Figure 1.5 represents a collection of data fields and could be interpreted as the attribute values for the attributes EMPLOYEE.*Name,* EMPLOYEE.*Soc_Sec_No,* EMPLOYEE.*Address,* EMPLOYEE.*Skill,* and EMPLOYEE.*Annual_Salary,* respectively. All occurrences of such records are grouped together and stored in a file. The storage medium could be manual (a file folder or a ledger) or computer oriented (magnetic tape, disk, drum, or optical disk).

Data for a record and its interpretation may also be stored together. This may be done by preceding each data value with the name of its attribute as shown in Figure 1.6. In this method of storage, the relative positions of the various attribute names and attribute value pairs within the record are not significant. However, where the data is stored as in Figure 1.5, the relative positions of the value for each of the attributes of the record **must** conform to the relative positions of the corresponding attribute used in the interpretation of the data.

The disadvantage of storing the name of the attribute along with the value, as shown in Figure 1.6, is the waste of storage space. The advantage is that the interpretation of the value is stored with the value in the file. However, the program using

Figure 1.6 Storing attribute names with values.

Attribute	**Value**
EMPLOYEE.*Name*	George Hall
EMPLOYEE.*Soc_Sec_No*	787394510
EMPLOYEE.*Address*	110 Woolsey Dr.
EMPLOYEE.*Skill*	cook
EMPLOYEE.*Annual_Salary*	42650.00
EMPLOYEE.*Name*	Denise Benoit
EMPLOYEE.*Skill*	busboy
EMPLOYEE.*Address*	357 Joseph Blvd.
EMPLOYEE.*Annual_Salary*	19700.00
EMPLOYEE.*Soc_Sec_No*	632749291

this data still requires information on the size of the descriptors used to store the attribute names and the size and type of the attribute values unless they, too, are stored. In addition, the program has to be aware of the file access method and the type of storage device employed. The volume of description required to interpret the data when it is stored using the method of Figure 1.5 is correspondingly greater. Such descriptors, being data about data, are called **metadata.**

Physical representation of a relationship is not quite as straightforward as the representation of the entity set. The representation of a relationship depends on the data model used by the database system. We discuss relationships further in the next chapter, where we introduce the various data models.

1.3 Abstraction and Data Integration

A user's program (the application program) interprets the world portrayed by the data, and this data represents a portion of the real world with which the program is concerned. Each program needs data relevant to its task. It is usual for a program to use some portion of data that is also used by other programs, and the simplest method of sharing common data is by duplicating it. In the early days of computerization, when each application was independently implemented (computerized), the practice was for each application programmer to design the file structure and for the application program to contain the metadata about the file organization and the access method to be used. Thus, each application program used its own data; the details concerning the structure of the data as well as the method of accessing and interpreting it were all embodied in the application program. Users' programs were also responsible for devising structures for data storage on secondary storage devices so that the data could be accessed efficiently. Consequently, users were required to choose an appropriate file access method. (We discuss files and access methods in Chapter 3.) A change in storage media required changes to these structures and access methods. Because the files were structured for one application, it was difficult to use the data in these files in new applications requiring data from several files belonging to different existing applications.

It might be necessary to duplicate data because of a different interpretation of the data or for the protection of some portion of the data from the general class of users. An employee's telephone number, for instance, could be made available to all users but not the employee's salary. Large-scale storage of redundant data is a waste of resources and results in inconsistency when some copies of the data are changed and others are not. A database system remedies these problems by centralizing the storage and management of data. The database management system has access to metadata, relieving users (or their application programs) of its maintenance and manipulation. The database system also provides the application programs or users with data in the form they require, with the database performing the appropriate translation of the actual data.

Consider a nondatabase operating environment consisting of a number of application programs as shown in Figure 1.7. Each such application has its own need of viewing the real world and the necessary data is stored in private files. Sharing is achieved in this environment by duplicating common data.

Figure 1.7 Nondatabase environment without any shared data.

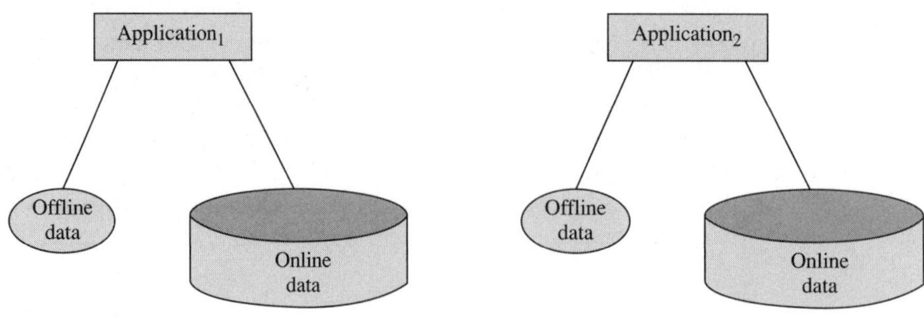

Consider two applications that require data on the entity set EMPLOYEE. The first application involves the public relations department sending each employee a newsletter and related material. This material is mailed to employees' homes, necessitating printing mailing labels. The application, therefore, is interested in the record type EMPLOYEE, which contains the values for the attributes EMPLOYEE.*Name* and EMPLOYEE.*Address*. This record type is the **view** of the real world as far as this application is concerned and can be described in pseudocode as shown in Figure 1.8.

The second application involves the payroll application for paycheck preparation. It requires the record type EMPLOYEE, which contains the values for the attributes EMPLOYEE.*Name*, EMPLOYEE.*Soc_Sec_No, EMPLOYEE.Address,* and EMPLOYEE.*Annual_Salary*. This record type is shown in Figure 1.9.

In a nondatabase environment, each application program is responsible for maintaining the currency of the data and a change in a data item must be effected in each copy of the data. Therefore, if an employee changes her or his address, each application program using the EMPLOYEE entity set with the attribute EMPLOYEE.*Address* would be required to update the address of that employee.

As shown in Figure 1.10, in a database environment data can be shared by these two applications. Their requirements can be integrated by the person (or a group of persons) who has the responsibility of centralized control. Such a person is referred to as the database administrator or DBA. The integrated version could appear as a record containing the following attributes: EMPLOYEE.*Name,* EMPLOYEE.*Soc_Sec_No,* EMPLOYEE.*Address, EMPLOYEE.Skill,* and EMPLOYEE.*Annual_Salary*. This integrated record type is shown in Figure 1.11. Note the inclusion of the

Figure 1.8 The view for the public relations application.

```
type EMPLOYEE = record
     EMPLOYEE.Name: string;
     EMPLOYEE.Address: string;
     end
```

Figure 1.9 The view for the payroll application.

type EMPLOYEE = *record*
EMPLOYEE.*Name: string;*
EMPLOYEE.*Soc_Sec_No: integer;*
EMPLOYEE.*Address: string;*
EMPLOYEE.*Annual_Salary: integer;*
end

attribute EMPLOYEE.*Skill,* which is not being used by either of the above described applications.

The integrated record EMPLOYEE described above can be considered a **conceptual record.** The views of the two applications it supports can be derived from it by using appropriate **mapping,** which in this case is done by simply hiding (i.e., masking out) the unnecessary attributes. The two views of this record as seen by the two applications are shown in Figure 1.12. Each application views only a portion of the conceptual record. The record each application is concerned with is called a **logical record.**

In addition to masking out the irrelevant attributes, it is possible to have a view that contains one or more attributes obtained by computation from the conceptual record. For instance, a new application that requires the monthly salary for each employee can be supported by the conceptual record of Figure 1.11. The monthly salary is derived by a simple computation on the data in the database for the attribute EMPLOYEE.*Annual_Salary*.

The application programs discussed above can continue to view the employee record in the same manner as before; however, they no longer are required to contain information about the file structure. Any change in the storage structure, storage

Figure 1.10 Database environment with shared data.

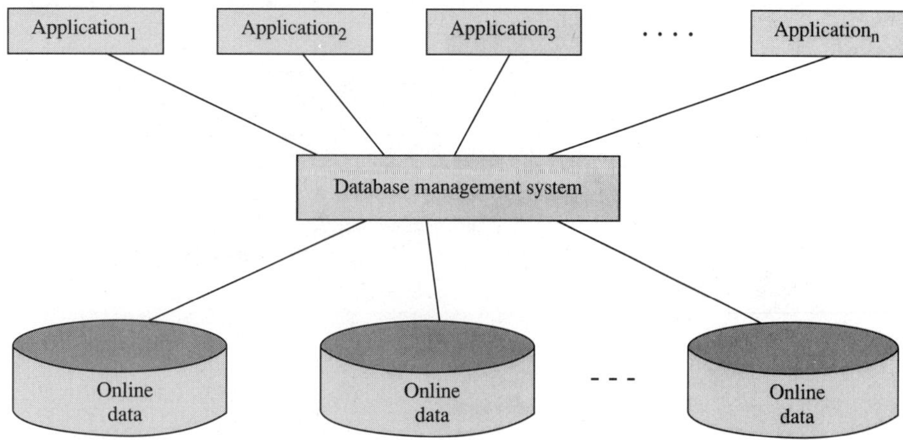

Figure 1.11 Integrated record definition.

type EMPLOYEE = *record*
EMPLOYEE.*Name: string;*
EMPLOYEE.*Soc_Sec_No: integer;*
EMPLOYEE.*Address: string;*
EMPLOYEE.*Skill: string;*
EMPLOYEE.*Annual_Salary: integer;*
end

device type, or access method is absorbed by the DBMS. Alteration of the application program is not required for such changes because data accessed by the application program is done via the DBMS.

Changes in the conceptual record do not affect the application programs. If a field such as EMPLOYEE.*Department* were added to the EMPLOYEE record and stored, the application programs discussed earlier would not require modifications. The database management system would simply be instructed to mask out this additional field from existing application programs. Similarly, the DBMS would insulate

Figure 1.12 Conceptual record and two views of it.

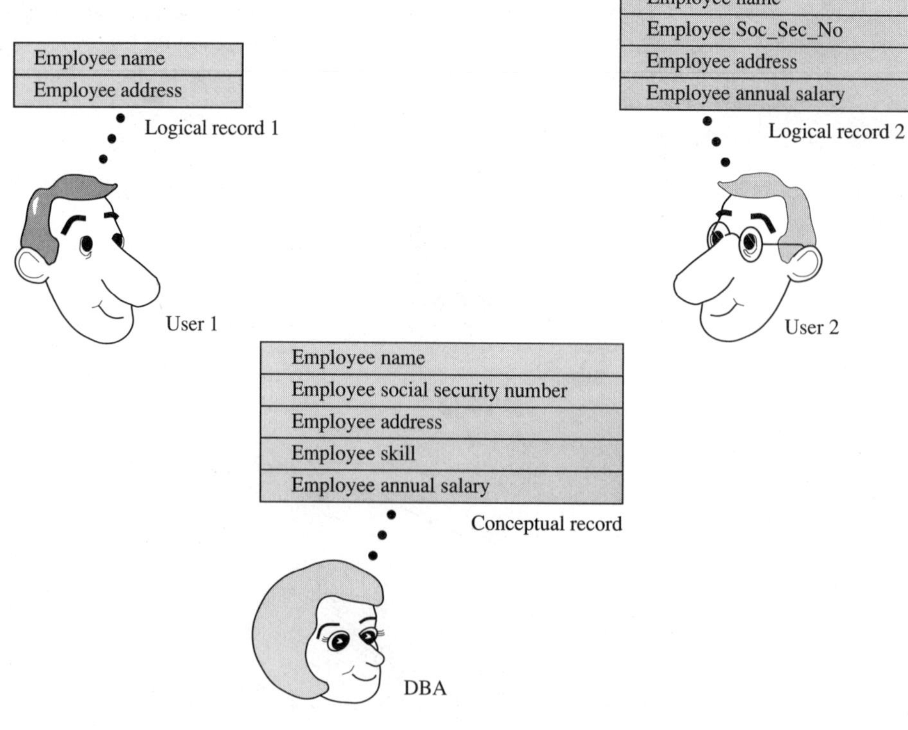

the application programs from any changes in the file structure or physical storage device storing the data.

Thus, in a nondatabase environment the logical record as viewed by the application program is identical to the conceptual record, and the physical record is determined and controlled by the application program. In a database environment, the logical record as viewed by the application program need not be the same as the conceptual record. In the above example, the logical record in each case is a simple subset of the conceptual record.

We have abstracted the data in three levels corresponding to three views as shown in Figure 1.13. The highest level, seen by the application program or user, is called the **external view, user view,** or simply **view.** The next level of abstraction is the sum total of users' views, called the **global view** or **conceptual view.** The

Figure 1.13 Three views of the data.

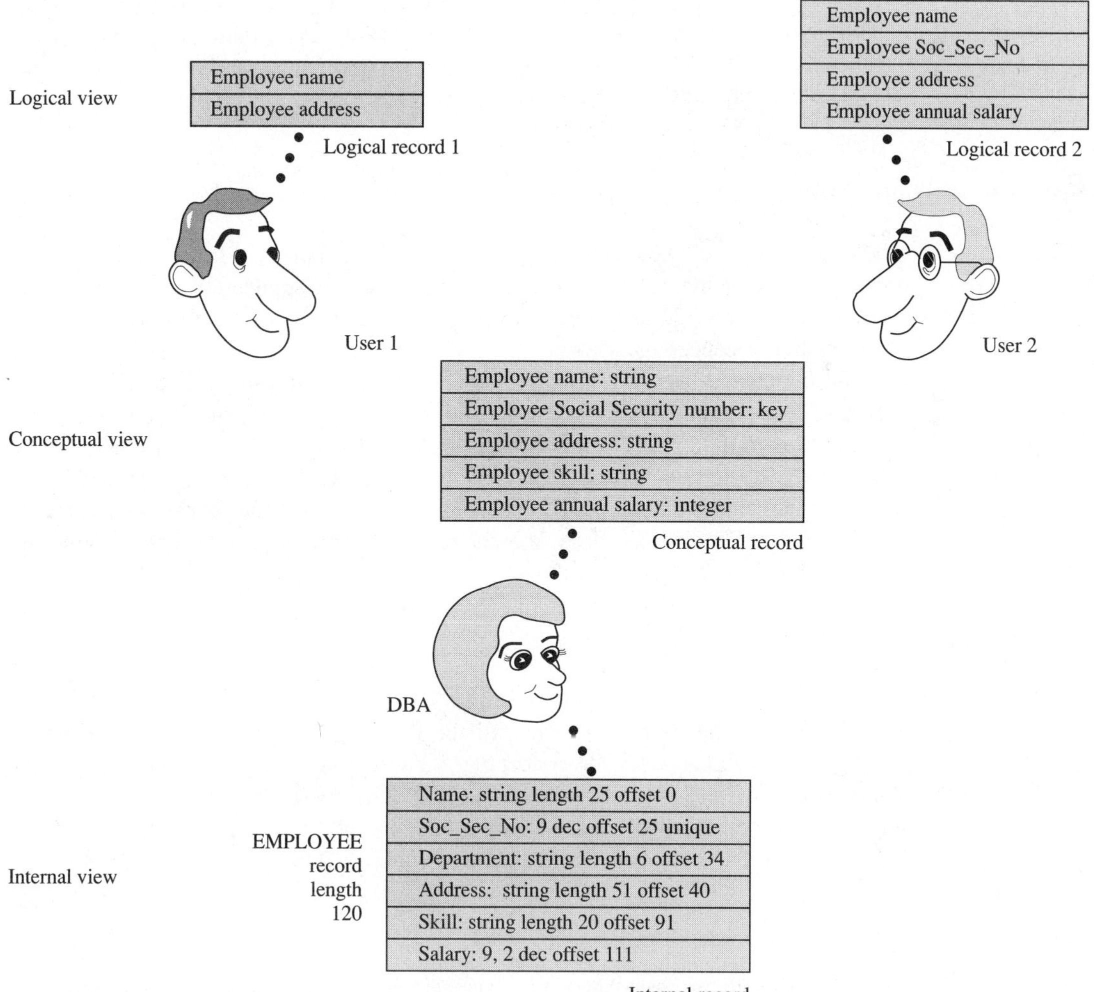

lowest level, a description of the actual method of storing the data, is the **internal view.** The database system can be designed using these levels of abstractions as described in the following section.

1.4 The Three-Level Architecture Proposal for a DBMS

In this section we describe the generalized architecture of a database system called the ANSI/SPARC[1] model. A large number of commercial systems and research database models fit this framework. The architecture, shown in Figure 1.14, is divided into three levels: the **external level,** the **conceptual level,** and the **internal level.**

The view at each of these levels is described by a **scheme.** A scheme is an outline or a plan that describes the records and relationships existing in the view. The word scheme, which means a systematic plan for attaining some goal, is used interchangeably in the database literature with the word **schema.** The word schemas is used in the database literature for the plural instead of schemata, the grammatically correct word. The scheme also describes the way in which entities at one level of abstraction can be mapped to the next level.

External or User View

The external or user view is at the highest level of database abstraction where only those portions of the database of concern to a user or application program are included. Any number of user views (some of which may be identical) may exist for a given global or conceptual view.

Each external view is described by means of a scheme called an **external schema.** The external schema consists of the definition of the logical records and the relationships in the external view. The external schema also contains the method of deriving the objects in the external view from the objects in the conceptual view. The objects includes entities, attributes, and relationships. (The terms view, scheme, and schema are sometimes used interchangeably when there is no confusion as to what is implied.)

Conceptual or Global View

At this level of database abstraction all the database entities and the relationships among them are included. One conceptual view represents the entire database. This conceptual view is defined by the **conceptual schema.** It describes all the records and relationships included in the conceptual view and, therefore, in the database. There is only one conceptual schema per database. This schema also contains the

[1] ANSI/SPARC: American National Standards Institute/Standards Planning and Requirements Committee

Figure 1.14 The three levels of architecture of a DBMS.

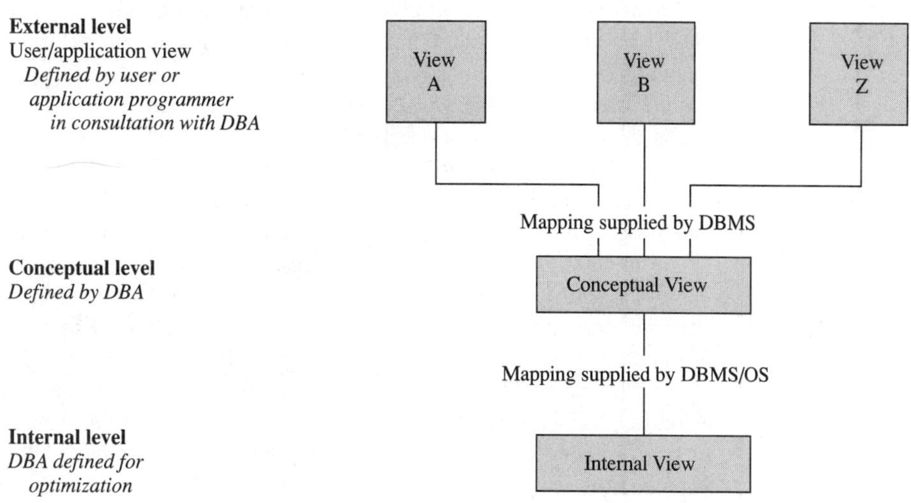

method of deriving the objects in the conceptual view from the objects in the internal view.

The description of data at this level is in a format independent of its physical representation. It also includes features that specify the checks to retain data consistency and integrity.

Internal View

We find this view at the lowest level of abstraction, closest to the physical storage method used. It indicates how the data will be stored and describes the data structures and access methods to be used by the database. The internal view is expressed by the **internal schema,** which contains the definition of the stored record, the method of representing the data fields, and the access aids used.

1.4.1 Mapping between Views

The **conceptual database** is the model or abstraction of the objects of concern to the database. Thus, the conceptual record of Figure 1.13 is the conceptual database and represents the abstraction of all the applications involving the entity set EMPLOYEE, for the present discussions. The view is the subset of the objects modeled in the conceptual database that is used by an application. There could be any number of views of a conceptual database. A view can be used to limit the portion of the database that is known and accessible to a given application.

Two mappings are required in a database system with three different views as shown in Figure 1.14. A mapping between the external and conceptual views gives the correspondence among the records and the relationships of the external and conceptual views. The external view is an abstraction of the conceptual view, which in its turn is an abstraction of the internal view. It describes the contents of the database as perceived by the user or application program of that view. The user of the external view sees and manipulates a record corresponding to the external view. There is a mapping from a particular logical record in the external view to one (or more) conceptual record(s) in the conceptual view. A number of differences could exist between the two. Names of the fields and records, for instance, may be different. A number of conceptual fields can be combined into a single logical field, for example, *Last_Name* and *First_Name* at the conceptual level but *Name* at the logical level. A given logical record could be derived from a number of conceptual records.

Similarly, there is a mapping from a conceptual record to an internal one. An internal record is a record at the internal level, not necessarily a stored record on a physical storage device. The internal record of Figure 1.14 may be split up into two or more physical records. The **physical database** is the data that is stored on secondary storage devices. It is made up of records with certain data structures and organized in files. Consequently, there is an additional mapping from the internal record to one or more stored records on secondary storage devices. This may have been implemented using some form of nonlinear addressing. The internal record is assumed to be linearly addressed. However, this complexity is managed by the DBMS and the user need not be aware of its presence nor be concerned with it.

Mapping between the conceptual and the internal levels specifies the method of deriving the conceptual record from the physical database. Again, differences similar to those that exist between external and conceptual views could exist between the conceptual and internal views. Such differences are indicated and resolved in the mapping.

Differences that could exist, besides the difference in names, include the following:

- Representation of numeric values could be different in the two views. One view could consider a field to be decimal, whereas the other view may regard the field as binary. A two-way transformation between such values can be easily incorporated in the mapping. If, however, the values are stored in a binary format, the range of values may be limited by the underlying hardware.
- Representation of string data can be considered by the two views to be coded differently. One view may perceive the string data to be in ASCII code, the other view may consider the data to be in EBCDIC code. Again, two-way transformation can be provided.
- The value for a field in one view could be computed from the values in one or more fields of the other view. For example, the external view may use a field containing a person's age, whereas the conceptual view contains the date of birth. The age value could be derived from the date of birth by using a date function available from the operating system. Another example of a computed field would be where an external view requires the value of the hours worked during a week in a field, whereas the conceptual view contains fields representing the hours worked each day of the week. The former can be derived from the latter by simple addition. These two examples of transformation between the external and conceptual views are not bidirectional. One cannot uniquely reflect a change in the total hours worked during a week to hours worked during each day of the week. Therefore, a user's attempt to modify the corresponding external fields will not be allowed by the DBMS.

Such mapping between the conceptual and internal levels is a correspon(that indicates how each conceptual record is to be stored and the characteristics and size of each field of the record. Changing the storage structure of the record involves changing the conceptual view to internal view mapping so that the conceptual view does not require any alteration.

The conceptual view can assume that the database contains a sequence of records for each conceptual record type. These records could be accessed sequentially or randomly. The actual storage could have been done to optimize performance. A conceptual record may be split into two records, with the less frequently used record (part of the original record) on a slower storage device and the more frequently used, record, on a faster device. The stored record could be in a physical sequence, or one or more indices may be implemented for faster access to record occurrences by the index fields. Pointers may exist in the physical records to access the next record occurrence in various orders. These structures are hidden from the conceptual view by the mapping between the two.

1.4.2 Data Independence

Three levels of abstraction, along with the mappings from internal to conceptual and from conceptual to external, provide two distinct levels of data independence: **logical data independence** and **physical data independence.**

Logical data independence indicates that the conceptual schema can be changed without affecting the existing external schemas. The change would be absorbed by the mapping between the external and conceptual levels. Logical data independence also insulates application programs from operations such as combining two records into one or splitting an existing record into two or more records.

Physical data independence indicates that the physical storage structures or devices used for storing the data could be changed without necessitating a change in the conceptual view or any of the external views. The change would be absorbed by the mapping between the conceptual and internal levels.

Logical data independence is achieved by providing the external level or user view of the database. The application programs or users see the database as described by their respective external views. The DBMS provides a mapping from this view to the conceptual view. The view at the conceptual level of the database is the sum total of the community view (current and anticipated) of the database There will be many external views, but only one conceptual view of a database. The users are only interested in that portion of the database that is described by their external view. It is an abstraction of the physically stored data and the user manipulates this abstraction.

Figure 1.15 gives the external views of the users from the public relations and payroll departments. Each of these external views is represented in a high-level language declaration in accordance with the normal rules of such languages. Figure 1.16 represents the conceptual level definition, using a similar facility for data definition. For simplicity, we have used the same names for both the external records and their components and the conceptual records and their components. However, the names used in each external view could be different and a correspondence is indicated between the names used in the external level and those in the conceptual level. Consequently, the way to derive the external view of the application program for the

Figure 1.15 External schemes of (a) user in public relations department and (b) user in payroll department.

type EMPLOYEE = *record*
EMPLOYEE.*Name: string;*
EMPLOYEE.*Address: string;*
end

(a)

type EMPLOYEE = *record*
EMPLOYEE.*Name: string;*
EMPLOYEE.*Soc_Sec_No: integer unique;*
EMPLOYEE.*Address: string;*
EMPLOYEE.*Salary: integer;*
end

(b)

public relations department given in Figure 1.15a from the conceptual view given in Figure 1.16 is to map the first and fourth fields of the record EMPLOYEE in the conceptual scheme into the first and second field of the record EMPLOYEE of the external scheme.

Figure 1.17 presents the internal level definition corresponding to the conceptual record type defined in Figure 1.16. The scheme indicates that the record EMPLOYEE is a record of length 120 bytes. There are six fields in this record and the scheme gives their sizes, types, and relative position from the beginning of the record. It also indicates that for faster access in random order, an index is to be built using the values from the primary key field EMPLOYEE.*Soc_Sec_No*.

Consider a change in the conceptual view such as merging two records into one or adding fields to an existing record. This would require a change in the mapping (for external views that are based on the records undergoing changes) from the external view to the conceptual view so as to leave the external view unchanged. However, not all changes in the conceptual schema can be absorbed by the adjustment of the mapping. Some changes, such as the deletion of a conceptual view field or rec-

Figure 1.16 Conceptual schema portion of database corresponding to Figure 1.15.

type EMPLOYEE = *record*
EMPLOYEE.*Name: string;*
EMPLOYEE.*Soc_Sec_No: integer primary key;*
EMPLOYEE.*Department: string;*
EMPLOYEE.*Address: string;*
EMPLOYEE.*Skill: string;*
EMPLOYEE.*Annual_Salary: integer;*
end

Figure 1.17 Internal schema of the portion of database corresponding to Figure 1.16.

```
type EMPLOYEE = record length 120
    EMPLOYEE.Name: string length 25 offset 0;
    EMPLOYEE.Soc_Sec_No: integer positive
                         9 dec digits offset 25
                         unique
                         use for index;
    EMPLOYEE.Department: string length 6 offset 34;
    EMPLOYEE.Address: string length 51 offset 40;
    EMPLOYEE.Skill: string length 20 offset 91;
    EMPLOYEE.Salary: integer positive 9,2 dec
                           digits offset 111;
    end
```

ord, may require changes in the external view and application programs using this external view.

Physical data independence is achieved by the presence of the internal level of the database and the mapping or transformation from the conceptual level of the database to the internal level. Conceptual level to internal level mapping, therefore, provides a means to go from the conceptual view (conceptual records) to the internal view and thence to the stored data in the database (physical records). If there is a need to change the file organization or the type of physical device used as a result of growth in the database or new technology, a change is required in the transformation functions between the physical and conceptual levels. This change is necessary to maintain the conceptual level invariant. Altering the physical database organization, however, can affect the response and efficiency of existing application programs. This may mean that while some application programs run faster, others may be slowed down. Regardless, no changes are required in the application programs themselves and they will run correctly with the new physical data organization.

The physical data independence criterion requires that the conceptual level does not specify storage structures or the access methods (indexing, hashing method, etc.) used to retrieve the data from the physical storage medium. Making the conceptual schema physically dataindependent means that the external schema, which is defined on the conceptual schema, is in turn physically dataindependent.

Another aspect of data independence allows different interpretations of the same data. The storage of data is in bits and may change from EBCDIC to ASCII coding, SI (metric) to imperial units of measure, or the data may be compressed to save storage space without affecting the application programs. In addition, a data field required by an application may be derived from one or several fields from one or more records of the database. As mentioned earlier, a field such as EMPLOYEE.*Age* may be derived from the stored field EMPLOYEE.*Birthdate* and from the calendar function DATE usually provided by the operating system. This is an example of a **virtual field.** Another such virtual field could be *Total_Hours_Worked_For_Week,* which is derived from the total of the seven entries for *Hours_Worked_During_Week* (record of hours worked on each day of the week). Note that unlike a real field, a virtual field may not be directly modified by a user.

1.5 Components of a DBMS

Let us now examine the components and structure of a database management system. A DBMS is a complex software system that is used to manage, store, and manipulate data and the metadata used to describe the data. It is utilized by a large variety of users, from the very naive to the most sophisticated, to retrieve and manipulate data under its control. The users could be utilizing the database concurrently from online terminals and/or in a batch environment via application programs written in a high-level language. Before looking at the various components of the DBMS, let us classify its users and examine the facilities it provides for the definition and manipulation of data.

1.5.1 Classification of DBMS Users

The users of a database system can be classified in the following groups, depending on their degree of expertise or the mode of their interactions with the DBMS.

Naive Users

Users who need not be aware of the presence of the database system or any other system supporting their usage are considered naive users. A user of an automatic teller machine falls in this category. The user is instructed through each step of a transaction; he or she responds by pressing a coded key or entering a numeric value. The operations that can be performed by this class of users are very limited and affect a precise portion of the database; in the case of the user of the automatic teller machine, only one or more of her or his own accounts. Other such naive users are end users of the database who work through a menu-oriented application program where the type and range of response is always indicated to the user. Thus, a very competent database designer could be allowed to use a particular database system only as a naive user.

Online Users

These are users who may communicate with the database directly via an online terminal or indirectly via a user interface and application program. These users are aware of the presence of the database system and may have acquired a certain amount of expertise in the limited interaction they are permitted with the database through the intermediary of the application program. The more sophisticated of these users may also use a data manipulation language to manipulate the database directly. Online users can also be naive users requiring additional help, such as menus.

Application Programmers

Professional programmers who are responsible for developing application programs or user interfaces utilized by the naive and online users fall into this category. The application programs could be written in a general-purpose programming language such as Assembler, C, COBOL, FORTRAN, Pascal, or PL/I and include the commands required to manipulate the database.

Database Administrator

Centralized control of the database is exerted by a person or group of persons under the supervision of a high-level administrator. This person or group is referred to as the **database administrator (DBA).** They are the users who are most familiar with the database and are responsible for creating, modifying, and maintaining its three levels.

The DBA is the custodian of the data and controls the database structure. The DBA administers the three levels of the database and, in consultation with the overall user community, sets up the definition of the global view or conceptual level of the database. The DBA further specifies the external view of the various users and applications and is responsible for the definition and implementation of the internal level, including the storage structure and access methods to be used for the optimum performance of the DBMS. Changes to any of the three levels necessitated by changes or growth in the organization and/or emerging technology are under the control of the DBA. Mappings between the internal and the conceptual levels, as well as between the conceptual and external levels, are also defined by the DBA. Ensuring that appropriate measures are in place to maintain the integrity of the database and that the database is not accessible to unauthorized users is another responsibility. The DBA is responsible for granting permission to the users of the database and stores the profile of each user in the database. This profile describes the permissible activities of a user on that portion of the database accessible to the user via one or more user views. The user profile can be used by the database system to verify that a particular user can perform a given operation on the database.

The DBA is also responsible for defining procedures to recover the database from failures due to human, natural, or hardware causes with minimal loss of data. This recovery procedure should enable the organization to continue to function and the intact portion of the database should continue to be available.

1.5.2 DBMS Facilities

Two main types of facilities are provided by a DBMS:

- The data definition facility or data definition language (DDL).
- The data manipulation facility or data manipulation language (DML).

Data Definition Language

Database management systems provide a facility known as **data definition language (DDL),** which can be used to define the conceptual scheme and also give some details about how to implement this scheme in the physical devices used to store the data. This definition includes all the entity sets and their associated attributes as well as the relationships among the entity sets. The definition also includes any constraints that have to be maintained, including the constraints on the value that can be assigned to a given attribute and the constraints on the values assigned to different attributes in the same or different records. These definitions, which can be described as metadata about the data in the database, are expressed in the DDL of the DBMS and maintained in a compiled form (usually as a set of tables). The compiled form of the definitions is known as a **data dictionary, directory,** or **system catalog.** The data dictionary contains information on the data stored in the database and is consulted by the DBMS before any data manipulation operation.

The database management system maintains the information on the file structure, the method used to efficiently access the relevant data (i.e., the access method). It also provides a method whereby the application programs indicate their data requirements. The application program could use a subset of the conceptual data definition language or a separate language. The database system also contains mapping functions that allow it to interpret the stored data for the application program. (Thus, the stored data is transformed into a form compatible with the application program.)

The internal schema is specified in a somewhat similar data definition language called data storage definition language. The definition of the internal view is compiled and maintained by the DBMS. The compiled internal schema specifies the implementation details of the internal database, including the access methods employed. This information is handled by the DBMS; the user need not be aware of these details.

Data Manipulation Language

The language used to manipulate data in the database is called **data manipulation language (DML).** Data manipulation involves retrieval of data from the database, insertion of new data into the database, and deletion or modification of existing data. The first of these data manipulation operations is called a **query.** A query is a statement in the DML that requests the retrieval of data from the database. The subset of the DML used to pose a query is known as a **query language;** however, we use the terms DML and query language synonymously.

The DML provides commands to select and retrieve data from the database. Commands are also provided to insert, update, and delete records. They could be used in an interactive mode or embedded in conventional programming languages such as Assembler, COBOL, FORTRAN, Pascal, or PL/I. The data manipulation functions provided by the DBMS can be invoked in application programs directly by procedure calls or by preprocessor statements. The latter would be replaced by appropriate procedure calls by either a preprocessor or the compiler. An example of a procedure call and a preprocessor statement is given below:

Procedure call: Call Retrieve (EMPLOYEE.*Name*, EMPLOYEE.*Address*)
Preprocessor statement: %select EMPLOYEE.*Name*, EMPLOYEE.*Address* *from EMPLOYEE;*

These preprocessor statements, indicated by the presence of the leading % symbol, would be replaced by data manipulation language statements in the compiled version of the application program. Commands in the conventional languages allow permissible operations on the database such as data retrieval, addition, modification, or deletion.

The DML can be procedural; the user indicates not only what to retrieve but how to go about retrieving it. If the DML is nonprocedural, the user has to indicate only what is to be retrieved. The DBMS in this case tries to optimize the exact order of retrieving the various components to make up the required response.

Data definition of the external view in most current DBMSs is done outside the application program or interactive session. Data manipulation is done by procedure calls to subroutines provided by a DBMS or via preprocessor statements. In an integrated environment, data definition and manipulation are achieved using a uniform set of constructs that forms part of the user's programming environment.

1.5.3 Structure of a DBMS

For our purposes, we may assume that the database management system is structured and interfaces with various users as shown in Figure 1.18. The major components of this system are described below.

Data Definition Language Compiler

The DDL **compiler** converts the data definition statements into a set of tables. These tables contain the metadata concerning the database and are in a form that can be used by other components of the DBMS.

Data Manager

The **data manager** is the central software component of the DBMS. It is sometimes referred to as the database control system. One of the functions of the data manager is to convert operations in the user's queries coming directly via the query processor or indirectly via an application program from the user's logical view to a physical file system. The data manager is responsible for interfacing with the file system. In addition, the tasks of enforcing constraints to maintain the consistency and integrity of the data, as well as its security, are also performed by the data manager. Synchronizing the simultaneous operations performed by concurrent users is under the control of the data manager. It is also entrusted with backup and recovery operations. We discuss backup and recovery, concurrency control, and security and integrity in Chapters 11, 12, and 13, respectively.

Figure 1.18 Structure of a database management system.

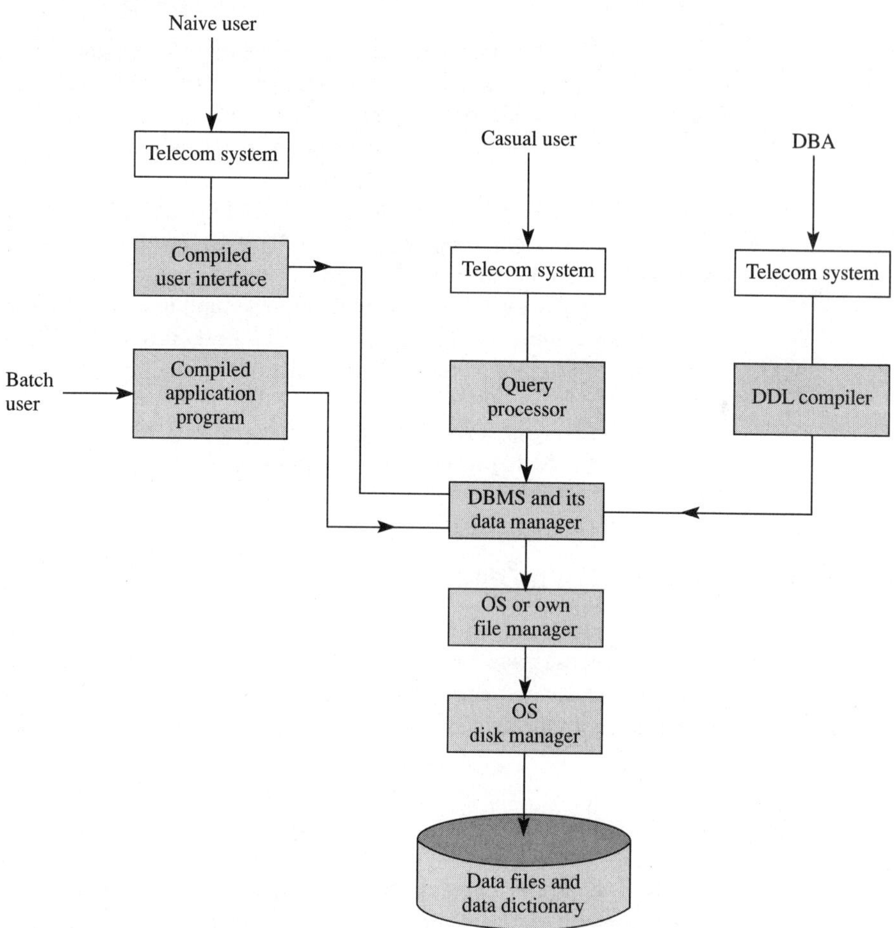

File Manager

Responsibility for the structure of the files and managing the file space rests with the **file manager.** It is also responsible for locating the block containing the required record, requesting this block from the disk manager, and transmitting the required record to the data manager. The file manager can be implemented using an interface to the existing file subsystem provided by the operating system of the host computer or it can include a file subsystem written especially for the DBMS.

Disk Manager

The **disk manager** is part of the operating system of the host computer and all physical input and output operations are performed by it. The disk manager transfers the block or page requested by the file manager so that the latter need not be concerned with the physical characteristics of the underlying storage media.

Query Processor

The database user retrieves data by formulating a query in the data manipulation language provided with the database. The **query processor** is used to interpret the online user's query and convert it into an efficient series of operations in a form capable of being sent to the data manager for execution. The query processor uses the data dictionary to find the structure of the relevant portion of the database and uses this information in modifying the query and preparing an optimal plan to access the database.

We now focus on the common method of using the database in an application program written in a high-level language (HLL) as illustrated in Figure 1.19. The data manipulation statements in the application program are replaced during a precompilation stage by a subroutine call to invoke the run-time system. The data manipulation statements are subsequently compiled separately into a sequence of optimized operations on the database that can be performed by the data manager. Many of the same optimization functions used by the query processors are also used in the compilation of the data manipulation statements. During execution, when a subroutine call inserted in place of the data manipulation statements is encountered, control transfers to the run-time system. This system in turn transfers control to the compiled

Figure 1.19 Processing database applications in HLL.

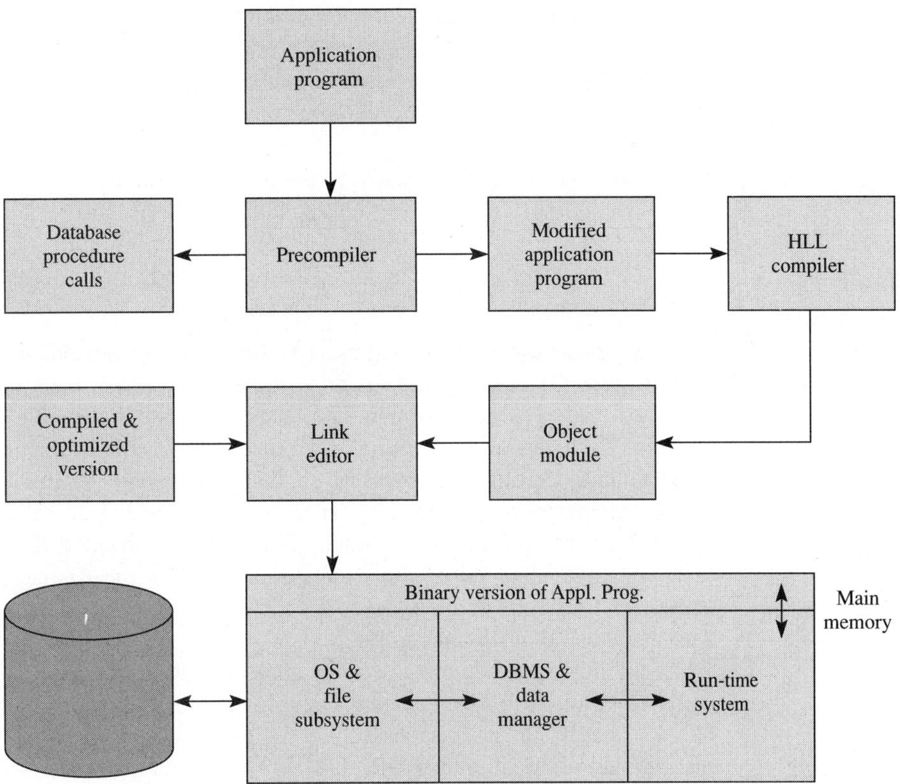

version of the original data manipulation statements. These data manipulation operations are executed by the data manager. The data manager transfers data to or from a work area indicated in the subroutine call and control returns to the application program.

For online users who manipulate the database through the intermediary of a user interface (such as a form-based or menu-driven system) and a supporting application program written in a high-level language, the interaction is indirect. A user action that requires a database operation causes the application program to request the service via its run-time system and the data manager.

Batch users of the database also interact with the database via their application program, its run-time system, and the data manager.

Telecommunication System

Online users of a computer system, whether remote or local, communicate with it by sending and receiving messages over communication lines. These messages are routed via an independent software system called a telecommunication system or a communication control program. Examples of these programs are CICS, IDMS-DC, TALKMASTER, and IERCOMM. The telecommunication system is not part of the DBMS but the DBMS works closely with the system; the subject is covered extensively in (Cyps 78). The online user may communicate with the database directly or indirectly via a user interface (menudriven or formbased) and an application program. Messages from the user are routed by the telecommunication system to the appropriate target and responses are sent back to the user.

Data Files

Data files contain the data portion of the database.

Data Dictionary

Information pertaining to the structure and usage of data contained in the database, the metadata, is maintained in a **data dictionary.** The term **system catalog** also describes this metadata. The data dictionary, which is a database itself, documents the data. Each database user can consult the data dictionary to learn what each piece of data and the various synonyms of the data fields mean.

In an integrated system (i.e., in a system where the data dictionary is part of the DBMS) the data dictionary stores information concerning the external, conceptual, and internal levels of the database. It contains the source of each data-field value, the frequency of its use, and an audit trail concerning updates, including the who and when of each update.

Currently data dictionary systems are available as add-ons to the DBMS. Standards have yet to be evolved for integrating the data dictionary facility with the DBMS so that the two databases, one for metadata and the other for data, can be manipulated using an unified DDL/DML.

Figure 1.20 Steps in data access.

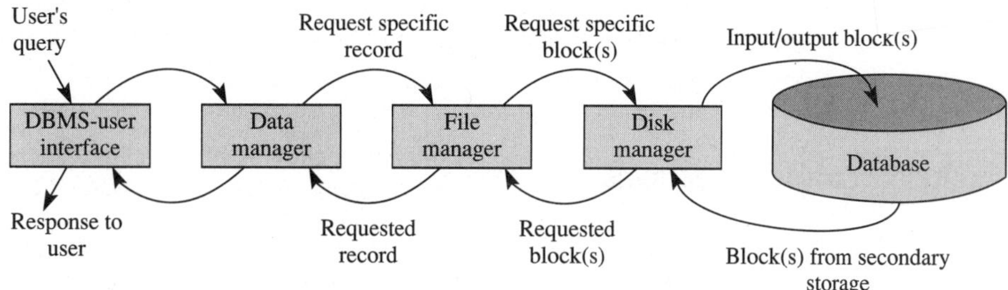

Access Aids

To improve the performance of a DBMS, a set of access aids in the form of indexes are usually provided in a database system. Commands are provided to build and destroy additional temporary indexes.

1.5.4 Database Access

Any access to the stored data is done by the data manager. The steps involved in database access can be summarized as shown in Figure 1.20.

A user's request for data is received by the data manager, which determines the physical record required. The decision as to which physical record is needed may require some preliminary consultation of the database and/or the data dictionary prior to the access of the actual data itself.

The data manager sends the request for a specific physical record to the file manager. The file manager decides which physical block of secondary storage devices contains the required record and sends the request for the appropriate block to the disk manager. A **block** is a unit of physical input/output operations between primary and secondary storage. The disk manager retrieves the block and sends it to the file manager, which sends the required record to the data manager.

1.6 Advantages and Disadvantages of a DBMS

Let us consider the pros and cons of using a DBMS.

1.6.1 Advantages of a DBMS

One of the main advantages of using a database system is that the organization can exert, via the DBA, centralized management and control over the data. The database administrator is the focus of the centralized control. Any application requiring a change in the structure of a data record requires an arrangement with the DBA, who makes the necessary modifications. Such modifications do not affect other applications or users of the record in question. Therefore, these changes meet another requirement of the DBMS: data independence, the advantages of which were discussed in section 1.4.2.

Reduction of Redundancies

Centralized control of data by the DBA avoids unnecessary duplication of data and effectively reduces the total amount of data storage required. It also eliminates the extra processing necessary to trace the required data in a large mass of data. Another advantage of avoiding duplication is the elimination of the inconsistencies that tend to be present in redundant data files. Any redundancies that exist in the DBMS are controlled and the system ensures that these multiple copies are consistent.

Shared Data

A database allows the sharing of data under its control by any number of application programs or users. In the example discussed earlier, the applications for the public relations and payroll departments could share the data contained for the record type EMPLOYEE described in Figure 1.11.

Integrity

Centralized control can also ensure that adequate checks are incorporated in the DBMS to provide data integrity. Data integrity means that the data contained in the database is both accurate and consistent. Therefore, data values being entered for storage could be checked to ensure that they fall within a specified range and are of the correct format. For example, the value for the age of an employee may be in the range of 16 and 75. Another integrity check that should be incorporated in the database is to ensure that if there is a reference to certain object, that object must exist. In the case of an automatic teller machine, for example, a user is not allowed to transfer funds from a nonexistent savings account to a checking account.

Security

Data is of vital importance to an organization and may be confidential. Such confidential data must not be accessed by unauthorized persons. The DBA who has the ultimate responsibility for the data in the DBMS can ensure that proper access procedures are followed, including proper authentication schemes for access to the DBMS and additional checks before permitting access to sensitive data. Different levels of security could be implemented for various types of data and operations. The enforcement of security could be datavalue dependent (e.g., a manager has access to the salary details of employees in his or her department only), as well as data-type dependent (but the manager cannot access the medical history of any employees, including those in his or her department).

Conflict Resolution

Since the database is under the control of the DBA, she or he should resolve the conflicting requirements of various users and applications. In essence, the DBA chooses the best file structure and access method to get optimal performance for the response-critical applications, while permitting less critical applications to continue to use the database, albeit with a relatively slower response.

Data Independence

Data independence, as discussed in section 1.4.2, is usually considered from two points of view: physical data independence and logical data independence. Physical data independence allows changes in the physical storage devices or organization of the files to be made without requiring changes in the conceptual view or any of the external views and hence in the application programs using the database. Thus, the files may migrate from one type of physical media to another or the file structure may change without any need for changes in the application programs. Logical data independence implies that application programs need not be changed if fields are added to an existing record; nor do they have to be changed if fields not used by application programs are deleted. Logical data independence indicates that the conceptual schema can be changed without affecting the existing external schemas. Data independence is advantageous in the database environment since it allows for changes at one level of the database without affecting other levels. These changes are absorbed by the mappings between the levels.

1.6.2 Disadvantages of a DBMS

A significant disadvantage of the DBMS system is cost.[2] In addition to the cost of purchasing or developing the software, the hardware has to be upgraded to allow for the extensive programs and the work spaces required for their execution and storage. The processing overhead introduced by the DBMS to implement security, integrity, and sharing of the data causes a degradation of the response and through-put times. An additional cost is that of migration from a traditionally separate application environment to an integrated one.

While centralization reduces duplication, the lack of duplication requires that the database be adequately backedup so that in the case of failure the data can be recovered. Backup and recovery operations are fairly complex in a DBMS environ-

[2]The costs of acquiring and using a database system are considerably lower for database systems on microprocessor-based personal workstations.

Figure 1.21 Pros and cons of a DBMS.

Advantages

Centralized control
Data independence allows dynamic changes and growth potential
Data duplication eliminated with controlled redundancy
Data quality enhanced
Security enforcement possible

Disadvantages

Problems associated with centralization
Cost of software/hardware and migration
Complexity of backup and recovery

ment, and this is exacerbated in a concurrent multiuser database system. Furthermore, a database system requires a certain amount of controlled redundancies and duplication to enable access to related data items.

Centralization also means that the data is accessible from a single source, namely the database. This increases the potential severity of security breaches and disruption of the operation of the organization because of downtimes and failures. The replacement of a monolithic centralized database by a federation of independent and cooperating distributed databases resolves some of the problems resulting from failures and downtimes.

The pros and cons of a DBMS system are summarized in Figure 1.21.

1.7 Summary

Data are facts from which a conclusion can be drawn; for this reason, humans record data. Data is required in the operation of any organization, and the same or similar data may be required in various facets of its functioning.

Entity sets are the categories of objects of interest to an organization for which the organization maintains data. To store the data about an entity set, a reasonable model of the entity is made by listing the characteristics or attributes that are of relevance to the database application. In order to uniquely identify a single instance of an entity set, a primary key is devised either from the attributes that are used to model the entity set or by adding such an attribute. The values for each attribute of an instance of an entity set are grouped together and this collection is called a record type. A file is a collection of identical record type occurrences pertaining to an entity set.

A database system is an integrated collection of related files along with the details about their definition, interpretation, manipulation, and maintenance. It is an attempt to satisfy the data needs of the various applications in an organization without unnecessary duplication. The DBMS not only makes the integrated collection of reliable and accurate data available to multiple applications and users, but also exerts centralized control, prevents fraudulent or unauthorized users from accessing the data, and ensures privacy.

The DBMS provides users with a method of abstracting their data requirements and removes the drudgery of specifying the details of the storage and maintenance of data. The DBMS insulates users from changes that occur in the database. Two levels of data independence are provided by the system. Physical independence allows changes in the physical level of data storage without affecting the conceptual view. Logical independence allows the conceptual view to be changed without affecting the external view.

A DBMS is a complex software system consisting of a number of components. It provides the user with a data definition language and a data manipulation language. The user defines the external and conceptual views by using the DDL and manipulates the data contained in the database by using the DML.

The data manager is the component of the DBMS that provides an interface between the user (via the query processor or the compiled application program) and the file system. It is also responsible for controlling the simultaneous use of the database and maintaining its integrity and security. Responsibility for recovery of the database after any failure lies with the data manager.

The database administrator defines and maintains the three levels of the database as well as the mapping between levels to insulate the higher levels from changes that occur in the lower levels. The DBA is responsible for implementing measures for ensuring the security, integrity, and recovery of the database.

Key Terms

database
database system
database management system (DBMS)
entities
entity type
entity set
relationship
attributes
domain
key
primary key
superkey
candidate key
alternate key
secondary key
relationship set
record type
record occurrence
field
file
metadata
view
conceptual record
mapping
logical record
external view
user view
global view
conceptual view
internal view
external level
conceptual level
internal level
schema
external schema
conceptual schema
internal schema
conceptual database
physical database
logical data independence
physical data independence
virtual field
database administrator (DBA)
data definition language (DDL)
data dictionary
directory
system catalog
data manipulation language (DML)
query
query language
compiler
data manager
file manager
disk manager
query processor
data files
block

Exercises

1.1 Explain the differences between a file-oriented system and a database-oriented system.

1.2 Consider the application program for the support of an automatic teller machine. How does such a program communicate with the user and the database?

1.3 Define the following terms:

metadata
data independence
database administrator
query processor
data manager
external view

1.4 Give the mappings required to derive (a) the conceptual record of Figure 1.16 from the internal record of Figure 1.17, and (b) the external records of Figure 1.15 from the conceptual record of Figure 1.16.

1.5 Suppose the field EMPLOYEE.*Address* of the internal record of Figure 1.17 is replaced by the following fields:

EMPLOYEE.*Street_Number: string length* 7 *offset* 40;
EMPLOYEE.*Street: string length* 20 *offset* 47;
EMPLOYEE.*City: string length* 16 *offset* 67;
EMPLOYEE.*State: string length* 2 *offset* 83;
EMPLOYEE.*Zip: string length* 5 *offset* 85;

What changes are required in the mappings of Exercise 1.4?

1.6 Consider an airline reservation database system in which travel agents are allowed online access to make reservations on any flight. Is it possible for two travel agents located in different cities to book their respective clients the last seat on the same flight? Explain your answer.

1.7 What problems are caused by data redundancies? Can data redundancies be completely eliminated when the database approach is used? Why or why not?

1.8 Why is data important to an enterprise? How does an enterprise that has better control of its data have a competitive edge over other organizations?

1.9 Choose from the following list an enterprise you are most familiar with: college or university, public library, hospital, fast-food restaurant, department store. What are the entities of interest to this enterprise? For each such entity set, list the attributes that could be used to model each of the entities. Are there any attributes (or collections of attributes) in each entity set that would uniquely identify an instance of the entity set? What are some of the applications that may be automated using the DBMS? Design the views of these applications and the conceptual view.

1.10 Softcraft Ltd. is a corporation involved in the design, development, and marketing of software products for a family of advanced personal computers. What entities are of interest to such an enterprise? Give a list of these entities and the relationships among them.

Bibliographic Notes

Bush (Bush 45) recognized the use of the computer in the analysis of large collections of data. Fry and Sibley (Fry 76) give the historic perspectives of the evolution of DBMS systems.

The Standards Planning and Requirements Committee (SPARC) of the American National Standards Institute (ANSI) via its Committee on Computers and Information Processing (ANSI/X3) established a Study Group on Database Management Systems in 1972. Its objectives were to determine if standardization was required in database systems. An interim report (ANSI 75, ANSI 76) proposed a framework for a database management system and its interfaces. The final report (ANSI 78) gave a description in greater detail of the generalized database system architecture and identified the interfaces.

Bibliography

(ANSI 75) ANSI/X3/SPARC Study Group on DBMS, Interim Report, vol. 7, no. 2. ACM SIGMOD, 1975.

(ANSI 76) The ANSI/SPARC DBMS Model: Proc. of 2nd SHARE Working Conf. on DBMS, Montreal, 1976. D. A. Jardine (ed.). New York. North-Holland, 1977.

(ANSI 78) "The ANSI/X3/SPARC DBMS Framework: Report of the Study Group on DBMS," D. C. Tscichritzis and A. Kings (eds.). Information Systems, 1978.

(Bush 45) V. Bush, "As We May Think," *Atlantic Monthly,* July 1945, pp. 101–108.

(Cyps 78) R. J. Cypser, "Communication Architecture for Distributed Systems," Reading, MA: Addison-Wesley, 1978.

(Fry 76) J. P. Fry & E. H. Sibley, "Evolution of Data-Base Management Systems," *Computing Surveys* 8(1), March 1976, pp. 7–42.

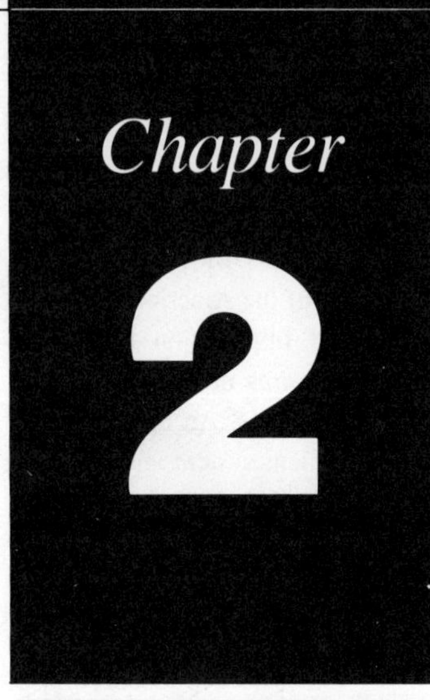

Data Models

Contents

In this chapter we look at the method of representing or modeling concrete and abstract entities. We introduce the concept of association among various attributes of an entity and the relationships among these entities. We also briefly look at the data models used in database applications. They differ in the method used to represent the relationships among entities.

2.1 Introduction

A model is an abstraction process that hides superfluous details while highlighting details pertinent to the applications at hand. A **data model** is a mechanism that provides this abstraction for database applications. Data modeling is used for representing entities of interest and their relationships in the database. It allows the conceptualization of the association between various entities and their attributes. A number of models for data representation have been developed. As with programming languages, there is no one ''best'' choice for all applications. Most data representation models provide mechanisms to structure data for the entities being modeled and allow a set of operations to be defined on them. The models can also enforce a set of constraints to maintain the integrity of the data. These models differ in their method of representing the associations amongst entities and attributes. The main models that we will study are the hierarchical, network, and relational models. Database management systems based on these models or variations thereof, are available from various software houses and are used to maintain corporate databases. In addition to these widely used models, others, such as the entity-relationship model, have been developed by researchers.

2.2 Data Associations

Information is obtained from raw data by using the context in which the data is obtained and made available, and the applicable conventions for its usage. For example, if we want to record the phone numbers of our friends, we usually keep a list as shown in Figure 2.1a. If we had simply written the list of the phone numbers as in Figure 2.1b, we might not be able to associate a number with a given friend. The only time we sometimes note only the phone number is when it is the only one on the list and is to be used within a very short time.

The association between Bill's name and his phone number is obtained by writing the name and number on the same line, and this mechanism, a simple data structure, is used to retrieve the corresponding information. It can also be used to modify the information if Bill changes his phone number.

When a large amount of data is stored in a database, we have to formalize the storage mechanism that will be used to obtain the correct information from the data. We have to establish a means of showing the relationship among various sets of data represented in the database. A relationship between two sets, X and Y, is a correspondence or mapping between members of the sets. A possible relationship that may exist between any two sets may be one-to-one, one-to-many, or many-to-many as shown in Figure 2.2.

Figure 2.1 Examples of telephone lists.

Bill	377-9219		371-5933
Jill	371-5933		377-9219
	(a)		(b)

2.2.1 Entities, Attributes, and Associations

Entities are distinguishable objects of concern and are modeled using their characteristics or attributes. Associations exist between different attributes of an entity. An **association** between two attributes indicates that the values of the associated attributes are interdependent. This correspondence between attributes of an entity is a property of the information that is used in modeling the object. It indicates that there is a constraint regarding the value that can be assigned to one of these attributes when a given value is assigned to the other.

We distinguish between the association that exists among the attributes of an entity, called an **attribute association,** and that which exists between entities, called a **relationship.**

Consider the employees of an organization. The organization maintains certain information about each employee, such as name, date of birth, a unique identifier such as an employee identification number and/or Social Security number, address, name and relationship the employee's dependents, and employment history, consisting of the positions held and the corresponding salary.

If we consider the association between an employee identification number and his or her Social Security number, we find that for a given employee identification

Figure 2.2 Different types of relationships between sets.

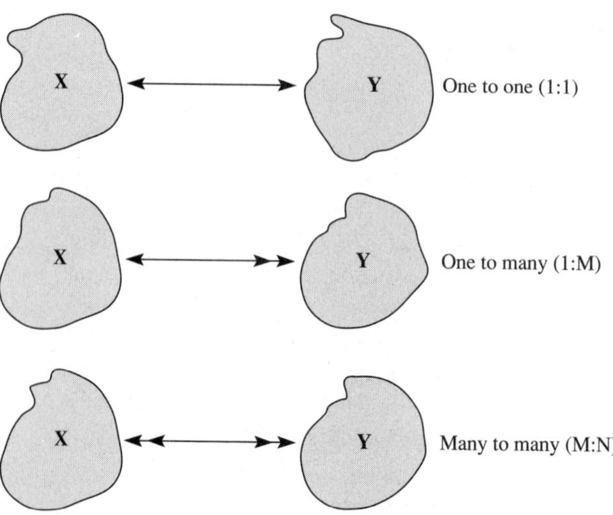

Figure 2.3 One-to-one association between attributes.

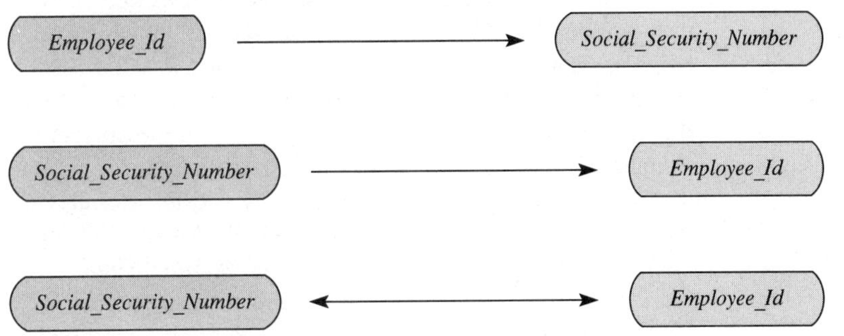

number there can exist only one Social Security number. Consequently, the association from the employee identification number to the Social Security number is unique. Similarly, the association from the Social Security number to the employee identification number is unique. The association between these attributes is therefore one to one. We can show this one-to-one association pictorially as in Figure 2.3. Here the attributes are shown as ovals and the association between the attributes is represented by a direct line. The arrow points to the dependent attribute in the attribute association.

Now consider the association between the attributes *Social_Security_Number* and *Employee_Name*. There can be only one *Employee_Name* associated with a given *Social_Security_Number*. Names are typically not unique. (This was demonstrated when the Nobel prize committee reached the wrong person while trying to contact the winner of the 1987 Nobel prize in chemistry. There were two persons with the same name in Los Angeles.) In a large organization, more than one employee could have the same name. A given *Employee_Name* has associated with it one or more *Social_Security_Numbers;* however, a given *Social_Security_Number* has only one corresponding name. These associations are shown in Figure 2.4. Here the double arrow indicates that for a given value of the attribute on the left side,

Figure 2.4 One-to-many association between attributes.

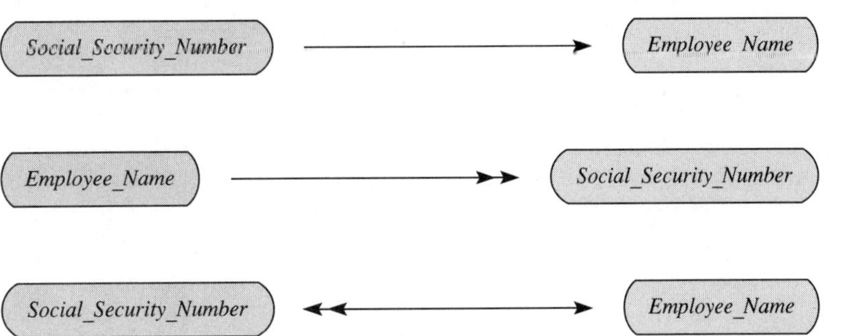

there could be one or more values for the attribute on the right side. The association between these attributes is one-to-many.

Consider the entity part with the attributes *Part#* and *Color*. *Part#* is a unique part number and *Color* represents the colors in which that part is available, there being a choice of one or more. In this instance the association from the attribute *Part#* to attribute *Color* is one-to-many. There could be many parts with a given color, thereby making the association between the attributes *Part#* and *Color* many-to-many. We show these associations in Figure 2.5.

Let us return to the employee entity and its attributes: *Employee_Id, Employee_Name, Address, Phone, Skill, Dependent_Name, Kinship_to_Employee, Position_Held, Position_Start_Date, Salary, Salary_Start_Date*.

There is one value for the attribute *Employee_Id* for a given instance of the entity type EMPLOYEE. It corresponds to the property that one employee is assigned a unique identifier. Similarly, there is one value for the attribute *Employee_Name* for one instance of the entity type EMPLOYEE. The value of the attribute *Employee_Name* depends on the value of the attribute *Employee_Id*. We show this dependence by the following notation:

Employee_Id → *Employee_Name*

to indicate that the (value of the) attribute *Employee_Name* is uniquely determined by the (value of the) attribute *Employee_Id*.

There could be many values of the attribute pair *Dependent_Name, Kinship_to_Employee* for a given instance of the entity EMPLOYEE to indicate that each employee could have many dependents. The multiple values of these attribute pairs depend on the value of the attribute *Employee_Id*. We show this dependence by the following notation:

Employee_Id →→ *(Dependent_Name,Kinship_to_Employee)*

Similarly, an employee could have held different positions with the organization and would have received increments in salary giving rise to the following associations from *Employee_Id:*

Employee_Id →→ *(Position_Held, Position_Start_Date)*
Employee_Id →→ *(Salary, Salary_Start_Date)*

An employee could have had many salaries for a given position and in the event been promoted without a salary increase, could have had many positions for a given

Figure 2.5 Many-to-many association.

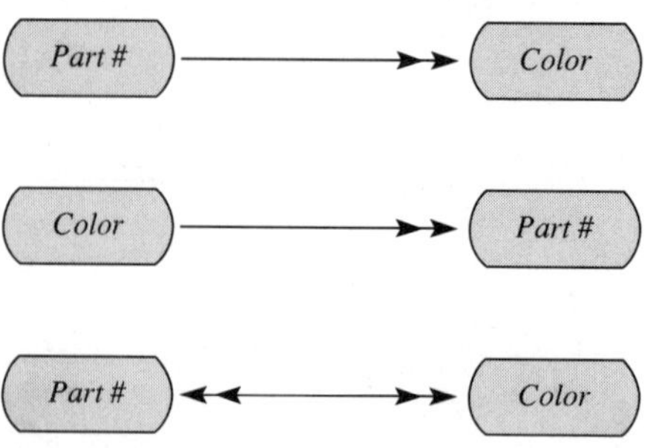

salary. Consequently, the association between *Position_Held* and *Salary* is many to many. We show this dependence by the following notation:

Position_Held ←←→→ *Salary*

The association of these attributes is shown in Figure 2.6.

In Figure 2.7, we show the associations among the attributes of an instance of the EMPLOYEE entity. The number 12345678 identifies the employee Jill Jones, who lives at 50 Main. She has a single phone number (371-5933) and two dependents, Bill Jones, her spouse, and her son Bob Jones. She has the skills of an electrical engineer and an administrator. She was a junior engineer from December 15, 1984 and an engineer as of January 20, 1986. Her starting salary was $38,000.00 with an increment on December 15, 1985 to $39,200.00 and again on May 15, 1986 to $42,000.00.

So far, we have considered only the associations between attributes belonging to the same entity type. The definition of a given entity, however, is relative to the point of view used. [One case is illustrated with respect to the EMPLOYEE entity in Section 2.2.3 and Figure 2.16, where the attributes *(Dependent_Name, Kinship_to_Employee)* are removed from the EMPLOYEE entity and a one-to-many relationship is established.] Consequently, there could be associations between any two attributes regardless of their entities. We can approach the design of a database by considering the attributes of interest without concerning ourselves with the associated entities. We look at the associations among these attributes and design the database, grouping

Figure 2.6 Association between attributes.

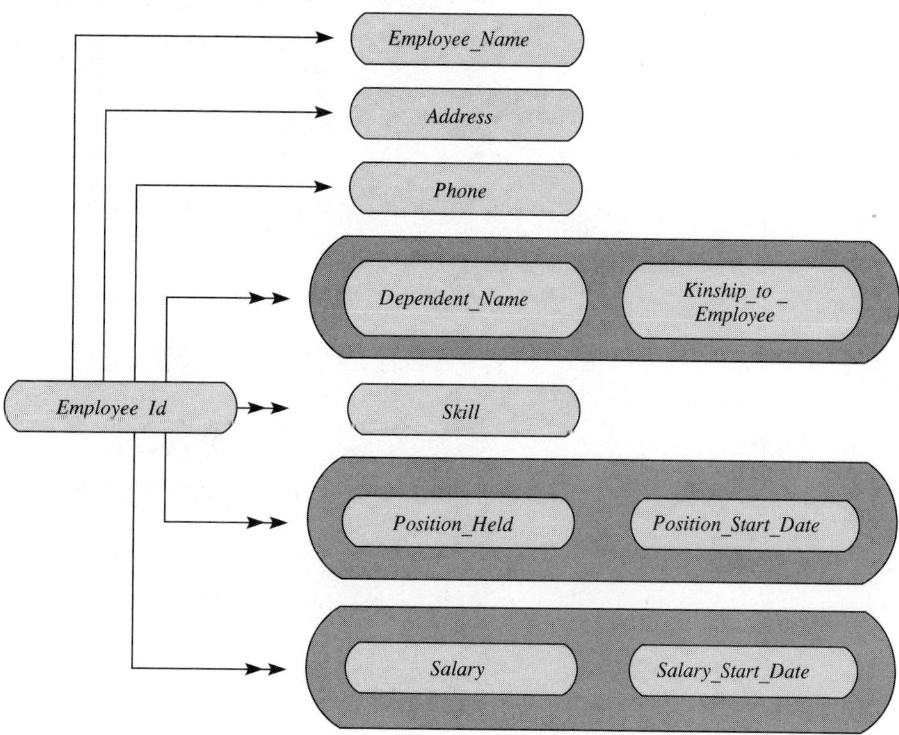

Figure 2.7 An instance of the entity set EMPLOYEE.

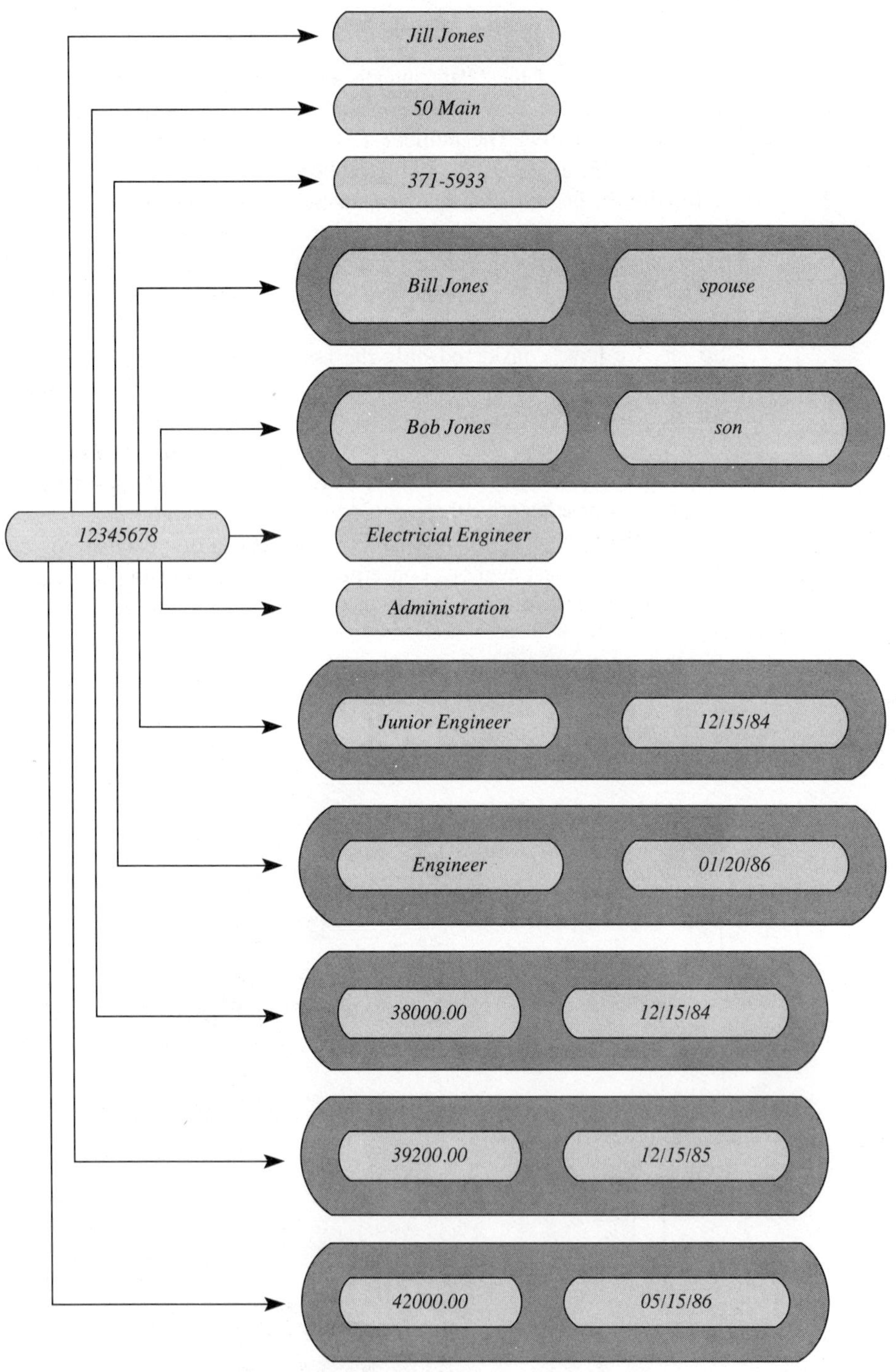

together those attributes that have a desirable association. Such an approach, called the synthesis approach, is discussed in Chapter 7.

Formally, the association or interdependence between attributes is called **functional dependency,** defined below.

Definition: **Functional Dependency:**

Given two sets of attributes X and Y, Y is said to be functionally dependent on X if a given value for each attribute in X uniquely determines the value of the attributes in Y. X is called the **determinant** of the functional dependency (FD) and the FD is denoted as $X \rightarrow Y$.

The process of identifying functional dependencies and selecting those attributes that should be grouped together in a given record is central to the process of database design. We deal with this topic in Chapter 6.

The primary key concept can be explained using the concept of functional dependency between attributes. Let X and Y be two sets of attributes of an entity type. If $X \rightarrow Y$ and if this dependency holds for all attributes Y in the entity and for all instances of the entity type, then X is a **candidate key.** For the entity type EMPLOYEE, the attribute *Employee_Id* is an example of a candidate key. Another candidate key for EMPLOYEE is the attribute *Social_Security_Number*. One of these candidate keys can be chosen as the **primary key.**

2.2.2 Relationships among Entities

In addition to the associations that exist between the attributes of an entity, relationships exist among different entities. Relationships are used to model the interactions that exist among entities and the constraint that specifies the number of instances of one entity that is associated with the others. Even though a relationship may involve more than two entities, we concentrate on the relationship between two entities because it is the most common type encountered in database applications. Such a relationship is known as a **binary relationship.** It may be one-to-one (1:1), one-to-many (1:M), or many-to-many (M:N). The 1:1 relationship between entity sets E_1 and E_2 indicates that for each entity in either set there is at most one entity in the second set that is associated with it. The 1:M relationship from entity set E_1 to E_2 indicates that for an occurrence of the entity from the set E_1, there could be zero, one, or more entities from the entity set E_2 associated with it. Each entity in E_2 is associated with at most one entity in the entity set E_1. In the M:N relationship between entity sets E_1 and E_2, there is no restriction as to the number of entities in one set associated with an entity in the other set.

To illustrate these different types of relationships, consider the following entity sets: DEPARTMENT, MANAGER, EMPLOYEE, and PROJECT.

The relationship between a DEPARTMENT and a MANAGER is usually one-to-one; there is only one manager per department and a manager manages only one department. This relationship between entities is shown in Figure 2.8. Each entity is

Figure 2.8 One-to-one relationship.

represented by a rectangle and the relationship between them is indicated by a direct line. The relationship from MANAGER to DEPARTMENT and from DEPARTMENT to MANAGER is both 1:1. Note that a one-to-one relationship between two entity sets does not imply that for an occurrence of an entity from one set at any time there must be an occurrence of an entity in the other set. In the case of an organization, there could be times when a department is without a manager or when an employee who is classified as a manager may be without a department to manage. Figure 2.9 shows some instances of one-to-one relationships between the entities DEPARTMENT and MANAGER. The sets of all instances of the entities are represented by the ovals.

A one-to-many relationship exists from the entity MANAGER to the entity EMPLOYEE because there are several employees reporting to the manager. As we just pointed out, there could be an occurrence of the entity type MANAGER having zero occurrences of the entity type EMPLOYEE reporting to him or her. A reverse relationship, from EMPLOYEE to MANAGER, would be many to one, since many employees may be supervised by a single manager. However, given an instance of the entity set EMPLOYEE, there could be only one instance of the entity set MANAGER to whom that employee reports (assuming that no employee reports to more than one manager). These relationships between entities are illustrated in Figure 2.10. Figure 2.11 shows some instances of these relationships.

The relationship between the entity EMPLOYEE and the entity PROJECT can be derived as follows: Each employee could be involved in a number of different projects, and a number of employees could be working on a given project. This relationship between EMPLOYEE and PROJECT is many-to-many. It is illustrated in Figure 2.12. Figure 2.13 shows some instances of such a relationship.

Figure 2.9 One-to-one relationships.

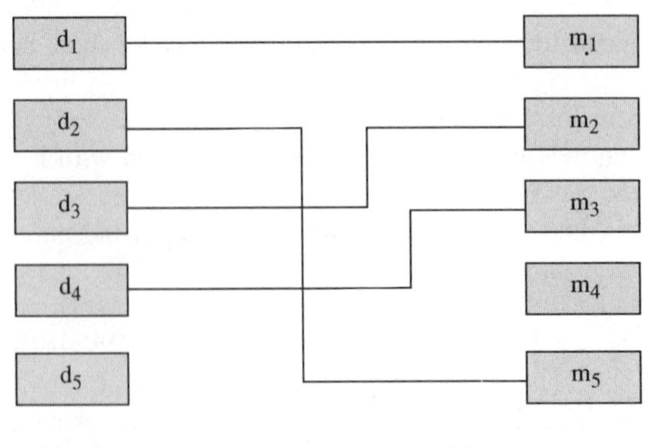

Figure 2.10 One-to-many relationship.

Figure 2.11 One-to-many relationships from MANAGER to EMPLOYEE and many-to-one reverse relationships.

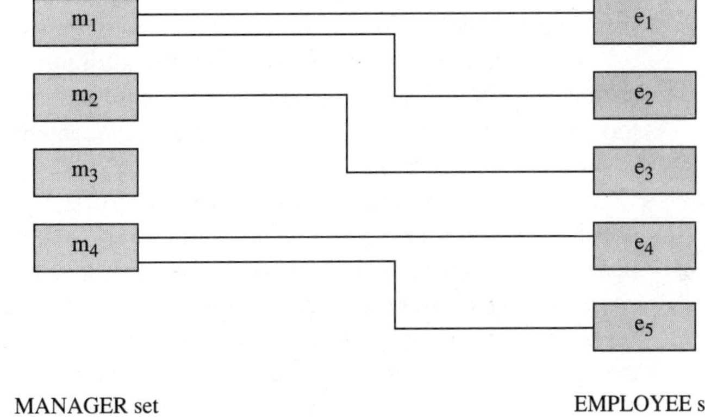

Figure 2.12 Many-to-many relationship.

Figure 2.13 Many-to-many relationships between EMPLOYEE and PROJECT.

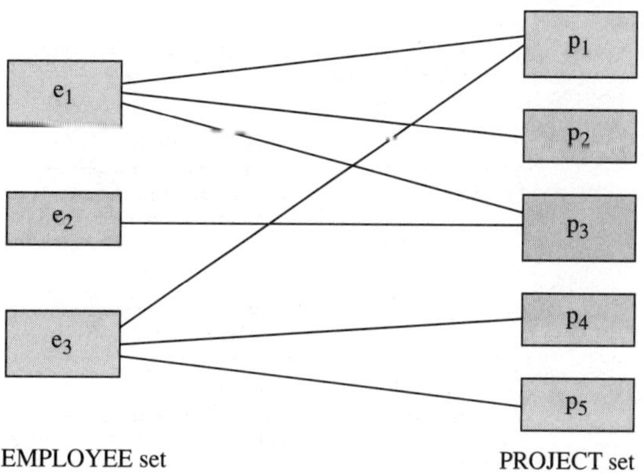

Figure 2.14 A one-to-many association between attributes of EMPLOYEE.

2.2.3 Representation of Associations and Relationships

In database modeling we have to represent both the attribute associations and the entity relationships. These representations are determined by the database management system's underlying data model.

One common way of representing the attribute associations is by grouping the attributes together. Such a grouping is a record and a representation of an entity. We look at this briefly below. The relationship between entities is represented in a variety of ways by the different data models.

When the association between sets of attributes is one-to-many, we can represent it by storing the attributes in a variable-size record. One case is the entity EMPLOYEE of Figure 2.6 and the one-to-many association between the attribute *Employee_Id* and *(Dependent_Name, Kinship_to_Employee)* as shown in Figure 2.14. Figure 2.15 is an example showing the record of Figure 2.7 with the multiple values of the attributes *Dependent_Name, Kinship_to_Employee,* and so on, repeated a number of times. The multiple sets of values for a set of attributes is known as a **repeating group.** Each repeating group is associated with a single value of the attribute *Employee_Id*.

The distinction between attribute association and entity relationship is difficult to make, especially when the perception of the object being modeled is modified. This observation leads to another method of representing a one-to-many association between sets of attributes. In this approach we separate each set of the entity's attributes having a one-to-many association into another entity. We then establish a one-

Figure 2.15 Representing a record.

repeating group
12345678 ¦ Jill Jones ¦ 50 Main ¦ 371-5933 | Bill Jones ¦ spouse ¦

repeating group / repeating group
Bob Jones ¦ son | Electrical Engineer ¦ Administration | Junior –

repeating group
Engineer ¦ 12/15/84 ¦ Engineer ¦ 01/20/86 | 38000.00 ¦

12/15/84 ¦ 39200.00 ¦ 12/15/85 ¦ 42000.00 ¦ 05/15/86

Figure 2.16 Converting an association to a relationship.

to-many relationship between the newly created entity and the original one (minus the attributes contained in the newly created entity). Therefore, in the entity EMPLOYEE, the attributes for the dependents can either be viewed as attributes of the entity or, as illustrated in Figure 2.16, as a distinct entity DEPENDENTS having a relationship to the modified entity denoted as EMPLOYEE*. Here entity EMPLOYEE* does not contain the attributes *Dependent_Name* or *Kinship_to_Employee,* which are the attributes of DEPENDENTS.

2.3 Data Models Classification

Data models can be classified as file-based systems, traditional data models, or semantic data models.

File-Based Systems or Primitive Models

Entities or objects of interest are represented by records that are stored together in files. Relationships between objects are represented by using directories of various kinds. We will not discuss **file-based models** here since there is no accepted standard for this method. The subject of files and different access aids, however, is discussed in Chapter 3.

Traditional Data Models

Traditional data models are the hierarchical, network, and relational models. The **hierarchical model** evolved from the file-based system and the **network model** is a superset of the hierarchical model. The **relational data model** is based on the mathematical concept of relation. The concept of data models evolved about the same time as the proposal of the relational model. A brief introduction of these data models is given in Sections 2.6, 2.7, and 2.8. We implement an example using these models and compare the implementations in Section 2.9. We return to an in-depth study of these models in Chapters 4 (relational model), 8 (network model), and 9 (hierarchical model).

Semantic Data Models

This class of data models was influenced by the semantic networks developed by artificial intelligence researchers. Semantic networks were developed to organize and represent general knowledge. **Semantic data models** are able to express greater interdependencies among entities of interest. These interdependencies consist of both inclusion and exclusion, enabling the models to represent the semantics of the data in the database.

In Section 2.4 we encounter the entity-relationship data model. It provides a means for representing relationships among entities and is popular in high-level database design. Other data models in this class are beyond the scope of this text.

2.4 Entity-Relationship Model

The **entity-relationship (E-R) data model** grew out of the exercise of using commercially available DBMSs to model application databases. Earlier commercial systems were based on the hierarchical and network approach. The entity-relationship model is a generalization of these models. It allows the representation of explicit constraints as well as relationships. Even though the E-R model has some means of describing the physical database model, it is basically useful in the design and communication of the logical database model. In this model, objects of similar structures are collected into an entity set. The relationship between entity sets is represented by a named E-R relationship and is 1:1, 1:M, or M:N, mapping from one entity set to another. The database structure, employing the E-R model is usually shown pictorially using **entity-relationship (E-R) diagrams.** The entities and the relationships between them are shown in Figure 2.17 using the following conventions:

- An entity set is shown as a rectangle.
- A diamond represents the relationship among a number of entities, which are connected to the diamond by lines.
- The attributes, shown as ovals, are connected to the entities or relationships by lines.
- Diamonds, ovals, and rectangles are labeled. The type of relationship existing between the entities is represented by giving the cardinality of the relationship on the line joining the relationship to the entity.

Figures 2.17, 2.21, and 2.22 depict a number of entity-relationship diagrams. In Figure 2.17, the E-R diagram shows a many-to-many relationship between entities

Figure 2.17 Entity-relationship diagram.

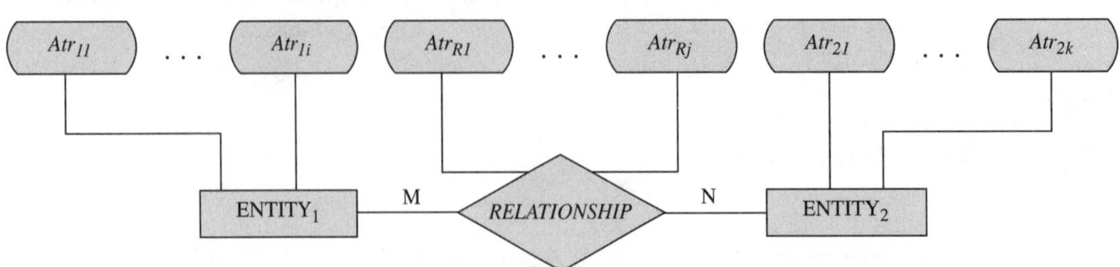

$ENTITY_1$ and $ENTITY_2$ having the attributes (Atr_{11}, . . ., Atr_{1i}) and (Atr_{21}, . . ., Atr_{2k}), respectively. The attributes of the relationship are (Atr_{R1}, . . ., Atr_{Rj}). The relationship *ENROLLMENT* in Figure 2.21 is many to many. In Figure 2.22, the relationship *MARRIAGE* is one-to-one and *REPORTS_TO* is one-to-many.

Before discussing the E-R model in more detail, we reexamine the two components of the E-R model: entities and relationships.

2.4.1 Entities

As discussed in Chapter 1, an entity is an object that is of interest to an organization. Objects of similar types are characterized by the same set of attributes or properties. Such similar objects form an entity set or entity type. Two objects are mutually distinguishable and this fact is represented in the entity set by giving them unique identifiers.

Consider an organization such as a hotel. Some of the objects of concern to it are its employees, rooms, guests, restaurants, and menus. These collections of similar entities form the entity sets, EMPLOYEE, ROOM, GUEST_LIST, RESTAURANT, MENUS.

Given an entity set, we can determine whether or not an object belongs to it. An object may belong to more than one entity set. For example, an individual may be part of the entity set STUDENT, the entity set PART_TIME_EMPLOYEE, and the entity set PERSON. Entities interact with each other to establish relationships of various kinds.

Objects are represented by their attributes and, as objects are interdistinguishable, a subset of these attributes forms a primary key or key for uniquely identifying an instance of an entity. Entity types that have primary keys are called **strong entities.** The entity set EMPLOYEE discussed in Section 2.2 would qualify as a strong entity because it has an attribute *Employee_Id* that uniquely identifies an instance of the entity EMPLOYEE; no two instances of the entity have the same value for the attribute *Employee_Id.* Figure 2.18 shows some examples of strong entities. Only the attributes that form the primary keys are shown.

Entities may not be distinguished by their attributes but by their relationship to another entity. Recall the representation of the entity EMPLOYEE wherein the 1:M association involving the attributes *(Dependent_Name, Kinship_to_Employee)* is removed as a separate entity, DEPENDENTS. We then establish a relationship, *DEDUCTIONS,* between the modified entity EMPLOYEE* and DEPENDENTS as

Figure 2.18 Strong entities.

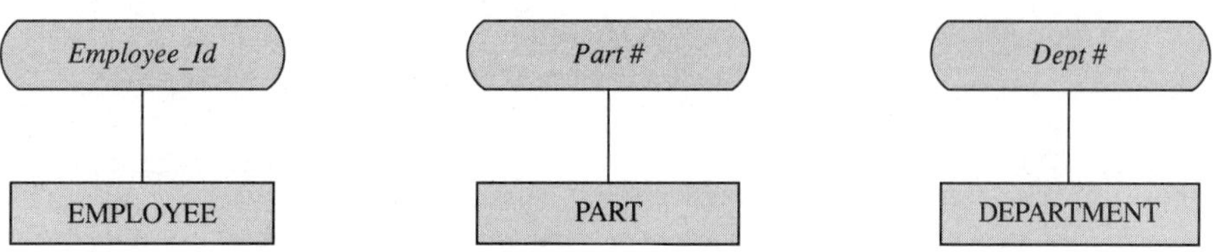

Figure 2.19 Converting an attribute association to a relationship.

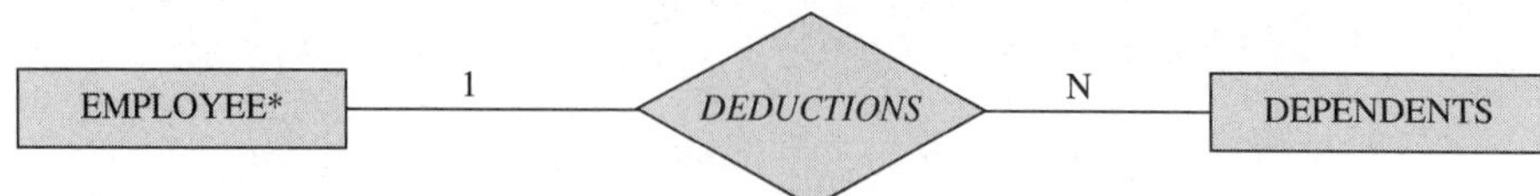

shown in Figure 2.19. In this case, the instances of the entity from the set DEPENDENTS are distinguishable only by their relationship with an instance of an entity from the entity set EMPLOYEE. The relationship set *DEDUCTIONS* is an example of an **identifying relationship** and the entity set DEPENDENTS is an example of a **weak entity.**

Instances of weak entity sets associated with the same instance of the strong entity must be distinguishable from each other by a subset of the attributes of the weak entity (the subset may be the entire weak entity). This subset of attributes is called the **discriminator** of the weak entity set. For instance, the EMPLOYEE 12345678 (Jill Jones) in Figure 2.7 has two DEPENDENTS, Bill Jones, spouse and Bob Jones, son. These are distinct and can be distinguished from each other. The organization could have another Jones in its employ (with given name Jim and *Employee_Id* = 12345679), who has dependents Lydia Jones, spouse and Bob Jones, son. This is illustrated in Figure 2.20. Note also that by adding attributes such as *Social_Security_Number* of the dependent to the weak entity it can be converted into a strong entity set. However, there may be no need to do so in a given application if there is an identifying relationship.

The two instances (Bob Jones, son) of the weak entity set DEPENDENTS associated with different instances of the strong entity set EMPLOYEE are not distinguishable from each other. They are nonetheless distinct because they are associated with different instances of the strong entity set EMPLOYEE. The primary key of a weak entity set is thus formed by using the primary key of the strong entity set to which it is related, along with the discriminator of the weak entity. We rule out the case where a dependent such as Bob Jones is the son of two different employees, namely his mother and father, since only one of them will claim him as a deduction!

Figure 2.20 Instances of a 1:M converted relationship.

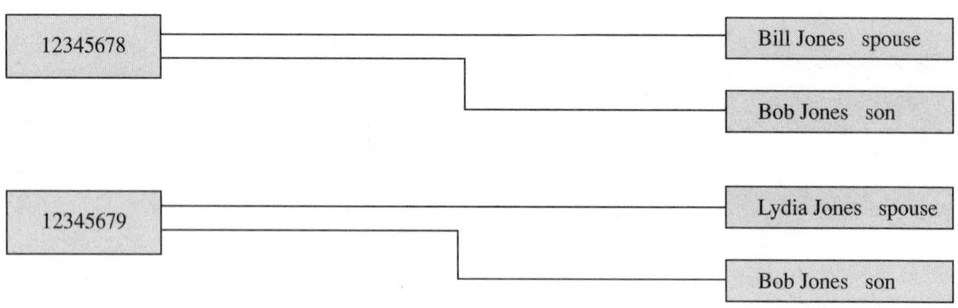

Figure 2.21 A binary relationship between different entity sets.

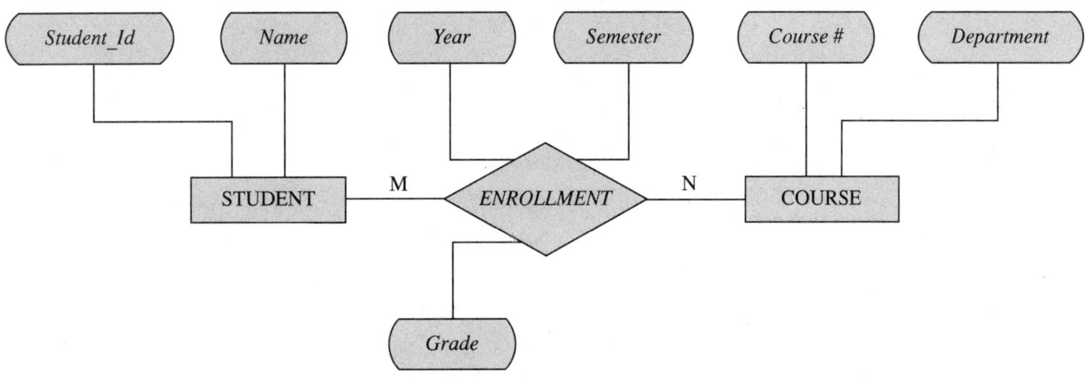

However, if we allow this possibility, the relationship between EMPLOYEE* and DEPENDENTS becomes many to many.

2.4.2 Relationships

An association among entities is called a relationship. We looked at a relationship indirectly when we converted a 1:M association into a strong entity, a weak entity, and a relationship. A collection of relationships of the same type is called a **relationship set.** A relationship is a binary relationship if the number of entity sets involved in the relationship is two. In Figure 2.21, *ENROLLMENT* is an example of a binary relationship involving two distinct entity sets. However, the entities need not be from distinct entity sets. Figure 2.22 illustrates binary relationships that involve the same entity sets. A marriage, for example, is a relation between a man and woman that is modeled by a relationship set *MARRIAGE* between two instances of entities derived from the entity set PERSON.

A relationship that involves N entities is called an **N-ary relationship.** In Figure 2.23, *COMPUTING* is an example of a **ternary relationship** involving three entity sets. *COMPUTING* represents the relationship involving a student using a particular computing system to do the computations for a given course.

Figure 2.22 Binary relationships involving the same entity sets.

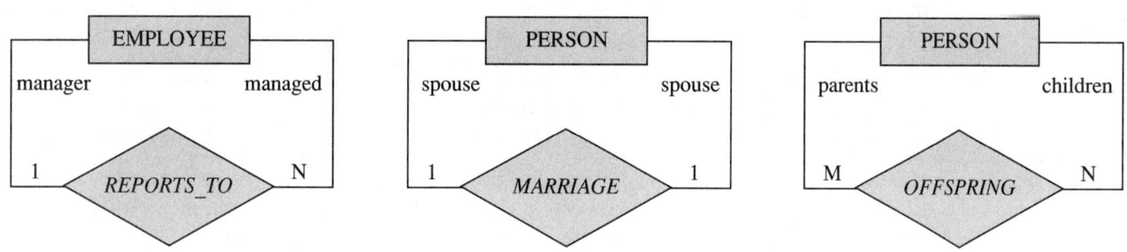

Figure 2.23 A ternary relationship.

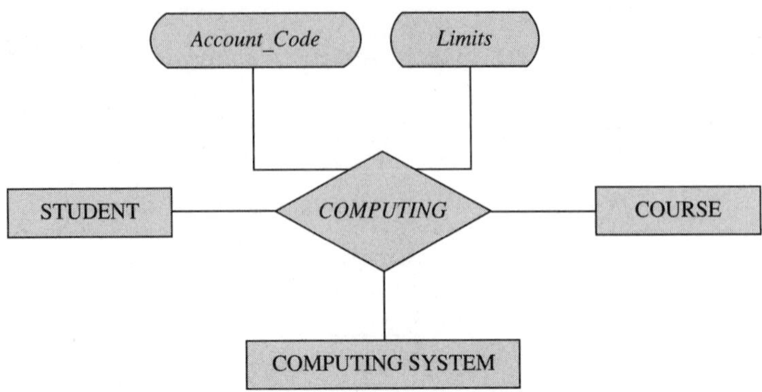

A relationship set or simply a relationship is formally defined as follows:

Definition:

Given the entity sets $E_1, E_2, \ldots, E_k$, not necessarily distinct, then the relationship **R** is a subset of the set defined as:

$$R \subseteq \{ e_1, e_2, \ldots, e_k \text{ such that } e_i \in E_i, i = 1 \text{ to } k \}$$

A relationship can be characterized by a number of attributes. In the case of the relationship *MARRIAGE,* we can identify the attributes *Date_of_Marriage* and *Place_of_Marriage*. Similarly, in the many-to-many relationship ENROLLMENT of Figure 2.21, the attributes of the relationship are *Year, Semester,* and *Grade*. The attributes of the ternary relationship *COMPUTING* of Figure 2.23 are *Account_Code* and *Limits* to indicate the accounting code and the computing limits assigned to a specific student for a given course on a particular computing system.

In a relationship the roles of the entities are important. This is particularly significant when some of the entities in the relationship are not distinct. Consequently, in an occurrence of a relationship from the relationship set *MARRIAGE* involving two members from the entity set PERSON, the role of one of the entities is that of a husband and the role of the other is that of a wife. Another role that can be assigned in a more symmetrical manner in this relationship is that of spouse, as shown in Figure 2.22. In some relationships the roles are implied and need not be specified. For example, in the binary relationship *ASSIGNED_TO* between the entity sets EMPLOYEE and DEPARTMENT, the roles of the two entities are implicit.

Identification of a relationship is done by using the primary keys of the entities involved in it. Therefore, in the relationship **R** involving entity sets $E_1, E_2, \ldots,$ E_k, having primary keys $p_1, p_2, \ldots, p_k$ respectively, the unique identifier of an instance of the relationship **R** is given by the composite attribute $(p_1, p_2, \ldots, p_k)$.

The composite attribute ($p_1, p_2, \ldots, p_k$) forms the primary key of the relationship **R.** An instance of the relationship **R** is represented by concatenating its attributes ($r_1, r_2, \ldots, r_m$) with the primary keys of the instances of the entities involved in the relationship. Figure 2.27 represents such a relationship.

2.4.3 Representation of Entities

Consider an application such as a hotel and its restaurants. Here we use a simplified version of the strong entity set EMPLOYEE with the following attributes: ***Empl_No,*** *Name, Skill.* The primary key for this entity is ***Empl_No.***

The entity set EMPLOYEE can be described as follows:

entity set EMPLOYEE
    Empl_No: **numeric;** (* primary key*)
    Name: **string;**
    Skill: **string;**

We represent the entity set EMPLOYEE by a table that can, for the sake of simplicity, be named EMPLOYEE. This table contains a column for each of its attributes and a row for each instance of the entity. We add a new instance of the entity EMPLOYEE by adding a row to this table. We also delete or modify rows to reflect changes that occur when employees leave or upgrade their skills. Figure 2.24 depicts an EMPLOYEE table. (We assume that each employee has but one skill.)

The weak entity DEPENDENTS, having as before the attributes *Dependent_Name* and *Kinship_to_Employee,* is dependent on the strong entity EMPLOYEE. We represent the weak entity by the table DEPENDENTS, which contains a column for the primary key of the strong entity EMPLOYEE. The DEPENDENTS table in Figure 2.25 includes instances of the weak entities (Rick, spouse) and (Chloe, daughter), which are dependent on EMPLOYEE 123459.

In general, to represent a weak entity such as W with the attributes $w_1, w_2, w_3, \ldots, w_n$ such that the weak entity is dependent on strong entity S with the primary key $s_1, s_2, \ldots, s_p$, we use a table with a column for each of the above attributes.

Figure 2.24 The EMPLOYEE table.

EMPLOYEE

Empl_No	*Name*	*Skill*
123456	Ron	waiter
123457	Jon	bartender
123458	Don	busboy
123459	Pam	hostess
123460	Pat	bellboy
123461	Ian	maître d'

Figure 2.25 The DEPENDENTS table.

DEPENDENTS

Empl_No	*Name*	*Kinship_to_Employee*
123459	Rick	spouse
123459	Chloe	daughter
123458	Cathy	spouse

2.4.4 Representation of Relationship Set

The entity-relationship diagrams are useful in representing the relationships among entities. They show the logical model of the database. In Figure 2.26, an E-R diagram shows the relationship between the entity sets EMPLOYEE and POSITION. The relationship set is called *DUTY_ALLOCATION* and its attributes are *Date* and *Shift*.

A relationship set involving entity sets E_1, E_2, . . . , E_n can be represented via a record containing the primary key of each of the entities E_i and the attributes of the relationship. Where the relationship has no attributes, only the primary keys of the entity involved are used to represent the relationship set.

Data for an E-R relationship could be represented by a number of tables. Each of the entities involved in the relationship is represented by a table, as is the relationship among these entities. The relationship *DUTY_ALLOCATION* between the entities EMPLOYEE and POSITION, shown in Figure 2.26, is represented by three tables displayed in Figure 2.27.

The table EMPLOYEE contains data about the entities representing the hotel employees. POSITION contains data on the duties to be performed by the hotel's employees in the restaurants run by the hotel. A relationship set is also represented by a table. *DUTY_ALLOCATION* is represented by the table DUTY_ALLOCATION, which contains the primary keys of the entities EMPLOYEE and POSITION along with the attributes of the relationship *Date* and *Shift*.

Figure 2.26 E-R diagram showing *DUTY_ALLOCATION* relationship between entity sets EMPLOYEE and POSITION.

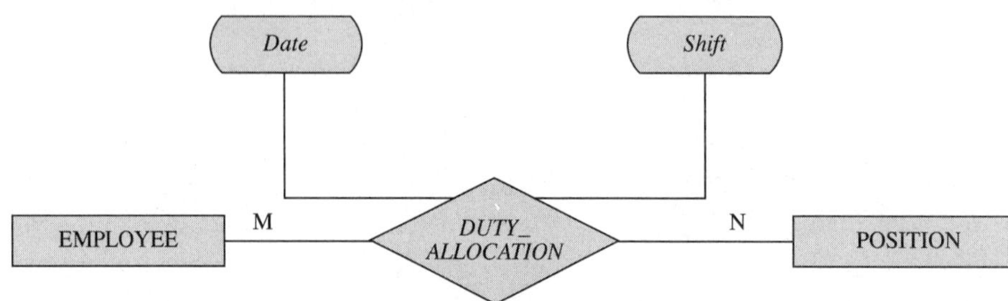

Figure 2.27 Representation of a relationship.

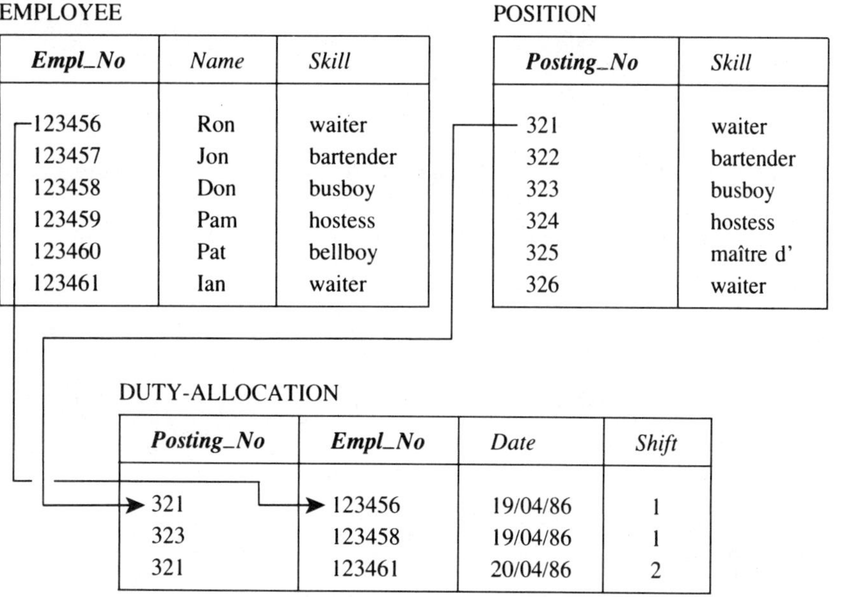

EMPLOYEE

Empl_No	*Name*	*Skill*
123456	Ron	waiter
123457	Jon	bartender
123458	Don	busboy
123459	Pam	hostess
123460	Pat	bellboy
123461	Ian	waiter

POSITION

Posting_No	*Skill*
321	waiter
322	bartender
323	busboy
324	hostess
325	maître d'
326	waiter

DUTY-ALLOCATION

Posting_No	*Empl_No*	*Date*	*Shift*
321	123456	19/04/86	1
323	123458	19/04/86	1
321	123461	20/04/86	2

2.4.5 Generalization and Aggregation

Abstraction is the simplification mechanism used to hide superfluous details of a set of objects, it allows one to concentrate on the properties that are of interest to the application. As such, car is an abstraction of a personal transportation vehicle but does not reveal details about model, year, color, and so on. Vehicle itself is an abstraction that includes the types car, truck, and bus.

There are two main abstraction mechanisms used to model information: generalization and aggregation. **Generalization** is the abstracting process of viewing sets of objects as a single general class by concentrating on the general characteristics of the constituent sets while suppressing or ignoring their differences. It is the union of a number of lower-level entity types for the purpose of producing a higher-level entity type. For instance, student is a generalization of graduate or undergraduate, full-time or part-time students. Similarly, employee is a generalization of the classes of objects cook, waiter, cashier, maître d'. Generalization is an *IS_A* relationship; therefore, manager *IS_An* employee, cook *IS_An* employee, waiter *IS_An* employee, and so forth. **Specialization** is the abstracting process of introducing new characteristics to an existing class of objects to create one or more new classes of objects. This involves taking a higher-level entity and, using additional characteristics, generating lower-level entities. The lower-level entities also inherit the characteristics of the higher-level entity. In applying the characteristic *size* to car we can create a full-size, mid-size, compact, or subcompact car. Specialization may be seen as the reverse process of generalization: additional specific properties are introduced at a lower level in a hierarchy of objects. Both processes are illustrated in Figure 2.28 wherein the lower levels of the hierarchy are disjoint.

Figure 2.28 Generalization and specialization.

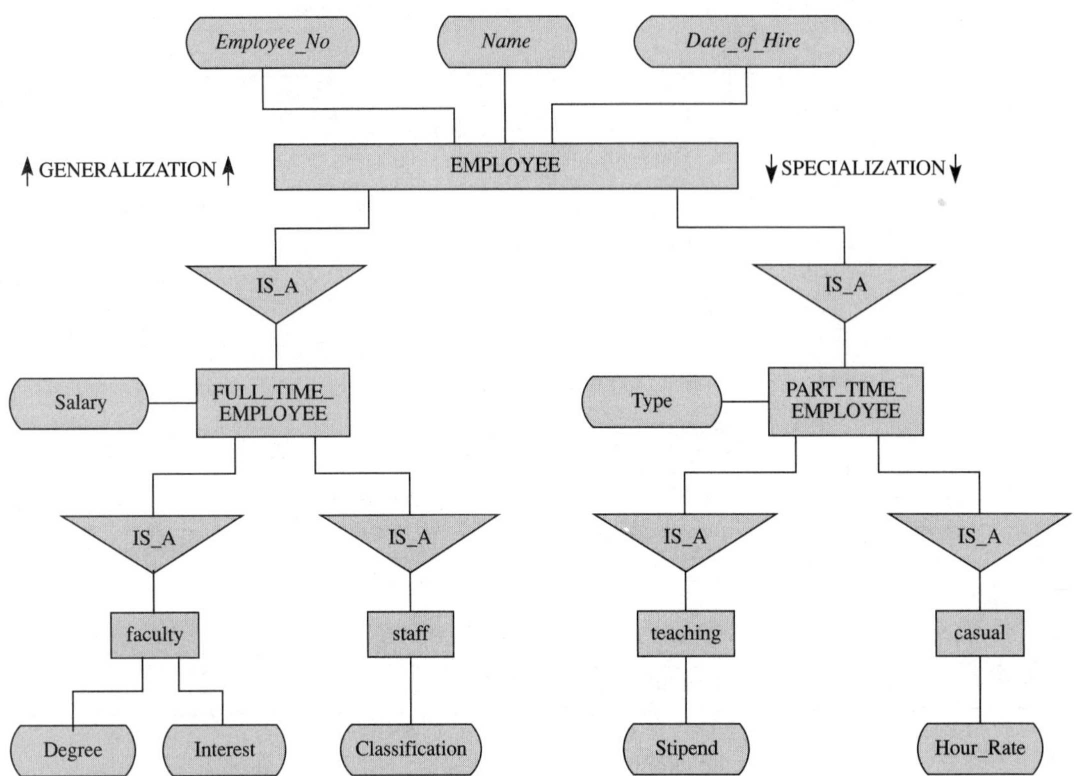

The entity set EMPLOYEE is a generalization of the entity sets FULL_TIME_EMPLOYEE and PART_TIME_EMPLOYEE. The former is a generalization of the entity sets faculty and staff; the latter, that of the entity sets TEACHING and CASUAL. FACULTY and STAFF inherit the attribute *Salary* of the entity set FULL_TIME_EMPLOYEE and the latter, in turn, inherits the attributes of EMPLOYEE. FULL_TIME_EMPLOYEE is a specialization of the entity set EMPLOYEE and is differentiated by the additional attribute *Salary*. Similarly, PART_TIME_EMPLOYEE is a specialization differentiated by the presence of the attribute *Type*.

In designing a database to model a segment of the real world, the data modeling scheme must be able to represent generalization. It allows the model to represent generic entities and treat a class of objects uniformly by assigning attributes common to the class of objects and specifying relationships in which the generic objects participate.

Generalization forms a hierarchy of entities and can be represented by a hierarchy of tables as shown in Figure 2.29. Here the primary key of each entity corresponds to entries in different tables and directs one to the appropriate row of related tables.

Another method of representing a generalization hierarchy is to have the lowest-level entities inherit the attributes of the entities of higher levels. The top and intermediate-level entities are not included as only those of the lowest level are repre-

Figure 2.29 Tabular representation of a generalization hierarchy.

EMPLOYEE

Empl_No	*Name*	*Date_of_Hire*
23456	Sheila	81/04/27
23457	Jerry	85/07/16
23458	Pavan	86/02/27
23459	Rajen	87/03/16
23460	Lettie	88/01/31
23461	Drew	88/09/20

FULL_TIME

Empl_No	*Salary*
23456	57000
23457	48000
23458	24500

PART_TIME

Empl_No	*Type*
23459	permanent
23460	sessional
23461	sessional

FACULTY

Empl_No	*Degree*	*Interest*
23456	MSc	ecology
23457	PhD	physics

STAFF

Empl_No	*Classification*
23458	secretary 6

TEACHING

Empl_No	*Stipend*
23460	5000
23461	5000

CASUAL

Empl_No	*Hour_Rate*
23459	14.25

sented in tabular form. For instance, the attributes of the entity set FACULTY would be {***Empl_No***, *Name, Date_of_Hire, Salary, Degree, Interest*}. A sample table representation for this entity set is given in Figure 2.30. A separate table would be required for each lowest-level entity in the hierarchy. The number of different tables required to represent these entities would be equal to the number of entities at the lowest level of the generalization hierarchy.

Figure 2.30 Tabular representation of entity set FACULTY with inherited attributes.

FACULTY

Empl_No	*Name*	*Date_of_Hire*	*Salary*	*Degree*	*Interest*
23456	Sheila	81/04/27	57000	MSc	ecology
23457	Jerry	85/07/16	48000	PhD	physics

Aggregation is the process of compiling information on an object, thereby abstracting a higher-level object. In this manner, the entity person is derived by aggregating the characteristics name, address, and Social Security number. Another form of aggregation is abstracting a relationship between objects and viewing the relationship as an object. As such, the *ENROLLMENT* relationship between entities student and course could be viewed as entity REGISTRATION. Examples of aggregations are shown in Figure 2.31.

Consider the ternary relationship *COMPUTING* of Figure 2.23. Here we have a relationship among the entities STUDENT, COURSE, and COMPUTING SYSTEM.

Figure 2.31 Examples of aggregation.

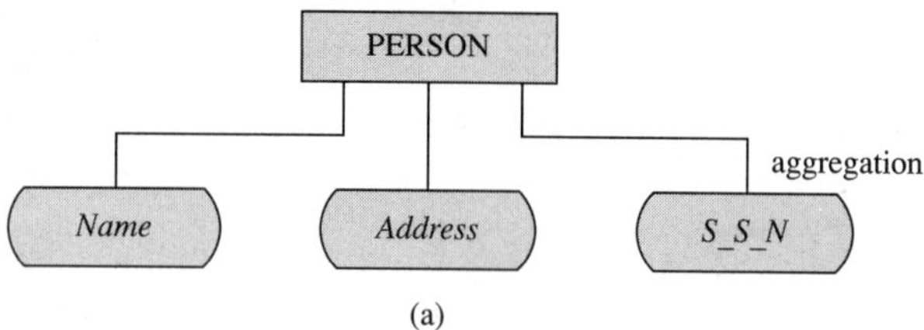

(a)

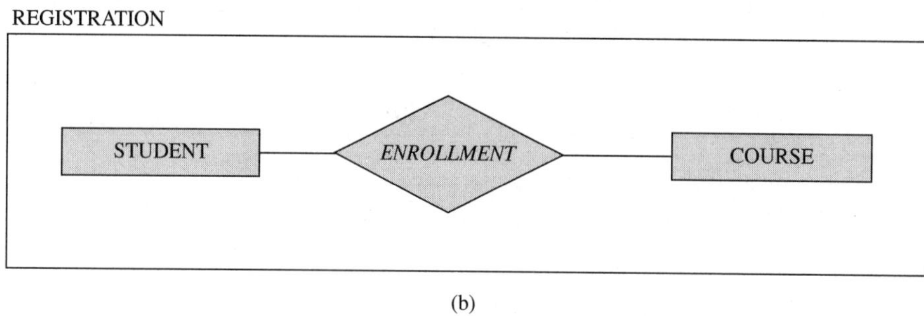

(b)

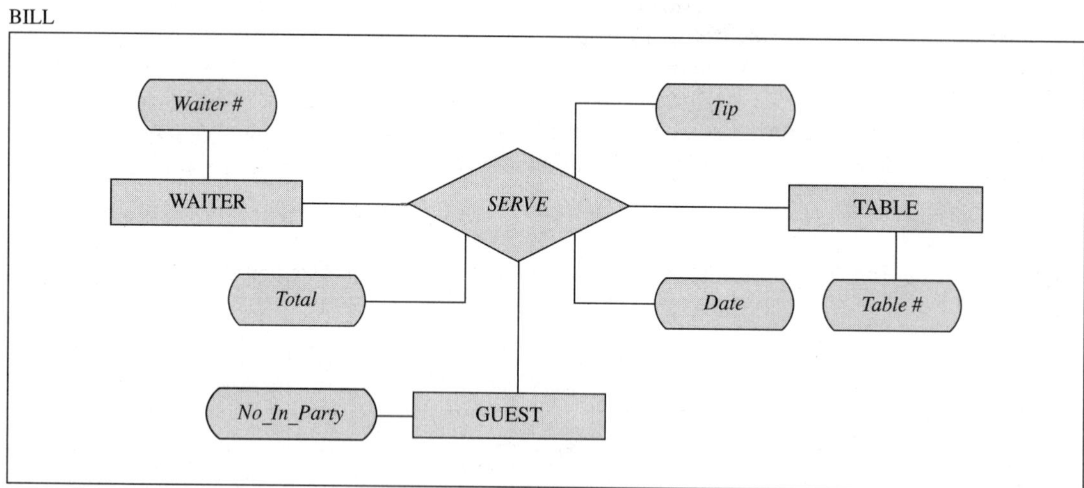

(c)

A student registered in a given course uses one of several computing systems to complete assignments and projects. The relationship between the entities STUDENT and COURSE could be the aggregated entity REGISTRATION (Figure 2.31b), as discussed above. In this case, we could view the ternary relationship of Figure 2.23 as one between registration and the entity computing system. Another method of aggregating is to consider a relationship consisting of the entity COMPUTING SYSTEMs being assigned to COURSEs. This relationship can be aggregated as a new entity and a relationship established between it and STUDENT. Note that the difference between a relationship involving an aggregation and one with the three entities lies in the number of relationships. In the former case we have two relationships; in the latter, only one exists. The approach to be taken depends on what we want to express. We would use the ternary relationship to express the fact that a STUDENT or COURSE cannot be independently related to a COMPUTING SYSTEM.

Let us investigate the relationship among the entities WAITER, TABLE, and GUEST shown in Figure 2.31c. These entities are of concern to a restaurant. There is a relationship, *SERVE,* among these entities; i.e., a waiter is assigned to serve guests at a given table. The waiters could be assigned unique identifiers. For example, a waiter is an employee and the employee number uniquely identifies an employee and hence a waiter. A table could be assigned a number; however, this may be more informal, since on occasion two or more tables are put together to accommodate a group of guests. The guests, even though identifiable by their features and other unique identifiers such as *Social_Security_Number* or driver's license number, are not distinguishable for this application. Thus the *SERVE* relationship can best be handled by an aggregation. The aggregation can be called a BILL (Figure 2.31c), and requires an introduction of an unique bill number for identification. In addition, the following attributes from the SERVE relationship and the entities involved in the relationship can be used for the aggregated entity: unique bill number, waiter identifier, table identifier, date, number of guests in party, total, tip.

2.5 A Comparative Example

In this section we describe a small database modeling problem and provide a E-R model for it. We give its implementation in each of the other three modeling schemes in Sections 2.6, 2.7, and 2.8.

Consider a database for the Universal Hockey League (UHL), a professional ice hockey league with teams worldwide. It consists of a number of divisions and numerous franchises under each division. The database records statistics on teams, players, and divisions of the league.

A franchise may relocate to another city and may become part of a different division. Players are under contract to a franchise and are obliged to move with it. This relationship between a franchise and a division is called a team. We use the word team synonymously with franchise. Consequently, we can view a franchise as consisting of a collection of players, coaches, and a general manager. Players are required to play for a given franchise for the entire season.

First we present the entity relationship diagram. We convert the E-R diagram to relational, network, and hierarchical models in Sections 2.6, 2.7, and 2.8.

E-R Model for the Universal Hockey League (UHL)

We limit ourselves to the entities DIVISION, FRANCHISE, and PLAYERS. The attributes of interest for each of these are as follows:

entity set DIVISION
Division_Name: **string;** (* unique identifier *)

entity set FRANCHISE
Franchise_Name: **string;** (* unique identifier *)
Year_Established: **integer;** (* yyyy *)

entity set PLAYERS
Name: string; (* assumed to be an unique identifier *)
Birth_Place: **string;**
Birth_Date: **string;** (*in yyyymmdd format: year,month,date*)

In addition to the above entities we have the following relationships. A player plays during a season (which we assume is a calendar year) for a given team. We distinguish the player's involvement as being a goalie or one of the forwards. (Here we are making a simplifying assumption: All players on the team who are not goalies are called forwards. Thus players who play defense are considered forwards in our model.) Since goalie is a specialized position, a player plays either in the goalie position or a forward position, but never in both. The entity PLAYER is in fact a generalization of the entities GOALIE and FORWARD. However, for this example we are not using any distinguishing attributes, so we will not consider such specialization (see Exercise 2.11). Consequently we have two relationships between a player and a team, *FORWARD* and *GOAL*. These relationships are many-to-many since a number of players play during a given season for a franchise and a given player over his lifetime plays for different franchises. We assume that a player plays the entire season for a single franchise and is not traded during the season. As a franchise may relocate and change divisions, the relationship between a franchise and division is also many-to-many.

The attributes of these relationships are:

relationship set *FORWARD*
Year: **integer;**
Goals: **integer;** (* number of goals scored by the player *)
Assists: **integer;** (* number of assists made by the player *)

relationship set *GOAL*
Year: **integer;**
Goals_Against_Avg: **integer;** (* average number of goals scored*)
Shutouts: **integer;** (* games where no goals were allowed*)

A *TEAM* is a relationship between a DIVISION and a FRANCHISE and for a given season may be in only one city. The attributes of the relationship are:

relationship set *TEAM*
Year: **integer;**
City: **string;**
Points: **integer;** (* cumulative value: 2 points for a win, 1 point for a tie, 0 point for a loss*)

The E-R diagram to model this database application is shown in Figure 2.32.

Figure 2.32 E-R diagram for the UHL database.

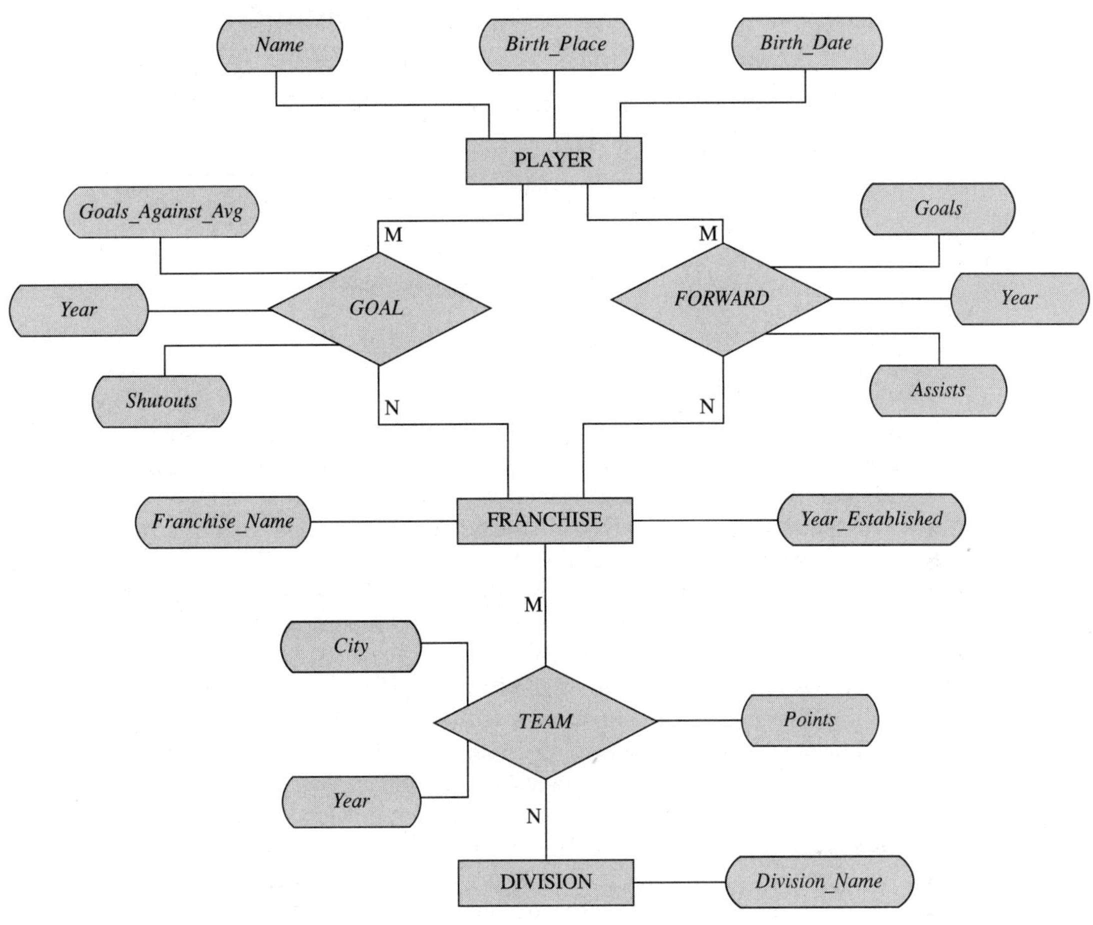

2.6 Relational Data Model

The relational data model, after more than a decade, has emerged from the research, development, test and trial stages as a commercial product. Software systems using this approach are available for all sizes of computer systems. This model has the advantage of being simple in principle; users can express their queries in a powerful query language. It is expected that many existing database applications will be retrofitted to use this approach.

In this model, the relation is the only construct required to represent the associations among the attributes of an entity as well as the relationships among different entities. One of the main reasons for introducing this model was to increase the productivity of the application programmer by eliminating the need to change application programs when a change is made to the database. Users need not know the exact physical structures to use the database and are protected from any changes made to these structures. They are, however, still required to know how the data has

Figure 2.33 A tabular representation of relations.

EMPLOYEE

Empl_No	*Name*	*Skill*
123456	Ron	waiter
123457	Jon	bartender
123458	Don	busboy
123459	Pam	hostess
123460	Pat	bellboy
123461	Ian	waiter

POSITION

Posting_No	*Skill*
321	waiter
322	bartender
323	busboy
324	hostess
325	maître d'
326	waiter

been partitioned into the various relations. While it is possible to infer access paths from the relational model, as we will see later, the relational approach does require the user to provide logical navigation through the database for the query.

The relation is the only data structure used in the relational data model to represent both entities and the relationships between them. A relation may be visualized as a named table. Figure 2.33 shows the two relations EMPLOYEE and POSITION using a tabular structure. Each column of the table corresponds to an attribute of the relation and is named.

Rows of the relation are referred to as **tuples** of the relation and the columns are its **attributes.** Each attribute of a relation has a distinct name. The values for an attribute or a column are drawn from a set of values known as a **domain.** The domain of an attribute contains the set of values that the attribute may assume. In the relational model, note that no two rows of a relation are identical and the ordering of the rows is not significant.

A relation represented by a table having n columns, defined on the domains D_1, $D_2, \ldots, D_n$ is a subset of the cartesian product $D_1 \times D_2 \times \ldots D_n$.

A relationship is represented, as in the E-R model, by combining the primary keys of the entities involved in a relation and its attributes, if any.

A correspondence between two relations is implied by the data values of attributes in the relation defined on common domains. Such correspondence is used in navigating through the relational database. In the example in Figure 2.33 both the EMPLOYEE and POSITION relations contain the identically named attribute[1] *Skill* defined on a common domain. Consequently we can join these two relations to form the relation, POSITION_ELIGIBILITY (Figure 2.34) using the common values of the attribute *Skill*. Joining the two relations involves taking two rows, one from each table, such that the value of *Skill* in the two rows is identical, and then concatenating these rows. Note that in Figure 2.34 the first attribute *Skill* is from the EMPLOYEE relation and the second is from the POSITION relation. Qualifying these attributes in POSITION_ELIGIBILITY by their respective relation names would allow us to more strictly adhere to the relational model where names of attributes in the same relation are distinct.

[1]The names of these attributes are identical in this instance to remind us that they have a common domain.

Figure 2.34 The relation obtained after joining the two relations of Figure 2.33

POSITION_ELIGIBILITY

Empl_No	*Name*	EMPLOYEE. *Skill*	***Posting_No***	POSITION. *Skill*
123456	Ron	waiter	321	waiter
123456	Ron	waiter	326	waiter
123457	Jon	bartender	322	bartender
123458	Don	busboy	323	busboy
123459	Pam	hostess	324	hostess
123461	Ian	waiter	321	waiter
123461	Ian	waiter	326	waiter

Relational Model for the UHL

Using the relational model, each of the entities in the UHL can be represented by a relation. The description of the relation is given by a **relation scheme.** A relation scheme is like a type declaration in a programming language. It indicates the attributes included in the scheme, their order, and their domain. However, we will ignore the domain for the present.

Each relation scheme is named and we indicate this name by boldface capital letters. We have a relation scheme for each of the PLAYER, FRANCHISE, and DIVISION relations. These relation schemes are similar to the corresponding entities in the E-R model:

PLAYER (***Name,*** *Birth_Place, Birth_Date*)
FRANCHISE (***Franchise_Name,*** *Year_Established*)
DIVISION (***Division_Name***)

Relationships between entities are also represented by relations.

The relationship *GOAL* is represented by a relation whose scheme includes the primary keys *Name* and *Franchise_Name,* respectively, of the entities PLAYER and FRANCHISE. In addition, it contains the attributes corresponding to those of the relationship, namely *Year, Goals_Against_Avg,* and *Shutouts*. Therefore, the relation scheme for GOAL is:

GOAL(***Name, Franchise_Name,*** *Year, Goals_Against_Avg, Shutouts*)

FORWARD is also represented by a relation scheme with attributes that consist of the same primary keys *Name* and *Franchise_Name*. It contains, as well the attributes *Year, Goals* and *Assists*. Accordingly, the relation scheme for FORWARD is:

FORWARD (***Name, Franchise_Name,*** *Year, goals, Assists*)

TEAM is represented by a relation scheme with attributes consisting of the primary keys *Franchise_Name* and *Division_Name,* respectively, of the entities FRANCHISE and DIVISION. It also contains the attributes corresponding to those of the relationship, namely *Year, City,* and *Points*. The relation scheme for TEAM is:

TEAM (***Franchise_Name, Division_Name,*** *Year, City, Points*)

Figure 2.35 Parts of relations from the UHL relation database.

PLAYER

Name	*Birth_Place*	*Birth_Date*
Zax Viviteer	Prague, Czec	1962-04-29
Barn Kurri	Detroit, Mich	1964-07-17
Todd Smith	Roseau, Minn	1963-05-09
Dave Fisher	Edmonton, Canada	1959-10-28
Ozzy Xavier	Kiruna, Sweden	1965-02-19
Gaston Vabr	Montreal, Canada	1958-05-12
Ken Dorky	Chicago, Ill	1958-05-13
Brian Lafontaine	Paris, France	1960-07-03
Bruce McTavish	Rio, Brazil	1966-10-27
Dave O'Connell	Dublin, Ireland	1967-03-16
Johnny Brent	Boston, Mass	1964-12-23

FRANCHISE

Franchise_Name	*Year_Established*
Bullets	1975
Rodeos	1921
Zippers	1917
Blades	1982
Flashers	1967

DIVISION

Division_Name
Northern
Southern
European
World

FORWARD

Name	*Franchise_Name*	*Year*	*Goals*	*Assists*
Barn Kurri	Bullets	1986	40	67
Bruce McTavish	Bullets	1986	30	37
Todd Smith	Rodeos	1986	17	24
Ozzy Xavier	Blades	1986	56	119
Ozzy Xavier	Flashers	1985	36	49
Gaston Vabr	Flashers	1986	16	22
Zax Viviteer	Blades	1986	80	162
Dave O'Connell	Zippers	1986	12	59
Brian Lafontaine	Zippers	1985	10	40
Brian Lafontaine	Zippers	1986	22	73

Sample tuples from these relations, which have the same names as the corresponding schemes, are shown in the tables of Figure 2.35.

We return to in-depth discussions of the relational data model in Chapter 4.

Figure 2.35 Continued

GOAL

Name	*Franchise_Name*	*Year*	*Goals_Against_Avg*	*Shutouts*
Ken Dorky	Blades	1986	1.21	7
Dave Fisher	Zippers	1986	4.02	4
Johnny Brent	Flashers	1986	7.61	0
Dave Fisher	Flashers	1985	3.05	5

TEAM

Franchise_Name	*Division_Name*	*Year*	*City*	*Points*
Flashers	Northern	1986	St. Louis	93
Blades	Northern	1986	Edmonton	97
Zippers	European	1985	Paris	82
Zippers	Northern	1986	Montreal	99
Rodeos	Southern	1986	Rio	65
Bullets	World	1986	Tokyo	79

2.7 Network Data Model

The network data model was formalized in the late 1960s by the Database Task Group of the Conference on Data System Languages (DBTG/CODASYL). Their first report (CODA 71), which has been revised a number of times, contained detailed specifications for the network data model (a model conforming to these specifications is also known as the DBTG data model). The specifications contained in the report and its subsequent revisions have been subjected to much debate and criticism. Many of the current database applications have been built on commercial DBMS systems using the DBTG model.

The DBTG model uses two different data structures to represent the database entities and relationships between the entities, namely record type and set type. A **record type** is used to represent an entity type. It is made up of a number of data items that represent the attributes of the entity.

A **set type** is used to represent a directed relationship between two record types, the so-called **owner record type,** and the **member record type.** The set type, like the record type, is named and specifies that there is a one-to-many relationship (1:M) between the owner and member record types. The set type can have more than one record type as its member, but only one record type is allowed to be the owner in a given set type. A database could have one or more occurrences of each of its record and set types. An occurrence of a set type consists of an occurrence of the owner record type and any number of occurrences of each of its member record types. A record type cannot be a member of two distinct occurrences of the same set type.

To avoid the confusion inherent in the use of the word ''set'' to describe the mechanism for showing relationships in the DBTG-network model, a more precise terminology has been suggested. Such terms as co-set, fan set, owner-coupled set, CODASYL set, and DBTG set are used to refer to a set.

Bachman (Bach 69) introduced a graphical means called a data structure diagram to denote the logical relationship implied by the set. Here a labeled rectangle represents the corresponding entity or record type. An arrow that connects two labeled rectangles represents a set type. The arrow direction is from the owner record type to the member record type. Figure 2.36 shows two record types (DEPARTMENT and EMPLOYEE) and the set type *DEPT_EMP*, with DEPARTMENT as the owner record type and EMPLOYEE as the member record type.

The data structure diagrams have been extended to include field names in the record type rectangle, and the arrow is used to clearly identify the data fields involved in the set association. A one-to-many (1:M) relationship is shown by a set type arrow that starts from the owner field in the owner record type. The arrow points to the member field within the member record type. The fields that support the relationship are clearly identified.

Each entity type in an E-R diagram is represented by a logical record type with the same name. The attributes of the entity are represented by data fields of the record. We use the term **logical record** to indicate that the actual implementation may be quite different.

The conversion of the E-R diagram into a network database consists of converting each 1:M binary relationship into a set (a 1:1 binary relationship being a special case of a 1:M relationship). If there is a 1:M binary relationship R_1 from entity type E_1 to entity type E_2, then the binary relationship is represented by a set. An instance of this would be S_1 with with an instance of the record type corresponding to entity E_1 as the owner and one or more instances of the record type corresponding to entity E_2 as the member. If a relationship has attributes, unless the attributes can be assigned to the member record type, they have to be maintained in a separate logical record type created for this purpose. The introduction of this additional record type requires that the original set be converted into two symmetrical sets, with the record corresponding to the attributes of the relationship as the member in both the sets and the records corresponding to the entities as the owners.

Each many-to-many relationship is handled by introducing a new record type to represent the relationship wherein the attributes, if any, of the relationship are stored. We then create two symmetrical 1:M sets with the member in each of the sets being the newly introduced record type. The conversion of a many-to-many relationship into two one-to-many sets using a common member record type is shown in Figure 2.37.

Figure 2.36 A DBTG set.

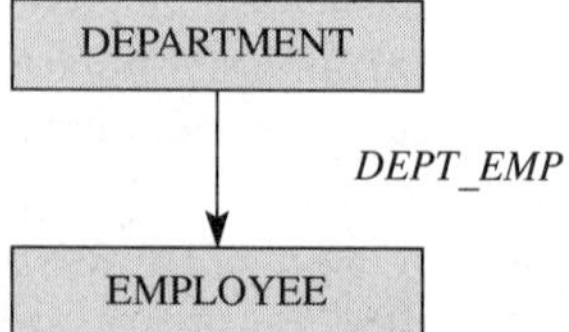

Figure 2.37 Conversion of an M:N relationship into two 1:M DBTG sets.

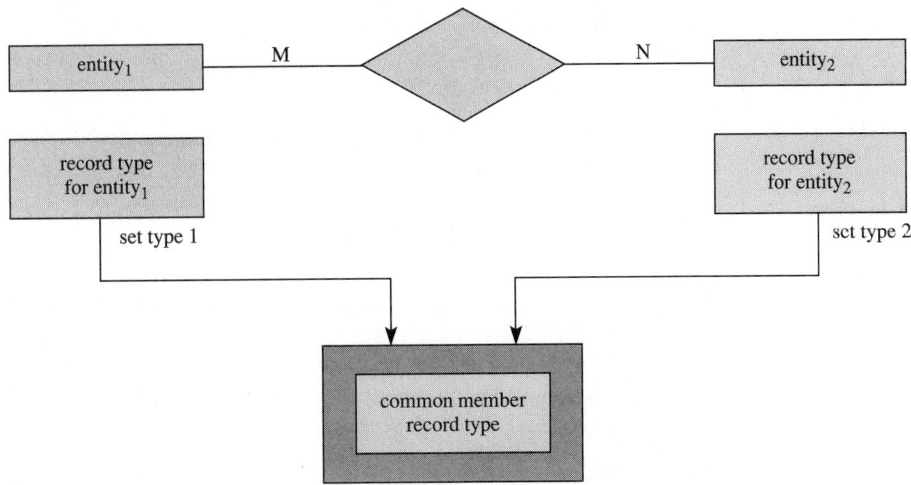

In the network model, the relationships as well as the navigation through the database are predefined at database creation time.

When a relationship involving a weak entity set is converted to a network set, it is possible that several identical occurrences of the logical record type corresponding to a weak entity could exist. These identical occurrences are distinguished by their membership in different occurrences of the sets (similar to the method of distinguishing identical weak entities by their relationship with unique strong entities).

Network Model for the UHL

Each entity type in the E-R diagram of Figure 2.32 is represented by a logical record type with the same name. The attributes of the entity are represented by data fields of the record. The logical record types corresponding to the entities PLAYER, FRANCHISE, and DIVISION are given by:

PLAYER *(Name, Birth_Place, Birth_Date)*
FRANCHISE *(Franchise_Name, Year_Established)*
DIVISION *(Division_Name)*

Furthermore, for the E-R diagram of Figure 2.32, we create logical record types for the attributes of each relationship and these record types are named for the corresponding relationship, i.e., *GOAL, FORWARD,* and *TEAM*. These logical record types are expressed as:

GOAL *(Year, Goals_Against_Avg, Shutouts)*
FORWARD *(Year, Goals, Assists)*
TEAM *(Year, City, Points)*

Since the relationships in the E-R diagram of Figure 2.32 are many to many, we handle this by creating two symmetrical 1:M sets with the attribute, if any, being the member record type of each of these symmetrical sets. Corresponding to the relationship *GOAL,* we create the logical record type GOAL, and the sets *Fr_G* and *P_G*. The record types FRANCHISE and PLAYER are owners and the record type GOAL is the common member in these sets.

The data structure diagram for the database for the UHL is shown in Figure 2.38. The sets included are:

- *P_G* and *Fr_G,* corresponding to the many-to-many relationship *GOAL* between the entities PLAYERS and FRANCHISE. GOAL is the common member record type, the owner record types being PLAYER (of the set *P_G*) and FRANCHISE (of the set *Fr_G*). The attributes of the relationship are the fields of the record type GOAL.
- *P_F* and *Fr_F,* corresponding to the many-to-many relationship *FORWARD* between the entities PLAYERS and FRANCHISE. The member record type is FORWARD, with PLAYER (of the set *P_F*) and FRANCHISE (of the set *Fr_F*) being the owner record types. The fields of the common member record type FORWARD are the attributes of the relationship.
- *Fr_T* and *D_T,* corresponding to the many-to-many relationship *TEAM* between the entities FRANCHISE and DIVISION. TEAM is the member record type; the owner record types are FRANCHISE (of the set *Fr_T*) and DIVISION (of the set *D_T*). The attributes of the relationship are the fields of the record type TEAM, the common member of *Fr_T* and *D_T*.

Figure 2.39 features a sample of the data contained in some of these logical record types and some of the sets in which these records are involved as member or owner. The common records, which are shaded, are the links in establishing a many-to-many relationship. The connecting lines between two records indicate the exis-

Figure 2.38 Network model for the UHL database.

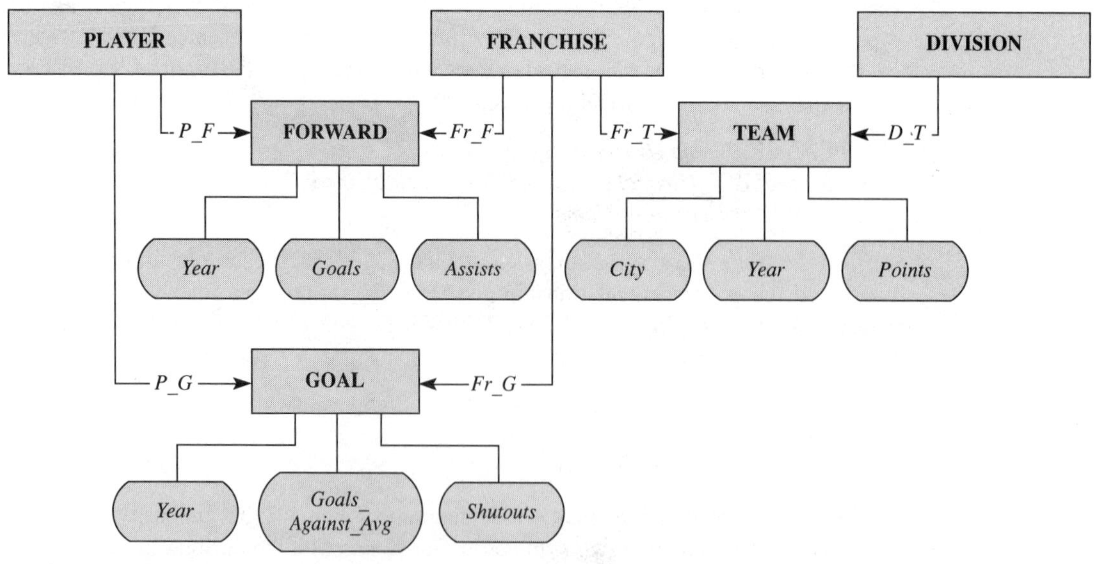

Figure 2.39 Part of the data in the network database of the UHL.

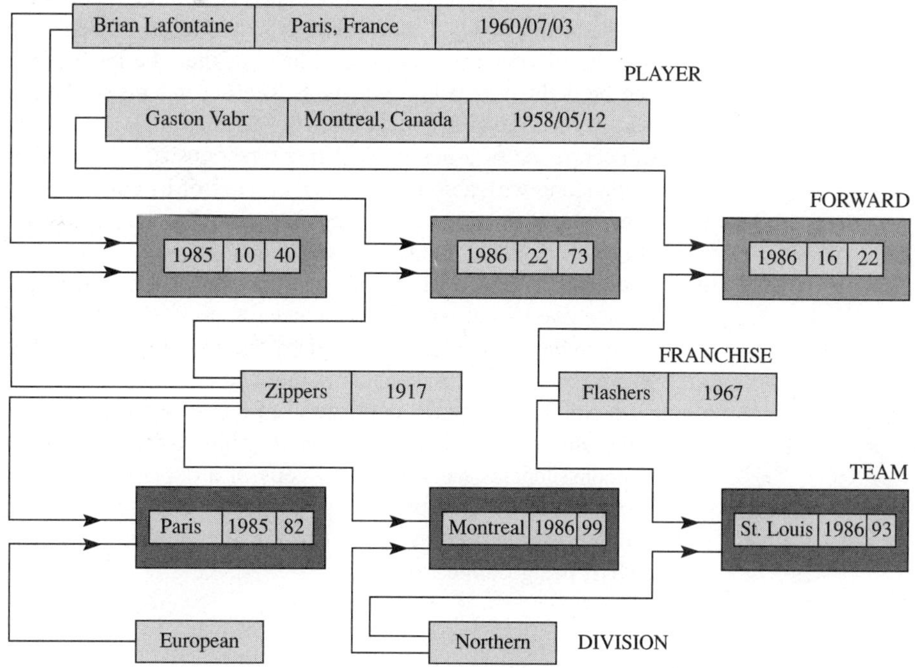

tence of an owner/member relationship between the record occurrences and some mechanism to go from one to the other. For instance, the occurrence (Brian Lafontaine, Paris, France, 1960-07-03) of the logical record type PLAYER is the owner in the set occurrence P_F. The members of this set occurrence owned by him are the FORWARD logical record occurrences (1985, 10, 40) and (1986, 22, 73). These are also owned by the franchise Zippers and establish the relationship between the player and the franchise.

We return to detailed discussions of the network model in Chapter 8.

2.8 Hierarchical Model

A tree may be defined as a set of nodes such that there is one specially designated node called the root (node) and the remaining nodes are partitioned into disjoint sets, each of which in turn is a tree, the subtrees of the root. If the relative order of the subtrees is significant, the tree is an ordered tree.

Like an organization chart or a family tree, a hierarchy is an ordered tree and is easy to understand. At the root of the tree is the single parent; the parent can have none, one, or more children. (Note that in comparing the hierarchical tree with a family tree, we are ignoring one of the parents; in other words, both the parents are represented implicitly by the single parent.)

In a hierarchical database, the data is organized in a hierarchical or ordered tree structure and the database is a collection of such disjoint trees (sometimes referred to as a **forest** or **spanning trees**). The nodes of the tree represent record types. Each tree effectively represents a root record type and all of its dependent record types. If we define the root record type to be at level 0, then the level of its dependent record types can be defined as being at level 1. The dependents of the record types at level 1 are said to be at level 2, and so on.

An occurrence of a hierarchical tree type consists of one occurrence of the root record type along with zero or more occurrences of its dependent subtree types. Each dependent subtree is, in turn, hierarchical and consists of a record type as its root node. In a hierarchical model, no dependent record can occur without its parent record occurrence. Furthermore, no dependent record occurrence may be connected to more than one parent record occurrence.

A hierarchical model can represent a one-to-many relationship between two entities where the two are respectively parent and child. However, to represent a many-to-many relationship requires duplication of one of the record types corresponding to one of the entities involved in this relationship. Note that such duplications could lead to inconsistencies when only one copy of a duplicated record is updated.

Another method of representing a many-to-many relationship by the use of a virtual record is presented in Chapter 9. For the present, we implement the database for the UHL using duplication.

Hierarchical Model for the UHL

Each entity in the E-R model for the UHL can be represented by a record type. The UHL database can be represented in the hierarchical model by a number of hierarchies. The first one used is the normal organizational hierarchy of the league and is displayed in Figure 2.40a. The record type YEAR_CITY_POINTS is created with

Figure 2.40 Hierarchical model for the UHL database.

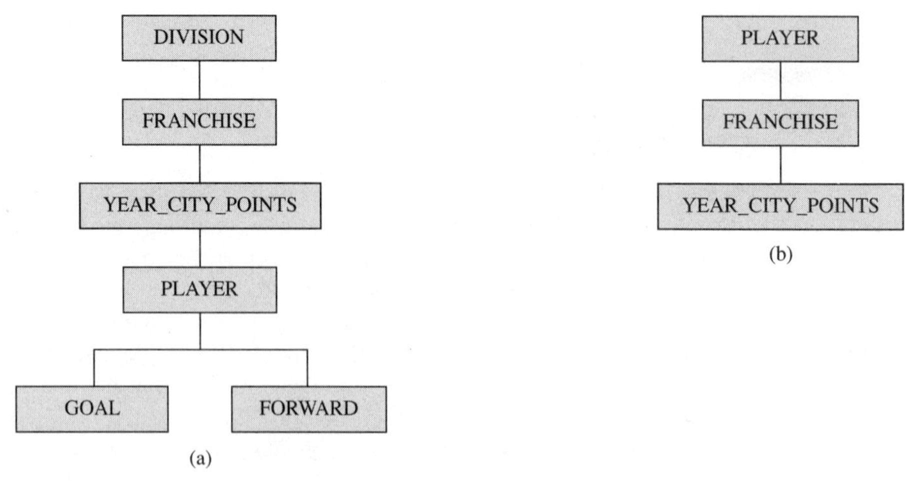

the attributes of the relationship *TEAM*. The record types GOAL and FORWARD represent all the attributes of the relationship *GOAL* and *FORWARD*, respectively, except the attribute year, which is inherited from the ancestor YEAR_CITY_POINTS. Note that a given occurrence of the PLAYER record type will have a single dependent record in either the GOAL hierarchy or the FORWARD hierarchy. Since we need to quickly locate the franchise of which a player is a member, we use a second hierarchy rooted with the record type PLAYER, shown in Figure 2.40b.

As we see in Figure 2.40, representing the many-to-many relationship between the players and the franchise requires the introduction of certain redundancies and inefficiencies. Furthermore, we cannot follow the player hierarchy to find out the player's score in a given year. This involves, first, finding the franchises to which a player belonged from the PLAYER hierarchy. Second, we have to refer to the DIVISION hierarchy to find this FRANCHISE and, for the required year, find the player and his score.

In the hierarchical model, we can have duplications of certain record occurrences as well. For example, if a franchise was in two different divisions, we would have two identical records for the same franchise. The parent record (DIVISION) would distinguish the fact that the franchise was in different divisions in different years. The TEAM relationship is represented only indirectly in the hierarchical model shown in Figure 2.40.

Part of the hierarchical database for the UHL is given in Figure 2.41. It shows that the Zipper franchise was in the European division and was located in Paris in 1985. In 1986 the franchise was in the the Northern division and was relocated to Montreal. This information is represented by duplication of the record for the franchise. For the year 1986 the players in the Blades franchise were Ozzy Xavier, Zax Viviteer, and Ken Dorky.

Since the late 1960s and early 1970s, the hierarchical model has been widely used in database applications. The most prominent commercial implementations are the IMS system from IBM (IBM 75) and the SYSTEM 2000 from MRI Systems Corporation (MRI 74). We return to detailed discussions of the hierarchical model in Chapter 9.

2.9 A Comparison

Having designed an E-R diagram for a database application, the relational representation of the model is relatively straightforward. Each entity type in the E-R diagram is represented by a relation wherein each attribute of the entity becomes an attribute of the relation. Each instance of the entity is represented by a tuple of the relation. A weak entity can also be represented by a relation but must include the primary key of the identifying strong entity. Each relationship in the E-R diagram is also represented by a relation, the attributes of this relation being the primary keys of the entities involved in the relationship plus the attributes of the relationship. Each instance of the relationship set among the entities is represented by a tuple of this relation.

Converting an E-R diagram to a network model can be accomplished as follows. Each entity type in the E-R diagram is represented by a record type and each instance

Figure 2.41 Part of the data in the hierarchical database of the UHL.

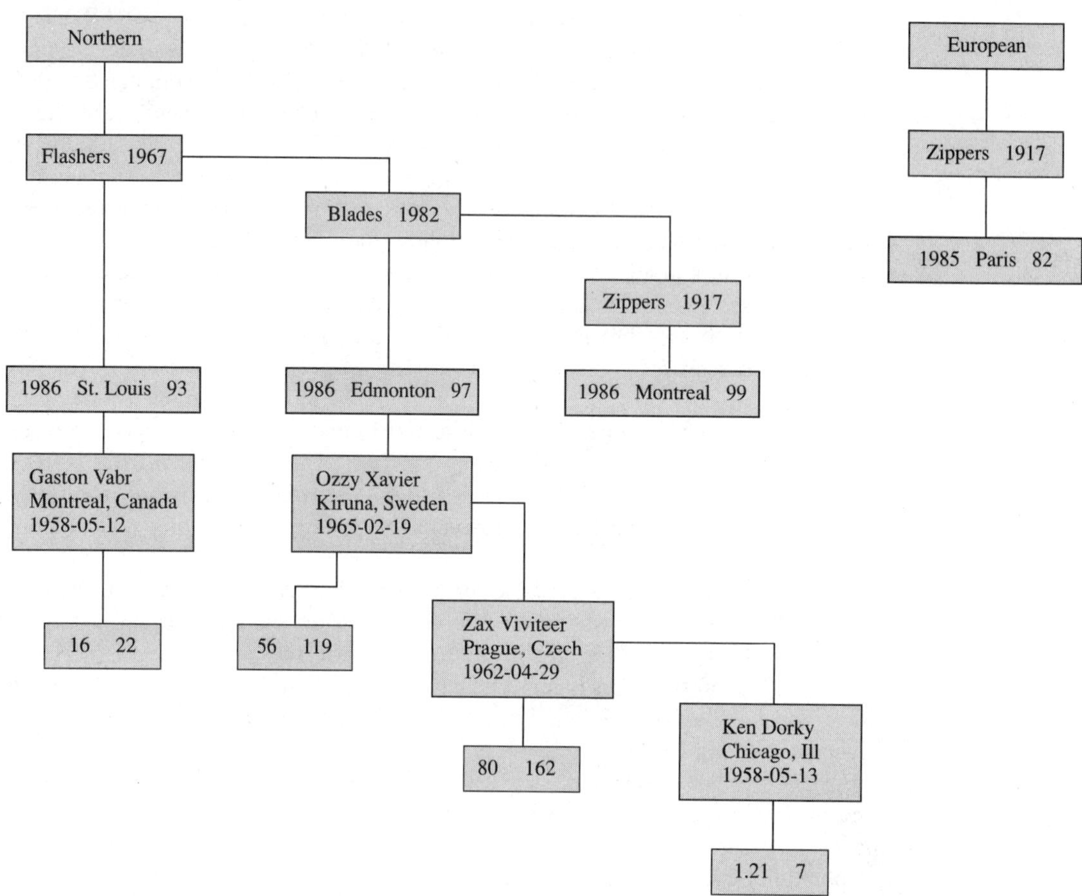

of the entity is represented by a record occurrence. A weak entity can be represented as a separate record type. In this case, the identifying relationship is represented as a set type wherein the record type corresponding to the weak entity type forms the member and the record type corresponding to the strong entity is the owner. A 1:1 or 1:N relationship is represented as a set type. An M:N relationship requires introducing an **intermediate record type.** This record type is a common member in two set types, one of which is owned by each of the record types involved in the M:N relationship.

Converting an E-R diagram to a hierarchical model can be accomplished as follows. Each entity type in the E-R diagram is represented by a record type. A 1:N relationship is represented as a hierarchy type where the record type corresponding to the one side of the relationship is the parent (a 1:1 relationship is a special case of the 1:N relationship). A weak entity can be represented as a separate record type. This record type becomes a dependent in a hierarchy where the record type, corresponding to the strong entity in the identifying relationship, is the parent. An M:N relationship requires introducing duplicate record types or using multiple hierarchies and introducing virtual records.

In the network model, it is possible that several identical occurrences of the same logical record type could exist. These multiple identical occurrences are distinguished by their membership in different occurrences of the sets. Similarly, in the hierarchical model, identical occurrences of a record type are distinguished by their associations with different ancestor record type occurrences. The tuples of a relation are, however, unique because if the relation represents a relationship between entities, the relationships between occurrences of the entities are explicitly recorded in the tuples by inclusion of the corresponding primary keys.

The relational model allows for a fairly straightforward method of **selecting** certain entities or relationships. This is done by selecting those tuples of the relation corresponding to the entity or relationship that meet certain selection conditions. For instance, all franchises for which the player Ozzy Xavier played could be derived by choosing tuples from the relation FORWARD (Figure 2.35) with *Name* = Ozzy Xavier. Similarly, all players who scored more than 50 goals in 1986 could be selected from the FORWARD relation. Likewise, finding all cities in which Ozzy Xavier played can be done by first selecting the tuples from FORWARD with the value of *Name* = Ozzy Xavier. These selected tuples are then joined (concatenated) with those in the table TEAM such that the values of *Franchise_Name* and *Year* in both is the same.

In the network model, the selection operation on a record type is similar to that in the relational model. However, the operation corresponding to the join operation of the relational model is handled differently. This involves following the owner-to-member or the member-to-owner pointers. Therefore, in order to identify all franchises for which Ozzy Xavier played, we would first find the record for Ozzy Xavier in the player record type. We would then follow the pointers in the set *P_F* to the occurrences of the member record type FORWARD for his score, and last, follow the pointers to the owner of each such occurrence in the set *Fr_F* to find the FRANCHISE. Since the player Ozzy Xavier is not a goalie, the set *P_G* for the occurrence of his record in record type PLAYER would be empty. Consequently, following the set *P_G* and then the owner in the set *Fr_G* for this player would not be possible.

Selection operations for the record type corresponding to the root of a hierarchical tree are similar to operations for its counterpart in the relational and network models. As in the case of the network model, we have to traverse pointers from parent to child since there is no method of traveling from descendant to parent. However, a virtual scheme using a virtual record concept (to be discussed in chapter 9) introduces this reverse-navigation facility.

The process of joining relations in the case of the relational model or following the pointers from owner to member, from member to owner, or from parent to child is known as **navigating** through the database. Navigation through relations that represent an M:N relationship is just as simple as through a 1:M relationship. This leads us to conclude that it is easier to specify how to manipulate a relational database than a network or hierarchical one. This in turn leads to a query language for the relational model that is correct, clear, and effective in specifying the required operations. Unfortunately, the join operation is inherently inefficient and demands a considerable amount of processing and retrieval of unnecessary data. The structure for the network and hierarchical models can be implemented efficiently. Such an implementation would mean that navigating through these databases, though awkward, requires the retrieval of relatively little unnecessary data.

2.10 Summary

In this chapter we previewed the major data modeling concepts and the data models used in current DBMSs. The E-R model is used increasingly as a tool for database applications modeling.

A number of data representation models have been developed over the years. As in the case of programming languages, one concludes that there is no one "best" choice for all applications. These models differ in their method of representing the associations between entities and attributes.

Traditional data models are hierarchical, network, or relational models. The hierarchical model evolved from the file-based system; the network model is a superset of the hierarchical model. The relational data model is based on the mathematical relational concept. The data model concept evolved at about the same time as the relational data model.

The entity-relationship data model, which is popular for high-level database design, provides a means of representing relationships between entities. The entity relationship data model was developed using commercially available DBMSs to model application databases.

The DBTG proposal was the first data model to be formalized in the late 1960s. Many current database applications have been built on commercial DBMSs using this approach.

Key Terms

data model
association
attribute association
relationship
functional dependency
determinant
candidate key
primary key
binary relationship
repeating group
file-based model
hierarchical model
network model
relational data model
semantic data model
entity-relationship (E-R) data model
entity-relationship (E-R) diagram
strong entity
identifying relationship
weak entity
discriminator
relationship set
N-ary relationship
ternary relationship
abstraction
generalization
specialization
aggregation
tuple
attribute
domain
relation scheme
record type
set type
owner record type
member record type
logical record
forest
spanning trees
selecting
intermediate record type
navigating

Exercises

2.1 Define the following terms:

(a) association
(b) relationship

(c) aggregation
(d) specialization
(e) generalization

2.2 Choose from the following list an organization you are most familiar with: college or university, public library, hospital, fast-food restaurant, department store. Determine, as in Exercise 1.9, the entities of interest and the relationships that exist between these entities. Draw the E-R diagram for the organization. Construct a tabular representation of the entities and relationships.

2.3 Are weak entities necessary? What is the distinction between a weak entity and a strong one? Can a weak entity be converted to a strong entity?

2.4 Using the EMPLOYEE entity of Figure 2.6, convert each of the one-to-many associations into a weak entity and a relationship. Identify the discriminator of each weak entity and the attributes of each relationship.

2.5 Convert the E-R diagram that you prepared for Exercise 2.2 into a network database model. List the record types and the set types in your model. Indicate for each set type the owner and member record types.

2.6 Convert the E-R diagram that you prepared for Exercise 2.2 into a hierarchical database model. List the record types and the hierarchy. Indicate how you can handle the situation where a record type occurs in more than one hierarchy or occurs more than once in the same hierarchy.

2.7 Explain the distinction between the representation of association and relationship in the network and hierarchical models.

2.8 The People's Bank offer five types of accounts: loan, checking, premium savings, daily interest saving, and money market. It operates a number of branches and a client of the bank can have any number of accounts. Accounts can be joint, i.e., more than one client may be able to operate a given account. Identify the entities of interest and show their attributes. What relationships exist among these entities? Draw the corresponding E-R diagram.

2.9 Give a sample of each of the tables that would be required for the E-R diagram of Exercise 2.8.

2.10 Complete the network sets and the hierarchical trees for the portion of the data for the Universal Hockey League given in the tables of Figure 2.35. Comment on the relative merits of the three models from the point of view of data duplication and ease of retrieval.

2.11 Suppose that in the database design for the UHL of Section 2.5, we wished to maintain the career statistics for each player. (The total goals and assists over the lifetime—career—of a player are to be maintained in addition to the season statistics.) Draw the modified E-R diagram and give the corresponding database design using the relational, network, or hierarchical model.

2.12 In each of the database designs given in Section 2.8, how would you find out if a certain player played as a forward or as a goalie? Introduce two *IS_A* relationships between players and entities FORWARD_POSITION and GOAL_POSITION and draw an E-R diagram for a database application that requires keeping the player's career statistics as well as the statistics indicated in the text.

2.13 Explain why navigation is simpler in the relational data model than in the hierarchical data model.

Bibliographic Notes

Senko (Senk 77), in a survey article, gave details of some of the models discussed in this chapter. The entity-relationship data model (Chen 76) grew out of the exercise of using commercially available DBMS to model application databases. Recently the E-R model has been enriched and used in conceptual view design (Buss 83).

The DBTG proposal was the first data model to be formalized. The first report (which has been revised a number of times), issued by the Database Task Group of the Conference on Data System Languages (DBTG/CODASYL) (CODA 71) contained detailed specifications for the network data model (a model conforming to these specifications is also known as the DBTG data model). The specifications contained in the first report and subsequent revisions have been subjected to much debate and criticism (Tayl 76). Many of the current database applications have been built on commercial DBMSs using this approach.

Bachman (Bach 69) introduced a graphical means called the data structure diagram to denote the logical relationship implied by the DBTG set. The data structure diagrams have been extended to include field names in the record type rectangle and the arrow is used to clearly identify the data fields involved in the set association (Brad 78).

In the network model, the relationships are predefined at database creation time; however, dynamic relationships as in the relational model have been proposed (Brad 78).

The hierarchical model has been widely used in many existing database systems since the late 1960s and early 1970s, due to the promotion of the IMS system by IBM (IBM 75) and SYSTEM 2000 by MRI Systems Corporation (MRI 74).

The relational data model (Codd 70) is a model for representing the association between the attributes of an entity and the association between different entities using the relation as a construct. One of the main reasons for the introduction of this model was to increase the productivity of the application programmer (Codd 82).

The relational model had its roots in the binary relations for data storage, namely the relational data file of Levien and Maron (Levi 67) and the TRAMP system of Ash and Sibley (Ash 68). The generalization of the binary relation to an n-ary relation was proposed by Codd (Codd 70). He gave a definition of the n-ary relation for use in large shared data banks and outlined the advantages of this approach.

Codd's paper was instrumental in setting the direction of research in relational database systems. After more than a decade of development and trials, relational data management systems are on the market. Examples of these are SYSTEM R, DB2, SQL/DS, ORACLE, INGRES, RAPPORT, QBE, and Knowledgeman.

The universal relational model aims at relieving the user of providing even the logical navigation through the database (Maie 84). Another concept missing from the relational model was that of specifying constraints between some relations; this problem has been addressed in (Codd 79).

Textbook-level discussions of data models can be found in (Tsic 82), (Kort 86), (Maie 83), (Ullm 82), (Date 86) and (Brod 84a).

Bibliography

(ANSI 75) ANSI/X3/SPARC Study Group on Database Management Systems, Interim Report, FDT (ACM SIGMOD bulletin), vol. 7(2), 1975.

(Ash 68) W. L. Ash & E. H. Sibley, "TRAMP: A Relational Memory with Deductive Capabilities," Proc. ACM 23rd National Conf. August 1968. Princeton, N.K.: Brandon Systems Press, 1968, pp. 143–156.

(Bach 69) C. W. Bachman, "Data Structure Diagrams," *Data Base* (ACM) 1(2), 1969, pp. 4–10.

(Brad 78) J. Bradley, "An Extended Owner-Coupled Set Data Model in Predicate Calculus for Database Management," *ACM TODS* 3(4), 1978, pp. 385–416.

(Brod 84a) M. J. Brodie, J. Mylopoulos, & J. W. Schmidt, *On Conceptual Modelling,* New York: Springer-Verlag, 1984.

(Brod 84b) M. J. Brodie, "On the Development of Data Models," in (Brod 84a), pp. 19–47.

(Buss 83) U. Bussolati, S. Ceri, V. De Antonellis, & B. Zonta, "Views: Conceptual Design," in *Methodology and Tools for Data Base Design* ed. S. Ceri, Amsterdam: North Holland, 1983, pp. 25–55.

(Cahe 83) R. G. G. Cahell, "Design and Implementation of a Relational-Entity-Datum Data Model," Technical Report CSL-83-4, XEROX PARC, Palo Alto, CA: May 1983.

(Chen 76) P. P. Chen, "The ER Model Toward a Unified View of Data,' *ACM TODS* 1(1), 1976, pp. 9–36.

(Chen 80) P. P. Chen, ed., "Entity-Relationship Approach to System Analysis and Design," North Holland, Mass., 1980.

(CODA 71) CODASYL Database Task Group Report, April 1971, ACM, New York, 1971.

(Codd 70) E. F. Codd, "A Relational Mode of Data for Large Shared Data Banks,' *CACM,* 13(2), 1970, pp. 377–387.

(Codd 79) E. F. Codd, "Extending the Database Relation Model to Capture More Meaning," *ACM TODS* 4, 1979, pp. 392–434.

(Codd 82) E. F. Codd, "Relational Database: A Practical Foundation For Productivity," The 1981 ACM Turing Award Lecture, in CACM, 25(2), 1982, pp. 109–117.

(Date 86) C. J. Date, *An Introduction to Database Systems,* vol. 1, 4th ed. Reading, MA: Addison-Wesley, 1986.

(Feld 69) J. A. Feldman & P. D. Rovner, "An Algol-Based Associative Language," *CACM* 12(8), August 1969, pp. 439–447.

(Find 79) N. V. Findler, ed., *Associative Networks: Representation and Use of Knowledge by Computer,"* New York: Academic Press, 1979.

(Grif 82) R. L. Griffith, "Three Principles of Representation for Semantic Networks," *ACM TODS* 7(3), 1982, pp. 417–442.

(Hamm 81) M. Hammer & D. McLeod, "Database Description with SDM: A Semantic Database Model," *ACM TODS* 6(3), 1981, pp. 351–386.

(IBM 75) Information Management System Publications, GH70-1260, White Plains, NY: IBM, 1975.

(Jard 77) D. A. Jardine, ed, "The ANSI/SPARC DBMS Model," Proceedings of the Second SHARE Working Conference on Database Management Systems, Montreal, Canada, 1976. Amsterdam: North-Holland, 1977.

(Kers 67) L. Kerschberg, A. Klug, & D. C. Tsichritzis, "A Taxonomy of Data Models," in *Systems for Large Databases,* ed. (P. C. Lockermann & E. J. Neuhold.) Amsterdam: North-Holland, 1967, pp. 43–64.

(Knut 68) D. E. Knuth, "The Art of Computer Programming," vol. 1. Reading, MA: Addison-Wesley, 1968.

(Kort 86) H. F. Korth & A. Silberschatz, *Database System Concepts,* New York: McGraw-Hill, 1986.

(Levi 67) R. E. Levien M. E. Maron, "A Computer System for Inference Execution and Data Retrieval," *CACM* 10(11), Nov. 1967, pp. 715–721.

(Maie 83) D. Maier, *The Theory of Relational Databases,* Rockville, MD: Computer Science Press, 1983.

(Maie 84) D. Maier, J. D. Ullman, & M. Y. Vardi, "On the Foundation of the Universal Relation Model," *ACM TODS* 9(2), 1984, pp. 283–308.

(MR 174) Systems 2000 Publications, A-1, C-1, F-1, G-1, I-1, P-1, R-1. Austin, TX: MRI Systems Corp., 1974.

(Mylo 80) J. Mylopoulos, P. A. Bernstein, & H. K. T. Eong, "A Language Facility for Database Intensive Applications," *ACM TODS* 5(2), 1980, pp. 185–207.

(Senk 77) M. E. Senko, "Data Structures and Data Accessing in Database Systems, Past, Present and Future," *IBM Systems Journal,* vol. 16, 1977, pp. 16, 208–257.

(Smit 77) J. M. Smith, D. C. P. Smith, "Database Abstractions: Aggregation and Generalization," *ACM TODS* 2(2), 1977, pp. 105–133.

(Su 79) S. Y. W. Su & D. H. Lo, "A Semantic Association Model for Conceptual Database Design," Proc. of Int. Conf. on Entity-Relationship Approach to System Analysis and Design, Los Angeles, CA, December 1979, pp. 147–171.

(Tayl 76), R. W. Taylor, R. L. Frank, "CODASYL Database Management System," *ACM Computing Surveys* 8(1), 1976, pp. 67–104.

(Teic 77) D. Teichroew & E. A. Hershey III, "PSL/PSA: A Computer-Aided Technique for Structured Documentation and Analysis of Information Processing System," *IEEE Trans. on Software Eng*. 3(1), 1977, pp. 41–48.

(Teor 86) T. J. Teory, D. Yang, & J. P. Fry, "A Logical Design Methodology for Relational Databases Using the Extended Entity-Relationship Model," *ACM Computing Survey* 18(2), June 1986, pp. 197–222.

(Tsic 78) D. C. Tsichritzis & A. Klug, eds, "The ANSI/X3/SPARC DBMS Framework Report of the Study Group on Database Management Systems," *Information Systems* 3, 1978, pp. 173–191.

(Tsic 82) D. C. Tsichritzis & F. H. Lochovsky, *Data Models,* Englewood Cliffs, NJ: Prentice-Hall, 1982.

(Ullm 82) J. D. Ullman, *Principles of Database Systems,* Rockville, MD: Computer Science Press, 1982.

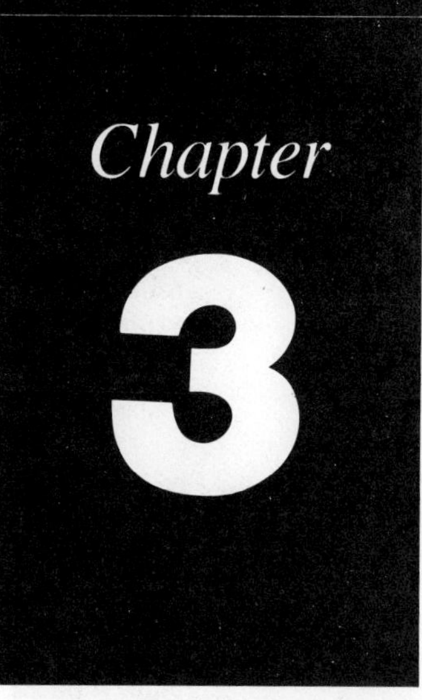

File Organization

Contents

In this chapter we focus on a number of methods used to organize files and the issues involved in the choice of a method. File organization deals with the structure of data in secondary storage devices. In designing the structure the designer is concerned with the access time involved in the retrieval of records based on primary or secondary keys, as well as the techniques involved in updating data. We discuss the following file organization schemes: sequential, index sequential, multilist, direct, extendable hashing, and tree structured. The general principles involved in these schemes are presented, although we do not discuss the implementation issues under a specific operating system.

3.1 Introduction

Just as lists, arrays, trees, and other data structures are used to implement data organization in main memory, a number of strategies are used to support the organization of data in secondary memory. We can expect, as in main memory data organization, that there is no universal secondary data organization strategy suitable under all usage conditions. As discussed earlier, certain attribute (or field) values can uniquely identify a record, i.e., these attributes makeup the primary key of the record. Other attribute values identify not one but a set of records. These attributes are called secondary or nonprimary keys. In this chapter we consider both primary key and nonprimary key retrieval and updates, bearing in mind that there are space/time trade-offs for all structures.

Traditionally the term **file** has been used to refer to the folder that holds related material in ordered storage for quick reference. We use the same word, file, to describe the object as well as its contents. The order of the file is an arrangement of its contents according to one's expected needs for future reference. For example, if we have a file of birth dates of persons we know, we may wish to arrange them by date. We could also arrange them alphabetically by family or first name. The choice of arrangement depends on the reason for the file. If we wish to consult the file periodically to discover upcoming birthdays, chronological order would be chosen. If, however, we wish to know the date of Bill's birthday, we would opt for the alphabetical ordering on first names. What are we to do when we have both types of requirements? We could, for example, maintain a copy of the file in chronological order and another in lexical order. In this case, the contents would be the same but the order would be different. We would rarely remove (or delete) a person's birth date from the file; rather, we would add new names and dates to the file. We may need to change someone's name. In all of these cases both copies of the file would be changed. It is impossible to change both files at the same instance, i.e., we first alter one copy and then the other. Can we, while the changes are being made, make use of either file? Imagine what would happen when a number of copies and a large number of users exist. The method of creating a copy for each application is replete with problems. A possible solution is to maintain the file in some physical order and allow access in some other order, i.e., the logical access order is different from the physical access order. This concept is very important because the same file could then be used to support different access orders.

To further classify the contents, a file should be labeled. We can label the file described above as a file of Birth_Dates. Similarly, we can create suitably named files for other things such as Recipes, Bills, and so on. We could keep all these files in a box. The box, by definition, is also a file—it is a file of files. We could treat the secondary storage medium as this box (a file of files). In this chapter we look at techniques for managing files. The same techniques are applicable to the file of files.

3.1.1 Storage Device Characteristics

Presently, the common secondary storage media used to store data are disk and tape. Tape is generally used for archival data. The storage medium used in a disk is a **disk pack.** A disk pack, shown in Figure 3.1, is made up of a number of surfaces. Data is read and written from the disk pack by means of transducers called **read/write heads.** The number of read/write heads depends on the type of disk drive. If we trace the projection of one head on the surface associated with it as the disk rotates, we would create a circular figure called a **track.** The tracks at the same position on every surface of the disk form the surface of an imaginary cylinder. In disk terminology, therefore, a **cylinder** consists of the tracks under the heads on each of its surfaces.

In one type of disk drive each track on each surface has a dedicated stationary head, which does not move. Such a disk drive is called a **fixed head drive.** The other type of disk drive is a **moving head drive,** wherein a single head is used for each surface. When data from a given track is to be read, the head is moved to the track. Figure 3.2 shows the cross section of a fixed head drive and Figure 3.3 shows that of a moving head drive.

The disk stores data along concentric tracks. It takes some time for the read/write head of a moving head disk drive to move from track (or cylinder) i to track (or cylinder) j. This is called the **seek time.** (For a fixed head disk, the seek time is 0.) In the case of a moving head drive, the seek time depends on the distance between the current head and the target head positions. Typical values are from 10 to 50 msec (msec = 1/1000 sec). If a file consists of c consecutive cylinders and we assume uniform and random distribution of requests for the different cylinders, we can show that the average distance (in cylinders) the head moves is c/3 (proof for this is given in Appendix 3.2 at the end of the text). Before data can be read or written the disk has to rotate so that the head is positioned at some point relative to

Figure 3.1 Structure of a disk pack with read/write heads.

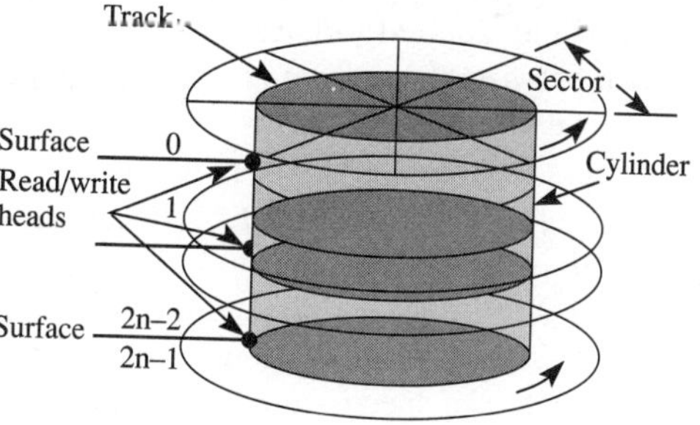

Figure 3.2 Fixed head disk with read/write head per track.

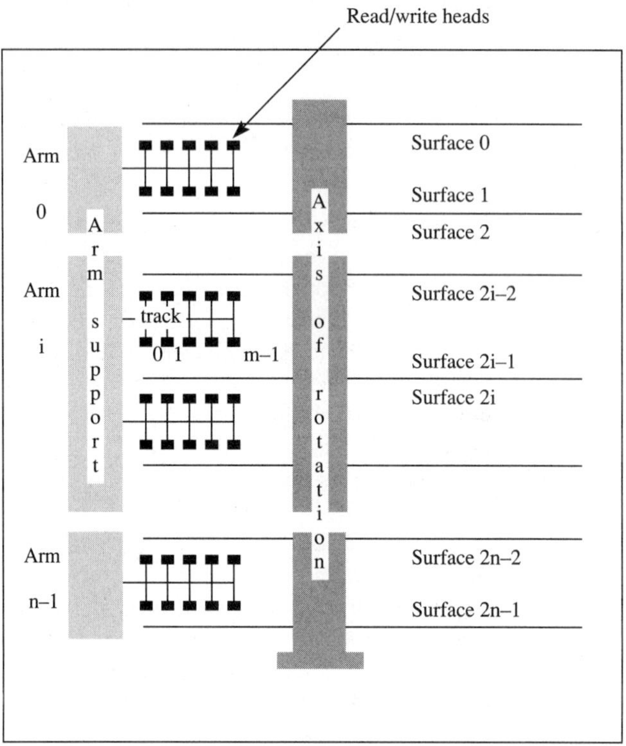

a marked start point. The time needed for the reading or writing to start depends on the rotational delay. On the average, the rotational delay is half the rotation time, that is, the time for the disk to rotate once. The rotational delay is called **latency time.** For a drive that rotates at 3600 revolutions per minute, the average latency time is 8.33 msec. The **access time,** therefore, depends on the seek time and the latency time.

On magnetic tapes, data blocks are separated by **interblock gaps (IBG).** The IBG can be attributed to the deceleration/ acceleration (stop/start) that takes place between successive block reads. This only happens when, after a single access, time is needed to process the data before a second read. When continuously scanning over the data, there is no need to stop/start after reading each block. The IBG is also scanned at the faster rate. The typical value for the IBG is 0.6 inch. The access time, i.e., the time required to locate the target block on a magnetic tape, depends on the distance between the current and target blocks.

As we see from the above, the access time depends on the distance between the current and target positions for both types of storage devices. This time can be optimized by suitably placing records. It can also be affected by the file organization employed.

We can abstract the disk storage medium in terms of a two-dimensional array and the tape as a one-dimensional array of data blocks (see Figure 3.4). Note that in both cases we can specify a unique address for a block (or physical record). We will

Figure 3.3 Moving head disk with a single read/write head per surface.

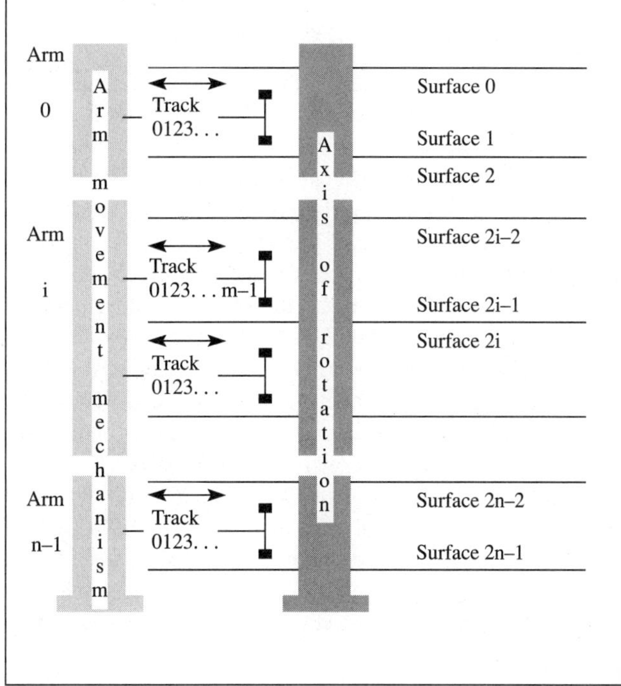

omit details of these physical mediums on which the files are stored. These details can be found in most elementary texts in computer organization. It is sufficient to say that some file organizations may be unsuitable for some mediums.

A block of data may contain one or more logical records (henceforth, unless otherwise stated, a record denotes a logical record), or a single record may be split across more than one block (Figure 3.5). Therefore, in addition to the block address, we require data on the start position, length, and pointer to continuation block for

Figure 3.4 Abstraction of secondary storage medium.

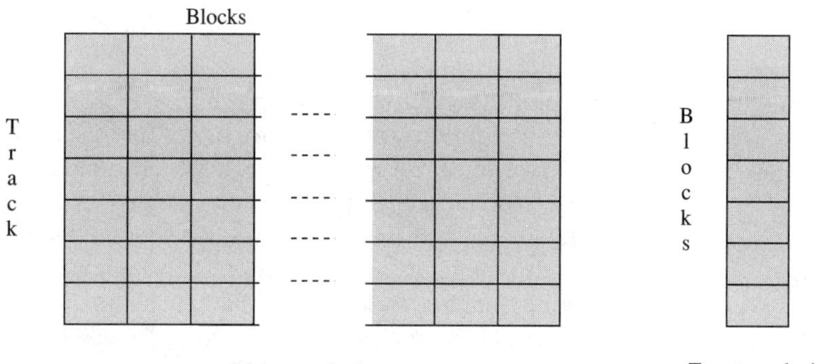

Figure 3.5 Organization of records on blocks (shaded area marks unused space).

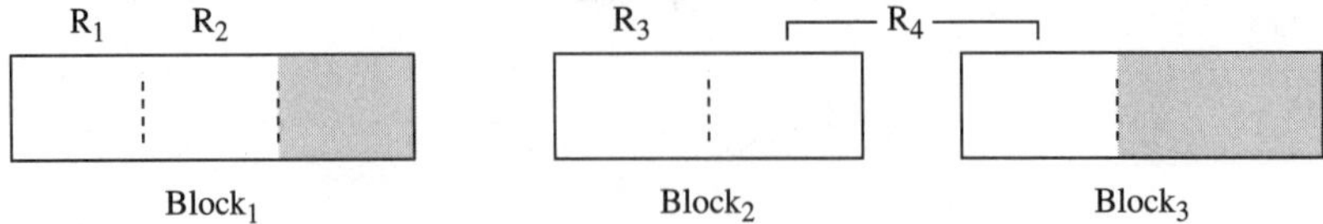

every record. As different blocks may be assigned to different files, a mapping must be maintained to record the particular files to which the blocks are assigned.

The importance of the study of file organization methods is that different methods have different properties and hence efficiencies for different applications. A major factor that determines the overall system performance is response time for data on secondary storage. This time depends not only on physical device characteristics, but also on the data arrangement and request sequencing. In general, the response cost has two components: access time and data transfer time. **Data transfer time** is the time needed to move data from the secondary storage device to processor memory; access time is the time needed to position the read/write head at the required position. The data transfer time depends on physical device characteristics and cannot be optimized. In the case of reading a 1KB (kilobyte = 1024 bytes) block of data from a device that can transfer it at 100KB/sec (KB/sec = kilobyte/second), the data transfer time is 10 msec. The response time, while influenced by physical characteristics, depends on the distance between current and target positions and, therefore, on data organization.

3.1.2 The Constituents of a File

Data is organized on a secondary storage medium in the context of a logical unit, the file. Some areas on the storage medium are designated by the file manager (FM) subsystem of the operating system (OS) for a specific file. The FM designates areas on the storage medium for every file, records information concerning the particular area each file occupies, and uses it whenever access to a file is required. Note that on the storage medium there is no distinction among the files. Although a file is mapped onto some physical areas of a storage medium, we consider a file to be made up of some logical units known as records. A record is used to store data about some entity of interest.

Example 3.1

We want to store birth date information. Obviously we shall use a record for every person whose data we store; that is, if there are 10 persons, we shall create 10 records. Although we are primarily interested in the birth date, it would not be of much use unless we could associate the date with a person. We shall therefore store data about a person's name (first and last) and date of birth. *First_Name, Last_Name,* and *Birth_Date* are the fields that constitute a record. Note that when we speak of a record we use the term field instead of attribute. We will use these terms interchangeably. ■

Before we go on to more formal material, let us examine the attribute *Birth_Date* in greater detail. We are all well aware that every date is not a legal date, eg, January 33, 1959. Furthermore, a future date could not be a valid value for this file. If we want to restrict the values that can be assigned to some attribute for a given record, we must define the set of legal values for that attribute. We refer to this set of legal values as the domain of an attribute.

Until now, we have been informally discussing certain concepts related to data organization on secondary storage. We shall now set these concepts in more formal terms.

A file F is a collection or "bag" of records, that is, $F = \{r_1, r_2, \ldots, r_n\}$, where the r_i's are used to represent the records in a file F containing n records. File F, in general, is not a set of records because duplicate records may be permitted. A "bag" permits duplicate occurrences although it may be difficult to visualize many situations where this would occur.

As discussed earlier, an attribute is used to capture some characteristic or property of an entity. A record r_i is a set of <attribute (or field), value> pairs defined on the set of attributes $A = \{A_{i1}, \ldots, A_{im}\}$ over the set of corresponding domains $D = \{D_{i1}, \ldots, D_{im}\}$. It is not necessary that D_{ij} and D_{ik}, $j \neq k$, be distinct domains, as different attributes can be defined on the same domain.

The record r_i can be represented as the set $r_i = \{(A_{i1}, v_{i1}), \ldots, (A_{im}, v_{im})\}$, where each $v_{ij} \in D_{ij}$, for $j = 1, \ldots, m$. If every record of a file contains <attribute,value> pairs for the same set of attributes, the file is said to contain **homogeneous records.** If the attribute-value pairs are similarly ordered in all the records of the file, i.e., for all r_i, $(A_{11} = A_{21} = \ldots = A_{n1})$, $(A_{12} = A_{22} = \ldots\ A_{n2})$, $\ldots, (A_{1m} = A_{2m} = \ldots = A_{nm})$, then the fact that the attribute order is known can be used to achieve efficiency in record representation. It is in fact usual to represent a record using positional notation, i.e., $r_i = (v_{i1}, \ldots, v_{im})$, where the attributes are discerned from the position of the associated value. This is how we represented a record in Figure 2.15. The order of the attributes has no semantic importance. For a data record using positional notation to make sense, the mapping between position and attribute names must be known. Although the attribute name may not be specifically incorporated in the record, we can logically associate the appropriate attribute name with the values stored.

Example 3.2

In the above example, the attribute order in each record of the file is given as *Birth_Date,* followed by *Last_Name* and then *First_Name*. On an access to a record we are presented with a sequence of bytes that we map, logically, to our three attributes. The first k bytes represent the *Birth_Date,* the succeeding k′ bytes the *Last_Name,* and the remaining k″ bytes the *First_Name*. Given the sequence of bytes, their decoding mechanism, and the values k, k′, and k″, we can interpret the sequence of bytes that constitutes the record. ■

A file that contains nonhomogeneous records needs to store the attribute names (or identification codes) within the records.

3.1.3 Formal Specification of Storage of a File

All storage organizations are ultimately constituted from bytes. Let us call the set of all possible bytes BYTES. We can define an attribute value, a record, and a file in terms of a sequence of bytes. The length of a sequence, s, is written as #s. An informal treatment of sequences is given in Appendix 3.1 at the end of the text.

An attribute value or simply an attribute is some sequence of bytes[1]:

ATTRIBUTE : : = sequence of BYTES

The values for different attributes and also the different values for some attributes would not all be encoded using equal-length sequences. We have to specify the length of the sequence. For attributes that can accept variable-length sequences as values, we specify the minimum (#min) and maximum (#max) sequence lengths. Fixed-length values have #min = #max. Thus we have:

ATTRIBUTE : : = sequence of BYTES of length (#min . . #max)

A record is defined in terms of some bag of attribute values. Physically a record is defined as:

RECORD : : = sequence of BYTES

However, logically we think of a record as:

RECORD : : = sequence of ATTRIBUTES

Records are stored on the physical medium in blocks. For simplicity we assume fixed-length blocks. Then we have:

FL_BLOCK : : = array [1 . . BLOCK_SIZE] of BYTES
FL_BLOCK : : = sequence of RECORD

The first definition pertains to physical blocks and the second to logical blocks. The first definition allows a logical record to span over physical blocks.

Similarly, we define the file:

FILE : : = sequence of FL_BLOCK

(Note that from the definition of FL_BLOCK, we may physically consider a file to be just a sequence of BYTES, or logically as a sequence of RECORD.)

The emphasis on "sequence of BYTES" is deliberate, for this precisely represents the fact that all data is stored in the form of bytes (or bits). This is important, too, for if we have a sequence and we wish to map it into a given logical structure, we should know (1) the beginning point of the sequence and (2) a definition of the logical structure into sequences of bytes. This has implications for searching without transferring data between the secondary medium and main memory. A processing element associated with the read/write head of a storage device can decide that it has located some desired sequence only if it knows the starting point. These are encoded or physically embedded in actual storage devices.

[1]Note that some attributes are Boolean and need less than one byte; however, many implementations use an entire byte to store a single Boolean valued attribute.

A number of initialization operations must be performed by the file manager before the initial access is made to a file. This is usually done by issuing an open file (or in Pascal, a reset/rewrite command). This initiates some internal housekeeping by the file manager. The creation of a number of buffers of appropriate size and initializing pointers (one each for blocks and records within blocks) would be necessary. We shall name these pointers BLOCK_PTR and RECORD_PTR, respectively.

Assume that we have issued an open command for some file; then we can assume that BLOCK_PTR = 1 and RECORD_PTR = 1. The number of blocks in the file is given by #file_block and the number of records in the block BLOCK_PTR is given by #record(BLOCK_PTR). Algorithm 3.1 for get_record follows. Here we ensure that we do not attempt to access a record past the last record of a block or access a block past the last block in the file. Provided that the pointers are correctly set, the next record is made available. If we had already accessed the last record in the block, the block pointer is incremented and the record pointer within the block is reset to 1. (Note that this algorithm is much more simple than what happens in reality. First, it is implicit that somehow the data from the secondary storage is already available. In practice, the blocks would have to be read off the secondary storage. Second, the sizes (# . . .) are made available from some system record

Algorithm **3.1**

Algorithm to Get a Record

Input: initialized values for BLOCK_PTR, RECORD_PTR, #file_block(number of blocks in the file) and #record(BLOCK_PTR) (number of records in the block)

Output: next record in file or end_of_file error condition

```
return_flag : = true
  while return_flag do
  if BLOCK_PTR > #file_block then begin
      error end_of_file (''reading after end'')
      return_flag : = false
      end
    else if RECORD_PTR ≤ #record(BLOCK_PTR) then begin
           record : = file(BLOCK_PTR,RECORD_PTR)
           RECORD_PTR : = RECORD_PTR + 1
           return_flag : = false
           end
       else begin
           BLOCK_PTR : = BLOCK_PTR + 1
           RECORD_PTR : = 1
           end
```

area. Thus, the algorithm should be taken as giving the general picture.) The successful execution of get_record logically (not physically) alters the file:

file' := file − record

The above expression specifies that the record is no longer available from the logical file. A sequence of get records would not fetch the already obtained record unless we reposition BLOCK_PTR and RECORD_PTR, for instance, by issuing an open or rewind command.

We can specify similar algorithms for insertion, deletion, and modification. Let us consider insertion. Suppose we have already identified the block into which the new record is to be inserted. In the simple scheme of things, the BLOCK_PTR and RECORD_PTR have been correctly set. We can specify the insertion as:

file(BLOCK_PTR,RECORD_PTR) := file(BLOCK_PTR,RECORD_PTR) + record,

where record is the record to be inserted. The operation + indicates the insertion of the record in the block specified by BLOCK_PTR at the position specified by RECORD_PTR. This would be perfectly correct if the block could accept any number of records. However, this is not so. If the block cannot accept the record, we must either reject the insertion or devise some scheme to make believe that the block is larger than it really is. In the latter scheme we implicitly or explicitly chain together blocks to logically extend a given block. The implicit method inserts the record in the next block with sufficient free space; this method is the same as that used in some of the hashing schemes to handle collision. Explicitly, we can either predesignate a block (or set of blocks) or point to a block that would accept the overflow record(s). In this scheme the original block is called the **primary block** and the block for the overflow record is the **overflow block.** Another possibility would be to ask the file manager to allocate a new block in which the overflow record(s) would be accepted.

In the above discussion, we have conveniently forgotten to look into our records. How is the sequence of bytes that constitutes the record interpreted? It is usual to specify the structure of the record within a program. This allows the physical sequence of bytes to be mapped into the logical sequence of attributes that we have defined. In Example 3.2, we defined a file that stored birth dates as *Birth_Date, Last_Name, First_Name,* or was it specified as *Birth_Date, First_Name, Last_Name,* or some other sequence? Two programs with the above different record structures would still be able to read the same data file. Remember that in the physical sense, we just stored a sequence of bytes. The results from one of the programs would be very interesting. For example, if the size for the two name attributes was the same, one program would have interchanged the first with the last name of every person. In this simple case we might be able to identify the malfunctioning program, but can we be sure that this would be the situation in all cases? The moral of the discussion is that for every file created, a repository of its structure is necessary.

3.1.4 Operations on Files: Logical Access

Having looked at the storage structure of a file and operations on it, we now consider both physical and logical sequencing or ordering of its records. Assume that we are

Figure 3.6 Physical and logical file.

Name	GPA
Abe	2.00
Anne	3.85
.	
.	
David	3.55
.	
.	
John	3.70
Marc	3.90
Mary	3.95
.	
.	
Zeon	3.65

(a) Physical file

first record retrieved
Mary 3.95
next record retrieved
Marc 3.90
last record retrieved
Abe 2.00
(b) Logical access

given a file containing data on student names and grade point averages (GPA). The records in the file are stored in lexicographic order. A subset of the records of the file is shown in Figure 3.6a. We can access the records in their physical (stored) order or we can do so in some other order, such as in decreasing GPA order. We assume that a logical access method is available that allows us to retrieve records in decreasing GPA order. For data in our file, the first record fetched will be that of Mary with a GPA of 3.95, as shown in the first entry in Figure 3.6b. The next record obtained will be that of Marc. The records are being fetched in their logical sequence (that of decreasing GPA) and not in their stored (or physical) sequence. After we access the last record in the file, a call for the next record in the file causes the end_of_file exception.

To reiterate, the records r_i of a file F may be accessed in some given logical sequence while being stored on the physical storage medium in another (physical) sequence. Access can be considered to be a mapping from file F and a pointer i to a record:

$$\text{ACCESS} : (F,i) \rightarrow r_i$$

The record, r, may be allocated space on the physical medium and stored as follows:

$$\text{STORE} : (F,j,r) \rightarrow \text{location}_j$$

The ACCESS mapping function needs to know where record r_j is stored to allow access to the record. Ideally, the STORE mapping function should not have to know how the records are accessed. The fact is, however, that in order to allow efficient access in a desired logical sequence, the store function needs additional information.

In addition to the ACCESS function, we need the following functions to access records relative to the current record accessed and the first and the last record of the file. These functions may be termed FIRST, LAST, NEXT, and PREVIOUS. If we assume that the logical sequence of the file F is $\{r_1, r_2, \ldots, r_n\}$ (the physical sequence may be same as the logical sequence), then

FIRST: $F \rightarrow r_1$ NEXT: $(F,r_i) \rightarrow r_{i+1}$ if $i \neq n$
LAST: $F \rightarrow r_n$ NEXT: $(F,r_n) \rightarrow$ ERROR (end_of_file)
PREVIOUS: $(F,r_i) \rightarrow r_{i-1}$ if $i > 1$
PREVIOUS: $(F,r_1) \rightarrow$ ERROR (beginning_of_file)

We sometimes do not require access to every attribute of a record, simply to a subset. Similarly, we may access only those records that satisfy some given condition. In general, we can specify access or retrieve operations on a file as:

<target_list | qualification>

where the target_list is the list of attributes for which the values of records satisfying the specified qualification clause are to be retrieved. The qualification clause is a Boolean expression, a sequence of terms connected with Boolean operators as defined below:

<qualification> : : = <term> [<Boolean_operator> <qualification>]
<term> : : = [<negation>] <attribute> <relational operator> <constant>
<relational operator> : : = '='|'≠'|'>'|'≥'|'<'|'≤'
<Boolean operator> : : = AND|OR
<negation> : : = NOT

In principle, we can retrieve records from a file based on the value of any attribute. However, it is common to retrieve records based on some subset of the attributes, designated as key attributes. The file is organized so that retrievals based on these key attributes will be efficient. Remember that certain attributes, **primary keys,** may be used to uniquely identify records in a file, while other attributes, secondary or nonprimary keys, can identify a set of records.

Example 3.3

In Figure 3.6, assume that the names are unique, i.e., the name can be used to identify a record. As such, name would be the primary key for the GPA file.

In the Birth_Date file we recorded information about the birth dates of persons we know. We can assume that the combination of *First_Name* and *Last_Name* uniquely identifies a record, i.e., that every person we know has a unique name. Suppose that a person's *First_Name* and *Birth_Date* also uniquely identify a record. In other words, some persons have a common birth date and a few of the persons have the same first name, but no two persons with the same first name have the same birth date (at least for this example). Thus we can assume that either one of the two combinations <*First_Name, Last_Name*> or <*First_Name, Birth_Date*> can be used as a primary key.

Let us choose the <*First_Name, Last_Name*> combination as our primary key. We can choose any or all of the attributes *First_Name, Last_Name,* and *Birth_Date* as secondary keys. For simplicity, we choose *Birth_Date*. Now, since we allow the possibility of more than one person with the same birth date, we expect to retrieve zero, one, or several records when we use *Birth_Date* to access this file. Accessing the file using the <*First_Name, Last_Name*> combination would retrieve at most one record. ■

The data contained within the file may have to be changed. The changes could be the addition (or insertion) of new records, the removal (or deletion) of an existing one, or the changing (or modifying) of some of the contents of an existing one. The insertion, deletion, and modification operations are collectively known as **update operations.** Update operations can also be expressed in terms of *target_list* and *qualification_list*. The *target_list* permits assignment statements in the form of attribute := expression. Insert operations have an empty qualification clause.

An update is a mapping from one (old) version of a file to another (new) version of it, i.e., $F \rightarrow F'$. Assume that #F_record represents the number of records in the file F. An update may include any of the following four possible procedures:

U_1. Insert records in their proper logical sequence. Let $F = \{r_1, \ldots, r_{k-1}, r_{k+1}, \ldots\}$ and #F_record = n, then

$$\text{INSERT}: (F, r_k) \rightarrow F'$$

where $F' = \{r_1, \ldots, r_{k-1}, r_k, r_{k+1}, \ldots\}$ and #F′_record = n+1.

The operation is accomplished logically by copying records $r_1, \ldots, r_{k-1}$ into file F′, then storing record r_k and copying the remaining records, $r_k, r_{k+1}, \ldots$ into F′.

U_2. Delete one or more existing records from the file. Let $F = \{r_1, \ldots, r_{k-1}, r_k, r_{k+1}, \ldots\}$ and #F_record = n, then

$$\text{DELETE}: (F, r_k) \rightarrow F'$$

where $F' = \{r_1, \ldots, r_{k-1}, r_{k+1}, \ldots\}$ and #F′_record = n − 1.

The operation is accomplished logically by copying records $r_1 \ldots, r_{k-1}$ into file F′, ignoring record r_k, and then copying the remaining records, $r_k, r_{k+1}, \ldots$ into F′.

U_3. Modify the data values in some existing record. This is akin to deleting record r_i and inserting r_i', where r_i' is the modified record.

$$\text{MODIFY}: (F, r_i) \rightarrow F'$$

Let $F = \{r_1, \ldots, r_i, \ldots, r_{k-1}, r_k, r_{k+1}, \ldots\}$ and
$F' = \{r_1, \ldots, r_i', \ldots, r_{k-1}, r_k, r_{k+1}, \ldots\}$

The operation is accomplished logically by copying records $r_1, \ldots, r_{i-1}$ into the file F′, modifying record r_i to r_i' and copying it to file F′, and then copying the remaining records, $r_{i+1}, \ldots$ into F′. Note that the relative positions of the records remain unchanged.

U_4. Modify the data values in existing records (it is common to assume that the record length remains the same).

$$\text{MODIFY}: (F, A_i, v_i, v_i') \rightarrow F'$$

This modifies data values in *all* records that have value v_i for the attribute A_i. The operation is accomplished logically as follows: Copy a record r_j, such that the value of attribute $A_i \neq v_i$, into the file F′; or modify a record r_k, such that the value of attribute $A_i = v_i$, to r_k' where the value of attribute A_i is modified to v_i' and copy the modified record to file F′.

Remember that update operations may also cause exceptions, such as when we try to delete or modify a nonexistent record. In most applications insertion of a duplicate record creates an exception condition. Updates to primary key attributes of a record are either disallowed or handled by a deletion followed by an insertion. The reason for this two-step operation is to ensure that the change was intended.

We mentioned earlier that access is usually required only on certain attributes. Our logical record may then be considered as composed of two distinct parts; KEYS and ATTS, where both are sequences of ATTRIBUTES:

```
RECORD ::= <KEYS> <ATTS>
KEYS   ::= sequence of ATTRIBUTE
ATTS   ::= sequence of ATTRIBUTE
```

This is more than just some whimsical rearrangement. It is a deliberate splitting of the key from the nonkey attributes. Now when a search is performed using some key attribute, we need only search the area where the key attributes are stored. We can, if we wish, store the key attributes and nonkey attributes in physically separate areas. The advantage will come when the size of the storage required by the key attributes is significantly smaller then the storage required for the complete record. We could store the key attributes and nonkey attributes in different, marked areas on the same block and use the read head, as it scans the surface, to locate records with certain key values. This is what is done on some disk storage technologies, wherein only a single key attribute is used.

3.1.5 Primary Key Retrieval

In this section we present an overview of the logical (or access mappings) and physical (or store mappings) file organizations commonly supported by the file management systems of operating systems. We consider here the sequential, indexed-sequential, and direct file organizations. We are not concerned with their implementations under individual operating systems, only with general principles.

In a **sequential file,** records are stored in ascending or descending primary key order. The logical sequence is the same as the physical sequence. The difference between a serial and a sequential file is that in a **serial file,** records are stored in no particular order. No logical sequence of records applies; the physical order is merely the order in which the records were added to the file.

The advent of disks made it possible to move randomly through a file. To access a given record, however, we must know its physical location. In a sequential file the records are stored in a physical sequence depending on the primary key value. Additional information giving the physical location for a given key value is needed to move directly to a random record. For example, at the beginning of a book, the contents section indicates the starting page number (physical location) for each chapter or section (key values). A similar concept can be used with a sequential file. In an **index-sequential file** the physical location of a record in the sequential file is maintained in a set of indexes. These indexes provide fast and random access to the records in the file.

In **direct file** organizations the physical location of a record is based on some relationship with its primary key value. The physical location is given directly or indirectly by a hash address. In the next sections, we shall look at each of the above file organizations.

3.2 Serial Files

We stated earlier that in a serial file records are stored in no particular logical order; therefore, the serial file is equivalent to an unordered sequence. Let us take, for instance, a deck of shuffled playing cards and spread some of the cards facedown from left to right on a tabletop. We shall call these cards on the table a cardfile. We are allowed to pick one card at a time from the cardfile, starting from the left. The card picked (the record just read) is placed faceup. We can assume that we have some pointer that points to the next card to be picked; the last faceup card acts as a pointer. If we pick a card and then another, the first and second cards picked bear no logical relationship with each other. For instance, if we treat all cards belonging to a given suit as logically related, it is not always the case that the two cards picked belong to the same suit. The cards can only be picked in their physical sequence. A card on the table may be referred to as the last card of the cardfile. The next card is placed to the immediate right of it, i.e., appended after the last card. Our layout of the cards simulates a serial file (see Figure 3.7)

A serial file is generated by appending records at the end, and if the records are randomly appended as in the case of a shuffled deck of cards, the logical ordering of the file with respect to a given key bears no correspondence to the physical sequence. The updates of type U_3 (updating an individual record) and U_4 (updating a group of records meeting certain criteria) can be done in place if we assume that the records are of fixed length and modifications do not change their size. The retrieval of a particular record entails searching the file from the beginning to end, if necessary. On average, the search requires the examination of half the records in the file.

The deletion of a record can be handled in a number of ways. All records following the deleted record can be moved forward or the last record in the file can be brought in to replace the deleted record. Both of these options require many additional accesses up to the end of file. A more practical alternative is to logically delete a record, that is, mark the record as having been deleted. In future insertions or file reorganizations, the space occupied by a deleted record can be reclaimed. In the case of insertions, this requires that every record of the file be checked until we find one that has been deleted and marked as such. A new record could be inserted in the space occupied by the first such deleted record.

A serial file is also referred to as a **nonkeyed sequential file.** In a serial file, The entire file has to be processed in searching for a nonexisting record, whereas in a sequential file, on average, only half the file has to be searched. A serial file is

Figure 3.7 Example of a serial file.

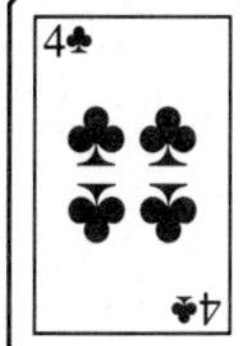

• • •

typically used to maintain records chronologically; one such application is to record transactions.

3.3 Sequential Files

In a sequential file, records are maintained in the logical sequence of their primary key values. The processing of a sequential file is conceptually simple but inefficient for random access. However, if access to the file is strictly sequential, a sequential file is suitable. A sequential file could be stored on a sequential storage device such as a magnetic tape.

Search for a given record in a sequential file requires, on average, access to half the records in the file. Consider a system where the file is stored on a direct access device such as a disk. Suppose the key value is separated from the rest of the record and a pointer is used to indicate the location of the record. In such a system, the device may scan over the key values at rotation speeds and only read in the desired record. A binary[2] or logarithmic search technique may also be used to search for a record. In this method, the cylinder on which the required record is stored is located by a series of decreasing head movements. The search, having been localized to a cylinder, may require the reading of half the tracks, on average, in the case where keys are embedded in the physical records, or require only a scan over the tracks in the case where keys are also stored separately.

Updating usually requires the creation of a new file. To maintain file sequence, records are copied to the point where amendment is required. The changes are then made and copied into the new file. Following this, the remaining records in the original file are copied to the new file. This method of updating a sequential file creates an automatic backup copy. It permits updates of the type U_1 through U_4.

Addition can be handled in a manner similar to updating. Adding a record necessitates the shifting of all records from the appropriate point to the end of file to create space for the new record. Inversely, deletion of a record requires a compression of the file space, achieved by the shifting of records. Changes to an existing record may also require shifting if the record size expands or shrinks.

The basic advantage offered by a sequential file is the ease of access to the next record, the simplicity of organization, and the absence of auxiliary data structures. However, replies to simple queries are time consuming for large files. Updates, as seen above, usually require the creation of a new file. A single update is an expensive proposition if a new file must be created. To reduce the cost per update, all such requests are batched, sorted in the order of the sequential file, and then used to update the sequential file in a single pass. Such a file, containing the updates to be made to a sequential file, is sometimes referred to as a **transaction file.**

In the batched mode of updating, a transaction file of update records is made and then sorted in the sequence of the sequential file. The update process requires the examination of each individual record in the original sequential file (the **old master file**). Records requiring no changes are copied directly to a new file (the **new**

[2]Factors such as seek and latency time rule out the use of binary search in favor of some form of indexing scheme for disk-based files.

Figure 3.8 A file with empty spaces for record insertions (the figure shows some fixed-length records and unused space).

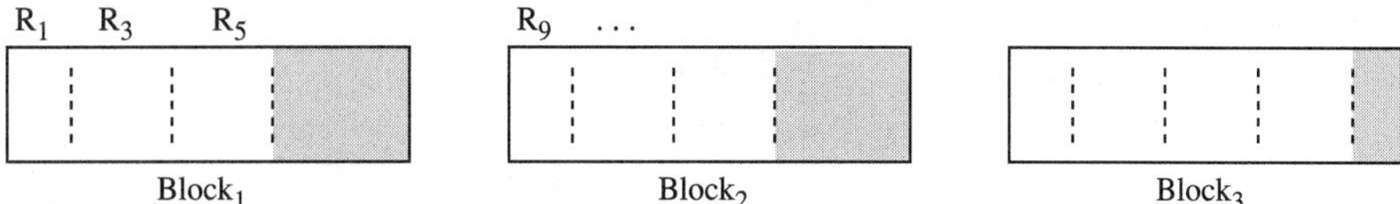

master file); records requiring one or more changes are written into the new master file only after all necessary changes have been made. Insertions of new records are made in the proper sequence: They are written into the new master file at the appropriate place. Records to be deleted are not copied to the new master file. A big advantage of this method of update is the creation of an automatic backup copy. The new master file can always be recreated by processing the old master file and the transaction file.

A possible method of reducing the creation of a new file at each update run is to create the original file with ''holes'' (space left for the addition of new records, as shown in Figure 3.8). As such, if a block could hold k records, then at initial creation it is made to contain only L * k records, where $0 < L \leq 1$ is known as the loading factor. Additional space may also be earmarked for records that may ''overflow'' their blocks, e.g., If the record r_i logically belongs to block B_i but the physical block B_i does not contain the requisite free space. This additional free space is known as the overflow area. A similar technique is employed in index-sequential files.

3.4 Index-Sequential Files

The retrieval of a record from a sequential file, on average, requires access to half the records in the file, making such enquiries not only inefficient but very time consuming for large files. To improve the query response time of a sequential file, a type of indexing technique can be added.

An index is a set of <key, address> pairs. Indexing associates a set of objects to a set of orderable quantities, which are usually smaller in number or their properties provide a mechanism for faster search. The purpose of indexing is to expedite the search process. Indexes created from a sequential (or sorted) set of primary keys are referred to as index sequential. Although the indices and the data blocks are held together physically, we distinguish between them logically. We shall use the term **index file** to describe the indexes and **data file** to refer to the data records. The index is usually small enough to be read into the processor memory.

A sequential (or sorted on primary keys) file that is indexed is called an index-sequential file. The index provides for random access to records, while the sequential nature of the file provides easy access to the subsequent records as well as sequential processing. An additional feature of this file system is the overflow area. This feature provides additional space for record addition without necessitating the creation of a new file.

Figure 3.9 Implicit index for starting page numbers of words in a dictionary.

Words starting with letter	Page#	Index Entries
A	3	3
B	43	43
C	85	85
E	159	−1000
.		159
.		.
.		.
X	807	807
Y	808	808
Z	811	811

(a) <Key, address> pairs (b) Implicit index

3.4.1 Implicit Index

The index file can be simplified or its storage requirements reduced if only the address part of the <key, address> pair is held in the index. This, however, necessitates holding the address of every possible key in the key range, including addresses of records not in the file. The addresses of nonexistent records can be set to an impossibly high or low value to indicate their absence from the file. If the number of such missing records in the range of stored key values is small, the saving obtained by not storing the key is considerable. Figure 3.9b is an example of an **implicit index** corresponding to the **explicit index** given in Figure 3.9a. Note that the record with a key of D is not in the file. This fact is indicated with a negative pointer value. This scheme requires that the value of the key be implicit in the position of the entry in the index. In this example, the first key is A, the second, B, and so on. In such a scheme, the maintenance of the index becomes simpler. The space requirement depends on the proportion of existent records to the key range.

3.4.2 Limit Indexing

Because data on a direct access storage device is stored as a block of records on tracks and the entire contents of each track[3] are read into main memory for processing, it is not necessary to use full indexing. In a **limit indexing** or partial indexing scheme, a single entry per track is maintained in the index. It is possible to group together a number of storage locations and identify these by a single address. In this manner, the storage on a track, a group of tracks, a cylinder, a group of cylinders,

[3]In the case of a sector-oriented direct access storage device, the track is divided into a number of sectors and the basic unit of transfer is a sector. Limit indexing may be either with respect to a track or with respect to a sector within a track.

Figure 3.10 Group formations for limit indexing.

Group	*Group Size*	*Keys in Group*	*Sequential Index*
G_1	s_1	$K_1, K_2, \ldots, K_{s1}$	K_{s1}
G_2	s_2	$K_{s1+1}, \ldots, K_{s1+s2}$	K_{s1+s2}
.	.	. .	
.	.	. .	.
G_m	s_m	$K_{n-sm+1}, \ldots, K_n$	K_n

and so on can be grouped together and referred to by a single address. Certain operating systems permit such logical grouping to form what is referred to as a **block** or a **bucket.** The index may then have one entry per block.

Consider a set of sorted keys $<K_1, K_2, \ldots, K_n>$, with $K_1 < K_2 < \ldots < K_n$, divided into m groups of sizes $<s_1, s_2, \ldots, s_m>$ with the sorted order of the keys being maintained within each group. Each group is identified by the key with the largest value in that group and called the **sequential index key.** Figure 3.10 illustrates the keys in the groups, their sizes, and the index key. In an index-sequential file the groups correspond to blocks.

Example 3.4 Consider a file with records having keys of 037, 039, 048, 052, 057, 065, 073, 081, 090, 103, 141, 157, 235, 241, 267, 299. We can create, for instance, six groups as shown in the Figure. The addition of a record that lies between 090 and 141, let us say with the key of 095, will be appended in group 3.

Example of limit indexing.

Group	*Group Size*	*Keys in Group*	*Sequential Index*
1	3	037, 039, 048	048
2	6	052,057,065,073,081,090	090
3	2	103, 141	141
4	1	157	157
5	2	235, 241	241
6	2	267, 299	299

■

Within a sequential index the sequential index keys are maintained in sorted order. Let us assume an ascending order, as shown in Example 3.4. In the search for a record, its key K_r is first compared with the sequential index keys. If K_r is greater than a sequential index key, it is compared with the next sequential index key. The process is continued until a sequential index key greater or equal to K_r is found.

If the group corresponding to the first index key greater than K_r is, let us say, G_s, then the logical position of record corresponding to the key K_r is in group G_s. This is because K_r is greater than the largest key in group G_{s-1} but smaller than or equal to the largest key in group G_s. The key K_r is then compared to the keys in the group G_s to find a match.

This search procedure based on a set of ordered indexes, (the largest keys of different groups of sorted keys) is called an **index-sequential search.** It is shown in Algorithm 3.2.

In Algorithm 3.2 we assume that the index is available in memory and the entries are INDEXKEY and ADDRESS. This first entry in the index gives us the first sequential index key value and the location address of the associated block. We compare the given search key value with that of successive index key value entries until we get to the desired entry. This would be a block suitable for holding a record with the search key value. LOCATION returns the address of the block to which the record corresponding to SEARCHKEY belongs (logically).

In some systems, instead of the largest keys of the different groups being maintained in the sequential index, the smallest keys are kept. This requires that the key K_r be compared with the group keys until the group with the key $G_i > K_r$ is located. Then K_r may be contained in the preceding group, G_{i-1}.

Number of Comparisons

Assume that the groups are of the same size, i.e., $s_1 = s_2 = \ldots = s_m = s$. Then the number of records $n = m*s$ where there are m groups. In every group, more than one key value may exist; therefore, when searching for a record with a given key value, we have to check this key value against those of the records in the group. The number of comparisons associated with index-sequential search for different keys is presented in Figure 3.11. Part a of the figure shows the index and the number of

Algorithm **3.2**

Index-Sequential Search Algorithm

Input: Index table, and SEARCHKEY the key of record to be retrieved

Output: The address of block for the record with key equal to SEARCHKEY

{Assumption: The last index entry has a key value that cannot be exceeded}

```
get first index entry, <INDEXKEY, ADDRESS>
while INDEXKEY < SEARCHKEY do
    get next index entry
LOCATION := ADDRESS
```

{the record associated with the SEARCHKEY logically belongs in the block with the address LOCATION, and this address can be used to lookup, insert, delete, or modify the record.}

Figure 3.11 Index key comparisons.

Index	*Address of Block*	*Number of Comparisons*
K_s	A_1	1
K_{2s}	A_2	2
.	.	.
.	.	.
K_n	A_m	m

(a)

Block at Address	*Record Key*	*Number of Comparisons*	
A_1	K_1	1	(2)
	K_2	2	(3)
	.	.	.
	K_s	s	(s+1)
A_2	K_{s+1}	1	(3)
	K_{s+2}	2	(4)
	.	.	.
	.	.	.
A_m	.	.	.
	K_n	s	(s+m)

(b)

comparisons required to sequentially search for a key in the index. Part b indicates the block structure and the number of comparisons required for the sequential search for a record with a given key. The total number of comparisons made in searching for a key is the sum of the comparisons for the index and the block, given within parentheses in Figure 3.11b.

For key K_i the total number of comparisons is given by:

$$\lceil i/s \rceil + (i - 1) \bmod s + 1$$

and the average number of comparisons is given by

$$1 + (m + s)/2$$

Example 3.5

Assume a file of 10,000 records distributed over 100 blocks, i.e., every block has 100 records. Also assume that every record is equally likely to be accessed. In trying to locate a particular record, we first examine the index, which is assumed to be within a single block. To locate the block containing the required record, we have to examine each index entry. The number of comparisons required are:

Search for	*# Comparisons*
First entry	1
Second entry	2
Third entry	3
.	
.	
.	
99th entry	99
100th entry	100

The total number of comparisons made is 100 * (101)/2 = 5050 and the average number of comparisons per access is 50.5. By similar reasoning, we know that the average number of comparisons required for the actual record from the data block (it also contains 100 entries) is also 50.5. Therefore, the average number of comparisons required is 101. This value agrees with the value calculated using the expression 1 + (m + s)/2, since in our example the block size, s, is 100 and the number of blocks, m, is 100. ■

It is normal to organize a file with several logical records per track (we can even consider a lower division of a track into a number of sectors and assign several logical records per sector). If the records are held in key sequence, it is sufficient to index only the highest record key within each track (or sector). The index entries, then, consist of <track number, highest key in track> pairs. A record (with a given search key) is located by reading the index into main memory and comparing its key with the index entries to locate the track. The record is then searched for within the track.

At the beginning of this chapter we abstracted a disk as a two dimensional array with tracks and blocks (sectors). Instead of labeling all the tracks uniquely, we can group them in sets. One such grouping is formed around cylinders. Let c be the number of cylinders on which n records are organized in an indexed sequential organization. Each cylinder contains m tracks for storing records and each track contains s records. Let us also assume that n = cms. Assuming that access to all records is equally likely, the average number of comparisons is given by (c + m + s + 3)/2.

Example 3.6 Assume that a file occupies 100 cylinders of 20 tracks each. Each track holds 20 records. Then the average number of comparisons to locate a given record is (100 + 20 + 20 + 3)/2 = 71.5. ■

The above expressions are for average number of comparisons. They do not indicate the number of disk accesses made in the retrieval of a record. Expressions for disk accesses are given in Section 3.4.4.

3.4.3 Multilevel Indexing Schemes: Basic Technique

In a full indexing scheme, the address of every record is maintained in the index. For a small file, this index would be small and can be processed very efficiently in main memory. For a large file, the index's size would pose problems. It is possible to create a hierarchy of indexes with the lowest level index pointing to the records, while the higher level indexes point to the indexes below them (Figure 3.12). The higher level indices are small and can be moved to main memory, allowing the search to be localized to one of the larger lower level indices.

Figure 3.12 Hierarchy of indexes.

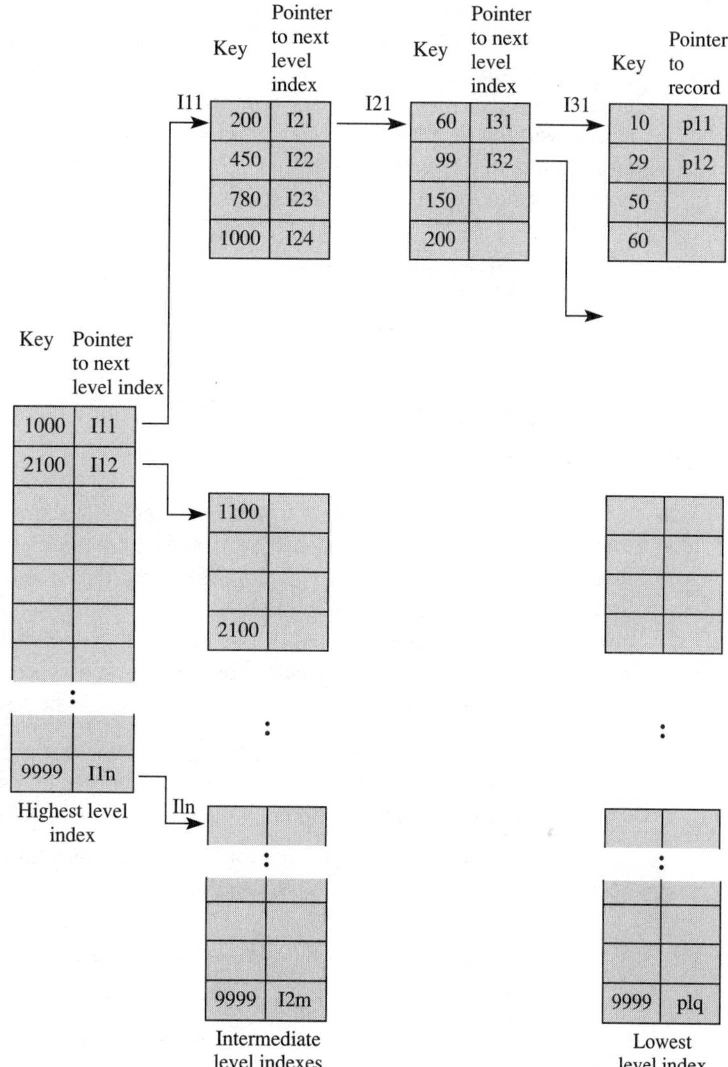

The lowest level index consists of the <key, address> pair for each record in the file; this is costly in terms of space. Updates of records require changes to the index file as well as the data file. Insertion of a record requires that its <key, address> pair be inserted in the index at the correct point, while deletion of a record requires that the <key, address> pair be removed from the index. Therefore, maintenance of the index is also expensive. In the simplest case, updates of variable length records require that changes be made to the address field of the record entry. In a variation of this scheme, the address value in the lowest level index entry points to a block of records and the key value represents the highest key value of records in this block. Another variation of this scheme is described in the next section.

3.4.4 Structure of Index Sequential Files

An index-sequential file consists of the data plus one or more levels of indexes. When inserting a record, we have to maintain the sequence of records and this may necessitate shifting subsequent records. For a large file this is a costly and inefficient process. Instead, the records that overflow their logical area are shifted into a designated overflow area and a pointer is provided in the logical area or associated index entry points to the overflow location. This is illustrated below. Record 615 is inserted in the original logical block causing a record to be moved to an overflow block.

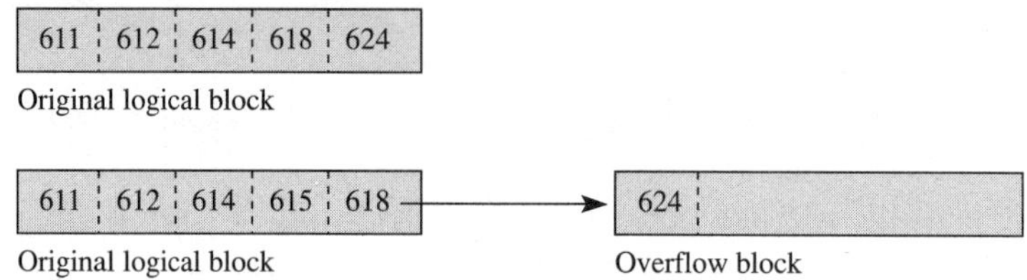

Multiple records belonging to the same logical area may be chained to maintain logical sequencing. When records are forced into the overflow areas as a result of insertion, the insertion process is simplified, but the search time is increased. Deletion of records from index-sequential files creates logical gaps; the records are not physically removed but only flagged as having been deleted. If there were a number of deletions, we may have a great amount of unused space.

An index-sequential file is therefore made up of the following components:

1. A primary data storage area. In certain systems this area may have unused spaces embedded within it to permit addition of records. It may also include records that have been marked as having been deleted.
2. Overflow area(s). This permits the addition of records to the files. A number of schemes exist for the incorporation of records in these areas into the expected logical sequence.
3. A hierarchy of indices. In a random enquiry or update, the physical location of the desired record is obtained by accessing these indices.

The primary data area contains the records written by the users' programs. The records are written in data blocks in ascending key sequence. These data blocks are in turn stored in ascending sequence in the primary data area. The data blocks are sequenced by the highest key of the logical records contained in them.

When using a disk device to store the index-sequential files, the data is stored on the cylinders, each of which is made up of a number of tracks. Some of these tracks are reserved for a prime data area and others are used for an overflow area associated with the prime data area on the cylinder.

A **track index** is written and maintained by the file system. Each cylinder of the index-sequential file has its own track index. The track index contains an entry for each prime data track in the cylinder as well as an entry to indicate if any records have overflowed from the track. Each prime track may be considered as a logical block.

Each track index entry is made up of the following items:

1. The address of the prime data track to which the entry refers.
2. The highest key of a record in the prime data track.
3. The highest key of a logical record in that data track, including records in the overflow areas (i.e., it is the highest key of an overflow record, if there were one or more, associated with that track).
4. The address of a record with the lowest key in the overflow area associated with that track (the address of the first record in the overflow chain).

Items 1 and 2 make up the normal track index entry and items 3 and 4 make up the overflow track index entry. If there were no overflow from a given track, items 2 and 3 would contain the same key value and item 4 would be set to a null value. If more than one record were required to be stored in an overflow area, these records will be chained so they can be reached from the first track overflow record. The structure of these track index entries for the cylinder is shown in Figure 3.13.

The address of the prime track entry in the normal track index does not change, nor does the highest key value of the logical block. The highest key value entry in the prime data track and the address of the first overflow record changes when a new record inserted in the prime data track causes an existing record to be bumped into the overflow area. (This is illustrated in Figure 3.14b). The last digit in the pointer refers to the record number on the track.

Figure 3.13 Typical cylinder organization.

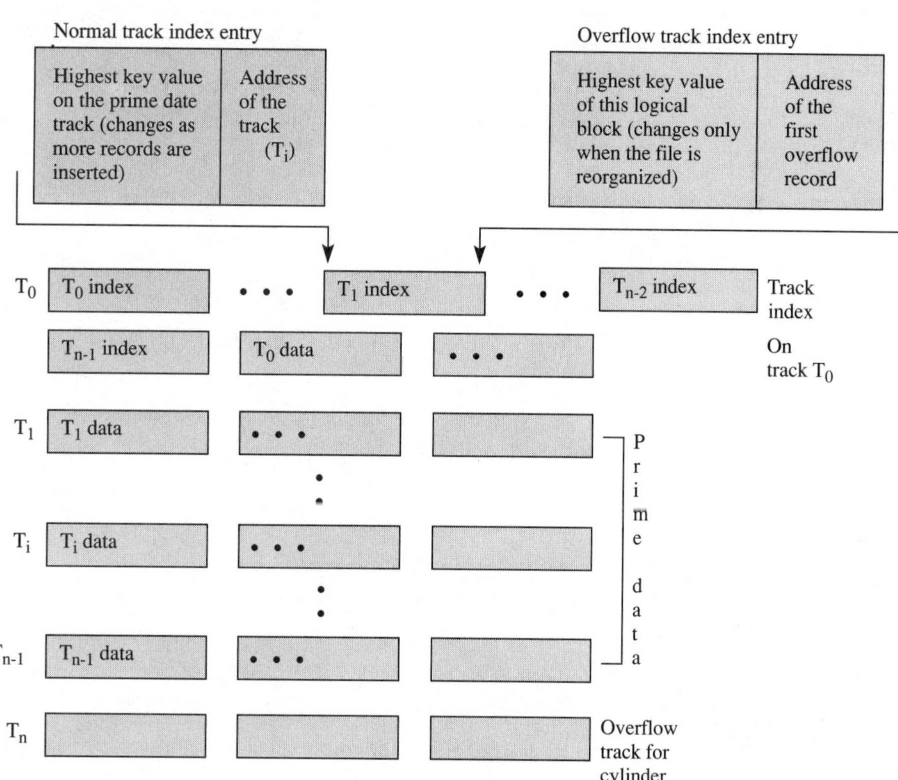

Figure 3.14 Structure of an index-sequential file.

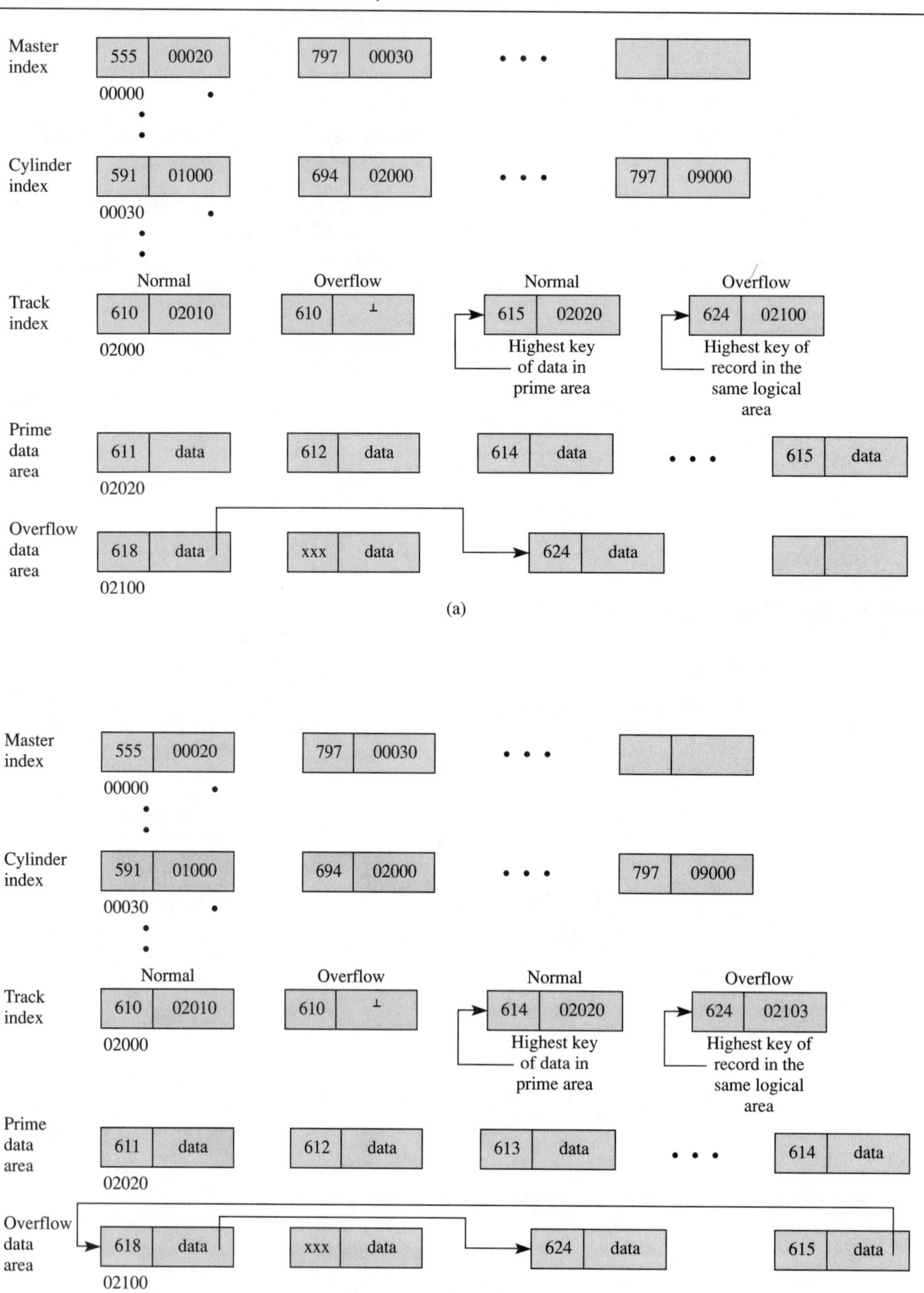

The track index entries are used by the file system to determine the track address of a given logical record. The cylinder's overflow area is used to store records that are forced off the prime data track when new records are inserted. The records in the overflow area are unblocked and stored in the order of their insertions or placement rather than, in key sequence. The logical sequence of records is maintained by prefixing a sequence link to each logical record. The access to records in an overflow area is via these links and therefore inefficient.

A file with records in overflow areas and with deleted records needs reorganization. (It has to be recreated.) Deleted records are not physically deleted, but marked as having been deleted. The space and the contents are physically undisturbed. Such marked records are retrieved by the file manager, and it is up to the application program to ascertain their status. Normally, on subsequent insertions, a marked record is not forced off the prime area to the overflow area. The only exception is when a record having the highest key value in a cylinder is marked as deleted. When such a record is forced off the prime data track due to subsequent insertions, it is written in the overflow area. Additional independent overflow areas are used when a cylinder overflow area becomes full.

The structure of an index-sequential file, including the index, prime data, and overflow areas is shown in Figure 3.14. The address is given as the cylinder address followed by the track address, both being two digits in this example. The final digit represents a record number. The index area of the file contains a cylinder index (shown in the figure as being stored in record 0 of cylinder 00, track 03) and may contain a master index (shown on cylinder 00, track 00). It does not contain the track index (which is stored on the cylinders themselves). Each cylinder in the prime data area has an entry in the cylinder index. The entry contains the address of the track index in that cylinder and the highest key stored on that cylinder. The cylinder index is used by the file system to determine the cylinder on which a record might or should be and the address of the track index for the cylinder.

An index-sequential file may be updated in sequential or random mode. In sequential mode, the insertion of new records in their proper sequence (update type U_1) requires the creation of a new file, so it is performed only if a very large number of new records are being added. Under certain file managers new records may be added to the end of the file in sequential mode only if there is enough space in the prime data areas, not the overflow areas. In random mode all types of updates can be performed on an existing file.

Retrieval from an index-sequential file may be sequential or random. In sequential mode, it may be possible to specify both a start and an end point. This is very useful for processing grouped data. The records, including those in the overflow area, are available in their logical sequence. All pointers between the overflow records in a sequence are handled automatically by the FM to retain the logical sequence. In random processing mode any arbitrary record may be accessed. **Skip-sequential processing,** wherein the records not needed for processing are skipped over, is also made very easy and efficient. For low hit rates, whole tracks and cylinders may be skipped. In a sequential file in which keys are stored separately from data, it is possible to skip records but every key must be read.

Number of Disk Accesses

Let us now consider the number of disk accesses required when searching for a given record. We again assume uniform distribution of records within blocks, tracks, and cylinders. Let there be L levels of indexing and the size of the index at a level, for instance j, be I_j blocks. Assume that each block is on a different track and access to a block consequently requires one disk access. Then, at each level, as we have assumed uniform distribution, we expect on average that half the number of index blocks will be accessed (in a sequential search). Therefore, the average total number of index blocks accessed is:

$$\sum_{j=1}^{L} \left\lceil \frac{I_j}{2} \right\rceil$$

In addition, we need to access the block on which the actual record resides. If the record is in a prime area, only one block has to be accessed; otherwise number O (≥ 0) overflow blocks are also accessed. As such, the total number of blocks accessed on average is:

$$\sum_{j=1}^{L} \left\lceil \frac{I_j}{2} \right\rceil + \begin{bmatrix} 1 \text{ if data on prime area} \\ 0 \text{ if data not on prime area} \end{bmatrix}$$

3.4.5 VSAM

The major disadvantage of the index-sequential organization is that as the file grows, performance deteriorates rapidly because of overflows and consequently there arises the need for periodic reorganization. Reorganization is an expensive process and the file becomes unavailable during reorganization. The **virtual storage access method (VSAM)** is IBM's advanced version of the index-sequential organization that avoids these disadvantages. The system is immune to the characteristics of the storage me-

Figure 3.15 Index and data blocks of a VSAM control interval.

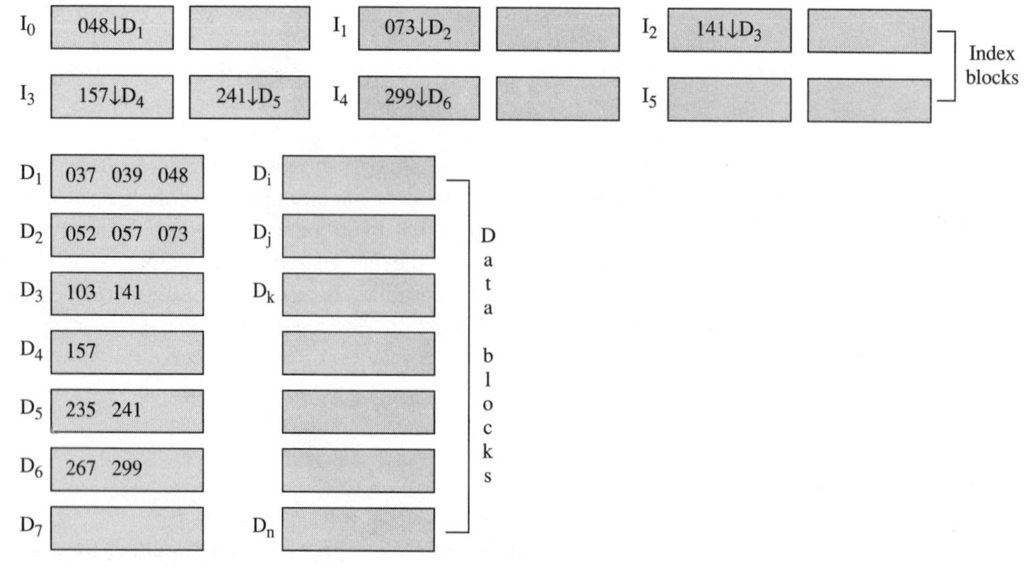

dium, which could be considered as a pool of blocks. The VSAM files are made up of two components: the index and data. However, unlike index-sequential organization, overflows are handled in a different manner. The VSAM index and data are assigned to distinct blocks of virtual storage called a **control interval.** To allow for growth, each time a data block overflows it is divided into two blocks and appropriate changes are made to the indexes to reflect this division.

Figure 3.15 shows the structure of a control interval of a VSAM file. The index block and the data blocks are included in a control interval. We can consider the control interval to serve the same purpose that the track does in the index-sequential organization. Higher level indices also exist in VSAM; however, these are not shown in Figure 3.15. The control interval contains a number of empty index and data blocks, which are used when a data block overflows. The index entry I_1 indicates that the highest key value of a record in data block D_2 is 73; the pointer to data block D_2 is indicated by $\downarrow D_2$. The method of handling overflow is illustrated in Example 3.7.

Example 3.7

Suppose the records to be added have the key values of 55 and 60. These records will logically be added into data block D_2. However, since D_2 has a block size of 4, only one record can be added without an overflow. The solution used in VSAM is to split the logical block D_2 into two blocks, let us say D_2 and D_7. The records are inserted in the correct logical sequence. Furthermore, the index entry I_1 is divided into two index entries as shown below:

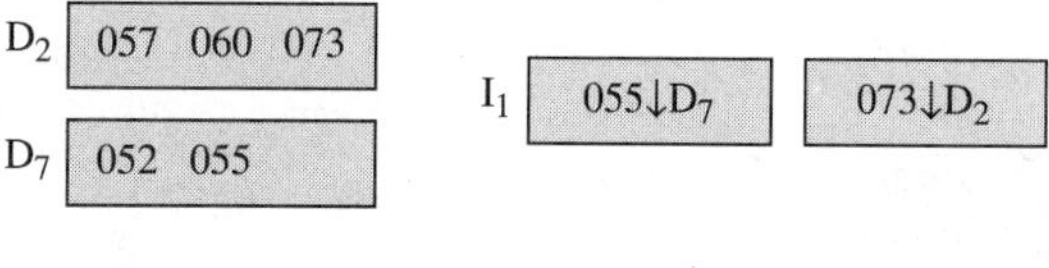

■

In VSAM, a number of control intervals are grouped together into a **control area.** An index exists for each control area. A control interval can be viewed as a track and a control area as a cylinder of the index-sequential organization.

Each control interval also contains control information that can be used in conjunction with routines provided in VSAM to allow retrieval of records, using either the key value or the relative position of a record. The relative position can either be the relative position in bytes from the start of the file or, in the case of fixed-length records, the relative number of the record.

3.5 Direct File

In the index-sequential file organization considered in the previous sections, the mapping from the search-key value to the storage location is via index entries. In direct

Figure 3.16 Mapping from a key value to an address value.

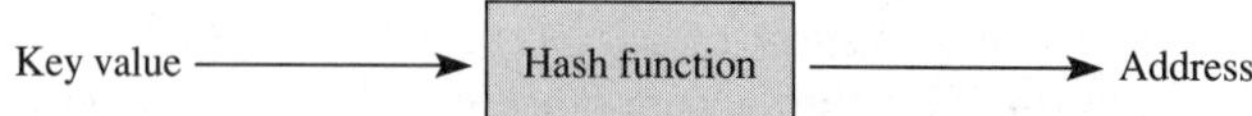

file organizations, the key value is mapped directly to the storage location. The usual method of direct mapping is by performing some arithmetic manipulation of the key value. This process is called **hashing.**

Let us consider a hash function *h* that maps the key value k to the value *h*(k). The value *h*(k) is used as an address and for our application we require that this value be in some range. If our address area for the records lies between S_1 and S_2, the requirement for the hash function *h*(k) is that for all values of k it should generate values between S_1 and S_2 (see Figure 3.16).

It is obvious that a hash function that maps many different key values to a single address or one that does not map the key values uniformly is a bad hash function. A **collision** is said to occur when two distinct key values are mapped to the same storage location. Collision is handled in a number of ways. The colliding records may be assigned to the next available space, or they may be assigned to an overflow area. We can immediately see that with hashing schemes there are no indexes to traverse. With well-designed hashing functions where collisions are few, this is a great advantage.

Another problem that we have to resolve is to decide what address is represented by *h*(k). Let the addresses generated by the hash function be addresses of buckets in which the <key, address> pair values of records are stored. Figure 3.17 shows the buckets containing the <key, address> pairs that allow a reorganization of the actual data file and actual record address without affecting the hash functions. A limited number of collisions could be handled automatically by the use of a bucket of sufficient capacity. Obviously the space required for the buckets will be, in general, much smaller than the actual data file. Consequently, its reorganization will not be that expensive. Once the bucket address is generated from the key by the hash function, a search in the bucket is also required to locate the address of the required record. However, since the bucket size is small, this overhead is small.

The use of the bucket reduces the problem associated with collisions. In spite of this, a bucket may become full and the resulting overflow could be handled by providing overflow buckets and using a pointer from the normal bucket to an entry in the overflow bucket. All such overflow entries are linked. Multiple overflow from the same bucket results in a long list and slows down the retrieval of these records. In an alternate scheme, the address generated by the hash function is a bucket address and the bucket is used to store the records directly instead of using a pointer to the block containing the record.

Let s represent the value:

$$s = \text{upper bucket address value} - \text{lower bucket address value} + 1$$

Here, s gives the number of buckets. Assume that we have some mechanism to convert key values to numeric ones. Then a simple hashing function is:

$$h(\text{k}) = \text{k mod s}$$

where k is the numeric representation of the key and *h*(k) produces a bucket address. A moment's thought tells us that this method would perform well in some cases and

Figure 3.17 Bucket and block organization for hashing.

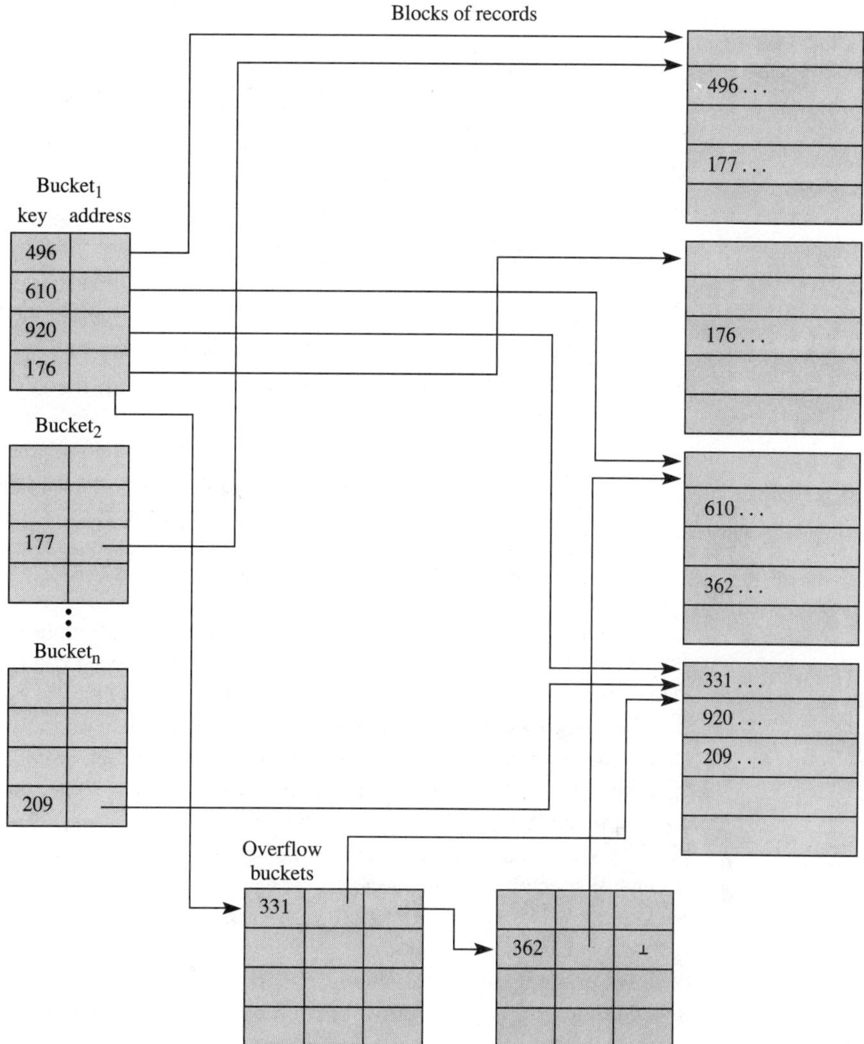

not in others. It has been shown, however, that the choice of a prime number for s is usually satisfactory. A combination of multiplicative and divisive methods can be used to advantage in many practical situations.

There are innumerable ways of converting a key to a numeric value. Most keys are numeric, others may be either alphabetic or alphanumeric. In the latter two cases, we can use the bit representation of the alphabet to generate the numeric equivalent key. A number of simple hashing methods are given below. Many hashing functions can be devised from these and other ways.

1. Use the low order part of the key. For keys that are consecutive integers with few gaps, this method can be used to map the keys to the available range.
2. End folding. For long keys, we identify start, middle, and end regions, such that the sum of the lengths of the start and end regions equals the length of the

middle region. The start and end digits are concatenated and the concatenated string of digits is added to the middle region digits. This new number, mod s, where s is the upper limit of the hash function, gives the bucket address:

123456	**123456789012**	**654321**

For the above key (converted to integer value if required) the end folding gives the two values to be added as: 123456654321 and 123456789012.

3. Square all or part of the key and take a part from the result. The whole or some defined part of the key is squared and a number of digits are selected from the square as being part of the hash result. A variation is the multiplicative scheme where one part of the key is multiplied by the remaining part and a number of digits are selected from the result.
4. Division. As stated in the beginning of this section, the key can be divided by a number, usually a prime, and the remainder is taken as the bucket address. A simple check with, for instance, a divisor of 100 tells us that the last two digits of any key will remain unchanged. In applications where keys may be in some multiples, this would produce a poor result. Therefore, division by a prime number is recommended. For many applications, division by odd numbers that have no divisors less than about 19 gives satisfactory results.

We can conclude from the above discussion that a number of possible methods for generating a hash function exist. In general it has been found that hash functions using division or multiplication perform quite well under most conditions.

Let us now consider the retrieve, insert, and delete operations using hashing to locate our records. Let K be the set of keys and A be the set of bucket addresses so that the hashing function h is a function from K to A. The hash value h(k) is the address of the bucket that contains the <key, address> pair for the record with key k. Here we assume the size of the bucket is chosen such that overflow would not occur. A special dummy record is always assumed to be the last record in each bucket and it is used in the search to indicate a failure. The bucket with address h(k) is examined for the <k, address> pair. If there is no match, the record with key k does not exist. If the operation was either a simple retrieval or a deletion, this results in a notfound message (or error condition). For insertions, the <k, address> pair is inserted in this bucket. The record is, of course, inserted in the file at the location given by the address. If the <k, address> pair exists, then for an insertion this would be an attempt to insert a duplicate record (which may or may not be permitted in the application). In the case of a deletion, we would delete the actual record as well as the bucket entry. Algorithm 3.3 specifies the sequence of steps.

As mentioned earlier, we require that the hash function uniformly distribute the keys in the buckets. This seems to be a reasonable approach until we examine certain details more closely. Although we may know the range of key values, do we also know their distribution characteristics? Note that not all key values are likely to occur. Different distributions require different hash functions to satisfy the uniformity requirement. The hash value is also required to lie within the range of addresses for the buckets, i.e., this range is prespecified. These considerations preclude any changes to the hash function once it has been implemented. Over a volatile file we can choose our range of addresses, A, to be large, but we waste valuable space. If

Algorithm **3.3**

Algorithm for Search, Delete, Insert Using Hashing

{To find, delete, or insert a record with key labeled SEARCHKEY; the operation types (OPTYPE) are FIND, DELETE or INSERT. If a record has to be inserted, we assume that the address of the block (INSERTADDR) in which the record will be inserted is specified by the file manager.}

```
i := h (SEARCHKEY)
{The hash function h will convert nonnumeric keys too. The hash value is
numeric and lies in the bucket address range.}

read bucket with address i into memory.
{Bucket entries are <key, address> pairs. The last key in each bucket is a
dummy and cannot be exceeded. It is used for detecting the last entry.}

get first <key,address> pair

while key ≠ SEARCHKEY and key ≠ DUMMY do
            get next <key,address> pair

found := key = SEARCHKEY {found is Boolean}
  case (OPTYPE) of
   'INSERT' :if found then error ('Record Already Exists')
              else
               begin {insert record}
                insert record in data block at INSERTADDR
                insert <SEARCHKEY, INSERTADDR> pair in bucket
                end{insert}
    'FIND': if not found then error ('Record Does Not Exist')
              else
               begin
                a := address
                get data from block a
                search for record within block
                end{find}
   'DELETE' : if not found then error ('Record Does Not Exist')
              else
               begin
                a := address
                delete <SEARCHKEY,address> entry from bucket
                get data from block a
                delete the appropriate record from block
                end {delete}
   end{case}
```

A is too small, the buckets will be large, containing a larger proportion of key values, and the performance will degrade. File reorganization is an expensive proposition. What we want is to be able to modify the hash function as and when required. There are a number of techniques to do this, referred to as **dynamic hashing.** We look at a simple technique called extendable hashing.

3.5.1 Extendable Hashing

Extendable hashing handles file growth and shrinkage by splitting or coalescing buckets, i.e., the number of buckets or the bucket address range changes with the file. Since the hash function, once implemented, can only generate values in some predefined range, the extendable hashing scheme requires that the hash function generates values over a very large range. Instead of using these values as addresses to buckets, some variable number of bits from these values are used as a key for entries in a bucket address table (Figure 3.18). In other words, another level of indirection is introduced. The entries in the bucket address table (BAT) are <*length* (of key), *key, bucket address*> triplets.

Let the hash function generate an a bit long value, $b_1b_2 \ldots b_a$. A number of high order bits are used as a pseudosearch key into the bucket address table. The number of bits to be used for each match is determined from the entries in the BAT table. Each *key* in the BAT table is of different length and the length is specified by the corresponding entry in the *length* field. For a given entry in the BAT table, if the value of the length field is $p (p \leq a)$, the p high order bit sequence $b_1b_2 \ldots b_p$ of the hash function generated value becomes the search key and is matched against the key entry in the BAT table. A match gives the *bucket address* where the required search key can be found.

Insertion

When a record is inserted, we follow the same procedure as in the simple hashing scheme. The only difference is when a bucket is full. We refer to it as the *original* bucket (with bucket address given by *original_address*). A new bucket is created; let us call it the *new* bucket (with bucket address given by *new_address).* Let us assume that the key was p bits long. Now since we have two buckets where there was one before, the *length* value has to be increased by one. Thus, the old key $b_1b_2 \ldots b_p$ is replaced by the new keys $b_1b_2 \ldots b_pb_{p+1}$ with the bit b_{p+1} being either 0 or 1. The *key* for the old bucket becomes $b_1b_2 \ldots b_p0$ and for the new bucket $b_1b_2 \ldots b_p1$. We divide the entries from the *original* bucket into the *original* and *new* buckets. In this manner, all keys with their high order bits equal to $b_1b_2 \ldots b_p0$ are placed in the *original* bucket and all keys with their high order bits equal to $b_1b_2 \ldots b_p1$ are placed in the *new* bucket. We modify the BAT entry <p, $b_1b_2 \ldots b_p$, *original_address*> for *original* bucket to become <$p + 1$, $b_1b_2 \ldots b_p0$, *original_*

Figure 3.18 Using extendable hashing.

Key value → Hash function → *a* bit value → Search BAT → Bucket_i address → Search Bucket_i → Record address →

address and insert a new entry $\langle p + 1, b_1b_2 \ldots b_p1, \textit{new\_address} \rangle$ in the bucket address table.

An example of insertion is illustrated in Example 3.8. Note that in this version of extendable hashing we allow multiple pointers to the same bucket, thus economizing on the number of buckets.

Example 3.8

Consider a numerical key and a division-based hash function. Suppose the hash function consists of dividing the key value by 31 and using high order bits of the remainder as a pseudosearch key in the BAT. Figure A gives the successive steps in generating the entries in the BAT and the buckets as records with following key values are inserted, in the given order:

176, 227, 371, 741, 629, 913, 345, 547, 806

After inserting 176, 227, 371, 741 the bucket b_1 becomes full (see part i) causing the bucket to split when 629 is inserted. This requires the entries in the bucket b1 to be redistributed and the address value in the BAT to be modified as shown in part ii. Insertion of 806 causes the bucket b2 and an entry in the BAT to split as shown in part iii. ■

Figure A Structure and usage of BAT in extendable hashing.

(i)

Bucket address table

Length	Key	Bucket address
1	1	b_1
1	0	b_1

Bucket b_1

Key	Record address
176	p_{176}
227	p_{227}
371	p_{371}
741	p_{741}

(ii)

Bucket address table

Length	Key	Bucket address
1	1	b_1
1	0	b_2

Bucket b_1

Key	Record address
176	p_{176}
371	p_{371}
741	p_{741}
547	p_{547}

Bucket b_2

Key	Record address
227	p_{227}
629	p_{629}
913	p_{913}
345	p_{345}

(iii)

Bucket address table

Length	Key	Bucket address
1	1	b_1
2	00	b_2
2	00	b_3

Bucket b_1

Key	Record address
176	p_{176}
371	p_{371}
741	p_{741}
547	p_{547}

Bucket b_2

Key	Record address
345	p_{345}
806	p_{806}
	$\perp$
	$\perp$

Bucket b_3

Key	Record address
227	p_{227}
629	p_{629}
913	p_{913}
	$\perp$

Deletion

When a bucket becomes empty after a deletion, it can be deleted together with its corresponding entry from the bucket address table. An alternate scheme, wherein two paired buckets are merged into a single bucket when the amount of entries in these buckets falls below some small number, can also be used. However, in the current discussion we only delete a bucket when it becomes empty. Let the entry in the bucket address table be:

$$<g, b_1b_2 \ldots b_{g-1}0, A_z>$$

Then we also modify the entry $<g, b_1b_2 \ldots b_{g-1}1, A_y>$ in the table to become:

$$<g-1, b_1b_2 \ldots b_{g-1}, A_y>$$

If no such entry exists in the BAT, the first entry is simply deleted. An example of deletion is illustrated in Example 3.9. Note that in this version of extendable hashing we avoid multiple pointers to the same bucket.

Example 3.9

Consider a numerical key of seven decimal digits with a multiplicative hash function that generates a product of the four high order digits by the three lower order digits. The key, the hash function generated values, and the corresponding binary equivalent of these values are given below:

Key	*H(key)*	*H(key) in binary*
1544542	836848	$1100\ 1100\ 0100\ 1111\ 0000_2$
1329632	839928	$1100\ 1101\ 0000\ 1111\ 1000_2$
1022821	839062	$1100\ 1100\ 1101\ 1001\ 0110_2$
0892941	839372	$1100\ 1100\ 1110\ 1100\ 1100_2$
1458576	839808	$1100\ 1101\ 0000\ 1000\ 0000_2$

Consider a bucket capacity of 4 and assume that the records are inserted in the order shown above with a minimum key length of 7 bits. Thus, after the first four records are inserted, an entry in the BAT and the corresponding bucket are as shown in part i of the Figure B.

When the record 145876 is to be inserted its key gives the hash value, which for a length of 7 high order bits matches an entry in the BAT. This entry, however, points to bucket b_i which is already full. This means that the bucket is split and the key length is increased to 8 bits. The entries in b_i are redistributed between b_i and a new bucket, b_j as shown in part ii of Figure B.

Subsequent deletion of the records with keys 1544542, 0892941, and 1022821 causes bucket b_i to become empty. This leads to the deletion of the BAT entry 11001100, compression of the entry 11001101 to 1100110, and a change in the length field to 7, as shown in part iii of Figure B.

Figure B

Example of extendable hashing.

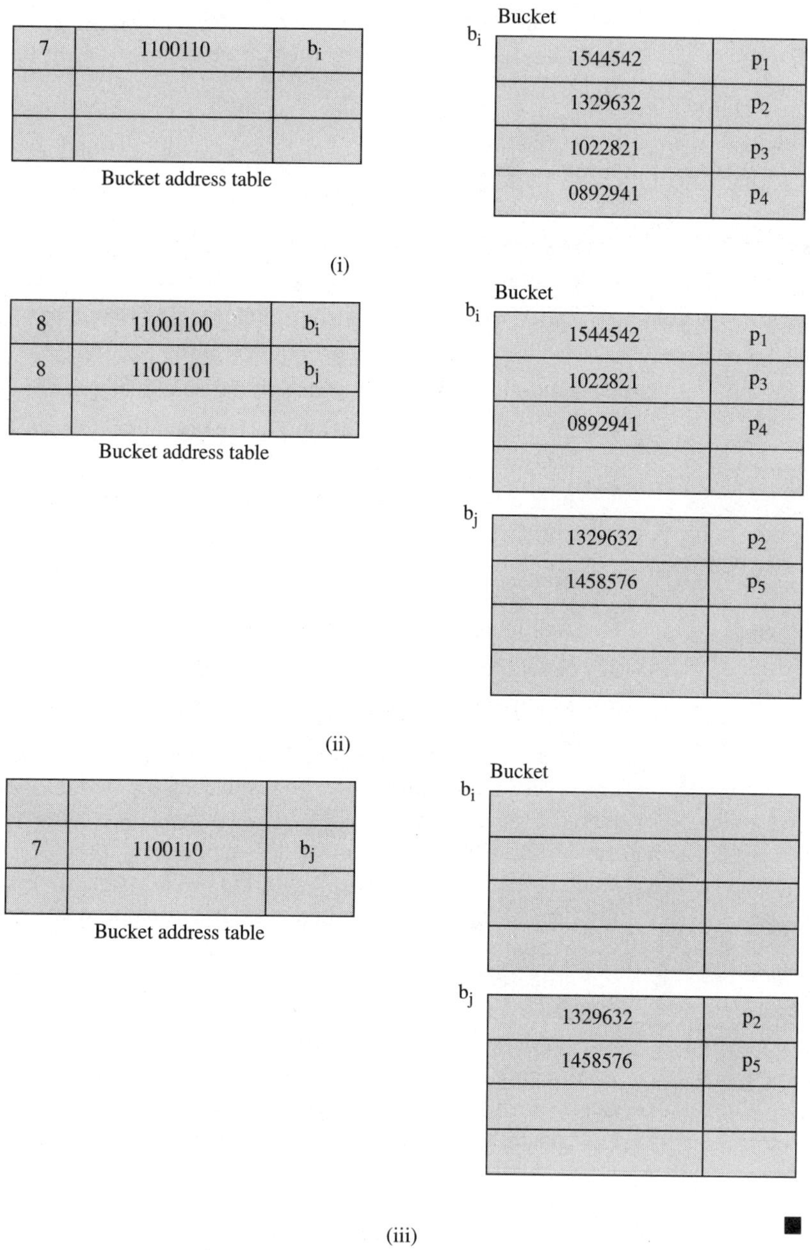

(i)

7	1100110	b_i

Bucket address table

Bucket b_i

1544542	p_1
1329632	p_2
1022821	p_3
0892941	p_4

(ii)

8	11001100	b_i
8	11001101	b_j

Bucket address table

Bucket b_i

1544542	p_1
1022821	p_3
0892941	p_4

b_j

1329632	p_2
1458576	p_5

(iii)

7	1100110	b_j

Bucket address table

Bucket b_i

b_j

1329632	p_2
1458576	p_5

■

3.6 Secondary Key Retrieval

In the previous sections we have considered the retrieval and update of data based on the primary key. In the following sections we consider file organizations that facilitate secondary key retrieval. Secondary key retrieval is characterized by the multiplicity of records satisfying a given key value. As such, there is no longer a one-to-one correspondence between key values and records. File organizations for secondary key retrieval are used in conjunction with methods for primary key retrieval.

Query and Update Types

Queries are in general formulated to retrieve records based on one or multiple key values. In the latter case, the retrieval expression contains key values punctuated with Boolean operators.

Query Types:

1. Find all employees working in the computer science department.
2. Find all employees working in the computer science department who are analysts.
3. Find all students who are taking the files and database course, but not the artificial intelligence course.

Update types:

1. Add records in proper sequence.
2. Delete records satisfying some condition.
3. Modify attribute values of records, satisfying some condition.

The above queries and updates can be simply but inefficiently handled by scanning every record in the file. A number of file organizations permit faster and more efficient retrieval. The choice between them, just as in the case of primary key retrieval, is solely dependent on the application. Faster access to the records is provided by the use of indexes and/or the linking together in lists or some other suitable structure of logically related records. It is usual to relate records based on <attribute, value> pairs.

The secondary key structures support access to all records that satisfy some <attribute, value> pair. Logically, as shown in Figure 3.19a, the secondary key access file is made up of a set of records containing (attribute, value, record_list). Here record_list is a list of records that contain the <attribute, value> pair. For example, in the following secondary key access file entry, the records $R_{ij_1}, \ldots, R_{ij_n}$ contain the value v_{ij} for the attribute A_i:

$$\{<A_i, v_{ij}>,(R_{ij_1}, \ldots, R_{ij_n})\}$$

The R_{ij_k}'s are used to represent the associated records and may be either the primary key values, some unique system assigned identifiers, or unique physical addresses.

In general, the record_list $(R_{ij_1}, \ldots, R_{ij_n})$ may be maintained as a number of separate stored lists, for instance, h_{ij}, such that we have

$$<A_i, v_{ij}, n_{ij}, h_{ij}> (P_{ij_1}, \ldots, P_{ij_{h_{ij}}})$$

where n_{ij} is the number of records with value v_{ij} for the attribute A_i (i.e., n_{ij} is the number of records in the record_list $R_{ij_1}, \ldots, R_{ij_n}$) and P_{ij_k} is the pointer to the kth stored list, for all $k = 1, \ldots, h_{ij}$. The average length of each stored list is n_{ij}/h_{ij}.

Physically, as shown in Figure 3.19b, the names of the attributes may be separated from the values and record_list and kept in a directory. Each entry in the

Figure 3.19 Structure of the directory and index.

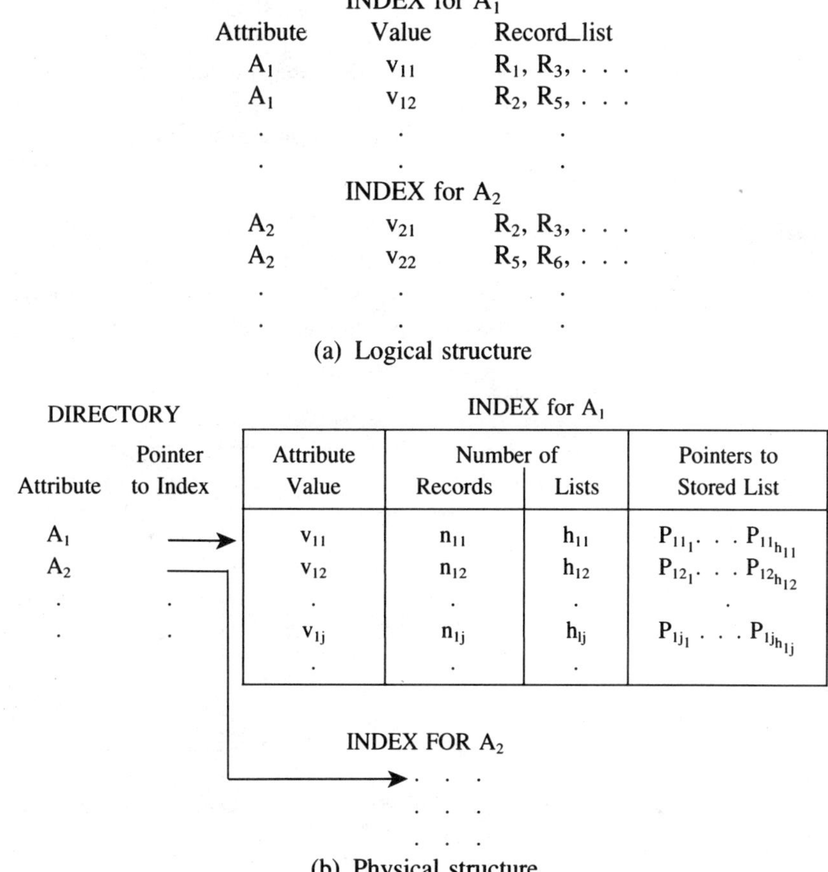

directory is associated with a given attribute and points to a structure containing the set of associated (value, record_list) pairs. For the moment, we can think of the structure containing the (value, record_list) pairs as a sequential file, referring to it as the value-access file or as the attribute index. There are two common methods of organizing the value-access file: the inverted index method and the multilist. We discuss these organizations in the following sections.

3.6.1 Inverted Index Files

The **inverted index file** (or simply the **inverted file**) contains the list of all records satisfying the particular <attribute, value> pair in the index, wherein h_{ij} (the number of separate stored lists) is equal to n_{ij} (the number of records with the given attribute value) and each P_{jk_m} points to a list of records of length one (P_{jk_m} is in effect R_{ij}, a pointer to the record instead of to a record list). In other words, a pointer for every record with the given value v_{ij} for the attribute A_i is kept in the index. This pointer could be in the form of an address, the primary key value, or a unique record number.

Query processing does not require access to the primary data areas until some of the records satisfying the query need to be furnished. For Boolean queries, the retrieved lists of record pointers may be manipulated to minimize the number of primary data area accesses. Also, the user can be made aware of the number of records satisfying a query before the data records are accessed. This gives us an opportunity to modify the query if our expectation of the number is different.

Example 3.10 Consider an automobile dealership that records the interior and exterior color and engine size availability of the models it sells. The inverted list for each value of the attribute is given in Figure C. Here we use the model name to identify the corresponding automobile model record.

Figure C Inverted index for Example 3.10.

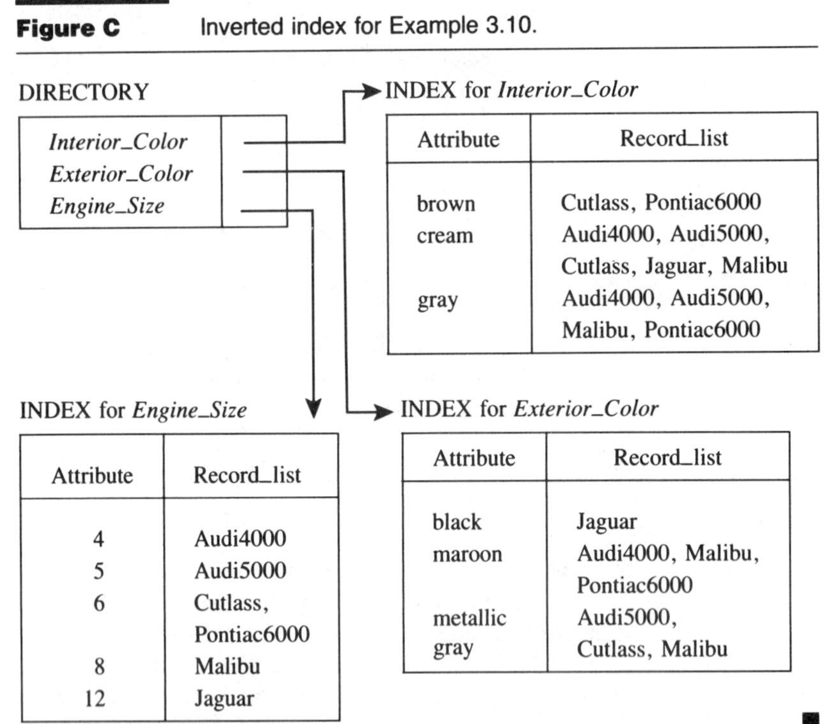

DIRECTORY

Interior_Color
Exterior_Color
Engine_Size

INDEX for *Interior_Color*

Attribute	Record_list
brown	Cutlass, Pontiac6000
cream	Audi4000, Audi5000, Cutlass, Jaguar, Malibu
gray	Audi4000, Audi5000, Malibu, Pontiac6000

INDEX for *Engine_Size*

Attribute	Record_list
4	Audi4000
5	Audi5000
6	Cutlass, Pontiac6000
8	Malibu
12	Jaguar

INDEX for *Exterior_Color*

Attribute	Record_list
black	Jaguar
maroon	Audi4000, Malibu, Pontiac6000
metallic gray	Audi5000, Cutlass, Malibu

■

Complete inversion requires that every attribute of a record be treated as a key and the record addresses associated with every attribute value be stored in inverted lists. Partially inverted files store record addresses associated with all values of only certain attributes.

Logically, the inverted index structure can be visualized as tabular with a variable number of entries in each row. This variable number of entries makes the index difficult to maintain. Inverted files thus have a built-in advantage when the query volume is much greater than the update volume or when the updates can be batched. Inverted organizations are used mostly in document/reference retrieval systems and less frequently in general purpose database management systems.

Query processing involves searching the directory for the attribute entry and then through the associated value access file to the associated attribute value entries. For Boolean queries, this results in the retrieval of a number of record_lists. For conjunctive clauses, an intersection, and for disjunctive clauses a union of the record_lists is made.

Example 3.11

Return to the automobile dealership example above. A customer requires a car with metallic gray exterior and gray interior. This query can be expressed as:

Find car models where *Interior_Color* = 'gray' and
Exterior_Color = 'metallic gray'.

We first search the directory (see Figure C) to locate the attribute entry for *Interior_Colors,* and then search the *Interior_Color* index for the attribute value gray. We obtain the list <Audi4000, Audi5000, Malibu, Pontiac600> of models that come with gray interior trim. We repeat the search process for the *Exterior_Color* attribute, obtaining the list of models with metallic gray exteriors: <Audi5000, Cutlass, Malibu>. An intersection of the two lists gives <Audi5000, Malibu> as the list of models that satisfy the query. ■

Insertion of a record requires that its identifiers be inserted in the record lists, associated with the values of its attributes. Deletion of a record entails the removal of the record identifier entry from every record list in which its entry exists. Modifying the attribute value of a record necessitates changes to the affected index. Clearly, index maintenance is a computationally expensive process.

Example 3.12

The dealership has been informed that the Pontiac6000 will from now on be available with only five cylinders instead of six. The update is performed by searching the directory for the index for the attribute *Engine_Size*. In the *Engine_Size* index, the entry corresponding to the attribute value six cylinders is retrieved and Pontiac6000 is deleted from the record_list. The entry for five cylinder models is then retrieved and Pontiac6000 is inserted into the record list. The old and updated indexes for the attribute *Engine_Size* are shown in Figure D.

Figure D

Update of inverted index.

Old
Engine_Size Index

Attribute	Record_list
4	Audi4000
5	Audi5000
6	Cutlass, Pontiac6000
8	Malibu
12	Jaguar

New
Engine_Size Index

Attribute	Record_list
4	Audi4000
5	Audi5000, Pontiac6000
6	Cutlass
8	Malibu
12	Jaguar

■

Figure 3.20 A simple implementation of an inverted index.

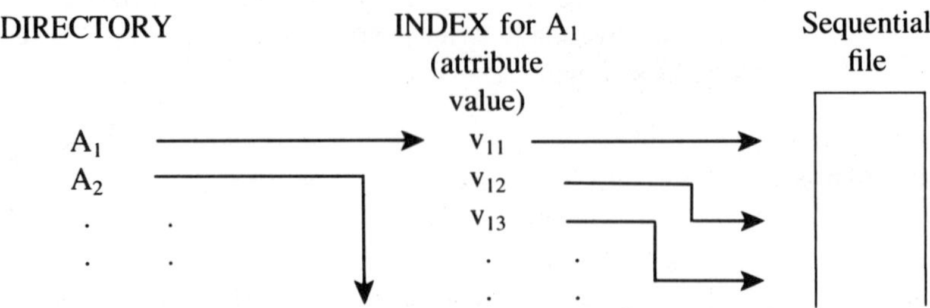

A simple implementation of an inverted list to maintain the record_list for each value for a given attribute as a sequential file is shown in Figure 3.20. The index contains a <value, pointer> pair, where the pointer points to the starting position of the associated record_list in the sequential file.

3.6.2 Multilist Files

In a **multilist file** there is only one stored list for every <attribute, value> pair. Therefore, the index of a multilist file contains only the single address P_{ij} for the <attribute,value> pair $<A_i, v_{ij}>$; $h_{ij} = 1$. There is only one stored list of length n_{ij}. The records in the stored list are linked together in the form of a list. Thus, the record list of a multilist file is implemented as a list of records. One exists for every <attribute, value> pair (as the name suggests), with each stored record containing a pointer indicating the succeeding member of every list to which it belongs. A pointer to the first member of every list is maintained in the index. The length of each list can also be maintained in the index (this is illustrated in Figure 3.22a).

Figure 3.21 gives, in pseudo-Pascal, the definition of a record, all of whose attributes participate in multilists. The pointer field associated with each attribute can

Figure 3.21 Pseudo-Pascal definition of a stored record in a multilist file.

```
attribute_rec_type_i = record
    value : attribute_type_i;
    next : pointer {pointer to next record}
    end;
    .
    .

stored_record = record
    attribute_1 : attribute_rec_type_1;
        .
    attribute_j : array[1..m] of attribute_rec_type_i;
        .
    attribute_n : attribute_rec_type_n;
    end;
```

Figure 3.22 Multilist file.

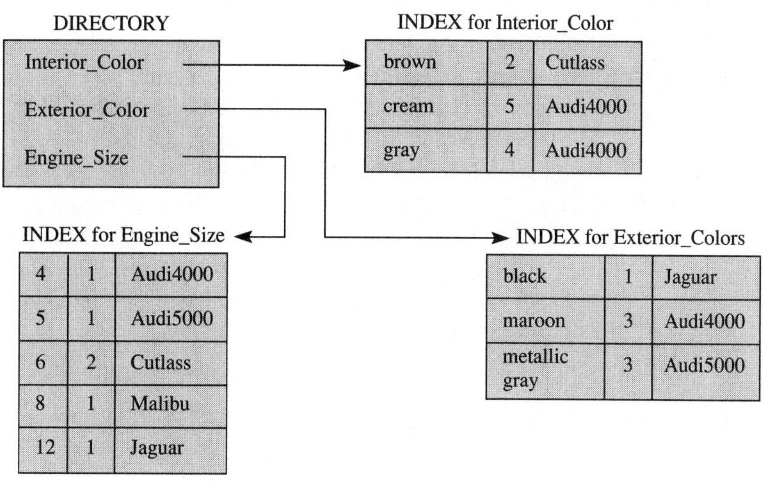

(a)

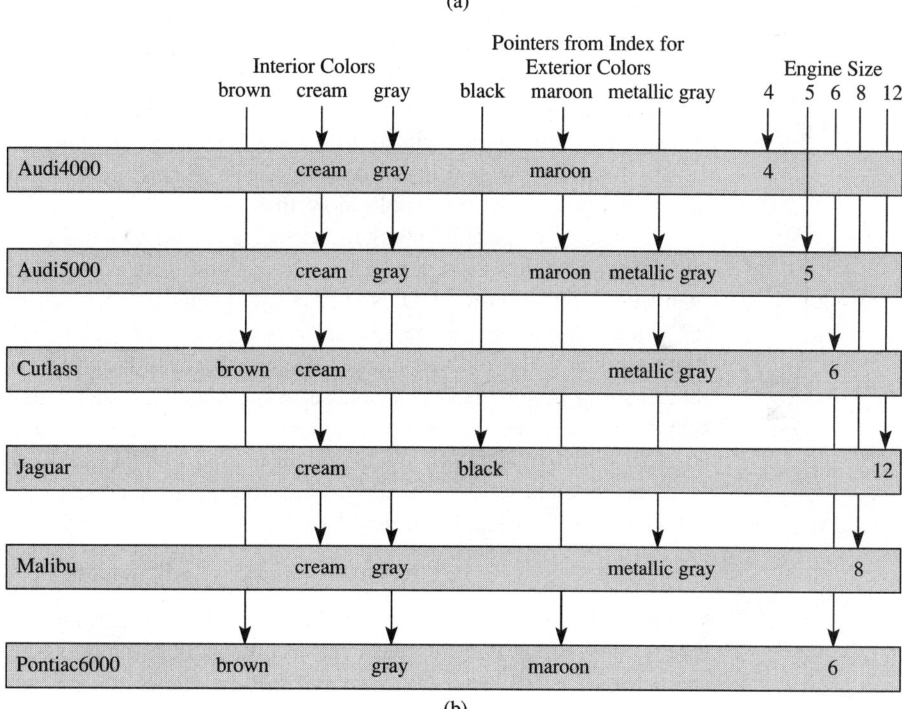

(b)

store the pointer to the next record with the same value. If an attribute has multiple values (e.g., the same model car in the automobile dealership example comes in many interior and exterior colors and engine sizes), the attribute may be stored as an array of size m, as indicated for the *attribute_j* in Figure 3.21.

A simple method of creating multilist files is to insert new records at the front of the list. Searching for a specific record with a given value for an attribute requires traversal through that list. On average half the list has to be scanned. The advantage of such a scheme is that maintenance is simple. The list can also be maintained in a particular order, increasing the insertion costs but reducing the search costs. If a multilist index is created for every attribute, then every record will be part of a multitude of lists. It is not always necessary, however, to retrieve information based on every attribute value; lists need only be created for a few of the attributes.

For the automobile dealership example, the multilist file for interior and exterior colors and engine sizes is shown in Figure 3.22. The directory and the index entries are given in part a and the actual records showing the multilists are shown in part b. As before, we use the model as symbolic pointers. Note that within the record for Cutlass corresponding to the attribute value for *Interior_Color* = brown, there is a pointer to the record for Pontiac6000. Similarly, for the value cream there is a pointer to the record for Jaguar.

Search in Multilist Files

For conjunctive queries (e.g., $\text{attribute}_1 = \text{value}_1 \wedge \text{attribute}_2 = \text{value}_2 \wedge \ldots$), a search over the shortest list is made, every record accessed being examined to see if it satisfies the conjuncts. Those records satisfying all the conjuncts are included in the response. We illustrate this in Example 3.13a.

For disjunctive queries (e.g., $\text{attribute}_1 = \text{value}_1 \vee \text{attribute}_2 = \text{value}_2 \vee \ldots$), all of the lists associated with the attributes in the condition have to be traversed. If we are not concerned with duplicate record retrieval, then all records are accessed, some of them possibly more than once.

Efficiency considerations demand that a record that has already been accessed should not be accessed again. This may suggest that a list of accessed records be maintained, possibly in a DO_NoT_Access_a Gain (DONTAG) list. This DONTAG list could become very large. Actually, we need only maintain a DONTAG list of those records that *would* be accessed again, because they are also members of the other lists to be traversed in response to the query. Having retrieved a record, it is easy to check if the record also satisfies any of the other conjuncts in the query. If so, then for every conjunct it satisfies, it is added to the DONTAG list. A moment of thought should tell us that just adding the record address to the DONTAG list is not sufficient. Consider the query

$$\text{Get records where } A \vee B \vee C$$

where A, B and C are some simple clauses of the form attribute = constant. Assume that we have already retrieved all the records satisfying the clause A. We have also created a DONTAG list. Next we traverse the list of records satisfying B and the next record, R_i, to be retrieved is in the DONTAG list. Having accessed R_i before, we would not need to do so again if and only if we knew the next member in B's list following R_i. Therefore in the DONTAG list we have to maintain the following information for each attribute appearing in the query:

<accessed-record, attribute, value, next-record-in-list>

Let us satisfy ourselves as to why we need the attribute and value information. Consider the above query. When a record has satisfied all the terms A, B, and C, then it would be entered onto the DONTAG list. The address of the next record for the lists, corresponding to B as well as C, will be added to the DONTAG list. Now, when processing for B, which of the records in the DONTAG list is the next record for B and which is for C? This justifies the inclusion of the attribute. Consider the situation where a record can possess multiple values for the same attribute, and we have the query: Get records where $A_1 = v_1 \lor A_1 = v_2$. We can see that the value also needs to be stored in such situations. We illustrate the use of the DONTAG list in Example 3.13b.

Example 3.13

(a) Consider the conjunctive query: Find cars with *Interior_Color* = cream $\land$ *Exterior_Color* = metallic gray.

For this conjunctive query, we consult the index entries for *Interior_Color* = cream and *Exterior_Color* = metallic gray and note that the first entry is of length 5, whereas the second one is of length 3. Therefore, we use the second list to retrieve the records for Audi5000, Cutlass, and Malibu to find that only two of these satisfy both the conjuncts.

(b) Consider the disjunctive query: Find cars with *Interior_Color* = cream $\lor$ *Interior_Color* = gray.

We process this query by using the *Interior_Color* index for the color cream and retrieve the first record for Audi4000. We examine the record and find that it also comes with gray *Interior_Color*. The next record in this list is Audi5000. We enter the following in the DONTAG list: <Audi4000, *Interior Color*, gray, Audi5000>. We retrieve the next record in the *Interior_Color* = cream list, namely Audi5000, and find that it also comes with gray *Interior Color*. The next record for the list for *Interior_Color* = gray is Malibu. We enter <Audi5000, Interior_Color, gray, Malibu> in the DONTAG list. We next process the records for Cutlass and, as it does not come in the *Interior Color* gray, we do not make any entry in the DONTAG list. The record for Cutlass does not satisfy the second query predicate; consequently we will not be reaccessing it. We process Jaguar and again make no entry in the DONTAG list. Finally we get the last record in the *Interior_Color* = cream list, namely Malibu, and find that it also comes with gray *Interior_Color*. The next record in the list for *Interior_Color* = gray is Pontiac6000 so we make the following entry in the DONTAG list: <Malibu, *Interior_Color*, gray, Pontiac6000>. Since Malibu is the last entry in the list for *Interior_Color* = cream, we have retrieved all records satisfying the first term in the query.

Contents of DONTAG List After Processing
First Term of the Disjunctive Query
of Example 3.14b

<Audi4000, *Interior_Color*, gray, Audi5000>
<Audi5000, *Interior_Color*, gray, Malibu>
<Malibu, *Interior_Color*, gray, Pontiac6000>

Now we start the list for the second query predicate. We consult the directory for *Interior_Color* = gray and find that the first record in the list is Audi4000. Before we retrieve this record, we consult the DONTAG list and discover that we already retrieved the record for Audi4000. We do not retrieve that record and find from the entry for Audi4000 that the next record in the list for *Interior_Color* = gray is Audi5000. Before actually retrieving this record we consult the DONTAG list again and discover that the record for Audi5000 has been processed and the next record in the list for *Interior_Color* = gray is Malibu. However, since there is an entry for Malibu in the DONTAG list, it was already retrieved. From this entry for Malibu in the DONTAG list we find the next record in the list for *Interior_Color* = gray to be Pontiac6000. There being no entry for Pontiac6000 in the DONTAG list, we retrieve and process it. Since there are no more records in the list for *Interior_Color* = gray, we have accessed all records. In this way we ensure that each record satisfying more than one term in the disjunct will be retrieved only once. ■

Maintenance of Multilist Files

The deletion of records entails the removal of the record from the various lists. In some implementations of the multilist where the record is not physically removed but only flagged to indicate its deletion, no change is involved. While the record is still physically part of the lists, it is not so logically. If a record is both deleted and physically removed, all the lists of which the record forms a part have to be altered as well. In any case, the length of each of the lists in which the record was involved is decremented.

A record must first be located before a change can be made to its data values. If the value to be changed belongs to a secondary key field, we would have to alter the relevant list. This entails that the list be traversed with the old value, the record removed from the list, the value changed, and the record added to the list for the new value. If data values in a number of fields are changed, this may require the traversal and update of many lists. The process is simpler if records are double-chained with pointers to both successor and predecessor records.

The performance of a multilist file is satisfactory when the individual lists are short. Regarding conjunctive queries, if the length of the lists are included in the index, the shortest list is used for record retrieval. However, the number of records actually satisfying all terms of the query may be a very small fraction of those retrieved. The use of the DONTAG list avoids reaccessing the same records in the case of disjunctive queries. When the lists become lengthy, it is desirable to break each list up into a number of sublists as in the case of the cellular lists discussed in the next section.

3.6.3 Cellular Lists

Lists in a multilist file can become lengthy. The fact that the stored records may be distributed among many physical (disk) storage units, or within the same storage unit in some manageable cluster of cylinders (the cluster may be a single cylinder), or some other manageable storage area, could be used to advantage by partitioning

Figure 3.23 Cellular list.

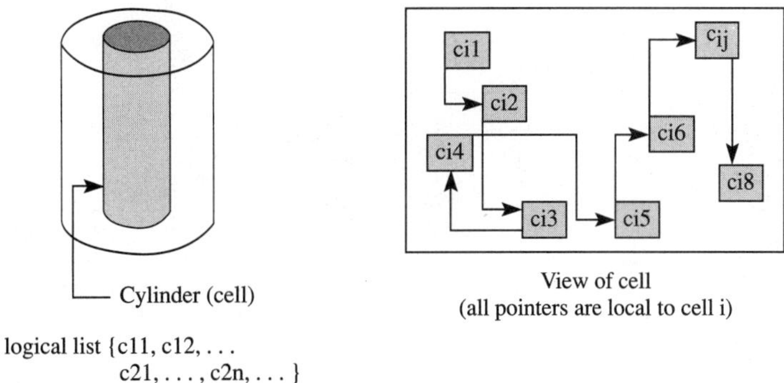

the lists along these boundaries (or cells). Thus, in a **cellular list** organization the lists are limited to be within a physical area of storage, referred to as a **cell.** Figure 3.23 is an example of a cellular list. The lists are limited to a single cylinder of a movable-head-disk-type storage device. The number of stored lists, h_{ij}, for a given <attribute, value> pair $<A_i, v_{ij}>$, may be more than 1, $1 \leq h_{ij} \leq n_{ij}$.

The number of stored lists still does not approach the inverted file case, except where there is only a single record in every cell. However, there are more stored lists than in the multilist case. The processing complexity lies between the inverted and multilist cases. Such an organization is particularly useful if the cell size is chosen so that the lists may be traversed in internal memory. In the case of paged systems, this may equal the page size. In multiprocessor systems, different processors may traverse lists within different cells in parallel to improve response times.

Let us reconsider the index structure of Figure 3.19 to explain the three file structures examined so far. In an inverted index the number of groups chosen is equal to the number of records, i.e., $h_{ij} = n_{ij}$. Each group is of length one and each pointer points to a single record. In a multilist file, $h_{ij} = 1$ and only one list of length n_{ij} exists for value v_{ij} of attribute A_i. With a cellular multilist, there are h_{ij} lists for value v_{ij} of attribute A_i, each list being limited to a convenient size to maximize the response time. The size of the list may be determined by the characteristics of the physical storage device. In the case of a disk-type device, the list may be limited to a single cylinder.

3.6.4 Ring Files

The last records of the lists in a multilist file points to a null record. In **ring files** the last record entry in each list points back to the index entry. Therefore, from any point within the list a forward traversal of the links would bring us to the index entry. The index entries contain the value for the attribute, making it unnecessary to store the attribute-value in the physical records. This makes for a smaller record. Figure 3.24 shows a number of rings for the car dealership data, shown in Figure C of example 3.10.

In DBMSs using the network data model, a set is implemented as a ring by linking the member record occurrences in a ring that starts at the owner record oc-

Figure 3.24 Ring file.

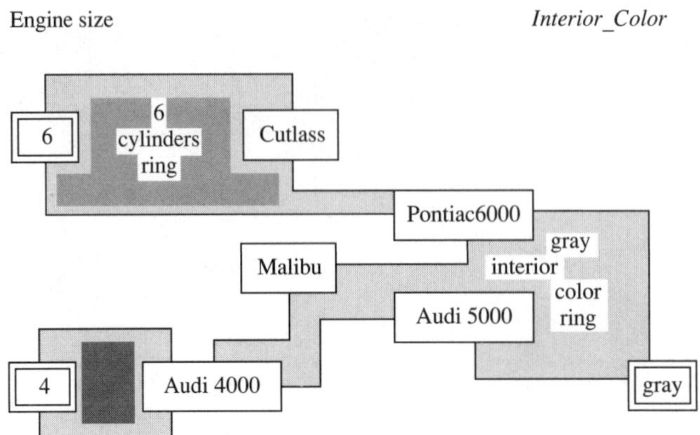

currence. The owner record occurrence points to the first member record occurrence. The members are linked together and the last member occurrence points back to the owner record occurrence.

3.7 Indexing Using Tree Structures

In the previous sections we considered some primary and secondary key indexing schemes. Here we consider two tree-based indexing schemes that are widely used in practical systems as the basis for both primary and secondary key indexing.

3.7.1 Introduction

In a tree-based indexing scheme the search generally starts at the root node. Depending on the conditions that are satisfied at the node under examination, a branch is made to one of several nodes, and the procedure is repeated until we find a match or encounter a **leaf node** (i.e., there are no more nodes beyond this node). There are several kinds of trees: binary, m-way, height-balanced, and so on. In this section we concern ourselves principally with the B^+-tree and for informational purposes, its ancestor the B-tree. The VSAM file discussed earlier is a version of the B^+-tree. For more detailed coverage of trees, consult a text on data structures.

Let us consider a file of records $R_1, R_2, \ldots, R_n$. Each record R_i, is identified by a key k_i. The record R_i contains other data in addition to the key k_i that does not affect the indexing in any way.

A multilevel index file featuring some pertinent details is shown in Figure 3.25. The indices at various levels are shown as ovals and the address to the next index level is represented as a pointer. The index is similar to a tree. The leaf nodes are the blocks containing the actual records and are shown as rectangles in the figure. (Instead of the actual records, the leaf nodes may contain pointers to storage areas

Figure 3.25 Multilevel index shown as a tree.

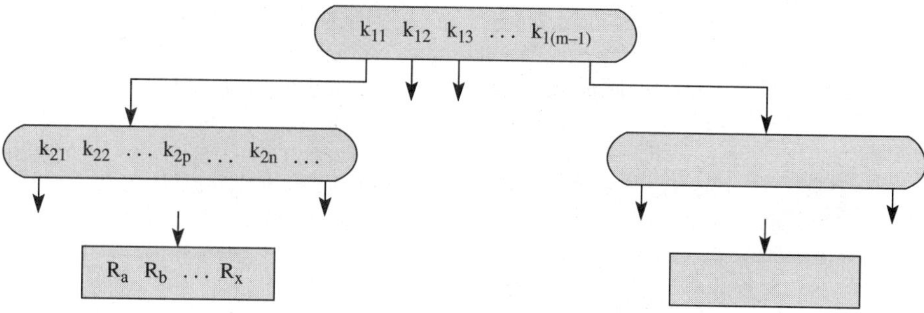

containing the actual records, or pointers directly to the actual records.) The similarity between the indexing schemes considered in the previous sections and the tree schemes ends here. The major disadvantage of index-sequential organization is that as the database grows, performance deteriorates rapidly due to overflows and consequently there arises the need for periodic reorganization. Reorganization is not only an expensive process but makes the file unavailable while it takes place. The tree structure overcomes this problem by splitting a node whenever it overflows. We illustrate this scheme in Section 3.7.3.

3.7.2 Tree Schemes

Each node of the tree except the leaf nodes, can be considered to consist of the following information:

$$[n, T_{i1}, k_{i1}, T_{i2}, k_{i2}, \ldots, T_{in}, k_{in}, T_{i(n+1)}]$$

where the k_{ij}'s are key values and the T_{ij}'s are pointers. For an **m-order tree** the following conditions are true:

- $n < m$
- $k_{i1} \leq k_{i2} \leq \ldots \leq k_{in}$ (we assume that $k_{i0} = -\infty$, $k_{i(n+1)} = +\infty$)
- each of the pointers, T_{ij}, $1 \leq j \leq (n+1)$, points to a subtree containing values less than k_{ij} and greater than or equal to $k_{i(j-1)}$

It is clear from the node structure and the condition $n < m$ that for an m-order tree, the maximum number of pointers in a node is m (or the maximum number of keys contained in a node is $m - 1$). The minimum number of pointers that may exist in a node is $\lceil m/2 \rceil$ (or the minimum number of keys contained in a node is $\lceil m/2 \rceil - 1$ keys). This minimum condition is enforced to avoid the situation in which a large number of nodes exist and each has very few keys. Such a situation not only increases the storage space for the index nodes but also the height of the tree. The minimum criterion is not enforced, for obvious reasons, for the root node.

The leaf nodes of the **B$^+$-tree** are quite similar to the nonleaf (or internal) nodes, except that the pointers in the leaf nodes do not point to subtrees. (They cannot, because they are the leaf nodes.) The pointers T_{Lj}, $1 \leq j \leq n$ (note, not n + 1), in the leaf nodes point to storage areas containing either records having a key value k_{lj}, or pointers to records, each of which has a key value k_{lj}. The number of key values in each leaf node is at least $\lceil(m - 1)/2\rceil$ and at most m − 1.

Note that unlike the index-sequential file, the B^+-tree need not be a clustering index. That is, records may or may not be arranged in storage according to their key values.

The pointer $T_{L(n+1)}$ is used to chain the leaf nodes in a sequential order. This allows for sequential processing of the underlying file of records.

The following conditions are satisfied by the nodes of a B^+-tree (and also by the nodes of the older B-tree scheme):

1. The height of the tree is ≥ 1.
2. The root has at least two children.
3. All nodes other than the root node and the leaf nodes have at least $\lceil m/2\rceil$ children, where m is the order of the tree.
4. All leaf nodes are at the same level.

Example 3.14

Assume that we are given a file containing the following records:

Book#	*Subject Area*
2	Files
3	Database
4	Artificial intelligence
5	Files
7	Discrete structures
8	Software engineering
9	Programming methodology
.	.
.	.
.	.
40	Operating systems
50	Graphics
51	Database
52	Data structures

A B^+-tree of order 4 on Book# is shown in Figure E.

■

Figure E A B^+-tree (showing only some of the leaf nodes). Each P_i is a pointer to the storage area containing records (or pointers) for the key Book# = i; ⊥ represents a null pointer.

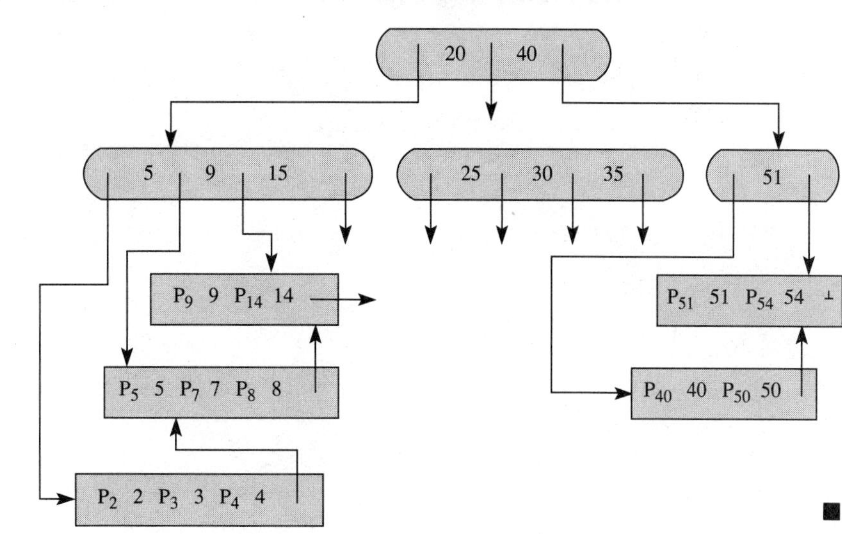

3.7.3 Operations

The nonleaf nodes of the B^+-tree act as a traversal map with the leaf nodes containing the actual records or the key values with pointers to the storage location containing the records. Therefore, all operations require access to the leaf nodes.

Search

The search algorithm for the B^+-tree is given in below. The number of nodes accessed is equal to the height of the tree. Once the required leaf node is reached, we can retrieve the pointer for the storage location containing the records; knowing the storage location, we can retrieve the required record(s).

Insertion and Deletion

The insertion and deletion of records with a given key first requires a search of the tree. Below, we discuss the insertion (or deletion) of record keys from the trees. We assume that the records themselves would be inserted in (or deleted from) the pertinent storage locations. Insertion and deletion that violates the conditions on the number of keys in a node requires the redistribution of keys among a node, its sibling, and their parent.

Algorithm 3.4 **Searching B^+-tree.**

Input: K_s, the search key

Output: found, (a Boolean value), and
A, the address of record if found

```
{nodes content: [n, T1, k1, T2, k2, . . . , Tn, kn, Tn+1] kn+1 = ∞
is assumed}

get root_node
while not leaf_node do
  begin
   i := 1
   while not (i>n or Ks<ki) do
     i := i + 1
     {Ti points to the sub-tree that may contain Ks}
   get sub-tree Ti
   end {while not leaf_node}
{search leaf node for key Ks}
{content of leaf node: [n, P1, k1, P2, k2, . . . , Pn, kn, Pn+1]}
i := 1
found := false
while not (found or i>n) do
   begin
    found := Ks = ki
    if found then
      A := Pi
      else i := i + 1
    end {while not (found or i>n)}
```

Insertion

If, after insertion of the key, the node has more than m-1 keys, the node is said to **overflow.** Overflow can be handled by **redistribution** if the number of entries in the left or right sibling of the node is less than the maximum. Such redistribution includes the key from the parent node and hence, the key value in the parent node may change. If there are no sibling nodes with space to receive the overflow keys, the node is split into two nodes, with the middle key inserted in the parent of the node being split. Such insertion into the parent node may in turn require redistribution or splitting and an increase in the height of the tree. Example 3.15 illustrates the insertion scheme.

The search for the key value, K_I, to be inserted locates the leaf node in which the key belongs. This node may be full or have space for the key. In the latter case, the key is inserted in its rightful place, maintaining the key order. In the former case, we would now have a node, let us say T_L, with m (instead of m-1) key values, assuming an m-order tree. The set of m values is split into two sets. The set of keys:

$$\{k_1, k_2, \ldots, k_{\lceil m/2 \rceil - 1}\}$$

is written in the existing node T_L, and the remaining set of keys:

$$\{k_{\lceil m/2 \rceil}, k_{\lceil m/2 \rceil + 1}, \ldots, k_m\}$$

in a new node, let us say T_N. The new node is inserted into the leaf node chain.

The key $k_{\lceil m/2 \rceil}$ (the smallest key in the new node) and a pointer to the node T_N are passed to the parent node for insertion. Let us represent the key $k_{\lceil m/2 \rceil}$ by k′. Let the contents of the parent node before the insertion of k′ be

$$[n, T_1, k_1, \ldots, T_L, k_L, \ldots, T_n, k_n, T_{n+1}]$$

where T_L is the pointer to the child node that split; that child node originally contained keys smaller than k_L. The node pointed to by T_L now contains keys smaller than k′, while the node T_N contains keys greater than or equal to k′ but smaller than k_L. The logical place for the insertion of the pair $<T_N, k'>$ is between the pair $<T_L, k_L>$. The parent node contents after the insertion of $<k', T_N>$ are:

$$[n, T_1, k_1, \ldots, T_L, k', T_N, k_L, \ldots, T_n, k_n, T_{n+1}]$$

The insertion of $<k', T_N>$ may itself cause a redistribution or a node split. The values would be distributed between the old and new node and a key value sent to its parent node for insertion, as before.

Example 3.15 In the B^+-tree of Example 3.14, let us insert an entry for Book# 1. The original contents of the leaf node (with the label PT_o) in which the key would be inserted are:

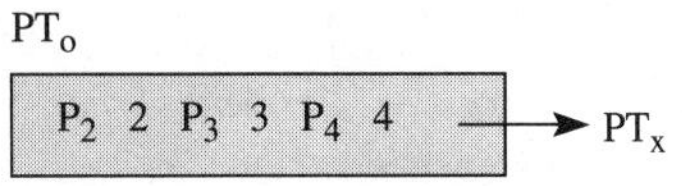

PT_o

P_2 2 P_3 3 P_4 4 → PT_x

This node does not have a left sibling and the right sibling is already full. Hence, insertion of the key 1 would cause a split. Let the new node be PT_N. The contents of these nodes are shown below:

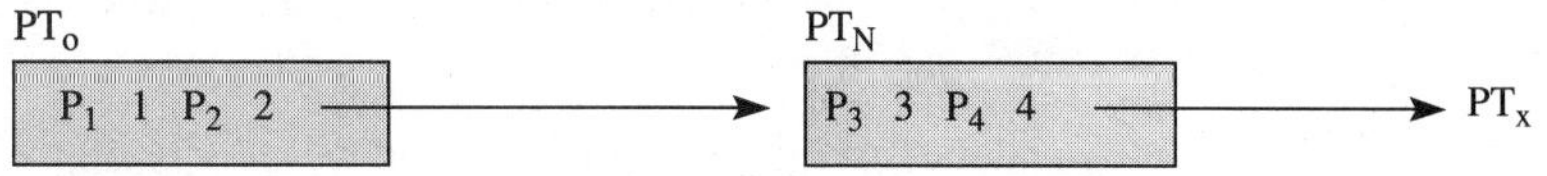

PT_o: P_1 1 P_2 2 → PT_N: P_3 3 P_4 4 → PT_x

The pair $<3, PT_N>$ are passed to the parent node (reproduced below) for insertion as indicated:

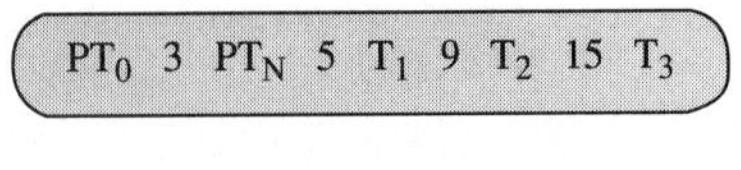

PT_0 3 PT_N 5 T_1 9 T_2 15 T_3

The insertion causes a split of this node into the following two nodes with the key value 5, along with a pointer passed to the parent of the node:

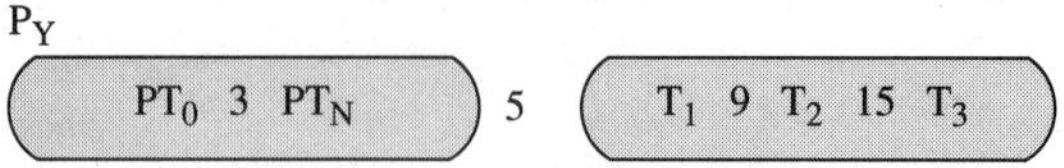

Let the address of the new node be P_Y. Then the pair <5, P_Y> is passed to the parent node (in this case the root) for insertion. The relevant portion of the resultant B^+-tree is shown in Figure F.

Figure F The B^+-tree of Example 3.14 after insertion of the key for Book# 1.

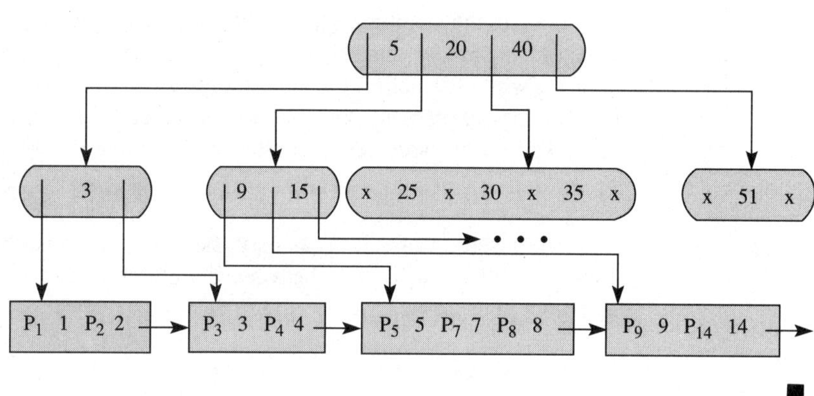

■

Deletion

When a key is deleted, the leaf node may end up with less than $\lceil(m-1)/2\rceil$ keys. This situation may also be handled by moving a key to the node from one of its left or right sibling nodes, and redistributing the keys in the parent node. However, if the siblings have no keys that could be spared, such redistribution is not possible. In this case, the node is merged with a sibling along with the deletion of a key from the parent node. The loss of the key from the parent node may in turn cause further redistribution or merging at this higher level of the tree.

The leaf node containing the key to be deleted is found and the key entry in the node deleted. If the resultant node (let us refer to it as TD) is empty or has fewer than $\lceil(m-1)/2\rceil$ keys,

1. The data from the sibling node could be redistributed, i.e., the sibling has more than the minimum number of keys and one of these keys is enough to bring the number of keys in node TD to be equal to $\lceil(m-1)/2\rceil$.
2. Or, the node TD is merged with the sibling to become a single node. This is possible if the sibling has only the minimum number of keys. The merger of the two nodes would still make the number of keys in the new node less than the maximum.

In the former case the key entry in the parent node will be changed to reflect the redistribution, and in the latter case the associated entry in the parent node would also be deleted.

Example 3.16

Let us delete the entry for Book# 5 from the tree shown in Example 3.14. The resultant tree is shown in part i of Figure G. Note that the key value 5 is maintained in the internal node.

Figure G (i) The B^+-tree that results after the deletion of key 5 from the tree of Example 3.14. (ii) The B^+-tree after the deletion of key 7.

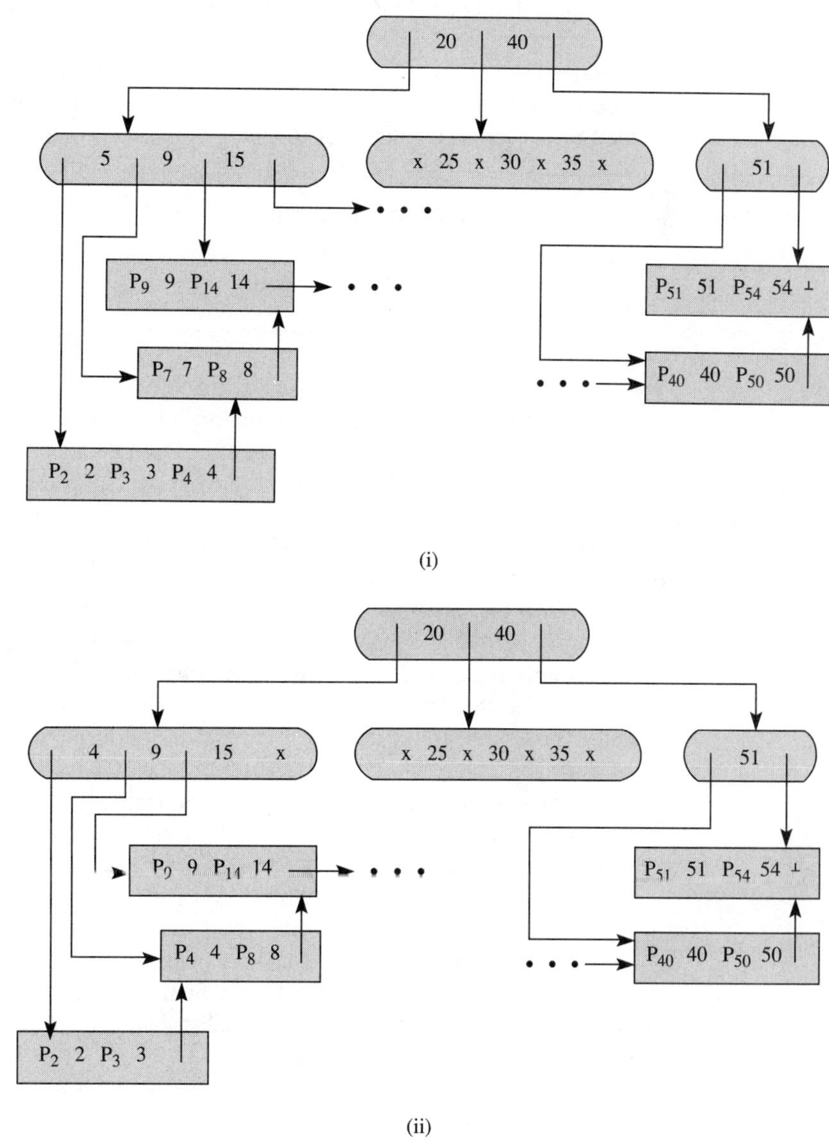

If we now delete key 7 from the B^+-tree of Figure G, the leaf node containing key 7 would have less than the minimum number of keys. The left sibling of this node contains P_2 2 P_3 3 P_4 4 × and can spare a key. This key and the appropriate pointers are moved to the about-to-be-underflow node. The resultant tree is shown in part ii of Figure G. Note that the index entry of the parent node reflects the redistribution. ■

3.7.4 Capacity

The upper and lower limits of the capacity of a B^+-tree of order m may be calculated by considering each node of the tree to be maximally (m − 1 keys) or minimally full ($\lceil m/2 \rceil - 1$ keys). We assume that the height of the tree is h. The two situations are depicted in Figure 3.26. As every key must occur in the leaf node and the leaf nodes may also contain a minimum of $\lceil (m-1)/2 \rceil$ and a maximum of (m − 1) keys, we have

$$2*\lceil (m-1)/2 \rceil * \lceil m/2 \rceil^{h-2} < N < (m-1) * m^{h-1}$$

3.7.5 B-trees

In the previous sections we looked at the B^+-tree, a descendant of the B-tree. The B^+-tree differs from the B-tree in the organization of the nodes. In the **B-tree,** the leaf nodes do not contain any information. During lookup, if the leaf node is reached without a match, the key does not exist (thus the leaf nodes are called **failure nodes**). Note that because the leaf nodes do not contain any information, they may be implemented in the parent node as null pointers. Because the leaf nodes do not contain pointers to the storage areas where the records reside, the pointers are included with the keys in the internal nodes. We may consider each k_i to represent a <key-value, address> pair. The advantage of the B-tree over the B^+-tree is that the key values appear only once in the tree, with consequent savings in space. We therefore require fewer nodes than in a corresponding B^+-tree. Another advantage is that it is no longer necessary to traverse up to the leaf nodes during lookup operations. Searches, on average, require fewer node accesses.

Whereas retrieval of the next record is relatively easy in the B^+-tree, this is not the case in the B-tree unless the internal nodes of the B-tree are linked in a sequential order. The deletions in a B^+-tree are always made in the leaf nodes. In a B-tree, however, a value can be deleted from any node, making deletions more complicated than in a B^+-tree.

Insertions in a B^+-tree are always made in the leaf nodes. In the B-tree, however, insertions are made at the lowest nonleaf node. Insertions (or deletions) may cause node splits (coalescing or key redistribution) and thereby affect the height of the tree in both cases.

The capacity of the B-tree can be calculated in a *manner* similar to that used for the B^+-tree. Note that the order of the tree is dictated by physical storage (buffer)

Figure 3.26 Capacity of a B$^+$-tree.

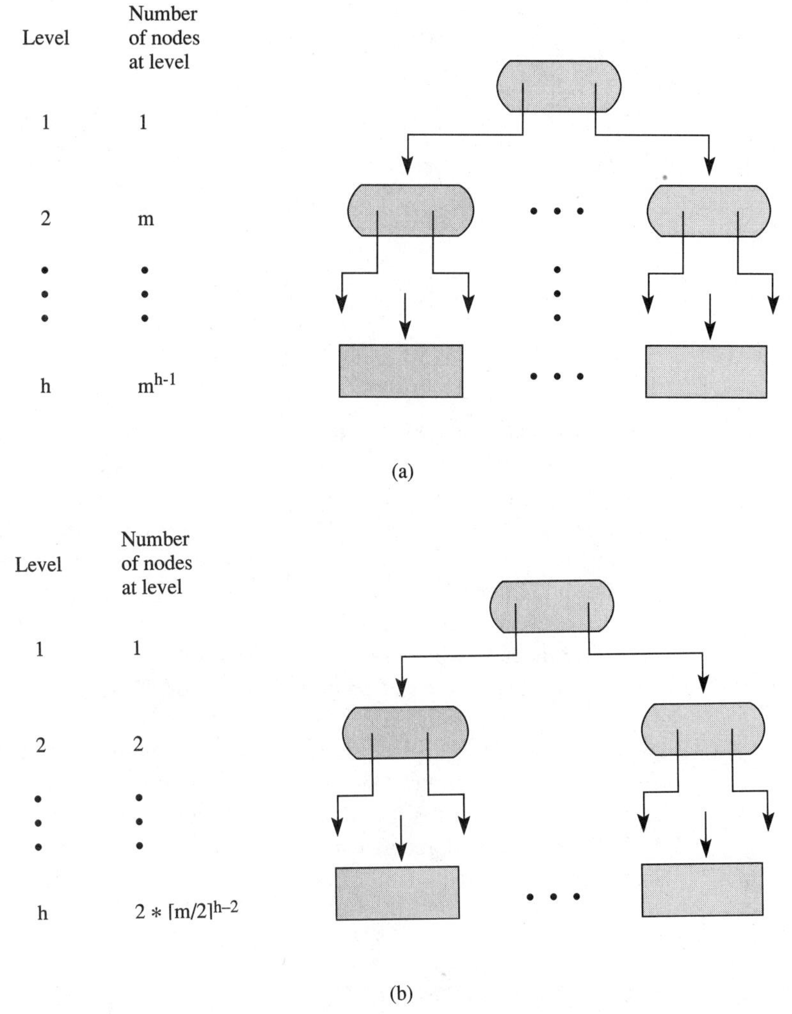

availability, among other factors. For the same buffer size, the order of the B-tree would be less than that of the B$^+$-tree.

3.8 Logical and Physical Pointers

Some of the file organizations considered in the previous sections required the use of pointers in their implementations. In many situations the use of pointers in file design arises. So far, we have not addressed the issue in any detail. What are these pointers and how are they implemented? We know, for example, that in the multilist file the pointers give us the address of the succeeding record. Are all pointers physical addresses? If they are, then any movement of the records or the file itself on the disks

Figure 3.27 Deriving address for clustered storage.

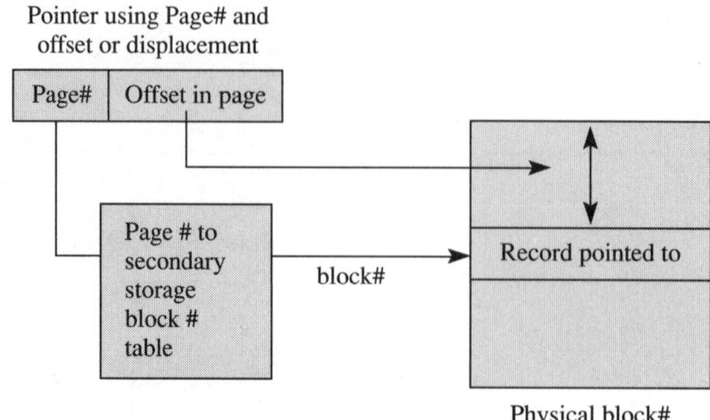

would necessitate changes to their values. Then should all pointers be implemented as logical addresses (i.e., by some key of the record)? This requires that there exist a mapping scheme from the key to the physical address. If this mapping is provided by an index, it entails additional accesses for each logical pointer access. Similarly, this applies for the hashing of the key values, except in unlikely hash functions that produce no collisions.

It is possible to use addresses based on page or bucket numbers and displacement within page where each page or bucket contains a set of blocks, i.e., a page contains a large number of records. The physical location of each of these file pages can be stored in a small table; this table can be brought into main memory when the file is in use. The displacement is used as a modifier, and the logical to physical address mapping can be done as shown in Figure 3.27 without additional secondary storage accesses. When the file is moved around on the disks, the only requirement is that the cluster of records in the page are moved together so that their displacements are not altered.

3.9 Record Placement

We began this chapter by stating that the time needed to access data on secondary storage could be optimized by minimizing the component of response time that we called the access time. In the sections above, we considered how access is facilitated by employing certain file organizations. The primary consideration in all organizations is access to the next or some particular logical record. Our main concern has been with access methods. We stated that the response time could also be optimized by suitable **record placement.**

A suitable placement strategy necessitates the knowledge or estimation of access frequencies or probabilities. We want the records to be placed in such a manner that the average head movement is minimal. It has been proven that the cost is minimal when the most frequent (or likely) records are grouped together in blocks and the blocks arranged such that the block access probabilities form an organ pipe arrangement. This type of arrangement results when we sequence block placement in non-

Figure 3.28 Organ pipe arrangement.

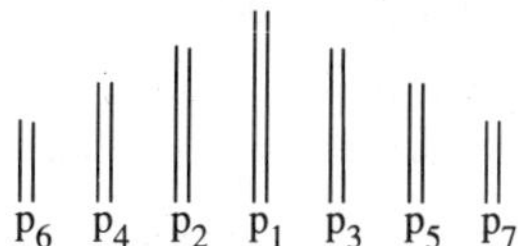

increasing access probability order. We first place the block with the highest access probability at some point and the other blocks in nonincreasing access probability order, alternately to the left or to the right of the already-placed blocks. Let us consider, for instance, n blocks and let the access probability of the *i*th block be p_i, where $p_1 \geq p_2 \geq \ldots \geq p_n$. The resultant optimal placement of blocks is shown in Figure 3.28. The optimal record placement strategy is applicable, even to the file organizations considered earlier in this chapter.

3.10 Concluding Remarks

In this chapter we looked at some common file organizations. They occur quite often in systems and applications work. As we have seen, no one organization can efficiently support all applications and types of access. It may be necessary to design a file that supports different organizations for different key fields, depending on the application requirements. However, it is not wise to design elaborate organizations for rare types of access. In file design, particular emphasis is placed on usage and factors of growth. We should also be aware of the space/time tradeoff in file design. Speeding up some accesses is always accompanied by increased storage demands. The simplest serial file has minimal wastage of storage space or overheads. However, as we have seen, access and updates are expensive. The other file organizations improve performance of certain operations, but require additional storage space.

In the index-sequential file the records are ordered with respect to the primary key. In this way it is possible to allow random and sequential access to any record. An index-sequential scheme, however, becomes inefficient if there are a large number of insertions and consequent overflows, and it requires periodic maintenance. For a file that is growing rapidly, index-sequential organization may be inappropriate. B^+-tree indexing, with its built-in maintenance, allows growth without the penalty of performance degradation. Both types of indexing allow random search followed by sequential search. However, the records in the case of the B^+-tree file may not be clustered and therefore it is possible that a disk access may be required to retrieve each record. Range queries, wherein records have a range of key values, can be handled by these file organizations.

With direct access supported by hashing, random access to any record is obtained in a fixed time but if the records are not clustered on the key used for hashing, sequential or range queries can only be handled as a series of independent requests. The hashing function maps a key value into a bucket address. With a good hashing function sequential keys need not be mapped to the same or consecutive buckets. However, having obtained the first bucket address, we have no way of knowing which bucket will contain the next key.

The steps involved in designing a file system for secondary key retrieval to reduce search time can be summarized as follows:

1. Determine the most likely secondary search keys.
2. Make an appropriate index for each such secondary key and generate the entries for each value of the key.

Consider the index structure of Figure 3.19b, an inverted index. The number of groups chosen is equal to the number of records $h_{ij} = n_{ij}$ and each pointer is directed to a single record. In a multilist file, $h_{ij} = 1$ and only one list of length n_{ij} exists for value v_{ij} of attribute A_i. With a cellular multilist, there are h_{ij} lists for value v_{ij} of attribute A_i, each list being limited to a convenient size, such as the cylinder of a disk drive, to maximize the response time.

Remember that with a multitude of indexes, the space occupied by them could exceed the space occupied by the actual data file.

When the same file is required for different applications or when a set of files are required by these applications, it becomes impossible to fully satisfy the requirements of every application. While it is not impossible to support secondary structures that can meet all requirements, any updates would require changes to all of them. These updates would be prohibitively expensive. Furthermore, different applications entail different logical relationships between data. Earlier in this book we introduced database systems. Just as file management systems remove the programmer/user from the knotty details of bits, bytes, and blocks, database management systems provide independence from details of data organization and access strategies.

With large random access memories available on the smallest of microcomputers, we hope that the file organizations considered in this chapter would only be the concern of system designers when dealing with very large files.

3.11 Summary

A file is a collection or bag of records. Having stored the records in a file, it is necessary to access these records using either a primary or secondary key. The type and frequency of access required determines the type of file organization to be used for a given set of records. In this chapter we looked at some common file organizations, examining the following: serial, sequential, index sequential, multilist, ring list, cellular list, direct, and tree-structured.

In a serial file, records are stored in no particular order and therefore the serial file is equivalent to an unordered sequence. Such a file is generated by appending records at the end of the file. The search for a record in a sequential file entails examining each record until it is found. Updates to records can be done in place if the records are of fixed length and the updates do not change the size of the records. Deletion of a record can be performed either by compressing the file or marking the record as deleted, and logically ignoring such records.

In a sequential file, records are maintained in the logical sequence of their primary key value. The search for a given record requires, on average, access to half the records in the file. Update operations, including the appending of a new record, require the creation of a new file. Updates could be batched and a transaction file of updates used to create a new master file from the existing one. This scheme automatically creates a backup copy of the file.

Access to a sequential file can be enhanced by creating an index. The index provides random access to records and the sequential nature of the file provides easy access to the next record. To avoid frequent reorganization, an index-sequential file uses overflow areas. This scheme provides space for the addition of records without the need for the creation of a new file. In index-sequential organization, it is the usual practice to have a hierarchy of indexes with the lowest level index pointing to the records while the higher level ones point to the index below them. Updates to an index-sequential file may entail modifications to the index in addition to the file. In VSAM the solution to the update overhead is found by providing free blocks for the indexes and records.

In direct file organization the key value is mapped directly or indirectly to a storage location, avoiding the use of indices. The usual method of direct mapping is by some arithmetical manipulation of the key value; the process is called hashing. However, hashing schemes usually give rise to collisions when two or more distinct key values are mapped to the same value. Collisions are handled in a number of ways. The colliding records may be assigned to the next available free space, or they may be assigned to an overflow area. In using the hash function to generate a value, which is the address of a bucket where the <key, address> pair values of records are stored, we can handle limited collisions as well as reorganization of the file without affecting the hash function. In extendable hashing, the database size changes are handled by splitting or coalescing buckets.

Secondary key retrieval is characterized by the multiplicity of records satisfying a given key value. Fast access to records is provided by the use of indexes and/or linking together logically related records in some suitable structure.

An inverted file contains the list of all records, satisfying the particular <attribute, value> pair in the index. The list contains a pointer to every record with a given value for the attribute.

In a multilist file the logically related records are linked together in the form of a list. A pointer to the first member of every list is maintained in the index. In a cellular list organization, lists are limited to a physical area of storage, referred to as a cell. In a ring file the last record of a linked list of records points back to the index entry.

Tree-based data organization schemes are used both for primary and secondary key retrieval. We considered the B^+-tree scheme, wherein each node of the tree except the leaf node contains a set of keys and pointers pointing to subtrees. The leaf nodes of the B^+-tree are similar to the nonleaf or internal nodes, except that the pointers in the leaf node point directly or indirectly to storage areas containing the required records. We also examined the method of performing the search and update operations using the B^+-tree and compared the B^+-tree with the B-tree.

Finally, we considered the implementation of pointers and the placement of records based on their probability of access.

Key Terms

file
disk pack
read/write heads
track
cylinder
fixed head drive
moving head drive
seek time
latency time
access time
interblock gaps (IBG)
data transfer time

homogeneous records
primary block
overflow block
update operations
sequential file
serial file
index-sequential file
direct file
nonkeyed sequential file
transaction file
old master file
new master file
index file
data file
implicit index
explicit index
limit indexing
block
bucket
sequential index key
index-sequential search
track index
skip-sequential processing
virtual storage access method (VSAM)
control interval
control area
hashing
collision
dynamic hashing
extendable hashing
inverted index file
inverted file
multilist file
cellular list
cell
ring file
leaf node
m-order tree
B^+-tree
overflow
redistribution
B-tree
failure nodes
record placement

Exercises

3.1 Access methods are measured by access and storage efficiencies. Define each term and its major objectives. Which is the most important consideration in a batch environment? In an online environment? Give reasons.

3.2 Discuss the differences between the following file organizations:

(a) serial
(b) index-sequential
(c) hashed
(d) inverted

Compare their storage and access efficiencies. To what type of application is each of the organizations suited?

3.3 We are given a file of 1 million records, each record being 200 bytes long, of which 10 bytes are for the key field. A physical block is 1000 bytes long and block addresses are 5 bytes long.

(a) Using a hashed file organization with 1000 buckets, calculate the bucket size in blocks. Assume all blocks contain the average number of records. What is the average number of accesses needed to search for a record that exists in the file?
(b) Using an index-sequential file with one level of indexing and assuming that all file blocks are as full as possible (with no overflow), how many blocks are needed for the index? If we employ a binary search on the index, how many accesses are required on average to find a record?
(c) If we use a B^+-tree and assume that all blocks are as full as possible, how many index blocks are needed? What is the height of the tree?
(d) Repeat part (c) if all blocks are half full.

3.4 We are given a file of 10 million records, each record being 100 bytes long, of which 5 bytes are for the key field. A physical block is 10000 bytes long and block addresses are 5 bytes long.

(a) Using a hashed file organization with 10,000 buckets, calculate the bucket size in blocks; assume all buckets are half full. What is the average number of accesses needed to search for a record that exists in the file?

(b) Using an index-sequential file with two levels of indexing and assuming that all data blocks are half full, how many blocks are needed for the index? If we employ a binary search on the index, how many accesses are required on average to find a record?

(c) If we use a B^+-tree of order 500, how many index blocks are needed? What is the height of the tree? How many disk accesses are required to find a record?

3.5 A file of 1,000,000 fixed-length records, each 200 bytes long, is stored on a magnetic tape. The tape handler characteristics are a 100KB/sec transfer rate and a start/stop time of 25 msec. Compare the time required to read all the records if the block size is chosen as (a) 5000 bytes, (b) 50,000 bytes and the tape has to be stopped after reading a block. Ignore the time used for processing after a block is read.

3.6 Records of 250 bytes are stored in blocks with a blocking factor of 20. A drive using a 3600-foot tape having a recording density of 6400 bpi (bytes per inch), an interblock gap size of 0.5 inch, a read/write speed of 200 kilobytes per second, and a start-stop time of 0.010 seconds is being used. How many records can the tape hold? What percentage of the tape is wasted? How long will it take to read the file from the tape without stopping? How much time is spent in reading the file if only one block is read at a time?

3.7 Given a record length of 32 bytes, a recording density of 1600 bpi, and an interblock gap size of 0.6 inch, calculate the blocking factor to have 80% of a 1600-foot tape holding data.

3.8 A file of 100,000 fixed-length records, each 100 bytes long, is stored on a magnetic tape. The tape handler characteristics are a 40KB/sec transfer rate and a start/stop time of 20 msec. The file is recorded at 1600 bpi and the interblock gap is 1/2 inch. Find the length of the tape required and compare the times required to read all the records if the block size is chosen as (a) 100 bytes, and (b) 10,000 bytes.

3.9 Consider a hash function h(k) = k mod 17 for a direct access file using extendable hashing. Assume that the bucket capacity is four records. Show the structure of the file including the bucket address table after the insertion of the following records: 87,13, 53, 82, 48, 921, 872, 284, 36, 128, 172.

3.10 In a multilist organization, give efficient algorithms to process the following queries:

(a) get all records with $Key_1 = x$ and $Key_2 = y$
(b) get all records with $Key_1 = x$ or $Key_2 = y$

If a ring organization is used instead, what complications are introduced into the processing of the above queries?

3.11 The following file contains student records. The Rec# is the address used to retrieve the record using a direct access function on the primary key (Id).

(a) Generate a directory for a multilist that has indexes for Dept, Advisor, and Status. Fill in the appropriate record number values in the Ptr field provided within the file.

(b) Using this multilist directory and the data file, indicate how you will answer the query to retrieve all records for students who are in the COMP department, or who have SMITH F. as an advisor, or whose status is F2, without accessing redundant records.

(c) Using the above data and assuming that there are three records per cell, generate a directory for a cellular multilist file with entries for Dept, Advisor, and Status.

Rec#	Name	Id	Dept	Ptr	Advisor	Ptr	Status	Ptr
1	MICROSLAW Kalik	3634592	COMP		SMITH F.		F2	
2	PASSASLO Joseph	3894336	PHYS		JONES A.		F3	
3	PRONOVOST Pierre	6888954	ELEC		WAGNER B.		I1	
4	LOANNIDES Lambi	3518445	CHEM		ACIAN R.		F3	
5	MACIOCIA Charles	7564019	ENGL		BROST A.		P2	
6	CHO BYUNG Chu	2566984	CHEM		JONES A.		F2	
7	CANNON Joe	7868286	PHYS		JONES A.		F3	
8	BERGERON Daniel	2736849	COMP		JONES A.		I2	
9	ABOND Daniel	7382943	ELEC		WEGNER B.		I3	
10	HAMMERBELL Abraham	6792839	COMP		SMITH F.		P2	
11	LANGEVIN Joseph	2768736	ENGL		NEWELL J.		P3	
12	PELLERIN George	6689184	COMP		WEGNER B.		F2	
13	ROBERT Louis	3707939	COMP		MARTIN R.		P1	
14	SHARPE George	9877546	CHEM		SMITH F.		I2	
15	PETIT Guy	2742619	ELEC		SMITH F.		I3	

3.12 What are the advantages and disadvantages of the index-sequential file?

3.13 Consider a cylinder of an index-sequential file as shown below. Only the key values are shown. The following changes are made to this cylinder:

add ID, **add** FW, **add** KP, **delete** FV, **add** FU, **delete** IQ, **add** JK, **add** IS, add IT, add JR

Here **add** indicates that a record is to be inserted into the file and **delete** indicates that the record is to be deleted from the file. Only the key values are given. The changes occur in the order specified. ⊥ indicates null pointers.

	HA	Block1	Block2	Block3	Block4	Block5	Block6
	2900	Tr.Index	FP	FR	FT	FV	FZ
P	2901	GB	GE	GH	GK	GM	GR
r	2902	GV	GY	HB	HC	HF	HI
i A	2903	HL	HO	HQ	HT	HX	IA
m r	2904	IC	IG	IJ	IM	IQ	IY
e e	2905	IZ	JB	JF	JJ	JN	JQ
a	2906	KA	KD	KG	KL	KO	KS
	2907	KT	KV	KY	KZ	LB	LF
Overflow	2908	⊥	⊥	⊥	⊥	⊥	⊥
Area	2909	⊥	⊥	⊥	⊥	⊥	⊥

Show the initial and final values of the track index. Also show the contents of the cylinder after all of the above changes have been made.

3.14 A software development company's employee records contain the following information:

ID (10), Name (25), Position (10), Age (2), Qualifications (9), Projects (10 repeated)

The value in the parentheses is the size of each entry in bytes. An employee can be involved in a number of projects at the same time; thus, this field is repeated. An internal coding mechanism groups qualifications into three types, each requiring 3 bytes to encode. The age of employees is divided into 10 groups. The total number of employees is 500 and, at any given time, up to 100 projects are handled. The file is to be maintained on disk with a physical block size of 4096 bytes. The pointer size for addresses is 4 bytes.

(a) Design file organizations for each of the access methods listed below that at least satisfy the retrieval/query transactions, also specified below, as efficiently as possible. Diagram the organization and discuss how your file organization satisfies the retrieval requirements.

Access methods: Index-sequential, inverted, and B^+-tree.
Retrieval requirements (specified in %):

1. List employees by name in alphabetical order (10%).
2. Print data for employees in some age group and with certain qualifications (50%).
3. Print names and current projects of employees with certain qualifications and holding certain positions (40%).

(b) Compare your design with organizations based on a single type of access method with respect to space and access time. In the derivation of the access time, use the following terms:

Block access time (random): t_R
Block Access time (next in sequence): t_S

Method	*Space*	*Total Access Time*		
		A	***B***	***C***
Your Design				
Index-sequential				
Inverted				
B^+-tree				

(c) Which access method minimizes total access time for all three application types? (Be sure to take transaction frequencies into account.) If accesses for application B also required the changing of age and qualifications, would this method still be the most efficient? Justify your answer.

3.15 The manufacturer's specifications for a disk drive are:

Number of surfaces	20
Number of tracks/surface	800
Number of sectors/track	20
Number of bytes/sector	512
Rotational speed	6000 rpm
Time to move arm to adjacent cylinder	5 msec
Average time to move arm to any cylinder	20 msec

(a) How many cylinders will be required to store 100,000 records each 100 bytes long if no logical record is split across sector boundaries?

(b) If the key plus cylinder-cum-track addresses require 8 bytes, when the above file is created as an indexed-sequential file with cylinder and track indexing, estimate the average time to locate a record. Assume that there are no overflow records and that the search of an index or sector, after having been transferred to main memory, is negligible.

3.16 Consider the cylinder of an index-sequential file as shown below. Each cylinder has six surfaces and a surface has four sectors. Each sector can hold three records. Surface 05 is used for the overflow records. (⊥ indicates null pointers)

Cyl.	Surface	Sectors 1	2	3	4
41					
	00	Tr.Index	A_1,A_4	A_5,A_6,A_9	A_{10},A_{13}
	01	A_{17},A_{18}	A_{20}	A_{28},A_{29}	A_{30},A_{31},A_{36}
	02	A_{42},A_{43}	A_{45},A_{46},A_{48}	A_{51},A_{52},A_{56}	A_{59},A_{61}
	03	A_{75},A_{76},A_{78}	A_{79},A_{80}	A_{83}	A_{89},A_{91}
	04	A_{93},A_{94}	A_{96},A_{98}	A_{100}	A_{120},A_{125}
	05	⊥	⊥	⊥	⊥

Give a track index that captures the current state of the cylinder. Also give the status of the cylinder and track index after the following operations have been performed:

I A_{34}, I A_{41}, I A_{95}, D A_{83}, I A_3, I A_{82}, I A_{84}, I A_{33}, D A_{36}, I A_2, D A_4, I A_{122}, D A_{125}, I A_{124}, I A_{54}, D A_{61}, I A_{60}

where I represents the insert, and D the delete, operation.

3.17 Create an index-sequential file using three cylinders, each of which has eight tracks. Up to four records can be stored in each track. Make appropriate provisions for overflow. The file is created initially with the following records in the order given:

132, 38, 87, 64, 88, 40, 759, 12, 459, 45, 362, 85, 835, 638, 414, 820, 41, 91, 29, 194, 517, 491, 524, 294, 43, 185, 791, 139, 59, 44, 11, 414, 37, 184, 472, 39, 88, 42, 758, 460, 412, 48, 415

Indicate the reorganization of the file if the following records are subsequently deleted and added. D preceding the key indicates that the record is to be deleted; A indicates that it has to be added:

D91, A92, D44, A43, A47, A46

3.18 Comment on the differences between index-sequential files and B^+-tree file organizations. Compare them for use wherever an indexed access may be required.

3.19 Give algorithms for the insertion and deletion of records in a B^+-tree.

3.20 In a B-tree file, pointers to the blocks containing the records exist even in the index level nodes. How does this alter the algorithms for insertion and deletion that you wrote for Exercise 3.19? Comment on the relative advantages and disadvantages of B-trees and B^+-trees.

3.21 The accompanying figure shows the B^+-tree index and the leaf nodes of a B^+-tree of order 3. The blocks containing the leaf nodes hold the actual records. (Only the key values are shown in the figure.) Each block must hold at least three and at most five records. Show the structure of the index after the following records are inserted or deleted. D preceding the key indicates that the record is to be deleted; **A** indicates that it has to be added:

D91, **A**98, **D**44, **A**43, **A**47, **A**46

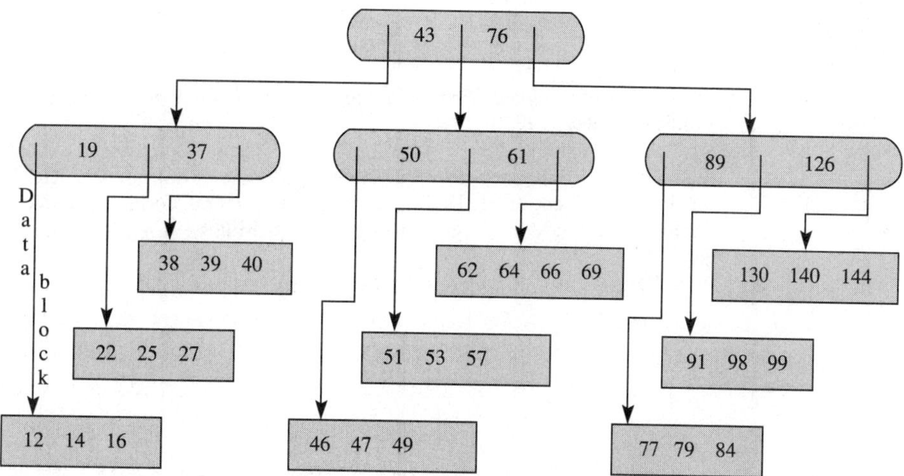

Bibliographic Notes

Discussion of storage devices and data organization methods is found in computer manufacturers manuals. A discussion on blocking and buffering techniques appears in (Wate 76). The handling of sequential files is the subject of many a textbook on programming; see also (Dwye 81). (Lum 71) presents hashing techniques as does (Litw 80). Index sequential files are the subject of a number of IBM manuals (IBM 1, IBM 2). Extendable hashing is discussed in (Fagi 79). B-tree indexes are presented in (Baye 72). A number of textbooks cover the areas of files and data structures, including (Ghos 86), (Harb 88), (Hans 82), (Horo 82), and (Knut 73). The discussion in this chapter is based to a great extent on (Goya 87).

Bibliography

(Baye 72) R. Bayer, ''Symmetric Binary B-trees: Data Structure and Maintenance Algorithms,'' *Acta Informatica,* 1(4), 1972, pp. 290–306.

(Come 79) D. Comer, ''The Ubiquitous B-tree'', *ACM Computing Surveys''* 11-(2), June 1979, pp. 121–137.

(Desa 89) B. C. Desai, ''Performance of a Composite Attribute and Join Index,'' *IEEE Trans. on Software Engineering* 15-(2), February 1989, pp. 142–152.

(Dwye 81) B. Dwyer, ''One More Time—How to Update a Master File,'' *Communications of the ACM* 24 (1), 1981, pp. 3–8.

(Fagi 79) R. Fagin, J. Nievergelt, N. Pippenger, & H. R. Strong, ''Extendible Hashing—A Fast Access Method for Dynamic Files,'' *ACM Trans. on Database Systems,* 4-(3), September 1979, pp.315–344.

(Ghos 86) S. P. Ghosh, *Data Base Organization for Data Management,* 2nd ed. Orlando, FL: Academic Press, 1986.

(Goya 87) P. Goyal, ''File Organization,'' *Computer Science Report,* Concordia University, Montreal, 1987.

(Hans 82) O. Hanson, *Design of Computer Data Files,* Rockville, MD: Computer Science Press, 1982.

(Harb 88) T. R. Harbon, *File Systems Structures and Algorithms*. Englewood Cliffs, NJ: Prentice-Hall, 1988.

(Horo 82) E. Horowitz & S. Sahni, *Fundamentals of Data Structures,* 2nd ed. Rockville, MD: Computer Science Press, 1982.

(IBM 1) ''Introduction to IBM Direct Access Storage Devices and Organization Methods,'' IBM Manual GC 20164910.

(IBM 2) "OS/VS1 and VS2 Access Method Services," IBM Manuals GC 263840 and GC 263841.

(Knut 73a) D. Knuth, *The Art of Computer Programming: Seminumerical Algorithms,* Reading, MA: AddisonWesley, 1973.

(Knut 73b) D. Knuth, *The Art of Computer Programming: Searching and Sorting,* Reading, MA: AddisonWesley, 1973.

(Litw 80) W. Litwin, "Linear Hashing: A New Tool for File and Table Addressing," Proceedings of the International Conference on Very Large Data Bases, 1980, pp. 212–223.

(Lum 71) V. Y. Lum, P. S. T. Yuen, & M. Dodd, "Key to Address Transform Techniques: A Fundamental Performance Study on Large Existing Formatted Files," *Communications of the ACM,* 14, pp. 228–239.

(Wate 76) S. J. Waters, "Hit Ratios," *Computer Journal* 19, 1976, pp. 21–24.

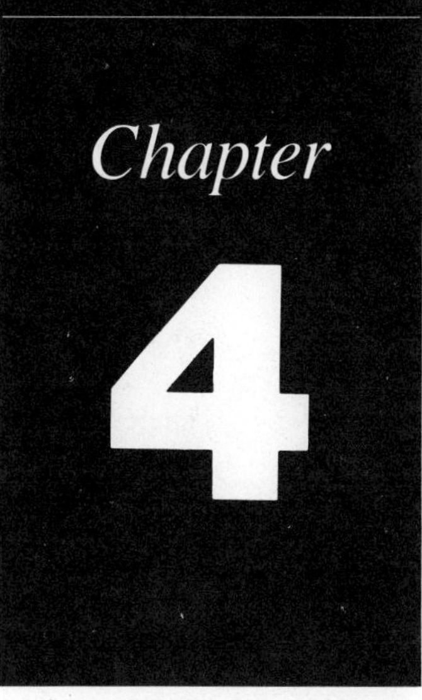

The Relational Model

Contents

The data models introduced in Chapter 2 differed only in the manner in which relationships among data are represented. In this chapter we concentrate on the relational data model (RDM), which was formally introduced in 1970. Since that time, it has undergone extensive study. The relational model frees the user from details of storage structures and access methods. It is also conceptually simple and, more importantly, based on sound theoretical principles that provide formal tools to tackle problems arising in database design and maintenance.

Numerous different formulations of the RDM have been presented and recently interest has been shown in its formalization. We shall, however, take a semiformal approach.

4.1 Introduction

In practice we can distinguish between entities and the relationships that exist between them. In modeling, we represent an entity set in the database by a set of its properties. However, only those properties of the entity type of interest to the application are used in the model. A data model allows the capturing of these properties using its data structures. Note that the association between the properties is only implicitly captured, i.e., we do not state what kind of association exists between the properties.

Furthermore, we may wish to retrieve or update the stored data and for this purpose a data model supports certain operations. The data may also need to conform to certain consistency and integrity rules, as in the case of a bank's rule that a customer's account balance remain nonnegative (i.e., ≥ 0). These constraints are specified as integrity rules.

The relational data model, like all data models, consists of three basic components:

- a set of domains and a set of relations
- operations on relations
- integrity rules

Each of these components is illustrated in the following examples.

Example 4.1 In this simple example we model certain properties of a number of database management systems (DBMSs). Let us assume that we want to maintain a database of these DBMSs. This database will register their names, the particular data models employed, and the company that developed and markets the DBMSs. Some of these DBMSs are shown in the table SOME_DBMS in Figure A. ■

Figure A Sample relation SOME _DBMS *(Name, Data_Model, Company)*

SOME_DBMS

Name	*Data_Model*	*Company*
Data	Network	WXY Inc.
Data-R	Relational	WXY Inc.
ISS	Hierarchical	BCD Systems
ISS/R	Relational	BCD Systems
ISS/R-PC	Relational	BCD Systems
Tables	Relational	ABC Relational Systems Inc.

■

From our knowledge of the relational model gained in Chapter 2, we can identify SOME_DBMS as a relation with the attributes *Name, Data_Model,* and *Company*. The fact that a relation has certain attributes is specified by its scheme, usually written as **RELATION_SCHEME_NAME**(*Attribute_Name*$_1$, *Attribute_Name*$_2$, . . .). Each attribute is defined over a set of values known as its domain. For our sample relation, the scheme can be specified as **SOME_DBMS**(***Name,*** *Data_Model, Company*). The relation SOME_DBMS shown in Figure A in Example 4.1 consists of six tuples, i.e., the **cardinality** of the relation SOME_DBMS is six. The number of attributes in the relation scheme is called its **degree** or **arity.** The degree of the scheme **SOME_DBMS** is three. Each tuple captures the association among the properties name, data model, and company of a DBMS package. Here the attribute *Name* can be used to uniquely identify a given DBMS and the corresponding tuple in the relation.

Just as we are able to model an entity and its properties by a relation, we can model relationships between entities using a relation. This is illustrated in Example 4.2. In Section 4.2 we shall study the relational database structures in a more formal manner.

Example 4.2

Certain DBMSs of Example 4.1 are used in particular applications. The application can be modeled using the budget code of the application as an identifying attribute or key and the name of the application. Some tuples for the relation APPLICATION(*App_Name,* ***Budget_Code***) are shown in part i of Figure B. The E-R diagram of the relationship between APPLICATION and SOME_DBMS, named *WHERE_USED*, is shown in part ii of the figure. We can record the information about this relationship in the relation WHERE_USED by pairing the keys from the entities SOME_DBMS and APPLICATION. This relationship can be expressed as a relation, some tuples of which are shown in part iii of Figure B. ■

Figure B Relationship between entities.

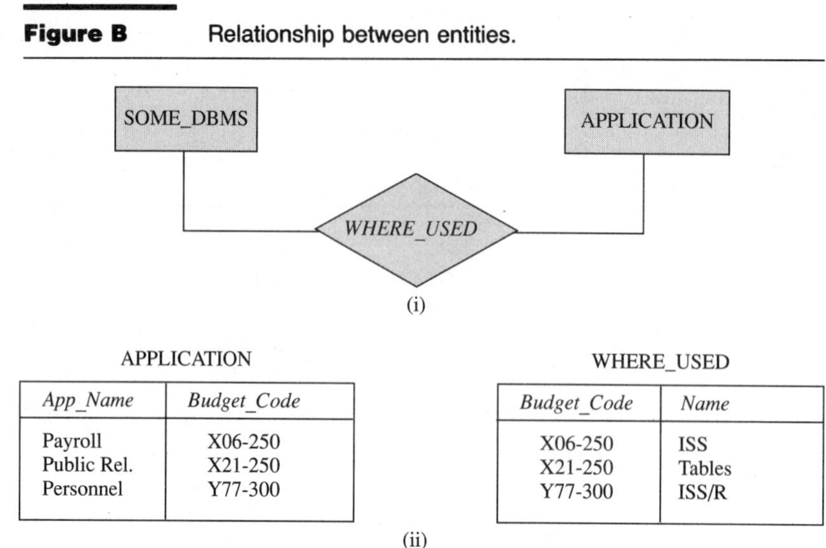

APPLICATION

App_Name	*Budget_Code*
Payroll	X06-250
Public Rel.	X21-250
Personnel	Y77-300

WHERE_USED

Budget_Code	*Name*
X06-250	ISS
X21-250	Tables
Y77-300	ISS/R

The relational operations define a set of data manipulation operations. The information recorded in the relation SOME_DBMS is of limited value by itself. Normally, we want to operate on the relation so that we can find, for example, the name of the DBMSs produced by a particular company. Another query that requires operation on more than one relation is illustrated in Example 4.3.

Example 4.3

Software packages are continually being modified. The modification may be performed to improve the product or remove errors that may have been encountered during its use. The modified package retains its name, but a new version or release number is assigned to it.

Let us record the name, release number, and year of release of the version for the DBMSs in the relation VERSION. Some tuples of the relation VERSION are shown in Figure C with the attributes given as *Name, Release,* and *Year*.

Figure C VERSION relation.

Name	*Release*	*Year*
ISS	1.0	1975
ISS	2.0	1979
ISS/R	1.0	1984
ISS/R-PC	1.0	1985
Data	1.0	1976
Data	2.0	1980
Data-R	2.0	1981
Data	3.0	1985
Data-R	3.0	1986
Tables	1.0	1987

Figure D Join of relations SOME_DBMS and VERSION.

VERSION. *Name*	*Release*	*Year*	SOME_DBMS. *Name*	*Data_Model*	*Company*
ISS	1.0	1975	ISS	Hierarchical	BCD Systems
ISS	2.0	1979	ISS	Hierarchical	BCD Systems
ISS/R	1.0	1984	ISS/R	Relational	BCD Systems
ISS/R-PC	1.0	1985	ISS/R-PC	Relational	BCD Systems
Data	1.0	1976	Data	Network	WXY Inc.
Data	2.0	1980	Data	Network	WXY Inc.
Data-R	2.0	1981	Data-R	Relational	WXY Inc.
Data	3.0	1985	Data	Network	WXY Inc.
Data-R	3.0	1986	Data-R	Relational	WXY Inc.
Tables	1.0	1987	Tables	Relational	ABC

Figure E (i) Join of selected tuples of relation SOME_DBMS with relation VERSION and (ii) Join of relation SOME_DBMS with selected tuples of relation VERSION.

VERSION. *Name*	*Release*	*Year*	SOME_DBMS. *Name*	*Data_Model*	*Company*
ISS/R	1.0	1984	ISS/R	Relational	BCD Systems
ISS/R-PC	1.0	1985	ISS/R-PC	Relational	BCD Systems
Data-R	2.0	1981	Data-R	Relational	WXY Inc.
Data-R	3.0	1986	Data-R	Relational	WXY Inc.
Tables	1.0	1987	Tables	Relational	ABC

(i)

VERSION. *Name*	*Release*	*Year*	SOME_DBMS. *Name*	*Data_Model*	*Company*
ISS/R-PC	1.0	1985	ISS/R-PC	Relational	BCD Systems
Data	3.0	1985	Data	Network	WXY Inc.
Data-R	3.0	1986	Data-R	Relational	WXY Inc.
Tables	1.0	1987	Tables	Relational	ABC

(ii)

Now consider the query "Find the names of the companies that released relational DBMSs versions after 1984." This particular query requires that we join the two relations SOME_DBMS and VERSION on the common attribute *Name*. The result of the join is shown in Figure D. The required rows of the table of Figure D are then identified to respond to the above query. Note that in joining the rows of the two tables, we only join those rows or tuples that have the same value for the attribute *Name* that is common to both these relations. As we will see in Section 4.3.2, the relations shown in Figures D and E, are the result of the so-called equi-join operations. ■

The number of tuples in the join of SOME_DBMS and VERSION is the same as those in VERSION because a tuple in SOME_DBMS has the same value of the *Name* attribute as a tuple in VERSION. Note that the two occurrences of the attribute *Name* in the join can be distinguished by preceding each with the corresponding relation name. The first attribute is labeled VERSION.*Name* and the second similarly named attribute is called SOME_DBMS.*Name*.

Figure D in Example 4.3 demonstrates that many of the tuples in the resulting tables are not required for answering the query. We could have approached the selection on the table of Figure A in Example 4.1, choosing only relational DBMSs and thereby giving a joined table as shown in Figure Ei in Example 4.3. But if we had selected only those rows or tuples from Figure B in Example 4.2, released after 1984, and joined this reduced set of tuples with the table SOME_DBMS, we would get a smaller table as illustrated in Figure Eii in Example 4.3. The response to the query is obtained by selecting only those tuples from one of the tables in Figure E that satisfy the two conditions of the query (in other words, taking a "horizontal subset" of the tables of Figure E). The resulting tuples are given in Figure 4.1a. The names of the companies are obtained by taking a "vertical subset" of the table on the column *Company* (in other words, **projecting** the table of Figure 4.1a on the column *Company*). The result is shown in Figure 4.1b. The method of determining which operation to perform first is the topic of query optimization, which we discuss in Chapter 10.

The **join** is just one way in which data in a relational database can be manipulated. Several kinds of data manipulation languages have been defined for the relational model. Most relational data manipulation languages are more assertional than procedural. In a purely assertional data manipulation language the target data are specified by stating their properties instead of describing how they can be retrieved. The majority of languages are based on a combination of relational algebra and re-

Figure 4.1 (a) Selecting only some tuples from the join of relation SOME_DBMS relation VERSION and (b) projecting on the column *Company*.

VERSION. *Name*	*Release*	*Year*	SOME_DBMS. *Name*	*Data_Model*	*Company*
ISS/R-PC	1.0	1985	ISS/R-PC	Relational	BCD Systems
Data-R	3.0	1986	Data-R	Relational	WXY Inc.
Tables	1.0	1987	Tables	Relational	ABC

(a)

Company
BCD Systems
WXY Inc.
ABC

(b)

lational calculus. We look at these in more depth in Sections 4.3 and 4.4, respectively.

Example 4.4 looks at the relational rules that define certain properties that the database must satisfy.

Example 4.4

If we intend to keep only information on currently available DBMS packages in our database, we could specify that in our VERSION relation the release year of a version not go beyond the current year. We could also specify that the DBMS name be unique. With the unique name and tuple properties, it is apparent that the name determines the company that produces the DBMS and its data model. We may conclude that *Name* uniquely determines *Company* and *Name* uniquely determines *Data_Model*. ■

This unique identification is an integrity constraint, which ensures that each instance of an entity is distinguishable. Functional dependency is also a form of constraint, as it specifies which combination of values is legal. Certain constraints are defined in terms of functional dependencies between the attributes and form the basis of the normalization theory (see Chapters 6 and 7). The entity and referential integrity rules are two general rules that all relational databases are expected to satisfy. Both rules will be studied in Section 4.2.8. Additional rules may also be defined for the application in hand.

Relational database theory borrows heavily from set algebra; therefore a brief review of set concepts is given in the following section. Some data manipulation languages make use of first-order predicate calculus and the relevant material is briefly covered in Section 4.4. The material presented here is not exhaustive but should be sufficient to understand the relational model.

4.1.1 A Brief Review of Set Theory

A **set** is well-defined collection of objects. It is commonly represented by a list of its elements (called **members**) or by the specification of some membership condition. The **intension** of a set defines the permissible occurrences by specifying a membership condition. The **extension** of the set specifies one of numerous possible occurrences by explicitly listing the set members. These two methods of defining a set are illustrated in the following example.

Example 4.5

Intension of set G: $\{g | g$ is an odd positive integer less than $20\}$

Extension of set G: $\{1,3,5,7,9,11,13,15,17,19\}$ ■

A set is determined by its members. The number 3 is a member of the set G and this is denoted by $3 \in G$. Given an object g and the set G exactly one of the statements "g is a member of G" (written as $g \in G$) or "g is not a member of G" (written as $g \notin G$) is true.

Operations on sets include the union, intersection, cartesian product, and difference operations. The **union** of two sets G and H (written $G \cup H$) is the set that contains all elements belonging either to set G or to set H. If sets G and H have any elements in common, the union will not duplicate those members. The **intersection** of the sets G and H (written $G \cap H$) is the set composed of all elements belonging to both G and H. If G and H are two sets, then G is included in H, written as $G \subseteq H$, if and only if each member of G is also a member of H. Should there be an element h such that $h \in H$ but $h \notin G$, then G is a proper subset of H, written as $G \subset H$.

Example 4.6

If we let set G represent the companies that produce a hierarchical database and set H represent those that produce a relational database then, from the SOME_DBMS relation of Figure A in example 4.1 we have:

$$G = \{\text{BCD}\}$$
$$H = \{\text{WXY Inc., BCD, ABC}\}$$
$$G \cup H = \{\text{WXY Inc., BCD, ABC}\}$$
$$G \cap H = \{\text{BCD}\}$$

Note that $G \cap H \subseteq G$ and $G \cap H \subseteq H$ and in the above example $G \subset H$. ■

The **cartesian product** of two sets G and H (denoted by $G \times H$) is defined in terms of ordered pairs or 2-tuples. An ordered pair is conventionally denoted by enclosing it in parentheses, e.g., (g,h). The product $G \times H$ is the set consisting of all ordered pairs (g,h) for which $g \in G$ and $h \in H$. (Note that here the symbols g and h are being used as variables.) Example 4.7 shows the cartesian product of the sets J and K.

Example 4.7

Let J = {BCD, ABC}, and
K = {Hierarchical, Relational}
J × K = {(BCD,Hierarchical), (BCD,Relational),
(ABC,Hierarchical), (ABC, Relational)}
K × J = {(Hierarchical,BCD), (Relational,BCD),
(Hierarchical,ABC), (Relational,ABC)} ■

Note that the individual n-tuples in the cartesian product are ordered. Therefore, $J \times K$ and $K \times J$ are entirely different sets, as illustrated in Example 4.7.

The **difference** of two sets G and H (denoted $G - H$) is the set that contains all elements that are members of G but not of H.

Example 4.8

If G = {BCD}, and
H = {WXY Inc., BCD, ABC} then the sets $G - H$ and $H - G$ are

$G - H = \phi$ (the null set)
$H - G = \{$WXY Inc., ABC$\}$ ■

In set theory, relations between sets can be of many kinds, such as a subset of ($\subset$), complement of ($\neg$), and so on. Pairing relations can also be defined in terms of some specific criterion. We can, for instance, pair the application name and the budget code for the application. In fact, this is what we did in the example relation APPLICATION of Figure Bi of Example 4.2. Pairing relations in general can be defined on sets of the same or different kinds. If G and H are sets of objects, $g \in G$ and $h \in H$, then the possible pairing relations of degree 2 are:

$$(g,g) \qquad (g,h) \qquad (h,g) \qquad (h,h)$$

Each is a relation. We can see that a pairing relation must be a subset of the cartesian product of the sets involved in the relationship. In the four relationships above, these cartesian products are $G \times G$, $G \times H$, $H \times G$, and $H \times H$, respectively.

Example 4.9

The pairs of DBMSs produced by one company:

{(Data, Data-R), (ISS, ISS/R), (ISS,ISS/R-PC), (ISS/R,ISS/R-PC), (ISS/R, ISS), (Data-R, Data), (ISS/R-PC,ISS), (ISS/R-PC,ISS/R)}

We can see that this is a subset of *Name* × *Name*. ■

4.2 Relational Database

In this section we cover the terminology, notation, and structural aspects of relational databases. We first look at the basic building blocks of relational systems: the attributes and the domains on which they are defined. Later we specify the meaning of tuples and then look at relations and their schemes.

4.2.1 Attributes and Domains

An object or entity is characterized by its properties (or attributes). In conventional file systems the term field refers to the smallest item of data with some practical meaning, i.e., a field is used to capture some specific property of the object. In relational database systems, attributes correspond to fields. For a given application, an attribute may only be allowed to take a value from a set of the permissible values. This set of allowable values for the attribute is the domain of the attribute. In Examples 4.10 and 4.11 we illustrate the definition of domains.

Example 4.10

If persons can only be between 0 and 255 years of age, then the attribute *Age* will be defined over the domain P_Age where
P_Age: $\{x \mid x \text{ a positive integer} \wedge 0 \leq x \leq 255\}$ ■

Note that the value of 255 in Example 4.10 may appear to have been arbitrarily chosen. The range in fact neatly fits into a 8-bit byte. In practical database design, as in this example, the choices are never arbitrary but depend on the system requirements.

Example 4.11 In the development of a software package, an estimate of the number of lines of code is made and this can only be a positive integer greater than zero. We can therefore define a domain consisting of only positive integers for this application. ■

Definition: **Domain:**

We define a domain, D_i, as a set of values of the same data type.

The domain D_i, a set having "homogeneous" members, is conceptually similar to the data type concept in programming languages. A domain, like a data type, may be unstructured (atomic) or structured. Domain D_i is said to be simple if all its elements are nondecomposable (i.e., atomic). (When we use the term decomposable, we mean in terms of the DBMS.) In typical DBMSs, **atomic domains** are general sets, such as the sets of integers, real numbers, character strings, and so on. Atomic domains are sometimes referred to as **application-independent domains** because these general sets are not dependent on a particular application. We can also define **application-dependent domains** by specifying the values permitted in the particular database. **Structured** or **composite domains** can be specified as consisting of nonatomic values. The domain for the attribute *Address,* for instance, which specifies street number, street name, city, state, and zip or postal code is considered a composite domain.

It is unfortunate that many of the currently available commercial relational database systems do not support the concept of domains. Such support of both application-independent and user-defined domains specified as types in programming languages allows for the validation of the value assigned to an attribute.

Attributes are defined on some underlying domain. That is, they can assume values from the set of values in the domain. Attributes defined on the same domain are comparable, as these attributes draw their values from the same set. It is meaningless to compare attributes defined on different domains, as exemplified below.

Example 4.12 Assume that in a given city house numbers are between 0 and 255. The domain H_Number for the attribute *House_Numbers* can be defined to be the set of values from 0 to 255. The attribute *House_Numbers* is defined over the same domain as *Age* (Example 4.10) and without any additional constraints, they are comparable. Semantically, we say that the domain of *Age* represents a value that is a measure of a number of years and the domain H_Number represents a part of an address. Therefore, comparing the age in years of persons with the house number part of an address is meaningless. Consequently, we have to consider the domain of *House_Numbers* as distinct from the domain of Age, and these domains are not compatible. ■

It is possible, however, to relax the above rule for two semantically compatible domains D_i and D_j where $D_i \cap D_j \neq \phi$. Then attribute A_i defined on domain D_i and attribute A_j defined on D_j can be compared if $a_i \in D_i \cap D_j$ and $a_j \in D_i \cap D_j$. Here, a_i and a_j are the values of attributes A_i and A_j, respectively.

It has become traditional to denote attributes by uppercase letters from the beginning of the alphabet. Thus, *A*, *B*, *C*, . . . , with or without subscripts denote attributes. In applications, however, attributes are given meaningful names. Sets of attributes are denoted by uppercase letters from the end of the alphabets such as . . . , X, Y, Z.

Using the concept of attributes and domains, we can now define a tuple.

4.2.2 Tuples

An entity type having n attributes can be represented by an ordered set of these attributes called an **n-tuple.** Assume that these n attributes take values from the domains $D_1, \ldots, D_n$. The representation of the entity must then be a member of the set $D_1 \times D_2 \times \ldots \times D_n$, as the resulting set of this cartesian product contains all the possible ordered n-tuples.

Example 4.13 A job applicant may be characterized for a particular application by her or his name, age, and profession. An applicant, John Doe, who is 55 years old and is an analyst, may be represented as a 3-tuple: "John Doe, 55, analyst" (Figure F). This is a possible ordered triple obtained from the cartesian product of the domain for attributes *Name, Age,* and *Profession.* The implication of this 3-tuple is that an instance of the entity type has the value John Doe for its attribute *Name,* the value 55 for *Age,* and the value analyst for *Profession.* ■

Figure F Representation of a association among attributes.

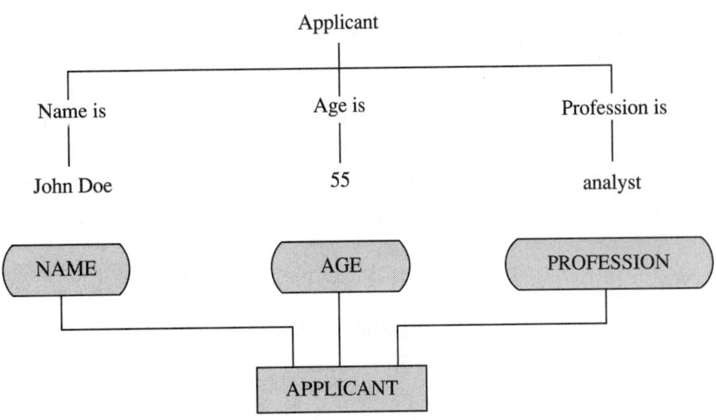

A tuple is comparable to a record in conventional file systems and is used for handling entities and relationships between entities. Tuples are generally denoted by lowercase letters r, s, t, . . . of the alphabet. An n-tuple t can be specified as

$$t = (a_1, \ldots, a_n)$$

where each a_i for $1 \le i \le n$ is a value in the domain D_i, and is the value of the attribute A_i in the tuple t. While it is required that the attribute names be different for unambiguous identification, no such restriction exists for domains. We may have the same domain for different attributes.

In the tuple representation above, the order of the attributes is significant, implicitly understood, and fixed (i.e., time invariant). If, however, we associate the attribute names with the corresponding values, we can relax the ordering requirement. Although the ordered set (a_1, a_2) is not equal to (a_2, a_1), we shall treat the sets $\{(A_1:a_1), (A_2:a_2)\}$ and $\{(A_2:a_2), (A_1:a_1)\}$ as the same. Formally, we view a tuple as a mapping from attribute names to values in the domains of the attributes.

Thus, a tuple can be represented in a number of ways, some of which are shown below:

$t = (a_1, \ldots, a_n)$	attribute value order must be constant
$t = (a_1, \ldots, a_n \mid A_1, \ldots, A_n)$	attribute value can be deduced from relative ordering of the names of the attribute
$t = (\mid A_1, \ldots, A_n \mid \mid a_1, \ldots, a_n \mid)$	
$t = ((A_1:a_1), \ldots, (A_n:a_n))$	
$t = ((A_1 \mid a_1), \ldots, (A_n \mid a_n))$	

In the above formulations the a_i's are values drawn from D_i, the domain of A_i. It is usual to denote the value of a tuple t over an attribute A_i as $t[A_i]$, i.e., $t[A_i] = a_i$. It is known as the projection of the tuple t over A_i.

We can define a simple projection (or attribute restriction) operation on a given tuple. Let us represent the set of attributes of the tuple t by X, i.e., $X = \{A_1, \ldots, A_n\}$. Let $Y = \{A_k, \ldots, A_m\}$ be a nonempty proper subset of X. Then the **projection** of the tuple t over Y, denoted t[Y], is given by:

$$t[Y] = ((A_i:a_i) \mid a_i = t[A_i], k \le i \le m, A_i \epsilon X)$$

(We assume that the set of attributes and the tuple values can be rearranged such that the attributes in set Y are consecutively ordered within X.)

Example 4.14

For the applicant tuple of Example 4.13, let t = (John Doe, 55, analyst). We then have the following projections:

t[*Name, Profession*] = (John Doe, analyst)
t[*Name, Age*] = (John Doe, 55)
t[*Age, Profession*] = (55, analyst)
t[*Name*] = (John Doe)
t[*Age*] = (55)
t[*Profession*] = (analyst)

In addition, we could use a projection to reorder the attrubutes as follows:

t[*Name, Profession, Age*] = (John Doe, analyst, 55) ■

4.2.3 Relations and Their Schemes

A relation consists of a homogeneous set of tuples. In the case of the SOME_DBMS relation of Figure A, Example 4.1, all the tuples have a similar structure and contain the same set of attributes. From another point of view, a relation is a subset of the cartesian product of the domains.

Example 4.15 Let the set of job applicant names be S_1 = {Smith, Doe}, the set of job applicant ages be S_2 = {32,47,55}, and S the set of applicants, which expresses a correspondence between name and age, be {(Smith, 32), (Doe,55)}. Now S is a subset of the cartesian product of the sets S_1 and S_2, where $S_1 \times S_2$ = {(Smith,32), (Smith,47), (Smith, 55), (Doe,32), (Doe,47), (Doe,55)}. ■

Since each tuple in a relation represents an identifiable instance of an object type, duplicate tuples are not allowed. (This also follows from the definition of a relation in terms of sets.) Note that the set of tuples in the relation are not static but can vary with time. In our discussion of tuples, the set of attributes on which the tuples are defined is the invariant. This is called the scheme of the relation or the relation scheme.

The relation has two parts: a **relation scheme** (or header), and a time-varying set of tuples (or body). The semantics of the specific relationships among the attributes, as we have seen, are not represented in the relation. The attribute names are specified in a relation scheme, i.e., the syntax is specified. The ordering of the attributes in the scheme is immaterial; however, the tuple layout matches this ordering. The entity job applicant of Example 4.13 can be represented by a relation such as APPLICANT(**Name,** *Age, Profession*). Examples of relation schemes used so far in this chapter are given below in Example 4.16.

Example 4.16 Examples of relation schemes:

SOME_DBMS (***Name,*** *Data_Model, Company*)
VERSION (***Name, Version#,*** *Year*)
WHERE_USED (***DBMS_Name, Application_Name***)
APPLICANT (***Name,*** *Age, Profession*) ■

We can formally define a relation in terms of set concepts. A mathematical relation is a set that expresses a correspondence between two or more sets and is a subset of the cartesian product of the sets. For example, a binary relation expresses a correspondence between two sets. This is illustrated below.

On a more formal basis we represent the relation scheme as $\mathbf{R}(A_1, \ldots, A_n)$, the domain of each attribute A_i by D_i for $1 \le i \le n$, and define the relation R over the set of attributes **R**, denoted R(**R**), as a set of n-tuples such that:

$$R(\mathbf{R}) \subseteq D_1 \times D_2 \ldots \times D_n$$

The value n (the number of attributes in the relation) is known as the degree or arity of the relation. A relation of degree one is called an unary relation, of degree two a binary relation, and of degree n an n-ary relation.[1] Attribute names could be considered a convenience rather than a formal requirement. However, when a number of attributes of a relation are defined on the same domain, the importance of unique attribute names becomes evident. Codd (Codd 70) originally described the relational model referring only to domains.

We formally represent a relation R as a 4-tuple:

$$R(T_R, AN_R, n, m)$$

where T_R represents the set of tuples, $m = |T_R|$ is the cardinality of the relation (i.e., the number of tuples in the relation), AN_R represents the set of attribute names, and $n = |AN_R|$ is the cardinality of the set of attribute names (the degree or arity of the relation).

In the above definition of a relation, we have specified the relation having these constituents: a set of tuples, a scheme (or set of attribute names), the degree, and the cardinality of the relation. The last two are conceptual values as they can be obtained from the set of attributes and tuples, respectively.

It is therefore more usual to represent the relation R defined on a relation scheme **R** in terms of just the scheme and set of tuples. The set of tuples of a relation, unless there is confusion, can be expressed by the name of the relation. We shall use an uppercase letter to represent both the relation name and its set of tuples and a bold uppercase letter for the relation's scheme and its set of attributes. This gives us a shorter form of the representation of a relation as simply R(**R**). The degree (or arity) of the relation is given by the number of attributes in scheme **R**, i.e., |**R**|, while the cardinality of the relation is given by the number of tuples in R and is indicated by |R|. As such, R(**R**) represents the relation R defined on scheme **R** having the set of tuples R.

We discuss other methods of representing a relation in the following section.

4.2.4 Relation Representation

Conceptually, a relation can be represented as a table. Remember that the contents of a relation are positionally independent, while a table gives the impression of positional addressing. Each column of the table represents an attribute and each row represents a tuple of the relation. Figure 4.2 shows the tabular representation of the APPLICANT relation of Example 4.13.

It is a myth that a relation is just a flat file. A table is just one of the conceptual representations of a relation. It is possible to store the relations using, for instance, inverted files.

As seen in Section 4.2.2, a tuple may be represented either as a labeled n-tuple or as an ordered n-tuple. The labeled n-tuples are represented using distinct attribute names $A_1, \ldots, A_n$ and the values $a_1, \ldots, a_n$ from the corresponding domains. The labeled n-tuples consist of unordered attribute value pairs: $(A_1{:}a_1, \ldots,$

[1]A domain can be thought of as a unary relation.

Figure 4.2 Example representation of a relation as a table.

APPLICANT:

Name	*Age*	*Profession*
John Doe	55	Analyst
Mirian Taylor	31	Programmer
Abe Malcolm	28	Receptionist
Adrian Cook	33	Programmer
Liz Smith	32	Manager

$A_n : a_n$). Ordered n-tuples are represented simply as (a_1, . . . , a_n), where the values appear in the same order as their domains in the cartesian product of which the relation is a subset.

4.2.5 Keys

In the relational model, we represent the entity by a relation and use a tuple to represent an instance of the entity. Different instances of an entity type are distinguishable and this fact is established in a relation by the requirement that no two tuples of the same relation can be the same. It is possible that only a subset of the attributes of the entity, and therefore the relation, may be sufficient to distinguish between the tuples. However, for certain relations, such a subset may be the complete set of attributes. In the instance of an EMPLOYEE relation, values of an attribute such as *Emp#* may be sufficient to distinguish between employee tuples. Such a subset of attributes, let us say X of a relation R(**R**), X ⊆ **R,** with the following time-independent properties is called the key of the relation:

- **Unique identification:** In each tuple of R, the values of X uniquely identify that tuple. To elaborate, if s and t represent any two tuples of a relation and if the values s[X] and t[X] for the attributes in X in the tuples s and t are the same, then s and t must be the same tuple. Therefore, $s[X] = t[X] \Rightarrow s = t$. Here the symbol $\Rightarrow$ is used to indicate that the left-hand side logically implies the right-hand side.
- **Nonredundancy:** No proper subset of X has the unique identification property, i.e., no attribute K ∈ X can be discarded without violating the unique identification property.

Since duplicate tuples are not permitted in a relation, the combination of all attributes of the relation would always uniquely identify its tuples. There may be more than one key in a relation; all such keys are known as candidate keys. One of the candidate keys is chosen as the primary key; the others are known as alternate keys. An attribute that forms part of a candidate key of a relation is called a **prime attribute.**

Example 4.17 In many applications, arbitrary attributes are assigned to the objects and these attributes play the role of keys. *Emp#* is such a key (the domain for the attribute *Emp#* is application specific and unique for a given application). A Social Security number in the U.S. and a Social Insurance number in Canada also identify a person uniquely in these countries. Both numbers are of nine digits and are assigned to individuals without any coordination between these countries. It is likely that the same number may identify two different individuals. Furthermore, there are many individuals who, having lived and worked in both countries, have been assigned different values for their Social Security numbers and Social Insurance numbers. ■

4.2.6 Relationship

The key property and the fact that every tuple must have a key are used to capture relationships between entities.

Example 4.18 An employee may perform different roles in the software development teams working on different products. John Doe may be an analyst in the development team for product "Super File System" and manager of the team for product "$B^{++}1$". The different job requirements are given in the relation JOB_FUNCTION. ■

ASSIGNMENT is a relationship in Figure 4.3a between the entities Employee, Product and Job_Function. A possible representation of this relationship is by using the entities involved in the relationship:

ASSIGNMENT (Employee, Product, Job_Function)

Using the unique identification properties of keys we can replace the Employee, Product, and Job_Function entities in ASSIGNMENT by their keys. The keys act as surrogates for their respective entities. We can represent, let us say, the scheduled duties of an employee by the relation scheme:

ASSIGNMENT (*Emp#*, *Prod#*, *Job#*)

ASSIGNMENT is a relation that establishes a relationship among three "owner" relations. Such a relation may be thought of as an **associative relation.** The key of the associative relation is always the union of the key attributes of the owner relations. Thus the key of the relation **ASSIGNMENT** is the combination of the attributes ***Emp#***, ***Prod#***, ***Job#***.

The attributes ***Emp#***, ***Prod#***, and ***Job#*** in the relation ASSIGNMENT are known as **foreign keys.** A foreign key is an attribute or set of attributes of a relation, let us say R(**R**), such that the value of each attribute in this set is that of a primary key of relation S(**S**) (**R** and **S** need not be distinct). For instance, we could not have a tuple in the ASSIGNMENT relation of Figure 3 with the value 127 for the attribute *Emp#* unless there were a tuple in the EMPLOYEE relation with that value for *Emp#*. We look at rules applicable to primary and foreign keys in Section 4.2.8.

Figure 4.3 (a) E-R diagram for employee role in development teams; (b) corr schemes; and (c) sample relations.

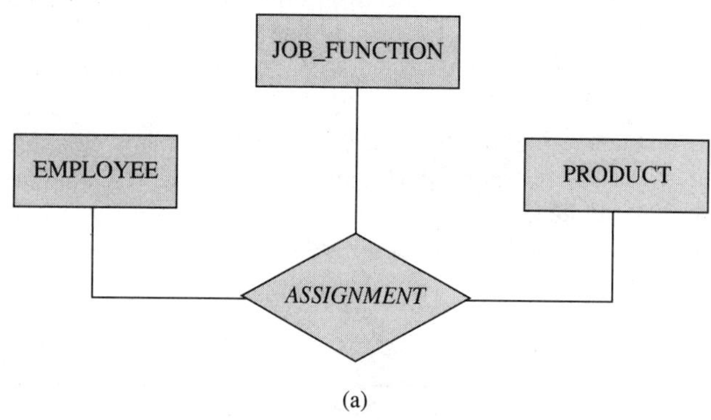

(a)

EMPLOYEE *(Emp#, Emp_Name, Profession)*
PRODUCT *(Prod#, Prod_Name, Prod_Details)*
JOB_FUNCTION *(Job#, Title)*
ASSIGNMENT *(Emp#, Prod#, Job#)*

(b)

EMPLOYEE:

Emp#	*Name*	*Profession*
101	Jones	Analyst
103	Smith	Programmer
104	Lalonde	Receptionist
106	Byron	Receptionist
107	Evan	VP R & D
110	Drew	VP Operations
112	Smith	Manager

PRODUCT:

Prod#	*Prod_Name*	*Prod_Details*
HEAP1	HEAP_SORT	ISS module
BINS9	BINARY_SEARCH	ISS/R module
FM6	FILE_MANAGER	ISS/R-PC subsys
B++1	B++_TREE	ISS/R turbo sys
B++2	B++_TREE	ISS/R-PC turbo

JOB_FUNCTION:

Job#	*Title*
1000	CEO
900	President
800	Manager
700	Chief Programmer
600	Analyst

ASSIGNMENT:

Emp#	*Prod#*	*Job#*
107	HEAP1	800
101	HEAP1	600
110	BINS9	800
103	HEAP1	700
101	BINS9	700
110	FM6	800
107	B++1	800

(c)

4.2.7 Relational Operations

Codd (Codd 72) defined a ''relationally complete'' set of operations and the collection of these, which take one or more relations as their operand(s), forms the basis of relational algebra (to be discussed in Section 4.3). In the same paper Codd included the formal definition of relational calculus (now known as tuple calculus). An alternative relational calculus called the domain calculus has also been proposed. (We study tuple and domain calculus in Section 4.4).

A number of operations are defined in these approaches to manipulate the relations. Relations can be derived from other relations (by taking a subset of the set of attributes) or a number of relations can be combined to define a new relation (by joining the relations). The transformation of relations is useful in obtaining results from the database.

Relational algebra, tuple calculus, and domain calculus form the underlying structure of the special-purpose languages provided by commercial database systems for data manipulation. A sampling of the commercially used data manipulation (or query) languages will be studied in Chapter 5.

4.2.8 Integrity Rules

The relational model includes two general integrity rules. These integrity rules implicitly or explicitly define the set of consistent database states, or changes of state, or both. Other integrity constraints can be specified, for example, in terms of dependencies during database design (see Chapter 6). In this section we restrict ourselves to the integrity rules formulated by Codd (Codd 70).

Integrity Rule 1 (Entity Integrity)

Earlier in this section we defined two properties for keys: unique identification and nonredundancy. Integrity rule 1 is concerned with primary key values. Before we formally state the rule, let us look at the effect of null values in prime attributes. A null value for an attribute is a value that is either not known at the time or does not apply to a given instance of the object. It may also be possible that a particular tuple does not have a value for an attribute; this fact could be represented by a null value.

If any attribute of a primary key (prime attribute) were permitted to have null values, then, because the attributes in the key must be nonredundant, the key cannot be used for unique identification of tuples. This contradicts the requirements for a primary key. Consider the relation P(**P**) in Figure 4.4a. The attribute *Id* is the pri-

Figure 4.4 (a) Relation without null values and (b) relation with null values.

P:

Id	*Name*
101	Jones
103	Smith
104	Lalonde
107	Evan
110	Drew
112	Smith

(a)

P:

Id	*Name*
101	Jones
@	Smith
104	Lalonde
107	Evan
110	Drew
@	Lalonde
@	Smith

(b)

mary key for P(**P**). If null values (represented as @) were permitted, as in Figure 4.4b, then the two tuples <@,Smith> are indistinguishable, even though they may represent two different instances of the entity type employee. Similarly, the tuples <@,Lalonde> and <104,Lalonde>, for all intents and purposes, are also indistinguishable and may be referring to the same person. As instances of entities are distinguishable, so must be their surrogates in the model.

Integrity rule 1 specifies that instances of the entities are distinguishable and thus no prime attribute (component of a primary key) value may be null. This rule is also referred to as the entity rule. We could state this rule formally as:

Definition: **Integrity Rule 1 (Entity Integrity):**

If attribute *A* of relation R(**R**) is a prime attribute of R(**R**), then *A* cannot accept null values.

Integrity Rule 2 (Referential Integrity)

Integrity rule 2 is concerned with foreign keys, i.e., with attributes of a relation having domains that are those of the primary key of another relation.

Relation (R) may contain references to another relation (S). Relations R and S need not be distinct. Suppose the reference in R is via a set of attributes that forms a primary key of the relation S. This set of attributes in R is a foreign key. A valid relationship between a tuple in R to one in S requires that the values of the attributes in the foreign key of R correspond to the primary key of a tuple in S. This ensures that the reference from a tuple of the relation R is made *unambiguously* to an existing tuple in the S relation. The referencing attribute(s) in the R relation can have null value(s); in this case, it is not referencing any tuple in the S relation. However, if the value is not null, it must exist as the primary attribute of a tuple of the S relation. If the referencing attribute in R has a value that is nonexistent in S, R is attempting to refer a nonexistent tuple and hence a nonexistent instance of the corresponding entity. This cannot be allowed. We illustrate this point in Example 4.19.

Example 4.19

Consider the example of employees and their ma[illegible] employ has a manager and as managers are also employees, we may represent managers by their employee numbers, if the employee number is a key of the relation employee. Figure G illustrates an example of such an employee relation. The *Manager* attribute represents the employee number of the manager. *Manager* is a foreign key; note that it is referring to the primary key of the same relation. An employee can only have a manager who is also an employee. The chief executive officer (CEO) of the company can have himself or herself as the manager or may take null values. Some employees may also be temporarily without managers, and this can be represented by the *Manager* taking null values.

Figure G Foreign keys.

Emp#	*Name*	*Manager*
101	Jones	@
103	Smith	110
104	Lalonde	107
107	Evan	110
110	Drew	112
112	Smith	112

(We can see that using a single null value for all cases can cause problems. Such problems are a topic of research and beyond the scope of this text.)

Definition: **Integrity Rule 2 (Referential Integrity):**

Given two relations R and S, suppose R refers to the relation S via a set of attributes that forms the primary key of S and this set of attributes forms a foreign key in R. Then the value of the foreign key in a tuple in R must either be equal to the primary key of a tuple of S or be entirely null.

If we have the attribute *A* of relation R(**R**) defined on domain D and the primary key of relation S(**S**) also defined on domain D, then the values of *A* in tuples of R(**R**) must be either null or equal to the value, let us say v, where v is the primary key value for a tuple in S(**S**). Note that R(**R**) and S(**S**) may be the same relation. The tuple in S(**S**) is called the **target** of the foreign key. The primary key of the referenced relation and the attributes in the foreign key of the referencing relation could be composite.

Referential integrity is very important. Because the foreign key is used as a surrogate for another entity, the rule enforces the existence of a tuple for the relation corresponding to the instance of the referred entity. In Example 4.19, we do not want a nonexisting employee to be manager. The integrity rule also implicitly defines the possible actions that could be taken whenever updates, insertions, and deletions are made.

If we delete a tuple that is a target of a foreign key reference, then three explicit possibilities exist to maintain database integrity:

- All tuples that contain references to the deleted tuple should also be deleted. This may cause, in turn, the deletion of other tuples. This option is referred to as a **domino** or **cascading deletion,** since one deletion leads to another.
- Only tuples that are not referenced by any other tuple can be deleted. A tuple referred by other tuples in the database cannot be deleted.
- The tuple is deleted. However, to avoid the domino effect, the pertinent foreign key attributes of all referencing tuples are set to null.

Similar actions are required when the primary key of a referenced relation is updated. An update of a primary key can be considered as a deletion followed by an insertion.

The choice of the option to use during a tuple deletion depends on the application. For example, in most cases it would be inappropriate to delete all employees under a given manager on the manager's departure; it would be more appropriate to replace it by null. Another example is when a department is closed. If employees were assigned to departments, then the employee tuples would contain the department key too. Deletion of department tuples should be disallowed until the employees have either been reassigned or their appropriate attribute values have been set to null. The insertion of a tuple with a foreign key reference or the update of the foreign key attributes of a relation require a check that the referenced relation exists.

Although the definition of the relational model specifies the two integrity rules, it is unfortunate that these concepts are not fully implemented in all commercial relational DBMSs. The concept of referential integrity enforcement would require an explicit statement as to what should be done when the primary key of a target tuple is updated or the target tuple is deleted.

4.3 Relational Algebra

Relational algebra is a collection of operations to manipulate relations. We have informally introduced some of these operations such as join (to combine related tuples from two relations), selection (to select particular tuples of a relation) and projection (to select particular attributes of a relation). The result of each of these operations is also a relation.

Relational algebra is a procedural language. It specifies the operations to be performed on existing relations to derive result relations. Furthermore, it defines the complete scheme for each of the result relations. The relational algebraic operations can be divided into basic set-oriented operations and relational-oriented operations. The former are the traditional set operations, the latter, those for performing joins, selection, projection, and division.

4.3.1 Basic Operations

Basic operations are the traditional set operations: union, difference, intersection, and cartesian product. Three of these four basic operations—union, intersection, and difference—require that operand relations be **union compatible.**[2] Two relations are union compatible if they have the same arity and one-to-one correspondence of the attributes with the corresponding attributes defined over the same domain. The cartesian product can be defined on any two relations. Two relations P(**P**) and Q(**Q**) are

[2]We assume that in the case of the union, difference, and intersection operations, the names of the attributes of the operand relations are the same and that the result relation inherits these names. If these names are not identical, some convention, for instance, using the names from the first operand relation, must be provided to assign names to the attributes of the result relation.

said to be union compatible if both **P** and **Q** are of the same degree n and the domains of the corresponding n attributes are identical, i.e., if $\mathbf{P} = \{P_1, \ldots, P_n\}$ and $\mathbf{Q} = \{Q_1, \ldots, Q_n\}$ then

$$\text{Dom}(P_i) = \text{Dom}(Q_i) \text{ for } i = \{1,2, \ldots, n\}$$

where $\text{Dom}(P_i)$ represents the domain of the attribute P_i.

Example 4.20 In the examples to follow, we utilize two relations P(**P**) and Q(**Q**) given in Figure H. R(**R**) is a computed result relation. We assume that the relations P(**P**) and Q(**Q**) in Figure H represent employees working on the development of software application packages J_1 and J_2, respectively.

Figure H Union Compatible Relations

P:

Id	*Name*
101	Jones
103	Smith
104	Lalonde
107	Evan
110	Drew
112	Smith

Q:

Id	*Name*
103	Smith
104	Lalonde
106	Byron
110	Drew

■

UNION (∪)

If we assume that P(**P**) and Q(**Q**) are two union-compatible relations, then the union of P(**P**) and Q(**Q**) is the **set-theoretic union** of P(**P**) and Q(**Q**). The resultant relation, R = P ∪ Q, has tuples drawn from P and Q such that

$$R = \{t \mid t \in P \lor t \in Q\} \text{ and}$$
$$\max(|P|,|Q|) \leq |R| \leq |P| + |Q|$$

The result relation R contains tuples that are in either P or Q or in both of them. The duplicate tuples are eliminated.

Remember that from our definition of union compatibility the degree of the relations P(**P**), Q(**Q**), and R(**R**) is the same. The cardinality of the resultant relation depends on the duplication of tuples in P and Q. From the above expression, we can see that if all the tuples in Q were contained in P, then R = P and |**R**| = |**P**|, while if the tuples in P and Q were disjoint, then |R| = |P| + |Q|.

Example 4.21 R, the union of P and Q given in Figure H in Example 4.20, is shown in Figure Ii. R represents employees working on the packages J_1 or J_2, or both of these packages. Since a relation does not have duplicate tuples, an em-

Figure I Results of (i) union, (ii) difference, and (iii) intersection operations.

R:

Id	*Name*
101	Jones
103	Smith
104	Lalonde
106	Byron
107	Evan
110	Drew
112	Smith

(i) $P \cup Q$

R:

Id	*Name*
101	Jones
107	Evan
112	Smith

(ii) $P - Q$

R:

Id	*Name*
103	Smith
104	Lalonde
110	Drew

(iii) $P \cap Q$

ployee working on both J_1 and J_2 will appear in the relation R only once. ■

Difference (−)

The difference operation removes common tuples from the first relation.

$$R = P - Q \text{ such that}$$
$$R = \{t \mid t \in P \wedge t \notin Q\} \quad \text{and}$$
$$0 \leq |R| \leq |P|$$

Example 4.22 R, the result of $P - Q$, gives employees working only on package J_1 (Figure Iii in Example 4.21). Employees working on both packages J_1 and J_2 have been removed. ■

Intersection (∩)

The intersection operation selects the common tuples from the two relations.

$$R = P \cap Q \text{ where}$$
$$R = \{t \mid t \in P \wedge t \in Q\} \quad \text{and}$$
$$0 \leq |R| \leq \min(|P|,|Q|)$$

Example 4.23 The resultant relation of $P \cap Q$ is the set of all employees working on both the packages (Figure Iiii of Example 4.21). ■

The intersection operation is really unnecessary. It can be very simply expressed as:

$$P \cap Q = P - (P - Q)$$

It is, however, more convenient to write an expression with a single intersection operation than one involving a pair of difference operations.

Note that in these examples the operand and the result relation schemes, including the attribute names, are identical i.e., $\mathbf{P} \equiv \mathbf{Q} \equiv \mathbf{R}$. If the attribute names of compatible relations are not identical, the naming of the attributes of the result relation will have to be resolved.

Cartesian Product (×)

The extended cartesian or simply the cartesian product of two relations is the concatenation of tuples belonging to the two relations. A new resultant relation scheme is created consisting of all possible combinations of the tuples.

$$R = P \times Q$$

where a tuple $r \in R$ is given by $\{t_1 \parallel t_2 \mid t_1 \in P \wedge t_2 \in Q\}$, i.e., the result relation is obtained by concatenating each tuple in relation P with each tuple in relation Q. Here, $\parallel$ represents the concatenation operation.

The scheme of the result relation is given by:

$$\mathbf{R} = \mathbf{P} \parallel \mathbf{Q}$$

The degree of the result relation is given by:

$$|\mathbf{R}| = |\mathbf{P}| + |\mathbf{Q}|$$

The cardinality of the result relation is given by:

$$|R| = |P| * |Q|$$

Example 4.24 The cartesian product of the PERSONNEL relation and SOFTWARE_PACKAGE relations of Figure Ji is shown in Figure Jii. Note that the relations P and Q from Figure H of Example 4.20 are a subset of the PERSONNEL relation. ■

Figure J (i) PERSONNEL(*Emp#*,*Name*) and SOFTWARE_PACKAGES(*S*) represent employees and software packages respectively; (ii) the Cartesian product of PERSONNEL and SOFTWARE_PACKAGES.

PERSONNEL:

Id	*Name*
101	Jones
103	Smith
104	Lalonde
106	Byron
107	Evan
110	Drew
112	Smith

SOFTWARE_PACKAGES:

S
J_1
J_2

(i)

P.*Id*	P.*Name*	*S*
101	Jones	J_1
101	Jones	J_2
103	Smith	J_1
103	Smith	J_2
104	Lalonde	J_1
104	Lalonde	J_2
106	Byron	J_1
106	Byron	J_2
107	Evan	J_1
107	Evan	J_2
110	Drew	J_1
110	Drew	J_2
112	Smith	J_1
112	Smith	J_2

(ii)

■

The union and intersection operations are associative and commutative; therefore, given relations R(**R**), S(**S**), T(**T**):

$$R \cup (S \cup T) = (R \cup S) \cup T = (S \cup R) \cup T = T \cup (S \cup R) = \ldots$$
$$R \cap (S \cap T) = (R \cap S) \cap T = \ldots$$

The difference operation, in general, is noncommutative and nonassociative.

$$R - S \neq S - R \quad \text{noncommutative}$$
$$R - (S - T) \neq (R - S) - T \quad \text{nonassociative}$$

4.3.2 Additional Relational Algebraic Operations

The basic set operations, which provide a very limited data manipulation facility, have been supplemented by the definition of the following operations: projection, selection, join, and division. These operations are represented by the symbols π, σ, $\bowtie$, and $\div$, respectively. Projection and selection are unary operations; join and division are binary.

Projection (π)

In Section 4.2.2 we defined the projection of a tuple. The projection of a relation is defined as a projection of all its tuples over some set of attributes, i.e., it yields a "vertical subset" of the relation. The projection operation is used to either reduce the number of attributes in the resultant relation or to reorder attributes. In the first case, the arity (or degree) of the relation is reduced. The projection operation is shown graphically in Figure 4.5. In Figure 4.5a we illustrate the possibility that when the number of attributes in the relation is reduced, the cardinality may also be reduced; this is due to the deletion of duplicate tuples in the projected relation. In Figure 4.5b we illustrate the rearrangment of the attributes of a relation. Figure 4.5c shows the projection of the relation PERSONNEL on the attribute *Name*. The cardinality of the result relation is also reduced due to the deletion of duplicate tuples.

We defined the projection of a tuple t_i over the attribute A, denoted $t_i[A]$ or $\pi_A(t_i)$, as (a), where a is the value of tuple t_i over the attribute A. Similarly, we

Figure 4.5 Projection: (a) graphical representation of reduction of degree or a relation; (b) graphical representation of re-ordering of attributes; (c) projection of relation PERSONNEL over attribute *Name.*

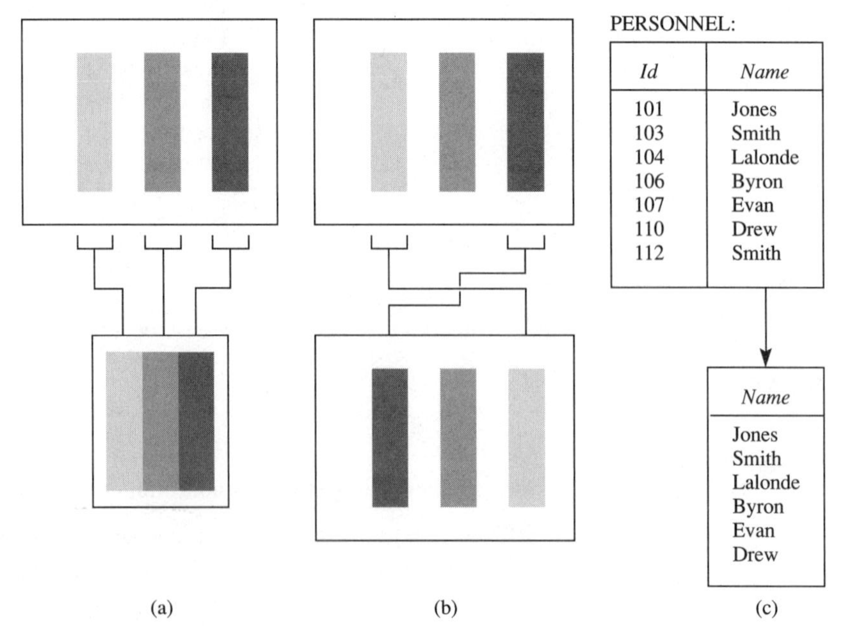

define the projection of a relation T(**T**), denoted by T[A] or π_A(T), on the attribute A. This is defined in terms of the projection for each tuple in $t_i \in$ T on the attribute A as:

$$T[A] = \{a_i \mid t_i\,[A] = a_i \wedge t_i \in T\}$$

where T[A] is a single attribute relation and $|T[A]| \leq |T|$. The cardinality $|T[A]|$ may be less than the cardinality $|T|$ because of the deletion of any duplicates in the result. A case in point is illustrated in Figure 4.5c.

Similarly, we can define the projection of a relation on a set of attribute names, X, as a concatenation of the projections for each attribute A in X for every tuple in the relation.

$$T[X] = \{ \underset{A \in X}{\|}\, t_i[A] \mid t_i \in T\}$$

where $\underset{A \in X}{\|}\, t_i[A]$ represents the concatenation of all $t_i[A]$ for all $A \in$ X.

Simply stated, the projection of a relation P(**P**) on the set of attribute names Y $\in$ **P** is the projection of each tuple of the relation P on the set of attribute names Y.

Note that the projection operation reduces the arity if the number of attributes in X is less than the arity of the relation. The projection operation may also reduce the cardinality of the result relation since duplicate tuples are removed. (Note that the projection operation produces a relation as the result. By definition, a relation cannot have duplicate tuples. In most commercial implementations of the relational model, however, the duplicates would still be present in the result.)

Selection (σ)

Suppose we want to find those employees in the relation PERSONNEL of Figure Ji of Example 4.24 with an *Id* less than 105. This is an operation that selects only some of the tuples of the relation. Such an operation is known as a selection operation. The selection operation is represented graphically in Figure 4.6a.

The projection operation yields a vertical subset of a relation. The action is defined over a subset of the attribute names but over all the tuples in the relation. The selection operation, however, yields a horizontal subset of a given relation, i.e., the action is defined over the complete set of attribute names but only a subset of the tuples are included in the result. To have a tuple included in the result relation, the specified selection conditions or predicates must be satisfied by it. The selection operation, represented by the symbol σ in this text, is sometimes known as the **restriction operation.**

Example 4.25

Consider the selection operation

$$\sigma_{Id < 105}\,(\text{PERSONNEL})$$

over the relation PERSONNEL of Figure J of Example 4.24. The selection is over the relation PERSONNEL and the predicate specifies that only those tuples in PERSONNEL are to be selected in which the value of the attribute *Id* is less than 105. Figure 4.6b presents PERSONNEL and the resulting relation. ■

Figure 4.6 (a) Graphical representation of selection that selects a subset of the tuples; (b) result of selection over PERSONNEL for *Id* < 105.

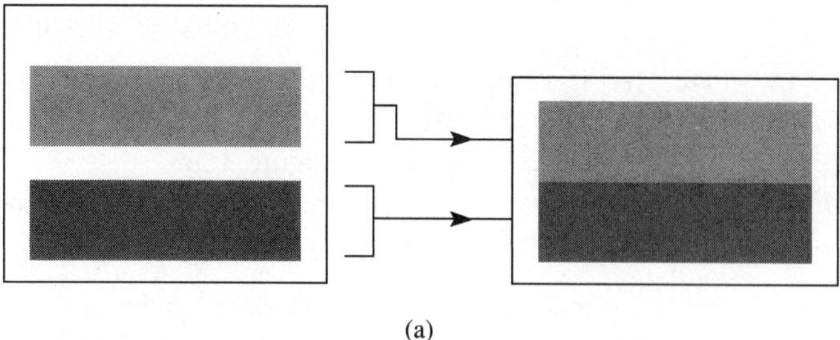

(a)

PERSONNEL:

Id	*Name*
101	Jones
103	Smith
104	Lalonde
106	Byron
107	Evan
110	Drew
112	Smith

Result of selection

Id	*Name*
101	Jones
103	Smith
104	Lalonde

(b)

Any finite number of predicates connected by Boolean operators may be specified in the selection operation. The predicates may define a comparison between two domain-compatible attributes or between an attribute and a constant value; if the comparison is between attribute A_1 and constant c_1, then $c_1 \in Dom(A_1)$.

Given a relation P and a predicate expression B, the selections of those tuples of relation P that satisfy the predicate B is a relation R written as:

$$R = \sigma_B(P)$$

The above expression could be read as "select those tuples t from P in which the predicate B(t) is true." The set of tuples in relation R are in this case defined as follows:

$$R = \{t \mid t \in P \wedge B\,(t)\}$$

Join (⋈)

The join operator, as the name suggests, allows the combining of two relations to form a single new relation. The tuples from the operand relations that participate in the operation and contribute to the result are related. The join operation allows the processing of relationships existing between the operand relations.

In Figure D of Example 4.3 we illustrated an example of a join of the relations SOME_DBMS and VERSION. We joined those tuples of the two relations that had the same value for the common attribute *Name* defined on a common domain. In this case, this common value was used to establish a relationship between these relations. Note that referential integrity dictates that a tuple in VERSION could not exist without a tuple in SOME_DBMS with the same value for the *Name* attribute. Join is basically the cartesian product of the relations followed by a selection operation.

Example 4.26

In Figure 4.3 we encountered the following relations:

ASSIGNMENT (***Emp#, Prod#, Job#***)
JOB_FUNCTION (***Job#***, *Title*)

Suppose we want to respond to the query "Get product number of assignments whose development teams have a chief programmer." This requires first computing the cartesian product of the ASSIGNMENT and JOB_FUNCTION relations. Let us name this product relation TEMP. This is followed by selecting those tuples of TEMP where the attribute *Title* has the value chief programmer and the value of the attribute *Job#* in ASSIGNMENT and JOB_FUNCTION are the same. The required result, shown below, is obtained by projecting these tuples on the attribute *Prod#*. The operations are specified below:

$$\text{TEMP} = (\text{ASSIGNMENT} \times \text{JOB\_FUNCTION})$$

$$\pi_{Prod\#}(\sigma_{Title\ =\ \text{'chief programmer'}\ \wedge\ \text{ASSIGNMENT}.Job\ =\ \text{JOB\_FUNCTION}.Job\#}(\text{TEMP}))$$

Prod#
HEAP1
BINS9

In another method of responding to this query, we can first select those tuples from the JOB_FUNCTION relation so that the value of the attribute *Title* is chief programmer. Let us call this set of tuples the relation TEMP1. We then compute the cartesian product of TEMP1 and ASSIGNMENT, calling the product TEMP2. This is followed by a projection on *Prod#* over TEMP2 to give us the required response. These operations are specified below:

$$\text{TEMP1} = (\sigma_{Title\ =\ \text{'}chief\text{ programmer'}}(\text{JOB\_FUNCTION}))$$

$$\text{TEMP2} = (\sigma_{\text{ASSIGNMENT}.Job\#\ =\ \text{JOB\_FUNCTION}.Job\#}(\text{ASSIGNMENT} \times \text{TEMP1}))$$

$\pi_{Prod\#}(\text{TEMP2})$ gives the required result. ■

Notice that in the selection operation that follows the cartesian product we take only those tuples where the value of the attributes ASSIGNMENT.*Job#* and JOB_FUNCTION.*Job#* are the same. These combined operations of cartesian product followed by selection are the join operation. Note that we have qualified the identically named attributes by the name of the corresponding relation to distinguish them.

In case of the join of a relation with itself, we would need to rename either the attributes of one of the copies of the relation or the relation name itself. We illustrate this in Example 4.27.

In general the join condition may have more than one term, necessitating the use of the subscript in the comparison operator. Now we shall define the different types of join operations.

Definition: **Theta join:**

The **theta join** of two relations P(**P**) and Q(**Q**) is defined as

$$R = P \bowtie_{B} Q$$

such that

$$R = \{t \mid t_1 \parallel t_2 \wedge t_1 \in P \wedge t_2 \in Q \wedge B\}$$

where B is a selection predicate consisting of terms of the form:

$$(t_1[A_i]\ \theta_i\ t_2[B_i]) \text{ for } i = 1, 2, \ldots, n$$

where θ_i is some comparison operator ($\theta_i \in \{=, \neq <, \leq, >, \geq\}$) and A_i and B_i are some domain-compatible attributes of the relation schemes **P** and **Q** respectively:

$$0 \leq |R| \leq |P|*|Q|$$
$$|\mathbf{R}| = |\mathbf{P}| + |\mathbf{Q}|$$

In the these discussions we use **P, Q, R,** and so on to represent both the relation scheme and the collection or bag of underlying domains of the attributes. We call it a bag of domains because more than one attribute may be defined on the same domain.

Typically, **P** ∩ **Q** may be null and this guarantees the uniqueness of attribute names in the result relation. When the same attribute name occurs in the two schemes we use qualified names.

Two common and very useful variants of the join are the **equi-join** and the **natural join.** In the equi-join the comparison operator $\theta_i(i = 1,2, \ldots, n)$ is always the equality operator (=). Similarly, in the natural join the comparison operator is always the equality operator. However, only one of the two sets of domain-compatible attributes is retained in the result relation of the natural join. It follows that if the attributes involved in the natural join are A_i from P and B_i from Q, for $i = 1, \ldots, n$, the natural join predicate is a conjunction of terms of the following form:

$$(t_1[A_i] = t_2[B_i]) \text{ for } i = 1, 2, \ldots, n$$

Domain compatibility requires that the domains of A_i and B_i be compatible, and for this reason relation schemes **P** and **Q** have attributes defined on common domains, i.e., **P** ∩ **Q** ≠ φ. Therefore, join attributes have common domains in the relation schemes P and Q. Consequently, only one set of the join attributes on these common domains needs to be preserved in the result relation. This is achieved by taking a projection after the join operation, thereby eliminating the dup butes. If the relations P and Q have attributes with the same domains b attribute names, then renaming or projection may be specified.

Example 4.27

In Figures D and E of Example 4.3 we encountered examples of the equi-join operation. Given the EMPLOYEE and SALARY relations of Figure Ki, if we have to find the salary of employees by name, we join the tuples in the relation EMPLOYEE with those in SALARY such that the value of the attribute *Id* in EMPLOYEE is the same as that in SALARY. The natural join takes the predicate expression to be EMPLOYEE.*Id* = SALARY.*Id* The result of the natural join is shown in Figure Ki. When using the natural join, we do not need to specify this predicate. The expression to specify the operation of finding the salary of employees by name is given as follows. Here we project the result of the natural join operation on the attributes *Name* and *Salary:*

$$\pi_{(Name, Salary)} \text{ (EMPLOYEE} \bowtie \text{SALARY)}$$

Figure K (i) The natural join of EMPLOYEE and SALARY relations; (ii) the joint of ASSIGNMENT with its renamed copy.

EMPLOYEE:

Id	*Name*
101	Jones
103	Smith
104	Lalonde
107	Evan

SALARY:

Id	*Salary*
101	67
103	55
104	75
107	80

EMPLOYEE ⋈ SALARY

Id	*Name*	*Salary*
101	Jones	67
103	Smith	55
104	Lalonde	75
107	Evan	80

(i)

ASSIGNMENT.*Emp#*	COASSIGN.*Emp#*
107	107
107	101
107	103
101	107
101	101
101	103
110	110
110	101
103	107
103	101
103	103
101	110

(ii)

Consider the ASSIGNMENT relation of Figure 4.3c. If we want to find the coworkers in all projects (but not necessarily doing the same job) we can join ASSIGNMENT with itself on the *Prod#* attribute. However, to have unique attribute names in the result relation, we can proceed as follows. Copy ASSIGNMENT into COASSIGN(***Emp#***, ***Prod#***, ***Job#***) and then perform the operation given below, using qualified attribute names. The result of the operation is shown in Figure Kb. Note that a simple join of ASSIGNMENT with itself, using the definition of natural join, gives the original relation:

$$\pi_{(\text{ASSIGNMENT}.Emp\#,\text{COASSIGN}.Emp\#)}(\text{ASSIGNMENT} \underset{\text{ASSIGNMENT}.Prod\# \,=\, \text{COASSIGN}.Prod\#}{\bowtie} \text{COASSIGN})$$ ■

Formally, the natural join of P(**P**) and Q(**Q**) is performed on the attributes of **P** and **Q** defined on common domains, i.e., **P** ∩ **Q.** The resultant relation consists of the attributes **P** ∪ **Q.**

In the cartesian product of two relations, we take a tuple from each relation and concatenate them to obtain a tuple in the result relation. Any duplication of attributes in the tuples, as well as duplicate tuples, remains. (Note that duplicate tuples are not generated in a cartesian product of two proper relations.) In a relational join, we select the subset of the product tuples that satisfy the join predicates. In an equi-join, the predicate involves equality constraints. In a natural join, which also involves equality constraints, the common attributes are not duplicated. In the majority of cases when we speak of a join, we are actually speaking about the natural join.

If two relations that are to be joined have no domain-compatible attributes, the natural join operation is equivalent to a simple cartesian product. If they have identical relation schemes, the natural join operation is an intersection operation.

We can summarize the above discussion on the various types of join operations using the cartesian product as follows:

- The equi-join and the theta join are horizontal subsets of the cartesian product. This is equivalent to applying a selection to the resulting tuple of the cartesian product. The selection is explicitly specified in the theta join and implicitly specified in the equi-join.
- The natural join is equivalent to an equi-join with a subsequent projection to eliminate the duplicate attributes. In this sense, a natural join is both a horizontal and vertical subset of the cartesian product.

Division (÷)

Before we define the division operation, let us consider an example.

Example 4.28 Given the relations P(**P**) and Q(**Q**) as shown in Figure Li, the result of dividing P by Q is the relation R and it has two tuples. For each tuple in R, its product with the tuples of Q must be in P. In our example (a_1,b_1) and (a_1,b_2) must both be tuples in P; the same is true for (a_5,b_1) and (a_5,b_2).

Figure L Examples of the division operation. (i) R = P ÷ Q; (ii) R = P ÷ Q (P is the same as in part i); (iii) R = P ÷ Q (P is the same as in part i); (iv) R = P ÷ Q (P is the same as in part i).

P(P):

A	B
a_1	b_1
a_1	b_2
a_2	b_1
a_3	b_1
a_4	b_2
a_5	b_1
a_5	b_2

Q(Q):

B
b_1
b_2

R(R) (result):

A
a_1
a_5

Has Both Properties Specified in Q!

(i)

Q(Q):

B
b_1

OK

then R(R) is:

A
a_1
a_2
a_3
a_5

(ii)

Q(Q):

B
b_1
b_2
b_3

OK

then R(R) is:

A

(iii)

Q(Q):

B

then R(R) is:

A
a_1
a_2
a_3
a_4
a_5

(iv)

Simply stated, the cartesian product of Q and R is a subset of P.

In Figure Lii, the result relation R has four tuples; the cartesian product of R and Q gives a resulting relation which is again a subset of P.

In Figure Liii, since there are no tuples in P with a value b_3 for the attribute B (i.e., $|\sigma_{B=b_3}(P)| = 0$), we have an empty relation R, which has a cardinality of zero.

In Figure Liv, the relation Q is empty. The result relation can be defined as the projection of P on the attributes in **P − Q.** However, it is usual to disallow division by an empty relation.

Finally, if relation P is an empty relation, then relation R is also an empty relation. ■

Let us treat the relation Q as representing one set of properties (the properties are defined on the scheme **Q,** each tuple in Q representing an instance of these properties) and the relation P as representing entities with these properties (entities are defined on **P − Q,** and the properties are, as before, defined on **Q**); note that **P** ∪ **Q** must be equal to **P.** Each tuple in P represents an object with some given property. (In Figure Li of Example 4.28, the relation P has 7 tuples. A tuple, for instance, (a_1,b_1) of P, represents the object a_1 with the property b_1.) The resultant relation R, then, is the set of entities that possesses all the properties specified in Q. The two entities a_1 and a_5 possess all the properties, i.e., b_1 and b_2. The other entities in P, a_2, a_3, and a_4, only possess one, not both, of the properties. The division operation is useful when a query involves the phrase *"for all objects having all the specified properties."* Note that both **P − Q** and **Q** in general represent a set of attributes. It should be clear that $\mathbf{Q} \subseteq \mathbf{P}$.

Example 4.29 Consider the relations of Figure M:

PRODUCT (*Prod#, Prod_Name, Prod_Details*)
DEVELOPED_BY (*Prod#, Emp#*)

The following method is used to find all employees who developed both the HEAPSORT and BINARY_SEARCH modules. We first find an intermediate relation, let us say TEMP, that contains the product numbers of these two modules. TEMP is obtained, as shown in the following equation, by a selection on these product names followed by a projection of the resulting relation on the attribute *Prod#:*

$$TEMP = \pi_{Prod\#}(\sigma_{(Prod\_Name\ =\ \text{'HEAPSORT'}\ \vee\ Prod\_Name\ =\ \text{'BINARY\_SEARCH'})}(\text{PRODUCT}))$$

The product and TEMP relations are shown in Figure Mi. We can then obtain the *Emp#* of employees involved in the development of these two modules by dividing the DEVELOPED_BY relation by TEMP:

$$\text{RESULT} = \text{DEVELOPED\_BY} \div \text{TEMP}$$

These operands and the result of the division are shown in Figure Mii. The overall operations can be written as shown below:

$$\text{DEVELOPED\_BY} \div (\pi_{Prod\#}(\sigma_{(Prod\_Name\ =\ \text{'HEAPSORT'}\ \vee\ Prod\_Name\ =\ \text{'BINARY\_SEARCH'})}(\text{PRODUCT}))$$

The result of the selection and projection is the set of tuples with the *Prod#* of the two modules HEAPSORT and BINARY_SEARCH. These tuples are

Figure M Finding employees who developed both HEAPSORT and BINARY_SEARCH. (i) $\pi_{Prod\#}$ ($\sigma_{(Prod\_Name\ =\ 'HEAPSORT'\ \vee\ Prod\_Name\ =\ 'BINARY\_SEARCH')}$ (PRODUCT)); (ii) DEVELOPED_BY ÷ TEMP

PRODUCT:

Prod#	*Prod_Name*	*Prod_Details*
HEAP1	HEAP_SORT	ISS module
BINS9	BINARY_SEARCH	ISS/R module
FM6	FILE_MANAGER	ISS/R-PC subsys
$B^{++}1$	B^{++}_TREE	ISS/R turbo sys
$B^{++}2$	B^{++}_TREE	ISSR-PC turbo

TEMP:

Prod#
HEAP1
BINS9

(i)

DEVELOPED_BY:

Prod#	*Emp#*
HEAP1	103
HEAP1	107
FM6	103
$B^{++}1$	109
BINS9	105
BINS9	107
BINS9	103

÷

TEMP

Prod#
HEAP1
BINS9

=

RESULT:

Emp#
103
107

(ii)

then used as a divisor; the result of the division is all employees involved in the development of both modules. This result is presented in Figure Mii.

If we had incorrectly formulated our query expression as:

$$\text{DEVELOPED\_BY} \bowtie (\pi_{Prod\#} (\sigma_{(Prod\_Name\ =\ \text{'HEAPSORT'}\ \vee\ Prod\_Name\ =\ \text{'BINARY\_SEARCH'})} (\text{PRODUCT}))$$

then we would find the *(Emp#, Prod#)* tuples for employees involved in the development of the HEAPSORT *or* BINARY_SEARCH modules, rather than employees involved in the development of both the modules. ■

4.3.3 Some Relational Algebra Queries

Let us illustrate the use of relational algebra to express a number of queries. For the examples in this section, we will consider a part of our database consisting of the following relations corresponding to the entities EMPLOYEE and PROJECT and the

Figure 4.7 Sample database

EMPLOYEE:

Emp#	*Name*
101	Jones
103	Smith
104	Lalonde
106	Byron
107	Evan
110	Drew
112	Smith

ASSIGNED_TO

Project#	*Emp#*
COMP453	101
COMP354	103
COMP343	104
COMP354	104
COMP231	106
COMP278	106
COMP353	106
COMP354	106
COMP453	106
COMP231	107
COMP353	107
COMP278	110
COMP353	112
COMP354	112

PROJECT:

Project#	*Project_Name*	*Chief_Architect*
COMP231	Pascal	107
COMP278	Pascal/Object	110
COMP353	Database	107
COMP354	Operating Sys	104
COMP453	Database	101

relationship *ASSIGNED_TO* between them. Some sample tuples from these relations are shown in Figure 4.7.

PROJECT ***(Project#**, Project_Name, Chief_Architect)*
EMPLOYEE ***(Emp#**, EmpName)*
ASSIGNED_TO ***(Project#, Emp#)***

Example 4.30 "Get *Emp#* of employees working on project COMP353." To evaluate this query, we select those tuples of relation ASSIGNED_TO such that the value of the *Project#* attribute is COMP353. We then project the result on the attribute *Emp#* to get the response relation. The query and the response relation are shown below:

$$\pi_{Emp\#}(\sigma_{Project\# \; = \; 'COMP353'} \text{ (ASSIGNED\_TO)})$$

Emp#
106
107
112

■

The following example entails a join of two relations.

Example 4.31

"Get details of employees (both number and name) working on project COMP353." The first part of the evaluation of this query is the same as in the query in Example 4.30. It is, however, followed by a natural join of the result with EMPLOYEE relation to gather the complete details about the employees working on project COMP353. The result and the the query are shown below:

$$\text{EMPLOYEE} \bowtie \pi_{Emp\#}(\sigma_{Project\# \,=\, \text{'COMP353'}}(\text{ASSIGNED\_TO}))$$

Emp#	*Name*
106	Byron
107	Evan
112	Smith

■

Example 4.32 requires using three relations to generate the required response.

Example 4.32

"Obtain details of employees working on the Database project." This query requires two joins. The first step is to find the number(s) of the project(s) named Database. This involves a selection of the relation PROJECT, followed by a projection on the attribute *Project#*. The result of this projection is joined with the ASSIGNED_TO relation to give tuples of the ASSIGNED _TO involving Database. This is projected on *Emp#* and subsequently joined with EMPLOYEE to get the required employee details. The query in relational algebra and the result are shown below:

$$\text{EMPLOYEE} \bowtie \pi_{Emp\#}(\text{ASSIGNED\_TO} \bowtie (\pi_{Project\#}(\sigma_{Project\_Name \,=\, \text{'Database'}}(\text{PROJECT}))))$$

Emp#	*Name*
101	Jones
106	Byron
107	Evan
112	Smith

■

The use of the division operation is illustrated in the following examples.

Example 4.33

"Gather details of employees working on both COMP353 and COMP354." In evaluating this query, we first create an unary relation with two tuples with the required project numbers. We select those tuples of ASSIGNED_TO where the project numbers are either COMP353 or COMP354 and then project the result on *Project#*. Next, we divide ASSIGNED_TO by the unary relation from the previous step to get another unary relation whose tuples correspond to those employees who are working on both projects. To collect the complete details about these employees, we join this last relation with EMPLOYEE. The query in relational algebra and the resulting relation are shown below:

$$\text{EMPLOYEE} \bowtie (\text{ASSIGNED\_TO} \div \pi_{Project\#}(\sigma_{(Project\# = \text{'COMP353'} \vee Project\# = \text{'COMP354'})}(\text{ASSIGNED\_TO})))$$

Emp#	*Name*
106	Byron
112	Smith

■

Example 4.34

"Find the employee numbers of employees who work on at least all of the projects that employee 107 works on." Here, we first find all of employee 107's project numbers. Having found this, we divide the relation ASSIGNED_TO by this unary relation to get a result that includes employee 107. To remove the tuple for 107, we find the difference. In the following expression, 107 is a shorthand method of writing a single tuple unary relation, obtained by $\pi_{Emp\#}(\sigma_{Emp\# = 107}(\text{ASSIGNED\_TO}))$. The query in relational algebra and the resulting relation are shown below:

$$(\text{ASSIGNED\_TO} \div \pi_{Project\#}(\sigma_{Emp\# = 107}(\text{ASSIGNED\_TO}))) - 107$$

Emp#
106

■

The use of the difference operation is illustrated in Example 4.35.

Example 4.35

"Find the employee numbers of employees who do not work on project COMP453." The evaluation here was done by first determining those employees who are working on project COMP453 (and other projects as well). We also find all employees assigned to projects. Both of these are obtained by projections on relation ASSIGNED_TO and will have no duplicate tuples. From the result of these projections we find the difference to arrive at the *Emp#* of employees not working on COMP453. The query expressed in relational algebra and the response to it are shown below:

$$\pi_{Emp\#}(\text{ASSIGNED\_TO}) - \pi_{Emp\#}(\sigma_{Project\# = \text{'COMP453'}}(\text{ASSIGNED\_TO}))$$

Emp#
103
104
107
110
112

■

The division operation which finds objects having all specified properties can be used to advantage in the following example.

Example 4.36

"Get the employee number of employees who work on all projects." The sequence to follow in evaluating this query is to first compile a list of all projects from the PROJECT relation by a simple projection on *Project#;* then divide the ASSIGNED_TO relation by it to derive a unary relation containing the required employee numbers:

$$\text{ASSIGNED\_TO} \div \pi_{Project\#}(\text{PROJECT})$$

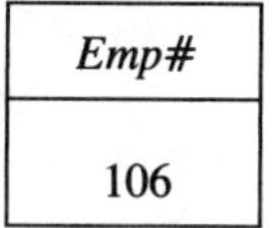

Emp#
106

■

A join involving a relation with itself is illustrated below.

Example 4.37

"List the employee numbers of employees other than employee 107 who work on at least one project that employee 107 works on." This is similar to the query in Example 4.36, except the list of projects is now comprised of those that include at least one project in which employee 107 is involved. This can be obtained by a selection and projection on the relation ASSIGNED _TO. Joining ASSIGNED_TO with the result relation gives us a relation that includes tuples for employee 107. Projecting this latest result relation on *Emp#* gives an unary relation, which includes a tuple for 107. This tuple is eliminated as in the query in Example 4.34 to give all employees who are involved in at least one project with employee 107.

$(\pi_{Emp\#}(\text{ASSIGNED\_TO} \bowtie \pi_{Project\#}(\sigma_{Emp\# = 107}(\text{ASSIGNED\_TO})))) - 107$

Emp#
106
112

■

4.4 Relational Calculus

Tuple and domain calculi are collectively referred to as relational calculus. As we have seen, queries in relational algebra are procedural. In general, a user should not have to be concerned with the details of how to obtain information. In relational calculus, a query is expressed as a formula consisting of a number of variables and an expression involving these variables. The formula describes the properties of the result relation to be obtained. There is no mechanism to specify how the formula should be evaluated. It is up to the DBMS to transform these nonprocedural queries into equivalent, efficient, procedural queries. In relational tuple calculus, the variables represent the tuples from specified relations; in relational domain calculus, the variables represent values drawn from specified domains.

Relational calculus is a query system wherein queries are expressed as variables and formulas on these variables. Such formulas describe the properties of the required result relation without specifying the method of evaluating it.

Relation calculus, which in effect means calculating with relations, is based on **predicate calculus,** which is calculating with predicates. The latter is a formal language used to symbolize logical arguments in mathematics. In the following paragraphs we briefly introduce predicate calculus; additional details are given in Chapter 16.

In formal logic the main subject matter is propositions. If, for instance, p and q are propositions, we can build other propositions "not p," "p or q," "p and q," and so on. In predicate calculus, propositions may be built not only out of other propositions but also out of elements that are not themselves propositions. In this manner we can build a proposition that specifies a certain property or characteristic of an object.

Propositions specifying a property consist of an expression that names an individual object (it may also be used to designate an object), and another expression, called the **predicate,** that stands for the property that the individual object possesses.

Example 4.38 Consider these statements:

BCD is a company
WXY is a company
Jill is an analyst
John is an analyst
Canada is a country
U.S.A. is a country

Each of these is a statement about an object having a certain feature or property. In these examples, the parts "is a company," "is an analyst," "is a country" are instances of predicates. Each describes some property or characteristic of an object. ■

A convenient method of writing the statements of Example 4.38 is to place the predicate first and follow it with the object enclosed in parentheses. Therefore, the statement "BCD is a company" can be written as "is a company(BCD)." Now we drop the "is a" part and write the first statement as "company(BCD)." Finally, if we use symbols for both the predicate and the object, we can rewrite the statements of Example 4.38 as P(x). The lowercase letters from the end of the alphabet (. . . x, y, z) denote variables, the beginning letters (a, b, c, . . .) denote constants, and uppercase letters denote predicates. P(x), where x is the argument, is a **one-place** or **monadic predicate.** DBMS(x) and COMPANY(y) are examples of monadic predicates. The variables x and y are replaceable by constants (or names of individual objects) such as DBMS(ISS).

The use of constants and variables is similar to that in some high-level languages. A constant specifies a particular value or object; a variable is used as a place holder for the values in an expression or procedure.

Example 4.39

Consider these statements:

Jill is taller than John
WXY is bigger than BCD
Canada is north of the U.S.A.

In these statements, the predicates "is taller than," "is bigger than," "is north of" require two objects and are called **two-place predicates.** ■

In general, we have predicates of degree n, where the predicate takes n arguments. In the case of bigger_than(WXY, BCD), the predicate BIGGER_THAN specifies the relation between WXY and BCD.

Example 4.40

Let DBMS_TYPE(x,y) specify the relation between DBMSs and their data model. The predicate DBMS_TYPE takes two arguments. ■

A predicate followed by its arguments is called an **atomic formula.** Examples of these are DBMS(x), COMPANY(y), and DBMS_TYPE(x,y).

We stated earlier that predicate calculus is a formal language. A language consists of symbols. We have already seen some of the primitive symbols, i.e., variables, constants, and predicates. We can also specify logical connectors such as "not" or negation, denoted by $\neg$, "or" ($\vee$), "and" ($\wedge$), and "implication" ($\rightarrow$).

Atomic formulas may be combined using the logical connectors to generate formulas such as $P(x) \wedge Q(y)$, $P(x) \vee Q(y)$, and so on. DBMS(ISS) $\wedge$ COMPANY(BCD), for instance, can represent "ISS is a DBMS and BCD is a company."

Other interesting formulas are formed with the use of quantifiers: universal or **"for all,"** denoted by $\forall$ and existential or **"for some,"** denoted by $\exists$. The notions expressed by the quantifiers assert that "everything has a certain property" (or deny that something lacks it) and that "something has a certain property" (or deny that everything lacks it). Therefore, $(\forall x)P(x)$ and $(\exists x)P(x)$ are used to specify that "for all x, x is P" (or simply that "everything is P") and "for some x, x is P" (or simply that "something is P").

"x is a DBMS" is an example of a formula. If the symbol x in the formula is replaced by the name of a DBMS, we have a declarative sentence that is either true or false. The phrase "x is a DBMS produced by company y" is a formula with two variables. If the occurrences of the variables x and y are replaced by the appropriate specific objects, the result is again a declarative sentence that is either true or false. For example, the declarative sentence "ISS is a DBMS produced by ABC" is false. The sentence "ISS is a DBMS produced by BCD" is true.

Example 4.41 $(\exists x)DBMS(x)$ is a formula that states that there is something that is a DBMS. We can also say that there exists something that possesses the property of being a DBMS. ■

It can be shown that the following are equivalent:

$$P(x) \land Q(x) \equiv \neg(\neg P(x) \lor \neg Q(x))$$
$$P(x) \lor Q(x) \equiv \neg(\neg P(x) \land \neg Q(x))$$

This pair of transformations is called De Morgan's law. A generalization of these transformations involving the quantifiers is obtained as follows:

$$\forall x(P(x)) \equiv \neg(\exists x)(\neg P(x))$$
$$\exists x(P(x)) \equiv \neg(\forall x)(\neg P(x))$$

Consequently, the quantifiers and the operations $\land$ and $\lor$ are connected and only one of these need be taken as the primitive.

In any formal system, it is necessary to specify which sentences (sequence of symbols) are acceptable. In the case of the English alphabet, not every sequence generated from it can be considered an English language sentence. In formal systems, the acceptable sentences (or formulas) are usually called **well-formed formulas (wffs).** The wff's should be those sequences of symbols that are unambiguous and make sense. This can be ensured by stating some rules for the construction of wffs. We will see rules in relational calculus used to ensure that only wffs are used.

Let x be any variable and W be a wff. Every occurrence of x in W is said to be **bound** by the quantifiers when occurring in the wffs $(\forall x)W$ and $(\exists x)W$. Any occurrence of a variable that is not bound is said to be **free.** For example, in $(\exists x)(P(x) \land Q(y))$, x is bound and y is free.

Free and bound variables may be compared with the global and local variables of programming languages. A bound variable is local to the quantified expression and dissimilar from the variable with the same name that is not within the quantified expression. In the following example,

$$\exists x(P_1) \land (P_2)$$

the variable x is bound in the expression P_1; however, any occurrence of x in P_2 is free and not the same variable as x in P_1.

A wff containing no free variables is said to be **closed** (otherwise **open**).

Given a wff in which we only have free variables, we can replace the variables by names of individual objects and, in so doing, obtain a proposition. DBMS(x) is such a wff, in which by replacing the variable x by some constant (or individual name) we obtain a proposition; e.g., DBMS(ISS), DBMS(Relational). When the variable is bound, for example, in $(\exists x)$DBMS(x), we already have a proposition that states "something is a DBMS."

Variables in relational calculus are like variables in programming languages in that they are restricted by their types. The declaration, for instance, that tuple variable t is defined on relation R signifies that t can only take a tuple value from the relation R. We may say that the relation R is the domain of the tuple variable t. Here a tuple variable can be equated to a record variable in Pascal (or similar high-level language). A record variable in Pascal takes on the value of a single record from among many records of its type. Similarly, in domain calculus, a domain variable d defined over a given domain D_i implies that the values associated with the variable d can only be elements from the domain D_i.

4.4.1 Tuple Calculus

Queries in **tuple calculus** are expressed by a tuple calculus expression. A tuple calculus expression is of the form

$$\{X \mid F(X)\}$$

where F is a formula involving X and X represents a set of tuple variables. The expression characterizes a set of tuples of X such that the formula F(X) is true. For the present we will assume that the formula involves predicates; however, we will examine the method of constructing and identifying valid formulae a little later.

For the examples in this section, we will continue to use the same database that we used for relational algebra. It consists of the following relations, some tuples of which are shown in Figure 4.7:

PROJECT (***Project#***, *Project_Name, Chief_Architect*)
EMPLOYEE (***Emp#***, *EmpName*)
ASSIGNED_TO (***Project#***, ***Emp#***)

Example 4.42 Consider the following query: "Obtain the employee numbers of employees working on project COMP353."

The result of this query is the set of tuples t such that there exists a tuple u in ASSIGNED_TO with value COMP353 for the *Project#*, and the same value for the *Emp#* attribute in both u and t. We can formulate this in the manner of the calculus expression above as:

$$\{t(Emp\#) \mid \exists u(u \in \text{ASSIGNED\_TO} \wedge u[Project\#] = \text{'COMP353'} \wedge t[Emp\#] = u[Emp\#])\}$$ ■

In this formulation, we specify the set of tuples t(*Emp#*) such that the predicate is true for each element of that set. The predicate specifies that there exists some tuple, u, in the relation ASSIGNED_TO such that it has the value COMP353 for the *Project#* attribute. Also, the value for the *Emp#* attributes of the result tuple t is the same as that for the tuple u.

Free variables appear to the left of the | (bar) symbol. The variable t is a free tuple variable in the above formula and assumes whatever attributes and corresponding values, assigned to it by the formula. The formula restricts t to the relation scheme (*Emp#*).

Example 4.43 Consider this query: "Obtain a list of employees (both numbers and names) working on the project COMP353," which can be rephrased as: "Obtain employee details for those employees assigned to the project COMP353."

To verify whether or not an employee is working on COMP353, we can compare the employee's *Emp#* with *Emp#* values of tuples in the relation ASSIGNED_TO. What we are really specifying is that "for the employee whose details we want, there exists a tuple in the relation ASSIGNED_TO for that employee with the value of the attribute *Project#* in that tuple being COMP353." This is a calculuslike formulation for our query. In the database we use surrogates to represent entities. For example, *Emp#* is used to represent an employee in the ASSIGNED_TO relation (*Project#* is used to represent a project). To check if an employee is working on some project, we would need to compare the employee's surrogate, *Emp#*, from EMPLOYEE, with the tuples of the ASSIGNED_TO relation containing the project's surrogate, *Project#*. Thus, the query can be reformulated as: "Get those tuples in employee relation such that there exists an ASSIGNED_TO tuple with ASSIGNED_TO.*Emp#* = EMPLOYEE.*Emp#* and ASSIGNED_TO.*Project#* = COMP353."

In tuple calculus this can be specified as:

$$\begin{aligned}\{t \mid \exists e(&e \in \text{EMPLOYEE} \wedge e[\mathit{Emp\#}] = t[\mathit{Emp\#}]\\ &\wedge e[\mathit{EmpName}] = t[\mathit{EmpName}]\\ &\wedge \exists u(u \in \text{ASSIGNED\_TO} \wedge u[\mathit{Emp\#}] = e[\mathit{Emp\#}]\\ &\qquad \wedge u[\mathit{Project\#}] = \text{'COMP353'}))\}\end{aligned}$$

The above may be simplified to the following form where the domain of the free variable t is the relation EMPLOYEE.

$$\begin{aligned}\{t \mid\ &t \in \text{EMPLOYEE}\\ &\wedge \exists u(u \in \text{ASSIGNED\_TO} \wedge u[\mathit{Emp\#}] = t[\mathit{Emp\#}]\\ &\qquad \wedge u[\mathit{Project\#}] = \text{'COMP353'}))\}\end{aligned}$$ ■

In the tuple calculus query formulations given above, we have only specified the characteristics of the desired result. The system is free to decide the operations and their execution order to satisfy the request. For comparison, a relational algebra like query would have to be stated as, "Select tuples from ASSIGNED_TO such that *Project#* = 'COMP353' and perform their join with the employee relation, projecting the results of the join over *Emp#* and *EmpName*." It is obvious that a calculus query is much simpler because it is devoid of procedural details.

Tuple Calculus Formulas

At this point it is useful to see how tuple calculus formulas are derived. A variable appearing in a formula is said to be free unless it is quantified by the existential (for some) quantifier, $\exists$ or the universal (for all) quantifier, $\forall$. Variables quantified by or are said to be bound.

In tuple calculus we define a qualified variable as t[*A*], where t is a tuple variable of some relation and *A* is an attribute of that relation. Two qualified variables, s[*A*] and t[*B*], are domain compatible if attributes *A* and *B* are domain compatible.

Tuple calculus formulas are built from **atoms.** An atom is either of the forms given below:

A_1. x $\in$ R, where R is a relation and x is a tuple variable.

A_2. x θ y or x θ c, where θ is one of the comparison operators $\{=, \neq, <, \leq, >, \geq\}$, x and y are domain-compatible qualified variables, and c is a domain compatible-constant.

For example, s[*A*] = t[*B*] is an atom in tuple calculus, where s and t are tuple variables.

Formulas (wffs) are built from atoms using the following rules:

B_1. An atom is a formula.

B_2. If f and g are formulas, then $\neg$f, (f), f $\vee$ g, f $\wedge$ g, f $\rightarrow$ g are also formulas.

B_3. If f(x) is a formula where x is free, then $\exists$x(f(x)) and $\forall$x(f(x)) are also formulas; however, x is now bound.

The logical implication expression f $\rightarrow$ g, meaning *if* f *then* g, is equivalent to $\neg$f $\vee$ g. Some well-formed formulas in tuple calculus are given below:

u $\in$ ASSIGNED_TO (declares u as a tuple variable; the domain of u is the relation ASSIGNED_TO)

u[*Project#*] = 'COMP353'

u $\in$ ASSIGNED_TO $\wedge$ u[*Project#*] = 'COMP353'

$\exists$u(u $\in$ ASSIGNED_TO $\wedge$ s $\in$ EMPLOYEE
$\wedge$ u[*Project#*] = 'COMP353'
$\wedge$ s[*Emp#*] = u[*Emp#*])
(here u is a bound variable, and s is a free variable)

$\exists$u,t (u $\in$ ASSIGNED_TO $\wedge$ s $\in$ EMPLOYEE $\wedge$ t $\in$ PROJECT
$\wedge$ t[*Project_Name*] = 'Database'
$\wedge$ u[*Project#*] = *t*[*Project#*]
$\wedge$ *s*[*Emp#*] = u[*Emp#*])

In the following examples we give some sample queries in tuple calculus using the relations shown in Figure 4.7.

Example 4.44 "Get complete details of employees working on a Database project," The query can be stated as given below. In this case, the tuple variable s is defined on the relation EMPLOYEE and it appears by itself to signify that we are interested in all attributes of its domain relation. We are saying that there exist tuples u and t on the domain relations ASSIGNED_TO and PROJECT, respectively, such that the conditions indicated below are true. The tuple t has for the *Project_Name* attribute a value of 'Database,' and the *Project#* in u and t are the same. The *Emp#* value of s and u are the same, as well. Note that $\exists$u,t(F(u,t)) is a shorthand notation for $\exists$u($\exists$t(F(u,t))).

$$\{s \mid s \in \text{EMPLOYEE} \\ \wedge \exists u, t(t \in \text{PROJECT} \wedge t[\textit{Project\_Name}] = \text{'Database'} \\ \wedge u \in \text{ASSIGNED\_TO} \wedge u[\textit{Project\#}] = t[\textit{Project\#}] \\ \wedge s[\textit{Emp\#}] = u[\textit{Emp\#}])\}$$

The query "Get complete details of employees working on all Database projects" can be expressed as follows:

$$\{s \mid s \in \text{EMPLOYEE} \\ \wedge \forall t(t \in \text{PROJECT} \wedge t[\textit{Project\_Name}] = \text{'Database'} \\ \rightarrow \exists u(u \in \text{ASSIGNED\_TO} \wedge u[\textit{Project\#}] = t[\textit{Project\#}] \\ \wedge s[\textit{Emp\#}] = u[\textit{Emp\#}])\}$$

An alternate method of writing this query without the logical implication is to replace f $\rightarrow$ g by its equivalent form $\neg$f $\vee$ g as follows:

$$\{s \mid s \in \text{EMPLOYEE} \\ \wedge \forall(t \notin \text{PROJECT} \vee t[\textit{Project\_Name}] \neq \text{'Database'} \\ \vee \exists u(u \in \text{ASSIGNED\_TO} \wedge u[\textit{Project\#}] = t[\textit{Project\#}] \\ \wedge s\,[\textit{Emp\#}] = u[\textit{Emp\#}])\}$$ ■

Any number of tuple variables can have the same relation as their domain as illustrated in the following example.

Example 4.45 "List the complete details about employees working on both COMP353 and COMP354." In this instance, we require that there exist two tuples u_1, u_2 of the relation ASSIGNED_TO with the values COMP353 and COMP354 for the attribute *Project#*. The *Emp#* attributes of s, u_1, and u_2 are equal.

$$\{s \mid s \in \text{EMPLOYEE} \wedge \exists u_1,u_2\ (u_1 \in \text{ASSIGNED\_TO} \\ \wedge u_2 \in \text{ASSIGNED\_TO} \wedge u_1[\textit{Emp\#}] = u_2[\textit{Emp \#}] \\ \wedge s[\textit{Emp\#}] = u_1[\textit{Emp\#}] \wedge u_1[\textit{Project\#}] = \text{'COMP353'} \\ \wedge u_2[\textit{Project\#}] = \text{'COMP354'})\}$$

We modify the above query to read "List the complete details about employees working on either COMP353 or COMP354 or both." Here we require that there exist tuples u_1 of the relation ASSIGNED_TO with the value COMP353 or u_2 of the same relation with the value COMP354 for the attribute *Project#*. The two "there exist" clauses are connected by the $\vee$ operator. The *Emp#* attribute of s and either u_1 or u_2, are equal.

$$\{s \mid s \in \text{EMPLOYEE} \land \exists u_1(u_1 \in \text{ASSIGNED\_TO} \land s[\textit{Emp\#}] = u_1[\textit{Emp\#}] \land u_1[\textit{Project\#}] = \text{'COMP353'} \lor \exists u_2(u_2 \in \text{ASSIGNED\_TO} \land s[\textit{Emp\#}] = u_2[\textit{Emp\#}] \land u_2[\textit{Project\#}] = \text{'COMP354'})\}$$

This query can be simplified to the following form:

$$\{s \mid s \in \text{EMPLOYEE} \land \exists u_1(u_1 \in \text{ASSIGNED\_TO} \land s\,[\textit{Emp\#}] = u_1[\textit{Emp\#}] \land (u_1[\textit{Project\#}] = \text{'COMP353'} \lor u_1[\textit{Project\#}] = \text{'COMP354'}))\}$$ ■

The following example illustrates the use of the universal quantifier.

Example 4.46

"Get the employee numbers of employees other than employee 107 who work on at least all those projects that employee 107 works on." Here a qualified variable, t[*Emp#*], is used to indicate that we are interested in finding the projection of tuple t on the attribute *Emp#*. The tuple t is from the relation ASSIGNED_TO, such that for all tuples u_1 from ASSIGNED_TO with $u_1[\textit{Emp\#}] = 107$, there exists a tuple $u_2 \in$ ASSIGNED_TO with $u_2[\textit{Emp\#}] \neq 107$. The value of the attribute *Project#* in u_2 is the same as in u_1 with identical values in the attribute *Emp#* of tuples t and u_2. The tuple expression for this query is given below:

$$\{t[\textit{Emp\#}] \mid t \in \text{ASSIGNED\_TO} \land \forall u_1(u_1 \in \text{ASSIGNED\_TO} \land u_1[\textit{Emp\#}] = 107 \rightarrow \exists u_2(u_2 \in \text{ASSIGNED\_TO} \land u_2[\textit{Emp\#}] \neq 107 \land u_1[\textit{Project\#}] = u_2[\textit{Project\#}] \land t[\textit{Emp\#}] = u_2[\textit{Emp\#}]))\}$$

Alternatively we can write this query without the logical implication by substituting its equivalent form $\neg f \lor g$ as follows:

$$\{t[\textit{Emp\#}] \mid t \in \text{ASSIGNED\_TO} \land \forall u_1(u_1 \notin \text{ASSIGNED\_TO} \lor u_1[\textit{Emp\#}] \neq 107 \lor \exists u_2(u_2 \in \text{ASSIGNED\_TO} \land u_2[\textit{Emp\#}] \neq 107 \land u_1[\textit{Project\#}] = u_2[\textit{Project\#}] \land t[\textit{Emp\#}] = u_2[\textit{Emp\#}]))\}$$

To avoid a procedural operation such as projection in a calculus query, we could define t to be on the relation scheme (*Emp#*) and rewrite this query expression as:

$$\{t(\textit{Emp\#}) \mid \forall u_1(u_1 \notin \text{ASSIGNED\_TO} \lor u_1\,[\textit{Emp\#}] \neq 107 \lor \exists u_2(u_2 \in \text{ASSIGNED\_TO} \land u_2[\textit{Emp\#}] \neq 107 \land u_1[\textit{Project\#}] = u_2[\textit{Project\#}] \land t[\textit{Emp\#}] = u_2[\text{Emp\#}]))\}$$ ■

Negation and its transformation is illustrated in Example 4.47.

Example 4.47

"Get employee numbers of employees who do not work on project COMP453." In this query we are interested in a qualified tuple variable, t[*Emp#*], t ∈ ASSIGNED_TO, to satisfy the following condition: There does not exist a tuple u in the same relation such that the *Project#* attribute of u has the value COMP453 with identical values in the attribute *Emp#* of tuples t and u. The tuple calculus expression for this query is given below:

$$\{t[[Emp\#]] \mid t \in \text{ASSIGNED\_TO} \wedge \neg\exists(u \in \text{ASSIGNED\_TO} \wedge u[[Project\#] = \text{'COMP453'} \wedge t[Emp\#] = u[Emp\#])\}$$

Alternatively, we can express this query in the following equivalent form:

$$\{t[Emp\#]] \mid t \in \text{ASSIGNED\_TO} \wedge \forall u(u \notin \text{ASSIGNED\_TO} \vee t[Emp\#] \neq u[Emp\#] \vee u[Project\#] \neq \text{'COMP453'})\}$$ ■

To find employees who work on all projects we use the universal quantifier and logical implication.

Example 4.48 "Compile a list of employee numbers of employees who work on all projects." The qualified tuple variable t[*Emp#*] satisfies the following predicates: For all tuples p from PROJECT, there exists a tuple u in ASSIGNED_TO such that the value of *Project#* in u and p are the same, and furthermore, the value of the qualified tuple variables t[*Emp#*] *and u*[*Emp#*] are the same.

$$\{t[Emp\#]] \mid t \in \text{ASSIGNED\_TO} \wedge \forall p(p \in \text{PROJECT} \rightarrow \exists u(u \in \text{ASSIGNED\_TO} \wedge p[Project\#] = u[Project\#] \wedge t[Emp\#] = u[Emp\#]))\}$$

The above can be rewritten as:

$$\{t[Emp\#]] \mid t \in \text{ASSIGNED\_TO} \wedge \forall p(p \notin \text{PROJECT} \vee \exists u(u \in \text{ASSIGNED\_TO} \wedge p[Project\#] = u[Project\#] \wedge t[Emp\#] = u[Emp\#]))\}$$ ■

The following example illustrates a method of finding employees who work at least one of a selected group of projects.

Example 4.49 "Get employee numbers of employees, not including employee 107, who work on at least one project that employee 107 works on." We are concerned here with a tuple t such that there exist tuples s and u in the relation ASSIGNED_TO, such that for the tuples s and u, the value of *Project#* is identical with the value of the attribute *Emp#;* in s, 107 and in t, not 107. The value of the attribute *Emp#* in t and u is the same. This query can be expressed in tuple calculus as follows:

$$\{t[Emp\#] \mid t \in \text{ASSIGNED\_TO} \land \exists s, u\,(s \in \text{ASSIGNED\_TO} \land u \in \text{ASSIGNED\_TO} \land s[Project\#] = u[Project\#] \land s[Emp\#] = 107 \land t[Emp\#] \neq 107 \land t[Emp\#] = u[Emp\#])\}$$ ■

We can use tuple calculus to define the division operation on the two relations P(**P**) and Q(**Q**), where $\mathbf{Q} \subseteq \mathbf{P}$:

$$R = P \div Q$$

The tuples in R are those projections of P on the set of attributes $\mathbf{P-Q}$ such that each tuple in the relation Q, when concatenated with all the tuples in R, gives the tuples in P. We can express this conditions for tuples in R as follows:

$$R = \{t \mid t \in P[\mathbf{P-Q}] \land \forall s(s \in Q \land (t \| s \in P)\}$$

To simplify the above, we can say that the tuples in R are those projection of tuples in P such that for all tuples s in Q there is a tuple u in P, which when projected on **Q** gives s and when projected on $\mathbf{P-Q}$ gives the tuples in R. In other words, the tuples in R are elements of the projection of P, on $\mathbf{P-Q}$, each of which when concatenated with all tuples s of Q is an element of P. We can express this modification to conditions for tuples in R as follows:

$$R = \{t \mid t \in P[\mathbf{P-Q}] \land \forall s(s \in Q \rightarrow \exists u(u \in P \land u[\mathbf{Q}] = s \land u[\mathbf{P-Q}] = t[\mathbf{P-Q}]))\}$$

From this second specification, we can express the division operation in terms of the other relational algebraic operations as:

$$R = P \div Q = \pi_{\mathbf{P-Q}}(P) - \pi_{\mathbf{P-Q}}((\pi_{\mathbf{P-Q}}(P) \times Q) - P)$$

We illustrate the above using the relations P(**P**) and Q(**Q**) shown in Figure Li of Example 4.28. The term $\pi_{\mathbf{P-Q}}(P)$ gives all objects in the relation P. Some of these objects do not have all the properties given in Q. The term $\pi_{\mathbf{P-Q}}(P) \times Q - P$ gives those tuples of P that will not participate in the result of the division. To find the objects that do not have all the properties in Q, we project these nonparticipating tuples on the attributes $\mathbf{P-Q}$. The result is obtained by subtracting these nonparticipating objects from all objects. These steps are illustrated in Figure 4.8.

4.4.2 Domain Calculus

As in tuple calculus, a **domain calculus** expression is of the form

$$\{X \mid F(X)\}$$

where F is a formula on X and X represents a set of domain variables. The expression characterizes X such that F(X) is true.

For the examples in this section, we continue to use the same database that we

Division operation is in terms of other relational algebraic operations.

A
a_1
a_2
a_3
a_4
a_5

Q

B
b_1
b_2

$\pi_{P-Q}(P) \times Q$

A	B
a_1	b_1
a_2	b_1
a_3	b_1
a_4	b_1
a_5	b_1
a_1	b_2
a_2	b_2
a_3	b_2
a_4	b_2
a_5	b_2

$\pi_{P-Q}(P) \times Q - P$

A	B
a_4	b_1
a_2	b_2
a_3	b_2

$\pi_{P-Q}(\pi_{P-Q}(P) \times Q - P)$

A
a_4
a_2
a_3

$\pi_{P-Q}(P) - \pi_{P-Q}(\pi_{P-Q}(P) \times Q - P)$

A
a_1
a_5

used for relational algebra and tuple calculus. It consists of the following relations, some tuples of which are shown in Figure 4.7:

PROJECT *(**Project#**, Project_Name, Chief_Architect)*
EMPLOYEE *(**Emp#**, EmpName)*
ASSIGNED_TO (***Project#**, **Emp#***)

Example 4.50

Consider the following query: "Get employee numbers for employees working on project COMP353." The method of converting this query into a domain calculus expression is by conjecturing the existence of p, a *Project#*. This *Project#* is such that the current value of the domain variables e (the domain of e being the domain of *Emp#*) and p (the domain of *p* being the domain of *Project#*) are in a tuple of the relation ASSIGNED_TO and the value of p is COMP353. We can formulate this in the manner of a domain calculus expression as follows:

$$\{e \mid \exists\, p\, (\langle e, p\rangle \in \text{ASSIGNED\_TO} \land p = \text{'COMP353'})\}$$

In the above formulation, we are specifying the set of domain values for the domain variable e such that the predicate is true. The predicate specifies that there exists a value of the domain variable p such that its current value along with the value of the domain variable e is in (the same tuple of) the relation ASSIGNED_TO. The specific value of p is the value COMP353.

Since we are interested in a particular known value of p, the quantifier can be dropped and the query simplified further to:

$$\{e \mid \langle e, p\rangle \in \text{ASSIGNED\_TO} \land p = \text{'COMP353'}\} \quad \blacksquare$$

We use two domain variables to retreive both the employee number and name as illustrated in the following example.

Example 4.51 Consider the query: "Get list of employees (both number and name) working on the project COMP353," which can be rephrased as: "Get employee details such that the employee is assigned to the project COMP353."

Here we are really specifying that "for the employee whose details we want, there exists a tuple in the relation ASSIGNED_TO for that employee for the COMP353 project." Now the value e that is associated with the value COMP353 in the ASSIGNED_TO tuple must also appear along with a value for m in a tuple of the employee relation. In domain calculus this can be specified as:

$$\{e_1, m \mid <e_1, m> \in \text{EMPLOYEE}) \land \exists e_2 (<p, e_2> (\text{ASSIGNED\_TO} \land p = \text{'COMP353'} \land e_1 = e_2)\}$$ ■

As in the case of tuple calculus, we have only specified the characteristics of the desired result; the system is free to decide the operations and their execution order to satisfy the request. Furthermore, a variable appearing in a formula is said to be free unless it is quantified by the existential quantifier $\exists$ or the universal quantifier $\forall$.

Domain Calculus Formulas

Domain calculus formulas are also built from atoms. As in tuple calculus, an atom is either of the form given below in A_1 or of the form in A_2. Here R(**R**) is a relation and X is the set of domain variables $\{x_1, x_2, \ldots, x_n\}$ in domain calculus, defined on a subset of the relation's attributes.

A_1. $X \subseteq \mathbf{R}$

A_2. $x\ \theta\ y$ or $x\ \theta\ c$, where ϵ is one of the comparison operators $\{=, \neq, <, \leq, >, \geq\}$, x and y are domain-compatible variables, and c is a domain-compatible constant.

For example, A = B is an atom in domain calculus.

Formulas (wffs) are built from atoms using the following rules:

B_1. An atom is a formula.

B_2. If f and g are formulas, then $\neg f$, (f), $f \lor g$, $f \land g$, $f \rightarrow g$ are also formulas.

B_3. If f(X) is a formula where X is free, then $\exists X(f(X))$ and $\forall X(f(X))$ are also formulas.

The expression $f \rightarrow g$, meaning *if* f *then* g, is equivalent to $\neg f \lor g$. Domain calculus expressions use the same operators as those in tuple calculus. The difference is that in domain calculus, instead of using tuple variables, we use domain variables to represent components of tuples. A tuple calculus expression can be converted to a domain calculus expression by replacing each tuple variable by n domain variables; here n is the arity of the tuple variable. Some well-formed domain calculus formula examples are given on the next page.

$<a,b> \in$ ASSIGNED_TO (declares a and b as domain variables defined on the domain of the attributes of the ASSIGNED_TO relation)

a = 'COMP353'

$<a,b> \in$ ASSIGNED_TO $\wedge$ a = 'COMP353'

$\exists a,b$ ($<a,b> \in$ ASSIGNED_TO $\wedge$ $<c,d> \in$ EMPLOYEE $\wedge$ a = 'COMP353' $\wedge$ b=c)

$\exists a,b,e,f$ ($<a,b> \in$ ASSIGNED_TO $\wedge$ $<c,d> \in$ EMPLOYEE
$\wedge$ $<e,f,g> \in$ PROJECT
$\wedge$ b = c $\wedge$ a = e $\wedge$ f = 'Database')

(Note that g is used as a placeholder, so that we know what domain the variable belongs to.)

Here we give some sample queries in domain calculus. We continue to use the relations given below and shown in Figure 4.7 for these queries:

PROJECT ***(Project#,** Project_Name, Chief_Architect)*
EMPLOYEE ***(Emp#,** EmpName)*
ASSIGNED_TO ***(Project#, Emp#)***

Furthermore, we use the domain variables $p_i \in$ Dom*(Project#)*, $n_i \in$ Dom*(Project_Name)*, $c_i \in$ Dom*(Chief_Architect)*, $e_i \in$ Dom*(Emp#)*, $m_i \in$ Dom*(EmpName)*, where Dom*(Project#)*, etc. are the domains of the corresponding attributes. The expression $<p_1,e_1> \in$ ASSIGNED_TO evaluates as true if and only if there exists a tuple in relation ASSIGNED_TO with the current value of the corresponding domain variables. As before we use the notation $\exists p_1,e_1(P)$ as shorthand for $\exists p_1 \exists e_1(P)$.

Example 4.52

The query "Compile the details of employees working on a Database project" can be stated as:

{e,m | $\exists p_1,e_1,p_2,n_2$ ($<p_1,e_1> \in$ ASSIGNED_TO
$\wedge$ $<e,m> \in$ EMPLOYEE
$\wedge$ $<p_2,n_2,c_2> \in$ PROJECT
$\wedge$ $e_1 = e \wedge p_1 = p_2 \wedge n_2$ = 'Database')} ■

Any number of domain variables can be defined on the domains of the attributes of a relation as illustrated below.

Example 4.53

Compile the details of employees working on both COMP353 and COMP354.

{e,m | $\exists p_1,e_1,p_2,e_2$ ($<e,m> \in$ EMPLOYEE
$\wedge$ $<p_1,e_1> \in$ ASSIGNED_TO
$\wedge$ $<p_2,e_2> \in$ ASSIGNED_TO
$\wedge$ $e = e_1 \wedge e = e_2$
$\wedge$ p_1 = 'COMP353' $\wedge$ p_2 = 'COMP354')} ■

The use of the universal quantifier and logical implication is demonstrated in Example 4.54.

Example 4.54

"Obtain the employee numbers of employees, other than employee 107, who work on at least all those projects that employee 107 works on."

$$\{e \mid \langle p,e\rangle \in ASSIGNED\_TO \ \forall\, p_1,e_1 \\ (\langle p_1,e_1\rangle \in ASSIGNED\_TO \wedge e_1 = 107 \\ \rightarrow (\exists p_2,e_2(\langle p_2,e_2\rangle \in ASSIGNED\_TO \\ \wedge\, e_2 \neq 107 \wedge p_1 = p_2 \wedge e = e_2))\}$$

An equivalent form of this query where the implication is replaced by the $\vee$ operator is given below:

$$\{e \mid \langle p,e\rangle \in ASSIGNED\_TO \wedge \\ \forall\, p_1,e_1(\langle p_1,e_1\rangle \notin ASSIGNED\_TO \vee e_1 \neq 107 \\ \vee (\exists p_2,e_2(\langle p_2,e_2\rangle \in ASSIGNED\_TO \\ \wedge\, e_2 \neq 107 \wedge p_1 = p_2 \wedge e = e_2))\} \ \blacksquare$$

Negation is illustrated in Example 4.55.

Example 4.55

"Get employee numbers of employees who do not work on the COMP453 project."

$$\{e \mid \exists p\, (\langle p,e\rangle \in ASSIGNED\_TO \\ \wedge \forall\, p_1,e_1\, (\langle p_1,e_1\rangle \notin ASSIGNED\_TO \\ \vee\, p_1 \neq COMP453 \vee e_1 \neq e))\} \ \blacksquare$$

Another example of the use of the universal qualifier and logical implication is given below.

Example 4.56

"What are the employee numbers of employees who work on all projects?"

$$\{e \mid \exists\, p(\langle p,e\rangle \in ASSIGNED\_TO \\ \wedge \forall\, p_1(\langle p_1,n_1,c_1\rangle \in PROJECT \\ \rightarrow \langle p_1,e\rangle \in ASSIGNED\_TO))\} \ \blacksquare$$

The domain calculus formula to find employees who are assigned to at least one of a selected group of projects is given in Example 4.57.

Example 4.57

"Get the employee numbers of employees, other than employee 107, who work on at least one project that employee 107 works on."

$$\{e \mid \exists\, p,p_1,e_1,p_2,e_2(<p,e> \in \text{ASSIGNED\_TO} \\ \wedge <p_1,e_1> \in \text{ASSIGNED\_TO} \\ \wedge <p_2,e_2> \in \text{ASSIGNED\_TO} \\ \wedge e_2 \neq 107 \wedge p_1 = p_2 \wedge e_1 = 107 \wedge e = e_2)\}$$ ■

4.5 Concluding Remarks on Data Manipulation

Consider tuple calculus expression:

$$\{x \mid x \notin R\}$$

Evaluating this expression generates tuples that are not in the relation R and entails generating an infinite number of tuples. If the domain of the tuple variable x were a relation scheme X, the tuples generated would be an indeterminate number of such tuples on the relation scheme X. However, in spite of this limitation, the number of tuples generated will be immense and the majority of these tuples are not likely to be in the actual database. In a database application an additional limitation is imposed: that all evaluating is done with respect to the content of the database at the time of the evaluation of the query. This further limitation generates, for the above expression, only those tuples that are in the database and not in the relation R. However, this evaluation is also prohibitively expensive in terms of computing resources used.

For relational calculus, by definition, infinite relations might be generated. In practice, this might be limited to finite relations because of condition imposed in the formula. It is therefore clear that the tuple relation calculus formulas are not only wffs, but they do not generate infinite relations. This in turn requires that the domain of the formula be clearly defined. The domain of a formula F(X), where X is a set of tuple variables, is the set of values either appearing explicitly in the formula or being referenced in it. The values that appear explicitly are constants and the values being referenced are from the relations appearing in the formula. Each such relation is assumed to be of finite cardinality. The purpose of defining the domain of a formula is to ensure that the result relation generated by evaluating the formula is also in the domain of the formula. This ensures that the result relation is finite and only tuples from the domain of the formula have to be examined in evaluating the expression. Such a tuple relational calculus expression is said to be **safe.**

The concept of safety can be applied to domain calculus expressions by defining a domain of a domain calculus expression and by ensuring that the result relation is within this domain. If we limit the relational calculus expressions to safe expressions, then tuple calculus and domain calculus are equivalent. Furthermore, both are equivalent to relational algebra. This means that for every safe relational calculus expression there exists a relational algebraic expression and vice versa. Also, we can write an equivalent domain calculus expression for a tuple calculus expression and vice versa.

Even though the final calculus expression for a query is more compact than an algebraic expression, it does not mean that calculus is a better interface, particularly with complex queries. It is natural to break such queries down into smaller steps (as in the case of the algebraic formulation; we presented a few examples of this in Section 4.3.3) and then compose the steps into a neat calculus formula. This may be the reason behind the success of SQL as a relational query language. SQL is clearly not assertional and includes intersection, union, and difference operations.

In Sections 4.3 and 4.4 we considered the features of relational data manipulation operations using relational algebra and relational calculus, respectively. The data manipulation language for the DBMS must supplement them with additional capabilities, such as relation creation, deletion, and modifications. Facilities are also provided for the insertion, deletion, and modification of tuples. These additional operations enables users to manipulate and update the data contained in the database. In the derivation operations, the attributes of one tuple are compared with attributes of another tuple or constants. In the alteration operations, the attribute values are altered or tuples are removed or inserted. As in the case of other relational operations, compatibility is also required in derivation and alteration operations.

A number of query languages based on the concepts of these sections have been developed. Three of these query languages (SQL, QUEL, and QBE) have gained wider acceptance than the others. SQL is in widespread use and, with an ANSI standard definition, has become the de facto query language for relational database systems. This in no way detracts from the elegance of QUEL. We consider all three languages in Chapter 5.

Relational Algebra vs. Relational Calculus

The relational algebra operations described in Section 4.3 allow the manipulation of relations and provide a means of formally expressing queries. The sequence of operations necessary to answer the query is also inherent in the relational algebraic expression. In other words, relational algebra is a procedural language. In Section 4.4 we considered two nonprocedural relational calculus query systems: tuple and domain calculus. In calculus queries we specify only the information required, not how it is obtained.

It can be proved that the expressive power of relational algebra and relational calculus are equivalent (Ullm 82). This means that any query that could be expressed in relational algebra could be expressed by formulas in relational calculus. Furthermore, any safe formula of relational calculus may be translated into a relational algebraic query.

There have been a number of proposed changes and additions to both relational algebra and calculus; for instance, the need for aggregation (average, count, and other such functions) and update operations in these query systems. Many researchers recognize this as omissions from the original formulation of relational algebra and calculus.

4.6 Physical Implementation Issues

So far, we have considered the relational model and the operations defined in the model. We have refrained from mentioning any implementation issues because, to the end user, these are of little concern. The relational algebra operations in some respects define what is to be done, but even then the DBMS can optimize the actual processing of the query and perform the operations in a different order (see Chapter

10 on query processing). In relational calculi we do not even specify the operations. To the users, the DBMS is a black box that insulates them from the details of file definitions and file management software as supported by the operating system. As we mentioned in Chapter 1, one function of the DBMS is to provide physical data independence.

The DBA cannot optimize the database for all possible query formulations. Thus, for every relation the anticipated volume of different types of queries, updates, and so on is estimated to come up with an anticipated usage pattern. Based on these statistics, decisions on physical organization are made. For example, it would be inappropriate to provide an access structure (say a B^+-tree) for every attribute of every relation; these secondary access structures have storage and search overheads.

The DBMS can make use of all the features of the file management system. As most DBMSs have versions that run on different machines and under different operating system environments, the DBMS may support file systems not available under the host machine environment. Thus, every DBMS defines the file and index structures it supports. The DBA chooses the most appropriate file organization. In the event of changes to usage patterns or to expedite the processing of certain queries, a reorganization can take place.

A large number of queries requires the joining of two relations. It may be appropriate to keep the joining tuples of the two relations either as linked records or physically grouped into a single record.

We may consider a relation to be implemented in terms of a single (or multiple) file(s) and a tuple of the relation to be a record (or collection of records). For the file, we may define a storage strategy, for example, sequential, indexed, or random, and for each attribute we can define additional access structures.

The more powerful DBMSs allow a great deal of implementation detail to be defined for the relations. The more common but less powerful DBMSs (mostly on microcomputers) allow very simple definitions, for example, indexing on certain attributes (this is usually a B^+-tree index). Some systems require the index to be regenerated after any modification to the indexing attribute values. Additional commands for sorting and other such operations are also supported. The typical file organization is plain sequential. (In fact, many micro-based DBMSs confuse a relation or table with a flat sequential file.)

A single relation may be stored in more than one file, i.e., some attributes in one, the rest in others. This is known as **fragmentation.** This may be done to improve the retrieval of certain attribute values; by reducing the size of the tuple in a given file more tuples can be fetched in a single physical access. The system associates the same internally generated identifier, called the **tuple identifier,** to the different fragments of each tuple. Based on these tuple identifiers a complete tuple is easy to reconstruct.

In addition to making use of the file system,[3] the DBMS must keep track of the details of each relation and its attribute defined in the database. All such information is kept in the directory. The directory can be implemented using a number of system-defined and -maintained relations. For each relation, the system may maintain a tuple in some system relation, recording the relation name, creator, date, size, storage

---

[3]To achieve satisfactory performance, many DBMSs develop their own file management systems and use disk input/output routines that directly access the secondary storage devices.

structure, and so on. For each attribute of the relation, the system may maintain a tuple recording the relation identifier, attribute name, type, size, and so forth. Different DBMSs keep different amounts of information in the directory relations. However, because the implementation is usually as relations, the same data manipulation language that the DBMS supports can be used to query these relations.

In this section we briefly examined some implementation issues. Implementors of databases and DBMSs must be aware that there exists much more detail than that contained in the model.

4.7 Summary

In this chapter we studied the relational data model, consisting of the relational data structure, relational operations, and the relational integrity rules. This model borrows heavily from set theory and is based on sound fundamental principles. Relational operations are applied to relations, and the result is a relation.

Conceptually, a relation can be represented as a table; each column of the table represents an attribute of the relation and each row represents a tuple of the relation. Mathematically a relation is a correspondence between a number of sets and is a subset of the cartesian product of these sets. The sets are the domains of the attributes of the relation.

Duplicate tuples are not permitted in a relation. Each tuple can be identified uniquely using a subset of the attributes of the relation. Such a minimum subset is called a key (primary) of the relation. The unique identification property of the key is used to capture relationships between entities. Such a relationship is represented by a relation that contains a key for each entity involved in the relationship.

Relational algebra is a procedural manipulation language. It specifies the operations and the order in which they are to be performed on tuples of relations. The result of these operations is also a relation. The relational algebraic operations are union, difference, cartesian product, intersection, projection, selection, join, and division.

Relational calculus consists of two distinct calculi, tuple calculus and domain calculus. In relational calculus queries are expressed using variables, a formula involving these variables, and compatible constants. The query expression specifies the result relation to be obtained without specifying the mechanism and the order used to evaluate the formula. It is up to the underlying database system to transform these nonprocedural queries into equivalent, efficient, procedural queries. In relational tuple calculus the variables represent tuples from specific relations; in domain calculus the variables represent values from specific domains.

Since relational calculus specifies queries as formulas, it is important that these formulas generate result relations of finite cardinality in an acceptable period of time. This in turn requires that the formulas be defined on a finite domain and the result be within that domain. The domain consists of relations and constants appearing in the formulas. Such formulas are called safe. With a safe formula, it is possible to convert a query expression from one representation to another.

In the next chapter we consider a number of commercial query languages based on relational algebra and calculus.

Key Terms

cardinality
degree
arity
projecting
join
set
members
intension
extension
union
intersection
cartesian product
difference
atomic domain
application-independent domain
application-dependent domain
structured domain
composite domain
n-tuple
projection
relation scheme
unique identification
nonredundancy
prime attribute
associative relation
foreign key
target
domino deletion
cascading deletion
union compatible
set-theoretic union
restriction operation
theta join
equi-join
natural join
relational calculus
predicate calculus
predicate
one-place predicate
monadic predicate
two-place predicate
atomic formula
well-formed formula (wff)
bound variable
free variable
closed
open
tuple calculus
atom
domain calculus
safe
fragmentation
tuple identifier

Exercises

4.1 For the relations P and Q shown in Figure N, perform the following operations and show the resulting relations.

(a) Find the projection of Q on the attributes (B,C).
(b) Find the natural join of P and Q on the common attributes.
(c) Divide P by the relation that is obtained by first selecting those tuples of Q where the value of B is either b_1 or b_2 and then projecting Q on the attributes (C,D).

Figure N For Exercise 4.1.

P

A	B	C	D
a_1	b_2	c_2	d_2
a_2	b_1	c_1	d_2
a_1	b_1	c_2	d_1
a_2	b_1	c_2	d_2
a_1	b_2	c_1	d_2
a_3	b_1	c_2	d_1
a_1	b_2	c_2	d_2
a_2	b_1	c_1	d_2
a_1	b_3	c_2	d_2

Q

B	C	D
b_1	c_1	d_2
b_3	c_1	d_2
b_2	c_2	d_1
b_1	c_1	d_2
b_3	c_2	d_2

4.2 Given the E-R diagram in Figure O, give the most suitable relational database scheme to implement this database. For each relation, choose a suitable name and list corresponding attributes, underlining the primary key. For each relation, also identify the foreign keys. Could any problems result as a consequence of tuple additions, deletions, or updates?

Figure O For Exercise 4.2.

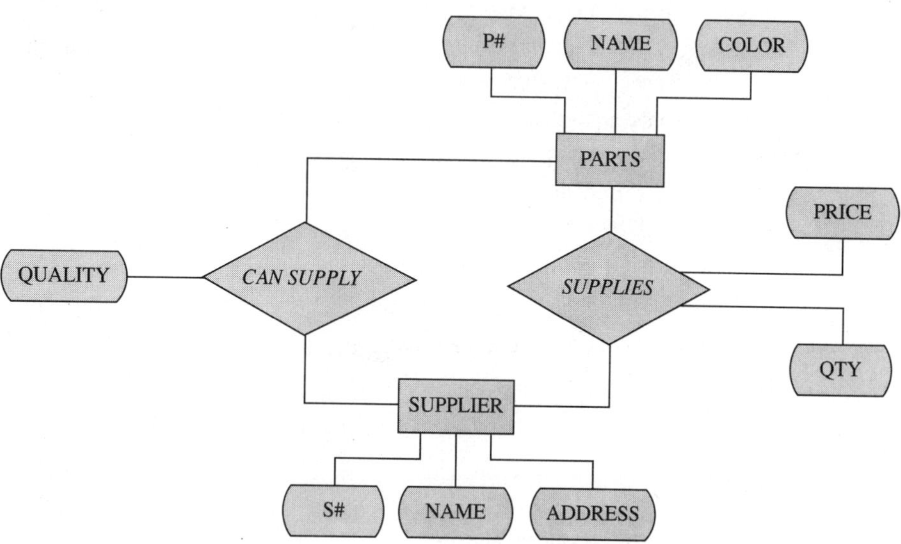

4.3 For the database of Figure O, write relational algebra and calculus expressions to pose the following queries:

(a) Get the supplier details and the price of bolts for all suppliers who supply 'bolts'.

(b) Find details of parts that suppliers who supply 'bolts' costing less than $0.01 are capable of supplying, with the parts being of a quality better than 'x'.

4.4 Given the relational schemes:

ENROLL *(S#, C#, Section)—S#* represents student number
TEACH *(Prof, C#, Section)—C#* represents course number
ADVISE *(Prof, S#)—Prof* is thesis advisor of S#
PRE_REQ *(C#, Pre_C#)—Pre_C#* is prerequisite course
GRADES *(S#, C#, Grade, Year)*
STUDENT *(S#, Sname)—Sname* is student name

Give queries expressed in relational algebra, tuple calculus, and domain calculus for the following queries:

(a) List all students taking courses with Smith or Jones.

(b) List all students taking at least one course that their advisor teaches.

(c) List those professors who teach more than one section of the same course.

(d) List the courses that student ''John Doe'' can enroll in, i.e., has passed the necessary prerequisite courses but not the course itself.

4.5 An orchestra database consists of the following relations:

CONDUCTS *(Conductor, Composition)*
REQUIRES *(Composition, Instrument)*
PLAYS *(Player, Instrument)*
LIKES *(Player, Composition)*

Give relational algebra, tuple calculus, and domain calculus queries for the following queries?

(a) List the players and their instruments who can be part of the orchestra when Letitia Melody conducts.
(b) From the above list of players, identify those who would like the composition they are to play.

4.6 Give the equivalent

(a) English statement,
(b) domain calculus, and
(c) algebra

expressions for the following tuple calculus query:

$$\{t | t \in rel_1 \wedge \exists s(s \in rel_2 \wedge (s.c = t.b))\}$$

given the relations $rel_1(A,B)$ and $rel_2(C,D)$.

4.7 Convert the following domain calculus query

$$\{<A,B> \mid <A,B> \in rel_1 \wedge B = 'B_1' \vee B = 'B_2'\}$$

into

(a) an English statement
(b) relational algebra
(c) tuple calculus.

4.8 Investigate the physical implementation details of a relational DBMS with which you are familiar. Under what circumstances would any file organization not supported by the system be beneficial?

4.9 An inverted file management system allows for the definition of inverted files and supports queries of the form "List records (or tuples) where the attribute_name has value x," and a Boolean combination of such queries. Discuss how the relational algebra operations can be handled using such a system.

4.10 Consider the queries in Examples 4.44 through 4.49. Rewrite the queries in tuple calculus; however, use the quantifier $\forall$ instead of $\exists$ and vice versa.

4.11 Consider the queries in Examples 4.52 through 4.57. Rewrite the queries in domain calculus; however, use the quantifier $\forall$ instead of $\exists$ and vice versa.

4.12 Using the relations ASSIGNED_TO, EMPLOYEE, and PROJECT given in the text, generate the following queries in relational algebra.

(a) Acquire details of the projects for each employee by name.
(b) Compile the names of projects to which employee 107 is assigned.
(c) Access all employees assigned to projects whose chief architect is employee 109.
(d) Derive the list of employees who are assigned to all projects on which employee 109 is the chief architect.
(e) Get all project names to which employee 107 is not assigned.
(f) Get complete details of employees who are assigned to projects not assigned to employee 107.

4.13 Repeat Exercise 4.12 using tuple calculus.

4.14 Repeat Exercise 4.12 using domain calculus.

4.15 Give the tuple calculus expressions for the relational algebraic operation of (a) the union of two relations P and Q, (b) the difference P − Q, (c) the projection of relation P on the attribute X, (d) the selection $\sigma_B(P)$, (e) the division of relation P by Q, i.e., P ÷ Q.

4.16 Consider the following relations concerning a driving school. The primary key of each relation is in boldface.

STUDENT : (***St_Name,*** *Class#, Th_Mark, Dr_Mark)*
STUDENT_DRIVING_TEACHER : (***St_Name,*** *Dr_T_Name)*
TEACHER_THEORY_CLASS : (***Class#,*** *Th_T_Name)*
TEACHER_VEHICLE : (***Dr_T_Name, License#)***
VEHICLE : (***License#,*** *Make, Model, Year)*

A student takes one theory class as well as driving lessons and at the end of the session receives marks for theory and driving. A teacher may teach theory, driving, or both. Write the following queries in relational algebra, domain calculus, and tuple calculus.

(a) Find the list of teachers who teach theory and give driving lessons on all the vehicles.
(b) Find the pairs of students satisfying the following conditions.

They have the same theory mark and
They have different theory teachers and
They have the same driving mark and
They have different driving teachers

(c) Find the list of students who are taught neither theory lessons nor driving lessons by "Johnson" (teacher).
(d) Find the list of students who have better marks than "John" in both theory and driving.
(f) Find the list of students who have more marks than the average theory mark of class 8 (Class#).
(g) Find the list of teachers who can drive all the vehicles.

4.17 Comment on the correctness of the following relational calculus solutions to the query: "Get employee numbers of employees who do not work on project COMP453."

(a) $\{t[Emp\#] \mid t \in \text{ASSIGNED\_TO} \wedge$
$\forall u(u \in \text{ASSIGNED\_TO} \wedge t\,[Emp\#] = u[Emp\#]$
$\wedge\, u[Project\#] \neq \text{'COMP453'})\}$

(b) $\{e \mid \exists p\, (\langle p,e\rangle \in \text{ASSIGNED\_TO}$
$\wedge \forall\, p_1,e_1\, (\langle p_1,e_1\rangle \in \text{ASSIGNED\_TO}$
$\wedge\, p_1 = \text{'COMP453'} \wedge e \neq e_1)))\}$

4.18 Comment on the correctness of the following relational calculus solutions to the query: "Compile a list of employee numbers of employees who work on all projects."

(a) $\{t[Emp\#] \mid t \in \text{ASSIGNED\_TO} \wedge$
$\exists p,u\, (p \in \text{PROJECT} \wedge u \in \text{ASSIGNED\_TO}$
$\wedge\, p[Project\#] = u\,[Project\#]$
$\wedge\, t\,[Emp\#] = u[Emp\#]$

(b) $\{e \mid \forall\, p_2(\langle p_2,n_2,c_2\rangle \in \text{PROJECT}$
$\wedge \langle p,e\rangle \in \text{ASSIGNED\_TO}$

$\rightarrow \exists\ p_1,e_1\ (<p_1,e_1> \in$ ASSIGNED_TO
$\wedge\ p_1 = p_2 \wedge e = e_1))\}$

(c) $\{e \mid \exists p\ (<p,e> \in$ ASSIGNED_TO
$\wedge \forall\ p_1,e_1\ (<p_1,e_1> \notin$ ASSIGNED_TO
$\vee\ p_1 \neq$ COMP453 $\vee\ e_1 \neq e))\}$

(d) $\{e \mid \exists p\ (<p,e> \in$ ASSIGNED_TO
$\wedge \forall\ p_1(<p_1,n_1,c_1> \in$ PROJECT
$\rightarrow <p_1,e> \in$ ASSIGNED_TO$))\}$

4.19 Comment on the correctness of the following relational calculus solution to the query: "Acquire the employee numbers of employees, other than employee 107, who work on at least one project that employee 107 works on."

$\{e \mid \exists p,p_1,e_1\ (<p,e> \in$ ASSIGNED_TO
$\wedge <p_1,e_1> \in$ ASSIGNED_TO
$\wedge\ p_1 = p \wedge e \neq e_1 \wedge e_1 = 107)\}$

Bibliographic Notes

The original concept of the use of relations to represent data was presented by Levien and Maron (Levi 67). The formal relational model as we know it today, however, was first proposed by E. F. Codd (Codd 70). Relational algebra was defined by Codd in his original paper and relational calculi in a subsequent paper (Codd 72). Since Codd's original article, the relational model has been extensively studied and is covered in most database texts, including Date (Date 86), Korth and Silberschatz (Kort 86), Maier (Maie 83), and Ullman (Ullm 82). Maier's text gives a comprehensive theoretical treatment of the relational model.

Bibliography

(Beer 77) C. Beeri, R. Fagin, & J. H. Howard, "A Complete Axiomisation for Functional and Multivalued Dependencies," Proc. ACM SIGMOD Record Conference, Toronto, Aug. 1977, pp. 47–61.

(Beer 78) C. Beeri, P. A. Bernstein, & N. Goodman, "A Sophisticate's Introduction to Database Normalization Theory," Proc. 4th International Conference on Very Large Data Bases, Berlin, 1978, pp. 113–123.

(Bern 76) P. A. Bernstein, "Synthesizing Third Normal Form Relations from Functional Dependencies," *ACM Transactions on Database Systems* 1(4), 1976, pp. 277–298.

(Brod 82) M. L. Brodie, & J. W. Schmidt, eds., "Final Report of the ANSI/X3/SPARC DBS-SG Relational Database Task Group," SPARC-81-690, *ACM SIGMOD Record* 12(4), 1982, pp. 1–62.

(Buss 83) V. Bussolati, S. Ceri, V. De Antenollis, & B. Zonta, "Views Conceptual Design," in S. Ceri, ed., *Methodology and Tools for Data Base Design*. North Holland, Amsterdam 1983, pp. 25–55.

(Codd 70) E. F. Codd, "A Relational Model for Large Shared Data Banks," *Communications of the ACM* 13(6), 1970, 377–387.

(Codd 72) E. F. Codd, "Relational Completeness of Data Base Sublanguages," in R. Randall, ed., *Data Base Systems*. Englewood Cliffs, NJ: Prentice-Hall, 1972, pp. 65–98.

(Codd 81) E. F. Codd, "Data Models in Database Management," *ACM SIGMOD Record* 11(2), 1981.

(Codd 82) E. F. Codd, "Relational Database: A Practical Foundation for Productivity," 1981 ACM Turing Award Lecture, *Communications of the ACM* 25(2), 1982, pp. 109–117.

(Date 86) C. J. Date, "An Introduction to Database Systems," 4th ed. Reading, Mass: Addison Wesley, 1986.

(Fagi 77) R. Fagin, ''Multivalued Dependencies and a New Normal Form for Relational Databases,'' *ACM Transactions of Database Systems* 2(3), 1977, pp. 262–278.

(Gall 78) H. Gallaire & J. Minker, *Logic and Databases*. New York: Plenum Press, 1978.

(Kort 86) H. F. Korth & A. Silberschatz, *Database System Concepts,* New York: McGraw-Hill, 1986.

(Kowa 79) R. Kowalski, *Logic for Problem Solving,* New York: North-Holland, 1979.

(Lacr 77) M. Lacroix & A. Pirotte, ''Domain-Oriented Relational Languages,'' Proc. 3rd International Conference on Very Large Data Bases, October 6-8, 1977. Tokyo, IEEE, New York, pp. 370–378.

(Levi 67) R. Levien, & M. E. Maron, ''A Computer System for Inference Execution and Data Retrieval, *Communications of the ACM* 10(11), 1967, pp. 715–721.

(Lum 79) V. Lum et al., 1978 New Orleans Data Base Design Workshop Report, IBM Yorktown Heights (RJ 2554), 1979.

(Maie 83) D. Maier, *The Theory of Relational Databases,''* Rockville, MD: Computer Science Press, 1983.

(Niem 84) T. Niemi & K. Jarvelin, ''A Straightforward Formalization of the Relational Model,'' *ACM SIGMOD Record* 14(1), 1984, pp. 15–38.

(Piro 82) A. Pirotte, ''A Precise Definition of Basic Relational Notions and of the Relational Algebra,'' *ACM SIGMOD Record* 13(1), 1982, pp. 30–45.

(Ullmn 82) J. D. Ullman, *Principles of Database Systems,* 2nd ed. Rockville, Md: Computer Science Press, 1982.

(Yang 86) C. C. Yang, *Relational Databases*. Englewood Cliffs, NJ: Prentice-Hall, 1986.

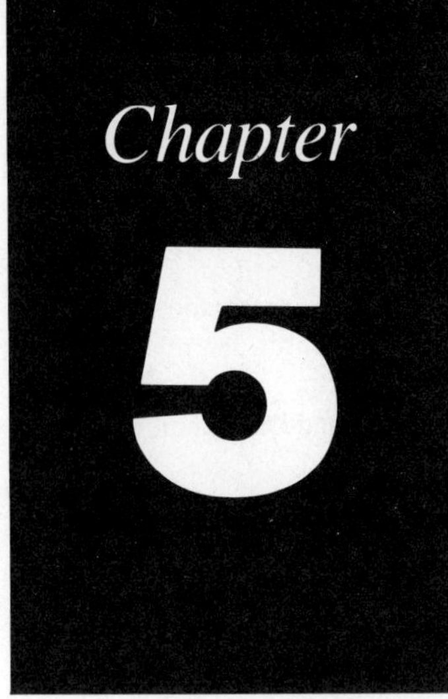

Chapter 5

Relational Database Manipulation

Contents

In this chapter we focus on a number of commercial data manipulation languages. We look at their main features and illustrate their usage.

5.1 Introduction

In the preceding chapter we looked at query languages for the relational model based on relational algebra or calculus. Data manipulation languages for commercial database systems, however, do not conform precisely to any of these languages. The commercial implementation of the query languages have some restrictions and omissions, as well as extensions. Most of the commercial languages, for example, support arithmetic, string and aggregate operators (such as average, maximum, etc.).

Relational algebra or relational calculi provide a powerful set of operations or means to specify queries, as we saw in Chapter 4. These operations form the basis for the data manipulation language component of a DBMS. The DBMS must also support data definition capabilities, with commands for the creation, deletion, and modification of relations, the insertion, deletion, and modification of tuples, and features to make it easier or more convenient to use.

In this chapter, although we do not provide detailed syntax or semantics, we demonstrate some of the features of Structured Query Language (SQL), Query Language (QUEL), and Query-By-Example (QBE). SQL is not truly non-procedural and uses features of relational algebra as well as relational calculus. QUEL is based on tuple calculus. QBE is a two-dimensional language based on domain calculus. None of these languages are purely procedural and consequently none of them quite follows the relational algebraic philosophy. Individual implementation of these languages, as with programming languages, has its own flavor.

In the examples of this chapter we use the relations discussed below, referring to the hotel and restaurants example presented in Chapter 2.

As we saw in Chapter 2, the aggregation BILL represents the *SERVE* relationship among the entities GUEST, TABLE, and WAITER. The aggregation BILL requires the introduction of a unique bill number for identification. In addition, the following attributes from the *SERVE* relationship and the entities involved in the relationship can be used for the aggregated entity: unique bill number, waiter identifier, table identifier, day, number of guests in party, total, tip. We have used day here as the name of one of the attributes instead of date, which is a reserved keyword in some commercial DMLs.

Now let us consider the relationship *ORDR*, shown in Figure 5.1, between the entities bill and menu. (Because ORDER is a reserved keyword in most query languages we use the name *ORDR* for this relationship.) A menu has a number of dishes with a price and description for each item. The guests order a number of dishes (more than one of the same dish may be consumed). The structure of the tables for the relations and the data type declarations are given below. Some tuples of these relations are shown in Figure 5.2.

MENU *(Dish#, Dish_Description, Price)*

Dish#: integer—unique identifier
Dish_Description: text—name and other details of dish
Price: real—price of the dish

Figure 5.1 The *ORDR* relationship.

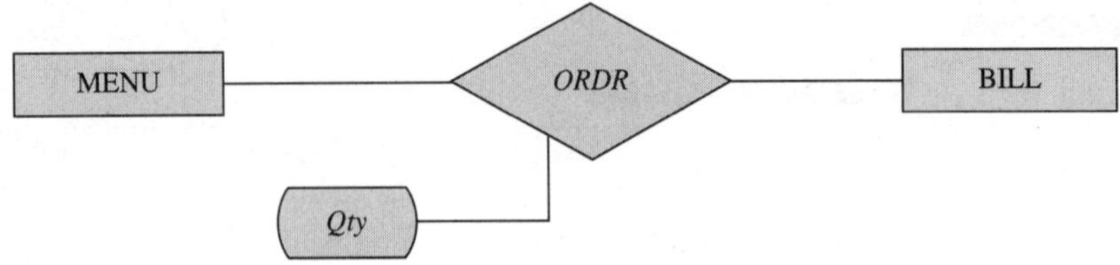

BILL *(Bill#, Day, Table#, Waiter#, Total, Tip)*

Bill#: integer—unique bill identifier
Day: date—in yyyymmdd unsigned decimal digits format
Table#: integer—table number
Waiter#: integer—employee identifier
Total: real—total amount
Tip: real

ORDR *(Bill#, Dish#, Qty)*

Bill#: integer—bill identifier
Dish#: integer—dish identifier
Qty: integer—number of dish ordered by client

The *DUTY_ALLOCATION* relationship (Figure 5.3) between various positions (POSITION) and employees (EMPLOYEE) in a restaurant can be described by the attributes *Day* and *Shift*. Each position in the restaurant is defined by a unique *Posting_No* and requires a (minimum) skill specified by *Skill*. The structure of the tables for these entities and the relationship is given below. Some tuples from these relations are given in Figure 5.4.

Figure 5.2 Some tuples from the MENU, BILL, and ORDR relations.

MENU

Dish#	*Dish_Description*	*Price*
50	Coffee	2.50
100	Scrambled eggs	7.50
200	Special du jour	19.50
250	Club sandwich	10.50
300	Pizza	14.50

ORDR

Bill#	*Dish#*	*Qty*
9234	50	2
9234	250	2
9235	300	1

BILL

Bill#	*Table#*	*Day*	*Waiter#*	*Total*	*Tip*
9234	12	19860419	123456	26.00	3.90
9235	17	19860420	123461	14.50	2.20

Figure 5.3 The *DUTY_ALLOCATION* relationship.

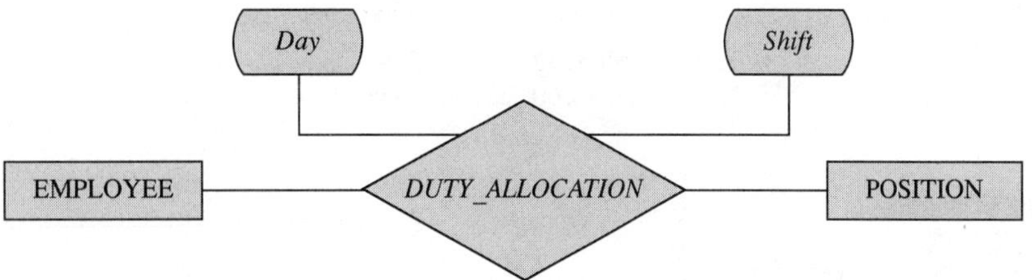

EMPLOYEE *(Empl_No, Name, Skill, Pay_Rate)*

Empl_No: integer—unique identifier
Name: string—employee's name
Skill: string—employee's skill
Pay_Rate: real—hourly pay rate

POSITION *(Posting_No, Skill)*

Posting_No: integer—unique position identifier
Skill: string—skill required for the position

Figure 5.4 Some Tuples from *EMPLOYEE, POSITION, DUTY_ALLOCATION relations.*

EMPLOYEE

Empl_No	*Name*	*Skill*	*Pay_Rate*
123456	Ron	waiter	7.50
123457	Jon	bartender	8.79
123458	Don	busboy	4.70
123459	Pam	hostess	4.90
123460	Pat	bellboy	4.70
123461	Ian	maître d'	9.00
123471	Pierre	chef	14.00
123472	Julie	chef	14.50

POSITION

Posting_No	*Skill*
321	waiter
322	bartender
323	busboy
324	hostess
325	maître d'
326	waiter
350	chef
351	chef

DUTY_ALLOCATION

Posting_No	*Empl_No*	*Day*	*Shift*
321	123456	19860419	1
322	123457	19860418	2
323	123458	19860418	1
321	123461	19860420	2
321	123461	19860419	2
350	123471	19860418	1
323	123458	19860420	3
351	123471	19860419	1

DUTY_ALLOCATION *(Posting_No, Empl_No, Day, Shift)*

Posting_No: integer—indicates the position assigned
Empl_No: integer—employee identifier
Day: date—in yyyymmdd format
Shift: integer—work day divided into shifts

5.2 SQL

Structured Query Language (SQL) originated with the System R project in 1974 at IBM's San Jose Research Center. The purpose of this project was to validate the feasibility of the relational model and to implement a DBMS based on this model. The results of this project are well documented in the database literature. In addition to contributing to the concept of query compilation and optimization and concurrency control mechanisms, the most salient result of this research project was the development of SQL. The System R project, concluded in 1979, was followed by the release of a number of commercial relational DBMS products from IBM. The first of these was SQL/DS for IBM's mid-range computers. Subsequently, DB2 was released for IBM's mainframe systems.

SQL (the original version was called SEQUEL and a predecessor of SEQUEL was named SQUARE) was the data definition and manipulation language for System R. SQL has emerged as the standard query language for relational DBMSs, and most of the commercial relational database management systems use SQL or a variant of SQL.

Response times and throughput in relational database applications have traditionally been slow, when compared to a similar application using network or hierarchical systems. This necessitated generating the best method for evaluating a query. A recent release of DB2 (version 2) promises a performance, measured in terms of throughput in real-time transaction processing, comparable to those available with the application using DBMSs based on other data models. This throughput, on IBM's 3090 600S six-processor running under the MVS/ESA operating system, is reported to be over 400 simple transactions per second and over 200 complex transactions per second. In addition, the new release of DB2 provides entity integrity, although full referential integrity is still not supported.

SQL is both the data definition and data manipulation language of a number of relational database systems (the IBM prototype System R, IBM's DB2 and SQL/DS, ORACLE, and many other commercial systems, including its recent introduction for INGRES), just as QUEL is for the INGRES RDBMS. SQL is based on tuple calculus, though not as closely as QUEL. SQL resembles relational algebra in some places and tuple calculus in others.

5.2.1 Data Definition: SQL

Data definition in SQL is via the **create** statement. The statement can be used to create a table, index, or view (i.e., a virtual table based on existing tables). To create a table, the create statement specifies the name of the table and the names and data types of each column of the table. Its format is:

create table <relation> (<attribute list>)

where the <attribute list> is specified as:

<attribute list> : : = <attribute name> (<data type>)[not null]
[,<attribute list>]

The data types supported by SQL depend on the particular implementation. However, the following data types are generally included: integer, decimal, real (i.e., floating point values), and character strings, both of fixed size and varying length. A number of ranges of values for the integer data type are generally supported, for example, integer and smallint. The decimal value declaration requires the specification of the total number of decimal digits for the value and (optionally), the number of digits to the right of the decimal point. The number of fractional decimal digits is assumed to be zero if only the total number of digits is specified.

<data type> : : = <integer>|<smallint>|<char(n)>|<varchar(n)>|
<float>|<decimal(p[,q])>

In addition, some implementations can support additional data types such as bit strings, graphical strings, logical, date, and time. Some DBMSs support the concept of date. One possible implementation of date could be as eight unsigned decimal digits representing the date in the yyyymmdd format. Here yyyy represents the year, mm represents the month and dd represents the day. Two dates can be compared to find the one that is larger and hence occurring later. The system ensures that only legal date values are inserted (19860536 for the date would be illegal) and functions are provided to perform operations such as adding a number of days to a date to come up with another date or subtracting a date from the current date to find the number of days, months, or years. Date constants are provided in either the format given above or as a character string in one of the following formats: mm/dd/yy; mm/dd/yyyy; dd-mmm-yy; dd-mmm-yyyy. In this text we represent a date constant as eight unsigned decimal digits in the format yyyymmdd.

The employee relation for the hotel database can be defined using the create table statement given below. Here, the *Empl_No* is specified to be **not null** to disallow this unique identifier from having a null value. SQL supports the concept of null values and, unless a column is declared with the not null option, it could be assigned a null value.

create table EMPLOYEE
 (*Empl_No* **integer not null,**
 Name **char**(25),
 Skill **char**(20),
 Pay_Rate **decimal**(10,2))

The definition of an existing relation can be altered by using the **alter** statement. This statement allows a new column to be added to an existing relation. The existing tuples of the altered relation are logically considered to be assigned the null value for the added column. The physical alteration occurs to a tuple only during an update of the record. The syntax of the alter statement and an example showing the attribute phone number added to the EMPLOYEE relation is given on the next page.

alter table existing-table-name
  add column-name data-type [, . . .]

alter table EMPLOYEE
  add *Phone_Number* **decimal** (10)

The **create index** statement allows the creation of an index for an already existing relation. The columns to be used in the generation of the index are also specified. The index is named and the ordering for each column used in the index can be specified as either ascending or descending. The **cluster** option could be specified to indicate that the records are to be placed in physical proximity to each other. The **unique** option specifies that only one record could exist at any time with a given value for the column(s) specified in the statement to create the index. (Even though this is just an access aid and a wrong place to declare the primary key.) Such columns, for instance, could form the primary key of the relation and hence duplicate tuples are not allowed. One case is the ORDR relation where the key is the combination of the attribute *Bill#, Dish#*. In the case of an existing relation, an attempt to create an index with the unique option will not succeed if the relation does not satisfy this uniqueness criterion. The syntax of the create index statement is shown below:

create [unique] index name-of-index
  on existing-table-name
    (column-name [**asc**ending or **desc**ending]
    [,column-name[order] . . .])
  [cluster]

The following statement causes an index called *empindex* to be built on the columns *Name* and *Pay_Rate*. The entries in the index are ascending by *Name* value and descending by *Pay_Rate*. In this example there are no restrictions on the number of records with the same *Name* and *Pay_Rate*.

create index *empindex*
  on EMPLOYEE (*Name* **asc,** *Pay_Rate* **desc);**

An existing relation or index could be deleted from the database by the **drop** SQL statement. The syntax of the drop statement is as follows:

drop table existing-table-name;
drop index existing-index-name;

5.3 Data Manipulation: SQL

In this section we present the data manipulation statements supported in SQL. Examples of their usage are given in subsequent sections. SQL provides the following basic data manipulation statements: select, update, delete, and insert.

Select Statement

The **select** statement, the only data retrieval statement in SQL, specifies the method of selecting the tuples of the relation(s). The tuples processed are from one or more relations specified by the from clause of the select statement; the selection predicates are specified by the where clause. The select statement could also specify the projection of the target tuples. Do not confuse the select verb of SQL with σ, the select operation of relational algebra. The difference is that the select statement entails selection, joins, and projection, whereas σ is a simple selection.

The syntax of the select statement is as follows:

select [distinct] <target list>
from <relation list>
[**where** <predicate>]

The **distinct** option is used in the select statement to eliminate duplicate tuples in the result. Without the distinct option duplicate tuples may appear in the result.

The <target list> is a method of specifying a projection operation of the result relation. It takes the form:

<target list> : : = <attribute name> [,<target list>]

The **from** clause specifies the relations to be used in the evaluation of the statement. It includes a relation list:

<relation list> : : = <relation name> [<tuple variable>]
[,<relation list>]

A tuple variable is an identifier; the domain of the tuple variable is the relation preceding it.

The **where** clause is used to specify the predicates involving the attributes of the relation appearing in the from clause.

An example of the use of a simple form of select to find the values for the attribute *Name* in the employee relation is given below:

select *Name*
from EMPLOYEE

The result of this select operation is a projection of the EMPLOYEE relation on the attribute *Name*. Unlike the theoretical version of projection, this projection contains duplicate tuples. The reason for not eliminating these duplicates is the large amount of processing time required to do so. If the theoretical equivalent is desired, however, the distinct clause is added to the select statement, as shown below:

select distinct *Name*
from EMPLOYEE

The predicates used to specify selection are added to a select statement by the use of the where clause. Additional features and examples of the select statement will be discussed in following sections.

Update Statement

The **update** statement is used to modify one or more records in a specified relation. The records to be modified are specified by a predicate in a where clause and the new value of the column(s) to be modified is specified by a **set** clause. The syntax of the update statement is shown on the next page.

update <relation> **set** <target_value_list>
[**where** <predicate>]

where the <target value list> is of the form:

<target value list> : : = <attribute name> = <value expression>
[,<target value list>]

The following statement changes the *Pay_Rate* of the employee Ron in the EMPLOYEE relation of Figure 5.4:

update EMPLOYEE
set *Pay_Rate* = 7.85
where *Name* = 'Ron'

Delete Statement

The **delete** statement is used to delete one or more records from a relation. The records to be deleted are specified by the predicate in the where clause. The syntax of the delete statement is given below:

delete <relation> [**where** <predicate>]

The following statement deletes the tuple for employee Ron in the EMPLOYEE relation of Figure 5.4.

delete EMPLOYEE
where *Name* = *'Ron'*

If the where clause is left out, all the tuples in the relation are deleted. In this case, the relation is still known to the database although it is an empty relation. A relation along with its tuples could be deleted by the drop statement.

Insert Statement

The **insert** statement is used to insert a new tuple into a specified relation. The value of each field of the record to be inserted is either specified by an expression or could come from selected records of existing relations. The format of the insert statement is given below:

insert into <relation>
values (<value list>)

where the <value list> takes the form:

<value list> : : = <value expression> [,<value list>]

In another form of the insert statement, a list of attribute names whose values are included in the <value list> are specified:

insert into <relation> (<target list>)
values (<value list>)

and the <target list> takes the form:

<target list> : : = <attribute name> [,<target list>]

The **value** clause can be replaced by a select statement, which is evaluated, and the result is inserted into the relation specified in the insert statement.

The following statement reinserts a tuple for the employee Ron in the EMPLOYEE relation of Figure 5.4:

insert into EMPLOEE
    values (123456, 'Ron', 'waiter', 7.50)

5.3.1 Basic Data Retrieval

The SQL mapping operation basically consists of a selection and join followed by a projection. The select verb of SQL is used to represent this mapping operation.

Example 5.1

Here we give two simple examples of the data retrieval operation.

(a) The *Posting_No* and *Empl_No* values from the DUTY_ALLOCATION relation can be retrieved by the SQL statement shown below. For the DUTY_ALLOCATION table of Figure 5.4, the statement produces the result shown in part i of Figure A.

select *Posting_No, Empl_No*
from DUTY_ALLOCATION

The above query resembles the relational algebra projection operation. This is not strictly a projection because duplicates are not removed, as shown in part i of Figure A. Duplicates may be removed by using the distinct option in the select statement, as indicated on page 218. The distinct option is applied to the entire result relation *(Posting_No, Empl_No)*. The result of this statement is shown in part ii of Figure A.

Figure A (i) A simple projection via select with duplicates tuples; (ii) Eliminating duplicate tuple by the distinct clause in the select statement.

Posting_No	*Empl_No*
321	123456
322	123457
323	123458
321	123461
321	123461
350	123471
351	123471

(i)

Posting_No	*Empl_No*
321	123456
322	123457
323	123458
321	123461
350	123471
351	123471

(ii)

```
select distinct Posting_No, Empl_No
from DUTY_ALLOCATION
```

(b) "Get complete details from DUTY_ALLOCATION."

```
select *
from DUTY_ALLOCATION
```

The asterisk character is used as shorthand for the full attribute list. The result of this statement is the entire DUTY_ALLOCATION relation shown in Figure 5.4. ■

5.3.2 Condition Specification

SQL supports the following Boolean and comparison operators: **and, or, not,** =, ≠ (not equal), >, ≥, >, ≤. These operators allow the formulation of more complex predicates, which are attached to the select statement by the where clause. Such predicates in the where clause specify the selection of specific tuples and/or a join of tuples from two relations (i.e., they provide the capability of the selection and join operations of relational algebra). If more than one of the Boolean operators appear together, not has the highest priority while **or** has the lowest. Parentheses may be used to indicate the desired order of evaluation.

Example 5.2 "Get DUTY_ALLOCATION details for *Empl_No* 123461 for the month of April 1986." This query is given on page 219. The result of the query is shown in part i of Figure B.

Figure B (i) Selecting specified tuples followed by projection; (ii) Ordering the result; (iii) Selecting tuples specified by disjunctive predicates.

Posting_No	*Shift*	*Day*
321	2	19860420
321	2	19860419

(i)

Posting_No	*Shift*	*Day*
321	2	19860419
321	2	19860420

(ii)

Posting_No	*Empl_No*	*Day*	*Shift*
321	123461	19860420	2
321	123461	19860419	2
323	123458	19860420	3

(iii)

select *Posting_No, Shift, Day*
from DUTY_ALLOCATION
where *Empl_No* = 123461 **and**
Day >19860401 **and**
Day ≤19860430

If the result had to be rearranged, the order clause could be specified as shown below. The result of this statement on our sample database is shown in part ii of Figure B.

select *Posting_No, Shift, Day*
from DUTY_ALLOCATION
where *Empl_No* = *123461*
order by *Day* **asc**

The following statement selects the posting information about employee 123461 for the month of April 1986, as well as for all employees for shift 3 regardless of dates. The result of this statement on our sample database is shown in part iii of Figure B.

select *
from DUTY_ALLOCATION
where (*Empl_No* = 123461 **and**
Day >19860401 **and**
Day ≤9860430) **or**
(*Shift* = 3) ■

5.3.3 Arithmetic and Aggregate Operators

SQL provides a full complement of arithmetic operators and functions. This includes functions to find the average, minimum, maximum, sum, and to count the number of occurrences.

Let us first consider the SQL facility to specify arithmetic operations on attribute values.

Example 5.3

Consider the relation SALARY(*Empl_No, Pay_Rate, Hours*), used for computing the weekly salary in our sample database. Part of this relation is shown in part i of Figure C. Consider the evaluation of the weekly salary (gross). This operation can be expressed in SQL as shown below. The result of this statement is shown in part ii of Figure C.

select *Empl_No, Pay_Rate*Hours*
from SALARY
where *Hours* > 0.0

Figure C (i) The SALARY relation; (ii) Result of computing the weekly salary.

SALARY:

Empl_No	*Pay_Rate*	*Hours*
123456	7.50	40.5
123457	8.79	42.5
123458	4.70	47.5
123459	4.90	0.0
123460	4.70	48.0
123461	9.00	48.0
123471	14.00	42.7
123472	14.50	45.5

(i)

result:

Empl_No	*Pay_Rate* Hours*
123456	303.50
123457	373.58
123458	223.25
123460	225.60
123461	432.00
123471	597.80
123472	659.75

(ii) ■

SQL also provides the following set of built-in functions. The operand of each of these functions is a column of an existing relation. Null values are ignored except in the case of count(∗). The functions are described below; examples are given in Example 5.4.

- **count:** This function must be used either with the distinct option of the select statement or as count(∗). When used with the distinct option, it counts the number of distinct values in the column. If the total number of rows in a relation is to be determined, count(∗) must be used.
- **sum:** The operand of this function must have a numeric value. It finds the sum of these values. If the distinct option is specified, the duplicate values are ignored in computing the result.
- **avg:** The operand of this function must have a numeric value. It finds the average of these values. If the distinct option is specified, the duplicate values are not used for computing the average.
- **min:** This function finds the minimum of the values in the column. The distinct option has no effect on this function.
- **max:** This function finds the maximum of the values in the column. The distinct option has no effect on this function.

In some of the following examples, the predicate has been omitted and the aggregate operations are carried out on the complete relation, except tuples that have null values in the argument. The distinct option may be specified with the argument to eliminate duplicates. Distinct must be specified with the arguments for count; count(*) is provided to count all rows without null or duplicate elimination.

Example 5.4

(a) "Get Average *Dish_Price*."

select avg *(Price)*
from MENU

For the menu relation shown in Figure 5.2, the result of this statement is 10.90.

(b) "Get minimum and maximum dish prices."

select min *(Price),* **max** *(Price)*
from MENU

For the menu relation shown in Figure 5.2, the result of this statement is 2.50 and 19.50.

(c) The average pay rate for employees can be derived using the following SQL statement.

select avg *(Pay_rate)*
from EMPLOYEE

For the EMPLOYEE relation shown in Figure 5.4 the result of this statement, as shown below, is a relation of arity and cardinality one:

result

avg (*Pay_Rate*)
8.51

(d) "Find the average pay rate for employees working as a chef.

select avg *(Pay_Rate)*
from EMPLOYEE
where *Skill* = 'chef'

For the employee relation shown in Figure 5.4, the result of this statement is 14.25.

(e) "Get the number of distinct pay rates from the EMPLOYEE relation."

select count(distinct *Pay_Rate)*
from EMPLOYEE

For the Employee relation shown in Figure 5.4, the result of this statement is 7. ■

5.3.4 SQL Join: Multiple Tables Queries

SQL does not have a direct representation of the join operation. However, the type of join can be specified by an appropriate predicate in the where clause of a select statement, wherein the relations to be joined are specified in the from clause. The join is performed by using the appropriate tuples of the participating relations, followed by selection and projection. Consider the following SQL statement. The relation name precedes the attribute name, the two being separated by a period. This method of qualifying is used to distinguish identical attribute names.

select $T_1.a_{11}, \ldots T_1.a_{1n}, T_2.a_{21}, \ldots, T_2.a_{2m}$
from T_1, T_2,
where $T_1.a_{1j} = T_2.a_{2k} \ldots$

This statement is evaluated[1] by performing a cartesian product of the tables T_1, T_2, and thence the tuples satisfying the where clause are selected. These tuples are then projected on the attributes $T_1.a_{11}$, . . . $T_1.a_{1n}$, $T_2.a_{21}$, . . . $T_2.a_{2m}$. The relational algebraic form of this statement is

$$\pi_{a_{11}, \ldots, a_{1n}, a_{21}, \ldots, a_{2m}} (T_1 \underset{a_{1j} = a_{2k} \ldots}{\bowtie} T_2)$$

In general the select statement represents the following relational algebraic operations where X is the cartesian product of the relations represented by the **from** list.

$$\pi_{\text{(represented by the target list)}}\sigma_{\text{(represented by the } \textbf{where} \text{ clause)}}(X))$$

Joins involving more than two relations can be similarly encoded in SQL. Queries of this form need data from more than one relation. In the case where the join involves a relation with itself, the query needs data from more than one record of the same relation.

Example 5.5

The following SQL query is used to retrieve the shift details for employee Ron:

> **select** *Posting_No, Day, Shift*
> **from** DUTY_ALLOCATION, EMPLOYEE
> **where** DUTY_ALLOCATION.*Empl_No* = EMPLOYEE.*Empl_no*
> **and** *Name* = 'Ron'

Note that attributes *Empl_No* have been qualified, since the names of these attributes are identical. The result of the query on the DUTY_ALLOCATION, EMPLOYEE tables of Figure 5.4 is the triple (321, 19860419, 1). ■

SQL uses the concept of tuple variable from relational calculus. In SQL a tuple variable is defined in the from clause of the select statement. The syntax of the declaration requires that the name of the tuple variable be declared after the relation name in the from clause, as shown below:

from relation_name$_1$ tv$_1$ [,relation_name$_2$ tv$_2$, . . .]

We use tuple variables in Example 5.6 to compare two tuples of the relation EMPLOYEE. The two tuple variables e_1, and e_2 are defined on the same relation.

Example 5.6

"Get employees whose rate of pay is more than or equal to the rate of pay of employee Pierre."

> **select** e_1.*Name*, e_1.Pay_Rate
> **from** EMPLOYEE e_1, EMPLOYEE e_2

[1]This is a conceptual explanation. The actual evaluation of the query may be optimized.

```
where e1.Pay_Rate > e2.Pay_Rate
    and e2.Name = 'Pierre'
```

The result of this query for the EMPLOYEE table shown in Figure 5.4 is the tuple (Julie, 14.50). ■

Now we turn to an example of a join involving one relation.

Example 5.7

"Compile all pairs of *Posting_Nos* requiring the same Skill."

```
select p1.Posting_No, p2.Posting_No
from POSITION p1 POSITION p2
where p1.Skill = p2.Skill
   and p1.Posting_No < p2.Posting_No
```

p_1. *Posting_No*	p_2. *Posting_No*
321	326
350	351

For the POSITION table of Figure 5.4, this SQL statement generates the result shown above. *Posting_Nos* 321 and 326 require a skill of waiter and *Posting_Nos* 350 and 351 require a skill of chef. The predicate p_1.*Posting_No* < p_2.*Posting_No* is used to avoid including tuples such as (326, 321), (350,350), (351,350), etc., in the result. ■

The following is an example that requires joining two relations.

Example 5.8

Consider the requirement to generate the eligibility of employees to fill a given position. Each position *(Posting_No)* requires a skill and only those employees who have this skill are eligible to fill that position. Thus to generate the position eligibility relation, we are required to join the relations EMPLOYEE and POSITION for equal values of the common attribute *Skill*. The following SQL statement implements the join. The result of the join is shown on the next page.

```
select EMPLOYEE.Empl_No,POSITION.Posting_No,POSITION.Skill
from EMPLOYEE, POSITION
where EMPLOYEE.Skill = POSITION.Skill
```

EMPLOYEE. *Empl_No*	POSITION. *Posting_No*	POSITION. *Skill*
123456	321	waiter
123456	326	waiter
123457	322	bartender
123458	323	busboy
123459	324	hostess
123461	325	maître d'
123471	350	chef
123471	351	chef
123472	350	chef
123472	351	chef

■

The following is an example of joining three relations.

Example 5.9

Consider the requirement to generate the itemized bill for table 12 for the date 19860419. This requires details from three relations, BILL, ORDR, and MENU. The itemized bill can be generated using the following query. The result is shown in Figure D.

Figure D Itemized bill

result

Bill#	*Dish_Description*	*Price*	*Qty*	*Price**Qty
9234	Coffee	2.50	2	5.00
9234	Club sandwich	10.50	2	21.00

```
select BILL.Bill#, MENU.Dish_Description, MENU.Price,
              ORDR.Qty, MENU.Price*ORDR.Qty
from BILL, MENU, ORDR
where BILL.Bill# = ORDR.Bill#
   and ORDR.Dish# = MENU.Dish
   and BILL.Table# = 12
   and BILL.Day = 19860419
```

A select statement can be nested in another select statement. The result of the nested select statement is a relation that can be used by the outer select statement. An alternate method of generating this itemized bill is by using the nested select statement (which forms a sub-query) as shown below:

```
select ORDR.Bill#, MENU.Dish_Description, MENU.Price,
              ORDR.Qty, MENU.Price*ORDR.Qty
```

from MENU, ORDR
where ORDR.*Dish#* = MENU.*Dish#*
and ORDR.*Bill#* =
(**select** BILL.*Bill#*
from BILL
where BILL.*Table#* = 12
and BILL.*Day* = 19860419) ■

5.3.5 Set Manipulation

SQL provides a number of set operators: any, in, all, exists, not exists, union, minus, intersect, and contains. These constructs, based on the operations used in relational calculus and relational algebra, are used for testing the membership of a value in a set of values, or the membership of a tuple in a set of tuples, or the membership of one set of values in another set of values. When using these operators, remember that the SQL statement ''select . . .'' returns a set of tuples (which is a set of values in cases where the target list is a single attribute). We describe these set manipulation operators below and illustrate them with a number of examples.

Any

The operator **any** allows the testing of a value against a set of values. The comparisons can be one of $\{<, \leq, >, \geq, =, \neq\}$, and are specified in SQL as the operators, <any, ≤any, >any, ≥any, =any, and ≠any (not equal to any). We refer to any one of these operators by the notation θany.

In general, the condition

c **θany (select X from . . .)**

evaluates to true if and only if the comparison ''c θany {at least one value from the result of the select X from . . . }''is true.[2] Let us illustrate this condition with the following example:

Example 5.10 Let the result of

select X
from rel
where P

be the set of values {'30', '40', '60', '70'}. Then the following statements, which compare the two sets on both sides of the θany operators, are valid and give the result indicated on the next page.

[2]The implementation of any and all leads to some confusion since ≠any actually is implemented, in some systems, to be not equal to some (any one of the set of values). For example {'50'} ≠any ({'30', '40', '50', '70'}) is evaluated to true since 50 ≠ 30. To justify this implementation, some is used as an alias for any in these systems! Such an implementation tends to give results that do not agree with the interpretation given here.

'50' =**any** ({'30', '40', '60', '70'}) is false
'50' =**any** ({'30', '40', '50', '70'}) is true
'69' <**any** ({'30', '40', '60', '70'}) is true
'29' >**any** ({'30', '40', '60', '70'}) is false
'31' >**any** ({'30', '40;', '60', '70'}) is true
'50' ≠**any** ({'30', '40', '60', '70'}) is true
'50' ≠**any** ({'30', '40', '50', '70'}) is false ■

Example 5.11 illustrates the use of θany operator.

Example 5.11

"Get the names and pay rates of employees with *Empl_No* less than 123460 whose rate of pay is more than the rate of pay of at least one employee with *Empl_No* greater than or equal to 123460." This query can be expressed as given below. Here we are using a nested form of the SQL query. The expression in the parentheses is evaluated first to give a set containing the *Pay_Rates* for employees with *Empl_No* greater than or equal to 123460. For the EMPLOYEE relation shown in Figure 5.4, this gives the set {4.70, 9.00, 14.00, 14.50} for the right-hand side of the >any test. For the EMPLOYEE relation shown in Figure 5.4, the result relation is shown below. Employee 123458 does not appear in the result since his pay rate of 4.70 is not greater than any value in the above set.

Result

Name	*Pay_Rate*
Ron	7.50
Jon	8.79
Pam	4.90

```
select Name, Pay_Rate
from EMPLOYEE
where Empl_No < 123460 and
      Pay_Rate >any
    (select Pay_Rate
       from EMPLOYEE
       where Empl_No ≥ 123460)
```
■

In the SQL query formulation used in Example 5.11, we used the nested queries. This is a powerful query formulation tool.

In

The operator **in,** equivalent to =**any,** tests for the membership of a value within a set. An example of its use is given in Example 5.12.

Example 5.12

"Get employees who are working either on the date 19860419 or 19860420."

```
select Empl_No
from DUTY_ALLOCATION
where Day in (19860419,19860420)
```

This query is equivalent to the following query involving two predicates connected with an or operator:

```
select Empl_No
from DUTY_ALLOCATION
where Day = 19860419
    or Day = 19860420
```

The same query can be expressed in another, albeit convoluted, way:

```
select Empl_No
from DUTY_ALLOCATION
where Day in
        (select Day
        from DUTY_ALLOCATION
        where Day =19860419 or Day =19860420)
```

The in test could also be replaced by =**any.** ■

Contains

The set operator in tests the membership of a single value within a set of values, but the operator **contains** is used to test for the containment of one set in another. For instance, the expression X contains Y tests whether or not set X is a superset of set Y and, consequently, X contains at least all those elements contained in Y. If set X contains set Y, the expression evaluates to true. An example of the use of contains is given below in Example 5.13.

This set operator is not always available in all implementations of SQL. However, it can be simulated using the **not exists** operator as shown below in Example 5.18b.

Example 5.13

"Find the names of employees who are assigned to all positions that require a chef's skill."

```
select e.Name
from EMPLOYEE e
where
        (select Posting_No
        from DUTY_ALLOCATION d
        where e.Empl_No = d.Empl_No)
        contains
```

```
(select p.Posting_No
from POSITION p
where p.Skill = 'chef')
```

Here the first nested subquery finds the positions where an employee is assigned. The second nested subquery finds the set of positions requiring a chef's skill. The main select statement considers each employee and for that employee finds all the positions and tests if this is a superset of the positions requiring a chef's skill. If this test evaluates to a true value, the attribute *Name* is output. For our sample database, the result of this query is (Pierre). ■

All

The set operator **all** is used, in general, to show that the condition

c θ**all (select X from . . .)**

evaluates to true. This is so, if and only if the comparison "c θ all the values from the result of **(select X from . . .)**" is true. We illustrate the various format of this condition in the following example:

Example 5.14 Let the result of:

```
select X
from rel
where P
```

be the set of values {'30', '40', '60', '70'}. Then each of the following statements is valid and produces the results indicated:

'50' =**all** ({'30', '40', '60', '70'}) is false
'29' <**all** ({'30', '40', '60', '70'}) is true
'50' ≠**all** ({'30', '40', '60', '70'}) is true
'70' >**all** ({'30', '40', '60', '70'}) is false
'70' ≥**all** ({'30', '40', '60', '70'}) is true ■

Example 5.15 below uses the all condition to find the employee with the lowest pay rate from the EMPLOYEE relation.

Example 5.15 "Find the employees with the lowest pay rate."

```
select Empl_No, Name, Pay_Rate
from EMPLOYEE
where Pay_Rate ≤all
      (select Pay_Rate
      from EMPLOYEE)
```

Empl_No	*Name*	*Pay_Rate*
123458	Don	4.70
123460	Pat	4.70

Here we use a nested version of the select statement. The second select statement produces the set of values {7.50, 8.79, 4.70, 4.90, 4.70, 9.0, 14.00, 14.50}. The first select uses this to compare the *Pay_Rate* of each record of EMPLOYEE to determine if it is ≤all of this set. The result of the query is shown above. ■

A variation of the above example is given below.

Example 5.16 "Get the names of chefs paid at the minimum *Pay_Rate*." We first find the pay rates for all chefs:

> **select** *Pay_Rate*
> **from** EMPLOYEE
> **where** *Skill* = 'chef'

This query returns a set of values and if we compare it with the pay rates of all chefs we get the desired result: (Pierre):

> **select** *Name*
> **from** EMPLOYEE
> **where** *Skill* = 'chef' **and**
> *Pay_Rate* ≤**all**
> (**select** *Pay_Rate*
> **from** EMPLOYEE
> **where** *Skill* = 'chef') ■

Not In

The set operator **not in** is equivalent to ≠all.

Not Contains

The set operator **not contains,** the complement of contains, is true if one set of values is not a superset of another set of values.

Exists

The set operator **exists** is the SQL version of the existential quantifier. The expression

exists (select X from . . .)

evaluates to true if and only if the result of "select X from . . . " is not empty.

Example 5.17 "Find the names and the rate of pay of all employees who are allocated a duty." This query can be expressed in SQL using the exists set operator.

```
select Name, Pay_Rate
from EMPLOYEE
where exists
(select *
from DUTY_ALLOCATION
where EMPLOYEE.Empl_No =
    DUTY_ALLOCATION.Empl_No)
```

Name	*Pay_Rate*
Ron	7.50
Jon	8.79
Don	4.70
Ian	9.00
Pierre	14.00

In this example, for each employee tuple from the EMPLOYEE relation, the exists clause is evaluated. If there is at least one tuple in DUTY_ALLOCATION for that employee, the second select statement will produce a nonempty result whereby the exists expression evaluates to the true value. There is a reference to the relation of the first from clause in the second select statement. This reference is made through the use of qualified column names. The result of this query for the relations shown in Figure 5.4 is given above. Notice that this query could be easily handled using a join. ■

Not Exists

The set operator **not exists** is the complement form of exists. The expression

not exists (select X from . . .)

evaluates to true if and only if the result of "select X from . . . " is empty.

The universal quantifier, $\forall$ is not directly implemented in SQL but can be indirectly implemented using the identity:

$$\forall x(f(x)) \equiv \neg\exists x(\neg f(x))$$

In other words, we implement the predicate, $\forall x(f(x))$, by not exist $x(\neg f(x))$. An example of the use of not exists to implement the universal quantifier is given in Example 5.18b.

Example 5.18

(a) "Find the names and the rate of pay of all employees who are not allocated a duty." This query can be expressed in SQL using the not exists set operator.

select *Name, Pay_Rate*
from EMPLOYEE
where not exists
(select *
from DUTY_ALLOCATION
where EMPLOYEE.*Empl_No* =
DUTY_ALLOCATION.*Empl_No*)

Name	*Pay_Rate*
Pam	4.90
Pat	4.70
Julie	14.50

In this example, for each employee tuple from the EMPLOYEE relation, the not exists clause is evaluated. If there is at least one tuple in DUTY_ALLOCATION for that employee, the second select statement produces a nonempty result whereby the not exists expression evaluates to the false value. The tuple is not included in the result, which is shown above.

The query can also be expressed using not in, as illustrated below:

select EMPLOYEE.*Name,* EMPLOYEE.*Pay_Rate*
from EMPLOYEE
where EMPLOYEE.*Empl_No* **not in**
(select DUTY_ALLOCATION.*Empl_No*
from DUTY_ALLOCATION)

(b) "Find the names of employees who are assigned to all positions that require a chef's skill." The tuple calculus expression for this query can be written as:

$$\{e[Name] | e \in \text{EMPLOYEE} \wedge \forall p(p \in \text{POSITION} \wedge p[Skill] = \text{'chef'} \rightarrow \exists d\,(d \in \text{DUTY\_ALLOCATION} \wedge d[Posting\_No] = p[Posting\_No] \wedge e[Empl\_No] = d[Empl\_No]))\}$$

Using $\forall x(f) \equiv \neg\exists x(\neg f)$, we can rewrite the tuple calculus expression as:

$$\{e[Name] | e \in \text{EMPLOYEE} \wedge \neg\exists p(\neg(p \in \text{POSITION} \wedge p[Skill] = \text{'chef'} \rightarrow \exists d\,(d \in \text{DUTY\_ALLOCATION} \wedge d[Posting\_No] = p[Posting\_No] \wedge e[Empl\_No]\ d[Empl\_No]))))\}$$

An alternate method of writing this query without the logical implication is to replace $f \rightarrow g$ by its equivalent form $\neg f \vee g$ to give the following expression:

$$\{e[Name] | e \in \text{EMPLOYEE} \wedge \neg\exists p(\neg(\neg(p \in \text{POSITION} \wedge p[Skill] = \text{'chef'}) \vee \exists d\,(d \in \text{DUTY\_ALLOCATION} \wedge d[Posting\_No] = p[Posting\_No] \wedge e[Empl\_No] = d[Empl\_No]))))\}$$

which is equivalent to:

$$\{e[Name] | e \in \text{EMPLOYEE} \wedge \neg\exists p(p \in \text{POSITION} \wedge p[Skill] = \text{'chef'} \wedge \neg\exists d\,(d \in \text{DUTY\_ALLOCATION} \wedge d[Posting\_No] = p[Posting\_No] \wedge e[Empl\_No] = d[Empl\_No]))\}$$

This expression can be converted to SQL using not exists:

```
select e.Name
from EMPLOYEE e
where not exists
        (select p.Posting_No
        from POSITION p
        where p.Skill = 'chef'
        and not exists
        (select d.Empl_No
        from DUTY_ALLOCATION d
        where d.Posting_No = p.Posting_No
        and e.Empl_No = d.Empl_No ))
```

Here the first (outer) nested subquery finds the positions requiring a chef's skill. For each such position, the second (inner) nested subquery finds if the employee whose name is to be output is assigned to that position. If the result of the second nested subquery is empty (i.e., the employee being considered is not assigned to a position requiring the skill of a chef), the second not exists evaluates to true, causing the first not exists to evaluate to false, and the employee is not selected. In effect, we are saying that for those employees whose names are to be output, if there exists a position requiring a skill of chef, then there exists a tuple in DUTY_ALLOCATION where this position is assigned to that employee. If these combined tests evaluate to a true value, the attribute *Name* of the employee is output. For our sample database, the result of this query is (Pierre). We will get identical results even if a tuple such as (350, 123472, 19860420,1) were inserted in the DUTY_ALLOCATION relation. ■

Union

The traditional set theory union operator is **union.** Duplicates are removed from the result of a union.

Example 5.19 "Get employees who are waiters or work at *Posting_No 321.*"

```
(select Empl_No
from EMPLOYEE
where Skill = 'waiter')
union
   (select Empl_No
   from DUTY_ALLOCATION
   where Posting_No = 321
```

■

Empl_No
123456
123461

Minus

The traditional set theory difference operator is **minus.**

Example 5.20

(a) "Get employee numbers of persons who work at *Posting_No* 321, but don't have the skill of waiter". This query, which uses the minus operator, and its results are shown below:

```
(select distinct Empl_No
from DUTY_ALLOCATION
where Posting_No = 321)
    minus
      (select Empl_No
      from EMPLOYEE
      where Skill = 'waiter')
```

Empl_No
123461

(b) "Get a list of employees not assigned a duty."

```
(select Empl_No
 from EMPLOYEE )
 minus
      (select Empl_No
      from DUTY_ALLOCATION)
```

■

Empl_No
123459
123460
123472

Intersect

The traditional set theory set intersection operator is **intersect.**

Example 5.21

"Get a list of the names of employees with the skill of chef who are assigned a duty."

```
select Name
from EMPLOYEE
where Empl_No in
   ((select Empl_No
   from EMPLOYEE
   where Skill = 'chef')
   intersect
(select Empl_No
from DUTY_ALLOCATION))
```

Name
Pierre

The result for the sample database of Figure 5.4 is given above. ■

5.3.6 Categorization

It is sometimes necessary to classify a relation into a number of groups. Each such group of tuples has a certain common property. Aggregation functions such as average, sum, and so on can be applied to each group instead of to the entire relation. SQL provides the **group by** function to allow data to be classified into categories. The aggregation functions are performed separately for each category or group. Each element in the list attached to the select clause of the select statement with the group by function must have a single value per group. The having option can be added to the group by function to specify a predicate to eliminate those elements that do not satisfy the predicate. The having option must have only one value for each group. The where clause could be used to specify predicates that would select those tuples of the relation to be considered in the categorization.

The having option usually appears with the group by function. If the having option appears without the group by function, the entire relation is treated as a single group.

Example 5.22

Consider the sample database given in Figures 5.2 and 5.4.

(a) The following SQL query generates the total charge for table 12 for the date 19860419. The result of this query for our database is the tuple (9234, 19860419, 26.00).

```
select BILL.Bill#, BILL.Day, sum(MENU.Price*ORDR.Qty)
from BILL, MENU, ORDR
where BILL.Bill# ORDR.Bill#
   and ORDR.Dish# = MENU.Dish#
   and BILL.Table# = 12
   and BILL.Day = 19860419
   group by BILL.Bill#, BILL.Day
```

We illustrate the group by function and the having option using the following queries requiring the categorization of a relation or selected tuples of the relation.

(b) "Get a count of different employees on each shift."

```
select Shift, count (distinct Empl_No)
from DUTY_ALLOCATION
group by Shift
```

Shift	count
1	4
2	3
3	1

For the DUTY_ALLOCATION relation of Figure 5.4, the result of this statement is as shown above.

(c) "Get employee numbers of all employees working on at least two dates."

```
select Empl_No
from DUTY_ALLOCATION
group by Empl_No
having count (*) > 1
```

Empl_No
123458
123461
123471

For the DUTY_ALLOCATION relation of Figure 5.4, the re
statement is as shown above.

(d) "Get employee numbers and dates for all employees working on 19860418 and at least one other date."

```
select Empl_No, Day
from DUTY_ALLOCATION
where Empl_No in
    (select Empl_No
    from DUTY_ALLOCATION
    where Empl_No in
        (select Empl_No
        from DUTY_ALLOCATION
        where Day = 19860418)
    group by Empl_No
    having count (*) > 1)
```

Empl_no	*Day*
123458	19860418
123458	19860420
123471	19860418
123471	19860419

For the DUTY_ALLOCATION relation of Figure 5.4, the result of this statement is as shown above. Here, the inner nested select statement is used to find those employees who are working on 19860418. For our sample relation it gives the set {123457, 123458, 123471}. The where clause of the second select statement is used to eliminate tuples of DUTY_ALLOCATION where the *Empl_No* is not in the set. Only the tuples not so eliminated are considered for the grouping. The having count(*) > 1 eliminates the group of employees working only on 19860418. The result of the second select statement is the set {123458, 123471}. The outer select statement is used to provide multiple *Day* values per group ■

5.3.7 Updates

SQL includes three update statements to modify the data. These are the **insert, update,** and **delete statements.** In Section 5.3, we saw the syntax of these statements. Here we give some examples of their usage.

Example 5.23

(a) "Insert a tuple in the BILL relation with *Bill#* 9234 for *Table#* 12 on *Day* 19860419, where the waiter is 123456."

```
insert into BILL (Bill#, Day, Waiter#, Table#)
    values (9234, 19860419, 123456, 12)
```

The attributes given in the statement above are ordered differently from those in the relation scheme. The values for these attributes are given in the value clause. The remaining attributes are set to null.

(b) "Insert a DUTY_ALLOCATION tuple for *Posting_No* 321, *Empl_No* 123456, *Shift* 2, and *Day* 86/04/22."

```
insert into DUTY_ALLOCATION
    values (321, 123456, 19860422, 2)
```

The same insertion can also be specified as:

```
insert into DUTY_ALLOCATION (Empl_No, Shift, Day,
                             Posting_No)
values (123456, 2, 19860422, 321) ■
```

Note that in the second format of the insert statement, the attribute names may appear in a different order than in the relation. The latter format of the insert statement is used where data values for all the attributes are not being specified. The attributes whose values are not explicitly specified are assigned the NULL value.

Example 5.24 (a) "Copy all tuples from DUTY_ALLOCATION into NEW_DUTY_ALLOCATION," is specified as shown below. Here the attributes of NEW_DUTY_ALLOCATION are those specified in a create statement for it. In this example these attributes are compatible to those in DUTY_ALLOCATION.

```
insert into NEW_DUTY_ALLOCATION:
    select *
    from DUTY_ALLOCATION
```

(b) "Create a relation of duty records for shift 1."

```
insert into SHIFT1_DUTY_ALLOCATION:
    select *
    from DUTY_ALLOCATION
    where Shift = 1
```

(c) "Increase the rate of pay of all employees by 10%."

```
update EMPLOYEE
set Pay_Rate = 1.1 * Pay_Rate
```

(d) "Increase the rate of pay of waiters by 10%."

```
update EMPLOYEE
set Pay_Rate = 1.1 * Pay_Rate
where Skill = 'waiter'
```

(e) "Remove employee record for *Empl_No* 123457."

```
delete EMPLOYEE
where Empl_No = 123457
```

(f) "Remove all EMPLOYEE records and retain the relation."

```
delete EMPLOYEE
```

(g) "Remove all EMPLOYEE records and drop the relation."

```
drop EMPLOYEE ■
```

5.4 Views: SQL

We have seen how users can manipulate the relations stored in the database. In examples presented so far, we have been manipulating the conceptual or ''physical''[3] relations. Such conceptual relations are sometimes referred to as **base relations.** Corresponding to each of these base relations there exists one (or more) physical record(s) in one (or more) data file(s). Sometimes, for security and other concerns, it is undesirable to have all users see the entire relation. It would also be beneficial if we could create useful relations for different groups of users, rather than have them all manipulate the base relations. Any relation that is not a part of the physical database, i.e., a virtual relation, is made available to the users as a **view.** It is possible to create views in SQL. A relation in a view is virtual since no corresponding physical relation exists. A view represents a different perspective of a base relation or relations.

The result of a query operation on one or more base relations is a relation. Therefore, if a user needs a particular view based on the base relations, it can be defined using a query expression. To be useful, we assign the view a name and relate it to the query expression:

create view <view name> **as** <query expression>

A view is a relation (virtual rather than base) and can be used in query expressions, that is, queries can be written using the view as a relation. Views generally are not stored, since the data in the base relations may change. The base relations on which a view is based are sometimes called the **existing relations.** The definition of a view in a **create view** statement is stored in the system catalog. Having been defined, it can be used as if the view really represented a real relation. However, such a virtual relation defined by a view is recomputed whenever a query refers to it.

Example 5.25

(a) For reasons of confidentiality, not all users are permitted to see the *Pay_Rate* of an employee. For such users the DBA can create a view, for example, EMP_VIEW defined as:

```
create view EMP_VIEW as
    (select Empl_No, Name, Skill
    from EMPLOYEE)
```

(b) A view can be created for a subset of the tuples of a relation, as in this example. For assigning employees to particular jobs, the manager requires a list of the employees who have not been assigned to any jobs:

```
create view FREE as
    (select Empl_No
    from EMPLOYEE)
```

[3]By physical we mean that the relation corresponds to some stored data. This data may not be stored as a table and may actually be split horizontally or vertically and reside on one or more storage devices (at one or more sites).

```
minus
(select Empl_No
from DUTY_ALLOCATION)
```

(c) The view in part b above can also be created using the following statements:

```
create view FREE as
    (select Empl_No
    from EMPLOYEE)
    where Empl_No ≠ any
    (select Empl_No
    from DUTY_ALLOCATION) ■
```

In the above examples, the names of the attributes in the views are implicitly taken from the base relation. The data types of the attribute of the view are inherited from the corresponding attributes in the base relation. We can, however, give new names to the attributes of the view. This is illustrated in the syntax of the create view statement given below:

```
create view VIEW_NAME
   (Name1, Name2, . . . )
   as ( select . . . )
```

Here the attributes in the view are given as *Name1, Name2, . . .* and these names are associated with the existing relation by order correspondence. The definition of a view is accomplished by means of a subquery involving a select statement as given in the syntax above. Since a view can be used in a select statement, a view can be defined on another existing view.

We could use French names for the relation and some of its attributes for the view defined in Example 5.24(a) above by modifying the view definition as follows:

```
create view EMPLOYE
    (Nom_de_Emp, Nom, Habileté)
    as (select Empl_No, Name, Skill
       from EMPLOYEE)
```

A view can be deleted by means of a **drop view** statement as shown below. When a view is deleted, all views defined on that view are dropped as well.

```
drop view FREE
```

The addition of a new attribute such as *Phone_Number* to the EMPLOYEE relation will not affect users, who view this relation through, let us say, EMP_VIEW. The definition of this view remains unchanged. Views allow a certain degree of logical data independence.

The addition of a new relation or restructuring the EMPLOYEE relation will not affect users either, although in the latter case the definition of the view will change but what the users manipulate will remain unchanged. In terms of ANSI/SPARC nomenclature, the view definition gives the external schema and the conceptual to external schema mapping. A change of the conceptual schema requires a change in this mapping, so that the external schema remains invariant. We illustrate this by the following example.

Suppose, as a result of changes in the needs of the user community of the database, the EMPLOYEE relation is split into two relations as shown below:

create table EMPLOYEE_INFO
(Empl_No **integer not null,**
Name **char**(25),
Skill **char**(20),
Phone_Number **decimal**(10))

create table EMPLOYEE_PAY_RATE
(Empl# **integer not null,**
Hourly_Rate **decimal**(10,2))

The users of the relation EMPLOYEE are now provided with the following view, which insulates them from this split:

create view EMPLOYEE *Empl_No,Name,Skill,Pay_Rate* **as**
(select *Empl_No, Name, Skill, Hourly_Rate*
from EMPLOYE_INFO, EMPLOYEE_PAY_RATE
where *Empl_No* = *Empl#*)

The users of the views EMP_VIEW, FREE, and QUALIFICATIONS (defined in Section 5.4.1) also continue to use the database exactly as before. However, the relations they are now using are views of a view, instead of views of a base relation. This change is transparent to the users. In this way views provide for both security and logical data independence.

5.4.1 Views and Update

The DBMS must be able to unambiguously determine the target tuples of an update operation. When a tuple in a view can be mapped to a tuple in a base relation, the update may be made. However, when the tuple in a view does not map to a single tuple, the update operation may not be determined unambiguously.

A tuple in a view can be theoretically updated, under the following constraints:

- Any update operation through a view requires that the user has appropriate authorization.
- If the definition of the view involves a simple query on a single base relation and includes the primary key, the following update operations are possible: a new tuple could be inserted into the database via a view, an existing tuple could be deleted via a view, and the value of a nonprime attribute could be modified. The simple query proviso rules out the possibility that the attributes in the view are derived using an aggregate function or a nonreversible operation. The definition of the reverse operation has to be stored with the view. For example, if the view uses the value of weight in pounds and the value in the base relation is stored in grams, the view attribute *Weight* is obtained by dividing the base value by 453.6 and the stored value, inserted via the view, is multiplied by the same amount.
- The insertion of a new record using a view requires that the primary attributes are included in the view, and the values for these are specified for the insertion (i.e., they are not null).

Views that involve a join may or may not be updatable. Such views are not updatable if they do not include the primary keys of the base relations. When the view includes the primary keys of the base relations, the target base tuples may be identifiable and hence updatable, provided the attributes included in the views are derived using reversible operations and both the forward (from the attribute in the base relation to the view) and reverse (from the attribute in the view to the base relation) operations are known to the DBMS.

The need for allowing a view to update a relation derived from the join of two relations can be illustrated by the following example.

Consider our EMPLOYEE(*Empl_No, Name, Skill, Pay_Rate*) relation. Suppose as a result of a reorganization of the database this relation is replaced by two relations EMPL(*Empl_No, Name, Skill*) and PAYRATE(*Empl#, Pay Rate*), defined as follows:

```
create table EMPL
    (Empl_No     integer not null,
    Name     char(25),
    Skill    char(20))
create table PAYRATE
    (Empl#     integer not null,
    Pay_Rate decimal(10,2))
```

Applications and users of the original relation EMPLOYEE continue using the database as before since they are now provided with the following view:

```
create view EMPLOYEE Empl_No, Name, Skill, Pay_Rate as
    (select Empl_No, Name, Skill, Hourly_Rate
        from EMPL, PAYRATE
            where Empl_No = Empl# )
```

The user of the EMPLOYEE relation should be insulated from this split and allowed to continue to use the database as they were accustomed to before the database reorganization. This would include making appropriate updates. If this view derived from a join could not be used to insert a tuple or make changes, then the users of the relation EMPLOYEE are not insulated from the database reorganization.

Some problems could arise when a new record is inserted in the database using a view instead of the base relation. One problem is that of assigning data values to attributes not included in the view. A method of resolving this is to insert null values for these attributes. However, this can be done only if the attributes in the base relation are defined without the not null option. If a value of a nonprimary attribute included in the view is not specified for insertion, then a null value is assigned to the corresponding attribute in the base relation. Such insertion into the base relation via the view can succeed provided the base attributes can accept a null value.

The other problem is the possibility of a record inserted by a view disappearing from that view. This is illustrated by the following example:

```
create view SOME_EMPLOYEE as
    (select (*)
    from EMPLOYEE
    where Empl_No < 123470)
```

The user of the view, SOME_EMPLOYEE, can insert the tuple (123481, 'Pavan', 'VP Developments', 50.00) in this relation. However, once inserted, this record will be inaccessible. Such anomalies could be avoided if the DBMS verifies that any record that is allowed to be inserted in the database satisfies the predicates of the view.

The view to be used in updates must include the primary attributes of the base relation, and these must have a nonnull value for insertion. If these conditions are not satisfied, the record to be inserted will have null values for the primary attributes. This cannot be allowed; in such cases the insertion will fail.

Any attribute in the view can be updated as long as the attribute is simple and not derived from a computation involving two or more base relation attributes. The view must, of course, include the primary attributes (or the attributes of a candidate key), otherwise the record to be updated cannot be determined and the update will fail.

The view EMP_VIEW of Example 5.25a can be used to insert a new record in the database. It is easy to see that no updates can be allowed through the following view, since it does not include the primary attribute:

create view QUALIFICATIONS **as**
 (**select** *Name, Skill*
  from EMPLOYEE)

When a view is defined on the natural join of a number of relations, the view, if used for updates, is required to include the primary keys of all base relations. Consider the view ELIGIBILITY*(Empl_No, Posting_No, Skill),* obtained as in Example 5.8 by a join of EMPLOYEE and POSITION. It contains the primary attributes of the two relations. A tuple such as (123481, 331, cashier) inserted using this view could succeed provided no tuples with *Empl_No* = 123481 *or Posting_No* = 331 exist in the EMPLOYEE and POSITION relations. The result of the insertion would be the tuples (1234581, null, cashier, null) and (331, cashier) in the two relations.

On the other hand, consider the view ITEMIZED_BILL*(Bill#, Dish_Description, Price, Qty, Price*Qty)* created by a query such as the one given in Example 5.9 and involving the relations BILL, MENU, and ORDR. This view does not contain the primary attributes of all its underlying relations. Consider the tuple (9234, Club sandwich, 10.50, 2, 21.00) of ITEMIZED_BILL. An attempt to update *Dish_Description* will fail because the *Dish#* cannot be determined uniquely. (The club sandwich may be offered as *Dish#* 100 on the lunch menu and as *Dish#* 400 on the room service menu with different prices and both items may be included on the same bill.) An attempt to update *Price*Qty* of the club sandwich from 21.00 to 27.00 cannot be unambiguously translated into a change in the base relations. Suppose a change in *Price*Qty* is given along with a change in *Price* and *Qty* to be 27.00, 9.00, 3, respectively. It is then possible to determine, in the current state of the example database, the actual tuples to be updated by examining all the tuples of ORDR, MENU and the previous values of the tuple of ITEMIZED_BILL. Even though this update is possible in this particular example, attempts to make such an update will fail in most DBMSs. Finally, updating *Bill#* can succeed, although it is debatable if such a change should be made through a view rather than the base relation BILL.

There remains a grey area in determining if an update to a view is theoretically sound under the following conditions: the view is derived from (a) a relation that is not in the proper normal form, or (b) the join of a number of relations. This is a current topic of research and most DBMSs treat updates via a view in an ad hoc manner, allowing updates to views that are either a proper horizontal subset (a selection) or a proper vertical subset (a projection) of a base relation. Many commercial DBMSs disallow updates through a view unless the view is based on a single relation and includes the primary attributes of the relation.

We summarize below the conditions under which most DBMSs determine whether an update is allowed through a view:

- Updates are allowed through a view defined using a simple query involving a single base relation and containing either the primary key or a candidate key of the base relation.
- Updates are not allowed through views involving multiple relations.
- Updates are not allowed through views involving aggregation or grouping operations.

5.5 Remarks

SQL supports the basic relational algebraic operations of union **(union),** difference **(minus),** cartesian product **(from),** and intersection **(intersect).** The **select** statement along with the **where** clause are used for selection. Projection is included in the **select** statement by specifying the attributes. Join is implemented by a cartesian product with the **where** clause indicating the joining attributes and the type of join.

SQL also provides for a wide variety of set operators to allow the expression of relational calculus types of predicates and the testing of the membership of a tuple in a set. In addition, the use of aggregate operators and categorization provide SQL with additional data manipulation features not included in relational algebra or calculus.

Unlike the theoretical languages, SQL provides statements for the definition and modification of data and indexes, and includes views.

Most commercial relational DBMSs support some form of the SQL data manipulation language, and this creates different dialects of SQL. SQL has been standardized; that is, a minimum compatible subset is specified as a standard. In addition, embedded versions of SQL are supported by many commercial DBMSs. This allows application programs written in a high-level language such as BASIC, C, COBOL, FORTRAN, Pascal, or PL/I to use the database accessing SQL by means of appropriate preprocessors (refer to Section 5.8).

5.6 QUEL

INGRES (INteractive GRaphics and REtrieval System) is a relational database system developed at the University of California at Berkeley. This project ran almost concurrently with the System R project at IBM's San Jose Research Center.

QUEL (QUEry Language), the data manipulation language for INGRES, is based on relational tuple calculus. Unlike SQL, it does not support relational algebraic operations such as intersection, minus, or union. QUEL does not support nested queries, i.e., the where clause is not allowed to use a subquery. However, equivalent queries could be formulated easily in QUEL.

The original version of INGRES is used extensively in the academic milieu and runs under UNIX on VAX systems, as well as workstations based on the MC68000 family of microprocessors. A commercial product, also named INGRES, is currently marketed by Relational Technology Inc., and runs on a variety of machines and operating systems.

The basic data retrieval statement in QUEL is the retrieve statement, used in conjunction with the range statement and the where clause. The range statement is used to define tuple variables and their domain. (The domain of a tuple variable is the relation from which the variable takes on values.) The where clause is used to specify the predicates as in SQL.

We will use the same relations for the restaurant database as in the previous sections to illustrate the features of QUEL.

5.6.1 Data Definition

The basic statements used to define relations and access aids in QUEL are create, range, index, destroy, and modify.

Create Statement

The create statement is used to create a new relation. Its syntax is:

create <relation name> (<attribute list>)

where <attribute list> is defined as:

<attribute list> : : = <attribute name> = <format>[,<attribute list>]

Example 5.26 The statement

create NEW_DUTY_ALLOCATION (*Posting_No* = i, *Empl_No* = i, *Shift* = i, *Day* = i)

will create a new relation called NEW_DUTY_ALLOCATION with attributes *Posting_No, Empl_No, Shift,* and *Day,* with all the attributes defined as integers. ■

Range Statement

Tuple variables (known as **range** variables in QUEL, although we will continue to refer to these by the familiar term) are defined using the **range** declaration statement. Its usage is:

range of <tuple variable> **is** <relation name>

This allows us to declare a tuple variable and restrict it to assume values that are tuples from the relation following the keyword **is.** This relation is the domain (the set of tuple values) of the tuple variable. A reference to the tuple variable is a reference to a tuple of the relation. The use of a tuple variable is similar to that in tuple calculus wherein a tuple variable is defined by writing

<tuple variable> ϵ <relation>

The use of a tuple variable is similar to the variable declaration in programming languages where a variable is allowed to have, at a given time, a value from a set of declared values (specified by the type). The tuple variable can thus be visualized as a place marker in our relation.

Example 5.27

range of d **is** DUTY_ALLOCATION
range of e **is** EMPLOYEE

The tuple variables d and e, at any given time, refer to a tuple in the DUTY ALLOCATION and EMPLOYEE relations, respectively. ■

In Chapter 4, we used RELATION_NAME[*Attribute_Name*] to refer to the values of an attribute of a relation. In QUEL this requires the use of qualified names:

RELATION_NAME.*Attribute_Name*, or
Tuple_Variable.*Attribute_Name*

The period is used to qualify the attribute by the relation. Note that in the convention followed in Chapter 4, a group of attribute names could be specified within brackets. There is no such simple grouping technique in QUEL.

Example 5.28

We assume that the tuple variable d has been declared as in Example 5.27. Then,

d.*Posting_No*

refers to the value of the *Posting_No* attrbitue of a tuple in the DUTY_ALLOCATION relation. ■

Index Statement

The indexes are defined for an existing relation using the **index** statement. It specifies the name of the secondary index to be built and the attributes from the relation that are used for indexing. The purpose of creating a secondary index is to increase the efficiency of secondary key retrieval. A relation could have any number of secondary indexes created for it in addition to the index created on the primary key. All indexes are destroyed when the relation is destroyed. Once created, an index is maintained and used automatically by the DBMS. The syntax of the index statement is as follows:

index on <relation name> **is** index_name
(attribute_name [,attribute_name, . . .])

Example 5.29

The following statement creates an additional index named *nameindex* for the EMPLOYEE relation using the *Name* attribute:

index on EMPLOYEE **is** *nameindex (Name)* ■

Destroy Statement

The **destroy** statement is used in QUEL to eliminate a relation, index, or view (discussed in Section 5.7.9). The syntax of the destroy statement is:

destroy <name[,name, . . .]>

where each name is the name of an existing relation, index, or view.

Example 5.30

The following statement destroys the index named *nameindex:*

destroy *nameindex* ■

Modify Statement

The **modify** statement is used to modify the storage structure of a relation from the current one to that specified in the statement. The storage structures supported in INGRES are B-tree, hash, ISAM, and heap. The compressed versions of these storage structures are also supported; the compression is on the physical storage medium. One example of a compression scheme is to suppress the trailing blanks of a character string. The syntax of the modify statement is as follows:

modify relation_name to storage_structure [**on** attribute1 [**order ascending|descending**] [, . . . ,]]

Here the name of the relation is specified by relation_name and the new storage structure by storage_structure. The **on** clause indicates the attribute(s) to be used for ordering the relation. The order can be specified optionally as ascending or descending; ascending being the default. If the on clause is not specified, ascending order of the relation by the first attribute is assumed.

Example 5.31

The following statement modifies the storage structure of the EMPLOYEE relation to a compressed hash (chash) structure with *Empl_No* as the hash key:

modify EMPLOYEE to chash on *Empl_No* ■

5.7 Data Manipulation: QUEL

The basic data retrieval statement in QUEL is **retrieve.** It is used for both projection and selection.

> **retrieve [unique]** (<target list>)
> [**where** <condition>]

In <target list> we specify the data items to be retrieved. The target list can be used to specify the attributes on which the result should be projected. If the unique option is specified, the relation is sorted on the first attribute in the target list and duplicate tuples are removed.

The **retrieve unique** command, except for the ordering, is equivalent to the calculus expression:

$$\{X \mid P(X)\}$$

where X represents the "target list" and the predicate(s) specify the "conditions" that must hold true. In fact, we can read the retrieve command as "get tuples with attributes specified in target list such that the tuples make the condition(s) true."

Example 5.32 Project the DUTY_ALLOCATION relation on the *Posting_No* and *Empl_No attributes*."

> **range of** d **is** DUTY_ALLOCATION
> **retrieve** (d.*Posting_No*, d.*Empl_No*)

Remember that according to the syntax of QUEL, the target list must be enclosed within parentheses. ■

The need to specify every attribute of the result relation can sometimes be tedious. The all keyword is used to represent all of the attributes of a tuple variable.

5.7.1 Condition Specification

Now let us see how we can specify conditions in QUEL. QUEL supports the following Boolean and comparison operators: **and, or, not,** =, ≠ (not equal)[4], >, ≥, <, ≤. Evaluation occurs in left-to-right order. When more than one Boolean operators are together, the evaluation order is based on the priority of the operators: not has the highest priority and or has the lowest. Parentheses may be used to change the order of evaluation.

[4]INGRES and SQL use != , <= , >= instead of ≠ ≤, ≥.

Example 5.34 The query

range of d **is** DUTY_ALLOCATION
retrieve (d.**all**) **where** d.*Empl_No* = 123471
and (d.*Day* = 19860418 **or**
d.*Day* = 19860419)

restricts the tuples in the result to only those DUTY_ALLOCATION tuples with the *Empl_No* attribute value of 123471, and *Day* is either 19860418 or 19860419. (This is equivalent to the use of the selection operation in relational algebra.) ■

We can specify complex qualification using the Boolean operators.

5.7.2 Renaming

The attribute names in the result relation can be changed from those in the base relation. This becomes necessary if the attribute name in the resulting relation would occur more than once or where a computation was performed. All attributes must have names, and remember that the result of a query is also a relation. In general, this attribute name assignment takes the form newname = <expression> and is included in the <target list>.

Example 5.35 "Get employee names and pay rates, renaming them as *Emp_Name* and *Hourly_Pay*."

range of e **is** EMPLOYEE
retrieve (*Emp_Name* = e.*Name*, *Hourly_Pay* = e.*Pay_Rate*) ■

5.7.3 Arithmetic Operators

The following arithmetic operators are supported in QUEL: +, −, *, /, ** (exponentiation), abs (absolute value), and mod (modular division). These operators together with the large library of computational functions (SIN, COS, SQRT, etc.) available to the users of INGRES make the system useful for performing arithmetic operations. Numeric data can thus be manipulated to derive additional information.

Example 5.36 Consider the weekly salary relation, part of which is shown in part i of figure E (this figure is a modified version of Figure C from Example 5.3). Consider the evaluation of the weekly salary (gross). This operation can be expressed in QUEL as on p. 248 and the result of this statement is shown

Figure E Modified form of Figure C.

SALARY:

Empl_No	*Pay_Rate*	*Hours*
123456	7.50	40.5
123457	8.79	42.5
123458	4.70	47.5
123459	4.90	0.0
123460	4.70	48.0
123461	9.00	48.0
123471	14.00	42.7
123472	14.50	45.5

(i)

result:

Empl_No	*Gross_Pay*
123456	303.50
123457	373.58
123458	223.25
123460	225.60
123461	432.00
123471	597.80
123472	659.75

(ii)

in part ii of Figure E (the second column heading has been renamed *Gross_Pay* instead of *Pay_Rate*Hours*):

range of s **is** SALARY
retrieve (s.*Empl_No*, *Gross_Pay* = s.*Pay_Rate**s.*Hours*)
  where s.*Hours* > 0.0 ■

5.7.4 Multiple Variable Queries

So far we have expressed queries using a single tuple variable and these queries required information from a single relation. However, when we are required to retrieve information stored in multiple relations we need to use multiple variables—one tuple variable for each relation. In this section we give examples of queries that require the use of multiple variables.

Example 5.37 "Get the name of the waiter for table 17, identified as *Waiter_Name*."

range of e **is** EMPLOYEE
range of b **is** BILL
retrieve (*Waiter_Name*= e.*Name*)
where e.*Empl_No* = b.*Waiter#* **and** b.*Table#* = 17 ■

In this query we get the identifier for waiter assigned to table 17 and compare it with the employee identifier of employee tuples (the attribute *Waiter#* in BILL refers to the same instance of the entity set employee as attribute *Empl_No* in EMPLOYEE). For the relations MENU and EMPLOYEE of Figures 5.2 and 5.4, the result of this query is the name Ian.

Example 5.38 "Get shift details of the employee named Pierre."

range of d **is** DUTY_ALLOCATION
range of e **is** EMPLOYEE
retrieve (d.*Posting_No*,d.*Shift*,d.*Day*)
where d.*Empl_No* = e.*Empl_No* **and** e.*Emp_Name* = 'Pierre' ■

The use of multiple variables is not restricted to different relations. Sometimes it becomes necessary to declare multiple tuple variables over the same relation. Thus if we want to compare the tuples of the same relation, we can have several tuple variables ranging over the relation. We demonstrate this in the following example.

Example 5.39 "Find employees whose rate of pay is more than that of employee Jon."

In this query, at any given time, we need data on two employees: one is fixed (the data for employee Jon) and the other will be another employee. Thus, we need one tuple variable that can be used to refer to the tuple for employee Jon, and another tuple variable for the other employee. (Imagine that this second tuple variable will be used to scan the complete relation, one tuple at a time.)

range of e **is** EMPLOYEE
range of e_1 **is** EMPLOYEE
retrieve (e.*Name*,e.*Pay_Rate*)
where e.*Pay_Rate* > e_1.*Pay_Rate*
and e_1.*Name* = 'Jon'

Name	*Pay_Rate*
Ian	9.00
Pierre	14.00
Julie	14.50

The tuple variable e_1 has the data for employee Jon while at any given instance the tuple variable e has data for another employee. The result of this query is shown in the example. ■

Example 5.40 "Get all pairs of *Empl_No* with the **same** *Posting_No*."

range of d **is** DUTY_ALLOCATION
range of d_1 **is** DUTY_ALLOCATION
retrieve (d.*Empl_No*, d_1.*Empl_No*)
where d.*Posting_No* = d_1.*Posting_No*
and (d.*Empl_No* < d_1.*Empl_No*) ■

Empl_No	*Empl_No*
123456	123461
123456	123461

In this query we need to compare two tuples of the DUTY_ALLOCATION relation. The condition (d.*Empl_No* < d_1.*Empl_No*) guarantees that only unique employee pairs are retrieved. Employee 123458, who is posted twice to *Posting_No* 323, is not in the result since the *Empl_No*s are the same. Also, by using this condition we avoid including symmetrical tuples in the result. Thus the tuple (123461, 123456) is excluded from the result. (In Example 5.39 we did not need to specify such a condition). Note, however, that the result shown above does have duplicate tuples because *Posting_No* 321 is associated with *Empl_No* 123456 twice in the relation DUTY_ALLOCATION. We could use the unique option in the retrieve statement to remove such duplicate tuples.

We next illustrate a query requiring the join of three relations:

Example 5.41 Consider the requirement to generate the itemized bill for table 12 for the date 19860419. This requires details from three relations, BILL, ORDR, and MENU. The itemized bill can be generated using the statements given below. The result of the query on the relations given in Figure 5.2 is also shown.

```
range of b is BILL
range of m is MENU
range of o is ORDR
retrieve (b.Bill#,m.Dish_Description,m.Price, o.Qty,
                    Dish_Total = m.Price*o.Qty)
where b.Bill# = o.Bill#
   and o.Dish# = m.Dish#
   and b.Table# = 12
   and b.Day = 19860419
```

Bill#	*Dish_Description*	*Price*	*Qty*	*Dish_Total*
9234	Coffee	2.50	2	5.00
9234	Club sandwich	10.50	2	21.00

■

QUEL does not allow nested retrieve statements (similar to the nested select statement) and hence unlike SQL this method cannot be used to generate the itemized bill.

5.7.5 Set Operations in QUEL

The set operations, for example union and intersection, are not supported by QUEL. A number of queries require us to use some of these operators. In relational calculus a tuple variable can be declared independent of the relation and thus can accept values from different relations. In QUEL a qualified tuple variable appears in the target list and since the tuple variable ranges over a single relation, we need some explicit mechanism for creating unions. The same holds true for the other operations. In Section 5.7.8 we introduce some of the data modification commands, and show how they can be used to encode the set operations indirectly.

5.7.6 Aggregation Operators in QUEL

QUEL provides a number of aggregation operators to be used in expressions. These allow a user to perform computations on the values of the relation's attributes.

The aggregation operators supported are any, avg, min, max, count, and sum, similar to the corresponding functions available in SQL. The operators **avg, count,** and **sum** have versions that eliminate duplicates before applying the operator. These "unique" versions are distinguished by the suffix u. The **any** aggregate operator can be used to check if any tuple satisfies a given qualification. The value returned by the **any** operator is 1 if the qualification is satisfied and 0 otherwise. The advantage of using the **any** operator as opposed to using the count operator is that if the qualification is satisfied, the processing of additional tuples is discontinued, resulting in a faster evaluation of the query. The format for using these operators is:

aggregation operator (<expression>)

The tuple variables appearing as arguments of an aggregate operator are always local to it and distinct from any tuple variable with the same name appearing external to the arguments of the aggregate operator. The aggregate operator could logically be considered to be processed separately, and a computed single value replaces it. We illustrate the use of some of these operators in the following examples.

Example 5.42

(a) "Obtain the average dish price."

range of r **is** MENU
retrieve *(Ave_Price* = **avg**(r.*Price))*

The term **avg**(r.*Price*) returns the average of the r.*Price* values. For our sample database the *Ave_Price* is 10.90.

(b) "Get minimum and maximum dish prices."

range of r **is** MENU
retrieve *(Minprice* = **min**(r.*Price),*
Maxprice = **max**(r.*Price*))

(c) "Get the average rate of pay for all employees and list it against each employees' names and rates of pay."

range of e **is** EMPLOYEE
retrieve (e.*Name,* e.*Pay_Rate, Avg_Pay* = **avg** (e.*Pay_Rate*))

The result of this query for our sample database is shown below:

Name	*Pay_Rate*	*Avg_Pay*
Ron	7.50	8.51
Jon	8.79	8.51
Don	4.70	8.51
Pam	4.90	8.51
Pat	4.70	8.51
Ian	9.00	8.51
Pierre	14.00	8.51
Julie	14.50	8.51

■

Note that in the query in Example 5.42c the aggregation operation is independent of the current tuple values. The average rate of pay from all employee tuples is returned by the avg operator. We see this important difference in the next few queries where the aggregates are themselves qualified.

Example 5.43

"Find the average rate of pay for employees with the skill of chef."

First attempt:

range of e **is** EMPLOYEE
retrieve (e.*Empl_No,* e.*Skill, Avgchef_Pay* =
    avg(e.*Pay_Rate* **where** e.*Skill* = 'chef'))

The result relation includes tuples with the above details for all employees including those who are not chefs. In the above query the qualification "e.*Skill* = 'chef'" applies only to the aggregate, not to the query. The aggregate qualification is local; it is not affected by and does not affect the rest of the query. Thus, the scheme of the result is *(Empl_No, Skill, Avgchef_Pay),* and each tuple of the result relation contains the same value for the *Avgchef_Pay* attribute.

Second attempt: The query

range of e **is** EMPLOYEE
retrieve (e.*Empl_No,* e.*Skill,*
        Avgchef_Pay = **avg**(e.*Pay_Rate))*
where e.*Skill* = 'chef'

gets employee number and skill for all employees who are chefs and the average rate of pay of all employees (not just chefs).

The correct query (to get the employee number, skill, and average salaries of employees who are chefs) should be formulated as given below in the third attempt. Here we are using two qualification clauses; one is for the computation of the average salary of employees with a skill of chef and the other is to ensure that the result contains only tuples for chefs.

Third attempt:

range of e **is** EMPLOYEE
retrieve (e.*Empl_No,* e.*Skill, Avgchef_Pay* =
    avg(e.*Pay_Rate* **where** e.*Skill* = 'chef'))
    where e.*Skill* = 'chef' ■

The use of count operator is illustrated in Example 5.44.

Example 5.44

"Get the total number of employees."

range of e **is** EMPLOYEE
retrieve (cnt = **count**(e.*Empl_No*))

Because we defined *Empl_No* as the key for the relation EMPLOYEE we expect no duplicate employee records and the unique version of count is unnecessary. ■

Another aggregation facility supported in QUEL is called the **aggregate function.** This facility allows data to be grouped into categories and aggregations to be performed separately on each group. The aggregate function is invoked by including the **by** clause in the expression for the aggregate operator:

by <by-list>

Unlike simple aggregates, aggregate functions are not local; the by-list links the function to the rest of the query. The tuple variable appearing in by-list is global to the query and is therefore restricted by the qualification of the entire query as well as by any aggregate qualification. The value of an aggregate function is a set of values.

The aggregate function any can be used as an existential quantifier. The use of it in any(. . .) = 1 or any(. . .) = 0 makes the quantification explicit, as illustrated in Example 5.45e.

Example 5.45

(a) "Obtain a count of employees on each shift."

```
range of e is DUTY_ALLOCATION
retrieve(cnt = count(e.Empl_No by e.Shift))
```

(b) "Find the number of employees on shift number 1."

```
range of e is DUTY_ALLOCATION
retrieve (cnt = count (e.Empl_No by e.Shift))
                        where e.Shift = 1
```

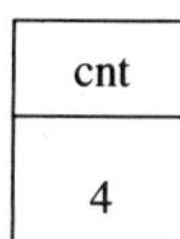

cnt
4

The tuple variable e is global and the by clause links it to the **where** clause, limiting the count to those for shift number 1. The result of this query for the sample database given in Figure 5.4 is as shown above.

A simpler formulation of this query, where the use of a local tuple variable is acceptable, is given below:

```
range of e is DUTY_ALLOCATION
retrieve (cnt = count (e.Empl_No where e.Shift = 1))
```

(c) "Determine the average *Pay_Rate* by skill."

```
range of e is EMPLOYEE
retrieve (e.Skill, Avg_Rate = avg(e.Pay_Rate
                                  by e.Skill))
```

Skill	*Avg_Rate*
waiter	7.50
bartender	8.79
busboy	4.70
hostess	4.90
bellboy	4.70
maître d'	9.00
chef	14.25

The query shows the global scope of the tuple variable used in the by clause. Here the use of the by clause causes the tuple variable associated with it to be global; it is the same as the one used outside the aggregate function. The tuple variable associated with e.*Pay_Rate* is strictly local. The avg function generates a number of values of average pay rate, namely one for each skill. However, a skill and its corresponding value is displayed only once, as shown above for the sample EMPLOYEE relation in Figure 5.4.

(d) "Obtain the average of the total pay rate for each skill."

```
range of e is EMPLOYEE
retrieve (Avg_of_Total = avg( sum (e.Pay_Rate
                              by e.Skill)))
```

The above query demonstrates the aggregate function nested in an aggregate operator. The sum aggregate function generates the sum of *Pay_Rates* by *Skill* giving the set {7.50, 8.79, 4.70, 4.90, 4.70, 9.00, 28.50} as its result for the sample EMPLOYEE relation of Figure 5.4.

The avg operator is applied to this set to get a single value, indicated below:

Avg_of_Total
9.73

Note that this query is not the same as the following, which generates the value 8.51, being the overall average value of the *Pay_Rate* for all employees:

```
retrieve(Overall_Avg_Rate = avg(EMPLOYEE.Pay_Rate) )
```

(e) "Get the names of employees who are assigned to *Posting_No* 321."

```
range of e is EMPLOYEE
range of d is DUTY_ALLOCATION
retrieve unique (e.Name)
where any (d.Empl_No by e.Empl_No
          where d.Posting_No = 321
          and d.Empl_No = e.Empl_No) = 1
```

In this example, the any aggregate function is evaluated over the argument attribute *Empl_No,* which is grouped using the by clause. The predicates specified by the where clause must be satisfied by each value of the argument. For our sample database, the result of the query is the employee names Ian and Ron.

The following can be used to find the names of employees who are not assigned to *Posting_No* 321:

```
range of e is EMPLOYEE
range of d is DUTY_ALLOCATION
retrieve unique (e.Name)
```

```
where any (d.Empl_No by e.Empl_No
              where d.Posting_No = 321
              and d.Empl_No = e.Empl_No) = 0
```

For our sample database, the result of the query is the employee names Don, Jon, Julie, Pam, Pat, Pierre. Note that the function count could have been used here instead of any giving the same result.

(f) "Get the *Empl_No* of the employees who are assigned a duty on at least one date in addition to 19860419." The first version for this query uses the count operator and accesses each tuple of the relation. The second version, which uses the any operator, will terminate the evaluation of the where clause when it accesses the first tuple satisfying the qualification. The result in each case is the employee numbers 123461 and 123471.

First version:

```
range of d is DUTY_ALLOCATION
retrieve (d.Empl_No)
where d.Day = 19860419
   and count(d.Day by d.Empl_No) > 1
```

Second version:

```
range of d is DUTY_ALLOCATION
retrieve (d.Empl_No)
where d.Day = 19860419
   and any(d.Day by d.Empl_No where d.Day ≠ 19860419) = 1
```

■

5.7.7 Retrieve into Temporary Relation

So far we have not considered what happens to the retrieved data; in an interactive environment the results would have been listed on the user's output device. It is also possible to assign the result of the retrieval to a relation. The format of such a retrieve command is:

```
retrieve into <new-relation > (<target list>)
    [where <condition>]
```

The new relation will be created with the correct attribute names and the result of the query put into this relation. The content of the new relation will be similar to a simple retrieve statement.

This scheme of using a relation to accept the result of a retrieve statement can be used in places where SQL uses a nested subquery, as illustrated in the next example.

Example 5.46 "Get total amount for Bill table 12 for the date 19860419." Here we create a temporary relation ITEMIZED_BILL and subsequently use it to find the total amount for the bill.

```
range of b is BILL
range of m is MENU
range of o is ORDR
retrieve into ITEMIZED_BILL(b.Bill#,m.Description,m.Price,
        o.Qty, Dish_Total = m.Price*o.Qty)
where b.Table# = 12
   and b.Day = 19860419
   and o.Dish# = m.Dish#
   and b.Bill# = o.Bill#
range of i is ITEMIZED_BILL
retrieve unique(i.Bill#, Total_Amount = sum(i.Dish_Total))
```
■

5.7.8 Updates

So far we have seen the QUEL data retrieval commands. Data in relations can also be changed using the three update commands append, replace, and delete. The format of the append command is:

append to <relation name> (<value list>)
[**where** <condition>]

and the value list takes the form

<value list> : : = <attribute name> = <value expression> [,<value list>]

Append is used to insert new tuples into a relation. The **replace** and **delete** commands are used to replace or delete existing tuples. Thus the append requires the use of a relation name and the replace and delete commands should use a tuple variable. The format of the replace and delete commands is:

replace <tuple variable> (<value list>)
[**where** <condition>]

delete <tuple variable>
[**where** <condition>]

Example 5.47

(a) "Append a tuple to DUTY_ALLOCATION for *Posting_No* = 322, *Empl_No* = 123457, *Shift* = 2, *Day* = 19860421."

```
append to DUTY_ALLOCATION
(Posting_No = 322, Empl_No = 123457, Shift = 2,
Day = 19860421)
```

(b) "Copy the DUTY_ALLOCATION relation into NEW_DUTY_ALLOCATION."

```
range of d is DUTY_ALLOCATION
append to NEW_DUTY_ALLOCATION (d.all)
```

In this example, all tuples from the DUTY_ALLOCATION relation are copied into NEW_DUTY_ALLOCATION.

(c) "Copy only the tuples for shift 1 into the NEW_DUTY_ALLOCATION."

range of d **is** DUTY_ALLOCATION
append to NEW_DUTY_ALLOCATION (d.all)
where d.Shift = 1 ■

Example 5.48 illustrates the use of the replace command.

Example 5.48

(a) "Increase the pay rate of all employees by 10%."

range of e **is** EMPLOYEE
replace e *(Pay_Rate* = 1.1 * e.*Pay_Rate)*

The value for the attribute *Pay_Rate* in each tuple is increased by 10%. The other attributes are unchanged.

(b) "Increase the pay rate of all waiters by 10%."

range of e **is** EMPLOYEE
replace e *(Pay_Rate* = 1.1 * e.*Pay_Rate)*
where e.*Skill* = 'waiter'

(c) To insert the total amount and the suggested tip into BILL with Bill# = 9234 from the relation ITEMIZED_BILL, we can use the following statements:

range of i **is** ITEMIZED_BILL
range of b **is** BILL
replace b
(*Total* = **sum**(i.*Dish_Total* **where** i.*Bill#* = 9234),
Tip = 0.15***sum**(i.*Dish_Total* **where** i.*Bill#* = 9234))
where b.*Bill#* = 9234 ■

Example 5.49 illustrates the delete command.

Example 5.49

"Remove the record for employee with *Empl_No* 123457."

range of e **is** EMPLOYEE
delete e
where e.*Empl_No* = 123457

and to delete all tuples from a relation:

range of e **is** EMPLOYEE
delete e

The result of the last command is an empty relation. ■

Now let us look at examples that illustrate the method of performing set unions and difference in QUEL.

Example 5.50

"Get all employees (employee numbers only) who are either waiters or work on *Posting_No* 321." This query requires that we obtain the union of the employee numbers obtained from the DUTY_ALLOCATION and EMPLOYEE relations As discussed in Section 5.7.5, QUEL does not support set operations. QUEL is based on relational calculus, so let us first write a calculus expression to help us formulate this query in QUEL:

$$\{t \mid \exists d(d \in \text{DUTY\_ALLOCATION} \wedge t[\mathit{Empl\_No}] = d[\mathit{Empl\_No}] \wedge d\,[\mathit{Posting\_No}] = 321) \vee \exists r(r \in \text{EMPLOYEE} \wedge t[\mathit{Empl\_No}] = r[\mathit{Empl\_No}] \wedge r[\mathit{Skill}] = \text{'waiter'})\}$$

An examination of this query shows that we create a relation over which we define the tuple variable t. We append to this relation the relevant *Empl_No* from the DUTY_ALLOCATION relation and the *Empl_No* from the EMPLOYEE relation. This is our clue for writing the QUEL query. The creation of a new relation and the appending of the appropriate *Empl_No* from the DUTY_ALLOCATION relation can be expressed as:

```
range of d is DUTY_ALLOCATION
retrieve into TEMP (d.Empl_No)
where d.Posting_No = 321
```

Now we append to our TEMP relation the employee numbers of all waiters:

```
range of r is EMPLOYEE
append to TEMP (Empl_No = r.Empl_No)
    where r.Skill = 'waiter'
```

The TEMP relation contains all employees (via the surrogate employee numbers) who work at *Posting_No* 321 or have the skill of waiter. If some persons work both at *Posting_No* 321 and have the skill of a waiter, their numbers will appear more than once in the relation TEMP. So as a final step we need to remove these duplicates by the following statements:

```
range of t is TEMP
retrieve unique (t.Empl_No)
```
■

Example 5.51 illustrates a method of implementing the difference operation.

Example 5.51

"Get employee numbers of persons who work at *Posting_No* 321 but who do not have the skill of waiter." We create a TEMP relation with the employee numbers of persons working at *Posting_No* 321 (as in Example 5.50):

range of d **is** DUTY_ALLOCATION
retrieve into TEMP (d.*Empl_No*)
where d.*Posting_No* = 321

Now we need to delete all tuples in TEMP corresponding to employees with the skill of waiter:

range of r **is** EMPLOYEE
range of t **is** TEMP
delete t
where t.*Empl_No* = r.*Empl_No* **and** r.*Skill* = 'waiter'

Now the temp relation consists of the desired tuples and can be retrieved as:

range of t **is** TEMP
retrieve unique (t.*Empl_No*) ■

5.7.9 Views

QUEL supports views in a manner similar to SQL. A view can be defined on an existing (or a base) relation. The syntax of a **define view** definition is as follows:

define view VIEW_NAME <target_list>
  [**where** <predicates>]

The target list specifies the attributes to be included in the virtual relation VIEW_NAME and must specify the names by which the virtual attributes will be referred.

As in the case of SQL, the data corresponding to a view are retrieved whenever a query refers to a view. Data retrieval is via a query modification as illustrated in the following example.

Example 5.52

range of e **is** EMPLOYEE
define view EMP_VIEW
(Emp_No = e.*Empl_No*
 Emp_Name = e.*Name*
 Emp_Profession = e.*Skill)*
  where e.*Empl_No* < 123460

A subsequent query to the view, for instance the one given below, is modified to refer to the existing base relation:

range of e **is** EMP_VIEW
retrieve (e.*Emp_no*, e.*Emp_Profession*)
where e.*Emp_No* > 123300

This query is converted to the following form, which refers to the base relation EMPLOYEE before any retrieval:

range of e **is** EMPLOYEE

retrieve *(Emp_No* = e.*Empl_No,*
Emp_Profession = e.*Skill)*
where e.*Empl_No* > 123300
and e.*Empl_No* < 123460 ■

Such query modifications produce an appropriate external scheme to conceptual scheme mapping in a orderly manner. Updates via view, create problems similar to the ones we discussed under SQL.

Once defined, a view can be used until it is destroyed by means of a destroy statement as follows:

destroy EMP_VIEW

5.7.10 Remarks

Other QUEL commands deal with database creation, database removal, interface to the file system, index organization, and index modification. These do not deal specifically with data manipulation, so we have not emphasized them here.

The commercial version of INGRES provides a form-based interface, a report writer, interactive as well as embedded SQL and QUEL with HLL interface to BASIC, C, COBOL, Pascal, and PL/I. The database response has been much improved (about one order) over the INGRES used in the academic milieu.

5.8 Embedded Data Manipulation Language

SQL and QUEL only provide facilities to define and retrieve data interactively. To extend the data manipulation operations of these languages, for example to separately process each tuple of a relation, these languages have to be used with a traditional high-level language (HLL). Such a language is called a **host language** and the program is called the **host program.** The use of a database system in applications written in an HLL requires that the DML statements be embedded in the host programs. All the statements and features that are available to an interactive user must be available to the application programmer using the HLL. The DML statements are distinguished by means of a special symbol or are invoked by means of a subroutine call.

One approach that is commonly used is to mark the DML statements and partially parse them during a precompilation step to look for statements and variables from the host HLL appearing in DML statements. Such variables are appropriately identified by looking for a variable declaration in the host program or by appropriately marking such variables (e.g., with a colon). In this way, it is possible to use identical names for both the HLL variables and the objects in the database.

The need for domain compatibility between host language variables and constants and database attributes has to be observed in the design and writing of HLL programs with embedded DML statements. Any data type mismatch between HLL variables and DML attributes must be resolved. One way to handle type mismatch is to do type conversion at run time. Such type conversions must either be established (e.g., converting temperatures given in Celsius to Fahrenheit) or provided by the user (e.g., the current rate of exchange between U.S. and Canadian currency).

In addition to executable DML statements, there is a need for declarative statements. Such declarative statements are used to declare names of relations, their attributes, and currency indicators (or cursors). Also, the program is informed of the status of the execution of a DML statement by appropriate status indicators, which have to be declared as well. We will not discuss status indicators here, but we recognize their importance in the HLL program to verify the status of the execution of the DML statement and take appropriate actions under various error conditions.

Let us illustrate the use of embedded DML statements by the following example. Note that the syntax and convention we are using are simply for illustration; they do not necessarily correspond to those used in any system known to the author. The SQL statements are indicated by the presence of the leading % symbol. The HLL variables Emp_Name, Emp_Skill, Emp_Id, Emp_Pay_Rate are declared to be compatible with the attributes of the EMPLOYEE relation. The EMPLOYEE relation is also declared in the HLL program and allows the precompiler to verify the data types of corresponding attributes and HLL variables match. The HLL variables in the SQL statements are indicated by preceding them with a colon.

We want to update the pay rate of selected employees in our database; each employees increase may be different. To implement this application in a high-level language, we read in the employee number and the percent pay rate of the employee. We retrieve the tuple for this employee and update the pay rate. Subsequently, we select each updated tuple of the EMPLOYEE relation and assign the value of the attributes to the HLL program variables using the %into statement. Finally, the values of these HLL variables are written out.

```
var {HLL variables}
 input_file: text;
 numb: integer;
 raise_pct: real;
var Emp_Name char(25), Emp_Skill char(25);
var Emp_Id decimal(6), Emp_Pay_Rate decimal(10,2);
record EMPLOYEE relation
     (Empl_No decimal(6),
      Name char(25),
      Skill char(25),
      Pay_Rate decimal(10,2));
readln(input_file, numb, raise_pct);
while not eof(input_file) do
  begin
   %update EMPLOYEE
     set Pay_Rate = Pay_Rate * :raise_pct
     where Empl_No = :numb
     readln(input_file, numb, raise_pct);
   end;
reset(input_file);
readln(input_file, numb, raise_pct);
while not eof(input_file) do
  begin
```

```
    %select Empl_No, Name, Pay_Rate
      into :Emp_Id :Emp_Name :Emp_Pay_Rate
     from EMPLOYEE
     where Empl_No = : numb
     writeln('Employee Number =' Emp_Id,
            'Employee Name =', Emp_Name,
            'Employee New Pay Rate =', Emp_Pay_Rate);
     readln(input_file, numb, raise_pct);
  end;
```

The need for currency indicators is illustrated by the following example. The select statement will generally retrieve a set of tuples. The elements of this set will be processed one at a time in the do-while loop. We can associate a currency indicator ptr1 with the relation EMPLOYEE by a declare statement. This currency indicator is used to step through elements of the set retrieved by the select statement. The do-while loop will terminate when the last element is processed.

```
var Emp_Name char(25), Emp_Skill char(25);
var Emp_Id decimal(6), Emp_Pay_Rate decimal(10,2);
 record EMPLOYEE relation
     (Empl_No decimal(6),
     Name char(25),
     Skill char(25),
     Pay_Rate decimal(10,2));
%var ptr1 currency-indicator for EMPLOYEE
     %select *
     from EMPLOYEE
     where Skill = 'chef'
%do while ptr1 ≠ end of set
     %assign using ptr1 to :Emp_Name :Emp_Skill :Emp_Id
                                    :Emp_Pay_Rate
     . . . other statements to process :Emp_Name :Skill
                          :Emp_Id :Pay_Rate
end while
```

Some DML statements do not require currency indicators. Examples of these are where a single tuple is retrieved, inserted, or updated. Deletion or updating of all tuples meeting certain predicates needs no currency indicators either. The following example shows the embedded SQL statements for adjusting the pay rates of employees with the skill of chef by the adjustment factor *Adj_Chef*. The latter is a host language variable indicated by the leading colon.

```
%update EMPLOYEE
%set Pay_Rate = Pay_Rate *:Adj_Chef
     %where Skill = 'chef'
```

As in the case of SQL, QUEL can be used in a form called EQUEL (embedded QUEL) in a high-level language. EQUEL allows application programs to access an INGRES database. The EQUEL statements are not precompiled nor optimized as in the case of embedded SQL. Rather, they are processed and optimized dynamically at runtime by INGRES.

5.9 A Critique: SQL, QUEL

SQL and QUEL are easier to use and more powerful as data sublanguages than the ones used in DBMSs based on the network and hierarchical models. However, these languages do not fully support some of the basic features of the relational data model: the concept of domains, entity and referential integrity and hence the concept of primary and foreign keys. Furthermore, these languages are redundant in the sense that the same query may be expressed in more than one way.

Redundancy is not a sin as long as different ways of expressing the same query yield the same results in approximately the same period of time. However, tests with a number of implementations of SQL, the most widely available query language for relational DBMSs, indicate a wide variation in response time. Furthermore, some forms of the query generate duplicate tuples whereas others do not.

Proponents of QUEL claim that it is more orthogonal and powerful than SQL. The term **orthogonal** is used in programming languages to mean that concepts and constructs are designed independently and can be used consistently in a uniform manner. In an orthogonal language, there are no special cases and few restrictions imposed on the use of the components of the language. The current SQL standard is viewed as one that tried to reconcile the various commercial implementations and came up with one that is, in effect, the lowest common denominator. An attempt is currently underway to upgrade the SQL standard.

The following illustrates the nonorthogonality of SQL. The first version is valid while the second, though symmetrical, is invalid. This is so because the nested select operand is required to be on the right-hand side of the θ operator.

First version:

```
select Name
from EMPLOYEE
where Pay_Rate >
      (select avg (Pay_Rate)
       from EMPLOYEE)
```

Second version:

```
select Name
from EMPLOYEE
where (select avg (Pay_Rate)
         from EMPLOYEE) ≤ Pay_Rate
```

As mentioned earlier, the select statement of SQL represents the following relational algebraic operations:

$$\text{projection}_{\text{(represented by the target list)}}\ (\text{selection}_{\text{(represented by the where clause)}}\ (\text{cartesian product of the relations represented by the from list}))$$

It is not possible to change the order of these operations in SQL. Consequently, the user has to express a query in this format, making the query less like a natural language query.

The treatment of nested select statements in various set operators such as exists, θany, θall, in, and contains is also nonuniform. Whereas a nested select statement producing a relation as the result is required in the case of exists, nested select is only permitted if the value produced in the case of one of the operators {=, ≠, >, ≥, <, ≤} is a relation of cardinality and degree one (a single value). On the other hand, the result of the nested select in the case of one of the set operators {**θany, θall, in, contains**} is required to be a relation of degree one and arbitrary cardinality.

Suppose we want to create a table that contains the names of employees, their pay rate, and, for comparison, the average pay rate. This can be expressed in QUEL as shown in Example 5.42c. However, an attempt to create such a table using the following SQL statement, though intuitively valid, will fail because such usage is illegal in SQL. The reason is that the select is a projection and the cardinality of *Name, Pay_Rate,* is not the same as the cardinality of **avg**(*Pay_Rate*).

```
select Name, Pay_Rate, avg(Pay_Rate)
from EMPLOYEE
```

However, the following is legal and produces a table of skill and the average pay rate for each skill:

```
select Skill, avg(Pay_Rate)
from EMPLOYEE
group by Skill
```

QUEL allows updates to involve values from two relations. As such, the pay rates of employee in the relation EMPLOYEE can be adjusted according to the values in a relation ADJUSTMENT shown below:

```
range of a is ADJUSTMENT
range of e is EMPLOYEE
replace (e.Pay_Rate = a.Raise * e.Pay_Rate)
    where e.Skill = a.Skill
```

ADJUSTMENT

Skill	*Raise*
waiter	1.08
bartender	1.07
busboy	1.12
hostess	1.09
maître d'	1.08
chef	1.09

A similar attempt to use a value from another relation, as illustrated below, is invalid in SQL:

```
update EMPLOYEE
set Pay_Rate = Pay_Rate *(select a.Raise
                          from ADJUSTMENT a
                          where EMPLOYEE.Skill = a.Skill)
```

However, in some implementations of SQL the following statement would produce the required adjustment in *Pay_Rates*. It should be obvious that for this statement to work correctly, the relation ADJUSTMENT must have a tuple corresponding to each value of *Skill* in EMPLOYEE.

```
update EMPLOYEE
set Pay_Rate = (select Pay_Rate * a.Raise
                from ADJUSTMENT a
                where EMPLOYEE.Skill = a.Skill)
```

The nonorthogonality of SQL in allowing nested query in some places and not in others is illustrated below. Whereas the select statement on the left is legal in SQL a similar form in the update statement on the right is not valid in all implementations of SQL.

```
select Name                      update EMPLOYEE
from EMPLOYEE                    set Pay_Rate = 1.3 * Pay_Rate
where Empl_No =                  where Empl_No in
    (select Empl_No                  (select Empl_No
     from DUTY_ALLOCATION             from DUTY_ALLOCATION
     where Shift = 3)                 where Shift = 3)
```

QUEL, on the other hand, has required the use of tuple variables in its query to date. This restriction has been modified and QUEL now allows the use of a relation name as the tuple variable. This was implemented by a query modification introducing the relation name as a tuple variable. However, as illustrated in the following query, using both a tuple variable and a relation name could produce an incorrect result:

```
range of e is EMPLOYEE
replace EMPLOYEE(Pay_Rate = 10.50)
where e.Empl_No = 123456
```

This query is modified by the introduction of a range statement:

```
range of e is EMPLOYEE
range of EMPLOYEE is EMPLOYEE
replace EMPLOYEE(Pay_Rate = 10.50)
where e.Empl_No = 123456
```

The result is unexpected since the query sets the pay rate of *all* employees to 10.50 if there exists an employee with the number 123456.

One of the more mystifying features of QUEL is the scope rule of tuple variables in aggregation operators and aggregate functions. In aggregation operators tuple variables are strictly local, whereas in aggregate functions the presence of the by clause requires that the tuple variable used in that clause has a global scope. Consider the query "Find the average *Pay_Rate* by *Skill*." The QUEL version of this query is shown in Example 5.45c. However, it may be expressed by a novice user using an additional tuple variable as follows:

```
range of e is EMPLOYEE
range of el is EMPLOYEE
retrieve (e.Skill, Avg_Rate = avg(el.Pay_Rate by e.Skill))
```

This query shows the global scope of the tuple variable used in the by clause, which is the same as that used outside the aggregate function. The tuple variable el is strictly local, causing the result to be computed on the cartesian product of EMPLOYEE with itself. This average value, as shown in Figure 5.5, is the same for all skills for our sample EMPLOYEE relation of Figure 5.4.

The correct result for the average pay rate by skill, when using an additional tuple variable, is obtained by adding a predicate in the aggregate function to select appropriate tuples of the cartesian product. This is illustrated in the following modified query:

> **range of** e is EMPLOYEE
> **range of** el **is** EMPLOYEE
> **retrieve** (e.*Skill, Avg_Rate* = **avg**(el.*Pay_Rate* **by** e.Skill
> **where** e.*Skill* = el.*Skill*))

The same result could have been obtained using the following query wherein only one tuple variable is used. Here the by clause causes the tuple variable e to be global and distinct from the local tuple variable in e.*Pay_Rate*.

> **range of** e **is** EMPLOYEE
> **retrieve** (e.*Skill, Avg_Rate* = **avg**(e.*Pay_Rate* **by** e.*Skill*))

The following is another example that illustrates the confusion in novice QUEL users due to a mixture of scope of tuple variables. Consider the query of finding, for each skill, the average pay rate of those employees whose pay rate is less than the average pay rate for their skill. Assume that the MORE_EMPLOYEE relation contains the tuples shown in Figure 5.6. Consider the following QUEL implementation of this query:

> **range of** e is MORE_EMPLOYEE
> **range of** e1 **is** MORE_EMPLOYEE
> **retrieve** (e.*Skill, Low_Avg_Rate* =
> **avg**(e.*Pay_Rate* **by** e.*Skill* **where** e.*Pay_Rate* <
> **avg**(el.*Pay_Rate* **where** el.*Skill* = e.*Skill*)))

The result of this QUEL query for our sample relation MORE_EMPLOYEE is shown in Figure 5.7. Here the use of the by clause in the first avg aggregate function causes the tuple variable e associated with it to be global and the same as one used outside the aggregate function in e.*Empl_No* and e.*Skill*. The identically named tuple variable e associated with the two occurrences of e.*Pay_Rate* in the first avg aggregate function are, on the other hand, local. The tuple variable e1 appearing in the

Figure 5.5 An attempt to compute average *Pay_Rate* by *Skill*.

Skill	*Avg_Rate*
waiter	8.51
bartender	8.51
busboy	8.51
hostess	8.51
bellboy	8.51
maître d'	8.51
chef	8.51

Figure 5.6 Tuples from MORE_EMPLOYEE relation.

MORE_EMPLOYEE

Empl_No	*Name*	*Skill*	*Pay_Rate*
123446	Art	waiter	7.75
123456	Ron	waiter	7.50
123466	Sam	waiter	7.25
123476	Ram	waiter	7.00
123486	Hon	waiter	6.75
123477	Tom	bartender	8.99
123457	Jon	bartender	8.79
123467	Mario	bartender	8.59
123448	Dan	busboy	4.60
123458	Don	busboy	4.70
123468	Dave	busboy	4.50
123459	Pam	hostess	4.90
123449	Mary	hostess	4.80
123460	Pat	bellboy	4.70
123450	Steve	bellboy	4.50
123461	Ian	maître d'	9.00
123451	Andre	maître d'	8.00
123471	Pierre	chef	14.00
123472	Julie	chef	14.50

avg aggregation operator is also local and the average is computed on the join of MORE_EMPLOYEE with itself. This average value, as seen earlier, will be the same for all skills and in this case equal to 7.41. Hence the query gives us the nonzero *Low_Avg_Rate* for those employees whose *Pay_Rate* is lower than the average pay rate of all employees. For skills wherein all employees' pay rates are higher than this

Figure 5.7 Attempt at computing the average *Pay_Rate* by *Skill* of employees whose *Pay_Rate* is below the average for their skills.

Skill	*Low Avg_Rate*
bartender	0.00
bellboy	4.60
busboy	4.60
chef	0.00
hostess	4.85
maître d'	0.00
waiter	7.00
chef	0.00

average pay rate, the result is derived as 0.0. The result relation produced by this query is evidently wrong. This would be not apparent to the user unless he or she had known the contents of the MORE_EMPLOYEE relation and had computed some sample results.

Let us modify the query as shown below. Here the by clause forces the tuple variable in both the aggregate functions to be global.

```
range of e is MORE_EMPLOYEE
range of el is MORE_EMPLOYEE
retrieve (e.Skill, Low_Avg_Rate =
    avg(e.Pay_Rate by e.Skill where e.Pay_Rate <
    avg(el.Pay_Rate by e.Skill where el.Skill = e.Skill) ) )
```

The second average is now computed using only those tuples of the join of MORE_EMPLOYEE with itself where the skill is the same as one outside the function. This indicates the correct tuples to choose for computing the low average pay rate. The result is shown in Figure 5.8.

We can simplify the last query as shown below. This simplified query gives the same result as shown in Figure 5.8.

```
range of e is MORE_EMPLOYEE
retrieve (e.Skill, Low_Avg_Rate =
            avg(e.Pay_Rate by e.Skill where e.Pay_Rate <
            avg(e.Pay_Rate by e.Skill) ) )
```

As illustrated above, a mixture of local and global scope of tuple variables in QUEL tends to create confusion and retrieve incorrect data.

The SQL version of this query is relatively simple as shown below:

```
select e.Skill, avg(e.Pay_Rate)
from MORE_EMPLOYEE e
where e.Pay_Rate < (select avg(el.Pay_Rate)
                    from MORE_EMPLOYEE el
                    where el.Skill = e.Skill)
group by e.Skill
```

Figure 5.8 Correct values by *Skill* of average *Pay_Rate* of employees below the average for their skills.

Skill	*Low Avg_Rate*
bartender	8.59
bellboy	4.50
busboy	4.50
chef	14.00
hostess	4.80
maître d'	8.00
waiter	6.88
chef	14.00

The above discussion illustrates that neither SQL nor QUEL are perfect for expressing all queries. A user has to know the "correct" versions without which the information gleaned from the DBMS may be incorrect. The user may have no way of ascertaining the correctness of the response.

The SQL standard is under review and as with all such standards will go through a number of versions. It is hoped that future standards will address some of the criticisms leveled at SQL.

5.10 QBE

Query-By-Example (QBE) was originally developed by M. M. Zloof at IBM's Yorktown Heights Research Laboratory and has now been marketed for various relational systems from IBM as part of their QMF (Query Management Facility). In QMF, QBE is implemented not as in the system developed by Zloof, but rather by translating the QBE queries into equivalent SQL queries. Other relational DBMSs such as DBASE IV, INGRES, and ORACLE have some form of example or form-based query system.

QBE is based on domain calculus and has a two-dimensional syntax. The queries are written in the horizontal and vertical dimensions of a table. Queries are formed by entering an example of a possible answer in a **skeleton** (empty) **table,** as shown in Figure 5.9. This example contains variables as in domain calculus and specifies the conditions that have to be satisfied by the response. Conditions specified on a single row of the table are generally considered to be **conjunctive** (i.e., "*and*ed"); conditions entered on separate rows are **disjunctive** (i.e., "*or*ed"). An empty skeleton is displayed by pressing a function key.

The skeleton table does not have column headings. The first column is used for the relation name.

To get a list of relations, we enter P. for the PRINT command in the first column of the column heading:

P.				

To get the attribute names for a given relation we enter the relation name followed by a P.

DUTY_ALLOCATION P.				

Figure 5.9 QBE skeleton table for writing QBE example query.

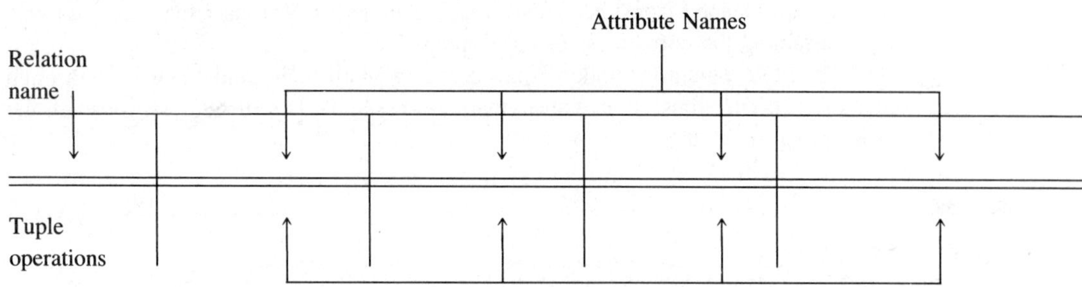

Having obtained a skeleton table, we specify queries by filling in the table with appropriate variables and constants. Variables are called **example elements.** Variable names are represented in QBE by preceding the name with an underscore. However, in this text, for ease in reading, the variables are denoted by underlined strings and in no way affect the interpretation of a query. It is usual to use example values from an attribute's domain as free variable names. The example value, chosen as a variable name, need not be in the database. Constants are nonunderlined strings. Therefore, <u>Waiter#</u> is a variable; Waiter# is a constant. <u>123456</u> is a variable; 123456 is a constant.

5.10.1 Basic Data Retrieval in QBE

The basic data retrieval command in QBE is the PRINT command indicated by P. with an optional variable name as shown below and in the following examples:

P.[<variable>]

Example 5.53 "Get employee position assignment." We first obtain the DUTY_ALLOCATION skeleton table. Next we enter variables or the example query.

DUTY_ALLOCATION	*Posting_No*	*Empl_No*	*Shift*	*Day*
	P.<u>P1</u>	P.<u>E1</u>		

This is the domain calculus query

$$\{p,e \mid \langle p,e,s,d \rangle \in DUTY\_ALLOCATION\} \quad \blacksquare$$

Duplicates in QBE are automatically eliminated. To suppress such elimination the variable name must include the ALL. keyword prefix. (In the above query it would be P.ALL.<u>P1</u>.)

Two alternative forms of expressing the same query are given below. In the first the domain values are used as variables and in the second we only specify the columns to be printed.

DUTY_ALLOCATION	*Posting_No*	*Empl_No*	*Shift*	*Day*
	P.325	P.123456		

DUTY_ALLOCATION	*Posting_No*	*Empl_No*	*Shift*	*Day*
	P.	P.		

Example 5.54 "Get full details of duty assignment." This query can be expressed in QBE by entering on a skeleton table for the DUTY_ALLOCATION relation the present or print directive followed by a variable name for all attributes of the relation. Such a sample is illustrated below:

DUTY_ALLOCATION	*Posting_No*	*Empl_No*	*Shift*	*Day*
	P.PI	P.EI	P.SI	P.DI

A simpler method of representing the same query is to enter a P. under the relation name as indicated below:

DUTY_ALLOCATION	*Posting_No*	*Empl_No*	*Shift*	*Day*
P.				

■

Predicates are introduced in queries by means of constants in appropriate columns as illustrated in the following example.

Example 5.55 Consider the query that requires all duty assignments for *Empl_No* 123456. The domain calculus version of this query, given below, can be translated readily into an example on the skeleton table. The condition *Empl_No* = 123456 is expressed by entering the value under the column for *Empl_No*.

The fact that all details are required is indicated by the P. under the relation name.

$$\{p,e,s,d \mid \langle p,e,s,d\rangle \in \text{DUTY\_ALLOCATION} \wedge e = 123456\}$$

DUTY_ALLOCATION	*Posting_No*	*Empl_No*	*Shift*	*Day*
P.		123456		

■

QBE supports the usual comparison operators: =, ≠ (not equal), <, ≤, >, ≥; = is normally omitted as seen in the previous example. The Boolean operators and, or, not are also supported. Conditions specified within a single row are *and*ed. For multiple conditions on the same column, k, to be *and*ed, QBE requires multiple rows with the same example element in the *k*th column of each row. To specify conditions to be *or*ed we use different rows with different example elements.

Example 5.56

"Get names of employees with the skill of chef earning more than $14.00 per hour." The above query reads "Get employee names where *Skill* = 'chef' and *Pay_Rate* > 14.00" and is the domain calculus query:

$$\{n \mid \langle e,n,s,p\rangle \in \text{EMPLOYEE} \wedge s = \text{'chef'} \wedge p > 14.00\}$$

This query requires two conditions to be true for the tuples that are retrieved. It can be expressed on the skeleton table as illustrated below:

EMPLOYEE	*Name*	*Skill*	*Pay_Rate*
	P.EX	'chef'	>14.00

■

In the above example not all attribute names of the employee relation were listed. It is possible in QBE to eliminate columns from the display if they are irrelevant to the query.

Example 5.57

"Get names of chefs who earn more than $10 per hour but less than $20 per hour." To specify a conjunctive predicate of the form $P_1(attr_i) \wedge P_2(attr_i) \wedge \ldots P_n(attr_i)$, QBE allows multiple columns for the same attribute in the skeleton table. Hence this query can be expressed as shown below:

EMPLOYEE	*Empl_No*	*Name*	*Skill*	*Pay_Rate*	*Pay_Rate*
		P.EX	chef	>10.00	<20.00

An alternate scheme with multiple rows with the same domain variable to express the conjunctive predicate can also be used. The query could be reexpressed as "Get employee names whose *Skill* = 'chef' with *Pay_Rate*>10 AND (the same) employee names whose *Skill* is also 'chef' with *Pay_Rate*<20." This is expressed in QBE by two rows with the same variable in the *Name* column as indicated below:

EMPLOYEE	*Empl_No*	*Name*	*Skill*	*Pay_Rate*
		P.EX	chef	>10.00
		EX	chef	<20.00

■

The following example illustrates a disjunctive predicate.

Example 5.58 "Get names of employees who are either chefs or earn more than $8 per hour." In this query, the conditions to be *or*ed are indicated by using two rows in the skeleton table with different variable names for the *Name* column.

EMPLOYEE	*Empl_No*	*Name*	*Skill*	*Pay_Rate*
		P.EX	chef	
		P.EY		>8.00

■

Data from multiple tables can be manipulated as shown in Example 5.59.

Example 5.59 "Get shift details for the employee named Ian." This query is "Print *Posting No, Shift* and *Day* (e.g., P1,S1,D1 respectively) for employee number EX where EX is the *Empl_No* for employee Ian. The response to the query involves a join of relations EMPLOYEE and DUTY_ALLOCATION. In QBE the join is implemented by utilizing the example element EX as a link between these relations. The link in QBE is used whenever a join would be used in relational algebra.

DUTY_ALLOCATION	*Posting_No*	*Empl_No*	*Shift*	*Day*
P.	P.P1	EX	P.S1	P.D1

EMPLOYEE	*Empl_No*	*Name*	*Skill*	*Pay_Rate*
	P.EX	Ian		

■

QBE also provides a "conditions" box to specify additional constraints. This is particularly helpful as it sometimes becomes impossible to specify all the constraints within the skeleton table. We illustrate the use of a condition box in the following example.

A number of variables can be defined over the same attribute of a relation. This is used in Example 5.60.

Example 5.60 "Get *Empl_No* of all pairs of chefs working on the same shift." The domain calculus version of this query is given below. Here f and s are domain variables on the domain of *Emp#* and x and y are domain variables on the domain of *Shift:*

$$\{f,s \mid <f,x> \epsilon \text{ DUTY\_ALLOCATION} \wedge <s,y> \epsilon \text{ DUTY\_ALLOCATION}$$
$$\wedge <ef,nf,sf,pf> \epsilon \text{ EMPLOYEE}$$
$$\wedge <es,ns,ss,ps> \epsilon \text{ EMPLOYEE}$$
$$\wedge x = y \wedge f < s \wedge f = ef \wedge s = es$$
$$\wedge ps = \text{'chef'} \wedge pf = \text{'chef'}\}$$

This calculus query states "Get employee numbers of chefs working on the same shift (x = y)." The conditions f = pf and s = es guarantee that we have the same employees from the two relations. Finally, to eliminate redundant pairs of the form (123471, 123472) and (123472, 123471) we impose the condition, f < s on the employee numbers. This calculus form of the query is converted into QBE as shown below:

DUTY_ALLOCATION	*Posting_No*	*Empl_No*	*Shift*	*Day*
		EX	SI	
		EY	SI	

EMPLOYEE	*Empl_No*	*Name*	*Skill*	*Pay_Rate*
	EF		chef	
	ES		chef	

RESULT	*First*	*Second*
	P.EX	P.EY

CONDITIONS
EX < EY **and** EF = EX **and** ES = EY

We could have used EX and EY instead of EF and ES respectively in the skeleton table for EMPLOYEE, eliminating the conditions EF = EX and ES = EY in the condition box to indicate that the skill of the employees are those of chefs. ■

5.10.2 Aggregation in QBE

QBE also provides min, max, cnt (count), sum, and avg aggregation functions. The latter three may be qualified by the UNQ. operator to eliminate duplicates. The ALL. qualifier must always be specified. We illustrate the use of these functions in Example 5.61.

MIN.ALL.
MAX.ALL.
CNT.[UNQ.]ALL.
SUM.[UNQ.]ALL.
AVG.[UNQ.]ALL.

Example 5.61

(a) "Get average dish price."

MENU	*Dish#*	*Dish_Description*	*Price*
			P.AVG.UNQ.ALL.CX

(b) "Get minimum and maximum dish prices."

MENU	*Dish#*	*Dish_Description*	*Price*
			P.MIN.ALL.CX P.MAX.ALL.CY

(c) "Get names and rate of pay compared with average rate of pay."

EMPLOYEE	*Empl_No*	*Name*	*Skill*	*Pay_Rate*
		P.EX		P.RX P.AVG.ALL.RY

(d) "Find names of employees with *Pay_Rate* less than the average *Pay_Rate*."

	P.EX	P.RX AVG.ALL.RY

CONDITIONS
RX < AVG.ALL.RY

■

5.10.3 Categorization in QBE

The equivalent of the SQL group by operator is obtained in QBE by preceding the variable with G.

Example 5.62 (a) "Get count of employees on each shift."

DUTY_ALLOCATION	*Empl_No*	*Shift*	*Day*
	P.CNT.ALL.EX	G.SX	

(b) "Get employee numbers of all employees assigned a duty on dates in addition to the date 19860419."

DUTY_ALLOCATION	*Empl_No*	*Day*
	EX P.G.EX	19860419

CONDITIONS
CNT.ALL.EX > 1

■

5.10.4 Updates

QBE includes the three update operations for inserting, modifying, and deleting. These are indicated on the skeleton table in the relation name column by I. (insert), U. (modify/replace), and D. (delete). For the U. update operation based on an old value, the user first specifies the old version and next the new version. We illustrate the syntax for specifying these operations in the following examples.

Example 5.63

(a) ''Insert a record into DUTY_ALLOCATION at *Posting_No* 321 for *Empl No* 123458, *Shift* 2, and *Day* 19860421.''

DUTY_ALLOCATION	*Posting_No*	*Empl_No*	*Shift*	*Day*
I.	321	123458	2	19860421

Here the I. in the relation name column indicates the insertion operation. The values for the columns are indicated on the skeleton of the table.

(b) ''Copy DUTY_ALLOCATION into NEW_DUTY_ALLOCATION.''

DUTY_ALLOCATION	*Posting_No*	*Empl_No*	*Shift*	*Day*
	PX	EX	SX	DX

NEW_DUTY_ALLOCATION	*Posting_No*	*Empl_No*	*Shift*	*Day*
I.	PX	EX	SX	DX

■

Here the I. in the relation name column for the NEW_DUTY_ALLOCATION table indicates the insertion operation. The similarly named variables in DUTY_ALLOCATION and NEW_DUTY_ALLOCATION indicate the source of the values to be used for the insertion.

(c) ''Copy into NEW_DUTY_ALLOCATION records for Shift 1 in DUTY _ALLOCATION.''

DUTY_ALLOCATION	*Posting_No*	*Empl_No*	*Shift*	*Day*
	PX	EX	SX	DX

NEW_DUTY_ALLOCATION	*Posting_No*	*Empl_No*	*Day*
I.	PX	EX	DX

(d) "Increase *Pay_Rate* of all employees by 10%."

EMPLOYEE	*Empl_No*	*Pay_Rate*
	EX	PX
U.	EX	1.1 * PX

Here U. in the relation name column indicates the update operation.

(e) "Increase *Pay_Rate* of employees with the skill of waiter by 10%."

EMPLOYEE	*Empl_No*	*Name*	*Skill*	*Pay_Rate*
	EX		waiter	PX
U.	EX			1.1 * PX

(f) "Assign all bellboys with a *Pay_Rate* of less than 5.00 and not working on third shift of 19860419 to *Posting_No* 327 for the third shift of 19860419."

EMPLOYEE	*Empl_No*	*Name*	*Skill*	*Pay_Rate*
	EX		bellboy	< 5.00

DUTY_ALLOCATION	*Posting_No*	*Empl_No*	*Shift*	*Day*
		EX	≠3	≠19860419
U.	327	EX	3	19860419

Another method of specifying the second table, which says that there does not exist a tuple in DUTY_ALLOCATION for the *Empl_No* EX such that the *Shift* is 3 and the *Day* is 19860419, is indicated below. Here we show that the tuple does not exist by using the not (¬) symbol in the relation name column with the same variable as in the EMPLOYEE relation and the other conditions specified in the *Shift* and the *Day* columns.

DUTY_ALLOCATION	*Posting_No*	*Empl_No*	*Shift*	*Day*
¬		EX	3	19860419
U.	327	EX	3	19860419

(g) "Delete employee record for *Emp#* 123459."

EMPLOYEE	*Empl_No*	*Name*	*Skill*	*Pay_Rate*
D.	123459			

Here the D. in the relation name column indicates the deletion operation.

(h) "Delete employee records for all employees."

EMPLOYEE	*Empl_No*	*Name*	*Skill*	*Pay_Rate*
D.				

(i) "Delete employee Ian and remove him from DUTY_ALLOCATION."

EMPLOYEE	*Empl_No*	*Name*	*Skill*	*Pay_Rate*
	EX	Ian		
D.	EX	Ian		

DUTY_ALLOCATION	*Posting_No*	*Empl_No*	*Shift*	*Day*
D.		EX		

In the first line of the EMPLOYEE skeleton we indicate that we are interested in the employee with the name of Ian and hence select these tuples. On the second line we indicate that these tuples are to be deleted. The use of the EX with D. in the DUTY_ALLOCATION skeleton indicates that tuples satisfying this predicate are to be deleted as well. ■

5.11 Concluding Remarks

In this chapter we considered some of the salient features of the more popular commercial data manipulation languages. We can see how they borrow heavily from relational algebra and calculus concepts. In query design, relatively little attention needs to be paid to evaluation. Users benefit greatly from this philosophy. In some ways data manipulation resembles programming and, like good programming, comes from practice. The requirement is that we be able to express exactly what we desire.

We can reflect on the complexity of what is achieved by some very simple queries. As is normal in most database systems, suppose that every relation is supported by an underlying file of records. Let us consider the SQL query

select R.A, S.D
from R, S
where R.B = S.C

Let the tuples of relations R and S be stored as records in the files FR and FS, respectively. The above query requires that starting with the first record of FR (tuple of R), we compare its field, B, with field C of every record of file FS, outputting field A value from FR and field D value from FS whenever the comparands are equal. For n records in file FR and m in file FS, this would require some m * n combinations. Even for moderate-sized relations this signifies a large number. In Chapter 10 we consider how we can optimize this query. More immediately, however, we should reflect on how to program this task in a file environment. In this case, the task of translating the query into a file processing program is easy. For more complex queries, the programming task is much more difficult. We can therefore appreciate the productivity improvements, among other benefits, of using a relational database system.

5.12 Summary

In this chapter we examined the commercial versions of languages used for relational database systems. These languages, unlike their theoretical counterparts, include facilities to define data as well as manipulate it.

SQL borrows both from relational algebra and tuple calculus. It is easy to use and contains only four data manipulation statements: select, update, insert, and delete. The data definition part of SQL consists of three statements: create, alter, and drop. Views can be created by using the create view statement.

QUEL is mainly based on tuple calculus and supports set operations only indirectly. Consequently, some queries that could be formulated easily using set operations require the use of temporary relations in QUEL.

QBE is a graphical query language based on domain calculus. Queries are formulated in QBE by generating on a skeleton table an example of what the user wishes to retrieve.

SQL has become the most popular and widely supported data manipulation language for relational database systems. Because of this force of the marketplace, SQL has emerged as the de facto standard for relational DBMSs.

Key Terms

Structured Query Language (SQL)
create
not null
alter
create index
cluster
unique
drop
select
distinct
from
where
update
set
delete
insert
value
and
or
not
count
sum
avg
min
max
any
in
contains
all
not in
not contains
exists
not exists
union
minus
intersect
group by
having
base relation
view
existing relation
create view
drop view
Query Language (QUEL)
range
is
index
destroy
modify
on
retrieve
retrieve unique
aggregate function
by
append
replace
define view
host language
host program
orthogonal
Query-By-Example (QBE)
skeleton table
conjunctive
disjunctive
example element

Exercises

5.1 For the queries of Exercise 4.4 in Chapter 4, give SQL, QUEL, and QBE query expressions.

5.2 For the queries of Exercise 4.5 in Chapter 4, give SQL and QUEL query expressions.

5.3 For the queries of Exercise 4.12 in Chapter 4, give SQL, QBE, and QUEL query expressions.

5.4 Express the following tuple calculus query in SQL and QUEL:

$$\{t|t \in rel_1 \wedge \exists s(s \in rel_2 \wedge (s.c = t.b))\}$$

given the relations rel_1(A,B) and rel_2(C,D).

5.5 Convert the following domain calculus query into SQL, QUEL and QBE:

$$\{<a,b> \mid <a,b> \in rel1 \wedge b = b_1' \vee b = 'b_2'\}$$

5.6 Given the following relations

CONSISTS_OF *(Module, Sub_Module)*
DEVELOPED_BY *(Module, Employee)*

give SQL and QUEL queries for the following:

(a) List all modules that use the HEAPSORT and BINARY_SEARCH modules.
(b) List employees who were involved in the development of all modules that use the HEAPSORT and BINARY_SEARCH modules.

If a module uses another module that uses either the HEAPSORT or BINARY_SEARCH modules, would your query list the employees who were involved? How should you express such a query?

5.7 Consider the relationship REGISTERED_GUEST_CHARGE between the entity REGISTERED_GUEST*(Room#, Name, Address)* and the view TOTAL_BILL as shown below with some tuples from this relation. Write the definition for TOTAL_BILL as a view of BILL in (a)SQL and (b)QUEL.

TOTAL_BILL

Bill#	*Day*	*Total*
9234	19860419	29.90
9235	19860420	16.70

REGISTERED_GUEST_CHARGE

Room#	*Bill#*
1267	9234
1492	9235

Use these relations to express a query in SQL and QUEL that gives the total charges attributable to a REGISTERED_GUEST.

5.8 Express the query, in SQL and QUEL to increase the pay rate of employees who work on the third shift at *Posting_No* 7 by 5% (use the relations defined in the chapter).

5.9 Create a view (in both SQL and QUEL) for employees assigned to a given table as a waiter. The user needs the table number, day (date), shift, and the waiter's name. The base relations BILL, DUTY_ALLOCATION, and EMPLOYEE given in Figures 5.2 and 5.4 should be used in the definition.

5.10 For the PROJECT, EMPLOYEE, and ASSIGNED_TO relations given in Chapter 4, express the following queries in SQL:

(a) Get *Emp#* of employees working on project numbered COMP353.
(b) Get details of employees (name and number) working on project COMP353.
(c) Get details of employees working on all database projects.
(d) Get details of employees working on both COMP353 and COMP354.
(e) Get employee numbers of employees who work on at least all those projects that employee 107 works on.

(f) Get employee numbers of employees who do not work on project COMP453.
(g) Get employee numbers of employees who work on all projects.
(h) Get employee numbers of employees who work on at least one project that employee 107 works on.

5.11 Repeat Exercise 5.10 using QUEL.

5.12 Repeat Exercise 5.10 using QBE.

5.13 Express the queries of Exercise 4.16 of Chapter 4 using SQL or QUEL.

5.14 Using SQL, get the *Empl_No, Skill,* and average chef's pay rate for the EMPLOYEE relation shown in Figure 5.4.

5.15 For the sample tuples given in Figures 5.2 and 5.4, evaluate the QBE queries given in Examples 5.53 through 5.59.

5.16 Repeat Exercise 5.15 for Examples 5.60 through 5.63.

5.17 Consider a database for the Universal Hockey League (UHL), discussed in Chapter 2, which records statistics on teams, players, and divisions of the league. Write the following queries in SQL and QUEL:

(a) Give the names of the players who played as forwards in 1987 in the franchise Blades.
(b) Find the names of all the goalies who played with the forward Ozzy Xavier over the span of his hockey career.
(c) List forwards and their franchises for those forwards who had at least 50 goals in the years 1985 and 1986. A player must have at least 50 goals in both the years but may have been with two different franchises.
(d) Give the complete details of players who played in the same franchises as Ozzy Xavier did over his career, but not necessarily in the same year or as a forward.
(e) Compile the list of goalies who played during their career for franchises in St. Louis, Edmonton, and Paris. A goalie should be listed if and only if he played in all three cities.

Bibliographic Notes

The query language QUEL was defined by Stonebraker et al. (Ston 76). It was also described in the paper by Wong and Youssefi (Wong 76) that described a method for the decomposition of the queries for query processing. The precursor of SQL, SEQUEL, was described by Chamberlin et al. (Cham 76). Commercial versions are described in manufacturers' reference manuals. QBE was proposed by Zloof (Zloo 77). The three languages are also described in varying detail in textbooks by Date (Date 86a), Korth and Silberschatz (Kort 86), Maier (Maie 83), and Ullman (Ullm 82). Semantics of updates and their application to relational databases are discussed in Desai et al. (Desa 87).

Bibliography

(Astr 75) M. M. Astrahan & D. D. Chamberlin, "Implementation of a Structured English Query Language," *CACM* 18(10), 1975, pp. 580–587.

(Astr 76) M. M. Astrahan, et al., "System R: A Relational Approach to Database Management," *ACM TODS* 1(2), 1976, pp. 97–137.

(Boyc 75) R. F. Boyce, D. D. Chamberlin, W. F. King, & M. M. Hammer, "Specifying Queries as Relational Expressions: The SQUARE Data Sublanguage," *CACM* 18(11), 1975, pp. 621–628.

(Cham 76) D. D. Chamberlin, et al., "SEQUEL 2: A Unified Approach to Data Definition, Manipulation and Control," *IBM J. of Res. and Dev.* 20(6), 1976, pp. 560–575.

(Codd 86) E. F. Codd, "An Evaluation Scheme for Database Management Systems That Are Claimed To Be Relational," Data Engineering Conf., 1986, pp. 720–729.

(Codd 88) E. F. Codd, "Fatal Flaws in SQL," *Datamation,* August 15, 1988, pp. 45–48, September 1, 1988, pp. 71–74.

(Date 86a) C. J. Date, "A Critique of the SQL Database Language," *ACM SIGMOD Record,* November, 1984, Vol 14-3, pp. 8–54.

(Date 86b) C. J. Date, *An Introduction to Database Systems* 4th ed. Reading, MA. Addison-Wesley, 1986.

(Date 87a) C. J. Date, *A Guide to the SQL Standard*. Reading, MA: Addison-Wesley, 1987.

(Date 87b) C. J. Date, "Where SQL Falls Short," *Datamation,* May 1, 1987, pp. 83–86.

(Desa 87) B. C. Desai, P. Goyal, F. Sadri, "Fact Structures and its Application to Updates in Relational Databases," *Information Systems* 12(2), 1987, pp. 215–221.

(Epst 77) R., Epstein, R., "A Tutorial on INGRES," ERL-M77-25, University of California, December 1977. Berkeley, CA:

(Held 75) C. D. Held, M. Stonebraker, & E. Wong, "INGRES: A Relational Database System," Proc. ACM Pacific 1975 Regional Conf., 1975, pp. 409–416.

(Kala 85) J. Kalash, et al., "INGRES Version 8 Reference Manual," in *UNIX 4.3*. Berkley, CA: University of California, December 1985.

(Kort 86) H. F. Korth & A. Silberschatz, *Database System Concepts,"* New York: McGraw-Hill, 1986.

(Lawr 88) A. Lawrence, "Living Up to the Hype," *Computing,* May 5, 1988, pp. 22–23.

(Maie 83) D. Maier, *The Theory of Relational Databases,* Rockville, MD: *Computer Science Press,* 1983.

(Moad 88) J. Moad, "DB2 Performance Gets Kick with Closer Ties to 3090S, ESA," *Datamation,* September 1988, pp. 19–20.

(ORAC 87) *SQL*Plus Reference Guide*. Belmont, CA: Oracle Corp., July 1987.

(Pasc 88) F. Pascal, "SQL Redundancy and DBMS Performance," *Database Programming and Design,* December 1988, pp. 22–28.

(RTI 88) *INGRES Reference Guide*. Alameda, CA: Relational Technology Inc., August 1988.

(Ston 76) M. Stonebraker, E. Wong, P. Kreps, & C. D. Held, "The Design and Implementation of INGRES," *ACM TODS* 1(3), 1976, pp. 189–222.

(Ullm 82) J. D. Ullman, *Principles of Database Systems* 2nd ed. Rockville, Md: Computer Science Press, 1982.

(Wong 76) E. Wong & K. Youssefi, "Decomposition—A Strategy for Query Processing," *ACM Transactions on Database Systems* 1, pp. 223–241.

(Wood 79) J. Woodfill, et al., "INGRES Version 6.2 Reference Manual," ERL Technical Memorandum M79-43. Berkeley, CA: University of California, 1979.

(Zloo 75) M. M. Zloof, "Query-By-Example: Operations on the Transitive Closure." Yorktown Heights, NY: IBM Research Report RC5526, 1975.

(Zloo 77) M. M. Zloof, "Query-By-Example: A Database Language," *IBM Systems Journal* 16(4), 1977, pp. 324–343.

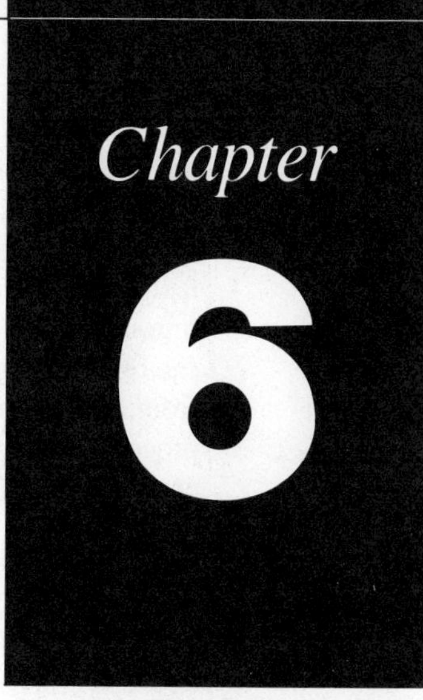

Relational Database Design

Contents

A relation in a relational database is based on a relation scheme, which consists of a number of attributes. A relational database is made up of a number of relations and the relational database scheme, in turn, consists of a number of relation schemes. In this chapter, we focus on the issues involved in the design of a database scheme using the relational model. Section 6.2 discusses the importance of having a consistent database without repetition of data and points out the anomalies that could be introduced in a database with an undesirable design. Section 6.3 presents the universal relation assumption. In Section 6.4 we look at some of the theoretical results from the functional dependency theory and present basic algorithms for the design process. In Section 6.5 we present the relational database design process. This process uses the functional dependencies among attributes to arrive at their desirable groupings. We discuss the first, second, third, and Boyce Codd normal forms and give algorithms for converting a relation in the first normal form into higher order normal forms. The next chapter introduces the synthesis approach to relational database design and higher order normal forms.

6.1 Relation Scheme and Relational Design

A relation scheme **R** is a plan that indicates the attributes involved in one or more relations. The scheme consists of a set **S** of attributes $\{A_1, A_2, \ldots, A_n\}$, where attribute A_i is defined on domain $\mathbf{D_i}$ for $1 \leq i \leq n$. We will use **R(S),** or **R** if there is no confusion, to indicate both the logical construction of the relation (its scheme) as well the name of this set **S** of attributes. Relation R on the relation scheme **R** is a finite set of mappings or tuples $\{t_1, t_2, \ldots, t_p\}$ such that for each $t_j \in R$, each of the attribute value $t_j(A_i)$ must be in the corresponding domain $\mathbf{D_i}$.

Example 6.1

Consider the relation SCHEDULE shown in Figure A. It contains the attributes *Prof, Course, Room, Max_Enrollment* (enrollment limit), *Day, Time*. Thus, the relation scheme for the relation SCHEDULE, say **SCHEDULE,**

Figure A The SCHEDULE relation.

Prof	*Course*	*Room*	*Max_Enrollment*	*Day*	*Time*
Smith	353	A532	40	mon	1145
Smith	353	A532	40	wed	1145
Smith	351	C320	60	tue	115
Smith	351	C320	60	thu	115
Clark	355	H940	300	tue	115
Clark	355	H940	300	thu	115
Turner	456	B278	45	mon	845
Turner	456	B278	45	wed	845
Jamieson	459	D110	45	tue	1015
Jamieson	459	D110	45	thu	1015

is *(Prof, Course, Room, Max_Enrollment, Day, Time)*. The domain of the attribute *Prof* (professors) is all the faculty members of the university; the domain of the attribute *Course* is the courses offered by the university; that of *Room* is all the rooms in the buildings of the university; that of *Max_Enrollment* is an integer value and indicates the maximum enrollment in the course (which is related to the capacity of the room, i.e., it should be less than or equal to the capacity of the room in which the course is scheduled). The domain of *Day* is {MON, TUE, WED, THU, FRI, SAT, SUN} and that of *Time* is the possible times of day. ■

The relation SCHEDULE of Figure A has ten tuples, the first one being *Prof* = Smith, *Course* = 353, *Room* = A532, *Max_Enrollment* = 40, *Day* = mon, *Time* = 1145. As mentioned earlier, the tabular representation of a relation is only for the purpose of illustration. Explicitly naming the columns of the table to show the mapping or association of an attribute and its value for a particular tuple avoids the requirement of a particular ordering of the attributes in the relation scheme and hence in the representation of the time-varying tuples of the relation. We will continue to represent relations as tables. We will also write the attributes of the relation in a particular order and show the tuples of the relation with the list of values for the corresponding attributes in the same order. The attribute names will be attached to the columns of the table when the tuples of a relation are shown in a table.

Since a relation is an abstraction of some portion of the real world that is being modeled in the database, and since the real world changes with time, the tuples of a relation also vary over time. Thus, tuples may be added, deleted, or updated over a period of time. However, the relation scheme itself does not change. (at least until the database is reorganized).

6.2 Anomalies in a Database: A Consequence of Bad Design

Consider the following relation scheme pertaining to the information about a student maintained by an university:

STDINF*(Name, Course,* *Phone_No, Major, Prof, Grade)*

Figure 6.1 shows some tuples of a relation on the relation scheme **STDINF *(Name, Course,*** *Phone_No, Major, Prof, Grade)*. The functional dependencies[1] among its attributes are shown in Figure 6.2. The key of the relation is *Name Course* and the relation has, in addition, the following functional dependencies {*Name* → *Phone_No, Name* → *Major, Name Course* → *Grade, Course* → *Prof*}.

Here the attribute *Phone_No,* which is not in any key of the relation scheme **STDINF,** is not functionally dependent on the whole key but only on part of the

[1]Recall the definition of functional dependency from Chapter 2, repeated here: Given attributes X and Y (each of which may contain one or more attributes), Y is said to be functionally dependent on X if a given value for each attribute in X uniquely determines the value of the attributes in Y. X is called the determinant of the functional dependency (FD) and the FD is denoted as X → Y.

Figure 6.1 Student data represented in relation STDINF.

Name	*Course*	*Phone_No*	*Major*	*Prof*	*Grade*
Jones	353	237-4539	Comp Sci	Smith	A
Ng	329	427-7390	Chemistry	Turner	B
Jones	328	237-4539	Comp Sci	Clark	B
Martin	456	388-5183	Physics	James	A
Dulles	293	371-6259	Decision Sci	Cook	C
Duke	491	823-7293	Mathematics	Lamb	B
Duke	356	823-7293	Mathematics	Bond	in prog
Jones	492	237-4539	Comp Sci	Cross	in prog
Baxter	379	839-0827	English	Broes	C

key, namely, the attribute *Name*. Similarly, the attributes *Major* and *Prof,* which are not in any key of the relation scheme **STDINF** either, are fully functionally dependent on the attributes *Name* and *Course,* respectively. Thus the determinants of these functional dependencies are again not the entire key but only part of the key of the relation. Only the attribute *Grade* is fully functionally dependent on the key ***Name Course.***

The relation scheme **STDINF** can lead to several undesirable problems:

- **Redundancy:** The aim of the database system is to reduce redundancy, meaning that information is to be stored only once. Storing information several times leads to the waste of storage space and an increase in the total size of the data stored. Updates to the database with such redundancies have the potential of becoming inconsistent, as explained below. In the relation of Figure 6.1, the *Major* and *Phone_No* of a student are stored several times in the database: once for each course that is or was taken by a student.
- **Update Anomalies:** Multiple copies of the same fact may lead to update anomalies or inconsistencies when an update is made and only some of the multiple copies are updated. Thus, a change in the *Phone_No* of Jones must be made, for consistency, in all tuples pertaining to the student Jones. If one of the

Figure 6.2 Function dependencies in **STDINF.**

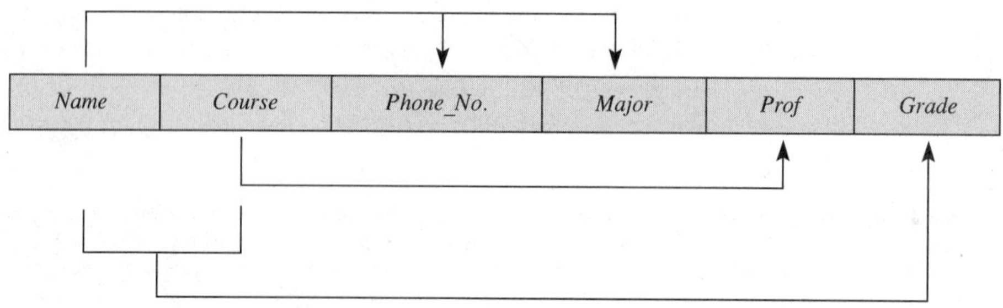

three tuples of Figure 6.2 is not changed to reflect the new *Phone_No* of Jones, there will be an inconsistency in the data.

- **Insertion Anomalies:** If this is the only relation in the database showing the association between a faculty member and the course he or she teaches, the fact that a given professor is teaching a given course cannot be entered in the database unless a student is registered in the course. Also, if another relation also establishes a relationship between a course and a professor who teaches that course (for example, the SCHEDULE relation of Figure A), the information stored in these relations has to be consistent.
- **Deletion Anomalies:** If the only student registered in a given course discontinues the course, the information as to which professor is offering the course will be lost if this is the only relation in the database showing the association between a faculty member and the course she or he teaches. If another relation in the database also establishes the relationship between a course and a professor who teaches that course, the deletion of the last tuple in STDINF for a given course will not cause the information about the course's teacher to be lost.

The problems of database inconsistency and redundancy of data are similar to the problems that exist in the hierarchical and network models. These problems are addressed in the network model by the introduction of virtual fields and in the hierarchical model by the introduction of virtual records. In the relational model, the above problems can be remedied by decomposition. We define **decomposition** as follows:

Definition: **Decomposition:**

The decomposition of a relation scheme $\mathbf{R} = (A_1, A_2, \ldots, A_n)$ is its replacement by a set of relation schemes $\{\mathbf{R_1}, \mathbf{R_2}, \ldots, \mathbf{R_m}\}$, such that $\mathbf{R_i} \subseteq \mathbf{R}$ for $1 \leq i \leq m$ and $\mathbf{R_1} \cup \mathbf{R_2} \cup \ldots \cup \mathbf{R_m} = \mathbf{R}$.

A relation scheme **R** can be decomposed into a collection of relation schemes $\{\mathbf{R_1}, \mathbf{R_2}, \mathbf{R_3}, \ldots, \mathbf{R_m}\}$ to eliminate some of the anomalies contained in the original relation **R**. Here the relation schemes $\mathbf{R_i}$ $(1 \leq i \leq m)$ are subsets of **R** and the intersection of $\mathbf{R_i} \cap \mathbf{R_j}$ for $i \neq j$ need not be empty. Furthermore, the union of $\mathbf{R_i}$ $(1 \leq i \leq m)$ is equal to **R**, i.e., $\mathbf{R} = \mathbf{R_1} \cup \mathbf{R_2} \cup \ldots \cup \mathbf{R_m}$.

The problems in the relation scheme **STDINF** can be resolved if we replace it with the following relation schemes:

STUDENT_INFO *(Name, Phone_No, Major)*
TRANSCRIPT *(Name, Course, Grade)*
TEACHER *(Course, Proof)*

The first relation scheme gives the phone number and the major of each student and such information will be stored only once for each student. Any change in the phone number will thus require a change in only one tuple of this relation.

The second relation scheme stores the grade of each student in each course that the student is or was enrolled in. (Note: In our database we assume that either the student takes the course only once, or if he or she has to repeat it to improve the grade, the TRANSCRIPT relation stores only the highest grade.)

The third relation scheme records the teacher of each course.

One of the disadvantages of replacing the original relation scheme **STDINF** with the three relation schemes is that the retrieval of certain information requires a natural join operation to be performed. For instance, to find the majors of student who obtained a grade of A in course 353 requires a join to be performed: (STUDENT_INFO $\bowtie$ TRANSCRIPT). The same information could be derived from the original relation STDINF by selection and projection.

When we replace the original relation scheme **STDINF** with the relation schemes **STUDENT_INFO, TRANSCRIPT,** and **TEACHER,** the consistency and referential integrity constraints have to be enforced. The referential integrity enforcement implies that if a tuple in the relation TRANSCRIPT exists, such as (Jones, 353, in prog), a tuple must exist in STUDENT_INFO with *Name* = Jones and, furthermore, a tuple must exist in TEACHER with *Course* = 353. The attribute *Name,* which forms part of the key of the relation TRANSCRIPT, is a key of the relation STUDENT_INFO. Such an attribute (or a group of attributes), which establishes a relationship between specific tuples (of the same or two distinct relations), is called a foreign key. Notice that the attribute *Course* in relation TRANSCRIPT is also a foreign key, since it is a key of the relation TEACHER.

Note that the decomposition of **STDINF** into the relation schemes **STUDENT**(*Name, Phone_No, Major, Grade*) and **COURSE**(*Course, Prof*) is a bad decomposition for the following reasons:

1. Redundancy and update anomaly, because the data for the attributes *Phone_No* and *Major* are repeated.
2. Loss of information, because we lose the fact that a student has a given grade in a particular course.

The rest of this chapter examines the problem of the design of the relational database and how to decide whether a given set of relations is better than another set.

6.3 Universal Relation

Let us consider the problem of designing a database. Such a design will be required to represent a finite number of entity sets. Each entity set will be represented by a number of its attributes. If we refer to the set of all attributes as the universal scheme **U** then a relation R(**U**) is called the **universal relation.** The universal relation is a single relation made up of all the attributes in the database. The term **universal relation assumption** is the assumption that all relations in a database are derived from the universal relation by appropriate projection. The attribute names in the universal relation scheme **U** have to be distinct to avoid obvious confusion. One reason for using the universal relation assumption is to allow the user to view the database using such a relation. Consequently, the user does not have to remember the relation schemes and which attributes are grouped together in each such scheme.

Consider the relation R_1 *(Course, Department)* in Figure 6.3: The attribute *Department* is used to indicate the department responsible for the course. For instance,

Figure 6.3 Relation R_1.

Course	*Department*
353	Comp Sci
355	Mathematics
456	Mathematics
221	Decision Sci

course 353 is offered by and is under the jurisdiction of the Comp(uter) Sci(ence) department.

The relation R_2*(Professor, Department)* of Figure 6.4 shows another role or interpretation of the attribute *Department;* here it is used to signify that a given professor is assigned to a given department. Thus, Smith is a member of the Comp Sci department. Note from Figures A, 6.3, and 6.4 that we are allowing for the incidence of a professor teaching a course in a outside department. Professor Clark of the Comp Sci department is teaching course 355 of the Mathematics department, and Professor Turner of the Chemistry department is teaching course 456, also of the Mathematics department.

The domain of the attribute *Department* in the relations R_1 and R_2 is the same, that is, all the departments in the university. Let us consider the representation of the data in the limited database indicated in Figures 6.3 and 6.4 as a universal relation U_1, where U_1 is defined as U_1*(Course, Department, Professor)*. The problem of using the universal relation U_1 becomes obvious when we try to represent the data from the relations R_1 and R_2 as shown in Figures 6.3 and 6.4. Here we have to decide whether or not data from different relations could appear in the same tuple of the universal relation. In Figure 6.5 we do not allow the data from different relations to appear in the same tuple of U_1, giving rise to a large number of empty or null values ($\perp$). These null values could signify one of three things: (1) the values, are not known, but they exist, (2) the values do not exist, or (3) the attribute does not apply. In case (1) we have to distinguish the null values by indicating them as $\perp_i$, and thus the two null values $\perp_i$ and $\perp_j$ (for $i \neq j$) are not equal and indicate that the values are not known to be the same.

In Figure 6.6, we have combined the data from the relations R_1 and R_2 in the same tuple of the universal relation U_2 with the scheme *(Course, Department, Pro-*

Figure 6.4 Relation R_2.

Professor	*Department*
Smith	Comp Sci
Clark	Comp Sci
Turner	Chemistry
Jamieson	Mathematics

Figure 6.5 Relation U_1.

Course	*Department*	*Professor*
353	Comp Sci	⊥
456	Mathematics	⊥
355	Mathematics	⊥
221	Decision Sci	⊥
⊥	Comp Sci	Smith
⊥	Comp Sci	Clark
⊥	Chemistry	Turner
⊥	Mathematics	Jamieson

fessor). Now the number of null values has been reduced at the expense of a certain amount of duplication. For instance, course 353 appears in two tuples of R_2 as being offered by the Comp Sci department.

When the roles that the attribute *Department* play in the relation R_1 and R_2 are explicitly expressed, we get the universal relation U_3 with the scheme *(Course, Crs_Dept, Fac_Dept, Professor)*. Here, *Crs_Dept* is the attribute *Department* in the relation R_1 renamed to indicate the department responsible for a given course and *Fac_Dept* is the attribute *Department* in the relation R_2 renamed to indicate the department of a professor. In Figure 6.7 we have allowed tuples from different relations to appear in a tuple of the universal relation. For symmetry, we express the cross product of the tuple of relations R_1 and R_2 in the universal relation U_3. This gives a representation that does not involve any null values but leads to an extensive amount of duplication of data and the associated problems of maintaining data consistency. A tuple in U_3 represents two independent facts. For example, the fourth tuple of U_3 represents the facts "221 is a course in Decision Sci" and "Smith is a professor in Comp Sci."

We can retrieve the original relations R_1 and R_2 by a projection operation as follows:

$$R_1 = \pi_{\{Course, Department\}}(U_1)$$
$$R_2 = \pi_{\{Professor,\ Department\}}(U_1)$$

Figure 6.6 Relation U_2.

Course	*Department*	*Professor*
353	Comp Sci	Smith
353	Comp Sci	Clark
456	Mathematics	Jamieson
355	Mathematics	Jamieson
221	Decision Sci	⊥
⊥	Chemistry	Turner

Figure 6.7 Relation U_3.

Course	*Crs_Dept*	*Fac_Dept*	*Professor*
353	Comp Sci	Comp Sci	Smith
456	Mathematics	Comp Sci	Smith
355	Mathematics	Comp Sci	Smith
221	Decision Sci	Comp Sci	Smith
353	Comp Sci	Comp Sci	Clark
456	Mathematics	Comp Sci	Clark
355	Mathematics	Comp Sci	Clark
221	Decision Sci	Comp Sci	Clark
353	Comp Sci	Chemistry	Turner
456	Mathematics	Chemistry	Turner
355	Mathematics	Chemistry	Turner
221	Decision Sci	Chemistry	Turner
353	Comp Sci	Mathematics	Jamieson
456	Mathematics	Mathematics	Jamieson
355	Mathematics	Mathematics	Jamieson
221	Decision Sci	Mathematics	Jamieson

However, we will get some tuples with null values that did not exist in the original R_1 and R_2 relations. These tuples are called **spurious tuples** and they have to be *ignored!* The above example of representing data by the universal relation shows some of the problems of this assumption.

The universal relation is obtained by including all database attributes in a single relation. There is controversy in the database community as to the validity of the universal assumption. However, it is helpful in encouraging some consistency in the use of attribute names in the database. A given attribute name appearing in the database must have the same meaning to make meaningful interpretation of the natural join operation. Without such universal meaning of an attribute, we will be forced to assume that multiple occurrences of an attribute in multiple relation schemes have different meanings and hence the interrelation connection cannot be made.

We will refer to the universal relation assumption in the synthesis approach to relational database design in the following chapter.

6.4 Functional Dependency

As we discussed in Chapter 2, functional dependencies are the consequence of the interrelationship among attributes of an entity represented by a relation or due to the relationship between entities that is also represented by a relation. Thus, if **R** represents an entity and the set **X** of attributes represents the key of **R,** then for any other set of attribute **Y** of **R,** $\mathbf{X} \rightarrow \mathbf{Y}$. This is because the key of a relation identifies a tuple and hence a particular instance of the corresponding entity. Two tuples of a relation having the same key must represent the same instance of the corresponding entity and since duplicate tuples are not allowed, these two tuples must indeed be the same tuple and the value of the attributes in **Y** must be determined by the key value. Similarly, if **R** represents a many-to-one relationship between two entities, say from E_1 to E_2, and if **X** contains attributes that form a key of E_1 and **Y** contains attributes that contain a key of E_2, again the FD **X** → **Y** will hold. But if **R** represents a one-to-one relationship between entity E_1 and E_2, the FD **Y** → **X** will hold in addition to the FD **X** → **Y**.

Let **R** be a relation scheme where each of its attribute A_i is defined on some domain $\mathbf{D_i}$ for $1 \le i \le n$. Let **X, Y, Z,** etc. be subsets of $\{A_1, A_2, \ldots, A_n\}$. We will write **X** ∪ **Y** as simply **XY**.

Let R be a relation on the relation scheme **R.** Then R satisfies the functional dependency **X** → **Y** if a given set of values for each attribute in **X** uniquely determines each of the values of the attributes in **Y. Y** is said to be functionally dependent on **X.** The functional dependency (FD) is denoted as **X** → **Y,** where **X** is the left-hand side or the determinant of the FD and **Y** is the right-hand side of the FD. We can say that the FD **X** → **Y** is satisfied on the relation R if the cardinality of $\pi_{\mathbf{Y}}(\sigma_{\mathbf{X}=x}(R))$ is at most one. In other words, if two tuples t_i and t_j of R have the same **X** value, the corresponding value of **Y** will be identical.

A functional dependency **X** → **Y** is said to be **trivial** if **Y** ⊆ **X.**

Example 6.2 In the relation SCHEDULE(*Prof, Course, Room, Max_Enrollment, Day, Time)* of Figure A, the FD *Course* → *Prof* is satisfied. However, the FD *Prof* → *Course* is not satisfied. ■

In order to verify if a given FD **X** → **Y** is satisfied by a relation R on a relation scheme **R,** we find any two tuples with the same **X** value; if the FD **X** → **Y** is satisfied in R, then the **Y** values in these tuples must be the same. We repeat this procedure until we have examined all such pairs of tuples with the same **X** value. A simpler approach involves ordering the tuples of R on the **X** values so that all tuples with the same **X** values are together. Then it is easy to verify if the corresponding **Y** values are also the same and verify if R satisfies the FD **X** → **Y.**

Figure 6.8 The SCHEDULE relation.

Prof	*Course*	*Room*	*Max_Enrollment*	*Day*	*Time*
Smith	353	A532	40	mon	1145
Smith	353	A532	40	wed	1145
Clark	355	H940	300	tue	115
Clark	355	H940	300	thu	115
Turner	456	B278	45	mon	845
Turner	456	B278	45	wed	845
Jamieson	459	D110	45	tue	1015
Jamieson	459	D110	45	thu	1015

The FD $\mathbf{X} \rightarrow \mathbf{Y}$ on a relation scheme must hold for all possible relations defined on the relation scheme **R.** Thus, we cannot look at a table representing a relation on the scheme **R** at a point in time and say, simply by inspection, that some FD $\mathbf{X} \rightarrow \mathbf{Y}$ holds. For example, if the relation SCHEDULE at some point in time contained the tuples as shown in Figure 6.8, we might erroneously conclude that the FD {*Prof* → *Course*} holds. The examination of the real world situation corresponding to the relation scheme **SCHEDULE** tells us that a particular professor may be teaching more than one course.

Example 6.3 In the relation scheme **STDINF** *(Name, Course, Phone_No, Major, Prof, Grade)*, the following functional dependencies are satisfied: {*Name* → *Phone_No, Name* → *Major, Name Course* → *Grade, Course* → *Prof*}. ■

6.4.1 Dependencies and Logical Implications

Given a relation scheme **R** and a set of functional dependencies **F,** let us consider a functional dependency $\mathbf{X} \rightarrow \mathbf{Y}$, which is not in **F. F** can be said to logically imply $\mathbf{X} \rightarrow \mathbf{Y}$ if for every relation R on the relation scheme **R** that satisfies the functional dependencies in **F,** R also satisfies $\mathbf{X} \rightarrow \mathbf{Y}$.

F logically implies $\mathbf{X} \rightarrow \mathbf{Y}$ is written as $\mathbf{F} \models \mathbf{X} \rightarrow \mathbf{Y}$.

Example 6.4 $\mathbf{R} = (A, B, C, D)$ and $\mathbf{F} = \{A \rightarrow B, A \rightarrow C, BC \rightarrow D\}$, then $\mathbf{F} \models A \rightarrow D$. ■

Inference Axioms

Suppose we have **F,** a set of functional dependencies. To determine whether a functional dependency $\mathbf{X} \rightarrow \mathbf{Y}$ is logically implied by **F** (i.e., $\mathbf{F} \models \mathbf{X} \rightarrow \mathbf{Y}$), we use a set of rules or axioms. The axioms are numbered **F1** through **F6** to indicate that they pertain to functional dependencies (as opposed to multivalued dependencies, which we examine in Chapter 7).

In the following discussions, we assume that we have a relation scheme $\mathbf{R}(A_1, A_2, A_3, \ldots, A_n)$; R is a relation on the relation scheme **R** and **W, X, Y, Z** are subsets of **R.** The symbol $\models$ used below is read as "logically implies."

- **F1: Reflexivity:** $(\mathbf{X} \rightarrow \mathbf{X}$ and $\mathbf{V} \subseteq \mathbf{Z})$
- **F2: Augmentation:** $(\mathbf{X} \rightarrow \mathbf{Y}) \models (\mathbf{XZ} \rightarrow \mathbf{Y}$, and $\mathbf{XZ} \rightarrow \mathbf{YZ})$
- **F3: Transitivity:** $(\mathbf{X} \rightarrow \mathbf{Y}$ and $\mathbf{Y} \rightarrow \mathbf{Z}) \models (\mathbf{X} \rightarrow \mathbf{Z})$
- **F4: Additivity:** $(\mathbf{X} \rightarrow \mathbf{Y}$ and $\mathbf{X} \rightarrow \mathbf{Z}) \models (\mathbf{X} \rightarrow \mathbf{YZ})$
- **F5: Projectivity:** $(\mathbf{X} \rightarrow \mathbf{YZ}) \models (\mathbf{X} \rightarrow \mathbf{Y}$ and $\mathbf{X} \rightarrow \mathbf{Z})$
- **F6: Pseudotransitivity:** $(\mathbf{X} \rightarrow \mathbf{Y}$ and $\mathbf{YZ} \rightarrow \mathbf{W}) \models (\mathbf{XZ} \rightarrow \mathbf{W})$

Example 6.5

We use the relation R of Figure B to illustrate the above inference axioms.

Reflexivity: This is obvious since any set of attributes implies the same set of attributes. The consequence of this axiom, along with **F5,** is that for any

Figure B Relation R on the scheme **R**(*A, B, C, D, E*).

R	*A*	*B*	*C*	*D*	*E*
	a_1	b_1	c_2	d_1	e_1
	a_2	b_2	c_1	d_2	e_2
	a_3	b_1	c_2	d_1	e_3
	a_3	b_3	c_3	d_3	e_4
	a_1	b_2	c_1	d_2	e_5
	a_4	b_4	c_4	d_4	e_6
	a_3	b_2	c_1	d_2	e_7
	a_5	b_4	c_4	d_4	e_8

$\mathbf{Y} \subseteq \mathbf{X}, \mathbf{X} \rightarrow \mathbf{Y}$. A FD $\mathbf{X} \rightarrow \mathbf{Y}$ is said to be a **trivial functional dependency** if $\mathbf{Y} \subseteq \mathbf{X}$.

Augmentation: This axiom indicates that the left-hand side alone or both sides of an FD can be augmented.

If the relation R satisfies the FD $\mathbf{X} \rightarrow \mathbf{Y}$, then for a given **X** value that appears in R, the number of tuples having some **Y** value that will be exactly 1. In other words, the cardinality of $\pi_{\mathbf{Y}}(\sigma_{\mathbf{X}=x}(R))$, written as $|\pi_{\mathbf{Y}}(\sigma_{\mathbf{X}=x}(R))|$, is equal to 1.

If $\mathbf{Z} \subseteq \mathbf{R}$, then $\sigma_{\mathbf{XZ}=xz}(R) \subseteq \sigma_{\mathbf{X}=x}(R)$, i.e., the set of tuples selected with a given value of **XZ** is a subset of the set of tuples selected for a given value of **X** alone. Now the number of tuples having a given **Y** value in $\sigma_{\mathbf{XZ}=xz}(R)$ will be a subset of the tuples having the same **Y** value in $\sigma_{\mathbf{X}=x}(R)$; since the latter is at most 1, the number of tuples having a given **Y** value in **XZ** will be at most 1. hence $\mathbf{XZ} \rightarrow \mathbf{Y}$.

It follows that $\mathbf{XZ} \rightarrow \mathbf{Y} \models \mathbf{XZ} \rightarrow \mathbf{YZ}$ and $\mathbf{X} \rightarrow \mathbf{Y} \models \mathbf{XZ} \rightarrow \mathbf{YV}$ for $\mathbf{V} \subseteq \mathbf{Z}$.

In Figure B, the FD $B \rightarrow C$ is satisfied and by augmentation we find that the FDs $AB \rightarrow C$, $BC \rightarrow C$, $BD \rightarrow C$, $BE \rightarrow C$ and $ABC \rightarrow C$, $BCD \rightarrow C$, etc. are also satisfied.

Additivity: The axiom indicates that if there are two FDs with the same left-hand side, the right-hand side of these FDs can be added to give an FD where the left-hand side is the original one and the right-hand side is the union of the right-hand sides of the two FDs. Thus, if $\mathbf{X} \rightarrow \mathbf{Y}$, then $\pi_{\mathbf{Y}}(\sigma_{\mathbf{X}=x}(R))$ has at most one tuple and similarly, if $\mathbf{X} \rightarrow \mathbf{Z}$, then $\pi_{\mathbf{Z}}(\sigma_{\mathbf{X}=x}(R))$ has at most one tuple. Hence, $\pi_{\mathbf{ZY}}(\sigma_{\mathbf{X}=x}(R))$ cannot have more than one tuple. The additivity axiom follows from these observations.

We note from Figure B that the FDs $B \rightarrow C$, $B \rightarrow D$, and consequently $B \rightarrow CD$ are all satisfied.

Projectivity: This axiom is the inverse of the additivity axiom; it splits up or projects an FD whose right-hand side is a union of attributes into a number of FDs. Each projected FD has the same left-hand side as the original FD and each contains a subset of the original right-hand side.

For the relation R of Figure B, the FD $B \rightarrow CD$ is satisfied and hence, by projectivity, $B \rightarrow C$ and $B \rightarrow D$.

Transitivity: For the relation R of Figure B, the FDs $B \rightarrow C$ and $C \rightarrow D$ are satisfied and hence, by transitivity, $B \rightarrow D$. Thus, when the value for B is b_1 in R, the value of C is c_2. Similarly, when the value of C is c_2, the value of D is d_1. When the value of B is b_1, the value of D is d_1.

Pseudotransitivity: This axiom follows from axioms **F2** and **F3.** Given **X → Y**, by **F2, XZ → YZ** and since **YZ → W** is given, then by **F3, XZ → W.**

The relation R of Figure B satisfies the FDs $C \rightarrow B$ and $AB \rightarrow E$, so by pseudotransitivity, the FD CA → E is also satisfied. ■

Inference rules **F1** through **F3** are variations of the Armstrong axioms, so called after W. W. Armstrong, who first proposed them (Arms 74). Example 6.5 gave informal arguments showing that each of the inference axioms **F1** through **F6** is sound (i.e., correct). This means that whenever an FD **X → Y** can be derived from a set of FDs **F** using these axioms, then **F** ⊨ **X → Y.** It has been shown that the converse also holds, even for the subset **F1** through **F3.** Whenever **F** ⊨ **X → Y, X → Y** can be derived from **F** using these inference axioms. These axioms form a complete axiom system for FDs. Rules **F4** through **F6** in particular can be derived from rules **F1** through **F3.**

6.4.2 Closure of a Set of Functional Dependencies

The set of functional dependencies that is logically implied by **F** is called the **closure** of **F** and is written as $\mathbf{F}^+$.

Definition: If **F** is a set of FDs on a relation scheme **R,** then $\mathbf{F}^+$, the closure of **F,** is the smallest set of FDs such that[2] $\mathbf{F}^+ \supseteq \mathbf{F}$ and no FD can be derived from **F** by using the inference axioms that are not contained in $\mathbf{F}^+$. If **R** is not specified, it is assumed to contain all the attributes that appear in **F**.

$\mathbf{F}^+$ is the set of FDs that are implied by the FDs in **F**, i.e., $\mathbf{F}^+ = \{\mathbf{X} \rightarrow \mathbf{Y} \mid \mathbf{F} \models \mathbf{X} \rightarrow \mathbf{Y}\}$.

An FD f in $\mathbf{F}^+$ is logically implied by **F** since any relation R on the relation scheme **R** that satisfies the FDs in **F** also satisfies the FD in $\mathbf{F}^+$ and, hence, f.

[2] $\mathbf{F}^+ \supseteq \mathbf{F}$ denotes that $\mathbf{F}^+$ contains **F.**

Example 6.6 Let $\mathbf{R} = (A, B, C, D)$ and $\mathbf{F} = \{A \rightarrow B, A \rightarrow C, BC \rightarrow D\}$. Since $A \rightarrow B$ and $A \rightarrow C$, then by **F4** $A \rightarrow BC$. Now since $BC \rightarrow D$, then by **F3** $A \rightarrow D$, i.e., $\mathbf{F} \models A \rightarrow D$ and thus $A \rightarrow D$ is in $\mathbf{F}^+$. ■

An example of an FD not implied by a given set of FDs is illustrated below.

Example 6.7 Let $\mathbf{F} = \{\mathbf{W} \rightarrow \mathbf{X}, \mathbf{X} \rightarrow \mathbf{Y}, \mathbf{W} \rightarrow \mathbf{XY}\}$. Then $\mathbf{F}^+$ includes the set $\{\mathbf{W} \rightarrow \mathbf{W}, \mathbf{X} \rightarrow \mathbf{X}, \mathbf{Y} \rightarrow \mathbf{Y}, \mathbf{W} \rightarrow \mathbf{X}, \mathbf{X} \rightarrow \mathbf{Y}, \mathbf{W} \rightarrow \mathbf{XY}, \mathbf{W} \rightarrow \mathbf{Y}\}$. The first three FDs follow from axiom **F1**; the next three FDs are in **F** and hence in $\mathbf{F}^+$. Since $\mathbf{W} \rightarrow \mathbf{XY}$, then by axiom **F5**, $\mathbf{W} \rightarrow \mathbf{X}$ and $\mathbf{W} \rightarrow \mathbf{Y}$. However, $\mathbf{F}^+$ does not contain an FD, e.g., $\mathbf{W} \rightarrow \mathbf{Z}$, because **Z** is not contained in the set of attributes that appear in **F**. ■

6.4.3 Testing if $F \models X \rightarrow Y$: Algorithm to Compute a Closure

To compute the closure $\mathbf{F}^+$ for a set of FD **F** is a lengthy process because the number of dependencies in $\mathbf{F}^+$, though finite, can be very large. The reason for computing $\mathbf{F}^+$ is to determine if the set of FDs $\mathbf{F} \models \mathbf{X} \rightarrow \mathbf{Y}$; this would be the case if and only if $\mathbf{X} \rightarrow \mathbf{Y} \in \mathbf{F}^+$. However, there is an alternative method to test if $\mathbf{F} \models \mathbf{X} \rightarrow \mathbf{Y}$ without generating $\mathbf{F}^+$. The method depends on generating $\mathbf{X}^+$, the closure of **X** under **F**.

Definition: The closure of **X** under a set of functional dependencies **F**, written as $\mathbf{X}^+$, is the set of attributes $\{A_1, A_2, \ldots, A_m\}$ such that the FD $\mathbf{X} \rightarrow A_i$ for $A_i \in \mathbf{X}^+$ follows from **F** by the inference axioms for functional dependencies.

$\mathbf{X}^+$, the closure of **X** with respect to the set of functional dependencies **F**, is the set of attributes $\{A_1, A_2, A_3, \ldots, A_m\}$ such that each of the FDs $\mathbf{X} \rightarrow A_i$, $1 \leq i \leq m$ can be derived from **F** by the inference axioms. Also, by the additivity axiom for functional dependency, $\mathbf{F} \models \mathbf{X} \rightarrow \mathbf{Y}$ if $\mathbf{Y} \subseteq \mathbf{X}^+$. (By the completeness of the axiom system, if $\mathbf{F} \models \mathbf{X} \rightarrow \mathbf{Y}$, then $\mathbf{Y} \subseteq \mathbf{X}^+$—see lemma below.)

Having found $\mathbf{X}^+$, we can test if $\mathbf{F} \models \mathbf{X} \rightarrow \mathbf{Y}$ by checking if $\mathbf{Y} \subseteq \mathbf{X}^+$: $\mathbf{X} \rightarrow \mathbf{Y}$ is logically implied by **F** if and only if $\mathbf{Y} \subseteq \mathbf{X}^+$.

We now present the algorithm to compute the closure $\mathbf{X}^+$ given a set of FDs **F** and a set of attributes **X**. The importance of computing the closure $\mathbf{X}^+$ is that it can be used to decide if any FD $\mathbf{X} \rightarrow \mathbf{Y}$ can be deduced from **F**. The following lemma establishes that if $\mathbf{Y} \subseteq \mathbf{X}^+$ then $\mathbf{F} \models \mathbf{X} \rightarrow \mathbf{Y}$.

Lemma: $\mathbf{F} \models \mathbf{X} \rightarrow \mathbf{Y}$ if and only if $\mathbf{Y} \subseteq \mathbf{X}^+$.

Proof: Suppose that $\mathbf{Y} \subseteq \mathbf{X}^+$. Then by the definition of $\mathbf{X}^+$, $\mathbf{X} \rightarrow A$ can be derived from **F** using the inference rules for each $A \in \mathbf{Y}$. By the soundness of these rules, $\mathbf{F} \models \mathbf{X} \rightarrow A$ for each $A \in \mathbf{Y}$ and by the additivity rule, $\mathbf{F} \models \mathbf{X} \rightarrow \mathbf{Y}$. Now suppose that $\mathbf{F} \models \mathbf{X} \rightarrow$

Algorithm **6.1**

Algorithm to Compute $\mathbf{X}^+$

Input: A set of functional dependencies **F** and a set of attributes **X**.

Output: The closure $\mathbf{X}^+$ of **X** under the FDs in **F**.

```
X+ := X; (* initialize X+ to X *)
change := true;
while change do
    begin
    change := false;
    for each FD W → Z in F do
        begin
        if W ⊆ X+ then do
                    begin
                    X+ := X+ ∪ Z;
                    change := true;
                    end
        end
    end
(* X+ now contains the closure of X under F *)
```

Y. Then by completeness of the inference rules, $\mathbf{X} \rightarrow \mathbf{Y}$ can be derived from **F** using them. By projectivity, $\mathbf{X} \rightarrow A$ can be derived for each $A \in \mathbf{Y}$. This clearly implies that $\mathbf{Y} \subseteq \mathbf{X}^+$ by the definition of $\mathbf{X}^+$.

Algorithm 6.1 to compute $\mathbf{X}^+$ follows. It starts with the set $\mathbf{X}^+$ initialized to **X**, the left-hand side of the FD $\mathbf{X} \rightarrow \mathbf{Y}$, which is to be tested for logical implication under **F**. For each FD $\mathbf{W} \rightarrow \mathbf{Z}$ in **F**, if $\mathbf{W} \subseteq \mathbf{X}^+$, the algorithm modifies $\mathbf{X}^+$ by forming a union of $\mathbf{X}^+$ and **Z**. The algorithm terminates when there is no change in $\mathbf{X}^+$.

Example 6.8

Let $\mathbf{X} = BCD$ and $\mathbf{F} = \{A \rightarrow BC,\ CD \rightarrow E,\ E \rightarrow C,\ D \rightarrow AEH,\ ABH \rightarrow BD,\ DH \rightarrow BC\}$. We want to compute the closure $\mathbf{X}^+$ of **X** under **F**.
We initialize $\mathbf{X}^+$ to **X**, i.e., $\mathbf{X}^+ := BCD$. Now since the left-hand side of the FD $CD \rightarrow E$ is a subset of $\mathbf{X}^+$, i.e., $CD \subseteq \mathbf{X}^+$, $\mathbf{X}^+$ is augmented by the right-hand side of the FD, i.e., E; thus $\mathbf{X}^+$ now becomes equal to $BCDE$. Similarly, since $D \subseteq \mathbf{X}^+$, the right-hand side of the FD $D \rightarrow AEH$ is added to $\mathbf{X}^+$, which now becomes $ABCDEH$. $\mathbf{X}^+$ cannot be augmented any further and Algorithm 6.1 ends with $\mathbf{X}^+$ equal to $ABCDEH$. ■

The time complexity of the closure algorithm can be derived as follows. Suppose the number of attributes in **F** is **a** and the number of FDs in **F** is **f** where each FD in **F** involves only one attribute on the right-hand side. Then the inner for loop will be executed at most **f** times, one for each FD in **F**, and each such execution can take the time proportional to **a** to check if one set is contained in another set. Thus the order of execution of the for loop is **O(af)**. In the worst case each execution of the while loop can increase the closure by one element and since there are **f** FDs, the while loop can be repeated at most **f** times. Hence the time complexity of the algorithm is $\mathbf{O(af^2)}$. The algorithm can be modified to run in time proportional to the number of symbols needed to represent the FDs in **F**. The modification takes into account the fact that the FDs whose right-hand sides are already added to $\mathbf{X}^+$ need not be reconsidered in the for loop. Furthermore, the FDs whose left-hand side lengths are greater than the current length of $\mathbf{X}^+$ need not be tested in the for loop. See the bibliographic notes for reference to a closure algorithm with these modifications.

6.4.4 Testing if an FD is in a Closure

As mentioned earlier, to find out whether $\mathbf{F} \models \mathbf{X} \rightarrow \mathbf{Y}$ without computing $\mathbf{F}^+$ requires the computation of $\mathbf{X}^+$ under the set of FDs **F**, and if $\mathbf{Y} \subseteq \mathbf{X}^+$ then **F** logically implies the functional dependency $\mathbf{X} \rightarrow \mathbf{Y}$, otherwise it does not. Algorithm 6.2 tests the membership of $\mathbf{X} \rightarrow \mathbf{Y}$ in $\mathbf{F}^+$ by this indirect scheme. It uses Algorithm 6.1 to compute the closure of **X** under **F**.

Example 6.9

Let $\mathbf{F} = \{A \rightarrow BC,\ CD \rightarrow E,\ E \rightarrow C,\ D \rightarrow AEH,\ ABH \rightarrow BD,\ DH \rightarrow BC\}$. We want to find if $\mathbf{F} \models BCD \rightarrow H$.

Having computed BCD^+ as being $ABCDEH$ we can clearly see that the FD $BCD \rightarrow H$ is implied by the FD **F** since $H \subseteq BCD^+$. ■

The time complexity of the membership algorithm is similar to the closure algorithm because the membership algorithm uses the closure algorithm.

6.4.5 Covers

Given a set of FDs **F**, $\mathbf{F}^+$ is the closure of **F** and contains all FDs that can be derived from **F**. As mentioned earlier, $\mathbf{F}^+$ can be very large; hence, we will look for a smaller set of FDs that are representative of the closure of **F**. Suppose we have another set of FDs **G**. We say that **F** and **G** are equivalent if the closure of **F** is identically equal to the closure of **G**, i.e., $\mathbf{F}^+ = \mathbf{G}^+$. If the sets of FDs **F** and **G** are equivalent, we can consider one to be representative of the other or one **covers** the other. Thus **F** covers **G** and **G** covers **F**.

Definition: Given two sets of FDs **F** and **G** over a relation scheme **R**, **F** and **G** are equivalent (i.e., $\mathbf{F} \equiv \mathbf{G}$) if the closure of **F** is identically equal to the closure of **G** (i.e., $\mathbf{F}^+ = \mathbf{G}^+$). If **F** and **G** are equivalent, then **F covers G** and **G covers F**.

Algorithm 6.2

Membership Algorithm

Input: A set of functional dependencies **F** and the functional dependency $\mathbf{X} \rightarrow \mathbf{Y}$.

Output: Is $\mathbf{X} \rightarrow \mathbf{Y} \in \mathbf{F}^+$ or not?

Compute $\mathbf{X}^+$ using Algorithm 6.1.
if $\mathbf{Y} \subseteq \mathbf{X}^+$ *then* $\mathbf{X} \rightarrow \mathbf{Y} \in \mathbf{F}^+ :=$ *true;*
else $\mathbf{X} \rightarrow \mathbf{Y} \in \mathbf{F}^+ :=$ *false.*

If **G** covers **F** and if no proper subset $\mathbf{G}'(\mathbf{G}' \subseteq \mathbf{G})$ covers **F**, **G** is called a **nonredundant cover.**

Definition: Given a set of FDs **F**, we say that it is nonredundant if no proper subset **F′** of **F** is equivalent to **F**, i.e., no **F′** exists such that $\mathbf{F}'^+ = \mathbf{F}^+$.

Given a functional dependency $\mathbf{X} \rightarrow \mathbf{Y}$, where $\mathbf{Y} = A_1A_2A_3 \ldots A_n$, the functional dependency $\mathbf{X} \rightarrow \mathbf{Y}$ can be replaced by an equivalent set of FDs $\{\mathbf{X} \rightarrow A_1, \mathbf{X} \rightarrow A_2, \mathbf{X} \rightarrow A_3, \ldots, \mathbf{X} \rightarrow A_n\}$ by using the inference axioms **F4** and **F5** (additivity and projectivity). A nontrivial FD of the form $\mathbf{X} \rightarrow A_i$ where the right-hand side has only one attribute is called a **simple** FD. Thus every set of FDs **F** can be replaced by an equivalent set of FDs G where G contains only simple FDs.

6.4.6 Nonredundant and Minimum Covers

Given **F**, a set of FDs, if a proper subset **F′** of **F** covers **F** (i.e., $\mathbf{F}' \subset \mathbf{F}$ and $\mathbf{F}'^+ = \mathbf{F}^+$), then **F** is redundant and we can remove some FD, say $\mathbf{X} \rightarrow \mathbf{Y}$, from **F** to find a nonredundant cover of **F.** Algorithm 6.3 finds a nonredundant cover of **F.** It does so by removing one FD $\mathbf{X} \rightarrow \mathbf{Y}$ from **F** and then checking if this FD is implied by the FD set $\{\mathbf{F} - (\mathbf{X} \rightarrow \mathbf{Y})\}$ by using Algorithms 6.1 and 6.2—finding the cover $\mathbf{X}^+$ under the set of FDs $\{\mathbf{F} - (\mathbf{X} \rightarrow \mathbf{Y})\}$. If $\{\mathbf{F} - (\mathbf{X} \rightarrow \mathbf{Y})\} \models \mathbf{X} \rightarrow \mathbf{Y}$, then $\mathbf{X} \rightarrow \mathbf{Y}$ can be removed from **F.** Algorithm 6.3 repeats this procedure for each FD that remains in **F.** Note that the nonredundant cover so obtained depends on the order in which the functional dependencies are considered. Thus, starting with a set **F** of functional dependencies we can derive more than one nonredundant cover. (See Exercise 6.7.)

Algorithm 6.3 Nonredundant Cover

Input: A set of FDs **F**.

Output: A nonredundant cover of **F**.

G := **F**; (* initialize **G** to **F** *)
for each FD $\mathbf{X} \rightarrow \mathbf{Y}$ in **G** *do*
  if $\mathbf{X} \rightarrow \mathbf{Y} \in \{\mathbf{F} - (\mathbf{X} \rightarrow \mathbf{Y})\}^+$ (* i.e., $\{\mathbf{F} - (\mathbf{X} \rightarrow \mathbf{Y})\} \models \mathbf{X} \rightarrow \mathbf{Y}$ *)
    then $\mathbf{F} := \{\mathbf{F} - (\mathbf{X} \rightarrow \mathbf{Y})\}$;
G := **F**; (* **G** is the nonredundant cover of **F** *)
end;

Example 6.10 If $\mathbf{F} = \{A \rightarrow BC, CD \rightarrow E, E \rightarrow C, D \rightarrow AEH, ABH \rightarrow BD, DH \rightarrow BC\}$ then the FDs $CD \rightarrow E$ and $DH \rightarrow BC$ are redundant. We find that $(CD)^+$ under $\{\mathbf{F} - (CD \rightarrow E)\}$ is equal to $ABCDEH$, and since the right-hand side of the FD $(CD \rightarrow E) \subseteq (CD)^+$ under $\{\mathbf{F} - (CD \rightarrow E)\}$, $\{\mathbf{F} - (CD \rightarrow E)\} \models CD \rightarrow E$. We now remove this redundant FD from **F** and then find that for the FD $(DH \rightarrow BC)$, $(DH)^+$ under $\{\mathbf{F} - (DH \rightarrow BC)\}$ is $ABCDEH$. Since the right-hand side of the FD $(DH \rightarrow BC) \subseteq (DH)^+$, the FD $(DH \rightarrow BC)$ is also redundant. No remaining FDs can be removed from the modified **F**. Thus a nonredundant cover for **F** is $\{A \rightarrow BC, E \rightarrow C, D \rightarrow AEH, ABH \rightarrow BD\}$. ■

If **F** is a set of FDs and if **G** is a nonredundant cover of **F**, then it is not true that **G** has the minimum number of FDs. In fact, there may exist a cover **G′** of **F** that has fewer FDs than **G**. Thus, a minimum cover **G′** of **F** has as small a number of FDs as any other cover of **F**. It is needless to add that a minimum cover **G′** of **F** has no redundant FDs; however, a nonredundant cover of **F** need not be minimal, as we see in Example 6.11. We will not discuss an algorithm to derive a minimum cover in this text. The interested reader is referred to the bibliographic notes at the end of the chapter.

6.4.7 Canonical Cover

A set of functional dependencies $\mathbf{F_c}$ is a **canonical cover** if every FD in $\mathbf{F_c}$ satisfies the following:

1. Each FD in $\mathbf{F_c}$ *is simple*. Recall that in a simple FD the right-hand side has a single attribute, i.e., each FD is of the form $\mathbf{X} \rightarrow A$.

2. For no FD $\mathbf{X} \rightarrow A$ with $\mathbf{Z} \subset \mathbf{X}$ is $\{(\mathbf{F_c} - (\mathbf{X} \rightarrow A)) \cup (\mathbf{Z} \rightarrow A)\} \models \mathbf{F_c}$. In other words, the left-hand side of each FD does not have any extraneous attributes, or the *FDs* in $\mathbf{F_c}$ are left reduced.
3. No FD $\mathbf{X} \rightarrow$ A is redundant, i.e., $\{\mathbf{F_c} - (\mathbf{X} \rightarrow A)\}$ does not logically imply $\mathbf{F_c}$.

A canonical cover is sometimes called **minimal.**

Given a set **F** of functional dependencies we can find a canonical set $\mathbf{F_c}$; obviously $\mathbf{F_c}$ covers **F.**

Example 6.11 If $\mathbf{F} = \{A \rightarrow BC, CD \rightarrow E, E \rightarrow C, D \rightarrow AEH, ABH \rightarrow BD, DH \rightarrow BC\}$, then a nonredundant cover for **F** is $\{A \rightarrow BC, E \rightarrow C, D \rightarrow AEH, ABH \rightarrow BD\}$. The FD $ABH \rightarrow BD$ can be decomposed into the FDs $ABH \rightarrow B$ and $ABH \rightarrow D$. Now, since the FD $A \rightarrow B$ is in **F,** we can left reduce these decomposed FDs into $AH \rightarrow B$ and $AH \rightarrow D$. We also notice that $AH \rightarrow B$ is redundant since the FD $A \rightarrow B$ is already in **F.** This gives us the canonical cover as $\{A \rightarrow B, A \rightarrow C, E \rightarrow C, D \rightarrow A, D \rightarrow E, D \rightarrow H, AH \rightarrow D\}$. ■

Note that if $\mathbf{F_c}$ is a canonical cover and if we form **G** using the additivity axiom (such that the FDs with the same left-hand sides are merged into a single FD with the right-hand sides combined), then $\mathbf{F_c}$ and **G** are equivalent. However, G will contain nonsimple FDs.

6.4.8 Functional Dependencies and Keys

Earlier we discussed the concept of uniquely identifying an entity within an entity set by a key, the key being a set of attributes of the entity. A relation scheme **R** has a similar concept, which can be explained using functional dependencies.

Definition: Given a relation scheme $\mathbf{R}\ \{A_1A_2A_3 \ldots A_n\}$ and a set of functional dependencies **F**, a key of **R** is a subset of **R** such that $\mathbf{K} \rightarrow A_1A_2A_3 \ldots A_n$ is in $\mathbf{F}^+$ and for any $\mathbf{Y} \subset \mathbf{K}$, $\mathbf{Y} \rightarrow A_1A_2A_3 \ldots A_n$ is not in $\mathbf{F}^+$.

The first requirement indicates that the dependency of all attributes of **R** on **K** is given explicitly in **F** or can be logically implied from **F.** The second requirement indicates that no proper subset of **K** can determine all the attributes of **R.** Thus, the key used here is minimal with respect to this property and the FD $\mathbf{K} \rightarrow \mathbf{R}$ is left reduced. A superset of **K** can then be called a superkey.

If there are two or more subsets of **R** such that the above conditions are satisfied, such subsets are called candidate keys. In such a case one of the candidate keys is designated as the primary key or simply as the key.

We do not allow any attribute in the key of a relation to have a null value.

Example 6.12 If **R** $(ABCDEH)$ and **F** $= \{A \rightarrow BC, CD \rightarrow E, E \rightarrow C, D \rightarrow AEH, ABH \rightarrow BD, DH \rightarrow BC\}$, then CD is a key of **R** because $CD \rightarrow ABCDEH$ is in $\mathbf{F}^+$ (since $(\mathbf{CD})^+$ under **F** is equal to $ABCDEH$ and $ABCDEH \subseteq ABCDEH$). Other candidate keys of **R** are AD and ED. ■

Full Functional Dependency

The concept of left-reduced FDs and fully functionally dependency is defined below and illustrated in Example 6.13.

> *Definition:* Given a relational scheme **R** and an FD **X → Y, Y** is **fully functionally dependent** on **X** if there is no **Z,** where **Z** is a proper subset of **X** such that **Z → Y.** The dependency **X → Y** is left reduced, there being no extraneous attributes in the left-hand side of the dependency.

Example 6.13 In the relation scheme **R** $(ABCDEH)$ with the FDs **F** $= \{A \rightarrow BC, CD \rightarrow E, E \rightarrow C, CD \rightarrow AH, ABH \rightarrow BD, DH \rightarrow BC\}$, the dependency $A \rightarrow BC$ is left reduced and BC is fully functionally dependent on A. However, the functional dependency $ABH \rightarrow D$ is not left reduced, the attribute B being extraneous in this dependency. ■

Prime Attribute and Nonprime Attribute

We defined the key of a relation scheme earlier. We distinguish the attributes that participate in any such key as indicated by the following definition.

> *Definition:* An attribute A in a relation scheme **R** is a **prime attribute** or simply **prime** if A is part of any candidate key of the relation. If A is not a part of any candidate key of **R,** A is called a **nonprime attribute** or simply **nonprime.**

Example 6.14 If **R** $(ABCDEH)$ and **F** $= \{A \rightarrow BC, CD \rightarrow E, E \rightarrow C, AH \rightarrow D\}$, then AH is the only candidate key of R. The attributes A and H are prime and the attributes B, C, D, and E are nonprime. ■

Partial Dependency

Let us introduce the concept of partial dependency below. We illustrate partial dependencies in Example 6.15.

Definition: Given a relation scheme **R** with the functional dependencies **F** defined on the attributes of **R** and **K** as a candidate key, if **X** is a proper subset of **K** and if $\mathbf{F} \models \mathbf{X} \rightarrow A$, then A is said to be **partially dependent** on **K.**

Example 6.15

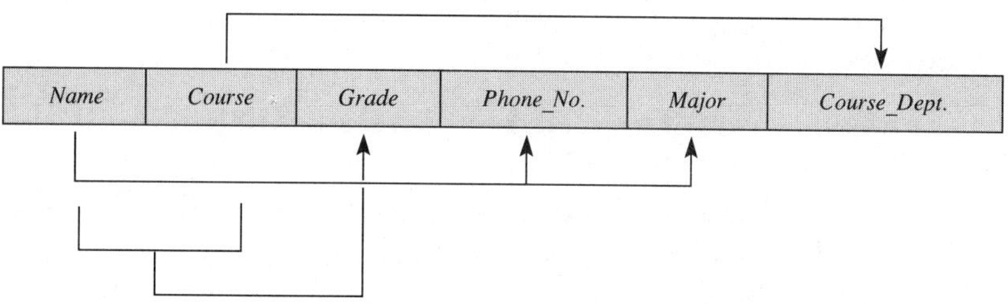

(a) In the relation scheme **STUDENT_COURSE_INFO(*Name, Course,*** *Grade, Phone_No, Major, Course_Dept)* with the FDs **F** = {*Name* → *Phone _NoMajor, Course* → *Course_Dept, NameCourse* → *Grade*}, *NameCourse* is a candidate key, *Name* and *Course* are prime attributes. *Grade* is fully functionally dependent on the candidate key. *Phone_No, Course_Dept,* and *Major* are partially dependent on the candidate key.
(b) Given **R** (A, B, C, D) and $\mathbf{F} = \{AB \rightarrow C, B \rightarrow D\}$, the key of this relation is AB and D is partially dependent on the key. ■

Transitive Dependency

Another type of dependency which we have to recognize in database design is introduced below and illustrated in Example 6.16.

Definition: Given a relation scheme **R** with the functional dependencies **F** defined on the attributes of **R,** let **X** and **Y** be subsets of **R** and let A be an attribute of **R** such that $\mathbf{X} \not\subset \mathbf{Y}, A \not\subset \mathbf{XY}$. If the set of functional dependencies $\{\mathbf{X} \rightarrow \mathbf{Y}, \mathbf{Y} \rightarrow A\}$ is implied by **F** (i.e., $\mathbf{F} \models \mathbf{X} \rightarrow \mathbf{Y} \rightarrow A$ and $\mathbf{F} \neg\models \mathbf{Y} \rightarrow \mathbf{X}$), then A is **transitively dependent** on **X.**

Example 6.16

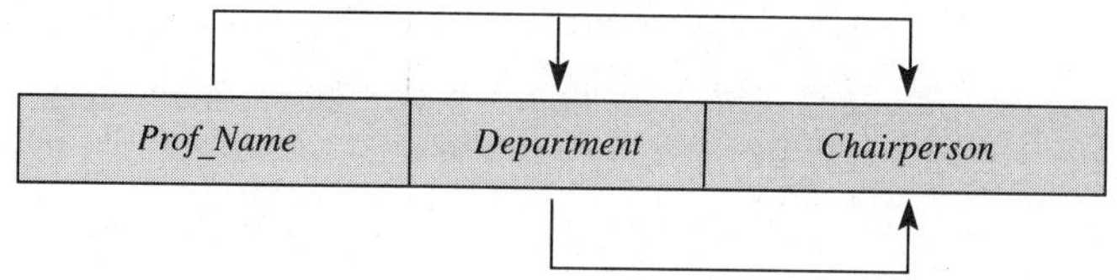

(a) In the relation scheme **PROF_INFO**(*Prof_Name, Department, Chairperson)* and the function dependencies **F** = {*Prof_Name* → *Department,*

Department → *Chairperson*}, *Prof_Name* is the key and *Chairperson* is transitively dependent on the key since *Prof_Name* → *Department* → *Chairperson*.

(b) Given **R** *(A, B, C, D, E)* and the function dependencies **F** = {$AB \rightarrow C$, $B \rightarrow D$, $C \rightarrow E$}, *AB* is the key and *E* is transitively dependent on the key since $AB \rightarrow C \rightarrow E$. ■

6.5 Relational Database Design

Relational database design, like database design using any other data model, is far from being a completely automated process[3] in the current state of database technology. It is an activity that requires the close attention of the database designer, who may be one individual, for example the DBA, or a team working with the DBA. This activity consists of identifying that portion of the enterprise for which the database application is being designed: the entity sets, their attributes, the domains on which the attributes are defined, and the constraints that these attributes have to satisfy. Then the design of the relational schemes can begin.

Two approaches are generally used in designing a relational database: the decomposition approach and the **synthesis** approach. The decomposition approach starts with one (the universal) relation and the associated set of constraints in the form of functional dependencies, multivalued dependencies, and join dependencies. A relation that has any undesirable properties in the form of insertion, deletion, or update anomalies is replaced by its projections. A number of desirable forms of projections have been identified, which we examine in the following sections. A number of algorithms for decomposing the input relation have been developed and reported in the database literature. We will examine some of these. These algorithms produce relations that are desirable from the point of view of some of the criteria described below. We discuss the synthesis approach, multivalued dependencies, and joint dependencies in Chapter 7.

The synthesis approach starts with a set of functional dependencies on a set of attributes. It then synthesizes relations of the third normal form.

Regardless of the approach used, the criteria for the design are the following:

- The design is **content preserving** if the original relation can be derived from the relations resulting from the design process. Since the join operation is used in deriving the original relation from its decomposed relations, this criterion is also called a lossless join decomposition. The design is minimally content preserving if there are no relations in addition to those included in the design which are required in recovering the original relation R.
- The relation design is **dependency preserving** if the original set of constraints can be derived from the dependencies in the output of the design process. The

[3]However, design aid tools do exist.

design is minimally dependency preserving if there are no extraneous dependencies in the output of the design process and the original dependencies cannot be derived from a subset of the dependencies in the output of the design process.

- The relation design is free from **interrelation join constraints** if there are no dependencies that can only be derived from the join of two or more relations in the output of the design process. This criterion is significant. If the design produces a database scheme in which some dependencies are only enforceable in a relation that is derived from the join of two or more relations, then in order to enforce these dependencies, joins will have to be produced. Consider for instance an FD $\mathbf{X} \rightarrow \mathbf{Y}$. Suppose the decomposition doesn't contain any relation $\mathbf{R}_i$ such that $\mathbf{XY} \in \mathbf{R}_i$, but it contains $\mathbf{R}_j$ and $\mathbf{R}_k$ such that $\mathbf{X} \in \mathbf{R}_j$ and $\mathbf{Y} \in \mathbf{R}_k$. Then the FD $\mathbf{X} \rightarrow \mathbf{Y}$ can only be enforced by joining $\mathbf{R}_j$ and $\mathbf{R}_k$. Since the join operation is a computationally expensive process, it is desirable that the database design be free of such interrelational joint constraints.

6.5.1 Recharacterizing Relational Database Schemes

Let us extend the relation scheme to include not only the set of attributes but also the set of functional dependencies among these attributes. We therefore indicate a relation scheme as $\mathbf{R}_i<\mathbf{S}_i, \mathbf{F}_i>$. Here $\mathbf{S}_i$ is a set of attributes $\{A_{i1}, A_{i2}, \ldots, A_{im}\}$ and $\mathbf{F}_i$ is a set of constraints on these attributes. Given **U,** a set of attributes each of which is defined over some designated domain, a relational database scheme is a collection of relation schemes $\boldsymbol{R} = \{\mathbf{R}_1, \mathbf{R}_2, \ldots, \mathbf{R}_p\}$ where each $\mathbf{R}_j = <\mathbf{S}_j = \{A_{j1}, A_{j1}, \ldots, A_{jm}\}, \mathbf{F}_j>$.

A relational database **D** on a relational database scheme $\boldsymbol{R}$ is a collection of relations $\{R_1, R_2, \ldots, R_p\}$ such that the relation R_i is defined on the relation scheme $\mathbf{R}_i<\mathbf{S}_i, \mathbf{F}_i>$.

As indicated, a relation scheme $\mathbf{R}<\mathbf{S}, \mathbf{F}>$ consists of two components: a set **S** of attributes and a set of constraints **F.** However, we will continue to use **R** to also denote **S,** the set of attributes. Thus, to define a subset of attributes, we may use $\mathbf{X} \subseteq \mathbf{R}$ to mean $\mathbf{X} \subseteq \mathbf{S}$. Also, unless there is confusion, we will simply use the term relation to denote a relation scheme as well as a relation on a relation scheme.

6.5.2 Normal Forms—Anomalies and Data Redundancies

A number of normal forms have been defined for classifying relations. Each normal form has associated with it a number of constraints on the kind of functional dependencies that could be associated with the relation. The normal forms are used to ensure that various types of anomalies and inconsistencies are not introduced into the database. Here we describe these normal forms, which are related either to the form of the relations or based on the type of functional dependencies that are allowed to exist among the attributes of the relations or among different relations.

Unnormalized Relation

Consider the table of Figure 6.9, which shows the preferences that faculty members have for teaching courses. As before, we allow the possibility of cross-departmental teaching. For instance, a faculty member in the Computer Science department may have a preference for a course in the Mathematics department, and so on. The table of Figure 6.9 is said to be **unnormalized.** Each row may contain multiple set of values for some of the columns; these multiple values in a single row are also called **nonatomic values.** In Figure 6.9 the row corresponding to the preferences of faculty in the Computer Science department has two professors. Professor Smith of the Computer Science department prefers to teach three different courses, and Professor Clark prefers four.

Definition: An unnormalized relation contains nonatomic *values.*

First Normal Form

The data of Figure 6.9 can be **normalized** into a relation, say CRS_PREF(*Prof, Course, Fac_Dept, Crs_Dept*), as shown in Figure 6.10. Note that we have shown

Figure 6.9 Course preferences.

Fac_Dept	*Prof*	*Course Preferences*	
		Course	*Course_Dept*
Comp Sci	Smith	353 379 221	Comp Sci Comp Sci Decision Sci
	Clark	353 351 379 456	Comp Sci Comp Sci Comp Sci Mathematics
Chemistry	Turner	353 456 272	Comp Sci Mathematics Chemistry
Mathematics	Jamieson	353 379 221 456 469	Comp Sci Comp Sci Decision Sci Mathematics Mathematics

Figure 6.10 The relation CRS_PREF.

Prof	*Course*	*Fac_Dept*	*Crs_Dept*
Smith	353	Comp Sci	Comp Sci
Smith	379	Comp Sci	Comp Sci
Smith	221	Comp Sci	Decision Sci
Clark	353	Comp Sci	Comp Sci
Clark	351	Comp Sci	Comp Sci
Clark	379	Comp Sci	Comp Sci
Clark	456	Comp Sci	Mathematics
Turner	353	Chemistry	Comp Sci
Turner	456	Chemistry	Mathematics
Turner	272	Chemistry	Chemistry
Jamieson	353	Mathematics	Comp Sci
Jamieson	379	Mathematics	Comp Sci
Jamieson	221	Mathematics	Decision Sci
Jamieson	456	Mathematics	Mathematics
Jamieson	469	Mathematics	Mathematics

the attributes in Figure 6.10 in a different order from those in Figure 6.9; however, as mentioned earlier, as long as the columns are labeled there is no significance in the order of the columns of a relation. Now, suppose the set of FDs that have to be satisfied is given by $\{Prof \rightarrow Fac\_Dept,\ Course, \rightarrow Crs\_Dept\}$; then the only key of the relation CRS_PREF is *(Prof, Course)*.

Definition: A relation scheme is said to be in **first normal form (1NF)** if the values in the domain of each attribute of the relation are atomic. In other words, only one value is associated with each attribute and the value is not a set of values or a list of values. A database scheme is in first normal form if every relation scheme included in the database scheme is in 1NF.

The first normal form pertains to the tabular format of the relation as shown in Figure 6.10.

The representation of the data for the courses that a faculty member would like to teach by the relation CRS_PREF has the following drawbacks. The fact that a given professor is assigned to a given department is repeated a number of times. The fact that a given course is offered by a given department is also repeated a number of times. These replications lead to some anomalies. For example, if a professor changes department, unless all the rows of Figure 6.10 where that professor appears are changed, we could have inconsistencies in the database. If the association between a course and its department is only kept in this relation, a new course cannot be entered (without null values) unless someone would like to teach it. Deletion of the only professor who teaches a given course will cause the loss of the information about the department to which the course belonged.

Second Normal Form

A second normal form does not permit partial dependency between a nonprime attribute and the relation key(s). The **STDINF** relation given in Section 6.2 involves partial dependency and hence it is not in the second normal form.

Definition: A relation scheme **R<S, F>** is in **second normal form (2NF)** if it is in the 1NF and if all nonprime attributes are fully functionally dependent on the relation key(s). A database scheme is in second normal form if every relation scheme included in the database scheme is in second normal form.

Even though second normal form does not permit partial dependency between a nonprime attribute and the relation key(s), it does not rule out the possibility that a nonprime attribute may also be functionally dependent on another nonprime attribute. This latter type of dependency between nonprime attributes also causes anomalies, as we see below.

Consider the TEACHES relation of Figure 6.11. It contains the attributes *Prof(essor), Course, Room, Room_Cap* (capacity of room), *Enrol_Lmt* (enrollment limit). The relation scheme for the relation TEACHES is *(Prof, Course, Room, Room Cap, Enrol_Lmt)*. The domain of the attribute *Prof* is all the faculty members of the university. The domain of the attribute *Course* is the courses offered by the university. The domain of *Room* is the rooms in the buildings of the university. The domain of *Room_Cap* is an integer value indicating the seating capacity of the room. The

Figure 6.11 The TEACHES relation.

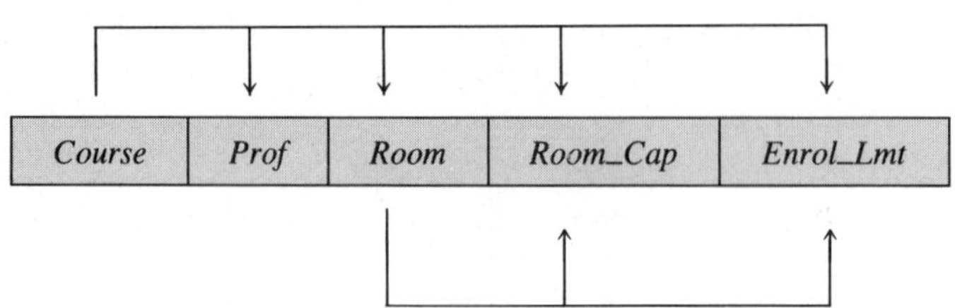

Course	*Prof*	*Room*	*Room_Cap*	*Enrol_Lmt*
353	Smith	A532	45	40
351	Smith	C320	100	60
355	Clark	H940	400	300
456	Turner	B278	50	45
459	Jamieson	D110	50	45

Figure 6.12 Decomposition of TEACHES relation: (a) COURSE_DETAILS; (b) ROOM-DETAILS; and (c) Decomposition of COURSE_DETAILS to eliminate transitive dependency.

Course	*Prof*	*Room*	*Enrol_Lmt*
353	Smith	A532	40
351	Smith	C320	60
355	Clark	H940	300
456	Turner	B278	45
459	Jamieson	D110	45

(a)

Room	*Room_Cap*
A532	45
C320	100
H940	400
B278	50
D110	50

(b)

Course	*Prof*	*Enrol_Lmt*
353	Smith	40
351	Smith	60
355	Clark	300
456	Turner	45
459	Jamieson	45

Course	*Room*
353	A532
351	C320
355	H940
456	B278
459	D110

(c)

domain of *Enrol_Lmt* is also an integer value and should be less than or equal to the corresponding value for *Room_Cap*.

The TEACHES relation is in first normal form since it contains only atomic values. However, as mentioned earlier, since the course is scheduled in a given room and since the room has the given maximum number of available seats, there is a functional dependency *Room* → *Room_Cap,* and hence by transitivity, *Course* → *Room* → *Room_Cap*. Thus, the functional dependencies in this relation are {*Course* → *(Prof, Room, Room_Cap, Enrol_Lmt), Room* → *Room_Cap*}. Also, there is another transitive dependency[4] *Room* → *Room_Cap* → *Enrol_Lmt*. The presence of these transitive dependencies in TEACHES will cause the following problems. The capacity of a room cannot be entered in the database unless a course is scheduled in that room; and the capacity of a room in which only one course is scheduled will be deleted if the only course scheduled in that room is deleted. Because the same room can appear more than once in the database, there could be inconsistencies between the multiple occurrences of the attribute pair *Room* and *Room_Cap*.

Consider the decomposition of the TEACHES relation into the relations COURSE_DETAILS *(Course, Prof, Room, Enrol_Lmt)* of Figure 6.12a and ROOM_DETAILS *(Room, Room_Cap)* of Figure 6.12b. The set of functional dependencies in COURSE DETAILS is given by {*Course* → *Prof, Course* → *Room, Course* → *Enrol_Lmt*} and the functional dependency in ROOM_DETAILS is {*Room* → *Room_Size*}. These relations do not have any partial dependencies: each of the attributes is fully

[4]Here we assume that *Enrol_Lmt* is the upper limit on registration for a course and is based solely on the room capacity.

functionally dependent on the key attribute, namely *Course* and *Room*, respectively. Hence, these relations are in second normal form. However, the relation COURSE_DETAILS has a transitive dependency since *Course* → *Room* → *Enrol_Lmt*. In addition there is an interrelation join dependency between the relation COURSE_DETAILS and ROOM_DETAILS to enforce the constraint that the *Enrol_Lmt* be less than or equal to the *Room_Cap*.

Third Normal Form

A relation scheme in third normal form does not allow partial or transitive dependencies. The decomposition of **STDINF** into **STUDENT_INFO TRANSCRIPT** and **TEACHER** gives third normal form relations.

Definition: A relation scheme **R<S, F>** is in **third normal form (3NF)** if for all nontrivial functional dependencies in $\mathbf{F}^+$ of the form **X** → *A*, either **X** contains a key (i.e., **X** is a superkey) or *A* is a prime attribute. A database scheme is in third normal form if every relation scheme included in the database scheme is in third normal form.

In a third normal form relation, every nonprime attribute is nontransitively and fully dependent on the every candidate key. A relation scheme **R** is *not* in third normal form if any functional dependency such as **X** → **Y** implied by **F** is in conflict with the above definition of third normal form. In this case one of the following must be true:

- **X** is a subset of a key of **R** and in this case **X** → *A* is a partial dependency.
- **X** is not a subset of any key of **R** and in this case there is a transitive dependency in $\mathbf{F}^+$. Since for a key **Z** of **RZ** → **X** with **X** not in **Z,** and **X** → *A* with *A* not in **X, Z** → **X** → *A* is a nontrivial chain of dependencies.

The problems with a relation scheme that is not in 3NF are discussed below.

If a relation scheme **R** contains a transitive dependency, **Z** → **X** → *A*, we cannot insert an **X** value in the relation along with an *A* value unless we have a **Z** value to go along with the **X** value. This means that we cannot independently record the fact that for each value of **X** there is one value of *A*. This is the insertion anomaly. Similarly, the deletion of a **Z** → **X** association also requires the deletion of an **X** → *A* association leading to the deletion anomaly. If a relation **R** contains a partial dependency, i.e., an attribute *A* depends on a subset **X** of the key **K** of R, then the association between **X** and *A* cannot be expressed unless the remaining parts of **K** are present in a tuple. Since **K** is a key, these parts cannot be null.

The 3NF scheme, like the 2NF scheme, does not allow partial dependencies. Furthermore, unlike the 2NF scheme, it does not allow any transitive dependencies.

The relation COURSE_DETAILS of Figure 6.12a has a transitive dependency because *Course* → *Room* → *Enrol_Lmt*. We can eliminate this transitive dependency by decomposing COURSE_DETAILS into the relations *(Course, Prof, Enrol_Lmt)* and *(Course, Room)*. These decomposed relations are shown in Figure 6.12c. Note that enforcing the constraint that *Enrol_Lmt* be less than the *Room_Cap* now requires a join of three relations!

Normalization through Decomposition (Based on FDs)

We noted above the presence of insertion and deletion anomalies when **R** contains a partial or transitive dependency. The insertion of values for **Z** and **X** without an *A* value may be handled by using a null value, provided the attribute *A* allows null values. If null values are not allowed for *A*, the **Z** to **X** association cannot be represented without a corresponding *A* value.

In this section we will examine how to start with a relation scheme **R** and a set of functional dependencies **F** such that **R** is not in third normal form with respect to the set **F**, and arrive at a resultant set of relation schemes that are a lossless join 3NF decomposition of **R**. The relation scheme **R** can be decomposed into a number of relation schemes by projection (the intent of the decomposition being to produce simpler schemes in 3NF).

Example 6.17

Consider the relation of Figure C, ENROLLMENT(***Student_Name, Course,*** *Phone_No, Department, Grade*). In this relation the key is *Student_Name, Course* and it has the following dependencies: {*Student_Name* → *Phone_No, Student_Name* → *Department, Student_Name Course* → *Grade*}. Here the nonprime attribute *Phone_No* is not fully functionally dependent on the key but only on part of the key, namely the attribute *Student_Name*. Similarly, the nonprime attribute *Department* is fully functionally dependent on the attribute *Student_Name*. These are examples of partial dependencies.

Figure C The ENROLLMENT relation.

Student_Name	*Course*	*Phone_No*	*Department*	*Grade*
Jones	353	237-4539	Comp Sci	A
Ng	329	427-7390	Chemistry	A
Jones	328	237-4539	Comp Sci	B
Martin	456	388-5183	Physics	C
Dulles	293	371-6259	Decision Sci	B
Duke	491	823-7293	Mathematics	C
Duke	353	823-7293	Mathematics	B
Jones	491	237-4539	Comp Sci	C
Evan	353	842-1729	Comp Sci	A+
Baxter	379	839-0827	English	B

■

The problem with the relation ENROLLMENT is that unless the student takes at least one course, we cannot enter data for the student. Note that we cannot enter a null value for the *Course* portion of a tuple since *Course* is part of the primary key

Figure 6.13 Decomposition of ENROLLMENT: (a) The STUDENT relation; (b) The ENROL relation.

Student_Name	*Phone_No*	*Department*
Jones	237-4539	Comp Sci
Ng	427-7390	Chemistry
Martin	388-5183	Physics
Dulles	371-6259	Decision Sci
Duke	823-7293	Mathematics
Evan	842-1729	Comp Sci
Baxter	830-0827	English

(a)

Student_Name	*Course*	*Grade*
Jones	353	A
Ng	329	A
Jones	328	B
Martin	456	C
Dulles	293	B
Duke	491	C
Duke	353	B
Jones	491	C
Evan	353	A+
Baxter	379	B

(b)

of the relation. The other problem with this relation is that the changes in the *Phone No* or *Department* of a student can lead to inconsistencies in the database.

We can rectify these problems in the ENROLLMENT relation by decomposing it into the following relations: STUDENT *(Student_Name, Phone_No, Department)* with the FDs {*Student_Name* → *Phone_No, Student_Name* → *Department*}, and ENROL *(Student_Name, Course, Grade)* with the FDs {*Student_Name Course* → *Grade*}. The relations STUDENT and ENROL are shown in Figure 6.13.

Example 6.18

Consider the relation MAJOR*(Student_Name, Major, Department)* of Figure D with the functional dependencies {*Student_Name* → *Major, Student_Name* → *Department, Major* → *Department*}. Since the attribute *Major* is not in the key, and because of the functional dependency of *Department* on *Major,* we have a transitive dependency in this relation.

Figure D The MAJOR relation.

Student_Name	*Major*	*Department*
Jones	Information Systems	Comp Sci
Ng	Biochemistry	Chemistry
Martin	Honors Physics	Physics
Dulles	Quantitative Methods	Decision Sci
Duke	Statistics	Mathematics
James	Systems Architecture	Comp Sci
Evan	Information Systems	Comp Sci
Baxter	Creative Writing	English

■

Figure 6.14 A decomposition MAJOR: (a) The STUDENT_MAJOR relation and (b)T DEPARTMENT relation.

Student_Name	*Major*
Jones	Information Systems
Ng	Biochemistry
Martin	Honors Physics
Dulles	Quantitative Methods
Duke	Statistics
James	Systems Architecture
Evan	Information Systems
Baxter	Creative Writing

(a)

Major	*Department*
Information Systems	Comp Sci
Biochemistry	Chemistry
Honors Physics	Physics
Quantitative Methods	Decision Sci
Statistics	Mathematics
Systems Architecture	Comp Sci
Creative Writing	English

(b)

The problem with the relation MAJOR is that unless a student is registered in one of the majors offered by a department, that major cannot be shown to be offered by the given department. Similarly, deleting the only student in a major loses the information of that major being offered by a given department.

This problem can be overcome by decomposing the relation MAJOR into the relations STUDENT_MAJOR*(Student_Name, Major)* with the functional dependency $\{Student\_Name \rightarrow Major\}$, and MAJOR_DEPT *(Major, Department)* with the functional dependency $\{Major \rightarrow Department\}$. These relations are shown in Figure 6.14.

The relations of Figures 6.13 and 6.14 do not exhibit the anomaly and inconsistency problems that were present in the relations of Figures C and D, respectively. Elimination of some of these anomalies is the motivation behind the decomposition of a scheme $\mathbf{R}\langle\mathbf{S}, \mathbf{F}\rangle$ (which suffers from anomalies and inconsistency problems) into relation schemes $\mathbf{R_1}$, $\mathbf{R_2}$, etc., each of which is not necessarily a disjoint subset of $\mathbf{R}$ so that the resulting relation schemes contain the same data as the original scheme.

6.5.3 Lossless Join and Dependency-Preserving Decomposition

A relation scheme **R** can be decomposed into a collection of relation schemes to eliminate some of the anomalies contained in the original relation scheme **R.** However, any such decomposition requires that the information contained in the original relation be maintained. This in turn requires that the decomposition be such that a join of the decomposed relations gives the same set of tuples as the original relation and that the dependencies of the original relation be preserved. Let us illustrate, with an example, a decomposition that violates these requirements.

Example 6.19 Consider the relation STUDENT_ADVISOR*(Name, Department, Advisor)* of Figure Ei with the functional dependencies $\mathbf{F}\{Name \rightarrow Department, Name \rightarrow Advisor, Advisor \rightarrow Department\}$. The decomposition of STUDENT

Figure E Example of a lossy decomposition: (i) The STUDENT_ADVISOR relation; (ii) STUDENT_DEPARTMENT; (iii) DEPARTMENT_ADVISOR; and (iv) Join of STUDENT_DEPARTMENT and DEPARTMENT_ADVISOR.

Name	*Department*	*Advisor*
Jones	Comp Sci	Smith
Ng	Chemistry	Turner
Martin	Physics	Bosky
Dulles	Decision Sci	Hall
Duke	Mathematics	James
James	Comp Sci	Clark
Evan	Comp Sci	Smith
Baxter	English	Bronte

(i)

Name	*Department*
Jones	Comp Sci
Ng	Chemistry
Martin	Physics
Dulles	Decision Sci
Duke	Mathematics
James	Comp Sci
Evan	Comp Sci
Baxter	English

(ii)

Department	*Advisor*
Comp Sci	Smith
Chemistry	Turner
Physics	Bosky
Decision Sci	Hall
Mathematics	James
Comp Sci	Clark
English	Bronte

(iii)

Name	*Department*	*Advisor*
Jones	Comp Sci	Smith
Jones	Comp Sci	Clark
Ng	Chemistry	Turner
Martin	Physics	Bosky
Dulles	Decision Sci	Hall
Duke	Mathematics	James
James	Comp Sci	Smith
James	Comp Sci	Clark
Evan	Comp Sci	Smith
Evan	Comp Sci	Clark
Baxter	English	Bronte

(iv)

ADVISOR into STUDENT_DEPARTMENT*(Name, Department)* and DEPARTMENT_ADVISOR *(Department, Advisor)* is given in Figures Eii and Eiii. The join of these decomposed relations is given in Figure Eiv and contains tuples that did not exist in the original relation of part i. The decomposition is called **lossy.** ■

The terms lossless and dependency preserving are defined below.

Definition: A decomposition of a relation scheme **R** <**S, F**> into the relation schemes $\mathbf{R_i}$ ($1 \leq i \leq n$) is said to be a **lossless join decomposition** or simply **lossless** if for every relation R(**R**) that satisfies the FDs in **F**, the natural join of the projections of R gives the original relation R; i.e.,

$$R = \pi_{R1}(R) \bowtie \pi_{R2}(R) \bowtie \ldots \bowtie \pi_{Rn}(R)$$

If $R \subset \pi_{R1}(R) \bowtie \pi_{R2}(R) \bowtie \ldots \bowtie \pi_{Rn}(R)$ then the decomposition is called **lossy.**[5]

The lossless join decomposition enables any relation to be recovered from its projections or decompositions by a series of natural joins. Such decomposed relations contain the same data as the original relation. Another property that the decomposition of a relation into smaller relations must preserve is that the set of functional dependencies of the original relation must be implied by the dependencies in the decompositions.

Definition: Given a relation scheme **R**<**S, F**> where **F** is the associated set of functional dependencies on the attributes in **S**, **R** is decomposed into the relation schemes $\mathbf{R_1}, \mathbf{R_2}, \ldots, \mathbf{R_n}$ with the functional dependencies $\mathbf{F_1}, \mathbf{F_2}, \ldots, \mathbf{F_n}$. Then this decomposition of **R** is **dependency-preserving** if the closure of $\mathbf{F'}$ (where $\mathbf{F'} = \mathbf{F_1} \cup \mathbf{F_2} \cup \ldots \cup \mathbf{F_n}$) is the identical to $\mathbf{F^+}$ (i.e., $\mathbf{F'^+} = \mathbf{F^+}$).

If we decompose a relation into relation schemes that do not preserve dependencies, the enforcement of the original FDs can only be accomplished by joining the decomposed relation. This operation has to be done for each update for verifying consistency. Note that the dependencies in the decomposition are always implied by the original set of FDs.

These observations are summarized in the following theorem; we will not give a formal proof of this theorem but illustrate it with examples. Formal proofs can be found in the references given in the bibliographic notes at the end of the chapter.

Theorem 6.1: A decomposition of relation scheme **R** <**(X, Y, Z), F**> into $\mathbf{R_1}$<**(X, Y),** $\mathbf{F_1}$> and $\mathbf{R_2}$<**(X, Z),** $\mathbf{F_2}$ $\mathbf{R_2}$ < **(X,Z),** $\mathbf{F_2}$ > is:

(a) dependency preserving if every functional dependency in **R** can be logically derived from the functional dependencies of $\mathbf{R_1}$ and $\mathbf{R_2}$, i.e., $(\mathbf{F_1} \cup \mathbf{F_2})^+ = \mathbf{F^+}$, and

(b) is lossless if the common attributes **X** of $\mathbf{R_1}$ and $\mathbf{R_2}$ form a superkey of at least one of these, i.e., $\mathbf{X \rightarrow Y}$ or $\mathbf{X \rightarrow Z}$.

[5] $R \subseteq \pi_{R1}(R) \bowtie \pi_{R2}(R) \bowtie \ldots \bowtie \pi_{Rn}(R)$ is always true.

Example 6.19 illustrated a decomposition that is both lossy and doesn't preserve the dependencies in the original relation. It is lossy because the common attribute *Department* is not a key of either of the resulting relations and consequently, the join of these projected relations produces tuples that are not in the original relation. The decomposition is not dependency-preserving because the FD *Name* $\rightarrow$ *Advisor* is not implied by the FDs of the decomposed relation.

Example 6.20 illustrates a lossless decomposition.

Example 6.20

Let $\mathbf{R}(A, B, C)$ and $\mathbf{F} = \{A \rightarrow B\}$. Then the decomposition of $\mathbf{R}$ into $\mathbf{R}_1(A, B)$ and $\mathbf{R}_2(A, C)$ is lossless because the FD $\{A \rightarrow B\}$ is contained in $\mathbf{R}_1$ and the common attribute A is a key of $\mathbf{R}_1$. ■

A decomposition which is lossy is given below.

Example 6.21

Let $\mathbf{R}(A, B, C)$ and $\mathbf{F} = \{A \rightarrow B\}$. Then the decomposition of $\mathbf{R}$ into $\mathbf{R}_1(A, B)$ and $\mathbf{R}_2(B, C)$ is not lossless because the common attribute B does not functionally determine either A or C, i.e. it is not a key of $\mathbf{R}_1$ or $\mathbf{R}_2$. ■

A decomposition which is both lossless and dependence preserving is given in Example 6.22.

Example 6.22

Given $\mathbf{R}(A, B, C, D)$ with the functional dependencies $\mathbf{F} = \{A \rightarrow B, A \rightarrow C, C \rightarrow D\}$, consider the decomposition of $\mathbf{R}$ into $\mathbf{R}_1(A, B, C)$ with the function dependencies $\mathbf{F}_1 = \{A \rightarrow B, A \rightarrow C\}$ and $\mathbf{R}_2(C, D)$ with the functional dependencies $\mathbf{F}_2 = \{C \rightarrow D\}$. In this decomposition all the original FDs can be logically derived from $\mathbf{F}_1$ and $\mathbf{F}_2$, hence the decomposition is dependency-preserving. Also, the common attribute C forms a key of $\mathbf{R}_2$. The decomposition of $\mathbf{R}$ into $\mathbf{R}_1$ and $\mathbf{R}_2$ is lossless. ■

Example 6.23 gives a lossy decomposition which also is not dependency preserving.

Example 6.23

Given $\mathbf{R}(A,B,C,D)$ with the functional dependencies $F = \{A \rightarrow B, A \rightarrow C, A \rightarrow D\}$, the decomposition of $\mathbf{R}$ into $\mathbf{R}_1(A,B,D)$ with the functional dependencies $\mathbf{F}_1 = \{A \rightarrow B, A \rightarrow D\}$ and $\mathbf{R}_2(B,C)$ with the functional dependencies $\mathbf{F}_2 = \{\}$ is lossy because the common attribute B is not a candidate key of either $\mathbf{R}_1$ or $\mathbf{R}_2$. In addition, the FD $A \rightarrow C$ is not implied by any FDs in $\mathbf{R}_1$ or $\mathbf{R}_2$. Thus, the decomposition is not dependency-preserving. ■

Now let us consider an example involving the decomposition of relations from the familiar university-related database. This decomposition, while lossless, is not dependency-preserving.

Example 6.24 Consider the relation scheme **CONCENTRATION** {*Student(S), Major_or_Minor(M_m), Field_of_Study(F_s), Advisor(A)*} with the functional dependencies **F** = {$(S, M_m, F_s) \rightarrow A$, $A \rightarrow F_s$}. Figure Fi illustrates some instances of tuples of a relations on this relation scheme. This relation can be decomposed by projection into the relation schemes $\mathbf{SM_mA}(S, M_m, A)$ and $\mathbf{F_sA}(F_s, A)$. The decomposition of the relation of part i into these two relations is shown in parts ii and iii. This decomposition is lossless because the common attribute A determines F_s. However, the decomposition does not preserve the dependencies; the only nontrivial dependency in the decomposition is $A \rightarrow F_s$, but it does not imply the dependency $(S, M_m, F_s) \rightarrow A$. This is an example of a decomposition that is lossless but not dependency-preserving.

Figure F Example of a lossless decomposition that is not dependency preserving: (i) The CONCENTRATION relation; (ii) The SM_mA relation; and (iii) The F_sA relation.

Student	*Major_or_Minor*	*Field_of_Study*	*Advisor*
Jones	Major	Comp Sci	Smith
Jones	Minor	Mathematics	Jamieson
Ng	Major	Chemistry	Turner
Ng	Minor	Comp Sci	Clark
Ng	Minor	Physics	Bosky
Martin	Major	Physics	Bosky
Martin	Minor	Chemistry	Turner
James	Major	Physics	Newton
James	Minor	Comp Sci	Clark

(i)

Student	M_m	*Advisor*
Jones	Major	Smith
Jones	Minor	Jamieson
Ng	Major	Turner
Ng	Minor	Clark
Ng	Minor	Bosky
Martin	Major	Bosky
Martin	Minor	Turner
James	Major	Newton
James	Minor	Clark

(ii)

Field_of_Study	*Advisor*
Comp Sci	Smith
Mathematics	Jamieson
Chemistry	Turner
Comp Sci	Clark
Physics	Bosky
Physics	Newton

(iii)

Note that the dependency $(S, M_m, F_s) \rightarrow A$ can be recovered from the join of the projected relations. ■

6.5.4 Algorithms to Check if a Decomposition is Lossless and Dependency-Preserving

We are given a relation scheme **R** and a set of functional dependencies **F.** Suppose **R** is decomposed into the relations $\mathbf{R_1}, \mathbf{R_2}, \ldots, \mathbf{R_n}$ with the functional dependencies $\mathbf{F_1}, \mathbf{F_2}, \ldots, \mathbf{F_n}$ respectively. We want to ascertain (a) if the decomposition is lossless and (b) if it is dependency-preserving. The following algorithms can be used to check for these requirements. Algorithm 6.4 can determine if a decomposition is lossless; Algorithm 6.5 can determine if the decomposition is dependency-preserving. Note that if the decomposition is into only two relations, it would be easier to test for lossless decomposition using Theorem 6.1. However, if the decomposition is into a number of relations, Algorithm 6.4 could be used. A decomposition could have one of these properties without having the other.

In Algorithm 6.4, we initialize the table element (i, j) with α_{Aj} if the attribute A_j is included in the decomposed relation R_i; otherwise we place the symbol β_{iAj}. The table is then used to verify if an arbitrary tuple with all αs, which is in the join of the decomposed relation, is also in the relation R. If this is the case, the decomposition is lossless; otherwise it is lossy. See the bibliographic notes for a reference to the proof of this algorithm.

We use algorithm 6.4 to verify that the decomposition in Example 6.25 is lossless.

Example 6.25

Given $\mathbf{R}(A,B,C,D)$ with the functional dependencies $\mathbf{F}$ $\{A \rightarrow B, A \rightarrow C, C \rightarrow D\}$, consider the dependency-preserving decomposition of **R** into $\mathbf{R_1}(A,B,C)$ and $\mathbf{R_2}(C,D)$. Let us verify whether it is lossless as well using Algorithm 6.4.

	A	*B*	*C*	*D*
R_1	α_A	α_B	α_C	β_{1D}
R_2	β_{2A}	β_{2B}	α_C	α_D

	A	*B*	*C*	*D*
R_1	α_A	α_B	α_C	α_D
R_2	β_{2A}	β_{2B}	α_C	α_D

We initialize the TABLE_LOSSY as shown on the left. Then we consider the FD $C \rightarrow D$ and find that the symbols in the *C* columns are the same. Because one of the symbols in the *D* column is an α, we make the other element (1, 4) in the *D* column the same. For the other FDs we are unable to find two rows with identical entries for the columns of the determinant, so there are no further changes and the final version of TABLE_LOSSY is as shown on the right. Finally we find a row in the table with αs in all columns, indicating that the decomposition is lossless. Because the common attribute, *C*, is a key of one of the projection, we could have used Theorem 6.1 to come to the same conclusion. ■

Algorithm 6.4 Algorithm to Check if a Decomposition is Lossless

Input: A relation scheme $\mathbf{R}(A_1, A_2, A_3, \ldots, A_k)$, decomposed into the relation schemes $\mathbf{R_1}, \mathbf{R_2}, \mathbf{R_3}, \ldots, \mathbf{R_i}, \ldots, \mathbf{R_n}$.

Output: Whether the decomposition is lossless or lossy.

```
(*A table, TABLE_LOSSY(1:n, 1:k) is used to test for the type of
decomposition. Row i is for relation scheme R_i of the decomposed relation
and column j is for attribute A_j in the original relation.*)
for each decomposed relation R_i do
  if an attribute A_j is included in R_i,
  then TABLE_LOSSY(i, j) := α_Aj (*place a symbol α_Aj in row i, column j
                                    of *)
  else TABLE_LOSSY(i, j) := β_iAj (* place a symbol β_iAj *)
change := true
while (change) do
  for each FD X → Y in F do
     if rows i and j exist such that the same symbol appears in each column
        corresponding to the attributes of X
       then if one of the symbols in the Y column is α_r
              then make the other α_r
              else if the symbols are β_pm and β_qm
                      then make both of them, say, β_pm;
       else change ;= false
i := 1
lossy := true
while (lossy and i ≤ n) do
  for each row i of TABLE_LOSSY
    if all symbols are αs
     then lossy := false
     else i := i +1;
```

Algorithm 6.4 is used in Example 6.26 to conclude that the given decomposition is lossy.

Example 6.26

Given R(A, B, C, D, E) with the functional dependencies F $\{AB \rightarrow CD, A \rightarrow E, C \rightarrow D\}$, the decomposition of **R** into $\mathbf{R_1}(A,B,C)$, $\mathbf{R_2}(B,C,D)$ and $\mathbf{R_3}(C,D,E)$ is lossy.

We initialize the TABLE_LOSSY as shown on the left. Now we consider the FDs $AB \rightarrow CD$, $A \rightarrow E$ in turn but since we find that there are no two rows with identical entries in the A columns, we are unable to make

	A	B	C	D	E
R_1	α_A	α_B	α_C	β_{1D}	β_{1E}
R_2	β_{2A}	α_B	α_C	α_D	β_{2E}
R_3	β_{3A}	β_{3B}	α_C	α_D	α_E

	A	B	C	D	E
R_1	α_A	α_B	α_C	α_D	β_{1E}
R_2	β_{2A}	α_B	α_C	α_D	β_{2E}
R_3	β_{3A}	β_{3B}	α_C	α_D	α_E

any changes to the table. When we consider the FD $C \rightarrow D$, we find that all rows of the column C, the determinant of the FD, are identical and this allows us to change the entries in the column D to α_D. No further changes are possible and the final version of the table is the same as the table on the right. Finally we find no rows in the table with all αs and conclude that the decomposition is lossy. ■

As we discussed earlier, a decomposition is dependency-preserving if the closure of $\mathbf{F}'$ (where $\mathbf{F}' = \mathbf{F_1} \cup \mathbf{F_2} \cup \ldots \cup \mathbf{F_n}$) is identical to $\mathbf{F}^+$. However, the task of computing the closure is time consuming and we would like to avoid it. With this in mind, we provide below an alternate method of checking for the preservation of the dependencies. This method takes each functional dependency $\mathbf{X} \rightarrow \mathbf{Y}$ in $\mathbf{F}$ and computes the closure $\mathbf{X}'^+$ of $\mathbf{X}$ with respect to $\mathbf{F}'$. If $\mathbf{Y} \subseteq \mathbf{X}'^+$, then $\mathbf{F}' \models \mathbf{X} \rightarrow \mathbf{Y}$. If we can show that all functional dependencies in $\mathbf{F}$ are logically implied by $\mathbf{F}'$, we can conclude that the decomposition is dependency-preserving. Obviously, if even a single dependency in $\mathbf{F}$ is not covered by $\mathbf{F}'$, the decomposition is not dependency-preserving. Algorithm 6.5 checks if a decomposition is dependency-preserving.

If the union of dependencies of the decomposed relations is the same as the original set of dependencies, then the decomposition is dependency-preserving. This is illustrated in the following example.

Example 6.27 Consider $\mathbf{R}(A,B,C,D)$ with the functional dependencies $\mathbf{F}$ $\{A \rightarrow B, A \rightarrow C, C \rightarrow D\}$ and its decomposition into $\mathbf{R_1}(A,B,C)$ with the functional dependencies $\mathbf{F_1} = \{A \rightarrow B, A \rightarrow C\}$ and $\mathbf{R_2}(C,D)$ with the functional dependencies $\mathbf{F_2} = \{C \rightarrow D\}$. This decomposition is dependency-preserving because all the original FDs can be logically derived from $\mathbf{F_1}$ and $\mathbf{F_2}$. (In this case each FD in $\mathbf{F}$ is included in $\mathbf{F}'$ (where $\mathbf{F}' = \mathbf{F_1} \cup \mathbf{F_2}$).) ■

The following example illustrates a decomposition which is not dependency-preserving.

Algorithm 6.5

Algorithm to Check if a Decomposition is Dependency Preserving

Input: A relation scheme and a set F of functional dependencies; a projection ($\mathbf{R_1}$, $\mathbf{R_2}$, . . ., $\mathbf{R_n}$) of **R** with the functional dependencies ($\mathbf{F_1}$, $\mathbf{F_2}$, . . ., $\mathbf{F_n}$).

Output: Whether the decomposition is dependency-preserving or not.

$\mathbf{F'^+\_=\_F^+}$:= *true;* (**Assume* $\mathbf{F'^+\_=\_F^+}$, used as a variable, is true *)
$\mathbf{F'} := \phi$;
for i := 1 **to** n *do*
  $\mathbf{F'} := \mathbf{F'} \cup \mathbf{F_i}$;
for each FD $\mathbf{X} \rightarrow \mathbf{Y} \in \mathbf{F}$ *and while* ($\mathbf{F'^+\_=\_F^+}$) *do*
  (* compute $\mathbf{X'^+}$, the closure of **X** under **F′**, using Algorithm 6.1))
  if $\mathbf{Y} \not\subset \mathbf{X'^+}$ *then* $\mathbf{F'^+\_=\_F^+}$ = *false;* (* i.e., the decomposition is not dependency-preserving *);

Example 6.28 $\mathbf{R}(A,B,C,D)$ with the functional dependencies F $\{A \rightarrow B, A \rightarrow C, A \rightarrow D\}$ is decomposed into $\mathbf{R_1}(A,B,D)$ with the functional dependencies $\mathbf{F_1} = \{A \rightarrow B, A \rightarrow D\}$ and $\mathbf{R_2}(B,C)$ with the functional dependencies $\mathbf{F_2} = \{\}$. This is not dependency-preserving because the FD $A \rightarrow C$ is not implied by any FDs in $\mathbf{R_1}$ or $\mathbf{R_2}$. ■

Now let us consider the decomposition of a relation from the university database.

Example 6.29 Consider the relation STUDENT_ADVISOR*(Name, Department, Advisor)* of Figure Ei with the functional dependencies **F** = {*Name → Department, Name → Advisor, Advisor → Department*}. Here, the decomposition of STUDENT_ADVISOR into STUDENT_PROFESSOR*(Name, Advisor)* with the functional dependency {*Name → Advisor*}, and DEPARTMENT_ADVISOR*(Department, Advisor)* with the functional dependency {*Advisor → Department* is dependency-preserving, because the dependency *Name → Department* is implied by *(Name → Advisor)* ∪ *(Advisor → Department);* in addition, the decomposition is lossless. ■

On the other hand, the following decomposition is not dependency-preserving.

Example 6.30 The decomposition of the relation CONCENTRATION of Figure F into the relations SM_mA and F_sA is not dependency-preserving because $\mathbf{F'} = A \rightarrow F_s$ and the FD $SM_mF_s \rightarrow A$ is not implied by **F′**. ■

6.5.5 Decomposition into Third Normal Form

Let us start from a normalized relation scheme $\mathbf{R}<\mathbf{S}, \mathbf{F}>$, where **S** is a set of attributes with atomic domains and **F** is a set of functional dependencies such that **R** is not in the 3NF. Since **R** is normalized, we know that it is in the **1NF** (note: here we do not insist that **R** be in the **2NF**). The reason why **R** is not in the **3NF** is that it has at least one FD $\mathbf{Y} \rightarrow A$, where A is a nonprime attribute that violates the 3NF requirements.

If $\mathbf{Y} \rightarrow A$ is a partial dependency (i.e., **Y** is a subset of a key of **R**), then **R** is not in the second normal form and these partial dependencies have to be removed by decomposition. To ensure that this decomposition is lossless and dependency-preserving, we decompose **R** into two relation schemes, say $\mathbf{R_1}<\mathbf{S_1}, \mathbf{F_1}>$ and $\mathbf{R_2}<\mathbf{S_2}, \mathbf{F_2}>$; here $\mathbf{S_1}$ is $\mathbf{S} - A$, $\mathbf{F_1}$ is $(\mathbf{F} - (\mathbf{Y} \rightarrow A))$, $\mathbf{S_2}$ is $\mathbf{Y}A$, and $\mathbf{F_2}$ is $\mathbf{Y} \rightarrow A$. This decomposition is lossless because **Y** is the common attribute in $\mathbf{R_1}$ and $\mathbf{R_2}$ and it forms a key of $\mathbf{R_2}$; it is dependency-preserving because the union of $\mathbf{F_1}$ and $\mathbf{F_2}$ is equal to **F**. The decomposition process can be hastened by removing from **R** any other nonprime attribute $A_1, A_2, \ldots$ such that $\mathbf{Y} \rightarrow AA_1A_2A_3 \ldots$ Thus **R** could be decomposed into $\mathbf{R_1}<(\mathbf{S} - AA_1A_2A_3 \ldots), \{\mathbf{F} - (\mathbf{Y} \rightarrow AA_1A_2A_3 \ldots)\}>$ and $\mathbf{R_2}<(YAA_1A_2A_3 \ldots), \mathbf{Y} \rightarrow AA_1A_2A_3 \ldots>$.

Now consider how we can handle the situation where $\mathbf{Y} \rightarrow A$ is a transitive dependency in **R** (if this type is the only offending form of dependency in the set **F**, then **R** is not only in the 1NF but it is also in the 2NF). If **K** is a key of **R**, then $\mathbf{K} \subseteq \mathbf{S}$. Now let $\mathbf{Y} \subseteq \mathbf{S}$ with $\mathbf{Y} \not\subset \mathbf{K}$ be a set of attributes so that for some nonprime attribute $A \in \mathbf{S}$ the FD $\mathbf{K} \rightarrow \mathbf{Y} \rightarrow A$ holds under **F** and **Y** is not a key of **R**. As before, the decomposition of **R** into $\mathbf{R_1}$ and $\mathbf{R_2}$ is done by removing from **R** the attribute A and forming a new relation $\mathbf{R_1}<(\mathbf{S} - A), \{\mathbf{F} - (\mathbf{Y} \rightarrow A)\}>$ and $\mathbf{R_2}<\mathbf{Y}A, \mathbf{Y} \rightarrow A>$.

The decomposition process, in the case of a transitive dependency, can be hastened by removing from the set of attributes $(\mathbf{R} - \mathbf{KY})$ any other nonprime attribute, e.g., A_i, such that $\mathbf{Y} \rightarrow A_i$. These other attributes will also be transitively dependent on the key **K** of **R**. Such further attributes A_i are also placed in the relation scheme $\mathbf{R_2}$ and removed from **R**. Thus we get the decomposition of **R** as $\mathbf{R_1}<(\mathbf{S} - AA_1A_2A_3 \ldots A_k), \{\mathbf{F} - (\mathbf{Y} \rightarrow AA_1A_2A_3 \ldots A_k)\}>$, and $\mathbf{R_2}<(\mathbf{Y}AA_1A_2A_3 \ldots A_k), \mathbf{Y} \rightarrow AA_1A_2A_3 \ldots A_k>$. As before, this decomposition is lossless because **Y** is the common attribute in $\mathbf{R_1}$ and $\mathbf{R_2}$ and it forms a key of $\mathbf{R_2}$. The decomposition is dependency-preserving because the union of $\mathbf{F_1}$ and $\mathbf{F_2}$ is equal to **F**.

If either $\mathbf{R_1}$ or $\mathbf{R_2}$ with the functional dependencies $\mathbf{F_1}$ and $\mathbf{F_2}$ is not in 3NF, we can continue the decomposition process until we get a database scheme, say $\mathbf{R_i}<\mathbf{S_i}, \mathbf{F_i}>, \mathbf{R_j}<\mathbf{S_j}, \mathbf{F_j}>, \mathbf{R_k}<\mathbf{S_k}, \mathbf{F_k}>, \ldots \mathbf{R_m}<\mathbf{S_m}, \mathbf{F_m}>$.

Algorithm 6.6 below is the formal method to decompose a normalized relation scheme $\mathbf{R}<\mathbf{S}, \mathbf{F}>$ into a number of 3NF relation schemes. The decomposition is lossless and dependency-preserving. The algorithm uses the canonical cover of the set of FDs **F** (see Section 6.4.7). The algorithm preserves dependency by building a relation scheme for each FD in the set of the canonical cover of **F**. The lossless join decomposition is assured in the algorithm by including in the decomposition a relation scheme that contains a candidate key of **R**. The algorithm also includes a relation scheme that contains all the attributes of **R** that are not involved in any FD in the

Algorithm 6.6

Lossless and Dependency-Preserving Third Normal Form Decomposition

Input: A relation scheme **R**, a set of canonical (minimal) functional dependencies $\mathbf{F_c}$, and **K**, a candidate key of **R**.

Output: A collection of third normal form relation schemes $(\mathbf{R_1}, \mathbf{R_2}, \ldots, \mathbf{R_n})$ that are dependency-preserving and lossless.

```
i := 0
Find all the attributes in R that are not involved in any FDs in F_c either on the
left or right side. If any such attributes {A} are found then
     begin
        i := i+1;
        form a relation R{A}; (*involving attributes not in any FDs*)
        R := R − {A}; (*remove the attributes {A} from R*)
if there is a dependency X → Y in F_c such that all the attributes that remain
        in R are included in it
   then
      begin
      i := i+1;
      output R as R_i{X, Y};
      end
   else
   begin
      for each FD X → A in F_c do
         begin
           i := i+1;
           form R_1<{X, A}, F{X → A}>
           end;
      combine all relation schemes corresponding to FDs with the same LHS
        (*i.e., <(X, A), {X → A}> and <(X,B), {X → B}>
        could be replaced by <(X, AB), {X → AB}>*)
          if none of left side of FD in
           F_j for 1 ≤ j ≤ i satisfies K ⊆ X
              then begin
                 i := i+1;
                 form R_i<{K}>; (*make sure that a relation contains
                   the candidate key of R*)
                 end;
      end;
```

canonical cover; this caters to any possible many-to-many association between these attributes.

Algorithm for Lossless and Dependency-Preserving Third Normal Form Decomposition

For this algorithm we assume that we have a canonical cover $\mathbf{F_c}$ for the set of FDs **F** for the relation scheme **R** and that **K** is a candidate key of **R.** Algorithm 6.6 produces a decomposition of **R** into a collection of relation schemes $\mathbf{R_1}$, $\mathbf{R_2}$, . . ., $\mathbf{R_n}$. Each relation scheme $\mathbf{R_i}$ is in third normal form with respect to the projection of $\mathbf{F_c}$ onto the scheme of **R**.

In Example 6.31 below, we give a decomposition into 3NF relation schemes which is both lossless and also dependency-preserving.

Example 6.31

Find a lossless join and dependency-preserving decomposition of the following relation scheme with the given set of functional dependencies:

SHIPPING *(Ship, Capacity, Date, Cargo, Value)*
Ship → *Capacity,*
ShipDate → *Cargo,*
CargoCapacity → *Value*

First find the canonical cover of the given set of FDs. The FDs are simple since each has a single attribute on the right-hand side. There are no redundant FDs in the set and none of the FDs contains extraneous attributes on the left-hand side. Hence the given set of FDs is in canonical form. A candidate key of the relation is *ShipDate*.

Now use Algorithm 6.6 to find a lossless and dependency-preserving decomposition of **SHIPPING.** Since all attributes appear in the canonical cover we need not form a relation for attributes not appearing in any FD. There is no single FD in the canonical cover that contains all remaining attributes in **SHIPPING,** so we proceed to form a relation for each FD in the canonical cover.

$\mathbf{R_1}$(*Ship, Capacity*) with the FD *Ship* → *Capacity*
$\mathbf{R_2}$(*Ship, Date, Cargo*) with the FD *ShipDate* → *Cargo*
$\mathbf{R_3}$(*Cargo, Capacity, Value*) with the FD *CargoCapacity* → *Value*

As a candidate key is included in the determinant of the FD of the decomposed relation scheme $\mathbf{R_2}$, we need not include another relation scheme with only a candidate key. The decomposition of **SHIPPING** into $\mathbf{R_1}$, $\mathbf{R_2}$, and $\mathbf{R_3}$ is both lossless and dependency-preserving. ■

In Example 6.32 we find a 3NF decomposition of a relation from the university database.

Example 6.32 Consider the relation scheme **STUDENT_INFO**(*Student*(S), Major(M), *Student_Department*(S_d), *Advisor*(A), *Course*(C), *Course_Department*(C_d), *Grade*(G), *Professor*(P), *Prof_Department*(P_d), *Room*(R), *Day*(D), *Time*(T)) with the following functional dependencies:

$S \rightarrow M$	each student is in an unique major
$S \rightarrow A$	each student has an unique advisor
$M \rightarrow S_d$	each major is offered in an unique department
$S \rightarrow S_d$	each student is in one department
$A \rightarrow S_d$	each advisor is in an unique department
$C \rightarrow C_d$	each course is offered by a single department
$C \rightarrow P$	each course is taught by one professor
$P \rightarrow P_d$	each professor is in an unique department
$RTD \rightarrow C$	each room has on a given day and time only one course scheduled in it
$RTD \rightarrow P$	each room has on a given day and time one professor teaching it it
$TPD \rightarrow R$	a given professor on a given day and time is in one room
$TSD \rightarrow R$	a given student on a given day and time is in one room
$TDC \rightarrow R$	a course can be in only one room on a given day and time
$TPD \rightarrow C$	on a given day and time a professor can be teaching only one course
$TSD \rightarrow C$	on a given day and time a student can be attending only one course
$SC \rightarrow G$	each student in a given course has a unique grade

A canonical cover of this set of functional dependencies will not contain the dependencies $\{S \rightarrow S_d, RTD \rightarrow P, TDC \rightarrow R, TPD \rightarrow C, TSD \rightarrow R\}$. The key of this relation scheme is TSD. The decomposition of this relation scheme into third normal form gives the following relation schemes:

$\mathbf{R_1}(SMA)$	with the FD $S \rightarrow MA$
$\mathbf{R_2}(MS_d)$	with the FD $M \rightarrow S_d$
$\mathbf{R_3}(AS_d)$	with the FD $A \rightarrow S_d$
$\mathbf{R_4}(CC_dP)$	with the FD $C \rightarrow C_dP$
$\mathbf{R_5}(PP_d)$	with the FD $P \rightarrow P_d$
$\mathbf{R_6}(RTDC)$	with the FD $RTD \rightarrow C$
$\mathbf{R_7}(TPDR)$	with the FD $TPD \rightarrow R$
$\mathbf{R_8}(TSDR)$	with the FD $TSD \rightarrow R$
$\mathbf{R_9}(SCG)$	with the FD $SC \rightarrow G$

(Note: Since all the attributes in the original relation scheme are involved with some FD we do not have to create a relation scheme with attributes not so involved. Also, the relation scheme $\mathbf{R_8}$ includes a candidate key; consequently we don't need to create an explicit relation scheme for the key.)
$\mathbf{R_1}$ through $\mathbf{R_9}$ form a lossless and dependency-preserving decomposition of **STUDENT_INFO** ■

Derivation of other canonical covers of this set of FDs and the corresponding relational schemes in 3NF is left as an exercise.

6.5.6 Boyce Codd Normal Form

Consider a relation scheme in third normal form that has a number of overlapping composite candidate keys. In particular consider the relation **GRADE**(*Name, Student#, Course, Grade*) of Figure 6.15. Here the functional dependencies are {*Name Course* → *Grade*, *Student#Course* → *Grade*, *Name* → *Student#*, *Student#* → *Name*}. Thus, each student has a unique name and a unique student number. The relation has two candidate keys, (*Name, Course*) and (*Student#, Course*). Each of these keys is a composite key and contains a common attribute *Course*. The relation scheme satisfies the criterion of the third normal form relation, i.e., for all functional dependencies $\mathbf{X} \rightarrow A$ in **GRADE,** when $A \notin \mathbf{X}$, either **X** is a superkey or *A* is prime. However, this relation has a disadvantage in the form of repetition of data. The association between a name and the corresponding student number is repeated; any change in one of these (for example, the change in the name to a compound name because of marriage) has to be reflected in all tuples, otherwise there will be inconsistency in the database. Furthermore, the student number cannot be associated with a student name unless the student has registered in a course, and this association is lost if the student drops all the courses he or she is registered in.

The problem in the relation GRADE is that it had two overlapping candidate keys. In the **Boyce Codd normal form** (BCNF), which is stronger than the third normal form, the intent is to avoid the above anomalies. This is done by ensuring that for all nontrivial FDs implied by the relation, the determinants of the FDs involve a candidate key.

Definition: A normalized relation scheme **R<S, F>** is in Boyce Codd normal form if for every nontrivial FD in $\mathbf{F}^+$ of the form $\mathbf{X} \rightarrow A$ where $\mathbf{X} \subseteq \mathbf{S}$ and $A \in \mathbf{S}$, **X** is a superkey of **R.**

Figure 6.15 The GRADE relation.

Name	*Student#*	*Course*	*Grade*
Jones	23714539	353	A
Ng	42717390	329	A
Jones	23714539	328	in prog
Martin	38815183	456	C
Dulles	37116259	293	B
Duke	82317293	491	C
Duke	82317293	353	in prog
Jones	23714539	491	C
Evan	11011978	353	A+
Baxter	83910827	379	in prog

A database scheme is in BCNF if every relation scheme in the database scheme is in BCNF. In other words, for a relation scheme **R<S, F>** to be in BCNF, for every FD in $\mathbf{F}^+$ of the form $\mathbf{X} \rightarrow A$ where $\mathbf{X} \subseteq \mathbf{S}$ and $A \in \mathbf{S}$, at least one of the following conditions hold:

- $\mathbf{X} \rightarrow A$ is a trivial FD and hence $A \in \mathbf{X}$, or
- $\mathbf{X} \rightarrow \mathbf{R}$, i.e., **X** is a superkey of **R.**

The above definition of the BCNF relation indicates that a relation in BCNF is also in 3NF. The BCNF imposes a stronger constraint on the types of FDs allowed in a relation. The only nontrival FDs allowed in the BCNF are those FDs whose determinants are candidate superkeys of the relation. In other words, even if *A* is a prime attribute, **X** must be a superkey to attain BCNF. In 3NF, **X** does not have to be a superkey, but in this case *A* must be a prime attribute. Effectively, 3NF allows nontrivial FDs whose determinant is not a superkey if the right-hand side is contained in a candidate key.

Example 6.33 The relation GRADE of Figure 6.15 is not in BCNF because the dependencies *Student#* → *Name* and *Name* → *Student#* are nontrivial and their determinants are not superkeys of GRADE. ■

The following is an example of a BCNF relation.

Example 6.34 Consider the relation scheme **STUDENT**(*SID, Name, Phone_No, Major*), where *SID* is an unique student identification number and where *Name*, and *Phone_No* are assumed to be unique for this example. The functional dependencies satisfied on the **STUDENT** relation scheme are {*SID* → *Major*, *Name* → *Major*, *Phone_No* → *Major*, *SID* → *Name*, *SID* → *Phone_No*, *Name* → *SID*, *Name* → *Phone_No*, *Phone_No* → *SID*, *Phone_No* → *Name*}. The relation **STUDENT** is in BCNF since each FD involves a candidate key as the determinant. ■

Lossless Join Decomposition into Boyce Codd Normal Form

We now give an algorithm that decomposes a relation scheme into a number of relation schemes, each of which is in Boyce Codd normal form. In Algorithm 6.7, **S** is a set of relation schemes. It is initialized with the original relation scheme, which may not be in the BCNF. At the end of the algorithm, **S** will contain a number of BCNF relation schemes. We start by finding a nonredundant cover **F′** of **F.** Then we look at the relation schemes in **S** and find a scheme, let us say $\mathbf{R_j}$, which is not in BCNF for a nontrivial FD $\mathbf{X} \rightarrow \mathbf{Y}$ in **F′.** Since $\mathbf{R_j}$ is not in BCNF, the conditions $\mathbf{XY} \subseteq \mathbf{R_j}$ and $\mathbf{X} \not\rightarrow \mathbf{R_j}$ will hold. We decompose $\mathbf{R_j}$ into two relations **XY** and $\mathbf{R_j} - \mathbf{Y}$. The algorithm terminates with all relations in the set being in BCNF.

The decomposition is lossless and the join of the resulting relations gives, the original relation. However, some of the dependencies in the original relation scheme

Algorithm 6.7

Lossless Boyce Codd Normal Form Decomposition Algorithm

Input: A relation scheme **R<U, F>** not in BCNF where **F** is a set of FD.

Output: Decomposition of **R(U)** into relation schemes $\mathbf{R_i(U_i)}$, $1 \le i \le n$ such that each $\mathbf{R_i(U_i)}$ is in BCNF and the decomposition is lossless.

```
begin
i := 0;
S := {R(U)};
all_BCNF := false;
Find F′ from F; (* here F′ is a nonredundant cover of F *)
while (¬ all_BCNF) do
   if there exists a nontrivial FD (X → Y) in F′⁺ such that
      XY ⊆ Rj and X ↛ Rj   (* Rj, a relation scheme in S, is not in BCNF,
                                i.e., X → Rj is not in F′⁺ *)
   then
      begin
         i := i+1;
         form relation Ri{X, Y} with the FD X → Y and add
               it to S
         Rj := Rj − Y;
      end;
   else  all_BCNF := true;
end;
```

may be lost. Also, the relation schemes so produced are not unique. The resulting set of decomposed schemes depends on the order in which the functional dependencies in the original relation is used.

We use Algorithm 6.7 to find BCNF decomposition of a number of relations in Examples 6.35 through 6.37.

Example 6.35

Find a BCNF decomposition of the relation scheme **SHIPPING** with the following set of functional dependencies:

SHIPPING(*Ship, Capacity, Date, Cargo, Value*)
Ship → *Capacity*
ShipDate → *Cargo*
CargoCapacity → *Value*

First find the nonredundant cover of the given set of FDs. There are no redundant FDs in the set, hence the given set of FDs is a nonredundant cover.

Now use Algorithm 6.7 to find a lossless decomposition of **SHIPPING.** Since there is an FD $Ship \rightarrow Capacity$ and since $Ship \nrightarrow$ **SHIPPING** we replace **SHIPPING** with the relation $\mathbf{R}_1$ *(Ship, Capacity)* formed with the FD in question and $\mathbf{R}_2$*(Ship, Date, Cargo, Value)*. Consider the relation $\mathbf{R}_2$: the FD $ShipDate \rightarrow Cargo$ is a nontrivial FD in the nonredundant cover. However, since $ShipDate \rightarrow ShipDateCargoValue$, the relation $\mathbf{R}_2$ is in BCNF and we have completed the decomposition.

$\mathbf{R}_1$*(Ship, Capacity)* with the FD $Ship \rightarrow Capacity$
$\mathbf{R}_2$*(Ship, Date, Cargo, Value)* with the FD $ShipDate \rightarrow Cargo$

The decomposition of **SHIPPING** into $\mathbf{R}_1$ and $\mathbf{R}_2$ is lossless but not dependency preserving because the FD $CargoCapacity \rightarrow Value$ is not implied by the set of FDs $\{Ship \rightarrow Capacity, ShipDate \rightarrow Cargo\}$.

Another BCNF decomposition of **SHIPPING** is obtained when we consider the FD $CargoCapacity \rightarrow Value$ first. This gives us the following decompositions:

$\mathbf{R}_1$*(Cargo, Capacity, Value)* with the FD $CargoCapacity \rightarrow Value$
$\mathbf{R}_2$*(Ship, Capacity)* with the FD $Ship \rightarrow Capacity$
$\mathbf{R}_3$*(Ship, Date, Cargo)* with the FD $ShipDate \rightarrow Cargo$

This decomposition is also dependency-preserving. ■

An example of a BCNF decomposition which is not dependency preserving is given below.

Example 6.36

Consider the relation scheme $<(ABCD), \{AB \rightarrow C, C \rightarrow A\}>$. None of the FDs are redundant, so the given set is a nonredundant cover. Using the FD $AB \rightarrow C$ we decompose this into the relation schemes: $<(ABC), \{AB \rightarrow C, C \rightarrow A\}>$ and $<(ABD), \{\ \}>$. The scheme $<(ABC), \{AB \rightarrow C, C \rightarrow A\}>$ can be further decomposed into the schemes $<(AC), \{C \rightarrow A\}>$ and $<(BC), \{\ \}>$. ■

In Example 6.37, we demonstrate the non-uniqueness of the BCNF decomposition.

Example 6.37

Consider the relation scheme **STUDENT_INFO**$\{S, M, S_d, A, C, C_d, G, P, P_d, R, D, T\}$ with the following functional dependencies $(S \rightarrow MA, M \rightarrow S_d, A \rightarrow S_d, C \rightarrow C_dP, P \rightarrow P_d, RDT \rightarrow C, TPD \rightarrow R, TSD \rightarrow R, SC \rightarrow G)$. The key of this relation is *TSD*. The decomposition of this relation into a number of BCNF relation schemes using Algorithm 6.7 gives the decomposition tree shown in Figure G. The left tree is obtained by considering the FDs in the order $S \rightarrow MA$, $S \rightarrow S_d$, $C \rightarrow C_d$, $C \rightarrow P$, and $RDT \rightarrow C$. This order gives the following set of BCNF relation schemes: (SMA), (SS_d), (CC_d), (CP), $(RDTC)$, and (SGP_dRDT). The right decomposition is obtained by considering the FD $SC \rightarrow G$ first.

Figure G Two Different Decomposition Trees.

$(SMS_dACC_dGPP_dRDT)$
$S \rightarrow MA$
(SMA), $(SS_dCC_dGPP_dRDT)$
$S \rightarrow S_d$
(SS_d), (SCC_dGPP_dRDT)
$C \rightarrow C_d$
(CC_d), $(SCGPP_dRDT)$
$C \rightarrow P$
(CP), $(SCGP_dRDT)$
$RDT \rightarrow C$
$(RDTC)$, (SGP_dRDT)
$RDT \rightarrow P_d$
$(RDTP_d)$, $(SGRDT)$

$(SMS_dACC_dGPP_dRDT)$
$SC \rightarrow G$
(SCG), $(SMS_dACC_dPP_dRDT)$
$TSD \rightarrow R$
$(TSDR)$, $(SMS_dACC_dPP_dDT)$
$P \rightarrow P_d$
(PP_d), (SMS_dACC_dPDT)
$C \rightarrow P$
(CP), (SMS_dACC_dDT)
$C \rightarrow C_d$
(CC_d), (SMS_dACDT)
$A \rightarrow S_d$
(AS_d), $(SMACDT)$
$S \rightarrow A$
(SA), $(SMCDT)$
$S \rightarrow M$
(SM), $(SCDT)$

■

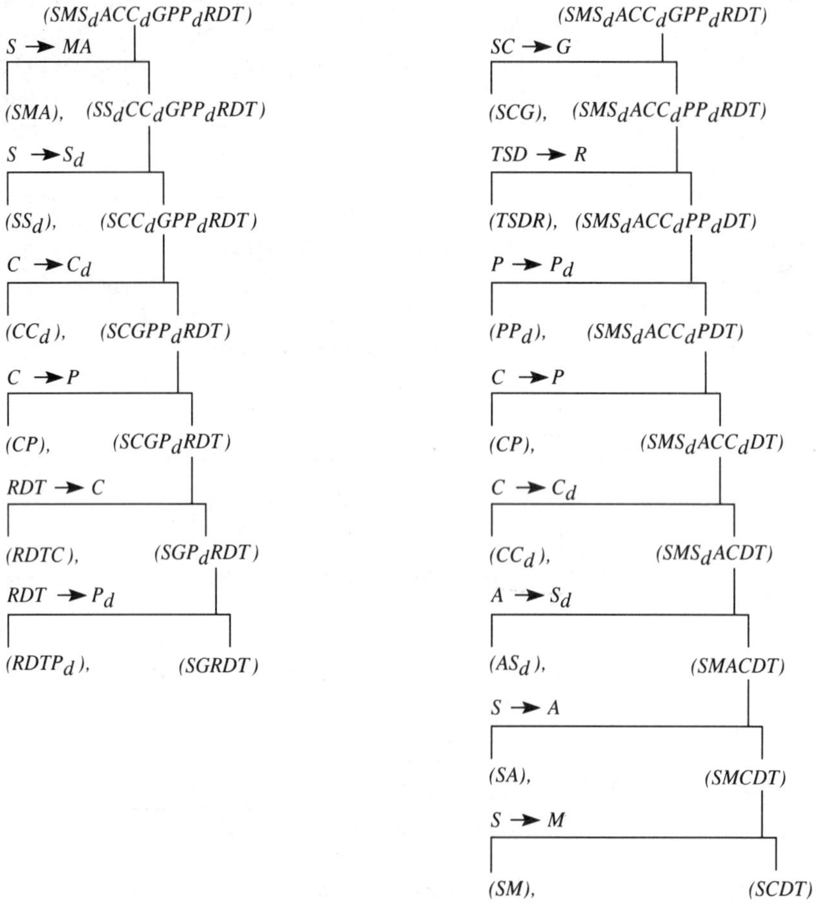

We see from the above example that for different orders of considering the FDs, we get different decomposition trees and hence different sets of resulting relation schemes. For Example 6.37, we illustrate in Figure G two different decomposition trees giving the following sets of relations: {*(SMA)*, (SS_d), (CC_d), *(CP)*, *(RDTC)*, (P_dRDT), *(SGRDT)*} and {*(SCG)*, *(TSDR)*, (PP_d), *(CP)*, (CC_d), (AS_d), *(SA)*, *(SM)*, *(SCDT)*}.

One other point we notice is that some of the original dependencies are no longer preserved in the decompositions given above. For instance, in both sets of relation schemes, the FD $M \rightarrow S_d$ is no longer represented. This means that we cannot ascertain, without one or more joins, that the corresponding fact is correctly represented in the database. At each step of the algorithm we are decomposing a relation into two relations, such that the common attribute is a key of one of these relations. Consequently, the decomposition algorithm produces a set of lossless BCNF relations.

We conclude with the observation that there are relation schemes **R<S, F>** such that no decomposition of **R** under **F** is dependency-preserving. This is a worse situation than one where some decompositions are dependency-preserving while others are not.

6.6 Concluding Remarks

Let us return to the relation STUDENT_ADVISOR*(Name, Department, Advisor)* of Figure Ei with the functional dependencies **F** = {*Name* → *Department, Name* → *Advisor, Advisor* → *Department*}. When we decomposed STUDENT_ADVISOR into STUDENT_DEPARTMENT*(Name, Department),* and DEPARTMENT_ADVISOR *(Department, Advisor),* giving the relations shown in Figures Eii and Eiii, we found that the decomposition was lossy. The common attribute, *Department,* is not a key of either of the decomposed relations. The join of these decomposed relations, given in Figure Eiv, contains tuples that did not exist in the original relation of Figure Ei. In addition the decomposition is not dependency-preserving. The FD *Name* → *Advisor* is not implied by the FDs of the decomposed relation nor could it be derived from their join.

We notice, however, that there are three independent relationships in the STUDENT_ADVISOR relation, and the only key is *NameAdvisor*. We can decompose it into three relations, ADVISOR_STUDENT*(Name, Advisor),* STUDENT_DEPARTMENT*(Name, Department),* and ADVISOR_DEPARTMENT*(Advisor, Department)*. This decomposition is useful in storing the independent relationships autonomously. The original relation can be obtained by joining these decomposed relations. The decomposition is lossless since the common attribute in these relations is a key of one of them. Furthermore, the decomposition is dependency preserving since each of the FDs is preserved in one of the relations.

Note that some of these independent relationships that are not involved with each other will be eliminated from the final result. For instance, a new student, Letitia, may join the Physics department without having an advisor. Similarly, a new professor, Jaffe, may join the Chemistry department and may not yet be advising students. The resulting relations are shown in parts a, b, and c of Figure 6.16. In the original relation, this data could only have been entered with null values for the unknown attribute.

The join of these relations to obtain the STUDENT_ADVISOR relation gives us the tuples shown in Figure E. The new tuples added in the decomposed relation participate in one of the joins, as shown in Figure Ed. However, these and other extraneous tuples are eliminated when the second join is performed. The tuples (Letitia, Physics) of STUDENT_DEPARTMENT and (Jaffe, Chemistry) of ADVISOR_DEPARTMENT are eliminated for this sequence of joins. Such tuples, which do not contribute to the result of the join operations, are called **dangling tuples.**

When we refer to the attributes *Name, Advisor,* and *Department* in a database containing the above three relations, we need to distinguish the various applications of the same symbol. A simple method of doing this is by preceding the attribute with the name of the relation. Another approach would be to use unique identifiers for each role that the attribute plays in the model.

Figure 6.16 Join of the decomposition of STUDENT_ADVISOR: (a) ADVISOR_STUDENT; (b) STUDENT_DEPARTMENT; (c) ADVISOR_DEPARTMENT; and (d) X = STUDENT DEPARTMENT $\bowtie$ ADVISOR_DEPARTMENT. Note: The marked tuples are eliminated when this result relation, X, is joined with ADVISOR_STUDENT, i.e., STUDENT ADVISOR = ADVISOR_STUDENT $\bowtie_{Name,Advisor.}$ X.

Name	*Advisor*
Jones	Smith
Ng	Turner
Martin	Bosky
Dulles	Hall
Duke	James
James	Clark
Evan	Smith
Baxter	Bronte

(a)

Name	*Department*
Jones	Comp Si
Ng	Chemistry
Martin	Physics
Dulles	Decision Sci
Duke	Mathematics
James	Comp Sci
Evan	Comp Sci
Letitia	Physics
Baxter	English

(b)

Advisor	*Department*
Smith	Comp Sci
Turner	Chemistry
Bosky	Physics
Hall	Decision Sci
James	Mathematics
Clark	Comp Sci
Bronte	English
Jaffe	Chemistry

(c)

Name	*Department*	*Advisor*	
Jones	Comp Sci	Smith	
Jones	Comp Sci	Clark	<
Ng	Chemistry	Turner	
Ng	Chemistry	Jaffe	<
Martin	Physics	Bosky	
Dulles	Decision Sci	Hall	
Duke	Mathematics	James	
James	Comp Sci	Smith	<
James	Comp Sci	Clark	
Evan	Comp Sci	Smith	
Evan	Comp Sci	Clark	<
Letitia	Physics	Brosky	<
Baxter	English	Bronte	

(d)

The goal of database design is to ensure that the data is represented in such a way that there is no redundancy and no extraneous data is generated. This means that we would generate relations in as high an order as possible. Since we cannot always guarantee that the BCNF relations will be dependency preserving when both lossless and dependency-preserving relations are required, we have to settle for the third normal form.

6.7 Summary

In this chapter we studied the issues involved in the design of a database application using the relational model. We discussed the importance of having a consistent database without repetition of data and pointed out the anomalies that could be introduced in a database with an undesirable design. The criteria to be addressed by the design process are redundancy, insertion anomalies, deletion anomalies, and update anomalies.

A relation scheme **R** is a method of indicating the attribute names involved in a relation. In addition the relation scheme **R** has a number of constraints that have to be satisfied to reflect the real world being modeled by the relation. These constraints are in the form of FDs. The approach we have used is to replace R by a set of more desirable relation schemes. In this chapter we considered the decomposition approach. The synthesis approach is discussed in Chapter 7.

The decomposition approach starts with one relation (the universal relation) and the associated set of constraints in the form of functional dependencies. The relation has a certain number of undesirable properties (in the form of insertion, deletion, or update anomalies) and it is replaced by its projections. A number of desirable forms of projections have been identified. In this chapter we discussed the following normal forms: 1NF, 2NF, 3NF, BCNF.

Any relation having constraints in the form of FDs only can be decomposed into relations in the third normal form; such a decomposition is lossless and preserves the dependencies. Any relation can also be decomposed losslessly into relations in the Boyce Codd normal form (and hence into the third normal form). However, such decomposition into the Boyce Codd normal form may not be dependency-preserving. The goal of the decomposition approach to the relational database design using FDs is to come up with a database scheme that is in BCNF, is lossless, and preserves the original set of FDs. If this goal is not possible, an alternate goal is to derive a database scheme that is in 3NF and is lossless and dependency-preserving.

Key Terms

decomposition
universal relation
universal relation assumption
spurious tuple
trivial functional dependency
closure
cover
nonredundant cover
simple
canonical cover
minimal
full functional dependency
prime attribute
nonprime attribute
partial dependency
transitive dependency
synthesis
content preserving
dependency-preserving
interrelation join constraints
unnormalized
nonatomic value
normalized
first normal form (1NF)
second normal form (2NF)
third normal form (3NF)
lossless join decomposition
lossless
lossy
Boyce Codd normal form (BCNF)
dangling tuple

Exercises

6.1 Given **R**{*ABCDE*} and **F** = {$A \rightarrow B$, $BC \rightarrow D$, $D \rightarrow BC$, $DE \rightarrow \phi$}. are there any redundant FDs in **F?** If so, remove them and decompose the relation **R** into 3NF relations.

6.2 Given **R**{*ABCDE*} and the set of FDs on **R** given by **F** = {$AB \rightarrow CD$, $ABC \rightarrow E$, $C \rightarrow A$}, what is $\mathbf{X}^+$, where **X** = {*ABC*}? What are the candidate keys of **R?** In what normal form is **R?**

6.3 Given **R**{*ABCDEF*} and the set of FDs on **R** given by **F** = {$ABC \rightarrow DE$, $AB \rightarrow D$, $DE \rightarrow ABCF$, $E \rightarrow C$}, in what normal form is **R?** If it is not in 3NF, decompose **R** and find a set of 3NF projections of **R.** Is this set lossless and dependency-preserving?

6.4 Given the relation scheme **R**{*Truck(T), Capacity (C), Date (Y), Cargo(G), Destination (D), Value(V)*} with the following FDs {$T \rightarrow C$, $TY \rightarrow G$, $TY \rightarrow D$, $CG \rightarrow V$}, is the decomposition of **R** into **R1**{*TCD*} and **R2**{*TGDVY*} dependency-preserving? Justify. Is this decomposition lossless? Justify. Find a lossless join and dependency-preserving decomposition of **R** into 3NF. If the 3NF decomposition is not in BCNF, find a BCNF decomposition of **R.**

6.5 Consider a relation scheme **R** with the following set of attributes and FDs: {*SID, Name, Date_of_Birth, Advisor, Department, Term, Year, Course, Grade*}, {*SID* → *NameDate_of_BirthAdvisorDepartment, Advisor* → *Department, SIDTermYearCourse* → *Grade*}. Find the candidate keys of **R.** Does a dependency-preserving and lossless join decomposition of **R** into a number of BCNF schemes exist? If so, find one such decomposition. Suppose **R** is decomposed into the relation schemes {*SID, Name, Date_of_Birth*}, {*SID, Advisor, Department*}, and {*SID, Term, Year, Course, Grade*}. Does this decomposition exhibit any redundancies or anomalies?

6.6 Prove that every set of functional dependencies **F** is covered by a set of simple functional dependencies **G,** wherein each functional dependency has no more than one attribute on the right-hand side.

6.7 Given the set of functional dependencies {$A \rightarrow BCD$, $CD \rightarrow E$, $E \rightarrow CD$, $D \rightarrow AH$, $ABH \rightarrow BD$, $DH \rightarrow BC$}, find a nonredundant cover. Is this the only nonredundant cover?

6.8 Given **R**{*ABCDEFGH*} with the FDs {$A \rightarrow BCDEFGH$, $BCD \rightarrow AEFGH$, $BCE \rightarrow ADEFGH$, $CE \rightarrow H$, $CD \rightarrow H$}, find a BCNF decomposition of **R.** Is it dependency-preserving?

6.9 Given **R** <{*A, B, C, D, E, F, G, H, I, J, K*}, {$I \rightarrow K$, $AI \rightarrow BFG$, $IC \rightarrow ADE$, $BIG \rightarrow CJ$, $K \rightarrow HA$}, find a canonical cover of this set of FDs. Find a dependency-preserving and lossless join 3NF decomposition of **R.** Is there a BCNF decomposition of **R** that is both dependency-preserving and also lossless? If so, find one such decomposition.

6.10 Given the relation **R** {*ABCDE*} with the FDs {$A \rightarrow BCDE$, $B \rightarrow ACDE$, $C \rightarrow ABDE$}, give the lossless decomposition of **R.**

6.11 Give an efficient algorithm to compute the closure of **X** under a set of FDs, using the scheme outlined in the text.

6.12 Does another canonical cover of the set of FDs of Example 6.32 exist? If so, derive it and show the corresponding relation schemes.

6.13 Given the relation **R** {*ABCDEF*} with the set H = {$A \rightarrow CE$, $B \rightarrow D$, $C \rightarrow ADE$, $BD \rightarrow F$}, find the closure of *BCD*.

6.14 Explain why there is renewed interest in unnormalized relations (called the non_1NF or NFNF). What are its advantages compared to normalized relations?

6.15 Discuss the advantages and disadvantages of representing hierarchical structured data from the real world as an unnormalized relation.

6.16 The Sky-High-Returns Mutual Fund (SMF) Corp. offers a number of different no-load mutual funds (F) for investment. It sells directly to the public through a number of branches (B). Each customer (C) is assigned to an agent (A) who is an employee of SMF and works out of only one branch. Any customer is allowed to buy any number of units (U) of any of the funds. Each fund is managed out of one of the branches and the portfolio (P) of the fund is directed by a board of managers (M). The board is made up of agents of SMF; however, agents from different branches may be involved in any number of boards at any branch. The unit value of each fund is decided at the end of the last business day of the month and all purchases and redemptions are done only after the unit price is determined at that time. The funds are charged a 5% per year management fee; the agents get 1% of this fee in addition to their regular salaries. Determine the entities and their attributes that have to be maintained if SMF is to design a database system to support its operations. What are the dependencies that have to be enforced? Make any additional assumptions that you may require.

6.17 Consider the TEACHES relation. Assume that *Room_Cap* $\not\rightarrow$ *Enrol_Lmt*. This means that two different courses allocated to the same room at different day and time could have different *Enrol_Lmt*s. In what normal form is TEACHES under this modified assumption? If it is not in 3NF form, find a lossless and dependency-preserving decomposition.

6.18 Consider the relation scheme **R**$(ABCDE)$ and the FDs $\{A \rightarrow B,\ C \rightarrow D,\ A \rightarrow E\}$. Is the decomposition of **R** into (ABC), (BCD), (CDE) lossless?

6.19 Find a 3NF decomposition of the following relation scheme: *(Faculty, Dean, Department, Chairperson, Professor, Rank, Student)*. The relation satisfies the following functional dependencies (and any others that are logically implied by these):

Faculty → *Dean*
Dean → *Faculty*
Department → *Chairperson*
Professor → *RankChairperson*
Department → *Faculty*
Student → *DepartmentFacultyDean*
ProfessorRank → *DepartmentFaculty*

6.20 What are the design goals of a good relational database design? Is it always possible to achieve these goals? If some of these goals are not achievable, what alternate goals should you aim for and why?

6.21 Use Algorithm 6.4 to determine if the decomposition of STUDENT_ADVISOR*(Name, Department, Advisor)* with the functional dependencies **F**{*Name* → *Department*, *Name* → *Advisor*, *Advisor* → *Department*} into ADVISOR_STUDENT*(Name, Advisor)*, STUDENT_DEPARTMENT *(Name, Department)*, and ADVISOR_DEPARTMENT*(Advisor, Department)* is lossless.

6.22 Consider the relation scheme **R**(A, B). With no information about the FDs involved, can you determine its normal form? Justify your answer.

6.23 Consider the relation scheme **R**(A, B, C, D) where A is a candidate key. With no information about the FDs involved, can you determine its normal form? Justify your answer.

6.24 Prove that the Armstrong axioms **F1** through **F3** are sound. (Hint: if $\mathbf{X} \rightarrow \mathbf{Y}$ is derived from **F** using the Armstrong axioms, then the dependency $\mathbf{X} \rightarrow \mathbf{Y}$ is satisfied in any relation that satisfies the dependencies in **F**.)

6.25 Prove that Algorithm 6.1 correctly computes $\mathbf{X}^+$.

6.26 Prove that $\mathbf{X} \rightarrow \mathbf{Y}$ follows from the inference axioms **F1** through **F3** if and only if $\mathbf{Y} \subseteq \mathbf{X}^+$.

Bibliographic Notes

Codd (Codd 70) studied functional dependencies and the third normal form. The 2NF, 3NF, and BCNF were introduced in (Codd 72) and (Codd 74), and the axioms for functional dependencies were developed by Armstrong (Arms 74). (Beer 77) gives a set of axioms for FDs and MVDs and proves the completeness and soundness of this set. The linear membership algorithm for functional dependencies was presented in (Beer 79). An algorithm to derive a minimum cover was given in (Maie 80).

The universal relation concept and associated problems were first discussed in (Kent 81). The formal proof of theorem on lossless join and dependency-preserving third normal form decomposition is given in (Bisk 79). The algorithm for testing for lossless join is based on (Aho 79). A more efficient algorithm is given in (Liu 80). An algorithm for testing the preservation of dependency is presented in (Beer 81). The complexity of finding whether a relation is in the BCNF is discussed in (Beer 79). Recent results from the NFNF (non_1NF) relations are presented in (Ozso 87) and (Roth 88).

Textbook discussions of the relational database design are included in (Date 85), (Lien 85), (Kort 86), and (Ullm 82). (Maie 83) gives a very detailed theoretical discussion of the relational database theory including relational database design.

Bibliography

(Aho 79) A. V. Aho, C. Beeri & J. D. Ullman, "The theory of Joins in Relational Databases," *ACM TODS* 9(2), June 1979, pp. 297–314. Corrigendum: *ACM TODS* 9(2), June 1979, p. 287.

(Arms 74) W. W. Armstrong, "Dependency Structures of Database Relationships," Proc. of the IFIP, 1974, pp. 580–583.

(Beer 77) C. Beeri, R. Fagin, & J. H. Howard, "A Complete Axiomatization for Functional and Multivalued Dependencies," Prov. of ACM SIGMOD International Symposium on Management of Data, 1977, pp. 47–61.

(Beer 79) C. Beeri, & P. A. Bernstein, "Computational problems Related to the Design of Normal Form Relational Schemes," *ACM TODS* 4(1), March 1979, pp. 113–124.

(Beer 80) C. Beeri, "On the Membership Problem for Functional and Multivalued Dependencies in Relational Databases," *ACM TODS* 5(3), September 1980, pp. 241–259.

(Beer 81) C. Beeri & P. Honeyman, "Preserving Functional Dependencies," *SIAM Journal of Computing* 10(3), pp. 647–656.

(Bisk 79) J. Biskup, U. Dayal, & P. A. Bernstein, "Synthesizing Independent Database Schemas," Prov. ACM SIGMOD International Symposium on Management of Data, 1979, pp. 143–152.

(Bros 88) V. Brosda, & G. Vossen, "Update and Retrieval in a Relational Database Through a Universal Schema interface," *ACM TODS* 13(4), December 1988, pp. 449–485.

(Codd 70) E. F. Codd, "A Relational Model for Large Shared Data Banks," *Communications of the ACM* 13(6), June 1970, pp. 377–387.

(Codd 72) E. F. Codd, "Further Normalization of the Data Base Relational Modd," in R. Rustin, ed., *Data Base Systems*. Englewood Cliffs, NJ: Prentice-Hall, 1972, pp. 33–64.

(Codd 74) E. F. Codd, "Recent Investigation in Relational Data Base Systems," Proc IFIP 74, 1974, pp. 1017–1021.

(Date 85) C. J. Date, *An Introduction to Database Systems,* vol. 1, 4th ed. Reading, MA: Addison-Wesley, 1985.

(Delo 78) C. Delobel, "Normalization and Hierarchical Dependencies in the Relational Data Model," *ACM TODS* 3(3), September 1978, pp. 201–22.

(Fagi 77) R. Fagin, "Multivalued Dependencies and a New Normal Form for Relational Databases," *ACM TODS* 2(3), September 1977, pp. 262–278.

(Fagi 79) R. Fagin, "Normal Forms and Relational Database Operators," ACM SIGMOD International Symposium on Management of Data, 1979, pp. 153–160.

(Fagi 81) R. Fagin "A Normal Form for Relational Databases that is Based on Domains and Keys," *ACM TODS* 6(3), September 1982, pp. 387–415.

(Kent 81) W., Kent, "Consequences of Assuming a Universal Relation," *ACM TODS* 6(4), December 1981, pp. 539–556.

(Kort 86) H. F. Korth & A. Silberschatz, *Database Systems Concepts*. New York: McGraw-Hill, 1986.

(Lien 81) Y. E. Lien, "Hierarchical Schemata for RElational Databases," *ACM TODS* 6(1), March 1981, pp. 48–69.

(Lien 85) Y. E. Lien, "Relational Database Design," in S. Bing Yao, ed., *Principles of Database Design*. Cliffs, NJ: Prentice-Hall 1985.

(Liu 80) L. Liu & A. Dembers, "An Algorithm for Testing Lossless Joins in Relational Databases," *Information Processing Letters* 11(1), pp. 73–76.

(Maie 80) D. Maier, "Minimum Covers in the Relational Database Model," *Journal of the ACM* 27(4), October 1980, pp. 664–674.

(Maie 83) D. Maier, *The Theory of Relational Databases*. Rockville, MD: Computer Science Press, 1983.

(Ozso 87) Z. M. Ozsoyoglu & Li-Yan Yuan, "A New Normal Form for Nested Relations," *ACM TODS* 12(1), March 1987, pp. 111–136.

(Riss 79) J. Rissanen, "Theory of Joins for Relational Databases—A Tutorial Survey," Prov. Seventh Symposium on Mathematical Foundations of Computer Science, Lecture Notes in Computer Science 64, New York: Springer-Verlag, pp. 537–551.

(Roth 88) M. A. Roth, H. F. Korth & A. Silberschatz, "Extended Algebra and Calculus for Nested Relational Databases," *ACM TODS* 13(4), December 1988, pp. 389–417.

(Ullm 82) Jeffrey D. Ullman, *Principles of Database Systems,* 2nd Rockville M: Computer Science Press, 1982.

(Zani 81) C. Zaniolo & M. A. Melkanoff, "On the Design of Relational Database Schemata," *ACM TODS* 6(1), March 1981, pp. 1–47.

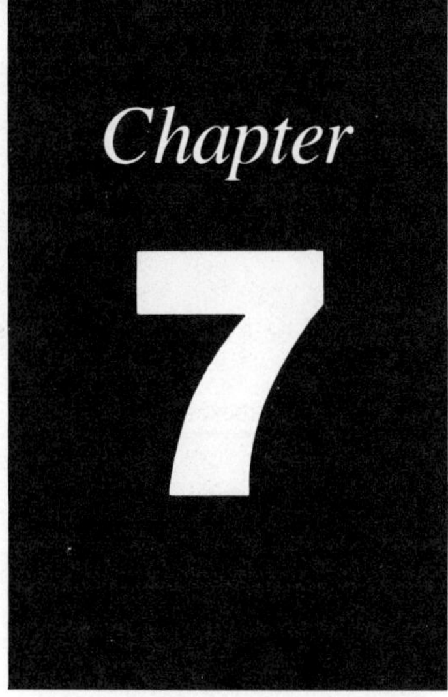

Synthesis Approach and Higher Order Normal Form

Contents

The first, second, third, and Boyce Codd normal forms and algorithms for converting a relation in first normal form into higher order normal forms were discussed in Chapter 6. In this chapter we continue our discussions of the issues involved in the design of a database application using the relational model. In Section 7.1, we examine the problems in the decomposition approach and present the synthesis approach to database design in Section 7.2. We then turn our attention to the higher order normal forms, examining the concept of multivalued dependency and axioms that involve both functional dependencies and multivalued dependencies. We discuss fourth normal form and a lossless decomposition algorithm for it. Next we introduce the concept of join dependency and a normal form for it. Finally, we introduce a scheme whereby all general constraints can be enforced via domain and key constraints and the associated normal form, called domain key normal form.

7.1 Problems in the Decomposition Approach

Any relation can be decomposed into a number of relations that are in third normal form. Such a decomposition is lossless and preserves the dependencies. Any relation can also be decomposed losslessly into relations in Boyce Codd normal form (and hence in third normal form). However, decomposition into Boyce Codd normal form may not be dependency preserving. A case was illustrated in Example 6.37 in Chapter 6, where among others, the FD $M \rightarrow S_d$ is no longer represented in any of the decomposed relation schemes. It is not always possible to find a BCNF decomposition that is both lossless and dependency preserving. In addition, the decomposition into BCNF is not unique. Many different BCNF relation schemes exist, as illustrated in Example 6.37.

The decomposition approach using the BCNF decomposition algorithm may produce interrelational join constraints. This happens when the attributes **XY** corresponding to one of the functional dependencies $\mathbf{X} \rightarrow \mathbf{Y}$ do not appear in any of the decomposed relation schemes. In the decomposed relation schemes of Example 6.37, to determine if the FD $M \rightarrow S_d$ is satisfied, we have to join the relations *(SMA)*, *(SSd)* for the left decomposition of Figure G in Example 6.37. In general, to find out if a functional dependency $\mathbf{X} \rightarrow \mathbf{Y}$ is maintained in the decomposed schemes requires joining several of the decomposed relations. Since join operations are computationally expensive, interrelational join constraints are undesirable.

However, a lossless and dependency preserving decomposition of a relation scheme into third normal form does not always give the minimum number of relation schemes. Furthermore, many different possible decompositions with the lossless and dependency preserving properties may be possible.

The goal of the decomposition approach to relational database design using FDs is to come up with a database scheme that is in BCNF, is lossless, and preserves the original set of FDs. If this goal is not achieved the alternate goal is to derive a database scheme that is in 3NF and is lossless and dependency preserving.

7.2 Normalization through Synthesis

In the decomposition approach to relational database design, we start with a relation (a universal relation) with undesirable properties and decompose it into a number of smaller relations to avoid these anomalies. Decomposition into third normal form using Algorithm 6.6 will be both lossless and dependency preserving. Decomposition into BCNF using Algorithm 6.7 will be lossless but may not be dependency preserving. Furthermore, decomposition into BCNF form is not unique.

The synthesis approach is an alternate approach to relational database design. Here we start with an universal relation scheme **U** that is not in third normal form and a set of functional dependencies **F** over **U,** and we create a database scheme $\mathbf{R} = \{\mathbf{R_1}, \mathbf{R_2}, \ldots, \mathbf{R_k}\}$. The scheme **R** is dependency preserving, i.e., all the dependencies in **F** are preserved and, in particular, if there is functional dependency $F_i \in \mathbf{F}$, there is a relation $\mathbf{R_i} \in \mathbf{R}$ such that the determinant of the FD F_i is a key of $\mathbf{R_i}$. Every relation $\mathbf{R_i}$ is in third normal form and there are no extraneous relations in the relation scheme **R** and hence no data duplications. In addition **R** is a lossless relation scheme if we ensure that at least one of the relations in **R** contains a key of **U.**

7.2.1 Functional Dependencies and Semantics

Functional dependencies are representations of the semantics of real world data in a model. We have to be careful that the semantics of the functional dependencies are preserved. We saw the importance of distinct names for attributes to indicate their semantic usage in the universal relation approach earlier.

Consider the attribute price of the entity set ***PART.*** Each part could have two prices associated with it, the wholesale or cost price and the retail or sale price. These price attributes are defined on the same domain. However, the wholesale and retail prices are not synonymous and are distinguished by using distinct names such as *Price_Wholesale* and *Price_Retail.*

Consider another example where different meanings are attached to an attribute defined on a given domain. The following example of functional dependencies involves the attribute *Department* defined on the domain consisting of all the departments of a university. The attribute *Department* appears a number of times: *Student → Department, Course → Department, Professor → Department.* However, the semantics of the use of this domain for the attribute *Department* is to indicate the department to which the student, course, or professor belongs and this could be distinct. This distinction is carried into the model by giving distinct names, let us say *S_Department, C_Department,* and *P_Department* to these distinct meanings assigned to the attribute. We write the above mentioned FDs as follows:

Student → S_Department
Course → C_Department
Professor → P_Department

7.2.2 Semantics of Nonfunctional Relationships

A nonfunctional relationship among attributes exists in a relation when some attributes are grouped together without any apparent dependencies existing between them. However, there is a relationship between these attributes that may become obvious if additional attributes are introduced. The FDs may not be apparent because the values for one set of attributes do not define unique values for another set of attributes. There may be no real functional dependency between these attributes but the database designer may want these attributes together. For example, the attributes *Professor, Interest,* and *Course* could be grouped together in the absence of apparent functional dependencies. However, this may be done to reflect the reality that a given professor has expertise and interest in a given area and that he or she can teach a given course requiring knowledge in that area. Such nonfunctional dependencies can be introduced by using the following scheme:

Professor Interest Course $\rightarrow \varnothing$

Here $\varnothing$ is a nonexistent attribute used only to show the nonfunctional relationship among the attributes of its determinant. To indicate additional nonfunctional relationships we can introduce additional nonexistent attributes $\varnothing_1, \varnothing_2, \ldots, \varnothing_n$.

These nonexistent attributes can be used to define the nonfunctional relationship during the database design process. Once a satisfactory database scheme is obtained these attributes can be discarded.

7.2.3 Synthesis Approach

Because the FDs determine whether or not a relation scheme is in third normal form, it would be easy to obtain a relation scheme in 3NF if the FDs are used to design the scheme. The synthesis approach uses the assumption that there is at least one functional relationship between two sets of attributes. If no such relationship in fact exists, the synthesis design approach introduces appropriate nonfunctional relationships. In the synthesis approach, the starting point of the relational database design process is a set of attributes (universal relation) and the set of functional (and nonfunctional) dependencies that have to be enforced among the attributes of this universal relation. The synthesis procedure then synthesizes a set of third normal form relation schemes, which preserves the required dependencies.

If the set of FDs used in the synthesis design process is a nonredundant cover, the number of relations synthesized will be minimum. In fact, it has been shown that the synthesis approach will produce the same set of relations regardless of the minimal cover used. (Recall that for a given set of FDs, it is possible to derive a number of covers.)

Example 7.1 Consider the universal relation **U**(A, B, C, D, E, H) and the set of FDs $\mathbf{F} = \{A \rightarrow BC, CD \rightarrow E, E \rightarrow C, D \rightarrow AEH, ABH \rightarrow BD, DH \rightarrow BC\}$. If a relation is synthesized for each FD in F, it will result in the following design:

$\mathbf{R}_1(ABC)$ with key A
$\mathbf{R}_2(CDE)$ with key CD
$\mathbf{R}_3(EC)$ with key E
$\mathbf{R}_4(DAEH)$ with key D
$\mathbf{R}_5(ABDH)$ with key ABH
$\mathbf{R}_6(DHBC)$ with key BC

However, **F** contains redundant FDs $CD \rightarrow E$ and $DH \rightarrow BC$. This means that the relations $\mathbf{R}_2$ and $\mathbf{R}_6$ are redundant and can be eliminated from the design. ■

If the FDs used in the synthesis approach are left reduced, i.e., there are no extraneous attributes on the left-hand side of the FDs, then we will not introduce any partial dependencies in the relations synthesized using such FDs.

Example 7.2 Consider $\mathbf{U}\{A,B,C,D\}$ with the set of FDs $\mathbf{F} = \{ABC \rightarrow D, A \rightarrow C\}$. The approach of using each FD in **F** to synthesize a relation gives the following relations:

$\mathbf{R}_1(ABCD)$ with key ABC
$\mathbf{R}_2(AC)$ with key A.

However, the relation $\mathbf{R}_1$ is not in 3NF since there is a partial dependency $AB \rightarrow D$. If the FD $A \rightarrow C$ were used to left reduce $ABC \rightarrow D$, we replace the latter by $AB \rightarrow D$ and hence obtain a synthesized design in the 3NF. ■

If two or more FDs have determinants that are functionally dependent on each other they are said to be **equivalent.** For instance, if we have set of attributes **X** and **Y** and if $\mathbf{X} \rightarrow \mathbf{Y}$ and $\mathbf{Y} \rightarrow \mathbf{X}$ then **X** and **Y** are equivalent, written as $\mathbf{X} \longleftrightarrow \mathbf{Y}$. In this case, instead of building two or more relations, one for each such FD, we can build only a single relation for each such group of FDs. Such a strategy produces an economic relational design.

Example 7.3 Let us return to the universal relation $\mathbf{U}\{A, B, C, D, E, H\}$ and the set of FDs $\mathbf{F} = \{A \rightarrow BC, CD \rightarrow E, E \rightarrow C, D \rightarrow AEH, ABH \rightarrow BD, DH \rightarrow BC\}$. We saw that the FDs $CD \rightarrow E$ and $DH \rightarrow BC$ are redundant and we can eliminate these. In addition, the FD $ABH \rightarrow BD$ is not left reduced, the attribute B being extraneous. This gives us, after reduction, the FDs $AH \rightarrow D$. Now, since $D \rightarrow AH$, we get the one-to-one dependency $AH \longleftrightarrow D$. Thus, AH and D are equivalent. We can combine these equivalent keys into one relation to give the following synthesized relational design:

$\mathbf{R}_1\{ABC\}$ with key A
$\mathbf{R}_2\{EC\}$ with key E
$\mathbf{R}_3\{ADEH\}$ with keys AH, D

Having determined the equivalent groups of FDs, we should eliminate any transitive dependencies that may exist. This will ensure that the relations produced will be in 3NF. ■

7.2.4 Synthesis Algorithm

The best known synthesis algorithm was proposed by Bernstein (Bern 76) and is sometimes called the Bernstein Synthesis algorithm. The algorithm starts with a universal relation and the functional dependencies to be enforced on it and produces a third normal form database scheme that is lossless and dependency preserving. The algorithm is called a synthesis algorithm because it constructs relation schemes from the FDs rather than decomposing a relation scheme into simpler relation schemes.

The synthesis algorithm uses a canonical cover of a set of (left-reduced) functional dependencies and groups the functional dependencies such that the determinant of the FDs in each group is the same. Recall that an FD is left reduced if the left-hand side does not contain any extraneous attributes. The algorithm then finds compound functional dependencies $(\mathbf{X_1},\mathbf{X_2}, \ldots, \mathbf{X_k}) \rightarrow \mathbf{Y}$ by using the equivalent determinant $\mathbf{X_i} \longleftrightarrow \mathbf{X_j}$ for $1 \leq i \leq k$ and $1 \leq j \leq k$. The characteristic of the compound functional dependency $(\mathbf{X_1}, \mathbf{X_2}, \ldots, \mathbf{X_k}) \rightarrow \mathbf{Y}$ is that $\mathbf{X_i} \rightarrow \mathbf{X_j}$ and $\mathbf{X_i} \rightarrow \mathbf{Y}$ for $1 \leq i \leq k$ and $1 \leq j \leq k$.

Let us illustrate the synthesis algorithm via the following example.

Example 7.4

Consider the universal relation **U**(A, B, C, D, E, F, G) with the functional dependencies:

$$
\begin{aligned}
BC &\rightarrow A \\
FG &\rightarrow BC \\
B &\rightarrow D \\
C &\rightarrow E \\
F &\rightarrow A \\
G &\rightarrow A \\
ABE &\rightarrow G \\
ACD &\rightarrow F
\end{aligned}
$$

In step 1 we find that the canonical cover of **F** includes the above FDs.

In step 2 we find that the groups contain one FD each.

In step 3 we discover that $BC \rightarrow FG$ and $FG \rightarrow BC$ are in the cover, hence we can combine these two groups into a single group $(BC, FG) \rightarrow A$.

G now becomes $(BC \rightarrow A, B \rightarrow D, \ldots ACD \rightarrow F)$.

J is $BC \rightarrow FG, FG \rightarrow BC$.

In step 4 we find that the minimum cover of **G** ∪ **J** does not contain $BC \rightarrow A$.

$(BCFG)$	with keys	(BC,FG)
(BD)	with key	(B)
(CE)	with key	(C)

(FA)	with key	(F)
(GA)	with key	(G)
(ABE)	with key	(ABE)
(ACD)	with key	(ACD).

Because the keys of **U** are BC or FG, contained in one of the relations above, the synthesis algorithm gives the final set of relations. ■

We now synthesize a set of 3NF relation for the STUDENT_INFO relation scheme discussed in Example 6.32.

Example 7.5 Consider the set of attributes in the relation scheme **STUDENT_INFO**$\{SMS_dACC_dGPP_dRDT\}$ with the following functional dependencies: $(S \rightarrow MA,\ M \rightarrow S_d,\ A \rightarrow S_d,\ C \rightarrow C_dP,\ P \rightarrow P_d,\ RTD \rightarrow C,\ TPD \rightarrow R,\ TSD \rightarrow R,\ SC \rightarrow G)$. The key of this relation is TSD.

In step 1 we find that the given set of FDs is minimal, i.e., **G** is the given set of FDs.

In step 2 the groups created are $(S \rightarrow M,\ S \rightarrow A)$, $(C \rightarrow C_d,\ C \rightarrow P)$, $(M \rightarrow S_d)$, $(A \rightarrow S_d)$, $(P \rightarrow P_d)$, $(SC \rightarrow G)$, $(RTD \rightarrow C)$, $(TPD \rightarrow R)$, $(TSD \rightarrow R)$.

In step 3 we find that $\mathbf{G}^+$ $RTD \longleftrightarrow TPD$ and hence we get **J** as being $RTD \rightarrow TPD$, $TPD \rightarrow RTD$. **G** reduces to $(S \rightarrow M,\ S \rightarrow A)$, $(C \rightarrow C_d,\ C \rightarrow P)$, $(M \rightarrow S_d)$, $(A \rightarrow S_d)$, $(P \rightarrow P_d)$, $(SC \rightarrow G)$, $(RTD \rightarrow C)$, $(TPD \rightarrow \phi)$, $(TSD \rightarrow R)$.

In step 4 we eliminate $TPD \rightarrow \phi$ to obtain $\mathbf{G_1}$ as being $S \rightarrow M$, $S \rightarrow A$, $C \rightarrow C_d$, $C \rightarrow P$, $M \rightarrow S_d$, $A \rightarrow S_d$, $P \rightarrow P_d$, $SC \rightarrow G$, $RTD \rightarrow C$, $TSD \rightarrow R$.

In step 5 we regroup $(S \rightarrow M,\ S \rightarrow A)$, $(C \rightarrow C_d,\ C \rightarrow P)$, $(M \rightarrow S_d)$, $(A \rightarrow S_d)$, $(P \rightarrow P_d)$, $(SC \rightarrow G)$, $(RTD \rightarrow C,\ RTD \rightarrow TPD,\ TPD \rightarrow RTD)$, $(TSD \rightarrow R)$.

In step 6 we get the following relation schemes:

Relation	*Key*
(SMA)	(S)
(CC_dP)	(C)
(MS_d)	(M)
(AS_d)	(A)
(PP_d)	(P)
(SCG)	(SC)
$(RTDPC)$	(RTD, TPD)
$(TSDR)$	(TSD)

Because the relation contains the key TSD the final relation scheme is as above. ■

Algorithm **7.1**

Synthesis Algorithm for Third Normal Form

Input: A universal database scheme **U**, a key **K** of **U**, and a set of simple left-reduced FDs **F**.

Output: A third normal form database scheme {**R**,**F′**}

1. (* Find a canonical cover *)
Find a canonical cover **G** of **F**. (* Use Algorithm 6.3 to first compute the nonredundant cover *)

Set **F′** to G.

2. (* Form groups with same determinant *)
Partition **G** into groups $\mathbf{H_1}$, $\mathbf{H_2}$, . . . such that all functional dependencies in each group have the same determinant.

3. (* Find and merge equivalent determinants *)
J : = ϕ; ;(* J will contain the FDs between equivalent keys *)
Examine each pair of groups $\mathbf{H_i}$, $\mathbf{H_j}$ with the determinant $\mathbf{X_i}$ and $\mathbf{X_j}$. If $\mathbf{X_i} \longleftrightarrow \mathbf{X_j}$, i.e., if $\mathbf{X_i} \rightarrow \mathbf{X_j}$ and $\mathbf{X_j} \rightarrow \mathbf{X_i}$ are in $\mathbf{G^+}$, then

$$\mathbf{J} := \mathbf{J} \cup \{\mathbf{X_i} \rightarrow \mathbf{X_j}, \mathbf{X_j} \rightarrow \mathbf{X_i}\};$$
$$\mathbf{H_i} := \mathbf{H_i} - \{\mathbf{X_i} \rightarrow A \mid A \in \mathbf{X_j}\};$$
$$\mathbf{H_j} := \mathbf{H_j} - \{\mathbf{X_j} \rightarrow B \mid B \in \mathbf{X_i}\};$$

merge $\mathbf{H_i}$ and $\mathbf{H_j}$ into a single group

(* Remove those FDs in $\mathbf{H_i}$, $\mathbf{H_j}$ that pertain to the FDs $\mathbf{X_i} \rightarrow \mathbf{X_j}$ and $\mathbf{X_j} \rightarrow \mathbf{X_i}$, respectively; thus we modify **G** as follows:

$$\mathbf{G} := \mathbf{G} - (\mathbf{X_i} \rightarrow \mathbf{X_j}) - (\mathbf{X_j} \rightarrow \mathbf{X_i});$$

i.e., remove from **G** the FDs $\mathbf{X_i} \rightarrow \mathbf{X_j}$ and/or $\mathbf{X_j} \rightarrow \mathbf{X_i}$ if they are in **G** *)

4. (* Eliminate transitive dependencies *)
Find a minimum set of FDs $\mathbf{G_1}$ of **G** such that

$$(\mathbf{G_1} \cup \mathbf{J})^+ = (\mathbf{G} \cup \mathbf{J})^+$$
Here $\mathbf{G_1} \subseteq \mathbf{G}$.
$$\mathbf{G_2} := \mathbf{G_1} \cup \mathbf{J};$$

5. Partition $\mathbf{G_2}$ into groups $\mathbf{H_1'}$, $\mathbf{H_2'}$, . . . where each group has the same or equivalent determinant (* here use **J** to find equivalent pairs $\mathbf{X_i} \longleftrightarrow \mathbf{X_j}$ *).

6. For each group $\mathbf{H_i'}$ with attributes ($\mathbf{X_i}$, $\mathbf{X_j}$, . . . , **Y**) corresponding to the FDs $\mathbf{X_i} \rightarrow \mathbf{X_j} \rightarrow \ldots \rightarrow \mathbf{X_l} \rightarrow \mathbf{Y}$ form a relation {$\mathbf{X_i X_j}$ . . . **Y**} with key ($\mathbf{X_i}$ or $\mathbf{X_j}$ or . . .) and add it to the relation scheme **R**.

7. (* Ensure that the relation scheme is lossless *)
If $\mathbf{K} \notin \mathbf{X_i}$, i.e., if a candidate key of **U** is not in one of the keys of the relations constructed, add the relation {**X**} to the relation scheme R.

If we compare the relation schemes obtained with this approach with the ones obtained in Example 6.32 using Algorithm 6.6 for the third normal form decomposition, we find that the synthesis approach gives one less scheme. Basically we have combined the FDs $RTD \rightarrow C$ and $TPD \rightarrow R$ into one relation scheme *(RTDPC)*. This particular relation scheme is not in BCNF since for the FD $C \rightarrow P$ in this relation, the determinant C of the FD is not a key of the relation. However, the relation *(RTDPC)* is in 3NF.

7.3 Multivalued Dependency

We discussed **multivalued dependency (MVD)** earlier with respect to the employee entity and the dependents, positions, and salary history of the employee. Figure 7.1 is an unnormalized relation showing the relation EMPLOYEE {*Employee_Name, Dependent(Name, Relationship), Position(Title, Date), Home_City, Home_Phone#*} and containing the information about employees. Each employee can have a number of dependents and would have occupied various positions in the organization. The relation has nonatomic values and hence, is not in normal form. We can normalize this relation as shown in in Figure 7.2. We see in Figure 7.2 that for a given value for *Employee_Name,* there are multiple values for the attributes *(Dependent_Name, Dependent_Relationship)* and *(Position_Title, Position_Date)*. The set of values for the attributes of *(Dependent_Name, Dependent_Relationship)* is not connected in any way to the values of the attributes in {EMPLOYEE − *Employee_Name* − *Depen-*

Figure 7.1 Unnormalized EMPLOYEE relation.

Employee_ Name	*Dependent*		*Positions*		*Home_ City*	*Home_ Phone*
	Name	*Relationship*	*Title*	*Date*		
Jill Jones	Bill Jones	spouse	J. Engineer	05/12/84	Lynn, MA	794-2356
			Engineer	10/06/86		
	Bob Jones	son	J. Engineer	05/12/84		
			Engineer	10/06/86		
Mark Smith	Ann Briggs	spouse	Programmer	09/15/83	Revere, MA	452-4729
			Analyst	06/06/86		
	Chloe Smith-Briggs	daughter	Programmer	09/15/83		
			Analyst	09/06/86		
	Mark Briggs-Smith	son	Programmer	09/15/83		
			Analyst	09/06/86		

Figure 7.2 Normalized EMPLOYEE relation.

Employee_ Name	*Dependent_ Name*	*Dependent_ Relationship*	*Position_ Title*	*Position_ Date*	*Home_ City*	*Home_ Phone#*
Jill Jones	Bill Jones	spouse	J. Engineer	05/12/84	Lynn, MA	794-2356
Jill Jones	Bill Jones	spouse	Engineer	10/06/86	Lynn, MA	794-2356
Jill Jones	Bob Jones	son	J. Engineer	05/12/84	Lynn, MA	794-2356
Jill Jones	Bob Jones	son	Engineer	19/06/86	Lynn, MA	794-2356
Mark Smith	Ann Briggs	spouse	Programmer	09/15/83	Revere, MA	452-4729
Mark Smith	Ann Briggs	spouse	Analyst	06/06/86	Revere, MA	45204729
Mark Smith	Chloe Smith-Briggs	daughter	Programmer	09/15/83	Revere, MA	452-4729
Mark Smith	Chloe Smith-Briggs	daughter	Analyst	06/06/86	Revere, MA	452-4729
Mark Smith	Mark Briggs-Smith	son	Programmer	09/15/83	Revere, MA	452-4729
Mark Smith	Mark Briggs-Smith	son	Analyst	06/06/86	Revere, MA	452-4729

dent}. Similarly, the set of values for the attributes of *(Position_Title, Position_Date)* is not connected in any way to the values of the attributes in {EMPLOYEE − *Employee Name* − *Positions*}.

For a second example of an **MVD,** look at the SCHEDULE relation described in Chapter 6 and shown, with some slight modifications in Figure 7.3. Notice that a course is scheduled a number of times during the week, and on each such meeting the room in which it meets may be different (not a frequent occurrence but nonetheless possible). Thus, the dependency between a course and a day is not simply functional but multivalued. Similarly, the dependency between a course and the room in which it meets is multivalued.

These multivalued dependencies can be indicated as follows:

Course $\twoheadrightarrow$ *RoomDayTime*

Figure 7.3 The SCHEDULE relation.

Prof	*Course*	*Room*	*Max_Enrollment*	*Day*	*Time*
Smith	353	A532	40	mon	1145
Smith	353	A534	40	wed	1245
Clark	355	H942	300	tue	115
Clark	355	H940	300	thu	115
Turner	456	B278	45	mon	845
Turner	456	B279	45	wed	845
Jamieson	459	D111	45	tue	1015
Jamieson	459	D110	45	thu	1015

However, a given course meets on a given day and time in but one room, i.e., there is a functional dependency:

CourseDayTime → *Room*

Multivalued dependencies arise when a relation R having a nonatomic attribute is converted to a normalized form. For each **X** value in such a relation, there will be a set of **Y** values associated with it. This association between the **X** and **Y** values does not depend on the values of the other attributes in the relation. Suppose we have two tuples t_1, t_2 in relation R defined on relation scheme **R** with the same **X** value. We exchange the **Y** values of these tuples and call the tuples so obtained t_3 and t_4. Then tuples t_3 and t_4 must also be in R.

In the SCHEDULE relation of Figure 7.3, there is a multivalued dependency between *Course* →→ *RoomDayTime*. Thus, if we exchange the {*Room, Day, Time*} value in tuples t_1 and t_2 with the same *Course* value (353) where

t_1 = |Smith | 353 |A532 | 40 | mon | 1145 |
t_2 = |Smith | 353 |A534 | 40 | wed | 1245 |

we get tuples t_3 and t_4 as follows:

t_3 = |Smith | 353 |A532 | 40 | mon | 1145 |
t_4 = |Smith | 353 |A534 | 40 | wed | 1245 |

Tuples t_3 and t_4 are in the database. (In fact, in this example tuple t_3 is the original tuple t_1 and tuple t_4 is the original tuple t_2!)

The multivalued dependency *Course* →→ {*Room, Day, Time*} does not mean that the multivalued dependencies *Course* →→ *Room, Course* →→ *Day*, and *Course* →→ *Time* will hold. Thus, corresponding to tuples t_1 and t_2 above, if we exchange just the *Room* values we get t_3' and t_4' which are not in the database.

t_3' = |Smith | 353 |A534 | 40 | mon | 1145 |
t_4' = |Smith | 353 |A532 | 40 | wed | 1245 |

Using Figure 7.2 we can verify that such an exchange of the **Y** values for a multivalued dependency **X** →→ **Y** in two tuples t_1 and t_2 with the same **X** value will always give tuples t_3 and t_4 which are in the database, even if the relation has multiple multivalued dependencies. However, tuples t_3 and t_4 need not be the original tuples t_1 and t_2. Exchanging the values of the attributes {*Dependent_Name, Dependent_Relationship*} in any two tuples t_1 and t_2 of Figure 7.2, gives us tuples t_3 and t_4 as shown below. Tuples t_3 and t_4 are in the database, but these tuples are not the original t_1 and t_2 tuples.

t_1 = |J J|Bill J |spouse|J. Eng|05/12/84|Lynn, MA|794-2356|
t_2 = |J J|Bob J|son |Eng |10/06/86|Lynn, MA|794-2356|

t_3 = |J J|Bill J |spouse|Eng |10/06/86|Lynn, MA|794-2356|
t_4 = |J J|Bob J|son |J. Eng|05/12/84|Lynn, MA|795-2356|

This property of multivalued dependency can be expressed formally by the definition given below.

Definition: Given a relation scheme **R**, let **X** and **Y** be subsets of attributes of **R** (**X** and **Y** need not be distinct). Then the multivalued dependency $\mathbf{X} \twoheadrightarrow \mathbf{Y}$ holds in a relation R defined on **R** if given two tuples t_1 and t_2 in R with $t_1(\mathbf{X}) = t_2(\mathbf{X})$; R contains two tuples t_3 and t_4 with the following characteristics:

·t_1 t_2, t_3, t_4 have the same **X** value, i.e.,

$$t_1(\mathbf{X}) = t_2(\mathbf{X}) = t_3(\mathbf{X}) = t_4(\mathbf{X})$$

·the **Y** values of t_1 and t_3 are the same and the **Y** values of t_2 and t_4 are the same, i.e.,

$$t_1(\mathbf{Y}) = t_3(\mathbf{Y}) \text{ and } t_2(\mathbf{Y}) = t_4(\mathbf{Y})$$

·the $\mathbf{R} - \mathbf{X} - \mathbf{Y}$ values of t_1 and t_4 are the same and the $\mathbf{R} - \mathbf{X} - \mathbf{Y}$ values of t_2 and t_3 are the same, i.e.,

$$t_1(\mathbf{R} - \mathbf{X} - \mathbf{Y}) = t_4(\mathbf{R} - \mathbf{X} - \mathbf{Y})$$
$$t_2(\mathbf{R} - \mathbf{X} - \mathbf{Y}) = t_3(\mathbf{R} - \mathbf{X} - \mathbf{Y})$$

Let us examine the problems that are created as a result of multivalued dependencies. Consider Figure 7.2 for the EMPLOYEE relation. It has two multivalued dependencies:

Employee_Name $\twoheadrightarrow$ *Dependent_NameDependent_Relationship*
Employee_Name $\twoheadrightarrow$ *Position_TitlePosition_Date*

Suppose employee Jill Jones gets a promotion on 12/15/86 to the position of manager. This involves adding two tuples to the database, one for each of her two dependents, to correctly register her employment history. A change in the value of an FD in a relation involving an MVD requires the change to be reflected in all tuples corresponding to that entity. In the EMPLOYEE relation of Figure 7.2 a change of the home address of an employee would have to be reflected in all tuples pertaining to that employee. Thus, if Jill Jones moves to Boston and her home phone number changes to 368-4384, a change is required in not one tuple but six tuples (after the addition of the two tuples for an additional position). Deletion requires that more than one tuple be deleted. For example, in the SCHEDULE relation, if course 355 is canceled, two tuples must be deleted from the table shown in Figure 7.3.

Summarizing, note that in multivalued dependencies the requirement is that if there is a certain tuple in a relation, then for consistency the relation must have additional tuple(s) with similar values. Updates to the database affect these sets of tuples or entail the insertion of more than one tuple. Failure to perform these multiple updates leads to inconsistencies in the database. To avoid these multiple updates, it is preferable to replace a relation having undesirable MVDs with a number of more "desirable" relation schemes. We illustrate more desirable schemes in Figure 7.4

Figure 7.4 Replacing the EMPLOYEE relation with three relations.

Employee_Name	*Dependent_Name*	*Dependent_Relationship*
Jill Jones	Bill Jones	spouse
Jill Jones	Bob Jones	son
Mark Smith	Ann Briggs	spouse
Mark Smith	Chloe Smith-Briggs	daughter
Mark Smith	Mark Briggs-Smith	son

Employee_ Name	*Position_ Title*	*Position_ Date*
Jill Jones	J. Engineer	05/12/84
Jill Jones	Engineer	10/06/86
Mark Smith	Programmer	09/15/83
Mark Smith	Analyst	06/06/86

Employee_ Name	*Home_ City*	*Home_ Phone#*
Jill Jones	Lynn, MA	794-2356
Mark Smith	Revere, MA	452-4729

for the EMPLOYEE relation of Figure 7.2.[1] Such a scheme avoids the necessity of multiple storage of the same information.

7.3.1 MVD and Normalization

In the normalization approach of a relation scheme with deletion, insertion, and update anomalies we have considered only functional dependencies so far. When the relation scheme to be normalized exhibits multivalued dependencies, we have to ensure that the resulting relation schemes do not exhibit any of these undesirable deletion, insertion, and update anomalies. A normal form called fourth normal form has been defined for relation schemes that have FDs as well as MVDs. The fourth normal form imposes constraints on the type of multivalued dependencies allowed in the relation scheme and is more restrictive than the BCNF.

The normalization of a relation scheme with MVDs requires, as in the case of normalization of relations with only FDs, that the decomposed relation schemes are both lossless and dependency preserving. The following property of the MVD will be used in the normalization approach.

[1]Recall our discussions on separating a repeating group from the representation of an entity set and replacing each such group by an identifying relationship and a weak entity. These were then represented by a relation containing the key of the strong entity along with the attributes of the weak entity (See Chapter 2).

Property of MVD

The following theorem for multivalued dependency is from Fagin (Fagi 77). We simply state it here. For the proof, see the bibliographic notes at the end of the chapter for the reference.

Theorem 7.1: If there is a multivalued dependency $\mathbf{X} \twoheadrightarrow \mathbf{Y}$ in a relation **R,** it also has an MVD $\mathbf{X} \twoheadrightarrow \mathbf{R} - \mathbf{XY}$ and **R** can be decomposed losslessly into two relations $\mathbf{R_1(X,Y)}$ and $\mathbf{R_2(X,Z)}$ where $\mathbf{Z} = \mathbf{R} - \mathbf{XY}$.

As a consequence of the above, a relation scheme with an MVD must be able to be decomposed losslessly. Consider a relation scheme **R**. Let **X, Y, Z** be subsets of **R,** not necessarily disjoint, such that $\mathbf{Z} = \mathbf{R} - \mathbf{XY}$. Let R be a relation on the relation scheme **R.** Relation R satisfies the MVD $\mathbf{X} \twoheadrightarrow \mathbf{Y}$ if and only if

$$R = \pi_{\mathbf{R1(XY)}}(R) \bowtie \pi_{\mathbf{R2(XZ)}}(R)$$

In other words, **R** decomposes losslessly into the relation scheme $\mathbf{R_1}$ and $\mathbf{R_2}$.

Definition: A **trivial multivalued dependency** is one that is satisfied by all relations R on a relation scheme **R** with $\mathbf{XY} \subseteq \mathbf{R}$. Thus, a MVD $\mathbf{X} \twoheadrightarrow \mathbf{Y}$ is trivial if $\mathbf{Y} \subseteq \mathbf{X}$ or $\mathbf{XY} = \mathbf{R}$. Obviously if $\mathbf{Y} = \phi$, then the MVD $\mathbf{X} \twoheadrightarrow \mathbf{Y}$ is trivial.

Example 7.6

(a) In the normalized EMPLOYEE relation of Figure 7.2 with the following dependencies:

Employee_Name → *Home_CityHome_Phone#*,
Employee_Name →→ *Dependent_NameDependent_Relationship*,
Employee_Name →→ *Position_TitlePosition_Date*.

the following MVDs are also satisfied:

Employee_Name →→ *Home_CityHome_Phone#Dependent_Name Dependent_Relationship*,
Employee_Name →→ *Home_CityHome_Phone#Position_Title Position_Date*.

(b) In Figure 7.4 the following MVDs are trivial:

Employee_Name →→ *Dependent_NameDependent_Relationship*
Employee_Name →→ *Position_TitlePosition_Date* ■

7.3.2 Axioms for Functional and Multivalued Dependencies

To design a relational database, given a relation scheme **R** with functional and multivalued dependencies, we need a set of rules or axioms that will allow us to determine all the dependencies implied by a given set of known dependencies. We need these axioms to verify whether a given relation scheme is legal (from the point of view of being lossless and dependency preserving) under a set of functional and multivalued dependencies. The first three of these axioms are the same as those we discussed for functional dependencies. As before, **W, X, Y, Z** are subsets of **R.**

F1: Reflexivity: X → X.
F2: Augmentation: (X → Y and V ⊆ Z) ⊨ (XZ → Y and XZ → VY)
F4: Additivity: (X → Y and X → Z) ⊨ X → YZ.
M1: Replication: X → Y ⊨ X →→ Y.

The replication axiom leads to the following versions of axioms F1 through F3 for multivalued dependencies:

M2: Reflexivity: X →→ X.
M3: Augmentation: X →→ Y ⊨ XZ →→ Y. If **(X →→ Y** and **V ⊆ W)** then **WX →→ VY.**
M4: Additivity or Union: (X →→ Y and **X →→ Z) ⊨ X →→ YZ.**
M5: Complementation: X →→ Y ⊨ X →→ (R − X − Y).
M6: Transitivity: (X →→ Y and **Y →→ Z) ⊨ X →→ (Z − Y).**

Note that unlike the transitivity rule for functional dependency, if **X →→ Y** and **Y →→ Z,** it does not always imply that **X →→ Z** (i.e., **X →→ Z** could be false).

M7: Coalescence: Given that **W ⊆ Y** and **Y ∩ Z = ϕ,** and if **X →→ Y** and **Z → W,** then **X → W.**

In addition to the above axioms, which have been shown to be sound and complete (refer to the bibliographic notes for reference to the formal proofs), the following rules are useful.

M8: Decomposition or Projectivity for the MVD: If **X →→ Y** and **X →→ Z,** then **X →→ (Y ∩ Z), X →→ (Y − Z),** and **X →→ (Z − Y).**

The decomposition rule for functional dependencies is much stronger than the corresponding one for the MVD; in the former, if **X → Y,** then **X →** A_i for A_i **∊ Y.** However, if **X →→ Y,** we can only say that **X →→** A, if we can find a **Z** such that **X →→Z** and **Y − Z =** A or **Z − Y =** A or **Y ∩ Z =** A.

M9: Mixed (Pseudo)Transitivity: If **X →→ Y** and **XY →→ Z** then **X →→ (Z − Y).**

7.3.3 Closure under MVDs

Given **D**, a set of FDs and MVDs, we can find a set of all functional and multivalued dependencies that can be derived from **D**. This set is the closure of **D**; to be consistent with the nomenclature for indicating the closure of a set of FDs it is indicated by $\mathbf{D}^+$. Computing the closure of **D**, like computing the closure of a set of FDs, is time consuming. However, instead of computing $\mathbf{D}^+$, we can use axioms **M1** through **M9** to ascertain if a given MVD is implied by a set of FDs and MVDs. With this goal in mind, we develop a method to determine if **D ⊨ X →→ Y.**

The Dependency Basis

Let **T** be a collection of sets closed under union, difference, and intersection. Given t_1 and t_2 are in **T** and $t_1\theta t_2$ is also in **T**, then **T** is said to be closed (with respect to θ). Here θ is one of the union, difference, or intersection operations for sets. Each member of **T** is made up of a subcollection **S** of nonempty, pairwise disjoint sets. The collection **S** is called the **basis** of **T**.

Given **U** a set of attributes $\mathbf{X} \subseteq \mathbf{U}$ and a set of dependencies **D**, we want to find all subsets of $\mathbf{U} - \mathbf{X}$ that are dependent on **X** by some MVD in $\mathbf{D}^+$. The complementation rule **(M5)**, the union rule **(M4)**, and the decomposition rule **(M8)** for multivalued dependencies imply that if the left-hand side of a set of MVDs is the same, then right-hand side is closed under Boolean operation (i.e., for MVDs of the form $\mathbf{X} \rightarrow\rightarrow \mathbf{Y}_i$, $1 \le i \le n$, the $\mathbf{Y}_i$s are closed under Boolean operation).

Algorithm 7.2 Computing the Dependency Basis of X

Input: **U**, a set of attributes; $\mathbf{X} \subseteq \mathbf{U}$ and **D**, a set of FDs and MVDs.

Output: The dependency basis $\{\mathbf{Y}_1, \mathbf{Y}_2, \ldots \mathbf{Y}_n\}$ of **X** under **D**.

1. Convert each FD $\mathbf{W} \rightarrow A$ to an MVD $\mathbf{W} \rightarrow\rightarrow A$ using rule **M1**.

2. (* Initialize the set **S** to the null set *) $\mathbf{S} = \phi$;

3. (* Apply rules **M3** and **M5** *)
For each MVD $\mathbf{W} \rightarrow\rightarrow \mathbf{Z}$ in **D** such that $\mathbf{W} \subseteq \mathbf{X}$ add $\mathbf{Z} - \mathbf{X}$ and $\mathbf{U} - \mathbf{Z} - \mathbf{X}$ to the set **S** as per rules **M3** and **M5**.

4. (* Now apply the decomposition rule **M8** to each pair of sets of attributes in set **S** such that they are not disjoint *)

For each pair of sets of attributes $\mathbf{Y}_1$ and $\mathbf{Y}_2$ in **S** such that $\mathbf{Y}_1 \cap \mathbf{Y}_2 \neq \phi$:
replace $\mathbf{Y}_1$ and $\mathbf{Y}_2$ by the nonempty sets $\mathbf{Y}_1 \cap \mathbf{Y}_2$, $\mathbf{Y}_1 - \mathbf{Y}_2$, and $\mathbf{Y}_2 - \mathbf{Y}_1$
(* i.e., discard the sets $\mathbf{Y}_1 - \mathbf{Y}_2$ and $\mathbf{Y}_2 - \mathbf{Y}_1$ if they are empty *).

5. (* Now look for MVD $\mathbf{W} \rightarrow\rightarrow \mathbf{Z}$ in **D** and **Y** in **S** such that $\mathbf{Y} \cap \mathbf{W} = \phi$ but $\mathbf{Y} \cap \mathbf{Z} \neq$ and $\mathbf{Y} - \mathbf{Z} \neq \phi$ and for such an MVD replace **Y** by $\mathbf{Y} - \mathbf{Z}$ and $\mathbf{Y} \cap \mathbf{Z}$ *)

For each MVD $\mathbf{W} \rightarrow\rightarrow \mathbf{Z} \in \mathbf{D}$ **and** $(\mathbf{Y} \in \mathbf{S})$
and $(\mathbf{Y} \cap \mathbf{W} = \phi)$
and $(\mathbf{Y} \cap \mathbf{Z} \neq \phi)$
and $(\mathbf{Y} - \mathbf{Z} \neq \phi)$
replace **Y** in **S** by $\mathbf{Y} \cap \mathbf{Z}$ and $\mathbf{Y} - \mathbf{Z}$;

6. (* **S** now contains the dependency basis of **X** *)
Output $\mathbf{S}\{\mathbf{Y}_1, \mathbf{Y}_2, \ldots, \mathbf{Y}_n\}$, the dependency basis of **X** under **D**.

Thus, given $\mathbf{X} \subseteq \mathbf{U}$ and a set $\mathbf{D}$ of dependencies, we can derive a set $\mathbf{Y_i}$, $1 \le i \le n$, such that

- $\mathbf{U - X = Y_1Y_2 \ldots Y_n}$,
- $\mathbf{Y_1, Y_2, \ldots Y_n}$ are **pairwise disjoint,** i.e., $\mathbf{Y_i \cap Y_j} = \phi$ for $i \neq j$, and
- For any MVD $\mathbf{X \twoheadrightarrow Z}$ in $\mathbf{D^+}$, $\mathbf{Z}$ is the union of some of the $\mathbf{Y_i}$s.

Definition: The set $\{\mathbf{Y_1, Y_2, \ldots Y_n}\}$, with the properties given above is referred to as the **dependency basis** of **X** with respect to **D** and is indicated by the nomenclature **DEP(X).**

An MVD $\mathbf{X \twoheadrightarrow Z}$ is in $\mathbf{D^+}$ if and only if $\mathbf{Z}$ is a union of some of the sets from DEP(**X**), the dependency basis of **X** relative to the set **D** of FDs and MVDs. It follows that for each set $\mathbf{Y_i} \in$ **DEP(X),** $\mathbf{X \twoheadrightarrow Y_i}$ is in $\mathbf{D^+}$.

The MVD $\mathbf{X \twoheadrightarrow Y_i}$ where $\mathbf{Y_i} \in$ DEP(**X**) is called a **simple MVD.**

We see that **DEP(X),** the dependency basis of **X,** serves a similar function in determining if any MVD $\mathbf{X \twoheadrightarrow Y}$ is implied by a set **D** of FDs and MVDs, as $\mathbf{X^+}$ was used to determine if any FD $\mathbf{X \rightarrow Y}$ was implied by a set of FDs **F.**

Algorithm 7.2 computes the dependency basis of **X.** It simply converts each FD into an MVD and then applies the rules of the MVD to decompose the MVDs into simpler MVDs. Careful implementation of the algorithm can be shown to take time proportional to n^3m to complete, where n is the number of attributes in **U** and m is the number of dependencies in **D.**

The following example illustrates the use of Algorithm 7.2

Example 7.7

Consider a database to store student information that contains the following attributes: students' names *(S)*, their majors *(M)*, the department they are registered in *(S_d)*, their advisers' name *(A)*, the courses they are taking *(C)*, the departments responsible for the course *(C_d)*, the final grades of the students in a course *(G)*, the teacher of the course *(P)*, the department of the teacher of the course *(P_d)*, and the room, day, and time *(RDT)* where the course is taught. Assume that the students' names and the advisers' names are unique. The database must satisfy the following set H of functional and multivalued dependencies:

$$
\begin{array}{lll}
S & \rightarrow & MA \\
M & \rightarrow & S_d \\
A & \rightarrow & S_d \\
C & \rightarrow & C_dP \\
P & \rightarrow & P_d \\
RTD & \rightarrow & C \\
TPD & \rightarrow & R \\
TSD & \rightarrow & R \\
SC & \rightarrow & G \\
C & \twoheadrightarrow & RTD \\
C & \twoheadrightarrow & SMG
\end{array}
$$

We want to compute DEP(C) using Algorithm 7.2. The first step will convert all FDs into MVDs.

Step 3 will give us the set **S** with the following sets of attributes:

$\{C_dP\}$, $\{RTD\}$, $\{SMG\}$, $\{SMAS_dP_dRTDG\}$, $\{SMAS_dP_dG\}$, $\{AS_dC_dPP_dRTD\}$.

Step 4 will split the sets in **S** to give the following sets in **S:**

$\{C_dP\}$, $\{RTD\}$, $\{SMG\}$, $\{AS_dP_d\}$.

Step 5 will complete the intersections and splitting to give **S** with the following sets, **DEP**(C), the dependency basis of C under the above set of FDs and MVDs:

$\{C_dP\}$, $\{RTD\}$, $\{SMG\}$, $\{S_d\}$, $\{A\}$, $\{P_d\}$

The dependency basis allows us to conclude that the MVDs $C \twoheadrightarrow SS_dAMG$, $C \twoheadrightarrow PP_dC_d$, etc., are in $\mathbf{H}^+$, since the right-hand side of each MVD is a union of sets from **DEP**(C). ■

7.3.4 Fourth Normal Form

A generalization of the Boyce Codd normal form to relation schemes which includes the multivalued dependencies is called fourth normal form and is defined as follows:

Definition: Given a relation scheme **R** such that the set **D** of FDs and MVDs are satisfied, consider a set of attributes **X** and **Y** where $\mathbf{X} \subseteq \mathbf{R}$, $\mathbf{Y} \subseteq \mathbf{R}$. The relation scheme **R** is in **fourth normal form (4NF)** if for all multivalued dependencies of the form $\mathbf{X} \twoheadrightarrow \mathbf{Y} \in \mathbf{D}^+$, either $\mathbf{X} \twoheadrightarrow \mathbf{Y}$ is a trivial MVD or **X** is a superkey of **R.** A database scheme is in 4NF if all relation schemes included in the database scheme are in 4NF.

If a relation scheme **R** with the set **D** of FDs and MVDs is in fourth normal form, it is also in BCNF. If this were not so, **R** would satisfy a functional dependency not involving the superkey as a determinant of the form $\mathbf{X} \rightarrow \mathbf{Y}$. However, by the rule **M1** $\mathbf{X} \rightarrow \mathbf{Y} \models \mathbf{X} \twoheadrightarrow \mathbf{Y}$. Again **X** here is not a superkey, but this contradicts the assertion that **R** is in fourth normal form.

7.3.5 Lossless Join Decomposition into Fourth Normal Form

Given a relation scheme that is not in fourth normal form, we would like to decompose it into a set of relations that are in fourth normal form and at the same time we want to preserve all the dependencies. Furthermore, we want the decomposition to be lossless. The latter requirement in the decomposition can be obtained using the property of a MVD given in Section 7.3.1 and restated in a different form in the next paragraph. However, the first requirement, that of dependency preservation, is not as simple to satisfy (as in the case of having only FDs) when we have both functional and multivalued dependencies.

The following property of a MVD can be used to perform a lossless decomposition of a relation **R** with both functional and multivalued dependencies. We are given a relation scheme **R** where **D** is a set of FDs and MVDs on the attributes of **R.** If **R** is decomposed into $\mathbf{R_1}$ and $\mathbf{R_2}$, the decomposition is a lossless join decomposition if and only if $\mathbf{D}^+$ contains one of the following MVDs:

$$(\mathbf{R_1} \cap \mathbf{R_2}) \twoheadrightarrow \mathbf{R_1} \text{ or } (\mathbf{R_1}\ \mathbf{R_2}) \twoheadrightarrow \mathbf{R_2}.$$

Recall that the requirement of a lossless join decomposition, when only FDs are involved, was $(\mathbf{R_1} \cap \mathbf{R_2}) \rightarrow \mathbf{R_1}$ or $(\mathbf{R_1} \cap \mathbf{R_2}) \rightarrow \mathbf{R_2}$.

The similarity between the Boyce Codd normal form and the fourth normal form extends to the decomposition algorithm of a relation scheme not in fourth normal form into a set of relations that are in fourth normal form. The adaptation of the decomposition algorithm for relation schemes with MVDs is given in Algorithm 7.3

Let us return to the normalized EMPLOYEE relation of Figure 7.2. It has the following set of FDs and MVDs: {*Employee_Name* $\twoheadrightarrow$ *Dependent_NameDependent Relationship, Employee_Name* $\twoheadrightarrow$ *Position_TitlePosition_Date, Employee_Name* $\rightarrow$ *Home_CityHome_Phone*}. Is this relation in fourth normal form? It will be if the attribute *Employee_Name* is a superkey of the EMPLOYEE relation. We have used relations where the name, for convenience, was taken as an unique identifier for a person, the relation about student and faculty members being other such examples. If *Employee_Name* were the key of the EMPLOYEE relation, then according to the

Algorithm **7.3**

Lossless Join Decomposition into Fourth Normal Form

Input: A relation scheme **R** not in 4NF and a set of FDs and MVDs **D**.

Output: Decomposition of **R** into a set **S** of relation schemes $\mathbf{R_i}$, $\mathbf{R_i} \subset \mathbf{S}$ for $1 \leq i \leq n$ such that each $\mathbf{R_i}$ is in 4NF and the decomposition is lossless.

i := 0;
S := $\mathbf{R_0}$ (* initialize **S** to $\mathbf{R_0} \equiv \mathbf{R}$ *)
for each nontrivial MVD ($\mathbf{X} \twoheadrightarrow \mathbf{Y}$) that holds on some scheme $\mathbf{R_j}$ in **S** such that **X** is not a superkey of $\mathbf{R_j}$ (* i.e., $\mathbf{X} \rightarrow \mathbf{R_j}$ is not in $\mathbf{D}^+$; we can further assume that $\mathbf{X} \cap \mathbf{Y} = \phi$ *) *do*
  begin
    i := i + 1;
    $\mathbf{R_j} := \mathbf{R_j} - \mathbf{Y}$
      (* remove the attributes **Y** from $\mathbf{R_j}$ *)
    $\mathbf{S} := \mathbf{S} \cup \mathbf{R_i}\{\mathbf{X}, \mathbf{Y}\}$;
      (* form relation $\mathbf{R_i}\{\mathbf{X}, \mathbf{Y}\}$ and add it to **S** *)
  end

definition of fourth normal form, the EMPLOYEE relation is in fourth normal form. However, recall the definitions for candidate key and superkey. A superkey of a relation R defined on a relation scheme **R** was defined as being a set of attributes **X** $\subseteq$ **R** such that, for two tuples t_1 and t_2 in R, $t_1(\mathbf{X}) \neq t_2(\mathbf{X})$. Thus, the values of the set of attributes in **X** uniquely identify a tuple in R. A key is a set **K** such that no proper subset **K′** of **K** can uniquely identify a tuple of R, i.e., $t_1(\mathbf{K'})$ may or may not be equal to $t_2(\mathbf{K'})$.

With the above definitions of superkey and key we see that the attribute *Employee_Name* is not a superkey of the relation EMPLOYEE and hence the relation is not in fourth normal form. As a matter of fact the candidate key of the EMPLOYEE relation is the entire relation! Note that even though *Employee_Name* is not a candidate key of the relation, it still uniquely identifies an instance of the entity EMPLOYEE. All characteristics of an instance of the entity are found by locating all tuples with this value for the *Employee_Name* attribute.

We noted the disadvantage in the form of anomalies in insertions, deletions, and updates for the EMPLOYEE relation as given in Figure 7.2. We can use Algorithm 7.3 to decompose the EMPLOYEE relation losslessly into a set of fourth normal form relations. The resulting relations are given in Figure 7.5. (Note that these rela-

Figure 7.5 Decomposition of the EMPLOYEE relation.

Employee_Name	*Dependent_Name*	*Dependent_Relationship*
Jill Jones	Bill Jones	spouse
Jill Jones	Bob Jones	son
Mark Smith	Ann Briggs	spouse
Mark Smith	Chloe Smith-Briggs	daughter
Mark Smith	Mark Briggs-Smith	son

(a)

Employee_Name	*Position_Title*	*Position_Date*
Jill Jones	J. Engineer	05/12/84
Jill Jones	Engineer	10/06/86
Mark Smith	Programmer	09/15/86
Mark Smith	Analyst	06/06/86

(b)

Employee_Name	*Home_City*	*Home_Phone#*
Jill Jones	Lynn, MA	794-2356
Mark Smith	Revere, MA	452-4729

(c)

tions are the same as the ones shown in Figure 7.4.) The relations of Figure 7.5a and b have the trivial multivalued dependency $\mathbf{X} \twoheadrightarrow \mathbf{Y}$ with $\mathbf{R} = \mathbf{XY}$. In addition, they are all key relations. A nontrivial MVD can be said to exist only if the relation has at least one attribute in addition to the two sets of attributes involved in the MVD.

7.3.6 Enforceability of Dependencies in the Fourth Normal Form

The fourth normal form decomposition algorithm produces a lossless relation scheme; however, it may not preserve all the dependencies in the original non-4NF relation scheme. In Example 7.8, we use one MVD at a time to decompose a non-4NF relation scheme into two relation schemes. Then we determine if each of these schemes is in 4NF. The following properties are used to find the dependencies that apply to the decomposed schemes.

Given $\mathbf{R}$ and the set of FDs and MVDs $\mathbf{D}$, let $\mathbf{R_1}$ be a projection of $\mathbf{R}$, i.e., $\mathbf{R_1} \subseteq \mathbf{R}$. The projection of $\mathbf{D}$ on $\mathbf{R_1}$ is derived as follows:

For each FD $\mathbf{X} \rightarrow \mathbf{Y}$ such that $\mathbf{D} \models \mathbf{X} \rightarrow \mathbf{Y}$, and if $\mathbf{X} \subseteq \mathbf{R_1}$, then $\mathbf{X} \rightarrow (\mathbf{Y} \cap \mathbf{R_1})$ holds in $\mathbf{R_1}$.

For each MVD $\mathbf{X} \twoheadrightarrow \mathbf{Y}$ such that $\mathbf{D} \models \mathbf{X} \twoheadrightarrow \mathbf{Y}$, and if $\mathbf{X} \subseteq \mathbf{R_1}$, then $\mathbf{X} \twoheadrightarrow (\mathbf{Y} \cap \mathbf{R_1})$ holds in $\mathbf{R_1}$.

Example 7.8 illustrates this method.

Example 7.8

Consider $\mathbf{R}(A, B, C, D, E, F, G)$ with the set $\mathbf{H}$ of FDs and MVDs given by $\mathbf{H}\{A \twoheadrightarrow B, B \twoheadrightarrow G, B \twoheadrightarrow EF, CD \rightarrow E\}$.

$\mathbf{R}$ is not in 4NF since for the nontrivial **MVD** $A \twoheadrightarrow B$, A is not a superkey of $\mathbf{R}$. We can take this MVD and decompose R into $\mathbf{R_1}(A, B)$ and $\mathbf{R}(A, C, D, E, F, G)$. $\mathbf{R_1}$ is in 4NF; however, the reduced relation $\mathbf{R}$ is not in 4NF.

Now the MVDs $A \twoheadrightarrow B$ and $B \twoheadrightarrow G$ give by axiom **M6** $A \twoheadrightarrow G - B$, which is equivalent to $A \twoheadrightarrow G$. Using this MVD, we decompose $\mathbf{R}$ into $\mathbf{R_2}(A, G)$ and $\mathbf{R}(A, C, D, E, F)$. $\mathbf{R_2}$ is in 4NF; however, the reduced relation $\mathbf{R}$ is still not in 4NF.

We now take the MVD $CD \twoheadrightarrow E$ (after converting the FD into an MVD) and decompose $\mathbf{R}$ into $\mathbf{R_3}(C, D, E)$ and $\mathbf{R}(A, C, D, F)$.

The MVDs $A \twoheadrightarrow B$, $B \twoheadrightarrow EF$ by axiom **M6** give $A \twoheadrightarrow EF - B$, which reduces to $A \twoheadrightarrow EF$ and when restricted to the current relation $\mathbf{R}$ gives $A \twoheadrightarrow F$. Decomposing $\mathbf{R}$ now gives $\mathbf{R_4}(A, F)$ and $\mathbf{R}(A, C, D)$.

$\mathbf{R}(A, C, D)$ is in 4NF since $A \twoheadrightarrow B \models A \twoheadrightarrow CDEFG$ and its restriction to current relation $\mathbf{R}$ gives A $\twoheadrightarrow$ CD.

However, we notice that the dependency $B \twoheadrightarrow G$ is not preserved. ■

Example 7.8 illustrates that the 4NF decomposition is not dependency preserving. Thus if lossless as well as dependency preserving decomposition is required, we may have to settle for simple 3NF relation schemes, unless the BCNF decomposition is lossless as well as dependency preserving. An approach that could be used to derive a dependency preserving decomposition is to eliminate each redundant dependency in **D**.[2] This process can be repeated until only nonredundant dependencies remain in **D.** However, the order in which the dependencies are checked for redundancy determines the resulting nonredundant cover of **D.** In this process, the MVDs should be eliminated before trying to eliminate FDs. The intuitive reason for this is that the FDs convey more semantics about the data than the MVDs.

Dependency preserving decomposition involving **D,** a set of FDs and MVDs, requires the derivation of the so-called 4NF cover of **D.** No efficient algorithms exist to date to compute such a cover. The algorithm to decompose a relation into a lossless and dependency-preserving 4NF relation is beyond the scope of this text. Interested readers should consult the references in the bibliographic notes. Attempts have been made to find a synthesis algorithm to construct a relation scheme from a set of FDs and MVDs. Here again, no satisfactory algorithm has emerged.

7.4 Normalization Using Join Dependency: Fifth Normal Form

A criterion of good database design is to reduce the data redundancy as much as possible. One way of doing this in a relational database design is to decompose one relation into multiple relations. However, the decomposition should be lossless and should maintain the dependencies of the original scheme. A relational database design is, as such, a compromise between the universal relation and a set of relations with desirable properties. The relational database design thus tries to find relations satisfying as high a normal form as possible. For instance, 3NF is preferable to 2NF, BCNF is preferable to 3NF, and so on.

However, recent research in relational database design theory has discovered higher and higher, hence more desirable normal forms. **Fifth normal form (5NF)** is a case in point. It is related to **join dependency,** which is the term used to indicate the property of a relation scheme that cannot be decomposed losslessly into two simpler relation schemes, but can be decomposed losslessly into three or more simpler relation schemes.

To understand join dependency, let us use the following dependencies from the database for an enterprise involved in developing computing products. It employs a number of workers and has a variety of projects.

Project $\twoheadrightarrow$ *Expertise*
(i.e., expertise needed for a given project)
Employee $\twoheadrightarrow$ *Expertise*
(i.e., expertise of the employee)
Employee $\twoheadrightarrow$ *Project*
(i.e., preferences of the employees to match their expertise)

[2]Elimination of redundant dependencies doesn't guarantee dependency-preserving decomposition, in general. However, with conflict-free MVDs, the lossless decomposition is also dependency preserving. Conflict-free MVD sets are equivalent to acyclic join dependencies (Lien 85, Scio 81).

Figure 7.6 PROJECT_ASSIGNMENT relation.

Employee	*Project*	*Expertise*
Smith	Query Systems	Database Systems
Smith	File systems	Operating Systems
Lalonde	Database Machine	Computer Architecture
Lalonde	Database Machine	VLSI Technology
Evan	Database Machine	VLSI Technology
Evan	Database Machine	Computer Architecture
Drew	SQL+ +	Relational Calculus
Drew	QUEL+ +	Relational Calculus
Shah	SQL+ +	Relational Calculus
Shah	QUEL+;+	Relational Calculus

These dependencies are the translation of the enterprise's need that the employees involved in a given project must have certain expertise. Because of the expertise of employees, they want to be involved in a given set of projects whose requirements match their interests. Let us look at the relation scheme **PROJECT_ASSIGNMENT***(Employee, Project, Expertise)*. A relation defined on this scheme is given in Figure 7.6. The relation scheme stores the employee's assignments based on the needs of the project, as well as the qualifications and preferences of the employee who can contribute to the project. A project may demand more than one type of expertise, and an employee may be an expert in more than one area. The project Query Systems needs only the expertise of Database Systems, while a project Database Machine needs the expertise of VLSI Technology as well as Computer Architecture. Further expertise of an employee, not needed for any project to which he or she is assigned, is not shown in this relation. Figure 7.6 illustrates the sample contents of a database defined on this relation scheme. Employees Lalonde and Evan are assigned to the project Database Machine; Employees Drew and Shah are assigned to projects SQL^{++} and $QUEL^{++}$. The relation exhibits the following nontrivial multivalued dependencies: *Project* $\twoheadrightarrow$ *Expertise* and *Project* $\twoheadrightarrow$ *Employee*. Note that the MVD *Employee* $\twoheadrightarrow$*Project* and, hence, *Employee* $\twoheadrightarrow$*Expertise* are not exhibited in this relation. This can be verified by exchanging the *Project* value for Smith, whereby we find that the resulting tuples are not in the database.

The relation PROJECT_ASSIGNMENT{*Employee, Project, Expertise*} having the MVD *Project* $\twoheadrightarrow$ *Expertise* (and by axiom **M5** *Project* $\twoheadrightarrow$ *Employee)* can be decomposed losslessly into relations PROJECT_REQUIREMENT{*Project, Expertise*} and PROJECT_REFERENCE{*Employee, Project*}. Figure 7.7 shows the decomposition of the relation of Figure 7.6. The join of PROJECT_REQUIREMENT and PROJECT_PREFERENCE gives the same data as in Figure 7.6.

Notice from Figure 7.7b that the relation PROJECT_PREFERENCE exhibits the (trivial) multivalued dependency *Employee* $\twoheadrightarrow$ *Project*. Such a multivalued dependency that is not exhibited in a relation but becomes evident in a projection of the relation is called an **embedded multivalued dependency.** Unlike multivalued dependencies, functional dependencies are never embedded. A functional dependency

Figure 7.7 Lossless decomposition of relation of Figure 7.6: (a) PROJECT_REQUIREMENT and (b) PROJECT_PREFERENCE.

Project	*Expertise*
Query Systems	Database Systems
File Systems	Operating Systems
Database Machine	Computer Architecture
Database Machine	VLSI Technology
SQL++	Relational Calculus
QUEL++	Relational Calculus

(a)

Employee	*Project*
Smith	Query Systems
Smith	File systems
Evan	Database Machine
Lalonde	Database Machine
Drew	SQL++
Shah	QUEL++
Drew	SQL++
Shah	QUEL++

(b)

$\mathbf{X} \rightarrow \mathbf{Y}$ that is evident in a projection of relation R is also evident in the relation R.

Consider a relation scheme **R** and let **X, Y,** and **Z** be sets of attributes of **R.** Here **X, Y, Z** need not be disjoint. A relation R over the relation scheme **R** satisfies the embedded multivalued dependency $\mathbf{X} \twoheadrightarrow \mathbf{Y}|\mathbf{Z}$ (i.e., **R** satisfies $\mathbf{X} \twoheadrightarrow \mathbf{Y}$ and hence, by axiom **M5,** $\mathbf{X} \twoheadrightarrow \mathbf{Z}$**),** if the projection of the relation R over **X, Y, Z** (i.e., $\pi_{\mathbf{X} \cup \mathbf{Y} \cup \mathbf{Z}}(\mathbf{R})$) satisfies the MVDs $\mathbf{X} \twoheadrightarrow \mathbf{Y}$ **and** $\mathbf{X} \twoheadrightarrow \mathbf{Z}$**.**

Now consider the relation scheme **NEW_PROJECT_ASSIGNMENT.** Perhaps after some modifications in the enterprise involved, there has been a turnover in employees and the expertise of new employees requires some changes in the assignment of projects. Figure 7.8 gives a sample table for a relation defined on the scheme **NEW_PROJECT_ASSIGNMENT.** As the figure indicates, we are assigning more than one employee to a given project. Each employee is assigned a specific role in this project, requiring knowledge that lies within her or his field of expertise. Thus, project Work Station, which requires expertise in User Interface, Artificial Intelligence, VLSI Technology, and Operating Systems, can be carried out by Brent,

Figure 7.8 NEW_PROJECT_ASSIGNMENT relation.

Employee	*Project*	*Expertise*
Brent	Work Station	User Interface
Brent	Work Station	Artificial Intelligence
Mann	Work Station	VLSI Technology
Smith	Work Station	Operating Systems
King	SQL 2	Relational Calculus
Ito	SQL 2	Relational Algebra
Ito	QBE++	Relational Calculus
Smith	Query Systems	Database Systems
Smith	File Systems	Operating Systems

Figure 7.9 Decomposition of relation of Figure 7.8.

Project	*Expertise*
Work Station	User interface
Work Station	Artificial Intelligence
Work Station	VLSI Technology
Work Station	Operating Systems
SQL 2	Relational Calculus
SQL 2	Relational Algebra
QBE+ +	Relational Calculus
Query Systems	Database Systems
File Systems	Operating Systems

(a)

Employee	*Expertise*
Brent	User Interface
Brent	Artificial Intelligence
Mann	VLSI Technology
King	Relational Calculus
Ito	Relational Algebra
Ito	Relational Calculus
Smith	Database Systems
Smith	Operating Systems

(b)

Employee	*Project*
Brent	Work Station
Mann	Work Station
King	SQL 2
Ito	SQL 2
Ito	QBE + +
Smith	File Systems
Smith	Query Systems
Smith	Work Station

(c)

Mann, and Smith combined. Brent is assigned the User Interface and Artificial Intelligence related role, Mann is assigned the VLSI Technology related role, and Smith is assigned the Operating Systems role. This flexibility was not exhibited in the data of Figure 7.6.

The relation of Figure 7.8 does not show any functional or multivalued dependencies; it is an all-key relation and therefore in fourth normal form. Unlike the relation **PROJECT_ASSIGNMENT,** the relation **NEW_PROJECT_ASSIGNMENT** cannot be decomposed losslessly into two relations. However, it can be decomposed losslessly into three relations. This decomposition is shown in Figure 7.9. Two of these relations, when joined, create a relation that contains extraneous tuples; thus the corresponding decomposition is not lossless. These superfluous tuples are removed when the resulting relation is joined with the third relation. Note that the MVDs, similar to those exhibited in Figure 7.6, are embedded in this example.

7.4.1 Join Dependencies

So far we have focused on the decomposition of a relation scheme with undesirable properties into two relation schemes (at each step of a multistep process) such that the decomposition is lossless. A join of these decomposed relation schemes will give the original scheme and, hence, the data. However, as we saw in the previous section, although it may not be possible to find a lossless decomposition of a relation scheme into two relation schemes, the same relation scheme can be decomposed losslessly into three relation schemes. This property is referred to as the join dependency **(JD).**

Definition: Given a relation scheme **R,** consider the following set of its projections: $\{\mathbf{R_1}, \mathbf{R_2}, \ldots \mathbf{R_n}\}$. A relation R(**R**) satisfies the join dependency $*[\mathbf{R_1}, \mathbf{R_2}, \ldots \mathbf{R_n}]$, if and only if the join of the projection of R on $\mathbf{R_i}$, $1 \leq i \leq n$, is equal to R.

$$R = \pi_{R1}(R) \bowtie \pi_{R2}(R) \bowtie \ldots \bowtie \pi_{Rn}(R)$$

In other words, join dependency is the assertion that the decomposition of R onto $\mathbf{R_1}, \ldots, \mathbf{R_n}$ is a lossless decomposition. A join dependency is trivial if one of the projections of **R** is **R** itself.

A necessary condition for a relation scheme **R** to satisfy a join dependency $*[\mathbf{R_1}, \mathbf{R_2}, \ldots \mathbf{R_n}]$ is that $\mathbf{R} = \mathbf{R_1} \cup \mathbf{R_2} \cup \ldots \cup \mathbf{R_n}$.

The relation scheme **PROJECT_ASSIGNMENT** satisfies the join dependency ***[PROJECT_REQUIREMENT, PROJECT_PREFERENCE],** since the join of PROJECT_REQUIREMENT and PROJECT_PREFERENCE gives the relation PROJECT_ASSIGNMENT losslessly. However, the relation NEW_PROJECT_ASSIGNMENT does not satisfy any of the following join dependencies:

[(Project,Expertise),(Employee,Expertise)*]
[(Project,Expertise),(Employee, Project)*]
[(Employee, Expertise),(Employee, Project)*]

Relation NEW_PROJECT_ASSIGNMENT, however, satisfies the join dependency:

[(Project,Expertise), (Employee,Expertise), (Employee, Project)*]

Since the relation scheme **NEW_PROJECT_ASSIGNMENT** does not satisfy any nontrivial MVD, then by Fagin's theorem (Theorem 7.1) it cannot be decomposed losslessly into two relations.

It is worthwhile pointing out that every MVD is equivalent to a join dependency; however, the converse is not true, i.e., there are join dependencies that are not equivalent to any nontrivial MVDs. The first part of this statement can be confirmed as follows: The relation R(**R**) satisfies the MVD $\mathbf{X} \twoheadrightarrow \mathbf{Y}$ if and only if the decomposition of R into **XY** and $\mathbf{R} - \mathbf{Y}$ is lossless. This is equivalent to saying that R(**R**) satisfies the JD $*[\mathbf{XY}, \mathbf{R} - \mathbf{Y}]$. Conversely, **R** satisfies the JD $*[\mathbf{R_1}, \mathbf{R2}]$ if $\mathbf{R_1} \cap \mathbf{R_2} \twoheadrightarrow \mathbf{R_1}$, or $\mathbf{R_1} \cap \mathbf{R_2} \twoheadrightarrow \mathbf{R_2}$. However, not all JDs are equivalent to MVD, as seen in Figures 7.8 and 7.9.

A join dependency on the relation scheme **R,** in addition to those for MVDs, could also be a result of key dependencies. This can occur when the decomposition of a relation involves a superkey and the relation can be reconstructed by joins, every join involving a superkey. Thus, if $\mathbf{R}(\mathbf{X_1}, \mathbf{X_2}, \ldots, \mathbf{X_m})$ and if $\mathbf{X_i}$s are the superkeys of **R,** then the join dependency $*[\mathbf{X_1}, \mathbf{X_2}, \ldots, \mathbf{X_m}]$, is due to the keys of R.

Join dependency expresses the fact that a set of relationships is independent, just as MVD indicates that a pair of relationships is independent. These independent relationships can be separated in different relations and their join will be lossless.

The join dependency in a relation scheme gives rise to another normal form, project-join normal form, discussed in the following section.

7.4.2 Project-Join Normal Form

Consider a relation scheme **R(U)** and a set of FDs $\{S_1 \rightarrow U, S_2 \rightarrow U, \ldots S_p \rightarrow U\}$. We name these FDs **key dependencies** or KDs since the determinant S_i in each FD is a superkey. The JD membership algorithm given below, determines if a JD is implied by a set of KDs. The algorithm terminates successfully if and only if the KDs $\models$ JD.

Example 7.9 determines the JDs implied by a given set of KDs.

Example 7.9 Let **R**(ABCDE) with the FDs **F** = {A → BCDE, C → ABDE and D → ABCE}. Let **R** satisfy the join dependencies *[ABE, CD, ABCD]. The FDs are KDs and we see that for the superkey (key) A, A $\subseteq$ ABE $\cap$ ABCD. We replace the set {ABE, CD, ABCD} with the set {ABCDE, CD}. Again we find that for the superkey (key) C, C $\subseteq$ ABCDE $\cap$ CD. We replace the set {ABCDE, CD} with the set {ABCDE}. Since this is the set of attributes in R we have shown that KD $\models$ JD. Similarly, we can show the KD implies the following JD: *[ABC,BCD, CDE]. ■

We can now define project-join normal form.

Definition: Consider a relation scheme **R** and a set **D** of dependencies (functional, multivalued, and join). The relation R is in **project-join normal form (PJ/NF)** with respect to **D** if for every join dependency $*[R_1, R_2, \ldots, R_n]$ that is applicable to R and is implied by **D**, either of the following holds: the join dependency is trivial, or every R_i is a superkey of **R.** A database is in project-join normal form if all relation schemes are in project-join normal form.

Project-join normal form is also referred to as fifth normal form (5NF) or as PJ/NF in the database literature.

Every fifth normal form relation scheme is also in fourth normal form and, hence, in BCNF and consequently in 3NF.

If a relation is in project-join normal form, then every functional dependency is determined by a key. Every multivalued dependency is also determined by a key. Furthermore, every JD is determined by one or more candidate keys. As a result, since all FDs, MVDs, and JDs are implied by keys, all that must be specified is the relation scheme and the set of keys. A database having all relations in PJ/NF and

Algorithm **7.4** **JD Membership Algorithm**

Input: JD$[X_1, X_2, X_3, \ldots X_q]$ and
KD$\{S_1 \rightarrow U, S_2 \rightarrow U, \ldots S_p \rightarrow U\}$

Output: Success or failure. Success indicates KD $\models$ JD.

```
H = {X1, X2, X3, . . . Xq}   (* initialize set H to be the JD
                                  to be checked *)
change : = true
while (change or number of members q in H > 1 ) do
  begin
    if Si ⊆ Xj ∩ Xk for 1 ≤ i ≤ p and Xj and Xk ∈ H and j ≠ k
      then begin
             delete Xj and Xk from H
             insert Xj ∪ Xk into H
             decrease q by 1
      else change : = false
  end
if U ∈ H
  then KD ⊨ JD is proven successfully
  else KD ⊨ JD is not proven
```

supporting the concept of key need no other consistency support mechanism, if there are no interrelational dependencies. However, when we convert a relation that is not in PJ/NF into a set of relations in PJ/NF, we could introduce interrelational dependencies.

Our example relation schemes **PROJECT_ASSIGNMENT** and **NEW_PROJECT_ASSIGNMENT** were not in fifth normal form, since each of them had nontrivial join dependencies. Their decompositions (respectively into {**PROJECT_REQUIREMENT, PROJECT_PREFERENCE,** and {*(Project, Expertise), (Employee, Expertise), (Employee, Project)*}) are in fifth normal form nonetheless.

Let us return to the **NEW_PROJECT_ASSIGNMENT** relation scheme. Here, we have three independent relationships:

Project $\twoheadrightarrow$ *Expertise*
Employee $\twoheadrightarrow$ *Expertise*
Employee $\twoheadrightarrow$ *Project*

There are other MVD relationships, for instance *Project* $\twoheadrightarrow$ *Employee,* that can be derived from the MVD *Employee* $\twoheadrightarrow$ *Project.*

It is not possible to insert, without null values, a project and the expertise needed for it unless we know the employees who could be assigned to the project. Similarly, it is not possible to record all types of expertise of an employee unless each type is called for in a project where that employee is required to use such expertise. The decomposition of the relation into {*(Project, Expertise), (Employee, Expertise), (Employee, Project)*} allows these independent relationships to be separated. It is then possible to independently maintain each separate relation. However, in the relation NEW_PROJECT_ASSIGNMENT, it is necessary to insert additional tuples when a tuple is inserted and the deletion of a tuple requires the deletion of other tuples.

Consider the relation STUDENT_INFO*(Name, Address, Department, Phone#)* with the FDs {*Name* $\rightarrow$ *Address, Name* $\rightarrow$ *Department, Name* $\rightarrow$ *Phone#)*. The decomposition of STUDENT_INFO into the following relation is lossless and dependency preserving: *(Name, Address), (Name, Department), (Name, Phone#)*. The original relation is in PJ/NF. However, since the only key of the original relation is *Name* and if the remaining attributes could have null values assigned to them, there is no advantage to decomposing the relation.

7.5 Domain Key Normal Form

Before discussing domain key normal form let us define two additional type of dependencies, domain constraints (DC) and key constraints (KC).

Definition: **Domain Constraint (DC):** Each attribute A_i of a relation scheme **R**$(A_1, A_2, A_i, \ldots)$, is assigned a domain constraint of the form IN(A_i, S_{Ai}). This means that the attribute A_i of relation R, defined on the relation scheme **R**, must have a value from the set S_{Ai}.

We have implicitly used domain constraint as part of integrity constraints.

Definition: **Key Constraint (KC):** For the relation scheme **R**$(A_1, A_2, A_\infty, \ldots)$, the key constraint, KEY(**K**), where **K** is a subset of **R**, is the restriction that no two tuples of relation **R** defined on the relation scheme **R** have the same values for the attributes in **K.**

We also define the concept of general constraints:

Definition: **General Constraints (GC):** A general constraint is expressed as a simple statement or predicate and specifies some special requirement. Each tuple of a relation must satisfy this predicate for it to be a valid tuple.

The domain key normal form (DK/NF), just like the previously discussed normal forms, requires that relations do not exhibit insertion and deletion anomalies.

However, unlike the other normal forms, DK/NF is not defined in terms of FDs, MVDs, or JDs. The central requirements of DK/NF are the basic concepts of domains, keys, and general constraints. We elaborate on each of these requirements in the following discussions. A relation scheme is in DK/NF if every general constraint can be inferred from the knowledge of the attributes involved in the scheme, their underlying domains, and the sets of attributes that form the keys. An insertion anomaly in the case of DK/NF occurs when a tuple is inserted in a relation and the resulting relation violates one or more general constraints. Similarly, a deletion anomaly occurs when a tuple from a relation is deleted and the remaining relation violates one or more general constraints. We illustrate these dependencies and general constraints in Example 7.10

Example 7.10

Consider the relation scheme **TRANSCRIPT** *(Student#, Course, Grade)*. Suppose the attributes *Student#* and *Course* are numeric, 8 and 3 digits long, respectively. The attribute *Grade* is a letter grade and could be A, B, C, D, P, F. The general constraint is that for *Courses* numbered 900 through 999, the *Grade* assigned is only P or F. For *Courses* 000 through 899, the *Grade* can only be A, B, C, D, F. The domain constraints for this relation are the following: *Student#* is required to be 8 digits long, *Course* is 3 digits long, and *Grade* has to be from the set {A, B, C, D, P, F}. The key constraint for the relation is that no two tuples can exist with the same values for the key attributes, which are *Student#* and *Course*. Obviously, *Student# Course* → *Grade*. Finally, the general constraint can be expressed by the following:

if Course ≥ *900*
then Grade ∈ *{P, F}*
else Grade ∈ *{A, B, C, D, F}*

The problem with this relation is that a tuple such as (12345678, 991, A), which satisfies all the DCs and KCs, can be inserted in the relation TRANSCRIPT of Figure A. However, since the tuple does not satisfy the general

Figure A The TRANSCRIPT relation.

Student#	*Course*	*Grade*
23714539	353	A
42717390	329	A
23714539	928	P
38815183	456	F
37116259	293	B
82317293	491	C
82317293	953	F
23714539	491	C
11011978	353	A
83910827	979	P

constraint, the relation TRANSCRIPT becomes illegal after the insertion. ■

We now give the formal definition of DK/NF.

Definition: A normalized relation scheme **R** **{S, Γ, σ}**, where **S** is the set of attributes, **Γ** is the set of DCs and KCs, and **σ** is the set of general constraints, is in **domain key normal form (DK/NF)** if **Γ** $\models$ **σ** for every constraint in **σ.**

A normalized relation is in DK/NF if the DCs and KCs imply the general constraints. The DK/NF is considered to be the highest form of normalization, since all insertion and deletion anomalies are eliminated and all general constraints can be verified by using only the DCs and KCs. For the TRANSCRIPT relation of Example 7.10, we can use the following decomposition to get two relations in DK/NF.

Example 7.11

The TRANSCRIPT relation of Example 7.10 can be decomposed into the following relations:

TRANSCRIPTS_REGULAR*(Student#, Course, Grade)* with the domain constraints *(Student#* being 8 digit, *Course* being 3 digit in the range 000 through 899, and Grade in the set {A, B, C, D, F}). The key as before is *Student#Course*.

TRANSCRIPTS_SPECIAL*(Student#, Course, Grade)* with the domain constraints (*Student#* being 8 digit, *Course* being 3 digit in the range 900 through 999, and Grade in the set {P, F}). The key as before is *Student# Course*. ■

An MVD can be expressed as a general constraint. To examine the insertion and deletion anomalies in such a situation, let us look at Example 7.12 using a software company.

Example 7.12

The work of the company is organized as projects and the employees are grouped as teams. A number of projects are assigned to each group and it is assumed that all employees in the group are involved with each project assigned to it. This is the general constraint for the relation TEAMWORK*(Group, Employee, Project)* as shown in Figure Bi. Assume that the domain of the attributes are a character string of length 20. The only key of the relation is the entire relation.

The insertion of a legal tuple, (B, Su, FILE_MANAGER), causes the relation TEAMWORK to become invalid. This is because the general constraint is no longer satisfied and requires the insertion of additional tuples.

Figure B The TEAMWORK relation and its DK/NF decompositions.

Group	*Employee*	*Project*
A	Jones	HEAP_SORT
A	Smith	HEAP_SORT
A	Lalonde	HEAP_SORT
A	Jones	BINARY_SEARCH
A	Smith	BINARY_SEARCH
A	Lalonde	BINARY_SEARCH
B	Evan	B++_TREE
B	Lalonde	B++_TREE
B	Smith	B++_TREE
B	Evan	FILE_MANAGER
B	Lalonde	FILE_MANAGER
B	Smith	FILE_MANAGER

(i)

Group	*Employee*
A	Jones
A	Smith
A	Lalonde
B	Evan
B	Lalonde
B	Smith

Group	*Project*
A	HEAP_SORT
A	BINARY_SEARCH
B	B++_TREE
B	FILE_MANAGER

(ii)

Similarly, the deletion of the tuple (A, Lalonde, FILE_MANAGER) makes the relation TEAMWORK violate the general constraint and requires the deletion of additional tuples.

In order to convert the relation into DK/NF, we can decompose it into the two relations TEAM*(Group, Employee)* and WORK*(Group, Project)*. This is shown in Figure Bii. ■

It has been shown that a relation in DK/NF is also in PJ/NF and, therefore, in 4NF and BCNF. The proof, found in (Fagi 81), is beyond the scope of this text.

The advantage of DK/NF relations is that all constraints could be satisfied by ensuring that tuples of the relations satisfy the corresponding domain and key constraints. Since this is easy to implement in a database system, relations in DK/NF are preferable. However, no simple algorithms exist to help in the design of DK/NF. Moreover, it appears unlikely that relation schemes with complex constraints could be converted to DK/NF.

The theory for join dependency is well developed; unfortunately, the results are negative. It has been concluded that JDs don't have a finite axiom system. Consequently, we have to be content with relations in 3NF or BCNF. Since we cannot always guarantee that BCNF relations will be dependency preserving when both lossless and dependency-preserving relations are required, we have to settle for third normal form.[5]

7.6 Summary

The decomposition approach we examined in Chapter 6 starts with a relation and the associated set of constraints in the form of functional dependencies. The relation has a certain number of undesirable properties (in the form of insertion, deletion, or update anomalies) and it is replaced by its projections. A number of desirable forms of projections have been identified. In Chapter 6 we discussed the following normal forms: 1NF, 2NF, 3NF, BCNF. Any relation having constraints in the form of FDs only can be decomposed into relations in third normal form; such a decomposition is lossless and preserves the dependencies. Any relation can also be decomposed losslessly into relations in Boyce Codd normal form (and hence into third normal form).

In this chapter we examined the synthesis approach to designing a 3NF database and the higher normal forms, 4NF, 5NF or PJ/NF, and DK/NF.

In the synthesis approach, the starting point of the relational database design process is a universal relation and the set of functional (and nonfunctional) dependencies that have to be enforced between the attributes of this universal relation. The synthesis procedure then synthesizes a set of third normal form relation schemes, which preserves the required dependencies.

Multivalued dependencies arise when **R,** having a nonatomic attribute, is converted to a normalized form. Thus, for each **X** value in such a relation, there will be a set of **Y** values associated with it. This association between the **X** and **Y** values does not depend on the values of the other attributes in the relation. A normal form called fourth normal form has been defined for relations that have FDs as well as MVDs. We discussed an algorithm for decomposing a relation into 4NF; however, like the BCNF decomposition algorithm, this algorithm does not always produce relation schemes that are dependency preserving. If dependency-preserving schemes are essential, in general, we will have to settle for 3NF.

The 5NF is related to what is called join dependency. This is the term used to indicate the property of a relation that can be decomposed losslessly into n simpler relations but cannot be decomposed losslessly into fewer relations. A relation in PJ/NF is also in 4NF.

In a DK/NF relation scheme, it is possible to enforce all general constraints from knowledge of the domains of the attributes and the key constraints. This is the highest and most desirable normal form, although it is not always possible to generate relation schemes in this form. Consequently, the database designer settles for a lower normal form that better meets the needs of the user community.

---

[5]When MVDs are conflict free, a unique 4NF decomposition can be obtained. It has been observed that conflict-free MVDs are natural enough to cover the "real world" situation.

Key Terms

equivalent
multivalued dependency (MVD)
trivial multivalued dependency
basis
pairwise disjoint
dependency basis
simple MVD
fourth normal form (4NF)
fifth normal form (5NF)
join dependency (JD)
embedded multivalued dependency
key dependency (KD)
project-joint normal form (PJ/NF)
domain constraint (DC)
key constraint (KC)
general constraint (GC)
domain key normal form (DK/NF)

Exercises

7.1 Given **U**{*ABCDE*} and F = $\{A \rightarrow B, BC \rightarrow D, D \rightarrow BC, DE \rightarrow \phi\}$, synthesize a set of 3NF relation schemes.

7.2 Given **U**{*ABCDEFGH*} with the FDs given by $\{A \rightarrow BCDEFGH, BCD \rightarrow AEFGH, BCE \rightarrow ADEFGH, CE \rightarrow H, CD \rightarrow H\}$, synthesize a set of lossless join relation schemes.

7.3 Given the relation **R** {*ABCDE*} with the FDs $\{A \rightarrow BCDE, B \rightarrow ACDE, C \rightarrow ABDE\}$, what are the join dependencies of **R?** Give the lossless decomposition of **R.**

7.4 Given the relation **R** {*ABCDEF*} with the set **H** = $\{A \rightarrow CE, B \rightarrow D, C \rightarrow ADE, BD \rightarrow\rightarrow F\}$, find the dependency basis of *BCD*.

7.5 Design a 3NF relation scheme for the database of Exercise 6.16 using the synthesis algorithm. Is the resulting database in BCNF?

7.6 Is it possible to decompose the relation STUDENT_ADVISOR(*Name, Department, Advisor*) with the functional dependencies **F**{*Name* → *Department, Name* → *Advisor, Advisor* → *Department*} illustrated in Figure E: of Example 6.19 into PJ/NF relation schemes? If so, give the projected relation schemes.

7.7 What are the difficulties in generating a relational design wherein all relations are in DK/NF?

7.8 Why is 4NF preferable to BCNF?

7.9 Show that axiom M7 is sound.

Bibliographic Notes

The universal relation concept and associated problems were first discussed in (Kent 81). The algorithm for synthesizing relation schemes from a given set of attributes and FDs was proposed and studied in (Bern 76).

MVDs were introduced by Fagin (Fagi 77) and independently by Delobel (Delo 78) and Zaniolo (Zani 81). Embedded MVDs were noted in (Fagi 77) and (Delo 78). Join dependencies were introduced formally by Rissanen (Riss 79) and examined further in (Aho 79). The project-join normal (Fagin 79) and the domain key normal (Fagi 81) forms were conceived by Fagin. The axioms for JD were proposed by Beeri and Vardi (Beer 79b) and also in (Scio 82). The algorithm for the dependency basis and its correctness and complexity issues were presented in (Beer 80). The DK/NF was proposed by Fagin in (Fagi 81), wherein he proves the theorem that states that a DK/NF is also in the PJ/NF, 4NF, and BCNF. Axiom systems for generalized and template constraints can be found in (Beer 84) and (Sadr 81).

Textbook discussions of the relational database design are included in (Date 85), (Lien 85), (Kort 86), and (Ullm 82). (Maie 83) gives a very detailed theoretical discussion of the relational database theory including relational database design.

Bibliography

(Aho 79) A. V. Aho, C. Beeri, & J. D. Ullman, "The Theory of Joins in Relational Databases," *ACM TODS* 4(3), September 1979, pp. 297–314.

(Arms 74) W. W. Armstrong, "Dependency Structures of Database Relationships." Proc. of the IFIP, 1974, pp. 580–583.

(Beer 77) C. Beeri, R. Fagin, & J. H. Howard, "A Complete Axiomatization for Functional and Multivalued Dependencies," Proc. of ACM SIGMOD International Symposium on Management of Data, 1977, pp. 47–61.

(Beer 79a) C. Beeri, & P. A. Bernstein, "Computational Problems Related to the Design of Normal Form Relational Schemes," *ACM TODS* 4(1), March 1979, pp. 113–124.

(Beer 79b) C. Beeri, & M. Y. Vardi, "On the Properties of Join Dependencies," in H. Gallaire et al., ed., *Advances in Database Theory,* vol. 1. New York: Plenum Press, 1979.

(Beer 80) C. Beeri, "On the Membership Problem for Functional and Multivalued Dependencies in Relational Databases," *ACM TODS* 5(3), September 1980, pp. 241–259.

(Beer 84) C. Beeri, & M. Y. Vardi, "Formal Systems for Tuple and Equality Generating Dependencies," *SIAM Journal of Computing* 13(1), pp. 76–98.

(Bern 76) P. A. Bernstein, "Synthesizing Third Normal Form Relations from Functional Dependencies," *ACM TODS* 1(4), March 1976, pp. 277–298.

(Bisk 79) J. Biskup, U. Dayal, & P. A. Bernstein, "Synthesizing Independent Database Schemas," Proc. ACM SIGMOD International Symposium on Management of Data, 1979, pp. 143–152.

(Codd 70) E. F., Codd, "A Relational Model for Large Shared Data Banks," *Communications of the ACM* 13(6), June 1970, pp. 377–387.

(Codd 72) E. F. Codd, E.F "Further Normalization of the Data Base Relational Model," in R. Rustin, ed., *Data Base Systems*. Englewood Cliffs, NJ: Prentice-Hall, 1972, pp. 33–64.

(Date 85) C. J. Date, *An Introduction to Database Systems,* vol. 1, 4th ed. Reading, MA: Addison-Wesley, 1985.

(Delo 78) C., Delobel, "Normalization and Hierarchical Dependencies in the Relational Data Model," *ACM TODS* 3(3), September 1978, pp. 201–22.

(Fagi 77) R. Fagin, "Multivalued Dependencies and a New Normal Form for Relational Databases," *ACM TODS* 2(3), September 1977, pp. 262–278.

(Fagi 79) R. Fagin, "Normal Forms and Relational Database Operators," ACM SIGMOD International Symposium on Management of Data, 1979, pp. 153–160.

(Fagi 81) R. Fagin, "A Normal Form for Relational Databases that is Based on Domains and Keys," *ACM TODS* 6(3), September 1982, pp. 387–415.

(Kent 81) W. Kent, "Consequences of Assuming a Universal Relation," *ACM TODS,* 6(4), December 1981, pp. 539–556.

(Kort 86) H. F. Korth, & A. Silberschatz, *Database Systems Concepts*. New York: McGraw-Hill, 1986.

(Lien 81) Y. E. Lien, "Hierarchical Schemata for Relational Databases," *ACM TODS,* 6(1), March 1981, pp. 48–69.

(Lien 85) Y. E. Lien, "Relational Database Design," in S. Bing Yao, ed., *Principles of Database Design*. Englewood Cliffs, NJ: Prentice-Hall, 1985.

(Maie 80) D. Maier, ''Minimum Covers in the Relational Database Model,'' *Journal of the ACM*. 27(4), October 1980, pp. 664–674.

(Maie 83) D. Maier, *The Theory of Relational Databases*. Rockville, MD: Computer Science Press, 1983.

(Riss 79) J. Rissanen, ''Theory of Joins for Relational Databases—A Tutorial survey,'' Proc. Seventh Symposium on Mathematical Foundations of Computer Science, Lecture Notes in Computer Science 64. Springer-Verlag, New York pp. 537–551.

(Sadr 81) F. Sadri, & J. D. Ullman, ''Template Dependencies: A Large Class of Dependencies in Relational Databases and Their Complete Axiomatization,'' *Journal of the ACM*. 29(2), April 1981, pp. 363–372.

(Scio 81) E. Sciore, ''Real World MVDs,'' Proc. of the ACM SIGMOD Conf., 1981, pp. 121–132.

(Scio 82) E. Sciore, ''A Complete Axiomatization of Full Join Dependencies,'' *Journal of the ACM*. 29(2), April 1982, pp. 373–393.

(Ullm 82) J. D. Ullman, *Principles of Database Systems,* 2nd ed. Rockville, MD: Computer Science Press, 1982.

(Zani 81) C. Zaniolo, & M. A. Melkanoff, ''On the Design of Relational Database Schemata,'' *ACM TODS*. 6(1), March 1981, pp. 1–47.

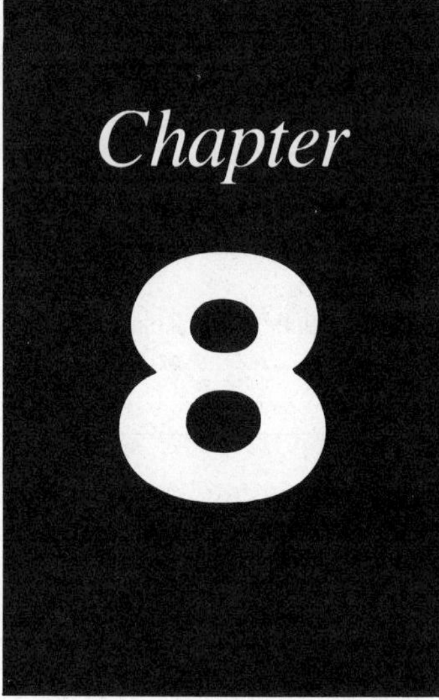

The Network Model

Contents

The Database Task Group (DBTG), a special group within the Conference on Data Systems Languages (CODASYL), issued a final report in 1971. The report was the first standard specification for a database system. A number of commercial database management systems were based on this report. The discussion of the network model in this text is, for the most part, based on the original DBTG draft; reference is made to the revised proposal when required.

8.1 The Network Data Model

The **network data model (NDM)** represents data for an entity set by a logical record type. The data for an instance of the entity set is represented by a record occurrence of the record type. Consider the entity set CLIENT which is of relevance to a public library. It is modeled by its attributes, *Client_No, Name,* and *Address.* (We use the word client instead of member to avoid confusion with the use of the word member in the network data model. We will use the word record synonymously with logical record unless we need to be explicit.)

CLIENT	*Client_No*	*Name*	*Address*

This record type can be defined as follows:

type CLIENT = *record*
Client_No: string;
Name: string;
Address: string;
end

Some occurrences of the record type CLIENT are shown in Figure 8.1a. The figure shows, for example, a client Smith with *Client_No* 234 and *Address* as Lynn.

The data for the entity set BOOK may be represented by the record type BOOK, which consists of the fields *Author, Title, Call_No:*

BOOK	*Author*	*Title*	*Call_No*

This record can be defined as:

type BOOK = *record*
Author: string;
Title: string;
Call_No: string;
end

Some occurrences of the record type BOOK are shown in Figure 8.1b. Note that in practice, a library maintains additional details about each title, including name of the publisher, place of publication, year of publication, size of the volume, date acquired, cost of acquisition, and so on. For simplicity we have ignored these details.

Figure 8.1 Occurrences of CLIENT and BOOK record types.

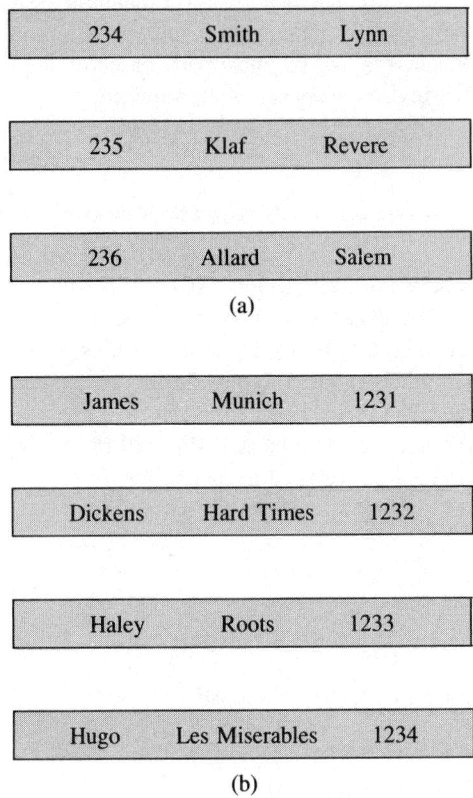

234 Smith Lynn
235 Klaf Revere
236 Allard Salem
(a)
James Munich 1231
Dickens Hard Times 1232
Haley Roots 1233
Hugo Les Miserables 1234
(b)

8.1.1 Expressing Relationship: The DBTG Set

The relationship of a client borrowing a book from the library may be represented by the entity relationship diagram of Figure 8.2a. The corresponding data structure diagram is shown in Figure 8.2b. In part a, we have the entity set CLIENT, which is related to the entity set BOOK in a one-to-many relationship; a client may have borrowed several books. Later we look at the possibility of a many-to-many relationship, where we show that a client has borrowed several books, as shown in part b, and also that a book (or a copy of the book) may have been borrowed by many clients, as shown in part c.

To express the relationship between the client and the borrowed book, the network model uses the set construct. The word *set* used here does not imply the mathematical meaning but indicates that there is a relationship between two record types. A set type represents a one-to-many relationship from the E–R model. An instance of the relationship is expressed by an instance or occurrence of the set type. A set consists of an owner record type and one or more member record type(s). The DBTG proposal of 1971 did not allow a record type to be both an owner and a member within the same set type. However, in the 1978 version of the proposal this restric-

Figure 8.2 Relationship between CLIENT and BOOK.

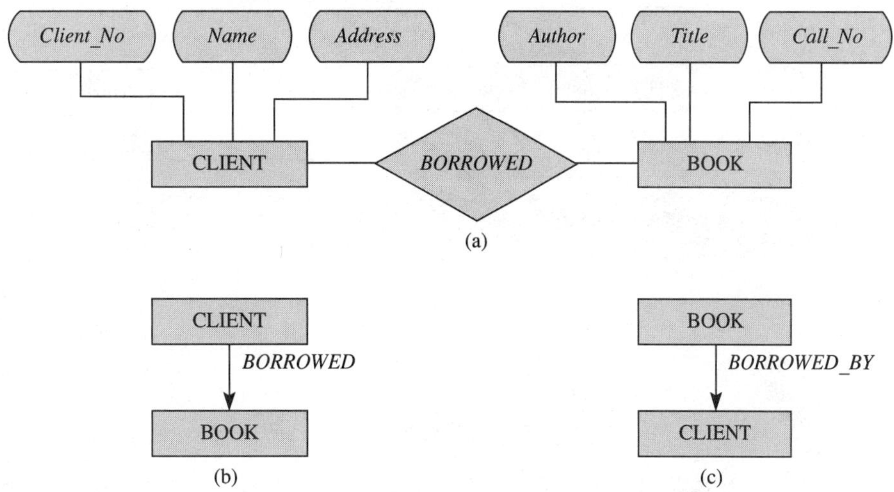

tion was eliminated. In the revised version, the records participating in a set type may be of the same type or of different types (We examine this aspect of the set construct in Section 8.4.) An occurrence of a set type consists of one occurrence of the owner record type and zero or more occurrences of the member record type(s).

The data structure diagram of Figure 8.2b represents the set *BORROWED;* the owner record type is CLIENT and the member record type is BOOK. The relationship between them is represented by the directed arc labeled with the name of the set; it is a functional link. The direction of the arc is from the owner to the member record type. The direction of the functionality is opposite to the direction of the arc. Each occurrence of the set *BORROWED* represents a relationship between a client and the books he or she borrows. If we want to represent the fact that a given book could have been borrowed by many clients, we must have, in addition to the set of Figure 8.2b, another set *BORROWED_BY,* as shown by the data structure diagram of Figure 8.2c. In the set *BORROWED_BY,* BOOK is the owner record type and CLIENT is the member record type.

Even though we can show a many-to-many relationship between two entities by data structure diagrams as in Figure 8.2b and c, its direct implementation is not allowed in the NDM. (We examine the reasons for this in Section 8.3 and show how a many-to-many relationship is implemented in the NDM.)

The set *BORROWED* can be defined as follows:

set is BORROWED
  owner is CLIENT
  member is BOOK
  end

Figure 8.3a gives some occurrences of the set type *BORROWED*. As we can see there is a one-to-many relationship expressed in this set; a CLIENT could borrow more than one book. If we allow the possibility that there could be more than one copy of the same book, then the relationship between CLIENT and BOOK becomes many-to-many; this is shown in Figure 8.3b.

Figure 8.3 Possible relationships between CLIENT and BOOK: (a) one-to-many relationship and (b) many-to-many relationship.

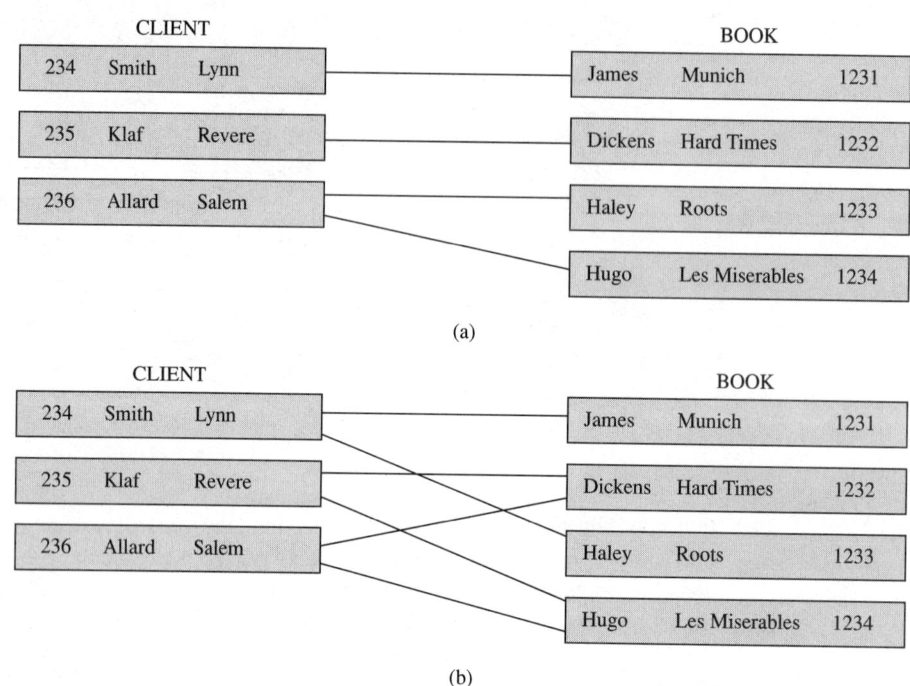

8.1.2 Multiple Level Set Construct

The set *BORROWED*, defined above, is an example of a single level set construct. The NDM does not impose any restrictions on the number of set types in which a given record type is involved as an owner or member. The only restriction is that a given occurrence of a record can participate in only one occurrence of a given set type. A multilevel set can be constructed as shown in the data structure diagram of Figure 8.4. Here we have the entity sets LIBRARY, BRANCH, DEPT_SECTION, and EMPLOYEE. The data for these entity sets can be represented by similarly named logical record types defined as follows:

```
type LIBRARY = record
        Lib_Name: string;
        Address: string;
        Phone_No: string;
        end
type BRANCH = record
        Br_Name: string;
        Address: string;
        Phone_No: string;
        end
```

Figure 8.4 Multilevel set construct.

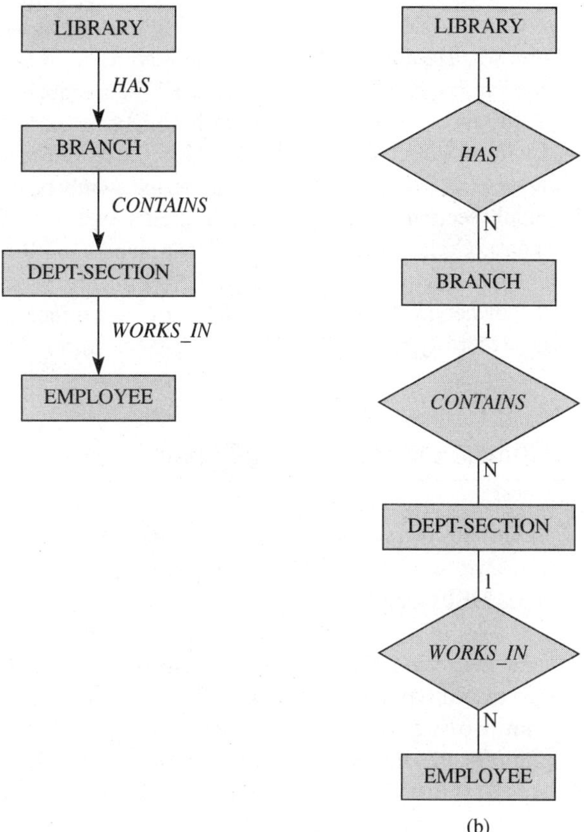


```
type DEPT_SECTION = record
        Ds_Name: string;
        Room_No: string;
        Phone_No: string;
        end
type EMPLOYEE = record
        Emp_Name: string;
        Home_Address: string;
        Phone_No: string;
        end
```

The LIBRARY has a number of BRANCHes, each BRANCH has a number of DEPT_SECTIONs, and each DEPT_SECTION has a number of EMPLOYEEs. There are therefore three levels in the data structure diagram shown in Figure 8.4b. The set *HAS* is owned by the LIBRARY record type and contains as members the record occurrences corresponding to all the BRANCHes of the library. On the next level we have the set type *CONTAINS*. An occurrence of the set type *CONTAINS* has as its owner an occurrence of the record type BRANCH, and the members are the record occurrences corresponding to DEPT_SECTIONs of that BRANCH. On the next level we find the set type *WORKS_IN;* here the owner is the record type DEPT SECTION and the member is the record type EMPLOYEE.

A simple database corresponding to the diagram of Figure 8.4 is shown in Figure 8.5. Here an occurrence of the record type LIBRARY, the MUC Public Library System, is the owner of the set *HAS*. The members of this set occurrence are the two occurrences of the record type BRANCH, Lynn and Revere. The record occurrence Lynn of the record type BRANCH is the owner of one of the occurrences of the set type *CONTAIN* and this set has as its members the record occurrences Adult_Sec (adult section), Childrn_Sec (children's section), Acqstn_Dept (acquisition department), Crcln_Dept (circulation department), and Ref_Dept (reference department) of the record type DEPT_SECTION. The record occurrence Adult_Sec, in its turn, is the owner in the set type *WORKS_IN* occurrence and has the record occurrence of the record type EMPLOYEE, for instance Barry, as its member.

8.1.3 Complex Multilevel Set Construct

Figure 8.6 is a portion of the library database example of Figure 8.4. However, here we have split the original record type DEPT_SECTION into two separate record types DEPT and SECTION.

We illustrate in this example that the DBTG proposal allows a set to have more than one record type as its member record type. For instance, the set *CONTAINS* has two record types as its members. This is not the same as replacing the set *CONTAINS* with two sets, for example, *CONT_SEC* and *CONT_DEPT*. The data structure diagram for this modification is shown in Figure 8.7.

At this point we might ask the following questions:

- Can the EMPLOYEE record occurrence Carrie in Figure 8.5 be a member of the two occurrences of the type set *WORKS_IN* where the owner records are the occurrences Adult_Sec and Childrn_Sec?

Figure 8.5 Sample database corresponding to Figure 8.4.

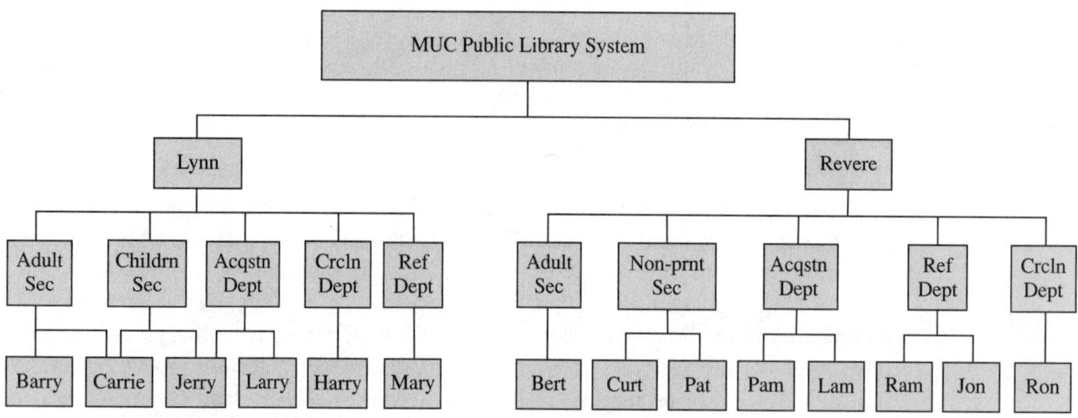

Figure 8.6 Complex multilevel set construct.

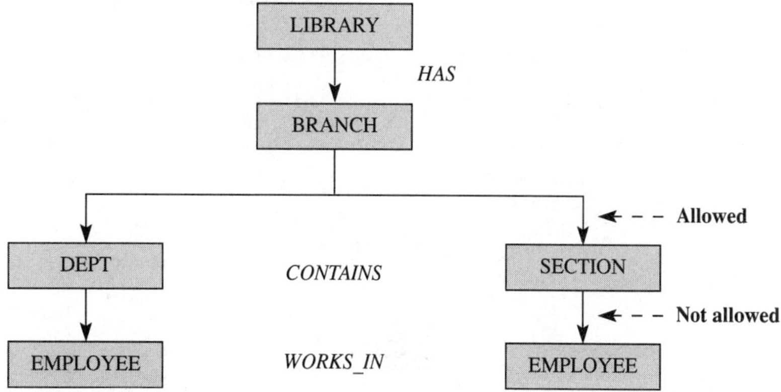

- Can the EMPLOYEE record occurrence Jerry be a member of the set *WORKS_IN* where the owner records are the occurrences Childrn_Sec of record type SECTION and Acqstn-Dept of record type DEPT?
- Can the set type *WORKS_IN* have as its owner record a record from two different record types, SECTION and DEPT?

From Figure 8.6 we also notice that the set type *WORKS_IN,* as it is shown, has two different record types as it owner record type. The DBTG proposal allows a given set type to include member records from more than one record type, but does not allow a set type to have the owner record coming from two different record types. Thus the set *WORKS_IN,* as indicated in Figure 8.6, is not allowed, The DBTG model requires that the intent of the design must be represented as two sets, for instance, *WORKS_IN_DEPT* and *WORKS_IN_SECT*. This modification is shown in the modified data structure diagram of Figure 8.7.

The network data model as proposed in the DBTG proposal has certain restrictions, which we discuss in the following section. These restrictions mean that the answer to each of the above questions is in the negative.

The data structure diagrams of Figures 8.7 and 8.8 illustrate the difference between a set type that can have records from two record types as its member record

Figure 8.7 One record type owner of two set types.

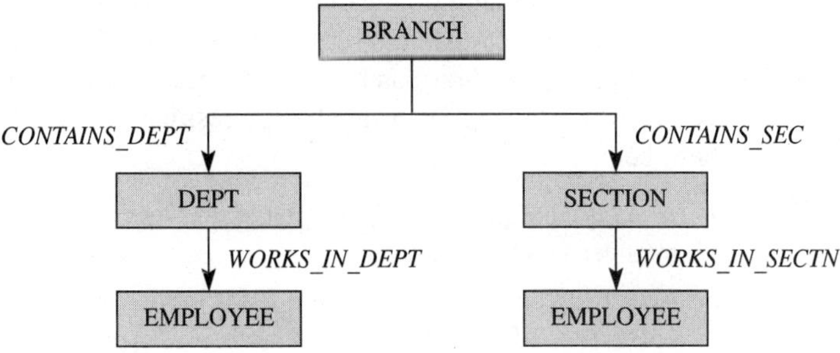

Figure 8.8 Complex multilevel set construct.

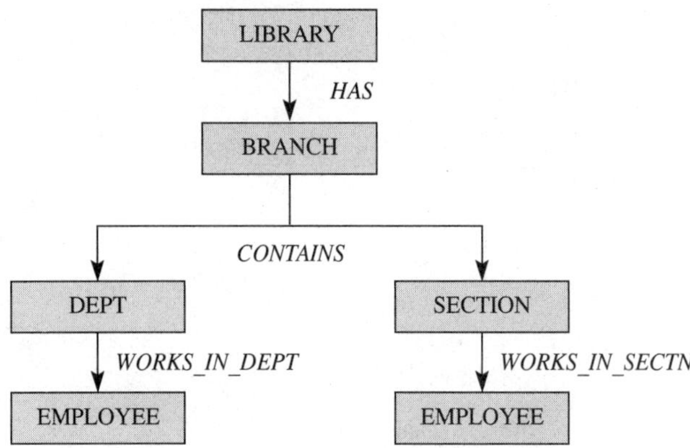

(in Figure 8.8 the set type *CONTAINS*) and a record from a given type as the owner of two or more set types (In Figure 8.7 the record type BRANCH is the owner in set types *CONTAINS_DEPT* and *CONTAINS_SEC*). Nevertheless, the restriction that a given record occurrence may be an owner or member of only one occurrence of a set type still must be observed in the DBTG proposal.

An example of a portion of database corresponding to the data structure diagram of Figure 8.7 is given in Figure 8.5. From this figure, we note that the record types DEPT and SECTION are owner record types in the sets *WORKS_IN_DEPT* and *WORKS_IN_SECTN* respectively. The record type EMPLOYEE is a member record type in both these set types. The instance of the record type corresponding to the employee Carrie is still not allowed to be a member of two occurrences of the set type *WORKS_IN_SECTN*. However, an instance of the record type Jerry can be a member in one occurrence of the set type *WORKS_IN_DEPT* and a member in one occurrence of another set type *WORKS_IN_SECTN*.

8.2 DBTG Set Construct and Restrictions

The DBTG network data model is based on the set construct. The set construct, among other things, defines the owner record type and the member record type(s). The set construct allows a one-to-many relationship to be expressed. The example in the previous section uses the set *WORKS_IN_DEPT* to represent the relation between a department of a library and the employees assigned to that department.

However, there are a number of restrictions in the DBTG proposals. We list these below:

- A set type is named and must have one owner record type and one or more member record types.
- A record occurrence of a given record type can be owner of only one occurrence of a set type where the record type is the owner.

- A record occurrence of a given record type can be a member of only one occurrence of a set type where the record is the member.
- A set type can have only one type of record as owner; however, one or more record types can be members of the set.
- A record type can be the owner record type in any number of set types.
- A record type can be the member record type in any number of set types.
- A given record type cannot be used as an owner and a member in the same set type.

The last restriction in the original DBTG proposal has been eliminated from the revised proposal. Under the revised proposal, the same record type can participate as both owner and member in the same set type. A given occurrence of the record type can therefore be both owner and member in the same set occurrence, or the owner in one set occurrence and a member in a different set occurrence. We examine the ramification of this change in the set construct in Section 8.4.

8.2.1 Implementation of the DBTG Set Construct

The record is a basic unit to represent data in the DBTG network database model. The implementation of the one-to-many relationships of a set is represented by linking the members of a given occurrence of a set to the owner record occurrence. The actual method of linking the member record occurrence to the owner is immaterial to the user of the database; however, for our discussion, we can assume that the set is implemented using a linked list. The list starts at the owner record occurrence and links all the member record occurrences with the pointer in the last member record occurrence leading back to the owner record. Figure 8.9 shows the implementation of the set occurrence *BORROWED* where the owner record is Klaf and the member records are the instances Dickens and Hugo. Note that for simplicity we have shown only one of the record fields of each record. This method of implementation assigns one pointer (link) in each record for each set type in which the record participates and, therefore, allows a record occurrence to participate in only one occurrence of a given set type. Any other method of implementing the set construct in a database management system based on the DBTG proposal is, in effect, equivalent to the linked list method.

Figure 8.9 Implementation of the DBTG SET.

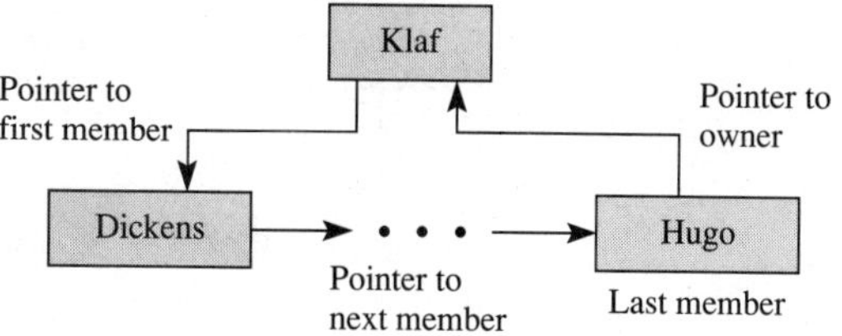

8.3 Expressing an M:N Relationship in DBTG

Let us now see how we can express the following relationship in the DBTG model. We would like to model a situation where an employee is able to help out in different departments depending on the workload. For example, during the evening, when there are more people in the library, it is common to increase the number of clerks at the circulation desk. An employee assigned to the acquisition department could also be designated to work in the circulation department. To allow for the possibility of an employee being assigned to work in more than one department, we need to express a many-to-many relationship. In this many-to-many relationship, a department has many employees and the employees are assigned to more than one department. This could be implemented indirectly by expressing two one-to-many relationships and using an intermediate record, the so-called intersection or common information-bearing record type. Such common information between the two original record types could, however, be null.

In the DBTG model we can express this M:N relationship by two set types. In one set type, the DEPT is the owner record type and the members are the record occurrences of the EMPLOYEE record type. In the second set type, the owner is an EMPLOYEE record occurrence and the members are the DEPT record occurrences. These sets are shown by the data structure diagram of Figure 8.10. However, the DBTG set construct does not allow the implementation of these sets. Suppose we allow an employee to work in more than one department. Then the record occurrence for that employee will appear as a member record in more than one occurrence of the set *WORKS_IN_DEPT*. This violates the DBTG restriction that a record occurrence can be a member of only one occurrence of a given set type. Similarly, for the set *ASSIGNED_TO* we find that since there are many EMPLOYEEs in a given DEPT a given occurrence of a record for that DEPT will be a member of more than one occurrence of this set type.

The above reasoning can be used to explain why we could not directly show the many-to-many relationship between a CLIENT and a BOOK as in Figures 8.2b and c.

The method for resolving this problem in the DBTG model is to introduce an intermediate record type between the two entity sets involved in the many-to-many relationship. This intermediate record type is sometimes called the **intersection record** or the **connection record.** This new record holds data common to the many-to-many relationship of the original entities represented by their respective record types.

Figure 8.10 Incorrect method of expression an M:N relationship in DBTG.

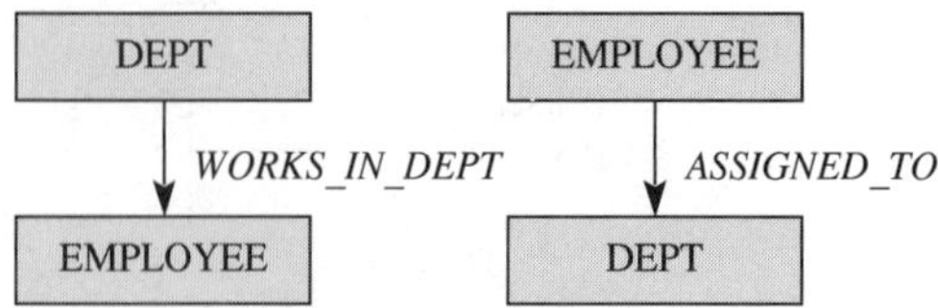

Therefore, to express the above M:N relationship we introduce the record type HOURS_ASSGND, which may be defined as follows:

type HOURS_ASSGND = *record*
Dept: string;
Employee: string;
Hours: integer;
end

A correct representation of the many-to-many relationship of Figure 8.10 is now expressed by introducing the sets *EMP_ASSGND* and *DEPT_ASSGND* with the record types DEPT and EMPLOYEE as owner and the intermediate record type HOURS_ASSGND as member in both the sets. A data structure diagram for this correct representation of the relationship is shown in Figure 8.11.

Figure 8.12 shows a possible method of implementing the M:N relationship using the intermediate record containing space for the common data and two pointers, one for each of the sets it is involved in. The common data here is the number of hours the employee is assigned to a given department. Sometimes the intermediate record contains duplicated information, e.g., department name and employee name, to facilitate the recovery and verification operations. The list of employees assigned to the Acqstn_Dept can be determined by the set *EMP_ASSGND,* where the owner is the record occurrence Acqstn_Dept (AD) and following the list containing the intermediate records AD J 40 and AD J 30. The record AD J 40 is owned by Jerry and the record AD L 30 is owned by Larry in the set type *DEPT_ASSGND,* indicating that employees Jerry and Larry work in the Acqstn_Dept. Similarly, we can see that employee Larry is assigned to the Acqstn_Dept for 30 hours and the Crcln_Dept for 10 hours. Since Larry is assigned to two departments, there are two occurrences of the intermediate record type containing the intersection data pertaining to Larry. Similarly, the circulation department has three employees assigned to it and, hence, the set occurrence of the set type *EMP_ASSGND* with the circulation department as the owner has three member record occurrences of the intermediate record type HOURS_ASSGND.

Suppose there is a need to express another M:N relationship, let us say between the employees and their participation in a number of activity clubs run by the library. This can be implemented by introducing another intermediate record type, let us say EMP_AFFILIATION, and two set types to establish this many-to-many relationship, as shown in Figure 8.13a. The corresponding sample database is shown in Figure 8.13b.

Figure 8.11 A correct representation of M:N relationship in DBTG.

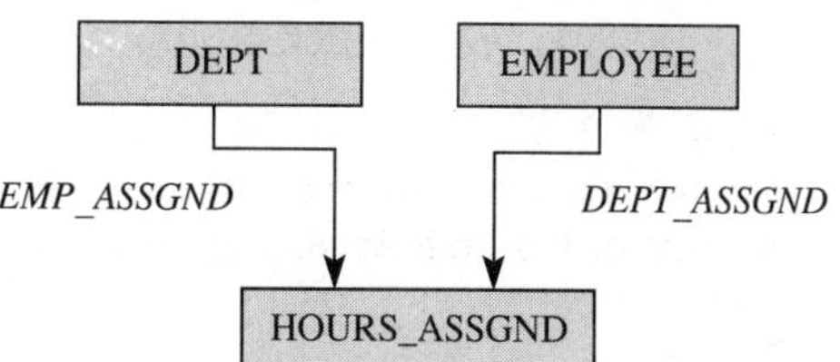

Figure 8.12 Sample database showing an M:N relationship.

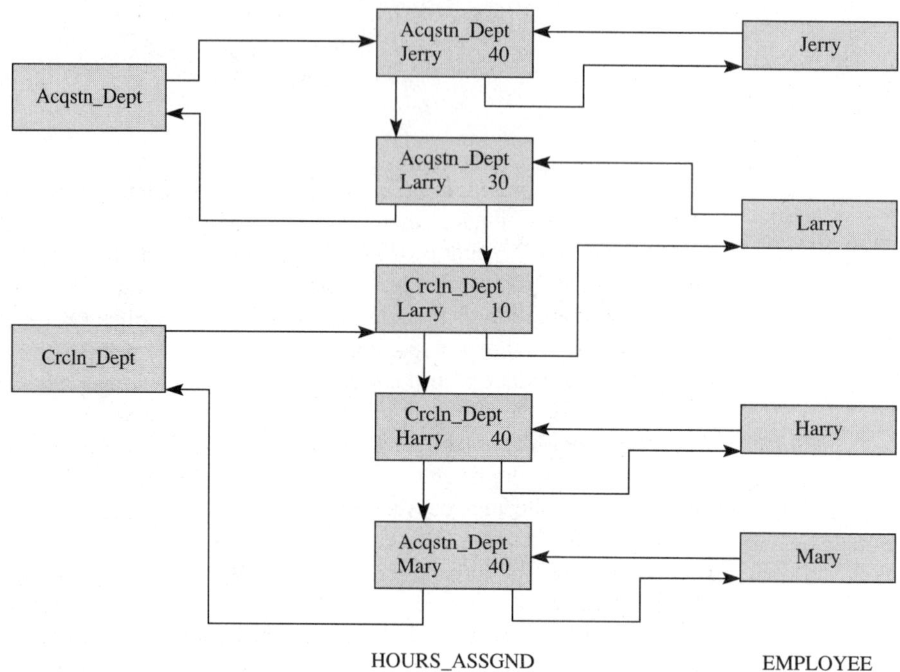

To express the fact that some books in the library may have several copies, we introduce a new record type, BOOK_COPY. This record contains information about the copy number of a particular book and indicates the branch it is assigned to and its current status. We establish a relationship between the record BOOK and BOOK_COPY using a set *COPY_STATUS*. The data structure diagram for this relationship is shown in Figure 8.14a. Figure 8.14b gives some examples.

```
type BOOK_COPY = record
            Call_No: string;
            Copy_No: integer;
            Branch_Id: string;
            Current_Status: string;
            end
set is COPY_STATUS
            owner is BOOK
            member is BOOK_COPY
            end
```

We now return to the many-to-many relationship we mentioned earlier in the E–R diagram of Figure 8.2a and which we implemented erroneously in Figures 8.2b and c. Some occurrences of this many-to-many relationship between a client and the books he or she may borrow is given in Figure 8.3b. To correctly implement this

Figure 8.13 Another example of an M:N relationship.

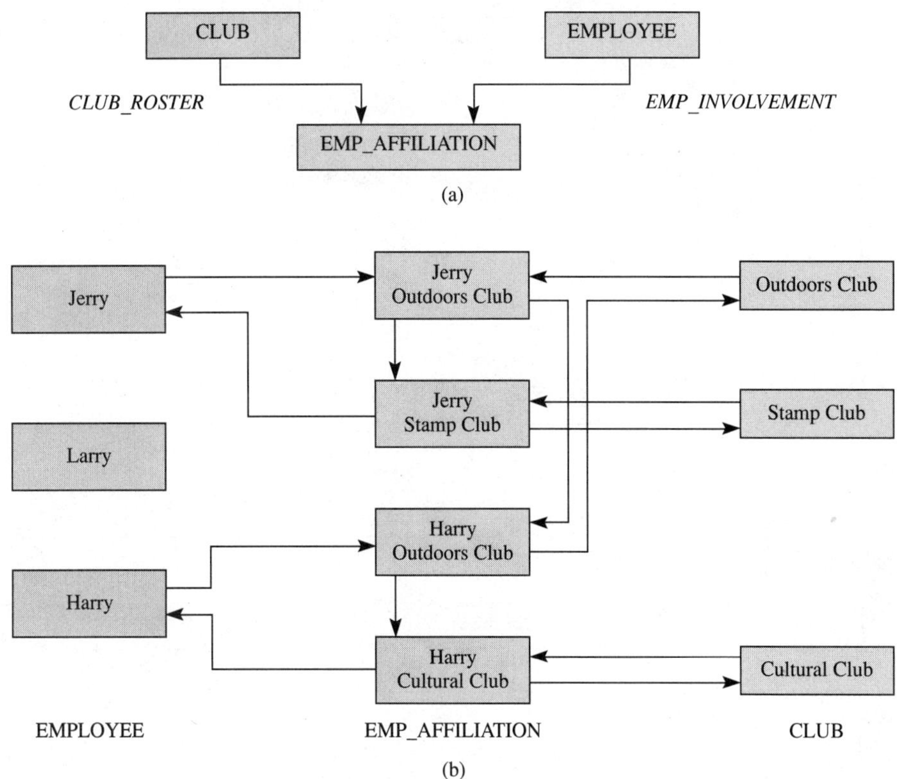

relationship, we introduce in addition to the CLIENT and the BOOK_COPY record an intermediate connector record BOOK_DUE defined as follows:

```
type  BOOK_DUE = record
                 Call_No: integer;
                 Copy_No: integer;
                 Client_No: string;
                 Due_Date: string;
                 end;
```

We also introduce two sets *BORROWED* and *BOOK_COPY_LENT* defined as follows:

```
set is  BORROWED
           owner is CLIENT
           member is BOOK_DUE
           end
set is  BOOK_COPY_LENT
           owner is BOOK_COPY
           member is BOOK_DUE
           end
```

Figure 8.14 Multiple copies of BOOKs.

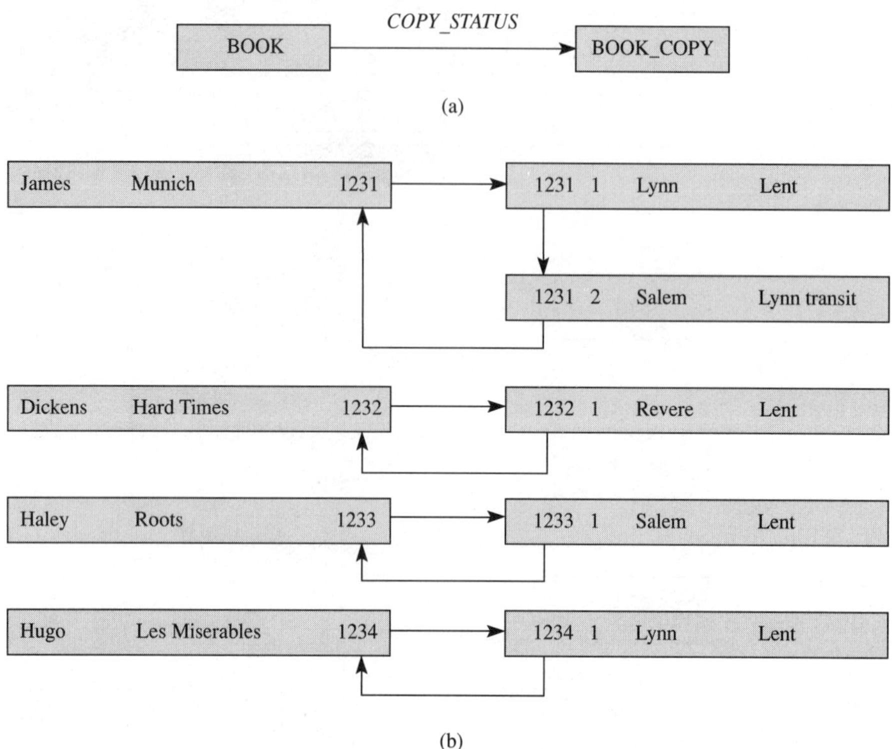

The many-to-many relationship of Figure 8.3b is expressed indirectly by using the one-to-many relationships between BOOK and BOOK_COPY, and CLIENT and BOOK_DUE; and a one-to-one relationship between BOOK_DUE and BOOK_COPY. These sets are shown in Figure 8.15. Each book could have a number of copies, which is shown by the set *COPY_STATUS* with owner record type being BOOK and member record type being BOOK_COPY. The BOOK_COPY taken out by a CLIENT is shown by the set *BORROWED*.

Figure 8.15 Many-to-many relationship of CLIENT and BOOKs.

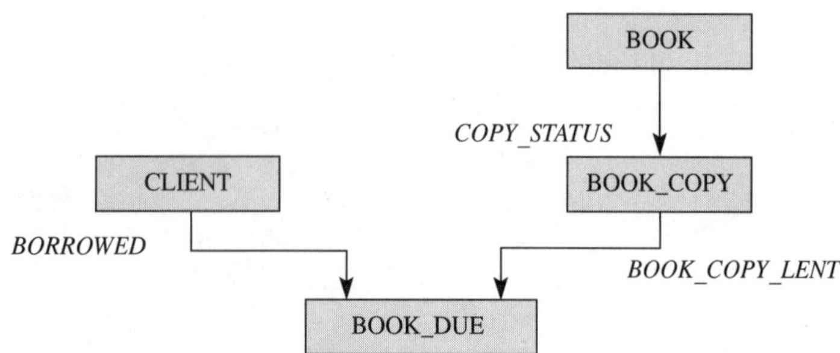

8.4 Cycles in DBTG

The original DBTG set construct prohibited the same type of record to be both an owner and a member in a given set type. However, relationships of this type, sometimes called intrarecord relationships, are required to model, for example, the organizational structure of an enterprise or the part explosion of a subassembly or an assembly, as shown in Figure 8.16. The DBTG set to express this relationship contains the same type of records as the owner and member record types: EMPLOYEEs for the former relationship and PARTs for the latter.

The 1978 modification of the DBTG proposal removed this restriction and allowed a set type to have the same record type as both a member and an owner. However, a given occurrence of a record could only be involved in one set occurrence as an owner and in one set occurrence as a member. This modification to the original DBTG set construct allows for the presence of cycles in the database.

A **cycle** is a path in a single-level or multilevel hierarchy of DBTG sets such that the path starting from a given record type leads back to the same record type while traversing the sets from an owner to a member. However, the return need not be to the same record occurrence.

When the same record type is declared to be both the owner record type and the member record type in the same set type, a cycle called the **single-level cycle** occurs. We illustrate this type of cycle in Figure 8.16 and discuss it in Section 8.4.1.

When a sequence of set types exists in the database such that the member record type in one set is the owner record type in the next set, a cycle called the **multilevel cycle** is said to be present. If we start with one record type, which is the owner record type in this sequence of set types, the final member record type reached as we go through this sequence of owner-member record types is the starting owner record type. (We illustrate the multilevel cycle in Figure 8.22 and focus on it in Section 8.4.2.)

8.4.1 Set Involving Only One Type of Record

Consider the set type *TEAM* (a work group or a play group) wherein the owner and member record types are EMPLOYEE. The owner of a set occurrence of this set

Figure 8.16 Single-level cycles.

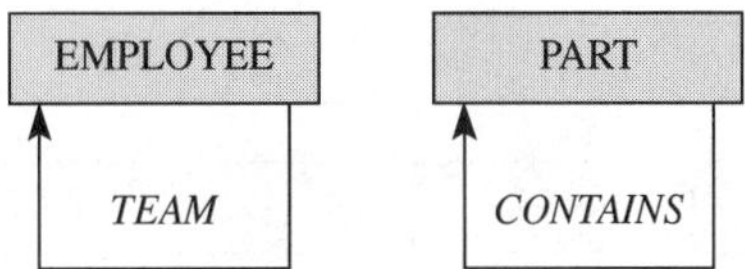

represents the team leader and the members of the set occurrence are the teammates. This set can be defined as follows:

set is *TEAM*
owner is EMPLOYEE
member is EMPLOYEE
end

Similarly, the set *CONTAINS,* defined below, forms a cycle involving the same record type.

set is *CONTAINS*
owner is PART
member is PART
end

Figure 8.17 shows the organizational structure of the work teams of a library branch. Barry is the team leader of one team. His *TEAM* consists of the EMPLOYEEs Carrie, Jerry, Larry, and Barry himself. We can modify the team organization of Figure 8.17 so that a team leader does not appear as a member of his or her own team. The modified database is shown in Figure 8.18.

However, this modification allows for the presence of loops in the database, which not only involves the same record type but also the same record occurrence. A **loop** is a path that starts with a given record occurrence as, let us say, an owner record type in a set occurrence. The path then winds through a number of member record occurrences. When it reaches a given member record occurrence, it establishes that member as an owner of another set occurrence of the same set type. The path continues through its member record occurrences. This procedure is repeated a number of times until the path returns to the starting record occurrence as a member record occurrence. Figure 8.19 shows a loop that starts with the EMPLOYEE record occurrence Barry and returns to the same record occurrence as a member in another occurrence of the set type *TEAM*. (Note: With the structure of *TEAM* as in Figure 8.17, we have a loop within a single set occurrence!)

Loops can be avoided in the NDM by the introduction of an intermediate record type to store the intersection or common data in the set involved. (It is likely that the intersection record type may be null, i.e., there are no data fields in this intermediate record type.) This intermediate record type can then be used to define two symmetrical sets; it is the member in each of the sets, as shown in Figure 8.20. Furthermore, such an intermediate record gives the flexibility of a many-to-many relationship being

Figure 8.17 Set with same type of record as owner and member.

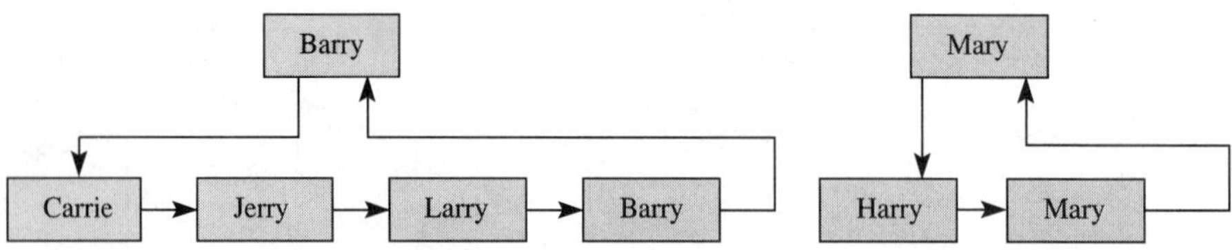

Figure 8.18 Modified organizational chart.

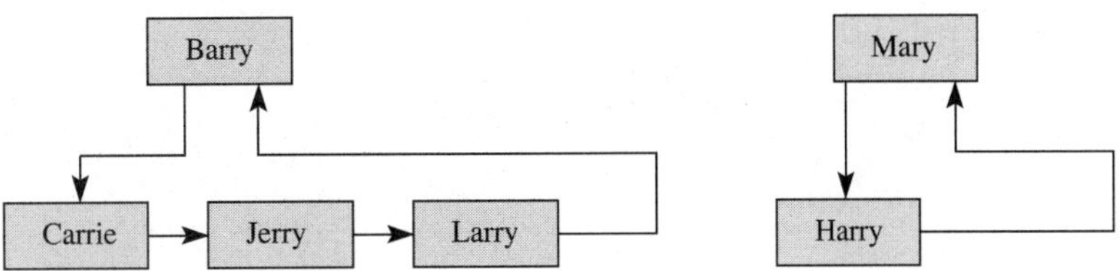

established between occurrences of records of the same record type, as discussed below.

The assignment of an employee to more than one occurrence of the set type *TEAM* is handled by the introduction of an intermediate record type to express the many-to-many relationship. The data structure diagram to represent this relationship is given in Figure 8.20. The intermediate record type is a member of the two sets, both owned by the EMPLOYEE type record. Compare this with the M:N relationship of Figure 8.11, where the owners of the sets involving the intersection record were of different types.

We can define the intersection record type as follows;

```
type TEAM_ASSG = record
                   Team_Leader: string;
                   Team_Mate: string;
                   Hours: integer;
                 end
```

Here the data items *Team_Leader* and *Team_Mate,* which are aliases for the data item *Emp_Name* in the record EMPLOYEE, are redundant and could have been introduced for verification and recovery as mentioned above.

Figure 8.19 Loops in database.

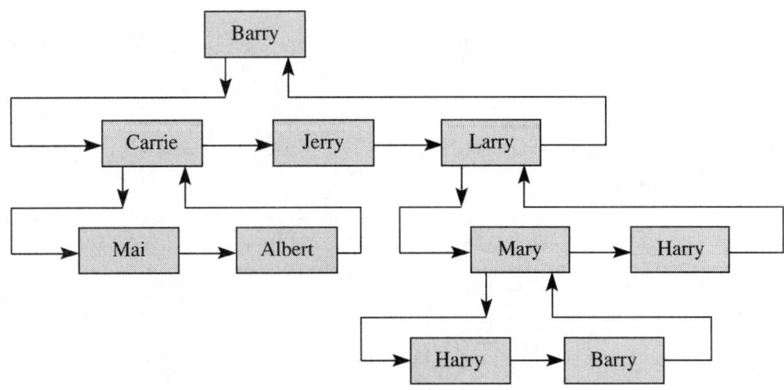

Figure 8.20 One record type with intersection record.

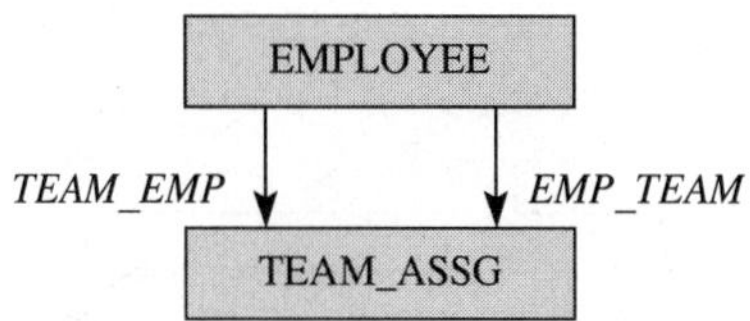

The sets *TEAM_EMP* and *EMP_TEAM* can be defined as follows:

sets *TEAM_EMP*
owner is EMPLOYEE
member is TEAM_ASSG
end
set is EMP_TEAM
owner is EMPLOYEE
member is TEAM_ASSG
end

A sample database involving this many-to-many relationship between occurrences of the record type EMPLOYEE is given in Figure 8.21. Here the owner of the two set occurrences of the set type *TEAM_EMP* are the records Barry and Harry of the record type EMPLOYEE. The members in the sets are the record occurrences {Barry Jerry 10, Barry Larry 15}, and {Harry Jerry 30, Harry Larry 25, Harry Mary 40} respectively. There are three occurrences of the set type *EMP_ASSG* with owners Jerry, Larry, and Mary. The corresponding members are the record occurrences {Barry Jerry 10, Harry Jerry 30}, {Barry Larry 15, Harry Larry 25}, and {Harry Mary 40}, respectively.

Figure 8.21 M:N relationship involving single record type.

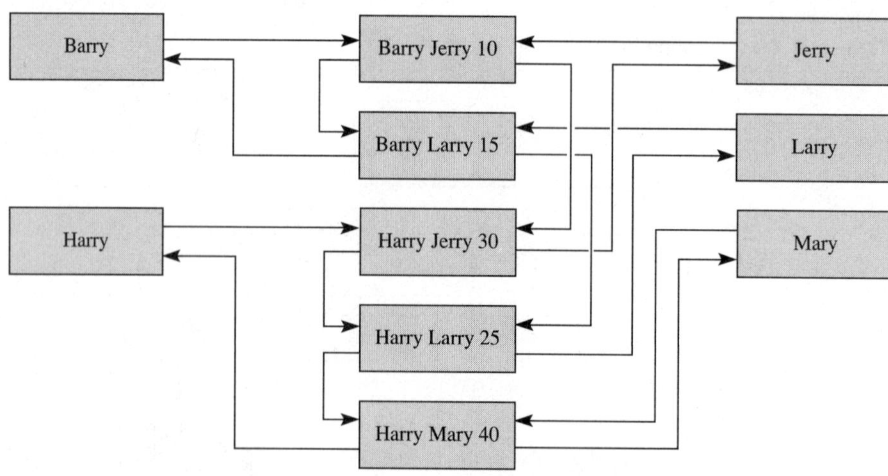

Figure 8.22 A cycle involving different record types.

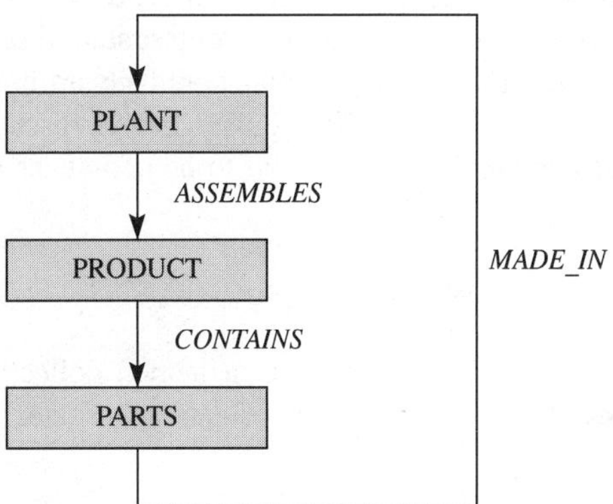

8.4.2 Sets Involving Different Record Types in a Cycle

Figure 8.22 is an example of a data structure diagram showing a cycle involving different record types. In this figure we indicate that a plant assembles a number of products. Each product is made from a number of parts and these parts are made in some plants.

With the automatic set insertion rule (described below in Section 8.5.4) it is obvious that no data can be inserted in a database with the above type of cycle. (See exercise 8.9.)

The designer of the database, using the NDM, can decide whether to include cycles in the database, provided the DBMS software correctly handles such cycles. As in the case of loops, the cycle can be eliminated with the introduction of one or more intermediate record types.

8.5 Data Description in the Network Model

Our discussion of the data description facility of a network database model closely follows the CODASYL model.

8.5.1 Record

A DBTG record is made up of smaller units of data called data-items, vectors, and repeating groups. Records of one type or several types are related via a set, and provide the basic unit of access in the database. In previous discussions we have used a number of records, such as CLIENT, EMPLOYEE, and so on.

Data-Item

Data-item is the DBTG term for field and is the smallest unit of named data. An occurrence of a data-item is a representation of a value. A data-item has a name and a type or format; the format could be arithmetic, string, or one specified by the implementer via a TYPE clause. In our discussions of the CLIENT record, we defined the data-item *Client_No* to be of integer type.

Data Aggregates

A record could also contain a named collection of data-items, called **data aggregates.** There are two kinds of data aggregates: vectors and repeating groups.

Vectors

The DBTG record is made up of basic units of data representation called data-items. It also allows a data-item to be repeated; this is called a **vector** in DBTG terminology. Suppose that the record type CLIENT contained an additional data-item for storing the phone number. However, two or more phone numbers, for instance, the home and business phone numbers, may be required to be stored for some clients. The phone number could then be described as a one-dimension array of data-items all of which have identical characteristics. Another example of using a vector can be in storing the positions in which an employee can work. For instance, in the logical record for the employee entity, we include a vector for position and each of its component contains the position in which he or she can work.

Repeating Groups

In the employee entity and the corresponding record illustrated in Figures 2.6 and 2.15, we need to store in the record for each employee, a number of dependents and the kinship of the dependent to the employee. This is an example of a **repeating group.** The repeating group is a collection of two or more data items, vectors, or repeating groups that occurs more than once within a record; a repeating group, thus, is nested. A repeating group can be considered to be a vector of records. We can represent the books borrowed by a client using a repeating group that contains the data–item *Call_No* and *Due_Date* defined below. The CLIENT record containing both a vector and a repeating group is defined as follows and shown in Figure 8.23:

```
type  BKS_BRWD = record
        Call_No: string;
        Due_Date: string;
        end;
type  CLIENT = record
          Name: string;
          Phone_No: array [1..2] of integer;
          Rptg_Grp1: array [1..15] of BKS_BRWD;
          end;
```

Figure 8.23 Example of vector and repeating group.

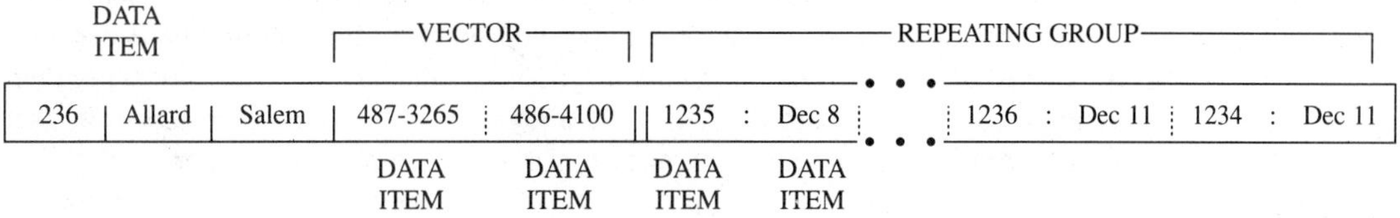

In the above example, the vector *Phone_No* may be used to store two phone numbers, which could be the home and business phone numbers. An alternate method of representing the data of the vector is by explicitly defining two data-items, *Home_Phone_No* and *Bus_Phone_No*. However, if the number of elements of the vectors is large, then this solution, even though more explicit as to the meaning of each component, is a bit awkward. Another method of representing the information contained in a repeating group is by means of a one-to-many set. For instance, the repeating group *Rptg_Grp1* can be replaced by a record and a set as follows. Note that in this case, the *Rptg_Grp1* is eliminated from the record type CLIENT.

```
type  BOOK_BRWD = record
          Call_No: string;
          Due_Date: string;
          end;
set is  BOOKS_BORROWED
          owner is CLIENT
          member is BOOK_BRWD
          end
```

Keys

The DBTG data description language allows keys to be declared in the declaration of a record type. A record key is a group of data-items or a single data-item used to identify a record or a group of records. A record type can have more than one record key declared for it. The record key can be used for direct retrieval of records by the database management system. A record key has an unique name associated with it.

A record type could also be declared to be ordered sequentially, the ordering options being ASCENDING or DESCENDING with respect to a record order key. A record could have more than one record order key declared for it and could be logically sorted in two or more different orders. The order can be used for sequential retrieval of the record type. The record order key is also a record key.

8.5.2 Set

The **DBTG set** is a named relationship between records of the same or different types. Each set has one owner record type and one or more member record types. Any record type may be declared as the owner of one or more set types. Any record type may be declared as a member of one or more set types. Therefore, a record type can be both an owner and a member in one or more set types. A record may be both owner and member in the same set type. However, a record cannot be a member or an owner of more than one occurrence of a given set type. If a record type is declared as the owner type as well as the member type in the declaration of the set type, then the same record can be both an owner and a member in the same occurrence of a set type, or it can be the owner in one occurrence and a member in another.

A set contains precisely one occurrence of the owner record and any number of occurrences of each of its member record types. A set containing only an occurrence of its owner record type is an empty set. This contradicts the definition of the mathematical set which, when empty, does not contain any element. The DBTG set occurrence always has an owner record occurrence even when empty. An empty DBTG set cannot exist without the owner record occurrence.

8.5.3 Order of Members in a Set

Each set type declared in the schema must have an ordering specified for it. This ordering indicates the logical ordering for the insertion of member records into the set. The ordering specified could be ascending or descending and is based on data items in each of the member record types. The ordering could also be given as the order of insertion, in the reverse order of insertion, or before or after a selected record.

The DBTG allows the user to specify the insertion point where a member record will be connected into an occurrence of a set type. The possible order that could be defined is first, last, next, prior, system default, sorted.

If we consider the set to be implemented via a doubly linked list, starting with the owner record occurrence, then the **order** can be explained as follows:

- **order first** indicates that the member records are to be inserted immediately following the owner record, thus giving a reverse chronological order. The member record most recently inserted into a set occurrence will be the first member in the set.
- **order last** indicates that the member records are to be inserted immediately before the owner record occurrence, thus giving a chronological order. The member record most recently inserted into the set will be the last member in the set.
- **order next** and **order prior** indicates that the member records are to be inserted relative to the currency indicator (discussed in Section 8.7.2) of the run unit for the set type. If the currency indicator is pointing to the owner record, order next is equivalent to order first and order prior is equivalent to **order last.**
- **sorted** indicates that the member records are to be maintained in a sorted sequence. If the sorting is based on the value of key items of the member record types, this is specified by the user.
- **system default** indicates that the DBMS maintains the member records in an order most convenient to it.

8.5.4 Set Membership

The set membership criteria consist of the insertion and retention status of a member record type with respect to a set. The insertion status indicates how the membership of a record occurrence, within a set occurrence of a set type of which it is a member, is established. If the status is **automatic,** the insertion of the record as a member in the appropriate occurrence of the set type is performed by the DBMS when a new occurrence of the record type is stored in the database. In the following example, we declare the set *BORROWED* to be owned by the record type CLIENT and to contain the record type BOOK_DUE as its member, the membership being defined as automatic. This ensures that the library will know exactly which client has borrowed a given volume.

```
type CLIENT = record
        Client_No: string;
        Name: string;
        Address: string;
        end
type BOOK_DUE = record
        Call_No: integer;
        Copy_No: integer;
        Client_No: string;
        Due_Date: string;
        end;
set is BORROWED
        owner is CLIENT
        member is BOOK_DUE automatic
        end
```

A **manual** membership status indicates that the membership is not automatic. In effect, with a manual membership, the selection of the appropriate occurrence of the set and the insertion of the record to become its member has to be done using appropriate data manipulation facilities. In the following example, the set *COLLECTION* owned by the record type BRANCH is declared to have the record type BOOK_COPY as member record, the membership being manual. Therefore, the application program is responsible for inserting an occurrence of the record type BOOK_COPY in the appropriate occurrence of the set type.

```
type BRANCH = record
        Br_Name: string;
        Address: string;
        Phone_No: string;
        end
type BOOK_COPY = record
        Call_No: string;
        Copy_No: integer;
        Branch_Id: string;
        Current_Status: string;
        end
```

```
set is COLLECTION
        owner is BRANCH
        member is BOOK_COPY manual
        end
```

The retention or removal status of a record indicates the continuance of the relationship of a member record occurrence with the set type once it becomes a member of an occurrence of the set type. The retention status could be defined as fixed, mandatory, or optional.

Fixed status indicates that once a record becomes a member of an occurrence of a set type, it will continue that relationship with that particular set occurrence until the record if deleted. *('til death do us part!)* When the owner of the record in a set is deleted, if the membership retention status had been defined as fixed, all member record occurrences are deleted along with the owner. In the following example, the set *CONTAINS* owned by the BRANCH record type has DEPT and SECTION as member record types; the membership insertion status is manual and the retention status is declared to be fixed. Thus, once a department or section is assigned to a given branch, it remains in that branch and, if the branch is closed, the department and the branch is deleted as well.

```
set is CONTAINS
        owner is BRANCH
        member is DEPT manual fixed
        member is SECTION manual fixed
        end
```

Mandatory status indicates that once a record becomes a member of an occurrence of a set type, it continues that relationship with an occurrence of that set type. The particular set occurrence of which the record occurrence is a member may change but the relationship in the set type must continue. When the membership status is defined as mandatory, an attempt to delete the owner record occurrence with a nonempty set will fail until all the members are moved to another set occurrence. In the following example, the set *WORKS_IN_DEPT* is owned by the record type dept and has as its members occurrences of the record type EMPLOYEE, the insertion and retention statuses being manual and mandatory, respectively. Thus, an occurrence of the employee record type is to be inserted in the appropriate set occurrence of the set type *WORKS_IN_DEPT*. Employees could, however, be moved from one department to another. Also, once a number of employees are assigned to a department, we cannot delete that department until we move all the employees to another department.

```
set is WORKS_IN_DEPT
        owner is DEPT
        member is employee manual mandatory
        end
```

Optional status allows a member record occurrence to discontinue a relationship in a set type. When the membership status is defined as optional, an attempt to delete the owner record occurrence will cause the members of the set occurrence owned by the owner record to be disconnected and the owner record occurrence to be deleted; the member record occurrence will continue to exist in the database. In the following example, the set type *COLLECTION* is owned by the record type BRANCH; the member record type is BOOK_COPY and the membership criteria of this record type is manual insertion and optional retention. Therefore, an application program will have to insert an occurrence of the member record type in the appropriate set occurrence. The retention is optional, which means that if a BRANCH type record occurrence were to be deleted from the database, all member record occurrences in the set occurrence of the set type COLLECTION owned by the branch record occurrence will be removed from the set before the owner record occurrence is deleted. The member record occurrence continues to exist in the database.

```
set is COLLECTION
        owner is BRANCH
        member is BOOK_COPY manual optional
        end
```

Figure 8.24 shows the meaning of the combination of the two membership statuses for a member record type in a set type.

We can add the status information for insertion and retention of the member BOOK DUE in the set borrowed as follows:

```
set is BORROWED
        owner is CLIENT
        member is BOOK_DUE automatic mandatory
        end
```

The insertion status is specified as automatic because a BOOK being borrowed must become the responsibility of a client. The retention status is specified as man-

Figure 8.24 Significance of membership status.

	FIXED	MANDATORY	OPTIONAL
AUTOMATIC	When a record is created, the DBMS places it in a set. The record stays there until it is deleted.	When a record is created, the DBMS places it in a set. The record can move from one occurrence of the set to another.	When a record is created, the DBMS places it in a set. The record can be moved to another occurrence of the set or removed and later reconnected.
MANUAL	The record has to be connected by appropriate data manipulation operations. Once it is connected it stays in the set occurrence until deleted.	The record has to be connected by appropriate data manipulation operations. The record can move from one set occurrence to another.	The record has to be connected by appropriate data manipulation operations. The record can be moved to another set occurrence or be removed and later reconnected.

datory because the library has to know which client has borrowed the book until it is returned. Also, the library does not allow clients to be deleted until they have returned the books they borrowed.

8.5.5 Structural Constraint

The data definition of a set could include a requirement that the value of a data-item in the member record occurrence be equal to a data-item in the owner record occurrence. An example of a member record type to allow such a constraint to be specified is shown in the declaration of the record type BOOK_DUE. BOOK_DUE participates in sets involving record types CLIENT and BOOK_COPY. The structural constraint that the value of the data-item BOOK_COPY. *Client_No* be equal to CLIENT. *Client_No* can be specified in the definition of the set *BORROWED* by the check statement as illustrated below.

```
set is BORROWED
        owner is CLIENT
        member is BOOK_DUE automatic mandatory
        check CLIENT.Client_No = BOOK_DUE.Client_No
        end
```

This requirement, called **structural constraint,** was added to the original DBTG proposal to provide a method of maintaining the integrity of data in the database.

8.5.6 Set Selection

For each set type specified in the database schema, the database contains several set occurrences. There must be a way to select the appropriate set occurrence when member record occurrences are to be added to or retrieved from a set. The set selection clause specified in the definition of the set defines the rules to be used by the DBMS for the purpose of selecting the appropriate set occurrence for inserting or accessing a member record. A separate **set selection** clause is required for each member record type in the set type. Set selection could be by structural constraint, key, application program, a procedure to be invoked for the selection, or by the DBMS. We show below set selection by structural constraint, which incorporates the feature of the check statement given above. With the following definition of the set *BORROWED,* the set occurrence to be selected will be the one where the *Client_No* of the owner record is equal to the *Client_No* in the record type BOOK_DUE.

```
set is BORROWED
        owner is CLIENT
        member is BOOK_DUE automatic mandatory
        set selection is structural CLIENT.Client_No =
                                        BOOK_DUE.Client_No
        end
```

To simplify the discussions of the data manipulation facility of the network data model, we will use the application program to select the appropriate set occurrence.

8.5.7 Singular Sets

The **singular set** is a special type of set with precisely one occurrence. The **system** is named as the owner of this type of set and is a convenient method of grouping together all occurrences of the member record type. For each such grouping of a record type we can declare a singular set. All clients to the public library, regardless of the branch they normally use, can be considered as being a member of the singular set *ALL_CLIENTS*.

```
set is ALL_CLIENTS
        owner is SYSTEM
        member is CLIENT
        end
```

Similarly, all employees and all books can be declared members of singular sets *ALL_EMPLOYEES* and *ALL_BOOKS*, respectively.

8.5.8 Area

In the original DBTG proposal the subdivision of a database was called the area. This construct was deleted in the revised version of the proposal since the concept is associated with the physical organization of the data. It would be inappropriate to specify physical details in the schema, which is a logical organization corresponding to the conceptual level.

8.6 Schema and Subschema

The schema is the logical description of the entire database. It includes the names and descriptions of all record types including all the associated data-items and aggregates and all set types including the singular sets. A portion of the schema for the database for the public library is shown below. The data structure diagram for this schema is shown in Figure 8.25. The schema is expressed in a simplified Pascal-like language; some of the details required by the DBTG proposals and its revisions have been omitted for simplicity.

```
Schema name is MUC_Public_Library
    type BRANCH = record
                Br_Name: string;
                Address: string;
                Phone_No: string;
                end
```

Figure 8.25 Data structure diagram for the library schema.

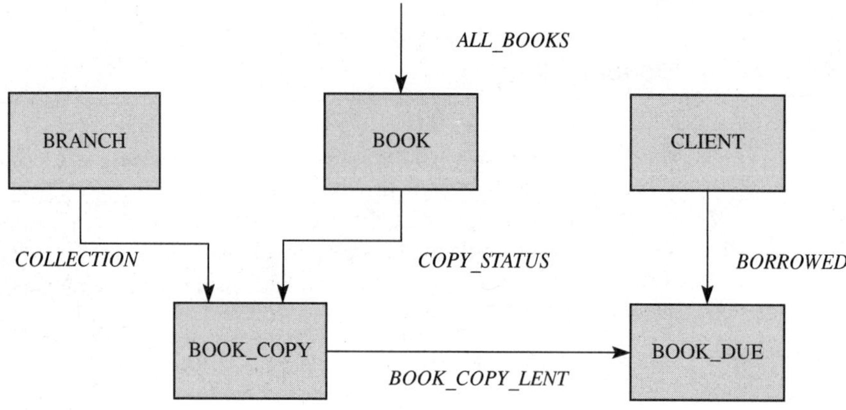


```
type BOOK = record
        Author: string;
        Title; string;
        Call_No: integer;
        end
type BOOK_COPY = record
        Call_No: string;
        Copy_No: integer;
        Branch_Id: string;
        Current_Status: string;
        end
type CLIENT = record
        Client_No: string;
        Name: string;
        Address: string;
        end
type BOOK_DUE = record
        Call_No: string;
        Copy_No: integer;
        Client_No: string;
        Due_Date: string;
        end;
set is BORROWED
        owner is CLIENT
        member is BOOK_DUE automatic mandatory
        end
set is BOOK_COPY_LENT
        owner is BOOK_COPY
        member is BOOK_DUE automatic optional
        end
```

set is COPY_STATUS
owner is BOOKS
member is BOOK_COPY *optional manual*
end
set is ALL_BOOKS
owner is SYSTEM
member is BOOK
end
set is COLLECTION
owner is BRANCH
member is BOOK_COPY *manual optional*
end

The subschema is a subset of the schema and corresponds to the ANSI/SPARC external schema. The subsetting of the schema is achieved by omitting from the subschema one or more data-items in a record, one or more record types, or one or more set types. In addition, aliases could be used for data-items, records, or sets. Furthermore, the data-items in the subschema may be given different data types from those defined for the corresponding data-items in the schema.

8.7 DBTG Data Manipulation Facility

The DBTG proposal included a data manipulation facility or language (DML). The facility included procedural statements, status and currency indicators, special registers, and conditions. The intent was to provide a number of operations or commands that could be embedded in a host language; the proposed host language was COBOL. For discussion here, we use a Pascal-like language as the host language. Before giving the details of the commands we consider some of the concepts used in the DBTG proposals to facilitate the understanding of the operations performed by the DBMS.

8.7.1 Run Unit

Run unit is a DBTG term that refers to each process or task (a program in execution is a process) that is running under the control of the DBMS. The process may be a user's application program containing DML commands or an interactive session with a user. Two or more users' processes may be concurrently executing the same application program or may be in an interactive session via on online terminal under the control of a teleprocessing monitor. The DBMS maintains separate records of the environment of each such run unit. An area of storage is set aside to provide an independent work space for each run unit. This work space is called the **user work area (UWA).** The UWA contains the processing environment of the run unit; the program being executed may be shared.

8.7.2 Currency Indicators

Each run unit must be allowed to access records that are part of the logical structure known to the run unit via its subschema. For each record type known to the run unit, the DBMS maintains a marker to indicate the current record position during the execution of the run unit. These record position markers or pointers are called **currency indicators.**

The DBMS maintains a number of currency indicators for each run unit. For each record type known to the run unit, there is a currency indicator called the **current record of a record type.** The currency indicator for a record type points to the record occurrence of the record type that was most recently referred by the most recent successfully executed DML command. For each set type known to a run unit there is an additional currency indicator called the **current record of a set type.** The currency indicator for the set type points to the record in the set type that was last referred by a successfully completed DML command. The currency indicator for the set type may be pointing to the owner record occurrence or member record occurrence, depending on the operation last performed. In case of a singular set, the null currency indicator for the set implies that the system is the owner. The most recently referred record by the last DML command executed successfully is also indicated by the **current of the run unit.**

The number of currency indicators associated with each run unit is, thus, one more than the number of record types and set types known to the run unit. The currency indicator for a particular set type or record type changes after a successful completion of the DML command that referred it, unless the command specified that one or more indicators remain unchanged.

Any currency indicator may have a null value if no reference to the corresponding record type or set type has been made.

8.7.3 Database Status Registers

In addition to the currency indicators, the DBMS maintains, for each run unit, a number of status indicators for the user's application program. The term used by the DBTG for these indicators is **special registers;** however, in reality these are not hardware registers. These status indicators, being part of the environment of the run unit, are maintained in the work area for the run unit (i.e., the UWA).

- ***DB-Status:*** This is the special register used by the DBMS to store the appropriate database status indicator during the execution of any DML command that refers to the database. The user program can access the DB-Status, but only the DBMS can change it. For our purposes here, we will assume that the DBMS places the value 0 into this register after the successful completion of a DML command. Thus, when the end-of-data condition is encountered during the sequential retrieval of a record type, the value returned in the DB-Status register will be nonzero.
- ***DB-Set-Name:*** When an error is detected during the execution of a DML command that refers to the database, the DBMS uses this register to store the name of the set type involved in the command.

- ***DB-Record-Name:*** This register is used by the DBMS to store the name of the current record type after the unsuccessful execution of a DML command that refers to the database.

8.7.4 Record Templates

The work area for a run unit, in addition to the above, contains storage space for each record type known to the run unit. Thus, for the record type CLIENT known to a run unit, a storage space is reserved in the work area; the name of this storage space is CLIENT. This storage for CLIENT is made up of the space for each data-item declared for the record type in the subschema used by the run unit. The names of the data-items in this space are the corresponding ones in the record type. The application program can use this space as a **record template** for data manipulation.

8.7.5 DML Commands

Here we give a list of DML commands and the operations performed by them. These commands, or a variation of them, are usually available in the DML of many DBMSs based on the DBTG model. We examine the usage of these commands in Section 8.8.

- **Find:** Locates the required occurrence of an existing record.
- **Get:** Accesses a record occurrence specified by the currency indicator of the record and places it into the template area for the record type in the UWA of the run unit.
- **Modify:** Changes or updates the value of one or more data-items in the current record of the run unit.
- **Store:** Causes a record to be stored from the template into the database.
- **Erase:** Destroys or removes one or more records from the database.
- **Connect:** Causes the current record stored in the database to become a member of one or more sets, wherein the record type of the record is defined as a member in the subschema.
- **Disconnect:** Removes the current record of the run unit from one or more sets, resulting in the discontinuance of one or more memberships.
- **Reconnect:** Removes the current record of the specified type from its existing set occurrence of the specified set type and connects it to the current set type.

8.8 Database Manipulation

To illustrate these DML statements we will consider and application program for a clerk at a library circulation desk. He or she is involved in the day-to-day work with only a portion of the database. The application program contains a subschema for

Figure 8.26 Data structure diagram for the subschema.

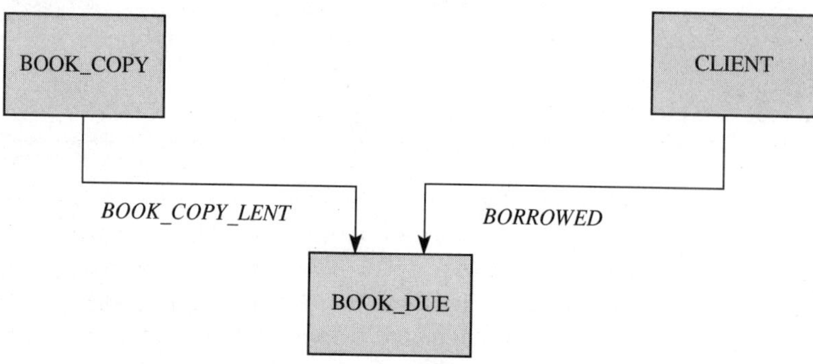

that portion of the database relevant to this user. We give the data structure diagram for this application in Figure 8.26 and the corresponding subschema below.

Subschema name is ***Circulation***
type BOOK_COPY = *record*
Call_No: string;
Copy_No: integer;
Branch_Id: string;
Current_Status: string;
end
type CLIENT = *record*
Client_No: string;
Name: string;
Address: string;
end
type BOOK_DUE = *record*
Call_No: string;
Copy_No: integer;
Client_No: string;
Due_Date: string;
end;
set is BORROWED
owner is CLIENT
member is BOOK_DUE *automatic mandatory*
end
set is BOOK_COPY_LENT
owner is BOOK_COPY
member is BOOK_DUE *automatic optional*
end

The DBTG proposal allows certain differences in the description of data between the schema and subschema, the DBMS performing the required transformation. For our purpose here, we used the same data descriptions as the schema.

Figure 8.27 Database contents.

234	Smith	Lynn
234	Klaf	Revere
236	Allard	Salem

CLIENT

1234	1	234	DEC 1
1237	1	234	DEC 1
1235	1	236	DEC 8
1236	1	236	DEC 11
1234	2	236	DEC 11

BOOK_COPY_LENT

1234	1	Lynn	LENT
1234	2	Revere	LENT
1235	1	Salem	LENT
1236	1	Salem	LENT
1237	2	Lynn	LENT
1237	1	Salem	LENT
1238	1	Lynn	IN
1238	2	Revere	IN
1238	3	Salem	IN

BOOK_COPY

The database contains the information for the records CLIENT, BOOK_COPY, and BOOK_DUE as shown in Figure 8.27

The DBMS maintains a currency indicator for each of the record types and set types and one for the run unit. We give these indicators in the form of a table in Figure 8.28. The initial values of the currency indicators for a run unit that uses the subschema shown above is given in the table. In this case there is one currency indicator for each of the record types BOOK_COPY, CLIENT, and BOOK_DUE; a currency indicator for each of the set types *BORROWED* and *BOOK_COPY_LENT;* in addition, there is an indicator for the run unit. The null values indicate that the database has not been accessed.

Figure 8.28 Initial values for the currency indicator for run unit using subscheme *Circulation.*

Indicator	Current Value
Run unit	null
BOOK_COPY	null
CLIENT	null
BOOK_DUE	null
BORROWED	null
BOOK_COPY_LENT	null

8.8.1 Operations on Records

Locating a Record and Setting the Currency Indicators

The find command is used to set the currency indicators and establish the specific occurrence of a record type for subsequent operations on the database. The DBTG proposal offered seven formats for specifying the record selection in the find command; we will use only a few of these. When a find command is successfully executed, the currency indicators for the run unit, the record type of the record, and the set type in which the record is either an owner or a member are updated. Consequently, the execution of the following statements will change the currency indicators as shown in Figure 8.29. The first statement sets the *Client_No* field of the UWA record template to the value 234 and the second statement locates the record type CLIENT occurrence in the database such that the value of that record occurrence for the data field *Client_No* is 234.

Client_No := 234;
find any CLIENT **using** *Client_No*

Retrieving a Record

Once a record has been located with the find command it could be retrieved using the get command. Therefore, the find command sets the currency indicators; the get command retrieves the data from the database and moves it into the record template in the UWA. To retrieve the address of a client with a *Client_No* of 234, we first locate the record occurrence and then move the data for that record occurrence into the template area for the record type CLIENT by using the get command. The following statements illustrate these operations:

Figure 8.29 Find *Client_No* = 234.

Indicator	Current Value
Run unit	234 Smith
BOOK_COPY	null
CLIENT	234 Smith
BOOK_DUE	null
BORROWED	234 Smith
BOOK_COPY_LENT	null

```
Client_No := 234;
find any CLIENT using Client_No
get CLIENT; (* move values into the scratch area for
                the record type CLIENT in UWA *)
```

Locating and Retrieving Duplicate Records

There could be many records having a given value in a specified data field. These could be located using another format or the find command as shown below.:

find duplicate <record name> **using** <record data-item>

The **duplicate** here indicates that the required record is to have the same value for the specified data-item as the current record of that type for the run unit.

To retrieve all BOOK_COPY at the Lynn branch of the library we could use the following sequence of statements. Here we use the DB_Status register provided by the DBMS in the while loop. As long as the find duplicate command completes itself successfully we execute the statements in the while loop.

```
BOOK_COPY.Branch_Id := Lynn;
find any BOOK_COPY using BOOK_COPY.Branch_Id;
while DB_Status = 0 do
    begin
      get BOOK_COPY;
      (* process the record *)
      find duplicate BOOK_COPY using BOOK_COPY.Branch_Id;
      end;
```

The order in which the records are retrieved in the above example depends on the order in which the records were stored in the database.

Updating a Record

The modify statement is used to update the value of one or more fields of a record. However, the record occurrence to be updated has to be located before the updating operation is performed. To update the value of a data-item in an existing database record, we first locate it using the find command with the clause **for update** to indicate to the DBMS that the record may be modified. It is not necessary to modify a record located with this clause. However, a record located without this clause may not be altered. Once the record occurrence is located, the new values for the fields to be modified are assigned to the corresponding fields in the record template. When this is done, the modify statement is executed to reflect the modification in the stored database.

To extend the loan period of the book with *Call_No* = 1234 borrowed by Smith with a *Client_No* = 234 from 12/1 to 12/11, we could use the following statements:

```
done := false;
Client_No := 234;
find for update any BOOK_DUE using Client_No
```

```
while DB_Status = 0 and not done do
        if Call_No = 1234 then
            begin
              Due_Date := 12/12;
              modify BOOK_DUE;
              done := true;
              end
            else find for update duplicate
                        BOOK_DUE using CLIENT_No;
```

Adding a Record Occurrence

The store command is used to store a new occurrence of a record type in the database. The new occurrence is first created in the template space for the record type in the UWA and then we execute the command:

store <record type>

This method allows a single record occurrence to be created and stored at one time. The following statements add the new CLIENT Gold to the database:

```
CLIENT.Client_No := 237;
CLIENT.Name := 'Gold';
CLIENT.Address := 'Lynn';
store CLIENT;
```

If the new record occurrence belongs to a record type associated with a set type, there must be a mechanism to place the record occurrence in the appropriate set occurrence. We discuss this in Section 8.8.2.

Deleting a Record Occurrence

An existing record occurrence may be deleted from the data base by use of the erase command. However, before the record is deleted, we have to locate it using the find command with the for update clause. As before, this informs the DBMS that the record may be updated, which in this case means deletion. The following statements delete the CLIENT Gold added in the previous example:

```
CLIENT.Client_No := 237;
find for update any CLIENT using CLIENT.Client_No;
if DB_Status = 0 then
          erase CLIENT
     else   error_routine;
```

In this example, we use the **DB_Status** register to verify that the find operation was successfully completed before executing the next statement.

In the case where a record occurrence to be deleted is associated with one or more set occurrences (obviously of different types) as an owner, appropriate operations must be carried out on the members of these sets before the record is deleted. One of the actions could be to move the member record occurrences to other set occurrences of the same set types (if the membership retention status for the member record type is mandatory or optional), or to remove the member record occurrences (if retention status is optional). If these operations are not performed, the DBMS will delete the record and the members of the sets of which the record is an owner would also be deleted or removed from the sets before the actual deletion. The **erase** statement has options that can be included to indicate the extent of deletion to be performed by the DBMS.

8.8.2 Operations on Sets

The DBTG set construct allows related records to be stored as a set. This construct also allows records to be retrieved via their association in one or more set types. A format of the find command can be used to locate the members in a set once we have located the owner record occurrence. Conversely, another format of the find command can be used to locate the owner record occurrence once the member record occurrence has been located.

Locating Records via Sets

To locate a member record occurrence of a member record type in a set, we first locate the appropriate set occurrence by locating the owner record occurrence. Once the owner record occurrence is located, we can locate the first member record occurrence of a given member type by the following format of the find statement:

find first <member record type> **within** <set type>

The following statements locate the first BOOK_DUE by CLIENT 234 in the set occurrence of set type *BORROWED* owned by 234. The first find statement locates the owner record occurrence and also sets the currency indicator for the set type *BORROWED*. The second find statement locates the first member occurrence of the record type BOOK_DUE.

```
CLIENT.Client_No := 234;
find any CLIENT using CLIENT.Client_No;
find first BOOK_DUE within BORROWED;
```

To locate all the books borrowed by the CLIENT 234 we could use the following program segment:

```
CLIENT.CLIENT_No := 234;
find any CLIENT using CLIENT.Client_No;
find first BOOK_DUE within BORROWED;
while DB_Status = 0 do
    begin
      (* process the current member record *)
      find next BOOK_DUE within BORROWED;
    end
```

In this example we located the first member record occurrence by the **find first within** statement and the subsequent member record occurrences using the **find next within** statement. The order in which the members are located depends on the order specified for the insertion of the members in the set definition.

The clerk at the circulation desk, in addition to checking out the books that have been borrowed by a client, can identify the branch from which a particular copy of a book was borrowed. The following program segment locates and retrieves the name of the branch from which client 234 borrowed the first book.

CLIENT.*Client_No* := 234;
find any CLIENT **using** CLIENT.*Client_No;*
find first BOOK_DUE **within** *BORROWED;*
find owner within *BOOK_COPY_LENT;*
get BOOK_COPY;
display ('Branch_Id is', BOOK_COPY.*Branch_Id*);

In this example, we located the first BOOK_DUE, representing the first book borrowed by 234 as before. After locating this book we located its owner in the set *BOOK_COPY_LENT*. The latter owner is an occurrence of the record type BOOK_COPY containing the branch information.

The find first within and the find next within commands for locating members of a set could be used with a singular set in exactly the same manner. However, since there is only one occurrence of a singular set of a given set type and it is owned by the system, there is no need to locate the owner record occurrence before issuing the find first command.

Set Manipulation

The DBTG data manipulation facility proposed a number of operations for manipulating sets. For instance, if a member record type is defined to have manual optional membership in a set type, the user could place a record occurrence of the record record type in a set occurrence. The user could also remove it from a set occurrence and then place it, if required, in another set occurrence at some later time.

For discussion purposes in this section, consider the subschema below, used by a clerk in the acquisition department of the library. The acquisition section of a library procures copies of new or existing books and assigns them to one or more branches; it may also transfer a copy of a book from one branch to another and remove a copy of a book from circulation.

Subschema name is **Acquisition**
    type BOOK = *record*
        Author: string;
        Title: string;
        Call_No: integer;
        end
    type BOOK_COPY = *record*
        Call_No: integer;
        Copy_No: integer;
        Branch_Id: string;
        Current_Status: string;
        end

```
set is COPY_STATUS
        owner is BOOK
        member is BOOK_COPY optional manual
        end
type BRANCH = record
        Br_Name: string;
        Address: string;
        Phone_No: string;
        end
set is COLLECTION
        owner is BRANCH
        member is BOOK_COPY manual optional
        end
```

Manual Set Manipulation

Let us see how to add a new title, *Anne of Green Gables* by Montgomery, to the collection. The steps involved are the following:

1. Add a record occurrence for the new title to the record type BOOK.
2. Add a record occurrence to the record type BOOK_COPY for every copy that is acquired.
3. Insert the newly created occurrences of BOOK_COPY into the *COPY_STATUS* set occurrence, where the newly inserted occurrence of BOOK is the owner.

The first step is performed using the following statements:

```
BOOK.Author := 'Montgomery';
BOOK.Title := 'Anne of Green Gables';
BOOK.Call_No := 1238;
store   BOOK;
```

Assuming that three copies are acquired and that one copy is to be assigned to each of the three branches of the library, the following statements perform this step.

```
BOOK_COPY.Call_No := 1238;
for i := 1 to 3 do
  begin
    BOOK_COPY.Copy_No := i;
    case i of
        1:BOOK_COPY.Branch_Id := 'Lynn';
        2:BOOK_COPY.Branch_Id := 'Revere';
        3:BOOK_COPY.Branch_Id := 'Salem'
        end
    BOOK_COPY.Current_Status := 'in transit';
    store BOOK_COPY;
    end
```

Note: In the above example, we have embedded the DML statements in an application program in a high level language.

At this point the database contains one record occurrence for the new book and three record occurrences, one for each copy of the book. Now we have to place each of these three occurrences of the record type BOOK_COPY in the set type *COPY_STATUS* wherein the owner is BOOK = 1238. The DBTG command to insert a new member into a set occurrence is the connect command, which specifies the record type that has to be inserted into the set type. The currency indicators have been appropriately initialized to point to the correct member record type occurrence and the correct owner record type occurrence.

The following statements insert the members of the record type BOOK_COPY in the set occurrence of the set type *COPY_STATUS* wherein the owner is BOOK = 1238:

```
BOOK.Call_No := 1238;
find any BOOK using BOOK.Call_No;
                (* establish the pointer for the set type
                                 COPY_STATUS *)
BOOK_COPY.Call_No := 1238;
find any BOOK_COPY using BOOK_COPY.Call_No
                retaining currency for COPY_STATUS;
while DB_Status = 0 do
    begin
      connect BOOK_COPY to COPY_STATUS;
      find duplicate BOOK_COPY using
          BOOK_COPY.Call_No
      retaining currency for COPY_STATUS;
      end
```

In the above program segment implementation we used the format of the find statement, which suppresses the updating of the currency indicator for the set type *COPY_STATUS*. Without the **retaining currency** clause, for example, the second find statement would have updated the currency indicator for the set type *COPY_STATUS* to point to the record occurrence of the record type BOOK_COPY. The reason for this is that the record type BOOK_COPY appears as a member of the set type *BOOK_COPY_STATUS* in the subschema.

An alternate method of connecting the record occurrences of the record type, wherein we locate the owner for each insertion, is given below:

```
BOOK.Call_No := 1238;
BOOK_COPY.Call_No := 1238;
find any BOOK_COPY using BOOK_COPY.Call_No;
          (* establish the currency indicator for the
                    record type BOOK_COPY *)
while DB_Status = 0 do
    begin
      find any BOOK using BOOK.Call_No;
      (* establish the currency indicator for the
          set type COPY_STATUS *)
      connect BOOK_COPY to COPY_STATUS;
      find duplicate BOOK_COPY using
          BOOK_COPY.Call_No;
      end
```

The reason we do not use the retaining clause in this case is that the find statement for the record type BOOK will set the currency indicator of the record type BOOK as well as the set type *COPY_STATUS* and run unit. However, it will not update the currency indicator for the record type BOOK_COPY.

We can combine the operation of storing the record occurrence for BOOK_COPY with connecting the occurrence in the appropriate set occurrence in the set type *COLLECTION,* as illustrated by the following program segment:

```
BOOK.Call_No := 1238;
BOOK_COPY.Call_No := 1238;
for i : = 1 to 3 do
  begin
    BOOK_COPY.Copy_No := i;
    case i of
         1:BOOK_COPY.Branch_Id := 'Lynn';
         2:BOOK_COPY.Branch_Id := 'Revere';
         3:BOOK_COPY.Branch_Id := 'Salem'
         end
    BOOK_COPY.Current_Status := 'in transit';
    store BOOK_COPY;
    BRANCH.Br_Name := BOOK_COPY.Branch_Id;
    find any BRANCH using BRANCH.Br_Name;
            (* establish the pointer for the set type
                  COLLECTION *)
    connect BOOK_COPY to COLLECTION;
    end
```

An occurrence of a record type declared in the set definition to be an optional member of a set could be removed using the disconnect statement. However, before this statement is issued the currency indicator for the record type must be updated to point to the specific occurrence of the record type that is to be removed from the set occurrence. The currency indicator of the set type must also be updated to point to the owner record occurrence of the set type wherein the record is a member.

To remove the *Copy_No* = 3 of the book with *Call_No* = 1238 from the set occurrence of the set type *COPY_STATUS,* we could use the following statements:

```
done := false;
BOOK.Call_No := 1238;
find for update any BOOK using BOOK.Call_No;
    (* establish the currency indicator for the set type
        COPY_STATUS *)
find first BOOK_COPY within COPY_STATUS;
    (* now find its member until Copy_No = 3 is found then
        disconnect it *)
while DB_Status = 0 and not done do
    if BOOK_COPY.Copy_No = 3 then
        begin
            disconnect BOOK_COPY from COPY_STATUS;
            done := true;
            end
```

```
        else
          find for update next BOOK_COPY within
            COPY_STATUS;
```

The above program segment removes the record occurrence from the set occurrence, although the record occurrence remains in the database. If we want to delete this record occurrence from the database, we have to issue the erase command after the record is disconnected from the set.

The following example illustrates the disconnection of a record from one set occurrence, followed by its reconnection in another set occurrence; both set occurrences are of the same set type. The program segment enables the acquisition clerk to transfer the *Copy_No* = 3 of the BOOK 1238 from the Salem to the Lynn branch.

```
BOOK.Call_No := 1238;
find any BOOK using BOOK.Call_No;
done := false;
find for update first BOOK_COPY within COPY_STATUS;
while DB_Status = 0 and not done do
    if BOOK_COPY.Copy_No = 3 then
     begin
         done := true;
         BOOK_COPY.Branch_Id := 'Lynn';
         end
     else
        find for update next
         BOOK_COPY within COPY_STATUS;
if done then
    begin
     BRANCH.Br_Name := 'Lynn';
     find any BRANCH using BRANCH.Br Name;
     if DB_Status = 0 then
      reconnect BOOK_COPY to COLLECTION
      else
           error routine 1;
     end
    else
      error routine 2
```

In this example, we first find the correct copy of the book via the set *COPY_STATUS* which has as its owner the occurrence of the record type BOOK with BOOK.*Call_No* = 1238. We locate the member of this set with the for update clause, since we will change the BOOK_COPY.*BRANCH_Id*. Once this member is located, we locate the appropriate owner in the set·*COLLECTION*, which in this case is the record occurrence with BRANCH.*Br_Name* = 'Lynn'. The successful find any BRANCH operation will set the currency indicators for the set type *COLLECTION* as well for the record type BRANCH to point to the BRANCH.*Br_Name* = 'Lynn'. The reconnect operation then removes the BOOK_COPY occurrence from its current owner (Salem branch) and reconnects it to the Lynn branch. We illustrate the need for an error routine to handle the situation in which the DBMS could not locate the appropriate record occurrence. such error routines, when the appropriate data base status registers are not set to their successful values, should be used in any application programs. For simplicity, we have omitted these tests in our discussion.

Automatic Set Manipulations

The sets *BORROWED* and *BOOK_COPY_LENT* have been defined in the schema and subschema with the automatic insertion clause. The retention clause is mandatory for the former set and fixed for the latter one. Thus, a new record occurrence of the record type BOOK_DUE is inserted automatically into the sets *BORROWED* and *BOOK_COPY_LENT* when the occurrence is created using the store operation. To ensure that the newly created record about to be stored is inserted in the correct occurrence(s) of the owner type record(s), the currency indicator(s) for the set type(s) must point to the appropriate owner record occurrence(s).

Suppose CLIENT 234 wants to borrow the newly acquired copy of the book *Anne of Green Gables*. The circulation clerk application program will create a new occurrence of the record type BOOK_DUE in the UWA; locate the record occurrence for the CLIENT and the BOOK_COPY; and then issue the store operation, which will cause the DBMS to automatically connect the new record occurrence of type BOOK_DUE to the two sets. The portion of the application program that performs these operations is given below. Here we first locate the record occurrence of the record type CLIENT with a *Client_No* = 234. Subsequently, the record occurrence of the record type BOOK_COPY is located with the update clause. These two record occurrences will be the owner in the two set occurrences in which a new occurrence of BOOK_DUE will be inserted. We create this new occurrence of the BOOK_DUE in the corresponding record template (assume that **DUE_DATE** is a predefined function that returns the due date). Finally, the new record is inserted in the database with the store statement, which also inserts it in the two sets indicated by the currency indicators.

```
CLIENT.Client_No := 234;
find any CLIENT using CLIENT.Client_No;
BOOK_COPY.Call_No := 1238;
BOOK_COPY.Branch_Id := 'Lynn';
find for update any BOOK_COPY using
                    BOOK_COPY.Call_No,
                        BOOK_COPY. Branch_Id;
BOOK_COPY.Current_Status := 'lent';
BOOK_DUE.Call_No := BOOK_COPY.Call_No;
BOOK_DUE.Copy_No := BOOK_COPY.Copy_No;
BOOK_DUE.Client_No := CLIENT.Client_No;
BOOK_DUE.Date := DUE_DATE;
store BOOK_DUE;
```

The mandatory retention clause for the sets *BORROWED* means that an occurrence of the owner record type CLIENT for the set could not be deleted from the database when it owns a nonempty set occurrence. Translating this into our library example, it means that a client may not discontinue her or his borrowing arrangement (membership) from the library until after returning all the items that were borrowed.

The CLIENT 234 returning the BOOK 1237 would require the circulation clerk to delete the appropriate BOOK_DUE record. The deletion of the record would detach the record from the two set occurrences. In the following application program section, we illustrate the location of the member record occurrence of the record type BOOK_DUE via the set occurrence of the set type *BORROWED* owned by CLIENT 234. We use this member record occurrence of BOOK_DUE in locating the owner record occurrence in the set *BOOK_COPY_LENT* and modify the data-item *Current_Status* of the record type BOOK_COPY. Before issuing the erase instruction we reestablish the currency indicator of the run unit to the record occurrence of BOOK_DUE by locating it as a member in *BOOK_COPY_LENT*.

```
done := false;
CLIENT.Client_No := 234;
find any CLIENT using CLIENT.Client_No;
find first BOOK_DUE within BORROWED;
while DB Status = 0 and not done do
    if BOOK_DUE.Call_No = 1237 then
      done := true
    else find next BOOK_DUE within BORROWED;
if done then
  begin
    find for update owner within BOOK_COPY_LENT;
    BOOK_COPY.CURRENT_Status := in;
    modify BOOK_COPY;
    find for update first BOOK_DUE within BOOK_COPY_LENT;
    disconnect BOOK_DUE from BOOK_COPY_LENT;
    erase BOOK_DUE;
    end
  else
    error routine
```

Deletion of an Owner Record Occurrence

The retention status for the sets BORROWED has been defined as mandatory. An attempt, as shown below, to delete the occurrence of the CLIENT 234, which is the owner of a nonempty set, will fail until all the members in the set are deleted.

```
CLIENT.CLIENT_No := 234;
find for update any Client using CLIENT.Client_No;
erase CLIENT;
```

However, if the retention status for the member record type in the set *BOOK_COPY_LENT* had been defined as fixed, an attempt to delete the occurrence of the owner record type BOOK_COPY (i.e., the record 1237 2 Lynn LENT) would have been successful. When the owner record occurrence is deleted in a set having member record types with the fixed retention status, the member record occurrences will be deleted as well. Furthermore, if the member records are themselves owner of set types with membership retention status fixed, the deletion will be done recursively. The deletion of the member records would have some very undesirable effects if the member record occurrences were members of other set types. In such a case, the preferable action for the DBMS would be to disconnect these member records from the owner record being deleted.

The retention status for the members of the set *BOOK_COPY_LENT* has been defined as optional. An attempt to delete a record occurrence of BOOK_COPY with a nonempty set would be successful. The member record occurrences in the set *BOOK_COPY_LENT* owned by the occurrence of BOOK_COPY are detached from the set occurrence prior to the deletion of the owner. These member record occurrences would continue to exist in the database.

8.9 Concluding Remarks

The NDM as defined in the DBTG was the first formally defined database model and led to the implementation of a large number of DBMSs from commercial software houses. These systems were designed to run on mainframe and midsize computers.

The advantage of the model is that the data structure diagrams give the user a clear pictorial means of understanding the database structure. The sets and the relationships between record types involved in the sets are predefined. These predefined relationships are usually implemented at the physical level with the use of link structure. This results in faster access to related records than is possible in the relational case using a simple join operation to navigate dynamically through the various relations.

The NDM builds indexes on user (DBA) specified key data-items for direct access to records or groups of records. Once one of the owner record occurrences is located by the use of a selection criterion based on a key, the record occurrences of the member record type(s) can be retrieved relatively quickly.

On the minus side, the query language is procedural and requires the user to navigate through the database by specifying sets, owners, and members. This in turn means that the user has to be cognizant of the structure of the database.

Notwithstanding the above, the model continues to be used extensively for corporate databases in many organizations.

With the current interest in the relational approach, a large number of network-based DBMSs are redesigned to offer the user an optional relational interface, thus combining convenience for the user and at the same time avoiding some of the inefficiencies of the relational approach.

8.10 Summary

The network data model represents entities by records and expresses relationships between entities by means of sets implemented by the use of pointers or links. The model allows the representation of an arbitrary relationship. The DBTG proposal places a number of restrictions on the use of the links.

The basic data definition structure of the DBTG proposal includes records and sets. Record types are representations of entity types and are made up of data-items, vectors, and repeating groups.

A set is a means of representing a one-to-many relationship between record types. A set is declared to have one record as the owner record type and one or more records as the member record type. One of the constraints imposed by the DBTG proposal, for ease of implementation, is that a given record occurrence could be an owner or a member in only one occurrence of a set type. This restriction means that a many-to-many relationship can only be represented by introducing an intermediate record type and representing the many-to-many relationships by two one-to-many relationships.

A set type can have an arbitrary number of occurrences. The order of insertions of the members in a set occurrence can be specified. The method of insertion of members can be automatic or manual. The fate of the member record occurrences in the database, when the owner is being deleted, can be specified by the retention clause in the set definition as fixed, mandatory, or optional.

The data manipulation facility of the DBTG proposal uses the concept of currency indicators to keep track of the records involved in the operations. The basic method of initializing the currency indicators and identifying records and sets is by means of the find command. Having initialized the currency indicator, other operations like connect, disconnect, erase, get, modify, reconnect, and store can be executed to manipulate the data.

Key Terms

network data model (NDM)
intersection record
connection record
cycle
single-level cycle
multilevel cycle
loop
data-item
data aggregate
vector
repeating group
DBTG set
order first
order last
order next
order prior
sorted
system default
automatic
manual
fixed
mandatory
optional
structural constraint
set selection
singular set
system
run unit
user work area (UWA)
currency indicator
current record of a record type
current record of a set type
current of the run unit
special register
record template
find
get
modify
store
erase
connect
disconnect
reconnect
duplicate
for update
find first within
find next within
retaining currency

Exercises

8.1 A school board or district has a number of schools under its jurisdiction. Each school has students and teachers. Teachers have certain qualifications and may have taught in other schools. Some teachers can teach in more than one school; however, a student attends only one school. Show how you would model the school system using the network model.

8.2 A school board has a number of committees. The members of the committees are the teachers and the parents of the students in the school system. Teachers are parents too, and their children attend school. Add parents and committees to the school system you modeled in Exercise 8.1.

8.3 Could you have cycles in the network implementation of the school system discussed in Exercises 8.1 and 8.2? Give examples if there are any.

8.4 Consider the *ENROLLMENT* relationship of Figure A between student and course, where *grade* is the grade of a student in a particular course. Model this relationship using the network model.

Figure A A relationship between STUDENT and COURSE.

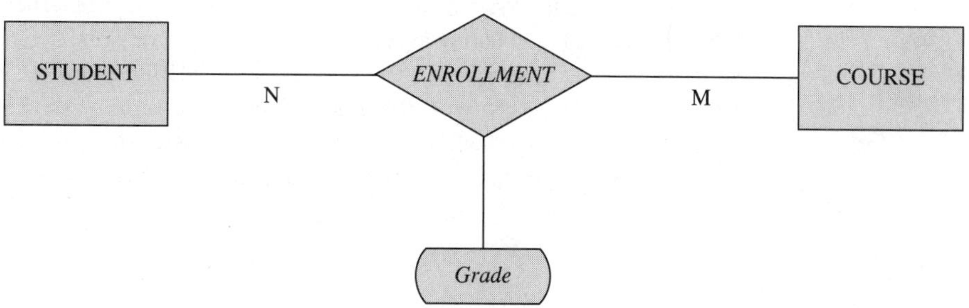

8.5 Write the schema for the school system described in Exercise 8.1.

8.6 Write the following queries for the school system of Exercise 8.1:

(a) Find all the teachers who teach in Riverdale High School.
(b) Find all schools where teacher Joe Doe teaches.

8.7 Consider the relations defined below:

SUPPLIER(*Supplier#,Company_Name,City*)
PARTS(*Part#,Weight*)
SUPPLY_PARTS(*Supplier#,Part#*)
PROJECTS(*Project#,Part#,Quantity*)
ORDERS(*Part#,Supplier#,Date_of_Delivery*)

Construct the corresponding network model and write the schema for the model. Use the schema description to write the following queries using the DML described in this chapter:

(a) Find all parts supplied by $supplier_1$.
(b) Find the cities where $supplier_1$ is located.
(c) Find another supplier who supplies at least one part supplied by $supplier_1$.
(d) Find all the projects for which $supplier_1$ might supply.
(e) Find all suppliers who can supply $part_1$.
(f) Find all projects where $part_1$ is used.

8.8 Which of the following statements are true for the network model?

(a) A record type can be both an owner and member in the same set type.
(b) A record type can be both an owner and member in the same set occurrence.
(c) A record type cannot be an owner in more than one set type.

(d) A set occurrence is empty when it has no member record occurrences.
(e) A set type can have only one record type as its member.
(f) A set can represent only a certain relationship between entities; however, not all possible relationships between entities can be conveyed through a set.
(g) Data independence and data integrity suffer due to the set concept.

8.9 Consider a network database with a schema corresponding to the data structure diagram of Figure 8.22, where all the sets have an automatic fixed membership status. Can data ever be inserted in such a database? Amplify your answer with adequate explanations.

8.10 Draw the data structure diagram of the complete library database system discussed in this chapter and comment on the statement that it is a purely hierarchical structure.

8.11 Consider the database for the UHL that we discussed in Chapter 2. Let us add to the database the requirement of keeping the statistics on the performance of the various lineups during a season. This extension is illustrated in Figure B. A lineup is the group of players from a franchise that plays together for certain shifts during a game. There can be a number of different lineups used during a game and lineups may change from game to game during a season. Here we have added the intersection record LINEUP and the sets P_L and Fr_L. Thus, the relationship between a player and lineup is one to many; similarly the relationship between a lineup and the franchise is also one to many. Give the modified schema for the database and write a pseudocode program to find the best lineup for each player.

Figure B Extended network model for UHL database.

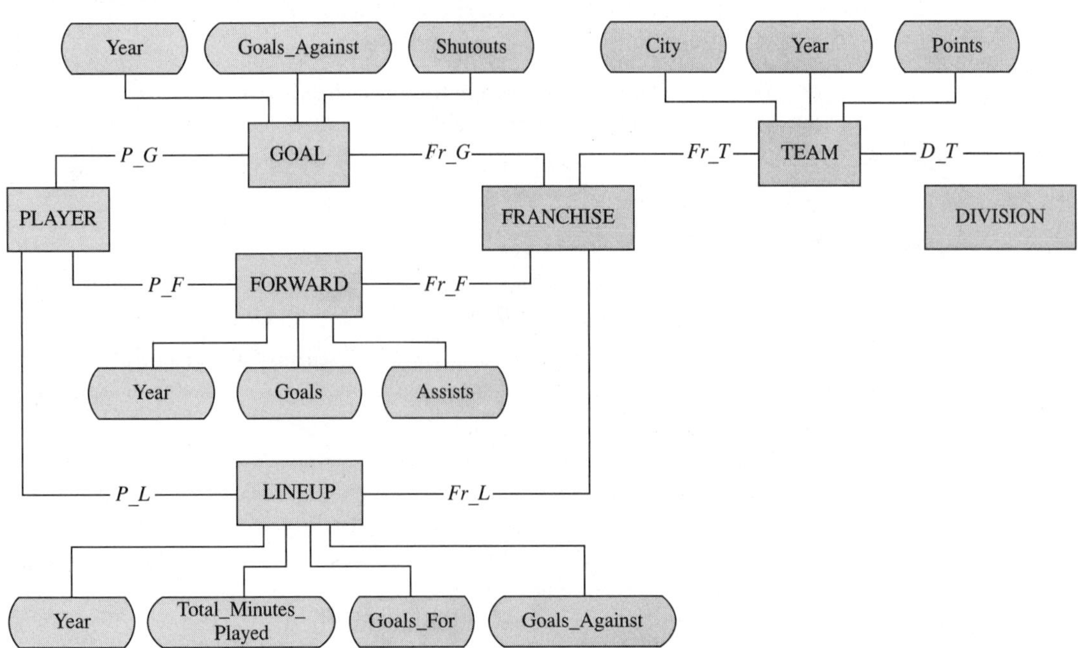

8.12 The following is an incomplete list of DBMSs marketed by various software houses. The names are registered trademarks of the respective companies. Choose one of these DBMSs and describe it in terms of the generalized features described in this chapter.

DBMS	Digital Equipment Corp.
DMS–11	Unisys
DMS–90	Unisys
DMS–1100	Unisys
IDMS	Cullinet
IDS II	Honeywell
IMAGE	Hewlett-Packard
TOTAL	Cincom

Bibliographic Notes

Several commercial database management systems based on what was to be the network approach were implemented in the late 1960s. The DBTG proposal evolved from these systems. The system that had the most influence on the proposal was the Integrated Data Store (IDS) system at General Electric (Bach 64). The IDS was the result of Bachman's early work and was developed under his supervision. Bachman is also credited with developing the data structure diagram for representing records and links used in the network data model (Bach 69). The data structure diagram, like the more recent E–R diagram, is an aid in the logical design of a database system.

The Database Task Group (DBTG) was set up as a special group within CODASYL. The DBTG group issued a final report in 1971 and this was the first standard specification for a database system. A number of commercial database management systems were based on this report. However, it has not been accepted as a standard by ANSI (American National Standards Institute). The DBTG was reconstituted as the Data Description Language Committee (DDLC), which produced a revised version of the scheme data description language (DDL). The ANSI-X3H2 committee received this report, modified it to some extent, and issued the 1981 DDL draft. This, too, has not been accepted to date because the draft lacks a data manipulation language to go with the DDL. In 1984, the X3H2 committee proposed NDL, a standard network database language based on the original DBTG specification. This too has yet to be standardized.

The DBTG proposal is discussed in the CODASYL DBTG 1971 report (CODA 71) and by Olle (Olle 78). Modifications to the original proposal and the DDL are presented in (Coda 78).

Since the DBTG proposal of 1971 there have been various modifications, not only by standards committees but also by software houses offering commercial DBMSs based on this model. Some examples are the DMS-1100 from Unisys (previously called Sperry Univac and which recently has merged with Burroughs) (Sper), TOTAL from Cincom (Cinc), and IDS II from Honeywell (Hone). Some of these systems are discussed in textbooks by Cardenas (Card 85), Date (Date 86), Kroenke (Kroe 83), Tsichritzis and Lochovsky (Tsic 77), and Ullman (Ullm 82).

Bibliography

(Bach 64) C. W. Bachman & S. S. Williams, ''A General Purpose Programming System for Random Access Memories,'' Proc. of the Fall Joint Computer Conference, vol 26. AFIPS Press, 1964, pp. 411–422.

(Back 69) C. W. Bachman, ''Data Structure Diagrams,'' *Journal of the ACM SIGBDP* 1(2), March 1969, pp. 4–10.

(Bach 73) C. W. Bachman, ''The Programmer as a Navigator,'' *CACM* 16(11), November 1973, pp. 653–658.

(Card 85) A. F. Cardenas, *Data Base Management Systems,* 2nd ed. Boston, MA: Allen and Bacon, 1985.

(Cinc) Reference manuals on TOTAL data base management systems available from Cincom Systems, Cincinnati, Ohio.

(Coda 71) CODASYL Date Base Task Group, April 1971 Report, ACM. New York: 1971.

(Coda 71) CODASYL Data Description Language Journal of Development, Dept. of Supply and Services, Ottawa, Ontario, 1978.

(Date 86) C. J. Date, *An Introduction to Database Systems,* vol. 1, 4th ed. Reading, MA: Addison-Wesley, 1986.

(Hone) Reference manuals on IDS II available from Honeywell Information Systems, Waltham, MA.

(Kroe 83) D. Kroenke, *Database Processing,* 2nd ed. Science Research Associates, Chicago, IL., 1983.

(Olle 78) T. W. Olle, *The Codasyl Approach to Data Base Management*. Chichester, England: Wiley Interscience, 1978.

(Sper) Reference manuals on Data Management System (DMS) 1100 for the Univac 1100 available from Sperry Univac, Blue Bell, PA.

(Tsic 77) D. C. Tsichritzis & F. H. Lochovsky, *Data Base Management Systems*. New York: Academic Press, 1977.

(Ulla 82) J. D. Ullman, *Principles of Database Systems,* 2nd ed. Rockville, MD: Computer Science Press, 1982.

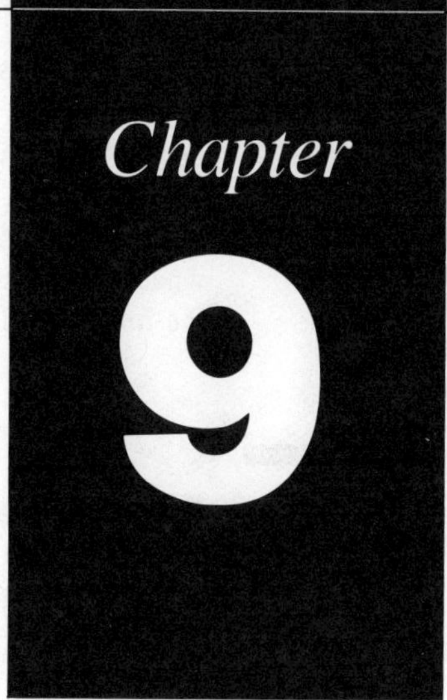

The Hierarchical Data Model

Contents

Like the network data model, the hierarchical data model uses records and pointers or links to represent entities and the relationships among them. However, unlike the network data model, the data structure used is a rooted tree with a strict parent-to-child ordering. We are not going to concentrate on any one of the commercially available DBMSs based on the hierarchical model, although the discussion is somewhat oriented toward features included in IBM's IMS database management system, the most prominent system of this type.

9.1 The Tree Concept

Trees in the form of a family tree or genealogical tree trace the ancestry of an individual and show the relationships among the parents, children, cousins, uncles, aunts, and siblings. A tree is thus a collection of nodes. One node is designated as the root node; the remaining nodes form trees or subtrees.

An **ordered tree** is a tree in which the relative order of the subtrees is significant. This relative order not only signifies the vertical placement or level of the subtrees but also the left to right ordering. Figures 9.1a and b give two examples of ordered trees with **R** as the root node and **A, B,** and **C** as its children nodes. Each of the nodes **A, B,** and **C,** in turn, are root nodes of subtrees with children nodes **(D, E), (F),** and **(G, H, J),** respectively. The significance in the ordering of the subtrees in these diagrams is discussed below.

Traversing an ordered tree can be done in a number of ways. The order of processing the nodes of the tree depends on whether or not one processes the node before the node's subtree and the order of processing the subtrees (left to right or right to left). The usual practice is the so-called **preorder traversal** in which the node is processed first, followed by the leftmost subtree not yet processed, as shown below:

```
Procedure Preorder (node);
    process node
    left_child := leftmost child node not processed yet
    while left_child ≠ null do
        begin
            Preorder (left_child)
            left_child := leftmost child node not
                              processed yet
            end
    end
```

The preorder processing of the ordered tree of Figure 9.1a will process the nodes in the sequence **R, A, D, E, B, F, C, G, H, J.**

The significance of the ordered tree becomes evident when we consider the sequence in which the nodes could be reached when using a given tree traversing strategy. For instance, the order in which the nodes of the hierarchical tree of Figure 9.1b are processed using the preorder processing strategy is not the same as the order for Figure 9.1a, even though the tree of part b contains the same nodes as the tree of part a.

Figure 9.1 Ordered tree where (c) illustrates hierarchical pointers and (d) illustrates child/sibling pointers.

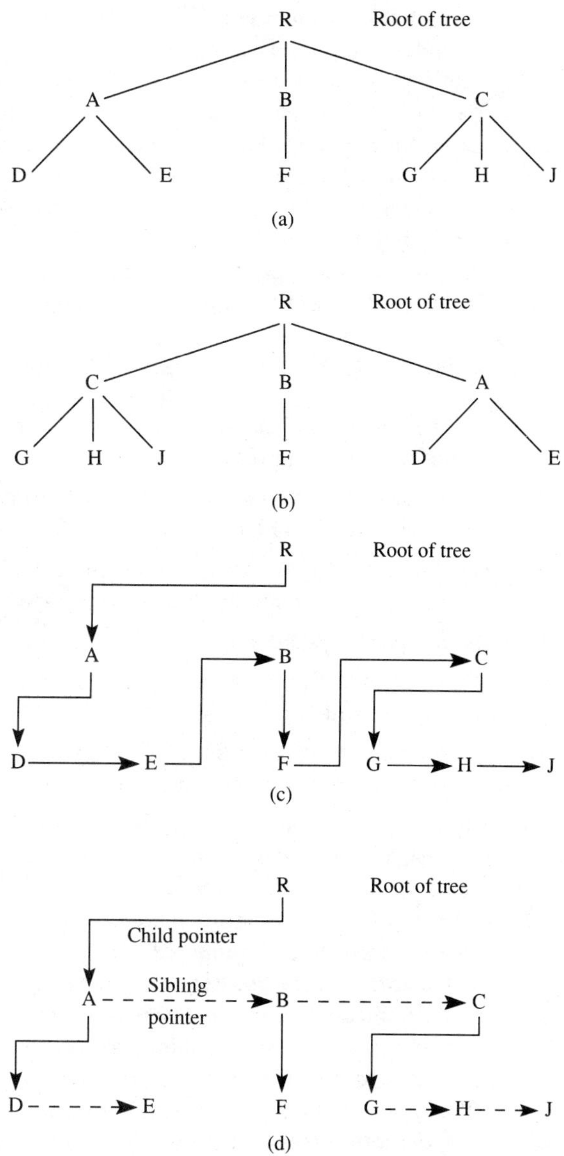

Two distinct methods can be used to implement the preorder sequence in the ordered tree. The first method, shown in Figure 9.1c uses hierarchical pointers to implement the ordered tree of part a. Here the pointer in each record points to the next record in the preorder sequence. The second method, shown in part d uses two types of pointers, the **child** and the **sibling pointers.** The child pointer is used to point to the leftmost child and the sibling pointer is used to point to the right sibling. The siblings are nodes that have the same parent and the right sibling of a node is the sibling that is immediately to the right of the node in question.

9.2 Hierarchical Data Model

The **hierarchical data model (HDM)** uses the tree concept to represent data and the relationship among data. The nodes of the tree are the record types representing the entity sets and are connected by pointers or links. The relationship between the entities is represented by the structure of the resulting ordered tree. A pointer or link as in the network data model represents a relationship between exactly two records. However, in the hierarchical model this relationship, as in the genealogical tree, is that of a parent and child. Furthermore, the hierarchical data model restricts each record type to only one parent record type. A parent record type can have any number of children record types. Two record types in a hierarchical tree can have at most one relationship between them and this relationship is that of one-to-one or one-to-many.

The hierarchical data model has the following constraints:

- Each hierarchical tree can have only one root record type and this record type does not have a parent record type.
- The root can have any number of child record types, each of which can itself be a root of a hierarchical (sub-) tree.
- Each child record type can have only one parent record type; thus a many-to-many relationship cannot be directly expressed between two record types.
- Data in a parent record applies to all its children records.
- Each occurrence of a record type can have any number of occurrences of each of its child record types.
- A child record occurrence must have a parent record occurrence; deleting a parent record occurrence requires deleting all its children record occurrences.
- A hierarchical tree can have any number of record occurrences for each record type at each level of the hierarchical tree.

In the implementation of the hierarchical data model the pointers are normally from a parent record to a child record only.

The hierarchical database can be represented using a structure similar to the data structure diagram used in the network data model. The records are represented by rectangular boxes and the relationships between records are represented by arcs pointing from a root toward the leaf. The arcs are not labeled, since the relationship is always that of a parent and a child. Such structure diagrams are called **tree structure diagrams, definition trees,** or **hierarchical definition trees.**

Figure 9.2 gives the E-R diagram of a part of the library example discussed earlier in Chapter 8. Figure 9.3 represents the hierarchical definition tree for the library database organized as a rooted tree with the root node being the record type LIBRARY. The relationship that can be represented by the tree is either one to one or one-to-many. In Figure 9.3 the parent record type BOOK of the hierarchical tree type *BOOK_TREE* has the child record type BOOK_COPY. The parent record type CLIENT of the hierarchical tree type *CLIENT_TREE* has BOOK_DUE as its child record type. The parent record type BRANCH of the hierarchical tree type *BRANCH_TREE* has the children record types DEPT_SECTION and EMPLOYEE.

Figure 9.2 E-R diagram for the library example.

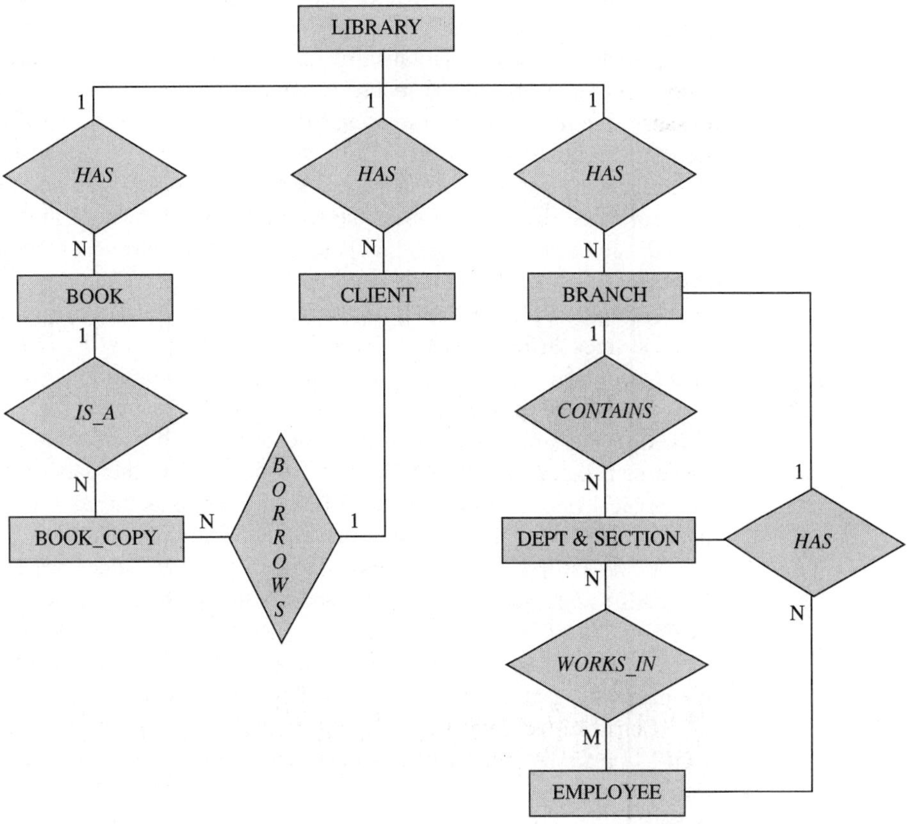

Figure 9.3 Library database using the hierarchical model.

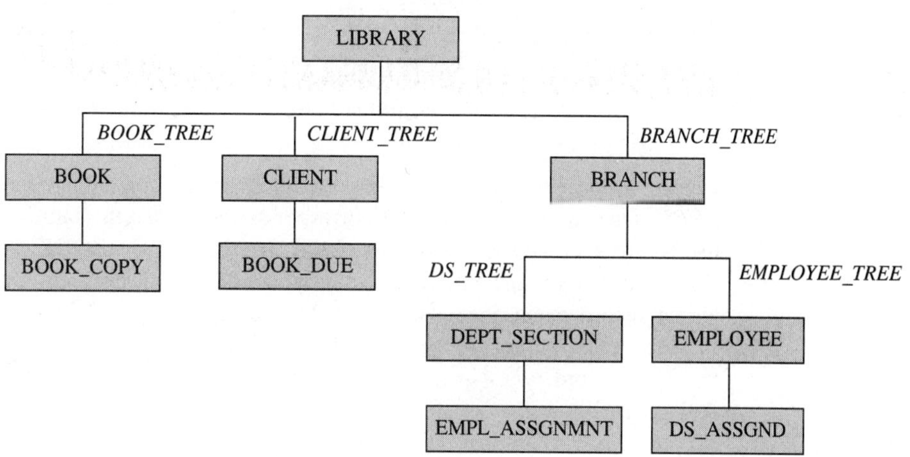

The record types DEPT_SECTION and EMPLOYEE in turn are the parents of the record types EMPL_ASSGNMNT (employee assignment) and *DS_ASSGND* (department or section assigned to), respectively. (Some instances of these hierarchical trees are given in Figures 9.4, 9.5 and 9.6.)

A many-to-many relationship can only be represented in the hierarchical data model by replication of the record concerned or by the use of **virtual records.** For instance, the many-to-many relationships between a BOOK and CLIENT or between DEPT_SECTION and EMPLOYEE, which were represented in the network model by introducing an intermediate record type and two sets, are represented in the hierarchical model by replication of the records or by the use of virtual records. Virtual records are basically pointers that point to the actual physical records in the database. We discuss virtual records in Section 9.2.1.

In Figure 9.3, LIBRARY is a dummy parent that holds together the three hierarchical trees *BOOK_TREE, CLIENT_TREE,* and *BRANCH_TREE.* A DBMS on a given computer system belonging to a library is supporting that library system, so there is no need to actually store a single occurrence of the record type LIBRARY. However, these disjointed trees can be considered to be connected to a single occurrence of the dummy LIBRARY node, and therefore the database contains a single hierarchical tree with this dummy LIBRARY node as the root node. Traversing this tree becomes equivalent to going through the entire database.

If the DBMS were to support the data for more than one library system, the LIBRARY node would actually exist and would form the root node of the subtrees *BOOK TREE, CLIENT_TREE,* and *BRANCH_TREE.* In this case, we would have a forest of trees and for each library system supported by the DBMS, there would exist in the database a tree with the corresponding library node as the root node.

Consider the following definitions for the record types BOOK and BOOK_COPY for the records in the first hierarchical tree, *BOOK_TREE:*

```
type BOOK = record
            Author: string;
            Title: string;
            Call_No: string;
            end

type BOOK_COPY = record
            Call_No: string;
            Copy_No: integer;
            Branch_Id: string;
            Current_Status: string;
            end
```

In Figure 9.4, we give some instances of the hierarchical trees for *BOOK_TREE.* One instance of the tree corresponds to the parent (James Munich 1231) of the record type BOOK; it has its child, the record type BOOK_COPY occurrence (1231 Copy 1 Lynn Lent). Another instance of this hierarchical tree consists of the parent record occurrence (Hugo Les Miserables 1234) and its two children record occurrences of the record type BOOK_COPY.

The record types in the second hierarchy with the root node CLIENT can be defined as follows:

Figure 9.4 Occurrences of *BOOK_TREE* hierarchical tree.

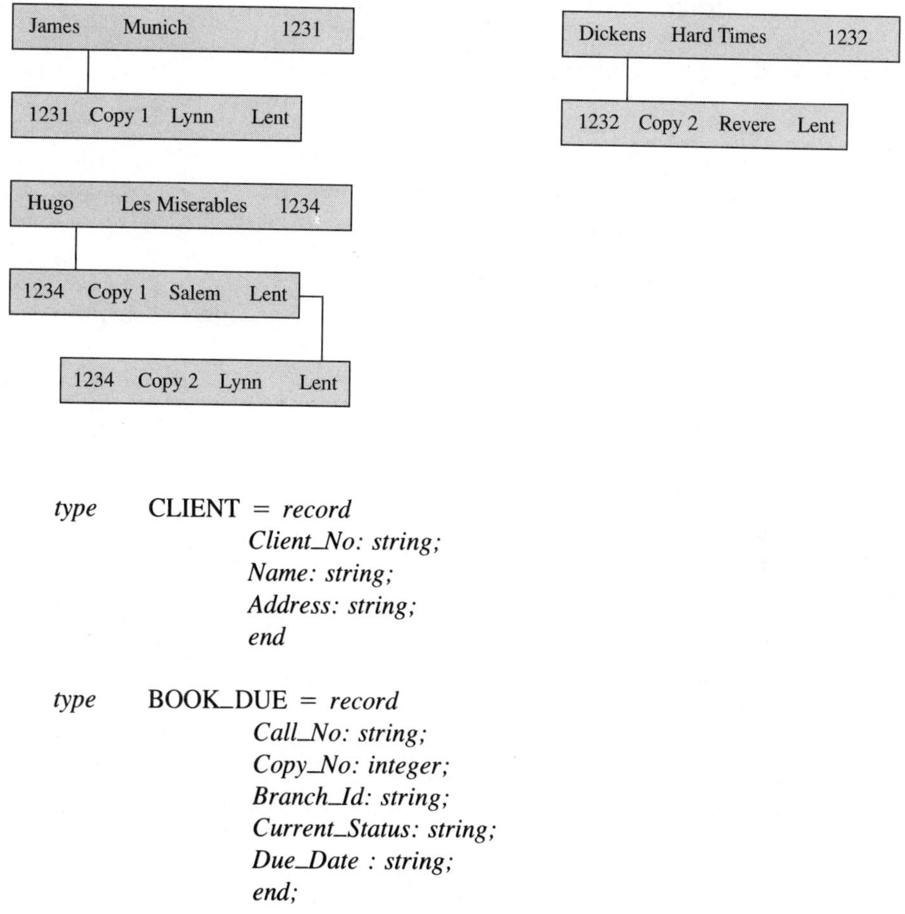


```
type    CLIENT = record
                Client_No: string;
                Name: string;
                Address: string;
                end

type    BOOK_DUE = record
                Call_No: string;
                Copy_No: integer;
                Branch_Id: string;
                Current_Status: string;
                Due_Date : string;
                end;
```

Figure 9.5 gives two occurrences of this hierarchy. The first tree corresponds to the CLIENT Smith who has borrowed two *BOOKs* with *Call_Nos* 1231 and 1234 with the *Due_Dates* of 12/06 and 12/15, respectively.

Figure 9.5 Occurrences of *CLIENT_TREE* hierarchical tree.

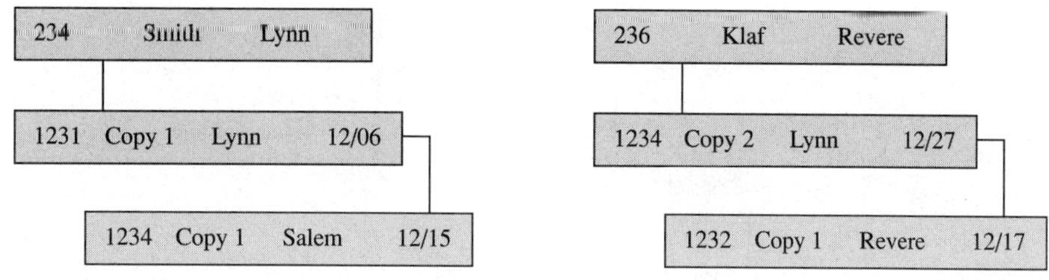

Consider the following definitions for the record types BRANCH, DEPT_SECTION, and EMPLOYEE in the hierarchical definition tree having BRANCH as the parent record type:

type BRANCH = *record*
Br_Name: string;
Address: string;
Phone_No: string;
end

type DEPT_SECTION = *record*
Ds_Name: string;
Room_No: string;
Phone_No: string;
end

type EMPLOYEE = *record*
Emp_Name: string;
Home_Address: string;
Phone_No: string;
end

Some instances of this hierarchical tree are given in Figure 9.6. For example, the Lynn branch has the following departments and sections: (DEPT_SECTION) Adult Sec (Adult Section), Child Sec (Children's Section), Acqstn Dept (Acquisition

Figure 9.6 Occurrences of BRANCH_TREE hierarchical tree.

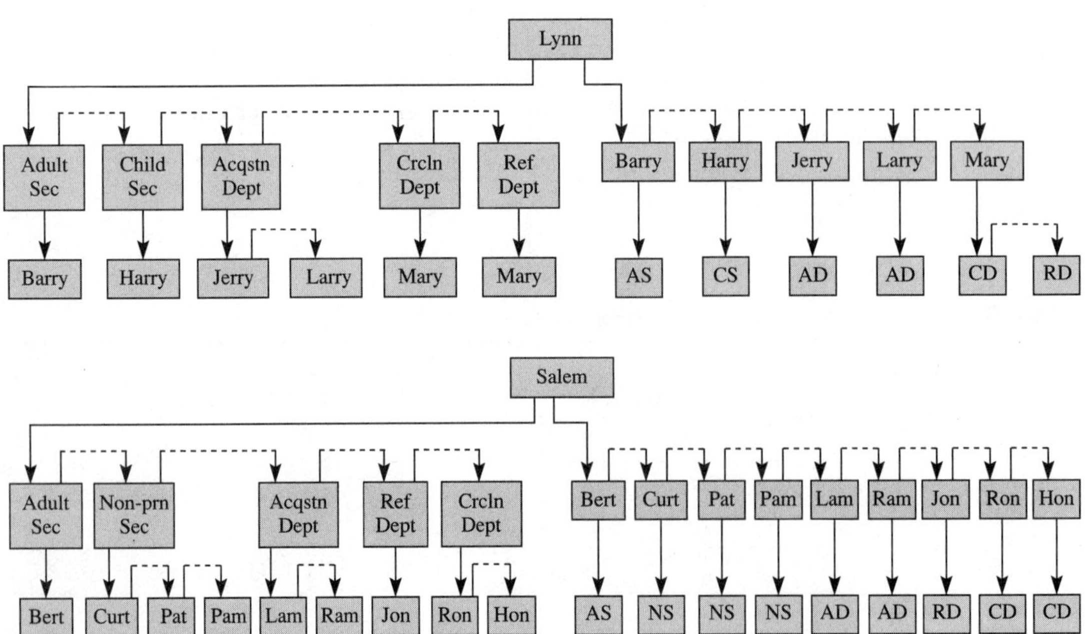

Department), Crcln Dept (Circulation Department), Ref Dept (Reference Department) and its employees (EMPLOYEE) are Barry, Harry, Jerry, Larry, and Mary. In Figure 9.6 we also show that the Lynn branch has Child Sec as one of its DEPT_SECTION. The Employee Harry is the instance of the record type EMPL_ASSGNMNT assigned to the Child_Sec. Similarly, employee Mary works in the Crcln Dept (CD) and Ref Dept (RD). We discuss the method of implementing the hierarchical subtrees *DS_TREE* and *EMPLOYEE_TREE* and the record types EMPL_ASSGNMNT and DS_ASSGND in Section 9.2.3.

9.2.1 Replication vs. Virtual Record

The hierarchical model, like the network model, cannot support a many-to-many relationship directly. In the network model the many-to-many relationship is implemented by introducing an intermediate record and two one-to-many relationships. The fact that a given employee may be assigned to more than one department during a work week is one instance of a many-to-many relationship in our library database. In the hierarchical model, the many-to-many relationship can be expressed using one of the following methods: **replication** or virtual record. When more than one employee works in a given department, then for the hierarchical tree with EMPLOYEE as the root node we have to replicate the record for the department and have this replicated record attached as a child to the corresponding occurrence of the EMPLOYEE record type. For example, in Figure 9.6 the Non_print Sec, shown as NS, is replicated and each of the replicated record occurrences becomes a child of the EMPLOYEE record occurrence for employees Curt, Pat, and Pam working in that DEPT_SECTION of the Salem branch. Similarly, if employee Mary is assigned to work in the Circulation department as well as the Reference department of the Lynn branch, the replication method would require that the record occurrence for the employee Mary is duplicated and one of these duplicate copies is included in the hierarchical tree occurrence of each of the departments mentioned above.

Replication of data would mean a waste of storage space and could lead to data inconsistencies when some copies of replicated data are not updated. The other method of representing the many-to-many relationship in the hierarchical data model is to use an indirect scheme similar to the network approach. In the hierarchical model the solution is to use the so-called virtual record. A virtual record is essentially a record containing a pointer to an occurrence of an actual physical record type. This physical record type is called the **logical parent** and the virtual record is the **logical child.** Each virtual record type has exactly one physical record type as its physical parent and one physical record type as its logical parent. In some cases, the virtual record is used to contain some information common to the relationship between the virtual record's logical and physical parents. This information is called the **intersection data.** The intersection data is concatenated with the information from the logical parent, which is an actual physical record indicated by the pointer in the virtual record. This concatenated information is made available to the user of the hierarchical database system. The virtual record scheme provides the hierarchical model with limited network capabilities; however, the data retrieval operations are basically of a hierarchical nature. For retrieval operations the user or the application program treats the database as though the virtual records are actual replications of the relevant logical parents.

9.2.2 Expressing a Many-to-Many Relationship

Let us consider the method that we can use to express the relationship between BOOK and CLIENT. As we discussed in Section 8.1.1 this is a many-to-many relationship because the library may have more than one copy (BOOK_COPY) of a given title. However, since only one client can borrow a given copy at a given time, the relationship between a CLIENT and a BOOK_COPY is one-to-one.

In the network model we converted the many-to-many relationship between BOOK and CLIENT into a one-to-many set between BOOK and BOOK_COPY. We then introduced an intermediate record BOOK_DUE to hold the common data between CLIENT and BOOK_COPY and the two one-to-one sets between CLIENT and BOOK_DUE and BOOK_COPY and BOOK_DUE.

In the hierarchical model we can easily express the one-to-many relationship between BOOK and BOOK_COPY as a hierarchy that can be represented by a tree as follows:

```
tree is BOOK_TREE
            BOOK is parent
            BOOK_COPY is child
            end
```

Examples of this hierarchical tree are shown in Figure 9.4.

Similarly, we can express the one-to-many relationship between a client and the items she or he borrows by a hierarchical tree *CLIENT_TREE* as follows:

```
tree is CLIENT_TREE
            CLIENT is parent
            BOOK_DUE is child
            end
```

Examples of this hierarchical tree are shown in Figure 9.5.

Suppose the relationship between a BOOK_COPY and a CLIENT who borrows it is expressed by replication as shown in Figures 9.4 and 9.5. The data in BOOK_DUE, except for *Due_Date,* is a duplication of the corresponding data in BOOK_COPY. If a virtual record is used for BOOK_DUE, we could indicate this by the following definition:

```
type  BOOK_DUE = record
            {Call_No: string;
             Copy_No: integer;
             Branch_Id: string;
             Current_Status: string;}
                virtual of logical parent
                     BOOK_COPY in BOOK_TREE;
              Due_Date: string;
            end
```

This indicates that the data items enclosed in the brackets of the record BOOK_DUE are virtual and are derived from the physical record BOOK_COPY, which is defined as the logical parent of the record BOOK_DUE, BOOK_DUE being its logical child. The data item *Due_Date* in this case is the intersection data in the rela-

Figure 9.7 Using virtual records.

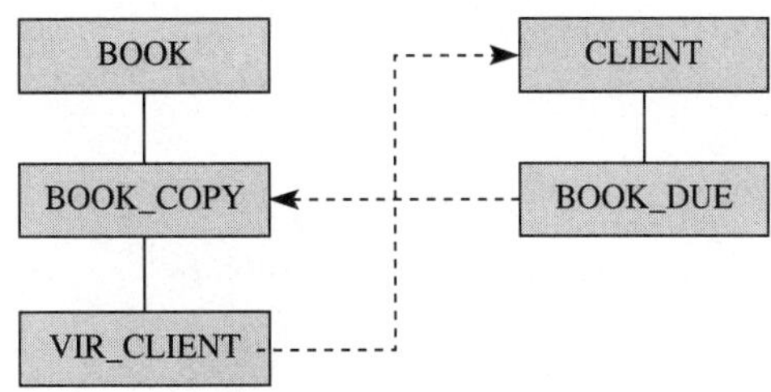

tionship between CLIENT and BOOK_COPY. Note that in the above example, the virtual record type BOOK_DUE in the hierarchical tree *CLIENT_TREE* contains data that is derived from a separate physical hierarchical tree, namely *BOOK_TREE*.

Similarly, to keep track of which CLIENT has borrowed a given BOOK_COPY, we can introduce a virtual record type VIR_CLIENT and a one-to-one relationship *BOOK_COPY_TREE* between BOOK_COPY and VIR_CLIENT as follows:

tree is BOOK_COPY_TREE
BOOK_COPY *is parent*
VIR_CLIENT *is child*
end

type VIR_CLIENT = *record*
{ *Client_No: string;*
Name: string;
Address: string;}
virtual of logical parent CLIENT *in CLIENT_TREE;*
end

Figure 9.7 now includes the modified section of the hierarchical structure diagram of Figure 9.3, showing the many-to-many relationship between BOOK and CLIENT.

The problem with this hierarchy is that to determine the author and title, etc., of the volumes borrowed by client Smith, we have to go through the following inefficient series of operations:

- Go from the required occurrence of the record type CLIENT to the first occurrence of its child record type BOOK_DUE.
- Follow the pointer to the logical parent of BOOK_DUE to an occurrence of BOOK COPY and note the *Call_No*.
- Search the occurrences of BOOK with the same *Call_No* and retrieve the details pertaining to the *Author,* etc.
- Repeat for each child occurrence of BOOK_DUE belonging to Smith.

Such queries can be handled more efficiently if we add another dependent record to *CLIENT_TREE,* such as VIR_BOOK, defined to be virtual of the logical parent BOOK as follows on the next page.

tree is CLIENT_TREE
CLIENT *is parent*
BOOK_DUE *is child*
VIR_BOOK *is child*
end

type VIR_BOOK = *record*
{*Author: string;*
Title: string;
Call_No: string;}
virtual of logical parent BOOK *in BOOK_TREE*
end

We thus establish a logical relationship directly to the BOOK physical record and the details about the volumes could be directly accessible from the logical parent occurrence of the record type. The final modified hierarchical structure diagram for the relationship between BOOK and CLIENT is shown in Figure 9.8

9.2.3 Another Example of a Many-to-Many Relationship

Consider the E-R diagram of Figure 9.9 which shows a many-to-many relationship between DEPT_SECTION and EMPLOYEE. Suppose that the database is required to respond efficiently to queries of the type:

FIND ALL EMPLOYEES IN DEPARTMENT A.
FIND ALL DEPARTMENTS WHERE EMPLOYEE X WORKS.

To respond to symmetrical queries of the above type efficiently, we express the many-to-many relationship between DEPT_SECTION and EMPLOYEE in the hierarchical model using virtual records. The hierarchical structure diagram corresponding to the E-R diagram of Figure 9.9 is shown in Figure 9.10, where EMPL_ASSGNMNT and DS_ASSGND are virtual records with logical parents EMPLOYEE and DEPT_SECTION respectively.

The tree *DS_TREE* has as its root node the record type DEPT_SECTION and has as its child record a virtual record EMPL_ASSGNMNT. The virtual record

Figure 9.8 Relationships between BOOK and CLIENT.

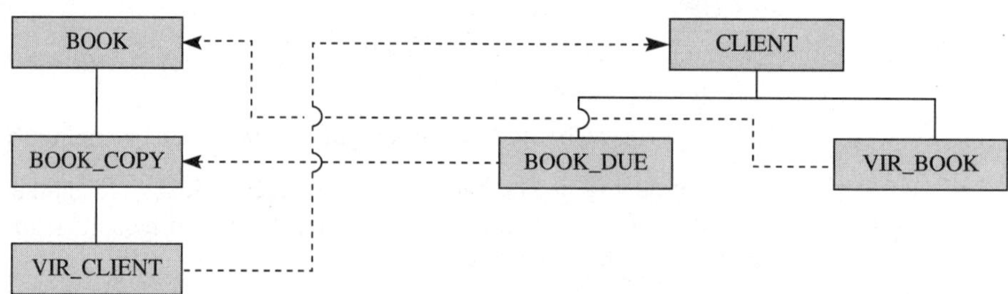

Figure 9.9 Relationship between DEPT_SECTION and EMPLOYEE.

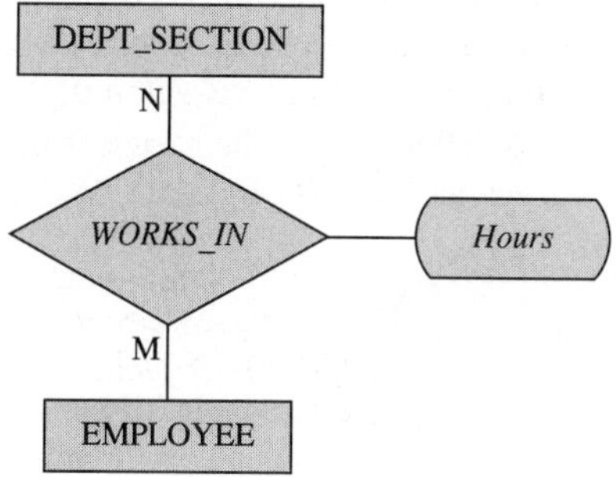

EMPL_ASSGNMNT is a logical child of the record type EMPLOYEE, which is its logical parent. This virtual record contains the intersection data *Hours,* which represents the hours worked during a work week by the employee for a given DEPT_SECTION. The tree *DS_TREE* and its parent and child record types are defined below.

```
tree is DS_TREE
            DEPT_SECTION is parent
            EMPL_ASSGNMNT is child
            end

type DEPT_SECTION = record
            Ds_Name: string
            Room_No: string:
            Phone_No: string
            end

type EMPL_ASSGNMNT = record
            {Emp_Name: string;
            Phone_No: string;}
            virtual of logical parent
              EMPLOYEE in BRANCH_TREE
            Hours: integer;
            end
```

The tree *EMPLOYEE_TREE* has as its root node the record type EMPLOYEE and has as its child record a virtual record DS_ASSGND. The virtual record DS_

Figure 9.10 Hierarchical structure diagram corresponding to Figure 9.9.

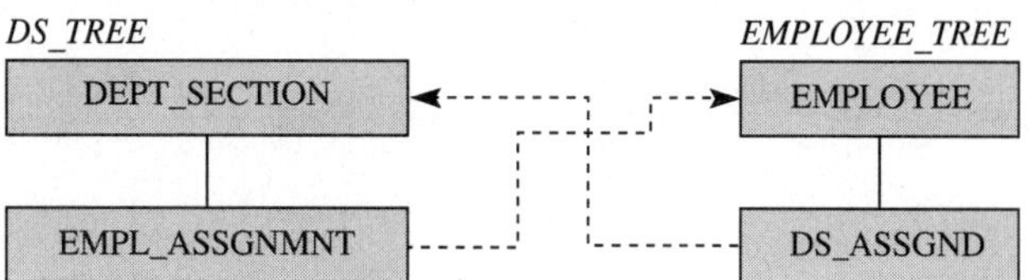

ASSGND is a logical child of the record type DEPT_SECTION. This virtual record contains the intersection data *Hours*, which represents the hours worked by the employee during a work week for a given DEPT_SECTION. The intersection data is a replication of that in the virtual record EMPL_ASSGNMNT. Unlike the examples of the virtual record discussed in Section 9.2.2, the virtual records EMPL_ASSGNMNT and DS_ASSGND have as their logical parent a record in the same physical hierarchical tree, namely, the *BRANCH_TREE* of Figure 9.3.

```
tree is EMPLOYEE_TREE
        EMPLOYEE is parent
        DS_ASSGND is child
        end

type EMPLOYEE = record
        Emp_Name: string;
        Home_Address: string;
        Phone_No: string;
        end

type DS_ASSGND = record
        {Ds_Name: string;
        Room_No: string;
        Phone_No: string;}
          virtual of logical parent
          DEPT_SECTION in BRANCH_TREE
        Hours: integer;
        end
```

Figure 9.11 gives some occurrences of the hierarchical trees *DS_TREE* and *EMPLOYEE_TREE*. The instance of *DS_TREE* rooted by the Acqstn Dept is shown

Figure 9.11 Sample occurrences of *DS_TREE* AND *EMPLOYEE_TREE*.

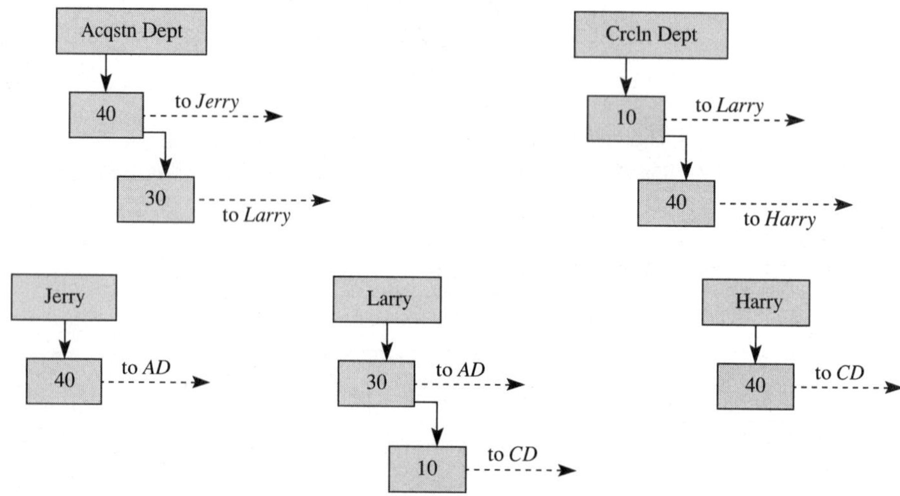

to have two occurrences of the dependent record type EMPL_ASSGNMNT. One of these contains the intersection data corresponding to employee Jerry and the other is for employee Larry. A pointer in each of these records, point to the logical parent.

The above example is an illustration of a **paired bidirectional logical relationship** of the hierarchical model. In such a relationship a many-to-many correspondence between two record types is resolved by introducing two virtual records with these record types as the logical parents. In the above example, the record types are DEPT_SECTION and EMPLOYEE. EMPL_ASSGNMNT is a virtual record that is a physical child of DEPT_SECTION and a logical child of EMPLOYEE; DS_ASSGND is a physical child of EMPLOYEE and a logical child of DEPT_SECTION. Each of these virtual record types contains appropriate pointers to the logical parents and the intersection data, *Hours,* may be replicated as we have done. The replicated data is stored in the two virtual record types and could lead to inconsistencies. Since the DBMS is aware of this controlled redundancy it has the responsibility for ensuring that whenever one of the replicated values in the intersection data is changed, its twin value is also changed.

9.3 Data Definition

The hierarchical database consists of a collection of hierarchical trees (or set of spanning trees) which are described using a database description facility. Figure 9.12 gives part of the hierarchical definition tree for our library database example. The corresponding data definition is given below. The trees described could be actual physically stored trees or logical trees derived from the physically stored trees. In the latter case, the logical trees can be considered to be user or external views. The logical trees are also hierarchical and derived from one or more physical trees and could contain virtual records. Defining a new logical tree thus may involve implementing pointers for the virtual records and as such is a reorganization of the physical database. Such a reorganization is performed by the DBA. A virtual record in a hierarchical tree can be materialized from its logical parent record. The latter may or may not be in the same physical hierarchical tree.

We used a Pascal-like convention to define the database, wherein we introduced the tree structure by listing the root of the tree and all its children record types. For the sake of clarity and simplicity, we avoided the introduction of implementation-related details such as specifying the number and types of pointers. In the commercially available database management products based on the hierarchical data model, the data definition requires the specification of these details.

Figure 9.12 Logical database as viewed by circulation clerk.

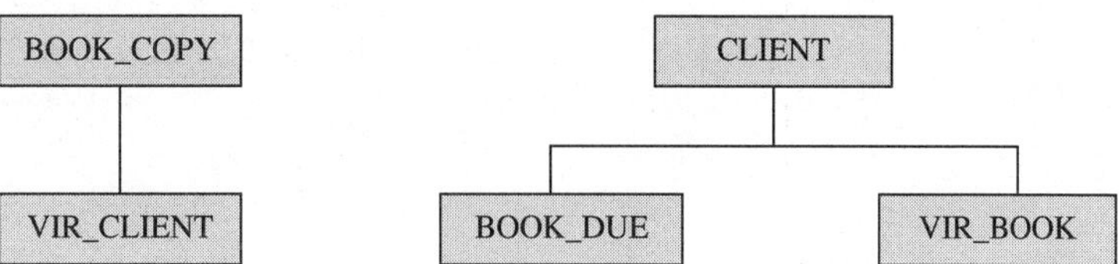

The ordering of the tree is according to the hierarchical structure diagram. This order is represented in the data definition by giving the leftmost child record type first.

Consider the logical database as viewed by the clerk at the circulation desk of the library. The hierarchical structure diagram of this view is given in Figure 9.12. The logical database could be described using the description (subschema) given below. In this description the fact that some portions of information in the virtual record are derived from the logical parent record type is not really required because the schema descriptor contains the relevant information; however, we leave this in as comments in our descriptors.

```
tree is BOOK_COPY_TREE
            BOOK_COPY is parent
            VIR_CLIENT is child
            end
type BOOK_COPY = record
            Call_No: string;
            Copy_No: integer;
            Branch_Id: string;
            Current_Status: string;
            end
type VIR_CLIENT = record
            {Client_No: string;
             Name: string;
             Address: string;}
                 (*virtual of logical parent
                     CLIENT in CLIENT_TREE;*)
            end
tree is CLIENT_TREE
            CLIENT is parent
            BOOK_DUE is child
            VIR_BOOK is child
            end
type CLIENT = record
            Client_No: string;
            Name: string;
            Address: string;
            end
type BOOK_DUE = record
            {Call_No: string;
             Copy_No: integer;
            Branch_Id: string;
            Current_Status: string;}
                 (*virtual of logical parent
                     BOOK_COPY in BOOK_TREE;*)
            Due_Date: string;
            end
```

```
type VIR_BOOK = record
         {Author: string;
         Title: string;
         Call_No: string;}
             (*virtual of logical parent
                BOOK in BOOK_COPY_TREE;*)
         end
```

9.4 Data Manipulation

To illustrate the data manipulation operations in the HDM, we use the logical database as viewed by the clerk at the circulation desk of the library. The hierarchical structure diagram of this view is given in Figure 9.12. The logical database is described in Section 9.3.

9.4.1 User Work Area in the HDM

For discussion of the data manipulation facility of the hierarchical data model, we assume that each user or application program (corresponding to the run unit of the DBTG proposal) has associated with it an area of memory. We refer to this area as the user work area (UWA). The UWA contains the processing environment of the run unit, which includes the following items:

- **Currency indicators:** In the case of the HDM we assume that the DBMS will maintain, for each hierarchical tree known to the run unit, via its logical database description, a set of pointers that indicate the records that have been last accessed by the run unit. We further assume that there is an indicator or pointer that points to the current record accessed by the run unit. In addition, we assume that the database management system maintains the current parent record of the current record. We assume that the hierarchical tree is traversed using the left-to-right preorder strategy, the ordering of the tree being that in the hierarchical structure diagram. Thus, once a record has been selected, the subsequent sequential retrieval will use the preorder strategy.
- **Record template:** For each record type known to the run unit, the UWA is assumed to contain the storage space that can be used as a template for data manipulation.
- **Status registers:** These are a set of indicators used to store the status of the run unit after the execution of a database operation. The run unit can examine these registers to determine whether an operation was completed successfully or not. For our purposes, we assume that there is a register called **DB-Status,** which will contain at the end of a DBMS operation a value of 0 if the operation was completed successfully or an error code if the command was not successful.

9.4.2 Basic Data Manipulation

The basic data retrieval command in the hierarchical data model is the **get** command, which unlike in the network data model need not be preceded by a find command. The command retrieves the appropriate occurrence of the record type, places it in the corresponding record type template in the UWA, and sets the currency indicators for the relevant hierarchical tree. In this instance, the currency indicators will be the current record of the run unit and the parent of the current record retrieved. The record occurrence to be retrieved is specified by indicating the condition to be met by the retrieved record. The hierarchical path to be used for the retrieval may also be given to retrieve a record. For instance, the condition specified in the get command may involve the parent (or one of the grandparents) of the record being retrieved.

The first format of the get command that we will discuss is the **get first.** This format is sometimes called **get unique** or **get leftmost.** Note that the hierarchical tree is traversed using the preorder scheme. Consequently, the get first command will retrieve the first record that meets this condition. The syntax of this format of the get command is as follows:

get first <record type> **where** <condition>

The **where** <condition> clause is optional and if it is omitted, the first record of the specified record type is retrieved and placed in the corresponding record template within the UWA. Once the command is successfully executed, the DB-Status register contains a value of 0 and the currency indicators are set. If the command is not executed successfully, i.e., if no record exists in the database that satisfies the specified condition, the the DB-Status will contain an error code.

For the sample database given in Figure 9.13b the following statements will locate the first record type BOOK_DUE for CLIENT Smith, and if the record is successfully located then the values for the data items *Call_No* and *Due_Date* are displayed:

get first BOOK_DUE **where** CLIENT.*Name* = 'Smith';
if **DB-Status** = 0 *then*
  display (BOOK_DUE.*Call_No,* BOOK_DUE.*Due_Date*);

The above statements for the sample database will display 1231 12/06.

9.4.3 Sequential Retrieval

The **get next** statement is used in the hierarchical database to do sequential processing in preorder. Once the position for a run unit is established in the database with a get first statement, the get next statement performs the retrieval in the forward sense. If the database contains disjoint hierarchical trees, we assume that the DBMS provides a dummy record and these disjoint trees are considered the children of the DBMS supplied unique dummy root record occurrence. The order of these disjoint hierarchical trees is their order in the data definition. For our example, we assume that there is a dummy record LIBRARY, which is the root of the hierarchical trees *BOOK*

Figure 9.13 (a) Sample database: *BOOK_COPY_TREE;* (b) sample database: *CLIENT_TREE.*

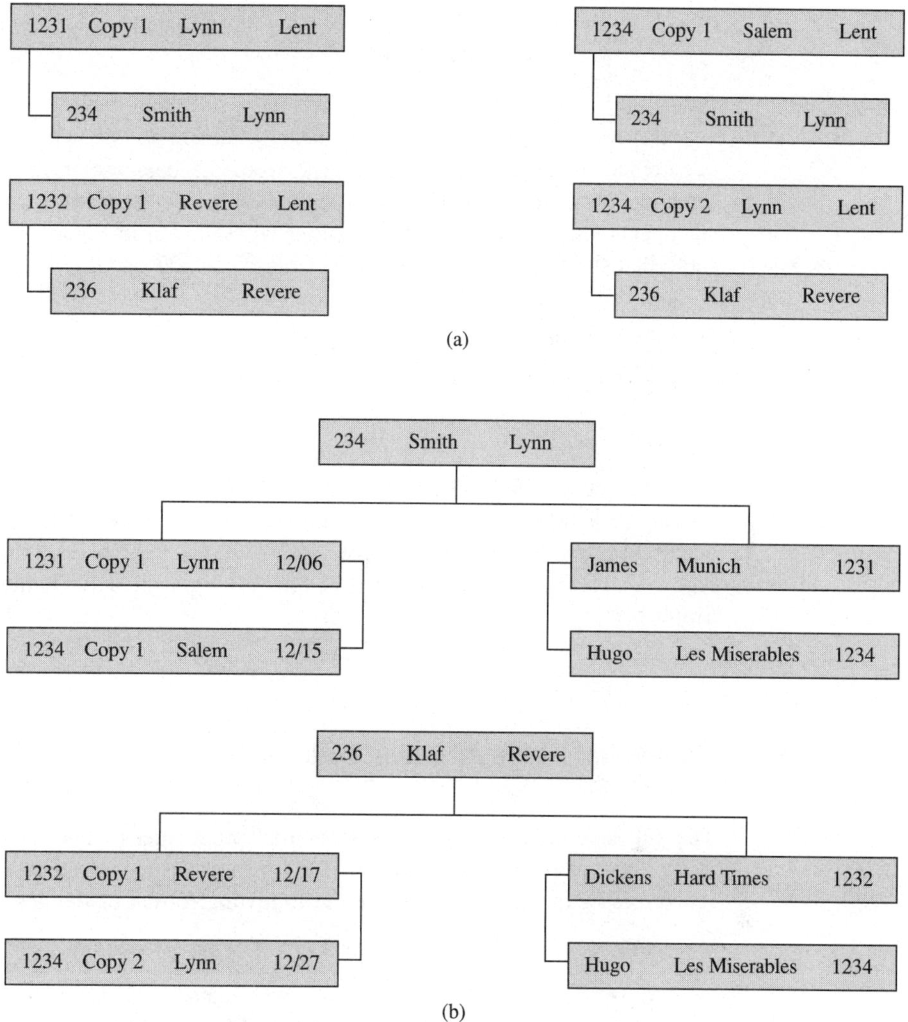

TREE, CLIENT_TREE, and *BRANCH_TREE*. The format of the get next statement is:

get next <record type> **where** <condition>

As in the **get first** statement, the **where** clause is optional; the <record type> specification is also optional. In case the **get first** statement appears without any options, the retrieval is of the next record in the database in preorder. If the <record type> is specified, the retrieval is of the next record of the specified type in the preorder. If both the <record type> and the **where** <condition> are included, the retrieval is the next record of the specified type that satisfies the <condition>.

Once we have located the first occurrence of the BOOK_DUE child of Smith, we can retrieve and display the subsequent occurrences using the following on the next page.

```
get first BOOK_DUE where CLIENT.Name = 'Smith';
while DB-Status = 0 do
    begin
    display (BOOK_DUE.Call_No, BOOK_DUE.Due_Date);
    get next BOOK_DUE
    end;
```

Repeated execution of the get next statement in the while loop retrieves all occurrence of the specified record type from the database in the forward preorder direction from the current location regardless of the ancestry of the record. These statements will display, for the sample database given in Figure 9.13b the following (note that the parent of BOOK_DUE.*Call_Nos* 1232 and 1234 in the following list is the CLIENT Klaf):

1231 12/06
1234 12/15
1232 12/17
1234 12/27

The record CLIENT in the logical database can be assumed to belong to a dummy root node LIBRARY as mentioned above. After retrieving the two record occurrences in the hierarchical tree for Smith, the search continues for the record type BOOK_DUE in the hierarchical tree belonging to Klaf, which is a sibling of Smith.

9.4.4 Sequential Retrieval within a Hierarchy

The get next statement performs sequential processing of the records of a database in the forward direction. However, if the retrieval is to be limited to a single occurrence of a hierarchical tree we use the following format of the get statement:

get next within parent <record type> **where** <condition>

As in the get next statement the where clause and the <record type> specification are optional. In case the **get next within parent** statement appears without any options, the retrieval is of the next record in the hierarchical tree or subtree belonging to the current parent as indicated by the currency indicator. If the <record type> is specified, the retrieval is of the next record of the specified type in preorder within the current parent. If both the <record type> and the **where** <condition> are included, the retrieval is of the next record of the specified type that satisfies the <condition> within the current parent.

Once we have located the root node of a hierarchical tree or subtree, we may need to retrieve all its dependent records. The following statements locate the hierarchical tree for the CLIENT Smith and then traverse it in preorder to retrieve the author and titles of all books borrowed by him:

```
get first CLIENT where CLIENT.Name = 'Smith';
if DB-Status = 0 then
    get next within parent (VIR_BOOK);
```

```
while DB-Status = 0 do
    begin
    display (VIR_BOOK.Author, VIR_BOOK.Title)
    get next within parent (VIR_BOOK);
    end;
```

The above statements will display, for the sample database given in Figure 9.13, the following:

James	Munich
Hugo	Les Miserables

9.5 Updates

Update operations on a hierarchical database are done using commands to insert new records in the database, delete existing records, or change the values of certain fields in existing records.

Before discussing these commands let us consider the view of the database as seen by a clerk in the acquisition department of the library. The logical portion of the database, as seen by this employee, is given in Figure 9.14 and the logical database definition is given below. The sample database contents are given in Figure 9.15. Note that there are no virtual records in this logical view.

```
tree is BOOK_TREE
            BOOK is parent
            BOOK_COPY is child
            end
type BOOK = record
            Author: string;
            Title: string;
            Call_No: string;
            end
type BOOK_COPY = record
            Call_No: string;
            Copy_No: integer;
            Branch_Id: string;
            Current_Status: string;
            end
```

Figure 9.14 Database view of acquisition clerk.

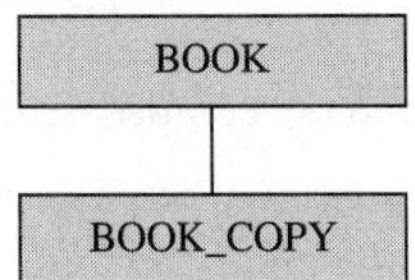

Figure 9.15 Sample database contents.

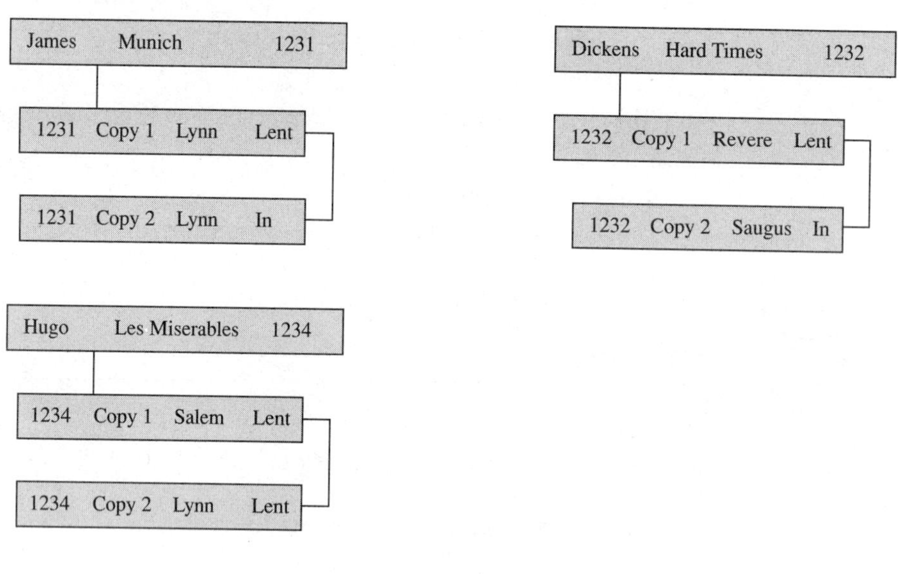

9.5.1 Insert

The format of the command to insert a new occurrence of a record type is given by:

insert <record type> **where** <condition>

When a new record is to be inserted in the database, the parentage of the record, unless it is at the root of a hierarchical tree, is specified with the where clause. Without the parentage information the DBMS will insert the record in the first possible position where the specified record type appears in the data definition. When the new record to be inserted is a child record type, we assume that it will be inserted in the first position in the preorder traversal, which will be to the left of the current leftmost child. The record to be inserted is first created in the record template in the UWA before the **insert** statement is executed.

The following statements create a new occurrence of the record type BOOK in the database:

BOOK.*Author* := 'Montgomery';
BOOK.*Title* := 'Anne of Green Gables';
BOOK.*Call_No* := 1235;
insert (BOOK);

Here we did not specify the parentage of the record type to be inserted because it is at the root of the hierarchical *BOOK_TREE*.

The following statements insert a copy of this new title into the database tree occurrence, corresponding to the new root record occurrence just inserted in the database. The parent record is specified in the where clause.

BOOK_COPY.*Call_No* := 1235;
BOOK_COPY.*Copy_No* := 1;

```
BOOK_COPY.Branch_Id := 'Lynn';
BOOK_COPY.Status := 'transit';
insert (BOOK_COPY)
    where (BOOK.Call_No = 1235);
```

Without the where <condition> clause, the record will be inserted in the database, but since a child record cannot exist in a hierarchical database without a parent record, it is connected to the first possible position where such a record could exist. For our sample database, assuming that Figure 9.15 is the preorder of the BOOK_TREE hierarchy, the new BOOK_COPY will be inserted in the tree with the (James Munich 1231) root node if the insert statement did not have the where clause.

9.5.2 Modification and Deletion

A record that is to be modified or deleted from the database must first be retrieved using a locking form of the get statement as follows:

get hold first <record type>

The need to hold the record arises when there are a number of concurrent run units using the database. A run unit issuing the **get hold** locks out the other programs from the record occurrence and thus avoids the anomalies associated with concurrent updates (see Chapter 12).

The following statements modify the BOOK_COPY.*Branch_Id* of the second copy of the BOOK (James Munich 1231) from Lynn to Salem.

```
get first (BOOK)
    where BOOK.Call_No = 1231;
get hold first BOOK_COPY
    where BOOK_COPY.Copy_No = 2;
BOOK_COPY.Branch_Id := 'Salem';
BOOK_COPY.Status := 'transit';
replace;
```

The first statement locates the root node of the hierarchical tree occurrence where the required BOOK is the parent. The next statement retrieves and locks the child record occurrence of BOOK_COPY where the BOOK_COPY.*Copy_No* is 2. The fields to be modified are changed in the next two statements within the record template. The last statement replaces the record occurrence of BOOK_COPY with the modified record. After execution of the **replace** statement, the lock on the record occurrence of BOOK_COPY is removed.

The following statements **delete** the BOOK_COPY record occurrence of the second copy of the BOOK (Dickens Hard Times 1232).

```
get first (BOOK)
    where BOOK.Call_No = 1232;
get hold first BOOK_COPY
    where BOOK_COPY.Copy_No = 2;
delete;
```

The first statement locates the root node of the hierarchy tree occurrence, where the required BOOK is the parent. The next statement retrieves and locks the child record occurrence of BOOK_COPY, where the BOOK_COPY.*Copy_No* is 2. The last statement deletes the record occurrence of BOOK_COPY.

When a record to be deleted is a parent record occurrence of a hierarchical tree or subtree, all the children (and grand children) record occurrences are also deleted. This action is similar to the deletion of the owner record occurrence of a set in DBTG with fixed membership, wherein all occurrences of the member records are also deleted.

9.5.3 Updates of Virtual Records

Let us return to the logical database as viewed by the clerk at the circulation desk, given in Figure 9.12. The logical database contains a number of virtual records. Some parts of these records (excluding the intersection data portion) are derived from their logical parent records, which are actual physical records. For the data retrieval operations, the logical database can be processed exactly as if the virtual record were really a physical one. In other words, the virtual records are materialized from their logical parent records. An update operation, however, could have an effect on the underlying physical records. Some of these operations are disallowed, while other operations could cause these logical parent records to be inserted, modified, or deleted. The operations that are allowed and their effects are determined by the rules for the insert, delete, and replace operations on the record type related to a virtual record. IMS uses options and associated rules that could be called physical, logical, or virtual for each of these update operations. The effects of these are, in a way, similar to the effects of the DBTG membership insertion and retention options we discussed in Chapter 8. We summarize some of the possibilities below. Details of these rules can be found in the application manuals of the commercially available DBMs based on the hierarchical approach.

Inserting a new occurrence of a CLIENT record is allowed because it is a physical record in the logical view. The following statements create a new occurrence of the record type CLIENT in the database.

CLIENT.*Client_No* : = '237';
CLIENT.*Name* : = 'Cook';
CLIENT.*Address* : = 'Peabody';
insert (CLIENT);

Here we need not specify the parentage of CLIENT because it is the root node of a hierarchical tree.

Inserting an instance of BOOK_DUE for a nonexistent CLIENT will not be allowed, since in the hierarchical data model a child record cannot exist without the parent record and such operations will fail.

Inserting an instance of BOOK_DUE for a nonexistent BOOK_COPY, depending on the rule specified for the logical parent BOOK_COPY, would fail or succeed. It will fail if the insert rule for BOOK_COPY is specified as physical. However, if the insert rule for BOOK_COPY is logical or virtual, then on insertion of BOOK_

DUE an occurrence of its logical parent is inserted in the physical database (assume that BOOK_COPY is a root node of a physical tree).

Consider the following statements to insert in the database information to indicate that Cook has borrowed copy 3 of a book with *Call_No* 1235 (entitled *Anne of Green Gables* by Montgomery) from the Lynn branch:

BOOK_DUE.*Call_No* = '123';
BOOK_DUE.*Copy_No* = 3;
BOOK_DUE.*Branch_Id* = 'Lynn';
BOOK_DUE.*Status* = 'Lent';
BOOK_DUE.*Due_Date* = 12/28;
insert (BOOK_DUE)
    where (CLIENT.*Client_No* = '237');

The last statement will succeed if an occurrence of the BOOK_COPY exists, and in this case the BOOK_COPY.*Status* is updated to lent. If no occurrence of the record BOOK_COPY exists, then depending on the rules specified for BOOK_COPY, the operation will succeed or fail. In the former case, an occurrence for BOOK_COPY will be inserted in the database. The information for this occurrence is available in the record BOOK_DUE.

Deleting a CLIENT may or may not succeed depending on the rules specified for CLIENT and whether there are any volumes outstanding with the CLIENT. If the rule specified for CLIENT is physical and if the client has a number of books on loan, the attempt to delete a client will fail. If the rule specified is either logical or virtual, the occurrence is made inaccessible as a CLIENT record occurrence. However, it remains accessible via VIR_CLIENT.

Finally, modification of certain fields in the records are not allowed. For example, the *Call_No* and the *Client_No* fields, which are used to establish the logical parent/child record occurrence association, cannot be modified.

Replacement of the other fields of CLIENT can always be done. However, replacement of a field of BOOK_DUE could affect the logical parent BOOK_COPY and would succeed if the option specified for BOOK_COPY is virtual.

9.6 Implementation of the Hierarchical Database

Each occurrence of a hierarchical tree can be stored as a variable length physical record, the nodes of the hierarchy being stored in preorder. In addition, the stored record contains a prefix field. This field contains control information including pointers, flags, locks, and counters, which are used by the DBMS to allow concurrent usage and enforce data integrity.

A number of methods could be used to store the hierarchical database system. The storage of the hierarchical trees in the physical medium affects not only the performance of the system but also the operations that can be performed on the database. For example, if each occurrence of the hierarchical tree is stored as a variable length record on a magnetic tape like device, the DBMS will allow only sequential retrieval and insertion or modification may be disallowed or performed only by recreating the entire database with the insertion and modification. Storage of

Figure 9.16 Hierarchical definition tree.

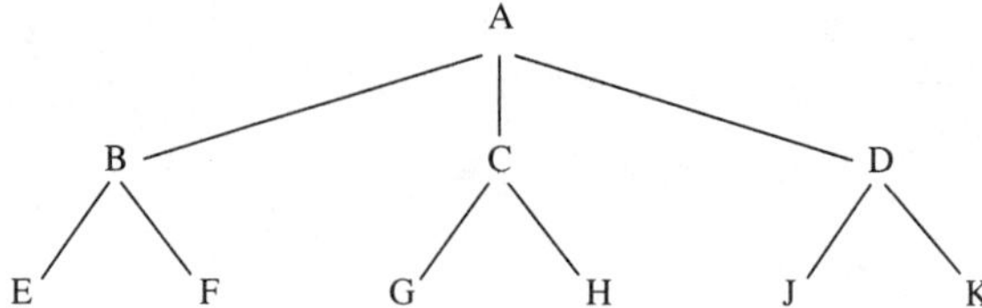

the database on a direct access device allows an index structure to be supported for the root nodes and allows direct access to an occurrence of a hierarchical tree.

The storage of one occurrence of the hierarchical definition tree of Figure 9.16 using the variable length record approach is given in Figure 9.17.

The hierarchy can also be represented using pointers of either preorder hierarchical type or child/sibling type. In the hierarchical type of pointer, each record occurrence has a pointer that points to the next record in the preorder sequence. In the child/sibling scheme each record has two types of pointers. The **sibling** pointer points to its right sibling (or twin). The **child** pointer points to its leftmost child record occurrence. A record has one sibling pointer and as many child pointers as the number of child types associated with the node corresponding to the record. Figure 9.16 gives the hierarchical definition tree and the one occurrence of this hierarchical definition tree is given in Figures 9.18 and 9.19. In Figure 9.18 the preorder hierarchical pointers are shown, whereas in Figure 9.19 we present the same database using the child/sibling pointers.

Figure 9.17 Sequential storage of hierarchical database.

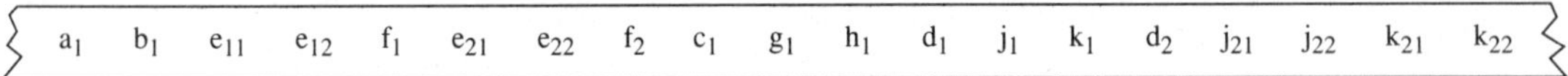

Figure 9.18 Preorder hierarchical pointers.

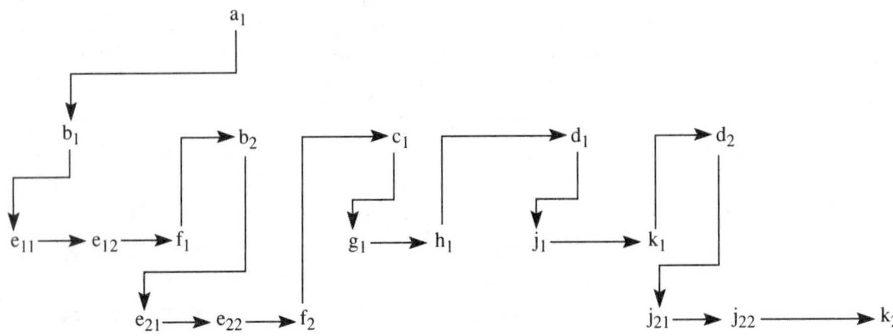

Figure 9.19 Child/sibling pointers.

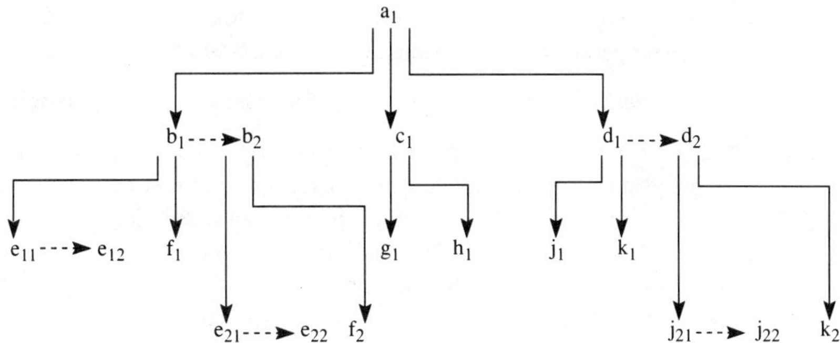

9.7 Additional Features of the Hierarchical DML

Consider the hierarchical definition tree of Figure 9.20. Access to a dependent record type is via a path beginning at the root node and after traversing through intermediate nodes, ending at the required record type. Such paths are called **hierarchical paths.** Access to record type E, in the hierarchical definition tree of Figure 9.20, requires a traversal through nodes A and B.

In addition to the data manipulation statement discussed earlier, the hierarchical data manipulation language needs a number of functions for better control of navigating through the database. This saves both processing and program development time.

One such feature is the use of control codes associated with the get statements. We will not give the exact syntax of these statements or describe them in detail, but we will highlight their usefulness. **Control codes** are associated with the get statement to perform additional functions. These include retrieving all records in a hierarchical path, locating first occurrence, locating last occurrence, and maintaining the currency indicators at a given level of the hierarchy or for the hierarchical path to this level.

Figure 9.20 A sample hierarchical definition tree.

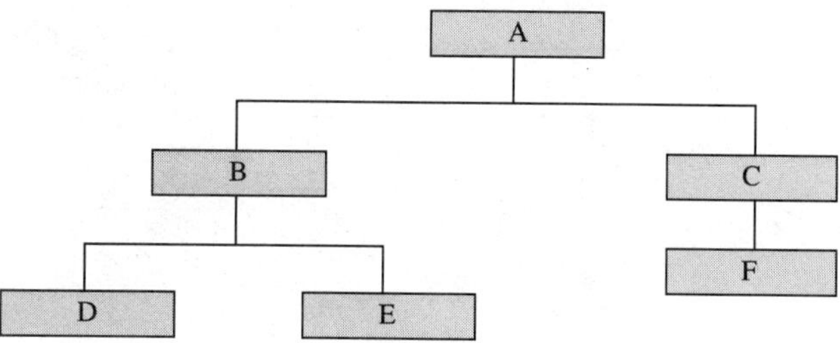

The need to retrieve all records in a hierarchical path can be illustrated by the following example. Suppose we need to find an occurrence of a record type E and also list its parentage. Instead of successively retrieving the correct occurrence of record type A, then record type B, and subsequently record type E, we can combine these operations in one statement as given below:

get next *D where A = A_1, ***D where** B = B_{11}, **where** E = E_{112}

Here the control code is specified by ***D** and it indicates that the corresponding occurrence of the record types in the hierarchical path are also to be retrieved and placed in the UWA in the appropriate record template.

If we wanted the last occurrence of record type D in a hierarchical path, the following version of the get statement could be used. Here the last sibling in the D record type is indicated by the ***L** control code.

get unique *L D **within parent** A = A_1 **and** B = B_{11}

A similar command to back up to the first sibling in a record type, while performing a sequential retrieval using the **get next within parent** statement, is provided by the ***F** command code.

Another feature of the hierarchical DML is the possibility of maintaining and navigating through multiple dependent record types at each level of a hierarchical path. To understand this facility, consider the database shown in Figure 9.21. Suppose we want to list the dependent record types of B_{11} in the order of D_{111}, E_{111}, D_{112}, E_{112}, and so on. The following statements would cause a problem:

get next where A = A_1, **where** B = B_{11}
get next within parent D
get next within parent E
get next within parent D

Figure 9.21 Data corresponding to the hierarchical definition tree of Figure 9.20.

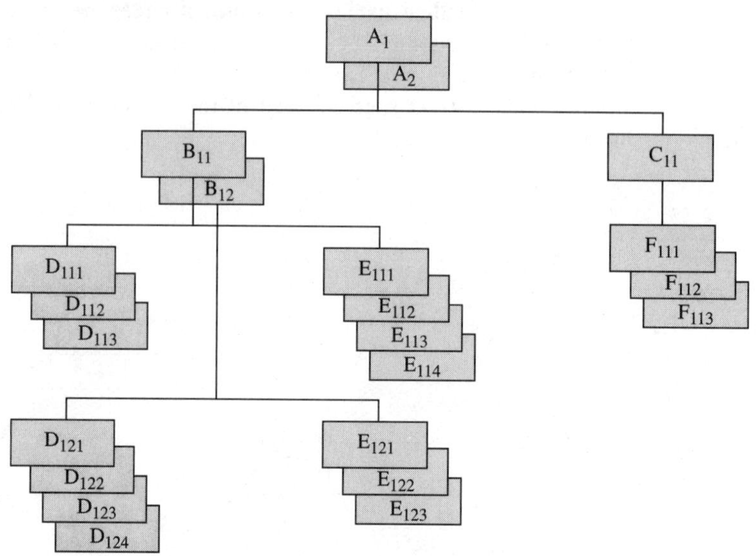

This is so because the database uses hierarchical pointers and for the second get request for record type D, it would access either the record occurrence D_{121} or return an error condition indicating that there are no more record types.

If we use multiple positioning, the position within the record type D would be maintained. Consequently, this would give us the correct occurrence, D_{112}, of the record type D.

9.8 Concluding Remarks

In the hierarchical model, we have to select the order of entities involved in the application into a hierarchy. This involves choosing the root node at each level. The ordering of the nodes at each level is also significant. Because we are unaware, at database design time, of the users' intent and range of needs, the number of different possible hierarchies with a sizable number of record types is enormous. Choosing among these hierarchies would be a formidable task. As a case in point, with two record types, the number of different hierarchies is two; with three record types, the number of different hierarchies is 12, and so on. Only some of these hierachies are suitable and the optimum for one application could turn out to be far from satisfactory for another application.

We face another problem in converting cyclic relationships into hierarchies. A cycle of relationship, for example,

BRANCH ⟷ DEPT_SECTION ⟷ EMPLOYEE ⟷ BRANCH

in the E-R diagram of Figure 9.2 cannot be expressed directly in the form of an ordered tree. However, we have resolved this cycle by the hierarchies:

BRANCH → DEPT_SECTION → EMPLOYEE
and
BRANCH → EMPLOYEE → DEPT_SECTION.

This resolution requires the use of replication or virtual records for the record types DEPT_SECTION and EMPLOYEE at the lowest level of the above hierarchies. In general, any set of relationships in E-R diagrams that forms a cycle can be converted to a number of rooted trees, using either replication or virtual records.

The hierarchical model inherently requires that the data in the database be structured in the form of a tree. However, some records in the database represent entities involved in more than one relationship. Furthermore, some of these relationships are of the many-to-many type. The implementation of these relationships using the hierarchical data model leads to a number of hierarchical trees that are unconnected except via a DBMS-supplied dummy root record. Such a collection of hierarchical trees is sometimes called a set of spanning trees. Hierarchical data manipulation facilities do not provide an easy means of accessing several hierarchical trees simultaneously. The virtual record facility allows the hierarchical data manipulation language to access data belonging to separate hierarchical trees. The virtual record facility also allow a record type to be included in several hierarchies without actual replication.

The paired bidirectional logical relationship, with its associated symmetrical virtual records, is one way to implement a many-to-many relationship. The database system is aware of the replication of the common data in such virtual records and the need to maintain consistency.

However, the virtual record scheme, even without any intersection data fields, requires physical support in the form of related pointers to and from the logical parent. Virtual records cannot be defined dynamically but require some database reorganization to be defined and implemented in conjunction with the DBA.

Performance considerations may require the hierarchical database to have an index not only on the key field of the root node of the hierarchical tree but also on other fields of the root node of a hierarchical tree or subtree. This type of index, called a **secondary index,** is particularly useful for logical parent records.

The hierarchical model is considered to have a built-in bias that is physically implemented. This bias may not be good for all applications. Consequently, a logical structure using secondary indexes is useful. The use of virtual records avoids replication, and provides a logical view of the database. Unfortunately, the implementation of this is not as straight forward as a view in the relation data model. The virtual record facility requires support of the underlying physical database and hence preplanning and involvement of the DBA at database design time. Consequently, new virtual records may not be defined. The update operations on the database and the records that are associated with a virtual record are much more complex than the operations on DBTG sets.

The hierarchical model, through one of its major implementations in the IMS system from IBM, has the lion's share of the current corporate databases. IMS has matured over the years and the applications have been tuned to an optimum level of performance. The results of attempts to move some of these applications to a relational model have been mixed. However, a number of companies are marketing products to provide a relational user front end, that interfaces with the existing hierarchical DBMS.

9.9 Summary

The hierarchical data model consists of a set of record types. The relationship between two record types is of the parent/child form, expressed using links or pointers. The records thus connected form an ordered tree, the so-called hierarchical definition tree.

The hierarchical model provides a straightforward and natural method of implementing a one-to-many relationship. However, a many-to-many relationship between record types cannot be expressed directly in the hierarchical model. Such a relationship can be expressed by using data replication or virtual records.

The disadvantages of data replication are waste of storage space and the problem of maintaining data consistencies. A virtual record is a mechanism to point to an occurrence of a physical record. Thus, instead of replicating a record occurrence, a single record occurrence is stored and a virtual record points to this record wherever the record is required. The virtual record can contain some data that is common to a relationship; such data is called the intersection data. The virtual record is the logical child of the physical record that it points to, which is its logical parent.

The database using the hierarchical model results in a number of hierarchical structure diagrams, each of which represents a hierarchical tree. These trees can be interrelated via the logical parent/child relationship to form a set of spanning trees. However, one can assume that the DBMS provides a single occurrence of a dummy record type and all the hierarchical trees can then be attached to this single dummy parent record. The roots of these trees can be treated as children of this dummy record.

The data manipulation facility of the hierarchical model provides functions similar to the network approach; however, the navigation to be provided is based on the hierarchical model. The get command is used to retrieve an occurrence of a specified record type that satisfies the specified conditions. The get next command is used for sequential processing and the get next within parent is used for sequential processing within a preselected hierarchy.

The database can be modified using the insert, replace, and delete operations. When records to be modified are virtual records, detailed rules have to be specified so that the modification, if allowed, leaves the database in a consistent state.

Key Terms

ordered tree
preorder traversal
child pointer
sibling pointer
hierarchical data model (HDM)
tree structure diagram
definition tree
hierarchical definition tree
virtual record
replication
logical parent
logical child
intersection data
paired bidirectional logical relationship
DB-Status
get
get first
get unique
get leftmost
where
get next
get next within parent
insert
get hold
replace
delete
hierarchical path
control codes
secondary index

Exercises

9.1 Write an algorithm to convert a network diagram into a hierarchical diagram.

9.2 Write an algorithm to convert a hierarchical diagram into a network diagram.

9.3 Consider the record types BOOK and CLIENT. Implement the relationship to model the waiting list of clients waiting to borrow a given BOOK.

9.4 Consider the record types BOOK_COPY and CLIENT. Implement the relationship to model the waiting list of clients waiting to borrow a given BOOK_COPY.

9.5 Comment on the statement that the HDM has limited network capabilities. Give an example of a network that cannot be represented in an HDM.

9.6 Why does the association between parent and child record type in the hierarchical data model *not* need the foreign key concept of the relational data model?

9.7 Figure A represents a hierarchical tree structure diagram for the hospitals in a certain area. Write the data description statements to define the structure.

Figure A Hospital database.

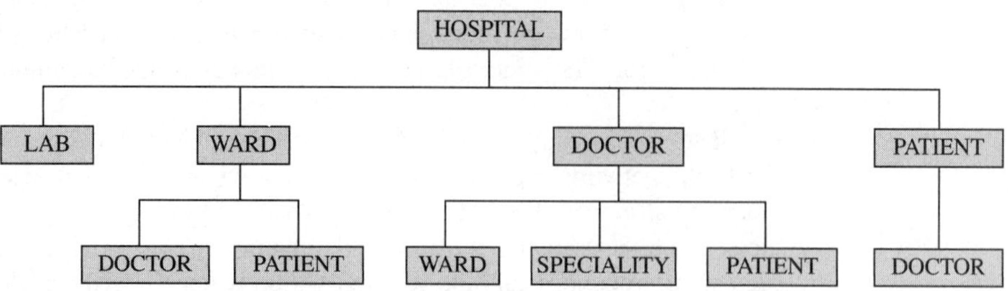

9.8 For the hierarchical data model of Figure A, write the data manipulation statements to perform the following operations:

(a) Display all hospitals that have a hematology lab.
(b) Display all wards that have a capacity in excess of 4.
(c) For a given patient, display all the doctors that the patient has consulted.
(d) Display all the doctors who have a specialty of pediatrics.
(e) Display the number of doctors consulted by a given patient.
(f) Add a doctor to the database belonging to a given hospital.

9.9 What modifications to the hierarchical tree structure diagram of Figure A will enable the query of Exercise 9.8d above to be handled efficiently?

9.10 What modification would you make to the diagram of Figure A if you were to allow a doctor to practice at more than one hospital?

9.11 In the HDM a record type is limited to only one physical parent and one logical parent. Would it be possible to represent a number many-to-many relationships between three record types? For example, can the E-R diagrams given in Figure 2.23 or Figure B be implemented?

Figure B E-R diagram for Exercise 9.11.

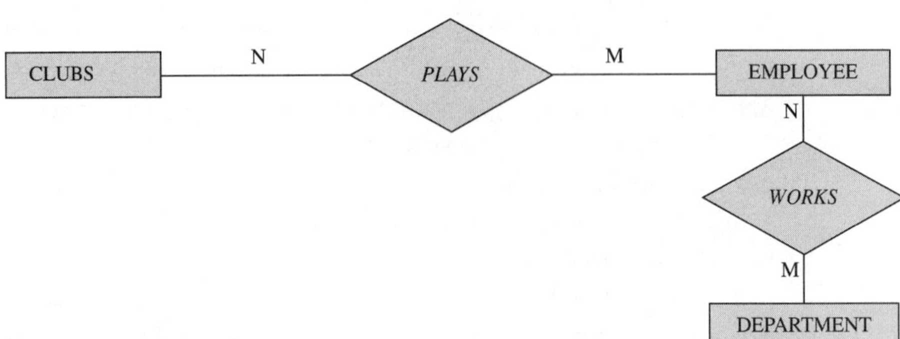

9.12 Consider the record types in a hierarchical definition tree as being relations, with the data items (or fields) being their attributes. Are these relations so derived in 1NF, 2NF, or 3NF? Do these relations have any update anomalies?

Bibliographic Notes

The hierarchical data model, like the DBTG data model, was proposed as a database management system and was not studied extensively as a data model per se. The most prominent commercially available DBMS using the hierarchical data models are the Information Management System (IMS) from IBM Corporation and MRI's System 2000. These are discussed extensively in the manuals available from these companies (IMS, MRI) and in a number of survey articles (Tsic 76) and textbooks (Card 85, Date 86, Kapp 86, Tsic 77, Tsic 82).

Bibliography

(Card 85) A. F. Cardenas, *Data Base Management Systems,* 2nd ed. Boston, MA: Allen and Bacon, 1985.

(Date 86) C. J. Date, *An Introduction to Database Systems,* 4th ed. Reading, MA: Addison-Wesley, 1986.

(IMS) Information Management System documentation, IBM Corp., White Plains, NY.

(Kapp 86) D. Kapp, & J. F. Leben, *IMS Programming Techniques: A Guide to Using DL/I,* 2nd ed. New York: Van Nostrand Reinhold, 1986.

(MRI) System 2000 documentation, MRI Systems Corporation, Austin, TX., 1974.

(Tsic 76) D. C. Tsichritzis, & F. H. Lochovsky,"Hierarchical Data Base Management: A Survey," *ACM Computing Survey* 8(1), March 1976, pp. 105–124.

(Tsic 77) D. C. Tsichritzis, & F. H. Lochovsky, *Data Base Management Systems*. New York: Academic Press, 1977.

(Tsic 82) D. C. Tsichritzis, & F. H. Lochovsky, *Data Models*. Englewood Cliffs, NJ: Prentice-Hall, 1982.

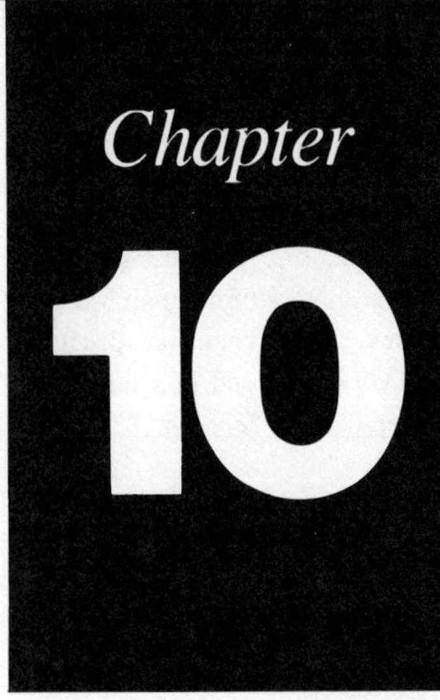

Query Processing

Contents

In this chapter we focus on different aspects of converting a user's query into a standard form and thence into a plan to be executed to generate a response.

10.1 Introduction

Query processing is the procedure of selecting the best plan or strategy to be used in responding to a database request. The plan is then executed to generate a response. The component of the DBMS responsible for generating this strategy is called a **query processor.**

Query processing is also referred to in database literature as **query optimization.** However, bear in mind that optimization here is mostly in the form of improvement in light of the inexact knowledge of the status of the database. The optimization done in practical systems is not necessarily the best. The optimal strategy may be too difficult to evaluate and could require much more computing to improve on it, which on average may not be dramatically different from the one afforded through a heuristic strategy.

Query processing is a stepwise process. The first step is to transform the query into a standard form. For instance, a query expressed in QBE is translated into SQL and subsequently into a relational algebraic expression. During this transformation process, the **parser** portion of the query processor checks the syntax and verifies if the relations and attributes used in the query are defined in the database. Having translated the query into a given form such as a relational algebraic expression, the optimization is performed by substituting equivalent expressions for those in the query. Such equivalent expressions, which we focus on in Section 10.4, are more efficiently evaluated than the ones in the transformed query. Substitution of such expressions also depends on factors such as the existence of certain database structures, whether or not a given file is sorted, the presence of different indexes, and so on. In the next step a number of strategies called **access plans** are generated for evaluating the transformed query. The physical characteristics of the data and any supporting access methods are taken into account in generating the alternate access plans. The cost of each access plan is estimated and the optimal one is chosen and executed.

We concentrate in this chapter on query processing for interactive usage on a relational database management system (RDBMS). A compiler would process database requests from batch programs. Techniques similar to the one to be discussed here could also be applied to compiled queries. The overhead involved in the query processing of an interactive query that is unlikely to be repeated should not be too high. Contrast this with the compilation of a batch query. A batch program is likely to be executed many times. Thus, a more intensive search for an optimal plan could be justified. However, the optimization of compiled queries is not guaranteed to remain optimal since the status of the database changes over time.

In the hierarchical and network models, the user specifies navigation though the database by indicating the low-level path to be followed through records. This path, for instance, leads from the parents to the children record types in a hierarchical database, or from the owners to the members record types (or from the members to the owners) of sets in the network database. Since these paths are already indicated, the onus of optimization is on the user. Nonetheless, even in these systems some form of query processing is possible. Such is the case when a query processor has information that the user does not have with respect to the current content of the database, the index present on various records, and the past statistics of the various operations.

The user interacts with a DBMS by submitting queries or update requests. These requests are expressed by the user in a simple language. The query language usually allows the same query to be expressed in a number of different ways, some of which may be more efficient than others. Regardless of this difference, the user expects the system to generate the response to the query in a reasonable period of time. In relational systems, for both types of requests, the required data for the response is described by their properties rather than their locations. The relational DBMS must select some optimal evaluation strategy and then execute it. This process of selecting an access plan (also known as a strategy) and executing it is query processing. In this chapter we shall see how query processing is handled in centralized database systems. We defer the discussion of query processing in distributed database systems until Chapter 15.

In centralized DBMSs an efficient query processor would try to minimize the utilization of computing resources by the DBMS. These resources are the storage space and processor time. The storage space consists of secondary stage as well as main memory. The secondary storage used is not only for the primary data, but also for storing indexes. The primary storage is used for storing the data and provides space used by the buffers. The processor time used includes the time spent by the input/output processor as well as the CPU. In a distributed environment, the communication channel is another resource and the costs of communication delays, setups, and transmission have to be considered.

Query processing strategies (see Figure 10.1), use general techniques for query modification. This includes expressing the query in an equivalent but more efficient form, substituting a query involving n-relations by a group of simpler queries (query decomposition), replacing a query involving views to one expressed on the base relations, or adding additional predicates to the query to enforce security. In addition, query processing strategies take into account the characteristics of the data and the expected sizes of both the intermediate and final results. Strategies are also included

Figure 10.1 Query processing strategy.

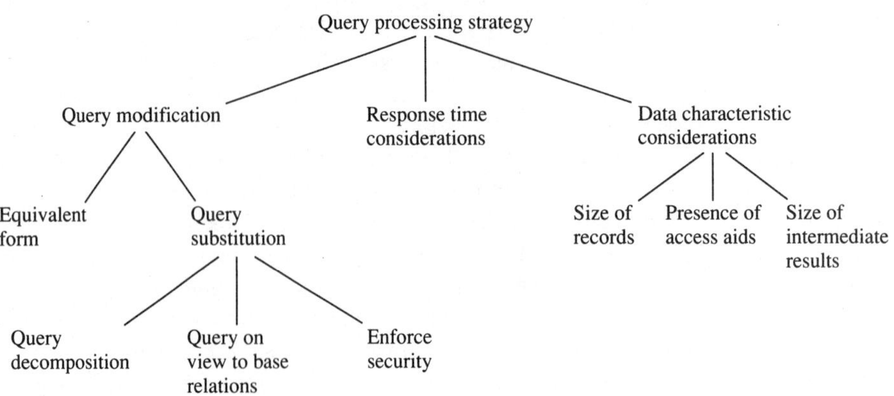

to enhance the query response time or reduce the cost of evaluating the query. It is unlikely that details of the precise sizes of relations and the distribution of data values in each attribute of every relation can be economically maintained. However, the query processing procedures estimate these values and use them in preparing a strategy for optimizing the query evaluation. The estimation cannot be exact and the optimization of costs may be computationally infeasible. Therefore, it is usual to employ a heuristic selection of evaluation strategies. The following are examples of such heuristic strategies: to reduce the size of relations participating in a query as early as possible by selection and projection, to use indices whenever possible, and to sort the intermediate relations to improve the efficiency of subsequent operations.

As we saw in Chapter 4, relational queries can be expressed in either relational algebra or calculus. It is possible to evaluate safe calculus expressions directly, although, under certain quantifiers, at high computational costs. The alternate approach involves translating the calculus expression into an equivalent relational algebraic expression. The algebraic expression can be executed directly. We first look at methods for evaluating relational algebraic expressions. At the end of the chapter we discuss processing relational calculus queries.

Another aspect of query processing is **query modification.** This is called for when the query is based on a view. Such queries have to be replaced by appropriate queries on the base relations. Examples of these were illustrated in Section 5.7.9. Additional modification may be necessary to impose restrictions enforcing data security and confidentiality. Thus a manager who is allowed access to the salary attributes of employees in her department would have queries involving the EMPLOYEE relation modified by a selection as shown below:

$$\sigma_{\text{DEPT} = \text{manager'sdepartment}}(\text{EMPLOYEE})$$

10.2 An Example

In the examples illustrated in this chapter, we consider part of a university database. We concentrate on that portion of the database consisting of the following four relations:

STUDENT (Std#, Std_Name)	student details
REGISTRATION *(Std#, Course#)*	courses the students are currently registered in
GRADE *(Std#, Course#, Grade)*	grade obtained in courses already completed by a student
COURSE *(Course#, Course_Name, Instructor)*	course details

We make the following assumptions regarding the size of the database. The STUDENT relation contains 40,000 tuples. The REGISTRATION relation represents the current courses in which a student is registered but has not completed. If we assume 10 courses per student for the academic year, we arrive at a total of 400,000 tuples in this relation. The GRADE relation represents the grade obtained by the student in completed courses. Using an average of 15 completed courses per student gives the number of tuples for this relation to be 600,000. The relation COURSE represents course offered and, ignoring the multiple sections of certain courses, represents 5,000 courses.

A given request can be expressed in a number of different ways in any language. Consider the query: "List the names of courses higher than COMP300 and all students registered in them."

The following are some different ways of stating this query in SQL and relational algebra. In SQL:

```
select Std_Name,Course_Name
from STUDENT, REGISTRATION, COURSE
where STUDENT.Std# = REGISTRATION.Std# and
      COURSE.Course# = REGISTRATION.Course# and
      REGISTRATION.Course# > COMP300
```

or

```
select Std_Name,c1.Course_Name
from STUDENT, REGISTRATION, COURSE c1
where STUDENT.Std# = REGISTRATION.Std# and
      REGISTRATION.Course# in
          (select c2.Course#
           from COURSE c2
           where c2.Course# > COMP300 and
                 c1.Course# = c2.Course# )
```

or

```
select Std_Name,c1.Course_Name
from STUDENT, COURSE c1
where STUDENT.Std# in
      (select REGISTRATION.Std#
       from REGISTRATION
       where REGISTRATION.Course# in
           (select    c2.Course#
            from COURSE c2
            where c2.Course# > COMP300 and
                c1.Course# = c2.Course# ))
```

In relational algebra:

$$\pi_{Std\_Name,Course\_Name}(\sigma_{Course\#>\mathrm{COMP300}}(\mathrm{STUDENT} \underset{Std\#}{\bowtie} \mathrm{REGISTRATION} \underset{Course\#}{\bowtie} \mathrm{COURSE}))$$

or

$$\pi_{Std\_Name,Course\_Name}(\mathrm{STUDENT} \underset{Std\#}{\bowtie} (\sigma_{Course\#>COMP300}(\mathrm{REGISTRATION} \underset{Course\#}{\bowtie} \mathrm{COURSE}))$$

or

$$\pi_{Std\_Name,Course\_Name}(\mathrm{STUDENT} \underset{Std\#}{\bowtie} (\sigma_{Course\#>COMP300}\ \mathrm{REGISTRATION}) \underset{Course\#}{\bowtie} (\sigma_{Course\#>COMP300}\ \mathrm{COURSE})$$

Some of these illustrated forms may be better than others as far as the use of computing resources is concerned. The DBMS must perform a transformation to convert a query from an undesirable form into an equivalent one that uses less resources and is therefore deemed better.

For the sample database, we get the following query processing costs for the different relational algebraic forms of the same query. Here, to simplify discussion, we compare costs in terms of the number of tuples processed. In an actual system, the cost would be given in terms of the processing cost and the I/O cost measured in terms of the number of block accesses required. This I/O cost depends, too, on the size of the relation and block.

Let us examine the cost for the first relational algebraic expression tabulated in Figure 10.2a. It involves a join of the relation STUDENT, containing 40,000 tuples, with REGISTRATION, having 400,000 tuples. In this case, the referential integrity constraint indicates that a tuple in REGISTRATION cannot exist unless there is a tuple in STUDENT with the same *Std#*. Therefore, the result would be equal to the number of tuples in REGISTRATION. If we use the brute force method of comparing each tuple of STUDENT with each tuple of REGISTRATION, this join is obtained by processing 40,000 * 400,000 tuples.

If the STUDENT and REGISTRATION relations are sorted on the joining attribute *Std#*, then the join can be obtained by processing 40,000 + 400,000 tuples. If indexes exist on the joining attribute, one per relation, then access to the tuples is not required unless the indexes indicate that there is a tuple in both relations with a common value for the joining attribute. We discuss these aspects in Section 9.8.

The second join is between the result of the first join and the tuples of COURSE involving a processing of 5,000 * 400,000 tuples. The result of this, again, would be 400,000 tuples. This is followed by a selection for *Course* > COMP300. If we assume that there are 500 courses whose course number is higher than COMP300, the result would involve, let us say, 40,000 tuples. The final result of the query is obtained by projecting these tuples on the attributes *Std_Name* and *Course_Name* and involves processing 40,000 tuples.

For the second relational algebraic form of the same query, the first join is between the relations REGISTRATION and COURSE. This entails the processing of 5,000 * 400,000 tuples for unsorted relations. If both these relations were sorted the join would involve processing 5,000 + 400,000 tuples. The result of this join is 400,000 tuples. We then select from the joined tuples those wherein the *Course#* is greater than COMP300, requiring the processing of 400,000 tuples to produce a result consisting of 40,000 tuples. This is subsequently joined with the tuples of the STUDENT relation, requiring processing 40,000 * 40,000 tuples or 40,000 + 40,000 tuples for unsorted and sorted cases, respectively. The final projection operation involves 40,000 tuples. These costs are tabulated in Figure 10.2b.

Let us now consider the third form of the relational algebraic query. The selection is done before each of the joins. The selection on COURSE entails the processing of 5,000 tuples to generate 500 tuples with *Course#* > COMP300. Similarly, the selection on REGISTRATION involves processing 400,000 tuples to select 40,000 tuples. The join of the STUDENT with the selected tuples of REGISTRATION involves processing 40,000 * 40,000 tuples to arrive at 40,000 resulting tuples. This result is joined with 500 tuples selected from COURSE and entails a processing of 500 * 40,000 tuples. The result is, as before, 40,000 tuples. We notice, however, that the amount of processing is considerably reduced. These costs are tabulated in Figure 10.2c.

Figure 10.2 Evaluating relational algebraic expressions. (a) Cost for evaluating the query in the first relational algebraic form; (b) Cost for evaluating the query in the second relational algebraic form; (c) Cost for evaluating the query in the third relational algebraic form.

$$\pi_{Std\_Name, Course\_Name}(\sigma_{Course\# > COMP300}\ (STUDENT \underset{Std\#}{\bowtie} REGISTRATION \underset{Course\#}{\bowtie} COURSE))$$

Operation	Processing cost if relations not sorted	sorted	Estimated size of result
Join of STUDENT and REGISTRATION	40,000 * 400,000	40,000 + 400,000	400,000 tuples
Join of this result with COURSE	5,000 * 400,000	5,000 + 400,000	400,000 tuples
Selection from result of *Course#* > COMP300	400,000	400,000	40,000 tuples
Projection on *Std_Name, Course_Name*	40,000	40,000	40,000 tuples

(a)

$$\pi_{Std\_Name, Course\_Name}(STUDENT \underset{Std\#}{\bowtie} (\sigma_{Course\# > COMP300}(REGISTRATION \underset{Course\#}{\bowtie} COURSE)))$$

Operation	Processing cost if relations not sorted	sorted	Estimated size of result
Join of REGISTRATION and COURSE	5,000 * 400,000	5,000 + 400,000	400,000 tuples
Selection from result of *COURSE#* > COMP300	400,000	400,000	40,000 tuples
Join of STUDENT and result above	40,000 * 40,000	40,000 + 40,000	40,000 tuples
Projection on *Std_Name, Course_Name*	40,000	40,000	40,000 tuples

(b)

The above illustrates a considerable processing (and I/O cost) reduction when one form of the query is used as opposed to another equivalent one. This indicates that some form of query processing is necessary if the DBMS is to provide an acceptable response. The intent of the query processor is to find a more efficient form of a user-supplied query expression. A query can be improved in a number of ways before its evaluation is performed. The improvements are basically concerned with minimizing, if not altogether removing, redundancy from expressions and results. This in turn involves simplifying and transforming the query, taking into account the characteristics of the data contained in the database. For example, relations may be supported by some access aid on certain attributes. Such access aids could be in the form of an index using a B^+-tree, ISAM, or a hash. Furthermore, the tuples of the

Figure 10.2 Continued

$\pi_{Std\_Name, Course\_Name}(\text{STUDENT} \underset{Std\#}{\bowtie} (\sigma_{Course\# > COMP300}\ (\text{REGISTRATION}) \underset{Course\#}{\bowtie} (\sigma_{Course\# > COMP300}\ \text{COURSE})$

Operation	Processing cost if relations not sorted	sorted	Estimated size of result
Selection from COURSE *Course#* > COMP300	5,000	5,000	500 tuples
Selection from REGISTRATION *Course#* > COMP300	400,000	400,000	40,000 tuples
Join of selected tuples from COURSE and REGISTRATION	500 * 400,000	500 + 40,000	40,000 tuples
Join of STUDENT with result above	40,000 * 40,000	40,000 + 40,000	40,000 tuples
Projection on *Std_Name, Course_Name*	40,000	40,000	40,000 tuples

(c)

relation may be stored in some particular order to aid their retrieval. The system must exploit these access aids and storage schemes to come up with an optimal access plan.

This system-performed optimization should be contrasted with the optimization performed by application programs. While the former is general, the latter is applicable only to certain queries known at application program implementation time. This chapter is concerned with some of the techniques adopted by the system in such optimizations.

10.3 General Strategies for Query Processing

10.3.1 Query Representation

Queries posed by users, while suited to people, are not in a form convenient for internal system use. The query processor represents the user query, transforming it from some query language supported by the DBMS into a standard internal form that it can manipulate. This form would be relational calculus, relational algebra, object graph, operator graph, or tableau.

The process of translating a query into internal form is similar to high-level programming language compilation. In compilation, the checking of variable declarations is done once at compile time, while in query processing of interactive queries, the verification of the existence of a relation (or attribute) has to be performed at the time of the initial analysis of the query. For internal use, it is convenient to represent queries using a procedural format. This rules out relational calculus and algebra for internal representation, even though these formats have been used in a number of query processors. We use operator graphs for internal representation of queries in this text.

Operator Graphs

An **operator graph** depicts how a sequence of operations can be performed. In operator graphs, operations are represented by nodes and the flow of data is shown by directed edges. The graph visually represents the query and is easily understood. Consider the query: ''List the names of students registered in the Database course.'' One possible algebraic formulation is:

$$\pi_{Std\_Name}(\sigma_{Course\_Name = 'Database'}(\text{STUDENT} \bowtie \text{REGISTRATION} \bowtie \text{COURSE})$$

An operator graph for the above sample query is shown in Figure 10.3.

Equivalence transformations such as the earlier application of the selection operation can be used to modify the graph. The graph clearly shows what the effect of such a transformation would be. For most simple queries, the graph resembles a tree. Later on we demonstrate how the graph can be used to discover redundancies in query expressions.

Steps in Query Processing

The steps involved in query processing are as follows:

1. **Convert to a standard starting point.** We would use a relational algebraic form and the operator graph as the starting point. We would also assume that the query expression is in **conjunctive normal form,** that is, the query is of the form $p_1 \vee p_2 \vee \ldots$, where each disjunct p_i is a conjunction of terms $t_{11} \wedge t_{12} \wedge \ldots$.

Figure 10.3 Example of an operator graph.

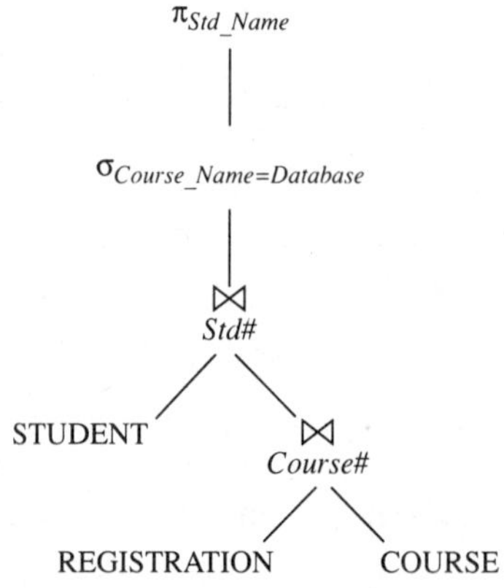

2. **Transform the query.** The query is transformed by replacing expressions in the query with those that are likely to enhance performance. Note that the choice of an equivalent form may be influenced by the existence of an index or the fact that a relation is sorted.
3. **Simplify the query.** The query is simplified by removing redundant and useless operations. We discuss query improvement in Section 10.7.
4. **Prepare alternate access plans.** The alternate access plans indicates the order in which the various operations will be performed and the cost of each such plan. The cost depends on whether or not the relations are sorted and the presence or absence of indexes. The optimal access plan is chosen.

Steps 2, 3, and 4 are usually done in conjunction with each other and use statistical information to derive the best possible form of the query and the associated access plan. The query transformations are carried out by applying standard processing strategies. We discuss some of these strategies for processing a query below and discuss some equivalent forms in Section 10.4.

10.3.2 General Processing Strategies

Recall Example 4.3, in which we illustrated the decrease in the size of join when a selection operation on one of the relations participating in the join was performed before the actual join. Since selection reduces the cardinality of a relation, the join would involve a relation with a smaller number of tuples and could be executed faster. There are a number of similar general strategies used in query processing to reduce the size of the intermediate and final results as well as processing costs. They are described below.

1. **Perform selection as early as possible.** Selection reduces the cardinality of the relation and, as a result, reduces the subsequent processing time.
2. **Combine a number of unary operations.** Consider the evaluation of $\pi_X(\sigma_Y(R))$, where $X, Y \subseteq \mathbf{R}$. Both the selection and projection operations can be done on the tuples of R simultaneously, requiring a single pass over these tuples and singular access to them. Similarly,

$$\sigma_{C1}(\sigma_{C2}(R)) \equiv \sigma_{C1 \wedge C2}(R), \qquad \pi_X(\pi_Y(R)) \equiv \pi_{X \cap Y}(R)$$

   If $X \subseteq Y$, then $\pi_X(\pi_Y(R)) \equiv \pi_X(R)$

3. **Convert the cartesian product with a certain subsequent selection into a join.** Consider the evaluation of $\sigma_Y(R * S)$, where Y is, let us say, $A\ \theta\ B$ and $A \in R$, $B \in S$. In this case, the cartesian product can be replaced by a theta join as follows:

$$R \underset{A\theta B}{\bowtie} S$$

4. **Compute common expressions once.** A common expression that appears more than once in a query may be computed once, stored, and then reused. This is advantageous only if the size of the relation resulting from the common expression is small enough to be either stored in main memory or accessed from secondary storage at a total cost less than that of recomputing it. Bear in

mind that when a number of operations are combined into a single one, as outlined above, common expressions could be masked.

5. **Preprocess the relations.** Before performing an operation such as a join, we can preprocess the relations. The preprocessing includes sorting and index creation on the join attributes. This step is particularly useful when the number of tuples in the operand relations is large.

10.4 Transformation into an Equivalent Expression

Earlier in this chapter we gave an example of a single query being formulated in different ways. This illustrated that the query specified by the user may not be in the best possible form. We saw in the previous section that a selection may reduce the size of a relation, while the size of the resulting join depends on that of the two relations taking part in it and the distribution of the values of the attributes involved in the join. The effort of performing the join can be as high as the product of the cardinality of the participating relations. We also noted that a possible query improvement strategy is to perform selections as early as possible. In this section we offer some of the possible equivalent transformations that could be applied in decreasing the cost of evaluating a query. Two expressions are considered to be equivalent if they produce the same result.

First, we consider the transformations that can be made without the benefit of any information on the relations and their schemes. They are based on the associative and commutative laws of relational algebra. We can use the commutative law in query transformation for a join, since the resulting relation has associated with it the names of the columns. Therefore, the order of columns in the resulting relation is insignificant. We state these general transformation rules below. R, S, T, . . . are relations on the relation schemes **R, S, T,** . . . and C, C1, C2, . . . are arbitrary conditions. Also, ∅ is an empty relation, that is, a relation with cardinality of zero, defined on an appropriate relation scheme.

$R \cup S \equiv S \cup R$	commutative law
$R \cap S \equiv S \cap R$	commutative law
$R \bowtie R \equiv R$	
$R \cup R \equiv R$	idempotent law
$R \cap R \equiv R$	idempotent law
$R - R \equiv \emptyset$	
$R \cup \emptyset \equiv R$	
$R \cap \emptyset \equiv \emptyset$	
$R \bowtie \emptyset \equiv \emptyset$	
$R - \emptyset \equiv R$	
$\emptyset - R \equiv \emptyset$	
$R \bowtie S \equiv S \bowtie R$	commutative law
$R * S \equiv S * R$	commutative law
$R \bowtie (S \bowtie T) \equiv (R \bowtie S) \bowtie T$	associative law
$R * (S * T) \equiv (R * S) * T$	associative law

We incorporate the above equivalences in the form of rules and illustrate them in the examples given below.

1. **Combine a cascade of selections.**

$$\sigma_{C1}(\sigma_{C2}(e)) \equiv \sigma_{C2}(\sigma_{C1}(e)) \equiv \sigma_{C1 \wedge C2}(e))$$

wherein e is an expression and C1 and C2 are predicates. If e is a single variable expression, then the conjunction of selection conditions can be evaluated at the same time.

Example 10.1

Consider the query: ''Get the full details of courses with course number COMP353 where the instructor is Smith.'' This query can be expressed in relational algebra as:

$$\sigma_{Course\# = \text{COMP353}}(\sigma_{Instructor = \text{'Smith'}}(\text{COURSE}))$$

or equivalently by:

$$\sigma_{Course\# = \text{COMP353} \wedge Instructor = \text{'Smith'}}(\text{COURSE}))$$

The latter expression can be evaluated by testing for the predicate

$$Course\# = \text{COMP353} \wedge Instructor = \text{'Smith'}$$

against each tuple of relation COURSE. ■

If e is a multivariable expression, say, of the form el $\bowtie$ e2, then the conditions Cl and C2 may be more appropriately evaluated against the subexpressions el and e2 (rule 5 below).

2. **Combine a cascade of projection into a single projection.**

$$\pi_X(\pi_Y(R)) \equiv \pi_X(R) \text{ where } X \subseteq Y$$

Example 10.2

Consider the query:

$$\pi_{Course\_Name}(\pi_{Course\_Name,Instructor}(\text{COURSE}))$$

This query can be stated as:

$$\pi_{Course\_Name}(\text{COURSE})$$ ■

3. **Commute selection and projection.**

$$\sigma_C(\pi_X(R)) \equiv \pi_X(\sigma_C(R))$$

and

$$\pi_X(\sigma_C(R)) \equiv \sigma_C(\pi_X(R))$$

However, if C involves attributes $Y \notin X$, then when commuting projection with selection we have to use the following equivalence:

$$\pi_X(\sigma_C(R)) \equiv \pi_X(\sigma_C(\pi_{X \cup Y}(R)))$$[1]

[1]From an implementation point of view, one wonders at the usefulness of this transformation. If projection and selection are done in separate steps, then the relation is accessed three times in the transformed version instead of twice. Admittedly, the selection operation deals with a smaller number of tuples, but its significance depends on the first projection. If projection and selection are combined in one access of the relation, the advantage of this transformation is doubtful.

4. **Use associative and commutative rules for joins and cartesian products.**

$R \bowtie S \equiv S \bowtie R$
$R \bowtie S \bowtie T \equiv R \bowtie (S \bowtie T) \equiv (R \bowtie S) \bowtie T \equiv (T \bowtie S) \bowtie R \equiv$
$R * S \equiv S * R$
$R * S * T \equiv R * (S * T) \equiv (R * S) * T \equiv (R * T) * S \equiv \ldots$

The order of the join and product is very important as it can substantially affect the size of the intermediate relations and, therefore, the total cost of generating the result relation.

Example 10.3

In Example 10.1, the expression

$$\sigma_{Course\# > \text{COMP300}} (\text{STUDENT} \underset{Std\#}{\bowtie} \text{REGISTRATION}) \underset{Course\#}{\bowtie} \text{COURSE})$$

can be replaced by the more efficient expression:

$$(\text{STUDENT} \underset{Std\#}{\bowtie} (\sigma_{Course\# > \text{COMP300}} \text{REGISTRATION}) \underset{Course\#}{\bowtie} (\sigma_{Course\# > \text{COMP300}} \text{COURSE})$$

The above expression is equivalent to the following:

$$((\sigma_{Course\# > \text{COMP300}} \text{REGISTRATION}) \underset{Course\#}{\bowtie} (\sigma_{Course\# > \text{COMP300}} \text{COURSE}) \underset{Std\#}{\bowtie} \text{STUDENT}) \blacksquare$$

5. **Perform selection before a join or cartesian product.** Consider $\sigma_C(R \bowtie S)$. If the attributes involved in the condition C are in the scheme of R and not in S, that is, attr(C) ∈ **R** and attr(C) ∉ **S,** then

$$\sigma_C(R \bowtie S) \equiv \sigma_C(R) \bowtie S$$

If the attributes involved in the condition C are in the scheme of S but not in R, i.e., attr(C) ∈ **S** and attr(C), ∉ **R,** then

$$\sigma_C(R \bowtie S) \equiv R \bowtie \sigma_C(S)$$

If the attributes involved in the condition C are in the scheme of **R** and **S,** i.e., attr(C) ∈ **R** and attr(C) ∈ **S,** then

$$\sigma_C(R \bowtie S) \equiv \sigma_C(R) \bowtie \sigma_C(S)$$

If C = C1 ∧ C2 and the attributes involved in the condition C1 are from **R,** i.e., attr(C1) ∈ **R,** and the attributes involved in the condition C2 are from **S,** i.e., attr(C2) ∈ **S,** then

$$\sigma_C(R \bowtie S) \equiv \sigma_{C1}(R) \bowtie \sigma_{C2}(S)$$

If C = C1 ∧ C2 ∧ C3 and the attributes involved in the condition C2 are only in **R,** i.e., attr(C2) ∈ **R** ∧ attr(C2) ∉ **S,** the attributes involved in the condition C3 are only in S, i.e., attr(C3) ∈ **S** ∧ attr(C3), ∉ **R,** and the attributes involved in the condition C1 are in **R** and **S,** then

$$\sigma_C(R \bowtie S) \equiv \sigma_{C1}(\sigma_{C2}(R) \bowtie \sigma_{C3}(S))$$

The above equivalences also apply when the cartesian product operation is substituted for the join.

Example 10.4 Consider the expression:

$$\sigma_{Std\# > 1234567 \wedge Course\# = \text{COMP353} \wedge Course\_Name = \text{'Database'}}(\text{GRADE} \bowtie \text{COURSE})$$

It is equivalent to:

$$\sigma_{Course\# = \text{COMP353}}((\sigma_{Std\# > 1234567}(\text{GRADE})) \bowtie (\sigma_{Course\_Name = \text{'Database'}}(\text{COURSE}))) \blacksquare$$

It is possible to combine projections with a binary operation that precedes or follows it. Only the attribute values specified in the projection need to be retained. The remaining ones can be eliminated as we evaluate the binary operation.

6. **Perform a modified projection before a join.** Note that when a projection operation is preceded by a join, it is possible to push the projection down before the join, but the projection acquires new attributes. This necessitates performing the original projection after the join. However, unless the cardinalites of intermediate relations are reduced, which would reduce the cost of the join operation and the subsequent size of the joined relation, the usefulness of pushing a projection before a join is questionable.

$$\pi_X(R \bowtie S) \equiv \pi_X(\pi_{R'}(R) \bowtie \pi_{S'}(S))$$

where $R' = \mathbf{R} \cap (X \cup \mathbf{S})$ and $S' = \mathbf{S} \cap (X \cup \mathbf{R})$, and **R, S** represent the set of attributes in these relation schemes. When $X \equiv \mathbf{R} \cup \mathbf{S} - \mathbf{R} \cap \mathbf{S}$, there is no improvement because $R' \equiv R$ and $S' \equiv S$.

Example 10.5 Consider the relations GRADE *(Std#, Course#, Grade)* and COURSE *(Course#, Course_Name, Instructor)*. The expression

$$\pi_{Std\#, Course\_Name}(\text{GRADE} \bowtie \text{COURSE})$$

is equivalent to:

$$\pi_{Std\#, Course\_Name}(\pi_{Std\#, Course\#}(\text{GRADE}) \bowtie \pi_{Course\#, Course\_Name}(\text{COURSE}))$$

However, consider the relations STUDENT *(Std#, Std_Name)* and REGISTRATION (Std#,Course#). The expression

$$\pi_{Std\_Name, Course\#}(\text{STUDENT} \bowtie \text{REGISTRATION})$$

is equivalent to:

$$\pi_{Std\_Name, Course\#}(\pi_{Std\#, Std\_Name}(\text{STUDENT}) \bowtie \pi_{Std\#, Course\#}(\text{REGISTRATION}))$$

which is equivalent to the original query:

$$\pi_{Std\_Name, Course\#}(\text{STUDENT} \bowtie \text{REGISTRATION})) \blacksquare$$

7. **Commuting projection with a cartesian product.** Consider the expression $\pi_X(R * S)$. This expression can be replaced by the following equivalent one under

these conditions: X1 is the set of attributes in X that is in the scheme of R, and X2 is the set of attributes in X that is in the scheme of S.

$$\pi_X(R * S) \equiv \pi_{X1}(R) * \pi_{X2}(S)$$

Example 10.6

Consider the relations STUDENT *(Std#, Std_Name)* and REGISTRATION *(Std#, Course#)*. The expression

$$\pi_{Course\#, Std\_Name}(\text{STUDENT} * \text{REGISTRATION})$$

is equivalent to:

$$\pi_{Std\_Name}(\text{STUDENT}) * \pi_{Course\#}(\text{REGISTRATION})$$ ■

8. **Commuting projection with a union.** Consider the expression $\pi_X(R \cup S)$. It can be substituted by the equivalent one given below provided the relations R and S are compatible. In other words, they are defined on similar relation schemes. Dissimilarities in the names of the attributes could be handled by appropriate renaming.

$$\pi_X(R \cup S) \equiv \pi_X(R) \cup \pi_X(S)$$

Example 10.7

Consider the relations STUDENT *(Std#, Std_Name)* and REGISTRATION *(Std#, Course#)*. The expression

$$\pi_{Std\#}(\text{STUDENT} \cup \text{REGISTRATION})$$

is equivalent to:

$$\pi_{Std\#}(\text{STUDENT}) \cup \pi_{Std\#}(\text{REGISTRATION})$$ ■

9. **Commute selection with a union.** Again, the relations R and S must be compatible and any difference in names of the attributes could be handled by appropriate renaming.

$$\sigma_C(R \cup S) = \sigma_C(R) \cup \sigma_C(S)$$

10. **Commute selection with a difference.** As in rules 8 and 9 above, relations R and S must be compatible and renaming would resolve any differences in the names of the attributes.

$$\sigma_C(R - S) = \sigma_C(R) - \sigma_C(S)$$

We could replace the relations R, S, etc. in each of the above rules by a relational expression. Note that the difference operation is not commutative.

In addition to the above rules, the semantics of the data may be used to generate a query that is more economical than the original query. We illustrate this in Example 10.8.

Example 10.8

Consider the university database. Suppose we want to find the list of active students (only the *Std#*). This can be expressed by the query:

$$\pi_{Std\#}(\text{STUDENT} \bowtie \text{REGISTRATION})$$

However, knowing that *Std#* is the foreign key corresponding to the primary key of STUDENT, we can replace the above query by the following, without involving a join:

$$\pi_{Std\#}\text{REGISTRATION} \quad ■$$

Finally, the query processor can use the knowledge of the relation schemes and functional dependencies to find additional equivalent forms for a query expression. Example 10.9 illustrates this.

Example 10.9 Given **R**(A,B,C) and **S**$(C,D,E \ldots; C \rightarrow D)$, the query $\sigma_{A=a1}(R \bowtie S)$ can be replaced by $(\sigma_{A=a1}\ R) \bowtie S$ and the query $\pi_{CD}(S) \bowtie \pi_{DE}(S)$ is equivalent to $\pi_{CDE}(S)$. ■

Having determined the rules for deriving different equivalence transformations, the question remains, "What can we do with the different equivalent forms of a query?" Also, which of these forms should the system choose to evaluate? These different forms could have varying sizes of intermediate and final results, which would affect input/output and processing costs and consequently response time. In the following section we discuss the methods used in estimating the size of the relations in the response.

10.5 Expected Size of Relations in the Response

The aim in centralized databases is to minimize disk (or secondary storage device) accesses, while in distributed databases, the goal has been communication cost reduction where long-haul communication links are used. Thus, the system would prefer the query form that meets the system's optimization goals.

In general, query processing involves the costs of processing, input/output, and communication in distributed systems. The goal could be to optimize one, a pair, or all of these costs. The costs are not known before the evaluation, but an estimate based on past statistics could be made to compare the different evaluations.

If access is required to all tuples of relation R with tuple size sz_R, then the number of bytes accessed are $|R| * sz_R$, which can be used as a cost estimate. It is, however, normal to access data from secondary storage in blocks (or pages). Let the blocking factor, which indicates the number of logical records per block, be bf_R. Then the number of blocks accessed to retrieve the tuples of relation R is given by

$$\text{number of block accesses} = \lceil |R|/bf_R \rceil \text{ blocks}$$

Communication cost is given in terms of setup cost and the number of bytes transmitted. Assuming that the setup cost is c_0 and the per byte transmission cost is c_1, and these costs are the same for all communication links, then

$$\text{communication cost} = c_0 + c_1 * |R| * sz_R$$

In this chapter we restrict ourselves to centralized database systems, for which the communication cost would be zero. We return to distributed query processing in Chapter 15.

Selection, projections, and joins affect the sizes of the resulting relations. The effect of projection is simple to calculate if the sizes of the attribute values are known. The effect of selections and joins is more involved.

We are interested in the size of the result relation for several reasons. First, the result relations could be intermediate relations and their size would be required to determine the cost of the succeeding part of the query expression. Second, the result relation may be too large to be stored in primary memory and would have to be written to secondary storage. We may want to compare the cost of this access with alternate equivalent query expressions.

Let us assume that the values of an attribute are uniformly distributed over its domain and that the distribution is independent of values in the other attributes. These assumptions are usually made for simplifying cost calculations, and it should be noted that these assumptions cannot be justified on any other grounds. In practice both uniform distribution and independence are unlikely to occur. In that case, the expressions become complicated and are beyond the scope of this text.

10.5.1 Selection

Let T = σ_C (R) represent the selection of relation R on condition C, and let C be a simple clause of the form R[A] = constant. Before we can estimate the size of the resultant relation we must possess some knowledge about the value distributions, that is, the number of times an attribute takes a particular value. We can simply assume that each value occurs with equal probability. Then the expected number of tuples in relation T is given by

$$|T| = \frac{1 * |R|}{|R[A]|}$$

where $|R[A]|$ is the number of distinct values for attribute A of relation R. The factor $1/|R[A]|$ is known as the **selectivity factor** and is usually represented by the symbol ρ (rho). As illustrated in Example 10.10, the nature of the data may allow an estimation of some selectivity factors.

Example 10.10 Recall that in the university database example, the assumption that each student is registered in 10 courses is a reasonable assumption. Therefore, we expect that

$$\sigma_{Std\# = 1234567}(\text{REGISTRATION})$$

will have ten tuples and

$$\sigma_{Course\# = \text{COMP453}}(\text{REGISTRATION})$$

will have 80 tuples if there are 5000 courses. We recognize that in reality, there will be considerable variations on these values. However, we can use them as estimates. ■

As discussed in Chapter 3, it is unfortunately not reasonable to assume uniform distribution of values in all cases. Uniform distribution assumption is widely used nonetheless for estimating costs in choosing a query processing strategy. We should therefore bear in mind that this is just an estimate.

Having generated the relation T (consisting of the tuples of relation R, satisfying the predicate C, involving the attribute A), suppose we need to estimate the number of distinct values for the attribute B in T. Note that $B \neq A$ and the number of distinct values for B in the relation T is given by $|T[B]|$.

We assume that the occurrence of a value in attribute B is unaffected by the values in A. In other words, the distributions are independent. Under these assumptions, it can be shown that this problem is equivalent to the so-called colored balls problem. In this problem we have n balls of m different colors. (Apart from color, all balls are identical.) Each color is represented by the same number of balls. We must determine the expected number of different colors represented by a random selection of t of these n balls.

It can be shown that the expected number of colors in these t balls is given by the following expression:

$$\text{expected number of colors} = m * \left[1 - \prod_{i=1}^{t} \frac{n((m-1)/m - i + 1}{n - i + 1} \right]$$

We can estimate $|T[B]|$, the expected number of different values for the attribute B in T, by the following substitution in the above expression: $n = |R|$, $m = |R[B]|$, and $t = |T|$.

However, the computation involved in evaluating this expression is considerable. As a result, a number of different approximations to the above expression have been proposed. We present below one of the more widely used approximations. This approximation is given by the following formula for different sizes of the relation T:

$$|T[B]| = \begin{bmatrix} |T| & \text{if } |T| < \dfrac{|R[B]|}{2} \\ \dfrac{(|T| + |R[B]|)}{3} & \text{if } \dfrac{|R[B]|}{2} \leq |T| \leq 2 * |R[B]| \\ |R[B]| & \text{if } |T| > 2 * |R[B]| \end{bmatrix}$$

The size of each tuple in relation T is the same as in relation R.

10.5.2 Projection

The cardinality of the resulting relation could be affected by a projection because duplicates would be deleted; however, most commercial database systems only delete duplicates as a result of explicit commands.

$$T = \pi_X (R)$$

where X is a set of attributes, $X \subseteq \mathbf{R}$.

When X is a single attribute, or contains the key attribute of R, and we represent the single or key attribute by A, then

$$|T| = |R[A]|$$

If A is a key attribute of R then $|T| = |R|$.
When X is a set of attributes, then

$$|T| = \prod_{A_i \in X} |R[A_i]|$$

In the above estimation of the result we are assuming that the relation is a cartesian product of the values of its attributes. Such an assumption is rarely justified. We can take this as the worse case estimate. The upper limit in the above expression is given as:

$$|T| \leq |R|$$

The size of the tuples of T is the sum of the size of the attributes in X.

10.5.3 Join

The join operation is very common in relational database systems. The size estimation for the result of a join is somewhat more complicated than that of selection because the cardinality of the result relation depends on the distribution of values in the joining attribute. Furthermore, the cost of evaluating a join is not reflected in the size of the result. The cost depends on the size of the relations being joined. We are, however, interested in estimating the size of the result, since it could be used in subsequent operations in evaluating a query.

Since the size of the result depends on the values of the joining attributes and the distribution of these values, we shall consider a number of special cases.

Let

$$T = R \underset{R.A = S \cdot B}{\bowtie} S$$

Estimating the cardinality of T is complex because it is difficult to estimate correctly the number of tuples of each relation that join with tuples of the other relation. In the worse case the join is equivalent to a cartesian product; this occurs when the operand relations do not share attributes defined on common domains. In such cases, the cardinality of the result relation is given by:

$$|T| \leq |R| * |S|$$

This value of cardinality is much too large for most practical databases. We consider a number of special cases below, assuming a uniform distribution of values.

1. Let $\{A\}$ represent the set of values that the attribute A takes in the relation R. The number of distinct values for attribute A is given by $|R[A]|$. We assume uniform distribution of these values and further assume that these values will also be in relation S. In this case, we could conclude that there are $|S|/|R[A]|$ tuples in S for each value for attribute A. Therefore, each tuple in R joins with $|S|/|R[A]|$ tuples in S and the number of tuples in T is given by:

$$|T| = \frac{|R| * |S|}{|R[A]|}$$

Let $\{B\}$ represent the set of values that attribute B takes in relation S. The number of distinct values for attribute B is given by $|S[B]|$. Again, using uniform distribution and further assuming that these values would also be in relation R, we could conclude that there are $|R|/|S[B]|$ tuples in R for each value for attribute B. This means that each tuple in S joins with $|R|/|S[B]|$ tuples in R, and it follows that the number of tuples in T is given by:

$$|T| = \frac{|R| * |S|}{|S[B]|}$$

If $\{A\} \neq \{B\}$, then $|R[A]| \neq |S[B]|$ and the values for $|T|$, obtained by the expressions $(|R| * |S|)/|R[A]|$ and $(|R| * |S|)/|S[B]|$, would be different. This indicates that there are tuples in R and S that do not participate in the join. Such tuples are called dangling tuples.

The greater, average, or the lesser of $(|R| * |S|)/|R[A]|$ and $(|R| * |S|)/|S[B]|$ could be taken as the estimate of the size of T.

2. If A is the key of R, then every tuple of S can only join with one tuple of R, i.e., the cardinality of the resultant relation cannot be greater than the cardinality of S:

$$|T| \leq |S|$$

3. Another possible derivation of an estimate, which takes into account the size of the domain and which estimates a much smaller value for the cardinality of the join, is as follows. The number of distinct values of A in R and B in S is $|R[A]|$ and $|S[B]|$, respectively. Assuming uniform distribution as before, each value of A in R (B in S) is associated with $|R|/|R[A]|$ tuples ($|S|/|S[B]|$). Thus, for each value of A (or B) in the join, we could derive the upper limit on the number of tuples in the join as given below:

$$\frac{|R| * |S|}{|R[A]| * |S[B]|} \text{ tuples}$$

The above will hold if the same set of values are in both R and S. Since the same set of values is unlikely to be in the two relations, the expected number of common domain values is much lower. This expected number depends on the probability of any value appearing in both the relations. The expected number of distinct values of A in R (or B in S) that takes part in the join is given by:

$$\frac{|R[A]| * |S[B]|}{|D|}$$

where $|D|$ is the cardinality of the domain of A and B. Therefore, the expected actual size of the join is given by:

$$|T| = \frac{|R[A]| * |S[B]|}{|D|} * \frac{|R| * |S|}{|R[A]| * |S[B]|}$$
$$= \frac{|R| * |S|}{|D|}$$

The size of tuples of T equals the sum of the sizes of tuples of R and S, minus the size of the joining attribute A (or B).

10.6 Statistics in Estimation

In the above discussions, we have estimated the size of the result. The cost of each of these operations depends on the storage organization and the indexes that may be present in the database. Additional indexes may be created, or the relation may be sorted to perform one of the above operations.

Estimation of the size of results could also be generated from statistics maintained by the DBMS. These statistics include the cardinality of the relations, the number of distinct values for each attribute, and the cardinality of joins with different relations. Such statistics could be recorded once a query is executed. For instance, having decided on the basis of the above estimates that the join of R and S be made, the database system generates this join. It can then determine the cardinality of the result and store this as an estimate.[2] Such an estimate will give a better indication of the costs and sizes than the estimate discussed in Section 10.5. However, if the database is modified in the interim, the result would be different than this recorded statistic. In such a case, the database could modify these statistics and record the amount of change in the statistics. The recording of such incremental changes would be useful in subsequent estimating to generate better results.

The overhead involved in generating and modifying such statistics dictates that those statistics be generated only during low load on the computing systems or by execution of specific utility programs. Examples of such utilities are RUNSTATS in DB2 and UPDATE STATISTICS in SQL/DS.

As a consequence of changes in the database, the result obtained by using outdated statistics may not be accurate. However, since these are only estimates, they are still useful in selecting a better query processing strategy.

10.7 Query Improvement

A query can be improved in a number of ways before its evaluation is performed. The improvements are basically concerned with minimizing, if not altogether removing, redundancy from expressions and results. Elimination of redundant expression is equivalent to pruning the query operator tree. The rules discussed in Section 10.4 are used in finding equivalent query expressions and the cost of each expression is evaluated. We illustrate the application of a few of these rules in a number of examples in this section.

Let us first consider the general strategy of performing selections and projections as early as possible.

Example 10.11 Consider the query: ''List the names of students registered in the Database course.'' The algebraic formulation of this query is given below and the corresponding query tree is given in Figure 10.3.

[2] The argument against recording such an estimate after each query is the additional locking required to update the statistics and concommitant locking overhead. It would also cause the serialization of queries modifying independent relations in the database.

$$\pi_{Std\_Name}(\sigma_{Course\_Name = \text{'Database'}}(\text{STUDENT} \bowtie \text{REGISTRATION} \bowtie \text{COURSE}))$$

Referring to Figure 10.3, we can see that if the operations were performed as stated, the selections and projections would be applied during the last stage of query evaluation. If the selection were to be applied to the COURSE relation, it would reduce the number of tuples of the COURSE relation that would take part in the joins. We therefore ''push down the tree'' any selection and projection operators. At the intermediate nodes, the operators are pushed into the appropriate branches. For example, if we push down the selection operator, because the relation STUDENT does not contain the *Course_Name* attribute, the selection is only applicable to the intermediate results from the other branch, as shown in Figure Ai. The selection can be pushed further down to the leaf nodes as shown in Figure Aii.

Figure A Example of pushing down the selection in an operator graph.

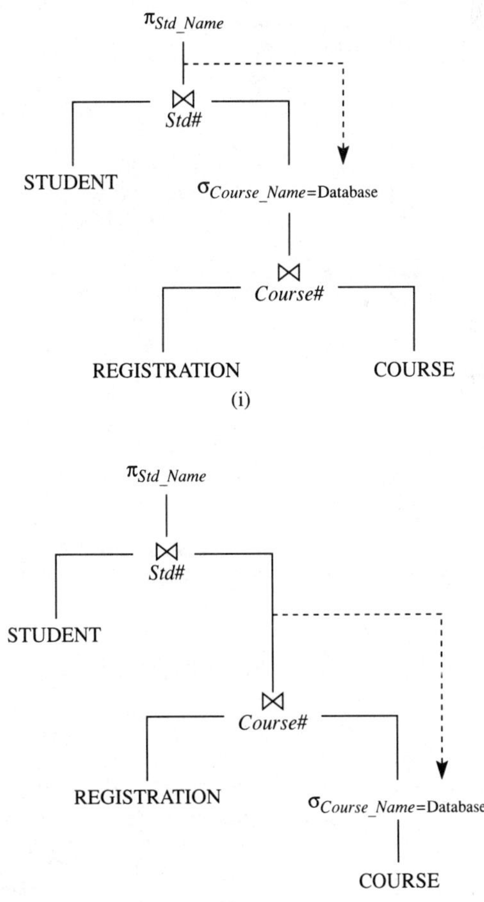

■

As we discussed under rule 6 in Section 10.4, a projection cannot be simply moved down. Given relations R and S defined on the relation schemes **R**(X,Y,Z) and **S**(X,Y,W), where W, X, Y, Z are sets of attributes, then

$$\pi_X(R \underset{Y}{\bowtie} S) \equiv \pi_X(\pi_{X,Y}(R) \underset{Y}{\bowtie} \pi_{X,Y}(S))$$

In other words, as the projection is pushed down, it acquires additional attributes. These additional attributes finally have to be eliminated by the original projection. This is illustrated in the following example.

Example 10.12 Consider the query: ''Compile a list of instructors and the grades they assign.'' The relational algebraic expression for this query is given below:

$$\pi_{Instructor,Grade}(\text{GRADE} \bowtie \text{COURSE})$$

The corresponding query tree is given in Figure Bi. To push the projection down the tree, we would have to include the common attribute *Course#* of GRADE and COURSE in both branches of the join operation as indicated in Figure Bii.

Figure B Pushing projection down the query tree.

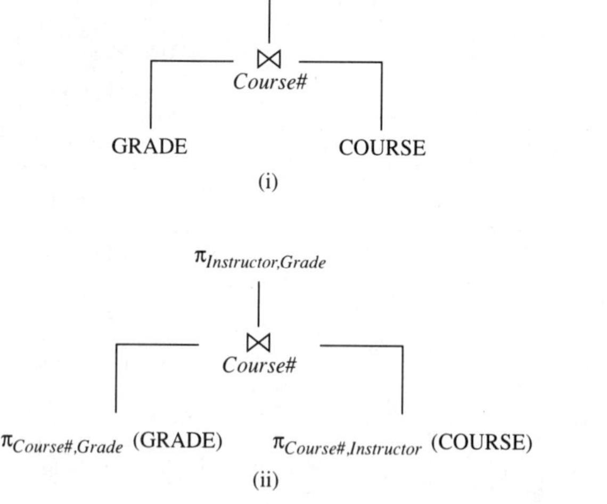

■

Example 10.13 illustrates the effect of pushing the projection operation down the query tree.

Example 10.13 Consider the query: ''List the names of the students in the Database course.'' The relational algebraic expression for this query is given below:

$$\pi_{Std\_Name}(\text{STUDENT} \underset{Std\#}{\bowtie} \pi_{Std\#,Course\#}(\text{REGISTRATION}$$

$$\underset{Course\#}{\bowtie} (\sigma_{Course\_Name = \text{'Database'}}(\text{COURSE})))$$

This expression can be simplified by moving the second projection further to the right in the expression, before the join on *Course#*. In the case of the relation REGISTRATION the projection is the entire relation and for COURSE the projection is on the attribute *Course#*. The modified expression is shown below:

$$\pi_{Std\_Name}(\text{STUDENT} \underset{Std\#}{\bowtie} (\text{REGISTRATION} \underset{Course\#}{\bowtie} \pi_{Course\#}(\sigma_{Course\_Name = \text{'Database'}}(\text{COURSE}))))$$

The effect of pushing the projection operation down the query tree is illustrated in Figures Ci and Cii. Since the projection on the attributes *Std#* and *Course#* of the relation REGISTRATION is the entire relation, the operation is redundant and dropped. *Course#* is the only attribute appearing

Figure C Effect of pushing down projection operator.

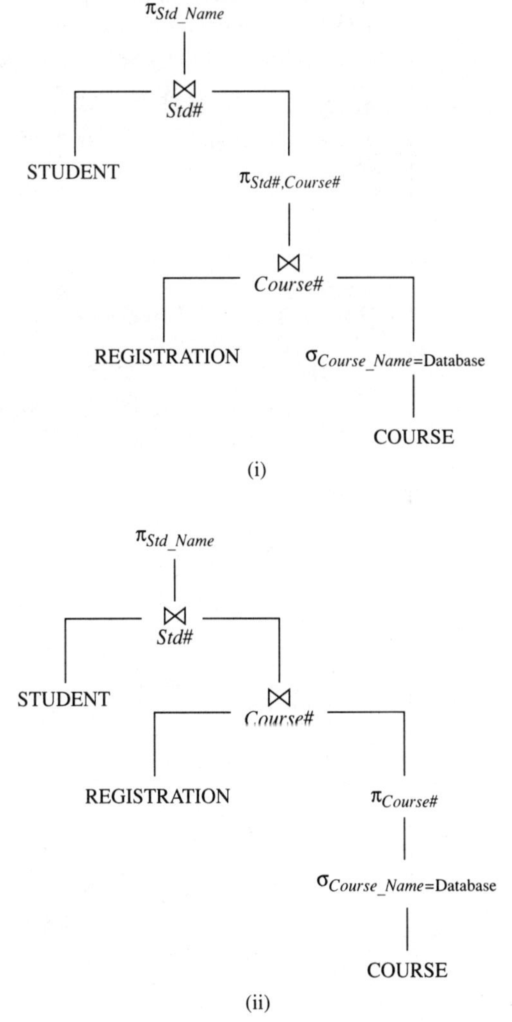

in the relation COURSE. Therefore in pushing the operation $\pi_{Std\#,Course\#}$ down, we drop the attribute *Std#*. Note that the projection and selection operations on the relation COURSE could be combined during a single pass over its tuples. ■

The other form of query improvement is the transformation of a redundant expression into a nonredundant one. Redundant expressions may have been entered by the user or may result during query transformation, as illustrated in Example 10.14.

Example 10.14 Consider the query: "Compile a list of the names of students who have not obtained a grade of C or higher in the Database course." A possible relational algebraic query is given in Figure Di and the corresponding operator graph is shown in Figure Dii.

The two subtrees of the difference operators are similar, the difference being that in the right subtree there is a selection on the GRADE relation. Moving the selection to be performed after the join on *Std#* (or just before the difference operation), we get the modified relational algebraic expression given below and the graph of Figure E.

$$\pi_{Std\_Name}(\text{STUDENT} \bowtie (\text{GRADE} \bowtie (\sigma_{Course\_Name = \text{'Database'}}(\text{COURSE}))) - \sigma_{Grade \geq C}(\text{STUDENT} \bowtie (\text{GRADE} \bowtie (\sigma_{Course\_Name = \text{'Database'}}(\text{COURSE}))))$$

Figure D (i) Relational algebraic query and (ii) corresponding query graph.

$$\pi_{Std\_Name}\ (\text{STUDENT} \bowtie (\text{GRADE} \bowtie (\sigma_{Course\_Name=\text{Database}}\ (\text{COURSE})))-(\text{STUDENT} \bowtie (\sigma_{Grade \geq C}\ \text{GRADE} \bowtie (\sigma_{Course\_Name=\text{Database}}\ (\text{COURSE})))))$$

(i)

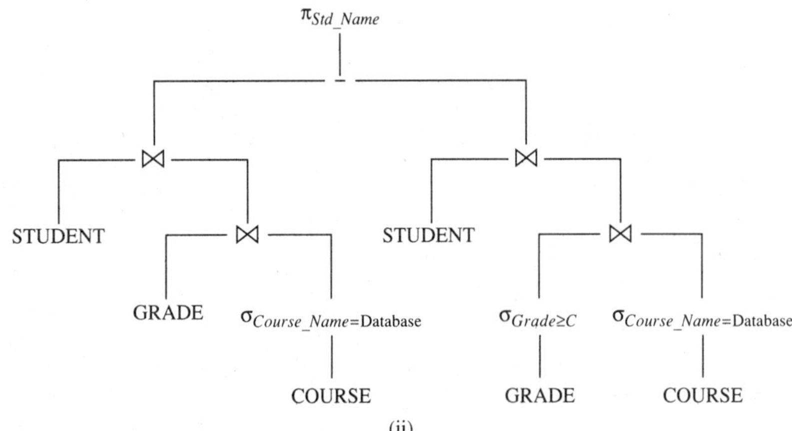

(ii)

Figure E Graph showing two identical subtrees.

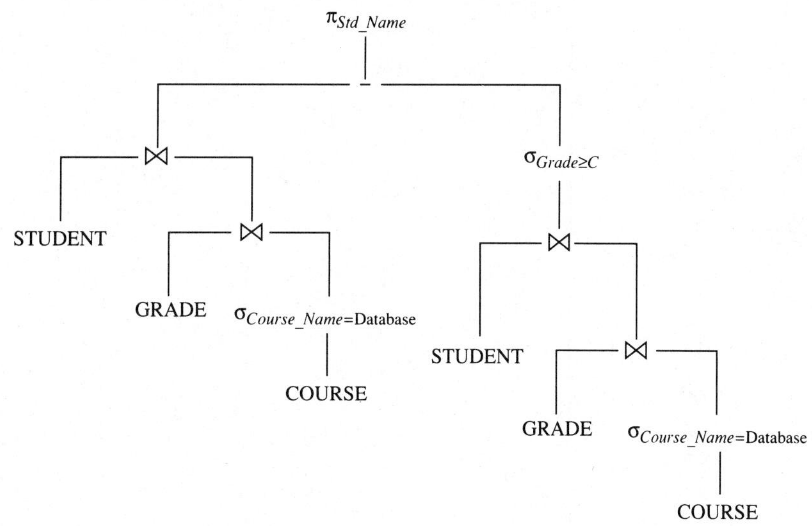

We can see that there are two identical subtress in the graph of Figure E, indicating a redundancy. We can remove the redundancy as shown in figure Fi and replace the difference operation by a selection. These changes are reflected in Figure Fii. Note that $R - \sigma_C(R) = \sigma_{\neg C}(R)$, where $\neg C$ is the negation of the predicate C.

Figure F Removing redundancy from the graph of Figure E.

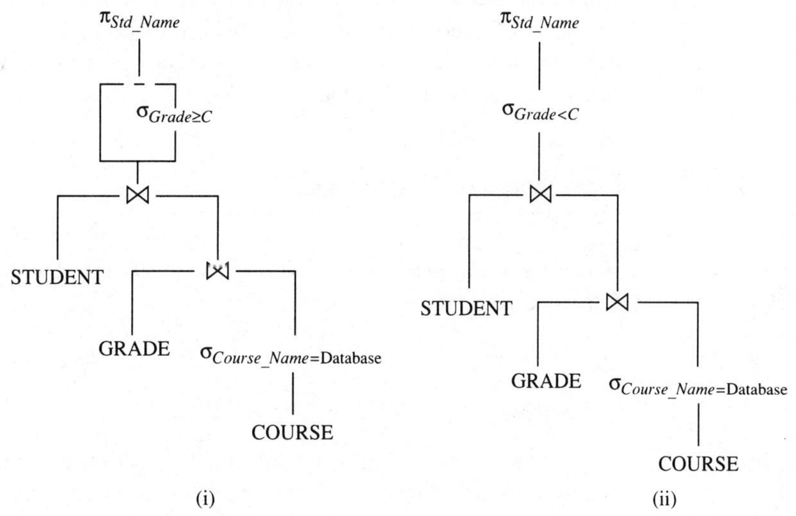

Figure G Final optimization for Example 10.14.

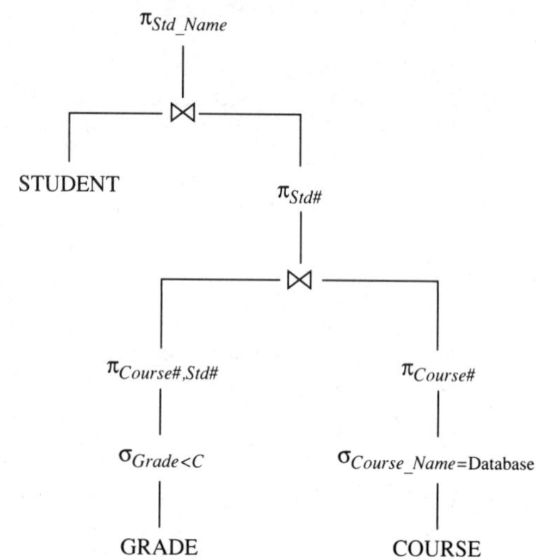

Finally, we can push down the selections and projections to give us the tree of Figure G. ■

10.8 Query Evaluation

We have presented a sampling of the many different query improvement strategies. Having found the best equivalent form of a query, the next step is to evaluate it. We classify the query evaluation approaches according to the number of relations involved in the query expression. Thus, we distinguish between the approach to be used when the query expression involves one, two, or many relations. These are known as one-variable, two-variable, and N-variable expressions, respectively. The last stage of query processing deals with the execution of access plans. A number of different query evaluation strategies have been proposed. Here we look at some commonly implemented techniques.

10.8.1 One-Variable Expressions

A **one-variable expression** involves the selection of tuples from a single relation. Let us consider the SQL query:

select al, . . ., ak
from R
where p

The simplest approach would involve reading in each tuple of the relation and testing it to ascertain if it satisfies the required predicates. This is illustrated below.

Sequential Access

Use **sequential access** to read in every tuple of the relation. If the tuple satisfies the qualification conditions, include the projection of the tuple on the target list attributes in the result relation. The algorithm is given below:

```
result := ∅ {empty}
for every r in R do
    if satisfies (p, r)
        then result := result + <r.al . . . r.ak>
```

where <r.al . . . r.ak> represents the tuple obtained by concatenating the projections of r onto the attributes in the target list.

If the relation has n tuples that are blocked as b tuples/block, then for sequential access to the tuples, the number of block accesses is $\lceil n/b \rceil$. In dealing with large relations, this is an inefficient approach, as illustrated in Example 10.15.

Example 10.15

Consider the REGISTRATION relation to evaluate the query: "Generate the list of students (*Std#* only) enrolled in COMP353." The SQL version of this query is:

select *Std#*
from REGISTRATION
where *Course#* = COMP353

We use sequential access to the tuples of REGISTRATION. Suppose there are 400 tuples per block of secondary storage devices. Reading in all tuples of REGISTRATION would involve access to 400,000/400 = 1,000 block accesses. ■

Access Aid

The number of tuples needing to be accessed could be reduced if the relation is sorted with respect to one or more attributes. In such cases, if the predicates involve one or more attributes on which the relation is sorted, then only some of the tuples need be accessed. Use of indexes can provide faster access to the required tuples.

Example 10.16

Let us reconsider the previous example of generating the list of students enrolled in COMP353. If the tuples of REGISTRATION are sorted in order based on *Course#* and the records are clustered with 400 tuples per block, we could do a binary search on these blocks. Locating the block containing the required course would limit access to about 10 blocks. This will be followed by access to at most one additional block. The last block accessed would be needed only if some 80 tuples with the required course number were not in the same block. This gives us a total of approximately 11 block accesses. ■

If the relation has an index, it may be used to improve evaluation performance when access is required to a subset of the tuples. Such indices could be on one attribute or they may involve a combination of attributes.

Example 10.17 Let us reconsider the previous example of generating the list of students enrolled in COMP353. If an index exists on the *Course#,* then access to the different levels of the index would involve (at most) two block accesses, followed by one to the appropriate tuples. If the tuples are clustered by *Course#,* then a maximum of two additional block accesses are required to generate the response. ■

10.8.2 Two-Variable Expressions

A **two-variable expression** involves either two distinct tuples from the same relation or two distinct relations. Here we concentrate on the latter case. One of the most common (and expensive) binary operations is the join operation. In this section we consider how the join, for instance R ⋈ S, can be evaluated.

Nested Loop Method

The **nested loop method** is a simple method in which every pair of tuples from the participating relations are accessed and tested for the join condition. The algorithm in the form of pseudocode is sketched below.

```
for i := 1 to |R| do            (* outer loop *)
   begin
      get ith tuple of R
      for j := 1 to |S| do       (* inner loop *)
      begin
         get jth tuple of S
         if join condition is satisfied then
            perform join of the ith tuple
            of R with the jth tuple of S
         end (* inner loop*)
   end (* outer loop *)
```

It should be clear that every tuple of the outer relation is matched with all of those of the inner relation.

The total number of secondary storage accesses required, assuming that each tuple requires an access, is given as $|R| + |R| * |S|$. The first term indicates the access to the tuple of the outer relation and for each such tuple, all the tuples of the inner relation must be accessed. It is preferable to have the smaller relation in the outer loop. We illustrate this in Example 10.18.

Example 10.18 Consider the problem of generating the class list, consisting of *Std#, Std_Name, Course#,* in the university database. This involves joining the STUDENT and REGISTRATION relations. The nested loop method would involve a total of 40,000 + 40,000 ∗ 400,000 disk accesses, assuming a disk access for each tuple. Obviously, if the larger relation were in the outer loop, the number of disk accesses would have been 400,000 + 400,000 ∗ 40,000. ■

Even in the case of small relations, the value $|R| + |R| * |S|$ is quite large. The order of the algorithm is $O(n^2)$.

We can substantially improve the performance of the nested loop method by considering physical device characteristics. Data is accessed from secondary storage in chunks called blocks or pages. So our first improvement to the algorithm would be to move away from comparing a single tuple of the outer relation with a single tuple of the inner, to comparing all tuples in a block of the outer relation with those from a block of the inner one. This strategy requires that there be space in the main memory for these blocks. The modified algorithm for a blocked nested loop is given below.

```
for each B blocks of R do          (* outer loop *)
  begin
    read B blocks of R
    for each block of S do  (* inner loop *)
      begin
        read block of S
        for each tuple of the B blocks of R do
          for each tuple in the block of S do
            if join condition is satisfied
             then
                  join the tuple of R with the tuple of S;
        end (* inner loop *)
    end (* outer loop *)
```

Suppose we use blocked (or paged) accesses with the blocking factors of relations R and S represented by bf_R and bf_S, respectively. B blocks of memory are available to store the blocks of relation R (the outer relation). Then the outer loop involves reading B blocks of R at a time. Each tuple in the block of the inner relation can be compared with tuples from these B blocks of the outer relation. This results in the total number of secondary memory accesses given by the following expression:

$$\lceil |R|/bf_R \rceil + \lceil (1/B) * \lceil |R|/bf_R \rceil \rceil * \lceil |S|/bf_S \rceil$$

If one of the relations (let us say R, the smaller of the two) can be kept entirely in memory, then the number of disk accesses required is $\lceil |R|/bf_R \rceil + \lceil |S|/bf_S \rceil$.

Example 10.19 Let us reconsider the problem of generating the class lists, consisting of *Std#, Std_Name, Course#,* in the university database. This involves joining the STUDENT and REGISTRATION relations. Let us suppose that the number of tuples per block, bf_S, for the STUDENT relation is 200, the bf_R for REGISTRATION is 400, and up to 5 blocks of the STUDENT relation can be kept in main memory. The nested loop using block access with STUDENT, the smaller relation in the outer loop, would involve a total of 40,200 disk accesses. If the smaller relation in the outer loop could be kept entirely in memory, then the number of disk accesses would be 1200. Note that this method requires sorting the result relation on the attribute *Course#* to obtain class lists. ■

Sort and Merge Method

Relations are assumed to be sorted in the **sort and merge method.** If they are not sorted, a preprocessing step in the query evaluation sorts them. These sorted relations can be scanned in ascending or descending order of the values of the join attributes. Tuples that satisfy the join predicate are merged. The process can be terminated as indicated in Algorithm 10.1 on page 491.

In the algorithm, we join the relation R with relation S and the join predicate is $R.A = S.B$. We assume that the relations have been sorted in ascending order with respect to the attributes A and B and that sufficient space for an appropriate number of buffers in available. The tuples are placed in the buffers by the file manager and the algorithm reads the tuples from these buffers. $R\uparrow$ and $S\uparrow$ are pointers that point to the corresponding tuples in the buffers. We assume that once the last tuple in a buffer has been read, the buffer is refilled. If the joining attributes are not the primary key of the relations, a many-to-many relationship could exist via the joining attributes. We use an array U where pointers to tuples of relation S that have the same attribute value as the current tuple of R are stored. These tuples join with the current tuple of the relation R and allow a single pass over the tuples of both the relations. A tuple whose pointer has been stored in this array locks the tuple so that the buffer containing it is not released. An attempt to read past the last tuple in the relation would raise the *eof* (end-of-file) condition. The algorithm could be easily modified to include cases where the join involves more than one attribute.

The number of accesses for Algorithm 10.1 is given by:

$$\lceil |R|/bf_R \rceil + \lceil |S|/bf_S \rceil + R_{CS} + S_{CS}$$

where R_{CS} and S_{CS} are the costs of sorting the relations, assumed to be equal to the number of accesses required during the sorting of the relations R and S, respectively. The sort costs depend on memory availability and the number of runs produced in the initial sort stage. For example, if we have enough memory to perform a max(N,M)-way merge, where the number of runs produced for R and S are N and M, respectively, then the number of accesses required for the join is as follows:

Initial read: $\lceil |R|/bf_R \rceil + \lceil |S|/bf_S \rceil$ blocks
Writes of the sorted runs: $\lceil |R|/bf_R \rceil + \lceil |S|/bf_S \rceil$ blocks
Read in merge phase: $\lceil |R|/bf_R \rceil + \lceil |S|/bf_S \rceil$ blocks
Writes of the join: $\lceil |T|/bf_T \rceil$ blocks

Note that T is the result relation and bf_T is the blocking factor for it. Similar calculations can be done for other memory sizes.

Algorithm 10.1 Sort-Merge to Include a Many-to-Many Relationship

Input: R, S, the two relations to be joined on attributes *A* and *B*, respectively.

Output: T, the relation that is the join of R and S (concatenation of the attributes of R and S, including the attributes *A* and *B*).

```
begin {sort-merge}
T := empty
sort R by A values and S by B values in ascending order
read (R)
read (S)
while not (eof(R) or eof(S)) do (* main while loop *)
begin
  while not(eof(R) or eof(S) or R↑.A ≠ S↑.B) do
                (* find a join value *)
  if R↑.A < S↑.B
    then read(R)
    else read(S)
  if not (eof(R) or eof(S))
     then
       begin (*join a R tuple with one or more S tuples*)
         n := 0
         R_current.A := R↑.A
         while S↑.B = R_current.A and not (eof(S)) do
           begin
             n := n+1
             U[n] := S↑
             read (S)
           end
         while R↑.A = R_current.A and not (eof(R)) do
           begin
             for i =1 to n do
               T := T + R↑ || U[i]↑
             read(R) (*does another tuple of R join with
                          the tuples whose pointers are in
                                        array U?*)
             end
         end
     end (*main while loop*)
  end (*sort-merge*)
```

If the relations are already sorted on the joining attributes, the merge-sort method is an efficient method for evaluating a join.

Join Selectivity and Use of Indexes

Consider the join:

$$R \underset{R.A=S.B}{\bowtie} S$$

Join selectivity of a relation R in a natural join with a relation S denoted by ρ_{RS} is the ratio of the distinct attribute values for attribute A participating in the join to the total number of distinct values for the same attribute in R, that is, $|R[A]|$. Similarly, ρ_{SR} is the join selectivity of the relation S in a natural join with the relation R.

Under the uniform distribution assumption, $\rho_{RS}*|R|$ tuples of R and $\rho_{SR}*|S|$ tuples of S would be involved in a natural join of relation R with S. The use of join selectivity statistics is an alternate and practical method of estimating the size of the join.

If the relation S has an index on the join attribute and if we assume uniform distribution, then the number of accesses required is given by $|R| + \rho_{SR}*|S|$, where ρ_{SR} is the join selectivity. The method of performing the join is as follows. We read in the tuples of R and for each attribute value of R.A we consult the index for S to determine if any tuples from S are involved in the join. If so, these tuples of S are retrieved and joined with the corresponding tuples of R. The tuples of S required to be retrieved would be $\rho_{SR}*|S|$.

Should the records of relations R be blocked, the number of block accesses is given by $|R|/bf_R$. If the records of relation S are stored in blocks, the number of block accesses required to access k records of S (where $k = \rho_{SR}*|S|$) is given by a formula that is derived from the colored balls problem. The optimal number of block accesses required to access k records randomly distributed in a file of n records ($n = |S|$) and stored as m blocks ($m = |S|/bf_S$) is given by the following expression:

$$y(k,m,n) = m * \left[1 - \prod_{i=1}^{k} \frac{n - n/m - i + 1}{n - i + 1}\right]$$

However, if indexes exist on the joining attributes for both relations, the use of these indexes provides a more efficient method of evaluating the join. In this case, we can determine if a given value that exists in one of the relations is also present in the other. If so, then the required tuples could be read and joined to produce the result tuples.

Only those tuples that are involved in the join are required, and therefore only $\rho_{RS}*|R|$ tuples of R and $\rho_{SR}*|S|$ tuples of S are retrieved. The total cost of the join, however, includes the cost of retrieving the indexes. The use of hash and join indexes to implement the join operation is discussed below.

Hash Method

Since we are using the **hash method** for evaluating a natural join, we can assume that the same hash function is applied to the attributes R.A and S.B. The buckets contain the pointers to the appropriate tuple of the relation. The pointers, sometimes called **tuple identifiers (or TID),** contain, in addition to a pointer indicating the storage location of the tuple, an identifier for the relation. Therefore, the structure of the TID is:

relation identifier || pointer to the tuple

Let us represent the hash values generated for the attribute values *Ar* and *Bs* of the relations R and S by h(*Ar*) and h(*Bs*), respectively. Now, if *Ar* = *Bs*, then h(*Ar*) = h(*Bs*). In other words, the hash function generates the same "bucket address" for the tuples of R and S that take part in the join. Ideally, if the hash function does not cause "collisions" we only need to take these tuples of R and S and generate a join. In reality collision would occur and we would need to compare the tuples before joining. We have, however, reduced the number of tuples that need to be compared. An alternate method of handling collision is to store the attribute value with the TIDs in the bucket. We assume this scheme in our discussions.

In performing the join using such a hash index, we read into main memory those hash buckets containing the attribute values and corresponding TIDs for the relations R and S. The joining values of the attributes are those that have TIDs for both the relations. These tuples are retrieved and the resulting joined tuple generated. Example 10.20 illustrates this method.

Example 10.20 Consider the problem of generating the list of courses *(Course#)* in which a student is currently registered. It involves joining the STUDENT relation with the REGISTRATION relation on the *Std#* attribute. Suppose the same hash function h(attribute) = attribute mod 97 is used to generate the bucket address for the common *Std#* attribute in these relations. The pointer values in the buckets in Figure H indicate the TIDs of the STUDENT and REGISTRATION relations.

Figure H Hash index for use in join operations.

STUDENT

$TID_{STUDENT}$	*Std#*	*Std_Name*
1000001	1234567	Jim
1000002	7654321	Jane
1000003	2345678	San
1000004	8765432	Ram

REGISTRATION

TID_{REGIST}	*Std#*	*Course#*
2000001	1234567	COMP353
2000002	1234567	COMP443
2000003	2345678	COMP201
2000004	8765432	COMP353
2000005	8765432	COMP441
2000006	7654321	COMP441

bucket

24

Attribute	TID
2345678	1000001
2345678	2000003

... 26

Attribute	TID
8765432	1000004
8765432	2000004
8765432	2000005

... 48

Attribute	TID
1234567	1000001
1234567	2000001
1234567	2000001
7654318	2000006

To determine the courses in which student 1234567 is registered, we generate the bucket address using 1234567 as the argument for the hash function and derive the address 48. Consulting bucket 48, we find that the values of the TIDs in REGISTRATION for this student are 2000001 and 2000002. Retrieving the tuples corresponding to these TIDs gives us the list of courses for the student as COMP353 and COMP443. ■

To determine the courses (*Course#* only) for all students necessitates a natural join of the STUDENT and REGISTRATION relations. This involves reading the hash buckets sequentially. For each attribute value, we read in the tuples participating in the join. For the attribute value 8765432, we need the tuples with the TIDS 1000004, 2000004, and 2000005. The first one is from the STUDENT relation and the last two are from the REGISTRATION relation.

The number of accesses to secondary storage required with such a hash index, with the relations being stored in blocks of size bf_R and bf_S, is given by $y_R + y_S +$ cost of accessing the hash index. Here, y_R and y_S are given as follows:

$$y_R(k_R, m_R, n_R) = m_R * \left[1 - \prod_{i=1}^{k_R} \frac{n_R - n_R / m_R - i + 1}{n_R - i + 1} \right]$$

$$y_S(k_S, m_S, n_S) = m_S * \left[1 - \prod_{i=1}^{k_S} \frac{n_S - n_S / m_S - i + 1}{n_S - i + 1} \right]$$

where $k_R = \rho_{RS} * |R|$, $n_R = |R|$, $m_R = \lceil |R|/bf_R \rceil$, and
$k_S = \rho_{SR} * |S|$, $n_S = |S|$, and $m_S = \lceil |S|/bf_S \rceil$

The size of the hash index is approximately equal to $(sz_A + sz_{TID}) * (|R| + |S|)$, where sz_A is the size in bytes of the attribute being joined and sz_{TID} is the size in bytes of the TID. The number of secondary storage accesses required to read in the hash index for a block size of sz_{b1} is $\lceil ((sz_A + sz_{TID}) * (|R| + |S|))/sz_{b1} \rceil$

If a hash index does not exist, the use of this method requires that such an index be generated to determine the tuples that would be involved in the join. We then need only to access the tuples of R and S once and write out the result. If the memory is not sufficiently large, we would need to store the hashed values on secondary storage and would require additional accesses.

Join Indexes

To provide more efficient join operations, join indexes have been proposed. A **join index** is a relation of arity two and conceptually can be thought to be obtained as follows: The TIDs of the tuples of the relations participating in a join are concatenated with the tuples. These augmented relations are joined and the resulting relation is then projected on the TIDs. For instance, the join index for:

$$R \underset{R.A = S \cdot B}{\bowtie} S$$

will only consist of tuples with the TID of R and S that participate in this natural join.

A join index is useful for joins that have to be performed often. The number of tuples in the join index for $R \bowtie S$ is equal to the cardinality of the join, namely $|R \bowtie S|$. The size of the tuples in a join index depends on the size of the TIDs.

Example 10.21

We return to the problem of generating the list of courses in which students are registered. Generating such a list involves joining the STUDENT relation with the REGISTRATION relation on the *Std#* attribute. Since this is assumed to be a frequently required operation, we can create a join index. We illustrate the join index on sample tuples in Figure I.

To find all courses *(Course#)* in which student 1234567 is registered, we note that the $TID_{STUDENT}$ for the tuple corresponding to this *Std#* has the value 100001. Now, consulting the join index STUDENT-REGISTRATION, we discover that the tuples with the TIDs 2000001 and 2000002 in the relation REGISTRATION will join with the tuple 100001. These TIDs lead us directly to the tuples in REGISTRATION involving student 1234567 and we find that this student is registered in courses COMP353 and COMP443.

Figure I Join index.

STUDENT

$TID_{STUDENT}$	*Std#*	*Std_Name*
1000001	1234567	Jim
1000002	7654321	Jane
1000003	2345678	San
1000004	8765432	Ram

Join Index: STUDENT-REGISTRATION

$TID_{STUDENT}$	TID_{REGIST}
1000001	2000001
1000001	2000002
1000002	2000006
1000003	2000003
1000004	2000004
1000004	2000005

REGISTRATION

TID_{REGIST}	*Std#*	*Course#*
2000001	1234567	COMP353
2000002	1234567	COMP443
2000003	2345678	COMP201
2000004	8765432	COMP353
2000005	8765432	COMP441
2000006	7654321	COMP441

■

The join index contains the TIDs for tuples of R and S that participate in the join and only these tuples have to be retrieved. If bf_{JI} is the blocking factor for the join index, the cost of accessing the join index is given by $|R \bowtie S|/bf_{JI}$. The cost of performing a join using join indexes is given by $|R \bowtie S|/bf_{JI} + y_R + y_S$, where $y_R + y_S$ are the optimal number of block accesses required to retrieve the tuples of R and S participating in the join.

10.8.3 N-Variable Expressions

An **n-variable expression** involves more than two variables. The strategy used here is to try to avoid accessing the same data more than once. One method of implementing such expressions is to simultaneously evaluate all terms of the query. Therefore, if a number of terms in the query require unary operations on the data accessed, these could be done in parallel. If the data accessed participates in binary operations, these binary operations are partially evaluated.

General n-variable queries can be reduced for evaluation by either tuple substitution or decomposition.

Tuple Substitution

In the **tuple substitution method** we substitute the tuples for one of the variables. Consequently, we reduce the query to $K_1 * (n-1)$-variable queries, where K_1 is the cardinality of the substituted variable. The process is repeated until we get a set of one-variable queries. This process is an extension of the nested loop approach and requires the processing of tuples equal to the cartesian product of all relations participating in the query.

Example 10.22 Consider the query: ''Compile a list giving the *Std#*s and *Std_Names* of students who, having failed the Database course, are taking it again.'' Note that we assume that the GRADE relation contains the best grade a student received in a given course. For a student who failed a course and subsequently passed it, the only tuple in the GRADE relation would be the one involving the second attempt!

The SQL and relational algebraic forms of this query are:

select *Std#*, *Std_Name*
from STUDENT s, REGISTRATION r, GRADE g, COURSE c
where s.*Std#* = r.*Std#* **and**
c.*Course_Name* = 'Database' **and**
g.*Std#* = s.*Std#* **and**
g.*Course#* = *c.Course#* **and**
g.*Grade* = F **and**
r.*Std#* = g.*Std#* **and**
r.*Course#* = c.*Course#*

$$\pi_{Std\#,Std\_Name}(\text{STUDENT} \bowtie \pi_{Std\#}(\text{REGISTRATION} \bowtie \pi_{Std\#,Course\#}(\sigma_{Grade=F \wedge Course\_Name=\text{'Database'}}(\text{GRADE} \bowtie \text{COURSE}))))$$

This query can be evaluated by substituting the value of each tuple of the four relations involved in the query. The number of tuples to be processed is approximately equal to 40,000 * 400,000 * 600,000 * 1,000. ■

Even though the substitution method will always work, it should be avoided because of the exponential increase in the number of tuples to be processed.

Figure 10.4 Moving selection and projection down the query tree.

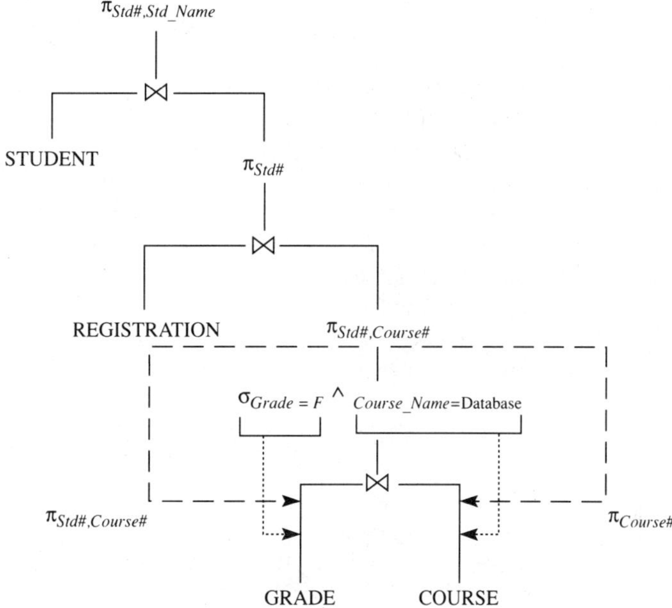

Note that we could use the optimization strategies discussed earlier to reduce the cost. One such operation involves moving the selection operations, as indicated in the query tree of Figure 10.4. This optimization scheme leads us to modify the tuple substitution scheme. In this modified scheme, the cardinality of one or more of the participating relations is reduced by selection or projection. For instance, instead of substituting all tuples of GRADE and COURSE, these relations could be scanned once and their cardinality restricted to those tuples that satisfy the query predicates.

Similar query modifications could be achieved in SQL or QUEL by a nested select statement or by using temporary relations, as illustrated below.

Using nested select in SQL:

```
select Std#, Std_Name
from STUDENT s
where s.Std# in
    (select r.Std#
    from REGISTRATION r
    where r.Course# =
        (select c.Course#
         from COURSE c
         where c.Course_Name = 'Database') and
         r.Std# =
        (select g.Std#
         from GRADE g
         where g.Grade = F and
              g.Course# =
```

```
(select cl.Course#
 from COURSE c1
 where cl.Course_Name = 'Database')))
```

Using temporary relations in QUEL:

```
range of c is COURSE
retrieve into COURSE_TEMP (c.Course#)
  where c.Course_Name = 'Database'
range of g is GRADE
retrieve into GRADE_TEMP1(g.Std#, g.Course#)
  where g.Grade = F
range of gl is GRADE_TEMP1
range of cl is COURSE_TEMP
retrieve into GRADE_TEMP2(g.Std#, g.Course#)
  where gl.Course# = cl.Course#
range of g2 is GRADE_TEMP2
range of r is REGISTRATION
retrieve into REGISTRATION_TEMP (r.Std#)
  where r.Std# = g2.Std# and
        r.Course# = g2.Course#
range of r1 is REGISTRATION_TEMP
range of s is STUDENT
retrieve s.Std#, s.Stud_Name
  where s.Std# = r1.Std#
```

Decomposition

Consider the SQL query:

select A1, A2, . . .
from X_1, X_2, X_3, . . . X_m, X_{m+1}, . . . X_n
where $C_1(X_1, X_2, \ldots X_m)$ **and**
$C2(X_m, X_{m+1}, \ldots X_n)$

Here C_1 and C_2 are predicates that involve the relations X_1, X_2, X_3, . . . X_m and X_m, X_{m+1}, . . . X_n, respectively. One method of evaluating this query is to evaluate a query with predicate C_2 seperately and assign the result into a temporary relation TEMP with the same relation scheme as X_m. This query is shown below:

insert into TEMP
from X_m, X_{m+1}, . . . X_n
where $C_2(X_m, X_{m+1}, \ldots X_n)$

Now the original query can be evaluated using the relation TEMP instead of X_m as indicated below:

select A1, A2, . . .
from X_1, X_2, X_3, . . ., TEMP
where $C_1(X_1, X_2, \ldots, \text{TEMP})$

This modified query is simpler than the original query and would involve a smaller relation TEMP instead of X_m.

In the **decomposition method,** we can consider the following special cases:

select A1, A2, . . .
from X_1, X_2, X_3, . . . X_m, X_{m+1}, . . . X_n
where $C_1(X_1, X_2, \ldots X_m)$ **and**
$C_2(X_{m+1}, \ldots X_n)$

This is a case of a disjoint predicate, which can be separately evaluated as shown below:

select *
from X_{m+1}, . . . X_n
where $C_2(X_{m+1}, \ldots X_n)$

If the above query produces an empty relation, then the original query would also produce an empty relation as a response. If the above query produces a non-empty relation, then the following query would provide the required response:

select A1, A2, . . .
from X_1, X_2, X_3, . . . X_m
where $C_1(X_1, X_2, \ldots X_m)$

Now consider the query of the following form:

select A1, A2, . . .
from X_1, X_2, X_3, . . . X_n
where $C_1(X_1, X_2, \ldots X_n)$ **and**
$C_2(X_n)$

In such cases, we can detach a one-variable query from the original one. This one-variable query could be independently evaluated to give us a result containing, let us say, k tuples. Now the original n-variable query can be replaced by k $(n-1)$-variable queries wherein the nth variable is replaced by its tuple values.

Let the predicate $C_2(X_n)$ applied to the variable X_n produce a set of tuples $\{t_{n1}, t_{n2}, \ldots, t_{nk}\}$. The original n-variable query could then be replaced by k $(n-1)$-variable queries of the following form:

select A1, A2, . . .
from X_1, X_2, X_3, . . . X_{n-1}
where $C_1(X_1, X_2, \ldots X_{n-1}, t_{ni})$

This is the tuple substitution operation of decomposition. Since the number of tuples in the relation X_n is much larger than k, the processing cost does not grow exponentially. The optimization strategy in this case is to select the variable to be detached and the sequencing of such detachment.

In the QUEL version of the query of Example 10.22, we have reduced the query into a number of single-variable subqueries, as shown in Figure 10.5. These subqueries could be evaluated independently or, if resources are available, in parallel. The results of the evaluation of these queries are the smaller relations GRAD_TEMP1 and COURSE_TEMP. The queries involving GRADE_TEMP1 and COURSE_TEMP can then be evaluated to yield GRADE_TEMP2. This is followed by using

Figure 10.5 Decomposition of query of Example 10.22.

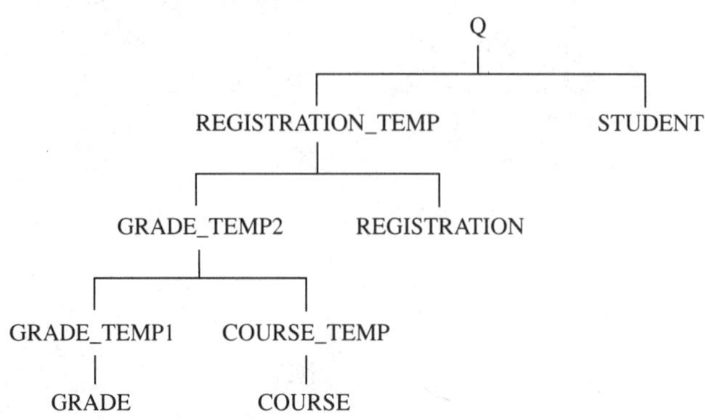

GRADE_TEMP2 and REGISTRATION to evaluate REGISTRATION_TEMP. The latter is used in the final stage of the query to compile the required list. In this decomposition, evaluation of GRADE_TEMP1 and COURSE_TEMP involves a one-variable query. GRADE_TEMP2 is a two-variable query, as are REGISTRATION TEMP and Q. Suppose there are 60,000 tuples in GRADE_TEMP1 with a grade of F (obtained after processing the 600,000 tuples of GRADE) and one tuple with the course name of Database (obtained after processing 5,000 tuples of COURSE). The number of tuples in GRADE_TEMP2 would be, let us say, 6. If only two of these students are reregistered, the tuple substitution at the point of evaluating Q involves finding only the names of these two students who have failed the Database course and are reregistered in the course. This tuple substitution results in the following:

retrieve *Std#, Stud_Name* **where** *Std#* = 1234567
retrieve *Std#, Stud_Name* **where** *Std#* = 7654321

In the decomposition approach, an n-variable query is replaced by a sequence of single variable queries. If this is impossible or undesirable, the query is split into two subqueries with a single common variable between them. Such subqueries could be recursively decomposed until they become single variable queries or irreducible. A query is reducible if it can be separated into two subqueries with a common variable, each of the subqueries having at least two variables. An irreducible subquery cannot be reduced and must be evaluated.

Some of the relations involved in the subqueries obtained by the reduction process can be reduced in cardinality by projection or selection. In this manner, the original query is replaced by a sequence of smaller queries. Figure 10.6 illustrates the decomposition of a query in the form of a tree.

The decomposition algorithm (Wong 76) consists of four subalgorithms refered to as reduction, subquery sequencing, tuple substitution, and variable selection. In the reduction subalgorithm, the query is separated into irreducible components. These are evaluated in an order determined by the subsequency subalgorithm. Each subquery is evaluated in order and the result of the evaluation is used in tuple substitution. Optimization is attempted by determining the sequence in which the subqueries are to be evaluated and selecting the variables for which the tuple substi-

Figure 10.6 Decomposition of a query in the form of a tree.

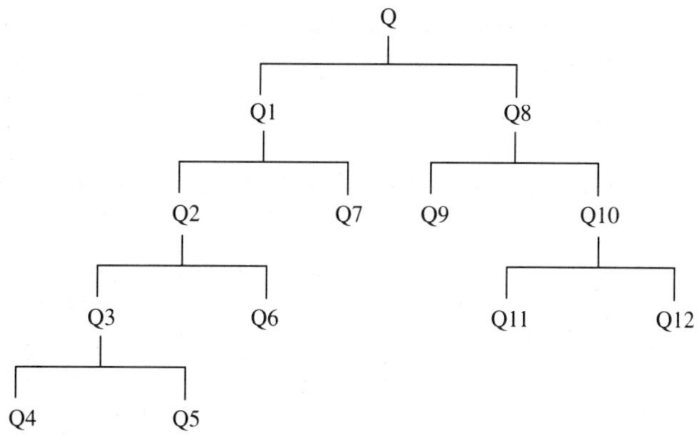

tution is to be performed. The objective of the optimization is to minimize the estimated costs.

Access Aids in N-Variable Expressions

The presence of access aids and the commonality of attributes can be used to advantage in the evaluations of multiple variable queries. Let us consider, for instance, the three-variable query, U = R ⋈ S ⋈ T. We can create indexes on the joining attributes in the join R ⋈ S for R and S ⋈ T for T, if they do not already exist. If these indexes have to be created, access to the relations R and T is involved, plus the cost of writing the indexes to secondary storage if insufficient space exists in main memory. Subsequently, the tuples of S are accessed. For each tuple of S, the required tuples from R and T are determined by using the values of the joining attribute and the indexes for R and T. In this manner, the three-way join could be evaluated.

The cost of this method is that of access to tuples of relation S and the required tuples of R and T, plus the cost of accessing the indexes. If the index must be created, the cost also entails the overhead of creating the indexes, plus access to each of the three relations followed by the selected tuples from the relations R and T.

10.8.4 Access Plan

Once the method of evaluating various operations is determined, the steps involved in combining the query components to deduce the final results have to be planned. Generating an optimal access plan is a stepwise process done in conjunction with the query transformation operation. In generating an access plan a decision has to be made regarding which indexes should be generated and which of the existing data structures should be used.

The database statistics also influence the selection of the sequence of operations to generate the intermediate and final result of the query and, hence, the optimal access plan. The optimal sequence of operations in evaluating the query minimizes access to secondary storage devices in the case of a centralized database system and minimizes communication costs in the case of a distributed system.

10.9 Evaluation of Calculus Expressions

A relational calculus query is nonprocedural; the result is described by specifying its properties. Calculus expressions can be interpreted using nested loop procedures. This method, however, is inefficient, requiring the processing of a number of tuples equal to the cartesian product of the participating relations.

The alternative is to first transform the relational calculus query into relational algebra and then evaluate the relational algebraic expression. The methods of evaluation discussed in the preceding sections can be applied to the transformed calculus queries.

The nonprocedural relational calculus query can be considered to consist of two parts: a target list and a qualification. The qualification, as we saw in Chapter 4, is a first-order predicate expression, and the target list is some list of free variables occurring in the predicate. The target list also specifies the structure of the result relation.

In this section we present a widely used method to translate a calculus query given in the disjunctive prenex normal form to an algebra query. A query is in **prenex normal form** if its qualification is of the form:

$$\forall \text{ [or } \exists] \; r_1 \in R_1 \; . \; . \; . \; \forall \text{ [or } \exists] \; r_n \in R_n \; (P)$$

where P is a quantifier-free predicate. Thus, in the prenex normal form, all the quantifiers are moved to the front of the expression. Note that either the universal or existential quantifier binds a variable in the above expression. A **disjunctive prenex normal form** query has the predicate P of the form:

$$P ::= P_1 \vee P_2 \vee \; . \; . \; . \; \vee P_k$$

where each disjunct P_i is a conjunction of terms:

$$P_i ::= T_{i1} \wedge \; . \; . \; . \; \wedge T_{im}$$

where T_{ij} are terms.

Let us consider the qualification clause of a query of the form:

$$\exists \; r_1 \in R_1 \; . \; . \; . \; \exists \; r_n \in R_n \; (P)$$

This can be transformed into the relational algebraic query:

$$\sigma_P \; (R_1 \bowtie R_2 \bowtie \; . \; . \; . \; \bowtie R_n)$$

preceded by a projection on the attributes specified in the target list of the query, plus the attribute required for the join.

Having converted the query into the relational algebraic form, we can apply the different simplification and improvement procedures considered in the previous sections. Example 10.23 illustrates the conversion of a tuple calculus query into a relational algebraic form.

Example 10.23 Consider the query: "Compile a list containing the names of students who have obtained a grade lower than C in the Database course." The tuple calculus expression for this query is given below:

$$\{t[Std\_Name] \mid t \in STUDENT \land \exists g,c(g \in GRADE \land c \in COURSE \land g[Std\#] = t[Std\#] \land g[Course\#] = c[Course\#] \land c[Course\_Name] = \text{'Database'} \land g[Grade] < C)\}$$

This could be converted into the following equivalent algebraic form query:

$$\pi_{Std\_Name}(\sigma_{Course\_Name = \text{Database} \land Grade < C \land Course\_Name = \text{'Database'}}(STUDENT \bowtie GRADE \bowtie COURSE)) \blacksquare$$

10.10 View Processing

In Section 10.1 we discussed the need for query modification when a query is expressed on a view. Such queries have to be replaced by appropriate queries on base relations. In the discussion so far we have considered the processing of queries assuming that the query is posed on base relations. In this section we briefly consider ways of transforming a query posed on views to an equivalent query on base relations.

Consider a SQL query based on a view, such as USERS_VIEW, as given below:

select <target_list(Q)>
from <from_list(Q)>
where <where_clause(Q)>

Here we have used <from_list(Q)>, <target_list(Q)>, and <where_clause(Q)> to indicate the names of the tuple variables used in the query. Since a view is defined by a SQL query, the query defining the view USERS_VIEW can be written as:

create view USERS_VIEW **as**
  select <target_list(V)>
  from <from_list(V)>
  where <where_clause(V)>

Here we have used <target_list(V)>, <from_list(V)>, and <where_clause(V)> to indicate the names of the attributes, tuple variables, and predicates used to generate the USERS_VIEW.

To process the user's query, we have to modify it to refer to the base relations. It is possible that the same tuple variable could be used in both the user's query and the definition of the view. Such multiple use of variable names should be replaced to differentiate them. Thus if the user's query and the view definition both use the tuple variable r, it is preferable to replace the tuple variable r in the view definition with a different tuple variable, for instance, r′.

Algorithm 10.2 transforms a query that involves views as well as base relations into one involving only base relations (given on page 504). The use of this algorithm in transforming a query based on views is illustrated in Example 10.24.

A relation V defined in the view need not be preserved in the modified user's

Algorithm **10.2** **Transform a Query on a View to the Base Relations**

Input: Query on a view

Output: > Query on the base relations

Let X be the set of common tuple variable names <from_list (V)> and <from_list (Q)>. For all names r in X, replace r in <target list (V)>, <from_list (V)>, and <where_clause (V)> by r′.

Delete V from <from_list (Q)> and append <from_list (V) to <from_list (Q)>.

Replace each attribute V.A in Q by its corresponding entry from <target_list (V)>.

Replace <where_clause (Q)> by <where_clause (Q)> **and** <where_clause (V)>, i.e., the new <where_clause> is a conjunction of the conditions of the view and query.

query provided all the relations and tuple variables appearing in the <from_list(V)> of the create view statement are appended to the user's query. The next stage in the query modification of the user's query is step 2 of the algorithm. In the subsequent steps of the query, all references to attributes of such deleted relations are replaced by the corresponding base relation attributes. Finally, the predicate in the view definition must be appended to the predicates in the user's query.

Example 10.24 Consider a database consisting of the following base relations:

EMPLOYEE*(Emp_Name, Salary, Dept, Position)*
PHONE#*(Emp_Name, Extension#)*

Consider a view defined as follows:

create view DEPT_EMP **as**
select e.*Emp_Name*,e. *Salary,* e.*Position*
from EMPLOYEE e EMPLOYEE el
where e.*Dept* = el.*Dept* **and**
  el.*Emp_Name* = 'Smith'

A query using this view is given below:

select e.*Emp_Name,* e.*Salary,* p.*Extension#*
from DEPT_EMP e PHONE# p
where e.*Position* = engineer **and**
  DEPT_EMP.*Emp_Name* = p.*Emp_Name*

The user's query uses the tuple variable e, which is also used in the statements to define the view. Therefore, the view variable e would be changed to, let us say, e′. We would also delete DEPT_EMP in the from clause of the user's query and append the from list from the view definition to the user's query. Next, we would replace DEPT_EMP.*Emp_Name* by e′.*Emp_Name* and e.*Position* by e′.*Position*. Finally, we would append the predicates from the definition of the view to the user's query. The modified user's query is given below:

> **select** e′.*Emp_Name*, e′.*Salary*, p.*Extension#*
> **from** PHONE# p EMPLOYEE e′ EMPLOYEE el
> **where** e′.*Position* = engineer **and**
> e′.*Emp_Name* = p. *Emp_Name* **and**
> e′.*Dept* = el.*Dept* **and**
> el.*Emp_Name* = 'Smith'

This modified query can now be optimized and evaluated using the techniques discussed earlier in this chapter. ■

10.11 A Typical Query Processor

We have presented a sampling of possible query optimization strategies. A query expression during the modification stage may be decomposed into several subqueries. Once the method of efficiently evaluating these components is determined, the steps involved in combining these components to deduce the final results have to be planned. An access plan, as represented in a query tree, describes the sequence of operations that are involved to generate the intermediate and final result of the query. It includes strategies such as determining what indexes should be generated and which of the existing data structures should be used.

A query may be embedded within an application program that may be executed repetitively. Should such a query be compiled, i.e., should the access plans be bound to it? Interactive queries tend to be ad hoc and cannot be expected to be repeated. DB2, for instance, compiles all queries, including the interactive queries. For the latter, DB2 discards the access plan after execution of the query.

Early **binding** (i.e., binding of the access plan at first invocation) is not recommended for compiled queries because there can be a significant hiatus between the binding and the query's eventual execution. During this hiatus, the original execution strategy may have become inefficient because of changes to data organization. Binding at execution allows the latest information to be utilized in the optimization process. This process is, however, not cheap, and for frequently run queries it may be beneficial to bind early and avoid the optimization overhead for each execution. A trade-off is made wherein the access plan is bound at compile time with a provision made to recompile such queries periodically and use the modified data structures.

An ad hoc query is submitted by a user using the direct interface (or monitor) to the DBMS. Queries can also be submitted by embedding them in high-level language programs. To facilitate this, it is usual to extend the high-level language or supplement it with additional features. For example, EQUEL is the version of QUEL that can be used in C programs on the INGRES relational database management system.

No matter how the query is entered into the system, a parser first converts the input stream of characters into tokens (internal code representation). The optimizer accepts this coded version of the query and performs query optimization. As we have seen in this chapter, this involves improving the query (removing redundancy) and generating a schedule or access plan. In the generation of the schedule, the optimizer would consider a large number of possible execution strategies based on available access aids and expected sizes of results. To assist in the selection of an appropriate strategy, some of the following statistical information is maintained in the data dictionary:

For each relation: number of tuples, number of blocks used to store these tuples, percent of total number of relevant database blocks used by the relation.

For each index: number of distinct data values and number of blocks used.

The optimization uses some of the strategies discussed earlier. However, to keep the overhead within limits, some shortcuts are commonly used, such as not considering a change in the order of evaluations of joins specified by the user's query. Joins are evaluated using either nested loop or sort-merge techniques. The sort-merge is normally preferred for large relations while the nested loop method is reserved for the smallest relations. Academic INGRES, for instance, uses the query decomposition strategy. It developes an access plan for one step, executes it, and uses the result of the execution to determine the subsequent access plans. Commercial INGRES, on the other hand, develops a complete access plan.

The access plan is submitted to the data manager, which retrieves the data and manipulates it to derive the result. The structure of a typical query processor is shown in Figure 10.7.

Figure 10.7 Structure of a query processor.

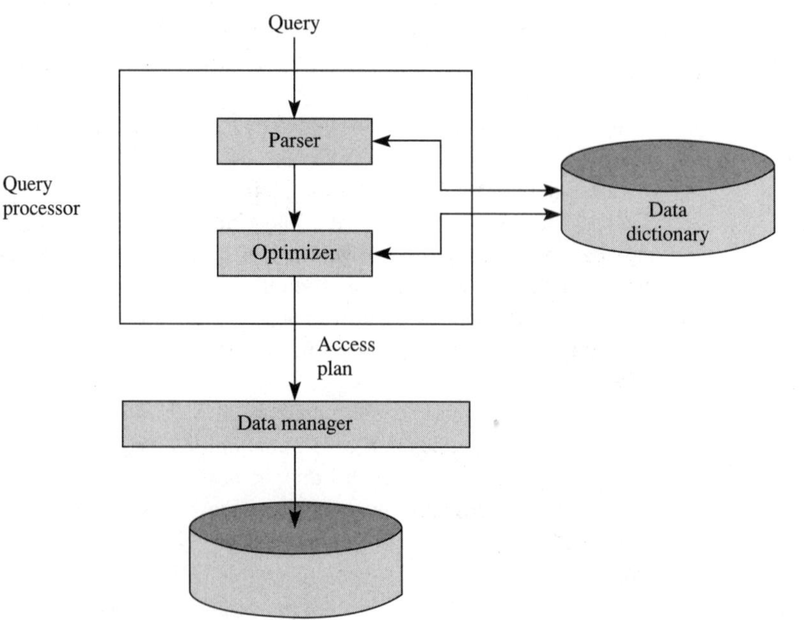

10.12 Summary

Query processing is the procedure of converting a user's query into an internal standard representation. The query is subsequently modified to an equivalent but more efficient to evaluate form. An access plan for evaluating the query is determined and executed. Converting queries using views into queries on base relations is also a responsibility of query processing.

The general strategy used in query modification is to try to execute the selection and projection operations as early as possible. Attempts are made to combine a number of unary operations, thereby avoiding the necessity of accessing the same data more than once. Common subexpressions are detected and attempts are made to evaluate such subexpressions only once. When the query involves more than two variables, attempts are made to break it down into a number of simpler, connected queries.

Joins, one of the most common operations used in relational databases, are evaluated using either the nested loop method or the sort-merge technique. Using indexes and sorting the relations also improves the execution of these operations. In deriving an access plan, an attempt is made to use existing indexes. In the absence of an index or if the relations are unsorted, the overhead of creating indexes and/or sorting the relations may be justified.

The query processor has access to the following statistical information maintained in the data dictionary: number of tuples in the relations, number of blocks used to store relations, number of distinct data values. These statistics are used in estimating the cost of alternate access plans, the best of which is chosen.

Key Terms

query processing
query processor
query optimization
parser
access plan
query modification
operator graph
conjunctive normal form
selectivity factor
one-variable expression
sequential access
two-variable expression
nested loop method
sort and merge method
join selectivity
hash method
tuple identifier (TID)
join index
n-variable expression
tuple substitution method
decomposition method
prenex normal form
disjunctive prenex normal form
binding

Exercises

10.1 Consider each of following relational operators: projection, selection, join. Suppose it is required to implement them so that duplicate tuples are removed. Prepare a pseudocode program to implement these using (a) sort-merge, (b) hashing.

10.2 Repeat Exercise 4.3 from Chapter 4, giving both an efficient relational algebra expression and the corresponding query tree.

10.3 Repeat Exercise 4.4 from Chapter 4, presenting both an efficient relational algebra expression and the corresponding query tree.

10.4 Repeat Exercise 4.12 from Chapter 4, giving both an optimal relational algebra expression and the corresponding query tree.

10.5 Consider the computation of the join R(*A,B,C*) and S(*B,C,D,*). Suppose R has 1,000 tuples stored 30 tuples per disk block and S has 10,000 tuples stored 40 tuples per disk block. There is space in the main memory for 3 buffers for relation R and 5 buffers for relation S. What is the number of disk accesses made if the relations are joined using the nested loop method?

10.6 Indicate if each of the following equivalences are valid, without any knowledge about the relation schemes of R and S. If valid, how could they be used in query modification to improve its evaluation?

(a) $\sigma_P(R - S) \equiv \sigma_P R - \sigma_P S$
(b) $\pi_P(R - S) \equiv \equiv \pi_P R - \pi_P S$

10.7 Given R(*A,B,C*), S(*B,C,D*), and T(*C,D,E*), draw the query tree for each of the following queries and apply optimization procedures to it.

(a) $\sigma_{B=b}(\pi_{ABC}(R \bowtie S) \cap \pi_{ABC}(R \bowtie T))$
(b) $\pi_{ABC}(\sigma_{B=b}(\pi_{AB}R) \bowtie \pi_{AB}S) - \pi_{ABC}(\sigma_{D=d}(R \bowtie T)))$

10.8 Consider the following query on the database discussed in this chapter:

```
select S.Std#, S.Std_Name
from STUDENT s,Grade g,Registration r,COURSE c,COURSE cl
where s.Std# = g.Std# and
      g.Course# = c.Course# and
      c.Course_Name = 'Database' and
      g.Grade = A and
      S.Std# = r.Std# and
      cl.Course# = r.Course# and
      cl.Course_Name = 'Database Design'
```

Assuming that the size of the relations are as indicated in the text, find the best strategy to evaluate this query.

10.9 Generate an optimal query tree for each query of Exercise 5.10 of Chapter 5.

10.10 Is it possible to use algebraic modification to convert the first relational algebraic version of the query in Section 10.2 to the third version? If so, depict a sequence of query trees showing each step of the modification process.

10.11 Consider the different access strategies (indexing and hashing). State how the availability of such access aids influences query processing.

10.12 Modify the algorithm for nested joins using block access wherein the join condition involves more than one attribute from each relation.

Bibliographic Notes

Wong and Youssefi (Wong 76) introduced the decomposition technique, Selinger et al. (Seli 79) describe access path selection, and Kim (Kim 82) describes join evaluation strategies. Techniques for query improvement are presented in Hall (Hall 76). Some join minimization techniques are presented in the textbooks by Maier (Maie 83) and Ullman (Ullm 82). Query evaluation algorithms are presented in Blasgen and Eswaren (Blas 77) and Yao (Yao 79). Join indexes for a two-variable join are presented in Valduriez (Vald 87). When two or more relations are to be joined, the use of a composite B-tree–based index has been shown to be advantageous (Desa, in press, Desa 89). A survey of query processing techniques is given by Jarke and Kock (Jark 84). The distributed query processing survey by Yu and Chang (Yu 84) also considers techniques useful in centralized database systems.

Bibliography

(Blas 77) M. W. Blasgen & K. P. Eswaren, "Storage and Access in Relational Databases," *IBM Systems Journal* 16, 1977.

(Desa 89) B. C. Desai, "Performance of a Composite Attribute and Join Index," *IEEE Trans. on Software Engineering* 15(2), February 1989, pp. 142–152.

(Desa) B. C. Desai, F. Sadri, & P. Goyal, "Composite B-tree: An Access Aid for Query Processing and Integrity Enforcement," *Computer Journal* (in press).

(Hall 76) P. A. Hall, "Optimization of a Single Relational Expression in a Relational Database System," *IBM Journal of Research and Development* 20, pp. 244–257.

(Jark 84) M. Jarke & J. Koch, "Query Optimization in Database Systems," *ACM Computing Surveys* (162), 1984, pp. 111–152.

(Kim 82) W. Kim, "On Optimizing SQL-Like Nested Query," *ACM Transactions on Database Systems* 3, pp. 443–469.

(Maie 83) D. Maier, *Theory of Relational Databases*. Rockville, MD: Computer Science Press, 1983.

(Seli 79) P. G. Selinger, M. M. Astrahan, D. D. Chamberlin, R. A. Lorie, & T. G. Price, "Access Path Selection in a Relational Database Management System," Proceedings ACM SIGMOD Intl. Conf. on Management of Data, 1979, pp. 23–34.

(Ullm 82) J. D. Ullman, *Principles of Database Systems*. Rockville, MD: Computer Science Press, 1982.

(Vald 87) P. Valduriez, "Join Indices," *ACM Transactions on Database Systems* 12(2), June 1987, pp. 218–246.

(Wong 76) E. Wong, & K. Youssefi, "Decomposition—A Strategy for Query Processing," *ACM Transactions on Database Systems* 1(3), 1976, pp. 223–241.

(Yao 79) S. B. Yao, "Optimization of Query Evaluation Algorithms," *ACM Transactions on Database Systems* 4(2), 1979, pp. 133–155.

(Yu 84) C. T. Yu & C. C. Chang, "Distributed Query Processing," *ACM Computing Surveys* 16(4), December 1984.

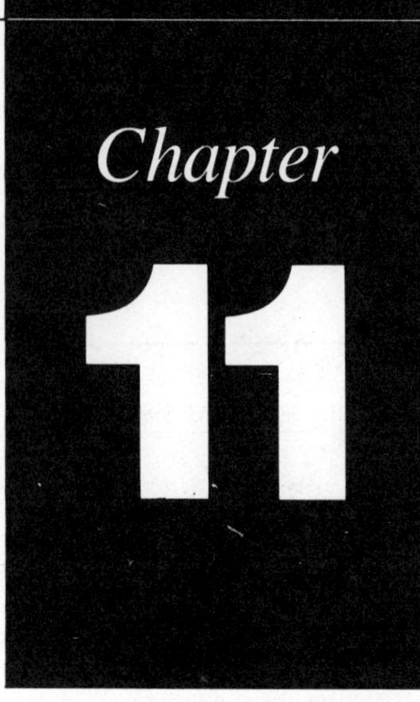

Recovery

Contents

A computer system is an electromechanical device subject to failures of various types. The reliability of the database system is linked to the reliability of the computer system on which it runs. In this chapter we discuss recovery of the data contained in a database system following failures of various types and present the different approaches to database recovery. The types of failures that the computer system is likely to be subjected to include failures of components or subsystems, software failures, power outages, accidents, unforeseen situations, and natural or man-made disasters. Database recovery techniques are methods of making the database fault tolerant. The aim of the recovery scheme is to allow database operations to be resumed after a failure with minimum loss of information at an economically justifiable cost. We concentrate on the recovery of centralized database systems in this chapter; recovery issues of a distributed system are presented in chapter 15.

11.1 Reliability

A system is considered **reliable** if it functions as per its specifications and produces a correct set of output values for a given set of input values. For a computer system, reliable operation is attained when all components of the system work according to specifications. The **failure** of a system occurs when the system does not function according to its specifications and fails to deliver the service for which it was intended. An **error** in the system occurs when a component of the system assumes a state that is not desirable; the fact that the state is undesirable is a subjective judgment. The component in question is said to be in an erroneous state and further use of the component will lead to a failure that cannot be attributed to any other factor. A **fault** is detected either when an error is propagated from one component to another or the failure of the component is observed. Sometimes it may not be possible to attribute a fault to a specific cause. Furthermore, errors such as logical errors in a program are latent as long as they do not manifest themselves as faults at some unspecified time. A fault is, in effect, the identified or assumed cause of an error. If an error is not propagated or perceived by another component of a system or by an user, it may not be considered as a failure.

Consider a bank teller who requests the balance of an account from the database system. If there is an unrecoverable parity error in trying to read the specific information, the system returns the response that it was unable to retrieve the required information; furthermore, the system reports to a system error log that the error occurred and that it was a parity error. The cause of the parity error could be a fault in the disk drive or memory location containing the required information; or the problem could be traced to poor interconnection or noise on the communication lines. We cannot rule out the fact that the parity checking unit itself may be defective.

For a database system (or for that matter, any other system) to work correctly, we need correct data, correct algorithms to manipulate the data, correct programs that implement these algorithms, and of course a computer system that functions correctly. Any source of errors in each of these components has to be identified and a method of correcting and recovering from these errors has to be designed in the system. To ensure that data is correct, validation checks have to be incorporated for data entry functions. For example, if the age of an employee is entered as too low or too high, the validation routine should ask for a confirmation of the data that was entered.

Fault-detection schemes of appropriate types have to be built into a reliable system. In addition, a reliable system has built into it appropriate recovery schemes that will correct the errors that have been detected, or eliminate a portion of the permanently failed system. Such elimination, however, may mean that the system may not be available until it is repaired.

A **fault-tolerant system,** in addition to the fault-detection scheme, has redundant components and subsystems built in. On detection of a fault, these redundant components are used to replace the faulty components. Such replacement makes it possible to keep the system available without any interruption of service, albeit, at a reduced level of performance and reliability.

We will not consider the aspects of correct algorithms or correct implementation of these algorithms in this text. However, we stress their paramount importance in the correct functioning of any system, including a database system.

Another aspect that has to be considered in database application is that of data consistency. Having correct data is important; however, the data must be consistent. This requires checks in the database system to ensure that any redundant data is consistent. For example, if the age of an employee is entered in the database, it must be consistent with the employee's date of birth and the current date.

Let us now try to informally define the concept of reliability of a system. **Reliability** is a measure used to indicate how successful a system is in providing the service it was intended for. Reliability is an important consideration in all systems designed for critical operations. It is considered during all stages of computer system design and implementation. To take into account the fact that physical devices have an inherent failure rate, these systems have built into them include various mechanisms to detect errors and correct many of them. A number of measures are used to define the reliability of a system. These include the **mean time between failures (MTBF),** the **mean time to repair (MTTR),** and the **system availability,** which is the fraction of time that a system performs according to its specifications.

There are two basic methods of increasing the reliability of a system. The first method uses fault avoidance and the second method tolerates faults and corrects them. In the fault-avoidance method, reliability is achieved by using reliable components and careful assembling techniques with comprehensive testing at each stage of design and assembly to eliminate all sources of hardware and software errors. In the fault-tolerance approach, the system incorporates protective redundancies, which can cater to faults occurring within the system and its components. These redundancies allow the system to perform according to its specifications (or within an acceptable level of degradation from these specifications). However, the use of redundancy in components and subsystems to make a system fault tolerant increases the number of components. A greater number of components in a system decreases its reliability unless the components are modular and the redundant components do not get in the way of the operation of the system's normal components. Modular construction effectively reduces the complexity of the system and the redundant components come into play only in case of an error.

Memory systems can have a simple parity check bit that can detect a single bit error correctly, but multiple bit errors can go undetected (or be detected incorrectly as a single bit error). However, memory systems can be made fault tolerant by additional parity bits to detect and correct errors in one or more bits. The degree to which such detection and correction schemes are used depends on the expected number of errors and the costs that can be economically justified.

Absolute reliability is hard to achieve at an economically acceptable cost (or at any cost), hence systems are designed with a level of reliability that is compatible with the use of the system and is economically justifiable.

In database systems, reliability of the system is achieved by using redundancy of data, including control data. In addition, failures are tolerated by using additional redundant data that can be used in recovery operations to return the database to an usable state after a failure.

11.1.1 Types of Failures

Hardware Failure

Failures that can occur in the hardware can be attributed to one of the following sources: design errors, inadequate quality control, overloading, and wearout.

Design errors: These could include a design that did not meet the required specifications of performance and/or reliability; the use of components that are of poor quality or insufficient capacity; poor error detection and correction schemes; and failure to take into account the errors that can occur in the error detection and correction subsystems.

Poor quality control (during fabrication): This could include poor connections, defective subsystems, and electrical and mechanical misalignments.

Overutilization and overloading: Using a component or subsystem beyond its capacity. This could be a design error or utilization error where mismatching subcomponents may be used, or due to unforeseen circumstances a system is simply used beyond its capacity.

Wearout: The system, especially its mechanical parts, tends to wear with usage causing it to divert from its design performance. Solid-state electrical parts do not wear out, but insulation on wire could undergo chemical changes with age and crack, leading to eventual failure.

Software Failure

The errors that can lead to a software failure are similar to those that lead to hardware failure, the only exception being wearout.

Design errors: Not all possible situations can be accounted for in the design process. This is particularly so in software design where it is hard to foresee all possible modes of operation, including the combinations and the sequence of usage of various components of a software system. However, the design should allow for the most serious types of errors to be detected and appropriate corrective action to be incorporated. In situations that could result in loss of life or property, the design must be fail-safe. An alternate approach to design in such a situation is to assign multiple design teams for the same project and an independent verification team to validate the design.

Poor quality control: This could include undetected errors in entering the program code. Incompatibility of various modules and conflict of conventions between versions of the operating system are other possible causes of failure in software.

Overutilization and overloading: A system designed to handle a certain load may be swamped when loading on it is exceeded. Buffers and stacks may overrun their boundaries or be shared erroneously.

Wearout: There are no known errors caused by wearout of software: software does not wear out. However, the usefulness of a software system may become obsolete due to the introduction of new versions with additional features.

Storage Medium Failure

Storage media can be classified as volatile, nonvolatile, and permanent or stable.

Volatile storage: An example of this type of storage is the semiconductor memory requiring an uninterruptable power source for correct operation. A volatile storage failure can occur due to the spontaneous shutdown of the computer system, sometimes referred to as a **system crash.** The cause of the shutdown could be a failure in the power supply unit or a loss of power. A system crash will result in the loss of the information stored in the volatile storage medium. One method of avoiding loss of data due to power outages is to provide for an uninterruptable power source (using batteries and/or standby electrical generators). Another source of data loss from volatile storage can be due to parity errors in more bits than could be corrected by the parity checking unit; such errors will cause partial loss of data.

Nonvolatile storage: Examples of this type of storage are magnetic tape and magnetic disk systems. These types of storage devices do not require power for maintaining the stored information. A power failure or system shutdown will not result in the loss of information stored on such devices. However, nonvolatile storage devices such as magnetic disks can experience a mechanical failure in the form of a **read/write head crash** (i.e., the read/write head comes in contact with the recording surface instead of being a small distance from it), which could result in some loss of information. It is vital that failures that cause the loss of ordinary data should not also cause the loss of the redundant data that is to be used for recovery of the ordinary data. One method of avoiding this double loss is to store the recovery data on separate storage devices. To avoid the loss of recovery data (primary recovery data), one can provide for a further set of recovery data (secondary recovery data), and so on. However, this multiple level of redundancy can only be carried to an economically justifiable level.

Permanent or **Stable storage:** Permanency of storage, in view of the possibility of failure of the storage medium, is achieved by redundancy. Thus, instead of having a single copy of the data on a nonvolatile storage medium, multiple copies of the data are stored. Each such copy is made on a separate nonvolatile storage device. Since these independent storage devices have independent failure modes, it is assumed that at least one of these multiple copies will survive any failure and be usable. The amount and type of data stored in stable storage depends on the recovery scheme used in the particular DBMS. The status of the database at a given point in time is called the **archive database** and such archive data is usually stored in stable storage. Recovery data that would be used to recover from the loss of volatile as well as nonvolatile storage is also stored on stable storage. Failure of permanent storage could be due to natural or man-made disasters. A manually assisted database regeneration is the only possible remedy to permanent storage failure. However, if multiple generations of archival database are kept, loss of the most recent generation, along with the loss of the nonvolatile storage, can be recovered from by reverting to the most recent previous generation and, if possible, manually regenerating the more recent data.

Implementation of Stable Storage

Stable storage is implemented by replicating the data on a number of separate nonvolatile storage devices and using a careful writing scheme (described below). Errors and failures occurring during transfer of information and leading to inconsistencies in the copies of data on stable storage can be arbitrated.

A write to the stable storage consists of writing the same block of data from volatile storage to distinct nonvolatile storage devices two or more times. If the writing of the block is done successfully, all copies of data will be identical and there will be no problems. If one or more errors are introduced in one or more copies, the correct data is assumed to be the copy that has no errors. If two or more sets of copies are found to be error free but the contents do not agree, the correct data is assumed to be the set that has the largest number of error-free copies. If there are the same number of copies in two or more such identical sets, then one of these sets is arbitrarily assumed to contain the correct data.

11.1.2 Types of Errors in Database Systems and Possible Detection Schemes

Errors in the use of the database can be traced to one of the following causes: user error, consistency error, system error, hardware failure, or external environmental conditions.

User error: This includes errors in application programs as well as errors made by online users of the database. One remedy is to allow online users limited access rights to the database, for example, read only. Any insertion or update operations require that appropriate validation check routines be built into the application programs and that these routines perform appropriate checks on the data entered. The routines will flag any values that are not valid and prompt the user to correct these errors.

Consistency error: The database system should include routines that check for consistency of data entered in the database. Due to oversight on the part of the DBA, some of the required consistency specifications may be left out, which could lead to inconsistency in the stored data. A simple distinction between validity and consistency errors should be made here. **Validity** establishes that the data is of the correct type and within the specified range; consistency establishes that it is reasonable with respect to itself or to the current values of other data-items in the database.

System error: This encompasses errors in the database system or the operating system, including situations such as **deadlocks** (see Section 12.8). Such errors are fairly hard to detect and require reprogramming the erroneous components of the system software or working with the DBMS vendor. Situations such as deadlocks are catered for in the DBMS by allowing appropriate locking facilities. Deadlocks are also catered to in the operating system by deadlock avoidance, prevention, or detection schemes.

Hardware failure: This refers to hardware malfunctions including storage system failures.

External environmental failure: Power failure is one possible type. Others are fire, flood, and other natural disasters, or malicious acts.

In addition to validity checks built into the application programs using a database, the database system usually contains a number of routines to recover from some of the above errors. These routines enforce consistency of the data entered in the database. The required consistencies that are to be enforced are indicated by the DBA.

11.1.3 Audit Trails

The concept of an audit trail is not new; recall the Greek myth about Theseus, who marked his trail into the labyrinth, where the monster Minotaur lived, with a ball of string. After killing Minotaur, Theseus used the trail marked by the string to find his way out of the labyrinth. The need for the reliability and relative permanency of such a trail is also illustrated in the children's story of Hansel and Gretel. They left a trail marked by bread crumbs, which were eaten by birds, and the pair were unable to find their way back home!

In accounting practice, each transaction is recorded in chronological order in a log called a journal before being entered to the appropriate accounts. Recording of the transactions is done in the form of double entry. For each transaction, there are debits to one or more accounts and credits to one or more accounts, and the sum of these debits and credits must be equal. Double entry helps in detecting errors and ensures the reliability of the accounting records.

The DBMS also has routines that maintain an **audit trail** or a **journal.** An audit trail or a journal is a record of an update operation made on the database. The audit trail records who (user or the application program and a transaction number), when (time and date), (from) where (location of the user and/or the terminal), and what (identification of the data affected, as well as a before-and-after image of that portion of the database that was affected by the update operation). In addition, a DBMS contains routines that make a backup copy of the data that is modified. This is done by taking a ''snapshot'' of the before-and-after image of that portion of the database that is modified. For obvious reasons, the backups are produced on a separate storage medium.

11.1.4 Recovery Schemes

Recovery schemes can be classified as forward or backward recovery. Database systems use the latter schemes to recover from errors.

Forward error recovery: In this scheme, when a particular error in the system is detected, the recovery system makes an accurate assessment of the state of the system and then makes appropriate adjustments based on the anticipated result had the system been error free. The adjustments obviously depend on the error, consequently the error types have to be anticipated by the designers of the recovery system. The aim of the adjustment is to restore the system so that the effects of the error are canceled and the system can continue to operate. This scheme is not applicable to unanticipated errors.

Backward error recovery: In this scheme no attempt is made to extrapolate what the state of the system would have been had the error not occurred. Instead, the system is reset to some previous correct state that is known to be free of any errors. The backward error recovery is a simulated reversal of time and does not try to anticipate the possible future state of a system.

11.2 Transactions

A single DBMS operation as viewed by an user, for example, to update the grade of a student in the relation ENROL *(Student_Name, Course, Grade),* involves more than one task. Since the data resides on a secondary nonvolatile storage medium, it will have to be brought into the volatile primary memory for manipulation. This requires that the data be transferred between secondary storage and primary storage. The transfer is usually performed in blocks of the implementation-specified size. The transfer task consists of locating the block in the secondary storage device containing the required tuple (which may be preceded by searching an index), obtaining the necessary locks on the block or the tuple involved in the update, and reading in this block. This task is followed by making the update to the tuple in memory, which in turn is followed by another transfer task, writing the tuple back to secondary device, and releasing the locks.

In order to reduce the number of accesses to disk, the blocks are read into blocks of main memory called **buffers.** We can thus assume that a program performs input/output using, for example, the get and put operations, and the system transfers the required block from secondary memory to main memory using the read and write operations. The block read (write) tasks need not be performed in case the system uses buffered input (output) and the required data (space) is already in the primary memory buffer. In such a case the get (put) operation of the program can input (output) the required data from (to) the appropriate buffer. If the required data is not in the buffer, the buffer manager does a read operation and obtains the required data, after which the data is input from the buffer to the program executing the get statement. If there is no more space left in the buffer, the put operation causes the buffer to be written to the secondary storage (with a write) and then the put operation transfers the data from main memory to the space made available in the buffer.

The above DBMS operation of changing the grade of a student in a given course initiated by a user and appearing to her or him as a single operation actually requires a number of distinct tasks or steps to be performed by the DBMS. This is illustrated by the skeleton program given on the next page.

```
Procedure Modify_Enrol (Student_Name, Course, New_Grade);
 define action update ENROL(Student_Name, Course, Grade)as
    {* action update ENROL is defined as the next two
         statements *}
  begin
    get for update ENROL where
         ENROL.Student_Name = Student_Name and
         ENROL.Course = Course;
    ENROL.Grade := New_Grade;
    end
  if error
  then
    rollback action update ENROL;{* do not output ENROL *}
  else
    commit action update ENROL;{* output ENROL *}
  end Modify_Enrol;
```

In this program the comment indicates the definition of the action **update** ENROL of the record for a given student in a given course; this action is being referenced later with the keywords *commit* and *rollback*. The statements defined for the update operation are assumed to modify a temporary copy of the selected portion of the database (the main memory copy of the block of nonvolatile storage containing the tuple for the relation ENROL). Here we are using *error* to indicate whether there are any errors during the execution of the statements defined for the action **update** ENROL. If there were any errors, we want to undo any changes made to the database by the statements defined for the update action. This involves simply discarding the temporary copy of the affected portion of the database. The database itself is not changed if a temporary copy of the database is being used. If there were no errors, we want the changes made by the update operations to become permanent by being reflected in the actual database.

Figure 11.1 shows the successive states of the database system at different points of the execution of this program, with the change of student Jones's grade in course Comp353 from **in progress** to **A,** as shown in part d of the figure. In case there are any errors by the program, it ignores any modifications and the record for Jones remains unchanged as shown in part e.

The program unit Modify_Enrol given above consists of a number of statements, each of which is executed one at a time (each of the statements is compiled into a number of machine instructions, which are executed one at a time, sequentially). Such sequential execution can be interrupted due to errors. (Interrupts to execute the statements of other concurrent programs can also occur, but we will ignore this type of interruption for the time being.) In case of errors, the program may be only partially executed. However, to preserve the consistency of the database we want to ensure that the program is executed as a single unit, the execution of which will not change the consistency of the database. Thus an interruption of a transaction following a system detected error will return the database to its state before the start of the transaction. Such a program unit, which operates on the database to perform a read operation or an update operation (which includes modification, insertion, and deletion), is called a transaction.

Figure 11.1 Database states for program of Section 11.2.

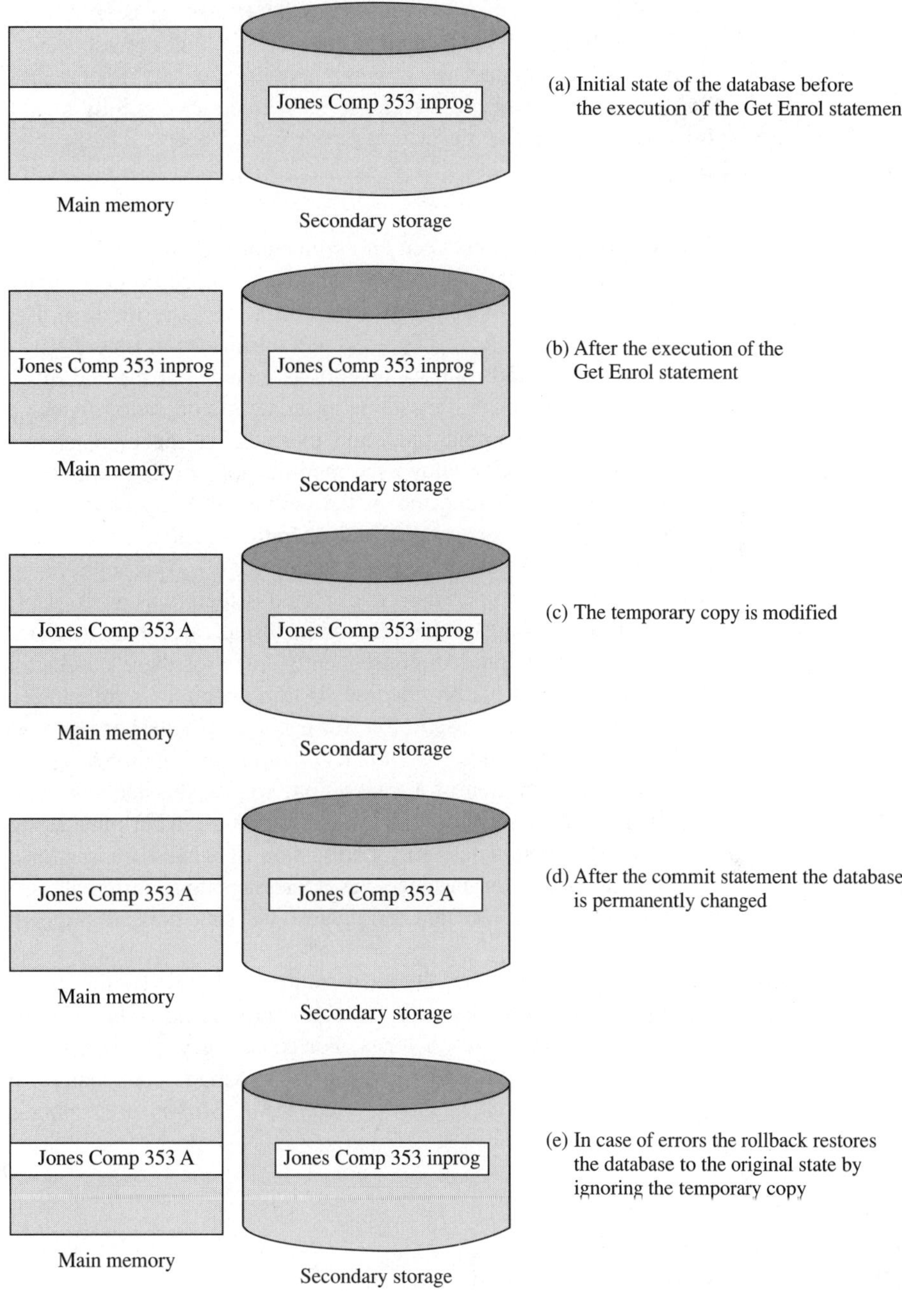

Definition: A **transaction** is a program unit whose execution may change the contents of a database. If the database was in a consistent state before a transaction, then on the completion of the execution of the program unit corresponding to the transaction, the database will be in a consistent state. This requires that the transaction be considered atomic: it is executed successfully or in case of errors, the user can view the transaction as not having been executed at all.

The relationship between an application program and a transaction is shown in Figure 11.2. The application program can be made up of a number of transactions, $T_1, T_2, \ldots, T_n$. Each such transaction T_i starts at the time T_{istart}. It commits (or rolls back) at time $T_{icommit}$ ($T_{irollback}$) and terminates at time T_{iend}.

The commit and rollback operations included at the end of a transaction ensure that the user can view a transaction as an atomic operation, which preserves database consistency. The commit operation executed at the completion of the modifying phase of the transaction allows the modifications made on the temporary copy of the database items to be reflected in the permanent copy of the database (later in this chapter we present recovery-related operations which are executed prior to making changes in the permanent copy of the database). The rollback operation (which is also called the undo operation) is executed if there was an error of some type during the modification phase of the transaction. It indicates that any modifications made by the transaction are ignored; consequently, none of these modifications is allowed to change the contents of the database. If transaction T_i is rolled back, the logic of the application program is responsible for deciding whether or not to execute transaction T_j (for $i < j \leq n$). *Once committed, a transaction cannot be rolled back.*

From the definition of a transaction, we see that the status of a transaction and the observation of its actions must not be visible from outside the transaction until the transaction terminates. Any notification of what a transaction is doing must not be communicated, for instance via a message to a terminal, until the transaction commits. Once a transaction terminates, the user may be notified of its success or failure.

There could be other DBMS operations viewed by the user as a single action but involve multiple changes. Consider the operation of changing the name of a student from Jones to Smith-Jones. For consistency, the DBMS application program that interfaces with the user must change the name in the relations STUDENT_INFO*(Student_Name, Phone_No, Major)* corresponding to the student

Figure 11.2 Application program and transactions.

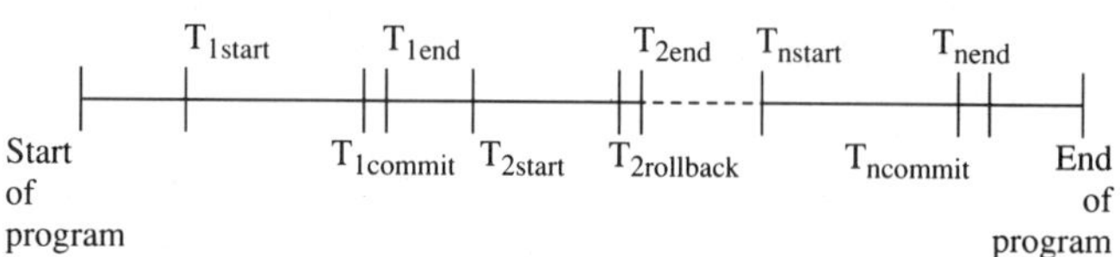

Jones and all tuples pertaining to this student in the relation ENROL(*Student_Name, Course, Grade*). A skeleton program to support this is given below.

```
Procedure Multiple_Modify Student_Name(Current_name, New_Name);
define action update STUDENT_INFO(Current_Name, New_Name) as
  begin
     get STUDENT_INFO where Student_Name = Current_name;
     STUDENT_INFO.Student_Name := New_Name;
     end;
define action update ENROL(Current_Name, New_Name) as
  begin
     while no_more_tuples_in ENROL do;
        begin
        get ENROL where ENROL.Student_Name = Current_Name;
        ENROL.Student_Name := New_Name;
        end;
     end;
if error
  then
     rollback (update STUDENT_INFO, update ENROL);
  else
     commit (update STUDENT_INFO, update ENROL);
end Multiple_Modify;
```

We see from the above skeleton program that modifying the student name involves a number of database accesses and changes. Because these changes can only occur one at a time, there is a period of time between the start of execution of this program and its termination during which the database is in an inconsistent state. For example, after the appropriate tuple in STUDENT_INFO is changed, we do not have referential integrity, there being no tuple in STUDENT_INFO corresponding to the tuples in ENROL for the student Jones (whose name has just been modified in STUDENT_INFO). Similarly, between the start of the update for the relation ENROL and its completion, some tuples have Smith-Jones as the value for the *Student_Name* attribute and others have Jones.

The point is that a database operation viewed by a user as a single operation in fact involves a number of database tasks, and there is no guarantee that the database is in a consistent state between these tasks. However, the user can view these tasks as a single operation (the so-called **atomic operation**), which will complete successfully or not at all. In the former case the changes are made and in the latter case the database remains unchanged. In either case, after the completion of the transaction, the database is in a consistent state.

11.2.1 States of a Transaction

A transaction can be considered to be an atomic operation by the user; in reality, however, it goes through a number of states during its lifetime. Figure 11.3 gives these states of the transaction, as well as the cause of a transition between these states.

Figure 11.3 Transaction states.

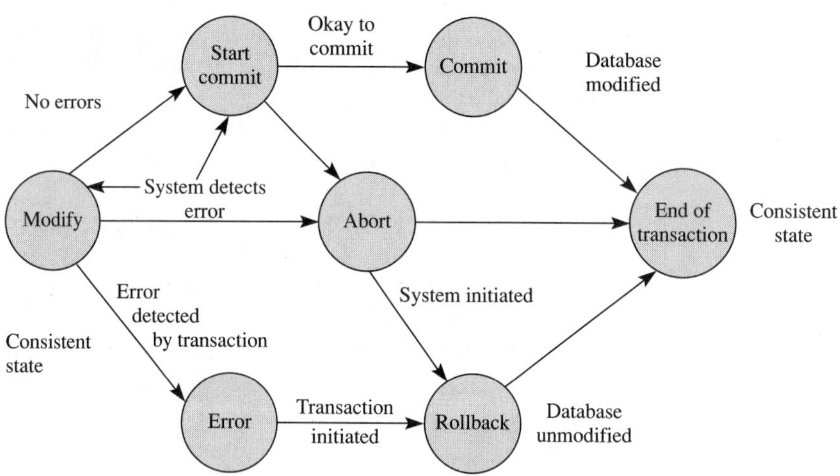

A transaction can end in three possible ways. It can end after a commit operation (a **successful termination**). It can detect an error during its processing and decide to abort itself by performing a rollback operation (a **suicidal termination**). The DBMS or the operating system can force it to be aborted for one reason or another (a **murderous termination**).

We assume that the database is in a consistent state before a transaction starts. A transaction starts when the first statement of the transaction is executed; it becomes active and we assume that it is in the modify state, when it modifies the database. At the end of the modify state, there is a transition into one of the following states: start to commit, abort, or error. If the transaction completes the modification state satisfactorily, it enters the start-to-commit state where it instructs the DBMS to reflect the changes made by it into the database. Once all the changes made by the transaction are propagated to the database, the transaction is said to be in the commit state and from there the transaction is terminated, the database once again being in a consistent state. In the interval of time between the start-to-commit state and the commit state, some of the data changed by the transaction in the buffers may or may not have been propagated to the database on the nonvolatile storage.

There is a possibility that all the modifications made by the transaction cannot be propagated to the database due to conflicts or hardware failures. In this case the system forces the transaction to the abort state. The abort state could also be entered from the modify state if there are system errors, for example, division by zero or an unrecoverable parity error. In case the transaction detects an error while in the modify state, it decides to terminate itself (suicide) and enters the error state and then, the rollback state. If the system aborts a transaction, it may have to initiate a rollback to undo partial changes made by the transaction. An aborted transaction that made no changes to the database is terminated without the need for a rollback, hence there are two paths in Figure 11.3 from the abort state to the end of the transaction. A transaction that, on the execution of its last statement, enters the start to commit state and from there the commit state is guaranteed that the modifications made by it are propagated to the database.

The transaction outcome can be either successful (if the transaction goes through the commit state), suicidal (if the transaction goes through the rollback state), or murdered (if the transaction goes through the abort state), as shown in Figure 11.3. In the last two cases, there is no trace of the transaction left in the database, and only the log indicates that the transaction was ever run.

Any messages given to the user by the transaction must be delayed till the end of the transaction, at which point the user can be notified as to the success or failure of the transaction and in the latter case, the reasons for the failure.

11.2.2 Properties of a Transaction

From the definition of a transaction, we see that the status of a transaction and the observation of its actions is not visible from outside until the transaction terminates. Any notification of what a transaction is doing must not be communicated, for instance via a message to a terminal, until the transaction is terminated. Nor should any partial changes made by an active transaction be visible from outside the transaction. Once a transaction ends, the user may be notified of its success or failure and the changes made by the transaction are accessible. In order for a transaction to achieve these characteristics, it should have the properties of atomicity, consistency, isolation, and durability. These properties, referred to as the ACID test, represent the transaction paradigm.

The **atomicity** property of a transaction implies that it will run to completion as an indivisible unit, at the end of which either no changes have occurred to the database or the database has been changed in a consistent manner. At the end of a transaction the updates made by the transaction will be accessible to other transactions and the processes outside the transaction.

The **consistency** property of a transaction implies that if the database was in a consistent state before the start of a transaction, then on termination of a transaction the database will also be in a consistent state.

The **isolation** property of a transaction indicates that actions performed by a transaction will be isolated or hidden from outside the transaction until the transaction terminates. This property gives the transaction a measure of relative independence.

The **durability** property of a transaction ensures that the commit action of a transaction, on its termination, will be reflected in the database. The permanence of the commit action of a transaction requires that any failures after the commit operation will not cause loss of the updates made by the transaction.

11.2.3 Failure Anticipation and Recovery

In designing a reliable system we try to anticipate different types of failures and provide for the means to recover without loss of information. Some very rare failures may not be catered to for economic reasons. Recovery from failures that are not thought of, overlooked, or ignored may not be possible. In common practice, the recovery system of a DBMS is designed to anticipate and recover from the following types of failure:

Failures without loss of data: This type of failure is due to errors that the transaction discovers before it reaches the start to commit state. It can also be due to the action of the system, which resets its state to that which existed before the start of the transaction. No loss of data is involved in this type of failure, especially in the case where the transactions are run in a batch mode; these transactions can be rerun later in the same sequence.

Failure with loss of volatile storage: Such a failure can occur as a result of software or hardware errors. The processing of an active transaction is terminated in an unpredictable manner before it reaches its commit or rollback state and the contents of the volatile memory are lost.

Failure with loss of nonvolatile storage: This is the sort of failure that can occur after the failure of a nonvolatile storage system; for example, a head crash on a disk drive or errors in writing to a nonvolatile device.

Failure with a loss of stable storage: This type involves loss of data stored on stable storage. The cause of the loss could be due to natural or man-made disasters. Recovery from this type of failure requires manual regeneration of the database. The probability of such a failure is reduced to a very small value by having multiple copies of data in stable storage, stored in physically secure environments in geographically dispersed locations.

11.3 Recovery in a Centralized DBMS

The basic technique to implement the database transaction paradigm in the presence of failures of various kinds is by using data redundancy in the form of logs, checkpoints and archival copies of the database.

11.3.1 Logs

The **log,** which is usually written to stable storage, contains the redundant data required to recover from volatile storage failures and also from errors discovered by the transaction or the database system. For each transaction the following data is recorded on the log:

- A start-of-transaction marker.
- The transaction identifier, which could include the who and where information referred to in Section 11.1.3.
- The record identifiers, which include the identifiers for the record occurrences.
- The operation(s) performed on the records (insert, delete, modify).
- The previous value(s) of the modified data. This information is required for undoing the changes made by a partially completed transaction; it is called the undo log. Where the modification made by the transaction is the insertion of a new record, the previous values can be assumed to be null.

- The updated value(s) of the modified record(s). This information is required for making sure that the changes made by a committed transaction are in fact reflected in the database and can be used to redo these modifications. This information is called the redo part of the log. In case the modification made by the transaction is the deletion of a record, the updated values can be assumed to be null.
- A commit transaction marker if the transaction is committed; otherwise an abort or rollback transaction marker.

The log is written before any updates are made to the database. This is called the **write-ahead log strategy.** In this strategy a transaction is not allowed to modify the physical database until the undo portion of the log (i.e. the portion of the log that contains the previous value(s) of the modified data) is written to stable storage. Furthermore, the log write-ahead strategy requires that a transaction is allowed to commit only after the redo portion of the log and the commit transaction marker are written to the log. In effect, both the undo and redo portion of the log will be written to stable storage before a transaction commit. Using this strategy, the partial updates made by an uncommitted transaction can be undone using the undo portion of the log, and a failure occurring between the writing of the log and the completion of updating the database corresponding to the actions implied by the log can be redone.

Let us see how the log information can be used in the case of a system crash with the loss of volatile information. Consider a number of transactions, as shown in Figure 11.4. The figure shows the system start-up at time t_0 and a number of concurrent transactions $T_0, T_1, \ldots, T_{i+6}$ are made on the database. Suppose a system crash occurs at time t_x.

We have stored the log information for transactions T_0 through T_{i+2} on stable storage, and we assume that this will be available when the system comes up after

Figure 11.4 DBMS operation to a system crash.

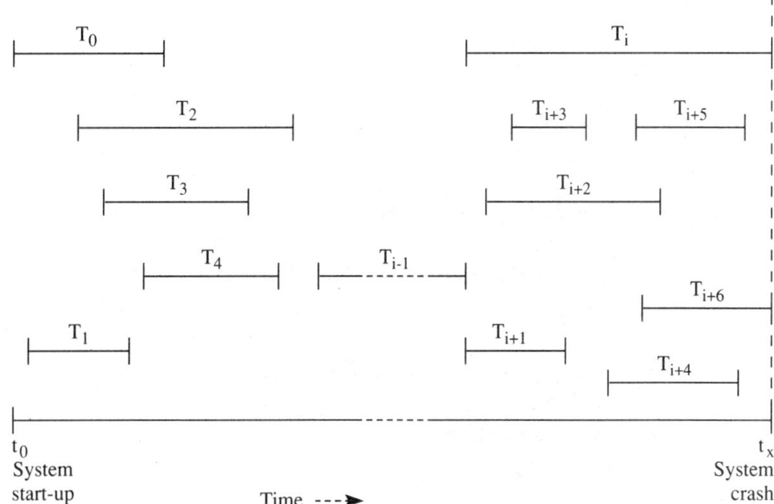

the crash. Furthermore, we assume that the database existing on the nonvolatile storage will also be available. It is clear that the transactions that were not committed at the time of the system crash will have to be undone. The changes made by these uncommitted transactions will have to be rolled back. The transactions that have not been committed can be found by examining the log, and those transactions that have a start of transaction marker but no commit or abort transaction marker are considered to have been active at the time of the crash. These transactions have to be rolled back to restore the database to a consistent state. In Figure 11.4 the transactions T_i and T_{i+6} started before the crash, but they had not been committed and, hence, are undone.

However, it is not clear from the log to what extent the changes made by committed transactions have actually been propagated to the database on the nonvolatile storage. The reason for this uncertainty is the fact that buffers (implemented in volatile storage) are used by the system to hold the modified data. Some of the changed data in these buffers may or may not have been propagated to the database on the nonvolatile storage. In the absence of any method of finding out the extent of the loss, we will be forced to redo the effects of all committed transactions. For Figure 11.4, this involves redoing the changes made by all transactions from time t_0. Under such a scenario, the longer the system operates without a crash, the longer it will take to recover from the crash.

In the above, we have assumed that the log information is available up to the time of the system crash in nonvolatile storage. However, the log information is also collected in buffers. In case of a system crash with loss of volatile information, the log information collected in buffers will also be lost and transactions that had been completed for some period prior to the system crash may be missing their respective end-of-transaction markers in the log. Such transactions, if rolled back, will likely be partially undone. The write-ahead log strategy avoids this type of recovery problem, since the log information is forced to be copied to stable storage before the transaction commits.

These problems point to the conclusion that some means must be devised to propagate to stable storage at regular intervals all the log information, as well as modifications to the database existing at a given time. Then the recovery operation after a system crash will not have to reprocess all transactions from the time of start-up of the system.

11.3.2 Checkpoints

In an on-line database system, for example an airline reservation system, there could be hundreds of transactions handled per minute. The log for this type of database contains a very large volume of information. A scheme called **checkpoint** is used to limit the volume of log information that has to be handled and processed in the event of a system failure involving the loss of volatile information. The checkpoint scheme is an additional component of the logging scheme described above.

In the case of a system crash, the log information being collected in buffers will be lost. A checkpoint operation, performed periodically, copies log information onto stable storage. The information and operations performed at each checkpoint consist of the following:

- A start-of-checkpoint record giving the identification that it is a checkpoint along with the time and date of the checkpoint is written to the log on a stable storage device.
- All log information from the buffers in the volatile storage is copied to the log on stable storage.
- All database updates from the buffers in the volatile storage are propagated to the physical database.
- An end-of-checkpoint record is written and the address of the checkpoint record is saved on a file accessible to the recovery routine on start-up after a system crash.

For all transactions active at checkpoint, their identifiers and their database modification actions, which at that time are reflected only in the database buffers, will be propagated to the appropriate storage.

The frequency of checkpointing is a design consideration of the recovery system. A checkpoint can be taken at fixed intervals of time (say, every 15 minutes). If this approach is used, a choice has to be made regarding what to do with the transactions that are active when the checkpoint signal is generated by a system timer. In one alternative, called **transaction-consistent checkpoint,** the transactions that are active when the system timer signals a checkpoint are allowed to complete, but no new transactions (requiring modifications to the database) are allowed to be started until the checkpoint is completed. This scheme, though attractive, makes the database unavailable at regular intervals and may not be acceptable for certain online applications. In addition, this approach is not appropriate for long transactions. In the second variation, called **action consistent checkpoint,** active transactions are allowed to complete the current step before the checkpoint and no new actions can be started on the database until the checkpoint is completed; during the checkpoint no actions are permitted on the database. Another alternative, called **transaction-oriented checkpoint,** is to take a checkpoint at the end of each transaction by forcing the log of the transaction onto stable storage. In effect, each commit transaction is a checkpoint.

How does the checkpoint information help in recovery? To answer this question, reconsider the set of transactions of Figure 11.4, shown in Figure 11.5, with the addition of a checkpoint being taken at time t_c.

Suppose, as before, the crash occurs at time t_x. Now the fact that a checkpoint was taken at time t_c indicates that at that time all log and data buffers were propagated to storage. Transactions $T_0, \ldots, T_{i-1}$ as well as transactions T_{i+1} and T_{i+3} were committed, and their modifications are reflected in the database. With the checkpoint scheme these transactions are not required to be redone during the recovery operation following a system crash occurring after time t_c. A transaction such as T_i (which started before checkpoint time t_c), as well as transaction T_{i+6} (which started after checkpoint time t_c), were not committed at the time of the crash and have to be rolled back. Transactions such as T_{i+4} and T_{i+5} which started after checkpoint time t_c and were committed before the system crash, have to be redone. Similarly, transactions such as T_{i+2}, which started before the checkpoint time and were committed before the system crash, will have to be redone. However, if the commit-transaction information is missing for any of the transactions T_{i+2}, T_{i+4}, or T_{i+5}, then they have to be undone.

Figure 11.5 Checkpointing.

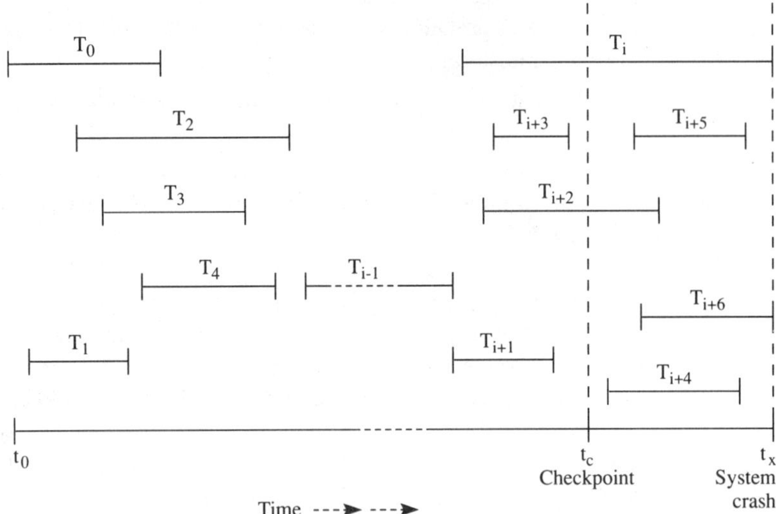

Let us now see how the system can perform a recovery at time t_x. Suppose all transactions that started before the checkpoint time but were not committed at that time, as well as the transactions started after the checkpoint time, are placed in an **undo** list, which is a list of transactions to be undone. The undo list for the transactions of Figure 11.5 is given below:

UNDO List: (T_i, T_{i+2}, T_{i+4}, T_{i+5}, T_{i+6})

Now the recovery system scans the log in a backward direction from the time t_x of system crash. If it finds that a transaction in the undo list has committed, that transaction is removed from the undo list and placed in the **redo** list. The redo list contains all the transactions that have to be redone. The reduced undo list and the redo list for the transactions of Figure 11.5 are given below:

REDO List: (T_{i+4}, T_{i+5}, T_{i+2})
UNDO List: (T_i, T_{i+6})

Obviously, all transactions that were committed before the checkpoint time need not be considered for the recovery operation. In this way the amount of work required to be done for recovery from a system crash is reduced. Without the checkpoint scheme, the redo list will contain all transactions except T_i and T_{i+6}. A system crash occurring during the checkpoint operation, requires recovery to be done using the most recent previous checkpoint.

The recovery scheme described above takes a pessimistic view about what has been propagated to the database at the time of a system crash with loss of volatile information. Such pessimism is adopted both for transactions committed after a checkpoint and transactions not committed since a checkpoint. It assumes that the transactions committed since the checkpoint have not been able to propagate their modifications to the database and the transactions still in progress have done so.

Note that in some systems, the term checkpoint is used to denote the correct state of system files recorded explicitly in a backup file and the term checkpointing is used to denote a mechanism used to restore the system files to a previous consistent state. However, in a system that uses the transaction paradigm, checkpoint is a strategy to minimize the search of the log and the amount of undo and redo required to recover from a system failure with loss of volatile storage.

11.3.3 Archival Database and Implementation of the Storage Hierarchy of a Database System

Figure 11.6 gives the different categories of data used in a database system. These storage types are sometimes called the storage hierarchy. It consists of the archival database, physical database, archival log, and current log.

Physical database: This is the online copy of the database that is stored in nonvolatile storage and used by all active transactions.

Current database: The current version of the database is made up of the physical database plus modifications implied by buffers in the volatile storage.

Figure 11.6 Database storage hierarchy.

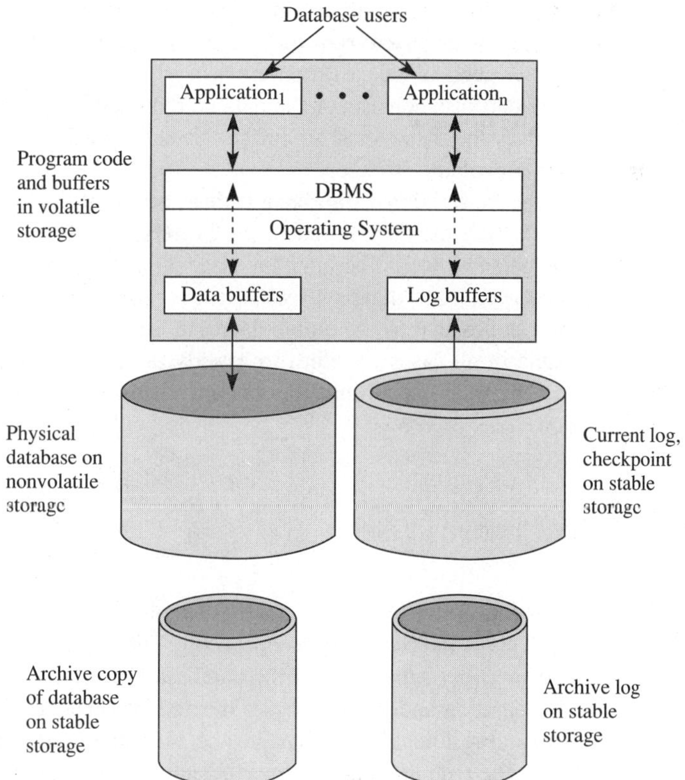

Archival database in stable storage: This is the copy of the database at a given time, stored on stable storage. It contains the entire database in a **quiescent** mode (i.e., no transactions were active when the database was copied to the stable storage) and could have been made by simple dump routines to dump the physical database (which in quiescent state would be the same as the current or online database) onto stable storage. The purpose of the archival database is to recover from failures that involve loss of nonvolatile storage. The archiving process is a relatively time-consuming operation and during this period the database is not accessible. Consequently, archiving is done at infrequent intervals. The frequency of archiving is a trade-off between the cost of archiving and that of recovery with the probability of a loss of nonvolatile data being the arbitrator. All transactions that have been executed on the database from the time of archiving have to be redone in a global recovery operation. No undoing is required in the global recovery operation since the archival database is a copy of the database in a quiescent state, and only the committed transactions since the time of archiving are applied to this database.

Current log: This contains the log information (including the checkpoint) required for recovery from system failures involving loss of volatile information.

Archival log: This log is used for failures involving loss of nonvolatile information. The log contains information on all transactions made on the database from the time of the archival copy. This log is written in chronological order. The recovery from loss of nonvolatile storage uses the archival copy of the database and the archival log to reconstruct the physical database to the time of the nonvolatile storage failure.

With the above storage hierarchy of a database, we can use the following terms to denote different combinations of this hierarchy.

The on-line or **current database** is made up of all the records (and the auxiliary structures such as indexes) that are accessible to the DBMS during its operation. The current database consists of the data stored in nonvolatile storage (physical database) as well as the data stored in buffers (in the volatile storage) and not yet propagated to the nonvolatile storage.

The **materialized database** is that portion of the database that is still intact after a failure. All the data stored in the buffers would have been lost and some portion of the database would be in an inconsistent state. The log information is to be applied to the materialized database by the recovery system to restore the database to as close a state as possible to the online database prior to the crash. Obviously, it will not be possible in all cases to return to exactly the same state as the precrash online database. The intent is to limit the amount of lost data and the loss of completed transactions.

11.3.4 Do, Undo, and Redo

A transaction on the current database transforms it from the current state to a new state. This is the so-called **do** operation. The undo and redo operations are functions of the recovery subsystem of the database system used in the recovery process. The undo operation undoes or reverses the actions (possibly partially executed) of a transaction and restores the database to the state that existed before the start of the transaction. The redo operation redoes the action of a transaction and restores the database to the state it would be in at the end of the transaction. The undo operation is also called into play when a transaction decides to terminate itself (suicidal termination). Figure 11.7 shows the transformation of the database as a result of a transaction do, redo, and undo.

The undo and redo operations for a given transaction are required to be **idempotent;** that is, for any transaction, performing one of these operations once is equivalent to performing it any number of times. Thus:

undo(any action) ≡ **undo(undo(** .. **undo**(any action) ..))
Redo(any action) ≡ **redo(redo(** .. **redo**(any action) ..))

The reason for the requirement that undo and redo be idempotent is that the recovery process, while in the process of undoing or redoing the actions of a transaction, may fail without a trace, and this type of failure can occur any number of times before the recovery is completed successfully.

Transaction Undo

A transaction that discovers an error while it is in progress and consequently needs to abort itself and roll back any changes made by it uses the **transaction undo** feature. A transaction also has to be undone when the DBMS forces the transaction to abort. A transaction undo removes all database changes, partial or otherwise, made by the transaction.

Figure 11.7 Do, undo, and redo operations.

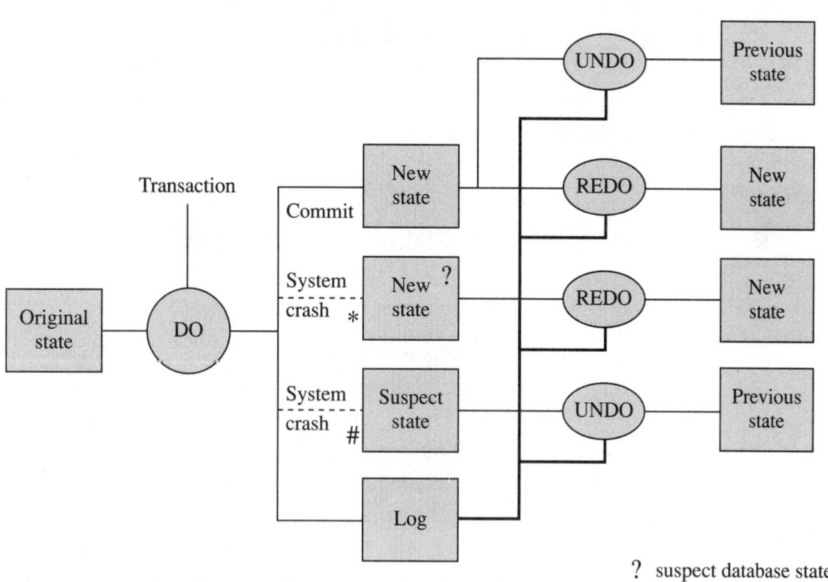

Transaction Redo

Transaction redo involves performing the changes made by a transaction that committed before a system crash. With the write-ahead log strategy, a committed transaction implies that the log for the transaction would have been written to nonvolatile storage, but the physical database may or may not have been modified before the system failure. A transaction redo modifies the physical database to the new values for a committed transaction. Since the redo operation is idempotent, redoing the partial or complete modifications made by a transaction to the physical database will not pose a problem for recovery.

Global Undo

Transactions that are partially complete at the time of a system crash with loss of volatile storage need to be undone by undoing any changes made by the transaction. The **global undo** operation, initiated by the recovery system, involves undoing the partial or otherwise updates made by all uncommitted transactions at the time of a system failure.

Global Redo

The **global redo** operation is required for recovery from failures involving nonvolatile storage loss. The archival copy of the database is used and all transactions committed since the time of the archival copy are redone to obtain a database updated to a point as close as possible to the time of the nonvolatile storage loss. The effects of the transaction in progress at the time of the nonvolatile loss will not be reflected in the recovered database. The archival copy of the database could be anywhere from months to days old and the number of transactions that have to be redone could be large. The log for the committed transactions needed for performing a global redo operation has to be stored on stable storage so that they are not lost with the loss of nonvolatile storage containing the physical database.

11.4 Reflecting Updates to the Database and Recovery

Let us assume that the physical database at the start of a transaction is equivalent to the current database, i.e., all modifications have been reflected in the database on the nonvolatile storage. Under this assumption, whenever a transaction is run against a database, we have a number of options as to the strategy that will be followed in reflecting the modifications made by the transaction as it is executed. The strategies we will explore are the following:

Update in place: In this approach the modifications appear in the database in the original locations and, in the case of a simple update, the new values will replace the old values.

Indirect update with careful replacement: In this approach the modifications are not made directly on the physical database. Two possibilities can be considered. The first scheme, called the **shadow page scheme,** makes the changes on a copy of that portion of the database being modified. The other scheme is called **update via log.** In this strategy of indirect update, the update operations of a transaction are logged and the log of a committed transaction is used to modify the physical database.

In the following sections we examine these update schemes in greater detail.

11.4.1 Update in Place

In this scheme (see Figure 11.8) the transaction updates the physical database and the modified record replaces the old record in the database on nonvolatile storage. The write-ahead log strategy is used and the log information about the transaction modifications are written before the corresponding *put*(x) operation, initiated by the transaction, is performed. Recall that the write-ahead log strategy has the following requirements:

1. Before a transaction is allowed to modify the database, at least the undo portion of the transaction log record is written to the stable storage.
2. A transaction is committed only after both the undo and the redo portion of the log are written to stable storage.

The sequence of operations for transaction T and the actions performed by the database are shown in Figure 11.9. The initiation of a transaction causes the start of the log of its activities; a start transaction along with the identification of the transaction is written out to the log. During the execution of the transaction, any output (in the form of a put by the transaction) is preceded by a log output to indicate the modification being made to the database. This output to the log consists of the record(s) being modified, old values of the data items in the case of an update, and the values of the data items. The old values will be used by the recovery system to undo the modifications made by a transaction in case a system crash occurs before the

Figure 11.8 Update in place scheme.

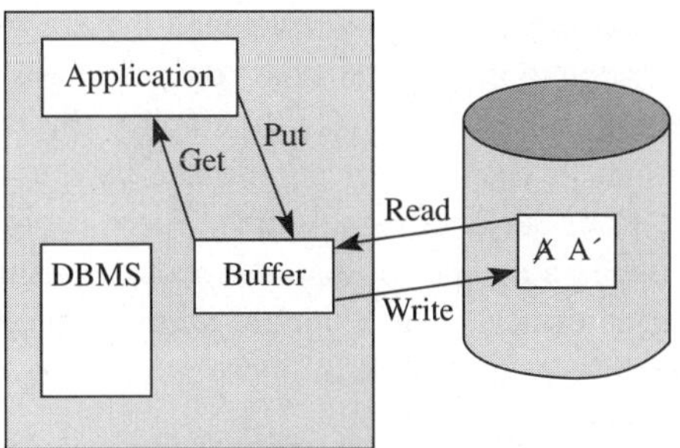

Figure 11.9 Direct update (write-ahead log).

Time	Transaction Step	Log Operation	Database Operation
t_0	Start of T	**Write**(start Transaction T)	
t_1	*get*(X)		**Read**(X)
t_2	*modify*(X)		
t_3	*put*(X)	**Write**(record X modified, old value of X, new value of X)	
t_4			**Write**(X)
t_5	*get*(Y)		**Read**(Y)
t_6	*modify*(Y)		
t_7	*put*(Y)	**Write**(record Y modified, old value of X, new value of X)	
t_8			**Write**(Y)
t_9	Start Commit	**Write**(Commit transaction T);	
t_{10}	End of T		

completion of the transaction. When a system crash occurs after a transaction commits, the new values will be used by the recovery system to redo the changes made by the transaction and thus ensure that the modifications made by a committed transaction are correctly reflected in the database.

The transaction shown in Figure 11.9 consists of reading in the value of some data item X and modifying it by a certain amount. The transaction then reads in the value of another data item Y and modifies it by an equal but opposite amount. The transaction may subtract, let us say, a quantity **n** from the inventory for part P_x and add this amount to quantities of that item shipped to customer C_y. For consistency this transaction must be completed atomically. A system crash occurring at any time before time t_9 will require that the transaction be undone. A system crash occurring after t_9, when the commit transaction marker is written to the log, requires that we redo the transaction to ensure that all of the changes made by this transaction are propagated to the physical database.

According to the write-ahead log strategy, the redo portion of the log need not be written to the log until the commit transaction is issued by the program performing the transaction. However, to simplify the log, we are combining the undo and redo portions of each modification made by a transaction in one log entry.

Consider another example where a program executes a number of transactions involving a number of distinct records. In this case, the transaction atomicity requirement is critical. The example involves projects, parts used by the projects, and an inventory of the parts. Suppose we have a number of parts $Part_1$, $Part_2$, . . . , and a number of projects $Proj_1$, $Proj_2$, ... Each project $Proj_i$ uses parts { . . . . , $Part_k$, . . . , }. Suppose the database contains the following relations:

PART(*Part#, Quantity_in_Stock)*
PROJECT(*Project#, Part#, Quantities_to_Date)*

Consider the execution of the program below which transfers 100 units of parts $Part_4$ to project $Proj_5$ and 10 units of parts $Part_1$ to project $Proj_2$. Here, each such transfer is considered as a separate transaction. If the quantity in stock of a part is less than the required quantities to be transferred, an error condition is said to exist and such a transaction is aborted (a suicidal end). The transfer of x quantity of $Part_i$ from inventory to project $Proj_j$ is considered to be a single atomic operation that either succeeds and performs the appropriate transfer or fails, in which case it does not leave a trace of partial execution (except in the log).

```
Program: Transfer_parts(input,output);
     var (* declarations are not given but should include
     all variables as well as database records to be used and
     the corresponding local declarations *)
  Procedure many_transactions
     begin
      while not eof do
      error := false;
      readln(projno, partno, quant);
      start_transaction(modifymode)
      get PART where Part_Number = partno;
      Quantity_in_Stock: = Quantity_in_Stock - quant;
      if Quantity_in_Stock < 0
        then error := true
        else begin
            put PART;
            get Project where Project_Number = projno
                 and  Part_Number = partno;
            Quantity_to_Date: = Quantity_to_Date + quant;
            put PROJECT;
            end;
      if error
        then abort_transaction
        else commit_transaction;
     end_transaction;
      end (* while *)
   end (* procedure *)
end.
```

With the update-in-place scheme, the new value of a record field overwrites the old value as shown in Figure 11.10 If a transaction involves multiple changes, a system crash causes the database to end up in an inconsistent state.

The update-in-place method goes against the well-established accounting practice of recording each and every transaction and never overwriting data. In accounting practice, a compensating transaction is used to make corrections when an error is discovered, and the fact that an error was made is also recorded.

Let us now see how the log information can be used in the recovery process if a system crash occurs before all the modifications made by a transaction are propa-

Figure 11.10 Modifications with update-in-place scheme.

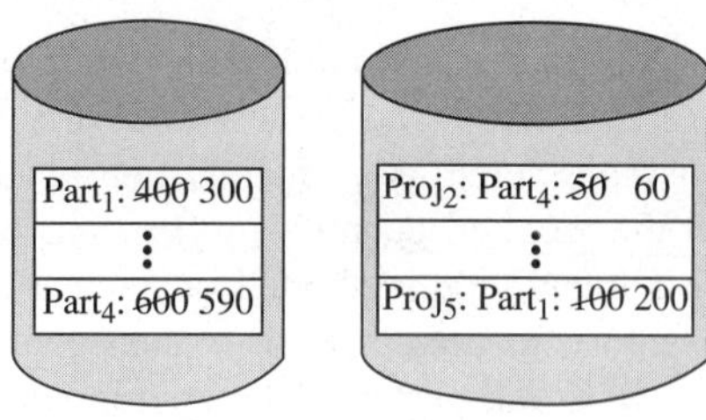

gated to the database. Suppose that before the program was run the inventory for parts $Part_1$ and $Part_4$ were 400 and 600 respectively; the quantity used by project $Proj_5$ of part $Part_1$ was 100 and the quantity used by project $Proj_2$ of part $Part_4$ was 10. The program above was run to transfer 100 units of $Part_1$ from inventory for use in $Proj_5$, followed by the transfer of 10 units of part $Part_4$ from inventory to $Proj_2$. The operations performed by the program are shown in Figure 11.11. The first operation is called transaction T_0; the second operation, T_1. *Quantity_in_Stock* is abbreviated as *Q_in_S* and *Quantity_to_Date* as *Q_to_D*.

Now suppose that while the program above was executing, there was a system crash with loss of volatile storage. Let us consider the various possibilities as to the progress made by the program and the sequence of recovery operations required using the information from the write-ahead log.

If the crash occurs just during or after step s_4, the log would have the following information for the transaction T_0:

Start of T_0
record *Part#* = $Part_1$,
    old value of *Q_in_S:* 400
    new value of *Q_in_S:* 300

The recovery process, when it examines the log, finds that the commit transaction marker for T_0 is missing and, hence, will undo the partially completed transaction T_0. To do this it will use the old value for the modified field of the part record identified by $Part_1$ to restore the *Quantity_in_Stock* field of the part record for $Part_1$ to the value 400 and restore the database to the consistent state that existed before the crash and before transaction T_0 was started.

If the crash occurs after step s_9 is completed, the recovery system will find an end-of-transaction marker for transaction T_0 in the log. The log entry will be as given below:

Start of T_0
record *Part#* = $Part_1$,
    old value of *Q_in_S:* 400
    new value of *Q_in_S:* 300
record *Project#* = $Proj_5$
    old value of *Q_to_D:* 100,
    new value of *Q_to_D:* 200
Commit T_0

Figure 11.11 The steps for two transactions.

Step	Transaction Action	Log Operation	Database Operation
s_0	Start of T_0	**Write**(start Transaction T_0)	
s_1	*get*($Part_1$)		**Read**($Part_1$)
s_2	modify(*Q_in_S* from 400 to 300)		
s_3	*put*($Part_1$)	**Write**(record for Part# = $Part_1$, old value of *Q_in_S:* 400, new value of *Q_in_S:* 300)	
s_4			**Write**($Part_1$)
s_5	*get*($Proj_5$)		**Read**($Proj_5$)
s_6	modify(*Q_to_D* from 100 to 200)		
s_7	*put*($Proj_5$)	**Write**(record for *Project#* = $Proj_5$, old value of *Q_to_D:* 100, new value of *Q_to_D:* 200)	
s_8			**Write**($Proj_5$)
s_9	Start Commit	**Write**(Commit transaction T_0);	
s_{10}	End of T_0		
$s_{10'}$	Start of T_1	**Write**(start Transaction T_1)	
s_{11}	*get*($Part_4$)		**Read**($Part_4$)
s_{12}	modify(*Q_in_S* from 600 to 590)		
s_{13}	*put* ($Part_4$)	**Write**(record Part# = $Part_4$, old value of *Q_in_S:* 600, new value of *Q_in_S:* 590)	
s_{14}			**Write**($Part_4$)
s_{15}	*get*($Proj_2$)		**Read**($Proj_2$)
s_{16}	modify(*Q_to_D* from 50 to 60)		
s_{17}	*put*($Proj_2$)	**Write**(record *Project#* = $Proj_2$, old value of *Q_to_D:* 50, new value of *Q_to_D:* 60)	
s_{18}			**Write**($Proj_2$)
s_{19}	Start Commit	**Write**(Commit transaction T_1);	
s_{20}	End of T_1		

However, since the log was written before the database, all modifications to the database may not have been propagated to the database. Thus to ensure that all modifications made by transaction T_0 are propagated to the database, the recovery system will redo the committed transaction. To do this it uses the new values of the appropriate fields of the records identified by *Part#* = $Part_1$ and *Project#* = $Proj_5$. This will restore the database to an up-to-date state, with the modifications of the committed transactions propagated to the database.

It is obvious that if the system crash occurs after step $s_{10'}$ but before step s_{19}, the recovery operation will require the undoing of modifications made by transaction T_1 and redoing those made by transaction T_0. Similarly, a crash occurring any time after step s_{19} will require the redoing of the modifications made by both transactions T_0 and T_1.

It is important to point out that the key to the recovery operation is the log, which is written to stable storage ahead of the update in place of the database; thus the log information survives any crash. However, the writing of the log may itself be interrupted by a system crash and log information may be incomplete. If the crash occurs sometime during step s_9, the commit transaction marker for transaction T_0 may not be safely written to the log, and this implies that the recovery system will undo the transaction even if all the modifications made by transaction T_0 have been propagated to the database.

In the above example, we have assumed that the DBMS propagates the modifications to the database as soon as the log entry for the modifications are written to stable storage. However, if the database system defers the propagations to the database until the commit step for the transaction, then in the event of a system crash the recovery tasks are modified slightly (see Exercise 11.17). If the transaction is rolled back by the user program, the rolling back operation involves writing a rollback marker to the log and inhibiting the propagation of the changes to the database. The propagation to the database will also be inhibited if the transaction is aborted by the system before it commits; the last log entry in that case would be an abort transaction marker.

In either of the two possible choices of propagating the changes to the database, the consistency criterion of the database requires that that portion of the database being modified by a transaction be accessible exclusively to the transaction, for the duration of the transaction.

11.4.2 Indirect Update and Careful Replacement

In the indirect update and careful replacement scheme, the database is not directly modified, but a copy is made of that portion of the database to be modified and all modifications are made on this copy. Once the transaction commits, the modified copy replaces the original.

In the most common scheme used, the **indirect page allocation** scheme, modifications to the database are directed to new blocks (pages) on nonvolatile storage (Figure 11.12). Each new block is a copy of the database block containing the records being modified. The old block of the database remains intact. When the transaction commits, the new blocks can be used to replace the old blocks in an atomic

Figure 11.12 Indirect page allocation scheme.

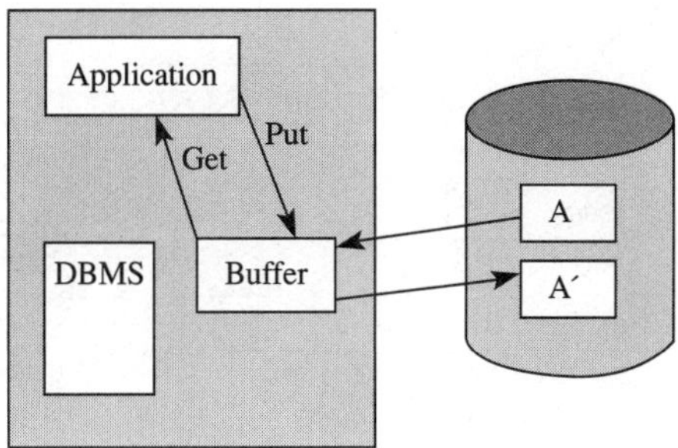

manner. In the case of a system crash, the old blocks are still available and the recovery operation is simplified.

In another form of indirect update, no changes are made to the database during a transaction. However, the modified values are written to a log on stable storage (recall the journal concept of accounting). When the transaction commits, the log is used to write the modifications onto the database. In this case, the rollback of a transaction entails discarding the log entries for the transaction. The recovery operation of a transaction is limited to redoing the modifications made by a transaction that are recorded in the log entry for that transaction. The undo recovery operation for the transaction does not need to undo any changes as far as the database on the nonvolatile storage is concerned since no changes were made for an uncommitted transaction.

Reflecting Updates to the Database via Shadow Page Scheme and Recovery

The shadow page scheme is one possible form of the indirect page allocation. Before we discuss this scheme, let us briefly review the paging scheme as used in the operating system for virtual memory management. The memory that is addressed by a process (a program in execution is a process) is called virtual memory. It is divided into pages that are assumed to be of a certain size, let us say 1024 (1K) bytes or more commonly 4096 (or 4K) bytes. The virtual or logical pages are mapped onto physical memory blocks of the same size as the pages, and the mapping is provided by means of a table known as a **page table.** The page table, shown in Figure 11.13, contains one entry for each logical page of the process's virtual address space. With this scheme, the consecutive logical pages need not be mapped onto consecutive physical blocks.

In the shadow page scheme, the database is considered to be made up of logical units of storage called pages. The pages are mapped into physical blocks of storage (of the same size as the logical pages) by means of a page table, with one entry for each logical page of the database. This entry contains the block number of the physical storage where this page is stored.

The shadow page scheme shown in Figure 11.14 uses two page tables for a transaction that is going to modify the database. The original page table is called the

Figure 11.13 Paging scheme.

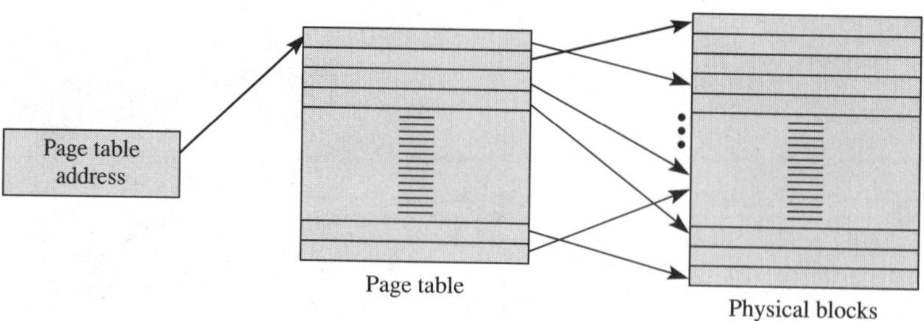

shadow page table and the transaction addresses the database using another page table known as the **current page table.** Initially, both page tables point to the same blocks of physical storage. The current page table entries may change during the life of the transaction. The changes are made whenever the transaction modifies the database by means of a write operation. The pages that are affected by a transaction are copied to new blocks of physical storage and these blocks, along with the blocks not modified, are accessible to the transaction via the current page table, as shown in Figure 11.14. The old version of the changes pages remains unchanged and these pages continue to be accessible via the shadow page table.

The shadow page table contains the entries that existed in the page table before the start of the transaction and points to blocks that were never changed by the transaction. The shadow page table remains unaltered by the transaction and is used for undoing the transaction.

Now let us see how the transaction accesses data during the time it is active. The transaction uses the current page table to access the database blocks for retrieval. Any modification made by the transaction involves a write operation to the database. The shadow page scheme handles the first write operation to a given page as follows:

Figure 11.14 Shadow page scheme.

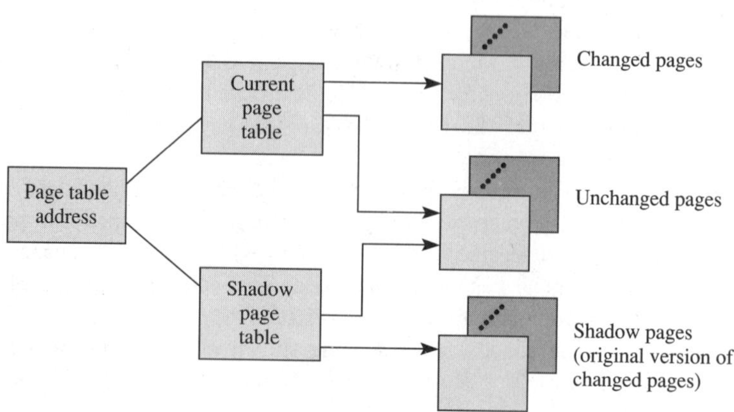

- A free block of nonvolatile storage is located from the pool of free blocks accessible by the database system.
- The block to be modified is copied onto this block.
- The original entry in the current page table is changed to point to this new block.
- The updates are propagated to the block pointed to by the current page table, which in this case would be the newly created block.

Subsequent write operations to a page already duplicated are handled via the current page table. Any changes made to the database are propagated to the blocks pointed to by the current page table. Once a transaction commits, all modifications made by the transaction and still in buffers are propagated to the physical database (i.e., the changes are written to the blocks pointed to by the current page table). The propagation is confirmed by adopting the current page table as the table containing the consistent database. The current page table or the active portion of it could be in volatile storage. In this case a commit transaction causes the current page table to be written to nonvolatile storage.

In the case of a system crash, before the transaction commits, the shadow page table and the corresponding blocks containing the old database, which was assumed to be in a consistent state, will continue to be accessible.

To recover from system crashes during the life of a transaction, all we have to do is revert to the shadow page table so that the database remains accessible after the crash. The only precaution to be taken is to store the shadow page table on stable storage and have a pointer that points to the address where the shadow page table is stored and that is accessible to the database through any system crash.

Committing a transaction in the shadow page scheme requires that all the modifications made by the transaction be propagated to physical storage and the current page table be copied to stable storage. Then the shadow page scheme reduces the problem of propagating a set of modified blocks to the database to that of changing a single pointer value contained in the page table address from the shadow page table address to the current page table address. This can be done in an atomic manner and is not interrupted by a system crash.

In the case of a system crash occurring any time between the start of a transaction and the last atomic step of modifying a single pointer from the shadow page to the current page, the old consistent database is accessible via the shadow page table and there is no need to undo a transaction. A system crash occurring after the last atomic operation will have no effect on the propagation of the changes made by the transaction; these changes will be preserved and there is no need for a redo operation.

The shadow blocks (i.e., the old version of the changed blocks) can be returned to the pool of available nonvolatile storage blocks to be used for further transactions.

The undo operation in the shadow page scheme consists of discarding the current page table and returning the changed blocks to a pool of available blocks.

The advantage of the shadow page scheme is that the recovery from system crash is relatively inexpensive and this is achieved without the overhead of logging.

Before we go on to another method of indirect update it is worth mentioning some of the drawbacks of the shadow page scheme. One of the main disadvantages of the shadow scheme is the problem of scattering. This problem is critical in database systems because over a period of time the database will be scattered over the physical memory and related records may require a very long access time. For example, two records that are required together and originally placed in blocks on the same cylinder of a disk may end up on the extreme cylinders on that same disk. Accessing these records together now involves moving the read/write head over the entire surface of the disk and, hence, a long access time.

The other problem with the shadow page scheme was already mentioned. When a transaction commits, the original version of the changed blocks pointed to by the shadow page table have to be returned to the pool of free blocks, otherwise such pages will become inaccessible. If this is not done successfully, when a transaction commits (perhaps due to a system crash), such blocks become inaccessible. A **garbage collection** operation to be performed periodically must reclaim such lost blocks.

Shadow paging for concurrent transactions requires additional bookkeeping and in such an environment some logging scheme is used as well.

Reflecting Updates to the Database via Logs and Recovery

In the update-via-log scheme, the transaction is generally not allowed to modify the database. All changes to the database are deferred until the transaction commits. However, as in the update-in-place scheme, all modifications made by the transaction are logged. Furthermore, since the database is not modified directly by the transaction, the old values do not have to be saved in the log. Once the transaction commits, the log is used to propagate the modifications to the database.

During the life of a transaction, all output operations to the database are intercepted, causing an entry to be made in the log for the transaction. This entry contains the identification of the items being updated along with the new values. When the transaction starts a commit operation, a commit transaction mark is written to the log. After this step, the log is used to modify the database.

A system crash occurring during the time when a transaction is active does not require an undo operation since the database was not directly changed by the transaction. A system crash occurring after the transaction commits can be recovered from the log maintained for the transaction.

Let us return to the example of transferring a part from inventory to a project, given in the program in section 11.4.1 on page 535. Figure 11.15 gives the log for the transactions corresponding to the transfer of 100 units of part $Part_1$ from inventory to project $Proj_5$, followed by a transaction corresponding to the transfer of 10 units of part $Part_4$ from inventory to project $Proj_2$. The log contains only redo information and the only operations performed during the life of a transaction on the physical database are reads.

Now let us assume various scenarios for a system crash. First, consider a system crash that occurs any time before step s_7; this step corresponds to the writing of the commit transactions T_0. This system crash will require the recovery system to undo the effect of transaction T_0, which in this case involves discarding the log for transaction T_0, which lacks the commit transaction marker. The values for the record corresponding to $Part_1$ and $Proj_5$ have not been propagated to the database.

If the system crash occurs after the completion of step s_8, when the system is restarted the recovery system will find the commit transaction marker for transaction T_0. It will redo the transaction to ensure that the effects of transaction T_0 are cor-

Figure 11.15 Entries for Indirect Update Log.

Step	Transaction Action	Log Operation	Database Operation
s_0	Start of T_0	**Write**(start Transaction T_0)	
s_1	*get*($Part_1$)		**Read**($Part_1$)
s_2	modify(*Q_in_S* from 400 to 300)		
s_3	*put*($Part_1$)	**Write**(record for *Part#* = $Part_1$, new value of *Q_in_S:* 300)	
s_4	*get*($Proj_5$)		**Read**($Proj_5$)
s_5	modify(*Q_to_D* from 100 to 200)		
s_6	*put*($Proj_5$)	**Write**(record for *Project#* = $Proj_5$, new value of *Q_to_D:* 200)	
s_7	Start Commit	**Write**(Commit transaction T_0);	
s_8	Commit/End of T_0		**Write**($Part_1$, $Proj_5$);
s_9	Start of T_1	**Write**(start Transaction T_1)	
s_{10}	*get*($Part_4$)		**Read**($Part_4$)
s_{11}	modify(*Q_in_S* from 600 to 590)		
s_{12}	*put* ($Part_4$)	**Write**(record *Part#* = $Part_4$, new value of *Q_in_S:* 590)	
s_{13}	*get*($Proj_2$)		**Read**($Proj_2$)
s_{14}	modify(*Q_to_D* from 50 to 60)		
s_{15}	*put*($Proj_2$)	**Write**(record *Project#* = $Proj_2$, new value of *Q_to_D*: 60)	
s_{16}	Start Commit	**Write** (Commit transaction T_1);	
s_{17}	Commit/End of T_1		**Write**($Part_4$, $Proj_2$)

rectly propagated to the database. The redo operation needs only the new values for the fields modified by the transaction in the records for $Part_1$ and $Proj_5$. After the redo operation, the database is restored to the state existing at the end of the transaction T_0.

A crash occurring during the recovery operation will not affect the subsequent recovery operation, since the redo operation is idempotent.

A crash occurring after step s_{17} requires the recovery system to redo both transactions T_0 and T_1.

The recovery system checks the log after a system crash. For those transactions that contain both a start transaction marker and an end transaction marker, it will initiate a redo transaction operation. A partially complete transaction in the system log is indicated by a start transaction marker without a corresponding end transaction marker. Such partially complete transactions are ignored by the recovery system since they will not have modified the database.

However, we must distinguish an update made by a partially complete transaction from a partial update made from the log of a committed transaction in the deferred update from the log phase. A partially completed update (updated during the end of transaction processing after a commit transaction is executed by the program controlling the transaction) cannot be undone with the deferred update using the log scheme; it can only be completed or redone. The only way it can be undone is by a compensating transaction to undo its effects (as is the case in standard accounting practice).

11.5 Buffer Management, Virtual Memory, and Recovery

The input and output operations required by a program, including a DBMS application program, are usually performed by a component of the operating system. These operations normally use buffers (reserved blocks of primary memory) to match the speed of the processor and the relatively fast primary memories with the slower secondary memories and to minimize, whenever possible, the number of input and output operations between the secondary and primary memories. The assignment and management of memory blocks is called **buffer management** and the component of the operating system that performs this task is usually called the **buffer manager.** The goal of the buffer manager is to ensure that as many data requests made by programs as possible are satisfied from data copied from secondary storage devices into the buffers. In effect, a program performs an input or an output operation using get or put statements; the buffer manager will be called on to respond to these input or output requests. It will check to see if the request for the data can be satisfied by reading from or writing to the existing buffers. If so, the input or output operation occurs between the program work area and buffers. If an input request cannot be satisfied, the buffer manager will have to do a physical transfer between the secondary memory and a free buffer and then make the data so placed in the buffer available to the program requesting the original input operation. A similar scenario will take place in the reverse order for an output. The buffer manager makes a new buffer available to the program performing a put operation. The buffer manager performs the physical transfer between the buffer and the secondary memory by means of read and write operations whenever there is an anticipated need for new buffers and none are available in a pool of free buffers for the current program. For sequential processing, the buffer manager can provide higher performance by prefetching the next block of data and by batching write operations into the commit phase of a transaction.

We have assumed so far that the buffer manager uses buffers in physical memory. However, in a computer system that uses a virtual memory management scheme, the buffers are in effect virtual memory buffers, there being an additional mapping between a virtual memory buffer and the physical memory, as shown in Figure 11.16. Since the physical memory is managed by the memory management component of the operating system, a virtual buffer input by the buffer manager may

Figure 11.16 DBMS buffers in virtual memory.

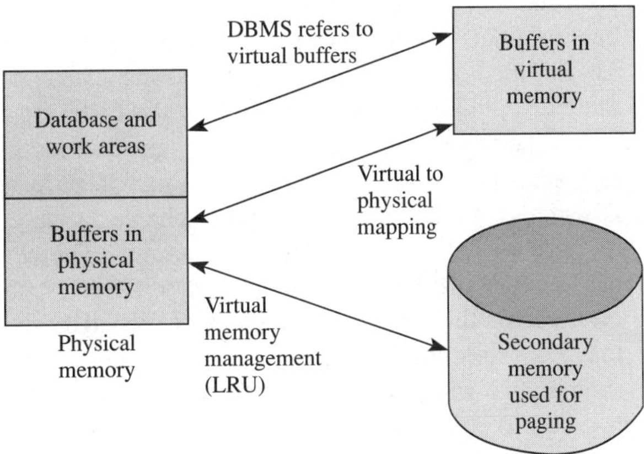

have been paged out by the memory manager in case there is insufficient space in the physical memory.

In a **virtual memory** management scheme, the buffers containing pages of the database undergoing modification by a transaction could be written out to secondary storage. The timing of this premature writing back of a buffer is independent of the state of the transaction and will be decided by the replacement policy used by the **memory manager,** which again is a component of the operating system. Thus, the page replacement scheme is entirely independent of the database requirements; these requirements being that records undergoing modifications by a partially completed transaction not be written back and records for a committed transaction be rewritten, especially in the case of the update in place scheme.

It has been found that the locality of reference property is applicable to database buffers. To decrease the number of buffer faults, the **least recently used (LRU)** algorithm is used for buffer replacement. However, the normal LRU algorithm is modified slightly and each transaction is allowed to maintain a certain number of pages in the buffer.

The buffering scheme can be used in the recovery system, since it effectively provides a temporary copy of a database page to which modifications can be directed and the original page can remain unchanged in the nonvolatile storage medium. Both the log and the data pages will be written to the buffer pages in virtual memory. The commit transaction operation can be considered a two-phase operation called a **two-phase commit.** The first phase is when the log buffers are written out (write-ahead log) and the second phase is when the data buffers are written. In case the data page is being used by another transaction, the writing of that page can be delayed. This will not cause a problem because the log is always forced during the first phase of the commit. With this scheme the undo log is not required, since no uncommitted modifications are reflected in the database.

In sequential processing of the database, the buffer manager prefetches the database pages. However, pages of data once used need not follow the locality property. A page once accessed is less likely to be accessed again. Hence, the buffer manager can use a modified LRU replacement algorithm, using not one but two LRU lists. One is for randomly accessed pages and the second one is for sequentially accessed pages. Buffers needed for sequential processing are obtained from the sequential LRU list (i.e., one of the sequential LRU pages is replaced to make room for the incoming page of data) if this list is longer than some established length; otherwise, the buffer is obtained from the LRU list.

Take the example of the program given in section 11.4.1 on p. 535 for transferring specified quantities of parts from inventory to projects. If the memory manager is using an LRU page replacement scheme, a committed transaction may not have its page written back long after it commits. The reason for this is that the program has many transactions, each needing different records, but these records may be clustered on the same physical block of secondary memory. A committing transaction may have used the same page as the page required by the next transaction. However, such a page will not be written back by the memory manager using the simple LRU page replacement scheme. This means that an update made by a committed transaction would not be reflected in the physical database, which would create havoc in the recovery scheme.

The write-ahead log protocol assumes that the undo log information for a transaction will be written to stable storage before the modifications made by a transaction are reflected in the database, and the redo portion of the log is written before the transaction commits. Under the memory and buffer managers of the operating system, we cannot assume that the buffers containing the log information are written ahead of the changes made to the database.

What this means is that the buffer manager, at least for those buffers used by the DBMS and its application programs, be under the control of the DBMS and the DBMS enforces the correct writing of the buffers assigned for the log and the data at an appropriate time. The terms **steal** and **force** are used to indicate the buffer control mechanism. Steal indicates that the modified pages of data in the buffers may be written to the database at any time (as in the case of the update-in-place scheme) and **not steal** means that the modified pages are kept in the buffer until the transaction commits. In the case of the not steal buffer control (wherein no changes are propagated to the database during the life of a transaction), we have to decide what is to be done when a transaction starts to commit. If during this end of transaction processing all modifications are actually propagated to the database, we are assuming that the buffers are being forced. If no such forced writing of the buffers can be assumed during the end of transaction processing, the updates cannot be presumed to have been propagated to the database. This requires that with the **no force** strategy, committed transactions have to be redone in the case of a system crash. With forcing no redone is required for committed transactions; the modifications made by the committed transactions can be safely assumed to have been propagated to the database.

11.6 Other Logging Schemes

In our discussion so far we have assumed that the logging scheme writes the following details in the log: the identification of the records being modified, the modified values of each record, and in some cases the old values of each record modified. This is the record-level logging. However, schemes can be used as described below.

Record-level logging: Instead of recording the entire page whenever a modification is done anywhere on a page, the log is kept of the before and the after image of the record that undergoes modification. Insertion of a new record can be handled by using null values for the before image and deletion of an existing record is indicated by using null values for the after image. The advantage of this scheme is the obvious; the amount of space needed for the log is much less.

Page-level logging: In this scheme the entire page is recorded in the log whenever a record within the page is modified; for the undo operation, the entire page before any modification is written to the log; and for the redo operation, the entire page after the modification is written to the log.

If a number of changes are made on the same page, a design decision has to be made regarding the number of page images that will be stored in the log. One choice is to have only one before image and one after image, the former being the image at the start of the transaction and the latter that at the end of the transaction. Another alternative is to have one before and one after image for each change. (if there are n changes made on a page, there will be 2n page images, the page image number 2i and 2i+1, for $1 \leq i \leq n - 1$, being the same! The order of i here is a chronological order.)

In a modification of the page-level logging scheme, instead of writing the before image of the page and the after image of the page to the log, a difference of these two in the form of an exclusive or is written in a compressed form to the log. Since only a few bytes of a page will be changed as a result of an update transaction on a record contained on the page, the exclusive or of the before and after images of the page will give a large number of zeros, which can be compressed using an appropriate data compression method.

Query language logging: In this approach the log entry of the data manipulation statements modifying the database, along with the parameters used by the statements, are recorded in the log. The parameters include the record identifiers and values of attributes of the record being modified. As in the case of record-level logging, appropriate null values can be used for the records being deleted. In case the update is made by a high level language program, these updates can be reduced to statements that operate on a single record; the latter would be recorded along with the parameters in the log. The redo recovery function requires reexecuting the logged data manipulation statements with their parameters. The undo recovery function requires generating reverse data manipulation statements corresponding to the logged statements and executing these reverse statements. To undo the effect of a delete statement requires the generation of an insert statement, and the parameter would be the identifier of the record to be inserted along with the before image of the record.

11.7 Cost Comparison

In this section we briefly compare the cost of the various recovery schemes we discussed, namely the update in place, the deferred update with shadow page scheme, and the deferred update using a log.

If an update-in-place scheme is used along with a buffer scheme where partially modified pages can be written at any time and all modified pages are written prior to a commit transaction, the cost of an undo operation is relatively high and the cost of a redo is very low. In this case each end of the transaction is a checkpoint because all modifications are forced to be written to nonvolatile storage. However, if all the modified pages are not forced to be written during the end of transaction processing, the costs of an undo and a redo are relatively higher. Furthermore, the end of a transaction is not a checkpoint in this scheme.

If an update-in-place scheme is used along with a not steal and force buffer scheme where partially modified pages are not allowed to be written at any time (the writing of such modified pages is delayed till the end of the transaction processing when all pages are written), then the costs of undo and redo are very low. Again each end of a transaction represents a checkpoint.

With an indirect update scheme where the end of the transaction forces all modified pages to be processed, the cost of the undo and redo are relatively lower.

If the database system defers the propagation of changes to the database until the commit operation, then in case the transaction is rolled back by the program controlling it, the changes made by the transaction need not be rolled back. The rollback operation in this case consists of not propagating the modifications made by the transaction to the database. The same procedure will apply if the system aborts the transaction.

11.8 Disaster Recovery

Disaster refers to circumstances that result in the loss of the physical database stored on the nonvolatile storage medium. This implies that there will also be a loss of the volatile storage, and the only reliable data are the data stored in stable storage. The data stored in stable storage consist of the archival copy of the database and the archival log of the transactions on the database represented in the archival copy.

The **disaster recovery** process requires a global redo. In a global redo the changes made by every transaction in the archival log are redone using the archival database as the initial version of the current database. The order of redoing the operations must be the same as the original order, hence the archival log must be chronologically ordered.

Since the archival database should be consistent, it must be a copy of the current database in a quiescent stage (i.e., no transaction can be allowed to run during the archiving process). The quiescent requirement dictates that the frequency of archiving be very low. The time required to archive a large database and the remote probability of a loss of nonvolatile storage result in performing archiving at quarterly or monthly intervals. The low frequency of archiving the database means that the number of transactions in the archival log will be large and this in turn leads to a lengthy recovery operation (of the order of days).

A method of reconciling the reluctance to archive and the heavy cost of infrequent archiving is to archive more often in an incremental manner. In effect, the database is archived in a quiescent mode very infrequently, but what is archived at more regular intervals is that portion of the database that was modified since the last incremental archiving. The archived copy can then be updated to the time of the incremental archiving without disrupting the online access of the database. This updating can be performed on a different computer system.

The recovery operation consists of redoing the changes made by committed transactions from the archive log on the archive database. A new consistent archive database copy can be generated during this recovery process.

11.9 Summary

In this chapter we discussed the recovery of the data contained in a database system after failures of various types. The reliability problem of the database system is linked to the reliability of the computer system on which it runs. The types of failures that the computer system is likely to be subject to include that of components or subsystems, software failures, power outages, accidents, unforeseen situations, and natural or man-made disasters. Database recovery techniques are methods of making the database fault tolerant. The aim of the recovery scheme is to allow database operations to be resumed after a failure with a minimum loss of information and at an economically justifiable cost.

In order for a database system to work correctly, we need correct data, correct algorithms to manipulate the data, correct programs that implement these algorithms, and of course a computer system that functions accurately. Any source of errors in each of these components has to be identified and a method of correcting and recovering from these errors has to be designed in the system.

A transaction is a program unit whose execution may change the contents of the database. If the database was in a consistent state before a transaction, then on completion of the execution of the program unit corresponding to the transaction the database will be in a consistent state. This requires that the transaction be considered atomic: it is executed successfully or, in case of errors, the user views the transaction as not having been executed at all.

A database recovery system is designed to recover from the following types of failures: failure without loss of data; failure with loss of volatile storage; failure with loss of nonvolatile storage; and failure with a loss of stable storage.

The basic technique to implement database recovery is by using data redundancy in the form of logs, checkpoints, and archival copies of the database.

The log contains the redundant data required to recover from volatile storage failures and also from errors discovered by the transaction or database system. For each transaction the following data is recorded on the log: the start of transaction marker, transaction identifier, record identifiers, the previous value(s) of the modified data, the updated values; and if the transaction is committed, a commit transaction marker, otherwise an abort or rollback transaction marker.

The checkpoint information is used to limit the amount of recovery operations to be done following a system crash resulting in the loss of volatile storage.

The archival database is the copy of the database at a given time stored to stable storage. It contains the entire database in a quiescent mode and is made by simple dump routines to dump the physical database to stable storage. The purpose of the archival database is to recover from failures that involve loss of nonvolatile storage. The archive log is used for recovery from failures involving loss of nonvolatile information. The log contains information on all transactions made on the database from the time of the archival copy, written in chronological order. Recovery from loss of nonvolatile storage uses the archival copy of the database and the archival log to reconstruct the physical database to the time of the nonvolatile storage failure.

Whenever a transaction is run against a database, a number of options can be used in reflecting the modifications made by the transactions. The options we have examined are update in place and indirect update with careful replacement: the shadow page scheme and the update via log scheme are two versions of the latter.

In the update-in-place scheme, the transaction updates the physical database and the modified record replaces the old record in the database. The write-ahead log strategy is used. The log information about the transaction modifications is written before update operations initiated by the transactions are performed.

The shadow page scheme uses two page tables for a transaction that is going to modify the database. The original page table is called the shadow page table; the transaction addresses the database using another table called the current page table. In the shadow page scheme, propagating a set of modified blocks to the database is achieved by changing a single pointer value contained in the page table address from the shadow page table address to the current page table address. This can be done in an atomic manner and is not interruptable by a system crash.

In the update via log scheme, the transaction is not allowed to modify the database. All changes to the database are deferred until the transaction commits. As in the update-in-place scheme, all modifications made by the transaction are logged. Since the database is not modified directly by the transaction, the old values do not have to be saved in the log. Once the transaction commits, the log is used to propagate the modifications to the database.

The recovery process from a failure resulting in the loss of nonvolatile storage requires a global redo, i.e., redoing the effect of every transaction in the archival log, the archival database being used as the initial version of the current database. The order of performing redo operations must be the same as the original order, hence the archival log file must be chronologically ordered.

Key Terms

reliable
failure
error
fault
fault-tolerant system
reliability
mean time between failures (MTBF)
mean time to repair (MTTR)
system availability
design error
poor quality control
overutilization
overloading
wearout
volatile storage
nonvolatile storage
system crash
permanent or stable storage
read/write head crash
archive database
user error
consistency error
system error
validity
deadlock
audit trail
journal
forward error recovery
backward error recovery
buffer
atomic operation
successful termination
suicidal termination
murderous termination
atomicity
consistency
isolation
durability
log
write-ahead log strategy
checkpoint
transaction-consistent checkpoint
action-consistent checkpoint
transaction-oriented checkpoint
undo
redo
quiescent
current database
materialized database
do
idempotent
transaction undo
transaction redo
global undo
global redo
update in place
indirect update
shadow page scheme
update via log
indirect page allocation
page table
shadow page table
current page table
buffer management
buffer manager
virtual memory
memory manager

least recently used (LRU)
two-phase commit
steal
not steal
force
no force
record-level logging
page-level logging
query language logging
disaster recovery

Exercises

11.1 What if anything can be done to recover the modifications made by partially completed transactions that are running at the time of a system crash? Can online transactions be recovered?

11.2 In a database system that uses an update-in-place scheme, how can the recovery system recover from a system crash if the write ahead protocol is used for the log information?

11.3 What modifications have to be made to a recovery scheme if the transactions are nested? (In a nested transaction one transaction is contained within another transaction.)

11.4 In the recovery technique known as forward error recovery, on the detection of a particular error in a system, the recovery procedure consists of adjusting the state of the system to recover from the error (without suffering the loss that could have occurred because of the error). Can such a technique be used in a DBMS to recover from system crashes with the loss of volatile storage?

11.5 Show how the backward error recovery technique is applied to a DBMS that uses the update-in-place scheme to recover from a system crash with a minimum loss of processing.

11.6 If the checkpoint frequency is too low, a system crash will lead to the loss of a large number of transactions and a long recovery operation; if the checkpoint frequency is too high, the cost of checkpointing is very high. Can you suggest a method of reducing the frequency of checkpointing without incurring a heavy recovery operation and at the same time reducing the number of lost transactions?

11.7 How can a recovery system deal with recovery of interactive transactions on online systems such as banking or airline reservations? Suggest a method to be used in such systems to restart active transactions after a system crash.

11.8 For a logging scheme based on a DML, give the kind of log entry required and indicate the undo and the redo part of the log.

11.9 If the write-ahead log scheme is being used, compare the strategy of writing the partial update made by a transaction to the database to the strategy of delaying all writes to the database till the commit.

11.11 How is the checkpoint information used in the recovery operation following a system crash?

11.11 Define the following terms:

Write-ahead log strategy
Transaction-consistent checkpoint
Action-consistent checkpoint
Transaction oriented checkpoint
Two-phase commit

11.12 From the point of view of recovery, compare the shadow page scheme with the update in place with forced and no steal buffering.

11.13 Explain why no undo operations need be done for recovery from loss of nonvolatile storage loss.

11.14 What type of software errors can cause a failure with loss of volatile storage?

11.15 What is the difference between transaction oriented checkpointing and the write-ahead log strategy?

11.16 What are the advantages and disadvantages of each of the methods of logging discussed in Section 11.6?

11.17 Consider the update-in-place scheme, where the database system defers the propagation of updates to the database until the transaction commits (see Section 11.4.1). Describe the recovery operations that have to be undertaken following a system crash with loss of volatile storage.

Bibliographic Notes

Some of the earliest work in recovery was reported in (Oppe 68), (Chan 72), (Bjor 73), and (Davi 73). Analytical models for recovery and rollback and discussions are presented in (Chan 75). The concept of transaction and its management is presented in (Gray 78). The recovery system for System R is presented in (Gray 81a); the shadow page scheme used in System R is described in an earlier paper (Lori 77). (Verh 78) is an early survey article on database recovery; (Haer 83) and (Kohl 81) are more recent survey articles based on the transaction paradigm. An efficient logging scheme for the undo operation is discussed in (Reut 80). (Teng 84) discusses the buffer management function to optimize database performance for the DB2 relational database system.

The concept of nested transaction was discussed by (Gray 81a); more recent discussions are presented in (Moss 85).

Textbooks discussing the recovery operation are (Bern 88), (Date 83), (Date 86), and (Kort 86). Reliability concepts are presented in (Wied 83).

Bibliography

(Bern 88) P. Bernstein, V. Hadzilacos, & N. Goodman, *Concurrency Control and Recovery in Database Systems*. Reading, MA: Addison-Wesley, 1988.

(Bjor 73) L. A. Bjork, ''Recovery Scenario for a DB/DC System,'' Proc. of the ACM Annual Conference, 1973, pp. 142–146.

(Chan 72) K. M. Chandy, & C. V. Ramamoorthy, ''Rollback and Recovery Strategies for Computer Programs,'' *IEEE* . C-21(6), June 1972, pp. 546–555.

(Chan 75) K. M. Chandy, J. C. Browne, C. W. Dissly, & W. R. Uhrig, ''Analytic Models for Rollback and Recovery Strategies in Data Base Systems,'' *IEEE* SE-1(1), March 1975, pp. 100–110.

(Date 83) C. J. Date, *An Introduction to Database Systems,* vol. 2, Reading, MA: Addison-Wesley, 1983.

(Date 86) C. J. Date, *An Introduction to Database Systems,* vol. 1,. 4th ed. Reading, MA: Addison-Wesley, 1986.

(Davi 73) J. C. Davies Jr., ''Recovery Semantics for a DB/DC System,'' Proc. of the ACM Annual Conference, 1973, pp. 136–141.

(Gior 76) N. J. Giordano, & M. S. Schwartz. ''Database Recovery at CMIC,'' Proc. ACM SIGMOD Conf. on Management of Data, June 1976, pp. 33–42.

(Gray 78) J. N. Gray, "Notes on Database Operating Systems," in R. Bayer et al., ed., Operating Systems: An Advanced Course. Berlin: Springer-Verlag, 1978.

(Gray 81) J. N. Gray, "The Transaction Concept: Virtues and Limitations," Proc. of the Intnl. Conf. on VLDB, 1981, pp. 144–154.

(Gray 81b) J. N. Gray, P. McJones, M. Blasgen, B. Lindsay, R. Lorie, T. Price, F. Putzolu, & I. Traiger, "The Recovery Manager of the System R Database Manager," *ACM Computing Surveys* 13(2), June 1981, pp. 223–242.

(Haer 83) T. Haerder, & A. Reuter, "Principles of Transaction(ru0,1n)Oriented Database Recovery," *ACM Computing Surveys* 15(4), December 1983, pp. 287–317.

(Kohl 81) K. H. Kohler, "A Survey of Techniques for Synchronization and Recovery in Decentralized Computer Systems," *ACM Computing Surveys* 13(2), June 1981, pp. 148–183.

(Kort 86) H. F. Korth, & A. Silberschatz, *Database System Concepts*. New York: McGraw-Hill, 1986.

(Lori 77) R. Lorie, "Physical Integrity in a Large Segmented Database," *ACM TODS* 2(1), March 1977, pp. 91–104.

(Lync 83) N. A. Lynch, "Multilevel Atomicity—A New Correctness Criterion for Database Concurrency Control," *ACM TODS* 8(4), December 1983, pp. 484–502.

(Moss 85) J. Moss, J. & B. Eliot, *Nested Transactions: An Approach to Reliable Distributed Computing*. Cambridge, MA: MIT Press, 1985.

(Oppe 68) G. Oppenheimer, K. P. Clancy, *Considerations of Software Protection and Recovery from Hardware Failures*. Washington, D.C.: FJCC, 1968.

(Reut 80) A. Reuter, "A Fast Transaction-Oriented Logging Scheme For UNDO Recovery," *IEEE* SE 6(4), July 1980, pp. 348–356.

(Seve 76) D. G. Severance, & G. M. Lohman, "Differential Files: Their Application to the Maintenance of Large Databases," *ACM TODS* 1(3), September 1976, pp. 256–267.

(Teng 84) J. Z. Teng, & R. A. Gumaer, "Managing IBM Database 2 Buffers to Maximize Performance," *IBM Systems Journal* 23(2), 1984, pp. 211–218.

(Verh 78) J. S. M. Verhofstad, "Recovery Techniques for Database Systems," *ACM Computing Surveys* 10(2), June 1978, pp. 167–195.

(Wied 83) Gio Wiederhold, *Database Design*, 2nd ed. New York: McGraw-Hill, 1983.

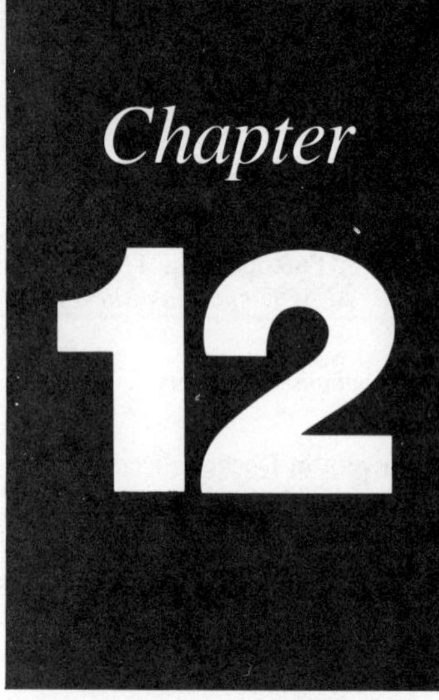

Concurrency Management

Contents

Concurrent execution of a number of transactions implies that the operations from these transactions may be interleaved. This is not the same as serial execution of the transactions where each transaction is run to completion before the next transaction is started. Concurrent access to a database by a number of transactions requires some type of concurrency control to preserve the consistency of the database, to ensure that the modifications made by the transactions are not lost, and to guard against transactions reading data that is inconsistent. The serializability criterion is used to test whether or not an interleaved execution of the operations from a number of concurrent transactions is correct. The serializability test consists of generating a precedence graph from a interleaved execution schedule. If the precedence graph is acyclic, the schedule is serializable, which means that the database will have the same state at the end of the schedule as some serial execution of the transactions. In this chapter, we introduce a number of concurrency control schemes.

12.1 Introduction

Larger computer systems are typically used by many users in a multiprogramming mode; programs are executed concurrently. One reason for the use of multiprogramming is to exploit the different characteristics of the various programs to maximize the utilization of the equipment; thus, while one program awaits the completion of an input/output operation, the processor can be used to do the computation of another program. Another reason for choosing multiprogramming is the need to share a resource by these different programs: a database is such a shared resource. The primary objective of the database system (at least on a large mainframe) is to allow many users and application programs to access data from the database in a concurrent manner.

One such shared database that is used in an online manner is the database for an airline reservations system, which is used by many agents accessing the database from their terminals. A database could also be accessed in a batch mode, exclusively or concurrently with the online access. The database for an airline reservations system, in addition to providing online access, could also be used by batch application programs that gather statistics and perform accounting operations.

The sharing of the database for read-only access does not cause any problem, but if one of the transactions running concurrently tries to modify some data-item, it could lead to inconsistencies. Furthermore, if more than one transaction is allowed to simultaneously modify a data-item in the database, it could lead to incorrect values for the data-item and an inconsistent database. Such would be the result even if each of the transactions were correct and a consistent database would remain so if each of these transactions were run one at a time. For example, suppose that two ticket agents access the airline reservations system simultaneously to see if a seat is available on a given flight; if both agents make a reservation against the last available seat on that flight, overbooking of the flight would result. This potential problem of leaving the database in an inconsistent state with concurrent usage requires that some kind of mutual exclusion be enforced so that the concurrently running transactions would be able to access only disjoint data for modifications.

We defined the concept of a transaction in the previous chapter as being a set of actions on the database that can be considered atomic from the point of view of the user. One method of enforcing mutual exclusion is by some type of locking mechanism that locks a shared resource (for example a data-item) used by a transaction for the duration of its usage by the transaction. The locked data-item can only be used by the transaction that locked it. The other concurrent transactions are locked out and have to wait their turn at using the data-item. However, a locking scheme must be fair. This requires that the lock manager, which is the DBMS subsystem managing the locks, must not cause some concurrent transaction to be permanently blocked from using the shared resource. This is referred to as avoiding the **starvation** or livelock situation. The other danger to be avoided is that of deadlock, wherein a number of transactions are waiting in a circular chain, each waiting for the release of resources held by the next transaction in the chain.

In other methods of concurrency control, some form of a priori ordering with a single or many versions of data is used. These methods are called timestamp ordering and multiversion schemes. The optimistic approach, on the other hand, assumes that the data-items used by concurrent transactions are most likely be disjoint.

Concurrency and Possible Problems

In the last chapter we stressed that a correct transaction, when completed, leaves the database in a consistent state provided that the database was in a consistent state at the start of the transaction. Nevertheless, during the life of a transaction, the database could be inconsistent, although if the inconsistencies are not accessible to other transactions, they would not cause a problem.

In the case of concurrent operations, where a number of transactions are running and using the database, we cannot make any assumptions about the order in which the statements belonging to different transactions will be executed. The order in which these statements are executed is called a **schedule.** Consider the two transactions in Figure 12.1. Each transaction reads some data-item, performs some operations on the data-item that could change its value, and then writes out the modified data-item.

In Figure 12.1 and in subsequent examples in this chapter, we assume that the read operation reads in the database value of the named variable to a local variable with an identical name. Any modifications by a transaction are made on this local copy. The modifications made by the transactions are indicated by the operators f_1 and f_2 in Figure 12.1. These modifications are not reflected in the database until the write operation is executed, at which point the modifications in the value of the

Figure 12.1 Two concurrent transactions.

Transaction T_1	Transaction T_2
Read(*Avg_Faculty_Salary*)	**Read**(*Avg_Staff_Salary*)
Avg_Faculty_Salary :=	*Avg_Staff_Salary* :=
f_1(*Avg_Faculty_Salary*)	f_2(*Avg_Staff_Salary*)
Write(*Avg_Faculty_Salary*)	**Write**(*Avg_Staff_Salary*)

Figure 12.2 Possible interleaving of concurrent transactions of Figure 12.1.

	Schedule 1		Schedule 2
	Read(*Avg_Faculty_Salary*)		**Read**(*Avg_Staff_Salary*)
	Avg_Faculty_Salary :=		*Avg_Staff_Salary* :=
T	f_1(*Avg_Faculty_Salary*)	T	f_2(*Avg_Staff_Salary*)
i	**Write**(*Avg_Faculty_Salary*)	i	**Read**(*Avg_Faculty_Salary*)
m	**Read**(*Avg_Staff_Salary*)	m	Avg_Faculty_Salary :=
e	*Avg_Staff_Salary* :=	e	f_1(*Avg_Faculty_Salary*)
↓	f_2(*Avg_Staff_Salary*)	↓	**Write**(*Avg_Faculty_Salary*)
	Write(*Avg_Staff_Salary*)		**Write**(*Avg_Staff_Salary*)

named variable are said to be committed. In effect the write operation is a signal for committing the modifications and reflecting the changes to the physical database.

Figure 12.2 gives two possible schedules for executing the transactions of Figure 12.1 in an interleaved manner. Since the transactions of Figure 12.1 are accessing and modifying distinct data-items, *(Avg_Faculty_Salary, Avg_Staff_Salary),* there is no problem in executing these transactions concurrently. In other words, regardless of the order of interleaving of the statements of these transactions, we will get a consistent database on the termination of these transactions.

12.1.1 Lost Update Problem

Consider the transactions of Figure 12.3. These transactions are accessing the same data-item *A*. Each of the transactions modifies the data-item and writes it back. Again let us consider a number of possible interleavings of the execution of the statements of these transactions. These schedules are given in Figure 12.4.

Starting with 200 as the initial value of *A*, let us see what the value of *A* would be if the transactions are run without any interleaving. In other words, the transactions are run to completion, without any interruptions, one at a time in a serial manner. If transaction T_3 is run first, then at the end of the transaction the value of *A* will have changed from 200 to 210. Running transaction T_4 after the completion of T_3 will change the value of *A* from 210 to 231. Running the transactions in the

Figure 12.3 Two transactions modifying the same data-item.

Transaction T_3	Transaction T_4
Read(A)	**Read**(A)
$A := A + 10$	$A := A * 1.1$
Write(A)	**Write**(A)

Figure 12.4 Two schedules for transactions of Figure 12.3.

Time ↓	Schedule 1	Transaction T_3	Transaction T_4	Value of A
	Read(A)		**Read**(A)	200
	$A := A * 1.1$		$A := A * 1.1$	
	Read(A)	**Read**(A)		
	$A := A + 10$	$A := A + 10$		
	Write(A)	**Write**(A)		210
	Write(A)		**Write**(A)	220

(a)

Time ↓	Schedule 2	Transaction T_3	Transaction T_4	Value of A
	Read(A)	**Read**(A)		200
	$A := A + 10$	$A := A + 10$		
	Read(A)		**Read**(A)	
	$A := A * 1.1$		$A := A * 1.1$	
	Write(A)		**Write**(A)	220
	Write(A)	**Write**(A)		210

(b)

order T_4 followed by T_3 result in a final value for A of 230. The result obtained with neither of the two interleaved execution schedules of Figure 12.4 agrees with either of the results of executing these same transactions serially. Obviously something is wrong!

In each of the schedules given in Figure 12.4, we have lost the update made by one of the transactions. In schedule 1, the update made by transaction T_3 is lost; in schedule 2, the update made by transaction T_4 is lost. Each schedule exhibits an example of the so-called **lost update** problem of the concurrent execution of a number of transactions.

It is obvious that the reason for the lost update problem is that even though we have been able to enforce that the changes made by one concurrent transaction are not accessible by the other transactions until it commits, we have not enforced the atomicity requirement. This demands that only one transaction can modify a given data-item at a given time and other transactions should be locked out from even viewing the unmodified value (in the database) until the modifications (being made to a local copy of the data) are committed to the database.

12.1.2 Inconsistent Read Problem

The lost update problem was caused by concurrent modifications of the same data-item. However, concurrency can also cause problems when only one transaction modifies a given set of data while that set of data is being used by other transactions.

Figure 12.5 Two transactions; one modified while the other reads.

Transaction T_5	Transaction T_6
Read(A)	$Sum := 0$
$A := A - 100$	**Read**(A)
Write(A)	$Sum := Sum + A$
Read(B)	**Read**(B)
$B := B + 100$	$Sum := Sum + B$
Write(B)	**Write**(Sum)

Consider the transactions of Figure 12.5. Suppose A and B represent some data-items containing integer valued data, for example, two accounts in a bank (or a quantity of some part X in two different locations, etc.). Let us assume that transaction T_5 transfers 100 units from A to B. Transaction T_6 is concurrently running and it wants to find the total of the current values of data-items A and B (the sum of the balance in case A and B represent two accounts, or the total quantity of part X in the two different locations, etc.).

Figure 12.6 gives a possible schedule for the concurrent execution of the transactions of Figure 12.5 with the initial value of A and B being 500 and 1000, respectively. We notice from the schedule that transaction T_6 uses the value of A before the transfer was made, but it uses the modified value of B after the transfer. The result is that transaction T_6 erroneously determines the total of A and B as being 1600 instead of 1500. We can also come up with another schedule of the concurrent exe-

Figure 12.6 Example of inconsistent reads.

Time	Schedule	Transaction T_5	Transaction T_6	Value of Database items A	B	Sum
↓	**Read**(A)	**Read**(A)		500	1100	—
	$Sum := 0$		Sum := 0			0
	Read (A)		**Read** (A)			
	$A := A - 100$	$A := A - 100$				
	Write(A)	**Write**(A)		400		
	$Sum := Sum + A$		$Sum := Sum + A$			500
	Read(B)	**Read**(B)				
	$B :=$ B + 100	$B := B + 100$				
	Write(B)	**Write**(B)			1100	
	Read(B)		**Read**(B)			
	$Sum := Sum + B$		$Sum := Sum + B$			
	Write(Sum)		**Write**(Sum)			1600

cution of these transactions that will give the total of A and B as 1400, and of course other schedules that will give the correct answer.

The reason we got an incorrect answer in the schedule of Figure 12.6 was because that transaction T_6 was using values of data-items A and B while they were being modified by transaction T_5. Locking out transaction T_6 from these data-items individually would not have solved the problem of this **inconsistent read.** The problem would have been resolved in this example only if transaction T_5 had not released the exclusive usage of the data-item A after locking data-item B. We discuss this scheme, called two-phase locking, in Section 12.4.1

12.1.3 The Phantom Phenomenon

The previous examples were deliberately simple to illustrate the points of the lost update and the inconsistent read problems. To illustrate the phantom phenomenon let us consider an organization where parts are purchased and kept in stock. The parts are withdrawn from stock and used by a number of projects. To check the extent of loss, for example due to pilferage, we want to see if the current quantity of some part purchased and received is equal to the current sum of the quantity of that part in stock, plus the current quantities in use by various projects. Let us assume that we have record types (relations in the case of a relational database system) called INVENTORY, RECEIVED, and USAGE. The fields of these records are as shown below. The record type INVENTORY keeps track of the quantity of a given part in stock at a given point in time. The record type RECEIVED contains, for a given part, the total units of that part that has been received to date. The record USAGE keeps track of the project for which a given part was used.

INVENTORY*(Part#, Quantity_in_Stock)*
RECEIVED*(Part#, Quantity_Received_to_Date)*
USAGE*(Project_No, Part#, Quantity_Used_to_Date)*

Consider transaction T_7 that will perform this auditing operation. It will, for example, proceed by locking each item in an exclusive mode before each step, as follows:

1. Lock the records of INVENTORY and for *Part#* = Part_1 find the *Quantity_in_Stock*.
2. Lock all existing records of USAGE and add the *Quantity_Used_to_Date* for Part_1 in any project that uses this part to *Quantity_in_Stock found in step 1*.
3. Lock the RECEIVED records and compare the value of the sum found with the *Received_to_Date value for* Part_1.
4. Release all locks.

Problems will be encountered if there is another transaction, T_8, which is run to reflect the receipt of additional quantities of Part_1. Transaction T_8 adds this quantity to the record corresponding to Part_1 of the record type RECEIVED and assigns these parts directly to a new project for which a new record of the record type USAGE is created. If transaction T_8 is scheduled to run between steps 2 and 3 above, then transaction T_7 will come up with an incorrect result (T_7 will show the loss in Part_1).

Here we see that the locking of records did not prevent the creation of a new record, which was created after the existing records had been locked. This new record for USAGE created by transaction T_8 is a **phantom** as far as transaction T_7 is concerned. It did not exist when transaction T_7 locked the records of USAGE.

However, the problem could be prevented if the locking of a set of records also prevents the addition of such phantom records. The locking of a record belonging to a record type must guarantee that no new record occurrences of the record type can be added until the lock is released. The other necessary precaution for the schedule above is to lock the record RECEIVED before releasing the lock on USAGE.

12.1.4 Semantics of Concurrent Transactions

In concurrent operations, where a number of transactions are running and modifying parts of the database, we not only have to hide the changes made by a transaction from other transactions, but we also have to make sure that only one transaction has exclusive access to these data-items for at least the duration of the original transaction's usage of the data-items. This requires that an appropriate locking mechanism be used to allow exclusive access of these data-items to the transaction requiring them. In the case of the transactions of Figure 12.3, no such locking was used with the consequence that the result is not the same as the result we would have obtained had these transactions run consequently.

Now let us see why the results obtained when we run two transactions, one after the other, need not be the same for different orderings. The modification operations performed by two transactions are not necessarily commutative. The operations $A := (A + 10) + 20$ give the same result as $A := (A + 20) + 10$ for the same initial value for A (which is assumed to be an integer valued data-item); this is so because the addition operation is commutative. Similarly, $(A * 10) * 20 = (A * 20) * 10$.

However, commuting the order of operations, as illustrated by the following expressions, does not always give the same result:

$$Salary := (Salary + 1000) * 1.1$$
$$Salary := (Salary * 1.1) + 1000$$

In the above example we have two transformations. In the first the *Salary* is initially modified by adding 1000 to it and then the result is augmented by 10% to give the revised *Salary*. In the second the *Salary* is first augmented by 10% and then 1000 is added to the result, which becomes the revised *Salary*. The reasonable approach, to make sure that the intended result is obtained in all cases (i.e. to make sure that transaction T_i is completed before transaction T_j is run), would be to code the operations in a single transaction and not to divide the operations into two or more transactions. Thus, if the above set of operations on *Salary* were written as two transactions as given below, we cannot be sure which of the above two results would be obtained with their concurrent execution.

Transaction T_i	Transaction T_j
Read *Salary*	**Read** *Salary*
$Salary := Salary * 1.1$	$Salary := Salary + 1000$
Write *Salary*	**Write** *Salary*

In effect, the division of a transaction into interdependent transactions run serially in the wrong order would give erroneous results. Furthermore, these interdependent transactions must not be run concurrently, otherwise the concurrent execution will lead to results that could be incorrect again and not agree with the result obtained by any serial execution of the same transactions. It is a logical error to divide a single set of operations into two or more transactions. We assume hereafter that transactions are semantically correct.

12.2 Serializability

Let us reconsider the transactions of Figure 12.3. We assume that these transactions are independent. An execution schedule of these transactions as shown in Figure 12.7 is called a **serial execution.** In a serial execution, each transaction runs to completion before any statements from any other transaction are executed. In Schedule A given in Figure 12.7a, transaction T_3 is run to completion before transaction T_4 is executed. In Schedule B, transaction T_4 is run to completion before transaction T_3 is started. If the initial value of A in the database were 200, Schedule A would result in the value of A being changed to 231. Similarly, Schedule B with the same initial value of A would give a result of 230.

This may seem odd, but in a shared environment, the result obtained by independent transactions that modify the same data-item always depends on the order in which these transactions are run; and any of these results is considered to be correct.

Figure 12.7 Two serial schedules.

Time ↓	Schedule A	Transaction T_3	Transaction T_4
	Read(A)	**Read**(A)	
	$A := A + 10$	$A := A + 10$	
	Write(A)	**Write**(A)	
	Read(A)		**Read**(A)
	$A := A * 1.1$		$A := A * 1.1$
	Write(A)		**Write**(A)

(a)

Time ↓	Schedule B	Transaction T_3	Transaction T_4
	Read(A)		**Read**(A)
	$A := A * 1.1$		$A := A * 1.1$
	Write(A)		**Write**(A)
	Read(A)	**Read**(A)	
	$A := A + 10$	$A := A + 10$	
	Write(A)	**Write**(A)	

(b)

If there are two transactions and if they refer to and use distinct data-items, the result obtained by the interleaved execution of the statements of these transactions would be the same regardless of the order in which these statements are executed (provided there are no other concurrent transactions that refer to any of these data-items). In this chapter, we assume that the concurrent transactions share some data-items, hence we are interested in a correct ordering of execution of the statements of these transactions.

A nonserial schedule wherein the operations from a set of concurrent transactions are interleaved is considered to be serializable if the execution of the operations in the schedule leaves the database in the same state as some serial execution of these transactions. With two transactions, we can have at most two distinct serial schedules, and starting with the same state of the database, each of these serial schedules could give a different final state of the database. Starting with an initial value of 200 for *A*, the serial schedule illustrated in Figure 12.7a would give the final value of *A* as 231, and for the serial schedule illustrated in part b the final value of *A* would be 230. If we have n concurrent transactions, it is possible to have n!, where n! = n * (n − 1) * (n − 2) * . . . * 3 * 2 * 1 distinct serial schedules, and possibly that many distinct resulting modifications to the database. For a serializable schedule, all we require is that the schedule gives a result that is the same as any one of these possibly distinct results.

When n transactions are run concurrently and in an interleaved manner, the number of possible schedules is much larger than n!. We would like to find out if a given interleaved schedule produces the same result as one of the serial schedules. If the answer is positive, then the given interleaved schedule is said to be serializable.

Definition: **Serializable Schedule:**

Given an interleaved execution of a set of n transactions; the following conditions hold for each transaction in the set:

- All transactions are correct in the sense that if any one of the transactions is executed by itself on a consistent database, the resulting database will be consistent.
- Any serial execution of the transactions is also correct and preserves the consistency of the database; the results obtained are correct. (This implies that the transactions are logically correct and that no two transactions are interdependent).

The given interleaved execution of these transactions is said to be serializable if it produces the same result as some serial execution of the transactions.

Since a serializable schedule gives the same result as some serial schedule and since that serial schedule is correct, then the serializable schedule is also correct. Thus, given any schedule, we can say it is correct if we can show that it is serializable.

Algorithm 12.1 given in Section 12.2.2 establishes the serializability of an arbitrarily interleaved execution of a set of transactions on a database. The algorithm does not consider the nature of the computations performed by a transaction nor the exact effect of each such computational operation on the database. In effect, the algorithm ignores the semantics of the operations performed by the transactions including the commuting property of algebraic or logical computations of the transactions. We may conclude from the algorithm that a given schedule is not serializable, when in effect it is, if some of the semantics and the algebraic commutability were not ignored. However, the algorithm will never lead us to conclude that a schedule is serializable, when it does not produce the same result as some serial schedule. The computation involved in analyzing each transaction and seeing if its operations could be safely interleaved with those of other concurrent transactions is not justified by the greater degree of concurrency of the resulting ''better'' serializable schedule.

In Algorithm 12.1 (p. 566) we make the following assumptions:

- Each transaction is a modifying transaction, i.e., it would change the value of at least one database item.
- For each such item A that a transaction modifies, it would first read the value a of the item from the database (this is the *read-before-write protocol*).
- Having read the value it would transform a to f(a), where f is some transaction-dependent computation or transformation.
- It would then write this new value to the database.

Before presenting the algorithm we present the notion of a precedence graph.

Figure 12.8 (a) A schedule and (b) an acyclic precedence graph.

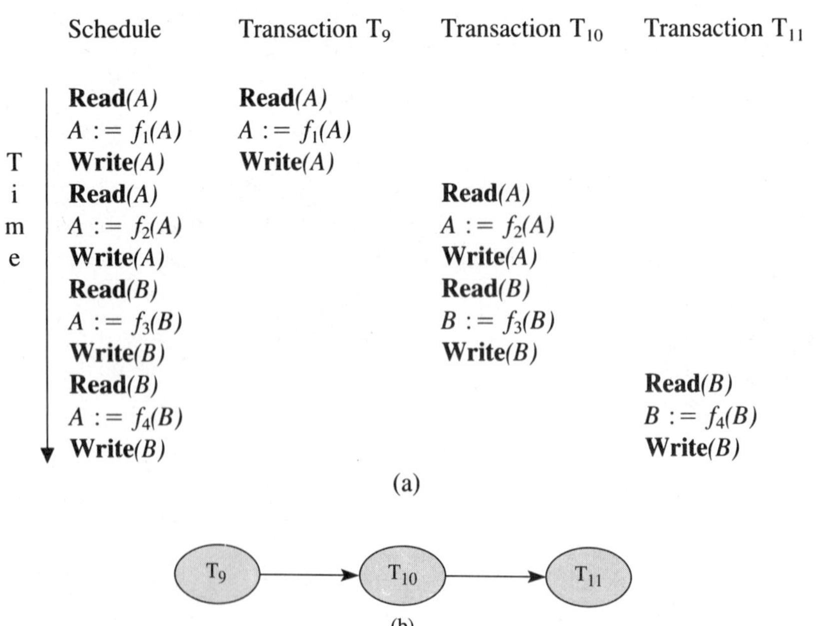

Time	Schedule	Transaction T_9	Transaction T_{10}	Transaction T_{11}
	Read(A)	**Read**(A)		
	$A := f_1(A)$	$A := f_1(A)$		
	Write(A)	**Write**(A)		
	Read(A)		**Read**(A)	
	$A := f_2(A)$		$A := f_2(A)$	
	Write(A)		**Write**(A)	
	Read(B)		**Read**(B)	
	$A := f_3(B)$		$B := f_3(B)$	
	Write(B)		**Write**(B)	
	Read(B)			**Read**(B)
	$A := f_4(B)$			$B := f_4(B)$
↓	**Write**(B)			**Write**(B)

(a)

(b)

12.2.1 Precedence Graph

Precedence graph G(V, E) consists of a set of nodes or vertices V and a set of directed arcs or edges E. Figure 12.8 gives an example of a schedule and the corresponding precedence graph. The schedule is for three transactions T_9, T_{10} and T_{11} and the corresponding precedence graph has the vertices T_9, T_{10} and T_{11}. There is an edge from T_9 to T_{10} and another edge from T_{10} to T_{11}. If T_9, T_{10} and T_{11} represent three transactions, the precedence graph represents the serial execution of these transactions.

In a **precedence graph,** a directed edge from a node T_i to a node T_j, $i \neq j$, indicates one of the following conditions regarding the read and write operations in transactions T_i and T_j with respect to some database item *A:*

- T_j performs the operation **Read(*A*)** to read the value written by T_i performing the operation **Write(*A*).**
- T_j performs the operation **Write(*A*)** after T_i performs thc operation **Read(*A*).**

If we limit ourselves to the read-before-write protocol only, we have to look for an edge corresponding to these conditions only.

In Figure 12.8a, all the statements in transaction T_9 are executed before transaction T_{10} is started. Similarly, all the operations of T_{10} are completed before starting T_{11}. The precedence graph corresponding to the schedule of part a is given in part b.

Figure 12.9a gives a schedule and Figure 12.9b gives the precedence graph for

Figure 12.9 (a) A schedule and (b) a cyclic precedence graph.

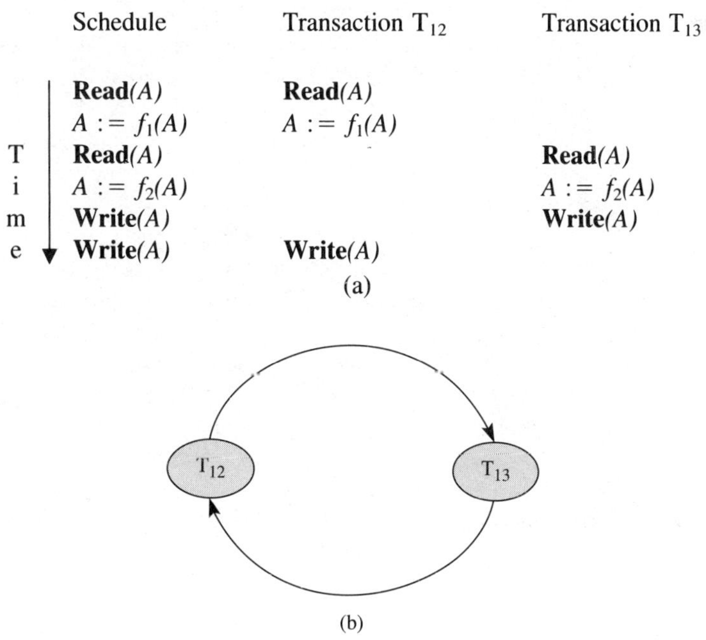

Time	Schedule	Transaction T_{12}	Transaction T_{13}
↓	**Read**(*A*)	**Read**(*A*)	
	$A := f_1(A)$	$A := f_1(A)$	
	Read(*A*)		**Read**(*A*)
	$A := f_2(A)$		$A := f_2(A)$
	Write(*A*)		**Write**(*A*)
	Write(*A*)	**Write**(*A*)	

(a)

(b)

transactions T_{12} and T_{13}. In the precedence graph there is an edge from T_{12} to T_{13} as well as an edge from T_{13} to T_{12}. The edge T_{13} to T_{12} is included because T_{12} executes a write operation after T_{13} executes a write operation for the same database item *A*. The edge T_{12} to T_{13} is included because T_{13} executes a write operation after T_{12} executes a read operation for the same database item *A*. We see that the precedence graph has a cycle, since we can start from one of the nodes of the graph and, following the directed edges, return to the starting node.

A precedence graph is said to be **acyclic** if there are no cycles in the graph. The graph of Figure 12.8b has no cycles. The graph of Figure 12.9b is **cyclic,** since it has a cycle.

The precedence graph for serializable schedule S must be acyclic, hence it can be converted to a serial schedule. To test for the serializability of the arbitrary schedule S for transactions $T_1, \ldots, T_k$ we convert the schedule into a precedence graph and then test the precedence graph for cycles. If no cycles are detected, the schedule is serializable; otherwise it is not. If there are n nodes in the graph for schedule S, the number of operations required to check if there is a cycle in the graph is proportional to n^2.

Algorithm 12.1 Serializibity Test

Input: Schedule S for the concurrent execution of transactions $T_1, \ldots, T_k$.

Output: A serial schedule for S if one exists.

Step 1: Create precedence graph G as follows. Transactions $T_1, \ldots, T_k$ are the nodes and each edge of the graph is inserted as follows: For a database item X used in the schedule find an operation **Write**(X) for some transaction T_i; if there is a subsequent (earliest) operation **Read**(X) in transaction T_j, $i \neq j$, insert an edge from T_i to T_j in the precedence graph, since T_i must be executed before T_j. For a database item X, if T_j executes a **Write**(X) after T_i, $i \neq j$, executes a **Read**(X) or a **Write**(X) operation, insert an edge from T_i to T_j in the precedence graph.

Step 2: If the graph G has a cycle (see Exercise 12.6), schedule S is nonserializable. If G is acyclic, then find, using the topological sort given below, a linear ordering of the transactions so that if there is an arc from T_i to T_j in G, T_i precedes T_j. Find a serial schedule as follows:

(a) Initialize the serial schedule as empty.

(b) Find a transaction T_i, such that there are no arcs entering T_i. T_i is the next transaction in the serial schedule.

(c) Remove T_i and all edges emitting from T_i: If the remaining set is nonempty, return to (b), otherwise the serial schedule is complete.

12.2.2 Serializability Algorithm: Read-before-Write Protocol

In the **read-before-write protocol** we assume that a transaction will read the data-item before it modifies it and after modifications, the modified value is written back to the database. In Algorithm 12.1, we give the method of testing whether a schedule is serializable. We create a precedence graph and test for a cycle in the graph. If we find a cycle, the schedule is nonserializable; otherwise we find a linear ordering of the transactions.

In Examples 12.1 and 12.2 we illustrate the application of this algorithm.

Example 12.1

Consider the schedule of Figure A. The precedence graph for this schedule is given in Figure B. The graph has three nodes corresponding to the three transactions T_{14}, T_{15}, and T_{16}. There is an arc from T_{14} to T_{15} because T_{14} writes data-item *A* before T_{15} reads it. Similarly, there is an arc from T_{15} to T_{16} because T_{15} writes data-item *B* before T_{16} reads it. Finally, there is an arc from T_{16} to T_{14} because T_{16} writes data-item *C* before T_{14} reads it. The precedence graph of Figure B has a cycle formed by the directed edges from T_{14} to T_{15}, from T_{15} to T_{16} and from T_{16} back to T_{14}. Hence, the schedule of Figure A is not serializable. We cannot execute the three transactions serially to get the same result as the given schedule.

Figure A An execution schedule involving three transactions.

Time	Schedule	Transaction T_{14}	Transaction T_{15}	Transaction T_{16}
↓	**Read**(A)	**Read**(A)		
	Read(B)		**Read**(B)	
	$A := f_1(A)$	$A := f_1(A)$		
	Read(C)			**Read**(C)
	$B := f_2(B)$		$B := f_2(B)$	
T	**Write**(B)		**Write**(B)	
i	$C := f_3(C)$			$C := f_3(C)$
m	**Write**(C)			**Write(C)**
e	**Write**(A)	**Write**(A)		
	Read(B)			**Read**(B)
	Read(A)		**Read**(A)	
	$A := f_4(A)$		$A := f_4(A)$	
	Read(C)	**Read**(C)		
	Write(A)		**Write**(A)	
	$C := f_5(C)$	$C := f_5(C)$		
	Write(C)	**Write**(C)		
	$B := f_6(B)$			$B := f_6(B)$
↓	**Write**(B)			**Write**(B)

Figure B A precedence graph with a cycle.

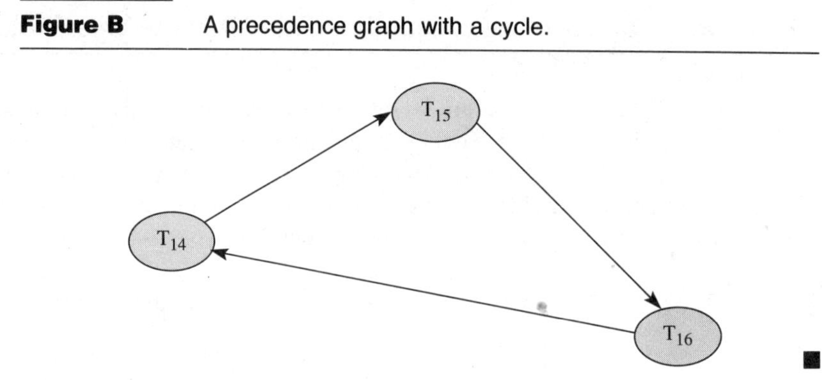

Example 12.2 presents a serializable schedule.

Example 12.2

Consider the schedule given in Figure C. The execution schedule of the figure is serializable because the precedence graph for this schedule given in Figure D, does not contain any cycles. The serial schedule is T_{17}, followed by T_{18}, followed by T_{19}.

Figure C An execution schedule involving three transactions.

Time	Schedule	Transaction T_{17}	Transaction T_{18}	Transaction T_{19}
	Read(A)	**Read**(A)		
	$A := f_1(A)$	$A := f_1(A)$		
	Read(C)	**Read**(C)		
	Write(A)	**Write**(A)		
	$A := f_2(C)$	$A := f_2(C)$		
	Read(B)		**Read**(B)	
T	**Write**(C)	**Write**(C)		
i	**Read**(A)		**Read**(A)	
m	**Read**(C)			**Read**(C)
e	$B := f_3(B)$		$B := f_3(B)$	
	Write(B)		**Write**(B)	
	$C := f_4(C)$			$C := f_4(C)$
	Read(B)			**Read**(B)
	Write(C)			**Write**(C)
	$A := f_5(A)$		$A := f_5(A)$	
	Write(A)		**Write**(A)	
	$B := f_6(B)$			$B := f_6(B)$
	Write(B)			**Write**(B)

Figure D Precedence graph for schedule of Figure C.

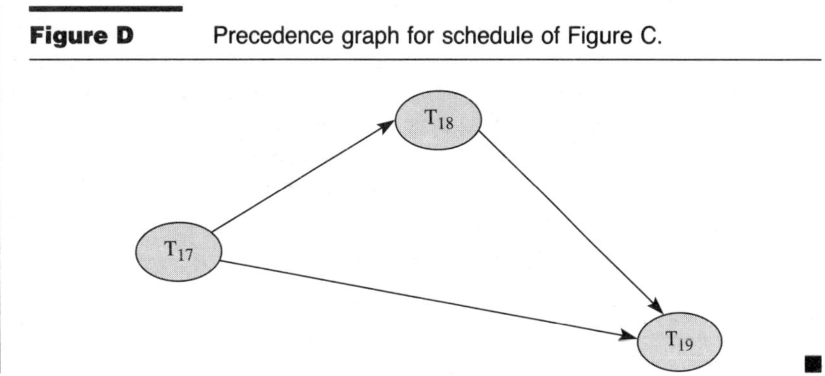

■

12.2.3 Serializability Algorithm: Read-Only and Write-Only Protocols

Algorithm 12.1 is for a set of transactions that follow the read-before-write protocol. Some transactions, in addition to having a set of data-items that are read before rewritten, have another set of data-items that are only read and a further set of data-items that are only written. In such a case some additional edges must be added to the graph. We will not treat this generalization in this text; refer to the bibliographic notes for further reading.

12.3 Concurrency Control

If all schedules in a concurrent environment are restricted to serializable schedules, the result obtained will be consistent with some serial execution of the transactions and will be considered correct. However, using only serial schedules unnecessarily limits the degree of concurrency. Furthermore, testing for serializability of a schedule is not only computationally expensive but it is an after-the-fact technique and impractical. Thus, one of the following **concurrency control** schemes is applied in a concurrent database environment to ensure that the schedules produced by concurrent transactions are serializable. The schemes we discuss are locking, timestamp-based order, optimistic scheduling, and the multiversion technique.

The intent of locking is to ensure serializability by ensuring mutual exclusion in accessing data-items. In the timestamp-based ordering scheme, the order of execution of the transactions is selected a priori by assigning each transaction an unique value. This value, usually based on the system clock, is called a timestamp. The values of the timestamp of the transactions determine the sequence in which transactions contesting for a given data-item will be executed. Conflicts in the timestamp scheme are resolved by abort and rollback. In the optimistic scheme it is recognized that the conflict between transactions, though possible, is in reality very rare, and it avoids all forms of locking. The price paid in the optimistic scheme is in verifying the validity of the assumptions that data used by a transaction has not changed and the abort and restart of a transaction for which it is ascertained that the data-items have changed between the time of reading and of writing. In the multiversion technique, a data-item is never written over; each write operation creates a new version of a data-item. Many versions of a data-item exist and these represent the historical evolution of the data-item. A transaction sees the data-item of its own epoch. Conflicts are resolved by rollback of a transaction that is too late to write out all values from its epoch. We examine each of these concurrency control schemes in the following sections. The problem of deadlock, which is possible in some of these schemes and/or their modifications, is discussed in Section 12.8.

12.4 Locking Scheme

From the point of view of locking, a database can be considered as being made up of a set of data-items. A **lock** is a variable associated with each such data-item. Manipulating the value of a lock is called **locking.** The value of a lock variable is used in the locking scheme to control the concurrent access and manipulation of the associated data-item. Locking the items being used by a transaction can prevent other concurrently running transactions from using these locked items. The locking is done by a subsystem of the database management system usually called the **lock manager.**

So that concurrency is not restricted unnecessarily, at least two types of locks are defined: exclusive lock and shared lock.

Exclusive lock: The exclusive lock is also called an update or a write lock. The intention of this mode of locking is to provide exclusive use of the data-item to one transaction. If a transaction T locks a data-item Q in an exclusive mode, no other transaction can access Q, not even to read Q, until the lock is released by transaction T.

Shared lock: The shared lock is also called a read lock. The intention of this mode of locking is to ensure that the data-item does not undergo any modifications while it is locked in this mode. Any number of transactions can concurrently lock and access a data-item in the shared mode, but none of these transactions can modify the data-item. A data-item locked in a shared mode cannot be locked in the exclusive mode until the shared lock is released by all transactions holding the lock. A data-item locked in the exclusive mode cannot be locked in the shared mode until the exclusive lock on the data-item is released.

The protocol of sharing is as follows. Each transaction, before accessing a data-item, requests that the data-item be locked in the appropriate mode. If the data-item is not locked, the lock request is honored by the lock manager. If the data-item is already locked, the request may or may not be granted, depending on the mode of locking requested and the current mode in which the data-item is locked. If the mode of locking requested is shared and if the data-item is already locked in the shared mode, the lock request can be granted. If the data-item is locked in an exclusive mode, then the lock request cannot be granted, regardless of the mode of the request. In this case the requesting transaction has to wait till the lock is released.

The compatibility of a lock request for a data-item with respect to its current state of locking is given in Figure 12.10. Here we are assuming that the request for locking is made by a transaction not already holding a lock on the data-item.

If transaction T_x makes a request to lock data item *A* in the shared mode and if *A* is not locked or if it is already locked in the shared mode, the lock request is granted. This means that a subsequent request from another transaction, T_y, to lock

Figure 12.10 Compatibility of locking.

Current state of locking of data-item

Lock mode of request		Unlocked	Shared	Exclusive
	Unlock	-	yes	yes
	Shared	yes	yes	no
	Exclusive	yes	no	no

data-item *A* in the exclusive mode would not be granted and transaction T_y will have to wait until *A* is unlocked. While *A* is locked in the shared mode, if transaction T_z makes a request to lock it in the shared mode, this request can be granted. Both T_x and T_z can concurrently use data-item *A*.

If transaction T_x makes a request to lock data-item *A* in the shared mode and if *A* is locked in the exclusive mode, the request made by transaction T_x cannot be granted. Similarly, a request by transaction T_z to lock *A* in the exclusive mode while it is already locked in the exclusive mode would also result in the request not being granted, and T_z would have to wait until the lock on *A* is released.

From the above we see that any lock request for a data-item can only be granted if it is compatible with the current mode of locking of the data-item. If the request is not compatible, the requesting transaction has to wait until the mode becomes compatible.

The releasing of a lock on a data-item changes its lock status. If the data-item was locked in an exclusive mode, the release of lock request by the transaction holding the exclusive lock on the data-item would result in the data-item being unlocked. Any transaction waiting for a release of the exclusive lock would have a chance of being granted its request for locking the data-item. If more than one transaction is waiting, it is assumed that the lock manager would use some fair scheduling technique to choose one of these waiting transactions.

If the data-item was locked in a shared mode, the release of lock request by the transaction holding the shared lock on the data-item may not result in the data-item being unlocked. This is because more than one transaction may be holding a shared lock on the data-item. Only when the transaction releasing the lock is the only transaction having the shared lock does the data-item become unlocked. The lock manager may keep a count of the number of transactions holding a shared lock on a data-item. It would increase this value by one when an additional transaction is granted a shared lock and decrease the value by one when a transaction holding a shared lock releases the lock. The data-item would then become unlocked when the number of transactions holding a shared lock on it becomes zero. This count could be stored in an appropriate data structure along with the data-item but it would be accessible only to the lock manager.

The lock manager must have a priority scheme whereby it decides whether to allow additional transactions to lock a data-item in the share-mode in the following situation:

- The data-item is already locked in the shared mode.
- There is at least one transaction waiting to lock the data-item in the exclusive mode.

Allowing a higher priority to share lock requests could result in possible starvation of the transactions waiting for an exclusive lock. Similarly, the lock manager has to deal with a situation where a data-item is locked in an exclusive mode and there are transactions waiting to lock the data-item in the shared mode and the exclusive mode.

In the following discussions we assume that a transaction makes a request to lock data-item A by executing the statement **Locks**(A) or **Lockx**(A). The former is for requesting a shared lock; the latter, an exclusive lock. A lock is released by simply executing an **Unlock**(A) statement. We assume that the transactions are correct. In other words, a transaction would not request a lock on a data-item for which it already holds a lock, nor would a transaction unlock a data-item if it does not hold a lock for it.

A transaction may have to hold onto the lock on a data-item beyond the point when it last needs it to preserve consistency and avoid the inconsistent read problems discussed in Section 12.1.2. We illustrate this point by reworking the example of Figure 12.5. Here each transaction request locks for the data-items A and B: transaction T_5 in exclusive mode and transaction T_6 in shared mode. The transactions with the lock requests are given in Figure 12.11. As shown there, the transactions attempt to release the locks on the data-items as soon as possible.

Now consider Figure 12.12, which gives a possible schedule of execution of the transactions of Figure 12.11. The locking scheme did not resolve the inconsistent read problem; the reason is that transactions T_5 and T_6 are performing an operation made up of many steps and all these have to be executed in an atomic manner. The database is in an inconsistent state after transaction T_5 has taken 100 units from A but not added it to B. Allowing transaction T_6 to read the values of A and B before transaction T_5 is complete leads to the inconsistent read problem.

A possible solution to the inconsistent read problem is shown in Figure 12.13. Here transactions T_5 and T_6 are rewritten as transactions T_{20} and T_{21}. The possible schedules of concurrent executions of these transactions are shown in Figures 12.14 and 12.15. Both of these solutions extend the period of time for which they keep

Figure 12.11 Two transactions of Figure 12.5 with lock requests.

Transaction T_5	Transaction T_6
Lockx(A)	**Lockx**(Sum)
Read(A)	$Sum := 0$
$A := A - 100$	**Locks**(A)
Write(A)	**Read**(A)
Unlock(A)	$Sum := Sum + A$
Lockx(B)	**Unlock**(A)
Read(B)	**Locks**(B)
$B := B + 100$	**Read**(B)
Write(B)	$Sum := Sum + B$
Unlock(B)	**Write**(Sum)
	Unlock(B)
	Unlock(Sum)

Figure 12.12 A possible schedule causing an inconsistent read.

Time	Schedule	Transaction T_5	Transaction T_6
	Lockx(*Sum*)		**Lockx**(*Sum*)
	Sum := 0		*Sum* := 0
	Locks(*A*)		**Locks**(*A*)
	Read(*A*)		**Read**(*A*)
	Sum := *Sum* + *A*		*Sum* := *Sum* + *A*
T	**Unlock**(*A*)		**Unlock**(*A*)
i	**Lockx**(*A*)	**Lockx**(*A*)	
m	**Read**(*A*)	**Read**(*A*)	
e	*A* := *A* − 100	*A* := *A* − 100	
	Write(*A*)	**Write**(*A*)	
	Unlock(*A*)	**Unlock**(*A*)	
	Lockx(*B*)	**Lockx**(*B*)	
	Read(*B*)	**Read**(*B*)	
	B := *B* + 100	*B* := *B* + 100	
	Write(*B*)	**Write**(*B*)	
	Unlock(*B*)	**Unlock**(*B*)	
	Locks(*B*)		**Locks**(*B*)
	Read(*B*)		**Read**(*B*)
	Sum := *Sum* + *B*		*Sum* := *Sum* + *B*
	Write(*Sum*)		**Write**(*Sum*)
	Unlock(*B*)		**Unlock**(*B*)
↓	**Unlock**(*Sum*)		**Unlock**(*Sum*)

Figure 12.13 Transactions locking all items before unlocking.

Transaction T_{20}	Transaction T_{21}
Lockx(*A*)	**Lockx**(*Sum*)
Read(*A*)	*Sum* := 0
A := *A* − 100	**Locks**(*A*)
Write(*A*)	**Read**(*A*)
Lockx(*B*)	*Sum* := *Sum* + *A*
Unlock(*A*)	**Locks**(*B*)
Read(*B*)	**Read**(*B*)
B := *B* + 100	*Sum* := *Sum* + *B*
Write(*B*)	**Write**(*Sum*)
Unlock(*B*)	**Unlock**(*B*)
	Unlock(*A*)
	Unlock(*Sum*)

Figure 12.14 A possible solution to the inconsistent read problem.

Time ↓	Schedule	Transaction T_{20}	Transaction T_{21}
	Lockx(*Sum*)		**Lockx**(*Sum*)
	Sum := 0		*Sum* := 0
	Locks(*A*)		**Locks**(*A*)
	Read(*A*)		**Read**(*A*)
	Sum := *Sum* + *A*		*Sum* := *Sum* + *A*
	Locks(*B*)		**Locks**(*B*)
	Read(*B*)		**Read**(*B*)
	Sum := *Sum* + *B*		*Sum* := Sum + B
	Write(*Sum*)		**Write**(*Sum*)
	Unlock(*B*)		**Unlock**(*B*)
	Unlock(*A*)		**Unlock**(*A*)
	Unlock(*Sum*)		**Unlock**(*Sum*)
	Lockx(*A*)	**Lockx**(*A*)	
	Read(*A*)	**Read**(*A*)	
	A := *A* − 100	*A* := *A* − 100	
	Write(*A*)	**Write**(*A*)	
	Lockx(*B*)	**Lockx**(*B*)	
	Unlock(*A*)	**Unlock**(*A*)	
	Read(*B*)	**Read**(*B*)	
	B := *B* + 100	*B* := *B* + 100	
	Write(*B*)	**Write**(*B*)	
	Unlock(*B*)	**Unlock**(*B*)	

some data-items locked even though the transactions no longer need these items. This extended locking forces a serialization of the two transactions and gives correct results.

12.4.1 Two-Phase Locking

The correctness of the schedules of Figures 12.14 and 12.15 and of the transactions in Figure 12.13 lead us to the observation that both these solutions involve transactions whose locking and unlocking operations are monotonic, in the sense that all locks are first acquired before any of the locks are released. Once a lock is released, no additional locks are requested. In other words, the release of the locks is delayed until all locks on all data-items required by the transaction have been acquired.

This method of locking is called **two-phase locking.** It has two phases, a **growing phase** wherein the number of locks increase from zero to the maximum for the transaction, and a **contracting phase** wherein the number of locks held decreases from the maximum to zero. Both of these phases are monotonic; the number of locks are only increasing in the first phase and decreasing in the second phase. Once a

Figure 12.15 Another solution to the inconsistent read problem.

Time	Schedule	Transaction T_{20}	Transaction T_{21}
	Lockx(*A*)	**Lockx**(*A*)	
	Read(*A*)	**Read**(*A*)	
	$A := A - 100$	$A := A - 100$	
	Write(*A*)	**Write**(*A*)	
T	**Lockx**(*B*)	**Lockx**(*B*)	
i	**Unlock**(*A*)	**Unlock**(*A*)	
m	**Read**(*B*)	**Read**(*B*)	
e	$B := B + 100$	$B := B + 100$	
	Write(*B*)	**Write**(*B*)	
	Unlock(*B*)	**Unlock**(*B*)	
	Lockx(*Sum*)		**Lockx***Sum*)
	$Sum := 0$		$Sum := 0$
	Locks(*A*)		**Locks**(*A*)
	Read(*A*)		**Read**(*A*)
	$Sum := Sum + A$		$Sum := Sum + A$
	Locks(*B*)		**Locks**(*B*)
	Read(*B*)		**Read**(*B*)
	$Sum := Sum + B$		$Sum := Sum + B$
	Write(*Sum*)		**Write**(*Sum*)
	Unlock(*B*)		**Unlock**(*B*)
	Unlock(*A*)		**Unlock**(*A*)
↓	**Unlock**(*Sum*)		**Unlock**(*Sum*)

transaction starts releasing locks, it is not allowed to request any further locks. In this way a transaction is obliged to request all locks it may need during its life before it releases any. This leads to a possible lower degree of concurrency.

The two-phase locking protocol ensures that the schedules involving transactions using this protocol will always be serializable. For instance, if S is a schedule containing the interleaved operations from a number of transactions, $T_1, T_2, \ldots, T_k$ and all the transactions are using the two-phase locking protocol, schedule S is serializable. This is because if the schedule is not serializable, the precedence graph for S will have a cycle made up of a subset of $\{T_1, T_2, \ldots, T_k\}$. Assume the cycle consists of $T_a \rightarrow T_b \rightarrow T_c \rightarrow \ldots T_x \rightarrow T_a$. This means that a lock operation by T_b is followed by an unlock operation by T_a; a lock operation by T_c is followed by an unlock operation by $T_b, \ldots$, and finally a lock operation by T_a is followed by an unlock operation by T_x. However, this is a contradiction of the assertion that T_a is using the two phase protocol. Thus the assumption that there was a cycle in the precedence graph is incorrect and hence S is serializable.

The transactions of Figure 12.13 use the two-phase locking protocol, and the schedules derived from the concurrent execution of these transactions given in Figures 12.14 and 12.15 are serializable. However, the transactions of Figure 12.11 do not follow the two-phase locking protocol and the schedule of Figure 12.12 is not serializable.

The observant reader will notice that the danger of deadlock exists in the two-phase locking protocol. We examine this problem in greater detail in Section 12.8.

12.4.2 Granularity of Locking

So far we have assumed that a data-item can be locked. However, we have not defined explicitly what the data-item is. If the size or **granularity** of the data-item is very large, for instance the entire database, then of course the overhead of locking is very small. The lock manager manages only one item. The drawback here is obvious. The concurrency is very low since only one transaction can run in an exclusive mode at a given time, even though it may need a very small portion of the database. On the other hand, if the granularity of the data-item is very small (for example, a data-item could be the field of a record), then the degree of concurrency can be fairly high, although the overhead of locking in this case can be considerable. A transaction that needs many records and fields will have to request many locks, all of which have to be managed by the lock manager. For the highest degree of flexibility, the locking scheme should allow multiple granularity of locking from a data field to the entire database.

When the data-item that is locked is, for example, a record type, then to avoid the phantom read problem, locking a record type requires not only that the existing record occurrences be locked but also implies that nonexisting records are also locked. In this manner it is possible to preclude the insertion of phantom records by other concurrent transactions.

To avoid locking too early and in situations where the transaction itself has to determine which data-items to lock, locks are requested dynamically by the transactions. This creates an additional overhead for the lock manager, which in addition to the locking overhead has to determine if there is a situation of deadlock. The methods of handling deadlocks are discussed in Section 12.8.

12.4.3 Hierarchy of Locks and Intention-Mode Locking

Some data structures used in the database are structured in the form of a tree. For example, the nodes of a B-tree index are hierarchically structured. A transaction may need to lock the entire B-tree or only a portion of it, i.e., a proper subtree. Similarly, the database may be considered to be a hierarchy consisting of the following nodes:

- the entire database
- some designated portion of the database
- a record type (or in the case of the relational database, a relation)
- an occurrence of a record (a tuple)
- a field of the record (an attribute)

The nodes of the hierarchy could depend on the data model being used by the DBMS. In the case of the hierarchical model, the hierarchies represent a tree and each node of the tree can be locked. In the case of the network model, locking could be based on sets. In the hierarchy shown in Figure 12.16, we generalize the nodes to be independent of the data model. The usual practice is to limit the locking granularity to the record occurrence level.

Having structured the database objects in a hierarchy, the corresponding locking scheme becomes a hierarchy; the lock manager allows each node of the hierarchy to be locked. A hierarchy of locks provides greater flexibility and efficiency in locking. Such a scheme allows multiple granularity of locking from a data field to the entire database. The descendants of a locked node are implicitly locked in the same mode (shared or exclusive) as the node. However, if a subtree is locked, the ancestor of the subtree is not allowed to be locked; this is because locking an ancestor of the subtree implicitly locks the subtree. An implicit lock on a node signifies that no other transaction is allowed to lock that node (either implicitly or explicitly) in an exclusive mode (and implicitly, any of the descendants).

Hierarchical organization of the database, however, increases the overhead in determining whether or not a request for a lock from a transaction can be accepted. Consider a portion of the database that is under the hierarchy specified by the node N. Suppose the transaction T_0 needs a share lock on this portion of the database. How can the lock manager know efficiently if any other transaction has locked some portion of the database rooted by node N, and if so, whether the mode is compatible with the request of transaction T_0? Checking each data-item under N is inefficient.

In the case of hierarchical structured locking, a new mode of locking, the **intention mode** is introduced. A transaction can lock a hierarchically structured data-item in the intention mode. This implies that the transaction intends to explicitly lock a lower portion of the hierarchy. In effect, intention locks are placed on all ancestors of a node until the node that is to be locked explicitly is reached.

To allow a higher degree of concurrency, the intention mode of locking is refined to intention share and intention exclusive modes. The intention mode simply indicates that the transaction intends to lock the lower level in some mode. If transaction T_a intends to lock the lower level in the share mode, the ancestor is locked in

Figure 12.16 Hierarchical structure of the database.

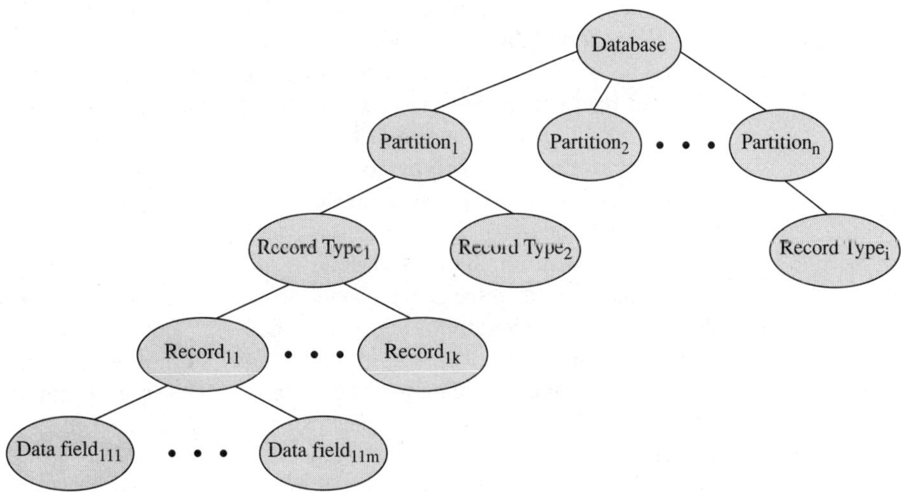

the **intention share mode** to indicate that the lower level is being locked in a share mode. Other transactions can access the node and all its lower levels, including the subtree being accessed by T_a; no transaction, however, can modify any portion of the database rooted at the node that was locked by T_a in the intention share mode. If transaction T_a intends to lock the lower level in the exclusive or share mode, then the ancestor is locked in the **intention exclusive mode** to indicate that the lower level is being locked in an exclusive or share mode. Another concurrent transaction, say T_b, needing to access any portion of this hierarchy in the exclusive or share mode can also lock this node in the intention exclusive mode. If T_b needs exclusive or share access to that portion of the subtree not being used by transaction T_a, it will place appropriate locks on it and can run concurrently with T_a. However, if T_b needs access to any portion of the subtree locked in the exclusive mode by T_a, then the explicit exclusive locks on these nodes will cause T_b to wait until T_a releases these explicit exclusive locks.

The intention lock locks a node to indicate that the lower level nodes are being locked either in the share or the exclusive mode, but it does no implicit locking of lower levels. Each lower level has to be locked explicitly in whichever mode required by the transaction. This adds a fairly large overhead if a transaction needs to access a subtree of the database and modify only a small portion of the subtree rooted at the intentionally locked node. The **share and intention exclusive mode** of locking is thus introduced. The share and intention exclusive mode differs from the other form of intention locking in so far as it implicitly locks all lower level nodes as well as the node in question. This mode allows access by other transactions to share that portion of the subtree not exclusively locked and gives higher concurrency than achievable with a simple exclusive lock. This avoids the overhead of locking the root node and all nodes in the path leading to the subtree to be modified in the intention exclusive mode, followed by locking the subtree to be modified in the exclusive mode. It is replaced by locking the root node in the share and intention exclusive mode (which will lock all descendants implicitly in the same mode), followed by locking the root node of the subtree to be modified in the exclusive mode.

We summarize below the possible modes in which a node of the database hierarchy could be locked and the effect of the locking on the descendants of the node. Figure 12.17 gives the relative privilege of these modes of locking. The exclusive mode has the highest privilege and the intention share mode has the lowest privilege.

S or shared lock: The node in question *and implicitly all its descendants* are locked in the share mode; all these nodes, locked explicitly or implicitly, are accessible for read-only access. No transaction can update the node or any of its descendants when the node is locked in the shared mode.

X or exclusive lock: The node in question *and implicitly all its descendants* are exclusively locked by a single transaction. No other transaction can concurrently access these nodes.

IS or intention share: The node is locked in the intention share mode, which means that it or its descendants cannot be exclusively locked. The descendant of the node may be individually locked in a shared or intention shared mode. The descendants of the node that is locked in the IS mode are not locked implicitly.

IX or intention exclusive: The node is locked in an intention exclusive mode. This means that the node itself cannot be exclusively locked; however, any of the descendants, if not already locked, can be locked in any of the locking modes. The descendants of the node that is locked in the IX mode are not locked implicitly.

Figure 12.17 Relative privilege of the locking modes.

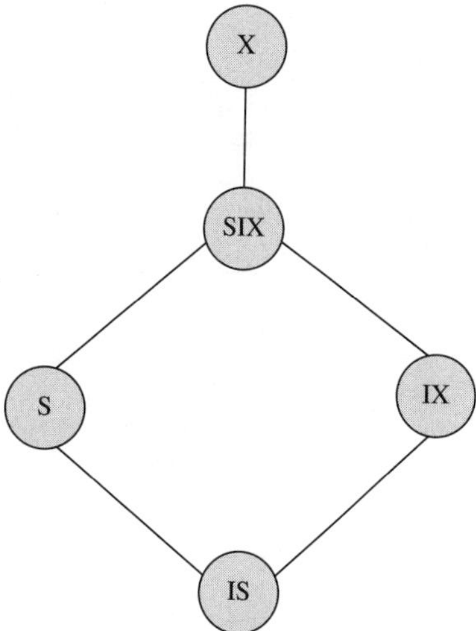

SIX or shared and intention exclusive: The node is locked in the shared and intention exclusive mode and all the descendants are implicitly locked in the shared mode. However, any of the descendants can be explicitly locked in the exclusive, intention exclusive, or shared and intention exclusive modes.

Relative Privilege of the Various Locking Modes

Figure 12.17 gives the relative privilege of the various modes of locking. The exclusive mode has the highest privilege: it locks out all other transactions from the portion of the database that is rooted at the node locked in the exclusive mode. All descendants of the node are implicitly locked in the exclusive mode. The intention share mode has the lowest privilege. The share mode is not comparable with the intention exclusive mode.

The advantage of the intention mode locking is that the lock manager knows that the lower level nodes of a node that is intentionally locked are or are being locked without having to examine all the lower level nodes. Furthermore, using the compatibility matrix shown in Figure 12.18 and discussed below, the lock manager can ascertain if a request for a lock can be granted.

Compatibility Matrix

Considering all the modes of locking described above, the compatibility between the current mode of locking for a node and the request of another transaction for locking the node in a given mode are given in Figure 12.18. The entry yes indicates that the request will be granted and the transaction can continue. The entry no indicates that the request cannot be granted and the requesting transaction will have to wait.

Figure 12.18 Access mode compatibility.

Current state of lock of the node

Request for locking	IS	IX	S	SIX	X	unlocked
IS	yes	yes	yes	yes	no	yes
IX	yes	yes	no	no	no	yes
S	yes	no	yes	no	no	yes
SIX	yes	no	no	no	no	yes
X	no	no	no	no	no	yes
UNLOCK	yes	yes	yes	yes	yes	yes

Locking Principle

With the above locking modes, the procedure to be followed in locking can be summarized as follows:

- A transaction is not allowed to request additional locks if it has released a lock (this is the two-phase locking protocol requirement).
- The access mode compatibility matrix determines if a lock request can be granted or if the requesting transaction has to wait.
- A transaction is required to request a lock in a root-to-leaf direction and to release locks in the leaf-to-root direction. Consequently, a transaction cannot unlock a node if it currently holds a lock on one of the descendants of the node. Similarly, a transaction cannot lock a node unless it already has a compatible lock on the ancestor of the node.
- A transaction can lock a node in the IS or S modes only if the transaction has successfully locked the ancestors of the node in the IX or IS modes.
- A transaction can lock a node in the IX, SIX, or X modes only if the transaction has successfully locked the ancestors of the node in the IX or SIX modes.
- The lock manager can lock a larger portion of the database than requested by a transaction and the duration of this lock could be for a period longer than needed by the transaction.

The above locking protocol ensures serializability. Let us consider a few examples to illustrate the locking procedures to be followed on a database stored in a hierarchical structure, as shown in Figure 12.19.

Example 12.3 To lock record occurrence R_{13} of Record $Type_1$ for retrieval only, the sequence of locking is as follows: (1) lock database in the IS mode, (2) lock $Partition_1$ in the IS mode, (3) lock Record $Type_1$ in the IS mode, (4) lock record R_{13} in the S mode. ■

Figure 12.19 Sample database storage structure.

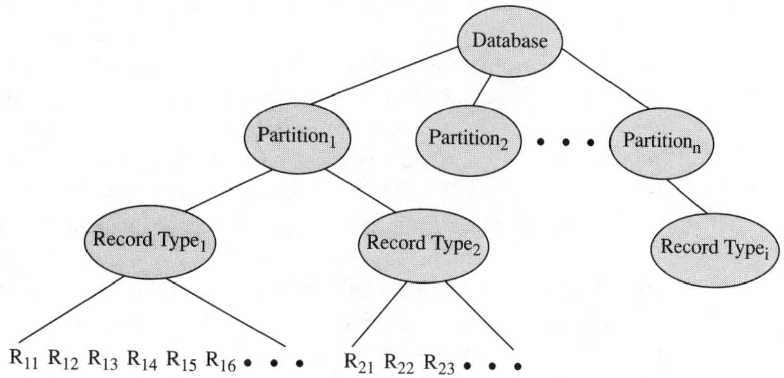

Exclusive locking can proceed as illustrated below.

Example 12.4 To lock the record occurrence R_{22} of Record Type$_2$, in the exclusive mode, the sequence of locking is as follows: (1) lock database in the IX mode, (2) lock Partition$_1$ in the IX mode, (3) lock Record Type$_2$ in the IX mode, (4) lock record R_{22} in the X mode. ■

Note that if two transactions are accessing records R_{ik} and R_{il}, for $k \neq l$, in the share and exclusive modes respectively, then both these transactions can be executed concurrently if the sequence of locking for the first transaction is IS, IS, IS, and S and for the second transaction IX, IX, IX, and X.

12.4.4 Tree-Locking Protocol

Let us assume that the storage structure of the database is in the form of a tree of data-items, as shown in Figure 12.19 Then a locking protocol called a **tree locking protocol** can be defined as follows:

- All locks are exclusive locks.
- Locking a node does not automatically lock any descendant of the locked node.
- The first item locked by a transaction can be any data-item including the root node.
- Except for the first data-item locked by a transaction, a node cannot be locked by a transaction unless the transaction has already successfully locked its parent.
- No items are locked twice by a transaction; thus, releasing a lock on a data-item implies that the transaction will not attempt another lock on the data-item.

A schedule for a set of transactions such that each transaction in the set uses the tree locking protocol can be shown to be serializable. Note that the transactions need not be two phase and they are allowed to unlock an item before locking another item. The only requirement is that the transaction must have a lock on the parent of the node being locked and that the item was not previously locked by the transaction.

Consider the database of Figure 12.19. A transaction, for instance T_a, can start off by locking the entire database. Then it proceeds to lock $Portion_1$, Record $Type_1$ and Record $Type_2$. At this point it unlocks the database and then locks record occurrences R_{11} and R_{21}, followed by unlocking $Portion_1$, and Record $Type_2$. Another transaction, T_b, can then proceed by first locking Record $Type_2$ followed by locking record occurrences R_{22}. The first transaction can now lock record occurrence R_{12}.

The advantage of the tree-locking protocol over the two-phase locking protocol is that a data-item can be released earlier by a transaction if the data-item (and of course, any of its yet unlocked descendants in the subtree rooted at the data-item) is not required by the transaction. In this way a greater amount of concurrency is feasible. However, since a descendant is not locked by the lock on a parent, the number of locks and associated locking overhead, including the resulting waits, is increased.

12.4.5 DAG Database Storage Structure

The use of indexes to obtain direct access to the records of the database causes the hierarchical storage structure to be converted into a **directed acyclic graph (DAG)** as shown in Figure 12.20. The locking protocol can be extended to a DAG structure; the only additional rule is that to lock a node in the IX, SIX, or X modes, all the parents of the node have to be locked in a compatible mode that is at least an IX mode. Thus, no other transaction can get a lock to any of the parents in the S, SIX, or X modes. This is illustrated in Example 12.5.

Example 12.5

To add a record occurrence to the Record $Type_1$, which uses an $index_1$ for direct access to the records, the sequence of locking is as follows: (1) lock the database in the IX mode, (2) lock $Portion_1$ in the IX mode, (3) lock Record $Type_1$ and $index_1$ in the X mode. With this method of locking, the phantom phenomenon is avoided at the expense of lower concurrency. ■

Figure 12.20 Sample DAG database storage structure.

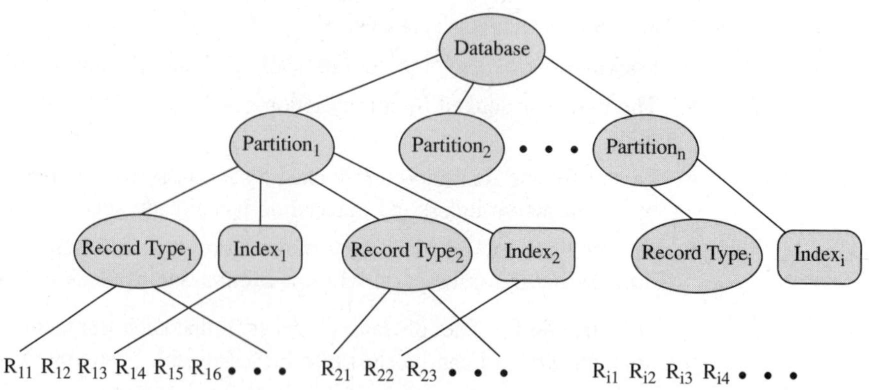

As in the case of two-phase locking, deadlock is possible in the locking scheme using hierarchical granularity of locking. Additional details regarding references to techniques to reduce and eliminate such deadlock are cited in the bibliographic notes.

12.5 Timestamp-Based Order

In the timestamp-based method, a serial order is created among the concurrent transaction by assigning to each transaction a unique nondecreasing number. The usual value assigned to each transaction is the system clock value at the start of the transaction, hence the name **timestamp ordering.** A variation of this scheme that is used in a distributed environment includes the site of a transaction appended to the system-wide clock value. This value can then be used in deciding the order in which the conflict between two transactions is resolved. A transaction with a smaller timestamp value is considered to be an ''older'' transaction than another transaction with a larger timestamp value.

The serializability that the system enforces is the chronological order of the timestamps of the concurrent transactions. If two transaction T_i and T_j with the time stamp values t_i and t_j respectively, such that $t_i < t_j$, are to run concurrently, then the schedule produced by the system is equivalent to running the older transaction T_i first, followed by the younger one, T_j.

The contention problem between two transactions in the timestamp ordering system is resolved by rolling back one of the conflicting transactions. A conflict is said to occur when an older transaction tries to read a value that is written by a younger transaction or when an older transaction tries to modify a value already read or written by a younger transaction. Both of these attempts signify that the older transaction was ''too late'' in performing the required read/write operations and it could be using values from different ''generations'' for different data-items.

In order for the system to determine if an older transaction is processing a value already read by or written by a younger transaction, each data-item has, in addition to the value of the item, two timestamps: a **write timestamp** and a **read timestamp.** Data-item X is thus represented by a triple X: $\{x, W_x, R_x\}$ where each component of the triple is interpreted as given below:

x, the value of the data-item X

W_x, the write timestamp value, the largest timestamp value of any transaction that was allowed to write a value of X.

R_x, the read timestamp value, the largest timestamp value of any transaction that was allowed to read the current value X.

Now let us see how these timestamp values find their way into the data structure of a data-item and how all these values are modified. A transaction T_a with the timesteamp value of t_a issues a read operation for the data-item X with the values $\{x, W_x, R_x\}$.

- This request will succeed if $t_a \geq W_x$, since transaction T_a is younger than the transaction that last wrote (or modified) the value of X. Transaction T_a is allowed to read the value x of X and if the value t_a is larger than R_x, then t_a becomes the new value of R_x.

- This request will fail if $t_a < W_x$, i.e., transaction T_a is an older transaction than the last transaction that wrote the value of X.

The failure of the read request is due to the fact that the older transaction was trying to read a value that had been overwritten by a younger transaction. Transaction T_a is too late to read the previous outdated value and any other values it has acquired are likely to be inconsistent with the updated value of X. It is thus safe to abort and roll back T_a. T_a is assigned a new timestamp and restarted.

A transaction T_a with the timestamp value of t_a issues a write operation for the data-item X with the values $\{x, W_x, R_x\}$.

- If $t_a \geq W_x$ and $t_a \geq R_x$, i.e. both the last transaction that updated the value of X and the last transaction that read the value of X are older than transaction T_a, then T_a is allowed to write the value of X and t_a becomes the current value of W_x, the write timestamp.
- If $t_a < R_x$, it means that a younger transaction is already using the current value of X and it would be an error to update the value of X. Transaction T_a is not allowed to modify the value of X. T_a is rolled back and its timestamp is reset to the current system-generated timestamp value and restarted.
- If $R_x \leq t_a < W_x$, this means that a younger transaction has already updated the value of X, and the value that T_a is writing must be based on an obsolete value of X and is obsolete. Transaction T_a is not allowed to modify the value of X; its write operation is ignored.

The reason for ignoring the write operation in the last alternative is as follows. In the serial order of transaction processing, transaction T_a with the timestamp of t_a wrote the value for the data-item X. This was followed by another write operation to the same data-item by a younger transaction with a timestamp of W_x. No transaction read the data-item between the writing by T_a and the time W_x. Hence, ignoring the

Figure 12.21 Transactions for Examples 12.6, 12.7, 12.9.

Transaction T_{22}	Transaction T_{23}
Sum := 0	*Sum* := 0
Read(*A*)	**Read**(*A*)
Sum := *Sum* + *A*	*A* := *A* − 100
Read(*B*)	**Write**(*A*)
Sum := *Sum* + *B*	*Sum* := *Sum* + *A*
Show(*Sum*)	**Read**(*B*)
	B := *B* + 100
	Write(*B*)
	Sum := *Sum* + *B*
	Show(*Sum*)

writing by T_a indicates that the value written by T_a was immediately overwritten by a younger transaction at time W_x.

Let us illustrate the timestamp ordering by considering transactions T_{22} and T_{23} given below in Figure 12.21. Each of these transactions has a local variable *Sum* and the intent is to show a user the sum of two data-items *A* and *B*. However, transaction T_{23} not only reads these values, it also transfers 100 units from *A* to *B* and writes the modified values to the database. Now let us suppose that $t_{23} > t_{22}$. This means that transaction T_{23} is younger than transaction T_{22}. Also, let the data-items *A* and *B* be stored as follows (here the W_i's and R_i's have some values assumed to be less than t_{22} and t_{23}):

A: 400, W_a, R_a *B:* 500, W_b, R_b

Example 12.6

Consider the transactions of Figure 12.21. In the schedule given in Figure E transactions T_{22} (t_{22}) and T_{23} (t_{23}) run concurrently and produce the correct result. A similar serializable schedule could have been obtained using the two phase locking protocol. (See Exercise 12.5.)

Figure E Serializable schedule based on timestamp scheme.

Step	Schedule	Transaction T_{22}	Transaction T_{23}
1	*Sum* := 0	*Sum* := 0	
2	**Read**(*A*)	**Read**(*A*)	
3	*Sum* := *Sum* + *A*	*Sum* := *Sum* + *A*	
4	*Sum* := 0		*Sum* := 0
5	**Read**(*A*)		**Read**(*A*)
6	*A* := *A* − 100		*A* := *A* − 100
7	**Write**(*A*)		**Write**(*A*)
8	**Read**(*B*)	**Read**(*B*)	
9	*Sum* := *Sum* + *B*	*Sum* := *Sum* + *B*	
10	**Show**(*Sum*)	**Show**(*Sum*)	
11	*Sum* := *Sum* + *A*		*Sum* := *Sum* + *A*
12	**Read**(*B*)		**Read**(*B*)
13	*B* := *B* + 100		*B* := *B* + 100
14	**Write**(*B*)		**Write**(*B*)
15	*Sum* := *Sum* + *B*		*Sum* := *Sum* + *B*
16	**Show**(*Sum*)		**Show**(*Sum*)

The steps of the schedule of Figure E cause the following modifications to the triple for *A* and *B:*

Initially	*A:* 400, W_a, R_a	*B:* 500, W_b, R_b
After step 2	*A:* 400, W_a, t_{22}	*B:* 500, W_b, R_b

After step 5	*A:* 400, W_a, t_{23}	*B:* 500, W_b, R_b
After step 7	*A:* 300, t_{23}, t_{23}	*B:* 500, W_b, R_b
After step 8	*A:* 300, t_{23}, t_{23}	*B:* 500, W_b, t_{22}
After step 10	the value displayed will be 900	
After step 12	*A:* 300, t_{23}, t_{23}	*B:* 500, W_b, t_{23}
After step 14	*A:* 300, t_{23}, t_{23}	*B:* 600, t_{23}, t_{23}

After step 14 the value displayed will be 900 ■

In the following example we illustrate a schedule where the older transaction is rolled back.

Example 12.7

Figure F Serializablę schedule produced after a rollback.

Step	Schedule	Transaction T_{22}	Transaction T_{23}
1	*Sum* := 0	*Sum* := 0	
2	*Sum* := 0		*Sum* := 0
3	**Read**(*A*)		**Read**(*A*)
4	*A* := *A* − 100		*A* := *A* − 100
5	**Write**(*A*)		**Write**(*A*)
6	**Read**(*A*)	**Read**(*A*)* causes a rollback of T_{22}	
7	*Sum* := *Sum* + *A*		*Sum* := *Sum* + *A*
8	**Read**(*B*)		**Read**(*B*)
9	*B* := *B* + 100		*B* := *B* + 100
10	**Write**(*B*)		**Write**(*B*)
11	*Sum* := *Sum* + *B*		*Sum* := *Sum* + *B*
12	**Show**(*Sum*)		**Show**(*Sum*)
13	*Sum* := 0	*Sum* := 0 with a timestamp $t_{22}'(> t_{23})$	
14	**Read**(*A*)	**Read**(*A*)	
15	*Sum* := *Sum* + *A*	*Sum* := *Sum* + *A*	
16	**Read**(*B*)	**Read**(*B*)	
17	*Sum* := *Sum* + *B*	*Sum* := *Sum* + *B*	
18	**Show**(*Sum*)	**Show**(*Sum*)	

Consider the schedule shown in Figure F. Transaction T_{22} is rolled back and rerun after step 6. When it is rolled back, a new timestamp value t_{22}' which would be greater than t_{23}, is assigned to it. The sequence of changes is given below:

Initially	*A:* 400, W_a, R_a	*B:* 500, W_b, R_b
After step 3	*A:* 400, W_a, t_{23}	*B:* 500, W_b, R_b
After step 5	*A:* 300, t_{23}, t_{23}	*B:* 500, W_b, R_b
After step 6	*A:* 300, t_{23}, t_{23}	*B:* 500, W_b, R_b*

(*causes a rollback of T_{22} which would be reassigned a new timestamp (t_{22}^1, $> t_{23}$) and would be reexecuted)

After step 8	*A*: 300, t_{23}, t_{23}	*B*: 500, W_b, t_{23}
After step 10	*A*: 300, t_{23}, t_{23}	*B*: 600, t_{23}, t_{23}

After step 12 the value displayed will be 900

After step 14	*A*: 300, t_{23}, t_{22}'	*B*: 600, t_{23}, t_{23}
After step 16	*A*: 300, t_{23}, t_{22}'	*B*: 600, t_{23}, t_{22}'

After step 18 the value displayed will be 900 ■

Example 12.8 below illustrates a case where the write operation of a transaction could be ignored.

Example 12.8

In the example illustrated in Figure G, we have three transactions, T_{24}, T_{25}, and T_{26} with timestamp values of t_{24}, t_{25}, and t_{26} respectively ($t_{24} < t_{25} < t_{26}$). Note that transactions T_{24} and T_{26} are write-only with respect to data-item *B*.

Figure G Another serializable schedule.

Step	Schedule	Transaction T_{24}	Transaction T_{25}	Transaction T_{26}
1	**Read**(*A*)	**Read**(*A*)		
2	*A* := *A* + 1	*A* := *A* + 1		
3	**Write**(*A*)	**Write**(*A*)		
4	**Read**(*C*)		**Read**(*C*)	
5	*C* := *C* * 3		*C* := C * 3	
6	**Read**(*C*)			**Read**(*C*)
7	**Write**(*C*)		**Write**(*C*)* causes a rollback of transaction T_{25}	
8	*C* := *C* * 2			*C* := *C* * 2
9	**Write**(*C*)			**Write**(*C*)
10	*B* := 100			*B* := 100
11	**Write**(*B*)			**Write**(*B*)
12	*B* := 150	*B* := 150		
13	**Write**(*B*)	**Write**(*B*)** causes the write operation to be ignored		
14	**Read**(*C*)		**Read**(*C*)	
15	*C* := *C* * 3		*C* := *C* * 3	
16	**Write**(*C*)		**Write**(*C*)	

Initially	*A*: 10, W_a, R_a	*B*: 50, W_b, R_b	*C*: 5, W_c, R_c
After step 1	*A*: 10, W_a, t_{24}	*B*: 50, W_b, R_b	*C*: 5, W_c, R_c
After step 3	*A*: 11, t_{24}, t_{24}	*B*: 50, W_b, R_b	*C*: 5, W_c, R_c
After step 4	*A*: 11, t_{24}, t_{24}	*B*: 50, W_b, R_b	*C*: 5, W_c, t_{25}
After step 5	*A*: 11, t_{24}, t_{24}	*B*: 50, W_b, R_b	*C*: 5, W_c, t_{25}

After step 6 A: 11, t_{24}, t_{24} B: 50, W_b, R_b C: 5, W_c, t_{26}

At step 7 transaction T_{25} with a timestamp value of t_{25} attempts to write the value of C; however, since the read timestamp value of C is t_{26}, which is greater than t_{25}, transaction T_{25} would be rolled back; the transaction would be reassigned a timestamp value of, say, $t_{25}'(> t_{26})$ and rerun at step 14.

After step 9 A: 11, t_{24}, t_{24} B: 50, W_b, R_b C: 10, t_{26}, t_{26}

After step 11 A: 11, t_{24}, t_{24} B: 100, t_{26}, R_b C: 10, t_{26}, t_{26}

At step 13, the attempt by transaction T_{24} to write a value of B is ignored since t_{24}, the timestamp of T_{24}, is less than the write timestamp (t_{26}) of B, and greater than the read timestamp value (R_b) of B.

After step 14 A: 11, t_{24}, t_{24} B: 100, t_{26}, R_b C: 10, t_{26}, t_{25}'

After step 16 A: 11, t_{24}, t_{24} B: 100, t_{26}, R_b C: 30, t_{25}', t_{25}' ■

It is obvious from the above examples that the timestamping scheme ensures serializability without waiting but causes transactions to be rolled back. Since there is no waiting there is no possibility of a deadlock. However, when transactions are rolled back, a **cascading rollback** may be needed. For instance, if transaction T_{22} had written a value for a data-item Q before it was rolled back, this data-item value must be restored to its old value. If another transaction, T′, had used the modified value of the data-item Q, transaction T′ has to be rolled back as well.

The cascading rollback could be avoided by disallowing the values modified by a transaction until the transaction commits. This adds additional overhead and requires waiting as in the case of the locking scheme. Furthermore, the waiting can cause a deadlock!

12.6 Optimistic Scheduling

In the locking scheme, a transaction does a two-pass operation. In the first pass it locks all the data-items it requires and if all locks are successfully acquired, it goes through the second pass of accessing and modifying the required data-items. In the **optimistic scheduling** scheme, the philosophy is to assume that all data-items can be successfully updated at the end of a transaction and to read in the values for data-items without any locking. Reading is done when required and if any data-item is found to be inconsistent (with respect to the value read in) at the end of a transaction, then the transaction is rolled back. Since a DBMS normally has a built-in rollback facility for recovery operations, the optimistic approach does not require any additional components. For most transactions, which access the database for read-only operations and modify disjoint sets of data-items, the optimistic scheduling scheme performs better than the two-pass locking approach.

In the optimistic approach, each transaction is made up of three phases: the read phase, the validation phase, and the write phase. The read phase is not constrained but the write phase is severely constrained; any conflicts could cause a transaction to be aborted and rolled back. Note that displaying a value of a data-item or a derived value of a set of data-items to a user is equivalent to a write operation (even though no items are modified). The optimistic technique uses a timestamp method to assign an unique identifier to each transaction, as well as for the end of the validation and write phases. The three phases are described below.

Read phase: This phase starts with the activation of a transaction and is considered to last until the commit. All data-items are read into local variables and any modifications that are made are only to these local copies.

Validation phase: For data-items that were read, the DBMS will verify that the values read are still the current values of the corresponding data-items. For data-items that are modified (a deletion and an insertion can be considered as modifications), the DBMS verifies that the modifications will not cause the database to become inconsistent. Any change in the value of data-items read or any possibility of inconsistencies due to modifications causes the transaction to be rolled back.

Write phase: If a transaction has passed the validation phase, the modifications made by the transaction are committed.

The three timestamps associated with the transactions are the following:

- **t_{si}:** The start timestamp for transaction T_i. We assume that a transaction starts its read phase when it starts.
- **t_{vi}:** The timestamp for transaction T_i when it finishes its read phase and starts its validation phase. This will occur when the transaction completes. All writes prior to the start of the validation phase will be to local copies of database items and these local copies will not be accessible to other concurrent transactions.
- **t_{wi}:** The timestamp for transaction T_i when it completes its write phase. The write phase will only start if the transaction completes the validation phase successfully. After the write phase, all modifications are reflected in the database.

A transaction such as T_j can complete its validation phase successfully if at least one of the following conditions is satisfied:

- For all transactions T_i such that $t_{si} < t_{sj}$, the condition $t_{wi} < t_{sj}$ holds. This condition ensures that all older transactions must have completed their write phases before the requesting transaction began.
- For all transactions T_i such that $t_{si} < t_{sj}$, i.e., for an older transactions, the data-items modified by T_i must be disjoint from the data-items read by transactions T_j. Furthermore, all older transactions must complete their write phase before time t_{vj}. Here t_{vj} is the time at which transaction T_j finishes its read phase and starts its validation phase. This ensures that a younger transaction's writes are not overwritten by an older transition's writes.
- For all transactions T_i such that $t_{si} < t_{sj}$, i.e., for all older transactions, the data-items modified must be disjoint from the data-items read or modified by transactions T_j. Furthermore, $t_{iv} < t_{jv}$, which ensures that the older transaction, T_i, completes its read phase before T_j completes its read phase. In this way the older transaction cannot influence the read or write phase of T_j.

Consider a schedule for a set of concurrent transactions. If each transaction in this set can complete its validation phase successfully with at least one of the above conditions, then the given schedule is serializable. Example 12.9 illustrates optimistic scheduling.

Example 12.9 Consider transactions T_{22} and T_{23} of Figure 12.21 and the schedule of Figure H. The initial value; of *A* and *B* are as follows:

A: 400 B: 500

The progress of the concurrent execution of transactions T_{22} and T_{23} causes the following actions:

At steps 7 and 14, the write is only local and the actual write to the database would be delayed until all reads are completed.

As step 10, before the value of *Sum* is displayed, the validation phase for transaction T_{22} would find that there are no outstanding writes from older transactions and its validation will be successful; the value of *Sum* would be displayed.

At step 16, before the value of *Sum* is displayed, the validation phase for transaction T_{23} would find that there are no outstanding writes from older transactions and its validation would be successful. Consequently the writes to *A* and *B* as well as the display of *Sum* would be completed.

Figure H Example of optimistic scheduling.

Step	Schedule	Transaction T_{22}	Transaction T_{23}
1	*Sum* := 0	*Sum* := 0	
2	*Sum* := 0		*Sum* := 0
3	**Read**(*A*)		**Read**(*A*)
4	*A* := *A* − 100		*A* := *A* − 100
5	**Read**(*A*)	**Read**(*A*)	
6	*Sum* := *Sum* + *A*	*Sum* := *Sum* + *A*	
7	**Write**(*A*)		**Write**(*A*)
8	**Read**(*B*)	**Read**(*B*)	
9	*Sum* := *Sum* + *B*	*Sum* := *Sum* + *B*	
10	**Show**(*Sum*)	**Show**(*Sum*)	
11	*Sum* := *Sum* + *A*		*Sum* := *Sum* + *A*
12	**Read**(*B*)		**Read**(*B*)
13	*B* := *B* + 100		*B* := *B* + 100
14	**Write**(*B*)		**Write**(*B*)
15	*Sum* := *Sum* + *B*		*Sum* := *Sum* + *B*
16	**Show**(*Sum*)		**Show**(*Sum*)

■

As the optimistic scheme does not use locks, it is deadlock free even though starvation can still occur. This is because a popular item, for instance an index, can be used by many transactions and each transaction could cause it to be modified as a result of insertions or deletions. An older transaction can thus fail its validation phase continuously. The method of solving this problem involves resorting to some form of locking.

12.7 Multiversion Techniques

In the concurrency control schemes discussed so far, the arbitration that produced serializable schedules was required when one or more of the concurrent transactions using a part of the database needed to modify the data-item. Any modifications to data required that the transaction have exclusive use of the data, and other transactions would be locked out or aborted until the lock on the data-item was released.

In a database system that uses the **multiversion** concurrency scheme, each write of a data-item, e.g., X, is achieved by making a new copy or version (hence the name multiversion) of data-item X. The multiversion scheme, which is also called a **time domain addressing** scheme, follows the accounting principle of never overwriting a transaction. Any changes are achieved by entering compensating transactions. In this way, a history of the evolution of the value of a data-item is recorded in the database. As far as the users are concerned, their transaction running on a system with multiversions will work in an identical manner as a single version system.

For data-item X the database could keep the multiversion in the form of a set of triples consisting of the value, the time entered, and the time modified as shown below:

Variable: {{value, time entered, time modified}, { . . . }, . . . }

X: $\{\{x_0, t_0, t_1\}, \{x_1, t_1, t_2\}, \ldots, \{x_n, t_n, t_p\}\}$

Here the value of the data-item X is initially x_0 and this value is entered in the database at time t_0. At time t_1, the value is modified to x_1. The value x_n entered at time t_n is the last update made to data-item X. Having many versions of a data-item, it is easy to know that the value of X from time t_0 to t_1 was x_0 and so on.

When a transaction needs to read a data-item such as X for which multiple versions exist, the DBMS selects one of the versions of the data-item. The value read by a transaction must be consistent with some serial execution of the transaction with a single version of the database. Thus, the concurrency control problem is transferred into the selection of the correct version from the multiple versions of a data-item.

With the multiversion technique, write operations can occur concurrently, since they do not overwrite each other. Furthermore, the read operation can read any version. This results in greater flexibility in scheduling concurrent transactions. Many schemes have been proposed for controlling concurrency using the multiversion approach. We discuss one such scheme based on timestamping below. Concurrency control ensures, among other things, that no new version of a data-item is created such that it is based on a version that already may have been used to create yet another version. In this way the phenomenon of lost update could be avoided.

In order to choose the correct version of data to be read by a given transaction, the multiversion timestamping scheme uses the timestamp ordering of the concurrent transactions and the time parameters associated with each version of the data-items to be used by a transaction. The timestamping of transactions was discussed earlier in Section 11.5. As mentioned above, there are two time values associated with each version of a data-item X. These are the write timestamp, W_x, and the read timestamp, R_x.

The write timestamp of a version of a data-item is the timestamp value of the transaction that wrote the version of the data-item. In other words, a value of the data-item X with the write timestamp value W_x was written by a transaction with a timestamp value of W_x. Note, that here we are ignoring the time lapse from the start of the transaction to the generation of the new version. The timestamps are in reality pseudotimes and a nondecreasing counter can be used instead of a timestamp with similar results.

The read timestamp of a version of a data-item is the timestamp value of the most recent transaction that successfully read the version of the data-item. A version of the data-item with the read timestamp of R_x was read by a transaction with a timestamp value of R_x. The read timestamp value is the same as the time of modification of the value of the data-item, if another version of the data-item exists; otherwise it remains the most recent version of the data-item. This is because a new version usually will not be created without first reading the current most recent version.

If a transaction T_i with a time stamp value of t_i writes a value x_i for the kth version of a data-item X, then the kth version of X will have the value x_i. W_{xk}, the write timestamp value, and R_{xk}, the read timestamp value of X_k will both be initialized to t_i.

A transaction needing to read the value of data-item X is directed to read that version of X that was the most recent version, with respect to the timestamp ordering of the transaction. We call this version the **relative-most-recent version.** Thus, if a transaction T_a with the timestamp value of t_a needs to read the value of data-item X, it will read the version X_j such that W_{xj} is the largest write timestamp value of all versions of X that is less than or equal to t_a. The read timestamp value of version X_j of X, read by transaction T_a, is updated to t_a if $t_a > R_{xj}$.

A transaction T_a, wanting to modify a data-item value will first read the relative-most-recent version X_j of data-item X. When it tries to write a new value of X, one of the following actions will be performed:

- A new version of X, e.g., version X_j', is created and stored with the value x_j' and with the timestamp values of $W_{xj}' = R_{xj}' = t_a$, if the current value of $R_{xj} \leq t_a$. This ensures that transaction T_a was the most recent transaction to read the value of version X_j, and no other transaction has read the value that was the basis of updating by T_a.
- Transaction T_a is aborted and rolled back if the current value of $R_{xj} > t_a$. The reason is that another younger transaction has read the value of version X_j and may have used it and/or modified it. Transaction T_a was too late and it should try to rerun to obtain the current most recent version of the value of X.

It is easy to see that the value of the write timestamp is the same as the time of generation of a new version of the value of a data-item, and the read timestamp value is the same as the time of modification of the value of the data-item.

A transaction T_a with a timestamp value of t_a, writing a new version of a data-item X without first reading, creates a new version of X with the write timestamp and read timestamp values of t_a.

It can be shown that any schedule generated according to the above requirements is serializable, and the result obtained by a set of concurrent transactions is the same as that obtained by some serial execution of the set with a single version of the data-items.

Example 12.10 Consider the schedule given in Figure I for two concurrent transactions T_{22} and T_{23} of Figure 12.21. Suppose the multiversion technique is used for concurrency control. Assume initially that a single version exists for data-items *A* and *B* with their initial values being:

$$A: \{\{ 400, W_a, R_a\}\} \text{ and } B: \{\{ 500, W_b, R_b\}\}$$

Transaction T_{22} has a timestamp value of t_{22}; transaction T_{23} has a timestamp value of t_{23}.

$$t_{22} < t_{23},\ W_a < t_{22},\ R_a < t_{22},\ W_b < t_{22},\ R_b < t_{22}$$

The modifications after the following steps are:

After step 3 *A*: $\{\{400, W_a, t_{23}\}\}$
B: $\{\{500, W_b, R_b\}\}$
After step 5 *A*: $\{\{400, W_a, t_{23}\}, \{300, t_{23}, t_{23}\}\}$
B: $\{\{500, W_b, R_b\}\}$
After step 6 *A*: $\{\{400, W_a, t_{23}\}, \{300, t_{23}, t_{23}\}\}$
B: $\{\{ 500, W_b, R_b\}\}$
After step 8 *A*: $\{\{400, W_a, t_{23}\}, \{300, t_{23}, t_{23}\}\}$
B: $\{\{500, W_b, t_{22}\}\}$
After step 10 the value shown by T_{22} is 900
After step 12 *A*: $\{\{400, W_a, t_{23}\}, \{300, t_{23}, t_{23}\}\}$
B: $\{\{500, W_b, t_{23}\}\}$
After step 14 *A*: $\{\{400, W_a, t_{23}\}, \{300, t_{23}, t_{23}\}\}$
B: $\{\{ 500, W_b, t_{23}\}, \{600, t_{23}, t_{23}\}\}$
After step 16 the value shown by T_{23} is 900

Figure I Schedule for the multiversion technique.

Step	Schedule	Transaction T_{22}	Transaction T_{23}
1	*Sum* := 0	*Sum* := 0	
2	*Sum* := 0		*Sum* := 0
3	**Read**(*A*)		**Read**(*A*)
4	*A* := *A* − 100		*A* := *A* − 100
5	**Write**(*A*)		**Write**(*A*)
6	**Read**(*A*)	**Read**(*A*)	
7	*Sum* := *Sum* + *A*	*Sum* := *Sum* + *A*	
8	**Read**(*B*)	**Read**(*B*)	
9	*Sum* := *Sum* + *B*	*Sum* := Sum + B	
10	**Show**(*Sum*)	**Show**(*Sum*)	
11	*Sum* := *Sum* + *A*		*Sum* := *Sum* + *A*
12	**Read**(*B*)		**Read**(*B*)
13	*B* := *B* + 100		*B* := *B* + 100
14	**Write**(*B*)		**Write**(*B*)
15	*Sum* := *Sum* + *B*		*Sum* := *Sum* + *B*
16	**Show**(*Sum*)		**Show**(*Sum*) ■

Note: If the value of timestamp t_{22} were larger than the value of timestamp t_{23} (i.e., transaction T_{22} was younger than transaction T_{23}), then at step 5 transaction T_{23} will be aborted and rolled back. (See Exercise 12.7.)

The multiversion scheme never causes a read operation to be delayed however, the overhead of the read operation is a search for the correct version of the value of the data-item and an update of the read timestamp of the version of the value read. This is advantageous if the majority of database operations are reads and only one version is likely to exist for most of the data-items. The locking overhead is traded for the overhead of updating the read timestamp. But this gets expensive when an entire file is to be processed and thousands of records are read, requiring the writing of the read timestamp for many records!

Another drawback of the multiversion scheme is that instead of forcing transactions that modify data-items to wait, it allows them to proceed with the caveat that any transaction could be rolled back if a younger transaction reads the same value as an older transaction and the older transaction is too late in modifying the value. Serializability is achieved by rollback, which could result in cascading and hence be quite expensive.

The deadlock problem is not possible in the timestamp-based multiversion scheme, though cascading rollback is possible. This problem can be avoided by not allowing other transactions to use the versions created by uncommitted transactions.

12.8 Deadlock and Its Resolution

In the concurrent mode of operation each concurrently running transaction may be allowed to exclusively claim one or more of a set of resources. Some of the problems with this mode of operations are that of deadlock and starvation, which we illustrate with the following examples. Here T_a, T_b, T_c, . . . , T_n are a set of concurrent transactions and r_a, r_b, r_c, . . . , r_m are a set of shared data-items (resources). Each transaction can claim any number of these data-items exclusively.

Suppose we have a situation where transaction T_a has claimed data-item r_a and is waiting for data-item r_b. Data-item r_b, however, has been claimed by transaction T_b, which in turn is waiting for data-item r_c. This chain of transactions holding some data-items and waiting for additional data-items continues until we come to transaction T_i, which has claimed data-item r_i and is waiting for data-item r_a. We know that data-item r_a is held by transaction T_a! If none of these transactions is willing to release the data-items they are holding, none of these transactions can proceed. This is deadlock.

The situation of starvation can occur if there is a transaction waiting for data-item r_i. However, the resource allocation method used by the system, along with the mix of transactions, is such that every time resource r_i, becomes available, it is assigned to some other transaction. This results in transaction T_i having to continue to wait. (Not unlike waiting for Godot.)

12.8.1 Deadlock Detection and Recovery

In the deadlock detection and recovery approach, the philosophy is to do nothing to avoid a deadlock. However, the system monitors the advance of the concurrent transactions and detects the symptoms of deadlock, namely, a chain of transactions all waiting for a resource that the next transaction in the chain has obtained in an exclusive mode.

The reason for this philosophy is that if deadlocks are rare, then the overhead of ensuring that there is no deadlock is very high, and the occasional deadlock and recovery from it is a small price to pay for doing nothing until a deadlock actually develops. In addition, deadlock avoidance schemes avoid all potential deadlocks, even those that do not translate into an actual deadlock.

In order for the system to detect a deadlock, it must have the following information:

- the current set of transactions
- the current allocations of data-items to each of the transactions
- the current set of data-items for which each of the transactions is waiting.

The system uses this information and applies an algorithm to determine if some proper subset of these transactions are in a deadlock state. If the system finds this to be the case, it attempts to recover from the deadlock by breaking the cyclic chain of waiting transactions.

We present below an algorithm for deadlock detection and a method of recovery.

Deadlock Detection

A deadlock is said to occur when there is a circular chain of transactions, each waiting for the release of a data-item held by the next transaction in the chain. The algorithm to detect a deadlock is based on the detection of such a circular chain in the current system **wait-for graph.** The wait-for graph is a directed graph and contains nodes and directed arcs; the nodes of the graph are active transactions. An arc of the graph is inserted between two nodes if there is a data-item required by the node at the tail of the arc, which is being held by the node at the head of the arc. If there is a transaction, such as T_i, waiting for a data-item that is currently allocated and held by transaction T_j, then there is a directed arc from the node for transaction T_i, to the node for transaction T_j.

Figure 12.22 gives examples of the wait-for graph. In part a we have the following situation:

- Transaction T_{27} is waiting for data-items locked by transactions T_{28} and T_{31}.
- Transaction T_{28} is waiting for data-items locked by transactions T_{29} and T_{30}.
- Transaction T_{29} is waiting for data-items locked by transactions T_{31} and T_{32}.
- Transaction T_{30} is waiting for data-items locked by transaction T_{31}.
- Transaction T_{32} is waiting for data-items locked by transaction T_{33}.
- Transaction T_{33} is waiting for data-items locked by transaction T_{31}.

In the wait-for graph of Figure 12.22a there are no cycles, hence the corresponding set of transactions is free from deadlock.

Figure 12.22b represents the state of the system after a certain period of time, when transaction T_{31} makes a request for a data-item held by transaction T_{28}. This request, assuming no previous requests depicted in the wait-for graph of part a have

Figure 12.22 Wait-for graph showing (a) no cycle and hence no deadlock; (b) a cycle and hence a deadlock.

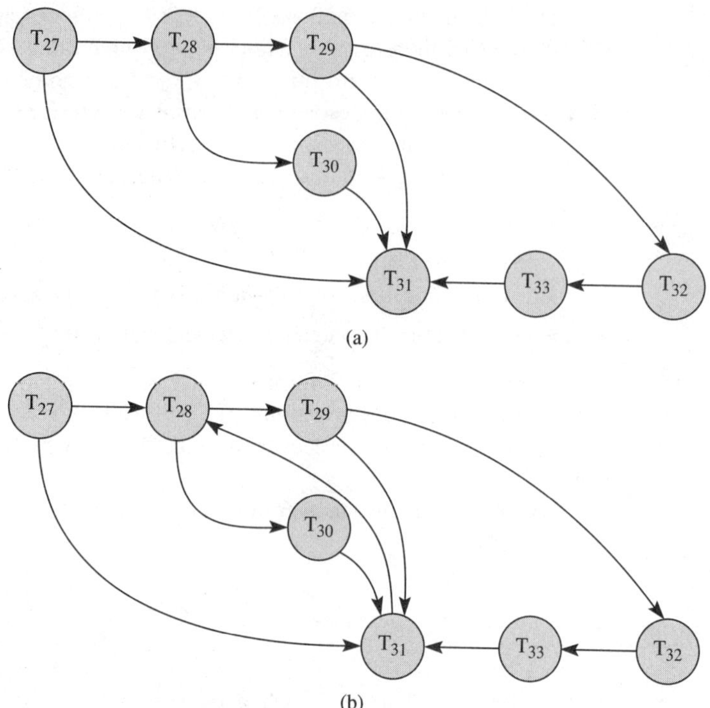

been satisfied, adds the arc from the node for transaction T_{31} to the node for transaction T_{28}. The addition of this arc causes the wait-for graph to have a number of cycles. One of these cycles is indicated by the arc from transaction T_{28} to transaction T_{30}, then, from transaction T_{30} to T_{31}, and finally from T_{31} back to T_{28}. Consequently part b represents a situation where a number of sets of transactions are deadlocked.

Since a cycle in the wait-for graph is a necessary and sufficient condition for deadlock to exist, the deadlock detection algorithm generates the wait-for graph at regular intervals and examines it for a chain. If the interval chosen is very small, deadlock detection will add considerable overhead; if the interval chosen is very large, there is a possibility that a deadlock will not be detected for a long period. The choice of interval depends on the frequency of deadlocks and the cost of not detecting the deadlocks for the chosen interval. The overhead of keeping the wait-for graph continuously, adding arcs as requests are blocked and removing them as locks are given up, would be very high.

The deadlock detection algorithm is given on page 598. In this algorithm we use a table called Wait_for table. It contains columns for each of the following: transaction IDs; the data-items for which they have acquired a lock; and the data-items they are waiting for (these wait-for items are currently locked in an incompatible mode by other transactions). The algorithm starts with the assumption that there is no deadlock. It locates a transaction, T_s, which is waiting for a data-item. If the data-item is currently locked by transaction T_r, the latter is in the wait-for graph. If

T_r in turn is waiting for a data item currently locked by transaction T_p, this transaction is also in the wait-for graph. In this way the algorithm finds all other transactions involved in a wait-for graph starting with transaction T_s. If the algorithm finally finds that there is a transaction T_q waiting for a data-item currently locked by T_s, the wait-for graph leads back to the starting transaction. Consequently the algorithm concludes that a cycle exists in the wait-for graph and there is a potential deadlock situation.

Example 12.11 Consider the wait-for table of Figure J. The wait-for graph for the transactions in this chain is given by Figure 12.22a. It has no cycles and hence there are no deadlocks. However, if transaction T_{31} makes a request for data-item C, the wait-for graph is converted into the one given in Figure 12.22b. This graph has a cycle that starts at transaction T_{28}, goes through transactions T_{30}, T_{31}; and back to T_{28}, and Algorithm 12.2 detects it. There are other cycles as well.

Figure J Wait-for table for Example 12.11.

Transaction_Id	Data_items_locked	Data_items_waiting_for
T_{27}	*B*	*C, A*
T_{28}	*C, M*	*H, G*
T_{29}	*H*	*D, E*
T_{30}	*G*	*A*
T_{31}	*A, E*	*(C)*
T_{32}	*D, I*	*F*
T_{33}	*F*	*E*

■

An adaptive system may initially choose a fairly infrequent interval to run the deadlock detection algorithm. Every time a deadlock is detected, the deadlock detection frequency could be increased, for example, to twice the previous frequency and every time no deadlock is detected, the frequency could be reduced, for example, to half the previous frequency. Of course an upper and lower limit to the frequency would have to be established.

Recovery from Deadlock

To recover from deadlock, the cycles in the wait-for graph must be broken. The common method of doing this is to roll back one or more transactions in the cycles

Algorithm 12.2 Deadlock Detection

Input and Data Structure Used: A table called Wait_for_Table that contains: transaction IDs, the data-items they have acquired a lock on, and the data-items they are waiting for (these wait-for items are currently locked in an incompatible mode by other transactions). A Boolean variable Deadlock_situation. A first-in, first-out stack, Transaction_stack, to hold transaction IDs: this stack will contain the transactions in a deadlocked chain if a deadlock is detected.

Output Whether the system is deadlocked and if so, the transactions in the cycle.

```
Initialize Deadlock_Situation to false;
Initialize Transaction_stack to empty;
for next transaction in table while not Deadlock_Situation
  begin
   Push next Transaction ID into Transaction_stack ;
    for next Data_item_waiting_for of
        transaction on top of Transaction_stack and
                  while not Deadlock_Situation
                         and not Transaction_stack empty
      begin
         D_next := next Data_item_waiting_for
         find Tran_ID of transaction which has locked D_next
         if Tran_ID is in stack
           then Deadlock_Situation := true
           else Push Tran_ID to Transaction_stack
         end
   Pop Transaction_stack
   end
```

until the system exhibits no further deadlock situation. The selection of the transactions to be rolled back is based on the following considerations:

- The progress of the transaction and the number of data-items it has used and modified. It is preferable to roll back a transaction that has just started or has not modified any data-item, rather than one that has run for a considerable time and/or has modified many data-items.
- The amount of computing remaining for the transaction and the number of data-items that have yet to be accessed by the transaction. It is preferable not to roll back a transaction if it has almost run to completion and/or it needs very few additional data-items before its termination.
- The relative cost of rolling back a transaction. Notwithstanding the above considerations, it is preferable to roll back a less important or noncritical transaction.

Once the selection of the transaction to be rolled back is made, the simplest scenario consists of rolling back the transaction to the start of the transaction, i.e., abort the transaction and restart it, *de nouveau*. If, however, additional logging is done by the system to maintain the state of all active transactions, the rollback need not be total, merely far enough to break the cycle indicating the deadlock situation. Nonetheless, this overhead may be excessive for many applications.

The process of deadlock recovery must also ensure that a given transaction is not continuously the one selected for rollback. If this is not avoided, the transaction will never (or at least for a period that looks like never) complete. This is starving a transaction!

12.8.2 Deadlock Avoidance

In the deadlock avoidance scheme, care is taken to ensure that a circular chain of processes holding some resources and waiting for additional ones held by other transactions in the chain never occurs. The two-phase locking protocol ensures serializability, but does not ensure a deadlock-free situation. This is illustrated in Example 12.12.

Example 12.12 Consider transactions T_{34} and T_{35} given in Figure K and the schedule of Figure L. These are two-phase transactions; however, a deadlock situation exists in Figure L, as transaction T_{34} waits for a data-item held by transaction T_{35}; later on, transaction T_{35} itself waits for a data-item held by T_{34}, which is already blocked from further progress.

Figure K Two-phase transactions.

Transaction T_{34}	Transaction T_{35}
Sum := 0	*Sum* := 0
Locks(*A*)	**Lockx**(*B*)
Read(*A*)	**Read**(*B*)
Sum := *Sum* + *A*	*B* := *B* + 100
Locks(*B*)	**Write**(*B*)
Read(*B*)	*Sum* := *Sum* + *B*
Sum := *Sum* + *B*	**Lockx**(*A*)
Show(*Sum*)	**Unlock**(*B*)
Unlock(*A*)	**Read**(*A*)
Unlock(*B*)	*A* := A − 100
	Write(*A*)
	Unlock(*A*)
	Sum := *Sum* + *A*
	Show(*Sum*)

Figure L Schedule leading to deadlock with two-phase transactions.

	Schedule	Transaction T_{34}	Transaction T_{35}
	Sum := 0	*Sum* := 0	
	Locks(A)	**Locks**(A)	
	Read(A)	**Read**(A)	
	Sum := *Sum* + *A*	*Sum* := *Sum* + *A*	
T	*Sum* := 0		*Sum* := 0
i	**Lockx**(B)		**Lockx**(B)
m	**Read**(B)		**Read**(B)
e	$B := B + 100$		$B := B + 100$
	Write(B)		**Write**(B)
	Sum := *Sum* + *B*		*Sum* := *Sum* + *B*
	Locks(B)	**Locks**(B)* transaction T_{34} will wait	
↓	**Lockx**(A)		**Lockx**(A)* T_{35} will wait

■

One of the simplest methods of avoiding a deadlock situation is to lock all data-items at the beginning of a transaction. This has to be done in an atomic manner, otherwise there could be a deadlock situation again. The main disadvantage of this scheme is that the degree of concurrency is lowered considerably. A transaction typically needs a given data-item for a very short interval. Locking all data-items for the entire duration of a transaction makes these data-items inaccessible to other concurrent transactions. This could be the case even though the transaction holding a lock on these data-items may not need them for a long time after it acquires a lock on them.

Another approach used in avoiding deadlock is assigning an order to the data-items and requiring the transactions to request locks in a given order, such as only ascending order. Thus, data-items may be ordered as having rank 1, 2, 3, and so on. A transaction T requiring data-items *A* (with a rank of i) and *B* (with a rank of j with j > i) must first request a lock for the data-item with the lowest rank, namely *A*. When it succeeds in getting the lock for *A*, only then can it request a lock for data-item *B*. All transactions follow such a protocol, even though within the body of the transaction the data-items are not required in the same order as the ranking of the data-items for lock requests. This scheme reduces the concurrency, but not to the same extent as the first scheme.

Another set of approaches to deadlock avoidance is to decide whether to wait or abort and roll back a transaction, if a transaction finds that the data-item it requests is locked in an incompatible mode by another transaction. The decision is controlled by timestamp values. Aborted and rolled back transactions retain their timestamp values and hence their "seniority." So, in subsequent situations, they would eventually get a "higher priority." We examine below two such approaches called wait-die and wound-wait.

Figure 12.23 Example of wait-die deadlock prevention scheme.

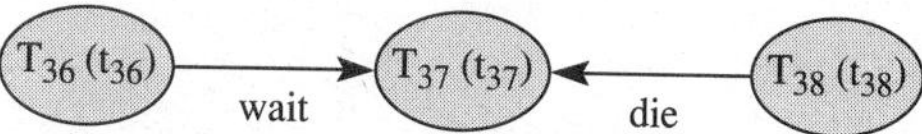

Wait-Die

One solution in a case of contention for a data-item is as follows:

- If the requesting transaction is older than the transaction that holds the lock on the requested data-item, the requesting transaction is allowed to wait.
- If the requesting transaction is younger than the transaction that holds the lock on the requested data-item, the requesting transaction is aborted and rolled back.

This is called the **wait-die** scheme of deadlock prevention.

If concurrent transactions T_{36}, T_{37}, and T_{38} (having timestamp values of t_{36}, t_{37}, and t_{38}, respectively, with $t_{36} < t_{37} < t_{38}$) have at some instance a wait-for graph, as shown in Figure 12.23, then transaction T_{36} would be allowed to wait, but transaction T_{38} would be aborted and rolled back.

Wound-Wait

An opposite approach to the wait-die scheme is called the **wound-wait** scheme. Here the decision whether to wait or abort is as follows:

- If a younger transaction holds a data-item requested by an older one, the younger transaction is the one that would be aborted and rolled back (the younger transaction is wounded by the older transaction and dies!).
- If a younger transaction requests a data-item held by an older transaction, the younger transaction is allowed to wait.

For the request shown in Figure 12.24, where transaction T_{39} has a smaller timestamp value than transaction T_{40}, the younger transaction T_{40} would be aborted and rolled back, thus freeing the data-item locked by it to be used by transaction T_{39}.

For the request shown in Figure 12.25, where transaction T_{41} has a smaller timestamp value than transaction T_{42}, the younger transaction T_{42} is allowed to wait for the completion of the older transaction T_{41}.

We observe that in neither the wait-die scheme nor the wound-wait scheme is it required to abort and roll back an older transaction. In this way the older transaction

Figure 12.24 Example of wounding request.

Figure 12.25 Example of waiting request.

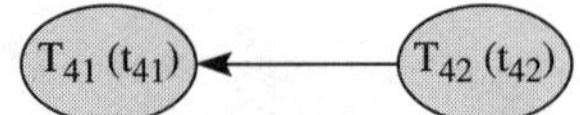

would eventually get all the data-items it needs and would run to completion. This implies that this scheme minimizes problem of starvation. However, the waiting that may be required by an older transaction could be significantly higher in the wait-die scheme. This because the older transaction has to wait for younger transactions to finish using popular data-items. On the other hand, in the wound-wait scheme, the older a transaction gets, the greater its probability of acquiring a data-item. An older transaction would force the abortion of any younger transaction that holds data-items it needs, but would only be aborted by a transaction older than itself. However, as a transaction gets older, the number of more senior transactions would decrease!

In the wait-die and the wound-wait schemes the first word of the scheme name indicates what the older transaction does when there is contention for a data-item. In the first scheme the older transaction waits for the younger transaction to finish; in the second scheme, the older transaction wounds the younger transaction, which releases the data-item for the older transaction. The second component indicates what a younger transaction does when there is a contention with an older transaction. In the first scheme the younger transaction is aborted and in the second, the younger transaction waits.

The number of aborts and rollbacks tend to be higher in the wait-die scheme than in the wound-wait scheme. This because, when a younger transaction such as T_y makes a requests for a data-item held by an older transaction, the younger transaction is aborted and rolled back. However, it is reinitiated with the original timestamp, which it retains. The reinitiated transaction T_y will make the same requests as in its last life, and it is likely that some of the data-items may still be held by older transactions. So transaction T_y dies again, to be born again, and so on. On the other hand, in the wound-wait scheme the younger transaction T_y is aborted by an older transaction because the younger transaction holds a data-item needed by the older transaction. When transaction T_y is reinitiated, it will request the same data-items as in its last life. However, these data-items may still be held by the older transaction, hence the younger transaction merely waits.

In addition to deadlock, the problem of starvation (where one or more transactions are forced to wait indefinitely) is also possible. For example, the situation can develop where, among the data-items required by some transaction, at least one of them is found to be locked by another concurrent transaction.

In conclusion, we note that the disadvantage of requesting all data-items at the beginning of a transaction, and the ordered data-item request method for deadlock avoidance, is the potential lower degree of concurrency. The advantage of these schemes is that there is no deadlock detection overhead. The disadvantage of the wait-die or wound-wait deadlock avoidance schemes is that the request for a data-item held by another transaction does not necessarily imply a deadlock. Hence, the abort required in either of these schemes may be unnecessary.

12.9 Atomicity, Concurrency, and Recovery

The atomic property of a transaction has to be preserved under concurrent execution. The atomicity requirement is an additional constraint to the serializability requirement, which we discussed earlier. Nevertheless, concurrency and failure of a transaction are both responsible for not preserving the atomicity requirements. These two requirements force the situation known as cascading rollback, described earlier. Consider a case where a write operation modifies the database, as in the update in place scheme (see Chapter 11). Following such write operations by a transaction and the subsequent unlocking of the data-items, the updated values are accessible to other concurrent transactions. However, the first transaction may have to be aborted and rolled back. This implies that all transactions that used any data-item written by a rolled-back transaction or any other data-item derived from such a data-item also have to be undone, resulting in cascading rollback.

The method of avoiding a cascading rollback is to prevent transactions from reading a data-item modified by an uncommitted transaction. One way of doing this is to extend all locks to the point of committing a transaction, though this reduces concurrency. Another approach requires that all writes to the database are to a log and considered as tentative. A transaction commits after it has done all its write operations. At the time of the commit, all tentative values are reflected in the database. Any transaction that needs a tentatively written data-item has to wait for the transaction to commit. Alternatively, if a transaction is allowed to use a tentative data value, it is marked for rollback in case the transaction that wrote the value is aborted.

The locking scheme of concurrency control can be considered to require the following steps: lock, read and/or write, unlock, commit. The timestamp scheme requires three steps, as follows: read, write, and commit. Optimistic scheduling also has three steps: read, validate, and write. The two latter schemes are preferable if the expected number of contentions and the resulting number of rollbacks is relatively low.

12.10 Summary

Concurrent access to a database by a number of transactions requires some type of control to preserve the consistency of the database; to ensure that the modifications made by the transactions are not lost; and to guard against transactions reading data that are inconsistent. A number of concurrency control schemes were discussed in this chapter.

Concurrent execution of transactions implies that the operations from these transactions may be interleaved. This is not the same as serial execution of the transactions, where each transaction is run to completion before the next transaction is started. The serializability criterion is used to test whether or not an interleaved execution of the operations from a number of concurrent transactions is correct. The serializability test consists of generating a precedence graph from a interleaved execution schedule. If the precedence graph is acyclic, the schedule is serializable, which means that the database will have the same state at the end of the schedule as some serial execution of the transactions.

The concurrency control scheme ensures that the schedule that can be produced by a set of concurrent transactions will be serializable. One of two approaches is usually used to ensure serializability: delaying one or more contending transactions, or aborting and restarting one or more of the contending transactions. The locking protocol uses the former approach. Timestamp-based ordering, optimistic scheduling, and the multiversion technique of concurrency control use the latter.

In the locking protocol, before a transaction can access a data-item, it is required to lock the data-item in an appropriate mode. It releases the lock on the data-item once it no longer needs it. In the locking scheme, the two-phase locking protocol is usually used. The principle characteristic of the two-phase locking protocol is that all locks are acquired before a transaction starts releasing any locks. This ensures serializability; however, deadlock is possible.

With hierarchically structured storage of the database and its data-items, a different granularity of locking is implied. Thus, locking an item may imply locking all items that are its descendants. To enhance the performance of a system with hierarchically structured data, additional modes of locking are introduced. Thus, in addition to read and write locks, intention locks are required. The locking protocol is modified to require a root-to-leaf direction of lock requests and the reverse direction of lock releases.

In timestamp-based ordering, each transaction is assigned an unique identifier, which is usually based on the system clock. This identifier is called a timestamp and the value of the time-stamp is used to schedule contending transactions. The rule is to ensure that a transaction with a smaller timestamp (older) is effectively executed before a larger (younger) transaction. Any variation from this rule is corrected by aborting a transaction, rolling back any modifications made by it, and starting it again.

In optimistic scheduling, the philosophy is that a contention between transactions will be very unlikely and any data-item used by a transaction is not likely to be used for modification by any other transaction. This assumption is valid for transactions that only read the data-item. If this assumption is found to be invalid for a given transaction, the transaction is aborted and rolled back.

In the multiversion technique, data is never written over; rather, whenever the value of a data-item is modified, a new version of the data-item is created. The result is that the history of the evolution of a data-item is maintained. A transaction is assigned an unique timestamp and is directed to read the appropriate version of a data-item. The write operation of a transaction, such as T, could cause a new version of the data-item to be generated. However, in case another transaction has already produced a new version of the data-item based on the version used by transaction T, an attempt to write a modified value for the data-item by transaction T causes transaction T to be aborted, rolled back, and restarted as a new and younger transaction.

Deadlock is a situation that arises when data-items are locked in different order by different transactions. A deadlock situation exists when there is a circular chain of transactions, each transaction in the chain waiting for a data-item already locked by the next transaction in the chain. Deadlock situations can be either avoided or detected and recovered from. One method of avoiding deadlock is to ask for all data-items at one time. An alternative is to assign a rank to each data-item and request locks for data-items in a given order. A third technique depends on selectively aborting some transactions and allowing others to wait. The selection is based on the timestamp of the contending transactions, and the decision as to which transactions to abort and which to allow to wait is determined according to the preemptive protocol being used. The wait-die and the wound-wait are two such preemptive protocols.

Deadlock detection depends on detecting the existence of a circular chain of transactions and then aborting or rolling back one transaction at a time until no further deadlocks are present. The wait-for graph is generated periodically by the system to enable it to detect a deadlock.

Key Terms

starvation
livelock
schedule
lost update
inconsistent read
phantom phenomenon
serial execution
serializable schedule
precedence graph
acyclic graph
cyclic graph
read-before-write protocol
concurrency control
lock
locking
lock manager
exclusive lock
shared lock
two-phase locking
growing phase
contracting phase
granularity
intention mode
intention share mode
intention exclusive mode
share and intention exclusive mode
tree-locking protocol
directed acyclic graph (DAG)
timestamp ordering
write timestamp
read timestamp
cascading rollback
optimistic scheduling
read phase
validation phase
write phase
multiversion
time-domain addressing
relative-most-recent version
wait-for graph
wait-die
wound-wait

Exercises

12.1 Consider two transactions as follows:

Transaction 1: $Fac\_Salary_i := 1.1 * Fac\_Salary_i + 1025.00$

Transaction 2: $Average\_Fac\_Salary := \sum_{i=1}^{N} Fac\_Salary_i / N$

What precaution, if any, would you suggest if these were to run concurrently? Write a pseudocode program for these transactions using an appropriate scheme to avoid undesirable results.

12.2 Consider that the adjustment of salary of the faculty members is done as follows, where Fac_Salary_i represents the salary of the ith faculty member:

Transaction 1: $Fac\_Salary_i := Fac\_Salary_i + 1025$
Transaction 2: $Fac\_Salary_i := Fac\_Salary_i * 1.1$

What precaution, if any, would you suggest if these were to run concurrently? Write a pseudocode program for these transactions using an appropriate scheme to avoid undesirable results.

12.3 Consider the schedule of Figure 12.8a. What is the value of A and B, if $f_1(A)$ is $A + 10$, $f_2(B)$ is $B * 1.2$, $f_3(B)$ is $B = 20$, and $f_4(A)$ is $A * 1.2$? Assume that the initial values of A and B are 1000 and 200, respectively.

12.4 Repeat Exercise 12.3 for the schedule of Figure 12.9a.

12.5 Consider the transactions of Figure 12.21. Rewrite the transactions using the two-phase protocol and produce a schedule that is serializable.

12.6 Write an algorithm to find a cycle in a precedence graph. (Hint: Use an approach similar to that of algorithm 12.1)

12.7 Consider the transactions of Figure 12.21 and the schedule of Figure I. What would happen at step 5 if $t_{22} > t_{23}$? Complete the schedule after step 5 and give the values for A and B after each step. Assume that the initial values are A: {400, W_a, R_a} and B: {500, W_b, R_b}.

12.8 Given the following schedule of Figure M, in a system where timestamp ordering is used, suppose transactions T_{22} and T_{23} had been assigned timestamps t_{22} and t_{23} respectively and *Sum* is a local variable. Any value read in from the database is copied into local variables with the same names as the corresponding database items. The database items are only changed with a write statement. If initially A: {400, W_a, R_a} and B: {500, W_b, R_b}, indicate their values after steps 3, 5, 7, 8, 12 and 14.

Figure M Schedule for Exercise 12.8.

Step	Schedule	Transaction T_{22}	Transaction T_{23}
1	*Sum* := 0	*Sum* := 0	
2	*Sum* := 0		*Sum* := 0
3	**Read**(*A*)		**Read**(*A*)
4	*A* := *A* − 100		*A* := *A* − 100
5	**Read**(*A*)	**Read**(*A*)	
6	*Sum* := *Sum* + *A*	*Sum* := *Sum* + *A*	
7	**Write**(*A*)		**Write**(*A*)
8	**Read**(*B*)	**Read**(*B*)	
9	*Sum* := *Sum* + *B*	*Sum* := *Sum* + *B*	
10	**Show**(*Sum*)	**Show**(*Sum*)	
11	*Sum* := *Sum* + *A*		*Sum* := *Sum* + *A*
12	**Read**(*B*)		**Read**(*B*)
13	*B* := *B* + 100		*B* := *B* + 100
14	**Write**(*B*)		**Write**(*B*)
15	*Sum* := *Sum* + *B*		*Sum* := *Sum* + *B*
16	**Show**(*Sum*)		**Show**(*Sum*)

12.9 We have three transactions, T_{24}, T_{25}, and T_{26}, with timestamp values of t_{24}, t_{25}, and t_{26}, respectively ($t_{24} < t_{25} < t_{26}$). The schedule for the concurrent execution of these transactions is given in Figure N. Assuming that initially A: a, W_a, R_a and B: b, W_b, R_b and C: c, W_c, R_c, show these values after each step if the timestamp-ordering scheme for concurrency control is used.

Figure N Schedule for Exercise 12.9.

Step	Schedule	Transaction T_{24}	Transaction T_{25}	Transaction T_{26}
1	**Read**(A)	**Read**(A)		
2	$A := f_1(A)$	$A := f_1(A)$		
3	**Read**(B)			**Read**(B)
4	**Write**(A)	**Write**(A)		
5	**Read**(C)		**Read**(C)	
6	$C := f_2(C)$		$C := f_2(C)$	
7	**Read**(C)			**Read**(C)
8	**Write**(C)		**Write**(C)	
9	**Read**(B)	**Read**(B)		
10	$B := f_3(B)$			$B := f_3(B)$
11	**Write**(B)			**Write**(B)
12	$B := f_4(B)$	$B := f_4(B)$		
13	**Write**(B)	**Write**(B)		

12.10 Suppose we want to add a record occurrence to record type R_1, (Figure 12.19) which uses indexes I_{11} and I_{12} for direct access to the records. Give the sequence of locking to perform this operation.

12.11 Algorithm 12.2 is inefficient because some transactions are processed many times. Give a modification to the algorithm to avoid this inefficiency.

12.12 In an adaptive deadlock detection scheme, why is it necessary to choose an upper and lower limit for the frequency of running the deadlock detection algorithm?

12.13 In the concurrency control scheme based on timestamp ordering, we have assumed that the timestamp value is based on a systemwide clock. Instead of using such a timestamp to determine the ordering, suppose a pseudorandom number generator was used. Show how you would modify the concept of older and younger transactions with this modification and give the modified wait-die and wound-wait protocols.

Bibliographic Notes

Gray in (Gray 79) presents comprehensive operating system requirements for a database system. The transaction concept and its limitations are discussed in (Gray 81). The serializability concept, the two-phase locking protocol, and its correctness is due to the early work by Eswaran et al. (Eswa 79) in connection with System R. The extension of the serializability test for read-only and write-only cases are discussed in (Papa 79). The algorithm for this case is developed in (Bern 79), and the text by Ullmann (Ullm 82) also treats this topic. Locking schemes, multigranularity, and intention-locking extensions are discussed in (Gray 75). Extensions to lock modes and deadlock avoidance are discussed in (Kort 82) and (Kort 83).

(Reed 79) presented the earliest known multiversion timestamping algorithm. The use of a pseudotimestamp was discussed in (Reed 83) and (Svob 80). It is shown in (Bern 83) that any schedule generated according to the timestamp concurrency control algorithm requirements is serializable, and the result obtained by a set of concurrent transactions is the same as obtained by some serial execution of the set of transactions with a single version of the data-items. The reader interested in the multiversion concurrency control algorithms based on locking is referred to (Baye 80) and (Ster 81). The extension of the locking scheme and locking with timestamp ordering (combination scheme) is discussed in (Bern 83). The combination scheme was discussed in (Chan 82). The tree-locking protocol for a database whose storage is tree structured is discussed in (Silb 80) and this protocol is generalized to the read-only and write-only locks in (Kade 80). (Bern 80) presents a number of different distributed database concurrency control schemes based on timestamping.

An optimistic method for concurrency control is presented in (Kung 81). (Rose 79) proposed the wait-die and wound-wait transaction retry schemes to avoid deadlocks in a distributed database system, although these schemes are applicable to a centralized database system as well.

The deadlock problem is surveyed in (Coff 71) and (Holt 72). (Islo 80) discusses the general deadlock problem and examines the problems unique to database systems, both centralized and distributed.

Bibliography

(Bass 88) M. A. Bassiouni, "Single-Site and Distributed Optimistic Protocols for Concurrency Control," *IEEE-SE* SE 14 (8), August 1988, pp. 1071–1080.

(Baye 80) H. Bayer, H. Heller, & A. Reiser, "Parallelism and Recovery in Database Systems," *ACM TODS* 5(4), June 1980, pp. 139–156.

(Bern 79) P. A. Bernstein, D. W. Shipman, & W. S. Wong, "Formal Aspects of Serializability in Database Concurrency Control," *IEEE-SE* SE 5 (3), May 1979, pp. 203–215.

(Bern 80) P. A. Bernstein, & N. Goodman, "Timestamp-Based Algorithms for Concurrency Control in Distributed Systems," Proc. 6th International Conf. on Very Large Data Bases, Montreal, October 1980, pp. 285–300.

(Bern 83) P. A. Bernstein, & N. Goodman, "Multiversion Concurrency Control—Theory and Algorithms," *ACM TODS* 8(4), Dec. 1983, pp. 465–483.

(Caso 81) M. A. Casonova, "The Concurrency Control Problem of Database Systems," *Lecture Notes in Computer Science,* vol. 116. New York: Springer-Verlag, 1981.

(Chan 82) A. Chan, S. Fox. W. T. K. Lin, A. Nori, & D. R. Ries, "The Implementation of an Integrated Concurrency Control and Recovery Scheme," Proc. ACM/SIGMOD Conf. on Management of Data, Orlando, Florida, June 1982, pp. 184–191.

(Coff 71) E. G. Coffman, M. J. Elphick, & A. Shoshani, "System Deadlocks," *ACM Computing Surveys* 3(2), June 1971, pp. 67–88.

(Eswa 79) K. P. Eswaran, J. N. Gray, R. A. Lorie, & I. L. Traiger, "The Notion of Consistency and Predicate Locks in a Database System," *CACM,* 19(11), November 1979, pp. 624–633.

(Gray 75) J. N. Gray, R. A. Lorie, & G. R. Putzolu, "Granularity of Locks in a Shared Data Base," Proc. of the VLDB, 1975, pp. 428–451.

(Gray 79) J. N. Gray, "Notes on Data Base Operating Systems," in R. Bayer, R. M. Graham, & G. Seegmuller, eds., *Operating Systems: An Advanced Course*. Berlin: Springer-Verlag, 1979.

(Gray 81) J. N. Gray, "The Transaction Concept: Virtues and Limitations," Proc of the 7th VLDB Conference, 1981, pp. 144–154.

(Holt 72) R. C. Holt, "Some Deadlock Properties of Computer Systems," *ACM Computing Surveys* 4(3), September 1972, pp. 179–196.

(Hunt 79) H. B. Hunt, & D. J. Rosenkrantz, "The Complexity of Testing Predicate Locks," Proc. ACM-SIGMOD 1979 International Conference on Management of Data, May 1979, pp. 127–133.

(Islo 80) S. S. Isloor, & T. A. Marsland, ''The Deadlock Problem: An Overview,'' *Computer* 13(9), September 1980, pp. 58–78.

(Kade 80) Z. Kadem, & A. Silberschatz, ''Non-Two Phase Locking Protocols with Shared and Exclusive Locks,'' Proc. 6th International Conf. on Very Large Data Bases, Montreal, October 1980, pp. 309–320.

(Kort 82) H. F. Korth, ''Deadlock Freedom Using Edge Locks,'' *ACM TODS* 7(4), December 1982, pp. 632–652.

(Kort 83) H. F. Korth, ''Locking Primitives in a Database System,'' *ACM JACM* 30(1), January 1983, pp. 55–79.

(Kung 79) H. T. Kung, & C. H. Papadimitriou, ''An Optimality Theory of Concurrency Control for Databases,'' Proc. ACM-SIGMOD 1979 International Conference on Management of Data, May 1979, pp. 116–126.

(Kung 81) H. T. Kung, & J. T. Robinson, ''On Optimistic Methods for Concurrency Control,'' *ACM Trans. on Database Systems* 6(2), June 1981, pp. 213–226.

(Lync 83) N. A. Lynch, ''Multilevel Atomicity—A New Correctness Criterion for Database Concurrency Control,'' *ACM TODS* 8(4), September 1983, pp. 484–502.

(Papa 79) C. H. Papadimitriou, ''The Serializability of Concurrent Database Updates,'' *JACM* 26(4), October 1979, pp. 150–157.

(Reed 79) D. P. Reed, ''Naming and Synchronization in a Decentralized Computer System,'' MIT/LCS/TR-205, Cambridge, MA: MIT, September 1979.

(Reed 83) D. P. Reed, ''Implementing Atomic Actions on Decentralized Data,'' *ACM Transactions on Computer Systems* 1(1), pp. 3–23.

(Rose 79) D. J. Rosenkrantz, R. E. Stearns, & P. M. Lewis II, ''System Level Concurrency Control for Distributed Data Base Systems,'' *ACM TODS* 3(2), March 1978, pp. 178–198.

(Silb 80) A. Silberschatz, & Z. Kadem, ''Consistency in Hierarchical Database Systems,'' *JACM,* 27(1), January 1980, pp. 72–80.

(Ster 81) R. E. Stern, & D. J. Rosenkrantz, ''Distributed Database Concurrency Controls Using Before-Values,'' Proc. ACM/SIGMOD Conf. on Management of Data, 1981, pp. 74–83.

(Svob 80) L. Svobodova, ''Management of Object Histories in the Swallow Repository,'' MIT/LCS/TR-243, Cambridge, MA: MIT, July, 1980.

(Ullm 82) J. D. Ullman, *Principles of Database Systems.* Rockville, MD: Computer Science Press, 1982.

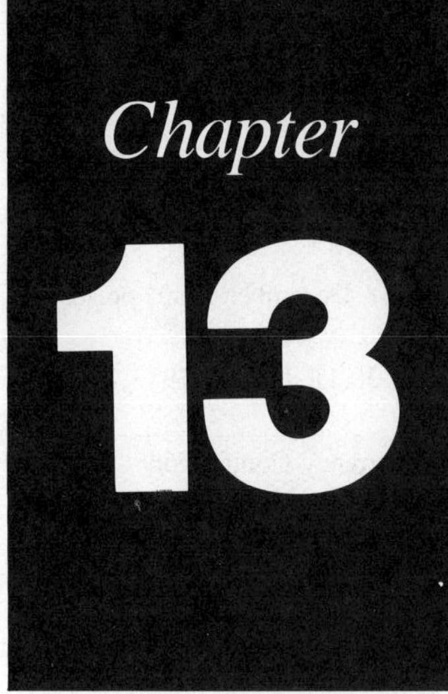

Database Security, Integrity, and Control

Contents

Security in a database involves both policies and mechanisms to protect the data and ensure that it is not accessed, altered, or deleted without proper authorization. Integrity implies that any properly authorized access, alteration, or deletion of the data in the database does not change the validity of the data. Security and integrity concepts, though distinct, are related. Implementation of both security and integrity requires that certain controls in the form of constraints must be built into the system. The DBA, in consultation with the security administrators, specifies these controls. The system enforces the controls by monitoring the actions of the users and limiting their actions within the constraints specified for them.

13.1 Introduction

It is generally recognized that access to up-to-date information is of vital importance to an organization. With the increasing amount of information under the control of DBMSs and the consequent dependence of organizations on databases, it is mandatory that these databases be secured from unauthorized access or manipulations. Data has to be protected in the database. There is a similar need for protection in a non-database environment, however, the database system must have features to enhance these manual confidentiality mechanisms. The database environment contains data from the most mundane to the most vital and this data is concurrently shared by a multitude of oneline users. Furthermore, modifications in a database mean that old values are no longer accessible; the fact that there was an old value for a given data item is not even evident unless steps are taken in processing to save the old value. Coupled with the trust and reliability with which users tend to treat the data in the database, the mechanisms of security and integrity are significant. The DBMS must have mechanisms to restrict users to only those pieces of data that are required for the functions they perform. In addition, the DBMS must restrict the type of actions that these users can perform on data that is accessible to them.

There are two dimensions for the protection of data in the database. First, a certain class of data is available only to those persons who are authorized to access it. This ensures that the confidentiality of the data is maintained. For example, the medical records of patients in a hospital are accessible only to health care officials.

Second, the data must be protected from accidental or intentional (malicious) corruption or destruction. For example, tampering with prescriptions could endanger lives. Data on national defense is vital to the security of a state. Manufacturing processes and techniques are vital to the competitive edge of a corporation. Disclosure of data regarding manufacturing processes or techniques would compromise the economical success of an enterprise. Destroying the customer mailing list of a retail sales organization could lead to the disruption of its operations.

In addition to the economic or strategic reasons for protecting data from unauthorized access, corruption, or destruction, there is a privacy dimension for data security and integrity. Tampering with the personal records of individuals is recognized in many countries as violating the privacy of the individual. Additionally, there are legal restrictions that data can only be used for the purpose for which it is collected.

Below are some informal definitions of the terms used in this chapter:

- **Privacy:** The ethical and legal rights that individuals have with regard to control over the dissemination and use of their personal information.

- **Database security:** Protection of the information contained in the database against unauthorized access, modification, or destruction.
- **Database integrity:** The mechanism that is applied to ensure that the data in the database is correct and consistent. The term **semantic integrity** is sometimes used to refer to the need for maintaining database consistency in the presence of user modifications. Semantic integrity is maintained either implicitly by the data model, or is specified explicitly by appropriate constraints on the data that can be entered by the user, and this data is checked by the DBMS. Entity and referential integrity constraints are implicit in the relational data model. Set insertion and retention rules are implicit in the network model. A record occurrence in the network model is restricted to be a member in only one occurrence of a set type. The requirement that an instance of a child type record cannot exist without the parent record occurrence is implicit in the hierarchical model. We discuss integrity issues further in Section 13.4.
- **Authorization:** The culmination of the administrative policies of the organization, expressed as a set of rules that can be used to determine which user has what type of access to which portion of the database. Persons who are in charge of specifying the authorization of different portions of the database are usually called **security administrators** or **authorizers.**

13.2 Security and Integrity Threats

Some types of threats can only be addressed using social, behavioral, and control mechanisms such as ethical training, expected conduct by the employees of an organization, and appropriate legislation. These threats include actions on the part of authorized users to perform actions such as deliberately adding unauthorized users, giving some users more access than required for their normal operations, divulging passwords, and threatening bribery and blackmail. However, in spite of the most stringent legislation and penalties for transgressions, there will always be lapses in any system, computerized or not. The intention of the DBMS is to make it unprofitable, economically or otherwise, for casual users to breach the security mechanism.

In addition to features required in the DBMS for security and integrity, additional requirements have to be supported by the operating system and the protocol for physical access to the computing system itself.

The operating system must ensure that files belonging to the database are not used directly without proper authorization. This authorization can consist of the user providing the proper passwords for the file. The operating system must also ensure that illegal users using public communication facilities are not allowed access to the system. Users must be required to use adequate identification and passwords (passwords must be sufficiently long and must be changed frequently to thwart intruders and hackers).

Access to the computing facility and the storage medium must be restricted to authorized persons only. There must be adequate physical protection, as in the case of any valuable asset. Disposal of old storage devices must be done in a proper manner. Any sensitive data resident on storage devices to be disposed of must be destroyed.

In a telecommunications environment, data may be accessed by eavesdroppers, wiretappers, and other illegal users. To prevent this type of threat, data transmitted over public communication channels should be in a ciphered form.

We can classify security and integrity threats in the categories of accidental, or intentional or malicious.

Accidental Security and Integrity Threats

- A user can get access to a portion of the database not normally accessible to that user due to a system error or an error on the part of another user. For example, if an application programmer accidentally omits appropriate verification routines, the resulting programs would compromise the database.
- Failures of various forms during normal operation, for example, transaction processing or storage media loss. Proper recovery procedures are normally used to recover from failures occurring during transaction processing. Lack of such procedures could lead to inconsistencies in the database as discussed in Chapter 11.
- Concurrent usage anomalies. Proper synchronization mechanisms are used to avoid data inconsistencies due to concurrent usage. We discussed these problems in Chapter 12.
- System error. A dial-in user may be assigned the identity of another dial-in user who was disconnected accidentally or who hung up without going through a log-off procedure.
- Improper authorization. The authorizer can accidentally give improper authorization to a user, which could lead to database security and/or integrity violations.
- Hardware failures. For example, memory protection hardware that fails could lead to software errors and culminate in database security and/or integrity violations.

Malicious or Intentional Security and Integrity Threats

- A computer system operator or system programmer can intentionally bypass the normal security and integrity mechanisms, alter or destroy the data in the database, or make unauthorized copies of sensitive data.
- An unauthorized user can get access to a secure terminal or to the password of an authorized user and compromise the database. Such users could also destroy the database files.
- Authorized users could pass on sensitive information under duress or for personal gain.
- System and application programmers could bypass normal security in their programs by directly accessing database files and making changes and copies for illegal use.
- An unauthorized person could get access to the computer system, physically or by using a communications channel, and compromise the database.

13.3 Defense Mechanisms

Four levels of defense are generally recognized for database security: human factors, physical security, administrative controls, and the security and integrity mechanisms built into the operating system and the DBMS.

Human Factors

At the outermost level are the human factors, which encompass the ethical, legal, and societal environments. An organization depends on these to provide a certain degree of protection. Thus, it is unethical for a person to obtain something by stealth, and it is illegal to forcibly enter the premises of an organization and hence the computing facility containing the database. Many countries have enacted legislation that makes it a crime to obtain unauthorized dial-in access into the computing system of an organization. Privacy laws also make it illegal to use information for purposes other than that for which it was collected.

An organization usually performs some type of clearance procedure for personnel who are going to be dealing with sensitive information, including that contained in a database. This clearance procedure can be a very informal one, in the form of the reliability and trust that an employee has earned in the eyes of management; or the clearance procedure could be a formal one.

The authorizer is responsible for granting proper database access authorization to the user community. Inadvertent assignment of authorization to a wrong class of users can result in possible security violations.

Physical Security

Physical security mechanisms include appropriate locks and keys and entry logs to computing facility and terminals.

Security of the physical storage devices (magnetic tapes, disk packs, etc.) within the organization and when being transmitted from one location to another must be maintained. Access to the computing facility must be guarded, since an unauthorized person can make copies of files by bypassing the normal security mechanism built into the DBMS and the operating system.

Authorized terminals from which database access is allowed have to be physically secure, otherwise unauthorized person may be able to glean information from the database using these terminals.

User identification and passwords have to be kept confidential, otherwise unauthorized users can ''borrow'' the identification and password of a more privileged user and compromise the database.

Administrative Controls

Administrative controls are the security and access control policies that determine what information will be accessible to what class of users, and the type of access that will be allowed to this class. We discuss this topic in Section 13.3.1.

DBMS and OS Security Mechanisms

The database depends on some of the protection features of the OS for security. Among the OS features required are:

- The proper mechanisms for the identification and verification of users. Each user is assigned an account number and a password. The OS ensures that access to the system is denied unless the number and password are valid. In addition, the DBMS could also require a number and password before allowing the user to perform any database operations.
- The protection of data and programs, both in primary and secondary memories. This is usually done by the OS to avoid direct access to the data in primary memory or to online files.

The DBMS has the following features for providing security and integrity: mechanisms to support concurrency; transaction management; audit and recovery data logging. In addition, the DBMS provides mechanisms for defining the authorizations for the user community and specifying semantic integrity constraints and checking.

13.3.1 Security Policies

To prevent the dissemination of sensitive information from the database to unauthorized users and thence to outside competitive or hostile agents, an organization must establish effective security policies. Database security policies are guidelines for present and future decisions regarding the maintenance of the database security. Database security mechanisms are the functions used to enforce database security policies. These functions could be implemented by a combination of one or more of the following: administrative control procedures, hardware functions, software functions, firmware functions.

The administrative control procedures are the implementation of security policies to provide protection, external to the database, operating systems, and computer hardware. An example of such administrative control procedures is to have application programs written by one team and validated by a separate team. Another administrative rule would require that passwords be a random string of alphanumeric characters, at least eight in length, and be changed regularly.

One of the first lower level decisions that has to be made is to choose the security features provided by the DBMS to adequately implement the security policies. The relative importance and sensitiveness of various parts of the database has to be determined. This will help determine the extent of protective features that can be economically justifiable for those parts of the database. As mentioned earlier, the intention is to make it economically unprofitable for the prospective data pirate.

The other policy decision that has to be made is whether the focus of security administration is integrated with the database administrator (DBA) and whether the security administration is centralized or decentralized. In the case of a decentralized security administration, the choice has to be made as to whether or not the owner of the data should also be the security administrator. In the case of shared data, the question of ownership of the database has to be settled by an administrative decision and the structure of the data has to be determined by the DBA (who could also be designated as owner). Procedures for modifications to the security control mechanism must also be enacted.

Access Control Policies

In addition to the administrative procedures, the lower level access control policies have to be determined in light of the security features provided by the DBMS and OS. Access control policies can be classified as follows:

- **Open vs. closed system:** In an open system, a user is allowed access to everything unless access is explicitly denied. In a closed system, a user is not allowed to access anything unless access is explicitly granted. A closed system enforces the **least privilege** or the **need-to-know** policy; an open system **maximizes sharing** of information and minimizes the portion that is not to be known.
- **Content-independent access control:** This policy is also called **name-dependent access control.** Access is allowed to those data objects whose names are known to the user. A data object can be a relation name and some of the associated attributes in the case of a relational database. In the case of a network database, it could be a set with the owner and member record types, with some of the associated data fields. Thus, access is independent of the contents of the data object. Consider the relation of Figure 13.1. All the employees in an organization may have content-independent access to the data object EMPLOYEE*(Employee_Name, Department, Room, Phone_No)*. The manager of the Personnel department, however, has content-independent access to the entire data object EMPLOYEE *(Employee_Name, Department, Room, Phone_No, Position, Salary)*.
- **Content-dependent access control:** In this policy the concept of least privilege can be extended to take into account the contents of the database and result in finer granularity of access control. The chairperson of a department can have content-independent access to EMPLOYEE*(Employee_Name, Department, Room, Phone_No)* and content-dependent access to EMPLOYEE*(Employee_*

Figure 13.1 The EMPLOYEE relation.

Employee_Name	*Department*	*Room*	*Phone_No*	*Position*	*Salary*
Smith	Comp Sci	A632	848-3876	Asst Prof	44500
Clark	Comp Sci	A651	848-3874	Asso Prof	49750
Turner	Chemistry	C643	848-2981	Professor	63050
Jamieson	Mathematics	M728	848-3829	Professor	61430
Bosky	Physics	P388	848-1286	Asso Prof	52800
Newton	Physics	P391	848-1291	Asst Prof	42750
Mann	Elect Eng	E389	848-8628	Asst Prof	44750

Figure 13.2 The HEAD relation.

Chairperson	*Secretary*	*Department*
Smith	Rolland	Comp Sci
Jamieson	Evans	Mathematics
Bosky	Fuhr	Physics
Turner	Horngren	Chemistry
Mann	Messer	Elect Eng

Name, Department, Room, Phone_No, Position, Salary), such that the EMPLOYEE.*Department* is the department where she is the chairperson. This can be implemented by a query modification as shown below:

select *(Employee_Name, Salary)*
from EMPLOYEE
where *Department* = Comp Sci

The above query can be modified as shown below, assuming that there is a relation HEAD with attributes *(Chairperson, Secretary,Department)* as shown in Figure 13.2.

select *(Employee_Name, Salary)*
from EMPLOYEE
where *Department* = (**select** *(Department)*
    from HEAD
    where *Chairperson* = user's name)

Access Operation Type Control Policies

Greater control over the use of data is obtained when the security policy distinguishes the type of access that is allowed to a data object. The classification of access to a data object known to the user can be as follows: read, update, insert, delete. Thus, everyone in an organization may be allowed access to the data object EMPLOYEE *(Employee_Name, Department, Room, Phone_No)* with the access type being read. The departmental secretary may be assigned update access to the EMPLOYEE.*Room* and EMPLOYEE.*Phone_No* data items, and this update access may be content dependent only to occurrences of the secretary's department. This can be implemented by a query modification as follows:

update EMPLOYEE
    Room = new room
    Phone_No = new phone number
    where *Employee_Name* = somename

The above query may be modified as follows to ensure that the departmental secretary modifies only the tuples for his own department's employees:

```
update EMPLOYEE
    Room = new room
    Phone_No = new phone number
    where Employee_Name = somename
    and where Department = (select (Department)
                            from HEAD
                            where Secretary = user's name)
```

The departmental chairperson may also be given update access to the EMPLOYEE.*Salary*. The personnel manager has read, update, insert, and delete access to the entire EMPLOYEE data object.

In addition to the above **access type control,** access control can be refined to include control over the context of access and the sequence of accesses as described below.

- **Access context control:** This type of access control is used to allow maximum access to statistical-type data without compromising confidentiality. Suppose the database contains a relation MED_HISTORY*(Employee_Name, Department, Visit Date, Diagnosis)* to record diagnoses for the employees who visit the company's health center (see Figure 13.3). A personnel manager may be allowed to access the attribute *Diagnosis* of this relation without simultaneous access to any other attributes. This enables the manager to determine the type of visits made to the health center and take appropriate actions to correct, say, some environmental problems. The personnel manager may also be allowed access to the attributes *Employee_Name, Department, Visit_Date* without simultaneous access to the attribute *Diagnosis* to verify whether an employee did in fact visit the health center and the number of visits made by a given employee or department, or on a given date.
- **Access control based on history of accesses:** To guard the confidentiality of information, it is not sufficient to depend solely on access context control, since a user can use a sequence of queries satisfying the access context control rules and yet be able to trace sensitive information to a single entity. We discuss the need for access control based on the history of accesses made by a user with respect to a statistical database in Section 13.5.

Figure 13.3 MED_HISTORY relation.

Employee_Name	*Department*	*Visit_Date*	*Diagnosis*
Smith	Comp Sci	12/03/86	bronchitis
Clark	Comp Sci	11/22/86	conjunctivitis
Fuhr	Physics	12/05/86	bronchitis
Roland	Comp Sci	12/15/86	psittacosis
Mann	Elect Eng	11/22/86	psittacosis
Horngren	Chemistry	12/05/86	shingles
Bosky	Physics	12/15/86	pleurisy

Information Flow Policies

Policies must be set up to prevent a flow of information from a secure program to an insecure program. One method of controlling the flow of information is to consider the programs to be running at different levels. A program assigned to run at a lower level of security is not allowed to access data produced by a program running at a higher level of security.

13.3.2 Authorization

As mentioned earlier, authorization is the culmination of the administrative policies of the organization, expressed as a set of rules that can be used to determine which user has what type of access of which portion of the database. The person who is in charge of specifying the authorization is usually called the authorizer. The authorizer can be distinct from the DBA and usually is the person who owns the data.

The authorization is usually maintained in the form of a table called an **access matrix.** Figure 13.4 gives an example of an access matrix. The access matrix con-

Figure 13.4 Access matrix

SUBJECTS	OBJECTS EMPLOYEE	 HEAD	 MED_HISTORY
Faculty	**read except** *Salary*	**read**	**read**[3]
Secretaries	**read except** *Salary* **update,**[1]*Room* **update,**[1]*Phone_No*	**read**	**read**[3]
Chairpersons	**read except** *Salary* **read**[2]		**read**[2] *Employee_Name, Date* **read**[3]
Physicians	**read except** *Salary*	**read**	**read** **write** **control**
Director of Personnel	**read** **write** **update** **control**	**read** **write** **update** **control**	**read** *Employee_Name, Date* **or read** *Diagnosis* but not together **read**[3]

[1]query modification **where** EMPLOYEE.*Department* = **select** *(Department)* **from** HEAD **where** *Secretary* = user's_name)

[2]query modification **where** EMPLOYEE.*Department* = **select** *(Department)* **from** HEAD **where** *Chairperson* = user's_name)

[3]query modification **where** MED_HISTORY.*Employee_Name* = user's_name

tains rows called **subjects** and columns termed **objects.** The entry in the matrix at the position corresponding to the intersection of a row and column indicate the **type of access** that the subject has with respect to the object.

Objects

An object is something that needs protection and one of the first steps in the authorization process is to select the objects to be used for security enforcement. A typical object in a database environment could be a unit of data that needs to be protected. However, the unit of data could be at some convenient size or granularity. Thus, a data field, a record, or a file could be considered an object. Another type of object that can be protected is a view or subscheme. Using views as objects and hence as units of protection automatically limits the amount of the database that can be accessed by a user.

The objects in the access matrix represent content-independent access control. However, to enforce content-dependent access control, some structure for conditions or access predicates are incorporated in the access matrix. Some examples of access predicates, expressed as query modifications, are shown in Figure 13.4.

Views as Objects

In addition to providing different ways of looking at the data in the database, views or subschemes can be used to enforce security. A user is allowed access to only that portion of the database defined by the user's view. A number of users may share a view. However, the user may create new views based on the views allowed. The advantage of this approach is that the number of objects accessible to a class of users and the entry for it in the authorization matrix is reduced to one per view. This reduces the size of the authorization matrix. The disadvantage is that the entire class of users have the same access rights.

Granularity

The usual practice is to choose the granularity of security enforcement. This could be a file, a record (relation), or a data item (attribute). The smaller the protected object, the finer the degree of specifying protection. However,. the finer granularity increases the size of the authorization matrix and the overhead in enforcing database security.

Subject

A subject is an active element in the security mechanism; it operates on objects. A subject is a user who is given some rights to access a data object. We can also treat a class of users or an application program as a subject. A user who belongs to or joins a class of users gets the access rights of that class of users. If a user belongs to more than one class of users, then the access rights for a given access made by the user depends on the class of user that is being used by that user for the access.

Access Types

The access allowed to a user could be for data manipulation or control. The manipulation operations are read, insert, delete, update. The control operations are add, drop, alter, and propagate access control. We define these operations below:

- **Read:** Allows reading only of the object.
- **Insert:** Allows inserting new occurrences of the object type, for example, a tuple in a relation. Insert access type requires that the subject has a read access as well. However, an insert access may not allow modification of existing data.
- **Delete:** Allows deleting an existing occurrence of the object type.
- **Update:** Allows the subject to change the value of the occurrence of the object. Some data-items in a record, such as the primary key attributes, however, may not be modified. For reasons discussed in Section 5.4.1, update through a view may or may not be allowed. An update authorization may not include a delete authorization as well.
- **Add:** Allows the subject to add new object types such as new relations (in relational systems), record and set types (in network systems), or record types and hierarchies (in hierarchical systems).
- **Drop:** Allows the subject to drop or delete existing object types from the database. Here we are referring to the deletion of a type and not of an occurrence.
- **Alter:** Allows the subject to add new data-items or attributes to an existing record type or relation; also allows the subject to drop existing data-items or attributes from existing record types or relations.
- **Propagate access control:** This is an additional right that determines if this subject is allowed to propagate the right over the object to other subjects. Thus, a subject S may be assigned an access right R over an object O, and in addition the right to grant this access right (or part of it) to another subject.

In the access matrix of Figure 13.4, we have indicated both content-independent access rights and content-dependent access rights; the latter have been indicated with query modification clauses.

In addition to the above access rights, a subject may have the privilege to create additional indexes for a record type or relation, execute certain application programs (another type of object), and so on.

Authorization Grant Tree

Consider a user subject. When the user has the propagate access control right over an object, he or she can pass all or part of her or his right to another subject, for instance another user. In a organization that uses the centralized security administration policy, the authorizer has all the access rights including the propagate access control right over the database. When the authorizer grants a user some rights this may be granted with the propagate access control as well. This leads to an **authorization grant tree,** as shown in Figure 13.5.

To properly revoke access rights, all paths in the access grant tree must start from the authorizer, otherwise the revocation cannot be guarded from unscrupulous

Figure 13.5 Authorization grant tree.

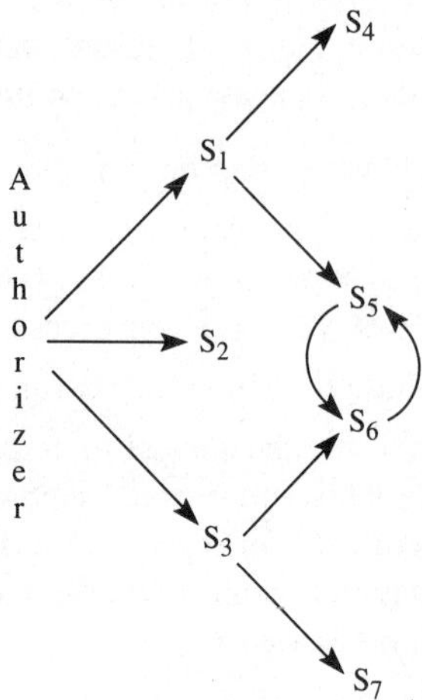

usage. With this proviso, revocation of the access rights of subject S_3 in Figure 13.5 means that subject S_7 also loses all rights. Subject S_6 retains those rights granted by S_5 and S_5 loses rights granted by S_6. We illustrate this pruned access grant tree in Figure 13.6.

Further revocation of access right of subject S_5 by S_1 causes S_6 to lose all access rights as well; this is illustrated in Figure 13.7.

Without the requirement that a direct path exists from the authorizer, the reader can verify that S_5, S_6, and S_7 would retain their access rights when the authorizer revokes the access right of subject S_3, as illustrated in Figure 13.8.

Figure 13.6 Authorization grant tree after revocation of access rights from S_3; S_6 retains the access right granted by S_5.

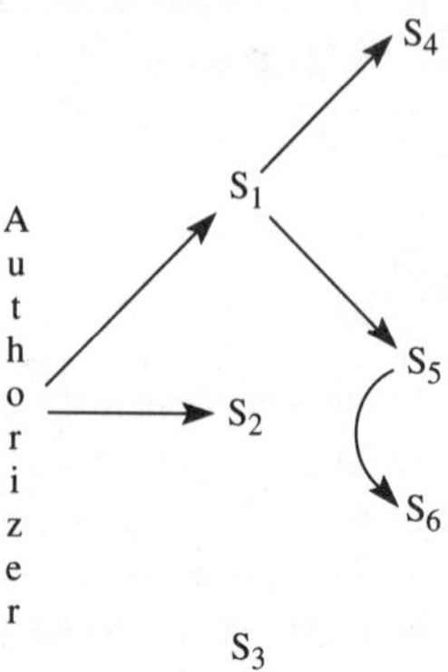

Figure 13.7 Authorization grant tree after revocation of access rights from S_5; S_6 also loses access rights.

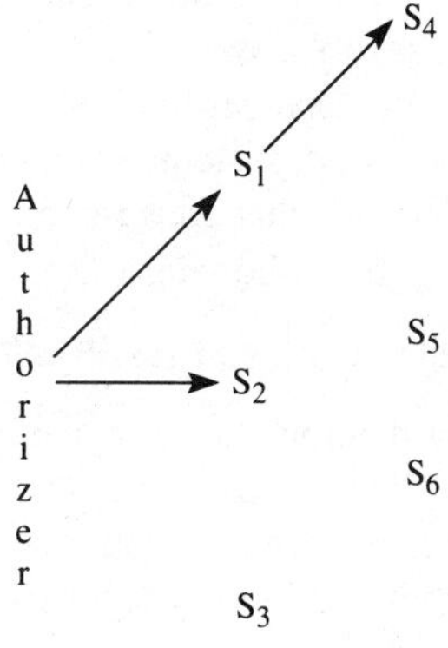

Authorization Facilities

The facility available to the authorizer (and to the users who can propagate access rights) to assign access rights could be in the form of a separate language or could be integrated with the data definition or the data manipulation language.

In the network model the access rights specifications are integrated with the data definition language. The subschema can be used to grant access to a subset of the database to an user. However, it does not provide a facility to indicate the operations that a user can perform on the portion of the database accessible to the user.

Figure 13.8 Authorization grant tree with access rights that cannot be properly revoked.

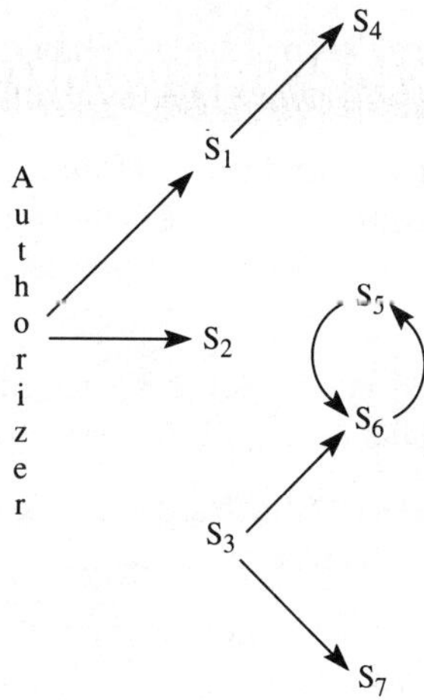

Another method of specifying the access privilege of a user is by means of a user profile. The profile for a user contains the objects and the associated access types allowed to that user as well as the application programs that the user can execute (i.e., types of transactions allowed to the user). The user profile is equivalent, in a sense, to a row of the access matrix. However, no null entries need be maintained in the user profile.

In a rule-based system, the access profile is given in the form of rules. For instance, to indicate that a user can have read access to the object EMPLOYEE could be specified by the following rule:

user 'Fuhr' **can read** EMPLOYEE

The data manipulation language can incorporate statements to grant and revoke access rights. This is the approach used in SQL to limit the operations a user can perform on the portion of a database defined by the user's view. The **grant** statement is used to grant access privileges and the **revoke** statement is used to revoke privileges. In the following example, the departmental secretaries are granted the access privilege of reading and updating a limited number of attributes from the EMPLOYEE relation. The tuples accessible to a given secretary are those belonging to his or her department.

```
grant select (Employee_Name, Room, Phone_No)
    update (Room, Phone_No) on table EMPLOYEE to
    'user_name' where EMPLOYEE.Department =
          select (Department) from HEAD where
              Secretary = 'user_name')
```

The following statements could be used to grant the personnel manager access rights to read, insert, update, or delete any tuple from the EMPLOYEE relation:

```
grant select, insert, update, delete on table EMPLOYEE to
        'personnel_manager'
```

The following form of grant allows the personnel manager to propagate the granted access rights or any subset of it to another user.

```
grant select, insert, update, delete on table EMPLOYEE to
        'personnel_manager' with grant option
```

The personnel manager can now propagate some of these access rights to the chairperson of the department by the following statement:

```
grant select, update on table EMPLOYEE to
    'chairperson_name' where EMPLOYEE.Department=
          select (Department) from HEAD where
              Chairperson = 'chairperson_name')
```

A limited number of attributes of the relation MED_HISTORY may be made accessible to the personnal manager by means of the following **grant** statement:

```
grant select(Date, Diagnosis) on table MED_HISTORY to
        'personnel_manager'
```

The limited access rights granted a secretary could be revoked by the following **revoke** statement:

revoke select update *(Room, Phone_No)* **on table** EMPLOYEE
from 'user_name'

QUEL uses the **define permit** statement to grant access authorization to a user. It specifies the operations allowed on specified attributes of a relation. The statement has provisions to optionally specify the terminal from which access is allowed and the time and day of the access. The syntax of the **define permit** statement is as follows:

define permit operations
on relation (attributes)
to user
at terminal_id
from time1 **to** time2
on day1 **to** day2
where predicates

A user may be allowed to create a new relation by means of the following access right:

grant createtab to 'user_name'

A user who can create a new relation is allowed all access rights to the relation including propagating any subset of these rights.

13.3.3 Identification and Authentication

The authorization mechanism prepares the user profile for a user and indicates the portion of the database accessible to that user and the mode of access allowed. The enforcement of the security policies in the database system requires that the system knows the identity of the user making the requests. This in turn requires that before making any request, the user has to **identify** herself or himself to the system and **authenticate** the identification to conform that the user is in fact the correct person. A number of methods can be used in this authentication: by something known only by the user, by something that only the user possesses, or by some physical/physiological characteristic of the user.

Something Known Only by the User

The simplest and most common authentication scheme used is a **password** to authenticate the user. The user enters the user name or number and then authenticates herself (himself) by the password. Typically, these identification/authentication steps are used once for the initial sign-on to the system. However, for sensitive data, this step could be repeated for each operation. The passwords themselves have to be guarded and a secure way of doing this is by storing only the encrypted form of the password. The encryption algorithm will not be of any use in deciphering the passwords. Thus, even if the file containing the enciphered passwords is stolen, it, along with the encryption algorithm, will not be useful. Application programs could also be designed to require the user to provide a password before allowing a sensitive operation.

Instead of a simple password, the system may ask the user one or more questions from a set of questions; only the user can correctly answer these questions. One such scheme involves generating a pseudorandom number *X* and prompting the user to respond with *T(X)*, where *T* is a prearranged simple transformation function. Since only the user and the system know what this prearranged transformation *T* is, anyone eavesdropping will only see *X* and *T(X)* and cannot easily discern *T*. Each authorized user in this method of authentication is supplied with unique transformation function.

Something in the User's Possession

In this scheme, each user could be given an appropriately encoded badge, card, or key to be used for identification purposes. A password or question-answering scheme as before can be used for the authentication purpose.

Some Characteristic of the User

In this scheme, the identification and authentication procedures are combined in one step, but require the use of special hardware and software to identify some physical or physiological characteristic of the user. These characteristics are known to be unique or have a very low probability of duplication in a population of a given size, and hence cannot be easily faked. Examples of such characteristics are fingerprints or the relative lengths of the fingers of a hand. Another scheme that has been proposed is the use of voiceprint; however, a simple technique like using a tape recording of the authorized user's voice can be used to impersonate the user.

13.3.4 Views/Subschemes in Security Enforcement

The content of the database is described by the conceptual scheme and the users' views are defined by the subschemes. The subscheme can be used in the name-dependent security enforcement policy to limit the portion of the database known to and hence accessible by a user. The network model as proposed in the DBTG uses the subschema as the major security enforcement mechanism. A user is not allowed access to anything that is not included in that user's subschema.

The following example illustrate creating a view for use by the departmental secretary consisting of the attributes *Employee_Name, Room,* and *Phone_No*. The tuples accessible are limited to the employees in the secretary's department.

```
create view EMP_ADDRESS (Name,Room_No, Phone) as
(select (e.Employee_Name,e.Room, e.Phone_No)
 from EMPLOYEE e
 where e.Department = (select (Department)
                        from HEAD
                        where Secretary = 'secretary_name'))
```

Having created this view, the secretary is granted appropriate access rights to any tuple of this relation and is allowed to update *Room_No, Phone* by means of the following grant statement:

grant select update *(Room_No, Phone)* **on table** EMP_ADDRESS to 'secretary_name'

13.3.5 Distributed Systems

Security enforcement in distributed systems can be enhanced by distribution. Sensitive information can be fragmented and stored at dispersed sites. The leakage of some portion of the fragmented data may be not as disastrous as the leakage of unfragmented data. Also, with distribution, different sites can have different levels of security. However, in this case, the more secure sites have to take into account the existence of less secure sites in transmitting data over the network. Since data will be transmitted over a communication channel, appropriate encryption schemes (discussed in Section 13.3.6) should be used.

The authorization functions in a distributed system have to be decentralized and a decision has to be made as to where to store the access matrix or access rules. One possible choice is to fragment the access matrix and store the appropriate fragments at the sites of the data fragments.

13.3.6 Cryptography and Encryption

Consider the secure transmission of this message:

"Mr. Watson, can you please come here."

One method of transmitting this message is to substitute a different character of the alphabet for each character in the message. If we ignore the space between words and the punctuation, and if the substitution is made by shifting each character by a different random amount, then the above message can be transformed into, e.g., the following string of characters:

"xhlkunsikevoabondwinhwoajahf."

Cryptography has been practiced since the days of the Roman Empire. With the increasing use of public communication facilities to transmit data, there is an increased need to make such transmissions secure. In a distributed environment, transmitting highly confidential information between geographically dispersed sites, in spite of the most stringent local security enforcement, could lead to leakage from eavesdropping and wiretapping.

This points to the need for the data to be encrypted before it is transmitted. At the receiving end, the received data is deciphered before it is used. The sender must know how to encrypt the data and the receiver must know how to decipher the coded message. Since the computers at both ends can be used to cipher and decipher the data, the code used for ciphering can be quite complex.

The simple enciphering method discussed at the beginning of this section turns out to be the most secure. This type of code has been used since the time of Julius Caesar and is called **Caesar code.** The **one-time code** is a Caesar *code* used only once, which makes it difficult for the interceptor of the coded message to break the code since he or she does not have an opportunity to intercept more than one sample of the coded message, apply the distribution characteristics of the language, and break the code. The other advantage of the one-time code is that breaking the code of a single transmission is not very helpful in deciphering subsequent coded messages, since each message will use a different code for encryption. However, the drawback is that there must be an initial transmittal of the code that is to be used to the recipient, and for absolute unbreakability, the code has to be as long as the message that is transmitted.

A enciphering scheme developed by the U.S. National Bureau of Standards (NBS) is called the **Data Encryption Standard (DES).** The NBS-DES scheme is based on the substitution of characters and rearrangement of their order and assumes the existence of secure encryption keys. This scheme, which has been implemented in hardware, is a relatively easy means to both encipher and decipher data. The algorithm is well known and publicized but the encryption key is kept secret, which makes it very difficult for anyone who does not know the key to decipher the message. However, the drawback in this scheme is that the encryption key has to be transmitted to the recipient before a message can be transmitted.

This difficulty has led to the search for encryption techniques called one-way or **trapdoor functions** having the following characteristics:

- It can change any message X into a message Y.
- It has an inverse function that changes Y back into X.
- Efficient algorithms can be devised to change X into Y and Y back into X.
- If the function and the algorithm to convert from X to Y is known, it is computationally infeasible to discover the inverse function; hence, the same enciphering and deciphering functions can be used over and over again.

The last property gives the function its name: the trapdoor function, easy to drop through but hard to get out of! The knowledge of an appropriate trapdoor function allows the use of a **public key** encryption scheme where both the encryption key and the encryption algorithm are public and readily available. This allows anyone to send a message in a coded form; however, the decryption key is secret and only the rightful recipient can decipher the coded message.

One of the best known trapdoor functions is the one proposed by Rivest et al. (Rive 78). Their encryption scheme, which is a form of a public key scheme, works as follows. Each member of a group wanting to securely communicate devises her or his own trapdoor function with its forward and reverse transformation algorithm. Thus, given a message N in a numeric form, D (E (N)) = N, where E is the forward algorithm for encryption and D is the inverse algorithm for deciphering.

A directory containing the forward encoding algorithm of each member of this group is published in a publicly accessible directory. The reverse algorithms are kept secret. Since the forward algorithms are public, anyone can consult the directory and using the published forward algorithm of a member of this group, encipher a message and send the enciphered message to the member. Only the intended recipient knows the reverse algorithm and will be able to decipher the coded message. The method of sending the message to a member P with forward algorithm E_P is as follows:

1. Convert the message M into numeric form N.
2. Compute $Y = E_p(N)$ and transmit Y to P over a public communication channel.
3. On receipt P will apply the secret reverse algorithm D_p on the message Y to compute N and thence M.

A method to sign the message can be incorporated if the functions D and E have the following additional property:

$$E(D(N)) = N$$

In order to "sign" a message, the sender R (who is required to be a member of the group listed in the published directory) uses his or her own secret inverse function D_r on the numeric form N of the message M, and then uses P's public key E_p and transmits the resulting message T over a public communication channel. Thus, the transmitted message T will be $E_p(D_r(N))$.

P, on receipt of T, first applies her or his own (secret) inverse function D_p and then the published forward function E_r of the sender to retrieve a "signed" message from R. Thus, P will decipher the message as being $E_r(D_p(T))$.

P now has a signed message from R. R cannot deny having sent P this message, since no one else could have created $D_r(N)$, because the function D_r is secret and $E_r(D_r(N))$ is N, which is the numeric form of the message M. P cannot modify the message to M′ and thence to N′, since P doesn't know the secret function D_r.

See (Rive 78) for their version of the trapdoor function, which is based on two prime factors of a large nonprime number.

13.4 Integrity

Security constraints guard against accidental or malicious tampering with data, whereas integrity constraints ensure that any properly authorized access, alteration, deletion, or insertion of the data in the database does not change the consistency and validity of the data. This requires that there is a need for guarding against invalid database operations. An operation here is used to indicate any action performed on behalf of a user or application program that modifies the state of the database. Such operations are the result of actions such as update, insert, or delete. In short, invalid changes have to be guarded against by the integrity subsystem, whereas illegal updates must be guarded against by the security subsystem.

Database integrity involves the correctness of data; this correctness has to be preserved in the presence of concurrent operations, errors in the user's operations and application programs, and failures in hardware and software. Two facets of maintaining the integrity of data in the presence of concurrent operations and failures of various types were discussed in Chapters 11 and 12. For example, the concurrency control mechanism ensures that two concurrent transactions are serializable. However, the integrity constraints must be applied to both these concurrent operations and these constraints ensure that each of these transactions, when run to completion, concurrently or in isolation, will not cause the database to become invalid. The recovery subsystem ensures that failures of various types, which may cause the loss of some of the actions of one or more transactions, will not cause the database to become inconsistent.

In this section we consider some types of constraints that the database has to enforce to maintain the consistency and validity of data. One aspect that has to be dealt with by the integrity subsystem is to ensure that only valid values can be assigned to each data-item. This is referred to as **domain integrity.** Another set of integrity constraints are the so-called structural and semantic constraints. Some of these types of constraints are addressed by the data models used and others are addressed in the design of the database by combining appropriate functional dependencies in different records. Some if not most of the functional dependencies can be expressed if the DBMS allows each record type or relation to have an associated primary key. We discuss these aspects below.

In traditional systems, application programs were responsible for the validation of data and maintaining the consistency of the data used by the programs. However, in a DBMS environment, depending on the application programs to perform these checks has the following drawbacks:

- Each application program must have correct validation and consistency check routines; a failure in one program could lead to database inconsistencies.
- Each application program must be aware of the semantics of the complete database to enforce the correct consistency checks; this is not always the case and unnecessarily burdens the application program writers.
- There will be considerable duplication of efforts.
- Integrity constraints are hard to understand when they are buried in the code of application programs.
- No consistency or validity checks are possible for direct database manipulation using a query language.

Centralizing the integrity checking directly under the DBMS reduces duplication and ensures the consistency and validity of the database. The centralized integrity constraints can be maintained in a system catalog (data dictionary) and can be accessible to the database users via the query language. This does not rule out an application program performing some specific checking, including input validation.

13.4.1 Domain or Data-Item Value Integrity Rules

One of the most common integrity constraints that is specified and validated is to define the domain for each attribute, or in the case of network or hierarchical models, to define the value set for each data-item. Domain integrity rules are simply the definition of the domains of the attributes or the value set for the data-items. The value that each attribute or data-item can be assigned is expressed as being one or more of the following forms: a data type, e.g., alphanumeric string or numeric; a range of values; or a value from a specified set. For instance, in the relation EMPLOYEE of Figure 13.1, the domain of the attribute *Salary* may be given as being between $12,000 and $300,000. The final *Grade* assigned to a student in a course can only be one of, say, A, B, C, D, or F.

A domain can be composite; for instance, the *Date* attribute in the relation MED_HISTORY is restricted to the form mm/dd/year, where mm is the month and is restricted to the range 01 through 12; dd is the date and is restricted to the range

01 through 31; and year is, say, 1986 through 2000. We can make the range of dd more precise by taking into account both the month and year.

Since online data entry is a common operation, validation of the entered values has to be performed to maintain the integrity of data. Traditionally the validation was performed by application programs. However, this approach has two drawbacks: first, it depends on the application programmer to include all validity checks, and second, each application program is duplicating some of these checks. Hence, it is preferable to centralize these operations and let the DBMS perform the validity checks. Note that some types of errors cannot be detected. For instance, a professor may incorrectly assign a grade of F instead of D to a student (an accidental error perhaps, because the keys for D and F are next to each other on the QWERTY keyboard). The validation procedure cannot detect this as an error, since F is a valid grade. Thus, integrity mechanisms can only ensure that the data is in the specified domain. Incorrect choices, as long as they do not violate any integrity constraints, are not considered to be errors.

Some domain constraints could be conditional. For example, the salary constraint in the EMPLOYEE relation, instead of being restricted to a given range could be restricted conditionally as follows:

if *Position* is Asst. Prof *Salary* must be between 35,000 and 45,000
  if *Position* is Asso. Prof *Salary* must be between 42,000 and 55,000
  if *Position* is Professor *Salary* must be between 53,000 and 200,000

The domain values supplied for an operation are validated against the domain constraints. Any violation of a domain integrity rule typically results in the operation being rejected with an appropriate message returned to the user for the correct value. Other possible choices of action to be undertaken by the DBMS on the detection of a domain constraint violation are: correct the value to a valid value; replace the value with a sentinel value that will be detected at audit time; roll back the transaction that issued the invalid value.

The validation procedure typically runs after each attempted modification; however, some integrity constraints may be validated only after the completion of a transaction. Consider the total quantities of some part in a plant. This value must not change unless there is a shipment or receipt of that part. If a transaction transfers 100 units of the part from inventory to a project in the plant, the total units of that part will be incorrect after the first operation of the transaction, which subtracts 100 units from the quantity on hand in inventory, and before the end of the second operation of the transaction, which adds 100 units to a project. The database is in an inconsistent state if the total for the part being transferred were to be computed after the first operation was completed.

In specifying the domain constraints, null values may or may not be allowed. Thus, it is usual not to allow null values for any attribute that forms part of a primary key of a relation.

The definition of the EMPLOYEE relation of Figure 13.1 can be given as shown below, where some of the domain constraints are included. The attribute *Employee_Name* is declared as a primary key that must not be null.

type EMPLOYEE = *relation*
  Employee_Name alphabetic string length 25 *unique null not allowed*
  Department alphabetic string length 15 *values* (CompSci, Chemistry, Electrical Engineering, Mathematics, Physics, . . .)

Room string alphanumeric length 4
Position alphabetic string length 15
Salary decimal of length 6 *digits value range* (10000 – 200000)
end

13.4.2 Implicit and Data Dependency Constraints

The simplest example of an **implicit** integrity constraint is that each record type must conform to the record declaration for that type. The data model used by the DBMS implicitly builds in certain integrity constraints, such as the one-to-many relationship between a parent record type and the children record types in the hierarchical model. The hierarchical model requires that the parent record type must exist for the child record type to be inserted in the database; the parent-to-child data structure is the implicit implementation of a one-to-many relationship. The insertion and the retention rules for set membership are examples of implicit structural integrity rules in the network model. A many-to-many relationship in the network model between record types A and B implicitly assumes the existence of two set types owned by the record types A and B with a common member record type.

These are structural constraints between the values of different data-items or fields and are the reflection of the functional and multivalued dependencies between the attributes of the entity being modeled in the database. Many functional dependencies can be implicitly represented in a database that allows the declaration of some attributes as a primary key. Having declared that a given set of attributes form a primary key of a relation, the update and insertion operations for that relation can be validated. For instance, duplicate tuples and update to attributes in the primary keys are disallowed.

Any general constraint that involves multiple relations is expensive in computation time. The conditional constraint of the valid range of *Salary* which was dependent on the *Position* of the employee involves a single relation.

Consider the relations STUDENT*(Student_Name, Major),* COURSE*(Course_No, Department)* and ENROLLMENT*(Student_Name, Course_No, Year, Term, Grade)*. A many-to-many relationship between students and courses is implemented in the relational model by the ENROLLMENT relation. However, a constraint that a student is not allowed to enroll in a course unless the course is scheduled and the student is a registered student at the university, involves multiple relations. Thus, the ENROLLMENT relation that represents a relationship between a course and a student requires that, for a given tuple in ENROLLMENT, the referenced tuples must exist in the relations STUDENT and COURSE; and a tuple in the relation STUDENT must have the same value for the attribute *Student_Name* as the given tuple in the relation ENROLLMENT; furthermore, the tuple in the relation COURSE must have the same value for the attribute *Course* as the given tuple in the relation ENROLLMENT. This is referred to as **referential integrity.**

There are similar integrity rules for other data models. In the network data model, a many-to-many relationship between record types A and B requires the presence of an intermediate record type, which is a member in two set types owned by record types A and B. Furthermore, a relationship can only exist between existing occurrences of each of these record types. Another example of referential integrity

Figure 13.9 Referential integrity in network model.

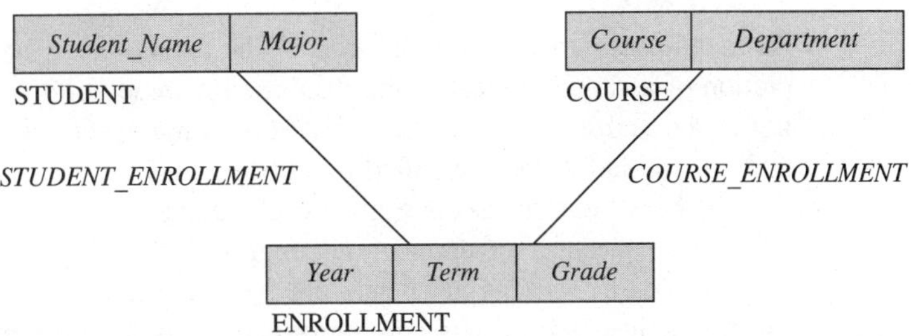

in the network model is that a member record type cannot exist without the presence of the owner record type in a set where the membership is automatic fixed. Consider a record type that is a member in one or more set types wherein the membership is specified to be automatic fixed. Inserting into the database a new occurrence of such a member record type requires that each of the owner record occurrences must exist and the appropriate set currency indicators point to these occurrences.

Let us see how the network model represents the relationship between students and courses. The many-to-many relationship between the record types student and course is represented in the network model by the sets *STUDENT_ENROLLMENT* and *COURSE_ENROLLMENT* as shown in Figure 13.9; ENROLLMENT is the common member record type in these sets. To maintain the integrity of the database, the deletion of a STUDENT (or COURSE) record occurrence should not be allowed if the set *STUDENT_ENROLLMENT* (or *COURSE_ENROLLMENT*) is not empty. Conversely, an occurrence of the set *STUDENT_ENROLLMENT* cannot exist without the existence of the record occurrence of its owner, i.e., STUDENT. An occurrence of the set *COURSE_ENROLLMENT* cannot exist without the existence of the record occurrence of its owner COURSE. An ENROLLMENT record cannot exist without the existence of both a STUDENT and a COURSE record occurrence.

The many-to-many relationship between students and courses can be represented in the hierarchical model by a hierarchical structure as shown in Figure 13.10. In a hierarchical model, the dependent record type does not exist independently of the parent record type. Also, if a data-item of some field of a record is declared to be an unique value, the insertion of another record with the same value in that field is not allowed at the same position in an occurrence of the hierarchical tree.

Figure 13.10 Referential integrity in hierarchical model.

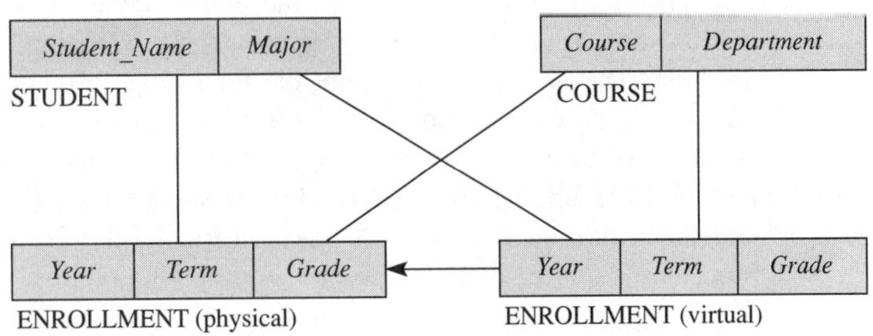

13.4.3 Violation of Integrity Constraints and Corrective Action

As mentioned earlier, the validation of the database can be done right after the completion of a single request to the database; at some point within a transaction, including at the end of a transaction; or at some time specified by the DBA or a database auditor (the latter may be called the **audit time**).

If the validation is done after each request to the database, a message can be returned to the user or application program indicating the problem, and the request will fail. If the validation checks are performed at some point within a transaction (including just before it is committed), there is a requirement to perform a maintenance operation in case of integrity violation. This would involve terminating the transaction and undoing any changes made by the transaction.

If the validation checks are done at audit time, it becomes difficult to assign the integrity violation to a single database request or a single transaction. An audit trail could be helpful in pinpointing the culprit; however, corrective actions have to be performed on transactions that were processed from the time of the integrity violation.

13.4.4 A General Model of Integrity

A general integrity constraint can be specified using a model that gives the following parameter for each constraint:

- **D:** The data object(s) to which the constraint applies.
- **O:** The database operation for which the constraint will be tested.
- **A:** The assertion or semantic constraint that must be satisfied by the occurrence of the data object(s).
- **C:** Predicates to be applied to the data object. The predicates select those occurrences of the data object to which the assertion **A** will be applied. If the condition holds for a given occurrence of **D,** it is a candidate for the constraint **A.**
- **P:** The procedure (sometimes called an **auxiliary procedure**) that will be triggered for execution when an integrity violation is found to be true (if the condition **A** is not true). The auxiliary procedure must take corrective action to maintain integrity.

Using this model, each constraint can be expressed as a five-tuple: **(D, O, A, C, P).**

The auxiliary procedure **P** in the above model is said to be triggered when a modification to the database causes an integrity violation, i.e., the constraint **A** does not hold. The procedure is responsible for taking corrective actions.

One type of operation that the auxiliary procedure can be called to take is to check some complex integrity requirements that cannot be specified by assertions. A method of triggering such a procedure would be by setting the assertion **A** to false and the condition **C** to true in the constraint rule. In addition, such an auxiliary procedure could be called to prepare appropriate audit trails, and so forth.

It has been proposed that an integrity mechanism called **trigger** be included in the new standard for SQL. A trigger is defined as follows:

define trigger trigger_name
on relation names
predicate(s)
action auxiliary procedure

We give below an example of trigger definition where the salary of employees is checked on insertion or update:

define trigger *salary_validation*
on relation EMPLOYEE
EMPLOYEE.*Salary* > 10000 **and** Employee.*Salary* < 200000
action Notify_Personnel_Manager

13.4.5 Expressing Integrity Constraints

Most DBMSs have some form of language constructs for expressing domain and key constraints. These constructs could be part of the data definition language, the data manipulation language, or a special language. However, the constructs for expressing complex constraints are only in the evolution stage. We gave a form for checking a general constraint in Section 13.4.4 and the **define trigger** statement proposed for SQL.

Since the DBMS is representing a given data model, it is aware of some of the integrity constraints implicitly built into the data model. It is informed of the record structure and other implicit integrity constraints by the declaration in the data definition language. For instance, in a hierarchical system the declaration of a record type gives its structure; in addition, some data fields may be declared as unique to specify a primary key of the record type. The hierarchies with the parent and dependent record type gives the relationship between record types. Additional rules, as mentioned in Chapter 9, may be specified which could result in the creation of logical or virtual parents and enforce appropriate referential integrity constraints and semantic consistencies.

The network data definition facility allows the definition of a primary key (by not allowing duplicates). The check clause in the data definition can be associated with each data-item that specifies the valid values or data type. The insertion and retention rules for sets define the semantics and referential integrity of the independent existence of the member record type occurrence vis-à-vis the owner record occurrence. The **check** clause is also used to specify other arbitrary constraints, and it may be formulated to enforce constraints between distinct record types, stipulating operations that will trigger the execution of an associated auxiliary procedure.

Relational data definition language also provides statements to allow specification of constraints. The **assert** statement is one such statement. The assert indicates that a constraint is specified involving relations in the **on clause.** The assertion to be enforced is given by predicates following the list of relations. However, current relational languages and DBMSs support such a statement only partially.

An assert statement can be used to specify referential integrity. The following assert statement ensures that only registered students are enrolled in existing courses:

assert Enrollment_Constraint **on** ENROLLMENT e STUDENT s COURSE c
e.*Student_Name* = s.*Student_Name* **and** e.*Course* = c.*Course*

13.5 Statistical Databases

A **statistical database** contains confidential information about individuals (or organizations), which is used to answer statistical queries concerning totals, averages, numbers with certain characteristics. Since the data is confidential, involving, say, the medical history or income of individuals, responses to queries should only involve nontrivial size subsets of the database.

In a statistical database the objective is to maximize the sharing of statistical information, yet preserve the privacy of individuals. The challenge is to make it difficult if not impossible for anyone to extract information about particular individuals from the answers to a set of queries that involve a large number of records. This security problem cannot be solved by normal access control strategy, since the aim of the database is to maximize sharing and allow all users full access to the data in the database.

To illustrate how individual values can be traced by a series of queries, let us look at the data of Figure 13.11. If this were a statistical database, the need for the unique identifier, such as *Employee_Name* in this database, would be to verify the correctness of the information. However, such unique identifiers will not be accessible to the users. (We assume that the persons who entered these unique identifiers and the rest of the information are reliable, or else the unique identifiers are in a coded form.) It is not possible to get a response from the database to a query that asks for the salary of one individual.

A query similar to the following, though of a statistical nature, would compromise the database since the response involves only one record in the database:

find average *Salary* **for all** EMP_SALARY
  where *Department* = Comp Sci.
  and *Position* = Asst Prof response 44500

Figure 13.11 The EMP_SALARY relation.

Employee_Name	*Department*	*Position*	*Salary*
Smith	Comp Sci	Asst Prof	44500
Clark	Comp Sci	Asso Prof	49750
Turner	Chemistry	Professor	63050
Jamieson	Mathematics	Professor	61430
Bosky	Physics	Asso Prof	52800
Newton	Physics	Asst Prof	42750
Mann	Elect Eng	Asst Prof	44750

This points out the constraint that the statistical database must not respond to a query if the number of records involved in arriving at the response for the query is very small, i.e., less than **s.** Notwithstanding the above condition, it is still possible for someone who has some knowledge about certain records in the database to compromise the database. For example, Clark, knowing her or his own salary and knowing that there are only two employees in the Computer Science department, can find Smith's salary using the following queries:

find average *Salary* **for all** EMP_SALARY
  where *Department* = Comp Sci: response 47125

Thus Smith's salary = 47125 * 2 − 49750 = 44500

If we limit queries so that only those queries that involve a large number of records are fielded by the database, Clark may use the following set of queries to compromise the database:

find average *Salary* **for all** EMP_SALARY: response 51290
find total number of EMP_SALARY: response 7
find average *Salary* **for** EMP_SALARY **not in** Comp Sci: response 52956

Thus knowing the details about Clark and the above responses, Smith's salary is computed as being:

$$51290 * 7 - 52956 * 5 - 49750 = 44500$$

In the above sequence of queries, each query by itself involved a large number of records. The database was compromised because the number of common records in the various queries in the above sequence was large. This leads us to the conclusion that if queries involve a very large set of records, e.g., greater than N − **s,** the response should be withheld (here N is the total number of records in the database).

Even if we restrict the DBMS to respond to only those queries such that the response involves records between **s** and N − **s,** it is still possible to compromise the database if the user has access to information pertaining to some specific records, as illustrated by the following sequence of queries. Here, we are assuming **s** is 2 and **N − s** is 5. This case of compromising the database involves the following set of queries:

find sum *Salary*
  where *Position* = Asst Prof **and** *Department* = Comp Sci
    or *Position* = Asso Prof **and** *Department* = Comp Sci
    or *Position* = Professor: response 218730
find sum *Salary*
  where *Position* = Asso Prof **and** *Department* = Comp Sci
    or *Position* = Professor: response 174230

Thus Smith's salary is computed as being 218730 − 174230 = 44500.

As shown above, it is possible for an unscrupulous user to extract information about individual records; however, the following techniques make this task difficult. One or more of the following strategies are usually used.

The first strategy is to reject queries that involve a very small number of records in the statistical database. Thus, if the response to the query involves only a few records, the use can infer the values for one individual using other generally available information of further queries. The method to thwart such attempts at breaching privacy is to reject queries unless the response involves a minimum number of records. Similarly, queries that involve a very large subset of the records in the database are also rejected.

However, as we saw rejecting queries, where the number of records involved in the response is either a very small subset(s) or a very large subset (**N** − s) is not sufficient when more than one query is used.

Thus, if the number of records involved in two queries q_1 and q_2 is n + 1, where $\mathbf{s} \leq n + 1 \leq \mathbf{N} - \mathbf{s}$, and if the number of common records (intersection records) in these two queries is, n, then the number of different records in the two queries is only 1. If the user has knowledge about one of these two nonintersecting records, information on the other record can be inferred, as shown in Figure 13.12. Additional outside information can lead to a compromise of the database when the intersecting number of records is less than n or greater than 1.

The method to prevent this type of inference is to reject queries if the number of intersection records with previous queries made by the user is very large. To implement this strategy the system must maintain a history of all records that were used in a query by a given user over a reasonable period of time. The amount of storage required to maintain this information will become very large and strain the capacity of the computing system. If this information is retained on only a few past queries, the system may be compromised and answer queries that it shouldn't. Another method of bypassing such precautions by the system is for the user to be in a pact with other users.

A third precaution is random falsification. In this approach, a small random amount of data is falsified. This falsification is statistically insignificant so that normal users will not suffer from erroneous statistics.

Another strategy that can be used in a large statistical database like a census database is to select a random sample of the database that will be used to answer any query. The random sample would be representative of the entire database. The user would get the correct statistical information without the possibility of the database being compromised.

A final strategy is to produce an audit trail of activities on the database. This trail will maintain the identity of the users and their interaction with the database. It can be used to find out after the fact if any user was trying to or had actually compromised the database. The very fact that this can be done would discourage such actions.

Figure 13.12 Statistical database compromise with response set intersection size being too large.

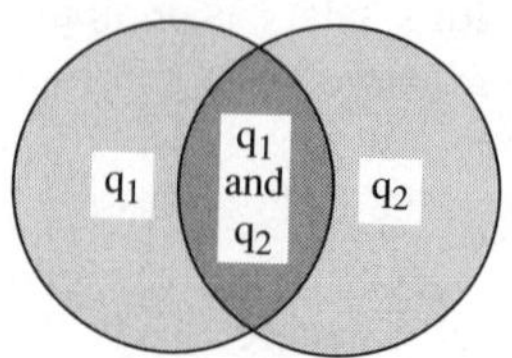

13.6 Auditing and Control

Auditing is a standard practice used in most organizations. It consists of an examination of the accounting and recordkeeping practices and other evidence to establish the soundness and validity of the underlying operations. The audit is done by an independent outside body called an auditor so as to be unbiased and objective. However, an appropriate continuous internal audit is required in any organization to ensure its health and continued existence.

The auditing process is relevant in the database environment to verify that the automated operations are properly implemented and executed. Since data entry and maintenance is done online, the history of the evolution of a piece of data is no longer available in the database, which will contain the latest values only. Contrast this with a traditional system where the evolution of a data object is preserved in the form of a trail of records on paper. Furthermore, the computing system, with its quiet and humanly invisible toil, can be used by crafty fraud artists to permanently destroy the evidence of their mischievous deeds. The maintenance of a secure audit trail becomes all the more necessary in the database environment.

In addition to the above, functions that were previously separated and controlled by distinct parts of an organization (for example, initiation of a transaction and recording the financial and operational part of the transaction) are integrated into the database environment. This integration of operations, while reducing redundancy, causes the loss of independent scrutiny and corrections. Furthermore, in an online system where a number of transactions are executed concurrently, it is very difficult to reproduce the same sequence of processing. All these factors point to a need for an audit trail in the database environment.

On the positive side, the computing system, with all its computing and recordkeeping power, also provides a great opportunity for improving the audit procedure. The auditing can now look into the complete database and, with minimum effort, perform a greater number of checking and cross-checking operations than was feasible with a manual system.

The audit trail to be maintained for audit purposes has some similarity with the data collected for recovery operations. Thus for each update operation, the before and after image of the data objects undergoing modification are recorded. All logons, read operations, and suspect or illegal operations are recorded. This information can be used to analyze the practice of the users of the database, detect any attempted violations, help correct errors in design or execution, and improve the control procedure.

The control of the database starts with the design of the database and the application programs that will be using the data. One of the first control principles is that of separating the responsibilities. This can be practiced by assigning separate teams for the design and implementation of the program and for its validation and installation. Any changes to the specifications or the actual program should be made and reviewed by different teams.

The integrity control mechanisms should be integrated in the database and the data entry function should be validated by the application programs. Careful design of the user interface could reduce the chances of data entry errors. The semantic integrity constraints should be enforced for all update operations. Finally, appropriate audit trails should be generated.

13.7 Summary

Security and integrity concepts are crucial since modifications in a database require the replacement of the old values, but the fact that there was an old value for a given data item is not evident. The DBMS security mechanism restricts users to only those pieces of data that are required for the functions they perform. Security mechanisms restrict the type of actions that these users can perform on the data that is accessible to them. The data must be protected from accidental or intentional (malicious) corruption or destruction. In addition there is a privacy dimension to data security and integrity.

Four levels of defense are generally recognized for database security: human factors, administrative controls, physical security, and the security and integrity mechanisms built into the operating system and the DBMS. Access control policies are classified as open vs. closed systems, content-independent access control, content-dependent access control, access operation type control, access context control, access control based on history of accesses, and information flow policies. The database depends on protection mechanisms such as user identification and validation as well as the memory and file protection features of the OS.

Authorization is the outcome of the administrative policies and is expressed as a set of rules that can be used to determine which user has what type of access to which portion of the database. The person who is in charge of specifying the authorization is called the authorizer. The authorization is usually maintained in the form of an access matrix, containing rows called the subjects and columns called the objects. An object is something that needs protection. The entry in the matrix at the position corresponding to the intersection of a row and column indicate the type of access that the subject has with respect to the object. Views or subschemes can be used to enforce security. A user is allowed access only to that portion of the database that is defined by the user's view. A user may be granted some rights with the propagate access control, which leads to the existence of an authorization grant tree. To revoke access rights, all paths in the grant tree must start from the authorizer, otherwise the revocation cannot be guarded against unscrupulous usage.

The facility available to the authorizer (and to the users who can propagate access rights) to assign access rights could be in the form of a separate language or could be integrated with the data definition or data manipulation language.

The user has to identify herself/himself to the system and authenticate the identification. Security enforcement in distributed systems can be enhanced by distribution; thus, sensitive information can be fragmented and stored at dispersed sites.

With the increasing use of public communication facilities to transmit information, there is a need for the data to be encrypted before it is transmitted and this requires that, at the receiving end, the received data be deciphered. A public key encryption scheme can be used. In this scheme both the encryption key and the encryption algorithm are public and readily available. However, the decryption key is secret; only the rightful recipient can decipher the coded message.

Security constraints guard against accidental or malicious tampering with data;

integrity constraints ensure that any properly authorized access, alteration, deletion, or insertion of the data in the database does not change the consistency and validity of the data. Database integrity involves the correctness of data and this correctness has to be preserved in the presence of concurrent operations, errors in the user's operations and application programs, and failures in hardware and software. One aspect to be dealt with by the integrity subsystem is to ensure that only valid values can be assigned to each data-item; this is referred to as domain integrity. Another set of integrity constraints are the so-called structural and semantic constraints. Some of these types of constraints are addressed by the data models and others are addressed in the design of the database by combining appropriate functional dependencies in different records. Many functional dependencies can be implicitly represented in a database that allows the declaration of some attributes as a primary key. Most DBMS have some form of language constructs for expressing integrity constraints.

In a statistical database the objective is to maximize sharing statistical information and yet preserve privacy of individual records. This security problem cannot be solved by normal access control strategy, since the aim of the database is to allow all users full access to the data. The means to prevent compromising a statistical database is to reject queries if the number of intersection records with previous queries made by the user is very large (or very small). If random falsification is used to protect confidentiality, it is statistically insignificant, so that normal users will not suffer from erroneous statistics. The maintenance of audit trails could discourage unscrupulous snooping.

The auditing process is also relevant in nonstatistical databases to verify if the automated operations are properly implemented and executed.

Key Terms

privacy
database security
database integrity
semantic integrity
authorization
security administrator
authorizer
open system
closed system
least privilege
need to know
maximize sharing
content-independent access control
name-dependent access control
content-dependent access control
access type control
access context control
access matrix
subject
object
propagate access control
authorization grant tree
password
identification
authentication
Caesar code
one-time code
Data Encryption Standard (DES)
trapdoor functions
public key
domain integrity
implicit constraint
referential integrity
auxiliary procedure
trigger
assert
on clause
statistical database

Exercises

13.1 Consider a case of computer-related fraud you are familiar with (or consult one of the references cited in the bibliographic notes). List the security and integrity constraints that should have been implemented. Could appropriate audit and control procedure have prevented the fraud?

13.2 Define two views for the MED_HISTORY database for the use of the personnel manager and the chairperson of the department so as not to compromise the confidentiality of the data contained in the relation.

13.3 Given that a view or a subschema can be used to enforce security, would it be possible in all cases to allow updates to be performed on a relation in a view (or records in a subscheme)? List cases where updates cannot be allowed and indicate what type of constraints could be violated if they were allowed.

13.4 Since it is possible to compromise the security of a statistical database by a sequence of queries, some form of access control based on the history of accesses is required. Is it possible to implement an access control mechanism that would prevent a number of users conspiring to compromise the database?

13.5 Can a user who has access both to the *Diagnosis* attribute and the rest of the attributes of the MED_HISTORY relation of Figure 13.3, but not simultaneously, compromise the confidential information? If so, give the queries used.

13.6 Consider the relations STUDENT*(Student_Name, Major)*, COURSE*(Course_No, Department)*, PREREQUISITE*(Course_No, Prerequisite_Course_No)* and ENROLLMENT*(Student_Name, Course_No, Year, Term, Grade)*. Suppose it is required that students be registered in only those courses for which they have passed all the prerequisite courses. Indicate how this could be implemented using the trigger mechanism.

13.7 Consider the MED_HISTORY relation of Figure 13.3. Suppose the personnel manager is allowed to access to the attributes *Employee_Name, Department,* and *Visit_Date*. He or she is also allowed access to the *Diagnosis* attribute, but not simultaneously with the other attributes. Is it possible for the personnel manager to compromise the confidentiality of the data in the relation? If so, what corrective actions are indicated?

Bibliographic Notes

(Hoff 69) provides an early discussion of the danger of the privacy problem and presents some early proposals for the safeguard. (Hoff 77) and (Mart 73) discuss the general problem of security in computer systems. Textbook discussions of database security and integrity problems are presented in (Date 83), (Fern 81), and (Mart 73).

The original proposal of the authorization mechanism for System R was presented in (Grif 76) and (Fagi 78). The paper by Fagin gives the proof of an algorithm for authorization grant tress. (Zloo 78) presents the security and integrity features in Query-by-Example. The approach used in INGRES to implement security was by query modification; this was presented in (Ston 74).

The concept of public key encryption was presented in (Diff 76). (Rive 78) presents a method to derive computationally secure trapdoor functions, public key encryption and decryption keys, and the associated algorithms. (Lemp 79) gives an excellent survey article on cryptology.

(Hoff 70) poses the earliest problem of compromising a statistical database. Several researchers, (Kam 77), (Dobk 79), and (Reis 79), have looked at the mathematical analysis of queries required to compromise a statistical database. (Denn 79) presents other methods of compromising a statistical database where minimum set size constraints are imposed on response sets.

An audit trail model is given in (Bjor 75). (Mair 78) is a textbook on electronic data processing auditing.

Bibliography

(Bjor 75) L. A. Bjork, Jr., ''Generalized Audit-Trail Requirements and Concepts for Data Base Applications,'' *IBM Systems Journal* 14(3), 1975, pp. 229–245.

(Date 83) C. J. Date, *An Introduction to Database Systems,* vol. 2. Reading, MA: Addison-Wesley, 1983.

(Denn 79) D. E. Denning, P. J. Denning & M. D. Schwartz, ''The Tracker: A Threat to Statistical Database Security,'' *ACM Transactions on Database Systems* 4(1), March 1979, pp. 76–96.

(Diff 76) W. Diffie & M. Hellman, ''New Directions in Cryptography,'' *IEEE Trans. Information Theory* IT-22(6), November 1976, pp. 644–654.

(Diff 77) W. Diffie & M. Hellman, ''Exhaustive Cryptanalysis of the NBS Data Encryption Standard,'' *Computer* 10(6), June 1977, pp. 74–84.

(Dobk 79) D. Dobkin, A. K. Jones & R. J. Lipton, ''Secure Databases: Protection against User Inferences,'' *ACM Transactions on Database Systems* 4(1), March 1979, pp. 97–106.

(Fagi 78) R. Fagin, ''On an Authorization Mechanism,'' *ACM Trans. on Database Systems* 3(3), September 1978, pp. 310–319.

(Fern 81) E. B. Fernandez, R. C. Summers & C. Wood, *Database Security and Integrity*. Reading, MA: Addison-Wesley, 1981.

(Grif 76) P. P. Griffiths & B. W. Wage, ''An Authorization Mechanism for a Relational Data Base System,'' *ACM Trans. on Database Systems* 1(3), September 1976, pp. 242–255.

(Hoff 69) L. J. Hoffman, ''Computers and Privacy: A Survey,'' *ACM Computing Survey* 1(2), June 1969, pp. 85–103.

(Hoff 70) L. J. Hoffman & W. F. Miller, ''Getting a Personal Dossier from a Statistical Data Bank,'' *Datamation* 16(5), 1970, pp. 74–75.

(Hoff 77) L. J. Hoffman, *Modern Methods for Security and Privacy,* Englewood Cliffs, NJ: Prentice-Hall, 1977.

(Kam 77) J. B. Kam & J. D. Ullman, ''A Model of Statistical Databases and their Security,'' *ACM Transactions on Database Systems* 2(1), January 1977, pp. 1–10.

(Lemp 79) A. Lempel, ''Cryptology in Transition,'' *ACM Computing Survey* 11(4), December 1979, pp. 285–303.

(Mair 78) W. C. Mair, D. R. Wood & K. W. Davis, ''Computer Control and Audit.'' Wellesley, MA: Institute of Internal Auditors, Q.E.D. Information Sciences, Inc., 1978.

(Mart 73) J. Martin, *Security, Accuracy, and Privacy in Computer Systems*. Englewood Cliffs, NJ: Prentice-Hall, 1973.

(Reis 79) S. P. Reiss, ''Security in Databases: A Combinatorial Study,'' *Journal of ACM,* 26(1), January 1979, pp. 45–57.

(Rive 78) R. L. Rivest, A. Shamir & L. Adleman, ''A Method for Obtaining Digital Signature and Public Key Cryptosystems,'' *CACM* 21(2), February 1978, pp. 120–126.

(Ston 74) M. R. Stonebraker & E. Wong, ''Access Control in a Relational Data Base Management by Query Modification,'' Proc. ACM National Conference, 1974, pp. 189–222.

(Worm 89) Special Section on the Internet Worm, Communications of the ACM, 32(6), June 1989, pp. 678–710.

(Zloo 78) M. M. Zloof, ''Security and Integrity within the Query-by-Example Database Management Language,'' *IBM Research Report* RC6982, Yorktown Heights, NY, February 1978.

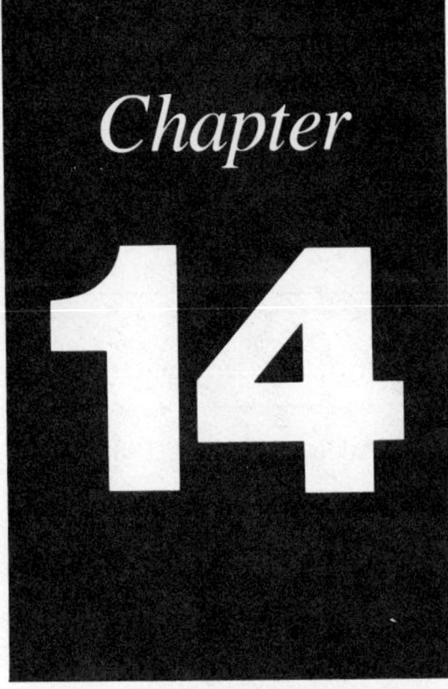

Database Design

Contents

Database design is an iterative process. A number of design methodologies have been developed.This chapter offers an informal discussion of the steps involved in designing a database.

14.1 The Organization and Its Information System

The information system of an organization consists of a number of subsystems involved in the collection, dissemination, and management of information. Some of these subsystems are manual, others are automated. A database system consisting of the data, DBMS software, hardware, and personnel is a component of such an information system.

Deciding to use a database system requires studying the organization and its needs. In the case of a small organization with few users, where the volume of data is small and there is no need for online query or update, a database system may not be necessary. In an organization with a large volume of data that changes rapidly, where there is a need for interactive queries and modifications, with a large number of users, and where decision making is distributed, the need for concurrent access to shared data is addressed by a database system.

In an organization where a large number of users and applications exist, the database system provides data independence, insulating these users and applications from changes. For the database to meets its objectives, its design must be complete and consistent. All the significant inputs should be used in the design process, including the inputs of the users. The external schema allows multiple views of the data contained in the database. Designing a database system requires gathering details about the applications and transactions that are to be supported and the classes of users that will use the system.

Figure 14.1 gives the system cycle for the design of a database system. It starts off with the definition of the problem and goes through a number of steps, culminating in the installation and operation of the system. In the following sections we examine the activities performed in each phase of this cycle.

14.2 Phase I: Definition of the Problem

The first step in the system cycle is the rough outline and scope of the project. Alternatives are examined and one of the alternatives is targeted for a feasibility study. Estimates of the costs, including initial setup and operational costs, and the risks versus the benefits are examined. The initial cost consists of acquiring the software and the hardware, converting from a manual or file-based system, and training the personnel. Time scales for the various stages of the development cycle are estimated. Approval of top management for a go-ahead is required.

Once it is decided that the organization wants to pursue the database solution for its information needs, the design of the database system begins.

Figure 14.1 Information system cycle.

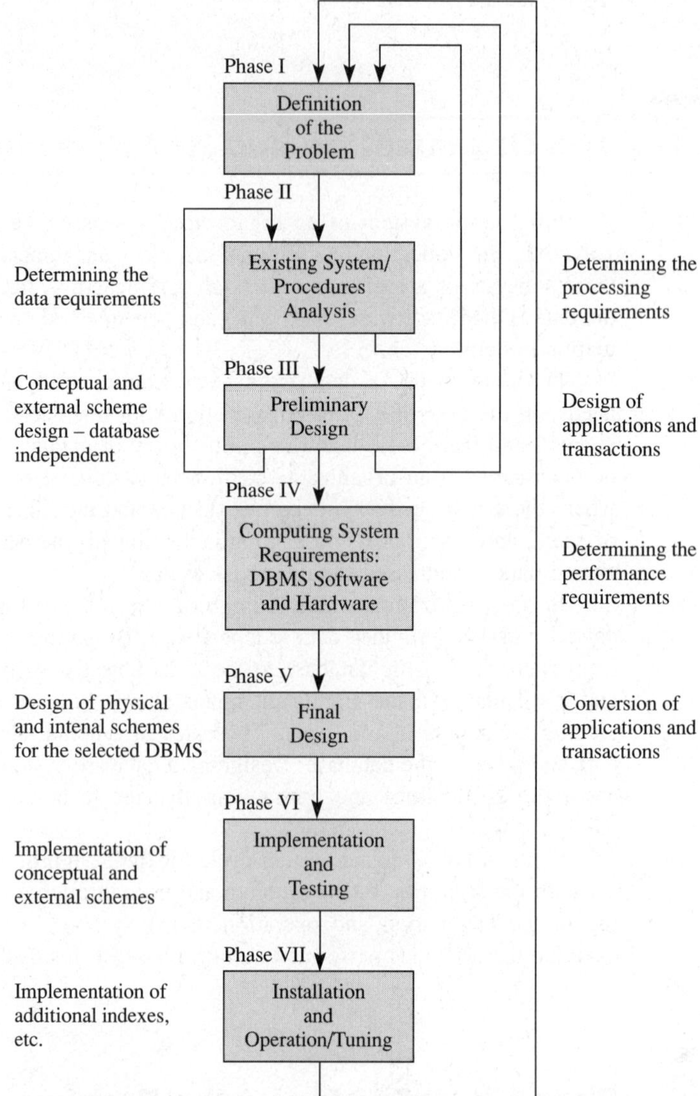

14.3 Phase II: Analysis of Existing System and Procedures

The second phase of the cycle is to perform a feasibility study of the proposed solution. An analysis of the existing system and procedures and the impact of the proposed system on the operations of the organization must be considered at this stage.

The study of the existing system and procedures is a very important phase of the design process. This study is in the form of observation of the existing system, existing procedures and practices, current communication channels (both formal and informal), and interviewing and/or surveying the users. The survey could be in the form of questionnaires. A detailed study of the system may reveal inefficiencies, duplications, and desired changes in procedures, as well as the effect of the database system on the existing system and procedures. The consideration of how these could be improved and/or replaced by more efficient or effective automated procedures is also essential.

Some design tools such as data flow diagrams may be used to graphically depict the data needs of the processes and how processes are interconnected. Information required to generate these diagrams can be gathered via interviews with users and existing procedural documentations.

Requirements that the system is to fulfil must be defined. These requirements refer to the functions of the system, activities that will be supported by it, and the data that will be required for these activities.

Factors that are considered in collecting and analyzing the requirements are the following: levels of management to be supported, the nature of functions to be served, and types of activities to be performed. A representative from each group of users is chosen for participation in collecting and verifying the requirements. The requirements could then be classed into two groups: information requirements and processing requirements.

Information requirements specify the information under the control of the proposed database system. These include the entities, their attributes, and relationships among them.

Processing requirements define the data-manipulation capabilities of the system and include their expected frequencies and required turnaround or response. Each process is listed along with its data requirements and its data manipulation operations. The processing requirements must be semantically correct and consistent, so that the processing does not violate any constraints imposed by the information requirements.

Integrity constraints are defined from the above two requirements. These requirements are generated from interaction with the targeted users of the database system. The conceptual schema would be generated from these requirements, specifying the entities and their relationships and including their attributes. For example, the payroll preparation function would require information about employees' salaries, pay rates, hours worked, and tax status (number of dependents, other valid deductions for tax computation). The payroll has to be prepared weekly, bimonthly, or monthly. The turnaround time is in hours.

The information and processing requirements form the entries in the data dictionary. The latter contains an entry for each data item used in the system. The entry defines each data item, provides any synonyms, and gives the characteristics of the data itcm and its domain.

Formal requirement specification methods have been developed and are mentioned in the bibliographic notes. These methods use hierarchical graphs and/or flow charts for gathering and documenting the requirements.

To summarize we list below the steps of this phase of the database design process:

- **Study of existing system and procedures:** This involves examining the current methods for recording and processing data.

- **Meetings with user groups:** One or more key users from each user group is invited to provide input in determining the data and processing needs for the group. A formal interview may be supplemented by a questionnaire.
- **Analysis of the procedures and information flow:** The information gathered is analyzed for consistency and problem areas are targeted for further study.
- **Modifications to improve efficiency:** Modification in the current procedures that could improve efficiency may be discovered. Such modifications have to be discussed with the groups concerned to elicit their cooperation.
- **Preparing the initial proposal and requirement specifications:** The initial proposal is prepared and may be discussed with the user group for any omissions and corrections made to the proposed requirements.

The output of this phase is:

- Data requirements
- Properties and interrelationships of the data
- Operation requirements
- Significant events and the operations and conditions causing transitions
- Constraints

The application programs and transactions are designed at this stage of the design process. The structure of the programs, their functions, and data needs (read and write sets) are determined, and the user interface is defined.

14.4 Phase III: Preliminary Design

A preliminary design of the proposed system is derived in the next step. This design is evaluated against the initial requirements. The users are consulted and required changes are made to the design.

The cycle of the steps consisting of the definition of the problem, procedure analysis, and preliminary design is repeated until a satisfactory design is obtained.

The design of the conceptual schema is initially DBMS independent and allows a better understanding of the information requirements and their interrelationships. It describes the contents of the database without reference to its implementation. It can be understood by the nonspecialist and can be used in documenting the proposed database. A data model such as the E-R model may be used for its graphical nature, simplicity, and expressiveness.

The requirement specifications would have established the entities and the relationships among them, as well as their attributes. The primary key of the entities, the cardinality of the relationship, and constraints are to be specified in the conceptual schema design.

Structure constraints such as normal forms for relations have to be enforced by the design. Two approaches to the design of the conceptual schema may be taken: **centralized schema design** or a **view-integration approach.** In the former, the requirement specifications for each class of users are merged into a single set of specifications. The conceptual schema is designed from this single set. Any conflicts that may exist in the individual requirement specifications are to be arbitrated by the

DBA. After designing the conceptual schema, the views of the user classes are defined.

In the view-integration approach, the requirement specifications for each class of users form the basis for designing their views. These views are then integrated into the conceptual schema for the database. Conflicts such as synonyms and homonyms are easy to resolve. Conflicts that cannot be resolved by a conceptual schema to view mapping have to be arbitrated. An instance of such a conflict is where one application uses a locally generated sequential employee number and another may use the social security number, conflict in which one application views an attribute such as *Length* as meters and another interprets it as yards may be easier to resolve.

Once such conflicts are resolved the views are appropriately integrated. The integration could be stepwise, where we start by integrating two similar views. Subsequently, at each step, an additional view is merged into the integrated conceptual schema. After the conceptual schema is defined, the individual views are defined.

In the **top-down approach** to conceptual schema design we start with the major entities of interest, their attributes, and their relationships for the database application. We add other attributes and may decide to split up the entities into a number of specialized entities and add the relationships among these specialized entities.

In the **bottom-up approach,** we start with a set of attributes. We group these attributes into entities and relationships among them. We also attempt to find higher level entities to generalize these entities and locate relationships at this higher level.

The processing requirements in the form of applications and transactions are designed and their response requirements are estimated. To determine the performance requirements, the data items to be read and written out (read and write sets) for each operation in the transaction or application have to be determined. This is used to derive the number and size of input/output for each transaction and application. The performance requirements for the system will influence the distribution of files on physical devices, the physical file structure, and the need for indexes.

14.5 Phase IV: Computing System Decision

This decision may be based on the existing environment. If the database is to be implemented on an existing computer system, the choice is limited to that for the DBMS. The existing system must be able to meet the storage and processing needs of the proposed DBMS. DBMSs are usually chosen from one of the commercial systems because of the cost of developing an in-house system. Features provided by different systems are also important. Some that should be considered are report generation facilities, utilities such as menu and form based user interface, features to support distribution of the database, communication facilities, and the like. Other considerations such as the expertise of the personnel and their preferences also come into play.

The structure of the data dictates the data model of the database. If the data is mainly hierarchical, the hierararchical model and a hierarchical DBMS may be appropriate. If the data exhibits a large number of interrelationships, the network or relational model would be preferable. Deciding on a model also narrows the choice of commercial DBMSs. Other factors that can influence the choice of a DBMS are the experience of the personnel, reputation of the vendor, and the availability of services from the vendor. Selecting the DBMS also dictates the data model.

New applications are increasingly implemented on relational DBMSs and non-relational DBMSs are retrofitted with a relational interface. The current trend for the same DBMS being able to run on different CPUs under different OSs allows some degree of independence between the choice of a DBMS and that of a computer system.

If the database is to be implemented on an existing system, it must be able to meet the processing requirements for the foreseeable features.

Factors that have to be considered in the choice of the computing system are capital costs, conversion and initial training costs, operating costs including those for personnel, and maintenance of the hardware and software.

14.6 Phase V: Final Design

The preliminary design of the database in Phase III is in database-independent form, for instance, using the E-R model. Once the DBMS is chosen, the (DBMS-independent) conceptual scheme is translated into the DBMS specific conceptual scheme and the views of the applications are derived from it as external views. The schemes are generated as programs in the DDL of the target DBMS.

The first step is to convert the conceptual and external schemes in the model of the database. We discussed the method of converting a design from the E-R model to one of the relational, network, or hierarchical models in Section 2.9. These conversions rules are summarized in Figure 14.2.

14.6.1 Designing the Conceptual Database—Relational DBMS

It is apparent from Figure 14.2 that converting the preliminary design in the E-R model to a relational model is a trivial task. An entity type is represented as a relation. A weak entity type is represented as a relation that includes the key of the identifying strong entity. A relationship is also represented as a relation and includes the primary keys of the entities involved in the relationship. In the case of a 1:N relationship, if it does not involve any attributes and if the entity on the "N side" does not participate in any other relationships, the 1:N relationship can be represented by appending the primary key of the "1 side" to the relation for the "N side." It is also possible to merge these two relations into one if performance requirements are not compromised.

An *IS_A* relationship representing a generalization-specialization hierarchy (superclass/subclass relationship) in the E-R diagram may be represented as a set of relations. Here a relation is created for the superclass entity and its key is used as a foreign key in each of the relations corresponding to the subclass entities. Another option is to have the subclass entities inherit the attributes of the superclass entity. (These options were illustrated in Figures 2.28 and 2.30, respectively.) In a third option, a single relation is created that includes the attributes of the entities at all levels of the generalization-specialization hierarchy. In this case null values are used

Figure 14.2 Conversion of E-R diagram to relational, network, and hierarchical models.

Concept in E-R Model	Conversion to Relational Model	Conversion to Network Model	Conversion to Hierarchical Model
Entity set	Relation	Record type	Record type
1:1 and 1:N binary relationship	As a relation including the primary keys of entities involved or by appending the primary key of the "1" side relation in the other relation.	As a set type where the owner record type is the "1 side."	As a hierarchy with the parent is the "1 side" record type.
M:N relationship	As a relation including the primary keys of the entities in the relationship.	Introduce an intermediate record type that is a common member of two set types owned by the record types corresponding to the M:N relationship.	For symmetric access use two hierarchies with either duplication or use of virtual records.
IS_A relationship	As a relation for the superclass and each of the subclasses with the primary key of the superclass included, or as a relation for each subclass with the attributes of the superclass included.	A 1:1 set type with mandatory membership. At most one member record type occurrence is enforced by the application program.	A hierarchy with at most one occurrence of the child record type. The constraint of at most one record occurrence at the child level is enforced by the application program.

for attributes that do not apply to a given instance of the entity. An additional attribute to indicate the type of the tuple could be used in case the generalization-specialization is disjoint. For an overlapping generalization-specialization, a Boolean attribute for each possible type may be included. In this way, the nonrelevant attributes may be ignored.

If care is taken in the preliminary design to normalize the records, the database will satisfy structural constraints. To meet the performance requirements, a number of indexes will have to be generated for each relation. The attributes used in generating the indexes depend on the types of access required.

14.6.2 Designing the Conceptual Database—Network DBMS

In the network model, the entity is represented as a record type. A weak entity is represented as a set type where the strong entity is the owner record type. Alternatively, the weak entity type may be represented as a repeating group within the record type for the strong entity. A 1:N relationship is represented as a set type where the record type corresponding to the "1 side" is the owner record type. The attribute of the relationship is combined with the attributes of the member record type. However, if the member record type participates in more than one set, the representation of the relationship requires the introduction of a record type to hold the attributes of the relationship. This newly introduced record type now becomes the common member in two sets. One is a 1:N set involving the original owner record type as owner and the new record type as member. The other is a 1:1 set involving the original member record type as an owner and the new record type as member. An N:M relationship is represented by two set types involving an intermediate record type as the member. The intermediate record type represents the attributes of the relationship.

The *IS_A* relationship representing a generalization-specialization hierarchy of the E-R diagram is represented by a 1:1 set type where set membership is mandatory. The fact that a set can have only one member occurrence is enforced by the application program.

14.6.3 Designing the Conceptual Database—Hierarchical DBMS

In the hierarchical model, each entity type is represented by a record type. A 1:1 or a 1:N relationship is represented as a hierarchy with the record type for the "1 side" being the parent. Optionally the child record type is represented as a part of the parent record type. A weak entity is represented as a child record type in a hierarchy where the record type for the strong entity is the parent or as a repeating group in the strong entity record type. An N:M relationship is represented by duplications or by use of virtual records.

The *IS_A* relationship representing a generalization-specialization hierarchy of the E-R diagram is represented by a 1:1 hierarchy, the constraint that there can be only one child record type occurrence being enforced by the application program.

14.6.4 Designing the Physical Database

The primary keys of the records included in the database are chosen during the preliminary logical database design. The physical design includes decisions regarding the following aspects of the physical database:

- The choice of clustering of records
- The choice of the file organization
- The choice of supporting indexes
- The provision of links between records

Here the intent is to choose appropriate storage structures and access aids for optimum performance of the database system. Direct access is required where the file has a high rate of insertions and deletions and indexed-sequential access is suitable for a stable file.

Performance is measured in response time for online queries such as airline reservations or banking applications, or turnaround time for application programs such as payroll preparation. Performance depends on the size of records, the amount of data and its distribution on a number of storage devices, the presence of various indexes or direct access mechanisms.

For a given system the file structures that may be used are usually dictated by the DBMS. The expected types and frequencies of data manipulation operations are used to determine access aids that would be effective. If an attribute such as address is normally used for retrieval in an online system, a direct access path based on this attribute may be implemented.

Special care is taken to define indexes in a relational system for attributes participating in join operations. The storage structure and indexes may have to be modified during the fine tuning of the system, once it becomes operational and supports day-to-day operations.

Physical storage strategy includes decisions regarding the partitioning of a record into vertical, horizontal, or mixed fragments. **Vertical fragmentation** is appropriate if some of the record's fields are accessed more frequently than others. By removing the less frequently used fields along with the primary key into a separate record on a different physical file, the volume of data transfer is reduced. This would also be applicable if the vertical fragments were rarely used simultaneously. **Horizontal fragmentation** is appropriate if some occurrences of a record are more frequently used than others.

A strategy used in a relational system is to store the join of two relations, or at least those attributes of the joined relations that are frequently required. However, this strategy requires that all update operations must maintain the consistency of the database by updating such duplicated attributes.

In a relational database, a number of indexes are created for each record. The records themselves may be stored in a serial manner. The attributes used for creating secondary indexes are determined from the processing requirements of the database. Alternately, performance requirements may dictate that if a relation is retrieved using its primary key, which is also used for join operations, the relation may be stored using direct file structure. If the relation is to be stored as a sequential file, the ordering is on the attribute that is used frequently in retrieving tuples from the relation or for performing join operations. If more than one such attribute is needed, the relation may be stored in a serial file and secondary indexes created for each such attribute. The advantages of a serial file are ease of growth and shrinkage of the file size.

In a network system, access to member record types can be improved by storing the members close to the owner record type. However, if a record type participates as a member in more than one set type, this scheme is possible for only one set, which has to be chosen judiciously. The remaining sets would be implemented with pointers and/or linked lists. Using pointers is the most common method of implementing a set construct of the network model. However, many network DBMSs allow the specification of the subsequent as well as the prior member and a pointer to the owner record from each member record. The owner record may be located efficiently using one or more indexes.

Performance in a network DBMS can be improved by the following strategies:

- Replicating attributes of the owner record in the member record. This avoids the necessity of locating the owner record to access the replicated attributes. Such replication requires that update operations modify these replicated attributes to maintain database consistency.
- Using direct access. This is specified by the calc option for an attribute of the record. The records are then stored in a direct access file and could be retrieved randomly using the value of the field.
- Assessing member records only through the owner record, specified by the via set option.
- Storing records in sequential order by specifying the field(s) to be used for the ordering.

In the hierarchical database, the storage structure allows efficient access via the root record type. The choice of the root record type will determine the performance of the system. Virtual parent-child hierarchies are implemented by pointers. A hierarchy can be partitioned and the root of each subtree can have direct access implemented for it. In this way it is possible to improve performance in the hierarchical system.

The physical database design is also an iterative process. Following the initial design, the performance of the system for a suitable mix of transactions is estimated. If the performance is not near the expected value, changes are made in the physical design. Possible problem areas could be the result of an improper choice of file organization for online transactions, storage of records required simultaneously on the same physical drive, improper type of storage unit, too many records in the overflow area of an indexed-sequential file, inappropriate bucket size for a direct access file, and so on. A number of strategies could be used to improve performance. This includes dividing a record into two or more records (e.g., relegating the little used fields into a separate record), combining two or more records into one (e.g., storing the join of two relations), or duplicating a file. These factors are considered and corrected until the performance requirements are achieved. The validity of the final design is confirmed in the next phase of the design process.

14.7 Phase VI: Implementation and Testing

In this phase the design is implemented and tested. Implementation consists of writing and compiling the code for the conceptual and external schemes in the DDL of the DBMS. The physical database is created and loaded with test data. The application programs and transactions are written using appropriate high-level languages with embedded DML statements or query language.

Once implemented, the system is put through a number of tests to verify its functioning. In a system where a large number of concurrent accesses and updates are made, errors are very difficult to locate. The test data and test pattern must be carefully planned to facilitate the location of the cause of errors.

Documentation of the system is also prepared. Documentation records procedures to be followed for regular operations and steps to be taken in the event of errors or failures. Procedures for backing up and restarting after failure of various types are outlined.

Once the system is found to be satisfactory, it is installed for use in day-to-day operations. Users are trained on the new system. It is usually given a dry run, which consists of using the new system along with the existing system. The operation of the system is monitored.

14.8 Phase VII: Operation and Tuning

In this phase of the design cycle, the design is completed and is ready for day-to-day operation. The users have been trained and the bugs have been removed. The system has been tried and the actual performance can now be measured. If the performance is not satisfactory, fine tuning is called for. This would entail using one or more of the following options: increasing the number of buffers, defining additional indexes, partitioning records, and/or clustering records that are likely to be accessed together.

14.9 Summary

In this chapter we informally examined the steps involved in the design of a database system. It begins with the identification of a problem area in the information handling capability of an organization. The feasibility of using a database system to resolve these problems is studied and where it is found that such an approach is warranted the design process starts. Once the information and processing requirements for the database system and the applications it supports are gathered, the preliminary design is undertaken. The preliminary database design is independent of any DBMS or its data model. These phases of the design problem are cyclic and may require going back to the initial step to resolve ambiguities in requirements or conflicts. The decision of which computing system and DBMS system to use can be made upon the completion of the preliminary design and the identification of the processing, storage, and performance needs. Once a decision is made on these aspects, the final design begins. It consists of mapping the preliminary design into the model of the selected DBMS and implementing the various schemes in the DDL of the DBMS. The physical database design is completed and the internal schema is defined. The application programs and the transactions are coded and the system is integrated and evaluated. At the end of the evaluation phase the system is made available for productive use and its performance is monitored.

Key Terms

information requirements
processing requirements
integrity constraints
centralized scheme design
view-integration approach
top-down approach
bottom-up approach
vertical fragmentation
horizontal fragmentation

Exercises

14.1 Videobec is the leading corporation in the growing video rental business. It has the largest number of stores and prides itself on having the most comprehensive list of video movies and games. It also rents VCRs and video cameras to its members. As a convenience, it repairs video equipment, the actual work being contracted out to a number of repair shops who reap 80% of the repair charge. Each of Videobec's stores is run by a manager and assistant manager who are full-time employees. In addition, each store hires its own part-time help who are paid on a hourly basis.

The membership privilege is extended to customers for a period of one year and is renewable, unless a member has been habitually tardy in returning items borrowed. A member is allowed to rent up to 12 movie titles, 6 video games, 1 VCR, and 1 video-camera simultaneously. Movies and games can be returned to any store, but a VCR or video camera has to be returned to the store from which it was borrowed. Members have access to the online catalogue of titles and may reserve titles. A reserved title has to be picked up before 6 P.M., after which time the reservation is automatically canceled. Items are charged per day and borrowed items have to be returned before noon. Any late return bears a charge of one additional day. A discount of 20% is awarded on weekdays for all items rented. A total discount of 33% is also given on movie rentals on weekdays when more than three titles are borrowed at one time.

Movies are held by Videobec in both VHS and Beta format. The catalogue of movies contains the title of the movie, the studio or producer, the director, two leading actors, the category of the movie, number of cassettes per copy, and charge per day. The video grames catalogue contains the name of the game, the game system, and the charge per day. Videobec carries multiple copies of the same title, and a store could have been assigned any number of copies of each title. A store that has more copies of a given title than assigned to it will return these at the end of each week to Videobec's head office, which redistributes them to appropriate stores.

You are required to design and implement the database for Videobec's operational data using an appropriate DBMS package. Prepare a report documenting your design, including an E-R model of the database. The implementation of the database is to be made using the chosen DBMS on an appropriate computer system.

Your database implementation should allow the following types of queries to be made:

- Add new titles, equipment, stores, members, employees, part-time employees, repair shops.
- Remove titles, equipment stores, members, employees, part-time employees, repair shops.
- Update appropriate attributes of titles, equipment, stores, members, employees, part-time employees, repair shops.
- Show status of a member, including titles borrowed and amount outstanding for items rented.

- Show status of movies, games, and equipment.
- Show payment to employees for the week.
- Show payment to repair shops for the month.
- Show income of a given store for the month.
- Reserve titles by members.
- Note return of items by members and additional charges outstanding (e.g., $1.00 per cassette not rewound).
- Show rental of items and initial charge for the first day of the rental.

Start with the E-R model of your system and note the attributes of each entity and relationship. Choose the DBMS and the computer system. Convert the E-R model to that of your DBMS. Implement the applications indicated above and design a set of tests for your system.

Many ambiguities in this case study will have to be resolved. This should be done via observation of an actual video store and discussions with its management. You may make appropriate assumptions but you must be able to defend them.

14.2 Do Drive is a small driving school that is growing and feels the need for a database system. The school offers driving lessons on three different vehicles—cars, trucks, and buses. To get a driving certificate from the school, which is a prerequisite for getting a driver's licenses, each student should score more than 75% in five theoretical courses (Defensive Driving, Automobile Mechanics, Highway Code, Safe Driving, and Maintenance) and more than 85% in practical driving. After 10 hours of practical driving, a student's performance is assessed. If the student fails, he or she will be asked to take two hours of additional driving. If the student fails one of the theoretical courses, he or she will be asked to appear for a supplementary test in that course.

The fee for the driving course is $300.00 for car, $700.00 for bus, and $1,000.00 for trucks. The fee for one supplementary test or one hour of extra driving, 10% of the course fee. Students can pay their fees in installments; however, the certificate is withheld while the student owes money to the school.

The school employs three types of employees: salaried employees for administration, teachers who offer theoretical courses, and instructors who give practical lessons. The salaried employees are paid a monthly salary. Each teacher is paid $300.00 per course section and each instructor is paid $100.00 per student.

You may make the following assumptions:

- A teacher can offer one or more courses. A teacher can also offer more than one section of the same course.
- An instructor can offer practical lessons to several students.
- An instructor can offer practical lesson on more than one type of vehicle.
- The school owns more than one vehicle of each type.

Once a student gets a certificate, the details pertaining to the student can be removed from the online database.

Typical operations to be supported by the database are listed below:

- Add new students, teachers, instructors, salaried employees, and vehicles.
- Remove existing students, teachers, instructors, salaried employees, and vehicles.
- Compute various types of statistics for the student population.
- Compute the payments for employees.
- Prepare the schedules for the courses and driving lessons.
- Keep track of payments made by students and amounts outstanding.

Design an E-R model for this database. Convert the model to a relation model listing the relational scheme, primary keys, and functional dependencies. Ensure that all relations are in at least the third normal form. Implement the relational model on a relational DBMS. If the DBMS does not support the concept of domain, your application programs and transactions must be able to support data validation.

14.3 You are hired to design a database system for Hotel Plein Air. The hotel owns a personal computer system and the database must be implemented on this system. The hotel has 100 guest rooms, a restaurant, a coffee shop, and a convention center/ballroom which may be divided into as many as four seminar rooms.

Each of the guest rooms has a description indicating its room number, type of beds, and its rate. Records are maintained for the regular guests of the hotel. The restaurant and the coffee shop have a certain seating capacity, and each has a number of menus. Registered guests may charge their restaurant bills to their room account. Registered guests' bills are updated every day and all charges made by these guests are entered on their room bill.

The hotel has a number of employees (assistant managers, chefs, waiters, maître d', bus-persons, maids, janitors, host/hostess, cashier, dishwashers, clerks, and a manager). All employees except the manager are paid on the basis of the number of hours worked. Each work position requires a minimum level of skill. Employees are assigned these positions for a given date and shift.

Design a database system for managing reservations, accounts, employee work assignments, and payroll preparation for the hotel. The system must have a friendly user interface, since the hotel is unwilling to train its employees extensively.

Bibliographic Notes

In this text, we did not discuss automated database design tools. However, a number of design tools for the more computationally intensive and time-consuming aspects of design are appearing on the market. Requirement analysis can be made manually using a graphical design tool such as data flow diagram (Gane 79) or hierarchical input process output (HIPO) (Jone 76), (Katz 79). Other commercial techniques such as structured analysis and design technique (SADT) (Ross 77a), (Ross 77b), developed by SofTech Inc., may also be used in establishing the requirements.

Scheme integration is surveyed in (Bati 87). In (Schk 78) the physical database design methodology is surveyed. (Marc 77) gives methods for segmenting records and deciding the blocking factor for the physical design. The following textbooks have extensive coverage of database design: (Atre 80), (Ceri 83), (Flem 89), (Furt 86), (Hawr 84), (Weid 83), and (Yao 82).

The projects given in the Exercises at the end of this chapter were used at Concordia University and were conceived by Profs. B. C. Desai, P. Goyal, T. Narayanan, and F. Sadri.

Bibliography

(Atre 80) S. Atre, *Database: Structured Techniques for Design, Performance, and Management*. New York: Wiley-Interscience, 1980.

(Bati 86) C. Batini, M. Lenzerini, & S. Navathe, "A Comparative Analysis of Methodologies for Database Schema Integration," *ACM Computing Surveys* 18(4), December 1986, pp. 323–364.

(Ceri 83) S. Ceri, ed. *Methodology and Tools for Data Base Design*. Amsterdam: North-Holland, 1983.

(Dewa 89) R. M. Dewan, & B. Gavish, ''Models for the Combined Logical and Physical Design of Databases,'' *IEEE Trans. on Computers* 38(7), July 1989, pp. 955–967.

(Flem 89) C. C. Fleming, & B. von Halle, *Handbook of Relational Database Design*. Reading, MA: Addison-Wesley, 1989.

(Furt 86) A. L. Furtado, & E. J. Neuhold, *Formal Techniques for Data Base Design*. Berlin: Springer-Verlag, 1986.

(Gane 79) C. P. Gane, & T. Sarson, *Structured Systems Analysis: Tools and Techniques*. Englewood Cliffs, NJ: Prentice Hall, 1979.

(Hawr 84) I. T. Hawryszkiewycz, *Database Design and Analysis*. Chicago: SRA, 1984.

(Jone 76) M. N. Jones, ''HIPO for Developing Specifications,'' *Datamation* March 1976, pp. 112–125.

(Katz 79) H. Katzan, Jr., *System Design and Documentation: An Introduction to the HIPO Method*. NY: Van Nostrand Reinhold, 1976.

(Loom 87) M. E. S. Loomis, *The Database Book*. NY: Macmillan, 1987.

(Marc 77) S. March, & D. Severance, ''The Determination of Efficient Record Segmentation and Blocking Factor for Shared Files,'' *ACM Trans. on Database Systems* 2(3), September 1977, pp. 279–296.

(Ross 77a) D. T. Ross, ''Structured Analysis (SA): A Language for Communicating Ideas,' *IEEE Trans. on Software Engineering* SE-3(1), January 1977, pp. 16–33.

(Ross 77b) D. T. Ross, & K. E. Schoman, Jr., ''Structured Analysis for Requirements Definition,'' *IEEE Trans. on Software Engineering* SE-3(1) January 1977, pp. 6–15.

(Schk 78) M. Schkolnick, M. ''A Survey of Physical Database Methodology and Techniques,'' Proc. of the Fourth International Conf. on Very Large Data Bases, West Berlin, 1978, pp. 474–487.

(Wied 83) G. Wiederhold, *Database Design*. NY: McGraw-Hill,1983.

(Yao 82) S. B. Yao, S. B. Navathe, J. L. Weldon, & T. L. Kunii, eds. ''Data Base Design Techniques I & II,'' Lecture Notes 132, 133. Berlin: Springer-Verlag, 1982.

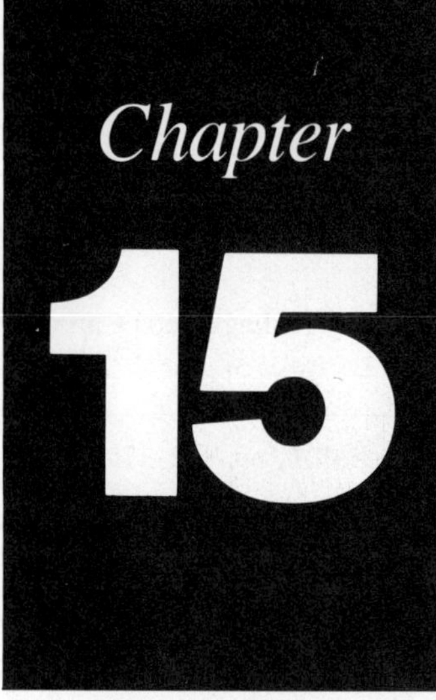

Distributed Databases

Contents

In this chapter we discuss some of the issues involved in the case of a distributed database. The components of such a database are located at a number of sites interconnected by means of a communications network. Each node consists of an independent computer system and its software. Advantages of distributing the database are the increased availability, reliability and the possibility of incremental growth. However, the costs and complexity of the system are higher. The partitioning of the database can be non-disjoint and some portions of the database could be replicated. Data distribution is covered in Section 15.3.

A query in a distributed database may need data from more than one node which entails communication costs. Distributed query processing is the topic of Section 15.5 wherein we introduce the semijoin operation. This operation is used to reduce the amount of data transmission. Consistency requirements are stressed in Section 15.6. Concurrency control in the case of a distributed database requires special treatment. A number of concurrency control alternatives are presented in Section 15.7. Section 15.8 introduces the failures peculiar to a distributed system and presents schemes for recovery from such failures. Distributed deadlock detection and prevention are covered in Section 15.9. Issues of security are the topic of Section 15.10. Examples of distributed systems are the subject of Section 15.11.

15.1 Introduction

Independent or decentralized systems were the norm in the earlier days of information management, the 1950s and early 1960s. There was duplication of hardware and facilities. Incompatible procedures and lack of management control were the consequences of the evolving nature of the field. The latter may also have been partly due to the lack of understanding of the computer as a tool. In the late 1960s and early 1970s, the trend was toward the use of large general-purpose computers, heralded by the introduction of the IBM System/360. The same facility served a multitude of users with differing needs, leading to conflict and lack of responsiveness. A centralized database system is one such shared facility.

In a centralized database system, the DBMS and the data reside at a single location, and control and processing is limited to this location. However, many organizations have geographically dispersed operations. A case in point is the MUC Library system discussed in Chapters 8 and 9. For such organizations, accessing data from a centralized database creates problems. Data of concern to a particular location, such as the Lynn branch, has to be obtained from the central site. The reliability of the system is compromised since loss of messages between sites or failure of the communication links may occur. The excessive load on the system at the central site would likely cause all accesses to be delayed. Furthermore, the single central site would exhibit a sizable load of transactions, requiring a very large computing system.

An organization located in a single building with quasi-independent operational divisions, each with its own information processing needs and using a centralized database on a local network, would have similar problems.

The current trend is toward a distributed system. This is a central system connected to intelligent remote devices, each of which can itself be a computer or interconnected, possibly heterogeneous, computers. The distribution of processing power creates a feasible environment for data distribution. All distributed data must still be accessible from each site. Thus, **distributed database** can be defined as consisting of a collection of data with different parts under the control of separate DBMSs, running on independent computer systems. All the computers are interconnected and each system has autonomous processing capability, serving local applications. Each system participates, as well, in the execution of one or more global applications. Such applications require data from more than one site.

We have to distinguish between a global or systemwide item and a local item in the distributed database system. The global item is the item as it would appear if the database were not distributed, corresponding to a conceptual data item. A local data item is a component or a copy of a global database item. We also distinguish between global and local transactions. A **global transaction** may involve the generation of a number of **subtransactions,** each of which may be executed at a different site. A transaction requiring data from its ''home'' site is a **local transaction.**

Example 15.1 Consider data item A for which two copies, A_1 and A_2, exist at sites S_1 and S_2. The operation of updating the value of A involves generating two subtransactions, T_{S1} and T_{S2}, each of which will perform the required operation at sites S_1 and S_2. ■

Teleprocessing techniques permit users to retrieve data from a remote central database. A straightforward extension permits retrieval from multiple remote databases. The implicit requirement is user knowledge of data availability and distribution. If a user desires access to some data that is moved around to different sites, the user needs to keep track of the data movement. In a general environment where each of the remote databases could have differing underlying models and be implemented on different database systems, the user would require knowledge of the properties of each of the accessed databases. Give the complexity of individual systems, this precludes effective routine access to multiple databases by most users. A distributed database hides the complexity of the underlying differences and allows such routine accesses.

Distributed database systems are capable of handling both local and global transactions. The system resolves all local database requests, access to data at other sites, and any requests it may receive from other sites. The system masks differences in the various local systems by providing a common networkwide view of the data. Through appropriate translation mechanisms, requests expressed on the common view can be translated to the local system view being accessed.

In addition to network and data distribution characteristics, the major issues in a **distributed database management system (DDBMS)** are query processing (including transaction processing), concurrency control, and recovery. We have considered these topics with respect to centralized DBMSs in earlier chapters. In this chapter we shall see how data and control distribution affect these issues.

15.1.1 Advantages and Disadvantages of the DDBMS

Distributed databases, like other distributed systems, offer advantages in:

- **Sharing:** Users at a given site are able to access data stored at other sites and at the same time retain control over the data at their own site.

- **Availability and reliability:** Even when a portion of a system (i.e., a local site) is down, the system remains available. With replicated data, the failure of one site still allows access to the replicated copy of the data from another site. The remaining sites continue to function. The greater accessibility enhances the reliability of the system.
- **Incremental growth:** As the organization grows, new sites can be added with little or no upheaval. Compare this to the situation in a centralized system, where growth entails upgrading with changes in hardware and software that affect the entire database.
- **Parallel evaluation:** A query involving data from several sites can be subdivided into subqueries and the parts evaluated in parallel.

Data distribution in DDBMs with redundant copies can be used to increase system availability and reliability. If data can be obtained from a site other than the one that has failed, then availability improves, and as the system can still run, reliability does too. Data distribution can, also, be used to decrease communication costs. If most of the data used at a given site is available locally, the communication cost compared with that of a remote centralized system is obviously reduced. These factors are also affected by the choice of network topology. While the nature of the network should be inconsequential to the database user, in reality this is not the case. Network characteristics have important effects on reliability, availability, and the cost and speed of response. In the next section we briefly look at some common network topologies.

The disadvantages of the distributed approach are its cost and complexity. A distributed system, which hides its distributed nature from the end user, is more complex than the centralized DBMS. Increased complexity means that the acquisition and maintenance costs of the system are higher than those for a centralized DBMS. The parallel nature of the system means that errors are harder to avoid and those in the applications are difficult to pinpoint. In addition, the distributed system, by its very nature, entails a large communication overhead in coordinating messages between sites. These messages not only clutter up the network, but degrade the system's performance as well. Out-of-sequence delivery or nondelivery of messages creates problems such as phantom deadlocks and blocked transactions. We examine these problems later in this chapter.

15.2 Networks

A network consisting of a number of dispersed sites interconnected over a large geographical area is referred to as **wide area** or **long haul network.** Wide area networks generally use shared telephone lines, microwaves, or satellites and are most likely relatively slow. Over a small geographical area, with a maximum distance of approximately 10 km, the interconnecting is referred to as a **local area network (LAN).** A LAN is likely to use dedicated lines in the form of a twisted pair, coaxial cable, or fiber optics and is likely to have a relatively higher transmission speed.

The sites participating in a distributed database system must be connected. Network design issues involve the choice of network topology, control and access methods, and transmission technology. The possible options for each of these aspects of networking are shown in Figure 15.1.

Figure 15.1 Network design issues.

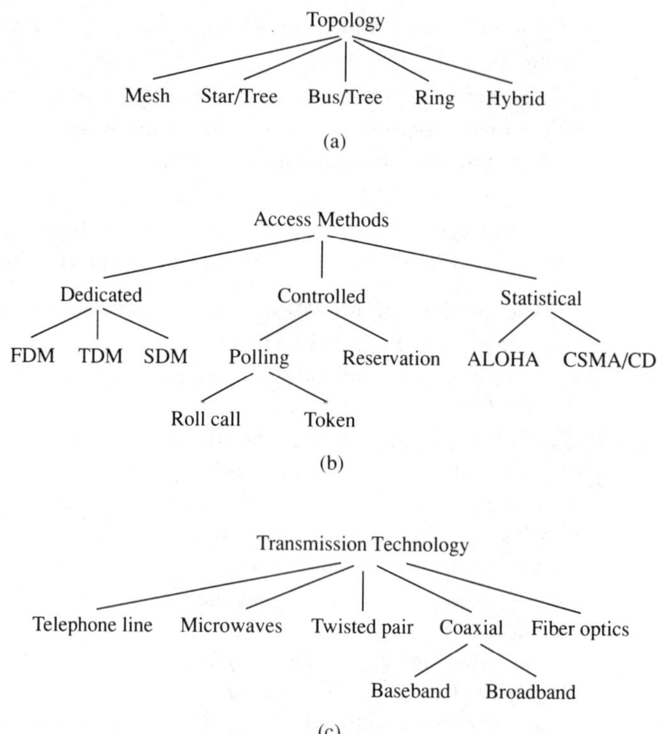

Network topology defines the structure of the network, as illustrated in Figure 15.2. In the **star topology,** all sites or nodes are connected to a central node, which is responsible for transmitting messages between the nodes. A star topology can be considered tree-based, if we consider the central node as the root node. In the **mesh connection,** the interconnecting could be variable or fully interconnected, where each node is connected directly to all other nodes. The nodes are connected by taps to a linear cable in the **bus network.** In **ring topology** each node is connected to the next by a point-to-point cable with the nodes forming a closed circuit.

A fully connected network (or mesh), in which every site is connected to all other sites, is very reliable, although expensive. Even when a link is down, a number of alternate paths exist. In practice, partially connected networks are more likely to occur. Based on traffic load and networking considerations, certain nodes are interconnected and this still allows some alternate paths between sites. In a partially connected network there may be links whose failures could partition the network.

The star network has a central node to which other nodes are connected. Some of these peripheral nodes may act as concentrators for nodes connected to them in a treelike fashion. The reliability of the system is critically dependent on the central node. Star networks or derivatives occur frequently in communication networks.

In ring topology, the nodes are connected to each other and form a closed loop. Data is transmitted in packets that circulate through the ring. The packets are inserted into the ring one at a time.

Figure 15.2 Network topologies.

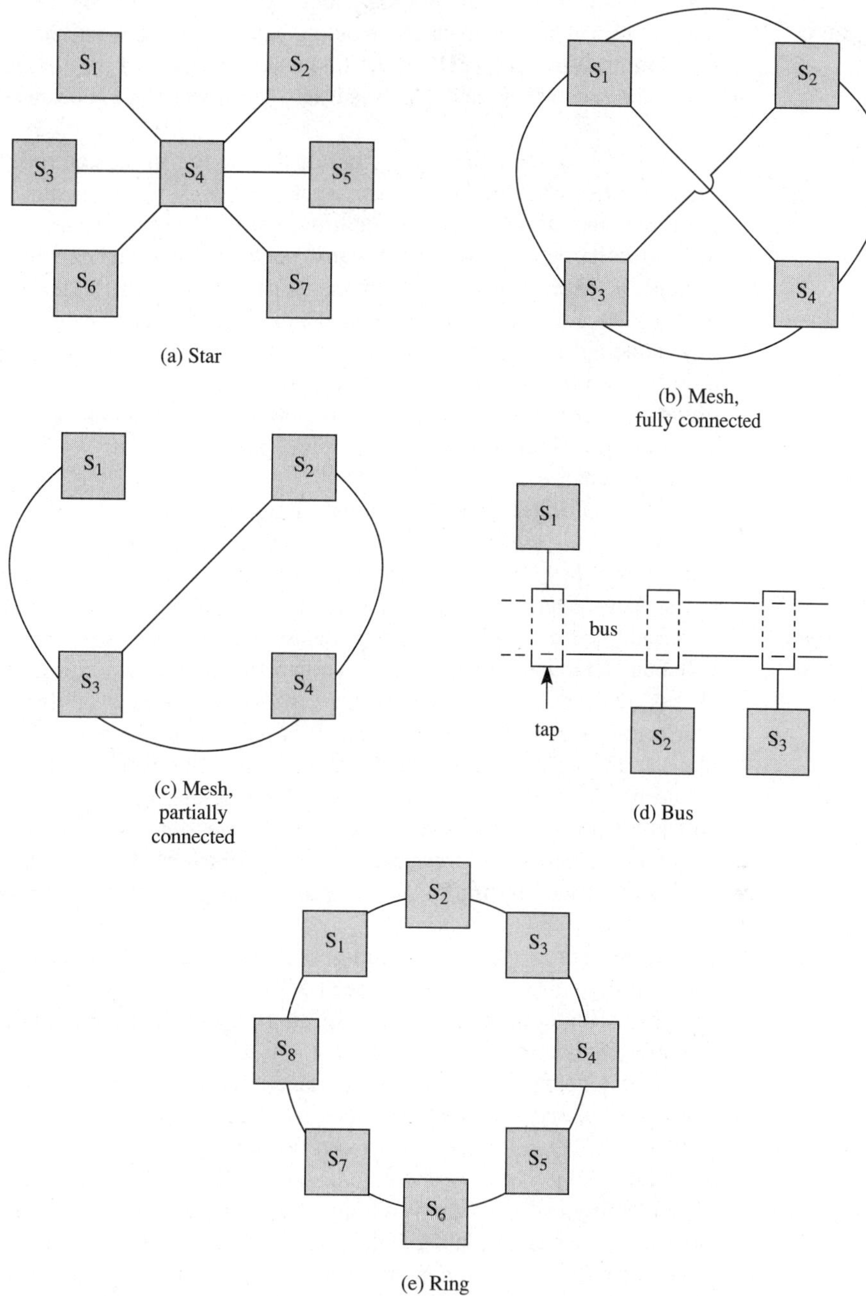

The control and access method defines how the nodes on the system get control of and utilize the transmission media. In the dedicated approach, the communication media is shared in a dedicated fashion, based on time or frequency. In **synchronous time-division multiplexing (SDM),** the different sites connected to a shared channel are assigned a time slot during which they take turns using the entire bandwidth of the channel. If a node does not have to transmit during its allocated time slot, the channel remains idle. In **time-division multiplexing (TDM)** the time slots are designated in a dynamic manner, avoiding idle periods on the channel. In **frequency division multiplexing (FDM),** the frequency spectrum of the communication channel is divided, as in radio and TV broadcasts. Each site communicates over a designated frequency.

Control can be either by polling or reservation in the controlled access scheme. In the **polling** scheme, the sites are usually polled by a central site, though distributed polling is also possible. A site requiring the use of the channel acknowledges when its address is polled and thereby gains control of the channel. In the token passing scheme, a **token** (a special bit stream) is passed from one node to another. A token-based scheme is a form of distributed polling and is used extensively in ring topology, although it could be used in others. The site requiring use of the channel waits until it receives the token. Once this happens, the site assumes control of the channel by retaining the token for as long as required. In the **reservation** scheme, a site gains control of the channel by requesting it and once the request is granted it has exclusive use of the channel.

The approach taken in the statistical access control scheme is to use the channel whenever a node has to transmit data and to detect collisions. A collision occurs when more than one node use the channel simultaneously. In the **ALOHA** scheme the senders detect the occurrence of a collision during transmission. The senders retransmit the data after a random delay. The **carrier sense multiple access with collision detection** scheme, better known by its acronym **CSMA/CD,** requires that all nodes listen before and during transmission to detect collision of simultaneous transmissions by more than one site. It is possible that more than one node will find that the channel is free and began to transmit. This would cause a collision, which would be detected since the nodes are listening during transmission. Detection of a collision causes the nodes to abort their transmission and delay retransmitting for a random time period, to prevent reoccurring collisions. In CSMA/CD, the time delay is also influenced by traffic on the channel, length of the transmission, and size of the network.

Transmission technology imposes physical constraints such as effective bandwidth and possible transmission speeds. The database system insulates the user from details of both topology and communication media characteristics, except in terms of response time.

Two topologies, bus and ring, have become popular in local area networks. Among bus-based systems, the **Ethernet** system has become the de facto standard. In Ethernet, the nodes are connected to a coaxial cable via transceiver taps as shown in Figure 15.3a. The access method used is CSMA/CD, which can be described as "listen before and while transmitting." The "listen before transmitting" is to determine if the bus is available; if it is being used, the node waits. Two nodes could simultaneously or within a short time find the bus to be quiet and start transmitting. "Listening while transmitting" allows for the discovery of collisions. In the event of a collision, the nodes involved abort transmission and reattempt after waiting a random period of time. The maximum speed of transmission on Ethernet is 10 Mbps (million bits per second) and the effective utilization is around 40%. Ethernet performance, shown in Figure 15.3b, is quite sensitive to utilization load. An increase in the number of collisions degrades performance.

Figure 15.3 Ethernet system: (a) Typical Ethernet configuration; (b) Throughput.

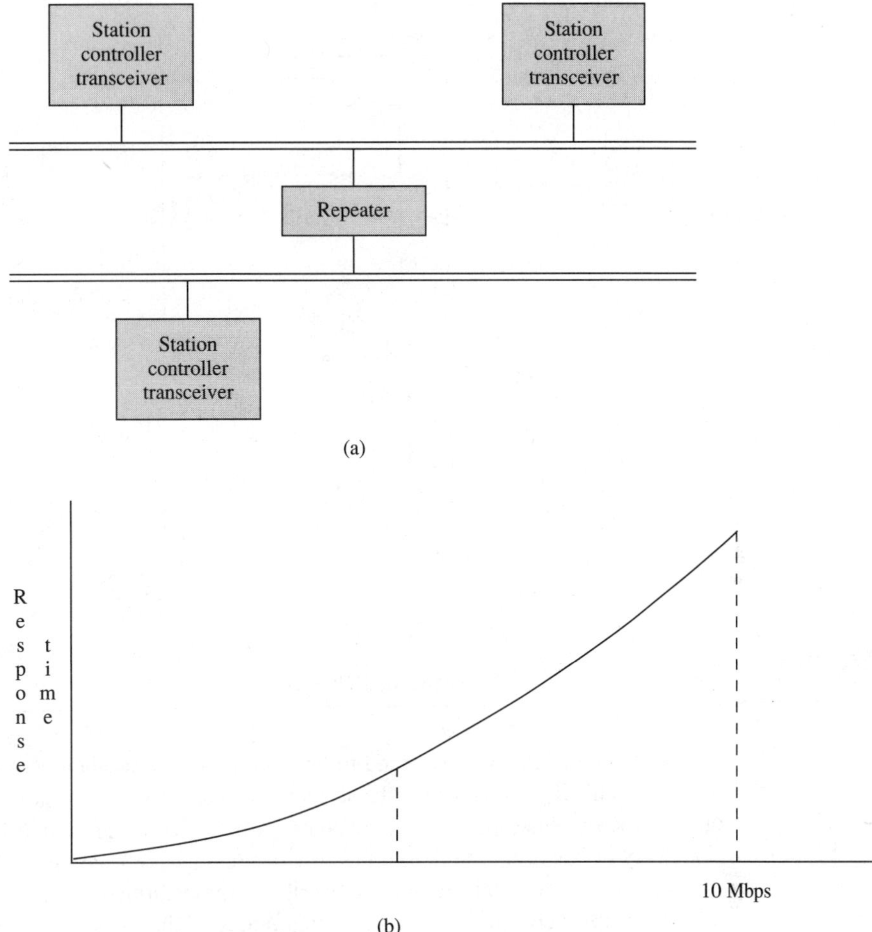

Slotted and token broadcast (or token passing) access methods are the more usual access methods employed on rings. In the token-based method, the node with the token has control of the ring. On finishing the task, the token is passed to the next node or broadcast on the ring for capture by another node.

Because the ring is susceptible to site or link failure, an alternate scheme called the **star ring,** using ''wiring concentrators,'' has been devised. This scheme, illustrated in Figure 15.4, ensures that the wiring lengths from operating nodes is constant. It allows for detecting and easily bypassing failed sites. Data from multiple rings can be selectively routed by use of a **bridge,** as shown in the figure. A ring can also contain a **gateway** to connect to external networks that might be using different communication protocols. The use of twisted pairs of wires allow speeds of up to 4 Mbps. Coaxial cables allow for speeds of up to 10 Mbps, while with fiber optics, speeds greater than 100 Mbps can be achieved.

Figure 15.4 Use of wiring concentrator in ring networks.

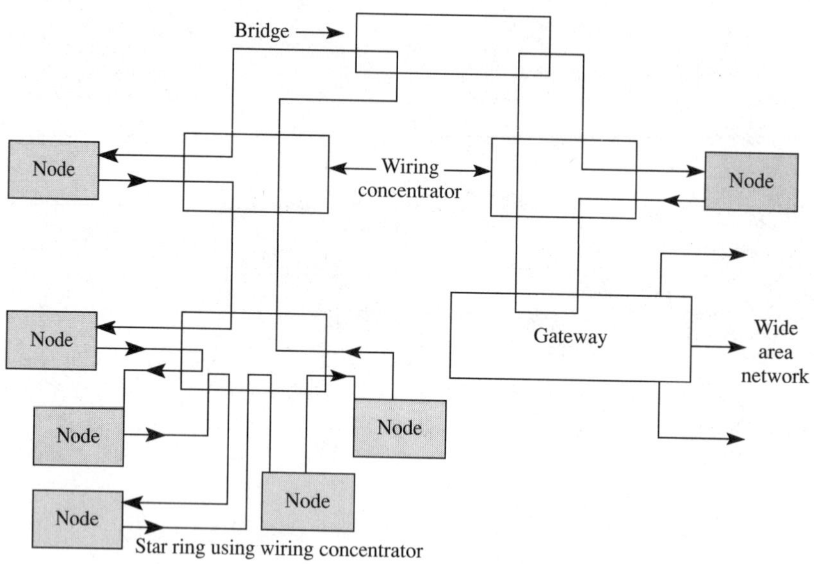

15.2.1 Failures and Distributed Databases

Distributed databases are designed to be operational even when certain failures occur in the system. Failure is said to have occurred when a site does not receive messages on a particular link, or when it receives garbled messages. Three kinds of failures can easily be identified: node failure, loss of message, or communication link failure.

A simple decentralized scheme to detect these failures could be based on periodic message exchanges between terminal nodes of the links with each site maintaining a table of "up" and "down" sites. A site that detects the failure of another site or of the link between the sites informs all other sites (including the failed site). This eventually forces a recovery procedure to start at the failed site. A site that is recovering from failure (has been down and is now ready to be up) requires that the system initiate special procedures to allow it to be reintegrated into the system. These procedures allow the site database state to become consistent with the rest of the database.

Communication link or node failures, in certain cases, can result in the database system becoming partitioned, i.e., become two or more independent systems. Example 15.2 illustrates such **network partitioning.**

Example 15.2

Consider the partially connected mesh structured communication network of Figure A. A failure in the link between nodes B and D will not cause any disruption in communication, since an alternate path exists. A failure of the link between A and D will divide the network into two partitions. A failure of node D will divide the network in three partitions.

Figure A Failures and network partitioning.

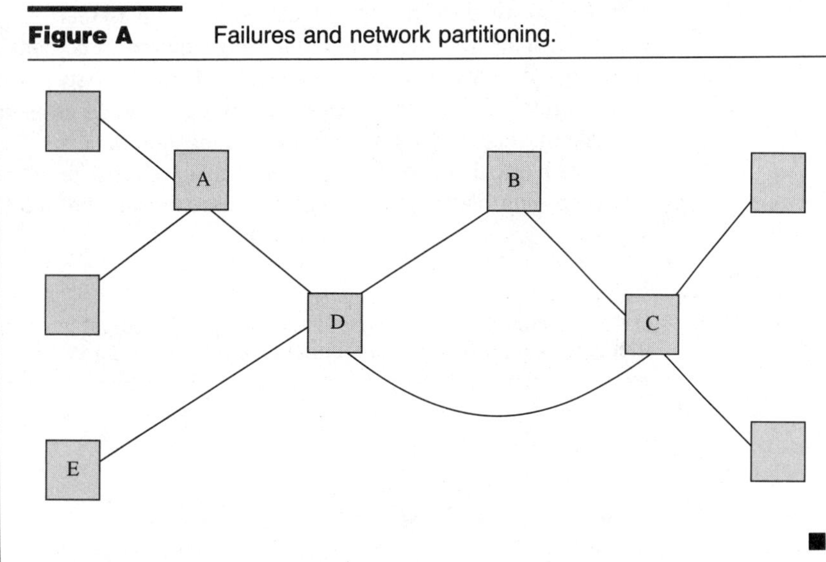

Each of the partitioned systems could operate by marking the sites in the other partitions as being down. A moment's thought should tell us that there is a considerable overhead in recovering from such a partitioning. Alternatively, the complete system has to be restarted from a consistent checkpoint before the partitioning occurred.

15.3 Data Distribution

One of the aims of a distributed database system is to maintain better control of the organization's data. The data is distributed at different sites and the distribution is based on the access patterns and costs. A comparison of the costs for different data placement options allows a selection of the best option. If a particular data item d_x stored at site S_1 is also accessed from site S_2, some possible options and corresponding cost considerations are:

1. The cost of accessing d_x at S_1 from S_2 and other sites.
2. The cost of storing d_x at S_2 instead of S_1 and the cost of accessing it from S_1 and other sites.
3. The cost of storing a copy of d_x at S_2 in addition to S_1 and the cost of accessing these from other sites. This is known as **replication,** with the copies at S_1 and S_2 being replicates.

Replication allows for increased local data availability. The advantages of local data availability are:

1. Access of a nonupdate type is cheaper.
2. Even if access to a remote site is not possible, access to local data is still available.

The major disadvantage of data replication is that the cost and complexity of updates increases, because all copies are required to be consistent with one another. However, local availability or unavailability are not issues that concern the user. One of the principal characteristics of distributed databases is **location transparency,** i.e., the insulation of the user from data location details.

It is likely that instead of access to a complete data relation, different sites need access to only portions of it. The relation can thus be divided into fragments. The

Figure 15.5 Data fragmentation: (a) A typical relation; (b) Horizontal fragmentation; (c) Vertical fragmentation; and (d) Horizontal-cum-vertical fragmentation.

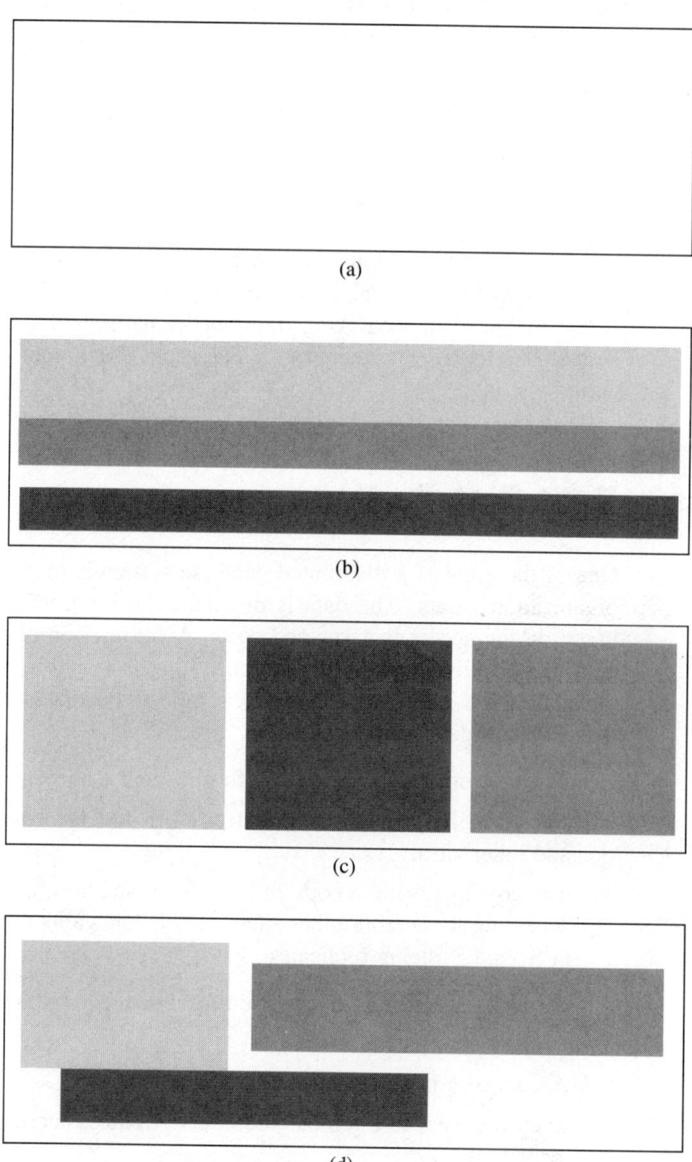

partitioning of relations is formally known as **fragmentation.** However, in the database literature, the term **disjoint fragmentation** is used to denote partitioning, and the term fragmentation refers to either disjoint or nondisjoint fragmentation.

A distributed database system insulates the user from knowledge of data fragmentation. This characteristic of distributed database systems is called **fragmentation transparency.** However, from our discussions on networks and data distribution, we realize that it may not always be possible to access all the data when communication link and node failures occur. The user may sense that some data is unavailable and consequently realize that data is partitioned.

To achieve locality of reference and reduced communication and redundancy costs, data is often fragmented. Fragmentation allows a subset of the relation's attributes or the subset of the relation's tuples to be defined at a given site to satisfy local applications. The idea of data fragmentation is displayed in Figure 15.5 and examples are given in Examples 15.3 and 15.7 and Figure E.

Example 15.3

Consider the MUC library system shown in Figure B. It has a number of branches and maintains a central acquisition, cataloging, and distribution center. A central catalog contains the title and a detailed description of each item. However, each branch maintains a local catalog and has access to the central catalog, as well as catalogs at other branches. In a manual system, the index card for items are duplicated at the central site and sent to each branch where they are stored in their local catalogs. Access to the central catalog or the catalog of another branch can only be had by calling on these locations. An alternate solution to this problem would be to include in each index card a list of all the branches at which a copy is maintained, and have a copy of the entire catalog stored at all branches. In a computerized distributed database system, the catalog is fragmented and maintained in a database at each branch.

Figure B The MUC library system.

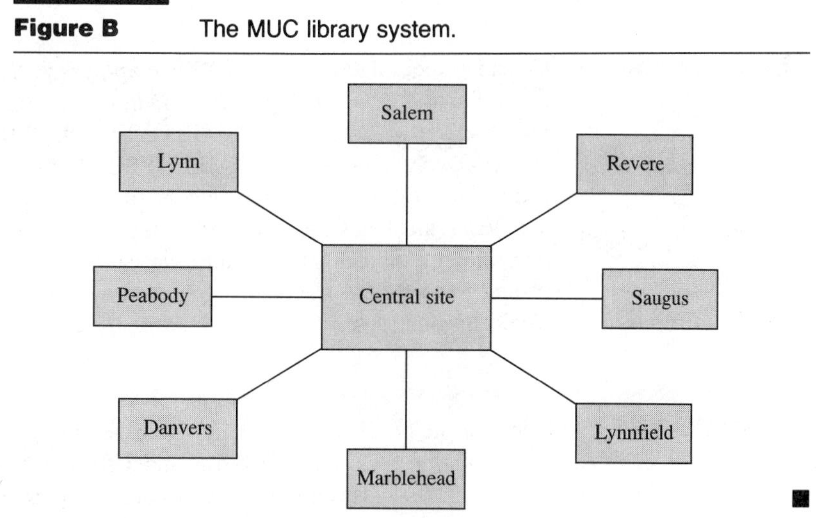

■

15.3.1 Fragmentation

A relation R defined on the scheme **R** can be broken down into the fragments R_1, R_2, . . ., R_n defined on the schemes $\mathbf{R_1}, \mathbf{R_2}, \ldots, \mathbf{R_n}$ such that it is always possible to obtain R from the fragments R_1, R_2, . . ., R_n. The fragmentation could be vertical, horizontal, or mixed, as described below.

Vertical Fragmentation

Vertical fragmentation is the projection of the original relation on different sets of attributes. Relations may be fragmented by decomposing the scheme of **R,** such that

$$\mathbf{R} = \bigcup_{i=1}^{n} \mathbf{R_i}$$

and

$$R_i = \pi_{\mathbf{R}_i}(R), \text{ for } i = 1, 2, \ldots, n$$

The original relation R can be reconstructed by a join of the fragments:

$$R = R_1 \bowtie R_2 \bowtie \ldots \bowtie R_n$$

It should be clear that for the original relation to be reconstructible, either:

1. For all fragments R_i ($i = 1, 2, \ldots, n$), there must exist another fragment R_j ($i \neq j, j = 1, 2, \ldots, n$), such that if we represent $R_i \cap R_j$ by X, then X is either a key of R_i or of R_j; or
2. System-generated TIDs (tuple identifiers) of the original relation must be duplicated in all fragments.

Examples 15.4 and 15.5 illustrate these methods of deriving the original relation from its fragments.

Example 15.4 Consider the relation EMPLOYEE(*Employee#, Name, Department, Degree, Phone#, Salary_Rate, Start_Date*). This relation can be partitioned into the vertical fragments EMPLOYEE_QUALIFICATION(*Employee#, Name, Degree, Phone#*) and EMPLOYEE_PAY(*Employee#, Name, Salary Rate, Start_Date*). The fragments are not disjoint because the *Employee#* and *Name* attributes are common in the fragments. If *Employee#* is a primary key of the original relation, we can derive the original relation by a natural join of these fragments, followed by the elimination of the duplicate *Name* attribute. ■

Example 15.5 Consider the relation MODULE_USE given in Figure C. Two vertical fragments of this relation, MODULE and USES, include the system-supplied attribute TIDs and could be joined to derive the original relation.

Figure C TIDs in vertical fragmentation.

relation: MODULE_USE

TID	MODULE	USES
t1	Query processor	SORT
t2	User interface	SORT

fragment: MODULE

TID	MODULE
t1	Query processor
t2	User interface

fragment: USES

TID	USES
t1	SORT
t2	SORT

■

TIDs may be used by the DDBMS as a physical pointer and are not visible to users. If the TIDs are visible, a user may use them in some manner and this constrains the DDBMS from changing the TIDs, for instance, when the data is reorganized. As a result, data independence, a goal of database systems, is compromised.

Note that with fragmentation, duplicate tuples may in reality be part of distinct tuples of the unfragmented relation. Such duplicate tuples should not be deleted from a fragment or, alternatively, the TIDs of the deleted tuples should somehow be maintained to reconstruct the original tuples. For example, consider the relation and its fragments given in Figure C. It is obvious that if one of the tuples in the fragment USES is deleted, say the tuple with TID t2, a join with the fragment MODULE will not result in the original relation. The reconstructed relation would lack the fact that the SORT module is also used by the user interface module. If we include the TIDs in the fragmented relation, there is no possibility of duplicate tuples. The original relation can be obtained using a join on the TIDs.

Horizontal Fragmentation

In **horizontal fragmentation** the tuples of a relation are assigned to different fragments, such that

$$R = \bigcup_{i=1}^{n} R_i$$

where each $R_i = \sigma_{C_i}(R)$ each C_i is some selection condition, and $\mathbf{R} = \mathbf{R_1} = \mathbf{R_2} = \ldots = \mathbf{R_n}$.

Example 15.6 In Figure D we graphically show a relation that is fragmented into a number of disjoint horizontal fragments, which are replicated and stored at a number of sites. The original relation could be obtained by a union operation.

Figure D Replications of disjoint horizontal fragments.

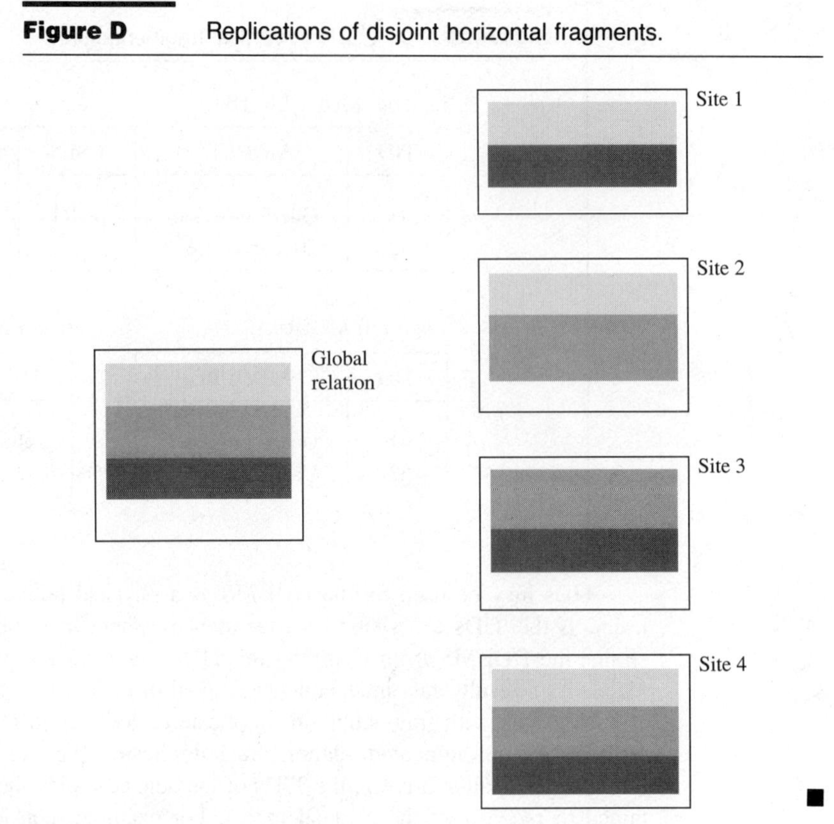

■

Figure 15.6 Data fragmentation tree.

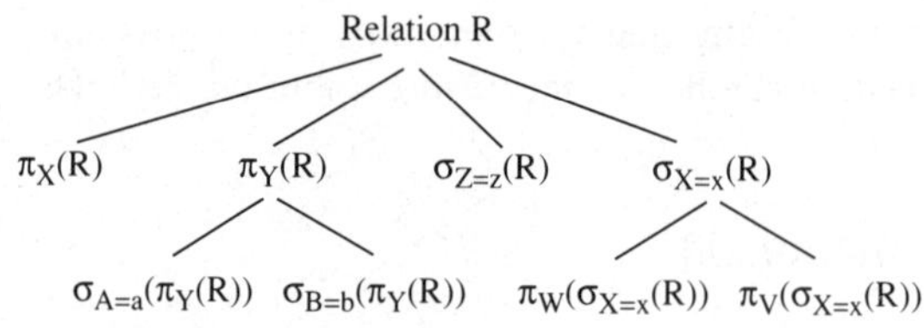

Mixed Fragmentation

Horizontal (or vertical) fragmentation of a relation, followed by further vertical (or horizontal) fragmentation of some of the fragments, is called **mixed fragmentation.** The original relation is obtained by a combination of join and union operations. Figure 15.6 illustrates a data fragmentation tree for a mixed fragmentation.

Example 15.7 The BOOK relation in the library database can be made up of the following attributes. *Book#, Call#, Copy#, First_Author_Name, Title, Volume, Publisher, Place_of_Publication, Date, Binding, Size, Number_of_Pages, Date_Acquired, Branch,* and *Cost*. Note that the attribute *Book#* is unique

Figure E Mixed fragmentation.

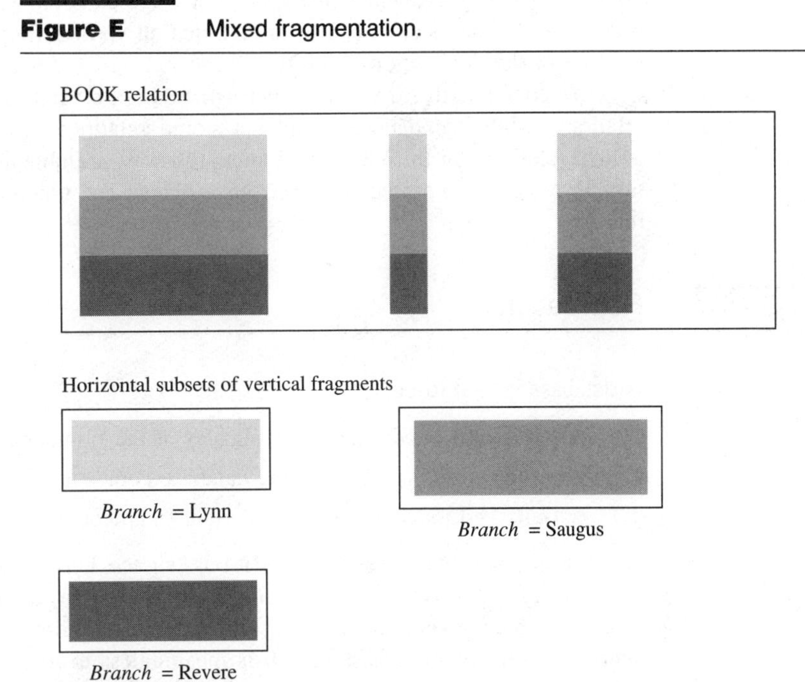

and forms a primary key of the relation. The attributes *Call#* and *Copy#* also form a key of the relation. The portion of this relation of interest to the general public is limited to *Call#, Copy#, First_Author_Name, Title,* and *Branch;* it forms a vertical fragment of the BOOK relation. The collection at a given branch forms the horizontal subset of this vertical fragment. This is illustrated graphically in Figure E. ■

Disjoint Fragmentation

In **disjoint vertical fragmentation** there are either no common attributes between any two vertical fragments or one fragment contains all the attributes of another, i.e., $R_i \cap R_j = \emptyset$ or R_i for all i and j. In **disjoint horizontal fragmentation** there are either no common tuples in any two fragments or one fragment contains all the tuples contained in another fragment, i.e., $R_i \cap R_j = \{\ \}$ or R_i for all i and j.

There is no partial overlap between the fragments. Replicates of a complete fragment are allowed in disjoint fragmentation. We point out that in disjoint vertical fragmentation with $\mathbf{R_i} \cap \mathbf{R_j} = \emptyset$, it is not possible to reconstruct the original relation unless each fragment contains the system generated TID.

Nondisjoint Fragmentation

In **nondisjoint horizontal fragmentation,** a tuple may be assigned to more than one fragment. With **nondisjoint vertical fragmentation,** an attribute may be assigned to more than one fragment. This differs from replication. Replicate fragments are exact copies of each other, while in nondisjoint fragmentation only portions of the fragments may be identical. It can be argued that all vertical fragmentation is nondisjoint because of the duplication of TIDs.

We conclude this discussion of fragmentation by stating that a user sees logical relations, while the database contains stored relations that could be fragments of logical relations. In this case, the logical relations are obtained, as discussed in Section 15.5.4, by some predefined sequence of join and union operations on the stored relations.

15.3.2 Replication

A database is said to be:

1. **strictly partitioned** when no replicates of the fragments are allowed
2. **fully redundant** when complete database copies are distributed at all sites
3. **partially redundant** when only certain fragments are replicated

For any reasonable set of applications, choice 1 for data replication would lead to relatively expensive query evaluation due to the unavailability of the data locally or at some nearby site. Choice 2 is very expensive in terms of storage space and the overhead to maintain consistency. It is meaningless to replicate data at nodes where it is unlikely to be accessed. Choice 3 is reasonable, allowing for reduced access time for frequently read local data or that from a nearby site. The choice allows for higher reliability and availability during site crashes. However, because of replication, updates are expensive.

Updates require access to all copies of the data item. Because the copies are distributed over different sites of the network, the sites must reach a consensus on the possibility of an update. Failed sites may not participate in the agreement, and sites may fail after the process has started. These issues are dealt with later in this chapter in sections on concurrency and recovery.

Although a major aim of database systems is to reduce if not eliminate redundancy, planned data redundancy can improve distributed database performance. For example, if a number of copies of a data item are available, a read operation can be directed to any one of these copies. A write operation, however, must update all copies, otherwise we would have inconsistent data. The system is required to ensure that any update operation is done on all replicates. This results in increased overhead—a price to be paid in distributed databases.

To summarize, replication improves the performance of simple read operations in a distributed system and improves its reliability. However, updates incur greater overhead and the requirement that all replicates of data be updated and consistent adds complexity to a distributed database system. This is especially true in the case of concurrent updates.

15.3.3 Transparency

In the preceding sections we discussed data distribution, fragmentation, and replication. Since it is possible for data to change, the number of copies could vary and these copies could migrate from one site to another. It is unreasonable to expect the user to know on which site the requested data resides, or the fragmentation criterion. This being so, the DDBMS is required to hide all such details from the user and provide:

- **Location transparency:** User does not need to know the location of the data.
- **Fragmentation transparency:** User need not be aware of the data fragmentation.
- **Replication transparency:** User is unaware of data replication.

In light of the above, a user accesses the database more or less as if it were completely local.

Example 15.8

Consider the fragmentation of the catalog information in the library database given in Example 15.7. A user who consults the database to find all the titles of books by Haley could pose the following query: "List all titles where first author is Haley." The response would return all titles by Haley, regardless of the branch to which a book is assigned. ■

In addition to providing a transparency to the user for reading, a DDBMS is required to provide an **update transparency.** This entails that all copies of the data item being updated, in all fragments that contain it, be modified. This involves concurrency control to ensure consistency and serializability. Failures of different types require rollback or recovery. We consider the problems of concurrency and recovery in Sections 15.7 and 15.8, respectively.

15.3.4 System Catalogs

System catalogs, or dictionaries, maintain metadata on database relations. In a distributed database system, information on locations, fragmentations, and replications is also added to the catalogs. The catalogs themselves, just like the database, may be distributed in any of the above three ways. That is, a catalog could be: (1) strictly partitioned, (2) fully redundant, or (3) partially redundant. Now let us consider the ramifications of each of these replication options.

During the transformation of a query from the user-specified form to an internal access plan, system catalogs are consulted at all stages. Choice 1 for catalog distribution would therefore be a poor strategy, requiring considerable communication between sites. Catalog maintenance is, however, very simple and the scheme allows for maximum site autonomy. Choice 2 would allow fast access for query resolution, but the catalogs would be costly to maintain. Choice 3 is a reasonable alternative, particularly when the complete catalog is available at a number of sites. For query resolution the user site accesses the nearest site with the complete catalog, or the one with the required catalog fragments. An advantage of schemes 2 and 3 is that there are always some sites on the system containing the catalog, allowing the system to function even when other sites have failed. The choice between 2 and 3 depends on retrieval and catalog update frequencies.

Catalog updates usually occur at the time of creation or deletion of relations and modification of attributes. In distributed databases, certain statistics pertaining to the characteristics of the data play an important role in determining access and query evaluation plans. These statistics, maintained in the system catalog, are likely to change regularly, entailing catalog updates. Some typical approaches to catalog distribution and maintenance problems are discussed below.

The R* system uses a distributed catalog. Local catalogs keep information on locally stored objects, including any fragments and replicates. The catalog at the **birth_site** of an object (site at which the object was first created) maintains the current storage sites of that object. Object movement causes this information to be updated. This scheme maintains complete site autonomy and is a type 1 scheme.

Distributed INGRES differentiates between local and global relations. Only global relations are accessible from all sites. A catalog of all global relations, the so-called **global catalog,** is maintained at all sites. The creation of a global relation requires its name and location to be broadcast to all sites. This is a type 2 scheme.

In the SDD-1 system, the catalog is a single relation that can be fragmented and replicated, allowing the entries to be distributed at data module sites. It is possible for local objects to have their catalog entries at a remote site. Consequently data definition operations may be nonlocal. This is a type 3 scheme. However, a fully replicated locator catalog is required at each site to keep track of the database catalog. A **locator catalog** contains information on the global scheme and details concerning fragmentation and replication.

Catalog details such as local-to-global name mappings, physical details concerning file organization and access methods, general and integrity constraint details, and database statistics could be stored locally. A site needing remote catalog information requests such information and stores it for later use. This scheme is called **caching the remote catalog.** It is not a replication of the remote catalog insofar as no attempt is made to maintain the consistency between the cached catalog and the remote one. The two are identical at the time of caching and this is indicated by both having identical version numbers. However, over time the remote catalog could be modified and its version number could change. This inconsistency is revealed when a query processed with a cached catalog is executed. At that time it is discovered that an out-of-date catalog has been used. This causes the query plan to be abandoned and the updated catalog to be transmitted to and cached at the site in question. The query is then reprocessed with the up-do-date remote catalog. SSD-1 and Distributed INGRES use this scheme of remote catalog caching.

15.4 Object Naming

In a distributed database system, we want to share data but we don't want too many restrictions on the user's choice of names. The system can adopt a **global naming** scheme such that all names are unique throughout the system. Two sites or users cannot use the same name for different data objects. This requirement for unique names can cause problems when a new site with an existing database is being integrated into the DDBMS. A unique name criterion would entail renaming objects in the database to be integrated as well as in the application programs that access them.

A drawback of the global name requirement is the loss of local autonomy, which allows users to choose appropriate local names even for global data items. Another deterrent is the bottleneck that would be created with the use of a single global name server, which has to be consulted for each name that is to be introduced in the database. The reliability of the system would also be compromised, since the entire system would be dependent on a single name server site for resolving naming conflicts.

For these reasons we stay away from a global naming scheme or the requirement that users choose systemwide unique names. Lifting such restrictions make it possible for different names to be used for the same data object, or the same name for different data objects. Although objects may not have unique names in the database, the DDBMS is required to differentiate between the objects.

Names used in queries or application programs are chosen by the end-users. To keep programming and query specification simple and invariant, regardless of the site from which they are executed, the network details must be transparent to the user. For instance, user A can enter the same query at site 1 or site 2 and anticipate the same results. Names selected by users have to be converted into system-unique names. This is done by consulting the local and/or the remote site catalog.

System R* maps end-user names (called **print names**) to internal systemwide names (SWNs). An SWN has the form:

creator@creator_site.object_name@birth_site

The birth_site is the site at which the object was first created, and because site names are chosen to be unique, an SWN is unique. An object X that was created in Washington by user John will have the SWN of:

John@Washington.X@Washington.

The same user could create, from Washington, an object named X at Montreal and this would receive the SWN of:

John@Washington.X@Montreal.

Note that the second data item is distinct from the first one. Also note that the user name is local; John@Washington is distinct from John@Montreal. In addition the name of an object includes its birth_site but this need not be its actual location. The data item could be moved to another site and be replicated at a number of sites.

To allow users to use print names, which are names of their choice for global data items, System R* creates these print names as synonyms for the corresponding SWNs. The synonyms are stored in the local catalog. The synonym-mapping scheme allows different print names for the same object and different objects having the same print names. The local catalog entry for an object includes its SWN, among other things. To find the catalog entry for an object, search the local catalog, followed by the birth_site catalog, then the site indicated by the birth_site catalog as currently holding the object.

Internal names can also be used to differentiate between fragments and replicates. If each fragment and replicate is assigned a number, these numbers can be concatenated with the name@birth_site to distinguish the different fragments or copies.

15.5 Distributed Query Processing

A query in a DDBMS may require data from more than one site. The transmission of this data entails communication costs. If some of the query operations can be executed at the site of the data, they may be performed in parallel. Section 15.5.1

elaborates on this aspect of distributed query processing. The semijoin operation, introduced in Section 15.5.2, is used to reduce the size of a relation that needs to be transmitted and hence the communication costs.

Consider a user at site S_1 that poses a query that requires data from another site, S_2, as well as its own. The response to the query can be built by one of the following:

1. Sending data from S_2 to S_1.
2. Resolving the query at S_2.
3. Resolving the query at another site, S_3.

The first choice is obvious. Option 2 requires that the query and relevant data be transmitted from S_1 to S_2, while option 3 requires that the relevant data from both S_1 and S_2 be sent to some other site, S_3 (strange as it may sound, in some circumstances this choice can be better than the other two). The optimal choice depends on the sizes of the relations and results; the communication costs between S_1 and S_2, S_1 and S_3, S_2 and S_1, S_2 and S_3; and the site where the result will be utilized. Here we concern ourselves only with communication cost. It is common to calculate communication cost in terms of the number and size of messages, i.e.,

$$\text{communication cost} = c_0 + c_1 * \text{size}$$

where c_0 is the setup constant, c_1 the cost per byte of transmitting data, and size the number of bytes of data transmitted. When the same message is broadcast to n sites, the factor c_1 can be replaced by c_n, where for point-to-point transmissions:

$$c_n = n * c_1$$

and for broadcast transmissions:

$$c_n = c_1$$

It becomes clear that if we want to optimize communication cost alone, we should consider both the total number of messages and the number of bytes transmitted.

The other point to be considered is data distribution. Access for read operations can be localized as far as possible. Consequently, communication costs can be incurred for update operations.

We consider the communication cost reduction techniques for one of the most common relational algebra operations, the join. The join is also one of the most expensive operations to perform. In the following join we ignore the joining attributes for convenience.

$$T = R \bowtie S$$

If these relations are stored at different sites, the join can be performed by transmitting tuples of one of the relations, on demand, to the site of the other relation; or one of the relations, in its entirety, to the site of the other relation; or both relations to a third site. The number of messages in the first choice is at least equal to the number of tuples in the relation. In the second, it is one and only one of the relations needs to be transmitted. In the third case the number of messages is two, and the size of each message transmitted is equal to the size of the corresponding relation.

Let us discuss the first method in more detail. If we have to transmit tuples on demand, why not ask for tuples that match some tuple in the other relation? For example, if we are to join the relations R and S, we can send a tuple of S and ask for all tuples of R that match this tuple of S. In this instance the number of messages is 2 * |S|. The size of each response depends on the number of tuples that match a given S tuple. If we assume that the number of tuples of R that join with a tuple of S is $\delta|R|$, where δ is some factor in the range [0,1], then the communication cost is given by:

$$|S| * (c_0 + c_1 * S_{sz}) + |S| * (c_0 + c_1 * \delta|R| * R_{sz})$$

Here R_{sz} and S_{sz} are the tuple sizes of relations R and S, respectively. The first factor is due to the tuples of S transmitted to the site of R. The second factor is due to the tuples of R returned in response to each tuple of S.

In the first and second methods of performing the join of R and S, having the choice of which relation to transmit doubles the number of possibilities to evaluate before a satisfactory determination of optimal costs can be made.

15.5.1 Parallelism in Distributed Query Processing

Consider the evaluation of a query involving a number of joins, as follows:

$$R \bowtie S \bowtie T \bowtie U$$

Suppose the relations R, S, T, U are stored at sites S_1, S_2, S_3, and S_4. Ignoring the differing costs due to the different sizes of these relations, the query can be evaluated in parallel by the following scheme. Relation S could be shipped to site S_1 where the first join $R \bowtie S$ is evaluated. Relation U is shipped to site S_3 where the join $T \bowtie U$ can be evaluated in parallel. In a bus-structured network, the transmission of these relations can be done in sequence, whereas in a mesh-structured network the transmission can occur in parallel.

At the conclusion of the first join, the result is transmitted to site S_3, where the final join of $(R \bowtie S)$ with $(T \bowtie U)$ is performed to evaluate $R \bowtie S \bowtie T \bowtie U$. Alternatively, the tuples of the first join can be transmitted to S_3 as they are produced at site S_1. Another alternative, where the result of the join is needed at site S, is to transmit to site S the tuples of the join $R \bowtie S$ from S_1 and the tuples of the join $T \bowtie U$ from S_3 as they are produced. This enables site S to concurrently compute the final join operation.

If the site where one of the relations involved in the join is also the site where the result of the join is required, that site should be used to evaluate one of the first joins and the final join. This scheme avoids retransmitting the result of the first of these joins.

15.5.2 Semijoin

Let us examine Example 15.9, which requires the join of two relations stored at different sites.

Example 15.9 Consider the two relations shown in Figure F. STUDENT is at site 1 and REGISTRATION is at site 2. Suppose a class list of each course is to be

Figure F Obtaining a join using a semijoin.

STUDENT

Std#	*Std_Name*
1234567	Jim
7654321	Jane
2345678	San
8765432	Ram
3920137	John
4729435	Ron
3927942	Aron
1934681	Rodney
8520183	Maria

Site 1

REGISTRATION

Std#	*Course#*
1234567	COMP353
1234567	COMP443
2345678	COMP201
8765432	COMP353
8765432	COMP441
7654321	COMP441

Site 2

X = $\pi_{Std\#}$ (REGISTRATION)

Std#
1234567
2345678
8765432
7654321

Y = STUDENT ⋉ REGISTRATION = STUDENT ⋈ X

Std#	*Std_Name*
1234567	Jim
7654321	Jane
2345678	San
8765432	Ram

STUDENT ⋈ REGISTRATION = Y ⋈ REGISTRATION

Std#	*Course#*	*Std_Name*
1234567	COMP353	Jim
1234567	COMP443	Jim
2345678	COMP201	San
8765432	COMP353	Ram
8765432	COMP441	Ram
7654321	COMP441	Jane

prepared, which involved joining the two relations. The join could be performed by first projecting REGISTRATION on *Std#* and transmitting the result, $\pi_{std\#}$ (REGISTRATION), to site 1. At site 1, we select those tuples of STUDENT that have the same value for the attribute *Std#* as a tuple in $\pi_{std\#}$ (REGISTRATION) by a join. The entire operation of first projecting the REGISTRATION and then performing this join is called a semijoin and denoted by ⋉. However, we do not obtain the desired result after the ⋉ operation. The semijoin operation reduces the number of tuples of STUDENT that have to be transmitted to site 2. The final result is obtained by a join of the reduced STUDENT relation and REGISTRATION. These steps are illustrated in Figure F. The class list can be obtained by sorting the resulting relation on *Course#*.

Note: It may be worthwhile to compute Y = STUDENT ⋉ REGISTRATION and Z = REGISTRATION ⋉ STUDENT and then obtain the final result by X ⋈ Z. ■

To reduce the communication cost in performing a join, the **semijoin** ($\ltimes$) operator has been introduced. Let P be the result of the semijoin:

$$P = R \ltimes S$$

Then P represents the set of tuples of R that join with some tuple(s) in S. P does not contain tuples of R that do not join with any tuple in S, thus P represents the reduced R that can be transmitted to a site of S for a join with it. If the join of R and S is highly selective, the size of P would only be a small proportion of the size of R. To get the join of R and S, we now join P with S, i.e.,

$$\begin{aligned} T &= P \bowtie S \\ &= (R \ltimes S) \bowtie S \\ &= (S \ltimes R) \bowtie R \\ &= (R \ltimes S) \bowtie (S \ltimes R) \end{aligned}$$

The semijoin is a reduction operator; R $\ltimes$ S can be read as R semijoin S or the reduction of R by S. Note that the semijoin operation is not associative. In Example 15.9, STUDENT $\ltimes$ REGISTRATION is not the same as REGISTRATION $\ltimes$ STUDENT. The former produces a reduction in the number of tuples of STUDENT; however, the latter is the same relation as REGISTRATION!

In distributed query processing, communication cost reduction is one of the objectives. The semijoin operation can be introduced to reduce the cardinality of large relations that are to be transmitted. Reduction in the number of tuples reduces the number and total size of the transmission and the total cost of communication.

It is wrong to assume that if $|R| > |S|$, then R should be reduced, as we shall see below.

To compute the join of R and S, we first compute the semijoin and then the join of one of the reduced relations with the other. The evaluation of the semijoin R $\ltimes$ S requires that we transmit $\pi_{R \cap S}(S)$ to the site of R. We do not need to transmit the whole of S. Let us refer to this projection of S and S′ and the size of the projected S as s′.

We use S′ to reduce R by computing R $\ltimes$ S′. Let us refer to the reduced R as R′ and the size of reduced R as r′. R′ is then transmitted to the site of S to compute the join (R′$\bowtie$ S). The communication cost incurred is:

$$2 * c_0 + c_1 * (s' + r')$$

Without the semijoin, we would have sent the whole of R to the site of S and the cost would have been:

$$c_0 + c_1 * |R| * R_{sz}$$

Therefore, the benefit of using the semijoin is:

$$c_1 * (|R| * R_{sz} - s' - r') - c_0$$

If the benefit is greater than zero, we prefer the semijoin over the traditional join.

The decision as to whether to reduce R or S can only be made after comparing the benefit of reducing R with that of reducing S. (We can also choose to reduce both.) We have already calculated the cost of reducing R; now let us do the same for S. As before, let us represent the size of $\pi_{R \cap S}(R)$ as r″ and the size of the reduced

S, after performing the semijoin S $\ltimes$ $\pi_{R \cap S}(R)$, as s″. Then the total communication cost incurred is:

$$2 * c_0 + c_1 * (s'' + r'')$$

Therefore, the optimal communication cost in evaluating R $\bowtie$ S using the semijoin technique is:

$$2 * c_0 + c_1 * \min (s' + r', s'' + r'')$$

The optimal cost of performing R $\bowtie$ S without the semijoin is:

$$c_0 + c_1 * \min (|R| * R_{sz}, |S| * S_{sz})$$

The semijoin technique is beneficial when:

$$c_0 + c_1 * \min (r' + s', r'' + s'') < c_1 * \min (|R| * R_{sz}, |S| * S_{sz})$$

Example 15.10 illustrates a numerical example to determine when the semijoin will be advantageous.

Example 15.10

Let us reconsider the join operation in Example 15.9. Suppose the result is required at site 2. Let us compare the communication costs of the semijoin with those of a simple join. Assume that the size of attributes are as follows: *Std#* = 7, *Std_Name* = 20.

The first semijoin incurs a communication cost of $c_0 + c_1 * 28$ and the transmission of the semijoin result incurs a communication cost of $c_0 + c_1 * 108$, for a total of $2 * c_0 + c_1 * 136$. For the joint operation the communication cost of transferring STUDENT to site 2 would be $c_0 + c_1 * 243$. The difference in cost is $c_1 * 107 - c_0$. If $c_0 < c_1/107$, then the semijoin operation is better from the point of view of communication costs. ■

In the above analysis, we have ignored the fact that the result of the join will be available at a different site when we reduce R rather than S. The same is true for the join operation (without using the semijoin) when we transmit S rather than R. In a complete analysis, the cost of transmitting the join result to the required site has to be taken into consideration.

The semijoin operation reduces the communication cost but not the I/O and processing costs. In fact, the latter two costs may increase.

15.5.3 Semijoin and Reduction of Relations

As we have seen, the semijoin operation reduces the size of the relations and this characteristic can be profitably utilized in query evaluation.

Definition: Full Reduction of Relation:

A relation that appears in the qualification clause of a query is said to be fully reduced if all of its tuples that do not satisfy the qualification have been eliminated.

In query evaluation, we can process the fully reduced relations instead of the original relations. The problem now becomes identifying all tuples that do not satisfy the qualification. A semijoin reduces a relation by eliminating tuples that will not take part in the join. Thus, we can use semijoin programs to reduce the participating relations. We cannot, however, claim that the relations are fully reduced.

Consider the qualification part of a query,

$$(\mathrm{R}.A = \mathrm{S}.B) \wedge (\mathrm{R}.C = \mathrm{T}.D) \wedge (\mathrm{R}.E = \mathrm{U}.F) \wedge (\mathrm{S}.G = \mathrm{V}.H) \wedge (\mathrm{S}.J = \mathrm{W}.K)$$

where the attributes A and B are defined on the same domain. Similarly, each of (C,D), (E,F), (G, H) and (J,K) are defined on the same domains. We can rename the attributes and rewrite the qualification part of the query as:

$$(\mathrm{R}.A = \mathrm{S}.A) \wedge (\mathrm{R}.C = \mathrm{T}.C) \wedge (\mathrm{R}.E = \mathrm{U}.E) \wedge (\mathrm{S}.G = \mathrm{V}.G) \wedge (\mathrm{S}.J = \mathrm{W}.J)$$

Each term of this expression can be evaluated by a join. A pictorial method of showing the order of evaluation of the joins involved is given in Figure 15.7a and is known as a **query graph.** The relations involved in the expression appear as nodes of the query graph. There is an edge in this graph between nodes R and S with the label A, if the clause (R.A = S.A) is in the expression. It has been shown (please see the bibliographic notes for reference) that the relations in a query whose qualification is either a tree or the equivalent of a tree graph can be fully reduced.

A query whose qualification part cannot be converted to a query graph in the form of a tree is called a **cyclic query.** (R.A = S.A) $\wedge$ (S.J = W.J) $\wedge$ (R.C =

Figure 15.7 Query graph: (a) tree query; (b) cyclic query.

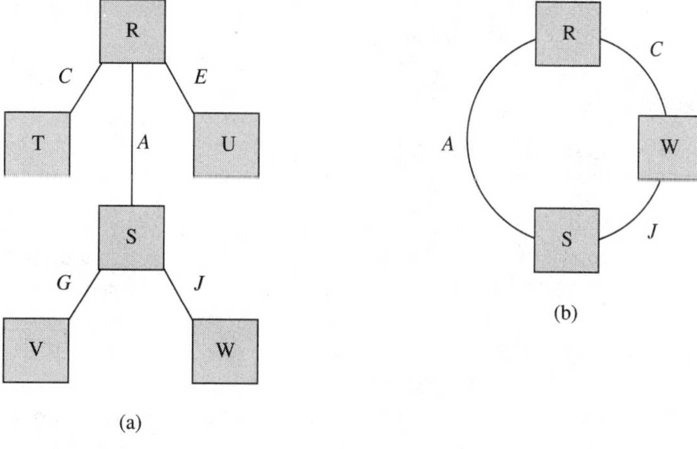

W.*C*) is an example of a cyclic query expression. The query graph for this query is given in Figure 15.7b. In the case of cyclic queries, it may not be possible to fully reduce all relations by semijoins.

15.5.4 Concluding Remarks

We have only considered the communication cost to date because it was not present in query processing in a centralized DBMS. The other two costs, I/O and processing costs, are similar to the centralized case. The other reason for focusing on communication costs is because of the traditional use of slow speed lines for connecting geographically dispersed sites. With slow speed lines, the communication cost dominates all other costs. On faster networks, which are more common for local area networks, communication and I/O costs are comparable and any optimization should attempt to optimize total costs.

In an earlier chapter on centralized database query processing, we considered ways of reducing the number of I/O pages accessed in processing a query. A common technique is the use of secondary access structures. In distributed systems, such access structures are sometimes inappropriate. We need to keep these indexes current. The processing of a query at multiple sites in parallel can reduce overall evaluation costs. Even when data is transmitted between sites, any possible local reduction, for example, due to selection or projection, is first made. After local reduction, the resultant relation or fragment becomes incompatible with the index. It has been shown that in some cases it may be advantageous to create a temporary index for query optimization. Such temporary indexes are discarded at the end of the query evaluation process.

Distributed query processing is also complicated by the presence of fragments. As we saw in the section on data distribution, some fragments are stored relations. The users see logical relations. A logical relation can be considered a query on stored relations. Such a query is composed of some sequence of joins and union operations on the stored fragments. The user query can thus be transformed into an expression containing operations on stored relations. For example, let R be some logical relation such that $R = R_1 \bowtie R_2$. Let the user query be $\sigma_P \pi_Q(R)$. We can replace the user query with $\sigma_P \pi_Q(R_1 \bowtie R_2)$ and subsequently apply query optimization operations to this modified one.

15.6 Consistency

In a distributed system, a transaction T_i requiring data items from a remote site S_j spawns a subtransaction (also called a transaction agent) T_{ij} at this remote site (Figure 15.8). Such subtransactions are executed independently at the respective sites. The site of the transaction can be considered the **coordinator site** and the sites where the spawned subtransactions run are called **participating sites.** The transaction T_i is referred to as the coordinator. In addition each site, as in a centralized database, contains a **transaction manager** that arbitrates resource requests from transactions running at the site. A request for a remote resource results in the spawning of a subtransaction at the remote site.

Figure 15.8 Query processing in the DDBMS.

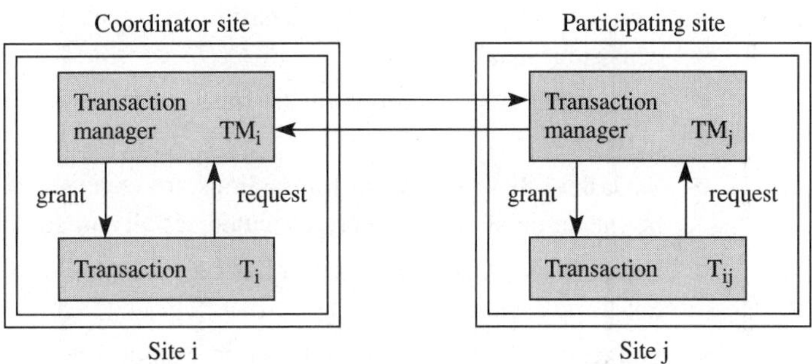

One such need for a subtransaction is when a transaction has to modify a data item and several copies of the data item exist at a number of different sites. Each data item could be modified by a subtransaction spawned at these remote sites, as indicated in Example 15.1.

All data in a database system must be consistent and must always satisfy certain a priori constraints. The DDBMS (DBMS, in a centralized system) must guarantee that these constraints are never violated. In practice, as we saw in Chapter 12, there are times when such constraints are violated; however, since the values of the data items not satisfying these constraints are not accessible during these times, the constraints never appear to be violated. Constraints of this type are also referred to as **invariants.** The system state is not only consistent, but it arrives at this consistent state from another consistent state as a result of external stimuli. Such is the case when a system in some consistent state is required to perform an action. Then the resultant state is not only consistent but also reflects the result of only that action. A system is required to be consistent with respect to its invariants and the externally applied stimuli.

We can say that an action F will change the state of the database:

state′ := F(state)

by changing the values of some entities in the write set of F (denoted F_w) depending on the values in the read set of F (denoted F_r). Thus, the action F needs only to read the referenced values in F_r and write the values in F_w.

While performing an action, the system state might be temporarily inconsistent. If the state is visible, our requirement for a consistent state is violated. An action, however trivial, will take some finite amount of time and during that time the state may be inconsistent (we use the word maybe because it the write set of the action is empty, it cannot leave the system in an inconsistent state). If we can make the transition from the old state to the new state instantaneously or not allow another action during the transition period, then we can guarantee that the visible state is always consistent.

An action F is atomic if all the writes are completed without making the database inconsistent, or none of the writes take place. When all the writes are successfully completed an action is said to have committed, otherwise it is said to have aborted.

As we discussed in Chapter 12, transactions are said to possess certain properties:

- **Consistency:** A transaction transforms a consistent database state into another consistent database state.
- **Atomicity:** All operations of the transaction are performed or none are performed.
- **Serializability:** If several transactions are executed concurrently, the result must be the same as if they were executed serially in some order.
- **Durability:** Once a transaction has been committed the results are guaranteed not to be lost.
- **Isolation:** An incomplete transaction cannot reveal its results.

These properties of a transaction are assured by using certain concurrency control and recovery techniques. Chapters 11 and 12 covered such techniques for centralized DBMSs. In the next two sections we briefly cover some techniques used in distributed DBMSs.

15.7 Concurrency Control

Concurrency control in a DDBMS has to take into account the existence of fragmentation and replication of data. Variations of the schemes used in centralized DBMSs are used in distributed concurrency control. A number of such schemes based on the locking and timestamp approaches are presented in this section.

Locking is the simplest concurrency control method. Locking enforces serial access to data. In centralized DBMSs, the lock requests go to a single lock manager, which can arbitrate any conflicts. In distributed systems, a centralized lock manager is not desirable due to the bottlenecks created at the central site. A centralized lock manager at a single site, furthermore, is vulnerable to failure, leading to the disruption of the entire system.

The locking scheme must be well formed. In other words, no transactions can access (read or write) a data item that it has not locked.

15.7.1 Distributed Locking

As discussed in Chapter 12, the different locking types can be applied to distributed locking. A centralized lock manager at a single site is relatively simple to implement. Here a transaction sends a message to the lock manager site requesting appropriate locks on specific data items. If the request for the locks could be granted immediately, the lock manager replies granting the request. If the request is incompatible with the current state of locking of the requested data items, the request is delayed. In the case of a read lock request, the data item from any site containing a copy of it, is locked in the share mode and then read. In the case of a write, all copies of the data items have to be modified and are locked in the exclusive mode. With a centralized lock manager, the detection of deadlock is straightforward, requiring the generation of a global wait-for graph (GWFG). The disadvantage of this scheme, in addition to the bottlenecks it creates, is the disruption of the entire system in case of the failure of the centralized lock manager site.

In the distributed method each lock manager is responsible for locking certain data items. The problem this scheme creates, however, is that of detection of deadlocks. Since lock requests are directed to a number of different sites, the nonexistence of a cycle in the **local wait-for graph** at each lock manager is not sufficient to conclude the absence of a deadlock. It is still necessary to generate a **global wait-for graph** to detect a deadlock.

Example 15.11 illustrates the type of locking required in a distributed system where data is fragmented as well as replicated.

Example 15.11

Consider transactions T_1 and T_2 of Figure G. Suppose the data is replicated and three copies of A are stored at sites S_1, S_2, and S_3. To execute these transactions, each spawns three local subtransactions, T_{1S1}, T_{1S2}, T_{1S3}, and T_{2S1}, T_{2S2}, T_{2S3} to be executed at sites S_1, S_2, and S_3, respectively. A possible execution schedule for these transactions is given in Figure H. As we see from Figure H, the final result obtained is incorrect because the schedule is not serializable. If each subtransaction of T_1 had run to completion before those of transaction T_2, the values in each replicate of A would have been 200. If each subtransaction of T_2 had run to completion before those of

Figure G Two modifying transactions.

Transaction T_1	Transaction T_2
Lockx(A)	**Lockx**(A)
A := 100	A := 200
Write(A)	**Write**(A)
Unlock(A)	**Unlock**(A)

Figure H A schedule for the transactions in Figure G.

	site S_1			site S_2		site S_3
Time	Transaction T_{1S1}	Transaction T_{2S1}	Transaction T_{1S2}	Transaction T_{2S2}	Transaction T_{1S3}	Transaction T_{2S3}
t_1	**Lockx**(A)			**Lockx**(A)	**Lockx**(A)	
t_2	A := 100			A := 200	A := 100	
t_3	**Write**(A)			**Write**(A)	**Write**(A)	
t_4	**Unlock**(A)			**Unlock**(A)	**Unlock**(A)	
t_5		**Lockx**(A)	**Lockx**(A)			**Lockx**(A)
t_6		A := 100	A := 200			A := 100
t_7		**Write**(A)	**Write**(A)			**Write**(A)
t_8		**Unlock**(A)	**Unlock**(A)			**Unlock**(A)

transaction T_1, each replicate of A would have the value 100. Consistency requires that transactions T_1 and T_2 be serializable and one of them be run to completion before the other. ■

Example 15.11 illustrates that allowing more than one transaction to write lock some subset of the replicates of a data item leads to inconsistency in the database. To achieve consistency, the write lock (exclusive mode locking) must be extended to all replicates of a data item. Reading can be achieved by locking a single replicate. A read lock can only be obtained if no transaction has locked the data item in the write mode.

Implementation of the locking mechanism can be effected as follows. A transaction T executing at site S does not know the total number of replicates of a data item nor the addresses of these sites. T, requiring a write lock on data item A, sends a message to all sites requesting the write lock. With n sites this involves n messages, unless a broadcast mode can be assumed. The sites having a replicate of the data item reply in the affirmative if the lock can be granted. The other sites indicate that they do not have a copy of the data item. Thus, up to 2n messages are involved before the transaction can proceed. Once the transaction decides to update the value of A, it would send up to n messages containing the updated value. Again, if a broadcast mode could be assumed, a single message could be used. If a transaction requires a read lock on a data item, say B, it could request the read lock from some known site that has a copy of B. If the site is not known, control messages have to be sent to a number of sites until one replies in the affirmative. The broadcast mode reduces the number of such control messages to one. In the latter case, the closest site having a copy of B would reply. The closeness criterion has to be determined a priori in the network.

Majority Locking

We can relax the requirement that all copies of a data item to be updated must be exclusively locked to the requirement that a majority of these copies must be locked for both the share (read) and exclusive (write) modes. This approach is called the **majority locking** strategy. Since a read lock is shareable, any number of transactions can simultaneously hold a read lock on a majority of the replicates of a data item. However, only one transaction can hold a write lock on a majority of these replicates. No transaction can majority lock a data item in the share mode if it is already majority locked in the exclusive mode.

To lock a data item in the read or write mode, a transaction must send out at least $\lceil(n + 1)/2\rceil$ messages and wait until it receives at least $\lceil(n + 1)/2\rceil$ affirmative replies. If the data item is to be updated, the transaction would have to send n messages with the updated value of the data item.

The number of messages required for an update in the majority approach is smaller than those required for locking all replicates. Compared to the approach requiring an exclusive lock on all replicates, the number of deadlocks and subsequent recoveries is smaller. In the lock-all approach, if two competing transactions obtain a write lock on at least one site, neither of them succeeds. In the majority approach, at least one transaction is able to obtain a write lock on a majority of sites. Note that in an update, all replicates have to be updated. A transaction, having obtained a write lock on a majority of replicates, locks out all other transactions and can subsequently succeed in locking all replicates for the update. The disadvantage of this scheme is that a majority of locks have to be acquired for reads.

Primary Site Locking

In the **primary site locking** approach, a single site is designated as the primary site for a given data item, regardless of the number of copies existing for that data item. All lock requests for the data item must be directed to this site, which will decide whether or not to grant the request. In the centralized approach, only one site is chosen as a primary site for all data items; in the distributed approach, different sites are chosen for different data items. The disadvantage of using a single site as the centralized coordinator for all locking is the bottleneck created by having to process all lock requests at a single site and the vulnerability of the entire system when the site fails. The distributed approach overcomes these problems. The choice of which site to choose as the primary site is flexible and the site that is chosen for managing the lock of a data item need not have a copy of that data item. A transaction T requiring a lock on a data item A sends the lock request to the primary site. The primary site will grant the request and could indicate in the grant message the address of the site of the replicate to be used by the transaction. If the primary site fails, the portion of the database controlled by the failed site is not available, in spite of the fact that the actual data may be stored at a site that has not failed.

Distributed Two-Phase Locking

Concurrent transactions in a distributed system must be serializable, in addition to obtaining appropriate locks. This requires, as in the case of the centralized system, **distributed two-phase locking.** A schedule in the case of a distributed system is serializable if it is equivalent to a schedule wherein all actions of one transaction precede those of another. Example 15.12 illustrates the need for two-phase locking to be generalized to a distributed database.

Example 15.12 Consider transactions T_1 and T_2 of Figure I. Suppose the data is distributed and A is stored at site S_1 and B at site S_2. To execute these transactions, each transaction spawns two local subtransaction, T_{1S1}, T_{1S2} and T_{2S1}, T_{2S2},

Figure I Two modifying transactions.

Transaction T_1	Transaction T_2
Lockx(A)	**Lockx**(A)
A := 100	A := 200
Write(A)	**Write**(A)
Unlock(A)	**Unlock**(A)
Lockx(B)	**Lockx**(B)
B := 1000	B := 2000
Write(B)	**Write**(B)
Unlock(B)	**Unlock**(B)

Figure J A schedule for the transactions of Figure I.

	site S_1		site S_2	
Time	Transaction T_{1S1}	Transaction T_{2S1}	Transaction T_{1S2}	Transaction T_{2S2}
t_1	**Lockx**(A)			**Lockx**(B)
t_2	A := 100			B := 2000
t_3	**Write**(A)			**Write**(B)
t_4	**Unlock**(A)			**Unlock**(B)
t_5		**Lockx**(A)	**Lockx**(B)	
t_6		A := 200	B := 1000	
t_7		**Write**(A)	**Write**(B)	
t_8		**Unlock**(A)	**Unlock**(B)	

respectively, to be executed at sites S_1 and S_2. A possible execution schedule for these transactions is given in Figure J. As we see from Figure J, the final result obtained is incorrect since the schedule is not serializable. If transaction T_1 had run to completion before transaction T_2, the values of A and B would have been 200 and 2000, respectively. Had transaction T_2 run to completion before transaction T_1, A and B would have the values 100 and 1000, respectively. ■

As in centralized two-phase locking, serializability requires that the locking in the distributed system also be two-phase. Recall that the two-phase locking scheme is required to have growing and shrinking phases. All lock requests made by a transaction or any of its subtransactions should be made in the growing phase and released in the shrinking phrase. Whenever a transaction issues an unlock instruction the shrinking phase starts indicating that all required locks are obtained. Where data is replicated, all subtransactions of a transaction that would modify the replicated data item would have to observe the two-phase locking protocol. Therefore, we cannot have one subtransaction release a lock and subsequently have another subtransaction request another lock. This requires that each subtransaction of a transaction notify all other subtransactions that it has acquired all its locks. The shrinking phase can start once all subtransactions have acquired all their locks.

In establishing the fact that all subtransactions have finished their growing phase, the number of messages involved is high. The possibility of failure in nodes and communication links and that of a rollback of some subtransactions in case of failure of others to complete normally indicates that the unlocking operations should be delayed until the distributed commit point of all subtransactions.

The distributed commit requires the exchange of a number of messages between the sites of subtransactions. It is done using a two-phase commit protocol discussed in Section 15.8.

15.7.2 Timestamp-Based Concurrency Control

Locking schemes suffer from two serious disadvantages: deadlock and low level of concurrency. Timestamp methods have been advocated as an alternative to locking.

The timestamp methods discussed in Chapter 12 can be extended to the distributed case. As in the case of the centralized timestamp methods, each copy of a data item in the distributed approach contains two timestamp values: the read timestamp and the write timestamp. Also, each transaction in the system is assigned a timestamp value that determines its serializability order. A transaction T with a timestamp value of t ensures that it does not read a value from the future (that is, the write timestamp of the data item must not be greater than value t) nor write a value that was already read by a younger transaction (i.e., the read timestamp of the data item must not be greater than value t). If the write timestamp of the data item to be read is greater than value t (written by a younger transaction) or if the read timestamp of the data item to be written is greater than value t (read by a younger transaction), transaction T must be aborted and restarted. If transaction T attempts to write a data item but finds that the read timestamp of the data item is less than t (an older transaction had read the value) and the write timestamp of the data item is greater than t (a younger transaction had already written a new value), transaction T is not required to be aborted. However, it does not update the data item (it was too slow to change the value of the data item). When more than one copy of a data item exists, a new value must be written in all of its copies. In this case, the two-phase commit protocol discussed in Section 15.8 must be used to make the new value permanent.

As in the centralized database system, a number of different timestamp-based schemes can be used. In these schemes a timestamp is used to associate some value with a transaction and give it an order in the set of all transactions being executed. In the serial execution of transactions, time plays an important role and timestamping seems to be the natural solution to the serializability problem.

If a system assigns a unique timestamp to a transaction, the timestamp identifies the transaction. The generation of timestamps in a centralized system requires the use of some monotonically increasing numbers. In distributed systems, each site generates a local timestamp and concatenates it with the site identifier. If the local timestamp is unique, its concatenation with the unique site identifier would make the (global) timestamp unique across the network. The site identifier must be the least significant digits of the timestamp so that the events can be ordered according to their occurrence and not their location, as illustrated in Example 15.13.

Example 15.13 Let two events be assigned the timestamps 200100 and 100200, where the first three digits of the timestamp identify the site and the last three digits the time at which the event occurred. Now even though the event with timestamp 100200 occurred later than the event with timestamp 200100, the timestamp comparison states otherwise. ■

The local timestamp can be generated by some local clock or counter. In the event a counter is used, a relatively busy site would rapidly outrun slower sites. The local clocks at different sites can also get out of step. These local timestamp-generating schemes can be kept fairly well synchronized by including the timestamp in the messages sent between sites. On receiving a message, a site compares its clock or counter with the timestamp contained in the message. If it finds its clock or counter to be slower, it sets it to some value greater than the message timestamp. In this way, an inactive site's counter or a slower clock will become synchronized with the others at the first message interaction with another site.

On the one hand, the number of messages required to be transmitted in the timestamp approach is smaller than in the locking approach. On the other hand, the number of transactions that are aborted to be restarted is relatively larger. This occurs in cases where more than one transaction attempts, simultaneously, to access the same data item. (If we can delay one of the conflicting operations, we can reduce the number of transactions that have to be aborted.)

15.8 Distributed Commitment and Recovery

In addition to the types of failures encountered in the centralized DBMSs, the recovery subsystem in a DDBMS has to contend with the loss of messages and failure of communication links and nodes. A distributed commit protocol known as two-phase commit is used to ensure data consistency. The recovery subsystem is used to restore the database to a consistent state on the restoration of the failed nodes or communication links.

In our discussion of transaction properties, we stated that not only should the transaction be serializable but that it should be atomic. This in turn implies that either all or none of the writes should be performed. In a distributed system, when the write requests have been issued there must be some way of ascertaining that all of them have indeed been performed. Where a site (or link) may have failed, recovery operations must be performed when the site or link is reconnected to the network. The recovery operations must guarantee that for committed (sub)transactions, the write operations are in fact correctly reflected in the database before the site comes online. If for some reason a subtransaction at a site cannot terminate normally, then all the other subtransactions spawned by its parent should be aborted.

In order for the atomic transactions to be recoverable,

- Updated data items should not become permanent until recovery data is transferred to stable storage.
- The original state of all updated data items should be available, at least until the updated data becomes permanent.

If there are no failures or abnormal conditions, such as denial of locks or deadlocks requiring the abortion of any of the subtransactions, the **distributed commit** protocol is relatively straightforward. Each subtransaction T_{ij} of transaction T_i sends a ready to commit or abort message to the coordinator. If the coordinator receives the ready to commit message from all subtransactions, it sends a commit message to all subtransactions. Once the commit message is received all subtransactions perform the appropriate commit action, which involves writing the recovery log including a commit (sub)transaction marker, and then making the updates to the data items permanent. If the coordinator receives an abort message from any subtransaction, it need not wait for any further messages and issues an abort message to all subtransactions. On receipt of an abort message, all subtransactions abort, after making appropriate entries in the recovery log.

Failures in a distributed system, in addition to the types of failure in a centralized system, include the following: lost message, node failure, and communication link failure. The latter two types may partition the network into two or more parts. These network failures create problems in the above simple method used in committing a transaction. One of the problems is that of **blocking** a subtransaction. A subtransaction is said to be blocked when it does not know what to do next. It cannot safely commit or abort, since it is cut off from the rest of the network. If it unilaterally decides to either commit or abort, there is a possibility that the system would be in an inconsistent state. This is illustrated in Example 15.14.

Example 15.14 Consider the subtransactions T_{11}, T_{12}, and T_{13} spawned at sites S_1, S_2, and S_3 of transaction T_1 at site S. Each of these subtransactions has been created to update the value of a replicated data item, *A*. If the communication links to site S_1 break down after T_{1S1} has sent a ready to commit message at step s_4 (Figure K), then it would not receive the commit message back from the coordinator. If T_{1S1} decides to abort, the value of *A* would be unchanged at site S_1. If the other two subtransactions had also indicated that they were ready to commit, the coordinator would have sent a commit message and the value of *A* at sites S_2 and S_3 would be updated. This means the database is inconsistent and T_{1S1} must not abort. If T_{1S1} decides to commit, the value of *A* would be changed at site S_1. However, if one of the other subtransactions had indicated that it was aborting, the coordinator would have issued an abort message. This would mean that the value of *A* in the copies at sites S_2 and S_3 would be unchanged. Thus, T_{1S1} must not commit. As a result of the possibility of inconsistency, regardless of what T_{1S1} does, it cannot proceed beyond step s_4. In other words, the subtransaction is blocked.

Figure K Blocked transaction.

Step	site S_1 Transaction T_{1S1}	site S_2 Transaction T_{1S2}	site S_3 Transaction T_{1S3}
s_1	**Lockx**(A)	**Lockx**(A)	**Lockx**(A)
s_2	**Read**(A)	**Read**(A)	**Read**(A)
s_3	A := A + 100	A := A + 100	A := A + 100
s_4	*ready_to_commit*		
failure of link to S_1			

■

Protocol for the two-phase commit, which allows recoverability of distributed transactions, is presented in the following section.

15.8.1 Two-Phase Commit

The voting phase and the decision phase are the two phases of the **two-phase commit** protocol. In the **voting phase,** the subtransactions are requested to vote on their readiness to commit or abort. In the **decision phase,** the decision as to whether all subtransactions should commit or abort is made and carried out. The transactions at a site interact with the transaction manager of the site, cooperating in the exchange of messages.

It is more convenient to use the process concept rather than the transaction concept in discussing the two-phase commit and deadlocks. Just like a transaction, a process is capable of requesting data items and releasing them. However, they have a better knowledge of their environment, including knowledge about the identity of the processes that are blocking them. The pseudocode for the processes at the participant and coordinator sites is given below. Note that part of the code belongs to the transaction manager (TM) and the remaining to the subtransactions or the coordinator.

The coordinator process starts by spawning a number, n, of subtransactions. Some of these would be at remote sites and others could be at the same site as the coordinator. The only difference is that a subtransaction at the same site does not have to communicate via the network. These subtransactions are run along with the respective TM as participant processes at a number of sites.

Participant Process

```
begin
acquire locks and make local changes
if normal end
  then status := okay to commit
  else status := should abort;
set timeout;
while (not request from coordinator for voting or not timeout)
      do {nothing};
if timeout
     then write recovery log, release all locks, and abort
if request from coordinator for voting
     then if status := should abort
             then begin
                    send abort to coordinator
                    write status on recovery log, release all locks, and abort
                    end;
                 else begin  {status := okay to commit}
                          send ready to commit, write status on recovery log
                          set timeout
                          while (not second_signal from coordinator or not
                          timeout)
                                  do nothing;
                          if receive commit from coordinator
                            then write recovery log, commit,
                                       release all locks, and send
                                          acknowledge to coordinator
                          if receive abort from coordinator
                            then write recovery log, release all locks,
                                       abort, and send acknowledge to coordinator
                          if timeout {blocked}
                            then begin
```

```
                send SOS_second_signal and wait for response
                activate recovery
                end
            end
    end
```

Coordinator Process

```
begin
  spawn n subtransactions
  write into recovery log request for voting, send to all
      subtransactions request for voting
  messages := 0;
  abortall := false;
  set timeout;
  while (messages ≠ n or not timeout or not abortall)
    do begin
         if receive ready to commit
           then messages := messages + 1;
         if receive abort
           then abortall := true;
         end;
  if timeout or abortall
   then begin
          second_signal := abort
          write global abort in log
          end
   else begin
          second_signal := commit
          write global commit in log
          end;
  send second_signal to all subtransactions;
  set timeout;
  acknowledge := 0;
  while (acknowledge ≠ n or not timeout)
    do begin
         if receive acknowledge from participant
          then acknowledge := acknowledge + 1;
         end;
    if timeout and acknowledge ≠ n
     then spawn SOS (second_signal) response process
     else write transaction complete in log
    end;
```

When the participant processes execute, they know whether the tasks assigned to them were completed successfully or not. If successful, they are willing to commit, otherwise they have to abort. Recall that the assigned database update is done only on a copy of the data items in each process's own workspace. These participant processes wait for a voting request from the coordinator process. If such a request is not received by a participant process, after a predetermined time period (timeout) it aborts after writing an appropriate recovery log. No changes are made to any data items in the database. If a request for voting is received before timeout, the participant process sends the appropriate status signal (okay to commit or should abort) to the coordinator process. On receipt of okay to commit signals from all the participant processes, the coordinator process sends a second signal to the participants to commit. On receipt of this commit signal, the participant process writes appropriate recovery log and commit markers onto stable storage at its site. Following this, it makes the changes permanent in the database.

If a participant process does not receive the second signal within a predetermined time period, it is said to be blocked. This could happen if the site goes down and then the recovery operation restores it and finds that the second signal was not received before the crash. A blocked participant process sends out an SOS signal, which is responded to by an SOS process. Such an SOS process could have been spawned by the coordinator process to help in the recovery of any site that failed after the vote was taken to commit or abort, but before the site could actually commit or abort. The SOS signal would also be emitted by a participant process if it did not receive the second signal (to commit or abort) from the coordinator, the signal being lost in the network.

A participant process that does not receive a request from the coordinator process for voting within a predefined time period will timeout. Timeouts result in the participant process having to write the recovery log, release all locks, and abort. In case the request for a voting message from the coordinator was lost, the coordinator would not receive any signal from such aborted participant processes. The coordinator process timeouts and therefore aborts all the other participant processes.

15.8.2 Recovery with Two-Phase Commit

The recovery log, in addition to the type of information indicated in the centralized case, includes the log of the messages transmitted between sites. Such a record would enable the recovery system to decide, when the site is reconnected to the network, on the extent of the site's interaction with the rest of the system. The recovery system would also be able to determine the fate of the subtransactions running at the site. It can then determine which subtransactions were committed, aborted, or blocked. Regarding the committed subtransactions, the recovery system would ensure that the changes are reflected in the database at the site. In the case of aborted transactions, any partial updates would be undone. As for the transactions that were blocked, an SOS signal would be sent to determine whether it should be committed or aborted.

Communication link failures in certain cases can result in the database system becoming partitioned. Each of the partitioned systems could operate by marking the sites in the other partitions as being down. A moment's thought should tell us that there may be no possibility of a smooth recovery from such a partitioning. In this case, the complete system has to be restarted from the period before the partitioning occurred with a manual assist to recover subsequent database modifications.

Site Recovery

When a failed site resumes operation, it consults the recovery log to find the transactions that were active at the time of the failure. For strictly local transactions, recovery actions similar to a centralized database requiring a simple undo or redo would be called for. Global transactions would be of two types: coordinator or participant.

Regarding all participant type transactions, if the log indicated that it had not sent the status message to the coordinator, then the latter would have aborted all subtransactions. The recovery operation would ensure that such participant transactions be aborted and no changes be reflected by such transactions in the database. Suppose the log for a participant type transaction indicates that it send an okay to commit status to the coordinator. This means that the global transaction could have been either committed or aborted. The recovery operation would ensure that the participant transaction, on restart, would send a SOS message to learn its fate from the SOS process. Once it receives the signal either to commit or abort, the recovery process performs a redo or undo operation. In the case of a participant for which the log indicates the receipt of a second signal from the coordinator (to commit or abort), the recovery process can take appropriate action and ensure that an acknowledge signal be sent to the coordinator.

For a coordinating transaction at the failed site, the recovery process examines the log to determine its status. If no request for a voting message was sent before the site failure, all participants would have aborted, whereupon the coordinating transaction can be aborted as well. If the coordinator sent a request for voting before the crash, the recovery process must retransmit this request for voting. Even though the pseudocode of the participant processes given above does not indicate this, they should treat the second request for voting as the first and proceed as if this were the first request for voting. The global transaction can then be completed as if nothing had happened. If the site failed after the coordinator sent the second signal for commit or abort, the recovery process would entail resending this signal. Participant sites that received this signal and acted accordingly would treat this as a repeat message, ensure that appropriate actions were taken (from their recovery logs), and send the required acknowledge signal. Participants that did not receive this second signal would be blocked and attempt to recover via SOS. The coordinator would not receive acknowledgement from these participants and therefore would spawn the SOS process, which would respond to these SOS signals and conclude the global transaction.

If the site failed after the coordinator wrote a complete transaction marker in the log, no further actions would be called for.

Lost Message

The type of recovery operation to be performed depends on the message that was lost. If the request to vote from the coordinator is lost, the participant would abort, which would eventually lead to the abortion of the global transaction. If the status message from any one of the participants is lost, the coordinator would timeout and abort the global transaction, including all the participant transactions. Should the second signal be lost, a participant would timeout and attempt a recovery via the SOS message. In the event that one of the acknowledge messages is lost, the coordinator would spawn the SOS response process. The coordinator would not know if the transaction is complete. An alternative approach is to have the coordinator send a request to the participants to retransmit the acknowledgements.

Communication Link Failure

Suppose the failure of the communication link occurs in such a way that a subset of the participant sites are partitioned without a coordinator. In this case, as far as the coordinator is concerned, this is equivalent to the failure of a number of participant sites. If the failure occurs before the partitioned participants were sent the voting message, the coordinator would have aborted the global transaction, including all nonpartitioned subtransactions. The partitioned participants would also abort after a timeout. If the failure occurs after the participants have reported their status, the coordinator would have decided either to commit or abort. The partitioned sites could recover, on reconnection, by sending an SOS.

15.9 Deadlocks in Distributed Systems

As in the case of a centralized system, deadlocks can occur in a distributed system, as illustrated in Example 15.15.

Example 15.15 Consider the transactions of Figure L, where data item A is resident at site S_1 and data item B is resident at site S_2. The schedule for the execution of the transactions is given in Figure M. The transactions are using two-phase

Figure L Two modifying transactions.

Transaction T_1	Transaction T_2
Lockx(A)	**Lockx**(B)
Read(A)	**Read**(B)
A := A − 100	B := B * 1.1
Write(A)	**Write**(B)
Lockx(B)	**Lockx**(A)
Read(B)	**Read**(A)
B := B + 100	A := A * 1.1
Write(B)	**Write**(A)
Unlock(A)	**Unlock**(B)
Unlock(B)	**Unlock**(A)

Figure M A schedule for the transactions in Figure L.

	site S_1		site S_2	
Step	Transaction T_{1S1}	Transaction T_{2S1}	Transaction T_{2S2}	Transaction T_{1S2}
s_1	**Lockx**(A)		**Lockx**(B)	
s_2	**Read**(A)		**Read**(B)	
s_3	A := A − 100		B := B * 1.1	
s_4	**Write**(A)		**Write**(B)	
s_5		**Lockx**(A)		**Lockx**(B)

Figure N A global wait-for graph.

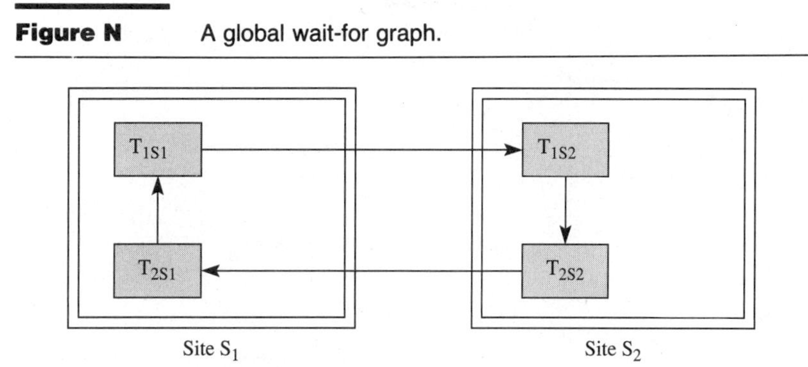

locking protocol and the schedule shows that the transactions will be deadlocked. The global wait-for graph for the situation at step s_5 of the schedule is shown in Figure N. ■

One simple method of recovering from a potential deadlock situation is to allow a transaction to wait for a finite amount of time for an incompatibly locked data item. If at the end of that time the resource is still locked, the transaction is aborted. The period of time should not be too short or too long. An unduly short period would likely cause the transaction to be aborted, since the resource may not be released. An unnecessarily long period would mean that these transactions would hold the resources already acquired, causing further transactions to deadlock. With this scheme, only transactions that are blocked are aborted.

The deadlock detection scheme allows deadlock to occur, but makes provision to detect the existence of a deadlock by the presence of a chain of transactions, each waiting for data items locked by the next transaction in the chain. The detection of deadlock in a distributed system requires the generation of not only a local wait-for graph (LWFG) for each site, but also a global wait-for graph (GWFG) for the entire system. Note that here we are assuming that a transaction can request one or more data items at a time and become blocked if it has at least one outstanding request for a data item. Under this assumption, a cycle in the global wait-for graph indicates a deadlock situation. Figure N shows the GWFG for the execution schedule of Figure M.

We see from Figure N that even though there are no cycles in the LWFG at each of two sites, there is a cycle in the GWFG and this indicates the existence of a deadlock. The disadvantage of the GWFG is the overhead required in generating such graphs. Furthermore, a deadlock detection site has to be chosen where the GWFG is created. This site becomes the location for detecting deadlocks and selecting the transactions that have to be aborted to recover from deadlock. One of the problems with such an approach is that if the messages indicating which transactions are waiting for which resources and the release of the resources by transactions are received out of order, then the deadlock detection site may conclude that there is a deadlock. However in reality no such deadlock exists. The erroneous deadlock that was detected is called a **phantom deadlock.** Example 15.16 shows how a phantom deadlock could result.

Example 15.16 Consider the GWFG of Figure O. Suppose the graph is maintained at site S. Suppose there is a request from T_8 for a data item locked by T_9 at about

Figure O A global wait-for graph.

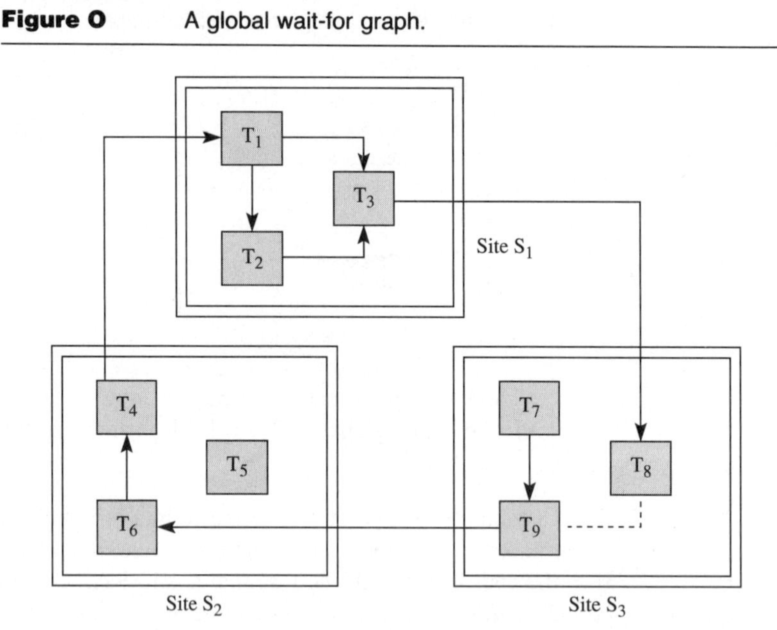

the same time as T_4 releases the data item it locked. The release of the data item allows T_6 to proceed and causes a removal of the edge (T_6,T_4). If the fact that the edge (T_6,T_4) is removed reaches site S after it learns of the addition of the edge (T_8,T_9), then a phantom deadlock would be detected. The cycles $(T_1,T_3,T_8,T_9,T_6,T_4,T_1)$ and $(T_1,T_2,T_3,T_8,T_9,T_6,T_4,T_1)$ do not, in fact, exist. ■

Instead of using a central site for deadlock detection, it is possible to use a distributed deadlock detection scheme. In one such approach, the LWFGs are broadcast to all sites. Each such site generates the portion of the GWFG that is of concern to it. If one of the site detects a deadlock, it tries to resolve it by aborting one or more of its transactions. The disadvantage of this approach is that the deadlock may not be detected for some time, and since the broadcast of the LWFGs is asynchronous, a phantom deadlock could be detected and lead to unnecessary transaction aborts.

Below we give another scheme, known as a probe computation algorithm, for distributed deadlock detection. It is from a class of algorithms called the **edge-chasing algorithms.** For other deadlock detection algorithms, refer to the bibliographic notes.

15.9.1 Deadlock Detection by Probe Computation

In the edge-chasing algorithms, the cycle in the GWFG is detected not by actually creating the graph but by sending messages along the edges of the graph. Such messages, called **probes,** are different from the other messages discussed above, and also distinct from resource requests and grant messages. As before, instead of referring to transactions, let us use the process concept, which encompasses the interaction between a transaction at a site with the TM at the site. Figure 15.9 shows an example of a number of such processes in a GWFG in a deadlock situation. Let us examine how probe computation is used to detect the deadlock.

An edge from a process in one site to a process in a distinct site is called an **intercontroller edge.** An **outgoing edge** for a process is an intercontroller edge that can be reached from the process by following edges in the local part of the GWFG. The probe is initiated by a blocked process and it is referred to as the initiator of the probe. A probe is made up of a three-tuple (i, j, k) and indicates that it is a probe for process T_i and the probe has been sent along the outgoing edge (T_j, T_k). Here process T_j is blocked by process T_k and T_i is blocked, directly or via a chain of intermediate processes, by T_j. If the initiator of the probe receives a matching probe, we can conclude that the blocked process is in a cycle in the GWFG. Thus, if process T_i, the initiator of a probe, receives a probe (i, x, i), it is in a cycle. An active process simply discards the probes. A blocked process propagates the probe along all its outgoing edges. This blocked process will send a probe (i, j, k) to the process at node k, along outgoing edge (T_j, T_k), under the following conditions: (a) the process T_j is blocked, (b) T_j is waiting for the process T_k, (c) T_i is blocked by T_j. Note that a site that has several blocked processes may initiate several probes. Similarly, several probes may be initiated in sequence by a blocked process if it has several outstanding requests. Each such probe is distinctly identifiable by the initiator.

Figure 15.9 Detection of deadlock using probe computation.

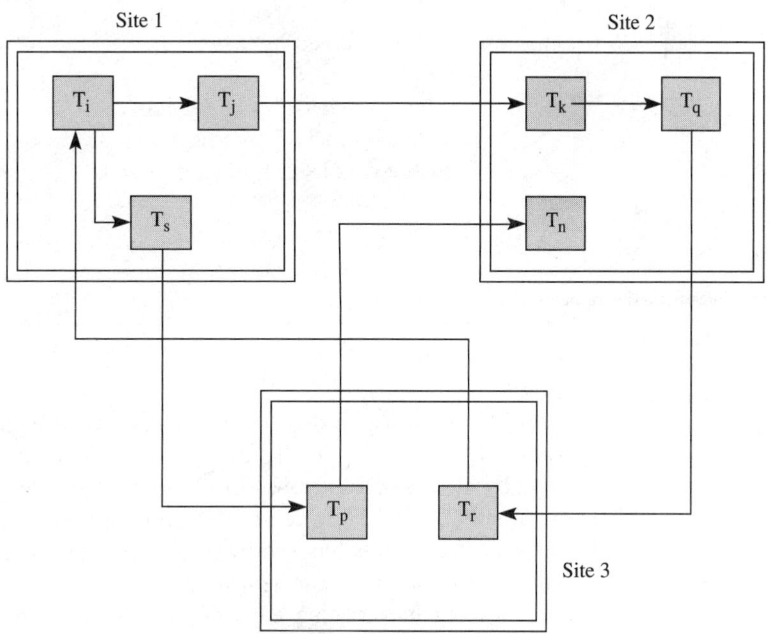

A blocked process, T_k, accepts only meaningful probes; others are discarded on receipt. A probe (i,j,k) is said to be meaningful under the following conditions: (a) the process T_k is blocked, and (b) it was unaware that T_i was dependent on it (that T_k is in a chain with T_i). Condition (b) ensures that nonmeaningful probes are suppressed and, consequently, only one probe per cycle is propagated. Receipt of a meaningful probe leads to the deduction that T_i is dependent on T_k and further probes (i,j,k) will be discarded (they will not longer be meaningful). On receipt of a meaningful probe, T_k sends, probes (i,p,q) on all its outgoing edges (T_p, T_q).

If a blocked process, T_i, receives a probe (i,j,i), we can deduce that it is deadlocked. The **probe computation** algorithms are given below and Example 15.17 illustrates its use in the detection of a distributed deadlock.

Algorithm 15.1

A Blocked Process Initiates Probe Computation

if process T_i is blocked and the deadlock is not local,
then for each distinct outgoing edge T_j, T_k
transmit a probe (i,j,k)

Algorithm 15.2

A Blocked Process Response to Probes Received

for each probe (x,y,z) received by T_i
if probe is meaningful
then if x = z (both x and z also being equal to i for some blocked process T_i)
then T_i is in a deadlock: initiate deadlock resolution
else for each distinct outgoing edge T_p, T_q
transmit a probe (x,p,q)

Example 15.17

Consider the situation depicted in the GWFG of Figure 15.9. We have processes T_i, T_j, T_k, T_q, T_r, T_i in a deadlock situation. The probe is initiated, say, by T_i. It sends a probe (i,j,k) along its outgoing edge (j,k) to process T_k at site 2. When T_k receives this probe it finds it meaningful since it was unaware that T_i was blocked by it. It knows that T_j is blocked by it since it has not released the data item requested by T_j. T_k, in turn, sends a probe (i,q,r) along its outgoing edge (T_q,T_r) to T_r at site 3. T_r finds this probe meaningful and, in turn, learns that T_i is dependent on it. T_r sends the probe (i,r,i) along its outgoing edge (r, i) to T_i. On receipt of this probe T_i learns that it is in a closed cycle in the GWFG. Note that a probe (i,s,p) along the outgoing edge (T_s,T_p) will be eventually ignored by process T_n and will not reach T_i. ■

15.9.2 Deadlock Prevention

The deadlock prevention method can be used in a distributed system. For instance, the timestamp method could be applied to prevent deadlock from occurring by aborting the transactions that could potentially cause deadlock. The wait-die scheme and the wound-wait scheme could be used to abort appropriate transactions as in the centralized system. The aborted transactions are reinitiated with the original timestamp to allow them to eventually run to completion. The timestamp method does not require that any messages be transmitted over the network; however being a deadlock prevention scheme it causes unnecessary transaction aborts.

15.10 Security and Protection

Security and protection problems are similar to those in the centralized database with remote access. However, the problem is exacerbated by the fact that there is increased communication, including site-to-site transfer of large amounts of data. This calls for appropriate identification and authentication of the user and the site. To prevent eavesdropping on the communication lines by intruders, these lines must be secure and the message should be encrypted.

The fact that data is replicated in the database means that a user can access any one of these replicated copies. Security dictates that the authorization rules for access and update of certain parts of this data be verified before user action is allowed. If the authorization rules are centralized, the authorization validation will generate traffic and the central site would become the bottleneck. Another approach is to replicate the authorization rules. Full replication allows local validation of user action at the time of compilation or execution of the user query. However, full replication adds unnecessary update overheads. Still another approach involves replicating, at a given site, only those authorization rules that pertain to the data items at the site. The maintenance problem is improved but validation of a user's action for a remote site can only be done at the remote site during an advance compilation or execution stage of the user's query. Considerable computing efforts are wasted, since a query is aborted on discovery that the query lacks authorization for particular data items.

15.11 Homogeneous and Heterogeneous Systems

In general, a distributed database system may be either **homogeneous** (i.e., all local database systems have the same underlying data model) or **heterogeneous** (i.e., local

Figure 15.10 Homogeneous and heterogeneous database systems.

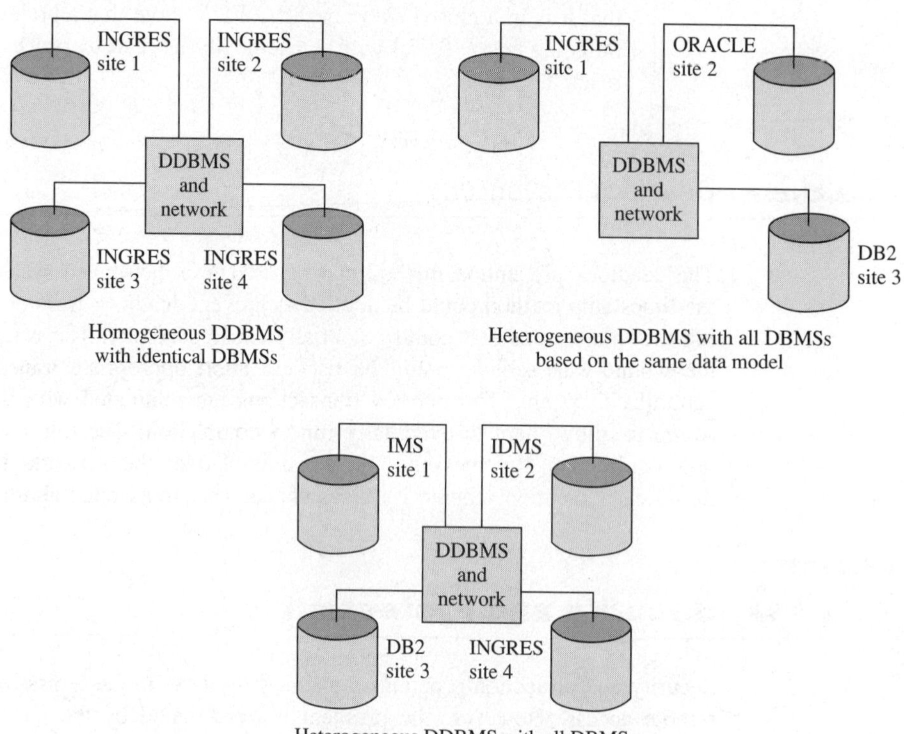

database systems at different sites may have different underlying data models). In fact, even with the same underlying data model there are substantial differences in individual DBMS implementations. A truly homogeneous database system is implemented with the same local DBMS at all sites. Figure 15.10 shows examples of homogeneous and heterogeneous systems.

We can differentiate between **local** and **global schemas.**[1] All data items that are visible at other nodes are specified in a global schema. This schema is specified using a common global model; translators between the local and global models and languages are provided. A distributed system with n different local systems and without the use of a global model would require n * (n–1) translators. Using a global model, we require only n translators to map between the global and local models (and vice-versa).

With the proliferation of microcomputers and microcomputer-based database systems and the growing networking of these systems, the existence of heterogeneous systems is bound to increase.

In the next section, we briefly consider some common DDBMSs. Note that these are mostly experimental systems. First we look at the homogeneous DDBMSs, followed by an example of a heterogeneous DDBMS.

[1]The term network schema is sometimes used to refer to the global schema. We prefer to use the term global schema to avoid confusion with the term applicable to the DBTG model.

15.11.1 The Homogeneous DDBMS

SDD–1: A System for Distributed Databases

The SDD–1, a prototype DDBMS, was developed by Computer Corporation of America in the late 1970s. SDD–1 supports the relational model. SDD–1 is a collection of three different types of virtual machines: transaction and data modules interconnected by the reliable network (Figure 15.11). The actual system runs on a number of DEC PDP–10s and PDP–20s using Arpanet. The Datacomputer database, a relational DBMS, is used at each site. Fragmentation is obtained in SDD–1 by first taking horizontal fragmentation and subsequently vertical fragmentation. The system catalog is also treated as ordinary data and can be fragmented and replicated. To allow any site to determine the locations of the catalog fragments, a higher level catalog known as a directory locater is fully replicated at each site.

Users interact with a given transaction module, which plans and controls the execution of the users' transactions. The transaction module is responsible for query translation, control of execution, and concurrency control. The transaction module converts a transaction into a parallel program that can be executed cooperatively at several data modules.

A data module manages all local data at a site. It provides data handling capabilities for transaction execution (e.g., move data from database to workspace, etc.).

Data modules and transaction modules are interconnected by the reliable network. All messages are guaranteed to be delivered by the network. It monitors sites and provides a global clock. The reliable network also ensures transaction atomicity by committing transactions at all sites or aborting at all sites.

In the SDD–1 system, the catalog is a single relation that can be fragmented and replicated, allowing the catalog entries to be distributed at data module sites. It

Figure 15.11 SDD-1 architecture.

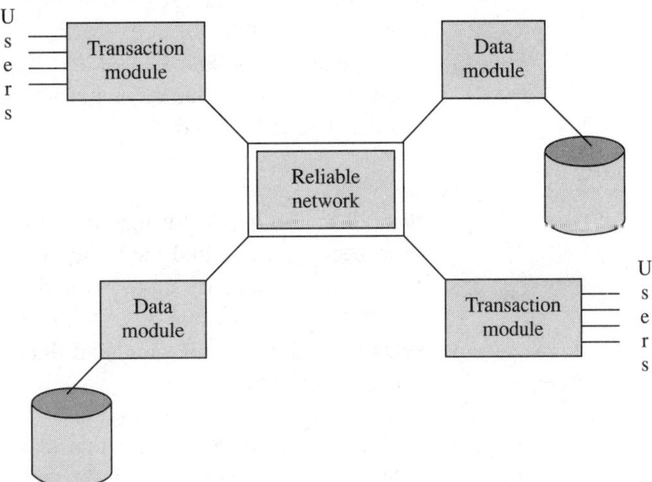

is therefore possible for local objects to have their catalog entries at a remote site. Consequently data definition operations may be nonlocal.

SDD–1 uses a centralized control scheme and a given transaction is supervised by a single transaction module. The transaction execution is in three phases, read, execute, and write. All reads for a transaction are performed at the beginning of the transaction; all writes are done at the end.

The read-set, the set of fragments to be read by the transaction, are determined by the TM. SDD–1 provides fragmentation transparencies and the set of fragments to be accessed for the read-set of the transaction are determined by it. This operation is called **materialization.** The TM then coordinates the data modules at various sites to transfer the required data into the workspace used by the transaction.

SDD–1 uses the **conservative timestamp** method for concurrency control. We briefly describe the conservative timestamp scheme here. The basic timestamp method, discussed in Chapter 12, suffers from costly restarts.

A pessimistic approach is taken by the conservative timestamp method, which causes possible delays until no conflict with a transaction can possibly happen. This is done by buffering younger transactions until all possible older transactions have been executed. At some point the system must decide that no older transaction is likely to be received. A simple implementation of the idea requires that a site send all requests to another site in timestamp order and that the network deliver messages in the order that they were sent. In this manner, if site j receives a message from site i with a timestamp t_{ik}, site j knows that it will not receive messages from site i with timestamps less than t_{ik}.

At site j, instead of keeping the timestamps of the last read or write operation on data item X, we now keep the oldest timestamp for the buffered read and write operations for data item X, say X_{RMIN} and X_{WMIN}, respectively. Site j, having received messages from all other sites, can proceed to execute an operation. The method is implemented as follows:

while not at least one request from each site wait.
READ
    if $X_{RMIN} < X_{WMIN}$
        then the read is older than any of the write requests on X, i.e., all older transactions that could update X have been executed and thus the read operation can be executed and X_{RMIN} updated.
        else there is at least one older update request and the read is buffered.
WRITE
    if $X_{WMIN} < X_{RMIN}$
        then all read requests for the current data value have been executed and the write operation can be executed; the value of X_{WMIN} is updated.
        else there is at least one older transaction that has still to read the current value and thus the write remains buffered.

This simple method suffers from the fact that at least one request must be received from each site. So that the system will not remain blocked, each active site that lacks an action request sends a null request message. In this manner, the buffer from each site would at least have a request, albeit null.

Major disadvantages of the conservative timestamp method are the long waiting periods and consequent low concurrency. The improvements suggested to overcome these shortcomings include the use of **transaction classes** and **conflict analysis graphs.**

All transactions are categorized into classes. Those transactions that are likely to conflict belong to the same class. A transaction's read requests can be termed its read-set and the write requests, its write-set. Two transactions conflict if the intersection of their write-sets or the read-set of one and the write-set of the other is nonempty. For instance, let the read and write sets of transaction T_1 be RS_1 and WS_1, respectively, and those for T_2 be RS_2 and WS_2. Then transactions T_1 and T_2 conflict if

$$RS_1 \cap WS_2 \neq \emptyset, \text{ or}$$
$$WS_1 \cap RS_2 \neq \emptyset, \text{ or}$$
$$WS_1 \cap WS_2 \neq \emptyset$$

Transaction requests waiting in buffers need only be compared with requests from conflicting transactions. Two requests from nonconflicting transactions can proceed concurrently, thus improving concurrency.

Whether or not transactions conflict can be decided using conflict graph analysis techniques in which arcs can be labeled to define the type of conflict (read-write or write-write).

The execute phase is performed by a compile-and-go approach. The access plan generated is executed and the supervision is by the TM at the site of the query. Program compilation uses semijoins extensively in optimization. The write phase begins by the distribution of the updated fragments to all data modules containing a replicate of an updated fragment. The updated fragments are made permanent by a write command issued by the coordinating TM.

Transaction atomicity is provided in SDD–1 by a four-phase commit protocol, which includes selection of backup coordinators to supervise the commit protocol in case of coordinator failure.

R*

R* (see Figure 15.12) is an experimental adaptation of the System R relational DBMS to the distributed environment. The architecture of R* is based on System R architecture. It is claimed that major modifications were made to the relation data storage (RSS*) and transaction manager (TM*) systems. A distributed communications (DC*) component was added.

R* runs under IBM's Customer Information Control System (CICS). CICS is responsible for handling online users and could entail running application programs or provide support for interactive queries. CICS is also responsible for intersite message communications and interfaces with another CICS at a remote site.

All requests are made at a single site, which becomes the **master site.** In common with System R, queries are compiled rather than interpreted. A distributed compilation scheme is used wherein the master site coordinates the global aspects of query compilation. The local decisions, including local data structure selections, are

Figure 15.12 R* architecture.

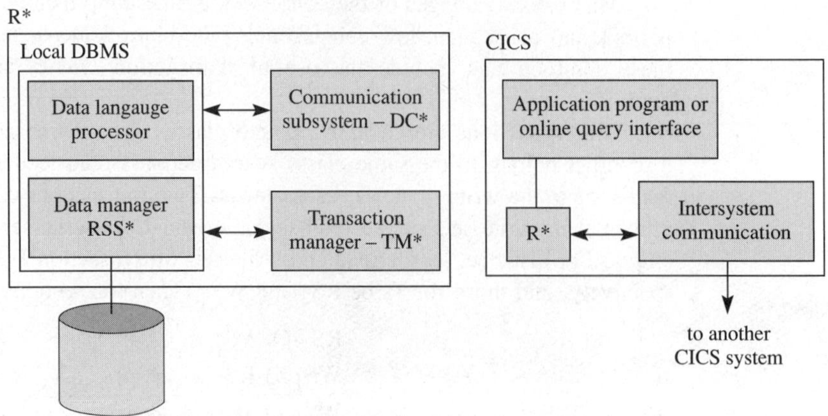

delegated to all the participating sites, called slave or **apprentice sites.** The master site produces a global plan that is broadcast to the apprentice sites along with the original SQL statement and catalog information used.

R* uses a distributed catalog. Local catalogs keep information on locally stored objects, including any fragments and replicates. The catalog at the birth_site (site at which the object was first created) of an object maintains the current storage sites of that object. Object movement causes this information to be updated. This scheme maintains complete site autonomy.

Each apprentice site takes the portions of the plan relevant to it and compiles it to produce an optimal local access plan. The sequence of actions is shown in Figure 15.13. Note that the master site can also be an apprentice site.

Transaction management, two-phase commit protocol, recovery, global and local deadlock detection and resolution are supported by the transaction manager. It also assigns unique names to the transactions. The run-time manager of RSS* executes calls to TM* and DC* (when data movement between sites is required).

R* uses the process concept wherein transactions are organized as processes, sharing common code and data structures, including lock tables. A master process is created for a single user or application program and all database requests are made through this process. In this scheme, creation and deletion of a process for each database manipulation is avoided. Similarly, for a remote database request, a process is created at the remote site. In this way, a hierarchy of processes can exist at a number of sites. The root of such a hierarchical tree is the process created at the master site.

15.11.2 The Heterogeneous DDBMS

The major problems in heterogeneous DDBMSs are concerned with the translation between different data manipulation languages, different data models, and the variety in data usage and definition. We can include in our definition of heterogeneous sys-

Figure 15.13 Distributed query compilation in R.*

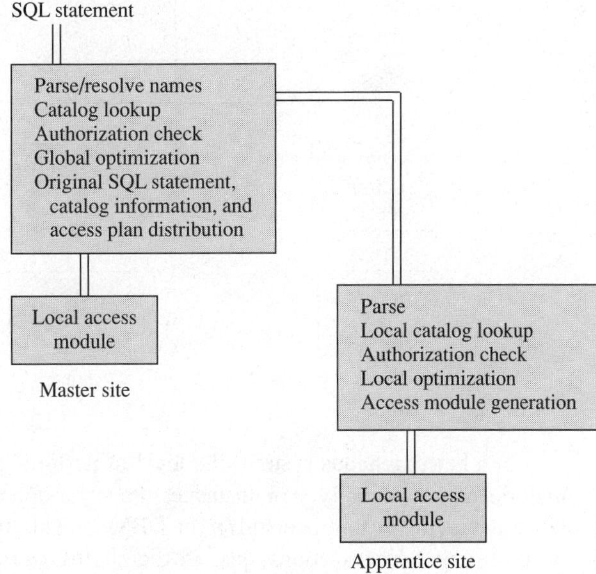

tems DBMSs which, while employing the same generic data model (relational, hierarchical, or network), are in essence different systems.

Earlier we mentioned possible conflicting situations that may arise in systems in which we aggregate preexisting systems. The possible conflicts are:

- **Name:** Same name used to describe different facts, or different names used for the same fact.
- **Structure:** Same fact described in two different schemes using different elements of a data model.
- **Abstraction:** Different levels of details.
- **Scale:** Different units of measurement for the same data item.

In addition to the above conflicts, others arise, such as disagreements in the data representing the same fact in separate databases due to measurement or entry errors. The conflicts cannot be resolved by force or mediation if the definitions in the component DBMSs are to remain unaltered—an important local autonomy consideration.

The problem of mapping between different data models and DMLs is solved by utilizing a common data model and DML. A DDBMS consists of k different DBMSs. Then, if we do not utilize a common data model we would need k * (k–1) translators—each system would need a translator to the remaining (k–1) systems. Using a common global data model, we need only 2 * k translators, one from each system to the common model and vice-versa. The characteristics that the common data model and its accompanying DML should possess include simple translation rules between it and the data models and DMLs of constituent DBMSs; and suitability to represent data and processing requirements of the DDBMS (e.g., fragmentation, replication, etc.).

Figure 15.14 MULTIBASE scheme architecture (adapted from [Land 82]).

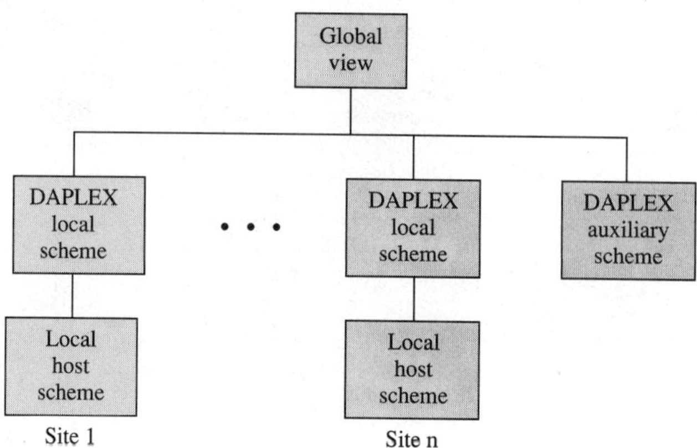

In a heterogeneous system, the level of performance of the various host DBMSs may differ considerably. For instance, the same operation on the same data may be done at varying costs under different DBMSs. This factor would be a consideration in allocating subtransactions, just as the nearness criteria is used when considering communication costs. In some cases, a particular host DBMS may not even be able to perform a specific operation. The above issues are addressed below in the section on MULTIBASE. If the DDBMS provides a single interface to external users, as is the common practice, then the network DML should be easy to learn and sufficiently powerful to satisfy all needs.

A few heterogeneous DDBMS prototypes have been built. Here we consider only one of them, a derivative of SDD–1.

Multibase

The MULTIBASE DDBMS,[2] developed by Computer Corporation of America, provides an integrated interface for retrieving data from preexisting, heterogeneous, distributed databases. Its aim is to present an integrated uniform interface. This is achieved by defining an integrated global schema and by utilizing a single global query language. Besides being read-only, MULTIBASE does not implement controls to ensure that when reading data from one site, other required data at another site is not being updated—because most systems do not make concurrency control services available to an external process. The global query language DAPLEX is based on the functional data model.[3] This model consists of entity sets and functions between them, and models object types of concern and their characteristics. The schema architecture is shown in Figure 15.14.

Resolving data and naming inconsistencies and any other incompatibilities in the preexisting databases are functions of the MULTIBASE system. For this reason an

[2]The discussion here is based on (Land 82).
[3]See (Ship 81) for details on DAPLEX and the functional data model.

integration schema called the auxiliary schema is specified. The auxiliary schema describes a DAPLEX auxiliary database that is maintained by an internal DBMS, which is part of MULTIBASE. It contains data unavailable in any of the host DBMSs, or data needed to solve incompatibilities. Examples of such data are the following: statistics to determine which data values should be used in case of conflict; conversion tables for performing data transformations that can't be done via simple arithmetic manipulations. Furthermore, if two sites have, say, EMPLOYEE data but only one site has an EMPLOYEE.*Phone_No,* the missing phone number data can be added to the auxiliary database. This is in addition to the global and local schema (both specified using DAPLEX) and a local host schema. The local host schema is the schema description in the local DBMS language.

Besides the language and schema definition systems, MULTIBASE also provides a query processing system. The query processing system incorporates the local data interface and local DBMS. At the global level are the query translator and query processor subsystems. The query translator transforms the global query into subqueries over the local and auxiliary schema. The global query processor chooses appropriate query optimization criteria and coordinates the local query executions. The optimization plan includes data movement between sites and the integration of the results from the sites.

Local queries are sent to the local sites and are subjected to local query optimization. These locally optimized queries are then translated into queries over the local host schema of the host DBMS.

Each of these tasks is performed at different levels. Figure 15.15 displays the MULTIBASE architecture, which shows the two major components, the **global data manager (GDM)** and **local database interface (LDI).** The user submits queries to the global data manager, which is responsible for global query translation and optimization. It receives results from the local sites and performs any processing necessary to output the result. At each local site is a local database interface module that

Figure 15.15 MULTIBASE architecture (adapted from [Land 82]).

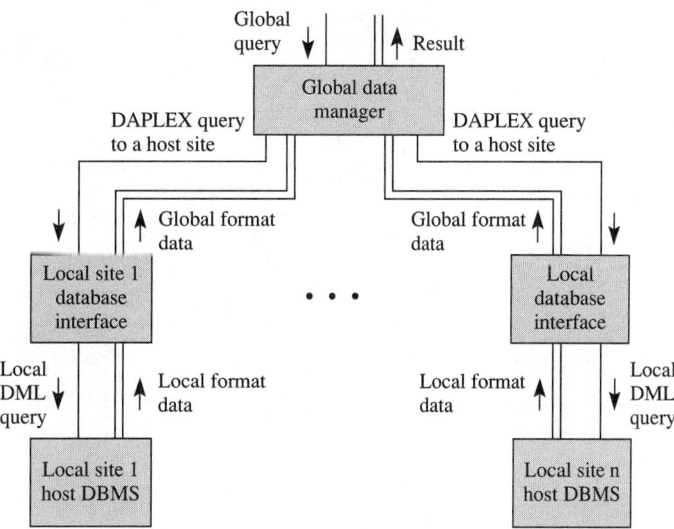

is responsible for DML translation and local query optimization, as well as reformatting local results to global format and returning them to the global data manager. The local database interface isolates the global data manager from the local site's DBMS and could be designed to augment the processing capability of the host DBMS.

The GDM is made up of the following subsystems, as shown in Figure 15.16: transformer, optimizer, decomposer, filter and monitor. We briefly describe the major tasks of each of these subsystems.

- **Transformer:** The transformer converts users' queries, expressed in DAPLEX on the global schema, into a DAPLEX query on local and auxiliary schemas. In this way the original query is modified to include mapping and conflict resolution information.
- **Optimizer, decomposer, filter:** These subsystems work in a cyclic fashion to define an overall strategy (optimizer), create DAPLEX single site queries (decomposer), and determine single site queries that can't be processed at the sites indicated by the overall strategy (filter). Output of the filter is resubmitted to the optimizer because if enough single site queries are unable to be executed at the planned sites, it may be worthwhile reevaluating the overall strategy. This cyclic processing caters to the DBMS difference that would not occur in a homogeneous DBMS.

Figure 15.16 Components of GDM (adapted from [Land 82]).

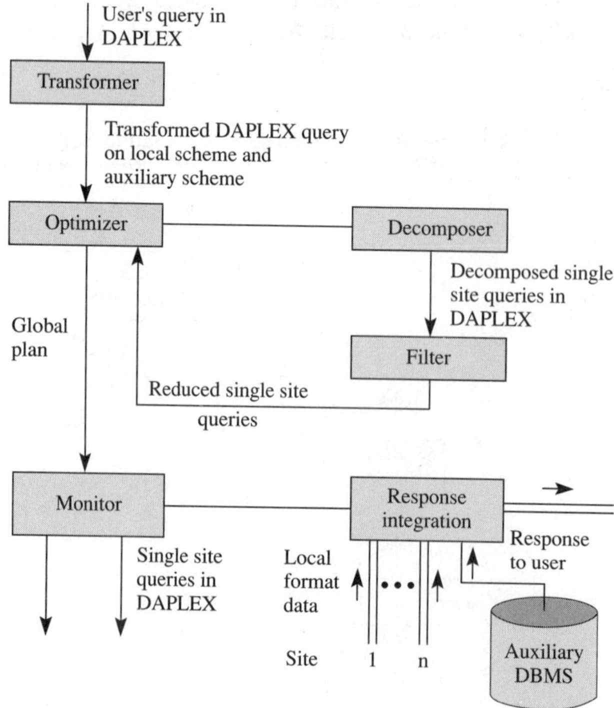

- **Monitor:** The monitor, as its name indicates, monitors the execution of the plan developed by the optimizer/decomposer/filter and communicated to the monitor by the optimizer. The monitor sends the single site DAPLEX queries to the corresponding LDIs. It also sends an internal query that may include reference to the auxiliary database and operations to compensate for operations for local database limitations. The monitor oversees the combination of local results and formats the output as requested by the user. (This is response integration, called internal DBMS in Multibase.)

The above components, plus the internal DBMS, are part of the GDM. There may be as few as one GDM for the entire system.

As described above, MULTIBASE provides a uniform interface and access language to the user of the heterogeneous databases. The local schema are integrated into a global schema and users see only this global schema. The system provides global as well as local query optimization.

15.12 Summary

A distributed database system consists of a collection of data in which separate parts of the collection are under the control of a separate DBMS running on an independent computer system. These independent computer systems are interconnected in a network. Each system is aware of the existence of the other systems and they communicate with each other via the network. Data can be replicated in a distributed system, increasing its accessibility and reliability. Since a query can be evaluated in parallel at different sites, the response can be faster in such a system.

The major issues involved in the DDBMS are that of data distribution, query processing, concurrency control, and deadlock detection and recovery.

Network design issues involved in the interconnecting of the different sites of the distributed system concern the choice of network topology, access method, and transmission technology.

In a distributed system, the data is distributed at a number of sites. The distribution is based on the expected access pattern and costs. The data can be partitioned. Such partitioning could be horizontal, vertical or both. Different DDBMSs allow different types of fragmentation. The DDBMS usually provides one or more of the following forms of transparencies, so that users need not concern themselves about them: location, fragmentation, and replication. The system catalog could be treated in a manner similar to ordinary data.

A query in a distributed system involves data from more than one site. An optimal query evaluation strategy involves determining the sites at which intermediate and final responses will be generated. The semijoin operation has been used to reduce communication costs.

The consistency and atomicity of a transaction requires the implementation of concurrency control and recovery techniques. Such techniques must take into account failures not only at local sites, but failures in the communication network. Consistency requirements dictate that all copies of a data item be modified. Usually a two-phase commit protocol is used.

Concurrency control schemes used in a centralized DBMS can be applied to control the concurrent execution of transactions in the DDBMS environment, with appropriate modifications. Detection of deadlock requires the generation of global wait-for graphs, either directly or indirectly. The deadlock prevention method based on schemes for a centralized system may be used. The problems of security and protection are similar to those of a centralized system.

Key Terms

distributed database
global transaction
subtransaction
local transaction
distributed database management system (DDBMS)
wide area network
long haul network
local area network (LAN)
star topology
mesh connection
bus network
ring topology
synchronous time-division multiplexing (SDM)
time-division multiplexing (TDM)
frequency division multiplexing (FDM)
polling
token
reservation
ALOHA
carrier sense multiple access with collision detection (CSMA/CD)
Ethernet
star ring
bridge
gateway
network partitioning
replication
location transparency
fragmentation
disjoint fragmentation
fragmentation transparency
vertical fragmentation
horizontal fragmentation
mixed fragmentation
disjoint vertical fragmentation
disjoint horizontal fragmentation
nondisjoint vertical fragmentation
nondisjoint horizontal fragmentation
replication transparency
update transparency
system catalog
birth_site
global catalog
locator catalog
caching the remote catalog
global naming
print name
systemwide name (SWN)
semijoin
reduction of relations
query graph
cyclic query
coordinator site
participating site
transaction manager
invariant
local wait-for graph (LWFG)
global wait-for graph (GWFG)
majority locking
primary site locking
distributed two-phase locking
distributed commit
blocking
two-phase commit
voting phase
decision phase
phantom deadlock
edge-chasing algorithms
probe
intercontroller edge
outgoing edge
probe computation
homogeneous system
heterogeneous system
local scheme
global scheme
materialization
conservative timestamp
transaction class
conflict analysis graph
master site
apprentice site
global data manager (GDM)
local database interface (LDI)
transformer
optimizer
decomposer
filter
monitor

Exercises

15.1 Explain why the query processing techniques discussed in this chapter would need to be modified for a distributed system running on a local area network. In your opinion, which of the three costs, communication, I/O, or CPU, are likely to dominate in a local area network environment? Justify your answer.

15.2 What are the advantages of horizontal fragmentation? How is query evaluation complicated or simplified by horizontal fragmentation? Design an algorithm to perform the join of two relations, R and S, both of which are horizontally fragmented. Account for the network to be either wide area or local area. Create some arbitrary data for the relations and their fragments. Distribute the fragments over a number of sites. Test your algorithm.

15.3 For exercise 2, modify your algorithm to use the semijoin technique.

15.4 Under what conditions is $R \ltimes S = S \ltimes R$?

15.5 How can the optimistic method presented in Chapter 12 be applied to concurrency control in a DDBMS? Discuss the relative advantages and disadvantages of the conservative timestamp and optimistic methods.

15.6 The validation phase of the optimistic method of a transaction may be checked against already committed transactions—the "committed validation technique," or the currently active (but not committed) transactions—the "active validation technique." Discuss the relative merits of these validation techniques for the optimistic concurrency control scheme for a DDBMS.

15.7 Using the library example discussed in Chapters 8 and 9, create a suitable distributed database. Indicate how the queries in those chapters would be handled.

15.8 Suppose a single copy of data items A and B is stored at sites S_1 and S_2, respectively. Consider the schedule for transactions T_1 and T_2 given in Figure P. Why is the schedule serializable, even though two-phase locking is not used?

Figure P Schedule for Exercise 15.8.

Time	site S_1		site S_2	
	Transaction	Transaction	Transaction	Transaction
t_1	T_{1S1}	T_{2S1}	T_{1S2}	T_{2S2}
t_2	**Lockx**(A)			**Lockx**(B)
t_3	**Read**(A)			**Read**(B)
t_4	A := A − 100			B := B − 200
t_5	**Write**(A)			**Write**(B)
t_6	**Unlock**(A)			**Unlock**(B)
t_7		**Lockx**(A)	**Lockx**(B)	
t_8		**Read**(A)	**Read**(B)	
t_9		A := A + 200	B := B + 100	
t_{10}		**Write**(A)	**Write**(B)	
t_{11}		**Unlock**(A)	**Unlock**(B)	

15.9 Consider a token approach to locking. Any number of read tokens can exist for a data item, but only one write token can exist, and that only if no read tokens are present. A transaction manager (TM) at a site can grant a read or write lock to a transaction at that site if the TM has a read or write token for the data item. Indicate the sequence of messages required between sites to allow transaction T running at site S to obtain a write lock on data item A.

15.10 Consider the following scheme to detect deadlock in a distributed database system. Each site maintains an LWFG with the addition of a node called T_{ex} (see Figure Q). T_{ex} is to depict

Figure Q LWFG at site S_i.

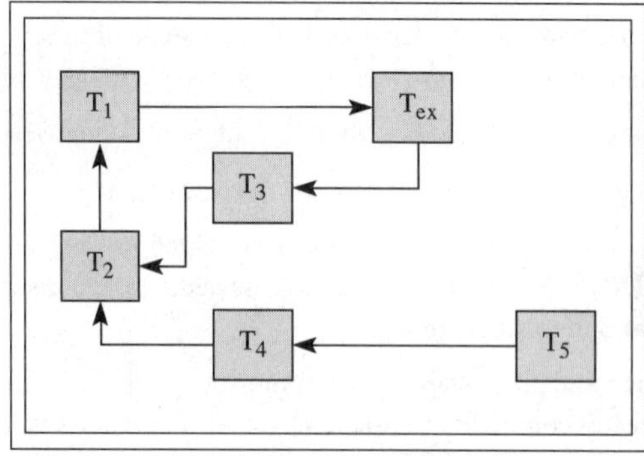

the situation in which a transaction at the site is waiting for a data item already locked by a transaction at a remote site. On detection of a cycle in the LWFG involving T_{ex}, site S_i sends its LWFG to, say, site S_j, containing the transaction that has locked the data item required by transaction T_1 at site S_i. The site uses this information to extend its LWFG to detect a global deadlock involving T_3 at site S_i. If deadlock is found, appropriate corrective action is taken. However, if S_j finds that there is a cycle involving a transaction in S_i but also involving its own special node T_{ex} with some site S_k, then S_j sends the extended wait-for graph to S_k for detection of a global deadlock. Comment on the feasibility of this scheme to detect global deadlocks. If the scheme does detect global deadlock, verify that such deadlocks are not phantoms.

Bibliographic Notes

Distributed database systems have been the subject of extensive study since the middle 1970s. A number of prototype systems were developed to explore the large number of problems that such systems encounter. Notable among the prototypes are SDD–1: A System for Distributed Databases, developed by Computer Corporation of America (Roth 80); System R,* developed by IBM (Will 81); and Distributed Ingres, developed at the University of California, Berkeley (Ston 77). MULTIBASE is presented in (Smit 81) and (Land 82).

The study of transactions management, including concurrency control, was influenced greatly by the works of Bernstein et al. (Bern 79), Eswaran et al. (Eswa 76), Gray et al. (Gray 75), and Stearns et al. (Stea 76). Excellent surveys of concurrency control are found in Bernstein and Goodman (Bern 81b, Bern 82). Concurrency control has also been covered by textbooks on distributed databases: Ceri and Pelgatti (Ceri 84) and Date (Date 83). Recent textbooks devoted exclusively to concurrency control are Bernstein, Hadzilacos and Goodman (Bern 87), and Papadimitriou (Papa 86).

Distributed query processing continues to be an extensive area of research. The papers by Wong (Wong 77), Hevener and Yao (Heve 79), Apers et al. (Aper 83), Bernstein and Chiu (Bern 81a) and Epstein and Stonebraker (Epst 80) set the direction of research. Bernstein and Chiu (Bern 81a) present an analysis of semijoins and show how tree form queries can be fully reduced using the semijoin, but semijoins are not adequate to fully reduce a cyclic query. Yu and Chang (Yu 84) present a survey of distributed query processing, while Ceri and Pelgatti (Ceri 84) give textbook coverage.

Data distribution and its effects on query processing is the subject of study in a number of the works cited above. Specific problems with data distribution are studied by Ceri et al. (Ceri 82, Ceri 83) and Navathe et al. (Nava 84).

Distributed deadlock detection is another area of active research. The survey papers by Knapp (Knap 87) and Elmagarmid (Elma 86) show the pitfalls in a number of published algorithms and give an excellent introduction to the subject. The proof of the edge-chasing algorithm given in this chapter is found in (Chan 82).

Bibliography

(Abad 89) A. El Abaddi & Sam Toueng, ''Maintaining Availability in Partitioned Replicated Databases,'' ACM Trans. on Database Systems, 14(2), June 1989, pp. 264–290.

(Agra 89) D. Agrawal and S. Sengupta, ''Modular Synchronization in Multiversion Databases: Version Control and Concurrency Control,'' *SIGMOD Record* 18(2), June 1989, pp. 408–417.

(Aper 83) P. Apers, A. Hevner, & S. B. Yao, ''Optimization Algorithms for Distributed Queries,'' *IEEE Transactions on Software Engineering* SE–9(1), January 1983, pp. 57–68.

(Bagr 89) R. Bagrodia, ''Process Synchronization: Design and Performance Evaluation of Distributed Algorithms,'' IEEE Trans. on Software Engineering, 15(9), September 1989, pp. 1053–1065.

(Bern 79) P. A. Bernstein, D. W. Shipman, & W. S. Wong, ''Formal Aspects of Serializability in Database Concurrency Control,'' *IEEE Transactions on Software Engineering* SE–5(3), 1979, pp. 203–216.

(Bern 80) P. A. Bernstein, D. W. Shipman, & J. B. Rothnie, ''Concurrency Control in a System for Distributed Databases (SDD–1),'' *ACM Transactions on Database Systems* 5(1), January 1980, pp. 18–51.

(Bern 81a) P. A. Bernstein & D. W. Chiu, ''Using Semijoins to Solve Relational Queries,'' *JACM* 28(1), January 1981, pp. 25–40.

(Bern 81b) P. A. Bernstein & N. Goodman, ''Concurrency Control in Distributed Database Systems,'' *ACM Computing Surveys* 13, 1981, pp. 185–221.

(Bern 82) P. A. Bernstein & N. Goodman, ''A Sophisticate's Introduction to Distributed Database Concurrency Control,'' Proceedings of the Eighth International Conference on Very Large Data Bases, 1982, pp. 62–76.

(Bern 87) P. A. Bernstein, V. Hadzilacos, & N. Goodman, *Concurrency Control and Recovery in Database Systems,* Reading, MA: Addison-Wesley, 1987.

(Ceri 82) S. Ceri, M. Negri, & G. Pelgatti, ''Horizontal Data Partitioning in Database Design,'' Proceedings of the ACM SIGMOD International Conference on Management of Data, Orlando, FL, 1982, pp. 128–136.

(Ceri 83) S. Ceri, S. Navathe, & G. Widerhold, ''Distribution Design of Logical Database Schemas,'' *IEEE Transactions on Software Engineering* SE–9(4), 1983, pp. 487–504.

(Ceri 84) S. Ceri & G. Pelgatti, *Distributed Databases—Principles and Systems.* New York: McGraw-Hill, 1984.

(Chan 82) K. M. Chandy & J. Misra, ''A Distributed Algorithm for Detecting Resource Deadlocks in Distributed Systems,'' Proc. of the ACM Symposium on Principles of Distributed Computing, Ottawa, Canada, 1982, pp. 157–164.

(Date 83) C. J. Date, *An Introduction to Database Systems,* vol. 2. Reading, MA: Addison-Wesley, 1983.

(Elma 86) A. K. Elmagarmid, ''A Survey of Distributed Deadlock Detection Algorithms,'' *ACM SIGMOD Record* 15(3), September 1986, pp. 37–45.

(Epst 80) R. Epstein & M. R. Stonebraker, ''Analysis of Distributed Database Processing Strategies,'' Proc. of the International Conf. on VLDB, 1980, pp. 92–100.

(Eswa 76) K. P. Eswaran, J. N. Gray, R. A. Lorie, & I. L. Traiger, "The Notions of Consistency and Predicate Locks in a Database System," *Communications of the ACM* 19(11), November 1976, pp. 624–633.

(Gray 75) J. N. Gray, R. A. Lorie, G. R. Putzula, & I. L. Traiger, "Granularity of Locks and Degrees of Consistency in a Shared Database," IBM Research Report RJ1654, 1975.

(Gray 81) J. N. Gray, "The Transaction Concept: Virtues and Limitations," Proceedings of the Seventh International Conference on Very Large Databases, 1981, pp. 144–154.

(Heve 79) A. R. Hevener & S. B. Yao, "Query Processing in a Distributed Database System," *IEEE Transactions on Software Engineering* SE–5(3), May 1979, pp. 177–187.

(Knap 87) E. Knapp, "Deadlock Detection in Distributed Databases," *Computing Surveys* 19(4), December 1987, pp. 303–328.

(Land 82) T. Landers & R. L. Rosenberg, "An Overview of Multibase," in H. J. Schneider, ed. *Distributed Data Bases*. New York, North Holland, 1982, pp. 153–188.

(Nava 84) S. Navathe, S. Ceri, G. Widerhold, & J. Dou, "Vertical Partitioning Algorithms for Database Design," *ACM Transactions on Database Systems* 9(4), December 1984, pp. 680–710.

(Papa 85) C. H. Papadimitriou & M. Yannakakis, "The Complexity of Reliable Concurrency Control," Proceedings of the Fourth ACM SIGACT-SIGMOD Symposium on the Principles of Database Systems, 1985, pp. 230–233.

(Papa 86) C. H. Papadimitriou, *The Theory of Concurrency Control*. Rockville, MD: Computer Science Press, 1986.

(Roth 80) J. B. Rothnie, P. A. Bernstein, S. Fox, N. Goodman, M. Hammer, T. A. Landers, C. Reeve, D. W. Shipman, & E. Wong, "Introduction to a System for Distributed Databases (SDD–1)," *ACM Transactions on Database Systems* 5, January 1980, pp. 1–17.

(Ship 81) D. W. Shipman, "The Functional Data Model and the Data Language DAPLEX," *ACM Transactions on Database Systems* 6(1), March 1981, pp. 140–173.

(Smit 81) J. M. Smith, P. Bernstein, U. Dayal, N. Goodman, T. Landers, K. W. T. Lin, & E. Wong, "Multibase-Integrating Heterogeneous Distributed Database Systems," NCC Conf. Proc. 50, May 1981, pp. 487–499.

(Stal 87) W. Stalling, *Local Networks, An Introduction,* 2nd ed. New York: Macmillan, 1987.

(Ston 77) M. Stonebraker & E. Neuhold, "A Distributed Database Version of INGRES," 1977 Berkeley Workshop on Distributed Data Management and Computer Networks, University of California, Berkeley, 1977, pp. 19–36.

(Will 81) R. Williams, D. Daniels, L. Haas, G. Lapis, B. Lindsay, P. Ng, R. Obermarck, P. Selinger, A. Walker, P. Wilms, & R. Yost, "R*: An Overview of the Architecture," IBM Technical Report, RJ 3325, San Jose, CA, 1981.

(Wong 77) E. Wong, "Retrieving Dispersed Data from SDD–1: A System for Distributed Databases." Proc. of the 2nd Berkeley Workshop on Distributed Data Management and Computer Networks, Berkeley, CA, 1977, pp. 217–235.

(Yu 84) C. T. Yu & C. C. Chang, "Distributed Query Processing," *ACM Computing Surveys* 16(4), December 1984, pp. 399–433.

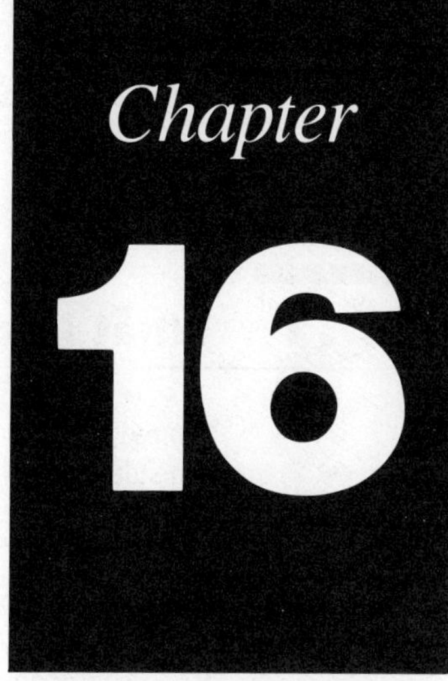

Current Topics in Database Research

Contents

In this chapter we present some highlights of the recent advances in database systems. We discuss knowledge base systems, deductive or logic databases, expert systems, and the object-oriented approach.

16.1 What Is a Knowledge Base System?

Knowledge is an abstract entity that can be characterized according to its use. We consider knowledge to be a justifiable belief and we use the pragmatic rather than the philosophical approach in a knowledge base system.

Using the analogy of a DBMS, we can define a **knowledge base management system (KBMS)** as a computer system used to manage and manipulate shared knowledge. A knowledge base system's manipulation facility includes a **reasoning[1] facility,** usually including aspects of one or more of the following forms of reasoning: deductive, inductive, or abductive. **Deductive reasoning** implies that a new fact can be inferred from a given set of facts or knowledge using known rules of inference. For instance, a given proposition can be found to be true or false in light of existing knowledge in the form of other propositions believed to be either true or false. **Inductive reasoning** is used to prove something by first proving a base fact and then the increment step; having proved these, we can prove a generalized fact. **Abductive reasoning** is used in generating a hypothesis to explain observations. Like deductive reasoning, it points to possible inferences from related concepts; however, unlike deductive reasoning, the number of inferences could be more than one. The likelihood of knowing which of these inferences corresponds to the current state of the system can be gleaned from the explanations generated by the system. These explanations can facilitate choosing among these alternatives and arriving at the final conclusion.

In addition to the reasoning facility, a knowledge base system may incorporate an **explanation facility** so that the user can verify whether the reasoning used by the system is consistent and complete. The reasoning facility also offers a form of tutoring to the uninitiated user. The so-called expert systems and the associated expert system generation facilities are one form of knowledge base systems that have emerged from research labs and are being marketed commercially. Since a KBMS includes reasoning capacity, there is a clear benefit in incorporating this reasoning power in database application programs in languages such as COBOL and Pascal.

Most knowledge base systems are still in the research stage. The first generation of commercial KBMSs are just beginning to emerge and integration of a KBMS with a DBMS is a current research problem. However, some headway has been made in the integration of expert systems in day-to-day database applications.

---

[1]We can define reasoning informally as the extraction of new knowledge from existing knowledge.

16.2 Knowledge Base and Database Systems: A Comparison

There is no consensus on the difference between a knowledge base system and a database system. In a DBMS, the starting point is a data model to represent the data and the interrelationships between them; similarly, the starting point of a KBMS is a **knowledge representation scheme.** The requirements for any knowledge representation scheme are adequacy, completeness, consistency, soundness, and validity. The scheme should provide some mechanism to organize knowledge in appropriate hierarchies or categories, thus allowing easy access to associated concepts. In addition, since knowledge can be expressed as rules and exceptions to rules, **exception-handling features** must be present in the knowledge representation scheme. Furthermore, the scheme should have some means of ensuring **knowledge independence.** Here, independence signifies that the knowledge stored in the system must be insulated from changes in usage in its physical or logical structure. This concept is similar to the data independence concept used in a DBMS. To date, little headway has been made in this aspect of a KBMS.

A KBMS is developed to solve problem for a finite domain or portion of the real world. In developing such a system, the designer selects significant objects and relationships among these objects. In addition to this domain-specific knowledge, general knowledge such as concepts of up, down, far, near, cold, hot, on top of, and besides must be incorporated in the KBMS. Another type of knowledge, which we call common sense, has yet to be successfully incorporated in the KBMS.

The DBMS and KBMS have similar architectures; both contain a component to model the information being managed by the system and have a subsystem to respond to queries. Both systems are used to model or represent a portion of the real world of interest to the application. A database system, in addition to storing facts in the form of data, has limited capability of establishing associations between these data. These associations could be preestablished as in the case of the network and hierarchical models, or established using common values of shared domains as in the relational model. A knowledge base system exhibits similar associative capability. However, this capability of establishing associations between data and thus a means of interpreting the information contained is at a much higher level in a knowledge base system, ideally at the level of a knowledgeable human agent.[2]

One difference between the DBMS and KBMS that has been proposed is that the knowledge base system handles a rather small amount of knowledge, whereas a DBMS efficiently (as measured by response performance) handles large amounts of shared data. However, this distinction is fallacious since the amount of knowledge has no known boundaries and what this says is that existing knowledge base systems handle a very small amount of knowledge. This does not mean that at some future date we couldn't develop knowledge base systems to efficiently handle much larger amounts of shared knowledge.

---

[2]The classical Turing test measures the performance of an intelligent system against a human being, the latter being the only measure we have for intelligent behavior.

In a knowledge base system, the emphasis is placed on a robust knowledge representation scheme and extensive reasoning capability. **Robust** signifies that the scheme is rich in expressive power and at the same time it is efficient. In a DBMS, emphasis is on efficient access and management of the data that model a portion of the real world. A knowledge base system is concerned with the meaning of information, whereas a DBMS is interested in the information contained in the data. However, these distinctions are not absolute.

For our purposes, we can adopt the following informal definition of a KBMS. The important point in this definition is that we are concerned with what the system does rather than how it is done.

Definition: A knowledge base management system is a computer system that manages the knowledge in a given domain or field of interest and exhibits reasoning power to the level of a human expert in this domain.

A KBMS, in addition, provides the user with an integrated language, which serves the purpose of the traditional DML of the existing DBMS and has the power of a high-level application language. A database can be viewed as a very basic knowledge base system insofar as it manages facts. It has been recognized that there should be an integration of the DBMS technology with the reasoning aspect in the development of shared knowledge bases. Database technology has already addressed the problems of improving system performance, concurrent access, distribution, and friendly interface; these features are equally pertinent in a KBMS. There will be a continuing need for current DBMSs and their functionalities coexisting with an integrated KBMS. However, the reasoning power of a KBMS can improve the ease of retrieval of pertinent information from a DBMS.

16.3 Knowledge and Its Representation

To solve a problem (i.e., carry out an intelligent activity) we need three components:[3]

- A model or a symbolic representation of the concepts of the domain of interest.
- A set of basic operations on this symbolic representation to generate one or more solutions to the problem.
- An evaluation method to select a solution from the set of possible candidates.

The representation scheme must be able to register the significant characteristics of the problem domain. These features of the problem domain must be easily accessible for appropriate manipulations.

[3]A. Newell & H. A. Simon, "Computer Science as Empirical Inquiry: Symbols and Search," *ACM 10th Turing Lecture—1975, CACM* 19(3), March 1976, pp. 113–126.

A natural language is an example of a symbolic representation scheme. Using this scheme, knowledge has been represented in folklore and more recently using the written word and recorded speech and image. These forms of representing knowledge have been developed over thousands of years. Natural language has very high expressive power. However, this form of representation, though suitable for humans, is either inappropriate or requires an enormous amount of resources for use in a computer-based system.

A knowledge base system contains knowledge about a particular domain. In addition, it contains a certain amount of general knowledge. The latter includes the pertinent world knowledge applicable to the domain and some degree of so-called commonsense knowledge. For instance, a knowledge base system containing information about diseases and diagnoses must have knowledge of the different units of measurements of mass, length, temperature, concepts of nearness, normal, higher, lower, faster, slower, and so on.

Just as beauty is in the eye of the beholder, meaning is not contained in the message, but is constructed around it by the recipient. For example, if we are presented with the statement "Jumbo is an elephant," we conjure up a picture of an elephant; we know that it is large, with a trunk and tusks and huge flapping ears. In order to make this addition to the simple statement, we recalled this common knowledge that we acquired during our life. If we are then presented with the statement "Jumbo lives in a teacup," we will think either (a) the statements are from a fairy tale or (b) the statements are inconsistent with what we know about elephants and cups in the real world. We know from experience that elephants are large animals, a normal teacup is too small to hold an elephant, and normally we don't put elephants in teacups!

One of the requirements of any knowledge representation scheme is that it must allow the associated knowledge about a concept or statement to be easily retrieved and employed to enable the knowledge base system to understand and reason. The concept of using association in retrieving information is a very old one; it can be traced back to the time of Aristotle. The use of association in database applications in the form of associative or intelligent memories has also been investigated. However, the use of associative memory[4] to model human memories for intelligent computer systems is more recent. The efficient access to associated knowledge in a particular situation need not be in a form similar to human memory; nevertheless, the result should be useful so that related concepts, associated both explicitly and implicitly, can be employed in inferences.

We not only know something, we know that we know it and have developed a certain degree of confidence in using the knowledge correctly (expertise). Our ability to read a map, our sense of orientation, and knowledge of these abilities give us the confidence to drive to an unknown city and find an address. Similarly, the knowledge base system must have knowledge about the knowledge representation scheme being used and how it can be manipulated in the reasoning process. Such knowledge, called **metaknowledge,** can be compared to the metadata used in a database system.

The knowledge base system must be able to deal with incomplete knowledge,

[4]An associative memory system has logic associated with each word or each bit of every word. This logic is used to simultaneously examine the contents of the entire memory and matching words are flagged.

as well as dynamically acquire new knowledge. These points are also applicable to DBMSs.

A knowledge representation scheme consists of two parts: data structures to represent the domain of the problem, and procedures to interpret the information contained therein to enable a knowledge base system to exhibit the behavior of a knowledgeable human expert. The knowledge to be maintained can be one of the following: objects, events, know-how, precedence and cause-and-effect relationships, and metaknowledge. Knowledge about objects can be considered factual knowledge such as: an elephant is a mammal, an elephant has a trunk and tusks, a bird has wings, a car has a steering wheel and pedals. Examples of knowledge about events are: John gave a book to Mary, Canada geese come back in spring. Know-how knowledge consists of the knowledge involved in doing something. For instance, driving a car involves using the accelerator pedal to activate the choke; turning the ignition key to engage the starter to start the engine; using the transmission and pedals to put the car in motion; and using the steering wheel to control the trajectory of this motion. Precedence knowledge in this case involves the correct ordering of the various operations. Animals, including humans, use know-how knowledge to perform repetitive operations. Walking, running, flying, or riding a bike require a considerable amount of computing; however, having learned these actions, animals do them without effort. Imparting the know-how knowledge in a knowledge base, and to robots, is not a trivial task. Metaknowledge, as discussed above, is knowledge about knowledge.

In the following sections we look at these knowledge representation schemes: semantic networks, first-order logic (predicate logic), frames, rule-based systems (production systems), and procedural representation.

16.3.1 Semantic Networks

The idea of a **semantic network** was introduced in the late 1960s to represent the semantics of English words and phrases as perceived by humans. The term semantic network refers not to one concept but a set of related concepts, extensions, and modifications. All these networks share a node-based data structure, the nodes being connected by arcs. Each arc denotes a relationship between the nodes and has a semantic or meaning associated with it, the common relationships being *IS_A*, *HAS*, *A_KIND_OF (AKO)*, and so on. The *IS_A* relationship denotes a member-to-class relationship (Jumbo is a elephant); the *AKO* relationship denotes a class-to-superclass relationship (an elephant is a kind of mammal). An associated set of inference procedures uses these structures in the reasoning process.

A semantic network (see Figure 16.1) can thus be classified as a system wherein concepts or objects are hierarchically classified either as trees, lattices, or graphs. In a tree hierarchy, each node has a single immediate parent node. A hierarchy with multiple higher order nodes can be represented by a lattice. The nodes of this network are the objects and the arcs represent the relationships between these objects. One such relationship is to provide inheritance of properties from one object to another. Such a relationship is usually called an *IS_A* link. Concepts such as John is a male, Jumbo is an elephant, Rags is a dog, a dog is a kind of mammal, a mammal is a kind of living organism, are examples of *IS_A* and *AKO* relationships. Here the

Figure 16.1 A semantic network.

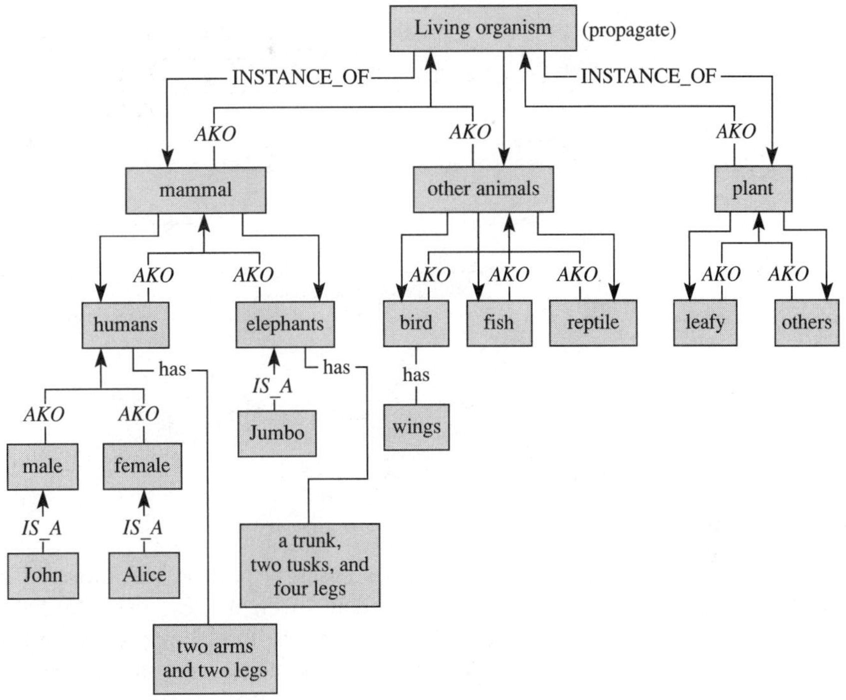

AKO link is used to describe a generalization relation between the concepts mammal and living organism, mammal being a subconcept of living organism. The *IS_A* link is used to identify an instance of a class. The *IS_A* and *AKO* links also represent a specialization relationship or a classification relationship in the reverse direction.

The *AKO* and *IS_A* links are associated with the **property inheritance mechanism.** Any property of a higher level node is inherited by all nodes connected to it by such a link. The property that all living organisms propagate is inherited by mammals, other animals, and plants. However, we may need to distinguish the properties of Indian elephants from those of African elephants; among Indian elephants, only the males have tusks. One method of showing these distinctions is illustrated in Figure 16.2. Furthermore, to represent exceptions, some mechanism must be used to allow cancellation of such inheritances. Thus, if Jumbo has lost one of its tusks, then it is an elephant with only one tusk. This is represented by canceling the inheritance of the general elephant properties for the node Jumbo and assigning its specific properties. Figure 16.2 also shows a mechanism for **overriding** inherited properties: Jumbo is an Asiatic male elephant with a trunk, four legs, and one tusk; the inherited property, two tusks, is canceled and explicitly overridden by a specific property, namely, one tusk.

The inheritance mechanism allows a more compact knowledge base since common properties are stored only once. The exception-handling features allow us to override some of these inherited properties.

Figure 16.2 Inheriting and overriding properties.

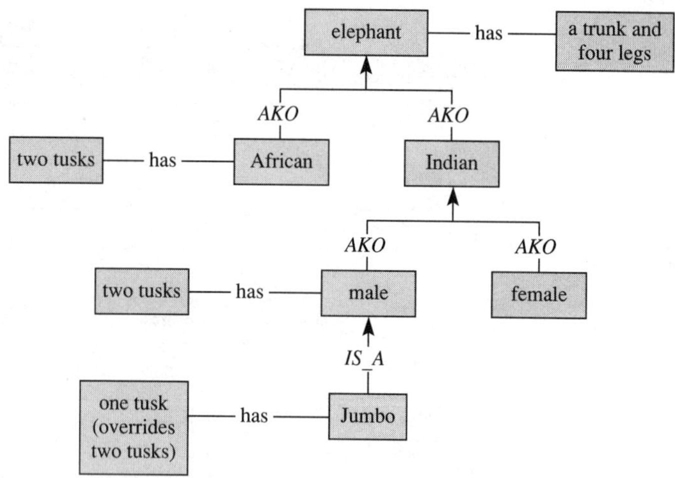

The *AKO* link can also be used to provide specialization or a classification or taxonomy in the reverse direction. In Figure 16.1 the *AKO* link provides a relationship between two generic nodes and the *IS_A* link provides it between a generic and an individual node. Thus, the generic nodes, human and mammal, are connected by an *AKO* arc to show the relationship that the human is a type of mammal. The relationship between a node representing an individual, Jumbo, and the generic node, elephant, is provided by an *IS_A* arc. In Figure 16.2, the node Jumbo inherits the properties of the elephant, Indian, and male nodes.

The semantics of an action, for instance, ''John gave Mary a book yesterday,'' can be represented as shown in Figure 16.3.

In addition to assigning the meaning to the arcs in the network, the use of a semantic network for knowledge representation requires that procedures using the semantic network correctly interpret the meaning of these arcs. The assigning of meaning to the arcs is ad hoc and a wide variation of network-based schemes have been proposed, along with procedures to interpret them. In spite of a lack of stan-

Figure 16.3 Assigning a meaning to an arc.

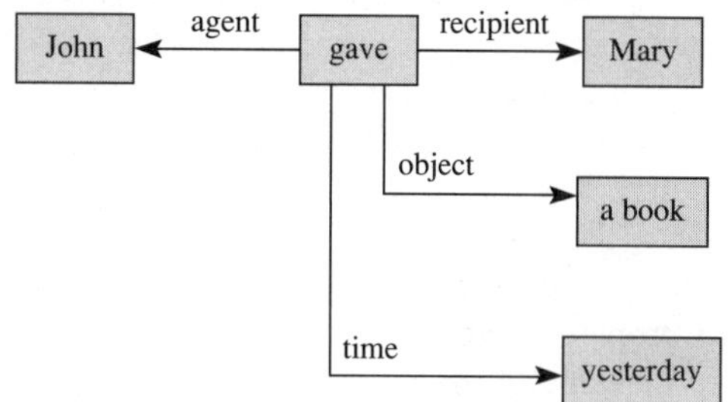

dardization, semantic networks are popular knowledge representation schemes. Their structure resembles the association perceived to be used by humans.

16.3.2 First-Order Logic (Predicate Logic)

A **proposition** is a declarative (or assertive) sentence, e.g., "It is snowing," "Rags is a dog." Declarative sentences are distinguished from interrogative and imperative sentences. An interrogative sentence asks a question; an imperative sentence is a directive or command.

Propositional logic is concerned with establishing the validity of a proposition in light of a given set of propositions. It establishes whether the proposition is true or false, relative to the given set. (The propositions in the set could be either true or false. It is, however, not in the realm of logic to establish the truthfulness of each statement in the given set of propositions.) Simple propositions can be combined using the sentential connectives and, or, not, implies, equivalent, and so on. An example of a combined proposition, which is always true, is the following: "If elephants are mammals, and if Jumbo is an elephant, then Jumbo is a mammal."

Propositional calculus is, in effect, computing with propositions. Given a set of propositions or axioms known to be true (or false), propositional calculus uses rules of inference to determine whether a given proposition is true or false. Let us use X, Y, Z, etc. to denote propositions; for instance, X may be the proposition "Jumbo is an elephant." The first rule of inference, called **modus ponens,** allows us to infer that proposition Y, "Jumbo is a mammal," is true under the condition that proposition X is true, and hence X logically implies Y (written as $X \rightarrow Y$). Thus, given that "Jumbo is an elephant" (X) is true, and "Jumbo is an elephant" implies "Jumbo is a mammal," which is also true, then "Jumbo is a mammal" is true. That is, if X and $X \rightarrow Y$ are both true, Y is also true. In the above example Y is the proposition "Jumbo is a mammal".

The second rule of inference is the **chain rule,** which allows us to infer a new implication from known implications; thus, if $X \rightarrow Y$ and $Y \rightarrow Z$, then $X \rightarrow Z$.

Mathematical logic, just like any other formal science, uses a language to express statements or formulas. The semantics of these statements are well defined. Mathematical logic also uses a theory of proofs so that statements can be proved to be correct or false. One method of proving the truthfulness or falsity of a proposition is called **reductio ad absurdum.** In this method the known propositions or axioms are appended with the negation of the proposition to be proved. If the resulting set is inconsistent, the proposition cannot be false. A major problem with this approach is that as the number of propositions increases, the number of combinations to be investigated increases in an exponential manner and the computation time becomes astronomical.

Propositions that specify a property consist of an expression that names an individual object and an expression, called the **predicate,** that stands for the property that the individual object possesses. We use the lowercase symbols from the end of the alphabet to denote variables, those from the beginning of the alphabet to denote constants, and uppercase letters to denote predicates. Thus P(x), where x is the argument, is a one-place or monadic predicate. DBMS(x) and COMPANY(y) are examples of monadic predicates; the variables x and y are replaceable by constants (or names of individual objects), like DBMS(ISS).

A predicate is a statement about an object or a relationship between two or more objects. Thus, in the propositions "Jumbo is an elephant," "an elephant is a mammal," "an elephant is bigger than a dog," "is an elephant," "is a mammal," "is bigger than" are predicates. The last predicate is applied to two arguments, whereas the first two have a single argument.

A one-place predicate, when applied to an object, gives a statement that is either true or false and thus divides or sorts the object into two disjoint sets or **sorts.** The predicate "is an elephant," when applied to the object Jumbo, forms a true statement: "Jumbo is an elephant." However, when it is applied to Robin, a bird, it forms "Robin is an elephant," a false statement.

Predicates can be combined using the operators $\wedge$ (and), $\vee$ (or), $\neg$ (negation), $\rightarrow$ (implication), or $\equiv$ (equivalence). Other interesting formulas are formed with the use of quantifiers: universal (or for all; denoted by the symbol $\forall$) and existential (or some; denoted by the symbol $\exists$). To express the term "for all objects" a certain property holds, we use the quantifier $\forall$. To express the term "there exists some object" with a certain property we use the quantifier $\exists$. Thus, $(\forall x)P(x)$ and $(\exists x)P(x)$ are used to specify that "for all x, x is P" (or simply that "everything is P") and "for some x, x is P" (or simply that "something is P"). Quantifiers are used to limit the range of values of a variable inside a predicate. The symbol $\forall$ is used to denote all values of the variable for which the predicate is valid. The symbol $\exists$ denotes the existence of some value of the variable for which the predicate is true. Well-formed formulas combine predicates with these operators. Parentheses can be used to resolve operation precedence ambiguities.

The only other primitive that we need to define is a function. A **function,** like a predicate, takes arguments and specifies some object; for example, the monadic function mother_of(x) specifies the individual who is the mother of the individual x. A function has a concept, similar to the one used in programming languages; i.e., a function has a number of arguments and returns a value that could be true, false, or have some other value related to the arguments. Note the difference between a predicate and a function. A function specifies an object that has some specified relationship (or property) to the argument objects, while a predicate specifies a property that the argument objects possess.

First-order logic can be used as a programming language. It consists of constants, variables, predicates, function symbols, logical connectives, and quantifiers. Traditionally, lowercase letters from the beginning of the alphabets are used to denote constants and lowercase letters from the end of the alphabets are used to denote variables. In first-order logic, we do not allow predicates to be used as variables. The concept of equality is defined as follows: two objects X and Y are considered equal, i.e., $X = Y$, if for all predicates P, $P(X) \equiv P(Y)$.

Predicate calculus is obtained by applying the rules of propositional calculus to predicates, using quantification, and adding to these the inference rules for quantifiers. If we further add the concepts of functions and equality, the result is a version of first-order logic or **first-order predicate calculus.**

A function is defined by a function symbol followed by its arguments: f(a), gcm(a,b), lcd(12,16), dad(Roy) fraction (7,8). The function lcd(12,16) is equal to 4, the function dad(Roy) has the value Frank, Roy's dad, and the function fraction(7,8) has the value 7/8.

A relation name can also be denoted by a predicate symbol. The relation PARENT(X,Y) is a two-place predicate symbol and indicates that Y is a parent of X. Some tuples from this relation are shown in Figure 16.4. Note that the relation PARENT(X,Y) is a form of a rule that states that Y is the parent of X.

First-order logic is complete since every true statement can be proven; in addition it is sound, since no false statement can be proven. The response to a query in a system using logic can be reduced to that of theorem proving. Some examples of wff in first-order logic are given in Example 16.1.

Example 16.1

The following are wffs:
brother(Roy,Jerry)
brother(Myrna,Roy)
brother(Jerry,Roy)
parent(y,x) $\wedge$ parent(z,x)
$\forall x(\forall y$ (parent(x,y) $\wedge$ female(y) $\rightarrow$ mother(x,y)) ■

The last example above indicates logic to state a rule. The rule is that for all (individuals) x and for all (individuals) y, if y is a parent of x and if y is a female, than y is a mother of x. The term ''for all and for all y'' can be abbreviated as ''for all x and y.''

A **Horn clause** is a wff of the form:

$$A \vee \neg B_1 \vee \neg B_2 \vee \neg B_3 \vee \ldots \vee \neg B_n$$

which can be written as:

$$B_1 \wedge B_2 \wedge B_3 \wedge \ldots \wedge B_n \rightarrow A$$

where A and B_is are nonnegated atomic formulas.

Figure 16.4 PARENT relation.

PARENT

X	Y
Roy	Frank
Jerry	Frank
Myrna	Ruth
Roy	Ruth
Lynn	Roy
Lynn	Rachel
Justin	Lynn
Janet	Myrna
Drew	Sheila
Pavan	Sheila
Sheila	Frank
Frank	George

In a Horn clause there is only one conclusion. PROLOG (PROgramming in LOGic) is a programming language based on the Horn clause. The human reasoning process is generally considered to be similar to the scheme used in logic. Logic results in a precise and flexible knowledge representation scheme that is easy to formulate and understand. The disadvantages of using logic are the lack of indexing or associative capability, the handling of dynamic and incomplete knowledge, and the intractability of computations involved in logic-based deductive inferences. In a logic-based knowledge representation, the processing is separated from the knowledge representation. The processing part, which determines the utility of the system, is usually implemented by theorem-proving techniques; however, this approach may not be useful for all applications. Another drawback of logic-based representation schemes is that heuristic or rule-of-thumb type knowledge may not be expressed in logic. In addition, the following assumptions have to be made in this processing (Gall 84), (Reit 84):

- **Closed world assumption (CWA),** which states that facts not known to be true are false.
- **Unique name assumption (UNA),** which states that objects are uniquely identified.
- **Domain closure assumption (DCA),** which states that no other objects or instances of objects other than the known ones exist.

16.3.3 Frames

The frame is another knowledge representation scheme used to represent the knowledge from a limited domain of stereotyped concepts or events. The concept of frames evolved from observations gleaned by psychologists as to the method humans use to interpret new situations. When confronted with an unknown object from a category of objects already experienced, we expect certain similarities and accept certain differences. We know how to handle these differences. We know what to expect and what to do if these expectations don't materialize. Thus, when we drive to a new city, we expect to see parks, buildings, streets, street signs. We know the usual locations of street signs and the correspondence between a street and a sign when a number of signs are posted on the same signposts. We also know what to do if a sign is missing at an intersection.

A **frame** (see Figure 16.5), is a data structure representing the collection of the expected and/or predicted description of a stereotype object, action, or event. Each important feature of the object is held in a slot. An optional procedure can be attached to a slot to introduce procedural information or specify consistency constraints. The frame also contains the object's relationship to other objects, these being represented by frames as well. The latter feature gives a frame a semantic network–like property. The description of the object includes a number of important features of the object and the relationships between other descriptors.

In addition to the predicted description of the various features of the object being represented, the frame may contain information such as the level of confidence assigned to the descriptor, the default values, alternate values (or their range) for descriptors, and variations in the descriptors that can be associated with the frame. The descriptors or slots can allow the inheritance of properties from a related frame. In

Figure 16.5 Frames

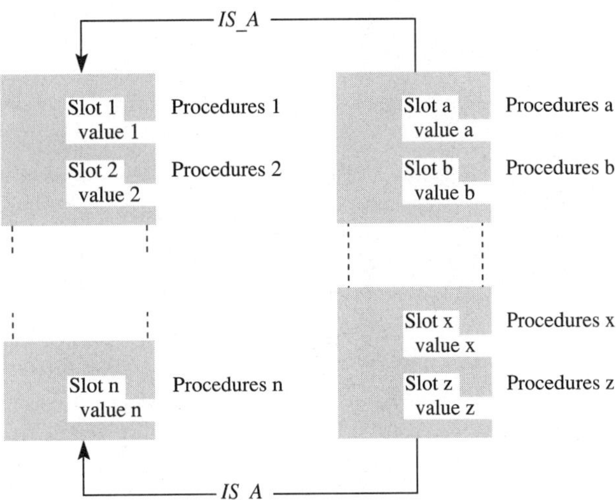

Figure 16.6, the frame *Bungalow* is a specialization of the frame *Building* and inherits from *Building* descriptors such as walls, doors, windows, roof. The slot or descriptor itself can be a frame. Thus, the descriptor *window* can have descriptors of its own, for example, *size* and *type*.

In addition, descriptors could have appropriate reasoning or inferencing procedures attached. These procedures are triggered or executed whenever the descriptors are filled in, modified, or matched to glean precompiled knowledge.

Frames have been used extensively to represent visual knowledge and knowledge about natural languages.

16.3.4 Rule-Based Systems (Production Systems)

The basic idea in **production systems** is the coupling of a condition with an appropriate action. Each such condition-action pair is called a **rule, production rule,** or simply a **production.** An example of a production is given below:

If condition **then** action

The condition part of a production expresses the conditions under which the rule is valid; the appropriate action to be taken is given by the action part. The action part of the rule changes the state of the system and can introduce new facts. The condition part of the rule is known as an **antecedent** and the action part, the **consequent.** An example of a production rule for the game of hockey, involving a team trailing by one goal in the ultimate minute of the game, can be expressed as a production rule as follows:

If trailing by one goal **and**
remaining time-to-play in game is less than one minute **and**
play is in opponent's zone
then replace goalie by forward.

Figure 16.6 Frame representation of different types of buildings.

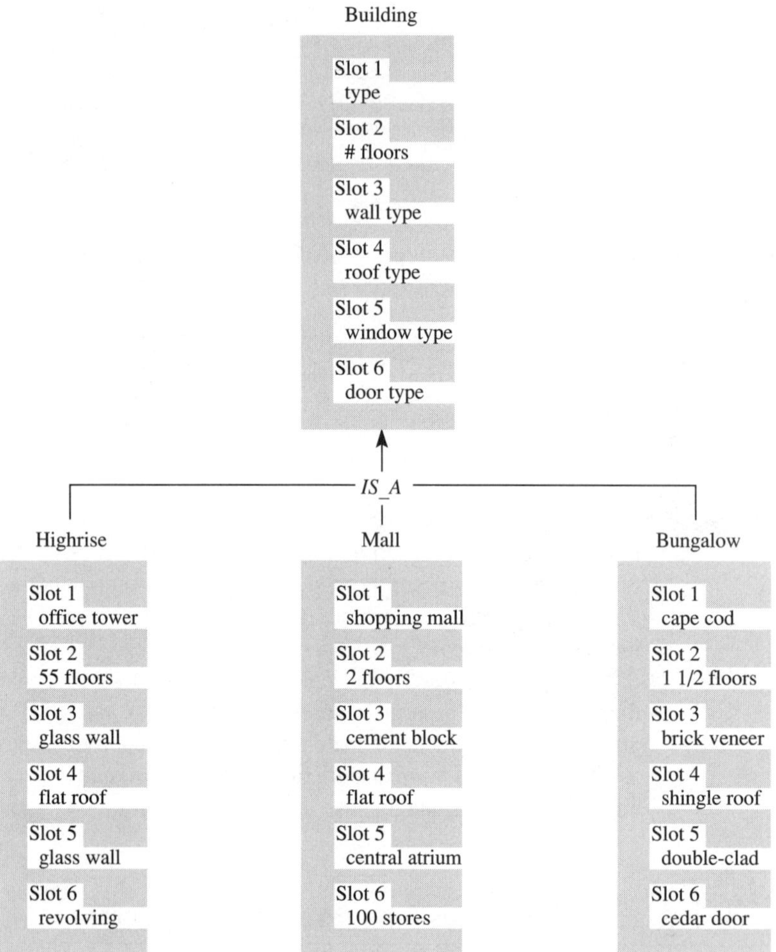

A production-based system consists of a set of production rules, a data structure that models the system's current state, and a control subsystem or interpreter that interprets the current state and controls its activity by initiating appropriate action. A rule is said to be **enabled** or **triggered** when the condition part of the rule is satisfied by the current state of the system. An enabled rule is said to be **fired** if the action part of a rule is executed. If the system status is such that more than one rule is triggered, the interpreter may be required to fire one or more of these simultaneously enabled rules; this is referred to as a **conflict resolution.** The conflict resolution can be enacted using its own set of productions. It uses criteria such as priority or ranking, prior selection, arbitrary or random choice, or doing all actions in parallel. The order in which the conditions are examined can be determined a priori or could be adjusted dynamically. The action part can be a single action or a set of procedures that will change the status of the system. The latter change can include disabling a subset of the existing productions and enabling other productions.

An example of a rule-based system is given below. This system examines the causes and the corrective actions to be performed after failing to start a car. The execution of each action will modify the state of the starting system under consideration and if there is more than one problem, all the corrective actions will have to be taken.

if starter cranks the engine very slowly
then problem may one or more of: extreme cold temperature, battery, cables, connections, voltage regulator, alternator; use jumper cable to start
if starter does not crank but solenoid operates
then check cables and tighten and clean terminals and check battery voltage
if problem is low battery voltage
then problem may be battery: check specific gravity and replace if not acceptable;
problem may be loose, worn, or broken alternator belt: do a visual inspection and if belt is okay, tighten belt, otherwise replace it;
problem may be cables: visual inspection, clean and tighten connections, and replace broken connectors or cables;
problem may be voltage regulator: check and replace;
problem may be alternator: check and repair or replace alternator;
problem may be shorts in electrical system: locate and correct
if problem loose or worn alternator belt
then tighten or replace alternator belt
if problem is battery
then check specific gravity and if acceptable charge otherwise replace battery
if problem is voltage regulator
then replace voltage regulator
if problem is alternator
then repair or replace alternator
if battery, cables, and connections are good, solenoid operates, but starter does not crank or cranks slowly
then replace the starter
if battery, cables, and connections are good but solenoid does not click
then check ignition switch to solenoid circuit and correct malfunctions
if battery, cables, connections, and ignition switch to solenoid circuit are good but solenoid does not click
then replace solenoid

if starter spins but does not crank the engine
then replace starter
if starter cranks the engine, smell of gas in the exhaust, but the engine does not fire
then check and dry ignition circuit and replace faulty parts
if starter cranks the engine but engine does not fire and no smell of gas
then check and correct problems with fuel lines, fuel pump, fuel filter, carburetor, fill tank

Since the action part of a rule can modify the state of the system, additional rules may have to be fired. There are two methods of matching rules to the current state of a system: forward chaining and backward chaining. In **forward chaining,** the initial set of facts are used to determine the rules that apply. If more than one rule applies, one of these is chosen. The search proceeds by firing this rule and arriving at a new set of facts. This procedure is repeated until a solution is reached. In **backward chaining,** all rules that have to be fired are first determined for the desired solution. These rules are then fired sequentially in the forward direction. We discuss this further in Section 16.5.

In a larger system, the production rules limit the interaction between rules and lead to inefficiencies. These inefficiencies become evident when a number of production rules have to be fired, but can only be executed one at a time. Each such firing is preceded by an interpretation of the current state of the system against the production rules. On average, half of these production rules have to be tested before each firing.

One approach used in a system with a very large set of production rules is to organize the condition part of the rules in a partitioned hierarchy or structured taxonomy. Here, taxonomy implies that the condition can be partitioned into disjoint sets and the condition in each such disjoint set can be organized hierarchically. Figure 16.7 represents the rules corresponding to the car starter system above, structured in a disjoint hierarchy. However, it may not be possible to do this in all applications.

A production system is a natural way of imparting some forms of expert knowledge in a modular and uniform way. Each production rule represents an independent slice of knowledge and how to use it. A rule can be added, changed, or deleted without affecting other production rules.

16.3.5 Procedural Representation

In the **procedural representation method,** the interpretation of so-called declarative knowledge is encapsulated in specialized procedures. Each such procedure processes a data structure representing certain semantics in the declarative data. The rationale is that what humans know can best be described as know-how knowledge. Such know-how knowledge is difficult to express in descriptive form. For example, knowledge that the engine is struggling or turning very slowly when being started is relative to what we already know as being its normal turning speed during starting. The heuristics as to what to do when confronted with such a situation can be built into

Figure 16.7 Hierarchically structured rules.

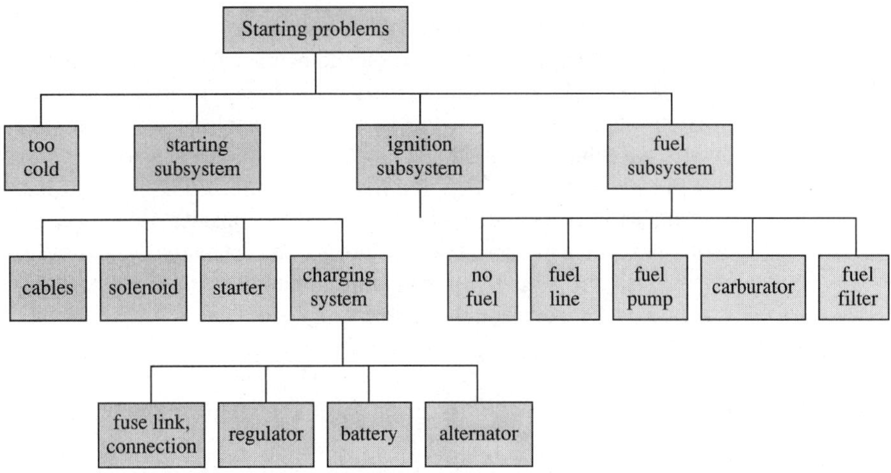

rules but could be expressed elegantly when built into procedures. The emphasis is on combining the data structures in these procedures along with the know-how of using the knowledge represented in these data structures. Instead of using irrelevant knowledge in the form of superfluous rules, the procedural representation uses specific knowledge for the problem at hand.

This approach, though not necessarily sound or complete, is pragmatic. It uses specialized procedures to limit the amount of processing involved in answering a query. The procedures, being ad hoc, have built-in heuristics to allow them to suitably direct the reasoning process. The disadvantage here is the complexity of the procedures and their interactions. Furthermore, there is an inherent difficulty in understanding, modifying, or augmenting the knowledge represented by these procedures.

16.4 Deductive Databases

There is a growing interest in the use of logic as a conceptual framework for database concepts. Mathematical logic can be used not only to formalize database concepts, but also to deduce facts implied by the facts stored in the database.

A **deductive database** is a marriage of a relational database system and logic programming. The term deductive highlights the fact that the system is able to make deductions from facts stored in the database using rules stored in the database. The two parts of the system are the **extensional database (EDB),** the set of facts in the form of the relations in the database, and the **intensional database (IDB),** the database derived by the set of rules imparting the deductive capability to the overall system. The relation gives explicit information; the rules elicit implicit information from this explicit information.

Deductive databases are also referred to as logic databases, deductive relational databases, and virtual relational databases. A relational database is a subset of a deductive database.

Up to now we have defined a relation as a set of tuples, i.e., by its extension. The set of tuples can be called the elementary facts, and the relation a base predicate. These sets of facts, which we have referred to as a database, are essentially an extensional database. In the extensional database we define the set of tuples that satisfy a relation. We can also define a relation intensionally by specifying some set of rules. These rules, defining the intensional database, are expressed as well-formed formulas in first-order logic. We can thus consider a database as consisting of a set of rules (or laws) and a set of tuples. The intensional database supplements the extensional one with rules that allow other facts to be derived from those explicitly stored in the extensional database.[5]

Example 16.2 Let the extensional database consist of a parent relation, i.e., a tuple (or fact) of the parent relation tells us the name of the parent of some person. If we also need grandparent names, we can either store the name of the grandparents or—from our knowledge of who the grandparents are—write a derivation rule: The grandparent of X is the person Y in that Z is the parent of X and Y is the parent of Z. ■

If we wanted to find the ancestors or cousins of a person we can specify these as rules. Obviously we save considerably on storage, but more importantly we increase the usability of our database.

Consider the relation PARENT(X,Y) given in Figure 16.4. It represents the fact that Y is a parent of X and is in the extensional database. To find the descendants of an individual, we have to specify a number of rules. The descendants can be specified as follows:

X is a descendant of Y if Y is a parent of X

X is a descendant of Y can be represented as DESC(X,Y), which can be interpreted as a relation DESC having two attributes X and Y. We can write this rule as an implication:

$$\text{PARENT(X,Y)} \rightarrow \text{DESC(X,Y)}$$

[5]We can go even further and consider a database as not having an extension but as consisting entirely of axioms. The extension counterpart could be a set of particularization axioms (to specify the CWA, UNA, and DCA) (Gall 84), (Reit 84).

Databases have been characterized by two basic approaches, the *model-theoretic view* (MTV) and the *proof-theoretic view* (PTV). In the MTV, the database is a model of a first-order theory and queries and integrity constraints are formulas to be evaluated on the model using the semantics of truth. *Model* here is in terms of some set of axioms (in the form of integrity constraints) and an interpretation that makes these axioms true. Queries are evaluated in the MTV under the CWA, UNA, and DCA. In the PTV, the database is a first-order theory (i.e., we try to spell everything out with formulas) and integrity constraints and queries are theorems to be proved. One difference between the MTV and the PTV is that with the former we can add data (a tuple) to the database and still have a model of the same theory (i.e., the model does not have to be changed) while with the latter a different theory would result.

The PTV is a formalization of the concept of the deductive database and not intended to be directly used as the basis of a DBMS implementation.

The above rule gives us the immediate descendants. However, we can find other descendants using a recursive rule:

If Z is a parent of X and a descendant of Y, then X is a descendant of Y

This rule can be expressed as:

$$\text{PARENT(X,Z)} \wedge \text{DESC(Z,Y)} \rightarrow \text{DESC(X,Y)}$$

The PARENT relation and the two rules can be used to derive the DESC relation and answer queries such as finding all the descendants of an individual.

Example 16.3

Consider the PARENT relation of Figure 16.4. We can find all the descendants using the above two rules. Initially the DESC relation is empty. We apply the first rule, PARENT(X,Y) → DESC (X,Y), and get the DESC relation (Figure A), which is the same as the PARENT relation.

Figure A DESC relation after the application of the first rule.

DESC

X	Y
Roy	Frank
Jerry	Frank
Myrna	Ruth
Roy	Ruth
Lynn	Roy
Lynn	Rachel
Justin	Lynn
Janet	Myrna
Drew	Sheila
Pavan	Sheila
Sheila	Frank
Frank	George

Now we apply the second rule. This involves the natural join of PARENT (X,Y) and DESC(Y,Z) followed by a projection on the attributes XZ. The new tuples, shown in Figure B, are generated for the DESC relations as a result of the join. (Note: we are renaming the variables in the figure.)

We repeat this step of applying the second rule until no new tuples are added to DESC. The new tuples generated after each application are shown in Figures C and D. No new tuples are generated after the third application of the second rule, so the resulting DESC relation gives all the descendants of a person.

To answer a query such as ''Find all the descendants of George,'' we do a selection on the DESC(X,Y), relation with the following query:

$$\pi_X(\sigma_{Y=\text{George}}\text{DESC})$$

Figure B After one application of the second rule.

PARENT

X	Y
Roy	Frank
Jerry	Frank
Myrna	Ruth
Roy	Ruth
Lynn	Roy
Lynn	Rachel
Justin	Lynn
Janet	Myrna
Drew	Sheila
Pavan	Sheila
Sheila	Frank
Frank	George

DESC

Y	Z
Roy	Frank
Jerry	Frank
Myrna	Ruth
Roy	Ruth
Lynn	Roy
Lynn	Rachel
Justin	Lynn
Janet	Myrna
Drew	Sheila
Pavan	Sheila
Sheila	Frank
Frank	George

new tuples for DESC

X	Z
Roy	George
Jerry	George
Lynn	Ruth
Lynn	Frank
Justin	Roy
Justin	Rachel
Janet	Ruth
Drew	Frank
Pavan	Frank
Sheila	George

Figure C After a second application of the second rule.

PARENT

X	Y
Roy	Frank
Jerry	Frank
Myrna	Ruth
Roy	Ruth
Lynn	Roy
Lynn	Rachel
Justin	Lynn
Janet	Myrna
Drew	Sheila
Pavan	Sheila
Sheila	Frank
Frank	George

DESC

Y	Z
Roy	Frank
Jerry	Frank
Myrna	Ruth
Roy	Ruth
Lynn	Roy
Lynn	Rachel
Justin	Lynn
Janet	Myrna
Drew	Sheila
Pavan	Sheila
Sheila	Frank
Frank	George
Roy	George
Jerry	George
Lynn	Ruth
Lynn	Frank
Justin	Roy
Justin	Rachel
Janet	Ruth
Drew	Frank
Pavan	Frank
Sheila	George

new tuples for DESC

X	Z
Justin	Ruth
Justin	Frank
Drew	George
Pavan	George
Lynn	George

Figure D After a third application of the second rule.

PARENT

X	Y
Roy	Frank
Jerry	Frank
Myrna	Ruth
Roy	Ruth
Lynn	Roy
Lynn	Rachel
Justin	Lynn
Janet	Myrna
Drew	Sheila
Pavan	Sheila
Sheila	Frank
Frank	George

DESC

Y	Z
Roy	Frank
Jerry	Frank
Myrna	Ruth
Roy	Ruth
Lynn	Roy
Lynn	Rachel
Justin	Lynn
Janet	Myrna
Drew	Sheila
Pavan	Sheila
Sheila	Frank
Frank	George
Roy	George
Jerry	George
Lynn	Ruth
Lynn	Frank
Justin	Roy
Justin	Rachel
Janet	Ruth
Drew	Frank
Pavan	Frank
Sheila	George
Justin	Ruth
Justin	Frank
Drew	George
Pavan	George
Lynn	George

new tuples for DESC

X	Z
Justin	George

For our sample PARENT relation, the result of this query is: Drew, Pavan, Lynn, Justin, Frank, Roy, Jerry, Sheila. ■

In Example 16.4 we use the database relation PRODUCT to find all constituents of a product.

Example 16.4 Consider the relation PRODUCT *(Prod_No, Sub_Prod_No)*. In this relation each subproduct is also a product. For each product, the relation gives all of its subproducts. If S is a subproduct of a product P, then S is its constituent. We can express this rule as follows:

$$\text{PRODUCT (P,S)} \rightarrow \text{CONSTITUENT (P,S)}$$

To find all products and their constituent products (at the lowest level), we require the following additional rule. This rule is recursive:

$$\text{PRODUCT (P,C)} \wedge \text{CONSTITUENT (C,S)} \rightarrow \text{CONSTITUENT (P,S)}$$

Here we are defining the rule that an object S is a constituent of an object P if it is a subproduct of P, or it is a constitutent of an object C, which is a subproduct of P. ■

Employees who work together can be derived as follows:

Example 16.5 Consider the relation ASSIGNED_TO *(Prod#,Emp#)*, which gives the employees assigned to a given project. We can find all employees who have worked together on a project by using the following rule:

$$\text{ASSIGNED\_TO } (P,E_1) \wedge \text{ASSIGNED\_TO } (P,E_2) \rightarrow \text{TOGETHER}(E_1,E_2)$$ ■

We can see that the above rules in the form of logic expressions allow us to express recursive queries. This adds to the power of database querying as well as specifying the intensional database.

If $P_1, \ldots, P_n$ and Q are atoms, then $\neg P_1 \vee \ldots \vee \neg P_n \vee Q$ (with a maximum of one unnegated atom) is a Horn clause. The Horn clause with one positive atom is said to contain one conclusion. The conclusion is also known as the head. The atoms $P_1, \ldots, P_n$, specify the conditions to be satisfied and are known as the body of the clause. A Horn clause with no positive atom has no conclusions. A Horn clause with no head may be thought of as integrity constraints, i.e., $P_1 \wedge \ldots \wedge P_n \rightarrow \bullet$ can be interpreted as: (P_1 and P_2 and . . . P_n) is a violation of an integrity constraint. For example, no individual can be both a father and a mother nor a brother and sister of another individual. This integrity constraint may be specified as:

$$\text{brother }(x,y) \wedge \text{sister}(x,y) \rightarrow \bullet$$

Horn clauses can be expressed easily in PROLOG. If the conditions $P_1, \ldots, P_n$, imply more than one conclusion, i.e., Q is of the form $Q_1 \vee \ldots \vee Q_m$, we write these as m Horn clauses.

In this section we have introduced a powerful extension to the relational database model. Coverage in greater depth is beyond the scope of this text. We give references to relevant literature in the bibliographic notes.

16.5 Expert Systems

Expert systems, also called knowledge base systems, are computer systems designed to implement the knowledge and reasoning used by experts in a particular domain to solve problems in that domain. Knowledge in these systems is obtained from interviews with human experts and represents known procedures, usual practice, heuristics, and rules of thumb. This knowledge is usually implemented as a set of rules, similar to those given in the car-starting example. These computer systems, as do the human experts, use logical inference procedures and compiled production rules (rules of thumb). The explicit domain knowledge, the so-called **institutional memory,** is accessible by the expert system and along with some form of reasoning gives it artificial intelligence. Unlike a human expert, this codified knowledge is of a more permanent nature.

The structure of an expert system, which is built around an appropriate representation of the domain knowledge of an expert, is shown in Figure 16.8. Many expert systems use productions or rules to represent the domain knowledge. The inference system uses the knowledge and applies inference procedures to infer facts not explicitly represented in the knowledge base to solve problems posed by the user. The inference system, in addition, provides the user with the steps used in the reasoning procedure to arrive at a solution to the problem. The user interface is responsible for presenting the user with an easy-to-use interface, and generates responses and understandable explanations to the queries posed by the user.

Abductive reasoning is used in expert systems for applications in areas such as medical or fault diagnostics. Medical diagnostics determines the likely cause for a patient's symptoms. The diagnosis may be multiple, there being a certain level of confidence associated with each possible diagnostic and each level having associated with it a subset of symptoms. Human judgment, along with suggested additional tests, may be required to confirm or rule out some of these multiple diagnoses. For instance, when a starting problem is encountered with the starter cranking the engine very slowly, the diagnosis is that there is a problem with one or more of the following components: extremely cold temperatures, alternator, battery, belt, cables, connections, fuse link, or regulator. Further tests in the form of visual inspection, specific gravity tests, battery voltage, voltage across the battery while the engine is running, or output current from the alternator are required to make a final diagnosis of the problem. In a rule-based expert system, the current known status of the system is matched with the rules and the actions corresponding to one or more of the matched rules are executed, i.e., the rules are fired. As a result of the firing, the state of the system changes.

However, not all expert systems deal with multiple answers or uncertainty. Production or rule-based systems can be deductive systems. Such is the case when the

Figure 16.8 An expert system.

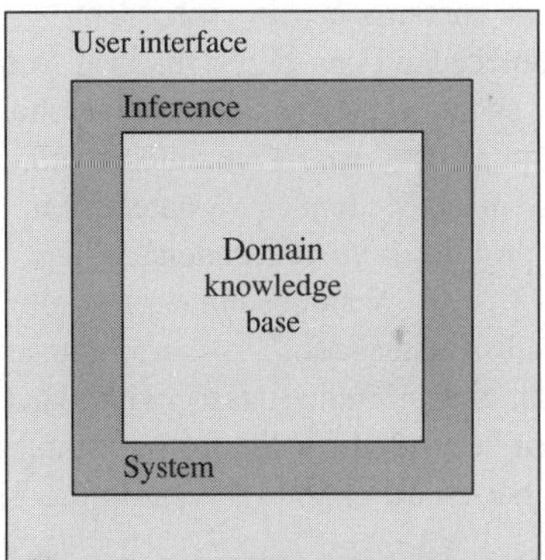

if part of the rules refer to one or more known facts (within the domain for which the expert system is being used) and the then part of the rules specify new facts that can be deduced from the known facts. The if part of the rule is the antecedent and the then part is the consequent.

An expert system can use the rules in a forward or backward direction. The former is called forward chaining; the latter, backward chaining. Consider the rules being used as follows:

$$\text{antecedent} \rightarrow \text{consequent}$$

Here we interpret the rule as follows: if the antecedent is true, then the consequent is also true. In forward chaining, each rule is fired when the rule is enabled by having its antecedent satisfied. As a result of the firing of a rule, the state of the system would change; the facts corresponding to the consequent of the fired rule would be added to the set of known facts. This in turn would enable and fire other rules. The direction of action is from the left-hand side of the rule to the right-hand side.

Consider a system containing the following rules:

$$a \rightarrow b,\ a \rightarrow f,\ b \wedge c \rightarrow d,\ e \wedge f \rightarrow j,\ d \wedge g \rightarrow h$$

Here the rule $e \wedge f \rightarrow j$ can be interpreted as: if currently e and f are true, then we can deduce that j is true as well.

Suppose it is currently known that (a, c, e, g) are true. We want to know whether h is true.

In this system the first rule, $a \rightarrow b$, will indicate that b is true, since a is known to be true. Augmenting this with the current known facts, we get the new known facts about the system as being (a, b, c, e, g). The second rule, $a \rightarrow f$, which can be fired simultaneously with the first rule, will augment the known facts by f. The next rule to be fired, $b \wedge c \rightarrow d$, augments the known facts by d; and the subsequent rule, $e \wedge f \rightarrow j$, augments the known facts by j. Finally the last rule, $d \wedge g \rightarrow h$, establishes the fact h. We see from this example that the firing of the rules $a \rightarrow f$ and $e \wedge f \rightarrow j$ were superfluous in proving h. The sequence of these steps is given in Figure 16.9. The rules being triggered and fired at each step are enclosed in parentheses.

In the backward chaining scheme, we hypothesize consequent n; then we try to verify this hypothesis by establishing the validity of a rule wherein n is a consequent. In other words, we prove a fact by showing that the antecedents corresponding to a rule where the hypothesized consequent appears on the right-hand sides are true. If the system contains a rule $\text{antecedent}_i \rightarrow \text{consequent}_i$, then consequent_i can be implied if antecedent_i can be established to be a fact. If the state of the system is such that antecedent_i is true, then we have shown consequent_i. Otherwise proving consequent_i requires that we prove antecedent_i.

Now, if $\text{antecedent}_{i-1} \wedge \text{antecedent}_{i-2} \rightarrow \text{antecedent}_i$, then proving consequent_i requires proving both antecedent_{i-1} and antecedent_{i-2}. If $\text{antecedent}_{i-1} \wedge \text{antecedent}_{i-2} \wedge \ldots \wedge \text{antecedent}_{i-j} \rightarrow \text{antecedent}_i$, then proving consequent_i requires proving all of $\text{antecedent}_{i-1}, \ldots, \text{antecedent}_{i-j}$.

Thus, the inference starts with what is required to be shown and the system finds what is needed for this to be established in a backward direction. This scheme is called backward chaining because the search is against the direction of the arrows

Figure 16.9 Forward chaining.

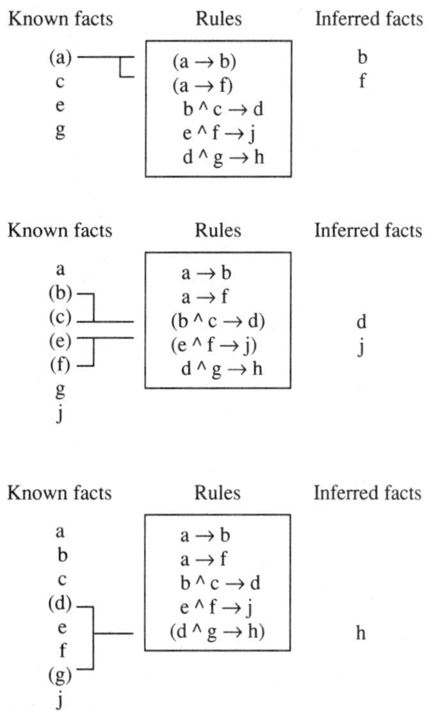

of the rules from the right-hand side to the left-hand side. Only rules that are pertinent to establishing the required facts are examined in a backward direction.

Let us take the previous example and try to establish the fact h using backward chaining. We hypothesize h and use the rule $d \wedge g \rightarrow h$ to establish that we need the facts d and g. Since g is already known, we have to establish d. To prove d, we use the rule $b \wedge c \rightarrow d$ and find that we need the facts b and c. Since c is known, we need to establish b, which requires by rule $a \rightarrow b$ that we need a. Since a is already known, we have proved h. The sequence of these steps is given in Figure 16.10.

This example illustrates that in backward chaining, only rules that are pertinent to establishing the required hypothesis or facts are examined; hence, the scheme is more efficient than the forward chaining scheme. When deciding whether to use forward or backward chaining, remember that for the given initial state and the desired goal, the chaining scheme that fans in will be more efficient than the one that fans out.

Production or rule-based systems can explain the reasoning process used to come to a given conclusion. The explanations entail showing the rules used in coming to the conclusion. Antecedent matching can be used to show why a given rule was used, and the consequent part can be used to show the conclusions reached and the subsequent actions taken.

Figure 16.10 Backward chaining.

Known fact	Rules	Facts needed to establish the required fact
a c e g Required fact h	a → b a → f b ^ c → d e ^ f → j (d ^ g → h)	d g

Known fact	Rules	Facts needed to establish the required fact
a c e g Required fact d	a → b a → f (b ^ c → d) e ^ f → j d ^ g → h	b c

Known fact	Rules	Facts needed to establish the required fact
a c e g Required fact b	(a → b) a → f b ^ c → d e ^ f → j d ^ g → h	a

16.6 Expert Database Systems: Integration of Expert Systems in Database Applications

Expert systems have been developed as stand-alone systems. A stand-alone expert system may be required to access data from a database as an ordinary application program. With an integrated approach, the expert system is integrated with the DBMS, as shown in Figure 16.11. In addition to traditional data, the system handles textual and graphical data as well as knowledge. (It must be pointed out that no such integrated system exists to date.) Such an integrated system will be called upon to perform the traditional DBMS functions and use the inference system in aspects of abductive, inductive, and deductive reasoning. The integrated system needs distribution and concurrent access, and at the same time provides enhanced integrity, security, and reliability.

There are obvious advantages in bringing rule-based knowledge representation and reasoning capability to database applications and traditional data processing tasks. The database can be used to store the known facts about objects and events as well as the rules required by the expert system. An ordinary database query not requiring any inference system service could be handled more efficiently by the traditional DML and database manager component of the multimedia database and

Figure 16.11 Integrated expert database system.

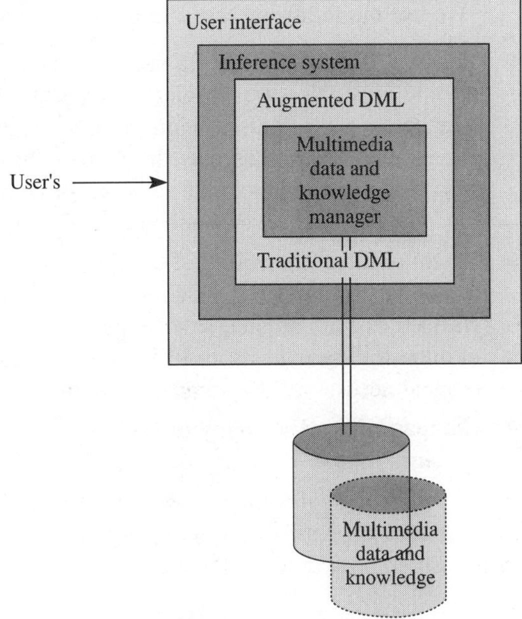

knowledge base system; the user interface can forward such queries directly to this subsystem.

The expert system component of such an integrated expert database system can be used to provide a means for interpreting the responses to queries, including responses that contain, for instance, null values. It can be used with appropriate knowledge to enhance the enforcement of integrity and security of the entire system.

16.7 Object Approach

In the object approach physical entities or abstract concepts of the real world are represented by objects. Objects are distinguished by identifiers and they encapsulate the characteristics or properties of the real world objects as well as their valid operations. The main difference between objects used in object-oriented programming and those in object-database is the persistence. Objects in object-oriented programming persist only for the duration of the program while those in object-database are of a more permanent nature.

It has been predicted that object-oriented programming will be the accepted software development approach of the '90s just as structured programming was the style used in the '70s. One of the results of the evolution of structured programming was the strongly typed requirement made popular by Pascal and the top-down modular approach.

Everyone has a different conception of **object-oriented programming (OOP)** and the **object model (OM).** One yardstick (meterstick!) used by almost everyone is that the OOP approach leads to software reusability. However, OOP by itself is not a panacea of reusability. Program components developed using OOP must have been designed for reusability, and reuse may require extension of the program module.

We use the following terms in discussing OOP:

- **Reusability:** The ability of a system to be used in an entirely new context from the one in which it was originally designed. This is the so-called **black box approach.** A black box (Figure 16.12) is anything that accepts certain inputs and produces certain outputs. It can be used as a building block in a more complex system wherein the same set or combination of inputs is required to produce the same set or combination of outputs.
- **Extendability:** The ability of easily modifying a system to accommodate additional requirements. However, the original requirements may not be changed; for the original set of inputs, the system would deliver the original set of outputs. The extendability characteristic allows the system to be used for the original needs, while accommodating the new requirements.
- **Compatibility:** The ability of the system to be easily combined with other systems.

Traditionally software has been developed using functional methods wherein the application is expressed by a set of algorithms, each of which may be implemented by a separate procedure. This scheme does not provide the following features:

- effective data abstraction facility
- scheme for information hiding
- concurrency and distribution
- easy means of adapting to changes

In a database environment, the data is separated from the programs that use it. The database provides a basic set of operations common to all objects in the database and additional operations, including the exact meaning of the data, are in the programs. The database is not aware of the existence of these programs.

Object-Oriented Systems

The simulation programming language SIMULA (Dahl 66) is considered to be the immediate ancestor of OOP. The Smalltalk programming system (Gold 83) developed this concept and coined the phrase **object-oriented approach (OOA).**

Figure 16.12 A black box with its inputs and outputs.

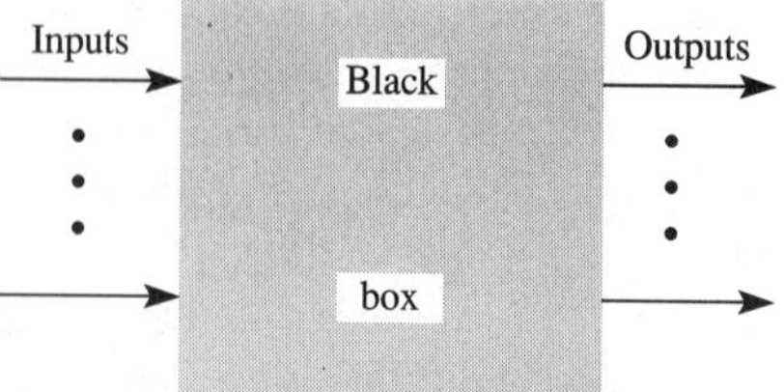

An **object** has a private memory and can manipulate the contents of this private memory as a result of the **messages** it accepts. The operations performed on the private memory are the **methods** of the object. Objects that respond to the same messages in the same way are grouped together; such a group is called a **class.** An object in Smalltalk is an **instance** of a class. A class could also be refined by adding further methods to create a **subclass.**

A message in Smalltalk is equivalent to a procedure call. It contains the name of the object to receive the message, the name of the message, and keyword arguments.

16.7.1 Concept of the Object

The first characteristic of the object-oriented approach is to change our point of view from inside the object that we are studying to outside. This change of perspective allows us to concentrate not on what the inner workings of an object are, but rather on what the object does. This is the so-called first principle of object approach, namely, to look at objects from the outside and determine what inputs they accept and what responses they provide for these inputs.

An object can be characterized as follows:

- It has a state that is recorded in private memory.
- It is characterized by the messages that it recognizes and the methods (procedures) used as a consequence of the message.
- It is denoted by a name.

Consider the university database example. Here we are interested in objects such as courses, students, enrollment, faculty, and so on. We could represent the enrollment by a relation, ENROLLMENT. The grades that students receive in the course in which they are enrolled could be assigned by using an application program with embedded query language. The application program could be used many times but it is considered separate from the database and stored and maintained separately. In an object-oriented approach, each of the above objects could be encapsulated with all possible operations that we may need to perform on the data of the object. These operations could be similar to the ones performed by the application programs. The data structures and the operations on these structures could be treated as objects. The data part of the object for ENROLLMENT would be similar to the corresponding relation.

An object can be considered a uniform abstraction or representation of the two capabilities of a computing system: storing and manipulating information. They are encapsulated in the object and everything can then be considered an object. However, for objects to be useful, they must be able to interact with other objects. This interaction is provided by message communication. The set of operations performed by an object is determined by the message to which it responds. This set of operations is sometimes called the object's **message interface** or **message protocol.**

Each object is cognizant of the messages it can understand. For each such message, it will carry out certain operations. These operations for each message make up a procedure or method and determine the response generated by the object to the accepted message.

Figure 16.13 Similarity of a black box and an object.

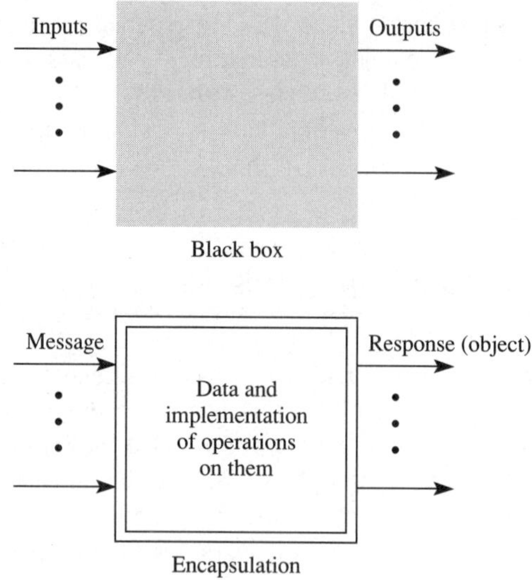

The messages that an object understands depends on the nature of the object. Objects for numbers understand a message that requests computation and reporting the result. An object representing a thesaurus would understand a message to provide the synonyms, antonyms, or homonyms for an entry in the thesaurus object.

The private memory of an object, which records the value of the data associated with an object, is made available to other objects via the response generated by the object. There is no way to open up an object and look inside it unless the object, via its behavior to messages accepted by it, allows such persual.

Objects are uniform in the method used for communicating, which is by message passing, and because no object is given special status. There is no distinction between objects supplied by the system and those created by a user.

The basic problem in OOP is to determine the kinds of objects that should be implemented. In addition, for each object, we have to determine the messages it will accept and the response provided by such messages. The choice of object depends on the application and use of the system. Sending a message in OOP is equivalent to calling a procedure in procedural language or providing inputs to a black box (see Figure 16.13).

16.7.2 Names and Identity

What's in a name?[6]

> Identity is such a simple and fundamental idea that it is hard to explain otherwise than through mere synonyms. To say that X and Y are identical is to say that they are the

[6]William Shakespeare, Romeo and Juliet, Act II scene 2.

> same thing. Everything is identical with itself and with nothing else. But despite its simplicity, identity invites confusion. E.g. it may be asked: Of what use is the notion of identity if identifying an object with itself is trivial and identifying with anything else is false?[7]

Having defined objects still leaves open the question of the ability to distinguish objects from each other. This ability must be distinct from the state of the object or its location and at the same time allow different objects to be shared. When talking of identifying something, we do not necessarily mean locating a name, but the object associated with the name.

Addressability is a scheme of locating an object or providing access to an object and is dependent on the environment. Consider Professor Smith. Her students address her in a way that is different from the way her children do, which in turn is different from the way her friends and acquaintances address her. However, Professor Smith is the same person and she knows it!

Addressability is external to an object. Consider the method used in FORTRAN to access a file. A file number is mapped into a logical file name, which is mapped into a physical file name and a physical file. The file has an identity of its own, which is compared to the physical file name to ensure that the correct file is accessed. This highlights the concept that **identity** is internal to the object.

Programming languages use variable names to distinguish objects, which last for the duration of the execution of the program or portion thereof. Such variable names are defined by users to represent the identity of an object. An object required by more than one program module is made global among these modules. The binding of an object, which in this case is a storage location in real or virtual memory, is done either at compilation time or run time. If the same program is rerun the same variable is used over again for the same purpose; this fact keeps us from realizing that these objects are only temporary. The addressing of an object is thus merged with the identity of the corresponding object. Objects that persist over different executions of a program or that are passed from one program to another use a file system.

The use of variable names without some built-in representation of identity and operator to test and manipulate this abstraction can cause problems. This is the case when the same transient objects are referred to by different variable names and accessed in different ways. The concept of COMMON in FORTRAN is used to share objects among different program units and could refer to the same object, such as storage location in real or virtual memory, using different variable names with possibly different data types. This creates a great number of errors that are hard to detect. The concept of EQUIVALENCE allows objects to be shared among variables of the same program module. Without a test for establishing the identity of the object, a problem is created. Pascal addressed this problem by introducing the variant record type. Smalltalk provides a simple identity test expression of the form X = = Y, where two variables, X and Y, are tested to determine if their identity is the same.

[7] W. V. Quine, *Methods of Logic,* 4th ed. Cambridge: Harvard University Press, 1982.

16.7.3 Database and Identity

Databases emerged to resolve the storage problem and facilitate the sharing of persistent objects. This required the support of the identity of an object not only in terms of its representation but also over time.

Every object is unique. However, we cannot, for example, distinguish between two 2d nails, nor do we bother to try. What is important for most applications is that they are 2d nails as opposed to 3d nails. In modeling a definite object for a particular application, we do not model all of its characteristics but only a subset of interest to the application. This subset may not be sufficient to bring out the uniqueness of the object. (For example, the 2d nails could have some characteristics that may identify one nail uniquely from another.) We also use some means to characterize abstract objects. It may also happen that the uniqueness of the object can only be established as a result of the object's relationship with another object.

Database systems use the concept of key attributes to distinguish individual records or tuples (persistent objects). The data values of the key attributes are thus mixed with the identity of the objects. This dictates that the value of the key attributes cannot be modified, even though they are descriptive data or artificially introduced data. The name of a department, for instance, is used as a key of the department and also used as a foreign key in the employee relation (object) to establish the relationship that an employee is assigned to a given department. Suppose the name of a department changes as a result of reorganization or modernization, say, from Quantitative Methods to Decision Science or from Personnel to Human Resources. This causes the problem of updating in the department object and all others referring to that object.

A change could be required in the choice of an identifier. Such a situation occurs when preexisting databases having similar classes of objects with different identifiers must be integrated. Two different divisions of a company, for instance, may use different identifiers for identifying employees. One division may use a locally generated sequential employee number; the other may choose the Social Security number. Another problem with this approach is that the individual attributes or any subset of attributes of a relation lack an identity.

In the object-oriented approach, a separate consistent mechanism is used to identify an object regardless of the actual method used in modeling the object or the attributes associated with the object (i.e., the descriptive data). An object system can then be defined to be made up of objects. In a consistent object system no two distinct objects have the same object identifiers, and for each existing object identifier there is a corresponding object. Two objects, O_1 and O_2, are identical if the identifiers for the objects are identical.

16.7.4 Implementation of Object Identifiers

The **object identifier** is best implemented using a system-generated surrogate. Such object identifiers, provided operations on them are allowed, need not be accessible to a user. The question as to what to do with an object identifier when the corresponding object ceases to exist is simply answered if the object is considered to be totally annihilated and no memory of such an object remains in some other object. If such a memory remains in the system, we have a problem of dangling pointers, which should not be allowed. The identifier of an object that ceases to exist may be reassigned depending on the implementation.

Object identifiers are useful for implementation and allow users to perform tests on the identity of an object. Nevertheless, they should not play a role in the model.

16.7.5 Object Class and Instantiation

As in traditional programming language, the notion of type is used to describe an object. It consists of two parts: the data and operation parts and their implementations, and the interface to the object that is visible from the outside. The data and the implementation of the operations on this data are private to the object. The operations that are implemented cater to the specified interface of the object.

Traditional programming language provides a number of data types such as integers, character strings, bit strings, floating point numbers, and so forth. These can be used as required by associating a name with an instance of this type. The instantiation can be static at compile time or dynamic at run time depending on the features provided by the language.

Similarly, in OOP, objects may be instantiated either statically at compile time or dynamically at run time. There could exist more than one object that recognizes and responds similarly to the same set of messages. These objects of the same object types are grouped together into a class of objects or simply as a class. Such objects have the same type of private memory, which is referred to by their methods using the same set of names. Each class has a name and is itself considered as an object belonging to a special system-defined class.

The collection of a group of identical objects into a class allows the sharing of common methods. The concept class thus groups together a set of externally visible operations, a set of corresponding hidden methods, and a set of private variables belonging to instances of the objects of the class. A new instance of an object in a class has its own private memory and shares the operations and the methods of the class.

16.7.6 Inheritance

In OOP, inheritance is used to allow different objects to share attributes and methods. One advantage of inheritance is lower development time due to program reusability.

In our university database (see Figure 16.14), The objects FACULTY and STUDENT are both specializations of the object PERSON and share some common traits. They both have a *Birthdate,* an *Address,* a *Home_Phone_Number, Next_of_Kin,* and so on. A number of operations could be performed on these items. For instance, one of these items could be updated. The program to implement these operations could be shared. Similarly, each of the objects STUDENT and FACULTY has certain special attributes, i.e., *Set_of_Grades* for STUDENT and *Salary* for FACULTY.

Figure 16.14 Objects in the university database.

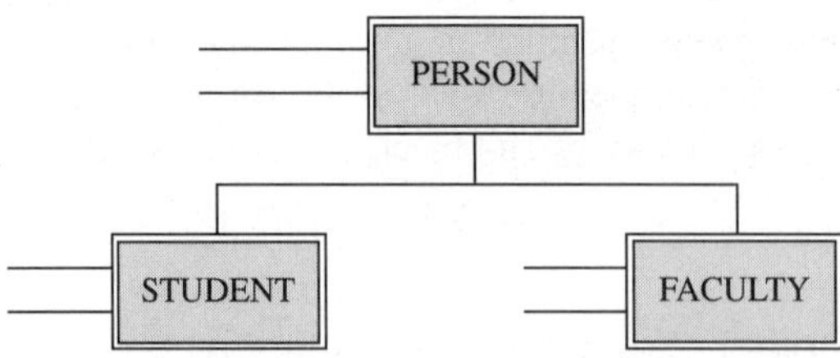

Class inheritance provides a method whereby a new class can be defined as a subclass of an existing class. It inherits not only the operations of the parent class but also its data structure (instance variable). It could be possible to add further data structures and operations on these structures in the subclass.

In **multiple inheritance** a subclass is considered to have not one parent class but multiple parent classes (Figure 16.15). Many of the OOP languages provide only single (or simple) inheritance. In the case of multiple inheritance, there would be the need to override one or more inherited methods and a method of resolving conflict in names of operations or instance variables. Conflict resolution would be by explicit disambuguation, default rules, or prefixing the name with that of the parent class.

If a class has to be modified in the presence of existing instances of objects of the class and its subclasses, there is a need for some form of **object independence.**

In **partial inheritance** the subclass inherits only a subset of the data structures and operations from the parent class and suppresses the remaining.

Class inheritance is a static mechanism. In **dynamic inheritance,** an object changes its response to a message when it accepts new parts from other objects or when it changes its environment. The latter concept is similar to a programming language where the environment can be changed dynamically, as in PL/1. Similarly, a given text changes its fonts when a new style sheet is attached to the document.

The direction of research and the very concept of an object depend on the roots of the researcher. Researchers are discovering new ways to use the old concepts.

Figure 16.15 Example of multiple inheritance.

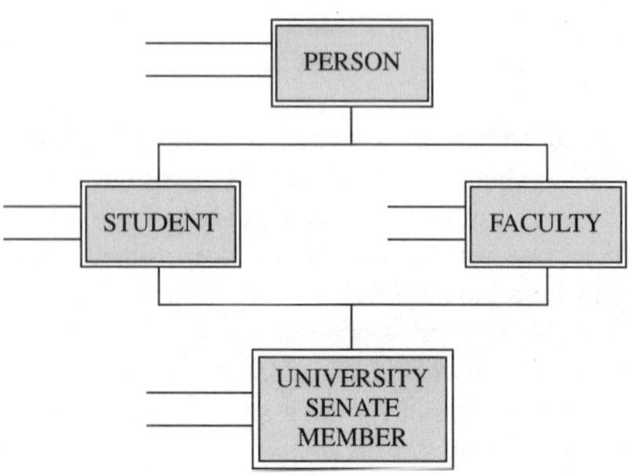

They are looking at five major areas: programming languages; concurrency control; object-based management; software management; and user interface and environment.

16.8 Object Databases

In databases, we concern ourselves with the management and sharing of a large amount of reliable and persistent data. The relational system is suitable for an ad hoc query expressed in a query language such as SQL. However, such query languages are not suitable for application development. The application development language must be suitably integrated with the relational query language and should have a similar model of the computation being performed. Unfortunately whereas relational query languages are set oriented, application languages tend to be record oriented. Object orientation, with the ability to treat everything as objects, including programs and data, is therefore a promising avenue of research.

The object model and the object approach have not been defined formally; consequently a large number of systems can rightly claim to be using the object model. The justification of the use of this approach in programming language is to provide an increased degree of abstraction. In the area of OS there is a constant need to reduce complexity in allowing concurrent tasks to share resources in an orderly manner and to communicate with each other. In the DBMS, there is a need to model complex entities such as CAD/CAM design data, office documents, and coauthored articles.

Along with the lack of a clear, well-defined and accepted object model, there is a lack of uniformity in the concept of an object-oriented database system. In a DBMS, the relationship between two record types may be statically established or based on the content. Relationships exist between classes due to the hierarchical structure and inheritance between subclass and superclass. In the object model, relationships may exist at object level via objects that know about each other and communicate via messages. However, content relationships between objects may not be allowed if the object paradigm is to be preserved. In a database system, all record instances share the same set of operations, which are implemented in the DBMS. In the object model, each object has its own set of operations and can be tailored to the object. However, to achieve efficiency, we use multiple inheritance, which creates its own set of problems. Database record instances are accessed based on the contents. In the object model, the contents of the object are encapsulated and not accessible; therefore, the identifiers are the only means of externally identifying an object instance.

Research projects in object databases can be classed as either an extension to existing systems or as an object-oriented DBMS (OODBMS). In the latter, the data model supports the object approach.

Extension to Existing Systems

POSTGRES (Ston 86a) (Ston 86b), designed by Stonebraker and his colleagues, extends the relational model by supporting abstract data types and procedures. The latter can be used to simulate objects.

Procedures in POSTGRES are global and unlike methods are not local to an object and thus are not able to provide encapsulation.

DAPLEX (Ship 81) is a query language used on a functional data model. PROBE (Mano 86) is a knowledge-oriented DBMS that uses an enhanced version of DAPLEX. PDM is the data model used in PROBE, which uses entities and functions in modeling. Entities are models of real objects and relationships among entities are represented by functions. In addition, the properties of entities and operations on them are also represented by functions.

Entities could be subtypes of other entities. They inherit their corresponding properties and operations. Values could be stored or computed by procedures.

OODBMS Approach

GEMSTONE (Cope 84) is an OODBMS that integrates concepts from programming languages and DBMSs. Objects in GEMSTONE are persistent without the concept of file in the system. In addition, objects have a unique and immutable identity.

ORION is the prototype of an object-oriented DBMS. It supports the shared objects and allows dynamic evolution of the schema. It addresses the problems in the creation and deletion of classes, the alteration of the class/subclass relationship, and those of addition and deletion of instance variables and methods. A set of rules for these alterations is discussed in (Bane 87).

IRIS (Fish 88) is an object-oriented research DBMS under development at Hewlett-Packard and is intended for integrating the needs of knowledge base systems. The IRIS object manager supports the object model, nonnormalized data, version control, user-defined functions, as well as abstractions such as aggregation, classification, generalization, and specialization. The IRIS storage manager currently supports the conventional relational database. The interaction with the system is via embedded languages such as C and LISP enriched with an object paradigm (see Figure 16.16). Interactive support is with Object SQL, which is conventional SQL with object-oriented features.

A class is called type in IRIS and represents a collection of objects that share common properties. A method is called a function in IRIS and objects belonging to the same type share common functions. Objects respond only to their functions. Objects are organized in a hierarchy and inherit properties and functions.

To define an object class Person we use the following declaration:

create type Person
(name **char required,**
address **char,**
department **char,**
phone# **char**)

To instantiate two instances of this object type:

create Person(*)
instance A1 ('Albert Smith', '10 Main', 'Comp Sci',
'345–1234'),
Joe('Joseph Birke', '35 Pine', 'Comp Sci', '529–3856')

Figure 16.16 Structure of the IRIS system (adapted from [Fish 87]).

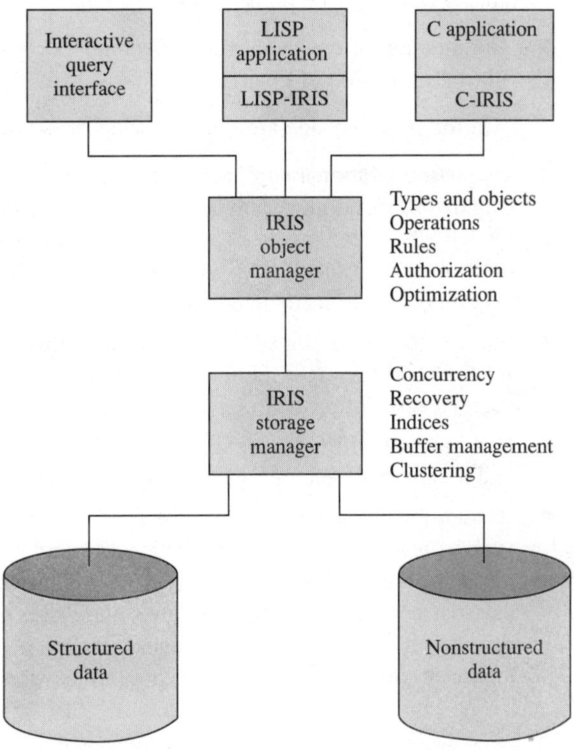

create type Student **subtype of** Person
(year **integer,**
major **char**)

Now an instant of the object type Student is created and values to the attribute name (inherited from Person), year, and major are assigned as follows:

create Student (name, year, major) ('Peter Watson', 2, 'Information Systems'')

16.8.1 Pros and Cons of the Object Approach in Databases

The following are the advantages of the OODBMS:

- The object approach allows modifications that are localized to a given level of an object hierarchy.
- The messages to which an object responds are encapsulated along with the properties of the object. This allows constraints of various complex forms to be

easily enforced. Since the operations allowed on an object are encapsulated, its interactions with other objects are known and hence predictable. This allows ease in extension of the system.

- The inheritance mechanism allows compact codes and the overriding features allow localization of changes.

On the negative side are the following drawbacks of the OODBMS:

- Unlike the relational approach, which started out with a formal theory and a framework for a query language, there is no formal or accepted framework of OODBMS. This lack of a formal framework and query system means that the development of OODBMS will most likely be Darwinian, with the most popular becoming the de facto standard.
- Since each object is a self-contained unit, there is no means of showing relationships among a number of objects. Interobject reference is used to show such an association indirectly.
- Performance will likely be a problem. Techniques such as associative access and architecture features such as tagged architecture have to be investigated.
- In traditional database systems the user must know what the schema contains, such as names of relations and attributes, and pose queries and design programs using this knowledge. In an OODBMS the user must know what each object class is, as well as its methods, messages, and responses. This is not a light requirement[8] and may be the biggest stumbling block in the use of the object approach unless an intelligent user interface is provided with the database.

16.9 Summary

In this chapter we defined a knowledge base system as a computer system used for the management and manipulation of shared knowledge. We compared a knowledge base system with a DBMS and pointed out the similarities and differences. We considered the different schemes used to represent knowledge: the semantic network, first-order logic, rule-based system, frames, and procedural representation.

Expert systems are knowledge base systems wherein the knowledge of experts in a limited domain of application is stored; this knowledge can be used by appropriate inference procedures to solve problems in the domain. The knowledge in expert systems is usually stored as rules. The expert system also generates explanations, which can be employed to illustrate the rules used to answer a user query. Expert systems use forward chaining or backward chaining in their inference procedures.

SIMULA, a programming language for computer simulation, introduced the concept of object class. Class in SIMULA is an abstract data type mechanism and the object-oriented programming language is based on this concept (Gold 83). Objects can be considered uniform abstractions or representations of the storage and manipulation capabilities of a computing system. The set of operations performed by

[8]A case in point is the UNIX operating system. It started off with a lean and utilitarian system with very attractive features but it has become a dinosaur. The online help facility is of no use to a novice and the manuals are too large and badly organized.

an object is determined by the message to which it responds; this set of operations is called the object's message protocol. Such a set of operations for each message is called a method and determines the response generated by the object. The collection of a group of identical objects into a class allows the sharing of common methods. In the object approach, inheritance is used to allow different objects to share attributes and methods.

Along with the lack of a clear, well-defined and accepted object model there is a lack of uniformity in the concept of an object-oriented database system. Object database can be classed as either an extension to an existing system or as an object-oriented DBMS (OODBMS) wherein the data model supports the object approach.

Key Terms

knowledge base management system (KBMS)
reasoning facility
deductive reasoning
inductive reasoning
abductive reasoning
explanation facility
knowledge representation scheme
exception-handling features
knowledge independence
robust
metaknowledge
semantic network
property inheritance mechanism
override
proposition
propositional logic
propositional calculus
modus ponens
chain rule
reductio ad absurdum
predicate
sorts
function
first-order logic predicate calculus
first-order predicate calculus
Horn clause
closed world assumption (CWA)
unique name assumption (UNA)
domain closure assumption (DCA)
frame
production system
rule
production rule
production
antecedent
consequent
enable
trigger
fire
conflict resolution
forward chaining
backward chaining
procedural representation method
deductive database
extensional database (EDB)
intensional database (IDB)
expert system
institutional memory
object-oriented programming (OOP)
object model (OM)
reusability
black box approach
extendability
compatibility
object-oriented approach (OOA)
object
message
method
class
instance
subclass
message interface
message protocol
addressability
identity
object identifier
class inheritance
multiple inheritance
object independence
partial inheritance
dynamic inheritance

Exercises

16.1 Write the production rules for an expert system to help in advising a client of a bank as to the type of account or accounts he or she should open.

16.2 Using the production rules of Figure E, show the order in which the rules will be fired in

Figure E Production rules for Exercises 16.2 and 16.3

$a \rightarrow b$
$b \wedge c \rightarrow d, m$
$b \wedge e \rightarrow c, f$
$b \wedge f \rightarrow s$
$d \wedge g \rightarrow n, r$
$d \wedge v \rightarrow x$
$h \wedge m \rightarrow g$
$s \wedge r \rightarrow b$
$m \wedge n \rightarrow v$

forward chaining to ascertain whether the fact x can be established under the assumption that (a, e, h) are true.

16.3 Using the production rules of Figure E, show the order in which the rules will be fired in backward chaining to establish if the fact x can be established under the assumption that (a, e, h) are true.

16.4 A smart pressing iron (see Figure F) consists of the following components: a heating element; a thermostat to control the heat setting; a motion-sensing probe to indicate if the iron is being used and a controller to turn the iron off if it has not been used in the last ten minutes; a manual reset button to reset the iron if it is turned off by the controller; a supply cord and a plug for connecting the iron to a standard 110 volt electric wall outlet. The iron resets automatically if it is unplugged. Write the production rules to indicate the likely cause of a problem if the iron heats intermittently.

Figure F Smart pressing iron for Exercise 16.4.

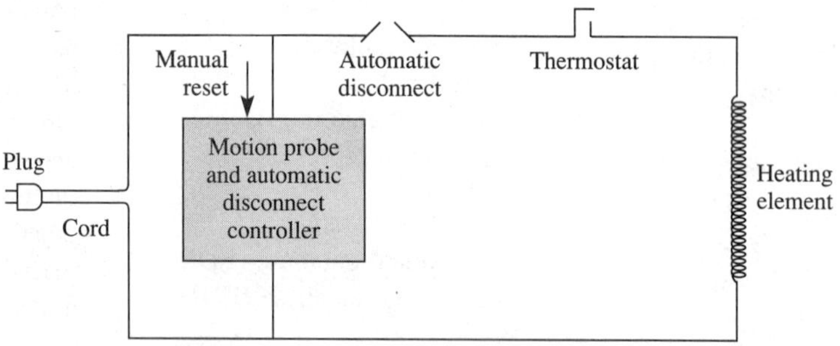

16.5 Design the knowledge base for an academic advisor expert system for advising new students who join your department.

16.6 Given the relation parent (x,y), where y is a parent of x, specify the rules to get

a. siblings (brothers or sisters)
b. ancestors (you may treat a person p as having an ancestor p)

What other facts would need to be recorded if we want to distinguish between brothers and sisters? How would you formulate the rules?

Bibliographic Notes

(Brod 86b) discusses the differences and similarities between a KBMS and a DBMS. (Brac 86) views a database from a knowledge level. (Find 79) is a collection of some later papers on the use of semantic networks in knowledge representation. (Korf 66) and (Quin 51) are introductory textbooks in mathematical logic. First-order logic is discussed in (Kowa 79). Frames are discussed in (Kuip 75) and (Mins 75). The relative merits of procedural representation and frames, wherein the procedures associated with the slots can incorporate aspects of know-how knowledge, are discussed in (Wino 75).

(Brod 86a) discusses the integration of AI techniques in databases. Logical databases are the subject of recent papers (Gall 84, Reit 84, and references given therein). A collection of papers also appears in (Gall 78). (Gray 84, Ullm 88) give a textbook-level introduction to the subject. (Smit 86) presents the architecture and functionality of an expert database system, which is an integration of an expert system with a DBMS. (Wate 86) contains an excellent textbook-level introduction to knowledge bases used for expert systems. (Wins 84) is an introductory text and (Barr 81) has emerged as a classical reference in AI. (Wate 86) and (Kers 86) contain bibliographies of existing expert systems.

POSTGRES is presented in (Ston 86a) and (Ston 86b). The description of the data model of PROBE is presented in (Mano 86). This data model is an extension of the DAPLEX (Ship 81) functional data model. VBASE (Andr 87) is a commercial OODBMS. Some of these systems are also claimed to be KBMSs.

Bibliography

(Alme 85) G. T. Almes, A. P. Black, E. D. Lazowska, & J. D. Noe, ''The Eden System: A Technical Review,'' *IEEE Transactions on Software Engineering* SE–11(1), pp. 43–59, 1985.

(Ande 86) T. L. Anderson, E. F. Eckland, & D. Maier, ''PROTEUS: Objectifying the DBMS User Interface,'' Proceedings, International Workshop on Object-Oriented Database Systems, Sept. 1986, pp. 133–145.

(Andr 87) T. Andrews & C. Harris, ''Combining Language and Database Advances in an Object-Oriented Development Environment,'' Proc. of OOPSLA, October 1987, pp. 430–440.

(Atki 86) M. P. Atkinson, A. Dearle, & R. Morrison, ''A Strongly Typed Persistent Object Store,'' Proceedings, International Workshop on Object-Oriented Database Systems, Sept. 1986, p. 206.

(Badr 88) B. R. Badrinath & K. Ramamrithan, ''Synchronizing Transactions on Objects,'' *IEEE Trans. on Software Engineering* 37(5), May 1988, pp. 541–547.

(Banc 86a) F. Bancilhon, ''A Logic-Programming/Object-Oriented Cocktail,'' *ACM SIGMOD Record* 15(3), 1986, pp. 11–21.

(Banc 86b) F. Bancilhon & S. Khoshafian, ''A Calculus for Complex Objects,'' Proceedings 5th ACM SIGACT-SIGMOD Symposium on Principles of Database Systems, March 1986, pp. 53–59.

(Banc 88) F. Bancilhon, ''Object-Oriented Database Systems,'' Proc. SICACT/SIGMOD/SIGACT Symposium of Principles of Database Systems, Austin, Texas, March 1988.

(Bane 87) J. Banerjee, et. al., ''Data Models Issues for Object-Oriented Applications,'' *ACM TOOIS* 5(1), January 1987, pp. 3–26.

(Bapa 86) K. V. Bapa Rao, ''An Object-Oriented Framework for Modeling Design Data,'' Proceedings, International Workshop on Object-Oriented Database Systems, Sept. 1986, p. 232.

(Barr 81) A. Barr & E. A. Feigenbaum eds., *The Handbook of Artificial Intelligence,* vol. 1. Los Alatos CA.: William Kaufman, 1981.

(Birt 73) G. M. Birtwhistle, O. J. Dahl, B. Myrhaug, & K. Nygaard, *SIMULA Begin.* Auerbach Publishers, 1973.

(Blac 85) A. P. Black, "Supporting Distributed Applications: Experience with Eden," Proceedings 10th ACM Symposium on Operating System Principles, 1985, pp. 181–193.

(Bobr 75) D. G. Bobrow & A. Collins, eds., *Representation and Understanding: Studies in Cognitive Science.* New York: Academic Press, 1975.

(Brac 83) R. J. Brachman, "What IS–A is and Isn't: An Analysis of Taxonomic Links in Semantic Network," *IEEE Computer* 16(10), 1983.

(Brac 86) R. J. Brachman & H. J. Levesque, "What Makes a Knowledge Base Knowledgeable? A View of Databases from the Knowledge Level," in L. Kerschberg, ed., *Expert Database Systems: Proceedings from the First International Workshop.* Menlo Park, CA: Benjamin/Cummings, 1986, pp. 69–78.

(Brod 84) M. L. Brodie, J. Mylopoulos, & J. W. Schmidt, eds., *On Conceptual Modelling: Perspective from Artificial Intelligence, Databases and Programming Languages.* New York: Springer-Verlag, 1986.

(Brod 86a) M. L. Brodie & J. Mylopoulos, eds., *On Knowledge Base Management Systems: Integrating Artificial Intelligence and Database Technologies.* New York: Springer-Verlag, 1986.

(Brod 86b) M. L. Brodie, R. Balzer, G. Wiederhold, R. Brachman, & J. Mylopoulos, "Knowledge Base Management Systems: Discussions from the Working Group" in L. Kerschberg, ed., *Expert Database Systems: Proceedings from the First International Workshop.* Menlo Park, CA: Benjamin/Cummings, 1986, pp. 19–23.

(Brod 86c) M. L. Brodie & J. Mylopoulos, "Knowledge Bases vs. Databases," in M. L. Brodie, & J. Mylopoulos, eds., *On Knowledge Base Management Systems: Integrating Artificial Intelligence and Database Technologies.* New York: Springer-Verlag, 1986, pp. 83–86.

(Card 85) L. Cardelli & P. Wegner, "On Understanding Types, Data Abstraction, and Polymorphism," *Computing Surveys* 17(4), December 1985, pp. 471–522.

(Care 86) M. J. Carey, D. J. DeWitt, D. Frank, G. Graefe, M. Muralikrishna, J. E. Richardson, & E. J. Shekita, "The Architecture of the EXODUS Extensible DBMS,' Proceedings, International Workshop on Object-Oriented Database Systems, Sept. 1986, pp. 52–65.

(Chen 76) P. P. Chen, "The Entity-Relationship Model—Towards a Unified View of Data," *ACM Transactions on Database Systems* 1(1), March 1976, pp. 9–36.

(Chri 86) S. Christodoulakis, F. Ho, & M. Theodoridou, "The Multimedia Object Presentation Manager of MINOS: Symmetric Approach," Proceedings, ACM SIGMOD '86, May 1986, pp. 295–310.

(Cope 84) G. Copeland & D. Maier, "Making Smalltalk a Data Base System," Proceedings, ACM SIGMOD '84, June 1984, pp. 316–325.

(Dahl 66) O. J. Dahl & K. Nygaard, "SIMULA, an ALGOL Bases Simulation Language," *Comm. of the ACM* 9(9), September 1966, pp. 671–678.

(Danf 88) S. Danforth, & C. Tomlinson, "Type Theories and Object-Oriented Programming," *ACM Computing Surveys* 20(1), March 1988, pp. 29–72.

(Dasg 85) P. Dasgupta, R. J. LeBlanc, & E. Spafford, "The Clouds Project: Designing and Implementing a Fault Tolerant, Distributed Operating System," Technical Report GIT-ICS 85/28, Georgia Institute of Technology, School of Information and Computer Science, 1985.

(Dasg 86) P. Dasgupta, "A Probe-Based Monitoring Scheme for an Object-Oriented Distributed Operating System," Proceedings, OOPSLA '86, September 1986, pp. 57–66.

(Ditt 86) K. R. Dittrich, "Object-Oriented Database Systems: The Notion and the Issues," Proceedings, International Workshop on Object-Oriented Database Systems, Sept. 1986, pp. 2–4.

(Dixo 89) G. N. Dixon, G. D. Parrington, S. K. Shrivastaua and S. M. Wheater, "The Treatment of Persistent Objects in Arjuna," *The Computer Journal,* 32(4), August 1989, pp. 323–332.

(East 86) G. M. Eastman, ''Three Uses of Object-Oriented Databases to Model Engineering Systems,'' Proceedings, International Workshop on Object-Oriented Database Systems, Sept. 1986, pp. 215–216.

(Find 79) N. V. Findler, ed., *Associative Networks: Representation and Use of Knowledge by Computers*. New York: Academic Press, 1979.

(Fish 87) D. H. Fishman, et al., ''Overview of the IRIS DBMS,'' *ACM TOOIS* 5(1), January 1987, pp. 48–69.

(Fish 88) D. H. Fishman, et al., *Overview of the IRIS DBMS*. Palo Alta, CA: 1988. H–P Labs, 1988.

(Fros 86) R. Frost, *Introduction to Knowledge Base Systems*. New York: Macmillan, 1986.

(Gall 78) H. Gallaire & J. Minker, *Logic and Databases*. New York: Plenum Press, 1978.

(Gall 84) H. Gallaire, J. Minker, & J.–M. Nicolas, ''Logic and Databases: A Deductive Approach,'' *ACM Computing Survey* 16(2), June 1984, pp. 153–185.

(Gold 83) A. Goldberg & D. Robson, *Smalltalk–80: The Language and Its Implementation*. Reading, MA: Addison-Wesley, 1983.

(Goya 87) P. Goyal, T. S. Narayanan, Y. Z. Qu, & F. Sadri, ''Requirements for an Object-Based Integrated Systems Environment,'' Technical Report CSD–87–007, Dept. of Computer Science, Concordia University, 1987.

(Gray 84) P. Gray, *Logic, Algebra and Databases*. Chichester, England: Ellis Horwood, 1984.

(Hamm 81) M. Hammer & D. McLeod, ''Database Description in SDM: A Semantic Database Model,'' *ACM Transactions on Database Systems* 6(3), 1981, pp. 351–386.

(Hard 86) T. Harder, ''New Approaches to Object Processing in Engineering Databases,'' Proceedings, International Workshop on Object-Oriented Database Systems, Sept. 1986, p. 217.

(Huds 86) S. E. Hudson & R. King, ''CACTIS: A Database System for Specifying Functionally Defined Data,'' Proceedings, International Workshop on Object-Oriented Database Systems, Sept. 1986, pp. 26–37.

(Isra 86) D. Israel, ''AI Knowledge Bases and Databases,'' in M. L. Brodie & J. Mylopoulous, eds., *On Knowledge Base Management Systems: Integrating Artificial Intelligence and Database Technologies*. New York: Springer-Verlag, 1986.

(Jone 79a) A. K. Jones, ''The Object Model: A Conceptual Tool for Structured Software,'' in R. Bayer, R. M. Graham, & G. Seagmuller), eds., *Operating Systems: An Advanced Course*. NY: Springer-Verlag, 1979, pp. 8–18.

(Jone 79b) A. K. Jones, R. J. Chandler, I. E. Durham, K. Schwans, & S. Vegdahl, ''StarOS: Multiprocessor Operating System for Support of Task Forces,'' Proceedings 7th ACM Symposium on Operating System Principles, Dec. 1979, pp. 117–129.

(Jones 86) M. B. Jones & R. F. Rashid, ''Mach and Matchmaker: Kernel and Language Support for Object-Oriented Distributed Systems,'' Proceedings, OOPSLA '86, Sept. 1986, pp. 67–77.

(Katz 86) R. H. Katz, E. Chang, & R. Bhateja, ''Version Modeling Concepts for Computer-Aided Design Databases,'' Proceedings, ACM SIGMOD '86, May 1986, pp. 379–386.

(Kers 86) L. Kerschberg, ed., *Expert Database Systems: Proc. from the First International Workshop*. Menlo Park, CA: Benjamin/Cummings, 1986.

(Keta 86) M. A. Ketabchi, ''Object-Oriented Data Models and Management of CAD Databases,'' Proceedings, International Workshop on Object-Oriented Database Systems, Sept. 1986, pp. 223–224.

(Khos 86) S. Khoshafian & G. P. Copeland ''Object Identity,'' Proceedings, OOPSLA '86, Sept. 1986, pp. 406–415.

(Kim 88) W. Kim & F. Lochovsky, *Object-Oriented Concepts and Databases*. Reading, MA: Addison-Wesley, 1988.

(Know 83) Special issue on knowledge representation. *IEEE Computer* 16(10), October 1983.

(Korf 66) R. R. Korfhage, *Logic and Algorithms*. New York: John Wiley, 1966.

(Kowa 79) R. Kowalski, *Logic for Problem Solving*. New York: North-Holland, 1979.

(Kuip 75) B. J. Kuipers, ''A Frame for Frames: Representing Knowledge for Recognition,'' in D. G. Bobrow

& A. Collins, eds., *Representation and Understanding: Studies in Cognitive Science*. New York: Academic Press, 1975, pp. 151–184.

(Lazo 81) E. D. Lazowska, H. M. Levy, G. T. Almes, M. J. Fischer, R. J. Fowler, & S. C. Vestal, ''The Architecture of the Eden System,'' Proceedings, 8th ACM Symposium on Operating System Principles, Dec. 1981, pp. 148–159.

(Lisk 83) B. Liskov & R. Scheifler, ''Guardians and Actions: Linguistic Support for Robust, Distributed programs,'' *ACM Transactions on Programming Languages and Systems* 5(3), 1983, pp. 381–404.

(Lloy 83) J. W. Lloyd, ''An Introduction to Deductive Database Systems,'' *Australian Computer Journal* 15(2), May 1983, pp. 52–57.

(Lori 86) H. Lorin, ''An Extended Approach to Objects,'' *Operating Systems Review* 20(1), Jan. 1986, pp. 6–11.

(Lyng 86) P. Lyngback & W. Kent, ''A Data Modeling Methodology for the Design and Implementation of Information Systems,'' Proceedings, International Workshop on Object-Oriented Database Systems, Sept. 1986, pp. 6–17.

(Maie 86a) D. Maier, J. Stein, A. Otis, A. Purdy, ''Development of an Object-Oriented DBMS,'' Proceedings, OOPSLA '86, Sept. 1986.

(Maie 86b) D. Maier & J. Stein, ''Indexing in an Object-Oriented DBMS,'' Proceedings, International Workshop on Object-Oriented Database Systems, Sept. 1986, pp. 171–182.

(Mano 86) F. Manola, & U. Dayal, ''PDM: An Object-Oriented Data Model,'' Proceedings, International Workshop on Object-Oriented Database Systems, Sept. 1986, pp. 18–25.

(Maye 87) B. Mayer, ''Reusability: The Case for Object-Oriented Design,'' *IEEE Software* 4(2), March 1987, pp. 50–64.

(Mend 78) E. Mendelson, *Introduction to Mathematical Logic,* 2nd ed. New York: Van Nostrand-Reinhold, 1978.

(Mins 75) M. Minsky, ''A Framework for Representing Knowledge,'' in P. Winston, ed., *The Psychology of Computer Vision*. New York: McGraw-Hill, 1975.

(Oren 86) J. A. Orenstein, ''Spatial Query Processing in an Object-Oriented Database System,'' Proceedings, ACM SIGMOD '86, May 1986, pp. 326–336.

(Peck 88) J. Peckham & F. Maryanski, ''Semantic Data Models,'' *Computing Survey* 20(3), September 1988, pp. 153–190.

(Popl 73) H. E. Pople, Jr., 'On the Mechanization of Abductive Logic,'' Proc. Third International Joint Conference on Artificial Intelligence, Stanford University, August 1973, pp. 147–152.

(Quin 51) W. V. O. Quine, *Mathematical Logic*. New York: Harper & Row, 1951.

(Reit 84) R. Reiter, ''Towards a Logical Reconstruction of Relational Database Theory,'' in M. L. Brodie, J. Mylopoulos, & J. W. Schmidt, eds., *On Conceptual Modelling: Perspective from Artificial Intelligence, Databases and Programming Languages*. New York: Springer-Verlag, 1986, pp. 191–238.

(Rent 82) T. Rentsch, ''Object-Oriented Programming,'' *SIGPLAN Notices* 17(9), September 1982, pp. 51–57.

(Rowe 86) L. A. Rowe, ''A Shared Object Hierarchy,'' Proceedings, International Workshop on Object-Oriented Database Systems, Sept. 1986, pp. 160–170.

(Schm 77) J. W. Schmidt, ''Some High Level Language Constructs for Data of Type Relation,'' *ACM Transactions on Database Systems* 2(3), September 1977, pp. 247–261.

(Schw 86) P. Schwarz, W. Chang, J. C. Freytag, G. Lohman, J. McPherson, C. Mohan, & H. Pirahesh, ''Extensibility in the Starburst Database System,'' Proceedings, International Workshop on Object-Oriented Database Systems, Sept. 1986, pp. 85–92.

(Ship 81) D. Shipman, ''The Functional Data Model and the Data Language DAPLEX,'' *ACM Transactions on Database Systems* 6(1), 1981, pp. 140–173.

(Smit 86) J. M. Smith, ''Expert Database Systems: A Database Perspective,'' in L. Kerschberg, ed., *Expert*

Database Systems: Proc. from the First International Workshop. Menlo Park, CA: Benjamin/Cummings, 1986, pp. 3–15.

(Snyd 86) A. Snyder, "Encapsulation and Inheritance in Object-Oriented Programming Languages," Proceedings, OOPSLA '88, Sept. 1986, pp. 38–45.

(Spec 85) A. Z. Spector, J. Butcher, D. S. Daniels, D. J. Duchamp, J. L. Eppinger, C. E. Fineman, A. Heddaya, & P. M. Schwarz, "Support for Distributed Transactions in the TABS Prototype," *IEEE Transactions on Software Engineering* SE 11(6), 1985, pp. 520–530.

(Ston 86a) M. R. Stonebraker, "Object Management in POSTGRES Using Procedures," Proceedings, International Workshop on Object-Oriented Database Systems, Sept. 1986, pp. 66–72.

(Ston 86b) M. R. Stonebraker & L. A. Rowe, "The Design of POSTGRES," Proceedings, ACM SIGMOD '86, May 1986, pp. 340–355.

(Tsic 88) D. Tsichritzis, ed., *Active Object Environment*. Geneva, Switzerland: University of Geneva, 1988.

(Ullm 88) J. D. Ullman, *Principles of Databases and Knowledge-Base Systems,* vol. 1. Rockville, MD: Computer Science Press, 1988.

(Vass 86) Y. Vassiliou, "Knowledge Based and Database Systems: Enhancements, Coupling or Integration?" in M. L. Brodie & J. Mylopoulos, eds., *On Knowledge Base Management Systems: Integrating Artificial Intelligence and Database Technologies*. New York: Springer-Verlag, 1986, pp. 87–91.

(Wate 86) D. A. Waterman, *A Guide to Expert Systems*. Reading, MA: Addison-Wesley, 1986.

(Wied 86) G. Wiederhold, "Knowledge versus Data," in M. L. Brodie & J. Mylopoulos, eds., *On Knowledge Base Management Systems: Integrating Artificial Intelligence and Database Technologies*. New York: Springer-Verlag, 1986, pp. 77–82.

(Wino 75) T. Winograd, "Frames Representations and the Declarative/Procedural Controversy," in D. G. Bobrow & A. Collins, eds., *Representation and Understanding: Studies in Cognitive Science*. New York: Academic Press, 1975, pp. 185–210.

(Wins 84) P. A. Winston, *Artificial Intelligence,* 2nd ed. Reading, MA: Addison-Wesley, 1984.

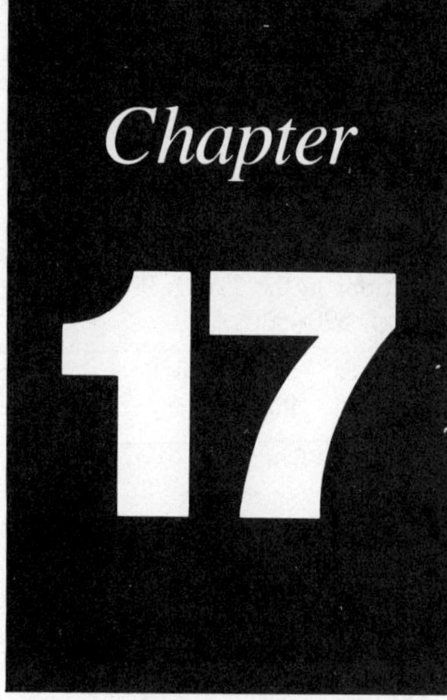

Database Machines

Contents

In this chapter we discuss a number of approaches used to relieve the main computer system of the burden of running the database management system and to handle the superfluous data not required for deriving the response to a user's query.

17.1 Introduction

In the traditional approach to database systems (see Figure 17.1), the data is stored on secondary storage devices and the ability to perform any logical or arithmetic computing operations is limited to the central processor. Data has to be moved from the secondary storage devices to the main memory attached to the central processor. Once the data is transferred to the main memory, the processor can access it and determine if the data is useful. Thus it is likely that a large quantity of superfluous data will also be retrieved and processed. It has been estimated that on the average, only 10% of the retrieved data is found to be pertinent. The utilization of indexes is one approach used to reduce this wasteful movement and processing of data. However, the indexes themselves take up considerable storage space and generate substantial traffic on the input/output channels as well as a heavy processing load on the processor.

17.2 Database Machine Taxonomy

The approach taken in **database machines** is to offload the database management functions onto a special processor and optionally add some level of computing capability closer to the data. The special processor relieves the main computer system of the task of managing the database; the extra level of computing capability makes it feasible to decide whether a given set of data will be useful in the evaluation of a query without having to transfer the data to a central processing unit.

A number of approaches to moving the computing power closer to the data have been proposed, and experimental systems for some of these proposals have been

Figure 17.1 Conventional approach.

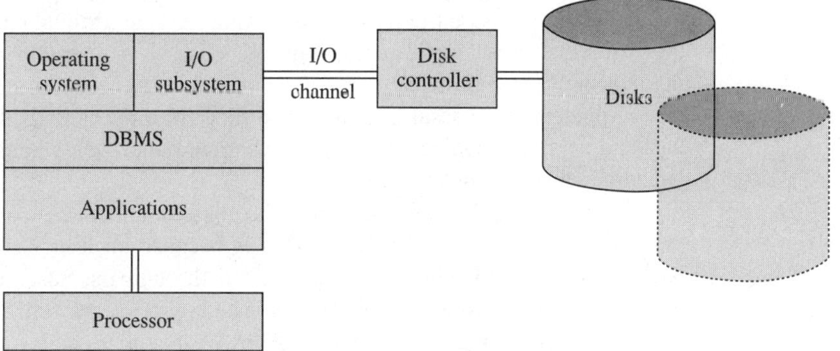

attempted. The references to some of these systems are given in the bibliographic notes. These approaches can be classified as one of the following: backend software approach; processor associated with memory or intelligent memory approach; special hardware approach. We briefly describe these approaches in the following sections.

17.2.1 Backend Software Approach

In the **backend software** approach, sometimes called the **backend computer** approach, the host computer where the applications are located is attached to a dedicated general-purpose computer and a conventional database management system runs on this backend computer. This dedicated backend computer is responsible for carrying out the database functions of locating and retrieving the required data as well as ensuring security, enforcing consistency criteria, and providing for recovery operations. This releases the host computer from database management functions. Superior performance can be achieved by parallel processing of the application programs and the database operations in distinct processors. A single backend computer can be attached to a single host or a number of hosts, not necessarily identical, can share a single backend computer.

A database request from an application program in the host computer is intercepted by special interface software, which sends the request to the dedicated backend database machine. The backend machine performs the required data access and processing operations to derive the response for the request and this response is sent back to the host.

The backend machine can be a conventional computer dedicated to running a conventional database management system. It can also be a system consisting of one or more specialized processors using traditional secondary storage devices or associative memories of one or more types. **Associative memory** has logic associated with each word or each bit of the memory. The logic is used to simultaneously examine the contents of the entire memory. Matching words are flagged and could be rapidly located for subsequent processing.

Regardless of the nature of the backend system, it is dedicated to performing the database functions in an optimal manner to achieve cost-effective performance. Higher performance is achieved by the parallelism inherent in such a system.

There are certain advantages and disadvantages in dedicating a separate system for the database functions. We already mentioned the higher performance attainable with such a system as a consequence of parallelism and specialization. The performance here is measured in terms of the overall system throughput and not necessarily the response for a single query. The response to a query in a backend approach involves an overhead in the form of communication between the host and the backend computers. As a result, the response time for a query is likely to be worse in the backend approach compared to the conventional approach where communication between computers is not required.

In the backend approach, since the data is under the control of a dedicated system, data security is enhanced. This is because no user has direct access to the backend system, all requests being handled through the host interface. Also, since no application programs run on the dedicated system, the reliability of the database system is improved; there is freedom from crashes that occur due to incorrect application programs. However, since the overall system has more components than a conventional system, the likelihood of failure is increased.

A dedicated database machine can be used to support the database operations for a number of host computers and/or workstations, as shown in Figure 17.2. Such an approach, where a number of hosts share one or more backend computers, permits cost-effective sharing of both the data and the database management functions. However, unless the dedicated database machine has the required capacity to handle this load, it will create a bottleneck. Furthermore, failure of this dedicated system would bring the operations of these hosts to a halt.

An alternative solution to relieve the bottleneck and to increase the reliability of the backend system is to incorporate multiple dedicated database machines in the database management functions, as shown in Figure 17.3. In this variation of the backend approach, a number of backend computers can be used to handle a very large database, the latter being distributed to optimize performance by allowing parallel retrieval and processing of data required simultaneously. However, with this scheme, the problems encountered are the following: the need to determine the dis-

Figure 17.2 Backend database computer approach.

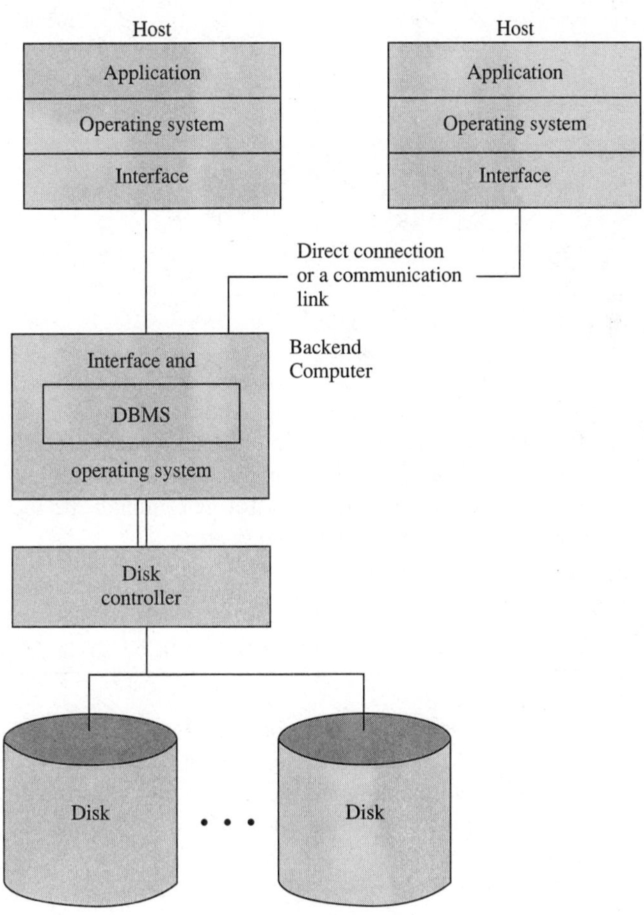

Figure 17.3 Multiple backend computers serving multiple hosts.

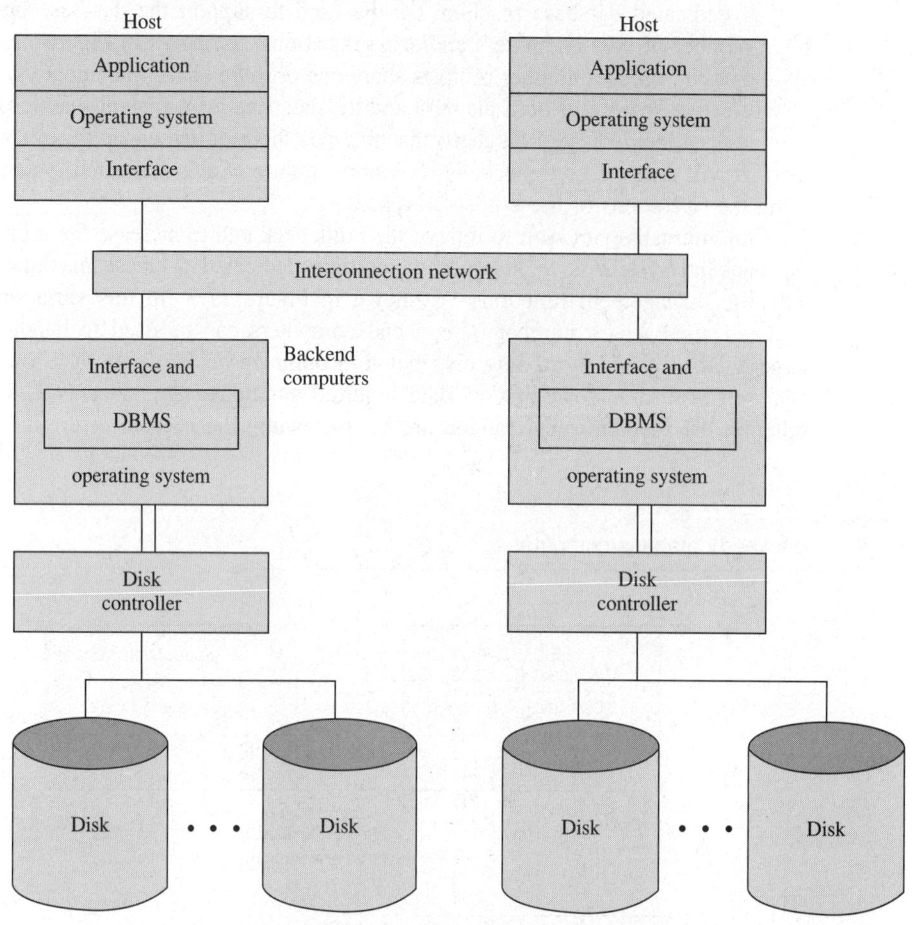

tribution of data on the multiple backend computers; the maintenance of the directory containing this information about the data distribution; if such a directory is not maintained, then the overhead for determining the location of required data; consistency enforcement if data is replicated.

17.2.2 Processor Associated with Memory or Intelligent Memory Approach

In the **intelligent memory** approach (see Figure 17.4), sufficient processing logic is associated with the secondary memory so that data can be processed before being transmitted to the host processor. The host runs the database management system. If sufficient processing capability is associated with the secondary storage device controller, it can intercept data from the secondary storage device to determine its usefulness. There is no need to move superfluous data to the host system running the database management system. The host could be a conventional system as in Figure

Figure 17.4 Associative memory approach.

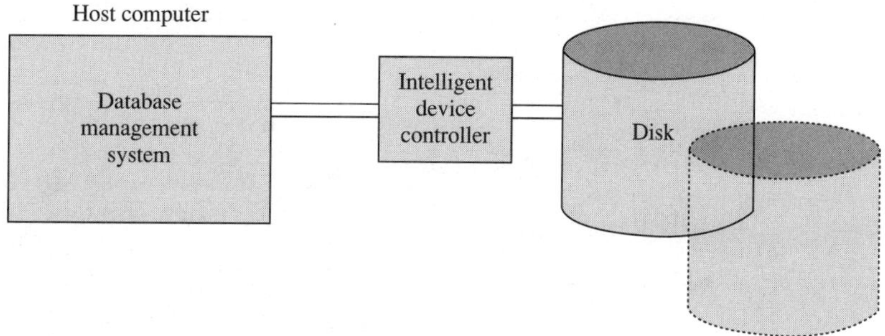

17.1, running the application as well as the DBMS, or it could be a dedicated back-end computer.

The processing capability associated with the secondary memory is provided by VLSI-based microprocessors and hence is cost effective. The storage device could be electromechanical in the form of rotating disks or drums, or it could be nonmechanical, e.g., magnetic bubble memories or charge-coupled devices. (In the following discussions, we assume that the storage devices are electromechanical; however, the same concepts can be applied to the nonmechanical devices.) The processing capability may be associated with a storage device in one of the following manners: processor per track of a fixed-head type storage device; processor per surface of a moving-head type storage device; processor per storage device; or multiprocessor and cache approach.

In the **processor-per-track** approach, a processor is associated with each track of the secondary storage device, the latter being a fixed-head disk or drum or other such device (Figure 17.5). This type of structure is also called a **cellular logic device,** since logic is associated with each cell of memory. Data from the track is processed by the associated processor and data from all tracks can be processed simultaneously. Thus, the entire contents of the storage device can be processed in one pass, which in the case of a rotating storage device is a single revolution. Since all data can be processed in a single pass, indexes are not needed.

The disadvantage of the processor-per-track scheme is that the data from all tracks of a single device is not necessarily required and the concurrent processing of the irrelevant data is unproductive. The cost of this type of storage device is high. However, with the ultralarge-scale integration (ULSI) of logic components, the cost is expected to decrease.

The **processor-per-surface** method is an attempt to associate processing power with each read/write head of a moving-head type secondary storage device (Figure 17.6). The amount of data that can be processed per pass by each processor is the same as in the processor-per-track approach; however, to process all the data from the storage device would take m passes or revolutions, where m is the number of tracks per surface. In the case of mechanical devices such as disks and drums, the movement of the head from track to track takes a finite amount of time and this will have to be accounted for in the total time required to process the data from the device. If the storage device is nonmechanical, the switching of the cells to be processed can be done at much faster electronic rates. To reduce the number of passes, indexes are necessary for these storage devices.

Figure 17.5 Fixed-head disk with read/write head and processor per track.

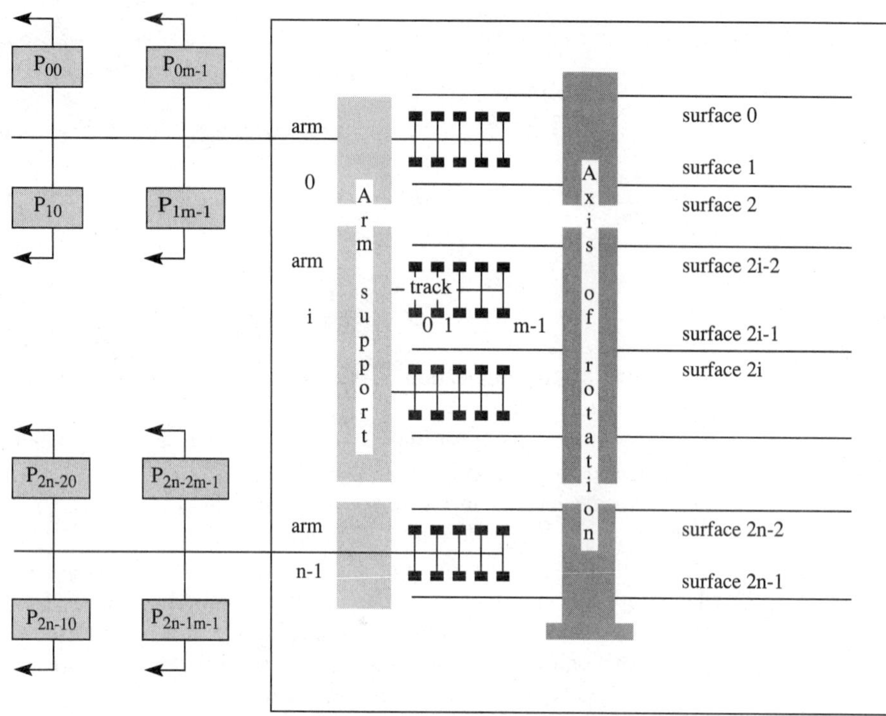

The **processor-per-device** approach is an attempt to further reduce the number of processing elements associated with the storage, and hence the cost. In this scheme there is a single processor associated with each storage device. The processor acts as a filter between the host computer and the device. Indexes are required to reduce the number of passes and the amount of data actually processed by this filter processor.

The **multiprocessor and cache** scheme (Figure 17.7) is an attempt to optimize the cost-performance factor by allowing the filter processors to be assigned to process the data from any one of a number of storage devices, or from a number of different tracks or cells of a single device. The data to be processed is placed in one of the n high-speed memory caches, there being m filter processors. The interconnection network is used to connect any one of the m processors to any of the n caches. Up to m caches can be processed simultaneously; the data in these caches could be from distinct devices or from the same device. With $n > m$, some of the empty caches could be filled while m caches are being processed and buffer the difference between the processing rate and the device access rate.

17.2.3 Special Hardware Approach

In the **special hardware** approach, instead of using a conventional computer as the engine in the backend for running the database management system, a specially de-

Figure 17.6 Moving head disk with a single read/write head and processor per surface.

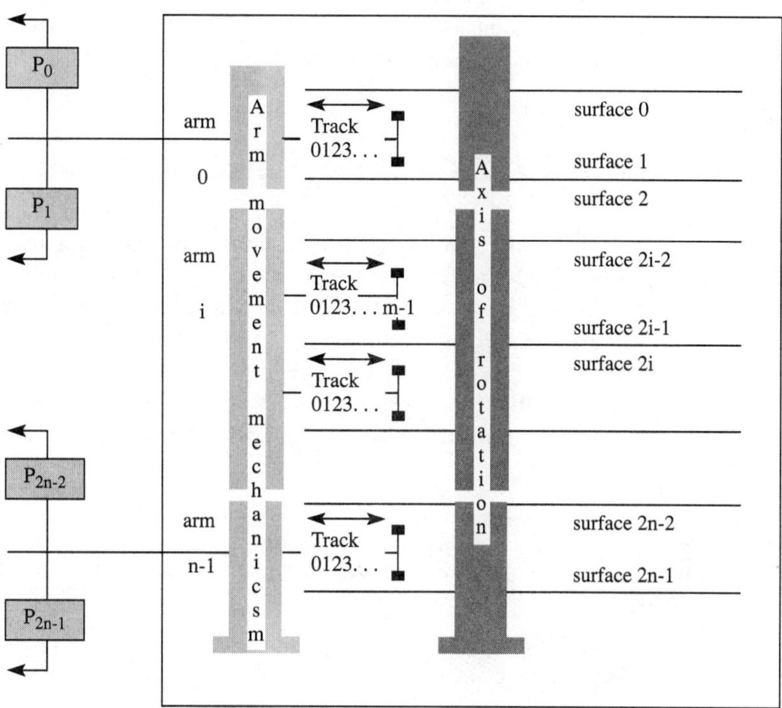

Figure 17.7 Multiprocessor and cache system.

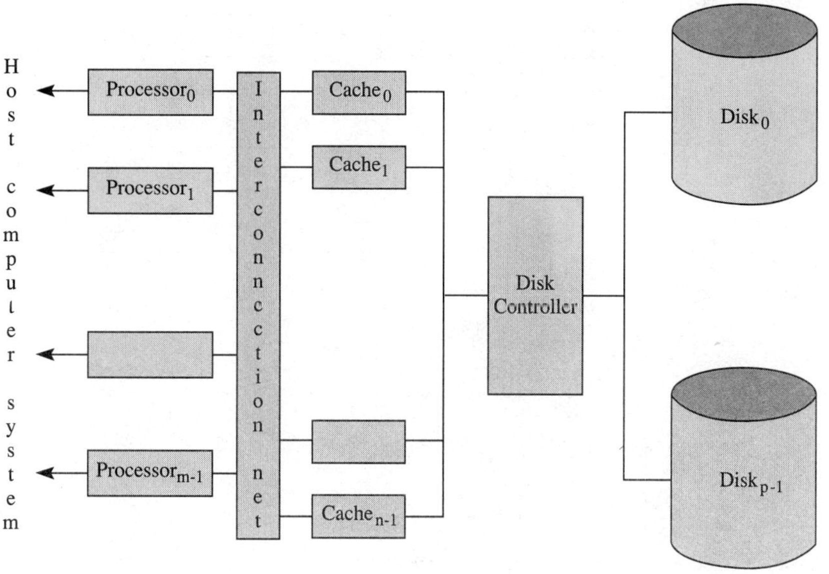

signed computer, usually called a database computer or database machine, is used to perform the database functions in hardware, firmware, and software. Since the database functions are performed by dedicated hardware components, the performance of the system is enhanced. A number of designs for database machines have been proposed; these are mentioned in the bibliographic notes.

17.3 DBC/1012 Overview and Features

In this section we describe the design of one current database computer, the DBC/1012 from Teradata Corporation. It is a self-contained database management system that interfaces directly to the input/output channel of the host computer. It can also be used as a local area network database server, servicing intelligent workstations.

The DBC/1012 (Figure 17.8) is an integrated system wherein the relational database management system is implemented in software, firmware, and hardware. It

Figure 17.8 Teradata DBC/1012 database computer (adapted from [Tera a]).

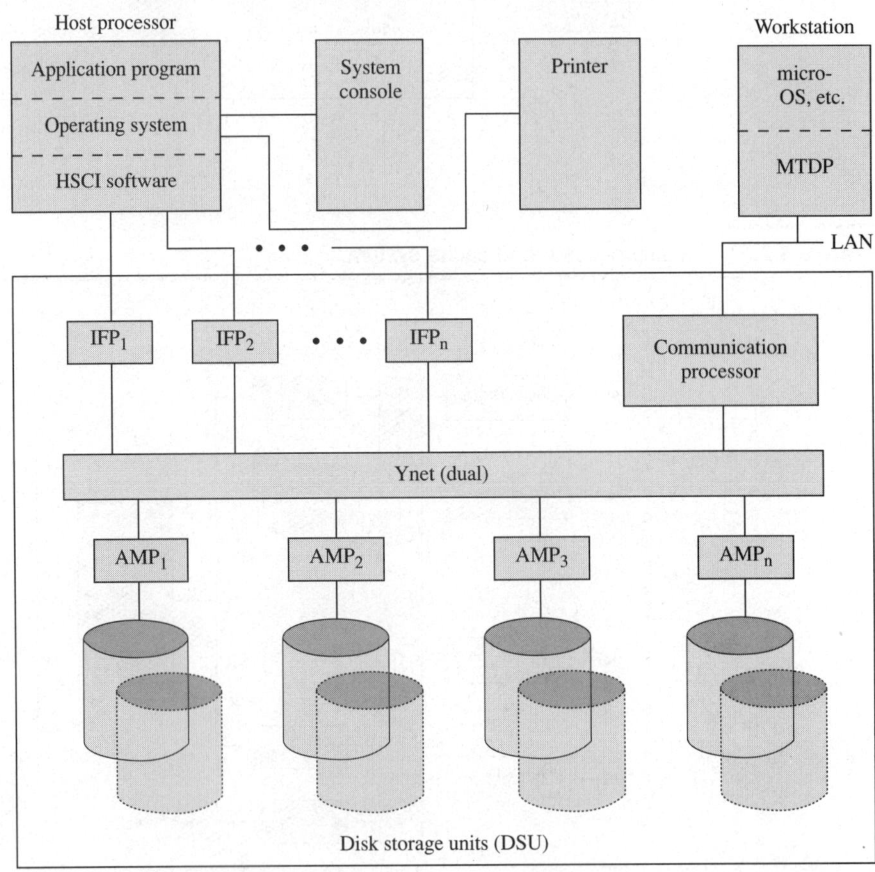

is a dedicated system and interfaces with one or more host computers as well as intelligent workstations connected to a LAN. It can be expanded modularly and consists of multiple microprocessors and direct-access storage devices; the database manipulation and control functions are implemented in the software and firmware. The interface and overall control function of the DBC/1012 is resident in one or more interface processors and/or communication processors. The system is made up of the following components: host system communication interface (HSCI); interface processors (IFP); processor interconnection network (Ynet); access module processor (AMP); disk storage unit (DSU); system console and printer; communication processor (COP). These components are described below.

Host System Communication Interface

The HSCI software, resident in the host computer, is responsible for supporting the database requests of the users and applications on the host system. The HSCI allows the users and applications to manipulate the database in the DBC/1012. It consists of the following components:

- A library of runtime service routines called call-level interface (CLI) routines.
- The Teradata director program (TDP), which manages the interaction of application programs and interactive users on the host system with the DBC/1012. The TDP is also responsible for input and output from the DBC/1012 via an IFP, as well as recovery and security.
- A set of routines called user-to-TDP communication (UTC), routines that manage the communication between applications and the TDP.

The CLI routines present a uniform protocol for converting requests from interactive users or programs into a form that can be communicated to the TDP via the UTC. The CLI routines are also responsible for handling the responses to these requests from the DBC/1012 and forwarding it to the user or application program.

Ynet

Processors interconnect in the DBC/1012 through the Ynet bus. This is an intelligent bus that implements the multiprocessor management, as well as interprocessor message routing and sorting functions in hardware. To provide reliable, fail-safe operations, the interconnection network consists of dual Ynet buses. The Ynet allows messages to be transmitted between the processors connected to it (IFPs, AMPs, and COP). The node module of the basic Ynet configuration, shown in Figure 17.9, is a three-level binary tree consisting of seven internal nodes and eight leaf nodes, the processor modules being connected at the leaf level. Only one of the dual Ynets is shown; the other network is identical. Each processor is connected to each of these Ynets. The data traveling up and down the network contains control information pertaining to the nature of the block of data and its destination. This control information enables the Ynet to route the block to the correct destination. The interconnection network is used as follows: A request from a user arrives at one of the IFP processors. The IFP processor determines the nature of the request and generates a

Figure 17.9 Basic configuration of the Ynet (adapted from [Tera a]).

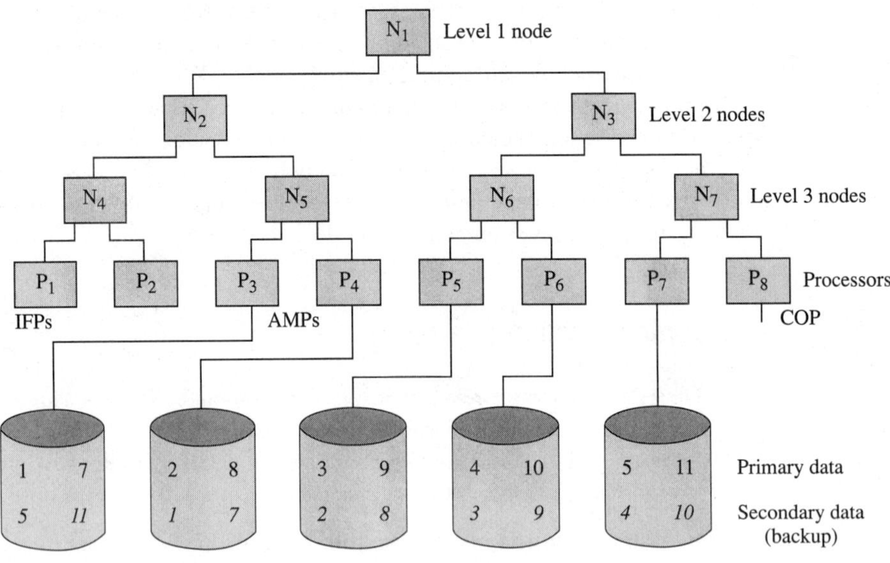

number of work steps to respond to this request. These work steps are encoded into data blocks that travel up the hierarchy from the IFP processor level to the node at level 3, and then down to one or more AMPs. The downward transmission uses a broadcast mode; the upward transmission is controlled by control information associated with the data block. Data retrieved by the AMPs travels up the network. Contention logic in the network is used to sort the data moving up from the AMPs. The control information in the data block is also used to sequence the arrival of blocks from AMPs to a given IFP in a certain order and achieve merge/sorting of the relevant data.

The following types of communication are provided by the Ynet: between any two processors; from one processor to a group of processors; from a group of processors to a single processor; or between processors to synchronize their operations on data. A Ynet can be expanded to support up to 968 processors.

IFP

The IFP (Figure 17.10) interfaces both with the host and the Ynets and manages the traffic between the two. The number of IFPs depends on this traffic and can be adjusted to match it. Each IFP is connected to both Ynets. The functions implemented in the IFPs are the following: host interface, session control, parser, dispatcher, and Ynet interface. These functions are implemented in hardware or software and are briefly described below.

The Ynet interface in the IFP controls the transmission of messages to and the receipt of responses from the AMPS. A message may be transmitted to a single AMP or to a group of them.

Figure 17.10 Interface processor (adapted from [Tera a]).

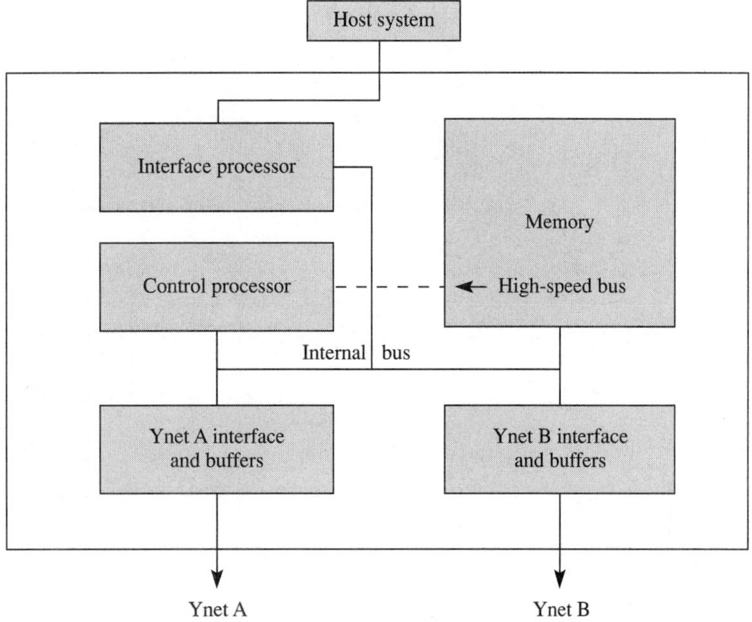

Session control involves processing the logon and logoff requests from the host. The messages to and from the TDP in the host are under the control of the host interface.

A DBC/SQL request from the host is semantically interpreted by the parser. This interpretation may need a reference to the system information stored in the data dictionary/directory to resolve symbolic references and determine integrity constraints. The parser generates a number of work steps required to process the request and sends these to the dispatcher.

The dispatcher controls the execution of work steps and also performs the assembly of the response to be sent to the host via a response control subsystem. The dispatcher schedules the execution of these work steps and passes them to the Ynet interface, which in turn sends them over the Ynet to one or more AMPs. The dispatcher is also responsible for monitoring the status of the work steps in the AMPS and interacting with the response control. The response control is responsible for the assembly and transmission of the response for a request from the host.

AMPs and DSUs

The access module processor (Figure 17.11) is very similar to the IFP and uses some of the same components. The AMPs receive requests for database access over the Ynet and respond by sending the required information back to the requesting IFP or COP over the Ynet. Each AMP is connected to both Ynets and could have a maximum of two data storage units. The database manager (DBM) subsystem is resident on each AMP in the DBC/1012 and is responsible for executing the functions of

Figure 17.11 Access module processor (adapted from [Tera a]).

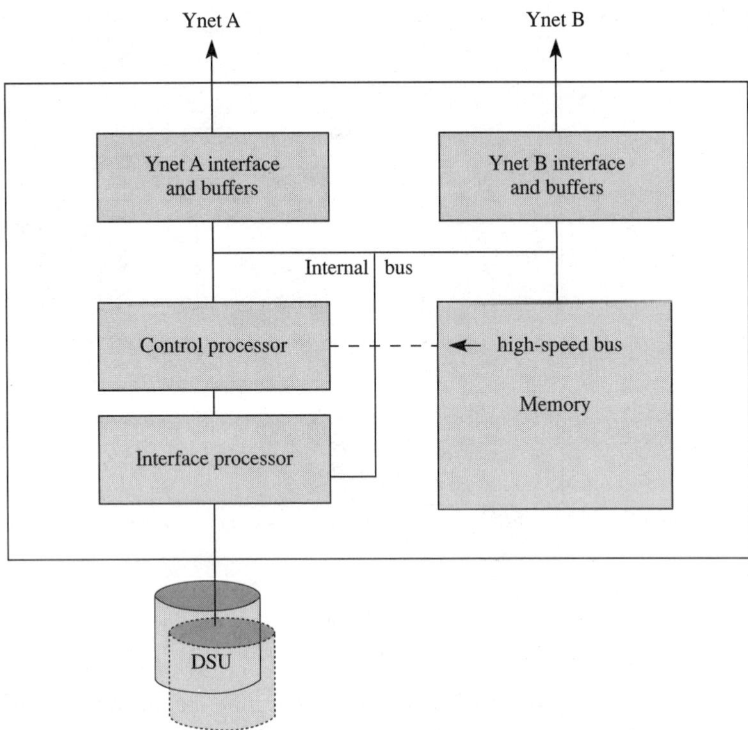

selecting, retrieving, or storing data onto the attached disk storage units (DSUs). The DSUs store the data in the system; the data is distributed and replicated over the DSUs to achieve both concurrency in access and reliability in case of the failure of a single DSU. The components of the AMPs are the Ynet interface, the database manager, and the disk interface. The Ynet interface is responsible for accepting requests from the IFPs or COPs via the Ynet and replying to them. The Ynet interface is also responsible for synchronizing the operation of the AMP with other AMPs and this allows data to be merge/sorted at the receiving IFP or COP.

The disk interface is responsible for controlling the I/O operations of the attached DSUs and communicates with them. Each disk contains space for use by the system in addition to the database; the latter could be either primary data or optional recovery data. The system area contains system software and system information such as tables and indexes. For each table created in the database, the DBA can specify if a second copy of the table is to be maintained for backup and recovery purposes. If a second copy is required, this data is maintained in another disk attached to a different AMP from that containing the primary copy. With this scheme, in the event the primary copy is inaccessible, the second copy can be used. The primary data and the secondary data are distributed. This distribution balances the load on the AMPs and allows concurrent access and processing of related data. This distribution is an imaginative method of achieving the efficiency of the multiprocessor and cache system.

The database manager is responsible for the definition, maintenance, and manipulation of the tables under control of the AMP, as well as participating in the recovery operations. The DBM receives the work steps from the dispatcher and processes them by appropriate selection, retrieval, insertion, deletion, or modification of data on the DSUs attached to the AMP. The DBM is also responsible for managing locks for concurrent requests and manages consistency by sending update messages to AMPs containing the secondary copy of data being modified. The database manager is also responsible for sending the response to the dispatcher in the IFPs or COPs. To facilitate data retrieval, the DBM uses two-level indexes (master index and cylinder index), processed using binary search.

Additional AMPs and DSUs can be modularly attached to the system to increase both capacity and performance. When additional AMPs and their DSUs are attached to the DBC/1012, the database is reconfigured by redistributing the existing tables from the existing AMPs onto the new AMPs.

COP and MTPD

When a host computer or intelligent workstation communicates with the DBC/1012 over a local area network (LAN), the communication processor (COP) is used to perform functions similar to those implemented in the IFP. The request to the DBC/1012 is via messages over the network. The COP is a special-purpose IFP; each COP is connected to both Ynets. The software resident in the host includes, in addition to the CLI routines and BTEQ (a batch facility to submit a job containing DBC/SQL statements as well as control statements for session control and output formatting), the Micro Teradata Director Program (MTDP) and the Micro Operating System Interface (MOSI). The MOSI is collection of routines for interfacing with the host operating system and the communication protocol routines used by the host.

The COP, like the IFP, contains the session control, parser, and dispatcher subsystems. These subsystems perform analogous tasks as in the IFP.

System Console and Printer

The system console, which is an IBM or compatible personal computer, is used for operator communication to monitor the status of the system, including its current configuration and performance. The console is also used in controlling the system and in diagnostic operations. The printer can be used to obtain a hard copy record of the operations of the console.

Data Dictionary/Directory

The data dictionary/directory (DD/D) contains information about the relations as well as views on these relations and the appropriate control information. The relation scheme consist of its attributes, the domains of these attributes, identification of the owner and creator of these relations, indexes to be maintained, a list of authorized users and their access rights. The scheme is maintained in the DD/D.

17.3.1 Operation of the DBC/1012

The database system in the DBC/1012 consists of the following components: session control, dispatcher, and database manager. Each IFP and COP is responsible for the first two components and in addition these processors interface with the host systems. The database manager is implemented on each AMP and is responsible for providing the transformation from the logical database organization to the physical level; the data is stored on the DSUs. The access aid used by the DBM is a two-level index consisting of a master index and a cylinder index; binary search is used on these indexes.

The user defines and manipulates the database using the following facilities:

- In DBC/SQL, the Teradata query language. This is the facility used to define and manipulate the database. Thus, the user can define relations or views on existing relations as well modify them using statements in DBC/SQL. Statements in DBC/SQL allow the user to control access to the database by establishing users and their access profiles.
- Interactively, by statements in the Interactive TEradata Query (ITEQ) language. This includes functions for retrieving metadata about the database; entering, editing, and executing DBC/SQL statements; and specifying the format of the output.
- In a batch mode, using a facility provided by the Batch TEradata Query (BTEQ) language, wherein a number of DBC/SQL statements along with BTEQ batch commands can be executed.
- By DBC/SQL statements included in application programs in a high-level language. These statements are converted by a language preprocessor into calls to CLI routines. After the compilation of the source program, these CLI routines are link-edited with the object code to generate a load module ready for execution. It is also possible to dynamically load the CLI routines at run time. At execution time, the CLI service routines generate a query request, which is communicated by a UTC routine to the TDP.
- In a natural query language such as INTELLECT or a fourth-generation language such as NOMAD.
- By using calls to CLI routines in a high-level language.
- By using a data directory/dictionary facility to access the meta information regarding the database objects.

The user's query requests are communicated to the TDP via UTC routines by the CLI service routines. The TDP is responsible for managing the communication between the application program or the user and the DBC/1012. On receiving a query request, the TDP creates a message for the IFP, which is communicated via the host to DBC/1012 interface. The CLI routines are also responsible for receiving the response to the DBC/SQL statements from the DBC, via the TDP, and forwarding it to the application program or user that originated the request.

17.3.2 System Facilities of the DBC/1012

The DBC/1012 provides a number of system facilities for database security, integrity, and concurrency control.

Security is implemented by means of a session protocol. A user is required to log on to the DBC/1012 to establish a session. The logon procedure identifies the user (or application program) and provides an account number and a password. A session is established once the logon parameters are accepted. A session ends when the user logs off. Unauthorized access or an attempt to access outside a session is denied and appropriately reported.

Concurrency is implemented by locking. The locking granularity could be the entire database, a relation, or a tuple. There are four modes of locking provided by DBC/1012: exclusive, write, read, and access. The access lock can be used by users who are not concerned with data consistency. The degree of concurrency is increased since the access lock allows read operations to be executed simultaneously against a data item locked in the write mode.

Recovery is implemented by the use of transient and permanent journals. The transient journal is a log of updates to the database. The log entry consist of the transaction identification and the before image or the modified data items. The transient journal is used to undo a single transaction error.

The permanent journal is an optional second method of recovery implemented in the DBC/1012. The DBA decides to log either the before image or the after image of data items in the log of the permanent journal. The log could be single or double; in the latter case redundancy in the log is provided by recording two copies of the before or after image.

Archiving (dump) is performed by making copies of the database and permanent journal at regular intervals. Checkpoint facility is part of the permanent journaling feature.

Recovery from failures is achieved by rollback or roll forward optionally to a specified checkpoint.

17.4 Summary

In the traditional approach to database systems, the DBMS runs on the same computer as the user programs. The data in this approach is stored on conventional rotating memories. It is necessary to move the data to the central processing unit for processing and to determine what portion of it is needed to respond to a user's query. We discussed a number of approaches that have been used to place some of the database management load on a separate system. In some of these approaches, some form of computing capability is provided near the data, which avoids moving superfluous data to the main processing unit. The processor per track or cellular logic, the processor per surface, the processor per device, and the multiprocessors and cache are attempts to provide processing close to the data. We also described one instance of a commercially available special-purpose computer that handles the database management functions.

Key Terms

database machines
backend software
backend computer
associative memory
intelligent memory
processor per track
cellular logic device
processor per surface
processor per device
multiprocessor and cache
special hardware

Bibliographic Notes

With the development of database management systems, the load placed on the system of second and third generation computers far exceeded their capabilities, which led to the concept of database computers. One of the first reports of a prototype development of backend database computers was the XDMS project of Bell Labs (Cana 74). Earlier, Slotnick (Slot 70) had proposed a logic-per-track storage device. The cellular logic device is a generalization of Slotnick's logic-per-track concept. Examples of this approach are the CASSM (Su 79), the RAP (Schu 78), and the RARES (Lin 76) projects. The processor-per-surface approach was used in the DBC project (Bane 78). DBC/1012 (Tera a) is an example of the processor-per-surface approach which, with the distribution of data on different AMPs, achieves the efficiency of the MPC approach. The DIRECT project (Dewi 81) is another example of the MPC approach. More recent systems are described in (Hsia 83), (MDBS); (Fish 84), (Jasmin); (Kits 85), (Grace); and (Dewi 86), (GAMMA).

(Mary 80) presents a tutorial on the software backend computer approach. With the increasing use of the relational model, there was an increase in emphasis on developing systems to improve the performance of the relational model in hardware (Babb 79), (Bane 78), (Dewi 81), (Lin 76), (Smit 79). The use of content-addressable memories is not cost effective and they remain controversial (Hawt 81). Commercial database machines continue to use conventional rotating memories.

Textbook-oriented discussions of database computers are presented in (Hsia 83) and (Su 88).

Bibliography

(Babb 79) E. Babb, "Implementing a Relational Database by Means of a Specialized Hardware," *ACM Trans. on Database Systems* 4(1), March 1979, pp. 1–29.

(Bane 78) J. Banerjee, D. K. Hsiao, & R. I. Baum, "Concepts and Capabilities of a Database Computer," *ACM Trans. on Database Systems* 3(4), 1978, pp. 347–384.

(Berr 79) P. B. Berra & E. Oliver, "The Role of the Associative Array Processor in Database Machine Architecture," *Computers* 12(3), March 1979, pp. 53–63.

(Cana 74) R. H. Canady, R. D. Harrison, E. L. Ivie, J. L. Ryder, I. A. Wehr, "A Backend Computer for Database Management," *Comm. of ACM* 17(10), October 1974, pp. 575–582.

(Date 83) C. J. Date, *An Introduction to Database systems,* vol. 2. Reading, Ma: Addison-Wesley, 1983.

(Dewi 81) D. J. DeWitt, "Direct—A Multiprocessor Organization for Supporting the Relational Database Management Systems," *IEEE Trans. on Computers* C–28, June 1979, pp. 395–406.

(Dewi 86) D. J. DeWitt, R. H. Gerber, G. Graefe, M. L. Heytens, K. B. Kumar, & M. Muralikrishna, "GAMMA: A Performance Dataflow Database Machine," Proc. of the 12th International Conf. On Very Large Data Bases, Kyoto, Japan, August 1986, pp. 315–344.

(Fish 84) D. H. Fishman, Ming-Yee Lai, & W. K. Wilkinson, "Overview of the Jasmin Database Machine," Proceedings of the ACM SIGMOD, 1984, pp. 234–239.

(Hawt 81) P. B. Hawthorn & D. J. DeWitt, "Performance Analysis of Alternative Database Machine Architectures," *IEEE Trans. on Software Eng.* SE–8, January 1982, pp. 61–74.

(Hsia 83) D. K. Hsiao, et al., "The Implementation of a Multibackend Database System (MDBS), Part 1—An Exercise in Database Software Engineering," in D. K. Hsiao, ed., *Advanced Database Machines*. Englewood, NJ: Prentice-Hall, 1983, pp. 300–326.

(Kerr 79) D. S. Kerr, "Data Base Machines with Large Content-Addressable Blocks and Structural Information Processor," *IEEE Computers* 12(3), March 1979, pp. 64–79.

(Kits 85) M. Kitsuregawa, M. Fushimi, H. Tanaka, & T. Moto-oka, "Memory Management Algorithm in Pipeland Merge Sorter," in D. DeWitt & H. Boral, eds., *"Proc. of the 4th International Workshop on Database Machines*. New York: Springer-Verlag, 1985, pp. 208–232.

(Lang 79) G. G. Langdon, "Database Machine, An Introduction," *IEEE Transactions on Computers* TC 28(6), June 1979, pp. 381–383.

(Lin 76) C. S. Lin, D. C. P. Smith, & J. M. Smith, "The Design of a Rotating Associative Memory for Relational Database Applications," *ACM Trans. on Database Systems* 1(1), March 1976, pp. 53–65.

(Mary 80) F. J. Maryanski, "Backend Database Systems," *ACM Computing Survey* 12(1), March 1980, pp. 3–26.

(Schu 78) S. A. Schuster, H. B. Nguyen, A. E. Ozkarahan, & C. K. Smith, "RAP.2—An Associative Processor for Databases and its Applications," *IEEE Transactions on Computers,* 1978, Vol C28(6) pp. 446–458.

(Slot 70) D. L. Slotnick, "Logic per Track Devices," in *Advances in Computers,* vol. 10. New York-Academic Press. 1970, pp. 291–296.

(Smit 79) D. C. P. Smith & J. M. Smith, "Relational Database Machines," *IEEE Computers* 12(3), March 1979. pp. 28–39.

(Su 79) S. Y. W. Su, "Cellular Logic Devices: Concepts and Applications," *IEEE Computers* 12(3), March 1979.

(Su 88) S. Y. W. Su, *Database Computers: Principles, Architectures and Techniques.*. New York: McGraw-Hill, 1988.

(Tera a) DBC/1012 Data Base Computer, Concepts and Facilities, C02–0001–04. Los Angeles, CA: Teradata Corporation.

(Tera b) DBC/1012 Data Base Computer, Reference Manual, C03–0001–06. CA: Teradata Corporation.

(Tera c) DBC/1012 Data Base Computer, User's Guide, C09–0001–07. Los Angeles, CA: Teradata Corporation.

(Tera d) DBC/1012 Data Base Computer, Systems Manual, C10–0001–06. Los Angeles, CA: Teradata Corporation.

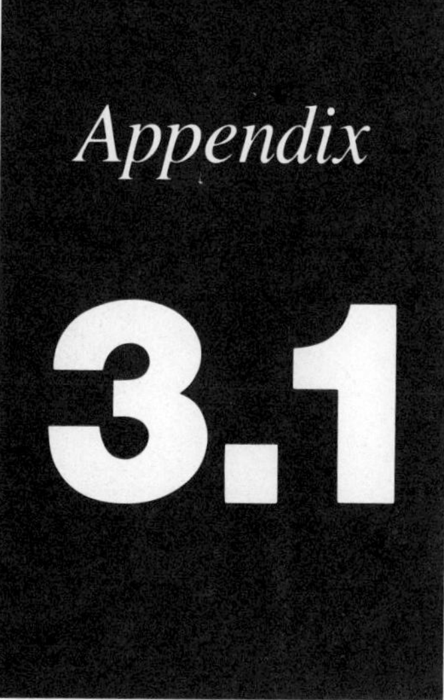

Appendix 3.1

Sequence

Let s be some sequence of elements. The kth element of the sequence is specified as s(k), the number of elements in the sequence as **#s.** To specify that e is an element of **s,** or not an element we write e $\in$ **s,** or e $\notin$ **s,** respectively.

To determine whether or not, e, is an element of sequence s, we have the program:

```
i := 1
while (i ≤ #s) and (s(i) ≠ e)
      i := i + 1
end while
if i > #s then return (false)
          else return (true)
```

This program sequentially accesses every element. Thus, if the element access requests are uniformly and randomly distributed, the average number of elements accessed for each find is **#s**/2.

We can insert an element in the sequence **s**

$$\mathbf{s}' := \mathbf{s} + \mathrm{e}$$

where **s′** represent the sequence after the insertion operation denoted by +, **#s′** = **#s**+1 and **s′**(**#s′**) = e. The intersection is always made at the end of the sequence. Thus, the insert program would be:

```
i := 1
while i ≤ #s do        { while not end of sequence do }
      s'(i) := s(i)    { copy s into s' }
      i := i + 1
end while
s'(i) := e             { insert element into s'       }
```

The deletion of an element e from **s** is:

$$s' := s - e$$

where $-$ indicates the deletion operation and s' is the new sequence after the deletion such that:

$$\#s' = \#s - 1, \text{ and}$$

$$\text{if } s(i) = e \text{ then } \begin{cases} s'(j) = s(j) & \text{for } j = 1,2,\ldots, i-1 \\ s'(j) = s(j+1) & \text{for } j = i, i+1, \ldots, \#s-1 \end{cases}$$

That is to say, one occurrence of e in the sequence is removed and the sequence rearranged, so that no gaps exist.

The last operation we define is replace (or modify):

$$s' := s \mathbin{\hat{}} e\%e'$$

which should be read as, "modify an occurrence of e in s to become e′", and where

$$\#s' = \#s, \text{ and}$$

$$\text{if } s(i) = e \text{ then } \begin{cases} s'(j) = s(j), & \text{for } j \neq i \\ s'(j) = e', & \text{for } j = i \end{cases}$$

So far, we have only considered unordered sequences. In an ordered sequence the elements satisfy some given order, viz.

$$s(i)\ \theta\ s(j), \quad \text{if } i > j$$

where $\theta \in [\geq, \leq]$ defines the ordering. Thus, for non-decreasing (or ascending) order we have :

$$s(i) \geq s(j), \quad \text{if } i > j$$

and for non-increasing (or descending) order, we have:

$$s(i) \leq s(j), \quad \text{if } i > j.$$

The operations on ordered sequences would need to be, suitably, modified. As such, the program for the find operation would be changed, as the if condition now becomes "s(i)≠e or i>**#s**. The element insert operation, now, has to maintain the order and the program becomes :

```
i := 1
while (s(i)θe and i ≤ #s) do
    s'(i) = s(i)
    i := i + 1
end while
if i ≤ #s then
        s'(i) := e
        for j := i to #s do s'(j+1) := s(j)
else s'(#s+1) := e
```

So far, we have been considering only atomic elements, these being the elements that cannot be further subdivided. The ordering could, thus, be simply specified on the elements.

For both ordered and unordered sequences, we may specify that every element of the sequence is distinguishable from all other elements in the sequence, as each is unique. This requires some changes to the operations. An element, e is, only, inserted in **s,** if e $\notin$ **s.** Deletion requires that e $\notin$ **s′**, and that the relational operator $\theta \in \{>,<\}$.

Lastly, we wish to consider the sequences of elements of which they themselves are a collection (elements or sequence). Consider a sequence s and **s**(i) is an element of **s.** However, **s**(i) is also a sequence, and thus, **s**(i)(j) represents the jth element of the ith element of s; we shall write this in the more convenient form **s**(i,j). It is simple to modify our operations to handle this situation. In ordered sequences, we have to decide which components of our elements would be chosen for the orderings. Earlier in our example on birth dates, we had considered ordering by date. What should one do if two persons have the same date of birth? Thus, in some ordered sequences a compound order may have to be defined :

$$\mathbf{s}(i,k_1)\ \theta_1\ \mathbf{s}(j,k_1) \wedge \mathbf{s}(i,k_2)\ \theta_2\ \mathbf{s}(j,k_2) \wedge \ldots.,$$

where $\theta_i \in \{\geq,\leq\}$ (for unique elements, we have $\theta_i \in \{>,<\}$.

Appendix 3.2

Average Seek Distance Computation

Let the file consist of N consecutive cylinders. For a given seek request, let i represent the current (or starting) cylinder, and j the destination cylinder.

The seek distance is $|i-j|$ cylinders, and the average seek distance is, therefore, given by:

$$\text{average seek distance} = \frac{1}{N^2}\sum_{i=1}^{N}\sum_{j=1}^{N}|i-j|$$

If we take the distance from the center, the above expression can be rewritten and simplified as follows:

$$\begin{aligned}\text{average seek distance} &= \frac{1}{N^2}\sum_{i=1}^{N} 2\sum_{j=1}^{i}(i-j)\\ &= \frac{1}{N^2}\sum_{i=1}^{N} 2\,(i-1 + i-2 + \ldots + i-1)\\ &\ \frac{1}{N^2}\sum_{i=1}^{N} 2\,(i^2 - 1 - 2 \ldots - i)\\ &= \frac{1}{N^2}\sum_{i=1}^{N} 2\,(i^2-(1+i)i/2)\\ &= \frac{1}{N^2}\sum_{i=1}^{N} 2\,(i^*(i-1)/2)\\ &= \frac{1}{N^2}\sum_{i=1}^{N}(i^2-i)\end{aligned}$$

$$= \frac{1}{N^2} (N*(N+1)*(2N+1)/6 \; - \; N*(N+1)/2)$$

$$= \frac{N^2 - 1}{3N}$$

For N >> 1, the average seek distance can be approximated by N/3.

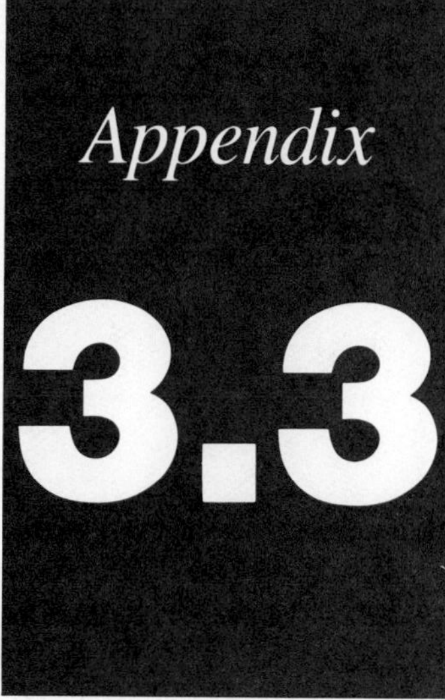

Appendix 3.3

Rotational Delay (Latency)

The circular track on a disk is divided into a number of sectors. Sectors may be hard or soft. Hard sectors are physically fixed and a physical gap exists between such sectors. Soft sectors are defined by the software system. The rotational delay is the time needed to position the read/write head on the correct sector.

Let the disk be rotating at s revolutions per minute. The time taken for the disk to rotate half a revolution is given by r_t where r_t is given by:

$$r_t = \frac{60 * 10^3}{2s} \text{ ms}$$

In the case of a hard sector type device, the sectors are physically implemented and the disk controller is able to detect the start of each sector. It takes, on the average, half a revolution before the correct sector is under the read/write head, and, hence, the average rotational delay, r_{th}, for this type of device is the same as r_t.

For the soft sector type device, let us assume that there are b sectors per track, and the start of a track is implemented physically on the disk. On the average, it would take k sectors to move past the head, before the start of track appears under the head; k being given by:

$$k = (b-1)/2$$

The average time needed before the start of track is detected is given by $2*k*r_t/b$, and the average rotational latency, r_{ts}, is given by:

$$r_{ts} = r_t * (2 - 1/b)$$

Appendix 3.4

Probabilities of Access

Let us consider the probability of accessing records in a block. Let n be the number of records per block and p be the probability that a block will be accessed (block hit ratio). We are assuming that the probability of accessing the blocks is uniform.

If we assume uniform access probabilities, then the probability of hitting a record in the block is p/n.

Thus, the probability that a given record in the block will not be accessed is $(1 - p/n)$, and the probability that no record in the block will be accessed is $(1 - p/n)^n$.

The probability of accessing at least one record in a block is thus given by $1 - (1 - p/n)^n$.

As n increases, the probability that no record in the block will be accessed approaches e^{-p}, and the probability of accessing at least one record in a block approaches $(1 - e^{-p})$.

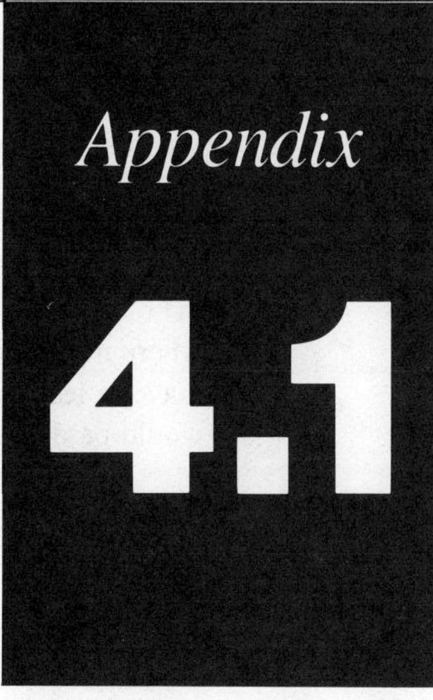

Appendix 4.1

Formal Definitions of Some Relational Algebraic Operations

Cartesian Product

We defined the extended cartesian product of two relations as the concatenation of tuples belonging to the two relations. Formally we can define a cartesian product of two relations $P(T_p,AN_p,n_p,m_p)$ and $Q(T_Q,AN_Q,n_Q,m_Q)$ as follows:

$R = P \times Q$ where

$t \in T_R$ where $t = t_1 \parallel t_2$ for all $t_1 \in T_P$ and $t_2 \in T_Q$,

$AN_R = AN_P \cup AN_Q$, assuming unique attribute names in AN_P and AN_Q,

$R = P \parallel Q$

$n_R = n_P + n_Q$, and

$m_R = m_p * m_Q$.

Projection

We define first the projection of a relation $P(T_P,AN_P,n_P,m_P)$ on a single attribute name, $A \in AN_P$. This is defined in terms of the extraction of a value for each tuple in P corresponding to the attribute *A*. The projection of tuple $t \in T_P$ over *A*, denoted by $t[A]$ or $\pi_A(t)$, is the value v corresponding to the attribute *A*. The projection of P over *A*, denoted by $P[A]$ or $\pi_A(P)$, is a single attribute relation $R(T_R,A, 1, m_R)$, where $m_R \leq m_P$ and $t \in T_R = \pi_A(tp)$ for all $t_P \in T_P$. The cardinality of R(i.e., m_R), may be less than the cardinality of P(i.e., m_P), as duplicate values of attribute *A* would be deleted.

We can then define the projection of a relation on a set of attributes, X, as a concatenation of extracted values for each attribute in X, for every tuple in the relation.

$$R = \pi_X(P)$$

such that

$$t \in T_R \text{ where } t = \pi_{A_1}(t_P) \parallel \pi_{A_2}(t_P) \parallel \ldots \parallel \pi_{A_k}(t_P) \text{ for all } t_P \in T_P$$
$$\text{where } \{A_1, A_2, \ldots, A_k\} = X \text{ and } X \subseteq AN_P$$

Thus, $\pi_X(P)$ the projection of a relation P on the set of attribute names $X \subseteq AN_P$, is the projection of each tuple $t_P \in T_P$ on the set of attribute names X. The result is a relation $R(T_R,X.n_R,m_R)$ such that:

$$R = \pi_X(P)$$
$$t_R \in T_R \text{ where } t_R = \pi_X(t_P) \text{ for all } t_P \in T_p$$
$$n_R \leq n_P \text{ and } m_R \leq m_P$$

If $|X| = |AN_P|$, i.e., the projection is over all attributes, however, the order of these could be rearranged, then the projection operation would rearrange the attributes of P.

Selection

Given a relation, $P(T_P, AN_P, n_P, m_P)$, and a predicate expression, B, the selection operation which gives a result relation, $R(T_R, AN_R, n_R, m_R)$, is given below:

$$R = \sigma_B(P)$$

$$\text{where } t \in T_R \leftrightarrow t \in T_P \wedge B(t)$$

$$n_R = n_P,$$
$$AN_R = AN_P, \text{ and}$$
$$m_R \leq m_P$$

Join A Formal Definition

The join of two relations $P(T_P,AN_P,n_P,m_P)$ and $Q(T_Q,AN_Q,n_Q,m_Q)$ giving a result relation $R(T_R,X,n_R,m_R)$ is defined, formally, as:

$$R = P \bowtie Q$$
$$t \in T_R \text{ where } t = t_1 \parallel t_2 \wedge t_1 \in T_P \wedge t_2 \in T_Q \wedge (\pi_{Ai}(t_1)\ \theta_i\ \pi_{Bi}(t_2))$$

where θ_i is some comparison operator ($\theta_i \in \{=, \neq, <, \leq, >, \geq\}$) and ($A_i \in AN_P$, $B_i \in AN_Q$, $(dom(A_i) = dom(B_i))$) for $i = 1, 2, \ldots, k$

$$0 \leq m_R \leq m_p * m_Q$$
$$n_R = n_P + n_Q$$
$$Q = AN_P \cup AN_Q$$

In general, $AN_P \cap AN_Q$ may be null and this guarantees uniqueness of attribute names in the result relation. Two common variants of the join are the equi-join and natural-join.

In the equi-join, the comparison operators $\theta_i (i = 1, 2, \ldots, n)$ are always the equality operator (=).

In the natural join the comparison operators θ are always the equality operators and $AN_P \cap AN_Q \neq \phi$. Thus, $|AN_P \cap AN_Q| = k$ join attributes are common in the relations P and Q and, consequently, only one set of the join attributes needs to be preserved in the result relation ($n_R = n_p + n_Q - k$ where k is the number of join attributes). Therefore, in natural join $X = (AN_P \cup AN_Q) - (AN_P \cap AN_Q)$.

Division

Formally, we can define the division operation on two relations $P(T_P, AN_P, n_P, m_P)$ and $Q(T_Q, AN_Q, n_Q, m_Q)$, where $AN_P \subseteq AN_Q$. We assume that the attributes which are common to P and Q are named A_i for $i = 1, 2, \ldots, |AN_Q|$.

$$R = P \div Q$$
where
$$t \in T_R = t \in \pi_{(AN_P - AN_Q)}(P)$$

(Such that for all $t_q \in T_Q$, there exists $t_P \in T_p = t_q \parallel t$.)

The division can also be expressed as:

$$R = P \div Q \text{ such that } t \in T_R = \pi_{(AN_P - AN_Q)}(\sigma_B(P)),$$

where the predicate expression B is given as a conjunction $C_1 \wedge C_2 \wedge \ldots \wedge C_i \wedge \ldots$ where each C_i is of the following form:

$$(\pi_{A_i}(t_P \in T_p) = \pi_{A_i}(t_P \in T_Q)) \text{ where } A_i \in AN_Q.$$

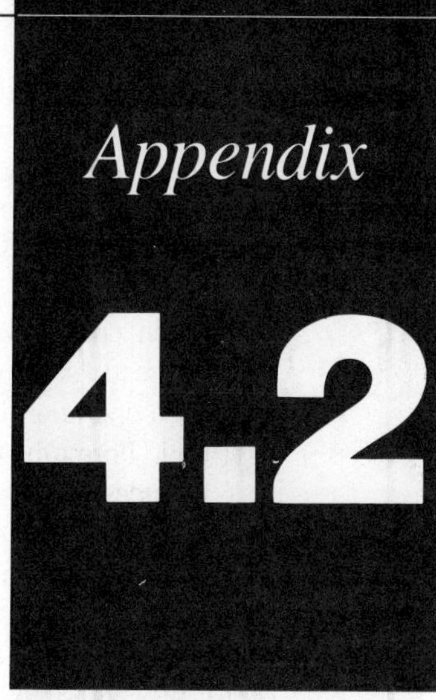

Appendix 4.2

Recursive Queries: Transitive Closure

Consider the relation: EMPLOYEE *(Emp#,Name,Manager)*. Here the attribute *Emp#* is a key of the EMPLOYEE relation. Every employee has a manager, and as managers are also employees, we may represent managers by their employee numbers. Figure A.4.1 illustrates an example of such an employee relation. The *Manager* attribute represents the employee number of the manager. *Manager* is a foreign key which is referring, in this case, to the primary key of the same relation. An employee can only have a manager who is also an employee.

Figure A.4.1 EMPLOYEE Relation.

Emp#	*Name*	*Manager*
101	Jones	@
103	Smith	110
104	Lalonde	107
107	Evan	110
110	Drew	112
112	Smith	112

The attribute *Manager* is a foreign key which establishes a relationship between one employee and another where one employee is the manager and the other is the managed. As a manager is an employee a given employee such as 112, may directly manage another employee such as 110, or indirectly manage an employee such as 103. Effectively, the relationship between employees is **recursive.**

We could use relational algebra to find all employees managed directly by a given employee. However, in finding all employees who are managed directly or indirectly by a given employee requires the implementation of some form of loop. This operation is called computing the **transitive closure** of the management hierarchy. Formally the transitive closure of a relation R is the smallest relation S that includes R and is transitive. This means that if S(a,b) and S(b,c) implies S(a,c).

This type of query cannot be implemented directly in relational algebra or the two forms of relational calculus.

Appendix 5.1

Syntax of SQL

The following is the syntax of the portion of SQL described in the text.

create table <relation> (<attribute list>)

where the <attribute list> is specified as:

<attribute list> ::= <attribute name> (<data type>) [not null] [,<attribute list>]

<data type> ::= <interger>|<smallint>|<char(n)>|<varchar(n)>|<float>|<decimal(p[,q]>

alter table existing-table-name
  add column-name data-type [, . . .]

create [unique] index name-of-index
  on existing-table-name
    (column-name [**asc** or **desc**]
      [,column-name[order] . . .])
    [**cluster**]

drop table existing-table-name;
drop index existing-index-name;

select [distinct] <target list>
  from <relation list>
  [**where** <predicate>]

- the **distinct** option is used in the **select** statement to eliminate duplicate tuples in the result. Without the **distinct** option duplicates tuples appear in the result,
- the <target list> is a method of specifying a projection operation of the result relation and it takes the form:

  <target list> ::= <attribute name> [,<target list>]

- the **from** clause specifies the relations to be used in the evaluation of the statement and includes a relation list

  <relation list> ::= <relation name> [tuple variable] [,<relation list>]

- the **where** clause is used to specify the predicates involving the attributes of the relation appearing in the **from** clause.

update <relation> **set** <target_value_list> [**where** <predicate>]
where the <target value list> is of the form:

<target value list> ::= <attribute name> = <value expression>
[,<target value list>]

delete <relation> [**where** <predicate>]

insert into <relation>
values<<value list>>
where the <value list> takes the form:

<value list> ::=<value expression> [,<value list>]
insert into <relation> (<target list>)
values<<value list>>
and the <target list> takes the form:

<target list> ::=<attribute name> [,<target list>]

The **value** clause can be replaced by a **select** statement, which is evaluated, and the result is inserted into the relation, specified in the **insert** statement.

SQL also provides the following set of built-in functions: **count, sum, avg, min, max.** The operand of each of these functions is a column of an existing relation. DISTINCT may be specified with the argument to eliminate redundant duplicates.

SQL provides a number of set operators. These are the **any, in, all, exists, not exist, union, minus, intersect,** and **contains** operators.

create view <view name> **as** <query expression>

drop view <view name>

Appendix

5.2

Syntax of QUEL

The following is the syntax of the portion of QUEL used in the text.

create <relation name> (<attribute list>)

where <attribute list> is defined as:

<attribute list> ::= <attribute name > = <format>[,<attribute list>]
range of <tuple variable> **is** <relation name>
index on <relation name> **is** index_name
(attribute_name [,attribute_name ,. . .])
destroy <name[,name,. . .]>
modify relation_name to storage_structure [**on** attribute] [**order ascending**|**descending**] [, . .]]
retrieve [unique] (<target list>)
[**where** <condition>]

QUEL provides a number of aggregation operators to be used in expressions. The aggregation operators supported are **any**, **avg**, **min**, **max**, **count**, and **sum.**

aggregation operator (<expression>)

retrieve into <new-relation> (<target list>)
[**where** <condition>]

append to <relation name> (<value list<)
[**where** <condition>]

are the value list takes the form

<value list> ::= <attribute name> = <value expression> [,<value list>]
replace <tuple variable> (<value list>)
[**where** <condition>]

delete <tuple variable>

define view VIEW_NAME <target_list>
[**where** <predicates>]
destroy VIEW_NAME

Index